KU-310-157

Programming

Principles and Practice
Using C++

Bjarne Stroustrup

Upper Saddle River, NJ • Boston • Indianapolis • San Francisco
New York • Toronto • Montreal • London • Munich • Paris • Madrid
Capetown • Sydney • Tokyo • Singapore • Mexico City

Many of the designations used by manufacturers and sellers to distinguish their products are claimed as trademarks. Where those designations appear in this book, and the publisher was aware of a trademark claim, the designations have been printed with initial capital letters or in all capitals.

A complete list of photo sources and credits appears on pages 1235–1236.

The author and publisher have taken care in the preparation of this book, but make no expressed or implied warranty of any kind and assume no responsibility for errors or omissions. No liability is assumed for incidental or consequential damages in connection with or arising out of the use of the information or programs contained herein.

The publisher offers excellent discounts on this book when ordered in quantity for bulk purchases or special sales, which may include electronic versions and/or custom covers and content particular to your business, training goals, marketing focus, and branding interests. For more information, please contact:

U.S. Corporate and Government Sales
(800) 382-3419
corpsales@pearsontechgroup.com

For sales outside the United States, please contact:

International Sales
international@pearsoned.com

Copyright © 2009 Pearson Education, Inc.

Stroustrup, Bjarne.
  Programming principles and practice using C++ / Bjarne Stroustrup.
     p.   cm.
  Includes bibliographical references and index.
  ISBN 978-0-321-54372-1 (pbk. : alk. paper) 1. C++ (Computer program language) I. Title.

  QA76.73.C153S82 2008
  005.13'3—dc22

                                                          2008032595

All rights reserved. Printed in the United States of America. This publication is protected by copyright, and permission must be obtained from the publisher prior to any prohibited reproduction, storage in a retrieval system, or transmission in any form or by any means, electronic, mechanical, photocopying, recording, or likewise. For information regarding permissions, write to:

   Pearson Education, Inc.
   Rights and Contracts Department
   501 Boylston Street, Suite 900
   Boston, MA 02116
   Fax (617) 671-3447

ISBN-13: 978-0-321-54372-1
ISBN-10:   0-321-54372-6
Text printed in the United States on recycled paper at Courier in Kendallville, Indiana.
First printing, December 2008

Programming

Contents

Preface

"Damn the torpedoes!
Full speed ahead."

—Admiral Farragut

Programming is the art of expressing solutions to problems so that a computer can execute those solutions. Much of the effort in programming is spent finding and refining solutions. Often, a problem is only fully understood through the process of programming a solution for it.

This book is for someone who has never programmed before but is willing to work hard to learn. It helps you understand the principles and acquire the practical skills of programming using the C++ programming language. My aim is for you to gain sufficient knowledge and experience to perform simple useful programming tasks using the best up-to-date techniques. How long will that take? As part of a first-year university course, you can work through this book in a semester (assuming that you have a workload of four courses of average difficulty). If you work by yourself, don't expect to spend less time than that (maybe 15 hours a week for 14 weeks).

Three months may seem a long time, but there's a lot to learn and you'll be writing your first simple programs after about an hour. Also, all learning is gradual: each chapter introduces new useful concepts and illustrates them with examples inspired by real-world uses. Your ability to express ideas in code – getting a computer to do what you want it to do – gradually and steadily increases as you go along. I never say, "Learn a month's worth of theory and then see if you can use it."

Why would you want to program? Our civilization runs on software. Without understanding software you are reduced to believing in "magic" and will be locked out of many of the most interesting, profitable, and socially useful technical fields of work. When I talk about programming, I think of the whole spectrum of computer programs from personal computer applications with GUIs (graphical user interfaces), through engineering calculations and embedded systems control applications (such as digital cameras, cars, and cell phones), to text manipulation applications as found in many humanities and business applications. Like mathematics, programming – when done well – is a valuable intellectual exercise that sharpens our ability to think. However, thanks to feedback from the computer, programming is more concrete than most forms of math, and therefore accessible to more people. It is a way to reach out and change the world – ideally for the better. Finally, programming can be great fun.

Why C++? You can't learn to program without a programming language, and C++ directly supports the key concepts and techniques used in real-world software. C++ is one of the most widely used programming languages, found in an unsurpassed range of application areas. You find C++ applications everywhere from the bottom of the oceans to the surface of Mars. C++ is precisely and comprehensively defined by a nonproprietary international standard. Quality and/or free implementations are available on every kind of computer. Most of the programming concepts that you will learn using C++ can be used directly in other languages, such as C, C#, Fortran, and Java. Finally, I simply like C++ as a language for writing elegant and efficient code.

This is not the easiest book on beginning programming; it is not meant to be. I just aim for it to be the easiest book from which you can learn the basics of real-world programming. That's quite an ambitious goal because much modern software relies on techniques considered advanced just a few years ago.

My fundamental assumption is that you want to write programs for the use of others, and to do so responsibly, providing a decent level of system quality; that is, I assume that you want to achieve a level of professionalism. Consequently, I chose the topics for this book to cover what is needed to get started with real-world programming, not just what is easy to teach and learn. If you need a technique to get basic work done right, I describe it, demonstrate concepts and language facilities needed to support the technique, provide exercises for it, and expect you to work on those exercises. If you just want to understand toy programs, you can get along with far less than I present. On the other hand, I won't waste your time with material of marginal practical importance. If an idea is explained here, it's because you'll almost certainly need it.

If your desire is to use the work of others without understanding how things are done and without adding significantly to the code yourself, this book is not for you. If so, please consider whether you would be better served by another book and another language. If that is approximately your view of programming, please also consider from where you got that view and whether it in fact is adequate for your needs. People often underestimate the complexity of programming as well as its value. I would hate for you to acquire a dislike for programming because of a mismatch between what you need and the part of the software reality I describe. There are many parts of the "information technology" world that do not require knowledge of programming. This book is aimed to serve those who do want to write or understand nontrivial programs.

Because of its structure and practical aims, this book can also be used as a second book on programming for someone who already knows a bit of C++ or for someone who programs in another language and wants to learn C++. If you fit into one of those categories, I refrain from guessing how long it will take you to read this book, but I do encourage you to do many of the exercises. This will help you to counteract the common problem of writing programs in older, familiar styles rather than adopting newer techniques where these are more appropriate. If you have learned C++ in one of the more traditional ways, you'll find something surprising and useful before you reach Chapter 7. Unless your name is Stroustrup, what I discuss here is not "your father's C++."

Programming is learned by writing programs. In this, programming is similar to other endeavors with a practical component. You cannot learn to swim, to play a musical instrument, or to drive a car just from reading a book – you must practice. Nor can you learn to program without reading and writing lots of code. This book focuses on code examples closely tied to explanatory text and diagrams. You need those to understand the ideals, concepts, and principles of programming and to master the language constructs used to express them. That's essential, but by itself, it will not give you the practical skills of programming. For that, you need to do the exercises and get used to the tools for writing, compiling, and running programs. You need to make your own mistakes and learn to correct them. There is no substitute for writing code. Besides, that's where the fun is!

On the other hand, there is more to programming – much more – than following a few rules and reading the manual. This book is emphatically not focused on "the syntax of C++." Understanding the fundamental ideals, principles, and techniques is the essence of a good programmer. Only well-designed code has a chance of becoming part of a correct, reliable, and maintainable system. Also, "the fundamentals" are what last: they will still be essential after today's languages and tools have evolved or been replaced.

What about computer science, software engineering, information technology, etc.? Is that all programming? Of course not! Programming is one of the fundamental topics that underlie everything in computer-related fields, and it has a natural place in a balanced course of computer science. I provide brief introductions to key concepts and techniques of algorithms, data structures, user interfaces, data processing, and software engineering. However, this book is not a substitute for a thorough and balanced study of those topics.

Code can be beautiful as well as useful. This book is written to help you see that, to understand what it means for code to be beautiful, and to help you to master the principles and acquire the practical skills to create such code. Good luck with programming!

A note to students

Of the 1000+ first-year students we have taught so far using drafts of this book at Texas A&M University, about 60% had programmed before and about 40% had never seen a line of code in their lives. Most succeeded, so you can do it, too.

You don't have to read this book as part of a course. I assume that the book will be widely used for self-study. However, whether you work your way through as part of a course or independently, try to work with others. Programming has an – unfair – reputation as a lonely activity. Most people work better and learn faster when they are part of a group with a common aim. Learning together and discussing problems with friends is not cheating! It is the most efficient – as well as most pleasant – way of making progress. If nothing else, working with friends forces you to articulate your ideas, which is just about the most efficient way of testing your understanding and making sure you remember. You don't actually have to personally discover the answer to every obscure language and programming environment problem. However, please don't cheat yourself by not doing the drills and a fair number of exercises (even if no teacher forces you to do them). Remember: programming is (among other things) a practical skill that you need to practice to master. If you don't write code (do several exercises for each chapter), reading this book will be a pointless theoretical exercise.

Most students – especially thoughtful good students – face times when they wonder whether their hard work is worthwhile. When (not if) this happens to you, take a break, reread the preface, and look at Chapter 1 ("Computers, People, and Programming") and Chapter 22 ("Ideals and History"). There, I try to articulate what I find exciting about programming and why I consider it a crucial tool for making a positive contribution to the world. If you wonder about my teaching philosophy and general approach, have a look at Chapter 0 ("Notes to the Reader").

You might find the weight of this book worrying, but it should reassure you that part of the reason for the heft is that I prefer to repeat an explanation or add an example rather than have you search for the one and only explanation. The other major part of the reason is that the second half of the book is reference material and "additional material" presented for you to explore only if you are interested in more information about a specific area of programming, such as embedded systems programming, text analysis, or numerical computation.

And please don't be too impatient. Learning any major new and valuable skill takes time and is worth it.

A note to teachers

No. This is not a traditional Computer Science 101 course. It is a book about how to construct working software. As such, it leaves out much of what a computer science student is traditionally exposed to (Turing completeness, state machines, discrete math, Chomsky grammars, etc.). Even hardware is ignored on the assumption that students have used computers in various ways since kindergarten. This book does not even try to mention most important CS topics. It is about programming (or more generally about how to develop software), and as such it goes into more detail about fewer topics than many traditional courses. It tries to do just one thing well, and computer science is not a one-course topic. If this book/course is used as part of a computer science, computer engineering, electrical engineering (many of our first students were EE majors), information science, or whatever program, I expect it to be taught alongside other courses as part of a well-rounded introduction.

Please read Chapter 0 ("Notes to the Reader") for an explanation of my teaching philosophy, general approach, etc. Please try to convey those ideas to your students along the way.

Support

The book's support website, **www.stroustrup.com/Programming**, contains a variety of materials supporting the teaching and learning of programming using this book. The material is likely to be improved with time, but for starters, you can find:

- Slides for lectures based on the book
- An instructor's guide
- Header files and implementations of libraries used in the book
- Code for examples in the book
- Solutions to selected exercises
- Potentially useful links
- Errata

Suggestions for improvements are always welcome.

Acknowledgments

I'd especially like to thank my late colleague and co-teacher Lawrence "Pete" Petersen for encouraging me to tackle the task of teaching beginners long before I'd otherwise have felt comfortable doing that, and for supplying the practical teaching experience to make the course succeed. Without him, the first version of the course would have been a failure. We worked together on the first versions of the course for which this book was designed and together taught it repeatedly, learning from our experiences, improving the course and the book. My use of "we" in this book initially meant "Pete and me."

Thanks to the students, teaching assistants, and peer teachers of ENGR 112 at Texas A&M University who directly and indirectly helped us construct this book, and to Walter Daugherity, who has also taught the course. Also thanks to Damian Dechev, Tracy Hammond, Arne Tolstrup Madsen, Gabriel Dos Reis, Nicholas Stroustrup, J. C. van Winkel, Greg Versoonder, Ronnie Ward, and Leor Zolman for constructive comments on drafts of this book. Thanks to Mogens Hansen for explaining about engine control software. Thanks to Al Aho, Stephen Edwards, Brian Kernighan, and Daisy Nguyen for helping me hide away from distractions to get writing done during the summers.

Thanks to the reviewers that Addison-Wesley found for me. Their comments, mostly based on teaching either C++ or Computer Science 101 at the college level, have been invaluable: Richard Enbody, David Gustafson, Ron McCarty, and K. Narayanaswamy. Also thanks to my editor, Peter Gordon, for many useful comments and (not least) for his patience. I'm very grateful to the production team assembled by Addison-Wesley; they added much to the quality of the book: Julie Grady (proofreader), Chris Keane (compositor), Rob Mauhar (illustrator), Julie Nahil (production editor), and Barbara Wood (copy editor).

In addition to my own unsystematic code checking, Bashar Anabtawi, Yinan Fan, and Yuriy Solodkyy checked all code fragments using Microsoft C++ 7.1 (2003) and 8.0 (2005) and GCC 3.4.4.

I would also like to thank Brian Kernighan and Doug McIlroy for setting a very high standard for writing about programming, and Dennis Ritchie and Kristen Nygaard for providing valuable lessons in practical language design.

0

Notes to the Reader

"When the terrain disagrees with the map,
trust the terrain."

— Swiss army proverb

This chapter is a grab bag of information; it aims to give you an idea of what to expect from the rest of the book. Please skim through it and read what you find interesting. A teacher will find most parts immediately useful. If you are reading this book without the benefit of a good teacher, please don't try to read and understand everything in this chapter; just look at "The structure of this book" and the first part of the "A philosophy of teaching and learning" sections. You may want to return and reread this chapter once you feel comfortable writing and executing small programs.

0.1 The structure of this book

This book consists of four parts and a collection of appendices:

- *Part I, "The Basics,"* presents the fundamental concepts and techniques of programming together with the C++ language and library facilities needed to get started writing code. This includes the type system, arithmetic operations, control structures, error handling, and the design, implementation, and use of functions and user-defined types.

- *Part II, "Input and Output,"* describes how to get numeric and text data from the keyboard and from files, and how to produce corresponding output to the screen and to files. Then, it shows how to present numeric data, text, and geometric shapes as graphical output, and how to get input into a program from a graphical user interface (GUI).

- *Part III, "Data and Algorithms,"* focuses on the C++ standard library's containers and algorithms framework (the STL, standard template library). It shows how containers (such as **vector**, **list**, and **map**) are implemented (using pointers, arrays, dynamic memory, exceptions, and templates) and used. It also demonstrates the design and use of standard library algorithms (such as **sort**, **find**, and **inner_product**).

- *Part IV, "Broadening the View,"* offers a perspective on programming through a discussion of ideals and history, through examples (such as matrix computation, text manipulation, testing, and embedded systems programming), and through a brief description of the C language.

- *Appendices* provide useful information that doesn't fit into a tutorial presentation, such as surveys of C++ language and standard library facilities, and descriptions of how to get started with an integrated development environment (IDE) and a graphical user interface (GUI) library.

Unfortunately, the world of programming doesn't really fall into four cleanly separated parts. Therefore, the "parts" of this book provide only a coarse classification of topics. We consider it a useful classification (obviously, or we wouldn't have used it), but reality has a way of escaping neat classifications. For example, we need to use input operations far sooner than we can give a thorough explanation of C++ standard I/O streams (input/output streams). Where the set of topics needed to present an idea conflicts with the overall classification, we explain the minimum needed for a good presentation, rather than just referring to the complete explanation elsewhere. Rigid classifications work much better for manuals than for tutorials.

The order of topics is determined by programming techniques, rather than programming language features; see §0.2. For a presentation organized around language features, see Appendix A.

To ease review and to help you if you miss a key point during a first reading where you have yet to discover which kind of information is crucial, we place three kinds of "alert markers" in the margin:

- Blue: concepts and techniques (this paragraph is an example of that)
- Green: advice
- Red: warning

0.1.1 General approach

In this book, we address you directly. That is simpler and clearer than the conventional "professional" indirect form of address, as found in most scientific papers. By "you" we mean "you, the reader," and by "we" we refer either to "ourselves, the author and teachers," or to you and us working together through a problem, as we might have done had we been in the same room.

This book is designed to be read chapter by chapter from the beginning to the end. Often, you'll want to go back to look at something a second or a third time. In fact, that's the only sensible approach, as you'll always dash past some details that you don't yet see the point in. In such cases, you'll eventually go back again. However, despite the index and the cross-references, this is not a book that you can open on any page and start reading with any expectation of success. Each section and each chapter assume understanding of what came before.

Each chapter is a reasonably self-contained unit, meant to be read in "one sitting" (logically, if not always feasible on a student's tight schedule). That's one major criterion for separating the text into chapters. Other criteria include that a chapter is a suitable unit for drills and exercises and that each chapter presents some specific concept, idea, or technique. This plurality of criteria has left a few chapters uncomfortably long, so please don't take "in one sitting" too literally. In particular, once you have thought about the review questions, done the drill, and worked on a few exercises, you'll often find that you have to go back to reread a few sections and that several days have gone by. We have clustered the chapters into "parts" focused on a major topic, such as input/output. These parts make good units of review.

Common praise for a textbook is "It answered all my questions just as I thought of them!" That's an ideal for minor technical questions, and early readers have observed the phenomenon with this book. However, that cannot be the whole ideal. We raise questions that a novice would probably not think of. We aim to ask and answer questions that you need to consider to write quality software for the use of others. Learning to ask the right (often hard) questions is an essential part of learning to think as a programmer. Asking only the easy and obvious questions would make you feel good, but it wouldn't help make you a programmer.

We try to respect your intelligence and to be considerate about your time. In our presentation, we aim for professionalism rather than cuteness, and we'd rather understate a point than hype it. We try not to exaggerate the importance of a programming technique or a language feature, but please don't underestimate a simple statement like "This is often useful." If we quietly emphasize that something is important, we mean that you'll sooner or later waste days if you don't master it. Our use of humor is more limited than we would have preferred, but experience shows that people's ideas of what is funny differ dramatically and that a failed attempt at humor can be confusing.

We do not pretend that our ideas or the tools offered are perfect. No tool, library, language, or technique is "the solution" to all of the many challenges facing a programmer. At best, it can help you to develop and express your solution. We try hard to avoid "white lies"; that is, we refrain from oversimplified explanations that are clear and easy to understand, but not true in the context of real languages and real problems. On the other hand, this book is not a reference; for more precise and complete descriptions of C++, see Bjarne Stroustrup, *The C++ Programming Language, Special Edition* (Addison-Wesley, 2000), and the ISO C++ standard.

0.1.2 Drills, exercises, etc.

Programming is not just an intellectual activity, so writing programs is necessary to master programming skills. We provide two levels of programming practice:

- *Drills:* A drill is a very simple exercise devised to develop practical, almost mechanical skills. A drill usually consists of a sequence of modifications of a single program. You should do every drill. A drill is not asking for deep understanding, cleverness, or initiative. We consider the drills part of the basic fabric of the book. If you haven't done the drills, you have not "done" the book.

- *Exercises:* Some exercises are trivial and others are very hard, but most are intended to leave some scope for initiative and imagination. If you are serious, you'll do quite a few exercises. At least do enough to know which are difficult for you. Then do a few more of those. That's how you'll learn the most. The exercises are meant to be manageable without exceptional cleverness, rather than to be tricky puzzles. However, we hope that we have provided exercises that are hard enough to challenge anybody and enough exercises to exhaust even the best student's available time. We do not expect you to do them all, but feel free to try.

In addition, we recommend that you (every student) take part in a small project (and more if time allows for it). A project is intended to produce a complete useful program. Ideally, a project is done by a small group of people (e.g., three people) working together for about a month while working through the chapters in Part III. Most people find the projects the most fun and what ties everything together.

Some people like to put the book aside and try some examples before reading to the end of a chapter; others prefer to read ahead to the end before trying to get code to run. To support readers with the former preference, we provide simple suggestions for practical work labeled **"Try this:"** at natural breaks in the text. A **Try this** is generally in the nature of a drill focused narrowly on the topic that precedes it. If you pass a **Try this** without trying – maybe because you are not near a computer or you find the text riveting – do return to it when you do the chapter drill; a **Try this** either complements the chapter drill or is a part of it.

At the end of each chapter you'll find a set of review questions. They are intended to point you to the key ideas explained in the chapter. One way to look at the review questions is as a complement to the exercises: the exercises focus on the practical aspects of programming, whereas the review questions try to help you articulate the ideas and concepts. In that, they resemble good interview questions.

The "Terms" section at the end of each chapter presents the basic vocabulary of programming and of C++. If you want to understand what people say about programming topics and to articulate your own ideas, you should know what each means.

Learning involves repetition. Our ideal is to make every important point at least twice and to reinforce it with exercises.

0.1.3 What comes after this book?

At the end of this book, will you be an expert at programming and at C++? Of course not! When done well, programming is a subtle, deep, and highly skilled art building on a variety of technical skills. You should no more expect to be an expert at programming in four months than you should expect to be an expert in biology, in math, in a natural language (such as Chinese, English, or Danish), or at playing the violin in four months – or in half a year, or a year. What you should hope for, and what you can expect if you approach this book seriously, is to have a really good start that allows you to write relatively simple useful programs, to be able to read more complex programs, and to have a good conceptual and practical background for further work.

The best follow-up to this initial course is to work on a real project developing code to be used by someone else. After that, or (even better) in parallel with a real project, read either a professional-level general textbook (such as Stroustrup, *The C++ Programming Language*), a more specialized book relating to the needs of your project (such as Qt for GUI, or ACE for distributed programming), or a textbook focusing on a particular aspect of C++ (such as Koenig and Moo, *Accelerated C++*; Sutter's *Exceptional C++*; or Gamma et al., *Design Patterns*). For complete references, see §0.6 or the Bibliography section at the back of the book.

Eventually, you should learn another programming language. We don't consider it possible to be a professional in the realm of software – even if you are not primarily a programmer – without knowing more than one language.

0.2 A philosophy of teaching and learning

What are we trying to help you learn? And how are we approaching the process of teaching? We try to present the minimal concepts, techniques, and tools for you to do effective practical programs, including

- Program organization
- Debugging and testing
- Class design
- Computation
- Function and algorithm design
- Graphics (two-dimensional only)
- Graphical user interfaces (GUIs)
- Text manipulation
- Regular expression matching
- Files and stream input and output (I/O)
- Memory management
- Scientific/numerical/engineering calculations
- Design and programming ideals
- The C++ standard library
- Software development strategies
- C-language programming techniques

Working our way through these topics, we cover the programming techniques called procedural programming (as with the C programming language), data abstraction, object-oriented programming, and generic programming. The main topic of this book is *programming*, that is, the ideals, techniques, and tools of expressing ideas in code. The C++ programming language is our main tool, so we describe many of C++'s facilities in some detail. But please remember that C++ is just a tool, rather than the main topic of this book. This is "programming using C++," not "C++ with a bit of programming theory."

Each topic we address serves at least two purposes: it presents a technique, concept, or principle and also a practical language or library feature. For example, we use the interface to a two-dimensional graphics system to illustrate the use of classes and inheritance. This allows us to be economical with space (and your time) and also to emphasize that programming is more than simply slinging code together to get a result as quickly as possible. The C++ standard library is a major source of such "double duty" examples – many even do triple duty. For example, we introduce the standard library **vector**, use it to illustrate widely useful design techniques, and show many of the programming techniques used to implement it. One of our aims is to show you how major library facilities are implemented and how they map to hardware. We insist that craftsmen must understand their tools, not just consider them "magical."

Some topics will be of greater interest to some programmers than to others. However, we encourage you not to prejudge your needs (how would you know what you'll need in the future?) and at least look at every chapter. If you read this book as part of a course, your teacher will guide your selection.

We characterize our approach as "depth-first." It is also "concrete-first" and "concept-based." First, we quickly (well, relatively quickly, Chapters 1–11) assemble a set of skills needed for writing small practical programs. In doing so, we present a lot of tools and techniques in minimal detail. We focus on simple concrete code examples because people grasp the concrete faster than the abstract. That's simply the way most humans learn. At this initial stage, you should not expect to understand every little detail. In particular, you'll find that trying something slightly different from what just worked can have "mysterious" effects. Do try, though! And please do the drills and exercises we provide. Just remember that early on you just don't have the concepts and skills to accurately estimate what's simple and what's complicated; expect surprises and learn from them.

We move fast in this initial phase – we want to get you to the point where you can write interesting programs as fast as possible. Someone will argue, "We must move slowly and carefully; we must walk before we can run!" But have you ever watched a baby learning to walk? Babies really do run by themselves before they learn the finer skills of slow, controlled walking. Similarly, you will dash ahead, occasionally stumbling, to get a feel of programming before slowing down to gain the necessary finer control and understanding. You must run before you can walk!

It is essential that you don't get stuck in an attempt to learn "everything" about some language detail or technique. For example, you could memorize all of C++'s built-in types and all the rules for their use. Of course you could, and doing so might make you feel knowledgeable. However, it would not make you a programmer. Skipping details will get you "burned" occasionally for lack of knowledge, but it is the fastest way to gain the perspective needed to write good programs. Note that our approach is essentially the one used by children learning their native language and also the most effective approach used to teach foreign languages. We encourage you to seek help from teachers, friends, colleagues, instructors, Mentors, etc. on the inevitable occasions when you are stuck. Be assured that nothing in these early chapters is fundamentally difficult. However, much will be unfamiliar and might therefore feel difficult at first.

Later, we build on the initial skills to broaden your base of knowledge and skills. We use examples and exercises to solidify your understanding, and to provide a conceptual base for programming.

We place a heavy emphasis on ideals and reasons. You need ideals to guide you when you look for practical solutions – to know when a solution is good and principled. You need to understand the reasons behind those ideals to understand why they should be your ideals, why aiming for them will help you and the users of your code. Nobody should be satisfied with "because that's the way it is" as an explanation. More importantly, an understanding of ideals and reasons allows you to generalize from what you know to new situations and to combine ideas and tools in novel ways to address new problems. Knowing "why" is an essential part of acquiring programming skills. Conversely, just memorizing lots of poorly understood rules and language facilities is limiting, a source of errors, and a massive waste of time. We consider your time precious and try not to waste it.

Many C++ language-technical details are banished to appendices and manuals, where you can look them up when needed. We assume that you have the initiative to search out information when needed. Use the index and the table of contents. Don't forget the online help facilities of your compiler, and the web. Remember, though, to consider every web resource highly suspect until you have reason to believe better of it. Many an authoritative-looking website is put up by a programming novice or someone with something to sell. Others are simply outdated. We provide a collection of links and information on our support website: **www.stroustrup.com/Programming**.

Please don't be too impatient for "realistic" examples. Our ideal example is the shortest and simplest code that directly illustrates a language facility, a concept, or a technique. Most real-world examples are far messier than ours, yet do not consist of more than a combination of what we demonstrate. Successful commercial programs with hundreds of thousands of lines of code are based on techniques that we illustrate in a dozen 50-line programs. The fastest way to understand real-world code is through a good understanding of the fundamentals.

On the other hand, we do not use "cute examples involving cuddly animals" to illustrate our points. We assume that you aim to write real programs to be used by real people, so every example that is not presented as language-technical is taken from a real-world use. Our basic tone is that of professionals addressing (future) professionals.

0.2.1 The order of topics

There are many ways to teach people how to program. Clearly, we don't subscribe to the popular "the way I learned to program is the best way to learn" theories. To ease learning, we early on present topics that would have been considered advanced only a few years ago. Our ideal is for the topics we present to be driven by problems you meet as you learn to program, to flow smoothly from topic to topic as you increase your understanding and practical skills. The major flow of this book is more like a story than a dictionary or a hierarchical order.

It is impossible to learn all the principles, techniques, and language facilities needed to write a program at once. Consequently, we have to choose a subset of principles, techniques, and features to start with. More generally, a textbook or a course must lead students through a series of subsets. We consider it our responsibility to select topics and to provide emphasis. We can't just present everything, so we must choose; what we leave out is at least as important as what we leave in – at each stage of the journey.

For contrast, it may be useful for you to see a list of (severely abbreviated) characterizations of approaches that we decided not to take:

- *"C first"*: This approach to learning C++ is wasteful of students' time and leads to poor programming practices by forcing students to approach problems with fewer facilities, techniques, and libraries than necessary. C++ provides stronger type checking than C, a standard library with better support for novices, and exceptions for error handling.

- *Bottom-up:* This approach distracts from learning good and effective programming practices. By forcing students to solve problems with insufficient support from the language and libraries, it promotes poor and wasteful programming practices.

- *"If you present something, you must present it fully"*: This approach implies a bottom-up approach (by drilling deeper and deeper into every topic touched). It bores novices with technical details they have no interest in and quite likely will not need for years to come. Once you can program, you can look up technical details in a manual. Manuals are good at that, whereas they are awful for initial learning of concepts.

- *Top-down:* This approach, working from first principles toward details, tends to distract readers from the practical aspects of programming and force them to concentrate on high-level concepts before they have any chance of appreciating their importance. For example, you simply can't appreciate proper software development principles before you have learned how easy it is to make a mistake in a program and how hard it can be to correct it.

- *"Abstract first":* Focusing on general principles and protecting the student from nasty real-world constraints can lead to a disdain for real-world problems, languages, tools, and hardware constraints. Often, this approach is supported by "teaching languages" that cannot be used later and (deliberately) insulate students from hardware and system concerns.

- *Software engineering principles first:* This approach and the abstract-first approach tend to share the problems of the top-down approach: without concrete examples and practical experience, you simply cannot appreciate the value of abstraction and proper software development practices.

- *"Object-oriented from day one":* Object-oriented programming is one of the best ways of organizing code and programming efforts, but it is not the only effective way. In particular, we feel that a grounding in the basics of types and algorithmic code is a prerequisite for appreciation of the design of classes and class hierarchies. We do use user-defined types (what some people would call "objects") from day one, but we don't show how to design a class until Chapter 6 and don't show a class hierarchy until Chapter 12.

- *"Just believe in magic":* This approach relies on demonstrations of powerful tools and techniques without introducing the novice to the underlying techniques and facilities. This leaves the student guessing – and usually guessing wrong – about why things are the way they are, what it costs to use them, and where they can be reasonably applied. This can lead to overrigid following of familiar patterns of work and become a barrier to further learning.

Naturally, we do not claim that these other approaches are never useful. In fact, we use several of these for specific subtopics where their strengths can be appreciated. However, as general approaches to learning programming aimed at real-world use, we reject them and apply our alternative: concrete-first and depth-first with an emphasis on concepts and techniques.

0.2.2 Programming and programming language

We teach programming first and treat our chosen programming language as secondary, as a tool. Our general approach can be used with any general-purpose programming language. Our primary aim is to help you learn general concepts, principles, and techniques. However, those cannot be appreciated in isolation. For example, details of syntax, the kinds of ideas that can be directly expressed, and tool support differ from programming language to programming language. However, many of the fundamental techniques for producing bug-free code, such as writing logically simple code (Chapters 5 and 6), establishing invariants (§9.4.3), and separating interfaces from implementation details (§9.7 and §14.1–2), vary little from programming language to programming language.

Programming and design techniques must be learned using a programming language. Design, code organization, and debugging are not skills you can acquire in the abstract. You need to write code in some programming language and gain practical experience with that. This implies that you must learn the basics of a programming language. We say "the basics" because the days when you could learn all of a major industrial language in a few weeks are gone for good. The parts of C++ we present were chosen as the subset that most directly supports the production of good code. Also, we present C++ features that you can't avoid encountering either because they are necessary for logical completeness or are common in the C++ community.

0.2.3 Portability

It is common to write C++ to run on a variety of machines. Major C++ applications run on machines we haven't ever heard of! We consider portability and the use of a variety of machine architectures and operating systems most important. Essentially every example in this book is not only ISO Standard C++, but also portable. Unless specifically stated, the code we present should work on every C++ implementation and has been tested on several machines and operating systems.

The details of how to compile, link, and run a C++ program differ from system to system. It would be tedious to mention the details of every system and every compiler each time we need to refer to an implementation issue. In Appendix E, we give the most basic information about getting started using Visual Studio and Microsoft C++ on a Windows machine.

If you have trouble with one of the popular, but rather elaborate, IDEs (integrated development environments), we suggest you try working from the command line; it's surprisingly simple. For example, here is the full set of commands needed to compile, link, and execute a simple program consisting of two source files, **my_file1.cpp** and **my_file2.cpp**, using the GNU C++ compiler, **g++**, on a Unix or Linux system:

```
g++ –o my_program my_file1.cpp my_file2.cpp
my_program
```

Yes, that really is all it takes.

0.3 Programming and computer science

Is programming all that there is to computer science? Of course not! The only reason we raise this question is that people have been known to be confused about this. We touch upon major topics from computer science, such as algorithms and data structures, but our aim is to teach programming: the design and implementation of programs. That is both more and less than most accepted notions of computer science:

- *More,* because programming involves many technical skills that are not usually considered part of any science
- *Less,* because we do not systematically present the foundation for the parts of computer science we use

The aim of this book is to be part of a course in computer science (if becoming a computer scientist is your aim), to be the foundation for the first of many courses in software construction and maintenance (if your aim is to become a programmer or a software engineer), and in general to be part of a greater whole.

We rely on computer science throughout and we emphasize principles, but we teach programming as a practical skill based on theory and experience, rather than as a science.

0.4 Creativity and problem solving

The primary aim of this book is to help you to express your ideas in code, not to teach you how to get those ideas. Along the way, we give many examples of how we can address a problem, usually through analysis of a problem followed by gradual refinement of a solution. We consider programming itself a form of problem solving: only through complete understanding of a problem and its solution can you express a correct program for it, and only through constructing and testing a program can you be certain that your understanding is complete. Thus, programming is inherently part of an effort to gain understanding. However, we aim to demonstrate this through examples, rather than through "preaching" or presentation of detailed prescriptions for problem solving.

0.5 Request for feedback

We don't think that the perfect textbook can exist; the needs of individuals differ too much for that. However, we'd like to make this book and its supporting materials as good as we can make them. For that, we need feedback; a good textbook cannot be written in isolation from its readers. Please send us reports on errors, typos, unclear text, missing explanations, etc. We'd also appreciate suggestions for better exercises, better examples, and topics to add, topics to delete, etc. Constructive comments will help future readers and we'll post errata on our support website: **www.stroustrup.com/Programming**.

0.6 References

Along with listing the publications mentioned in this chapter, this section also includes publications you might find helpful.

Austern, Matthew H. *Generic Programming and the STL: Using and Extending the C++ Standard Template Library*. Addison-Wesley, 1999. ISBN 0201309564.

Austern, Matthew H. (editor). "Technical Report on C++ Standard Library Extensions." ISO/IEC PDTR 19768.

Blanchette, Jasmin, and Mark Summerfield. *C++ GUI Programming with Qt 4*. Prentice Hall, 2006. ISBN 0131872493.

Gamma, Erich, Richard Helm, Ralph Johnson, and John M. Vlissides. *Design Patterns: Elements of Reusable Object-Oriented Software*. Addison-Wesley, 1994. ISBN 0201633612.

Goldthwaite, Lois (editor). "Technical Report on C++ Performance." ISO/IEC PDTR 18015.

Koenig, Andrew (editor). *The C++ Standard*. ISO/IEC 14882:2002. Wiley, 2003. ISBN 0470846747.

Koenig, Andrew, and Barbara Moo. *Accelerated C++: Practical Programming by Example*. Addison-Wesley, 2000. ISBN 020170353X.

Langer, Angelika, and Klaus Kreft. *Standard C++ IOStreams and Locales: Advanced Programmer's Guide and Reference*. Addison-Wesley, 2000. ISBN 0201183951.

Meyers, Scott. *Effective STL: 50 Specific Ways to Improve Your Use of the Standard Template Library*. Addison-Wesley, 2001. ISBN 0201749625.

Meyers, Scott. *Effective C++: 55 Specific Ways to Improve Your Programs and Designs (3rd Edition)*. Addison-Wesley, 2005. ISBN 0321334876.

Schmidt, Douglas C., and Stephen D. Huston. *C++ Network Programming, Volume 1: Mastering Complexity with ACE and Patterns*. Addison-Wesley, 2002. ISBN 0201604647.

Schmidt, Douglas C., and Stephen D. Huston. *C++ Network Programming, Volume 2: Systematic Reuse with ACE and Frameworks*. Addison-Wesley, 2003. ISBN 0201795256.

Stroustrup, Bjarne. *The Design and Evolution of C++*. Addison-Wesley, 1994. ISBN 0201543303.

Stroustrup, Bjarne. "Learning Standard C++ as a New Language." *C/C++ Users Journal*, May 1999.

Stroustrup, Bjarne. *The C++ Programming Language (Special Edition)*. Addison-Wesley, 2000. ISBN 0201700735.

Stroustrup, Bjarne. "C and C++: Siblings"; "C and C++: A Case for Compatibility"; and "C and C++: Case Studies in Compatibility." *C/C++ Users Journal*, July, Aug., Sept. 2002.

Sutter, Herb. *Exceptional C++: 47 Engineering Puzzles, Programming Problems, and Solutions*. Addison-Wesley, 2000. ISBN 0201615622.

A more comprehensive list of references can be found in the Bibliography section at the back of the book.

0.7 Biographies

You might reasonably ask, "Who are these guys who want to teach me how to program?" So here is some biographical information. I, Bjarne Stroustrup, wrote this book, and together with Lawrence "Pete" Petersen, I designed and taught the university-level beginner's (first-year) course that was developed concurrently with the book, using drafts of the book.

Bjarne Stroustrup

I'm the designer and original implementer of the C++ programming language. I have used the language, and many other programming languages, for a wide variety of programming tasks over the last 30 years or so. I just love elegant and efficient code used in challenging applications, such as robot control, graphics, games, text analysis, and networking. I have taught design, programming, and C++ to people of essentially all abilities and interests. I'm a founding member of the ISO standards committee for C++ where I serve as the chair of the working group for language evolution.

This is my first introductory book. My other books, such as *The C++ Programming Language* and *The Design and Evolution of C++*, were written for experienced programmers.

I was born into a blue-collar (working-class) family in Århus, Denmark, and got my master's degree in mathematics with computer science in my hometown university. My Ph.D. in computer science is from Cambridge University, England. I worked for AT&T for about 25 years, first in the famous Computer Science Research Center of Bell Labs — where Unix, C, C++, and so much else were invented — and later in AT&T Labs–Research.

I'm a member of the U.S. National Academy of Engineering, a Fellow of the ACM, an IEEE Fellow, a Bell Laboratories Fellow, and an AT&T Fellow. As the first computer scientist ever, I received the 2005 William Procter Prize for Scientific Achievement from Sigma Xi (the scientific research society).

I do have a life outside work. I'm married and have two children, one a medical doctor and one a Ph.D. student. I read a lot (including history, science fiction, crime, and current affairs) and like most kinds of music (including classical, rock, blues, and country). Good food with friends is an essential part of life, and I enjoy visiting interesting places and people, all over the world. To be able to enjoy the good food, I run.

For more information, see my home pages: www.research.att.com/~bs and www.cs.tamu.edu/people/faculty/bs. In particular, there you can find out how to pronounce my name.

Lawrence "Pete" Petersen

In late 2006, Pete introduced himself as follows: "I am a teacher. For almost 20 years, I have taught programming languages at Texas A&M. I have been selected by students for Teaching Excellence Awards five times and in 1996 received the Distinguished Teaching Award from the Alumni Association for the College of Engineering. I am a Fellow of the Wakonse Program for Teaching Excellence and a Fellow of the Academy for Educator Development.

As the son of an army officer, I was raised on the move. After completing a degree in philosophy at the University of Washington, I served in the army for 22 years as a Field Artillery Officer and as a Research Analyst for Operational Testing. I taught at the Field Artillery Officer's Advanced Course at Fort Sill, Oklahoma, from 1971 to 1973. In 1979 I helped organize a Test Officer's Training Course and taught it as lead instructor at nine different locations across the United States from 1978 to 1981 and from 1985 to 1989.

In 1991 I formed a small software company that produced management software for university departments until 1999. My interests are in teaching, designing, and programming software that real people can use. I completed master's degrees in industrial engineering at Georgia Tech and in education curriculum and instruction at Texas A&M. I also completed a master's program in microcomputers from NTS. My Ph.D. is in information and operations management from Texas A&M.

My wife, Barbara, and I live in Bryan, Texas. We like to travel, garden, and entertain; and we spend as much time as we can with our sons and their families, and especially with our grandchildren, Angelina, Carlos, Tess, Avery, Nicholas, and Jordan."

Sadly, Pete died of lung cancer in 2007. Without him, the course would never have succeeded.

Postscript

Most chapters provide a short "postscript" trying to give some perspective on the information presented in the chapter. We do that in the realization that the information can be – and often is – daunting and will only be fully comprehended after doing exercises, reading further chapters (which apply the ideas of the chapter), and a later review. Don't panic. Relax; this is natural and expected. You won't become an expert in a day, but you can become a reasonably competent programmer as you work your way through the book. On the way, you'll encounter much information, many examples, and many techniques that lots of programmers have found stimulating and fun.

1

Computers, People, and Programming

"Specialization is for insects."

—R. A. Heinlein

In this chapter, we present some of the things that we think make programming important, interesting, and fun. We also present a few fundamental ideas and ideals. We hope to debunk a couple of popular myths about programming and programmers. This is a chapter to skim for now and to return to later when you are struggling with some programming problem and wondering if it's all worth it.

1.1 Introduction

Like most learning, learning how to program is a chicken and egg problem: We want to get started, but we also want to know why what we are about to learn matters. We want to learn a practical skill, but also make sure it is not just a passing fad. We want to know that we are not going to waste our time, but don't want to be bored by still more hype and moralizing. For now, just read as much of this chapter as seems interesting and come back later when you feel the need to refresh your memory of why the technical details matter outside the classroom.

This chapter is a personal statement of what we find interesting and important about programming. It explains what motivates us to keep going in this field after decades. This is a chapter to read to get an idea of possible ultimate goals and an idea of what kind of person a programmer might be. A beginner's technical book inevitably contains much pretty basic stuff. In this chapter, we lift our eyes from the technical details and consider the big picture: Why is programming a worthwhile activity? What is the role of programming in our civilization? Where can a programmer make contributions to be proud of? Where does programming fit into the greater world of software development, deployment, and maintenance? When people talk about "computer science," "software engineering," "information technology," etc., where does programming fit into the picture? What does a programmer do? What skills does a good programmer have?

To a student, the most urgent reason for understanding an idea, a technique, or a chapter may be to pass a test with a good grade — but there has to be more to learning than that! To someone working in the software industry, the most urgent reason for understanding an idea, a technique, or a chapter may be to find something that can help with the current project and that will not annoy the boss who controls the next paycheck, promotions, and firings – but there has to be more to learning than that! We work best when we feel that our work in some small way makes the world a better place for people to live in. For tasks that we perform over a period of years (the "things" that professions and careers are made of), ideals and more abstract ideas are crucial.

Our civilization runs on software. Improving software and finding new uses for software are two of the ways an individual can help improve the lives of many. Programming plays an essential role in that.

1.2 Software

Good software is invisible. You can't see it, feel it, weigh it, or knock on it. *Software* is a collection of programs running on some computer. Sometimes, we can see the computer. Often, we can see only something that contains the computer, such as a telephone, a camera, a bread maker, a car, or a wind turbine. We can see what that software does. We can be annoyed or hurt if it doesn't do what it is supposed to do. We can be annoyed or hurt if what it is supposed to do doesn't suit our needs.

How many computers are there in the world? We don't know; billions at least. There may be more computers in the world than people. A 2004 estimate from ITU (International Telecommunication Union, a UN agency) lists 772 million PCs and most computers are not PCs.

How many computers do you (more or less directly) use every day? There are more than 30 computers in my car, two in my cell phone, one in my MP3 player, and one in my camera. Then there is my laptop (on which the page you are reading is being written) and my desktop machine. The air-conditioning controller that keeps the summer heat and humidity at bay is a simple computer. There is one controlling the computer science department's elevator. If you use a modern television, there will be at least one computer in there somewhere. A bit of web surfing gets you into direct contact with dozens – possibly hundreds – of servers through a telecommunications system consisting of many thousands of computers – telephone switches, routers, and so on.

No, I do not drive around with 30 laptops on the backseat of my car! The point is that most computers do not look like the popular image of a computer (with a screen, a keyboard, a mouse, etc.); they are small "parts" embedded in the kind of equipment we use. So, that car has nothing that looks like a computer, not even a screen to display maps and driving directions (though such gadgets are popular in other cars). However, its engine contains quite a few computers, doing things like fuel injection control and temperature monitoring. The power-assisted steering involves at least one computer, the radio and the security system contain some, and we suspect that even the open/close controls of the windows are computer controlled. Newer models even have computers that continuously monitor tire pressure.

How many computers do you depend on for what you do during a day? You eat; if you live in a modern city, getting the food to you is a major effort requiring minor miracles of planning, transport, and storage. The management of the distribution networks is of course computerized, as are the communication systems that stitch them all together. Modern farming is highly computerized; next to the cow barn you find computers used to monitor the herd (ages, health, milk production, etc.), farm equipment is increasingly computerized, and the number of forms required by the various branches of government can make any honest farmer cry. If something goes wrong, you can read all about it in your newspaper; of course, the articles in that paper were written on computers, set on the page by computers, and (if you still read the "dead tree edition") printed by computerized equipment − often after having been electronically transmitted to the printing plant. Books are produced in the same way. If you have to commute, the traffic flows are monitored by computers in a (usually vain) attempt to avoid traffic jams. You prefer to take the train? That train will also be computerized; some even operate without a driver, and the train's subsystems, such as announcements, braking, and ticketing, involve lots of computers. Today's entertainment industry (music, movies, television, stage shows) is among the largest users of computers. Even non-cartoon movies use (computer) animation heavily; music and photography also tend to be digital (i.e., using computers) for both recording and delivery. Should you become ill, the tests your doctor orders will involve computers, the medical records are often computerized, and most of the medical equipment you'll encounter if you are sent to a hospital to be cured contains computers. Unless you happen to be staying in a cottage in the woods without access to any electrically powered gadgets (including light bulbs), you use energy. Oil is found, extracted, processed, and distributed through a system using computers every step along the way, from the drill bit deep in the ground to your local gas (petrol) pump. If you pay for that gas with a credit card, you again exercise a whole host of computers. It is the same story for coal, gas, solar, and wind power.

The examples so far are all "operational"; they are directly involved in what you are doing. Once removed from that is the important and interesting area of design. The clothes you wear, the telephone you talk into, and the coffee machine that dispenses your favorite brew were designed and manufactured using computers. The superior quality of modern photographic lenses and the exquisite shapes in the design of modern everyday gadgets and utensils owe almost everything to computer-based design and production methods. The craftsmen/designers/artists/engineers who design our environment have been freed from many physical constraints previously considered fundamental. If you get ill, the medicines given to cure you will have been designed using computers.

Finally, research – science itself – relies heavily on computers. The telescopes that probe the secrets of distant stars could not be designed, built, or operated without computers, and the masses of data they produce couldn't be analyzed and understood without computers. An individual biology field researcher may not be heavily computerized (unless, of course, a camera, a digital tape recorder, a telephone, etc. are used), but back in the lab, the data has to be stored, analyzed, checked against computer models, and communicated to fellow scientists. Modern chemistry and biology – including medical research – use computers to an extent undreamed of a few years ago and still unimagined by most people. The human genome was sequenced by computers. Or – let's be precise – the human genome was sequenced by humans using computers. In all of these examples, we see computers as something that enables us to do something we would have had a harder time doing without computers.

Every one of those computers runs software. Without software, they would just be expensive lumps of silicon, metal, and plastic: doorstops, boat anchors, and space heaters. Every line of that software was written by some individual. Every one of those lines that was actually executed was minimally reasonable, if not correct. It's amazing that it all works! We are talking about billions of lines of code (program text) in hundreds of programming languages. Getting all that to work took a staggering amount of effort and involved an unimaginable number of skills. We want further improvements to essentially every service and gadget we depend on. Just think of any one service and gadget you rely on; what would you like to see improved? If nothing else, we want our services and gadgets smaller (or bigger), faster, more reliable, with more features, easier to use, with higher capacity, better looking, and cheaper. The likelihood is that the improvement you thought of requires some programming.

1.3 People

Computers are built by people for the use of people. A computer is a very generic tool; it can be used for an unimaginable range of tasks. It takes a program to make it useful to someone. In other words, a computer is just a piece of hardware until someone – some programmer – writes code for it to do something useful. We often forget about the software. Even more often, we forget about the programmer.

Hollywood and similar "popular culture" sources of disinformation have assigned largely negative images to programmers. For example, we have all seen the solitary, fat, ugly nerd with no social skills who is obsessed with video games and breaking into other people's computers. He (almost always a male) is as likely to want to destroy the world as he is to want to save it. Obviously, milder versions of such caricatures exist in real life, but in our experience they are no more frequent among software developers than they are among lawyers, police officers, car salesmen, journalists, artists, or politicians.

Think about the applications of computers you know from your own life. Were they done by a loner in a dark room? Of course not; the creation of a successful piece of software, computerized gadget, or system involves dozens, hundreds, or thousands of people performing a bewildering set of roles: for example, programmers, (program) designers, testers, animators, focus group managers, experimental psychologists, user interface designers, analysts, system administrators, customer relations people, sound engineers, project managers, quality engineers, statisticians, animators, hardware interface engineers, requirements engineers, safety officers, mathematicians, sales support personnel, troubleshooters, network designers, methodologists, software tools managers, software librarians, etc. The range of roles is huge and made even more bewildering by the titles varying from organization to organization: one organization's "engineer" may be another organization's "programmer" and yet another organization's "developer," "member of technical staff," or "architect." There are even organizations that let their employees pick their own titles. Not all of these roles directly involve programming. However, we have personally seen examples of people performing each of the roles mentioned while reading or writing code as an essential part of their job. Additionally, a programmer (performing any of these roles, and more) may over a short period of time interact with a wide range of people from application areas, such as biologists, engine designers, lawyers, car salesmen, medical researchers, historians, geologists, astronauts, airplane engineers, lumberyard managers, rocket scientists, bowling alley builders, journalists, and animators (yes, this is a list drawn from personal experience). Someone may also be a programmer at times and fill non-programming roles at other stages of a professional career.

The myth of a programmer being isolated is just that: a myth. People who like to work on their own choose areas of work where that is most feasible and usually complain bitterly about the number of "interruptions" and meetings. People who prefer to interact with other people have an easier time because modern software development is a team activity. The implication is that social and communication skills are essential and valued far more than the stereotypes indicate. On a short list of highly desirable skills for a programmer (however you realistically define *programmer*), you find the ability to communicate well – with people from a wide variety of backgrounds – informally, in meetings, in writing, and in formal presentations. We are convinced that until you have completed a team project or two, you have no idea of what programming is and whether you really like it. Among the things we like about programming are all the nice and interesting people we meet and the variety of places we get to visit as part of our professional lives.

One implication of all this is that people with a wide variety of skills, interests, and work habits are essential for producing good software. Our quality of life depends on those people — sometimes even our life itself. No one person could fill all the roles we mention here; no sensible person would want every role. The point is that you have a wider choice than you could possibly imagine; not that you have to make any particular choice. As an individual you will "drift" toward areas of work that match your skills, talents, and interests.

We talk about "programmers" and "programming," but obviously programming is only part of the overall picture. The people who design a ship or a cell phone don't think of themselves as programmers. Programming is an important part of software development, but not all there is to software development. Similarly, for most products, software development is an important part of product development, but not all there is to product development.

We do not assume that you — our reader — want to become a professional programmer and spend the rest of your working life writing code. Even the best programmers — especially the *best* programmers — spend most of their time *not* writing code. Understanding problems takes serious time and often requires significant intellectual effort. That intellectual challenge is what many programmers refer to when they say that programming is interesting. Many of the best programmers also have degrees in subjects not usually considered part of computer science. For example, if you work on software for genomic research, you will be much more effective if you understand some molecular biology. If you work on programs for analyzing medieval literature, you could be much better off reading a bit of that literature and maybe even knowing one or more of the relevant languages. In particular, a person with an "all I care about is computers and programming" attitude will be incapable of interacting with his or her non-programmer colleagues. Such a person will not only miss out on the best parts of human interactions (i.e., life) but also be a bad software developer.

So, what do we assume? Programming is an intellectually challenging set of skills that are part of many important and interesting technical disciplines. In addition, programming is an essential part of our world, so not knowing the basics of programming is like not knowing the basics of physics, history, biology, or literature. Someone totally ignorant of programming is reduced to believing in magic and is dangerous in many technical roles. If you read Dilbert, think of the pointy-haired boss as the kind of manager you don't want to meet or (far worse) become. In addition, programming can be fun.

But what do we assume you might use programming for? Maybe you will use programming as a key tool in your further studies and work without becoming a professional programmer. Maybe you will interact with other people professionally and personally in ways where a basic knowledge of programming will be an advantage, maybe as a designer, writer, manager, or scientist. Maybe you will do programming at a professional level as part of your studies or work. Even if you do become a professional programmer it is unlikely that you will do nothing but programming.

You might become an engineer focusing on computers or a computer scientist, but even then you will not "program all the time." Programming is a way of presenting ideas in code – a way of aiding problem solving. It is nothing – absolutely a waste of time – unless you have ideas that are worth presenting and problems worth solving.

This is a book about programming and we have promised to help you learn how to program, so why do we emphasize non-programming subjects and the limited role of programming? A good programmer understands the role of code and programming technique in a project. A good programmer is (at most times) a good team player and tries hard to understand how the code and its production best support the overall project. For example, imagine that I worked on a new MP3 player and all that I cared about was the beauty of my code and the number of neat features I could provide. I would probably insist on the largest, most powerful computer to run my code. I might disdain the theory of sound encoding because it is "not programming." I would stay in my lab, rather than go out to meet potential users, who undoubtedly would have bad tastes in music anyway and would not appreciate the latest advances in GUI (graphical user interface) programming. The likely result would be disaster for the project. A bigger computer would mean a costlier MP3 player and most likely a shorter battery life. Encoding is an essential part of handling music digitally, so failing to pay attention to advances in encoding techniques could lead to increased memory requirements for each song (encodings differ by as much as 100% for the same-quality output). A disregard for users' preferences – however odd and archaic they may seem to you – typically leads to the users choosing some other product. An essential part of writing a good program is to understand the needs of the users and the constraints that those needs place on the implementation (i.e., the code). To complete this caricature of a bad programmer, we just have to add a tendency to deliver late because of an obsession with details and an excessive confidence in the correctness of lightly tested code. We encourage you to become a good programmer, with a broad view of what it takes to produce good software. That's where both the value to society and the keys to personal satisfaction lie.

1.4 Computer science

Even by the broadest definition, programming is best seen as a part of something greater. We can see it as a subdiscipline of computer science, computer engineering, software engineering, information technology, or any other software-related discipline. We see programming as an enabling technology for those computer and information fields of science and engineering, as well as for physics, biology, medicine, history, literature, and any other academic or research field.

Consider computer science. A 1995 U.S. government "blue book" defines it like this: "The systematic study of computing systems and computation. The body of knowledge resulting from this discipline contains theories for understanding computing systems and methods; design methodology, algorithms, and tools; methods for the testing of concepts; methods of analysis and verification; and knowledge representation and implementation." As we would expect, the Wikipedia entry is less formal: "Computer science, or computing science, is the study of the theoretical foundations of information and computation and their implementation and application in computer systems. Computer science has many sub-fields; some emphasize the computation of specific results (such as computer graphics), while others (such as computational complexity theory) relate to properties of computational problems. Still others focus on the challenges in implementing computations. For example, programming language theory studies approaches to describing computations, while computer programming applies specific programming languages to solve specific computational problems."

Programming is a tool; it is a fundamental tool for expressing solutions to fundamental and practical problems so that they can be tested, improved through experiment, and used. Programming is where ideas and theories meet reality. This is where computer science can become an experimental discipline, rather than pure theory, and impact the world. In this context, as in many others, it is essential that programming is an expression of well-tried practices as well as the theories. It must not degenerate into mere hacking: just get some code written, any old way that meets an immediate need.

1.5 Computers are everywhere

Nobody knows everything there is to know about computers or software. This section just gives you a few examples. Maybe you'll see something you like. At least you might be convinced that the scope of computer use – and through that, programming – is far larger than any individual can fully grasp.

Most people think of a computer as a small gray box attached to a screen and a keyboard. Such computers tend to hide under tables and be good at games, messaging and email, and playing music. Other computers, called laptops, are used on planes by bored businessmen to look at spreadsheets, play games, and watch videos. This caricature is just the tip of the iceberg. Most computers work out of our sight and are part of the systems that keep our civilization going. Some fill rooms; others are smaller than a small coin. Many of the most interesting computers don't directly interact with a human through a keyboard, mouse, or similar gadget.

1.5.1 Screens and no screens

The idea of a computer as a fairly large square box with a screen and a keyboard is common and often hard to shake off. However, consider these two computers:

Both of these "gadgets" (which happen to be watches) are primarily computers. In fact, we conjecture that they are essentially the same model computer with different I/O (input/output) systems. The left one drives a small screen (similar to the screens on conventional computers, but smaller) and the second drives little electric motors controlling traditional clock hands and a disk of numbers for day-of-month readout. Their input systems are the four buttons (more easily seen on the right-hand watch) and a radio receiver, used for synchronization with very high-precision "atomic" clocks. Most of the programs controlling these two computers are shared between them.

1.5.2 Shipping

These two photos show a large marine diesel engine and the kind of huge ship that it may power:

Consider where computers and software play key roles here:

- *Design:* Of course, the ship and the engine were both designed using computers. The list of uses is almost endless and includes architectural and engineering drawings, general calculations, visualization of spaces and parts, and simulations of the performance of parts.

- *Construction:* A modern shipyard is heavily computerized. The assembly of a ship is carefully planned using computers, and the work is done guided by computers. Welding is done by robots. In particular, a modern double-hulled tanker couldn't be built without little welding robots to do the welding from within the space between the hulls. There just isn't room for a human in there. Cutting steel plates for a ship was one of the world's first CAD/CAM (computer-aided design and computer-aided manufacture) applications.

- *The engine:* The engine has electronic fuel injection and is controlled by a few dozen computers. For a 100,000-horsepower engine (like the one in the photo), that's a nontrivial task. For example, the engine management computers continuously adjust fuel mix to minimize the pollution that would result from a badly tuned engine. Many of the pumps associated with the engine (and other parts of the ship) are themselves computerized.

- *Management:* Ships sail where there is cargo to pick up and to deliver. The scheduling of fleets of ships is a continuing process (computerized, of course) so that routings change with the weather, with supply and demand, and with space and loading capacity of harbors. There are even websites where you can watch the position of major merchant vessels at any time. The ship in the photo happens to be a container vessel (the largest such in the world; 397m long and 56m wide), but other kinds of large modern ships are managed in similar ways.

- *Monitoring:* An oceangoing ship is largely autonomous; that is, its crew can handle most contingencies likely to arise before the next port. However, they are also part of a globe-spanning network. The crew has access to reasonably accurate weather information (from and through – computerized – satellites). They have GPS (global positioning system) and computer-controlled and computer-enhanced radar. If the crew needs a rest, most systems (including the engine, radar, etc.) can be monitored (via satellite) from a shipping-line control room. If anything unusual is spotted, or if the connection "back home" is broken, the crew is notified.

Consider the implication of a failure of one of the hundreds of computers explicitly mentioned or implied in this brief description. Chapter 25 ("Embedded Systems Programming") examines this in slightly more detail. Writing code for a modern ship is a skilled and interesting activity. It is also useful. The cost of transport is really amazingly low. You appreciate that when you buy something that wasn't manufactured locally. Sea transport has always been cheaper than land transport; these days one of the reasons is serious use of computers and information.

1.5.3 Telecommunications

These two photos show a telephone switch and a telephone (that also happens to be a camera, an MP3 player, an FM radio, and a web browser):

Consider where computers and software play key roles here. You pick up a telephone and dial, the person you dialed answers, and you talk. Or maybe you get to talk to an answering machine, or maybe you send a photo from your phone camera, or maybe you send a text message (hit "send" and let the phone do the dialing). Obviously the phone is a computer. This is especially obvious if the phone (like most mobile phones) has a screen and allows more than traditional "plain old telephone services," such as web browsing. Actually, such phones tend to contain several computers: one to manage the screen, one to talk to the phone system, and maybe more.

The part of the phone that manages the screen, does web browsing, etc. is probably the most familiar to computer users: it just runs a graphical user interface to "all the usual stuff." What is unknown to and largely unsuspected by most users is the huge system that the little phone talks to while doing its job. I dial a number in Texas, but you are on vacation in New York City, yet within seconds your phone rings and I hear your "Hello!" over the roar of city traffic. Many phones can perform that trick for essentially any two locations on earth and we just take it for granted. How did my phone find yours? How is the sound transmitted? How is the sound encoded into data packets? The answer could fill many books much thicker than this one, but it involves a combination of hardware and software on hundreds of computers scattered over the geographical area in question. If you are unlucky, a few telecommunications satellites (themselves computerized systems) are also involved – "unlucky" because we cannot perfectly compensate for the 20,000-mile detour out into space; the speed of light (and therefore the speed of your voice) is finite (light fiber cables are much better: shorter, faster, and carrying much more data). Most of this works remarkably well; the backbone telecommunications systems are 99.9999% reliable (for example, 20 minutes of downtime in 20 years – that's 20/20*365*24*60). The trouble we have tends to be in the communications between our mobile phone and the nearest main telephone switch.

There is software for connecting the phones, for chopping our spoken words into data packets to be sent over wires and radio links, for routing those messages, for recovering from all kinds of failures, for continuously monitoring the quality and reliability of the services, and of course for billing. Even keeping track of all the physical pieces of the system requires serious amounts of clever software: What talks to what? What parts go into a new system? When do you need to do some preventive maintenance?

Arguably the backbone telecommunications system of the world, consisting of semi-independent but interconnected systems, is the largest and most complicated man-made artifact. To make things a bit more real: remember, this is not just boring old telephony with a few new bells and whistles. The various infrastructures have merged. They are also what the internet (the web) runs on, what our banking and trading systems run on, and what carry our television programs to the broadcasting stations. So, we can add another couple of photos to illustrate telecommunications:

The room is the "trading floor" of the American stock exchange on New York's Wall Street and the map is a representation of parts of the internet backbones (a complete map would be too messy to be useful).

As it happens, we also like digital photography and the use of computers to draw specialized maps to visualize knowledge.

1.5.4 Medicine

These two photos show a CAT (computed axial tomography) scanner and an operating theater for computer-aided surgery (also called "robot-assisted surgery" or "robotic surgery"):

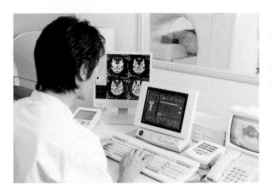 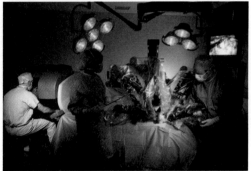

Consider where computers and software play key roles here. The scanners basically are computers; the pulses they send out are controlled by a computer, and the readings are nothing but gibberish until quite sophisticated algorithms are applied to convert them to something we recognize as a (three-dimensional) image of the relevant part of a human body. To do computerized surgery, we must go several steps further. A wide variety of imaging techniques are used to let the surgeon see the inside of the patient, to see the point of surgery with significant enlargement or in better light than would otherwise be possible. With the aid of a computer a surgeon can use tools that are too fine for a human hand to hold or in a place where a human hand could not reach without unnecessary cutting. The use of minimally invasive surgery (laparoscopic surgery) is a simple example of this that has minimized the pain and recovery time for millions of people. The computer can also help steady the surgeon's "hand" to allow for more delicate work than would otherwise be possible. Finally, a "robotic" system can be operated remotely, thus making it possible for a doctor to help someone remotely (over the internet). The computers and programming involved are mind-boggling, complex, and interesting. The user-interface, equipment control, and imaging challenges alone will keep thousands of researchers, engineers, and programmers busy for decades.

We heard of a discussion among a large group of medical doctors about which new tool had provided the most help to them in their work: The CAT scanner? The MRI scanner? The automated blood analysis machines? The high-resolution ultrasound machines? PDAs? After some discussion, a surprising "winner" of this "competition" emerged: instant access to patient records. Knowing the medical history of a patient (earlier illnesses, medicines tried earlier, allergies, hereditary problems, general health, current medication, etc.) simplifies the problem of diagnosis and minimizes the chance of mistakes.

1.5.5 Information

These two photos show an ordinary PC (well, two) and part of a server farm:

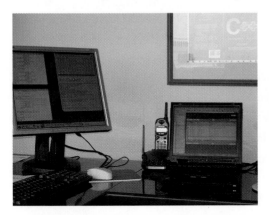 

We have focused on "gadgets" for the usual reason: you cannot see, feel, or hear software. We cannot present you with a photograph of a neat program, so we show you a "gadget" that runs one. However, much software deals directly with "information." So let's consider "ordinary uses" of "ordinary computers" running "ordinary software."

A "server farm" is a collection of computers providing web services. By using Google (a web search engine), we found the following information supplied by Wikipedia (a web dictionary). In 2004 it was estimated that Google's server farm had the following specs:

- 719 racks
- 63,272 machines
- 126,544 CPUs
- 253THz of processing power
- 126,544GB of RAM
- 5,062TB of hard drive space

A GB is a gigabyte, that is, about 1,000,000,000 characters. A TB, a terabyte, is about 1,000GB, that is, about 1,000,000,000,000 characters. These days, the "farms" are much bigger. This is a pretty extreme example, but every major company runs programs on the web to interact with its users/customers. Examples are Amazon (book and other sales), Amadeus (airline ticketing and automobile rental), and eBay (online auctions). Millions of little companies, organizations, and individuals also have a presence on the web. Most don't run their own software, but many do and much of that is not trivial.

The other, and more traditional, massive computing effort involves accounting, order processing, payroll, record keeping, billing, inventory management, personnel records, student records, patient records, etc. – the records that essentially every organization (commercial and noncommercial, governmental and private) keeps. These records are the backbone of their respective organizations. As a computing effort, processing such records seems simple: mostly some information (records) is just stored and retrieved and very little is done to it. Examples include

- Is my 12:30 flight to Chicago still on time?
- Has Gilbert Sullivan had the measles?
- Has the coffeemaker that Juan Valdez ordered been shipped?
- What kind of kitchen chair did Jack Sprat buy in 1996 (or so)?
- How many phone calls originated from the 212 area code in August of 2006?
- What was the number of coffeepots sold in January and for what total price?

The sheer scale of the databases involved makes these systems highly complex. To that add the need to respond quickly (often in less than two seconds for individual queries) and to be correct (at least most of the time). These days, it is not uncommon for people to talk about terabytes of data (a byte is the amount of memory needed to hold an ordinary character). That's traditional "data processing" and it is merging with "the web" because most access to the databases is now though web interfaces.

This kind of computer use is often referred to as *information processing*. It focuses on data – often lots of data. This leads to challenges in the organization and transmission of data and lots of interesting work on how to present vast amounts of data in a comprehensible form: "user interface" is a very important aspect of handling data. For example, think of analyzing a work of older literature (say, Chaucer's *Canterbury Tales* or Cervantes' *Don Quixote*) to figure out what the author actually wrote by comparing dozens of versions. We need to search through the texts with a variety of criteria supplied by the person doing the analysis and to display the results in a way that aids the discovery of salient points. Thinking of text analysis, publishing comes to mind: today, just about every article, book, brochure, newspaper, etc. is produced on a computer. Designing software to support that well is for most people still a problem that lacks a really good solution.

1.5.6 A vertical view

It is sometimes claimed that a paleontologist can reconstruct a complete dinosaur and describe its lifestyle and natural environment from studying a single small bone. That may be an exaggeration, but there is something to the idea of looking at a simple artifact and thinking about what it implies. Consider this photo showing the landscape of Mars taken by a camera on one of NASA's Mars Rovers:

If you want to do "rocket science," becoming a good programmer is one way. The various space programs employ lots of software designers, especially ones who can also understand some of the physics, math, electrical engineering, mechanical engineering, medical engineering, etc. that underlie the manned and unmanned space programs. Getting those two Rovers to drive around on Mars for over four years (their estimated design life was three months) is one of the greatest technological triumphs of our civilization.

The photo was transmitted to earth through a communication channel with a 25-minute transmission delay each way; there is a lot of clever programming and advanced math to make sure that the picture is transmitted using the minimal number of bits without losing any of them. On earth, the photo is then rendered using algorithms to restore color and minimize distortion due to the optics and electronic sensors.

The control programs for the Mars Rovers are of course programs – the Rovers drive autonomously for 24 hours at a time and follow instructions sent from earth the day before. The transmission is managed by programs.

The operating systems used for the various computers involved in the Rovers, the transmission, and the photo reconstruction are programs, as are the applications used to write this chapter. The computers on which these programs run are designed and produced using CAD/CAM (computer-aided design and computer-aided manufacture) programs. The chips that go into those computers are produced on computerized assembly lines constructed using precision tools, and those tools also use computers (and software) in their design and manufacture. The quality control for those long construction processes involves serious computation. All that code was written by humans in a high-level programming language and translated into machine code by a compiler, which is itself such a program. Many of these programs interact with users using GUI and exchange data using input/output streams.

Finally, a lot of programming goes into image processing (including the processing of the photos from the Mars Rovers), animation, and photo editing (there are versions of the Rover photos floating around on the web featuring "Martians").

1.5.7 So what?

What do all these "fancy and complicated" applications and software systems have to do with learning programming and using C++? The connection is simply that many programmers do get to work on projects like these. These are the kinds of things that good programming can help achieve. Also, every example used in this chapter involved C++ and at least some of the techniques we describe in this book. Yes, there are C++ programs in MP3 players, in ships, in wind turbines, on Mars, and in the human genome project. For more applications using C++, see www.research.att/~bs/applications.html.

1.6 Ideals for programmers

What do we want from our programs? What do we want in general, as opposed to a particular feature of a particular program? We want *correctness* and as part of that, *reliability*. If the program doesn't do what it is supposed to do, and do so in a way so that we can rely on it, it is at best a serious nuisance, at worst a danger. We want it to be *well designed* so that it addresses a real need well; it doesn't really matter that a program is correct if what it does is irrelevant to us or if it correctly does something in a way that annoys us. We also want it to be *affordable*; I might prefer a Rolls-Royce or an executive jet to my usual forms of transport, but unless I'm a zillionaire, cost will enter into my choices.

These are aspects of software (gadgets, systems) that can be appreciated from the outside, by non-programmers. They must be ideals for programmers and we must keep them in mind at all times, especially in the early phases of development, if we want to produce successful software. In addition, we must concern ourselves with ideals related to the code itself: our code must be *maintainable*; that is, its structure must be such that someone who didn't write it can understand it and make changes. A successful program "lives" for a long time (often for decades) and will be changed again and again. For example, it will be moved to new hardware, it will have new features added, it will be modified to use new I/O facilities (screens, video, sound), to interact using new natural languages, etc. Only a failed program will never be modified. To be maintainable, a program must be simple relative to its requirements, and the code must directly represent the ideas expressed. Complexity – the enemy of simplicity and maintainability – can be intrinsic to a problem (in that case we just have to deal with it), but it can also arise from poor expression of ideas in code. We must try to avoid that through good coding style – style matters!

This doesn't sound too difficult, but it is. Why? Programming is fundamentally simple: just tell the machine what it is supposed to do. So why can programming be most challenging? Computers are fundamentally simple; they can just do a few operations, such as adding two numbers and choosing the next instruction to execute based on a comparison of two numbers. The problem is that we don't want computers to do simple things. We want "the machine" to do things that are difficult enough for us to want help with them, but computers are nit-picking, unforgiving, dumb beasts. Furthermore, the world is more complex than we'd like to believe, so we don't really know the implications of what we request. We just want a program to "do something like this" and don't want to be bothered with technical details. We also tend to assume "common sense." Unfortunately, common sense isn't all that common among humans and is totally absent in computers (though some really well-designed programs can imitate it in specific, well-understood cases).

This line of thinking leads to the idea that "programming is understanding": when you can program a task, you understand it. Conversely, when you understand a task thoroughly, you can write a program to do it. In other words, we can see programming as part of an effort to thoroughly understand a topic. A program is a precise representation of our understanding of a topic.

When you program, you spend significant time trying to understand the task you are trying to automate.

We can describe the process of developing a program as having four stages:

- *Analysis:* What's the problem? What does the user want? What does the user need? What can the user afford? What kind of reliability do we need?

- *Design:* How do we solve the problem? What should be the overall structure of the system? Which parts does it consist of? How do those parts communicate with each other? How does the system communicate with its users?

- *Programming:* Express the solution to the problem (the design) in code. Write the code in a way that meets all constraints (time, space, money, reliability, and so on). Make sure that the code is correct and maintainable.

- *Testing:* Make sure the system works correctly under all circumstances required by systematically trying it out.

Programming plus testing is often called *implementation*. Obviously, this simple split of software development into four parts is a simplification. Thick books have been written on each of these four topics and more books still about how they relate to each other. One important thing to note is that these stages of development are not independent and do not occur strictly in sequence. We typically start with analysis, but feedback from testing can help improve the programming; problems with getting the program working may indicate a problem with the design; and working with the design may suggest aspects of the problem that hitherto had been overlooked in the analysis. Actually using the system typically exposes weaknesses of the analysis.

The crucial concept here is *feedback*. We learn from experience and modify our behavior based on what we learn. That's essential for effective software development. For any large project, we don't know everything there is to know about the problem and its solution before we start. We can try out ideas and get feedback by programming, but in the earlier stages of development it is easier (and faster) to get feedback by writing down design ideas, trying out those design ideas, and using scenarios on friends. The best design tool we know of is a blackboard (use a whiteboard instead if you prefer chemical smells over chalk dust). Never design alone if you can avoid it! Don't start coding before you have tried out your ideas by explaining them to someone. Discuss designs and programming techniques with friends, colleagues, potential users, and so on before you head for the keyboard. It is amazing how much you can learn from simply trying to articulate an idea. After all, a program is nothing more than an expression (in code) of some ideas.

Similarly, when you get stuck implementing a program, look up from the keyboard. Think about the problem itself, rather than your incomplete solution. Talk with someone: explain what you want to do and why it doesn't work. It's amazing how often you find the solution just by carefully explaining the problem to someone. Don't debug (find program errors) alone if you don't have to!

The focus of this book is implementation, and especially programming. We do not teach "problem solving" beyond giving you plenty of examples of problems and their solutions. Much of problem solving is recognizing a known problem and applying a known solution technique. Only when most subproblems are handled this way will you find the time to indulge in exciting and creative "out-of-the-box thinking." So, we focus on showing how to express ideas clearly in code.

Direct expression of ideas in code is a fundamental ideal of programming. That's really pretty obvious, but so far we are a bit short of good examples. We'll come back to this, repeatedly. When we want an integer in our code, we store it in an **int**, which provides the basic integer operations. When we want a string of characters, we store it in a **string**, which provides the most basic text manipulation operations. At the most fundamental level, the ideal is that when we have an idea, a concept, an entity, something we think of as a "thing," something we can draw on our whiteboard, something we can refer to in our discussions, something our (non–computer science) textbook talks about, then we want that something to exist in our program as a named entity (a type) providing the operations we think appropriate for it. If we want to do math, we want a **complex** type for complex numbers and a **Matrix** type for linear algebra. If we want to do graphics, we want a **Shape** type, a **Circle** type, a **Color** type, and a **Dialog_box**. When we want to deal with streams of data, say from a temperature sensor, we want an **istream** type ("**i**" for input). Obviously, every such type should provide the appropriate operations and only the appropriate operations. These are just a few examples from this book. Beyond that, we offer tools and techniques for you to build your own types to directly represent whatever concepts you want in your program.

Programming is part practical, part theory. If you are just practical, you will produce non-scalable, unmaintainable hacks. If you are just theoretical, you will produce unusable (or unaffordable) toys.

For a different kind of view of the ideals of programming and a few people who have contributed in major ways to software through work with programming languages, see Chapter 22, "Ideals and History."

Review

Review questions are intended to point you to the key ideas explained in a chapter. One way to look at them is as a complement to the exercises: the exercises focus on the practical aspects of programming, whereas the review questions try to help you articulate the ideas and concepts. In that, they resemble good interview questions.

1. What is software?
2. Why is software important?
3. Where is software important?
4. What could go wrong if some software fails? List some examples.
5. Where does software play an important role? List some examples.
6. What are some jobs related to software development? List some.
7. What's the difference between computer science and programming?
8. Where in the design, construction, and use of a ship is software used?
9. What is a server farm?
10. What kinds of queries do you ask online? List some.
11. What are some uses of software in science? List some.
12. What are some uses of software in medicine? List some.
13. What are some uses of software in entertainment? List some.
14. What general properties do we expect from good software?
15. What does a software developer look like?
16. What are the stages of software development?
17. Why can software development be difficult? List some reasons.
18. What are some uses of software that make your life easier?
19. What are some uses of software that make your life more difficult?

Terms

These terms present the basic vocabulary of programming and of C++. If you want to understand what people say about programming topics and to articulate your own ideas, you should know what each means.

affordability	customer	programmer
analysis	design	programming
blackboard	feedback	software
CAD/CAM	GUI	stereotype
communications	ideals	testing
correctness	implementation	user

Exercises

1. Pick an activity you do most days (such as going to class, eating dinner, or watching television). Make a list of ways computers are directly or indirectly involved.

2. Pick a profession, preferably one that you have some interest in or some knowledge of. Make a list of activities done by people in that profession that involve computers.

3. Swap your list from exercise 2 with a friend who picked a different profession and improve his or her list. When you have both done that, compare your results. Remember: There is no perfect solution to an open-ended exercise; improvements are always possible.

4. From your own experience, describe an activity that would not have been possible without computers.

5. Make a list of programs (software applications) that you have directly used. List only examples where you obviously interact with a program (such as when selecting a new song on an MP3 player) and not cases where there just might happen to be a computer involved (such as turning the steering wheel of your car).

6. Make a list of ten activities that people do that do not involve computers in any way, even indirectly. This may be harder than you think!

7. Identify five tasks for which computers are not used today, but for which you think they will be used for at some time in the future. Write a few sentences to elaborate on each one that you choose.

8. Write an explanation (at least 100 words, but fewer than 500) of why you would like to be a computer programmer. If, on the other hand, you are convinced that you would not like to be a programmer, explain that. In either case, present well-thought-out, logical arguments.

9. Write an explanation (at least 100 words, but fewer than 500) of what role other than programmer you'd like to play in the computer industry (independently of whether "programmer" is your first choice).

10. Do you think computers will ever develop to be conscious, thinking beings, capable of competing with humans? Write a short paragraph (at least 100 words) supporting your position.

11. List some characteristics that most successful programmers share. Then list some characteristics that programmers are popularly assumed to have.

12. Identify at least five kinds of applications for computer programs mentioned in this chapter and pick the one that you find the most interesting and that you would most likely want to participate in someday. Write a short paragraph (at least 100 words) explaining why you chose the one you did.

13. How much memory would it take to store (a) this page of text, (b) this chapter, (c) all of Shakespeare's work? Assume one byte of memory holds one character and just try to be precise to about 20%.

14. How much memory does your computer have? Main memory? Disk?

Postscript

Our civilization runs on software. Software is an area of unsurpassed diversity and opportunities for interesting, socially useful, and profitable work. When you approach software, do it in a principled and serious manner: you want to be part of the solution, not add to the problems.

We are obviously in awe of the range of software that permeates our technological civilization. Not all applications of software do good, of course, but that is another story. Here we wanted to emphasize how pervasive software is and how much of what we rely on in our daily lives depends on software. It was all written by people like us. All the scientists, mathematicians, engineers, programmers, etc. who built the software briefly mentioned here started like you are starting.

Now, let's get back to the down-to-earth business of learning the technical skills needed to program. If you start wondering if it is worth all your hard work (most thoughtful people wonder about that sometime), come back and reread this chapter, the Preface, and bits of Chapter 0 ("Notes to the Reader"). If you start wondering if you can handle it all, remember that millions have succeeded in becoming competent programmers, designers, software engineers, etc. You can, too.

Part I
The Basics

Hello, World!

"Programming is learned by writing programs."

—Brian Kernighan

Here, we present the simplest C++ program that actually does anything. The purpose of writing this program is to

- Let you try your programming environment
- Give you a first feel of how you can get a computer to do things for you

Thus, we present the notion of a program, the idea of translating a program from human-readable form to machine instructions using a compiler, and finally executing those machine instructions.

2.1 Programs

To get a computer to do something, you (or someone else) have to tell it exactly – in excruciating detail – what to do. Such a description of "what to do" is called a *program*, and *programming* is the activity of writing and testing such programs.

In a sense, we have all programmed before. After all, we have given descriptions of tasks to be done, such as "how to drive to the nearest cinema," "how to find the upstairs bathroom," and "how to heat a meal in the microwave." The difference between such descriptions and programs is one of degree of precision: humans tend to compensate for poor instructions by using common sense, but computers don't. For example, "turn right in the corridor, up the stairs, it'll be on your left" is probably a fine description of how to get to the upstairs bathroom. However, when you look at those simple instructions, you'll find the grammar sloppy and the instructions incomplete. A human easily compensates. For example, assume that you are sitting at the table and ask for directions to the bathroom. You don't need to be told to get up from your chair to get to the corridor, somehow walk around (and not across or under) the table, not to step on the cat, etc. You'll not have to be told not to bring your knife and fork or to remember to switch on the light so that you can see the stairs. Opening the door to the bathroom before entering is probably also something you don't have to be told.

In contrast, computers are *really* dumb. They have to have everything described precisely and in detail. Consider again "turn right in the corridor, up the stairs, it'll be on your left." Where is the corridor? What's a corridor? What is "turn right"? What stairs? How do I go up stairs? (One step at a time? Two steps? Slide up the banister?) What is my left? When will it be on my left? To be able to describe "things" precisely for a computer, we need a precisely defined language with a specific grammar (English is far too loosely structured for that) and a well-defined vocabulary for the kinds of actions we want performed. Such a language is called a *programming language*, and C++ is a programming language designed for a wide selection of programming tasks.

If you want greater philosophical detail about computers, programs, and programming, (re)read Chapter 1. Here, let's have a look at some code, starting with a very simple program and the tools and techniques you need to get it to run.

2.2 The classic first program

Here is a version of the classic first program. It writes "Hello, World!" to your screen:

```
// This program outputs the message "Hello, World!" to the monitor

#include ("std_lib_facilities.h")  < iostream >
              using namespace std;
int main()      // C++ programs start by executing the function main
{
        cout << "Hello, World!\n";     // output "Hello, World!"
        return 0;
}
```

Think of this text as a set of instructions that we give to the computer to execute, much as we would give a recipe to a cook to follow, or as a list of assembly instructions for us to follow to get a new toy working. Let's discuss what each line of this program does, starting with the line

```
        cout << "Hello, World!\n";     // output "Hello, World!"
```

That's the line that actually produces the output. It prints the characters **Hello, World!** followed by a newline; that is, after writing **Hello, World!**, the cursor will be placed at the start of the next line. A *cursor* is a little blinking character or line showing where you can type the next character.

In C++, string literals are delimited by double quotes ("); that is, **"Hello, World!\n"** is a string of characters. The **\n** is a "special character" indicating a newline. The name **cout** refers to a standard output stream. Characters "put into cout" using the output operator **<<** will appear on the screen. The name **cout** is pronounced "see-out" and is an abbreviation of "character **out**put stream." You'll find abbreviations rather common in programming. Naturally, an abbreviation can be a bit of a nuisance the first time you see it and have to remember it, but once you start using abbreviations repeatedly, they become second nature, and they are essential for keeping program text short and manageable.

The end of that line

```
    // output "Hello, World!"
```

is a comment. Anything written after the token // (that's the character /, called "slash," twice) on a line is a comment. Comments are ignored by the compiler and written for the benefit of programmers who read the code. Here, we used the comment to tell you what the beginning of that line actually did.

Comments are written to describe what the program is intended to do and in general to provide information useful for humans that can't be directly expressed in code. The person most likely to benefit from the comments in your code is you — when you come back to that code next week, or next year, and have forgotten exactly why you wrote the code the way you did. So, document your programs well. In §7.6.4, we'll discuss what makes good comments.

A program is written for two audiences. Naturally, we write code for computers to execute. However, we spend long hours reading and modifying the code. Thus, programmers are another audience for programs. So, writing code is also a form of human-to-human communication. In fact, it makes sense to consider the human readers of our code our primary audience: if they (we) don't find the code reasonably easy to understand, the code is unlikely to ever become correct. So, please don't forget: code is for reading — do all you can to make it readable. Anyway, the comments are for the benefit of human readers only; the computer doesn't look at the text in comments.

The first line of the program is a typical comment; it simply tells the human reader what the program is supposed to do:

```
// This program outputs the message "Hello, World!" to the monitor
```

Such comments are useful because the code itself says what the program does, not what we meant it to do. Also, we can usually explain (roughly) what a program should do to a human much more concisely than we can express it (in detail) in code to a computer. Often such a comment is the first part of the program we write. If nothing else, it reminds us what we are trying to do.

The next line

```
#include "std_lib_facilities.h"
```

is an "**#include** directive." It instructs the computer to make available ("to include") facilities from a file called **std_lib_facilities.h**. We wrote that file to simplify use of the facilities available in all implementations of C++ ("the C++ standard library"). We will explain its contents as we go along. It is perfectly ordinary standard C++, but it contains details that we'd rather not bother you with for another dozen chapters. For this program, the importance of **std_lib_facilities.h** is that we make the standard C++ stream I/O facilities available. Here, we just use the standard output stream, **cout**, and its output operator, **<<**. A file included using **#include** usually has the suffix **.h** and is called a *header* or a *header file*. A header contains definitions of terms, such as **cout**, that we use in our program.

How does a computer know where to start executing a program? It looks for a function called **main** and starts executing the instructions it finds there. Here is the function **main** of our "Hello, World!" program:

```
int main() // C++ programs start by executing the function main
{
      cout << "Hello, World!\n";     // output "Hello, World!"
      return 0;
}
```

Every C++ program must have a function called **main** to tell it where to start executing. A function is basically a named sequence of instructions for the computer to execute in the order in which they are written. A function has four parts:

- A *return type*, here **int** (meaning "integer"), which specifies what kind of result, if any, the function will return to whoever asked for it to be executed. The word **int** is a reserved word in C++ (a *keyword*), so **int** cannot be used as the name of anything else (see §A.3.1).
- A *name*, here **main**.
- A *parameter list* enclosed in parentheses (see §8.2 and §8.6), here (); in this case, the parameter list is empty.
- A *function body* enclosed in a set of "curly braces," { }, which lists the actions (called *statements*) that the function is to perform.

It follows that the minimal C++ program is simply

```
int main() { }
```

That's not of much use, though, because it doesn't do anything. The **main()** ("the main function") of our "Hello, World!" program has two statements in its body:

```
cout << "Hello, World!\n"; // output "Hello, World!"
return 0;
```

First it'll write **Hello, World!** to the screen, and then it will return a value **0** (zero) to whoever called it. Since **main()** is called by "the system," we won't use that return value. However, on some systems (notably Unix/Linux) it can be used to check whether the program succeeded. A zero (**0**) returned by **main()** indicates the program terminated successfully.

A part of a C++ program that specifies an action and isn't an **#include** directive (or some other preprocessor directive; see §4.4 and §A.17) is called a *statement*.

2.3 Compilation

C++ is a compiled language. That means that to get a program to run, you must first translate it from the human-readable form to something a machine can "understand." That translation is done by a program called a *compiler*. What you read and write is called *source code* or *program text*, and what the computer executes is called *executable*, *object code*, or *machine code*. Typically C++ source code files are given the suffix **.cpp** (e.g., **hello_world.cpp**) or **.h** (as in **std_lib_facilities.h**), and object code files are given the suffix **.obj** (on Windows) or **.o** (Unix). The plain word *code* is therefore ambiguous and can cause confusion; use it with care only when it is obvious what's meant by it. Unless otherwise specified, we use *code* to mean "source code" or even "the source code except the comments," because comments really are there just for us humans and are not seen by the compiler generating object code.

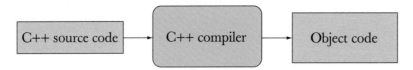

The compiler reads your source code and tries to make sense of what you wrote. It looks to see if your program is grammatically correct, if every word has a defined meaning, and if there is anything obviously wrong that can be detected without trying to actually execute the program. You'll find that computers are rather picky about syntax. Leaving out any detail of our program, such as an **#include** file, a semicolon, or a curly brace, will cause errors. Similarly, the compiler has absolutely zero tolerance for spelling mistakes. Let us illustrate this with a series of examples that each have a single small error. Each error is an example of a kind of mistake we often make:

```
// no #include here
int main()
{
        cout << "Hello, World!\n";
        return 0;
}
```

We didn't include something to tell the compiler what **cout** was, so the compiler complains. To correct that, let's add a header file:

```
#include "std_facilities.h"
int main()
{
        cout << "Hello, World!\n";
        return 0;
}
```

Unfortunately, the compiler again complains: we misspelled **std_lib_facilities.h**. The compiler also objects to this:

```
#include "std_lib_facilities.h"
int main()
{
        cout << "Hello, World!\n;
        return 0;
}
```

We didn't terminate the string with a ". The compiler also objects to this:

```
#include "std_lib_facilities.h"
integer main()
{
        cout << "Hello, World!\n";
        return 0;
}
```

The abbreviation **int** is used in C++ rather than the word **integer**. The compiler doesn't like this either:

```
#include "std_lib_facilities.h"
int main()
{
        cout < "Hello, World!\n";
        return 0;
}
```

We used < (the less-than operator) rather than << (the output operator). The compiler also objects to this:

```
#include "std_lib_facilities.h"
int main()
{
        cout << 'Hello, World!\n';
        return 0;
}
```

We used single quotes rather than double quotes to delimit the string. Finally, the compiler gives an error for this:

```
#include "std_lib_facilities.h"
int main()
{
        cout << "Hello, World!\n"
        return 0;
}
```

We forgot to terminate the output statement with a semicolon. Note that many C++ statements are terminated by a semicolon (;). The compiler needs those semicolons to know where one statement ends and the next begins. There is no really short, fully correct, and nontechnical way of summarizing where semicolons are needed. For now, just copy our pattern of use, which can be summarized as: "Put a semicolon after every expression that doesn't end with a right curly brace (})."

Why do we spend two pages of good space and minutes of your precious time showing you examples of trivial errors in a trivial program? To make the point that you – like all programmers – will spend a lot of time looking for errors in program source text. Most of the time, we look at text with errors in it. After all, if we were convinced that some code was correct, we'd typically be looking at some other code or taking the time off. It came as a major surprise to the early computer pioneers that they were making mistakes and had to devote a major portion of their time to finding them. It is still a surprise to most newcomers to programming.

When you program, you'll get quite annoyed with the compiler at times. Sometimes it appears to complain about unimportant details (such as a missing semicolon) or about things you consider "obviously right." However, the compiler is usually right: when it gives an error message and refuses to produce object code from your source code, there is something not quite right with your program; that is, the meaning of what you wrote isn't precisely defined by the C++ standard.

The compiler has no common sense (it isn't human) and is very picky about details. Since it has no common sense you wouldn't like it to try to guess what you meant by something that "looked OK" but didn't conform to the definition of C++. If it did and its guess was different from yours, you could end up spending a lot of time trying to figure out why the program didn't do what you thought you had told it to do. When all is said and done, the compiler saves us from a lot of self-inflicted problems. It saves us from many more problems than it causes. So, please remember: the compiler is your friend; possibly, the compiler is the best friend you have when you program.

2.4 Linking

A program usually consists of several separate parts, often developed by different people. For example, the "Hello, World!" program consists of the part we wrote plus parts of the C++ standard library. These separate parts (sometimes called *translation units*) must be compiled and the resulting object code files must be linked together to form an executable program. The program that links such parts together is (unsurprisingly) called a *linker*:

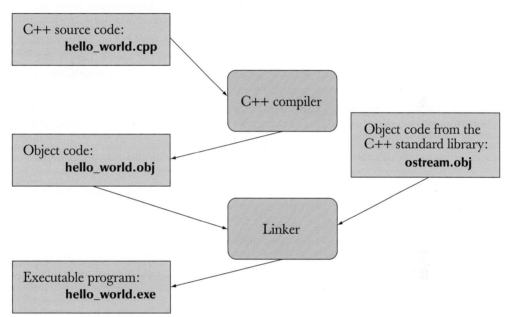

Please note that object code and executables are *not* portable among systems. For example, when you compile for a Windows machine, you get object code for Windows that will not run on a Linux machine.

A *library* is simply some code – usually written by others – that we access using declarations found in an **#include**d file. A *declaration* is a program statement specifying how a piece of code can be used; we'll examine declarations in detail later (e.g., §4.5.2).

Errors found by the compiler are called *compile-time errors*, errors found by the linker are called *link-time errors*, and errors not found until the program is run are called *run-time errors* or *logic errors*. Generally, compile-time errors are easier to understand and fix than link-time errors, and link-time errors are often easier to find and fix than run-time errors and logic errors. In Chapter 5 we discuss errors and the ways of handling them in greater detail.

2.5 Programming environments

To program, we use a programming language. We also use a compiler to translate our source code into object code and a linker to link our object code into an executable program. In addition, we use some program to enter our source code text into the computer and to edit it. These are just the first and most crucial tools that constitute our programmer's tool set or "program development environment."

If you work from a command-line window, as many professional programmers do, you will have to issue the compile and link commands yourself. If instead you use an IDE ("interactive development environment" or "integrated development environment"), as many professional programmers also do, a simple click on the correct button will do the job. See Appendix D for a description of how to compile and link on your C++ implementation.

IDEs usually include an editor with helpful features like color coding to help distinguish between comments, keywords, and other parts of your program source code, plus other facilities to help you debug your code, compile it, and run it. *Debugging* is the activity of finding errors in a program and removing them; you'll hear a lot about that along the way.

In this book, we use Visual C++ from Microsoft as our example program development environment. If we just say "the compiler" or refer to parts of "the IDE," that's the system we are referring to. However, you can use any system that provides an up-to-date, standards-conforming implementation of C++. Most of what we say will, with very minor modifications, be true for all implementations of C++, and the code will run everywhere. In our work, we use several different implementations.

 Drill

So far we have talked about programming, code, and tools (such as compilers). Now you have to get a program to run. This is a crucial point in this book and in learning to program. This is where you start to develop practical skills and good programming habits. The exercises for this chapter are focused on getting you acquainted with your software development environment. Once you get the "Hello, World!" program to run, you will have passed the first major milestone as a programmer.

The purpose of a drill is to establish or reinforce your practical programming skills and give you experience with programming environment tools. Typically, a drill is a sequence of modifications to a single program, "growing" it from something completely trivial to something that might be a useful part of a real program. A traditional set of exercises is designed to test your initiative, cleverness, or inventiveness. In contrast, a drill requires little invention from you. Typically, sequencing is crucial, and each individual step should be easy (or even trivial). Please don't try to be clever and skip steps; on average that will slow you down or even confuse you.

You might think you understand everything you read and everything your Mentor or instructor told you, but repetition and practice are necessary to develop programming skills. In this regard, programming is like athletics, music, dance, or any skill-based craft. Imagine people trying to compete in any of those fields without regular practice. You know how well they would perform. Constant practice — for professionals that means lifelong constant practice — is the only way to develop and maintain a high-level practical skill.

So, never skip the drills, no matter how tempted you are; they are essential to the learning process. Just start with the first step and proceed, testing each step as you go to make sure you are doing it right.

Don't be alarmed if you don't understand every detail of the syntax you are using, and don't be afraid to ask for help from instructors or friends. Keep going, do all of the drills and many of the exercises, and all will become clear in due time.

So, here is your first drill:

1. Go to Appendix D and follow the steps required to set up a project. Set up an empty, console C++ project called hello_world.
2. Type in **hello_world.cpp**, exactly as specified below, save it in your practice directory, and include it in your hello_world project.

```
#include "std_lib_facilities.h"
int main()        // C++ programs start by executing the function main
{
        cout << "Hello, World!\n";   // output "Hello, World!"
        keep_window_open();          // wait for a character to be entered
        return 0;
}
```

The call to **keep_window_open()** is needed on some Windows machines to prevent them from closing the window before you have a chance to read the output. This is a peculiarity/feature of Windows, not of C++. We defined **keep_window_open()** in **std_lib_facilities.h** to simplify writing simple text programs.

How do you find **std_lib_facilities.h**? If you are in a course, ask your instructor. If not, download it from our support site **www.stroustrup.com/Programming**. But what if you don't have an instructor and no access to the web? In that case (only), replace the **#include** directive with:

```
#include<iostream>
#include<string>
#include<vector>
```

```
#include<algorithm>
#include<cmath>
using namespace std;
inline void keep_window_open() { char ch; cin>>ch; }
```

This uses the standard library directly, will keep you going until Chapter 5, and will be explained in detail later (§8.7).

3. Compile and run the "Hello, World!" program. Quite likely, something didn't work quite right. It very rarely does for a first attempt to use a new programming language or a new programming environment. Find the problem and fix it! This is a point where asking for help from a more experienced person is sensible, but be sure to understand what you are shown so that you can do it all by yourself before proceeding further.

4. By now, you have probably encountered some errors and had to correct them. Now is the time to get a bit better acquainted with your compiler's error-detection and error-reporting facilities! Try the six errors from §2.3 to see how your programming environment reacts. Think of at least five more errors you might have made typing in your program (e.g., forget **keep_window_open**(), leave the Caps Lock key on while typing a word, or type a comma instead of a semicolon) and try each to see what happens when you try to compile and run those versions.

Review

The basic idea of these review questions is to give you a chance to see if you have noticed and understood the key points of the chapter. You may have to refer back to the text to answer a question; that's normal and expected. You may have to reread whole sections; that too is normal and expected. However, if you have to reread the whole chapter or have problems with every review question, you should consider whether your style of learning is effective. Are you reading too fast? Should you stop and do some of the **Try this** suggestions? Should you study with a friend so that you can discuss problems with the explanations in the text?

1. What is the purpose of the "Hello, World!" program?
2. Name the four parts of a function.
3. Name a function that must appear in every C++ program.
4. In the "Hello, World!" program, what is the purpose of the line **return 0;**?
5. What is the purpose of the compiler?
6. What is the purpose of the **#include** directive?
7. What does a **.h** suffix at the end of a file name signify in C++?
8. What does the linker do for your program?
9. What is the difference between a source file and an object file?
10. What is an IDE and what does it do for you?
11. If you understand everything in the textbook, why is it necessary to practice?

Most review questions have a clear answer in the chapter in which they appear. However, we do occasionally include questions to remind you of relevant information from other chapters and sometimes even relating to the world outside this book. We consider that fair; there is more to writing good software and thinking about the implications of doing so than fits into an individual chapter or book.

Terms

These terms present the basic vocabulary of programming and of C++. If you want to understand what people say about programming topics and to articulate your own ideas, you should know what each means.

//	executable	**main()**
<<	function	object code
C++	header	output
comment	IDE	program
compiler	**#include**	source code
compile-time error	library	statement
cout	linker	

You might like to gradually develop a glossary written in your own words. You can do that by repeating exercise 4 below for each chapter.

Exercises

We list drills separately from exercises; always complete the chapter drill before attempting an exercise. Doing so will save you time.

1. Change the program to output the two lines

   Hello, programming!
   Here we go!

2. Expanding on what you have learned, write a program that lists the instructions for a computer to find the upstairs bathroom, discussed in §2.1. Can you think of any more steps that a person would assume, but that a computer would not? Add them to your list. This is a good start in "thinking like a computer." Warning: For most people, "go to the bathroom" is a perfectly adequate instruction. For someone with no experience with houses or bathrooms (imagine a stone-age person, somehow transported into your dining room) the list of necessary instructions could be *very* long. Please don't use more than a page. For the benefit of the reader, you may add a short description of the layout of the house you are imagining.

3. Write a description of how to get from the front door of your dorm room, apartment, house, whatever, to the door of your classroom (assuming you

are attending some school; if you are not, pick another target). Have a friend try to follow the instructions and annotate them with improvements as he or she goes along. To keep friends, it may be a good idea to "field test" those instructions before giving them to a friend.

4. Find a good cookbook. Read the instructions for baking blueberry muffins (if you are in a country where "blueberry muffins" is a strange, exotic dish, use a more familiar dish instead). Please note that with a bit of help and instruction, most of the people in the world can bake delicious blueberry muffins. It is not considered advanced or difficult fine cooking. However, for the author, few exercises in this book are as difficult as this one. It is amazing what you can do with a bit of practice.

   • Rewrite those instructions so that each individual action is in its own numbered paragraph. Be careful to list all ingredients and all kitchen utensils used at each step. Be careful about crucial details, such as the desired oven temperature, preheating the oven, the preparation of the baking sheet, the way to time the cooking, and the need to protect your hands when removing the muffins from the oven.

   • Consider those instructions from the point of view of a cooking novice (if you are not one, get help from a friend who does not know how to cook). Fill in the steps that the book's author (almost certainly an experienced cook) left out for being obvious.

   • Build a glossary of terms used. (What's a muffin pan? What does preheat do? What do you mean by "oven"?)

   • Now bake some muffins and enjoy your results.

5. Write a definition for each of the terms from "Terms." First try to see if you can do it without looking at the chapter (not likely), then look through the chapter to find definitions. You might find the difference between your first attempt and the book's version interesting. You might consult some suitable online glossary, such as www.research.att.com/~bs/glossary.html. By writing your own definition before looking it up, you reinforce the learning you achieved through your reading. If you have to reread a section to form a definition, that just helps you to understand. Feel free to use your own words for the definitions, and make the definitions as detailed as you think reasonable. Often, an example after the main definition will be helpful. You may like to store the definitions in a file so that you can add to them from the "Terms" sections of later chapters.

Postscript

What's so important about the "Hello, World!" program? Its purpose is to get us acquainted with the basic tools of programming. We tend to do an extremely simple example, such as "Hello, World!," whenever we approach a new tool. That way, we separate our learning into two parts: first we learn the basics of our tools with a trivial program, and later we learn about more complicated programs without being distracted by our tools. Learning the tools and the language simultaneously is far harder than doing first one and then the other. This approach to simplifying learning a complex task by breaking it into a series of small (and more manageable) steps is not limited to programming and computers. It is common and useful in most areas of life, especially in those that involve some practical skill.

3

Objects, Types, and Values

"Fortune favors the prepared mind."

—Louis Pasteur

This chapter introduces the basics of storing and using data in a program. To do so, we first concentrate on reading in data from the keyboard. After establishing the fundamental notions of objects, types, values, and variables, we introduce several operators and give many examples of use of variables of types **char**, **int**, **double**, and **string**.

3.1 Input

The "Hello, World!" program just writes to the screen. It produces output. It does not read anything; it does not get input from its user. That's rather a bore. Real programs tend to produce results based on some input we give them, rather than just doing the same thing each time we execute them.

To read something, we need somewhere to read into; that is, we need somewhere in the computer's memory to place what we read. We call such a "place" an object. An *object* is a region of memory with a *type* that specifies what kind of information can be placed in it. A named object is called a *variable*. For example, character strings are put into **string** variables and integers are put into **int** variables. You can think of an object as a "box" into which you can put a value of the object's type:

int:

age: | 42 |

This would represent an object of type **int** named **age** containing the integer value **42**. Using a string variable, we can read a string from input and write it out again like this:

```
// read and write a first name
#include "std_lib_facilities.h"  < iostream >
using namespace std;  <string>
int main()
{
        cout << "Please enter your first name (followed by 'enter'):\n";
        string first_name;      // first_name is a variable of type string
        cin >> first_name;      // read characters into first_name
        cout << "Hello, " << first_name << "!\n";
}
```

The **#include** and the **main**() are familiar from Chapter 2. Since the **#include** is needed for all our programs (up to Chapter 12), we'll leave it out of our presentation to avoid distraction. Similarly, we'll sometimes present code that will work only if it is placed in **main**() or some other function by itself, like this:

> **cout << "Please enter your first name (followed by 'enter'):\n";**

We assume that you can figure out how to put such code into a complete program for testing.

The first line of **main**() simply writes out a message encouraging the user to enter a first name. Such a message is typically called a *prompt* because it prompts the user to take an action. The next lines define a variable of type **string** called **first_name**, read input from the keyboard into that variable, and write out a greeting. Let's look at those three lines in turn:

> **string first_name;** // first_name is a variable of type string

This sets aside an area of memory for holding a string of characters and gives it the name **first_name**:

string:

first_name: ⬚

A statement that introduces a new name into a program and sets aside memory for a variable is called a *definition*.

The next line reads characters from input (the keyboard) into that variable:

> **cin >> first_name;** // read characters into name

The name **cin** refers to the standard input stream (pronounced "see-in," for "character **in**put") defined in the standard library. The second operand of the **>>** operator ("get from") specifies where that input goes. So, if we type some first name, say **Nicholas**, followed by a newline, the string **"Nicholas"** becomes the value of **first_name**:

string:

first_name: | Nicholas |

The newline is necessary to get the machine's attention. Until a newline is entered (the Enter key is hit), the computer simply collects characters. That "delay" gives you the chance to change your mind, erase some characters, and replace them with others before hitting Enter. The newline will not be part of the string stored in memory.

Having gotten the input string into **first_name**, we can use it:

> **cout << "Hello, " << first_name << "!\n";**

This prints **Hello,** followed by **Nicholas** (the value of **first_name**) followed by **!** and a newline (**'\n'**) on the screen:

> **Hello, Nicholas!**

If we had liked repetition and extra typing, we could have written three separate output statements instead:

> **cout << "Hello, ";**
> **cout << first_name;**
> **cout << "!\n";**

However, we are indifferent typists, and – more importantly – strongly dislike needless repetition (because repetition provides opportunity for errors), so we combined those three output operations into a single statement.

Note the way we use quotes around the characters in **"Hello, "** but not in **first_name**. We use quotes when we want a literal string. When we don't quote, we refer to the value of something with a name. Consider:

> **cout << "first_name" << " is " << first_name;**

Here, **"first_name"** gives us the ten characters **first_name** and plain **first_name** gives us the value of the variable **first_name**, in this case, **Nicholas**. So, we get

> **first_name is Nicholas**

3.2 Variables

Basically, we can do nothing of interest with a computer without storing data in memory, the way we did it with the input string in the example above. The "places" in which we store data are called *objects*. To access an object we need a *name*. A named object is called a *variable* and has a specific *type* (such as **int** or **string**) that determines what can be put into the object (e.g., **123** can go into an **int** and **"Hello, World!\n"** can go into a **string**) and which operations can be applied (e.g., we can multiply **ints** using the * operator and compare **strings** using the **<=** operator). The data items we put into variables are called *values*. A statement that defines a variable is (unsurprisingly) called a *definition*, and a definition can (and usually should) provide an initial value. Consider

```
string name = "Annemarie";
int number_of_steps = 39;
```

You can visualize these variables like this:

int: **string:**

number_of_steps: `39`   **name:**   `Annemarie`

You cannot put values of the wrong type into a variable:

```
string name2 = 39;                  // error: 39 isn't a string
int number_of_steps = "Annemarie";  // error: "Annemarie" is not an int
```

The compiler remembers the type of each variable and makes sure that you use it according to its type, as specified in its definition.

C++ provides a rather large number of types (see §A.8). However, you can write perfectly good programs using only five of those:

```
int number_of_steps = 39;      // int for integers
double flying_time = 3.5;       // double for floating-point numbers
char decimal_point = '.';       // char for individual characters
string name = "Annemarie";      // string for character strings
bool tap_on = true;             // bool for logical variables
```

The reason for the name **double** is historical: **double** is short for "double-precision floating point." Floating point is the computer's approximation to the mathematical concept of a real number.

Note that each of these types has its own characteristic style of literals:

```
39              // int: an integer
3.5             // double: a floating-point number
'.'             // char: an individual character enclosed in single quotes
"Annemarie"     // string: a sequence of characters delimited by double quotes
true            // bool: either true or false
```

That is, a sequence of digits (such as **1234**, **2**, or **976**) denotes an integer, a single character in single quotes (such as **'1'**, **'@'**, or **'x'**) denotes a character, a sequence of digits with a decimal point (such as **1.234**, **0.12**, or **.98**) denotes a floating-point value, and a sequence of characters enclosed in double quotes (such as **"1234"**, **"Howdy!"**, or **"Annemarie"**) denotes a string. For a detailed description of literals see §A.2.

3.3 Input and type

The input operation **>>** ("get from") is sensitive to type; that is, it reads according to the type of variable you read into. For example:

```
// read name and age
int main()
{
      cout << "Please enter your first name and age\n";
      string first_name;      // string variable
      int age;                // integer variable
      cin >> first_name;      // read a string
      cin >> age;             // read an integer
      cout << "Hello, " << first_name << " (age " << age << ")\n";
}
```

So, if you type in **Carlos 22** the **>>** operator will read **Carlos** into **first_name**, **22** into **age**, and produce this output:

Hello, Carlos (age 22)

Why won't it read (all of) **Carlos 22** into **first_name**? Because, by convention, reading of strings is terminated by what is called *whitespace*, that is, space, newline, and tab characters. Otherwise, whitespace by default is ignored by **>>**. For example, you can add as many spaces as you like before a number to be read; **>>** will just skip past them and read the number.

If you type in **22 Carlos**, you'll see something that might be surprising until you think about it. The **22** will be read into **first_name** because, after all, **22** is a sequence of characters. On the other hand, **Carlos** isn't an integer, so it will not be read. The output will be **22** followed by some random number, such as **–96739** or **0**. Why? You didn't give **age** an initial value and you didn't succeed in reading a value into it. Therefore, you get some "garbage value" that happened to be in that part of memory when you started executing. In §10.6, we look at ways to handle "input format errors." For now, let's just initialize **age** so that we get a predictable value if the input fails:

```
// read name and age (2nd version)
int main()
{
      cout << "Please enter your first_name and age\n";
```

```
        string first_name = "???";    // string variable
                                      // ("???" means "don't know the name")
        int age = -1;      // integer variable (-1 means "don't know the age")
        cin >> first_name >> age;      // read a string followed by an integer
        cout << "Hello, " << first_name << " (age " << age << ")\n";
}
```

Now the input **22 Carlos** will output

> **Hello 22 (age -1)**

Note that we can read several values in a single input statement, just as we can write several values in a single output statement. Note also that **<<** is sensitive to type, just as **>>** is, so we can output the **int** variable **age** and the character literal **'\n'** as well as the **string** variable **first_name** and the string literals **"Hello, "** and **" (age "**.

A **string** read using **>>** is (by default) terminated by whitespace; that is, it reads a single word. But sometimes, we want to read more than one word. There are of course many ways of doing this. For example, we can read a name consisting of two words like this:

```
int main()
{
        cout << "Please enter your first and second names\n";
        string first;
        string second;
        cin >> first >> second;        // read two strings
        cout << "Hello, " << first << ' ' << second << '\n';
}
```

We simply used **>>** twice, once for each name. When we want to write the names to output we must insert a space between them.

TRY THIS

Get the "name and age" example to run. Then, modify it to write out the age in months: read the input in years and multiply (using the * operator) by 12. Read the age into a **double** to allow for children who can be very proud of being 5.5 years old rather than just 5.

3.4 Operations and operators

In addition to specifying what values can be stored in a variable, the type of a variable determines what operations we can apply to it and what they mean. For example:

```
int count;
cin >> count;              // >> reads an integer into count
string name;
cin >> name;               // >> reads a string into name

int c2 = count+2;          // + adds integers
string s2 = name + " Jr. ";   // + appends characters

int c3 = count-2;          // - subtracts integers
string s3 = name - "Jr. ";    // error: - isn't defined for strings
```

By "error" we mean that the compiler will reject a program trying to subtract strings. The compiler knows exactly which operations can be applied to each variable and can therefore prevent many mistakes. However, the compiler doesn't know which operations make sense to you for which values, so it will happily accept legal operations that yield results that may look absurd to you. For example:

```
int age = -100;
```

It may be obvious to you that you can't have a negative age (why not?) but nobody told the compiler, so it'll produce code for that definition.

Here is a table of useful operators for some common and useful types:

	bool	char	int	double	string
assignment	=	=	=	=	=
addition			+	+	
concatenation					+
subtraction			−	−	
multiplication			*	*	
division			/	/	
remainder (modulo)			%		
increment by 1			++	++	
decrement by 1			--	--	
increment by **n**			+= n	+= n	

	bool	char	int	double	string
add to end					+=
decrement by **n**			–= n	–= n	
multiply and assign			*=	*=	
divide and assign			/=	/=	
remainder and assign			%=		
read from **s** into **x**	s >> x	s >> x	s >> x	s >> x	s >> x
write **x** to **s**	s << x	s << x	s << x	s << x	s << x
equals	==	==	==	==	==
not equal	!=	!=	!=	!=	!=
greater than	>	>	>	>	>
greater than or equal	>=	>=	>=	>=	>=
less than	<	<	<	<	<
less than or equal	<=	<=	<=	<=	<=

A blank square indicates that an operation is not directly available for a type (though there may be indirect ways of using that operation; see §3.7). We'll explain these operations, and more, as we go along. The key points here are that there are a lot of useful operators and that their meaning tends to be the same for similar types.

Let's try an example involving floating-point numbers:

```
// simple program to exercise operators
#include <iostream>
#include <cmath>
using namespace std;
int main()
{
        cout << "Please enter a floating-point value: ";
        double n;
        cin >> n;
        cout << "n == " << n
                << "\nn+1 == " << n+1
                << "\nthree times n == " << 3*n
                << "\ntwice n == " << n+n
                << "\nn squared == " << n*n
                << "\nhalf of n == " << n/2
                << "\nsquare root of n == " << sqrt(n)
                << endl;        // another name for newline ("end of line")
}
```

Obviously, the usual arithmetic operations have their usual notation and meaning as we know them from primary school. Naturally, not everything we might want to do to a floating-point number, such as taking its square root, is available as an operator. Many operations are represented as named functions. In this case, we use **sqrt()** from the standard library to get the square root of **n**: **sqrt(n)**. The notation is familiar from math. We'll use functions along the way and discuss them in some detail in §4.5 and §8.5.

TRY THIS

Get this little program to run. Then, modify it to read an **int** rather than a **double**. Note that **sqrt()** is not defined for an **int** so assign **n** to a **double** and take **sqrt()** of that. Also, "exercise" some other operations. Note that for **ints** / is integer division and % is remainder (modulo), so that **5/2** is **2** (and not **2.5** or **3**) and **5%2** is **1**. The definitions of integer *, /, and % guarantee that for two positive **ints a** and **b** we have **a/b * b + a%b == a**.

Strings have fewer operators, but as we'll see in Chapter 23, they have plenty of named operations. However, the operators they do have can be used conventionally. For example:

```
// read first and second name
int main()
{
        cout << "Please enter your first and second names\n";
        string first;
        string second;
        cin >> first >> second;              // read two strings
        string name = first + ' ' + second;  // concatenate strings
        cout << "Hello, " << name << '\n';
}
```

For strings + means concatenation; that is, when **s1** and **s2** are strings, **s1+s2** is a string where the characters from **s1** are followed by the characters from **s2**. For example, if **s1** has the value **"Hello"** and **s2** the value **"World"** then **s1+s2** will have the value **"HelloWorld"**. Comparison of **strings** is particularly useful:

```
// read and compare names
int main()
{
        cout << "Please enter two names\n";
        string first;
        string second;
        cin >> first >> second;     // read two strings
        if (first == second) cout << "that's the same name twice\n";
```

```
    if (first < second)
        cout << first << " is alphabetically before " << second <<'\n';
    if (first > second)
        cout << first << " is alphabetically after " << second <<'\n';
}
```

Here, we used an **if**-statement, which will be explained in detail in §4.4.1.1, to select actions based on conditions.

3.5 Assignment and initialization

In many ways, the most interesting operator is assignment, represented as =. It gives a variable a new value. For example:

int a = 3;   // a starts out with the value 3

a: | 3 |

a = 4;   // a gets the value 4 ("becomes 4")

a: | 4 |

int b = a;   // b starts out with a copy of a's value (that is, 4)

a: | 4 |
b: | 4 |

b = a+5;   // b gets the value a+5 (that is, 9)

a: | 4 |
b: | 9 |

a = a+7;   // a gets the value a+7 (that is, 11)

a: | 11 |
b: | 9 |

That last assignment deserves notice. First of all it clearly shows that = does not mean equals — clearly, **a** doesn't equal **a+7**. It means assignment, that is, to place a new value in a variable. What is done for **a=a+7** is the following:

1. First, get the value of **a**; that's the integer 4.
2. Next, add 7 to that 4, yielding the integer 11.
3. Finally, put that 11 into **a**.

We can also illustrate assignments using strings:

string a = "alpha";   *// a starts out with the value "alpha"*

        a: **alpha**

a = "beta";   *// a gets the value "beta" (becomes "beta")*

        a: **beta**

string b = a;   *// b starts out with a copy of a's value (that is, "beta")*

        a: **beta**
        b: **beta**

b = a+"gamma";   *// b gets the value a+"gamma" (that is, "betagamma")*

        a: **beta**
        b: **betagamma**

a = a+"delta";   *// a gets the value a+"delta" (that is, "betadelta")*

        a: **betadelta**
        b: **betagamma**

Above, we use "starts out with" and "gets" to distinguish two similar, but logically distinct, operations:

- Initialization (giving a variable its initial value)
- Assignment (giving a variable a new value)

These operations are so similar that C++ allows us to use the same notation (the =) for both:

```
int y = 8;          // initialize y with 8
x = 9;              // assign 9 to x

string t = "howdy!";   // initialize t with "howdy!"
s = "G'day";           // assign "G'day" to s
```

However, logically assignment and initialization are different. You can tell the two apart by the type specification (like **int** or **string**) that always starts an initialization; an assignment does not have that. In principle, an initialization always finds the variable empty. On the other hand, an assignment (in principle) must clear out the old value from the variable before putting in the new value. You can think of the variable as a kind of small box and the value as a concrete thing, such as a coin, that you put into it. Before initialization, the box is empty, but after initialization it always holds a coin so that to put a new coin in, you (i.e., the assignment operator) first have to remove the old one ("destroy the old value") – and you cannot leave the box empty. Things are not quite this literal in the computer's memory, but it's not a bad way of thinking of what's going on.

3.5.1 An example: delete repeated words

Assignment is needed when we want to put a new value into an object. When you think of it, it is obvious that assignment is most useful when you do things many times. We need an assignment when we want to do something again with a different value. Let's have a look at a little program that detects adjacent repeated words in a sequence of words. Such code is part of most grammar checkers:

```
int main()
{
    string previous = " ";        // previous word; initialized to "not a word"
    string current;               // current word
    while (cin>>current) {        // read a stream of words
        if (previous == current)      // check if the word is the same as last
            cout << "repeated word: " << current << '\n';
        previous = current;
    }
}
```

This program is not the most helpful since it doesn't tell where the repeated word occurred in the text, but it'll do for now. We will look at this program line by line starting with

```
string current;     // current word
```

This is the string variable into which we immediately read the current (i.e., most recently read) word using

```
while (cin>>current)
```

This construct, called a **while**-statement, is interesting in its own right, and we'll examine it further in §4.4.2.1. The **while** says that the statement after (**cin>>current**) is to be repeated as long as the input operation **cin>>current** succeeds, and **cin>>current** will succeed as long as there are characters to read on the standard input. Remember that for a **string**, **>>** reads whitespace-separated words. You terminate this loop by giving the program an end-of-input character (usually referred to as *end of file*). On a Windows machine, that's Ctrl+Z (Control and Z pressed together) followed by an Enter (return). On a Unix or Linux machine that's Ctrl+D (Control and D pressed together).

So, what we do is to read a word into **current** and then compare it to the previous word (stored in **previous**). If they are the same, we say so:

```
if (previous == current)      // check if the word is the same as last
        cout << "repeated word: " << current << '\n';
```

Then we have to get ready to do this again for the next word. We do that by copying the **current** word into **previous**:

```
previous = current;
```

This handles all cases provided that we can get started. What should this code do for the first word where we have no previous word to compare? This problem is dealt with by the definition of **previous**:

```
string previous = " ";      // previous word; initialized to "not a word"
```

The " " contains only a single character (the space character, the one we get by hitting the space bar on our keyboard). The input operator **>>** skips whitespace, so we couldn't possibly read that from input. Therefore, the first time through the **while**-statement, the test

```
if (previous == current)
```

fails (as we want it to).

One way of understanding program flow is to "play computer," that is, to follow the program line for line, doing what it specifies. Just draw boxes on a piece of paper and write their values into them. Change the values stored as specified by the program.

TRY THIS

Execute this program yourself using a piece of paper. Use the input "**The cat cat jumped**". Even experienced programmers use this technique to visualize the actions of small sections of code that somehow don't seem completely obvious.

TRY THIS

Get the "repeated word detection program" to run. Test it with the sentence **"She she laughed He He He because what he did did not look very very good good"**. How many repeated words were there? Why? What is the definition of *word* used here? What is the definition of *repeated word*? (For example, is **"She she"** a repetition?)

3.6 Composite assignment operators

Incrementing a variable (that is, adding 1 to it) is so common in programs that C++ provides a special syntax for it. For example:

```
++counter
```

means

```
counter = counter + 1
```

There are many other common ways of changing the value of a variable based on its current value. For example, we might like to add 7 to it, to subtract 9, or to multiply it by 2. Such operations are also supported directly by C++. For example:

```
a += 7;      // means a = a+7
b –= 9;      // means b = b–9
c *= 2;      // means c = c*2
```

In general, for any binary operator **oper, a oper= b** means **a = a oper b** (§A.5). For starters, that rule gives us operators +=, –=, *=, /=, and %=. This provides a pleasantly compact notation that directly reflects our ideas. For example, in many application domains /= and %= are referred to as "scaling."

3.6.1 An example: count repeated words

Consider the example detecting repeated adjacent words above. We could improve that by giving an idea of where the repeated word was in the sequence. A simple variation of that idea simply counts the words and outputs the count for the repeated word:

```
int main()
{
```

```
int number_of_words = 0;
string previous = " ";      // not a word
string current;
while (cin>>current) {
        ++number_of_words;    // increase word count
        if (previous == current)
                cout << "word number " << number_of_words
                        << " repeated: "<< current << '\n';
        previous = current;
    }
}
```

We start our word counter at 0. Each time we see a word, we increment that counter:

```
++number_of_words;
```

That way, the first word becomes number 1, the next number 2, and so on. We could have accomplished the same by saying

```
number_of_words += 1;
```

or even

```
number_of_words = number_of_words+1;
```

but **++number_of_words** is shorter and expresses the idea of incrementing directly.

Note how similar this program is to the one from §3.5.1. Obviously, we just took the program from §3.5.1 and modified it a bit to serve our new purpose. That's a very common technique: when we need to solve a problem, we look for a similar problem and use our solution for that with suitable modification. Don't start from scratch unless you really have to. Using a previous version of a program as a base for modification often saves a lot of time, and we benefit from much of the effort that went into the original program.

3.7 Names

We name our variables so that we can remember them and refer to them from other parts of a program. What can be a name in C++? In a C++ program, a name starts with a letter and contains only letters, digits, and underscores. For example:

x
number_of_elements
Fourier_transform
z2
Polygon

The following are not names:

2x	// a name must start with a letter
timetomarket	// $ is not a letter, digit, or underscore
Start menu	// space is not a letter, digit, or underscore

When we say "not names" we mean that a C++ compiler will not accept them as names.

If you read system code or machine-generated code, you might see names starting with underscores, such as **_foo**. Never write those yourself; such names are reserved for implementation and system entities. By avoiding leading underscores, you will never find your names clashing with some name that the implementation generated.

Names are case sensitive; that is, uppercase and lowercase letters are distinct, so **x** and **X** are different names. This little program has at least four errors:

```
#include "std_lib_facilities.h"

int Main()
{
    String s = "Goodbye, cruel world! ";
    cOut << S << '\n';
}
```

It is usually not a good idea to define names that differ only in the case of a character, such as **one** and **One**; that will not confuse a compiler, but it can easily confuse a programmer.

TRY THIS

Compile the "Goodbye, cruel world!" program and examine the error messages. Did the compiler find all the errors? What did it suggest as the problems? Did the compiler get confused and diagnose more than four errors? Remove the errors one by one, starting with the lexically first, and see how the error messages change (and improve).

The C++ language reserves many (about 70) names as "keywords." We list them in §A.3.1. You can't use those to name your variables, types, functions, etc. For example:

    int if = 7;   // error: "if" is a keyword

You can use names of facilities in the standard library, such as **string**, but you shouldn't. Reuse of such a common name will cause trouble if you should ever want to use the standard library:

    int string = 7;   // this will lead to trouble

When you choose names for your variables, functions, types, etc., choose meaningful names; that is, choose names that will help people understand your program. Even you will have problems understanding what your program is supposed to do if you have littered it with variables with "easy to type" names like **x1**, **x2**, **s3**, and **p7**. Abbreviations and acronyms can confuse people, so use them sparingly. These acronyms were obvious to us when we wrote them, but we expect you'll have trouble with at least one:

    mtbf
    TLA
    myw
    NBV

We expect that in a few months, we'll also have trouble with at least one.

Short names, such as **x** and **i**, are meaningful when used conventionally; that is, **x** should be a local variable or a parameter (see §4.5 and §8.4) and **i** should be a loop index (see §4.4.2.3).

Don't use overly long names; they are hard to type, make lines so long that they don't fit on a screen, and are hard to read quickly. These are probably OK:

    partial_sum
    element_count
    stable_partition

These are probably too long:

    the_number_of_elements
    remaining_free_slots_in_symbol_table

Our "house style" is to use underscores to separate words in an identifier, such as **element_count**, rather than alternatives, such as **elementCount** and **Element-Count**. We never use names with all capital letters, such as **ALL_CAPITAL_LETTERS**, because that's conventionally reserved for macros (§27.8 and §A.17.2), which we avoid. We use an initial capital letter for types we define, such as **Square** and **Graph**. The C++ language and standard library don't use capital letters, so it's **int** rather than **Int** and **string** rather than **String**. Thus, our convention helps to minimize confusion between our types and the standard ones.

Avoid names that are easy to mistype, misread, or confuse. For example:

Name	names	nameS
foo	f00	fl
f1	fl	fi

The characters **0, o, O, 1, l, I** are particularly prone to cause trouble.

3.8 Types and objects

The notion of type is central to C++ and most other programming languages. Let's take a closer and slightly more technical look at types, specifically at the types of the objects in which we store our data during computation. It'll save time in the long run, and it may save you some confusion.

- A *type* defines a set of possible values and a set of operations (for an object).
- An *object* is some memory that holds a value of a given type.
- A *value* is a set of bits in memory interpreted according to a type.
- A *variable* is a named object.
- A *declaration* is a statement that gives a name to an object.
- A *definition* is a declaration that sets aside memory for an object.

Informally, we think of an object as a box into which we can put values of a given type. An **int** box can hold integers, such as **7**, **42**, and **−399**. A **string** box can hold character string values, such as **"Interoperability"**, **"tokens: !@#$%^&*"**, and **"Old McDonald had a farm"**. Graphically, we can think of it like this:

```
int a = 7;                          a: [    7    ]

int b = 9;                          b: [    9    ]

char c = 'a';                       c: [ a ]

double x = 1.2;                     x: [      1.2      ]

string s1 = "Hello, World!";        s1: [  13  | Hello, World! ]

string s2 = "1.2";                  s2: [  3  |   1.2   ]
```

The representation of a **string** is a bit more complicated than that of an **int** because a **string** keeps track of the number of characters it holds. Note that a **double** stores a number whereas a **string** stores characters. For example, x stores the number **1.2**, whereas **s2** stores the three characters **'1'**, **'.'**, and **'2'**. The quotes for character and string literals are not stored.

Every **int** is of the same size; that is, the compiler sets aside the same fixed amount of memory for each **int**. On a typical desktop computer, that amount is 4 bytes (32 bits). Similarly, **bools**, **chars**, and **doubles** are fixed size. You'll typically find that a desktop computer uses a byte (8 bits) for a **bool** or a **char** and 8 bytes for a **double**. Note that different types of objects take up different amounts of space. In particular, a **char** takes up less space than an **int**, and **string** differs from **double**, **int**, and **char** in that different strings take up different amounts of space.

The meaning of bits in memory is completely dependent on the type used to access it. Think of it this way: computer memory doesn't know about our types; it's just memory. The bits of memory get meaning only when we decide how that memory is to be interpreted. This is similar to what we do every day when we use numbers. What does **12.5** mean? We don't know. It could be **$12.5** or **12.5cm** or **12.5gallons**. Only when we supply the unit does the notation **12.5** mean anything.

For example, the very same bits of memory that represent the value **120** when looked upon as an **int** would be **'x'** when looked upon as a **char**. If looked at as a **string**, it wouldn't make sense at all and would become a run-time error if we tried to use it. We can illustrate this graphically like this, using 1 and 0 to indicate the value of bits in memory:

> **00000000 00000000 00000000 01111000**

This is the setting of the bits of an area of memory (a word) that could be read as an **int** (**120**) or as a **char** (**'x'**, looking at the rightmost 8 bits only). A **bit** is a unit of computer memory that can hold the value 0 or 1. For the meaning of *binary* numbers, see §A.2.1.1.

3.9 Type safety

Every object is given a type when it is defined. A program — or a part of a program — is type-safe when objects are used only according to the rules for their type. Unfortunately, there are ways of doing operations that are not type-safe. For example, using a variable before it has been initialized is not considered type-safe:

```
int main()
{
    double x;            // we "forgot" to initialize:
                         // the value of x is undefined
```

```
        double y = x;         // the value of y is undefined
        double z = 2.0+x;     // the meaning of + and the value of z are undefined
}
```

An implementation is even allowed to give a hardware error when the uninitialized **x** is used. Always initialize your variables! There are a few — very few — exceptions to this rule, such as a variable we immediately use as the target of an input operation, but always to initialize is a good habit that'll save you a lot of grief.

Complete type safety is the ideal and therefore the general rule for the language. Unfortunately, a C++ compiler cannot guarantee complete type safety, but we can avoid type safety violations through a combination of good coding practice and run-time checks. The ideal is never to use language features that the compiler cannot prove to be safe: static type safety. Unfortunately, that's too restrictive for most interesting uses of programming. The obvious fallback, that the compiler implicitly generates code that checks for type safety violations and catches all of them, is beyond C++. When we decide to do things that are (type) unsafe, we must do some checking ourselves. We'll point out such cases, as we get to them.

The ideal of type safety is incredibly important when writing code. That's why we spend time on it this early in the book. Please note the pitfalls and avoid them.

3.9.1 Safe conversions

In §3.4, we saw that we couldn't directly add **char**s or compare a **double** to an **int**. However, C++ provides an indirect way to do both. When needed, a **char** is converted to an **int** and an **int** is converted to a **double**. For example:

```
    char c = 'x';
    int i1 = c;
    int i2 = 'x';
```

Here both **i1** and **i2** get the value **120**, which is the integer value of the character '**x**' in the most popular 8-bit character set, ASCII. This is a simple and safe way of getting the numeric representation of a character. We call this **char**-to-**int** conversion safe because no information is lost; that is, we can copy the resulting **int** back into a **char** and get the original value:

```
    char c2 = i1;
    cout << c << ' ' << i1 << ' ' << c2 << '\n';
```

This will print

```
    x 120 x
```

In this sense – that a value is always converted to an equal value or (for **doubles**) to the best approximation of an equal value – these conversions are safe:

bool to **char**
bool to **int**
bool to **double**
char to **int**
char to **double**
int to **double**

The most useful conversion is **int** to **double** because it allows us to mix **ints** and **doubles** in expressions:

```
double d1 = 2.3;
double d2 = d1+2;     // 2 is converted to 2.0 before adding
if (d1 < 0)            // 0 is converted to 0.0 before comparison
      error("d1 is negative");
```

For a really large **int**, we can (for some computers) suffer a loss of precision when converting to **double**. This is a rare problem.

3.9.2 Unsafe conversions

Safe conversions are usually a boon to the programmer and simplify writing code. Unfortunately, C++ also allows for (implicit) unsafe conversions. By unsafe, we mean that a value can be implicitly turned into a value of another type that does not equal the original value. For example:

```
int main()
{
      int a = 20000;
      char c = a;     // try to squeeze a large int into a small char
      int b = c;
      if (a != b)      // != means "not equal"
            cout << "oops!: " << a << "!=" << b << '\n';
      else
            cout << "Wow! We have large characters\n";
}
```

Such conversions are also called "narrowing" conversions, because they put a value into an object that may be too small ("narrow") to hold it. Unfortunately, few compilers warn about the unsafe initialization of the **char** with an **int**. The problem is that an **int** is typically much larger than a **char**, so that it can (and in this case does) hold an **int** value that cannot be represented as a **char**. Try it to see what value **b** gets on your machine (**32** is a common result); better still, experiment:

```
int main()
{
    double d =0;
    while (cin>>d) {      // repeat the statements below
                          // as long as we type in numbers
        int i = d;        // try to squeeze a double into an int
        char c = i;       // try to squeeze an int into a char
        int i2 = c;       // get the integer value of the character
        cout << "d==" << d                  // the original double
             << " i=="<< i                  // converted to int
             << " i2==" << i2               // int value of char
             << " char(" << c << ")\n";     // the char
    }
}
```

The **while**-statement that we use to allow many values to be tried will be explained in §4.4.2.1.

TRY THIS

> Run this program with a variety of inputs. Try small values (e.g., **2** and **3**); try large values (larger than **127**, larger than **1000**); try negative values; try **56**; try **89**; try **128**; try non-integer values (e.g., **56.9** and **56.2**). In addition to showing how conversions from **double** to **int** and conversions from **int** to **char** are done on your machine, this program shows you what character (if any) your machine will print for a given integer value.

You'll find that many input values produce "unreasonable" results. Basically, we are trying to put a gallon into a pint pot (about 4 liters into a 500ml glass). All of the conversions

    double to **int**
    double to **char**
    double to **bool**
    int to **char**

int to **bool**
char to **bool**

are accepted by the compiler even though they are unsafe. They are unsafe in the sense that the value stored might differ from the value assigned. Why can this be a problem? Because often we don't suspect that an unsafe conversion is taking place. Consider:

```
double x = 2.7;
// lots of code
int y = x;      // y becomes 2
```

By the time we define **y** we may have forgotten that **x** was a **double**, or we may have temporarily forgotten that **double**-to-**int** conversion truncates (always rounds down) rather than using the conventional 4/5 rounding. What happens is perfectly predictable, but there is nothing in the **int y = x;** to remind us that information (the **.7**) is thrown away.

Conversions from **int** to **char** don't have problems with truncation – neither **int** nor **char** can represent a fraction of an integer. However, a **char** can hold only very small integer values. On a PC, a **char** is 1 byte whereas an **int** is 4 bytes:

char: ☐

int: ☐☐☐☐

So, we can't put a large number, such as 1000, into a **char** without loss of information: the value is "narrowed." For example:

```
int a = 1000;
char b = a;    // b becomes -24 (on some machines)
```

Not all **int** values have **char** equivalents, and the exact range of **char** values depends on the particular implementation. On a PC the range of **char** values is [-128:127], but only [0,127] can be used portably because not every computer is a PC, and different computers have different ranges for their **char** values, such as [0:255].

Why do people accept the problem of narrowing conversions? The major reason is history: C++ inherited narrowing conversions from its ancestor language, C, so from day one of C++, there existed much code that depended on narrowing conversions. Also, many such conversions don't actually cause problems because the values involved happen to be in range, and many programmers object to compilers "telling them what to do." In particular, the problems with unsafe conversions are often manageable in small programs and for experienced programmers. They can be a source of errors in larger programs, though, and a significant cause of problems for novice programmers. However, compilers can warn about narrowing conversions – and many do.

So what should you do if you think that a conversion might lead to a bad value? You simply check the value before assigning as we did in the first example in this section. See §5.6.4 and §7.5 for a simplified way of doing such checking.

Drill

After each step of this drill, run your program to make sure it is really doing what you expect it to. Keep a list of what mistakes you make so that you can try to avoid those in the future.

1. This drill is to write a program that produces a simple form letter based on user input. Begin by typing the code from §3.1 prompting a user to enter his or her first name and writing "Hello, **first_name**" where **first_name** is the name entered by the user. Then modify your code as follows: change the prompt to "Enter the name of the person you want to write to" and change the output to "Dear **first_name**,". Don't forget the comma.

2. Add an introductory line or two, like "How are you? I am fine. I miss you." Be sure to indent the first line. Add a few more lines of your choosing – it's your letter.

3. Now prompt the user for the name of another friend, and store it in **friend_name**. Add a line to your letter: "Have you seen **friend_name** lately?"

4. Declare a **char** variable called **friend_sex** and initialize its value to 0. Prompt the user to enter an **m** if the friend is male and an **f** if the friend is female. Assign the value entered to the variable **friend_sex**. Then use two **if**-statements to write the following:

   If the friend is male, write "If you see **friend_name** please ask him to call me."

   If the friend is female, write "If you see **friend_name** please ask her to call me."

5. Prompt the user to enter the age of the recipient and assign it to an **int** variable **age**. Have your program write "I hear you just had a birthday and you are **age** years old." If **age** is 0 or less or 110 or more, call **error("you're kidding!")**.

6. Add this to your letter:

If your friend is under 12, write "Next year you will be **age+1**."

If your friend is 17, write "Next year you will be able to vote."

If your friend is over 70, write "I hope you are enjoying retirement."

Check your program to make sure it responds appropriately to each kind of value.

7. Add "Yours sincerely," followed by two blank lines for a signature, followed by your name.

Review

1. What is meant by the term *prompt*?
2. Which operator do you use to read into a variable?
3. If you want the user to input an integer value into your program for a variable named **number**, what are two lines of code you could write to ask the user to do it and to input the value into your program?
4. What is **\n** called and what purpose does it serve?
5. What terminates input into a string?
6. What terminates input into an integer?
7. How would you write

```
cout << "Hello, ";
cout << first_name;
cout << "!\n";
```

as a single line of code?
8. What is an object?
9. What is a literal?
10. What kinds of literals are there?
11. What is a variable?
12. What are typical sizes for a **char**, an **int**, and a **double**?
13. What measures do we use for the size of small entities in memory, such as **ints** and **strings**?
14. What is the difference between = and ==?
15. What is a definition?
16. What is an initialization and how does it differ from an assignment?
17. What is string concatenation and how do you make it work in C++?
18. Which of the following are legal names in C++? If a name is not legal, why not?

This_little_pig	This_1_is fine	2_For_1_special
latest thing	the_$12_method	_this_is_ok
MiniMineMine	number	correct?

19. Give five examples of legal names that you shouldn't use because they are likely to cause confusion.
20. What are some good rules for choosing names?
21. What is type safety and why is it important?
22. Why can conversion from **double** to **int** be a bad thing?
23. Define a rule to help decide if a conversion from one type to another is safe or unsafe.

Terms

assignment	definition	operation
cin	increment	operator
concatenation	initialization	type
conversion	name	type safety
declaration	narrowing	value
decrement	object	variable

Exercises

1. If you haven't done so already, do the **Try this** exercises from this chapter.
2. Write a program in C++ that converts from miles to kilometers. Your program should have a reasonable prompt for the user to enter a number of miles. Hint: There are 1.609 kilometers to the mile.
3. Write a program that doesn't do anything, but declares a number of variables with legal and illegal names (such as **int double = 0;**), so that you can see how the compiler reacts.
4. Write a program that prompts the user to enter two integer values. Store these values in **int** variables named **val1** and **val2**. Write your program to determine the smallest, largest, sum, difference, product, and ratio of these values and report them to the user.
5. Modify the program above to ask the user to enter floating-point values and store them in **double** variables. Compare the outputs of the two programs for some inputs of your choice. Are the results the same? Should they be? What's the difference?
6. Write a program that prompts the user to enter three integer values, and then outputs the values in numerical sequence separated by commas. So, if the user enters the values 10 4 6, the output should be 4, 6, 10. If two values are the same, they should just be ordered together. So, the input 4 5 4 should give 4, 4, 5.
7. Do exercise 6, but with three string values. So, if the user enters the values "**Steinbeck**", "**Hemingway**", "**Fitzgerald**", the output should be "**Fitzgerald, Hemingway, Steinbeck**".

8. Write a program to test an integer value to determine if it is odd or even. As always, make sure your output is clear and complete. In other words, don't just output "yes" or "no." Your output should stand alone, like "The value 4 is an even number." Hint: See the remainder (modulo) operator in §3.4.

9. Write a program that converts spelled-out numbers such as "zero" and "two" into digits, such as 0 and 2. When the user inputs a number, the program should print out the corresponding digit. Do it for the values 0, 1, 2, 3, and 4 and write out "not a number I know" if the user enters something that doesn't correspond, such as "stupid computer!"

10. Write a program that takes an operation followed by two operands and outputs the result. For example:

> + 100 3.14
> * 4 5

Read the operation into a string called **operation** and use an **if**-statement to figure out which operation the user wants, for example, **if (operation=="+")**. Read the operands into variables of type **double**. Implement this for operations called +, –, *, /, plus, minus, mul, and div with their obvious meanings.

11. Write a program that prompts the user to enter some number of pennies (1-cent coins), nickels (5-cent coins), dimes (10-cent coins), quarters (25-cent coins), half dollars (50-cent coins), and one-dollar coins (100-cent coins). Query the user separately for the number of each size coin, e.g., "How many pennies do you have?" Then your program should print out something like this:

You have 23 pennies.

You have 17 nickels.

You have 14 dimes.

You have 7 quarters.

You have 3 half dollars.

The value of all of your coins is 573 cents.
You may have to use your imagination to get the numbers to add up right-justified, but try; it can be done. Make some improvements: if only one of a coin is reported, make the output grammatically correct, e.g., "14 dimes" and "1 dime" (not "1 dimes"). Also, report the sum in dollars and cents, i.e., $5.73 instead of 573 cents.

Postscript

Please don't underestimate the importance of the notion of type safety. Types are at the center of most notions of correct programs, and some of the most effective techniques for constructing programs rely on the design and use of types – as you'll see in Chapters 6 and 9, Parts II, III, and IV.

4

Computation

> "If it doesn't have to produce correct results,
> I can make it arbitrarily fast."

—Gerald M. Weinberg

This chapter presents the basics of computation. In particular, we discuss how to compute a value from a set of operands (*expression*), how to choose among alternative actions (*selection*), and how to repeat a computation for a series of values (*iteration*). We also show how a particular sub-computation can be named and specified separately (a *function*). Our primary concern is to express computations in ways that lead to correct and well-organized programs. To help you perform more realistic computations, we introduce the **vector** type to hold sequences of values.

4.1 Computation

From one point of view, all that a program ever does is to compute; that is, it takes some inputs and produces some output. After all, we call the hardware on which we run the program a computer. This view is accurate and reasonable as long as we take a broad view of what constitutes input and output:

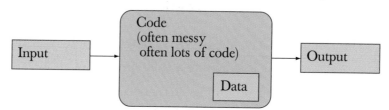

The input can come from a keyboard, from a mouse, from a touch screen, from files, from other input devices, from other programs, from other parts of a program. "Other input devices" is a category that contains most really interesting input sources: music keyboards, video recorders, network connections, temperature sensors, digital camera image sensors, etc. The variety is essentially infinite.

To deal with input, a program usually contains some data, sometimes referred to as its *data structures* or its *state*. For example, a calendar program may contain lists of holidays in various countries and a list of your appointments. Some of that data is part of the program from the start; other data is built up as the program reads input and collects useful information from it. For example, the calendar program will probably build your list of appointments from the input you give it. For the calendar, the main inputs are the requests to see the months and days you ask for (probably using mouse clicks) and the appointments you give it to keep track of (probably by typing information on your keyboard). The output is the display of calendars and appointments, plus the buttons and prompts for input that the calendar program writes on your screen.

Input comes from a wide variety of sources. Similarly, output can go to a wide variety of destinations. Output can be to a screen, to files, to other output devices, to other programs, and to other parts of a program. Examples of output devices include network interfaces, music synthesizers, electric motors, light generators, heaters, etc.

From a programming point of view the most important and interesting categories are "to/from another program" and "to/from other parts of a program." Most of the rest of this book could be seen as discussing that last category: how do we express a program as a set of cooperating parts and how can they share and exchange data? These are key questions in programming. We can illustrate that graphically:

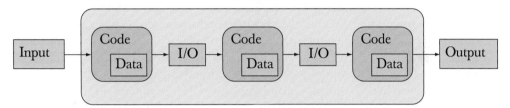

The abbreviation *I/O* stands for "input/output." In this case, the output from one part of code is the input for the next part. What such "parts of a program" share is data stored in main memory, on persistent storage devices (such as disks), or transmitted over network connections. By "parts of a program" we mean entities such as a function producing a result from a set of input arguments (e.g., a square root from a floating-point number), a function performing an action on a physical object (e.g., a function drawing a line on a screen), or a function modifying some table within the program (e.g., a function adding a name to a table of customers).

When we say "input" and "output" we generally mean information coming into and out of a computer, but as you see, we can also use the terms for information given to or produced by a part of a program. Inputs to a part of a program are often called *arguments* and outputs from a part of a program are often called *results*.

By *computation* we simply mean the act of producing some outputs based on some inputs, such as producing the result (output) **49** from the argument (input) **7** using the computation (function) **square** (see §4.5). As a possibly helpful curiosity, we note that until the 1950s a computer was defined as a person who did computations, such as an accountant, a navigator, or a physicist. Today, we simply delegate most computations to computers (machines) of various forms, of which the pocket calculator is among the simplest.

4.2 Objectives and tools

Our job as programmers is to express computations

- Correctly
- Simply
- Efficiently

Please note the order of those ideals: it doesn't matter how fast a program is if it gives the wrong results. Similarly, a correct and efficient program can be so complicated that it must be thrown away or completely rewritten to produce a new version (release). Remember, useful programs will always be modified to accommodate new needs, new hardware, etc. Therefore a program — and any part of a program — should be as simple as possible to perform its task. For example, assume that you have written the perfect program for teaching basic arithmetic to children in your local school, and that its internal structure is a mess. Which language did you use to communicate with the children? English? English and Spanish? What if I'd like to use it in Finland? In Kuwait? How would you change the (natural) language used for communication with a child? If the internal structure of the program is a mess, the logically simple (but in practice almost always very difficult) operation of changing the natural language used to communicate with users becomes insurmountable.

Concerns about correctness, simplicity, and efficiency become ours the minute we start writing code for others and accept the responsibility to do that well; that is, we must accept that responsibility when we decide to become professionals. In practical terms, this means that we can't just throw code together until it appears to work; we must concern ourselves with the structure of code. Paradoxically, concerns for structure and "quality of code" are often the fastest way of getting something to work. When programming is done well, such concerns minimize the need for the most frustrating part of programming: debugging; that is, good program structure during development can minimize the number of mistakes made and the time needed to search for such errors and to remove them.

Our main tool for organizing a program — and for organizing our thoughts as we program — is to break up a big computation into many little ones. This technique comes in two variations:

- *Abstraction:* Hide details that we don't need to use a facility ("implementation details") behind a convenient and general interface. For example, rather than considering the details of how to sort a phone book (thick books have been written about how to sort), we just call the sort algorithm from the C++ standard library. All we need to know to sort is how to invoke (call) that algorithm, so we can write **sort(b,e)** where **b** and **e** refer to the beginning and the end of the phone book, respectively. Another example is the way we use computer memory. Direct use of memory can be quite messy, so we access it through typed and named variables (§3.2), standard library **vectors** (§4.6, Chapters 17–19), **maps** (Chapter 21), etc.

- *"Divide and conquer":* Here we take a large problem and divide it into several little ones. For example, if we need to build a dictionary, we can separate that job into three: read the data, sort the data, and output the data. Each of the resulting problems is significantly smaller than the original.

Why does this help? After all, a program built out of parts is likely to be slightly larger than a program where everything is optimally merged together. The reason is that we are not very good at dealing with large problems. The way we actually deal with those — in programming and elsewhere — is to break them down into smaller problems, and we keep breaking those into even smaller parts until we get something simple enough to understand and solve. In terms of programming, you'll find that a 1000-line program has far more than ten times as many errors as a 100-line program, so we try to compose the 1000-line program out of parts with fewer than 100 lines. For large programs, say 10,000,000 lines, applying abstraction and divide-and-conquer is not just an option, it's an essential requirement. We simply cannot write and maintain large monolithic programs. One way of looking at the rest of this book is as a long series of examples of problems that need to be broken up into smaller parts together with the tools and techniques needed to do so.

When we consider dividing up a program, we must always consider what tools we have available to express the parts and their communications. A good library, supplying useful facilities for expressing ideas, can crucially affect the way we distribute functionality into different parts of a program. We cannot just sit back and "imagine" how best to partition a program; we must consider what libraries we have available to express the parts and their communication. It is early days yet, but not too soon to point out that if you can use an existing library, such as the C++ standard library, you can save yourself a lot of work, not just on programming but also on testing and documentation. The **iostreams** save us from having to directly deal with the hardware's input/output ports. This is a first example of partitioning a program using abstraction. Every new chapter will provide more examples.

Note the emphasis on structure and organization: you don't get good code just by writing a lot of statements. Why do we mention this now? At this stage you (or at least many readers) have little idea about what code is, and it will be months before you are ready to write code upon which other people could depend for their lives or livelihood. We mention it to help you get the emphasis of your learning right. It is very tempting to dash ahead, focusing on the parts of

programming that – like what is described in the rest of this chapter – are concrete and immediately useful and to ignore the "softer," more conceptual parts of
the art of software development. However, good programmers and system designers know (often having learned it the hard way) that concerns about structure lie at the heart of good software and that ignoring structure leads to
expensive messes. Without structure, you are (metaphorically speaking) building
with mud bricks. It can be done, but you'll never get to the fifth floor (mud
bricks lack the structural strength for that). If you have the ambition to build
something reasonably permanent, you pay attention to matters of code structure
and organization along the way, rather than having to come back and learn them
after failures.

4.3 Expressions

The most basic building block of programs is an expression. An expression computes a value from a number of operands. The simplest expression is simply a literal value, such as **10**, **'a'**, **3.14**, or **"Norah"**.

   Names of variables are also expressions. A variable represents the object of
which it is the name. Consider:

```
// compute area:
int length = 20;            // a literal integer (used to initialize a variable)
int width = 40;
int area = length*width;    // a multiplication
```

Here the literals **20** and **40** are used to initialize the variables **length** and **width**.
Then, **length** and **width** are multiplied; that is, we multiply the values found in
length and **width**. Here, **length** is simply shorthand for "the value found in the
object named **length**." Consider also

```
length = 99;   // assign 99 to length
```

Here, as the left-hand operand of the assignment, **length** means "the object
named **length**," so that the assignment expression is read "Put **99** into the object
named by **length**." We distinguish between **length** used on the left-hand side of
an assignment or an initialization ("the lvalue of **length**" or "the object named by
length") and **length** used on the right-hand side of an assignment or initialization
("the rvalue of **length**," "the value of the object named by **length**," or just "the
value of **length**"). In this context, we find it useful to visualize a variable as a box
labeled by its name:

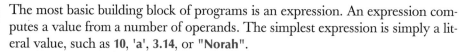

That is, **length** is the name of an object of type **int** containing the value **99**. Sometimes (as an lvalue) **length** refers to the box (object) and sometimes (as an rvalue) **length** refers to the value in that box.

We can make more complicated expressions by combining expressions using operators, such as + and *, in just the way that we are used to. When needed, we can use parentheses to group expressions:

    int perimeter = (length+width)*2;   // add then multiply

Without parentheses, we'd have had to say

    int perimeter = length*2+width*2;

which is clumsy, and we might even have made this mistake:

    int perimeter = length+width*2;   // add width*2 to length

This last error is logical and cannot be found by the compiler. All the compiler sees is a variable called **perimeter** initialized by a valid expression. If the result of that expression is nonsense, that's your problem. You know the mathematical definition of a perimeter, but the compiler doesn't.

The usual mathematical rules of operator precedence apply, so **length+width*2** means **length+(width*2)**. Similarly **a*b+c/d** means **(a*b)+(c/d)** and not **a*(b+c)/d**. See §A.5 for a precedence table.

The first rule for the use of parentheses is simply "If in doubt, parenthesize," but please do learn enough about expressions so that you are not in doubt about **a*b+c/d**. Overuse of parentheses, as in **(a*b)+(c/d)**, decreases readability.

Why should you care about readability? Because you and possibly others will read your code, and ugly code slows down reading and comprehension. Ugly code is not just hard to read, it is also much harder to get correct. Ugly code often hides logical errors. It is slower to read and makes it harder to convince yourself – and others – that ugly code is correct. Don't write absurdly complicated expressions such as

    a*b+c/d*(e–f/g)/h+7   // too complicated

and always try to choose meaningful names.

4.3.1 Constant expressions

Programs typically use a lot of constants. For example, a geometry program might use **pi** and an inch-to-centimeter conversion program will use a conversion factor such as **2.54**. Obviously, we want to use meaningful names for those constants (as we did for **pi**; we didn't say **3.14159**). Similarly, we don't want to change those constants accidentally. Consequently, C++ offers the notion of a symbolic constant, that is, a named object to which you can't give a new value after it has been initialized. For example:

```
const double pi = 3.14159;
pi = 7;              // error: assignment to const
int v = 2*pi/r;      // OK: we just read pi; we don't try to change it
```

Such constants are useful for keeping code readable. You might have recognized **3.14159** as an approximation to **pi** if you saw it in some code, but would you have recognized **299792458**? Also, if someone asked you to change some code to use **pi** with the precision of 12 digits for your computation, you could search for **3.14** in your code, but if someone incautiously had used **22/7**, you probably wouldn't find it. It would be much better just to change the definition of **pi** to use the more appropriate value:

```
const double pi = 3.14159265359;
```

Consequently, we prefer not to use literals (except very obvious ones, such as **0** and **1**) in most places in our code. Instead, we use constants with descriptive names. Non-obvious literals in code (outside **const** definitions) are derisively referred to as *magic constants*.

In some places, such as case labels (§4.4.1.3), C++ requires a *constant expression*, that is, an expression with an integer value composed exclusively of constants. For example:

```
const int max = 17;   // a literal is a constant expression
int val = 19;

max+2     // a constant expression (a const int plus a literal)
val+2     // not a constant expression: it uses a variable
```

And by the way, **299792458** is one of the fundamental constants of the universe: the speed of light in vacuum measured in meters per second. If you didn't instantly recognize that, why would you expect not to be confused and slowed down by other constants embedded in code? Avoid magic constants!

4.3.2 Operators

We just used the simplest operators. However, you will soon need more as you want to express more complex operations. Most operators are conventional, so we'll just explain them later as needed and you can look up details if and when you find a need. Here is a list of the most common operators:

	Name	Comment
f(a)	function call	pass **a** to **f** as an argument
++lval	pre-increment	increment and use the incremented value
−−lval	pre-decrement	decrement and use the decremented value
!a	not	result is **bool**
−a	unary minus	
a*b	multiply	
a/b	divide	
a%b	modulo (remainder)	only for integer types
a+b	add	
a−b	subtract	
out<<b	write **b** to **out**	where **out** is an **ostream**
in>>b	read from **in** into **b**	where **in** is an **istream**
a<b	less than	result is **bool**
a<=b	less than or equal	result is **bool**
a>b	greater than	result is **bool**
a>=b	greater than or equal	result is **bool**
a==b	equal	not to be confused with =
a!=b	not equal	result is **bool**
a && b	logical and	result is **bool**
a || b	logical or	result is **bool**
lval = a	assignment	not to be confused with ==
lval *= a	compound assignment	**lval = lval*a**; also for /, %, +, −

We used **lval** (short for "value that can appear on the left-hand side of an assignment") where the operator modifies an operand. You can find a complete list in §A.5.

For examples of the use of the logical operators **&&** (and), **||** (or), and **!** (not), see §5.5.1, §7.7, §7.8.2, and §10.4.

Note that **a<b<c** means **(a<b)<c** and that **a<b** evaluates to a Boolean value: **true** or **false**. So, **a<b<c** will be equivalent to either **true<c** or **false<c**. In particular, **a<b<c** does not mean "Is **b** between **a** and **c**?" as many have naively (and not unreasonably) assumed. Thus, **a<b<c** is basically a useless expression. Don't write such expressions with two comparison operations, and be very suspicious if you find such an expression in someone else's code − it is most likely an error.

An increment can be expressed in at least three ways:

```
++a
a+=1
a=a+1
```

Which notation should we use? Why? We prefer the first version, **++a**, because it more directly expresses the idea of incrementing. It says what we want to do (increment **a**) rather than how to do it (add **1** to **a** and then write the result to **a**). In general, a way of saying something in a program is better than another if it more directly expresses an idea. The result is more concise and easier for a reader to understand. If we wrote **a=a+1**, a reader could easily wonder whether we really meant to increment by **1**. Maybe we just mistyped **a=b+1**, **a=a+2**, or even **a=a−1**; with **++a** there are far fewer opportunities for such doubts. Please note that this is a logical argument about readability and correctness, not an argument about efficiency. Contrary to popular belief, modern compilers tend to generate exactly the same code from **a=a+1** as for **++a** when **a** is one of the built-in types. Similarly, we prefer **a *= scale** over **a = a*scale**.

4.3.3 Conversions

We can "mix" different types in expressions. For example, **2.5/2** is a **double** divided by an **int**. What does this mean? Do we do integer division or floating-point division? Integer division throws away the remainder; for example, **5/2** is **2**. Floating-point division is different in that there is no remainder to throw away; for example, **5.0/2.0** is **2.5**. It follows that the most obvious answer to the question "Is **2.5/2** integer division or floating-point division?" is "Floating-point, of course; otherwise we'd lose information." We would prefer the answer **1.25** rather than **1**, and **1.25** is what we get. The rule (for the types we have presented so far) is that if an operator has an operand of type **double**, we use floating-point arithmetic yielding a **double** result; otherwise, we use integer arithmetic yielding an **int** result. For example:

```
5/2     is       2 (not 2.5)
2.5/2   means    2.5/double(2), that is, 1.25
'a'+1   means    int('a')+1
```

In other words, if necessary, the compiler converts ("promotes") **int** operands to **doubles** or **char** operands to **int**. Once the result has been calculated, the compiler may have to convert it (again) to use it as an initializer or the right hand of an assignment. For example:

```
double d = 2.5;
int i = 2;

double d2 = d/i;    // d2 == 1.25
int i2 = d/i;       // i2 == 1
```

```
d2 = d/i;        // d2 == 1.25
i2 = d/i;        // i2 == 1
```

Beware that it is easy to forget about integer division in an expression that also contains floating-point operands. Consider the usual formula for converting degrees Celsius to degrees Fahrenheit: $f = 9/5 * c + 32$. We might write

```
double dc;
cin >> dc;
double df = 9/5*dc+32;      // beware!
```

Unfortunately, but quite logically, this does not represent an accurate temperature scale conversion: the value of **9/5** is **1** rather than the **1.8** we might have hoped for. To get the code mathematically correct, either **9** or **5** (or both) will have to be converted into a **double**. For example:

```
double dc;
cin >> dc;
double df = 9.0/5*dc+32;    // better
```

4.4 Statements

An expression computes a value from a set of operands using operators like the ones mentioned in §4.3. What do we do when we want to produce several values? When we want to do something many times? When we want to choose among alternatives? When we want to get input or produce output? In C++, as in many languages, you use language constructs called *statements* to express those things.

So far, we have seen two kinds of statements: expression statements and declarations. An expression statement is simply an expression followed by a semicolon. For example:

```
a = b;
++b;
```

Those are two expression statements. Note that the assignment **=** is an operator so that **a=b** is an expression and we need the terminating semicolon to make **a=b;** a statement. Why do we need those semicolons? The reason is largely technical. Consider

```
a = b ++ b;   // syntax error: missing semicolons
```

Without the semicolon, the compiler doesn't know whether we mean **a=b++; b;** or **a=b; ++b;**. This kind of problem is not restricted to computer languages; consider the exclamation "man eating tiger!" Who is eating whom? Punctuation exists to eliminate such problems, for example, "man-eating tiger!"

When statements follow each other, the computer executes them in the order in which they are written. For example:

```
int a = 7;
cout << a << '\n';
```

Here the declaration, with its initialization, is executed before the output expression statement.

In general, we want a statement to have some effect. Statements without effect are typically useless. For example:

```
1+2;      // do an addition, but don't use the sum
a*b;      // do a multiplication, but don't use the product
```

Such statements without effects are typically logical errors, and compilers often warn against them. Thus, expression statements are typically assignments, I/O statements, or function calls.

We will mention one more type of statement: the "empty statement." Consider the code:

```
if (x == 5);
{ y = 3; }
```

This looks like an error, and it almost certainly is. The **;** in the first line is not supposed to be there. But, unfortunately, this is a legal construct in C++. It is called an *empty statement*, a statement doing nothing. An empty statement before a semicolon is rarely useful. In this case, it has the unfortunate consequence of allowing what is almost certainly an error to be acceptable to the compiler, so it will not alert you to the error and you will have that much more difficulty finding it.

What will happen if this code is run? The compiler will test **x** to see if it has the value **5**. If this condition is true, the following statement (the empty statement) will be executed, with no effect. Then the program continues to the next line, assigning the value **3** to **y** (which is what you wanted to have happen if **x** equals **5**). If, on the other hand, **x** does not have the value **5**, the compiler will not execute the empty statement (still no effect) and will continue as before to assign the value **3** to **y** (which is not what you wanted to have happen unless **x** equals **5**). In other words, the **if**-statement doesn't matter; **y** is going to get the value **3** regardless. This is a common error for novice programmers, and it can be difficult to spot, so watch out for it.

The next section is devoted to statements used to alter the order of evaluation to allow us to express more interesting computations than those we get by just executing statements in the order in which they were written.

4.4.1 Selection

In programs, as in life, we often have to select among alternatives. In C++, that is done using either an **if**-statement or a **switch**-statement.

4.4.1.1 if-statements

The simplest form of selection is an **if**-statement, which selects between two alternatives. For example:

```
int main()
{
    int a = 0;
    int b = 0;
    cout << "Please enter two integers\n";
    cin >> a >> b;

    if (a<b)      // condition
            // 1st alternative (taken if condition is true):
            cout << "max(" << a << "," << b <<") is " << b <<"\n";

    else
            // 2nd alternative (taken if condition is false):
            cout << "max(" << a << "," << b <<") is " << a << "\n";
}
```

An **if**-statement chooses between two alternatives. If its condition is true, the first statement is executed; otherwise, the second statement is. This notion is simple. Most basic programming language features are. In fact, most basic facilities in a programming language are just new notation for things you learned in primary school — or even before that. For example, you were probably told in kindergarten that to cross the street at a traffic light, you had to wait for the light to turn green: "If the traffic light is green, go" and "If the traffic light is red, wait." In C++ that becomes something like

```
if (traffic_light==green) go();
```

and

    if (traffic_light==red) wait();

So, the basic notion is simple, but it is also easy to use **if**-statements in a too simpleminded manner. Consider what's wrong with this program (apart from leaving out the **#include** as usual):

```
// convert from inches to centimeters or centimeters to inches
// a suffix 'i' or 'c' indicates the unit of the input

int main()
{
        const double cm_per_inch = 2.54;   // number of centimeters in an inch
        int length = 1;                     // length in inches or centimeters
        char unit = 0;
        cout<< "Please enter a length followed by a unit (c or i):\n";
        cin >> length >> unit;

        if (unit == 'i')
                cout << length << "in == " << cm_per_inch*length << "cm\n";
        else
                cout << length << "cm == " << length/cm_per_inch << "in\n";
}
```

Actually, this program works roughly as advertised: enter **1i** and you get **1in == 2.54cm**; enter **2.54c** and you'll get **2.54cm == 1in**. Just try it; it's good practice.

The snag is that we didn't test for bad input. The program assumes that the user enters proper input. The condition **unit=='i'** distinguishes between the case where the unit is **'i'** and all other cases. It never looks for a **'c'**.

What if the user entered **15f** (for feet) "just to see what happens"? The condition (**unit == 'i'**) would fail and the program would execute the **else** part (the second alternative), converting from centimeters to inches. Presumably that was not what we wanted when we entered **'f'**.

We must always test our programs with "bad" input, because someone will eventually – intentionally or accidentally – enter bad input. A program should behave sensibly even if its users don't.

Here is an improved version:

```
// convert from inches to centimeters or centimeters to inches
// a suffix 'i' or 'c' indicates the unit of the input
// any other suffix is an error
```

```
int main()
{
        const double cm_per_inch = 2.54;   // number of centimeters in an inch
        int length = 1;                    // length in inches or centimeters
        char unit = ' ';                   // a space is not a unit
        cout<< "Please enter a length followed by a unit (c or i):\n";
        cin >> length >> unit;

        if (unit == 'i')
                cout << length << "in == " << cm_per_inch*length << "cm\n";
        else if (unit == 'c')
                cout << length << "cm == " << length/cm_per_inch << "in\n";
        else
                cout << "Sorry, I don't know a unit called '" << unit << "'\n";
}
```

We first test for **unit=='i'** and then for **unit=='c'** and if it isn't (either) we say, "Sorry." It may look as if we used an "**else-if**-statement," but there is no such thing in C++. Instead, we combined two **if**-statements. The general form of an **if**-statement is

> **if** (*expression*) *statement* **else** *statement*

That is, an **if** followed by an *expression* in parentheses followed by a *statement* followed by an **else** followed by a *statement*. What we did was to use an **if**-statement as the **else**-part of an **if**-statement:

> **if** (*expression*) *statement* **else if** (*expression*) *statement* **else** *statement*

For our program that gives this structure:

```
if (unit == 'i')
        . . .               // 1st alternative
else if (unit == 'c')
        . . .               // 2nd alternative
else
        . . .               // 3rd alternative
```

In this way, we can write arbitrarily complex tests and associate a statement with each alternative. However, please remember that one of the ideals for code is simplicity, rather than complexity. You don't demonstrate your cleverness by writing the most complex program. Rather, you demonstrate competence by writing the simplest code that does the job.

TRY THIS

Use the example above as a model for a program that converts yen, euros, and pounds into dollars. If you like realism, you can find conversion rates on the web.

4.4.1.2 switch-statements

Actually, the comparison of **unit** to **'i'** and to **'c'** is an example of the most common form of selection: a selection based on comparison of a value against several constants. Such selection is so common that C++ provides a special statement for it: the **switch**-statement. We can rewrite our example as

```
int main()
{
        const double cm_per_inch = 2.54;   // number of centimeters in an inch
        int length = 1;                    // length in inches or centimeters
        char unit = 'a';
        cout<< "Please enter a length followed by a unit (c or i):\n";
        cin >> length >> unit;
        switch (unit) {
        case 'i':
                cout << length << "in == " << cm_per_inch*length << "cm\n";
                break;
        case 'c':
                cout << length << "cm == " << length/cm_per_inch << "in\n";
                break;
        default:
                cout << "Sorry, I don't know a unit called '" << unit << "'\n";
                break;
        }
}
```

The **switch**-statement syntax is archaic but still clearer than nested **if**-statements, especially when we compare against many constants. The value presented in parentheses after the **switch** is compared to a set of constants. Each constant is presented as part of a **case** label. If the value equals the constant in a **case** label, the statement for that case is chosen. Each case is terminated by a **break**. If the value doesn't match any of the **case** labels, the statement identified by the **default** label is chosen. You don't have to provide a default, but it is a good idea to do so unless you are absolutely certain that you have listed every alternative. If you don't already know, programming will teach you that it's hard to be absolutely certain (and right) about anything.

4.4.1.3 Switch technicalities

Here are some technical details about **switch**-statements:

1. The value on which we switch must be of an integer, **char**, or enumeration (§9.5) type. In particular, you cannot switch on a **string**.
2. The values in the case labels must be constant expressions (§4.3.1). In particular, you cannot use a variable in a case label.
3. You cannot use the same value for two case labels.
4. You can use several case labels for a single case.
5. Don't forget to end each case with a **break**. Unfortunately, the compiler won't warn you if you forget.

For example:

```
int main()      // you can switch only on integers, etc.
{
    cout << "Do you like fish?\n";
    string s;
    cin >> s;
    switch (s) {    // error: the value must be of integer, char, or enum type
    case "no":
        // . . .
        break;
    case "yes":
        // . . .
        break;
    }
}
```

To select based on a **string** you have to use an **if**-statement or a **map** (Chapter 21).

A **switch**-statement generates optimized code for comparing against a set of constants. For larger sets of constants, this typically yields more-efficient code than a collection of **if**-statements. However, this means that the case label values must be constants and distinct. For example:

```
int main()        // case labels must be constants
{
    // define alternatives:
    int y = 'y';       // this is going to cause trouble
```

```
        const char n = 'n';
        const char m = '?';
        cout << "Do you like fish?\n";
        char a;
        cin >> a;
        switch (a) {
        case n:
            // . . .
            break;
        case y:         // error: variable in case label
            // . . .
            break;
        case m:
            // . . .
            break;
        case 'n':       // error: duplicate case label (n's value is 'n')
            // . . .
            break;
        default:
            // . . .
            break;
        }
    }
```

Often you want the same action for a set of values in a switch. It would be tedious to repeat the action so you can label a single action by a set of case labels.
For example:

```
    int main()  // you can label a statement with several case labels
    {
        cout << "Please enter a digit\n";
        char a;
        cin >> a;

        switch (a) {
        case '0': case '2': case '4': case '6': case '8':
            cout << "is even\n";
            break;
        case '1': case '3': case '5': case '7': case '9':
            cout << "is odd\n";
            break;
```

```
        default:
                cout << "is not a digit\n";
                break;
        }
    }
```

The most common error with **switch**-statements is to forget to terminate a **case** with a break. For example:

```
int main()  // example of bad code (a break is missing)
{
        const double cm_per_inch = 2.54;   // number of centimeters in an inch
        int length = 1;                     // length in inches or centimeters
        char unit = 'a';
        cout << "Please enter a length followed by a unit (c or i):\n";
        cin >> length >> unit;

        switch (unit) {
        case 'i':
                cout << length << "in == " << cm_per_inch*length << "cm\n";
        case 'c':
                cout << length << "cm == " << length/cm_per_inch << "in\n";
        }
}
```

Unfortunately, the compiler will accept this, and when you have finished case **'i'** you'll just "drop through" into case **'c'**, so that if you enter **2i** the program will output

```
2in == 5.08cm
2cm == 0.787402in
```

You have been warned!

TRY THIS

Rewrite your currency converter program from the previous **Try this** to use a **switch**-statement. Add conversions from yuan and kroner. Which version of the program is easier to write, understand, and modify? Why?

4.4.2 Iteration

We rarely do something only once. Therefore, programming languages provide convenient ways of doing something several times. This is called *repetition* or – especially when you do something to a series of elements of a data structure – *iteration*.

4.4.2.1 while-statements

As an example of iteration, consider the first program ever to run on a stored-program computer (the EDSAC). It was written and run by David Wheeler in the computer laboratory in Cambridge University, England, on May 6, 1949, to calculate and print a simple list of squares like this:

```
0       0
1       1
2       4
3       9
4       16
    . . .
98      9604
99      9801
```

Each line is a number followed by a "tab" character ('\t'), followed by the square of the number. A C++ version looks like this:

```cpp
// calculate and print a table of squares 0–99
int main()
{
    int i = 0;        // start from 0
    while (i<100) {
        cout << i << '\t' << square(i) << '\n';
        ++i ;    // increment i (that is, i becomes i+1)
    }
}
```

The notation **square(i)** simply means the square of **i**. We'll later explain how it gets to mean that (§4.5).

No, this first modern program wasn't actually written in C++, but the logic was as is shown here:

- We start with 0.
- We see if we have reached 100, and if so we are finished.

- Otherwise, we print the number and its square, separated by a tab ('\t'), increase the number, and try again.

Clearly, to do this we need

- A way to repeat some statement (to *loop*)
- A variable to keep track of how many times we have been through the loop (a *loop variable* or a *control variable*), here the **int** called **i**
- An initializer for the loop variable, here **0**
- A termination criterion, here, that we want to go through the loop 100 times
- Something to do each time around the loop (the *body* of the loop)

The language construct we used is called a **while**-statement. Just following its distinguishing keyword, **while**, it has a condition "on top" followed by its body:

```
while (i<100)          // the loop condition testing the loop variable i
{
    cout << i << '\t' << square(i) << '\n';
    ++i ;              // increment the loop variable i
}
```

The loop body is a block (delimited by curly braces) that writes out a row of the table and increments the loop variable, **i**. We start each pass through the loop by testing if **i<100**. If so, we are not yet finished and we can execute the loop body. If we have reached the end, that is, if **i** is **100**, we leave the **while**-statement and execute what comes next. In this program the end of the program is next, so we leave the program.

The loop variable for a **while**-statement must be defined and initialized outside (before) the **while**-statement. If we fail to define it, the compiler will give us an error. If we define it, but fail to initialize it, most compilers will warn us, saying something like "local variable **i** not set," but would be willing to let us execute the program if we insisted. Don't insist! Compilers are almost certainly right when they warn about uninitialized variables. Uninitialized variables are a common source of errors. In this case, we wrote

```
int i = 0;      // start from 0
```

so all is well.

Basically, writing a loop is simple. Getting it right for real-world problems can be tricky, though. In particular, it can be hard to express the condition correctly and to initialize all variables so that the loop starts correctly.

TRY THIS

The character **'b'** is **char('a'+1)**, **'c'** is **char('a'+2)**, etc. Use a loop to write out a table of characters with their corresponding integer values:

```
a       97
b       98
. . .
z       122
```

4.4.2.2 Blocks

Note how we grouped the two statements that the **while** had to execute:

```
while (i<100) {
        cout << i << '\t' << square(i) << '\n';
        ++i ;      // increment i (that is, i becomes i+1)
}
```

A sequence of statements delimited by curly braces { and } is called a *block* or a *compound statement*. A block is a kind of statement. The empty block { } is sometimes useful for expressing that nothing is to be done. For example:

```
if (a<=b) {         // do nothing
}
else {              // swap a and b
        int t = a;
        a = b;
        b = t;
}
```

4.4.2.3 for-statements

Iterating over a sequence of numbers is so common that C++, like most other programming languages, has a special syntax for it. A **for**-statement is like a **while**-statement except that the management of the control variable is concentrated at the top where it is easy to see and understand. We could have written the "first program" like this:

```
// calculate and print a table of squares 0–99
int main()
{
```

```
        for (int i = 0; i<100; ++i)
            cout << i << '\t' << square(i) << '\n';
}
```

This means "Execute the body with **i** starting at **0** incrementing **i** after each execution of the body until we reach **100**." A **for**-statement is always equivalent to some **while**-statement. In this case

```
for (int i = 0; i<100; ++i)
    cout << i << '\t' << square(i) << '\n';
```

means

```
{
    int = 0;            // the for-statement initializer
    while (i<100) {     // the for-statement condition
        cout << i << '\t' << square(i) << '\n';    // the for-statement body
        ++i;            // the for-statement increment
    }
}
```

Some novices prefer **while**-statements and some novices prefer **for**-statements. However, using a **for**-statement yields more easily understood and more maintainable code whenever a loop can be defined as a **for**-statement with a simple initializer, condition, and increment operation. Use a **while**-statement only when that's not the case.

Never modify the loop variable inside the body of a **for**-statement. That would violate every reader's reasonable assumption about what a loop is doing. Consider:

```
int main()
{
    for (int i = 0; i<100; ++i) {    // for i in the [0:100) range
        cout << i << '\t' << square(i) << '\n';
        ++i;    // what's going on here? It smells like an error!
    }
}
```

Anyone looking at this loop would reasonably assume that the body would be executed 100 times. However, it isn't. The **++i** in the body ensures that **i** is incremented twice each time around the loop so that we get an output only for the 50 even values of **i**. If we saw such code, we would assume it to be an error, probably caused by a sloppy conversion from a **while**-loop. If you want to increment by 2, say so:

```
// calculate and print a table of squares of even numbers in the [0:100) range
int main()
{
    for (int i = 0; i<100; i+=2)
        cout << i << '\t' << square(i) << '\n';
}
```

Please note that the cleaner, more explicit version is shorter than the messy one. That's typical.

TRY THIS

Rewrite the character value example from the previous **Try this** to use a for-loop. Then modify your program to also get a table of the integer values for uppercase letters and digits.

4.5 Functions

In the program above, what was **square(i)**? It is a call of a function. In particular, it is a call of the function called **square** with the argument **i**. A *function* is a named sequence of statements. A function can return a result (also called a return value). The standard library provides a lot of useful functions, such as the square root function **sqrt()** that we used in §3.4. However, we write many functions ourselves. Here is a plausible definition of **square**:

```
int square(int x)     // return the square of x
{
    return x*x;
}
```

The first line of this definition tells us that this is a function (that's what the parentheses mean), that it is called **square**, that it takes an **int** argument (here, called **x**), and that it returns an **int** (the type of the result always comes first in a function declaration); that is, we can use it like this:

```
int main()
{
    cout << square(2) << '\n';   // print 4
    cout << square(10) << '\n';  // print 100
}
```

We don't have to use the result of a function call (but if we didn't want the result, why would we call it?), but we do have to give a function exactly the arguments it requires. Consider:

```
square(2);              // probably a mistake: unused return value
int v1 = square();      // error: argument missing
int v2 = square;        // error: parentheses missing
int v3 = square(1,2);   // error: too many arguments
int v4 = square("two"); // error: wrong type of argument — int expected
```

Many compilers warn against unused results, and all give errors as indicated. You might think that a computer should be smart enough to figure out that by the string "two" you really meant the integer **2**. However, a C++ compiler deliberately isn't that smart. It is the compiler's job to do exactly what you tell it to do after verifying that your code is well formed according to the definition of C++. If the compiler guessed about what you meant, it would occasionally guess wrong, and you – or the users of your program – would be quite annoyed. You'll find it hard enough to predict what your code will do without having the compiler "help you" by second-guessing you.

The *function body* is the block (§4.4.2.2) that actually does the work.

```
{
        return x*x;   // return the square of x
}
```

For **square**, the work is trivial: we produce the square of the argument and return that as our result. Saying that in C++ is easier than saying it in English. That's typical for simple ideas. After all, a programming language is designed to state such simple ideas simply and precisely.

The syntax of a *function definition* can be described like this:

type identifier (parameter-list) function-body

That is, a type (the return type), followed by an identifier (the name of the function), followed by a list of parameters in parentheses, followed by the body of the function (the statements to be executed). The list of arguments required by the function is called a *parameter list* and its elements are called *parameters* (or *formal arguments*). The list of parameters can be empty, and if we don't want to return a result we give **void** (meaning "nothing") as the return type. For example:

```
void write_sorry()    // take no argument; return no value
{
     cout << "Sorry\n";
}
```

The language-technical aspects of functions will be examined more closely in Chapter 8.

4.5.1 Why bother with functions?

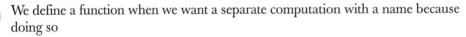

We define a function when we want a separate computation with a name because doing so

- Makes the computation logically separate
- Makes the program text clearer (by naming the computation)
- Makes it possible to use the function in more than one place in our program
- Eases testing

We'll see many examples of each of those reasons as we go along, and we'll occasionally mention a reason. Note that real-world programs use thousands of functions, some even hundred of thousands of functions. Obviously, we would never be able to write or understand such programs if their parts (e.g., computations) were not clearly separated and named. Also, you'll soon find that many functions are repeatedly useful and you'd soon tire of repeating their definitions. For example, you might be happy writing **x*x** and **7*7** and **(x+7)*(x+7)**, etc. rather than **square(x)** and **square(7)** and **square(x+7)**, etc. However, that's only because **square** is a very simple computation. Consider square root (called **sqrt** in C++): you prefer to write **sqrt(x)** and **sqrt(7)** and **sqrt(x+7)**, etc. rather than repeating the (somewhat complicated and many lines long) code for computing square root. Even better: you don't have to even look at the computation of square root because knowing that **sqrt(x)** gives the square root of **x** is sufficient.

In §8.5 we will address many function technicalities, but for now, we'll just give another example.

If we had wanted to make the loop in **main()** really simple, we could have written

```
void print_square(int v)
{
        cout << v << '\t' << v*v << '\n';
}

int main()
{
        for (int i = 0; i<100; ++i) print_square(i);
}
```

Why didn't we use that version using **print_square()**? That version is not significantly simpler than the version using **square()**, and note that

- **print_square()** is a rather specialized function that we could not expect to be able to use later, whereas **square()** is an obvious candidate for other uses
- **square()** hardly requires documentation, whereas **print_square()** obviously needs explanation

The underlying reason for both is that **print_square()** performs two logically separate actions:

- It prints.
- It calculates a square.

Programs are usually easier to write and to understand if each function performs a single logical action. Basically, the **square()** version is the better design.

Finally, why did we use **square(i)** rather than simply **i*i** in the first version of the problem? Well, one of the purposes of functions is to simplify code by separating out complicated calculations as named functions, and for the 1949 version of the program there was no hardware that directly implemented "multiply." Consequently, in the 1949 version of the program, **i*i** was actually a fairly complicated calculation, similar to what you'd do by hand using a piece a paper. Also, the writer of that original version, David Wheeler, was the inventor of the function (then called a subroutine) in modern computing, so it seemed appropriate to use it here.

TRY THIS

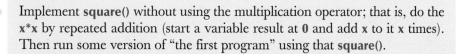

Implement **square()** without using the multiplication operator; that is, do the **x*x** by repeated addition (start a variable result at **0** and add **x** to it **x** times). Then run some version of "the first program" using that **square()**.

4.5.2 Function declarations

Did you notice that all the information needed to call a function was in the first line of its definition? For example:

```
int square(int x)
```

Given that, we know enough to say

```
int x = square(44);
```

We don't really need to look at the function body. In real programs, we most often don't want to look at a function body. Why would we want to look at the body of the standard library **sqrt()** function? We know it calculates the square root of its argument. Why would we want to see the body of our **square()** function? Of course we might just be curious. But almost all of the time, we are just interested in knowing how to call a function – seeing the definition would just be distracting. Fortunately, C++ provides a way of supplying that information separate from the complete function definition. It is called a *function declaration*:

```
int square(int);          // declaration of square
double sqrt(double);      // declaration of sqrt
```

Note the terminating semicolons. A semicolon is used in a function declaration instead of the body used in the corresponding function definition:

```
int square(int x)      // definition of square
{
      return x*x;
}
```

So, if you just want to use a function, you simply write – or more commonly **#include** – its declaration. The function definition can be elsewhere. We'll discuss where that "elsewhere" might be in §8.3 and §8.7. This distinction between declarations and definitions becomes essential in larger programs where we use declarations to keep most of the code out of sight to allow us to concentrate on a single part of a program at a time (§4.2).

4.6 Vector

To do just about anything of interest in a program, we need a collection of data to work on. For example, we might need a list of phone numbers, a list of members of a football team, a list of courses, a list of books read over the last year, a catalog of songs for download, a set of payment options for a car, a list of the weather forecasts for the next week, a list of prices for a camera in different web stores, etc. The possibilities are literally endless and therefore ubiquitous in programs. We'll get to see a variety of ways of storing collections of data (a variety of containers of data; see Chapters 20 and 21). Here we will start with one of the simplest, and arguably the most useful, ways of storing data: a **vector**.

A **vector** is simply a sequence of elements that you can access by an index. For example, here is a **vector** called **v**:

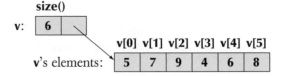

That is, the first element has index 0, the second index 1, and so on. We refer to an element by subscripting the name of the **vector** with the element's index, so here the value of **v[0]** is **5**, the value of **v[1]** is **7**, and so on. Indices for a **vector** always start with 0 and increase by 1. This should look familiar: the standard library **vector** is simply the C++ standard library's version of an old and well-known idea. I have drawn the vector so as to emphasize that it "knows its size"; that is, a **vector** doesn't just store its elements, it also stores its size.

We could make such a **vector** like this:

```
vector<int> v(6);    // vector of 6 ints
v[0] = 5;
v[1] = 7;
v[2] = 9;
v[3] = 4;
v[4] = 6;
v[5] = 8;
```

We see that to make a **vector** we need to specify the type of the elements and the initial number of elements. The element type comes after **vector** in angle brackets (**< >**), here **<int>**, and the initial number of elements comes after the name in parentheses, here **(6)**. Here is another example:

```
vector<string> philosopher(4);   // vector of 4 strings
philosopher [0] = "Kant";
philosopher [1] = "Plato";
philosopher [2] = "Hume";
philosopher [3] = "Kierkegaard";
```

Naturally, a **vector** will only accept elements of its declared element type:

```
philosopher[2] = 99;     // error: trying to assign an int to a string
v[2] = "Hume";           // error: trying to assign a string to an int
```

When we define a **vector** of a given size, its elements are given a default value according to the element type. For example:

```
vector<int> v(6);                // vector of 6 ints initialized to 0
vector<string> philosopher(4);   // vector of 4 strings initialized to ""
```

If you don't like the default, you can specify another. For example:

```
vector<double> vd(1000,-1.2);    // vector of 1000 doubles initialized to -1.2
```

Please note that you cannot simply refer to a nonexistent element of a **vector**:

```
vd[20000] = 4.7;            // run-time error
```

We will discuss run-time errors and subscripting in the next chapter.

4.6.1 Growing a vector

Often, we start a **vector** empty and grow it to its desired size as we read or compute the data we want in it. The key operation here is **push_back()**, which adds a new element to a **vector**. The new element becomes the last element of the **vector**. For example:

```
vector<double> v;     // start off empty; that is, v has no elements
```

```
v.push_back(2.7);     // add an element with the value 2.7 at end ("the back") of v
                      // v now has one element and v[0]==2.7
```

```
v.push_back(5.6);     // add an element with the value 5.6 at end of v
                      // v now has two elements and v[1]==5.6
```

```
v.push_back(7.9);     // add an element with the value 7.9 at end of v
                      // v now has three elements and v[2]==7.9
```

Note the syntax for a call of **push_back()**. It is called a *member function call*; **push_back()** is a member function of **vector** and must be called using this dot notation:

member-function-call:
    object_name **.** *member-function-name* (*argument-list*)

The size of a **vector** can be obtained by a call to another of **vector**'s member functions: **size()**. Initially **v.size()** was **0**, and after the third call of **push_back()**, **v.size()** has become 3. Size makes it easy to loop through all elements of a **vector**. For example:

```
for(int i=0; i<v.size(); ++i)
        cout << "v[" << i << "]==" <<v[i] << '\n';
```

Given the definition of **v** and the **push_back**()s above, this **for**-loop will print

```
v[0]==2.7
v[1]==5.6
v[2]==7.9
```

If you have programmed before, you will note that a **vector** is similar to an array in C and other languages. However, you need not specify the size (length) of a **vector** in advance, and you can add as many elements as you like. As we go along, you'll find that the C++ standard **vector** has other useful properties.

4.6.2 A numeric example

Let's look at a more realistic example. Often, we have a series of values that we want to read into our program so that we can do something with them. The "something" could be producing a graph of the values, calculating the mean and median, finding the largest element, sorting them, combining them with other data, searching for "interesting" values, comparing them to other data, etc. There is no limit to the range of computations we might perform on data, but first we need to get it into our computer's memory. Here is the basic technique for getting an unknown – possibly large – amount of data into a computer. As a concrete example, we chose to read in floating-point numbers representing temperatures:

```
// read some temperatures into a vector
int main()
{
    vector<double> temps;          // temperatures
    double temp;
    while (cin>>temp)              // read
        temps.push_back(temp);    // put into vector
    // . . . do something . . .
}
```

So, what goes on here? First we declare a **vector** to hold the data and a variable into which we can read each number as it comes from input:

```
vector<double> temps;          // temperatures
double temp;
```

This is where the type of input we expect is mentioned. We read and store **doubles**.

Next comes the actual read loop:

```
while (cin>>temp)                   // read
     temps.push_back(temp);    // put into vector
```

The **cin>>temp** reads a **double**, and that **double** is pushed into the **vector** (placed at the back). We have seen those individual operations before. What's new here is that we use the input operation, **cin>>temp**, as the condition for a **while**-loop. Basically, **cin>>temp** is true if a value was read correctly and false otherwise, so that **while**-loop will read all the **double**s we give it and stop when we give it anything else. For example, if you typed

    1.2 3.4 5.6 7.8 9.0 |

then **temps** would get the five elements **1.2**, **3.4**, **5.6**, **7.8**, **9.0** (in that order, for example, **temps[0]==1.2**). We used the character '**|**' to terminate the input − anything that isn't a **double** can be used. In §10.6 we discuss how to terminate input and how to deal with errors in input.

Once we get data into a **vector** we can easily manipulate it. As an example, let's calculate the mean and median temperatures:

```
// compute mean and median temperatures
int main()
{
     vector<double> temps;           // temperatures
     double temp;
     while (cin>>temp)               // read
          temps.push_back(temp);    // put into vector

     // compute mean temperature:
     double sum = 0;
     for (int i = 0; i< temps.size(); ++i) sum += temps[i];
     cout << "Average temperature: " << sum/temps.size() << endl;

     // compute median temperature:
     sort(temps.begin(),temps.end());   // sort temps
                                        // "from the beginning to the end"
     cout << "Median temperature: " << temps[temps.size()/2] << endl;
}
```

[handwritten annotations:] #include <algorithm> // for sort #include <iostream> #include <vector> using namespace std;

We calculate the average (the mean) by simply adding all the elements into sum, and then dividing the sum by the number of elements (that is, **temps.size()**):

```
// compute average temperature:
double sum = 0;
```

```
for (int i = 0; i< temps.size(); ++i) sum += temps[i];
cout << "Average temperature: " << sum/temps.size() << endl;
```

Note how the += operator comes in handy.

To calculate a median (a value chosen so that half of the values are lower and the other half are higher) we need to sort the elements. For that, we use the standard library sort algorithm, **sort()**:

```
// compute median temperature:
sort(temps.begin(),temps.end());   // sort "from the beginning to the end"
cout << "Median temperature: " << temps[temps.size()/2] << endl;
```

The standard library **sort()** takes two arguments: the beginning of the sequence of elements that it is to sort and the end of that sequence. We will explain the standard library algorithms much later (Chapter 20), but fortunately, a **vector** "knows" where its beginning and end are, so we don't need to worry about details: **temps.begin()** and **temps.end()** will do just fine. Note that **begin()** and **end()** are member functions of **vector**, just like **size()**, so we call them for their **vector** using dot. Once the temperatures are sorted, it's easy to find the median: we just pick the middle element, the one with index **temps.size()/2**. If you feel like being picky (and if you do, you are starting to think like a programmer), you could observe that the value we found may not be a median according to the definition we offered above. Exercise 2 at the end of this chapter is designed to solve that little problem.

4.6.3 A text example

We didn't present the temperature example because we were particularly interested in temperatures. Many people – such as meteorologists, agronomists, and oceanographers – are very interested in temperature data and values based on it, such as means and medians. However, we are not. From a programmer's point of view, what's interesting about this example is its generality: the **vector** and the simple operations on it can be used in a huge range of applications. It is fair to say that whatever you are interested in, if you need to analyze data, you'll use **vector** (or a similar data structure; see Chapter 21). As an example, let's build a simple dictionary:

```
// simple dictionary: list of sorted words
int main()
{
    vector<string> words;
    string temp;
    while (cin>>temp)              // read whitespace-separated words
        words.push_back(temp);     // put into vector
```

```
cout << "Number of words: " << words.size() << endl;

sort(words.begin(),words.end());    // sort "from beginning to end"

for (int i = 0; i< words.size(); ++i)
        if (i==0 || words[i−1]!=words[i])    // is this a new word?
            cout << words[i] << "\n";
}
```

If we feed some words to this program, it will write them out in order without repeating a word. For example, given

a man a plan panama

it will write

a
man
panama
plan

How do we stop reading string input? In other words, how do we terminate the input loop?

```
while (cin>>temp)                 // read
        words.push_back(temp);    // put into vector
```

When we read numbers (in §4.6.2), we just gave some input character that wasn't a number. We can't do that here because every (ordinary) character can be read into a **string**. Fortunately, there are characters that are "not ordinary." As mentioned in §3.5.1, Ctrl+Z terminates an input stream under Windows and Ctrl+D does that under Unix.

Most of this program is remarkably similar to what we did for the temperatures. In fact, we wrote the "dictionary program" by cutting and pasting from the "temperature program." The only thing that's new is the test

if (i==0 || words[i−1]!=words[i])   // is this a new word?

If you deleted that test the output would be

a
a

man
panama
plan

We didn't like the repetition, so we eliminated it using that test. What does the test do? It looks to see if the previous word we printed is different from the one we are about to print (**words[i–1]!=words[i]**) and if so, we print that word; otherwise, we do not. Obviously, we can't talk about a previous word when we are about to print the first word (**i==0**), so we first test for that and combine those two tests using the **||** (or) operator:

    if (i==0 || words[i–1]!=words[i])   *// is this a new word?*

Note that we can compare strings. We use **!=** (not equals) here; **==** (equals), **<** (less than), **<=** (less than or equal), **>** (greater than), and **>=** (greater than or equal) also work for strings. The **<**, **>**, etc. operators use the usual lexicographical ordering, so "**Ape**" comes before "**Apple**" and "**Chimpanzee**".

TRY THIS

Write a program that "bleeps" out words that you don't like; that is, you read in words using **cin** and print them again on **cout**. If a word is among a few you have defined, you write out **BLEEP** instead of that word. Start with one "disliked word" such as

    string disliked = "Broccoli";

When that works, add a few more.

4.7 Language features

The temperature and dictionary programs used most of the fundamental language features we presented in this chapter: iteration (the **for**-statement and the **while**-statement), selection (the **if**-statement), simple arithmetic (the **++** and **+=** operators), comparisons and logical operators (the **==**, **!=**, and **||** operators), variables, and functions (e.g., **main()**, **sort()**, and **size()**). In addition, we used standard library facilities, such as **vector** (a container of elements), **cout** (an output stream), and **sort()** (an algorithm).

   If you count, you'll find that we actually achieved quite a lot with rather few features. That's the ideal! Each programming language feature exists to express a fundamental idea, and we can combine them in a huge (really, infinite) number of ways to write useful programs. This is a key notion: a computer is not a gadget with a fixed function. Instead it is a machine that we can program to do any computation we can think of, and given that we can attach computers to gadgets that interact with the world outside the computer, we can in principle get it to do anything.

Drill

Go through this drill step by step. Do not try to speed up by skipping steps. Test each step by entering at least three pairs of values – more values would be better.

1. Write a program that consists of a **while**-loop that (each time around the loop) reads in two **ints** and then prints them. Exit the program when a terminating '|' is entered.
2. Change the program to write out **the smaller value is:** followed by the smaller of the numbers and **the larger value is:** followed by the larger value.
3. Augment the program so that it writes the line **the numbers are equal** (only) if they are equal.
4. Change the program so that it uses **doubles** instead of **ints**.
5. Change the program so that it writes out **the numbers are almost equal** after writing out which is the larger and the smaller if the two numbers differ by less than 1.0/10000000.
6. Now change the body of the loop so that it reads just one **double** each time around. Define two variables to keep track of which is the smallest and which is the largest value you have seen so far. Each time through the loop write out the value entered. If it's the smallest so far, write **the smallest so far** after the number. If it is the largest so far, write **the largest so far** after the number.
7. Add a unit to each **double** entered; that is, enter values such as **10cm**, **2.5in**, **5ft**, or **3.33m**. Accept the four units: **cm, m, in, ft**. Assume conversion factors **1m == 100cm, 1in == 2.54cm, 1ft == 12in**. Read the unit indicator into a string.
8. Reject values without units or with "illegal" representations of units, such as **y, yard, meter, km**, and **gallons**.
9. Keep track of the sum of values entered (as well as the smallest and the largest) and the number of values entered. When you see the final '|' print the smallest, the largest, the number of values, and the sum of values. Note that to keep the sum, you have to decide on a unit to use for that sum; use meters.
10. Keep all the values entered (converted into meters) in a **vector**. At the end, write out those values.

11. Before writing out the values from the **vector**, sort them (that'll make them come out in increasing order).

Review

1. What is a computation?
2. What do we mean by inputs and outputs to a computation? Give examples.
3. What are the three requirements a programmer should keep in mind when expressing computations?
4. What does an expression do?
5. What is the difference between a statement and an expression, as described in this chapter?
6. What is an lvalue? List the operators that require an lvalue. Why do these operators, and not the others, require an lvalue?
7. What is a constant expression?
8. What is a literal?
9. What is a symbolic constant and why do we use them?
10. What is a magic constant? Give examples.
11. What are some operators that we can use for integers and floating-point values?
12. What operators can be used on integers but not on floating-point numbers?
13. What are some operators that can be used for **strings**?
14. When would a programmer prefer a **switch**-statement to an **if**-statement?
15. What are some common problems with **switch**-statements?
16. What is the function of each part of the header line in a **for**-loop, and in what sequence are they executed?
17. When should the **for**-loop be used and when should the **while**-loop be used?
18. How do you print the numeric value of a **char**?
19. Describe what the line **char foo(int x)** means in a function definition.
20. When should you define a separate function for part of a program? List reasons.
21. What can you do to an **int** that you cannot do to a **string**?
22. What can you do to a **string** that you cannot do to an **int**?
23. What is the index of the third element of a **vector**?
24. How do you write a **for**-loop that prints every element of a **vector**?
25. What does **vector<char>alphabet(26);** do?
26. Describe what **push_back()** does to a **vector**.
27. What do **vector**'s member functions **begin()**, **end()**, and **size()** do?
28. What makes **vector** so popular/useful?
29. How do you sort the elements of a **vector**?

Terms

abstraction	**for**-statement	**push_back()**
begin()	function	repetition
computation	**if**-statement	rvalue
conditional statement	increment	selection
declaration	input	**size()**
definition	iteration	**sort()**
divide and conquer	loop	statement
else	lvalue	**switch**-statement
end()	member function	**vector**
expression	output	**while**-statement

Exercises

1. If you haven't already, do the **Try this** exercises from this chapter.

2. If we define the median of a sequence as "the number for which exactly half of the elements of the sequence come before it and exactly half come after it," fix the program in §4.6.2 so that it always prints out a median. Hint: A median need not be an element of the sequence.

3. Read a sequence of **double** values into a **vector**. Think of each value as the distance between two cities along a given route. Compute and print the total distance (the sum of all distances). Find and print the smallest and greatest distance between two neighboring cities. Find and print the mean distance between two neighboring cities.

4. Write a program to play a numbers guessing game. The user thinks of a number between 1 and 100 and your program asks questions to figure out what the number is (e.g., "Is the number you are thinking of less than 50?"). Your program should be able to identify the number after asking no more than seven questions. Hint: Use the < and <= operators and the **if-else** construct.

5. Write a program that performs as a very simple calculator. Your calculator should be able to handle the five basic math operations — add, subtract, multiply, divide, and modulus (remainder) — on two input values. Your program should prompt the user to enter three arguments: two **double** values and a character to represent an operation. If the entry arguments are **35.6**, **24.1**, and '**+**', the program output should be "**The sum of 35.6 and 24.1 is 59.7.**" In Chapter 6 we look at a much more sophisticated simple calculator.

6. Make a **vector** holding the ten string values "**zero**", "**one**", . . . "**nine**". Use that in a program that converts a digit to its corresponding spelled-out value; e.g., the input **7** gives the output **seven**. Have the same pro-

gram, using the same input loop, convert spelled-out numbers into their digit form; e.g., the input **seven** gives the output **7**.

7. Modify the "mini calculator" from exercise 5 to accept (just) single-digit numbers written as either digits or spelled out.

8. There is an old story that the emperor wanted to thank the inventor of the game of chess and asked the inventor to name his reward. The inventor asked for one grain of rice for the first square, 2 for the second, 4 for the third, and so on, doubling for each of the 64 squares. That may sound modest, but there wasn't that much rice in the empire! Write a program to calculate how many squares are required to give the inventor at least 1000 grains of rice, at least 1,000,000 grains, and at least 1,000,000,000 grains. You'll need a loop, of course, and probably an **int** to keep track of which square you are at, an **int** to keep the number of grains on the current square, and an **int** to keep track of the grains on all previous squares. We suggest that you write out the value of all your variables for each iteration of the loop so that you can see what's going on.

9. Try to calculate the number of rice grains that the inventor asked for in exercise 8 above. You'll find that the number is so large that it won't fit in an **int** or a **double**. Observe what happens when the number gets too large to represent as an **int** and as a **double**. What is the largest number of squares for which you can calculate the exact number of grains (using an **int**)? What is the largest number of squares for which you can calculate the approximate number of grains (using a **double**)?

10. Write a program that plays the game "Rock, Paper, Scissors." If you are not familiar with the game do some research (e.g., on the web using Google). Research is a common task for programmers. Use a **switch**-statement to solve this exercise. Also, the machine should give random answers (i.e., select the next rock, paper, or scissors randomly). Real randomness is too hard to provide just now, so just build a **vector** with a sequence of values to be used as "the next value." If you build the **vector** into the program, it will always play the same game, so maybe you should let the user enter some values. Try variations to make it less easy for the user to guess which move the machine will make next.

11. Create a program to find all the prime numbers between 1 and 100. One way to do this is to write a function that will check if a number is prime (i.e., see if the number can be divided by a prime number smaller than itself) using a **vector** of primes in order (so that if the **vector** is called **primes**, **primes[0]==2**, **primes[1]==3**, **primes[2]==5**, etc.). Then write a loop that goes from 1 to 100, checks each number to see if it is a prime, and stores each prime found in a **vector**. Write another loop that lists the primes you found. You might check your result by comparing your **vector** of prime numbers with **primes**. Consider 2 the first prime.

12. Modify the program described in the previous exercise to take an input value **max** and then find all prime numbers from **1** to **max**.

13. Create a program to find all the prime numbers between 1 and 100. There is a classic method for doing this, called the "Sieve of Eratosthenes." If you don't know that method, get on the web and look it up. Write your program using this method.

14. Modify the program described in the previous exercise to take an input value **max** and then find all prime numbers from **1** to **max**.

15. Write a program that takes an input value **n** and then finds the first **n** primes.

16. In the drill, you wrote a program that, given a series of numbers, found the max and min of that series. The number that appears the most times in a sequence is called the *mode*. Create a program that finds the mode of a set of positive integers.

17. Write a program that finds the min, max, and mode of a sequence of **strings**.

18. Write a program to solve quadratic equations. A quadratic equation is of the form

    ax2+bx+c=0

    If you don't know the quadratic formula for solving such an expression, do some research. Remember, researching how to solve a problem is often necessary before a programmer can teach the computer how to solve it. Use **doubles** for the user inputs for **a**, **b**, and **c**. Since there are two solutions to a quadratic equation, output both **x1** and **x2**.

19. Write a program where you first enter a set of name-and-value pairs, such as **Joe 17** and **Barbara 22**. For each pair, add the name to a **vector** called **names** and the number to a **vector** called **scores** (in corresponding positions, so that if **names[7]=="Joe"** then **scores[7]==18**). Terminate input by the line **No more** ("more" will make the attempt to read another integer fail). Check that each name is unique and terminate with an error message if a name is entered twice. Write out all the (name,score) pairs, one per line.

20. Modify the program from exercise 19 so that when you enter a name, the program will output the corresponding score or "**name not found**".

21. Modify the program from exercise 19 so that when you enter an integer, the program will output all the names with that score or "**score not found**".

Postscript

From a philosophical point of view, you can now do everything that can be done using a computer – the rest is details! Among other things, this shows the value of "details" and the importance of practical skills, because clearly you have barely started as a programmer. But we are serious. The tools presented in this chapter do allow you to express every computation: you have as many variables (including **vectors** and **strings**) as you want, you have arithmetic, comparisons, and you have selection and iteration. Every computation can be expressed using those primitives. You have text and numeric input and output, and every input or output can be expressed as text (even graphics). You can even organize your computations as sets of named functions. What is left for you to do is "just" to learn to write good programs, that is, to write programs that are correct, maintainable, and reasonably efficient. Importantly, you must try to learn to do so with a reasonable amount of effort.

5

Errors

"I realized that from now on a large part of my life would be spent finding and correcting my own mistakes."

—Maurice Wilkes, 1949

In this chapter, we discuss correctness of programs, errors, and error handling. If you are a genuine novice, you'll find the discussion a bit abstract at times and painfully detailed at other times. Can error handling really be this important? It is, and you'll learn that one way or another before you can write programs that others are willing to use. What we are trying to do is to show you what "thinking like a programmer" is about. It combines fairly abstract strategy with painstaking analysis of details and alternatives.

5.1 Introduction

We have referred to errors repeatedly in the previous chapters, and – having done the drills and some exercises – you have some idea why. Errors are simply unavoidable when you develop a program, yet the final program must be free of errors, or at least free of errors that we consider unacceptable for it.

There are many ways of classifying errors. For example:

- *Compile-time errors:* Errors found by the compiler. We can further classify compile-time errors based on which language rules they violate, for example:

  - Syntax errors
  - Type errors

- *Link-time errors:* Errors found by the linker when it is trying to combine object files into an executable program.

- *Run-time errors:* Errors found by checks in a running program. We can further classify run-time errors as

  - Errors detected by the computer (hardware and/or operating system)
  - Errors detected by a library (e.g., the standard library)
  - Errors detected by user code

- *Logic errors:* Errors found by the programmer looking for the causes of erroneous results.

It is tempting to say that our job as programmers is to eliminate all errors. That is of course the ideal, but often that's not feasible. In fact, for real-world programs it can be hard to know exactly what "all errors" means. If we kicked out the power cord from your computer while it executed your program, would that be an error that you were supposed to handle? In many cases, the answer is "Obviously not," but what if we were talking about a medical monitoring program or the control program for a telephone switch? In those cases, a user could reasonably expect that something in the system of which your program was a part will do something sensible even if your computer lost power or a cosmic ray damaged the memory holding your program. The key question becomes: "Is my program supposed to detect that error?" Unless we specifically say otherwise, we will assume that your program

1. Should produce the desired results for all legal inputs
2. Should give reasonable error messages for all illegal inputs
3. Need not worry about misbehaving hardware
4. Need not worry about misbehaving system software
5. Is allowed to terminate after finding an error

Essentially all programs for which assumptions 3, 4, or 5 do not hold can be considered advanced and beyond the scope of this book. However, assumptions 1 and 2 are included in the definition of basic professionalism, and professionalism is one of our goals. Even if we don't meet that ideal 100% of the time, it must be the ideal.

When we write programs, errors are natural and unavoidable; the question is: how do we deal with them? Our guess is that avoiding, finding, and correcting errors takes 90% or more of the effort when developing serious software. For safety-critical programs, the effort can be greater still. You can do much better for small programs; on the other hand, you can easily do worse if you're sloppy.

Basically, we offer three approaches to producing acceptable software:

* Organize software to minimize errors.
* Eliminate most of the errors we made through debugging and testing.
* Make sure the remaining errors are not serious.

None of these approaches can completely eliminate errors by itself; we have to use all three.

Experience matters immensely when it comes to producing reliable programs, that is, programs that can be relied on to do what they are supposed to do with an acceptable error rate. Please don't forget that the ideal is that our programs always do the right thing. We are usually able only to approximate that ideal, but that's no excuse for not trying very hard.

5.2 Sources of errors

Here are some sources of errors:

- *Poor specification:* If we are not specific about what a program should do, we are unlikely to adequately examine the "dark corners" and make sure that all cases are handled (i.e., that every input gives a correct answer or an adequate error message).

- *Incomplete programs:* During development, there are obviously cases that we haven't yet taken care of. That's unavoidable. What we must aim for is to know when we have handled all cases.

- *Unexpected arguments:* Functions take arguments. If a function is given an argument we don't handle, we have a problem. An example is calling the standard library square root function with –1.2: **sqrt(–1.2)**. Since **sqrt()** of a **double** returns a **double**, there is no possible correct return value. §5.5.3 discusses this kind of problem.

- *Unexpected input:* Programs typically read data (from a keyboard, from files, from GUIs, from network connections, etc.). A program makes many assumptions about such input, for example, that the user will input a number. What if the user inputs "aw, shut up!" rather than the expected integer? §5.6.3 and §10.6 discuss this kind of problem.

- *Unexpected state:* Most programs keep a lot of data ("state") around for use by different parts of the system. Examples are address lists, phone directories, and **vector**s of temperature readings. What if such data is incomplete or wrong? The various parts of the program must still manage. §26.3.5 discusses this kind of problem.

- *Logical errors:* That is, code that simply doesn't do what it was supposed to do; we'll just have to find and fix such problems. §6.6 and §6.9 give examples of finding such problems.

This list has a practical use. We can use it as a checklist when we are considering how far we have come with a program. No program is complete until we have considered all of these potential sources of errors. In fact, it is prudent to keep them in mind from the very start of a project, because it is most unlikely that a program that is just thrown together without thought about errors can have its errors found and removed without a serious rewrite.

5.3 Compile-time errors

When you are writing programs, your compiler is your first line of defense against errors. Before generating code, the compiler analyzes code to detect syntax errors and type errors. Only if it finds that the program completely conforms to the language specification will it allow you to proceed. Many of the errors that the compiler finds are simply "silly errors" caused by mistyping or incomplete edits of the source code. Others result from flaws in our understanding of the way parts of our program interact. To a beginner, the compiler often seems petty, but as you learn to use the language facilities – and especially the type system – to directly express your ideas, you'll come to appreciate the compiler's ability to detect problems that would otherwise have caused you hours of tedious searching for bugs.

As an example, we will look at some calls of this simple function:

```
int area(int length, int width);    // calculate area of a rectangle
```

5.3.1 Syntax errors

What if we were to call **area()** like this:

```
int s1 = area(7;      // error: ) missing
int s1 = area(7)      // error: ; missing
Int s3 = area(7);     // error: Int is not a type
int s4 = area('7);    // error: non-terminated character (' missing)
```

Each of those lines has a syntax error; that is, they are not well formed according to the C++ grammar, so the compiler will reject them. Unfortunately, syntax errors are not always easy to report in a way that you, the programmer, find easy to understand. That's because the compiler may have to read a bit further than the error to be sure that there really is an error. The effect of this is that even though syntax errors tend to be completely trivial (you'll often find it hard to believe you have made such a mistake once you find it), the reporting is often cryptic and occasionally refers to a line further on in the program. So, for syntax errors, if you don't see anything wrong with the line the compiler points to, also look at previous lines in the program.

Note that the compiler has no idea what you are trying to do, so it cannot report errors in terms of your intent, only in terms of what you did. For example, given the error in the declaration of **s3** above, a compiler is unlikely to say

"You misspelled **int**; don't capitalize the **i**."

Rather, it'll say something like

"syntax error: missing ';' before identifier 's3' "

" 's3' missing storage-class or type identifiers"

" '**Int**' missing storage-class or type identifiers"

Such messages tend to be cryptic, until you get used to them, and to use a vocabulary that can be hard to penetrate. Different compilers can give very different-

looking error messages for the same code. Fortunately, you soon get used to reading such stuff. After all, a quick look at those cryptic lines can be read as

"There was a syntax error before **s3**,
and it had something to do with the type of **Int** or **s3**."

Given that, it's not rocket science to find the problem.

TRY THIS

Try to compile those examples and see how the compiler responds.

5.3.2 Type errors

Once you have removed syntax errors, the compiler will start reporting type errors; that is, it will report mismatches between the types you declared (or forgot
to declare) for your variables, functions, etc. and the types of values or expressions you assign to them, pass as function arguments, etc. For example:

```
int x0 = arena(7);          // error: undeclared function
int x1 = area(7);           // error: wrong number of arguments
int x2 = area("seven",2);   // error: 1st argument has a wrong type
```

Let's consider these errors.

1. For **arena(7)**, we misspelled **area** as **arena**, so the compiler thinks we
   want to call a function called **arena**. (What else could it "think"? That's
   what we said.) Assuming there is no function called **arena()**, you'll get an
   error message complaining about an undeclared function. If there is a
   function called **arena**, and if that function accepts **7** as an argument, you
   have a worse problem: the program will compile but do something you
   didn't expect it to (that's a logical error; see §5.7).

2. For **area(7)**, the compiler detects the wrong number of arguments. In
   C++, every function call must provide the expected number of arguments, of the right types, and in the right order. When the type system is
   used appropriately, this can be a powerful tool for avoiding run-time errors (see §14.1).

3. For **area("seven",2)**, you might hope that the computer would look at
   "seven" and figure out that you meant the integer **7**. It won't. If a function needs an integer, you can't give it a string. C++ does support some
   implicit type conversions (see §3.9) but not **string** to **int**. The compiler
   does not try to guess what you meant. What would you have expected
   for **area("Hovel lane",2)**, **area("7,2")**, and **area("sieben","zwei")**?

These are just a few examples. There are many more errors that the compiler will find for you.

TRY THIS

> Try to compile those examples and see how the compiler responds. Try thinking of a few more errors yourself, and try those.

5.3.3 Non-errors

As you work with the compiler, you'll wish that it was smart enough to figure out what you meant; that is, you'd like some of the errors it reports not to be errors. That's natural. More surprisingly, as you gain experience, you'll begin to wish that the compiler would reject more code, rather than less. Consider:

```
int x4 = area(10,-7);       // OK: but what is a rectangle with a width of minus 7?
int x5 = area(10.7,9.3);    // OK: but calls area(10,9)
char x6 = area(100, 9999);  // OK, but truncates the result
```

For **x4** we get no error message from the compiler. From the compiler's point of view, **area(10,-7)** is fine: **area()** asks for two integers and you gave them to it; nobody said that those arguments had to be positive.

For **x5**, a good compiler will warn about the truncation of the **doubles 10.7** and **9.3** into the **ints 10** and **9** (see §3.9.2) However, the (ancient) language rules state that you can implicitly convert a **double** to an **int**, so the compiler is not allowed to reject the call **area(10.7,9.3)**.

The initialization of **x6** suffers from a variant of the same problem as the call **area(10.7,9.3)**. The **int** returned by **area(100,9999)**, probably **999900**, will be assigned to a **char**. The most likely result is for **x6** to get the "truncated" value **−36**. Again, a good compiler will give you a warning even though the (ancient) language rules prevent it from rejecting the code.

As you gain experience, you'll learn how to get the most out of the compiler's ability to detect errors and to dodge its known weaknesses. However, don't get overconfident: "my program compiled" doesn't mean that it will run. Even if it does run, it typically gives wrong results at first until you find the flaws in your logic.

5.4 Link-time errors

A program consists of several separately compiled parts, called *translation units*. Every function in a program must be declared with exactly the same type in every translation unit in which it is used. We use header files to ensure that; see §8.3. Every function must also be defined exactly once in a program. If either of these rules is violated, the linker will give an error. We discuss how to avoid link-time errors in §8.3. For now, here is an example of a program that might give a typical linker error:

```
int area(int length, int width);     // calculate area of a rectangle

int main()
{
    int x = area(2,3);
}
```

Unless we somehow have defined **area()** in another source file and linked the code generated from that source file to this code, the linker will complain that it didn't find a definition of **area()**.

The definition of **area()** must have exactly the same types (both the return type and the argument type) as we used in our file, that is:

```
int area(int x, int y) { /* . . . */ }     // "our" area()
```

Functions with the same name but different types will not match and will be ignored:

```
double area(double x, double y) { /* . . . */ }     // not "our" area()

int area(int x, int y, char unit) { /* . . . */ }        // not "our" area()
```

Note that a misspelled function name doesn't usually give a linker error. However, the compiler gives an error immediately when it sees a call to an undeclared function. That's good: compile-time errors are found earlier than link-time errors and are typically easier to fix.

The linkage rules for functions, as stated above, also hold for all other entities of a program, such as variables and types: there has to be exactly one definition of an entity with a given name, but there can be many declarations, and all have to agree exactly on its type.

5.5 Run-time errors

If your program has no compile-time errors and no link-time errors, it'll run. This is where the fun really starts. When you write the program you are able to detect errors, but it is not always easy to know what to do with an error once you catch it at run time. Consider:

```
int area(int length, int width)      // calculate area of a rectangle
{
        return length*width;
}


int framed_area(int x, int y)      // calculate area within frame
{
        return area(x-2,y-2);
}


int main()
{
        int x = -1;
        int y = 2;
        int z = 4;
        // . . .
        int area1 = area(x,y);
        int area2 = framed_area(1,z);
        int area3 = framed_area(y,z);
        double ratio = double(area1)/area3;      // convert to double to get
                                                 // floating-point division
}
```

We used the variables **x, y, z** (rather than using the values directly as arguments) to make the problems less obvious to the human reader and harder for the compiler to detect. However, these calls lead to negative values, representing areas, being assigned to **area1** and **area2**. Should we accept such erroneous results, which violate most notions of math and physics? If not, who should detect the errors: the caller of **area()** or the function itself? And how should such errors be reported?

Before answering those questions, look at the calculation of the **ratio** in the code above. It looks innocent enough. Did you notice something wrong with it? If not, look again: **area3** will be **0**, so that **double(area1)/area3** divides by zero. This leads to a hardware-detected error that terminates the program with some cryptic message relating to hardware. This is the kind of error that you – or your users – will have to deal with if you don't detect and deal sensibly with run-time errors. Most people have low tolerance for such "hardware violations" because to anyone not intimately familiar with the program all the information provided is "Something went wrong somewhere!" That's insufficient for any constructive action, so we feel angry and would like to yell at whoever supplied the program.

So, let's tackle the problem of argument errors with **area()**. We have two obvious alternatives:

    a. Let the caller of **area()** deal with bad arguments.

    b. Let **area()** (the called function) deal with bad arguments.

5.5.1 The caller deals with errors

Let's try the first alternative ("Let the user beware!") first. That's the one we'd have to choose if **area()** was a function in a library where we couldn't modify it. For better or worse, this is the most common answer.

Protecting the call of **area(x,y)** in **main()** is relatively easy:

```
if (x<=0) error("non-positive x");
if (y<=0) error("non-positive y");
int area1 = area(x,y);
```

Really, the only question is what to do if we find an error. Here, we have called a function **error()** which we will assume will do something sensible. In fact, in **std_lib_facilities.h** we supply an **error()** function that by default terminates the program with a system error message plus the string we passed as an argument to **error()**. If you prefer to write out your own error message or take other actions, you catch **runtime_error** (§5.6.2, §7.3, §7.8, §B.2.1). This suffices for most student programs and is an example of a style that can be used for more sophisticated error handling.

If we didn't need separate error messages about each argument, we would simplify:

```
if (x<=0 || y<=0) error("non-positive area() argument");    // || means "or"
int area1 = area(x,y);
```

To complete protecting **area()** from bad arguments, we have to deal with the calls through **framed_area()**. We could write:

```
if (z<=2)
        error("non-positive 2nd area() argument called by framed_area()");
int area2 = framed_area(1,z);
if (y<=2 || z<=2)
        error("non-positive area() argument called by framed_area()");
int area3 = framed_area(y,z);
```

This is messy, but there is also something fundamentally wrong. We could write this only by knowing exactly how **framed_area()** used **area()**. We had to know that **framed_area()** subtracted **2** from each argument. We shouldn't have to know such details! What if someone modified **framed_area()** to use **1** instead of **2**?

Someone doing that would have to look at every call of **framed_area()** and modify the error-checking code correspondingly. Such code is called "brittle" because it breaks easily. This is also an example of a "magic constant" (§4.3.1). We could make the code less brittle by giving the value subtracted by **framed_area()** a name:

```
const int frame_width = 2;
int framed_area(int x, int y)     // calculate area within frame
{
        return area(x–frame_width,y–frame_width);
}
```

That name could be used by code calling **frame_area()**:

```
if (1–frame_width<=0 || z–frame_width<=0)
        error("non-positive 2nd area() argument called by framed_area()");
int area2 = framed_area(1,z);
if (y–frame_width<=0 || z–frame_width<=0)
        error("non-positive area() argument called by framed_area()");
int area3 = framed_area(y,z);
```

Look at that code! Are you sure it is correct? Do you find it pretty? Is it easy to read? Actually, we find it ugly (and therefore error-prone). We have more than trebled the size of the code and exposed an implementation detail of **frame_area()**. There has to be a better way!

Look at the original code:

```
int area2 = framed_area(1,z);
int area3 = framed_area(y,z);
```

It may be wrong, but at least we can see what it is supposed to do. We can keep this code if we put the check inside **framed_area()**.

5.5.2 The callee deals with errors

Checking for valid arguments within **framed_area()** is easy, and **error()** can still be used to report a problem:

```
int framed_area(int x, int y)     // calculate area within frame
{
        const int frame_width = 2;
        if (x–frame_width<=0 || y–frame_width<=0)
                error("non-positive area() argument called by framed_area()");
        return area(x–frame_width,y–frame_width);
}
```

This is rather nice, and we no longer have to write a test for each call of **frame_area**(). For a useful function that we call 500 times in a large program, that can be a huge advantage. Furthermore, if anything to do with the error handling changes, we only have to modify the code in one place.

Note something interesting: we almost unconsciously slid from the "caller must check the arguments" approach to the "function must check its own arguments" approach (also called "the callee checks" because a called function is often called "a callee"). One benefit of the latter approach is that the argument-checking code is in one place. We don't have to search the whole program for calls. Furthermore, that one place is exactly where the arguments are to be used, so we have all the information needed easily available to do the check.

Let's apply this solution to **area**():

```
int area(int length, int width)       // calculate area of a rectangle
{
        if (length<=0 || width <=0) error("non-positive area() argument");
        return length*width;
}
```

This will catch all errors in calls to **area**(), so we no longer need to check in **framed_area**(). We might want to, though, to get a better – more specific – error message.

Checking arguments in the function seems so simple, so why don't people do that always? Inattention to error handling is one answer, sloppiness is another, but there are also respectable reasons:

- *We can't modify the function definition:* The function is in a library that for some reason can't be changed. Maybe it's used by others who don't share your notions of what constitutes good error handling. Maybe it's owned by someone else and you don't have the source code. Maybe it's in a library where new versions come regularly so that if you made a change, you'd have to change it again for each new release of the library.

- *The called function doesn't know what to do in case of error:* This is typically the case for library functions. The library writer can detect the error, but only you know what is to be done when an error occurs.

- *The called function doesn't know where it was called from:* When you get an error message, it tells you that something is wrong, but not how the executing program got to that point. Sometimes, you want an error message to be more specific.

- *Performance:* For a small function the cost of a check can be more than the cost of calculating the result. For example, that's the case with **area**(), where the check also more than doubles the size of the function (that is, the number of machine instructions that need to be executed, not just the length of the source code). For some programs, that can be critical, especially if the same information is checked repeatedly as functions call each other, passing information along more or less unchanged.

So what should you do? Check your arguments in a function unless you have a good reason not to.

After examining a few related topics, we'll return to the question of how to deal with bad arguments in §5.9.

5.5.3 Error reporting

Let's consider a slightly different question: once you have checked a set of arguments and found an error, what should you do? Sometimes you can return an "error value." For example:

```
// ask user for a yes-or-no answer;
// return 'b' to indicate a bad answer (i.e., not yes or no)
char ask_user(string question)
{
        cout << question << "? (yes or no)\n";
        string answer = " ";
        cin >> answer;
        if (answer =="y" || answer=="yes") return 'y';
        if (answer =="n" || answer=="no") return 'n';
        return 'b';     // 'b' for "bad answer"
}
```

```
// calculate area of a rectangle;
// return −1 to indicate a bad argument
int area(int length, int width)
{
        if (length<=0 || width <=0) return −1;
        return length*width;
}
```

That way, we can have the called function do the detailed checking, while letting each caller handle the error as desired. This approach seems like it could work, but it has a couple of problems that make it unusable in many cases:

- Now both the called function and all callers must test. The caller has only a simple test to do but must still write that test and decide what to do if it fails.

- A caller can forget to test. That can lead to unpredictable behavior further along in the program.

- Many functions do not have an "extra" return value that they can use to indicate an error. For example, a function that reads an integer from input (such as, **cin**'s operator **>>**) can obviously return any **int** value, so there is no **int** that it could return to indicate failure.

The second case above – a caller forgetting to test – can easily lead to surprises. For example:

```
int f(int x, int y, int z)
{
        int area1 = area(x,y);
        if (area1<=0) error("non-positive area");
        int area2 = framed_area(1,z);
        int area3 = framed_area(y,z);
        double ratio = double(area1)/area3;
        // . . .

}
```

Do you see the errors? This kind of error is hard to find because there is no obvious "wrong code" to look at: the error is the absence of a test.

TRY THIS

Test this program with a variety of values. Print out the values of **area1**, **area2**, **area3**, and **ratio**. Insert more tests until all errors are caught. How do you know that you caught all errors? This is not a trick question; in this particular example you can give a valid argument for having caught all errors.

There is another solution that deals with that problem: using exceptions.

5.6 Exceptions

Like most modern programming languages, C++ provides a mechanism to help deal with errors: exceptions. The fundamental idea is to separate detection of an error (which should be done in a called function) from the handling of an error (which should be done in the calling function) while ensuring that a detected error cannot be ignored; that is, exceptions provide a mechanism that allows us to combine the best of the various approaches to error handling we have explored so far. Nothing makes error handling easy, but exceptions make it easier.

The basic idea is that if a function finds an error that it cannot handle, it does not **return** normally; instead, it **throws** an exception indicating what went wrong. Any direct or indirect caller can **catch** the exception, that is, specify what to do if the called code used **throw**. A function expresses interest in exceptions by using a **try**-block (as described in the following subsections) listing the kinds of exceptions it wants to handle in the **catch**-parts of the **try**-block. If no caller catches an exception, the program terminates.

We'll come back to exceptions much later (Chapter 19) to see how to use them in slightly more advanced ways.

5.6.1 Bad arguments

Here is a version of **area()** using exceptions:

```
class Bad_area { };      // a type specifically for reporting errors from area()

// calculate area of a rectangle;
// throw a Bad_area exception in case of a bad argument
int area(int length, int width)
{
        if (length<=0 || width <=0) throw Bad_area();
        return length*width;
}
```

That is, if the arguments are OK, we return the area as always; if not, we get out of **area()** using the **throw**, hoping that some **catch** will provide an appropriate response. **Bad_area** is a new type we define with no other purpose than to provide something unique to **throw** from **area()** so that some **catch** can recognize it as the kind of exception thrown by **area()**. User-defined types (classes and enumeration) will be discussed in Chapter 9. The notation **Bad_area()** means "Make an object of type **Bad_area**," so **throw Bad_area()** means "Make an object of type **Bad_area** and **throw** it."

We can now write

```
int main()
try {
        int x = -1;
        int y = 2;
        int z = 4;
        // . . .
        int area1 = area(x,y);
        int area2 = framed_area(1,z);
        int area3 = framed_area(y,z);
        double ratio = area1/area3;
}
```

```
catch (Bad_area) {
    cout << "Oops! bad arguments to area()\n";
}
```

First note that this handles all calls to **area()**, both the one in **main()** and the two through **framed_area()**. Second, note how the handling of the error is cleanly separated from the detection of the error: **main()** knows nothing about which function did a **throw Bad_area()**, and **area()** knows nothing about which function (if any) cares to **catch** the **Bad_area** exceptions it **throws**. This separation is especially important in large programs written using many libraries. In such programs, nobody can "just deal with an error by putting some code where it's needed," because nobody would want to modify code in both the application and in all of the libraries.

5.6.2 Range errors

Most real-world code deals with collections of data; that is, it uses all kinds of tables, lists, etc. of data elements to do a job. In the context of C++, we often refer to "collections of data" as *containers*. The most common and useful standard library container is the **vector** we introduced in §4.6. A **vector** holds a number of elements, and we can determine that number by calling the **vector**'s **size()** member function. What happens if we try to use an element with an index (subscript) that isn't in the valid range **[0:v.size())**? The general notation **[low:high)** means indices from **low** to **high−1**, that is, including low but not high:

Before answering that question, we should pose another question and answer it:

> "Why would you do that?" After all, you know that a subscript for **v** should be in the range **[0,v.size())**, so just be sure that's so!

As it happens, that's easy to say but sometimes hard to do. Consider this plausible program:

```
vector<int> v;        // a vector ints
int i;
while (cin>>i) v.push_back(i);      // get values
for (int i = 0; i<=v.size(); ++i)        // print values
    cout << "v[" << i <<"] == " << v[i] << endl;
```

Do you see the error? Please try to spot it before reading on. It's not an uncommon error. We have made such errors ourselves — especially late at night when we were tired. Errors are always more common when you are tired or rushed. We use **0** and **size()** to try to make sure that **i** is always in range when we do **v[i]**.

Unfortunately, we made a mistake. Look at the **for**-loop: the termination condition is **i<=v.size()** rather than the correct **i<v.size()**. This has the unfortunate consequence that if we read in five integers we'll try to write out six. We try to read **v[5]**, which is one beyond the end of the **vector**. This kind of error is so common and "famous" that it has several names: it is an example of an *off-by-one error*, a *range error* because the index (subscript) wasn't in the range required by the **vector**, and a *bounds error* because the index was not within the limits (bounds) of the **vector**.

Here is a simpler version that produces the same effect:

```
vector<int> v(5);
int x = v[5];
```

However, we doubt that you'd have considered that realistic and worth serious attention.

So what actually happens when we make such a range error? The subscript operation of **vector** knows the size of the **vector**, so it can check (and the **vector** we are using does; see §4.6 and §19.4). If that check fails, the subscript operation throws an exception of type **out_of_range**. So, if the off-by-one code above had been part of a program that caught exceptions, we would at least have gotten a decent error message:

```
int main()
try {
        vector<int> v;          // a vector ints
        int x;
        while (cin>>x) v.push_back(x);        // set values
        for (int i = 0; i<=v.size(); ++i)        // print values
                cout << "v[" << i <<"] == " << v[i] << endl;
} catch (out_of_range_error) {
        cerr << "Oops! Range error\n";
        return 1;
} catch (...) {                    // catch all other exceptions
        cerr << "Exception: something went wrong\n";
        return 2;
}
```

Note that a range error is really a special case of the argument errors we discussed in §5.5.2. We didn't trust ourselves to consistently check the range of **vector** indices, so we told **vector**'s subscript operation to do it for us. For the reasons we outline, **vector**'s subscript function (called **vector::operator[]**) reports finding an error by throwing an exception. What else could it do? It has no idea what we would like to happen in case of a range error. The author of **vector** couldn't even know what programs his or her code would be part of.

5.6.3 Bad input

We'll postpone the detailed discussion of what to do with bad input until §10.6. However, once bad input is detected, it is dealt with using the same techniques and language features as argument errors and range errors. Here, we'll just show how you can tell if your input operations succeeded. Consider reading a floating-point number:

```
double d = 0;
cin >> d;
```

We can test if the last input operation succeeded by testing **cin**:

```
if (cin) {
        // all is well, and we can try reading again
}
else {
        // the last read didn't succeed, so we take some other action
}
```

There are several possible reasons for that input operation's failure. The one that should concern you right now is that there wasn't a **double** for **>>** to read.

During the early stages of development, we often want to indicate that we have found an error but aren't yet ready to do anything particularly clever about it; we just want to report the error and terminate the program. Later, maybe, we'll come back and do something more appropriate. For example:

```
double some_function()
{
        double d = 0;
        cin >> d;
        if (!cin) error("couldn't read a double in 'some_function()'");
        // do something useful
}
```

The string passed to **error**() can then be printed as a help to debugging or as a message to the user. How can we write **error**() so as to be useful in a lot of programs? It can't return a value because we wouldn't know what to do with that value; instead **error()** is supposed to terminate the program after getting its message written. In addition, we might want to take some minor action before exiting, such as keeping a window alive long enough for us to read the message. That's an obvious job for an exception (see §7.3).

The standard library defines a few exceptions, such as the **out_of_range** thrown by **vector**. It also supplies **runtime_error** which is pretty ideal for our needs because it holds a string that can be used by an error handler. So, we can write our simple **error()** like this: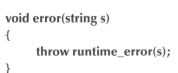

```
void error(string s)
{
        throw runtime_error(s);
}
```

When we want to deal with **runtime_error** we simply catch it. For simple programs, catching **runtime_error** in **main()** is ideal:

```
int main()
try {
        // our program
        return 0;        // 0 indicates success
}
catch (runtime_error& e) {
        cerr << "runtime error: " << e.what() << '\n';
        keep_window_open();
        return 1;        // 1 indicates failure
}
```

The call **e.what()** extracts the error message from the **runtime_error**. The & in

```
catch(runtime_error& e) {
```

is an indicator that we want to "pass the exception by reference." For now, please treat this as simply an irrelevant technicality. In §8.5.4–6, we explain what it means to pass something by reference.

Note that we used **cerr** rather than **cout** for our error output: **cerr** is exactly like **cout** except that it is meant for error output. By default both **cerr** and **cout** write to the screen, but **cerr** isn't optimized so it is more resilient to errors, and on some operating systems it can be diverted to a different target, such as a file. Using **cerr** also has the simple effect of documenting that what we write relates to errors. Consequently, we use **cerr** for error messages.

As it happens, **out_of_range** is not a **runtime_error**, so catching **runtime_error** does not deal with the **out_of_range** errors that we might get from misuse of **vectors** and other standard library container types. However, both **out_of_range** and **runtime_error** are "exceptions," so we can catch **exception** to deal with both:

```
int main()
try {
     // our program
     return 0;      // 0 indicates success
}
catch (exception& e) {
     cerr << "error: " << e.what() << '\n';
     keep_window_open();
     return 1;      // 1 indicates failure
}
catch (...) {
     cerr << "Oops: unknown exception!\n";
     keep_window_open();
     return 2;      // 2 indicates failure
}
```

We added **catch(...)** to handle exceptions of any type whatsoever.

Dealing with exceptions of both type **out_of_range** and type **runtime_error** through a single type **exception**, said to be a common base (supertype) of both, is a most useful and general technique that we will explore in Chapters 13–16.

Note again that the return value from **main()** is passed to "the system" that invoked the program. Some systems (such as Unix) often use that value, whereas others (such as Windows) typically ignore it. A zero indicates successful completion and a nonzero return value from **main()** indicates some sort of failure.

When you use **error()**, you'll often wish to pass two pieces of information along to describe the problem. In that case, just concatenate the strings describing those two pieces of information. This is so common that we provide a second version of **error()** for that:

```
void error(string s1, string s2)
{
     throw runtime_error(s1+s2);
}
```

This simple error handling will do for a while, until our needs increase significantly and our sophistication as designers and programmers increases correspondingly. Note that we can use **error()** independently of how many function calls we have done on the way to the error: **error()** will find its way to the nearest catch of **runtime_error**, typically the one in **main()**. For examples of the use of exceptions and **error()**, see §7.3 and §7.7. If you don't catch an exception, you'll get a default system error (an "uncaught exception" error).

TRY THIS

To see what an uncaught exception error looks like, run a small program that uses **error()** without catching any exceptions.

5.6.4 Narrowing errors

In §3.9.2 we saw a nasty kind of error: when we assign a value that's "too large to fit" to a variable, it is implicitly truncated. For example:

```
int x = 2.9;
char c = 1066;
```

Here **x** will get the value **2** rather than **2.9**, because **x** is an **int** and **int**s don't have values that are fractions of an integer, just whole integers (obviously). Similarly, if we use the common ASCII character set, **c** will get the value **42** (representing the character *), rather than **1066**, because there is no **char** with the value **1066** in that character set.

In §3.9.2 we saw how we could protect ourselves against such narrowing by testing. Given exceptions (and templates; see §19.3) we can write a function that tests and throws a **runtime_error** exception if an assignment or initialization would lead to a changed value. For example:

```
int x1 = narrow_cast<int>(2.9);      // throws
int x2 = narrow_cast<int>(2.0);      // OK
char c1 = narrow_cast<char>(1066);   // throws
char c2 = narrow_cast<char>(85);     // OK
```

The < . . . > brackets are the same as are used for **vector<int>**. They are used when we need to specify a type, rather than a value, to express an idea. They are called *template arguments*. We can use **narrow_cast** when we need to convert a value and we are not sure "if it will fit"; it is defined in **std_lib_facilities.h** and implemented using **error()**. The word *cast* means "type conversion" and indicates the operation's role in dealing with something that's broken (like a cast on a broken leg). Note that a cast doesn't change its operand; it produces a new value corresponding to its operand of the required type.

5.7 Logic errors

Once we have removed the initial compiler and linker errors, the program runs. Typically, what happens next is that no output is produced or that the output that the program produces is just wrong. This can occur for a number of reasons. Maybe your understanding of the underlying program logic is flawed; maybe you didn't write what you thought you wrote; or maybe you made some "silly error" in one of your control statements, or whatever. Logic errors are usually the most difficult to find and eliminate, because at this stage the computer does what you asked it to. Your job now is to figure out why that wasn't really what you meant. Basically, a computer is a very fast moron. It does exactly what you tell it to do, and that can be most humbling.

Let us try to illustrate this with a simple example. Consider this code for finding the lowest, highest, and average temperature values in a set of data:

```
int main()
{
        vector<double> temps;        // temperatures

        double temp = 0;
        double sum = 0;
        double high_temp = 0;
        double low_temp = 0;

        while (cin>>temp)            // read and put into temps
                temps.push_back(temp);

        for (int i = 0; i<temps.size(); ++i)
        {
                if(temps[i] > high_temp) high_temp = temps[i];    // find high
                if(temps[i] < low_temp) low_temp = temps[i];      // find low
                sum += temps[i];        // compute sum
        }

        cout << "High temperature: " << high_temp<< endl;
        cout << "Low temperature: " << low_temp << endl;
        cout << "Average temperature: " << sum/temps.size() << endl;
}
```

We tested this program by entering the hourly temperature values from the weather center in Lubbock, Texas, for February 16, 2004 (Texas still uses Fahrenheit):

−16.5,	−23.2,	−24.0,	−25.7,	−26.1,	−18.6,	−9.7,	−2.4,
7.5,	12.6,	23.8,	25.3,	28.0,	34.8,	36.7,	41.5,
40.3,	42.6,	39.7,	35.4,	12.6,	6.5,	−3.7,	−14.3

The output was

High temperature: 42.6
Low temperature: −26.1
Average temperature: 9.3

A naive programmer would conclude that the program works just fine. An irresponsible programmer would ship it to a customer. It would be prudent to test it again with another set of data. This time use the temperatures from July 23, 2004:

76.5,	73.5,	71.0,	73.6,	70.1,	73.5,	77.6,	85.3,
88.5,	91.7,	95.9,	99.2,	98.2,	100.6,	106.3,	112.4,
110.2,	103.6,	94.9,	91.7,	88.4,	85.2,	85.4,	87.7

This time, the output was

High temperature: 112.4
Low temperature: 0.0
Average temperature: 89.2

Oops, something is not quite right. Hard frost (0.0°F is about −18°C) in Lubbock in July would mean the end of the world! Did you spot the error? Since **low_temp** was initialized at **0.0**, it would remain **0.0** unless one of the temperatures in the data was below zero.

TRY THIS

Get this program to run. Check that our input really does produce that output. Try to "break" the program (i.e., get it to give wrong results) by giving it other input sets. What is the least amount of input you can give it to get it to fail?

Unfortunately, there are more errors in this program. What would happen if all of the temperatures were below zero? The initialization for **high_temp** has the equivalent problem to **low_temp**: **high_temp** will remain at **0.0** unless there is a higher temperature in the data. This program wouldn't work for the South Pole in winter either.

These errors are fairly typical; they will not cause any errors when you compile the program or cause wrong results for "reasonable" inputs. However, we forgot to think about what we should consider "reasonable." Here is an improved program:

```cpp
int main()
{
    double temp = 0;
    double sum = 0;
    double high_temp = –1000;    // initialize to impossibly low
    double low_temp = 1000;      // initialize to "impossibly high"
    int no_of_temps = 0;

    while (cin>>temp) {          // read temp
        ++no_of_temps;          // count temperatures
        sum += temp;            // compute sum
        if (temp > high_temp) high_temp = temp;   // find high
        if (temp < low_temp) low_temp = temp;     // find low
    }

    cout << "High temperature: " << high_temp<< endl;
    cout << "Low temperature: " << low_temp << endl;
    cout << "Average temperature: " << sum/no_of_temps << endl;
}
```

Does it work? How would you be certain? How would you precisely define "work"? Where did we get the values **1000** and **–1000**? Remember that we warned about "magic constants" (§5.5.1). Having **1000** and **–1000** as literal values in the middle of the program is bad style, but are the values also wrong? Are there places where the temperatures go below –1000°F (–573°C)? Are there places where the temperatures go above 1000°F (538°C)?

TRY THIS

Look it up. Check some information sources to pick good values for the **min_temp** (the "minimum temperature") and **max_temp** (the "maximum temperature") constants for our program. Those values will determine the limits of usefulness of our program.

5.8 Estimation

Imagine you have written a program that does a simple calculation, say, computing the area of a hexagon. You run it and it gives the area −34.56. You just know that's wrong. Why? Because no shape has a negative area. So, you fix that bug (whatever it was) and get 21.65685. Is that right? That's harder to say because we don't usually keep the formula for the area of a hexagon in our heads. What we must do before making fools of ourselves by delivering a program that produces ridiculous results is just to check that the answer is plausible. In this case, that's easy. A hexagon is much like a square. We scribble our regular hexagon on a piece of paper and eyeball it to be about the size of a 3-by-3 square. Such a square has the area 9. Bummer, our 21.65685 can't be right! So we work over our program again and get 9.65685. Now, that just might be right!

The general point here has nothing to do with hexagons. The point is that unless we have some idea of what a correct answer will be like − even ever so approximately − we don't have a clue whether our result is reasonable. Always ask yourself this question:

1. Is this answer to this particular problem plausible?

You should also ask the more general (and often far harder) question:

2. How would I recognize a plausible result?

Here, we are not asking, "What's the exact answer?" or "What's the correct answer?" That's what we are writing the program to tell us. All we want is to know that the answer is not ridiculous. Only when we know that we have a plausible answer does it make sense to proceed with further work.

Estimation is a noble art that combines common sense and some very simple arithmetic applied to a few facts. Some people are good at doing estimates in their heads, but we prefer scribbles "on the back of an envelope" because we find we get confused less often that way. What we call estimation here is an informal set of techniques that are sometimes (humorously) called *guesstimation* because they combine a bit of guessing with a bit of calculation.

TRY THIS

Our hexagon was regular with 2cm sides. Did we get that answer right? Just do the "back of the envelope" calculation. Take a piece a paper and scribble on it. Don't feel that's below you. Many famous scientists have been greatly admired for their ability to come up with an approximate answer using a pencil and the back of an envelope (or a napkin). This is an ability − a simple habit, really − that can save us a lot of time and confusion.

Often, making an estimate involves coming up with estimates of data that are needed for a proper calculation, but that we don't yet have. Imagine you have to test a program that estimates driving times between cities. Is a driving time of 15 hours and 33 minutes plausible for New York City to Denver? From London to Nice? Why or why not? What data do you have to "guess" to answer these questions? Often, a quick web search can be most helpful. For example, 2000 miles is not a bad guess on the road distance from New York City to Denver, and it would be hard (and illegal) to maintain an average speed of 130m/hr, so 15 hours is not plausible (15*130 is just a bit less than 2000). You can check: we overestimated both the distance and the average speed, but for a check of plausibility we don't have to be exactly right; we just have to guess well enough.

TRY THIS

Estimate those driving times. Also, estimate the corresponding flight times (using ordinary commercial air travel). Then, try to verify your estimates by using appropriate sources, such as maps and timetables. We'd use online sources.

5.9 Debugging

When you have written (drafted?) a program, it'll have errors. Small programs do occasionally compile and run correctly the first time you try. But if that happens for anything but a completely trivial program, you should at first be very, very suspicious. If it really did run correctly the first time, go tell your friends and celebrate – because this won't happen every year.

So, when you have written some code, you have to find and remove the errors. That process is usually called *debugging* and the errors *bugs*. The term *bug* is often claimed to have originated from a hardware failure caused by insects in the electronics in the days when computers were racks of vacuum tubes and relays filling rooms. Several people have been credited with the discovery and the application of the word *bug* to errors in software. The most famous of those is Grace Murray Hopper, the inventor of the COBOL programming language (§22.2.2.2). Whoever invented the term more than 50 years ago, *bug* is evocative and ubiquitous. The activity of deliberately searching for errors and removing them is called *debugging*.

Debugging works roughly like this:

1. Get the program to compile.
2. Get the program to link.
3. Get the program to do what it is supposed to do.

Basically, we go through this sequence again and again: hundreds of times, thousands of times, again and again for years for really large programs. Each time something doesn't work we have to find what caused the problem and fix it. I consider debugging the most tedious and time-wasting aspect of programming and will go to great lengths during design and programming to minimize the amount of time spent hunting for bugs. Others find that hunt thrilling and the essence of programming – it can be as addictive as any video game and keep a programmer glued to the terminal for days and nights (I can vouch for that from personal experience also).

Here is how *not* to debug:

```
while (the program doesn't appear to work) {      // pseudo code
        Randomly look through the program for something that "looks odd"
        Change it to look better
}
```

Why do we bother to mention this? It's obviously a poor algorithm with little guarantee of success. Unfortunately, that description is only a slight caricature of what many people find themselves doing late at night when feeling particularly lost and clueless, having tried "everything else."

The key question in debugging is

> *How would I know if the program actually worked correctly?*

If you can't answer that question, you are in for a long and tedious debug session, and most likely your users are in for some frustration. We keep returning to this point because anything that helps answer that question minimizes debugging and helps produce correct and maintainable programs. Basically, we'd like to design our programs so that bugs have nowhere to hide. That's typically too much to ask for, but we aim to structure programs to minimize the chance of error and maximize the chance of finding the errors that do creep in.

5.9.1 Practical debug advice

Start thinking about debugging before you write the first line of code. Once you have a lot of code written it's too late to try to simplify debugging.

Decide how to report errors: "Use **error**() and catch **exception** in **main**()" will be your default answer in this book.

Make the program easy to read so that you have a chance of spotting the bugs:

- Comment your code well. That doesn't simply mean "Add a lot of comments." You don't say in English what is better said in code. Rather, you say in the comments – as clearly and briefly as you can – what can't be said clearly in code:

- The name of the program
- The purpose of the program
- Who wrote this code and when
- Version numbers
- What complicated code fragments are supposed to do
- What the general design ideas are
- How the source code is organized
- What assumptions are made about inputs
- What parts of the code are still missing and what cases are still not handled

- Use meaningful names.

  - That doesn't simply mean "Use long names."

- Use a consistent layout of code.

  - Your IDE tries to help, but it can't do everything and you are the one responsible.
  - The style used in this book is a reasonable starting point.

- Break code into small functions, each expressing a logical action.

  - Try to avoid functions longer than a page or two; most functions will be much shorter.

- Avoid complicated code sequences.

  - Try to avoid nested loops, nested **if**-statements, complicated conditions, etc. Unfortunately, you sometimes need those, but remember that complicated code is where bugs can most easily hide.

- Use library facilities rather than your own code when you can.

  - A library is likely to be better thought out and better tested than what you could produce as an alternative while busily solving your main problem.

This is pretty abstract just now, but we'll show you example after example as we go along.

Get the program to compile. Obviously, your compiler is your best help here. Its error messages are usually helpful – even if we always wish for better ones – and, unless you are a real expert, assume that the compiler is always right; if you are a real expert, this book wasn't written for you. Occasionally, you will feel that the rules the compiler enforces are stupid and unnecessary (they rarely are) and that things could and ought to be simpler (indeed, but they are not). However, as they say, "a poor craftsman curses his tools." A good craftsman knows the strengths and weaknesses of his tools and adjusts his work accordingly. Here are some common compile-time errors:

- Is every string literal terminated?

```
cout << "Hello, << name << '\n';        // oops!
```

- Is every character literal terminated?

```
cout << "Hello, " << name << '\n;        // oops!
```

- Is every block terminated?

```
int f(int a)
{
        if (a>0) { /* do something */ else { /* do something else */ }
}        // oops!
```

- Is every set of parentheses matched?

```
if (a<=0        // oops!
        x = f(y);
```

The compiler generally reports this kind of error "late"; it doesn't know you meant to type a closing parenthesis after the 0.

- Is every name declared?

    - Did you include needed headers (for now, **#include "std_lib_facilities.h"**)?

    - Is every name declared before it's used?

    - Did you spell all names correctly?

```
int count;  /* . . . */ ++Count;        // oops!
char ch;    /* . . . */ Cin>>c;        // double oops!
```

- Did you terminate each expression statement with a semicolon?

```
x = sqrt(y)+2        // oops!
z = x+3;
```

We present more examples in this chapter's drills. Also, keep in mind the classification of errors from §5.2.

After the program compiles and links, next comes what is typically the hardest part: figuring out why the program doesn't do what it's supposed to. You look at the output and try to figure out how your code could have produced that. Actually, first you often look at a blank screen (or window), wondering how your program could have failed to produce any output. A common first problem with a Windows console mode program is that the console window disappears before you have had a chance to see the output (if any). One solution is to call **keep_window_open()** from our **std_lib_facilities.h** at the end of **main()**. Then the program will ask for input before exiting and you can look at the output produced before giving it the input that will let it close the window.

When looking for a bug, carefully follow the code statement by statement from the last point that you are sure it was correct. Pretend you're the computer executing the program. Does the output match your expectations? Of course not, or you wouldn't be debugging.

- Often, when you don't see the problem, the reason is that you "see" what you expect to see rather than what you wrote. Consider:

```
for (int i = 0; i<=max; ++j) {            // oops! (twice)
      for (int i=0; 0<max; ++i);          // print the elements of v
cout << "v[" << i << "]==" << v[i] << '\n';
```

This last example came from a real program written by experienced programmers (we expect it was written very late some night).

- Often when you do not see the problem, the reason is that there is too much code being executed between the point where the program produced the last good output and the next output (or lack of output). Most programming environments provide a way to execute ("step through") the statements of a program one by one. Eventually, you'll learn to use such facilities, but for simple problems and simple programs, you can just temporarily put in a few extra output statements (using **cerr**) to help you see what's going on. For example:

```
int my_fct(int a, double d)
{
      int res = 0;
      cerr << "my_fct(" << a << "," << d << ")\n";
      // . . . misbehaving code here . . .
      cerr << "my_fct() returns " << res << '\n';
      return res;
}
```

- Insert statements that check invariants (that is, conditions that should always hold; see §9.4.3) in sections of code suspected of harboring bugs. For example:

```
int my_complicated_function(int a, int b, int c)
// the arguments are positive and a < b < c
```

```
    {
        if (!(0<a && a<b && b<c)) // ! means "not" and && means "and"
            error("bad arguments for mcf");
        // . . .
    }
```

- If that doesn't have any effect, insert invariants in sections of code not suspected of harboring bugs; if you can't find a bug, you are almost certainly looking in the wrong place.

A statement that states (asserts) an invariant is called an *assertion* (or just an *assert*).

Interestingly enough, there are many effective ways of programming. Different people successfully use dramatically different techniques. Many differences in debugging technique come from differences in the kinds of programs people work on; others seem to have to do with differences in the ways people think. To the best of our knowledge, there is no one best way to debug. One thing should always be remembered, though: messy code can easily harbor bugs. By keeping your code as simple, logical, and well formatted as possible, you decrease your debug time.

5.10 Pre- and post-conditions

Now, let us return to the question of how to deal with bad arguments to a function. The call of a function is basically the best point to think about correct code and to catch errors: this is where a logically separate computation starts (and ends on the return). Look at what we did in the piece of advice above:

```
int my_complicated_function(int a, int b, int c)
// the arguments are positive and a < b < c
{
    if (!(0<a && a<b && b<c))        // ! means "not" and && means "and"
        error("bad arguments for mcf");
    // . . .
}
```

First, we stated (in a comment) what the function required of its arguments, and then we checked that this requirement held (throwing an exception if it did not).

This is a good basic strategy. A requirement of a function upon its argument is often called a *pre-condition*: it must be true for the function to perform its action correctly. The question is just what to do if the pre-condition is violated (doesn't hold). We basically have two choices:

1. Ignore it (hope/assume that all callers give correct arguments).
2. Check it (and report the error somehow).

Looking at it this way, argument types are just a way of having the compiler check the simplest pre-conditions for us and report them at compile time. For example:

```
int x = my_complicated_function(1, 2, "horsefeathers");
```

Here, the compiler will catch that the requirement ("pre-condition") that the third argument be an integer was violated. Basically, what we are talking about here is what to do with the requirements/pre-conditions that the compiler can't check.

Our suggestion is to always document pre-conditions in comments (so that a caller can see what a function expects). A function with no comments documented will be assumed to handle every possible argument value. But should we believe that callers read those comments and follow the rules? Sometimes we have to, but the "check the arguments in the callee" rule could be stated "Let a function check its pre-conditions." We should do that whenever we don't see a reason not to. The reasons most often given for not checking pre-conditions are:

- Nobody would give bad arguments.
- It would slow down my code.
- It is too complicated to check.

The first reason can be reasonable only when we happen to know "who" calls a function – and in real-world code that can be very hard to know.

The second reason is valid far less often than people think and should most often be ignored as an example of "premature optimization." You can always remove checks if they really turn out to be a burden. You cannot easily gain the correctness they ensure or get back the nights' sleep you lost looking for bugs those tests could have caught.

The third reason is the serious one. It is easy (once you are an experienced programmer) to find examples where checking a pre-condition would take significantly more work than executing the function. An example is a lookup in a dictionary: a pre-condition is that the dictionary entries are sorted – and verifying that a dictionary is sorted can be far more expensive than a lookup. Sometimes, it can also be difficult to express a pre-condition in code and to be sure that you expressed it correctly. However, when you write a function, always consider if you can write a quick check of the pre-conditions, and do so unless you have a good reason not to.

Writing pre-conditions (even as comments) also has a significant benefit for the quality of your programs: it forces you to think about what a function requires. If you can't state that simply and precisely in a couple of comment lines, you probably haven't thought hard enough about what you are doing. Experience shows that writing those pre-condition comments and the pre-condition tests helps you avoid many design mistakes. We did mention that we hated debugging; explicitly stating pre-conditions helps in avoiding design errors as well as catching usage errors early. Writing

```
int my_complicated_function(int a, int b, int c)
// the arguments are positive and a < b < c
{
        if (!(0<a && a<b && b<c))        // ! means "not" and && means "and"
            error("bad arguments for mcf");
        // . . .
}
```

saves you time and grief compared with the apparently simpler

```
int my_complicated_function(int a, int b, int c)
{
        // . . .
}
```

5.10.1 Post-conditions

Stating pre-conditions helps us improve our design and catch usage errors early. Can this idea of explicitly stating requirements be used elsewhere? Yes, one more place immediately springs to mind: the return value! After all, we typically have to state what a function returns; that is, if we return a value from a function we are *always* making a promise about the return value (how else would a caller know what to expect?). Let's look at our area function (from §5.6.1) again:

```
// calculate area of a rectangle;
// throw a Bad_area exception in case of a bad argument
int area(int length, int width)
{
        if (length<=0 || width <=0) throw Bad_area();
        return length*width;
}
```

It checks its pre-condition, but it doesn't state it in the comment (that may be OK for such a short function) and it assumes that the computation is correct (that's probably OK for such a trivial computation). However, we could be a bit more explicit:

```
int area(int length, int width)
// calculate area of a rectangle;
// pre-conditions: length and width are positive
```

```
// post-condition: returns a positive value that is the area
{
        if (length<=0 || width <=0) error("area() pre-condition");
        int a = length*width;
        if (a<=0) error("area() post-condition");
        return a;
}
```

We couldn't check the complete post-condition, but we checked the part that said that it should be positive.

TRY THIS

Find a pair of values so that the pre-condition of this version of area holds, but the post-condition doesn't.

Pre- and post-conditions provide basic sanity checks in code. As such they are closely connected to the notion of invariants (§9.4.3), correctness (§4.2, §5.2), and testing (Chapter 26).

5.11 Testing

How do we know when to stop debugging? Well, we keep debugging until we have found all the bugs — or at least we try to. How do we know that we have found the last bug? We don't. "The last bug" is a programmers' joke: there is no such creature; we never find "the last bug" in a large program. By the time we might have, we are busy modifying the program for some new use.

In addition to debugging we need a systematic way to search for errors. This is called *testing* and we'll get back to that in §7.3, the exercises in Chapter 10, and in Chapter 26. Basically, testing is executing a program with a large and systematically selected set of inputs and comparing the results to what was expected. A run with a given set of inputs is called a *test case*. Realistic programs can require millions of test cases. Basically, systematic testing cannot be done by humans typing in one test after another, so we'll have to wait a few chapters before we have the tools necessary to properly approach testing. However, in the meantime, remember that we have to approach testing with the attitude that finding errors is good. Consider:

Attitude 1:   I'm smarter than any program! I'll break that @#$%^ code!
Attitude 2:   I polished this code for two weeks. It's perfect!

Who do you think will find more errors? Of course, the very best is an experienced person with a bit of "attitude 1" who coolly, calmly, patiently, and systematically works through the possible failings of the program. Good testers are worth their weight in gold.

We try to be systematic in choosing our test cases and always try both correct and incorrect inputs. §7.3 gives the first example of this.

Drill

Below are 25 code fragments. Each is meant to be inserted into this "scaffolding":

```cpp
#include "std_lib_facilities.h"

int main()
try {
    <<your code here>>
    keep_window_open();
    return 0;
}
catch (exception& e) {
    cerr << "error: " << e.what() << '\n';
    keep_window_open();
    return 1;
}
catch (...) {
    cerr << "Oops: unknown exception!\n";
    keep_window_open();
    return 2;
}
```

Each has zero or more errors. Your task is to find and remove all errors in each program. When you have removed those bugs, the resulting program will compile, run, and write "Success!" Even if you think you have spotted an error, you still need to enter the (original, unimproved) program fragment and test it; you may have guessed wrong about what the error is, or there may be more errors in a fragment than you spotted. Also, one purpose of this drill is to give you a feel for how your compiler reacts to different kinds of errors. Do not enter the scaffolding 25 times – that's a job for cut and paste or some similar "mechanical" technique. Do not fix problems by simply deleting a statement; repair them by changing, adding, or deleting a few characters.

1. Cout << "Success!\n";
2. cout << "Success!\n;
3. cout << "Success" << !\n"
4. cout << success << endl;
5. string res = 7; vector<int> v(10); v[5] = res; cout << "Success!\n";
6. vector<int> v(10); v(5) = 7; if (v(5)!=7) cout << "Success!\n";
7. if (cond) cout << "Success!\n"; else cout << "Fail!\n";
8. bool c = false; if (c) cout << "Success!\n"; else cout << "Fail!\n";
9. string s = "ape"; boo c = "fool"<s; if (c) cout << "Success!\n";
10. string s = "ape"; if (s=="fool") cout << "Success!\n";
11. string s = "ape"; if (s=="fool") cout < "Success!\n";
12. string s = "ape"; if (s+"fool") cout < "Success!\n";
13. vector<char> v(5); for (int i=0; 0<v.size(); ++i) ; cout << "Success!\n";
14. vector<char> v(5); for (int i=0; i<=v.size(); ++i) ; cout << "Success!\n";
15. string s = "Success!\n"; for (int i=0; i<6; ++i) cout << s[i];
16. if (true) then cout << "Success!\n"; else cout << "Fail!\n";
17. int x = 2000; char c = x; if (c==2000) cout << "Success!\n";
18. string s = "Success!\n"; for (int i=0; i<10; ++i) cout << s[i];
19. vector v(5); for (int i=0; i<=v.size(); ++i) ; cout << "Success!\n";
20. int i=0; int j = 9; while (i<10) ++j; if (j<i) cout << "Success!\n";
21. int x = 2; double d = 5/(x–2); if (d==2*x+0.5) cout << "Success!\n";
22. string<char> s = "Success!\n"; for (int i=0; i<=10; ++i) cout << s[i];
23. int i=0; while (i<10) ++j; if (j<i) cout << "Success!\n";
24. int x = 4; double d = 5/(x–2); if (d=2*x+0.5) cout << "Success!\n";
25. cin << "Success!\n";

Review

1. Name four major types of errors and briefly define each one.
2. What kinds of errors can we ignore in student programs?
3. What guarantees should every completed project offer?
4. List three approaches we can take to eliminate errors in programs and produce acceptable software.
5. Why do we hate debugging?
6. What is a syntax error? Give five examples.
7. What is a type error? Give five examples.
8. What is a linker error? Give three examples.
9. What is a logic error? Give three examples.
10. List four potential sources of program errors discussed in the text.
11. How do you know if a result is plausible? What techniques do you have to answer such questions?
12. Compare and contrast having the caller of a function handle a run-time error vs. the called function's handling the run-time error.
13. Why is using exceptions a better idea than returning an "error value"?

14. How do you test if an input operation succeeded?
15. Describe the process of how exceptions are thrown and caught.
16. Why, with a **vector** called **v**, is **v[v.size()]** a range error? What would be the result of calling this?
17. Define *pre-condition* and *post-condition*; give an example (that is not the **area()** function from this chapter), preferably a computation that requires a loop.
18. When would you *not* test a pre-condition?
19. When would you *not* test a post-condition?
20. What are the steps in debugging a program?
21. Why does commenting help when debugging?
22. How does testing differ from debugging?

Terms

argument error	exception	requirement
assertion	invariant	run-time error
catch	link-time error	syntax error
compile-time error	logic error	testing
container	post-condition	**throw**
debugging	pre-condition	type error
error	range error	

Exercises

1. If you haven't already, do the **Try this** exercises from this chapter.
2. The following program takes in a temperature value in Celsius and converts it to Kelvin. This code has many errors in it. Find the errors, list them, and correct the code.

```
double ctok(double c)        // converts Celsius to Kelvin
{
        int k = c + 273.15;
        return int
}

int main()
{
        double c = 0;        // declare input variable
        cin >> d;            // retrieve temperature to input variable
        double k = ctok("c");   // convert temperature
        Cout << k << endl ;     // print out temperature
}
```

3. Absolute zero is the lowest temperature that can be reached; it is –273.15°C, or 0K. The above program, even when corrected, will produce erroneous results when given a temperature below this. Place a check in the main program that will produce an error if a temperature is given below –273.15°C.

4. Do exercise 3 again, but this time handle the error inside **ctok()**.

5. Add to the program so that it can also convert from Kelvin to Celsius.

6. Write a program that converts from Celsius to Fahrenheit and from Fahrenheit to Celsius (formula in §4.3.3). Use estimation (§5.8) to see if your results are plausible.

7. Quadratic equations are of the form

$$a \cdot x^2 + b \cdot x + c = 0$$

To solve these, one uses the quadratic formula:

$$x = \frac{-b \pm \sqrt{b^2 - 4ac}}{2a}$$

There is a problem though: if $b^2 - 4ac$ is less than zero, then it will fail. Write a program that can calculate x for a quadratic equation. Create a function that prints out the roots of a quadratic equation, given a, b, c, and have it throw an exception if $b^2 - 4ac$ is less than zero. Have the main function of the program call the function, and catch the exception if there is an error. When the program detects an equation with no real roots, have it print out a message. How do you know that your results are plausible? Can you check that they are correct?

8. Write a program that reads a series of numbers and stores them in a **vector<int>**. After the user inputs all the numbers he or she wishes to, ask how many of the numbers the user wants to sum. For an answer N, print the sum of the first N elements of the **vector**. For example:

"Please enter some numbers (press '|' at prompt to stop):"

12 23 13 24 15

"Please enter how many of the numbers you wish to sum, starting from the first:"

3

"The sum of the first **3** numbers: **12**, **23**, and **13** is **48**."

Handle all inputs. For example, make sure to give an error message if the user asks for a sum of more numbers than there are in the vector.

9. Modify the program from exercise 6 to write out an error if the result cannot be represented as an **int**.

10. Modify the program from exercise 8 to use **double** instead of **int**. Also, make a **vector** of **doubles** containing the N-1 differences between adjacent values and write out that **vector** of differences.

11. Write a program that writes out the first so many values of the Fibonacci series, that is, the series that starts with 1 1 2 3 5 8 13 21 34. The next number of the series is the sum of the two previous ones. Find the largest Fibonacci number that fits in an **int**.

12. Implement a little guessing game called (for some obscure reason) "Bulls and Cows." The program has a vector of four integers in the range 0 to 9 and it is the user's task to discover those numbers by repeated guesses. Say the number to be guessed is 1234 and the user guesses 1359; the response should be "1 bull and 1 cow" because the user got one digit (1) right and in the right position (a bull) and one digit (3) right but in the wrong position (a cow). The guessing continues until the user gets four bulls, that is, has the four digits correct and in the correct order.

13. The program is a bit tedious because the answer is hard-coded into the program. Make a version where the user can play repeatedly (without stopping and restarting the program) and each game has a new set of four digits. You can get four random digits by calling the random number generator **randint(10)** from **std_lib_facilities.h** four times. You will note that if you run that program repeatedly, it will pick the same sequence of four digits each time you start the program. To avoid that, ask the user to enter a number (any number) and call **srand(n)** where **n** is the number the user entered before calling **randint(10)**. Such an **n** is called a *seed*, and different seeds give different sequences of random numbers.

14. Read (day-of-the-week,value) pairs from standard input. For example:

Tuesday 23 Friday 56 Tuesday −3 Thursday 99

Collect all the values for each day of the week in a **vector<int>**. Write out the values of the seven day-of-the-week **vectors**. Print out the sum of the values in each **vector**. Ignore illegal days of the week, such as **Funday**, but accept common synonyms such as **Mon** and **monday**. Write out the number of rejected values.

Postscript

Do you think we overemphasize errors? As novice programmers we would have thought so. The obvious and natural reaction is "It simply can't be that bad!" Well, it is that bad. Many of the world's best brains have been astounded and confounded by the difficulty of writing correct programs. In our experience, good mathematicians are the people most likely to underestimate the problem of bugs, but we all quickly exceed our natural capacity for writing programs that are correct the first time. You have been warned! Fortunately, after 50 years or so, we have a lot of experience in organizing code to minimize problems, and techniques to find the bugs that we – despite our best efforts – inevitably leave in our programs as we first write them. The techniques and examples in this chapter are a good start.

6

Writing a Program

"Programming is understanding."

—Kristen Nygaard

Writing a program involves gradually refining your ideas
of what you want to do and how you want to express it.
In this chapter and the next, we will develop a program from a
first vague idea through stages of analysis, design, implementation, testing, redesign and re-implementation. Our aim is to give
you some idea of the kind of thinking that goes on when you develop a piece of code. In the process, we discuss program organization, user-defined types, and input processing.

6.1 A problem

Writing a program starts with a problem; that is, you have a problem that you'd like a program to help solve. Understanding that problem is key to a good program. After all, a program that solves the wrong problem is likely to be of little use to you, however elegant it may be. There are happy accidents when a program just happens to be useful for something for which it was never intended, but let's not rely on such rare luck. What we want is a program that simply and cleanly solves the problem we decided to solve.

At this stage, what would be a good program to look at? A program that

- Illustrates design and programming techniques
- Gives us a chance to explore the kinds of decisions that a programmer must make and the considerations that go into such decisions
- Doesn't require too many new programming language constructs
- Is complicated enough to require thought about its design
- Allows for many variations in its solution
- Solves an easily understood problem
- Solves a problem that's worth solving
- Has a solution that is small enough to completely present and completely comprehend

We chose "Get the computer to do ordinary arithmetic on expressions we type in"; that is, we want to write a simple calculator. Such programs are clearly useful; every desktop computer comes with such a program, and you can even buy computers specially built to run nothing but such programs: pocket calculators.

For example, if you enter

2+3.1*4

the program should respond

14.4

Unfortunately, such a calculator program doesn't give us anything we don't already have available on our computer, but that would be too much to ask from a first program.

6.2 Thinking about the problem

So how do we start? Basically, think a bit about the problem and how to solve it. First think about what the program should do and how you'd like to interact with it. Later, you can think about how the program could be written to do that. Try writing down a brief sketch of an idea for a solution, and see what's wrong with that first idea. Maybe discuss the problem and how to solve it with a friend. Trying to explain something to a friend is a marvelous way of figuring out what's wrong with ideas, even better than writing them down; paper (or a computer) doesn't talk back at you and challenge your assumptions. Ideally, design isn't a lonely activity.

Unfortunately, there isn't a general strategy for problem solving that works for all people and all problems. There are whole books that claim to help you be better at problem solving and another huge branch of literature that deals with program design. We won't go there. Instead, we'll present a page's worth of suggestions for a general strategy for the kind of smaller problems an individual might face. After that, we'll quickly proceed to try out these suggestions on our tiny calculator problem.

When reading our discussion of the calculator program, we recommend that you adopt a more than usually skeptical attitude. For realism, we evolve our program through a series of versions, presenting the reasoning that leads to each version along the way. Obviously, much of that reasoning must be incomplete or even faulty, or we would finish the chapter early. As we go along, we provide examples of the kinds of concerns and reasoning that designers and programmers deal with all the time. We don't reach a version of the program that we are happy with until the end of the next chapter.

Please keep in mind that for this chapter and the next, the way we get to the final version of the program — the journey through partial solutions, ideas, and mistakes — is at least as important as that final version and more important than the language-technical details we encounter along the way (we will get back to those later).

6.2.1 Stages of development

Here is a bit of terminology for program development. As you work on a problem you repeatedly go through these stages:

- *Analysis:* Figure out what should be done and write a description of your (current) understanding of that. Such a description is called a *set of requirements* or a *specification*. We will not go into details about how such requirements are developed and written down. That's beyond the scope of this book, but it becomes increasingly important as the size of problems increases.

- *Design:* Create an overall structure for the system, deciding which parts the implementation should have and how those parts should communicate. As part of the design consider which tools — such as libraries — can help you structure the program.

- *Implementation:* Write the code, debug it, and test that it actually does what it is supposed to do.

6.2.2 Strategy

Here are some suggestions that — when applied thoughtfully and with imagination — help with many programming projects:

- What is the problem to be solved? The first thing to do is to try to be specific about what you are trying to accomplish. This typically involves constructing a description of the problem or — if someone else gave you such a statement — trying to figure out what it really means. At this point you should take the user's point of view (not the programmer/implementer's view); that is, you should ask questions about what the program should do, not about how it is going to do it. Ask: "What can this program do for me?" and "How would I like to interact with this program?" Remember, most of us have lots of experience as users of computers on which to draw.

  - Is the problem statement clear? For real problems, it never is. Even for a student exercise, it can be hard to be sufficiently precise and specific. So we try to clarify it. It would be a pity if we solved the wrong problem. Another pitfall is to ask for too much. When we try to figure out what we want, we easily get too greedy/ambitious. It is almost always better to ask for less to make a program easier to specify, easier to understand, easier to use, and (hopefully) easier to implement. Once it works, we can always build a fancier "version 2.0" based on our experience.

- Does the problem seem manageable, given the time, skills, and tools available? There is little point in starting a project that you couldn't possibly complete. If there isn't sufficient time to implement (including testing) a program that does all that is required, it is usually wise not to start. Instead, acquire more resources (especially more time) or (best of all) modify the requirements to simplify your task.

- Try breaking the program into manageable parts. Even the smallest program for solving a real problem is large enough to be subdivided.

  - Do you know of any tools, libraries, etc. that might help? The answer is almost always yes. Even at the earliest stage of learning to program, you have parts of the C++ standard library. Later, you'll know large parts of that standard library and how to find more. You'll have graphics and GUI libraries, a matrix library, etc. Once you have gained a little experience, you will be able to find thousands of libraries by simple web searches. Remember: There is little value in reinventing the wheel when you are building software for real use. When learning to program it is a different matter; then, reinventing the wheel to see how that is done is often a good idea. Any time you save by using a good library can be spent on other parts of your problem, or on rest. How do you know that a library is appropriate for your task and of sufficient quality? That's a hard problem. Part of the solution is to ask colleagues, to ask in discussion groups, and to try small examples before committing to use a library.

  - Look for parts of a solution that can be separately described (and potentially used in several places in a program or even in other programs). To find such parts requires experience, so we provide many examples throughout this book. We have already used **vector**, **string**, and **iostreams** (**cin** and **cout**). This chapter gives the first complete examples of design, implementation, and use of program parts provided as user-defined types (**Token** and **Token_stream**). Chapters 8 and 13–15 present many more examples together with their design rationales. For now, consider an analogy: If we were to design a car, we would start by identifying parts, such as wheels, engine, seats, door handles, etc., on which we could work separately before assembling the complete car. There are tens of thousands of such parts of a modern car. A real-world program is no different in that respect, except of course that the parts are code. We would not try to build a car directly out of raw materials, such as iron, plastics, and wood. Nor would we try to build a major program directly out of (just) the expressions, statements, and types provided by the language. Designing and implementing such parts is a major theme of this book and of software development in general; see user-defined types (Chapter 9), class hierarchies (Chapter 14), and generic types (Chapter 20).

- Build a small, limited version of the program that solves a key part of the problem. When we start, we rarely know the problem well. We often think we do (don't we know what a calculator program is?), but we don't. Only a combination of thinking about the problem (analysis) and experimentation (design and implementation) gives us the solid under-standing that we need to write a good program. So, we build a small, limited version

    - To bring out problems in our understanding, ideas, and tools.
    - To see if details of the problem statement need changing to make the problem manageable. It is rare to find that we had anticipated every-thing when we analyzed the problem and made the initial design. We should take advantage of the feedback that writing code and testing give us.

    Sometimes, such a limited initial version aimed at experimentation is called a *prototype*. If (as is likely) our first version doesn't work or is so ugly and awkward that we don't want to work with it, we throw it away and make another limited version based on our experience. Repeat until we find a version that we are happy with. Do not proceed with a mess; messes just grow with time.

- Build a full-scale solution, ideally by using parts of the initial version. The ideal is to grow a program from working parts rather than writing all the code at once. The alternative is to hope that by some miracle an untested idea will work and do what we want.

6.3 Back to the calculator!

How do we want to interact with the calculator? That's easy: we know how to use **cin** and **cout**, but graphical user interfaces (GUIs) are not explained until Chapter 16, so we'll stick to the keyboard and a console window. Given expres-sions as input from the keyboard, we evaluate them and write out the resulting value to the screen. For example:

```
Expression: 2+2
Result: 4
Expression: 2+2*3
Result: 8
Expression: 2+3–25/5
Result: 0
```

The expressions, e.g., **2+2** and **2+2*3**, should be entered by the user; the rest is produced by the program. We chose to output "**Expression:** " to prompt the user. We could have chosen "**Please enter an expression followed by a newline**" but that seemed verbose and pointless. On the other hand a pleasantly short prompt, such as **>**, seemed too cryptic. Sketching out such examples of use early on is important. They provide a very practical definition of what the program should minimally do. When discussing design and analysis, such examples of use are called *use cases*.

When faced with the calculator problem for the first time, most people come up with a first idea like this for the main logic of the program:

> **read_a_line**
> **calculate**   *// do the work*
> **write_result**

This kind of "scribbles" clearly isn't code; it's called *pseudo code*. We tend to use it in the early stages of design when we are not yet certain exactly what our notation means. For example, is "calculate" a function call? If so, what would be its arguments? It is simply too early to answer such questions.

6.3.1 First attempt

At this point, we are not really ready to write the calculator program. We simply haven't thought hard enough, but thinking is hard work and — like most programmers — we are anxious to write some code. So let's take a chance, write a simple calculator, and see where it leads us. The first idea is something like

```
#include "std_lib_facilities.h"

int main()
{
    cout << "Please enter expression (we can handle + and -): ";
    int lval = 0;
    int rval;
    char op;
    int res;
    cin>>lval>>op>>rval;        // read something like 1 + 3

    if (op=='+')
            res = lval + rval;      // addition
    else if (op=='-')
            res = lval - rval;      // subtraction

    cout << "Result: " << res << '\n';
    keep_window_open();
```

```
        return 0;
}
```

That is, read a pair of values separated by an operator, such as **2+2**, compute the result (in this case **4**), and print the resulting value. We chose the variable names **lval** for left-hand value and **rval** for right-hand value.

This (sort of) works! So what if this program isn't quite complete? It feels great to get something running! Maybe this programming and computer science stuff is easier than the rumors say. Well, maybe, but let's not get too carried away by an early success. Let's

1. Clean up the code a bit
2. Add multiplication and division (e.g., **2*3**)
3. Add the ability to handle more than one operand (e.g., **1+2+3**)

In particular, we know that we should always check that our input is reasonable (in our hurry, we "forgot") and that testing a value against many constants is best done by a **switch**-statement rather than an **if**-statement.

The "chaining" of operations, such as **1+2+3+4**, we will handle by adding the values as they are read; that is, we start with **1**, see **+2** and add **2** to **1** (getting an intermediate result **3**), see **+3** and add that **3** to our intermediate result (**3**), and so on. After a few false starts and after correcting a few syntax and logic errors, we get:

```cpp
#include "std_lib_facilities.h"

int main()
{
    cout << "Please enter expression (we can handle +, −, *, and /): ";
    int lval = 0;
    int rval;
    char op;
    cin>>lval;          // read leftmost operand
    if (!cin) error("no first operand");
    while (cin>>op) {       // read operator and right-hand operand repeatedly
        cin>>rval;
        if (!cin) error("no second operand");
        switch(op) {
        case '+':
            lval += rval;   // add: lval = lval + rval
            break;
        case '−':
            lval −= rval;   // subtract: lval = lval − rval
            break;
```

```
        case '*':
                lval *= rval;    // multiply: lval = lval * rval
                break;
        case '/':
                lval /= rval;    // divide: lval = lval / rval
                break;
        default:                 // not another operator: print result
                cout << "Result: " << lval << '\n';
                keep_window_open();
                return 0;
        }
    }
    error("bad expression");
}
```

This isn't bad, but then we try **1+2*3** and see that the result is **9** and not the **7** our arithmetic teachers told us was the right answer. Similarly, **1–2*3** gives **–3** rather than the **–5** we expected. We are doing the operations in the wrong order: **1+2*3** is calculated as **(1+2)*3** rather than as the conventional 1+(2*3). Similarly, **1–2*3** is calculated as **(1–2)*3** rather than as the conventional 1–(2*3). Bummer! We might consider the convention that "multiplication binds tighter than addition" as a silly old convention, but hundreds of years of convention will not disappear just to simplify our programming.

6.3.2 Tokens

So (somehow), we have to "look ahead" on the line to see if there is a * (or a /). If so, we have to (somehow) adjust the evaluation order from the simple and obvious left-to-right order. Unfortunately, trying to barge ahead here, we immediately hit a couple of snags:

1. We don't actually require an expression to be on one line. For example:

    1

    +

    2

    works perfectly with our code so far.

2. How do we search for a * (or a /) among digits and plusses on several input lines?

3. How do we remember where a * was?

4. How do we handle evaluation that's not strictly left-to-right (e.g., **1+2*3**)?

Having decided to be super-optimists, we'll solve problems 1–3 first and not worry about 4 until later.

Also, we'll ask around for help. Surely someone will know a conventional way of reading "stuff," such as numbers and operators, from input and storing it in a way that lets us look at it in convenient ways. The conventional and very useful answer is "tokenize": first input characters are read and assembled into *tokens,* so if you type in

45+11.5/7

the program should produce a list of tokens representing

45
+
11.5
/
7

A *token* is a sequence of characters that represents something we consider a unit, such as a number or an operator. That's the way a C++ compiler deals with its source. Actually, "tokenizing" in some form or another is the way most analysis of text starts. Following the example of C++ expression, we see the need for three kinds of tokens:

- Floating-point-literals: as defined by C++, e.g., **3.14**, **0.274e2**, and **42**
- Operators: e.g., **+, −, *, /, %**
- Parentheses: **(,)**

The floating-point-literals look as if they may become a problem: reading **12** seems much easier than reading **12.3e−3**, but calculators do tend to do floating-point arithmetic. Similarly, we suspect that we'll have to accept parentheses to have our calculator deemed useful.

How do we represent such tokens in our program? We could try to keep track of where each token started (and ended), but that gets messy (especially if we allow expressions to span line boundaries). Also, if we keep a number as a string of characters, we later have to figure out what its value is; that is, if we see **42** and store the characters **4** and **2** somewhere, we then later have to figure out that those characters represent the numerical value **42** (i.e., **4*10+2**). The obvious − and conventional − solution is to represent each token as a *(kind,value)* pair. The *kind* tells us if a token is a number, an operator, or a parenthesis. For a number, and in this example only for a number, we use its numerical value as its *value.*

So how do we express the idea of a *(kind,value)* pair in code? We define a type **Token** to represent tokens. Why? Remember why we use types: they hold the data we need and give us useful operations on that data. For example, **ints** hold integers and give us addition, subtraction, multiplication, division, and remainder, whereas **strings** hold sequences of characters and give us concatenation and subscripting. The C++ language and its standard library give us many types such as **char**, **int**, **double**, **string**, **vector**, and **ostream**, but not a **Token** type. In fact, there is a huge number of types – thousands or tens of thousands – that we would like to have, but the language and its standard library do not supply them. Among our favorite types that are not supported are **Matrix** (see Chapter 24), **Date** (see Chapter 9), and infinite precision integers (try searching the web for "**Bignum**"). If you think about it for a second, you'll realize that a language cannot supply tens of thousands of types: who would define them, who would implement them, how would you find them, and how thick would the manual have to be? Like most modern languages, C++ escapes that problem by letting us define our own types (*user-defined types*) when we need them.

6.3.3 Implementing tokens

What should a token look like in our program? In other words, what would we like our **Token** type to be? A **Token** must be able to represent operators, such as **+** and **–**, and numeric values, such as **42** and **3.14**. The obvious implementation is something that can represent what "kind" a token is and hold the numeric value for tokens that have one:

Token:		**Token:**	
kind:	plus	kind:	number
value:		value:	3.14

There are many ways that this idea could be represented in C++ code. Here is the simplest that we found useful:

```
class Token {        // a very simple user-defined type
public:
        char kind;
        double value;
};
```

A **Token** is a type (like **int** or **char**), so it can be used to define variables and hold values. It has two parts (called *members*): **kind** and **value**. The keyword **class** means "user-defined type"; it indicates that a type with zero or more members is being defined. The first member, **kind**, is a character, **char**, so that it conveniently can hold '+' and '*' to represent + and *. We can use it to make types like this:

```
Token t;              // t is a Token
t.kind = '+';         // t represents a +
Token t2;             // t2 is another Token
```

```
t2.kind = '8';      // we use the digit 8 as the "kind" for numbers
t2.value = 3.14;
```

We use the member access notation, *object_name . member_name*, to access a member. You can read **t.kind** as "t's **kind**" and **t2.value** as "t2's **value**." We can copy **Token**s just as we can copy **int**s:

```
Token tt = t;       // copy initialization
if (tt.kind != t.kind) error("impossible!");
t = t2;             // assignment
cout << t.value;    // will print 3.14
```

Given **Token**, we can represent the expression **(1.5+4)*11** using seven tokens like this:

'('	'8'	'+'	'8'	')'	'*'	'8'
	1.5		4			11

Note that for simple tokens, such as **+**, we don't need the value, so we don't use its **value** member. We needed a character to mean "number" and picked **'8'** just because **'8'** obviously isn't an operator or a punctuation character. Using **'8'** to mean "number" is a bit cryptic, but it'll do for now.

Token is an example of a C++ user-defined type. A user-defined type can have member functions (operations) as well as data members. There can be many reasons for defining member functions. Here, we'll just provide two member functions to give us a more convenient way of initializing **Token**s:

```
class Token {
public:
        char kind;          // what kind of token
        double value;       // for numbers: a value
        Token(char ch)      // make a Token from a char
            :kind(ch), value(0) { }
        Token(char ch, double val)      // make a Token from a char and a double
            :kind(ch), value(val) { }
};
```

These two member functions are of a special kind called *constructors*. They have the same name as their type and are used to initialize ("construct") **Token** objects. For example:

```
Token t1('+');      // initialize t1 so that t1.kind = '+'
Token t2('8',11.5); // initialize t2 so that t2.kind = '8' and t2.value = 11.5
```

In the first constructor, **:kind(ch), value(0)** means "Initialize **kind** to **ch** and set **value** to **0**." In the second constructor, **:kind(ch), value(val)** means "Initialize **kind** to **ch** and set **value** to **val**." In both cases, nothing more needs to be done to construct the **Token**, so the body of the function is empty: { }. The special initializer syntax (a *member initializer list*) starting with a colon is used only in constructors.

Note that a constructor does not return a value. No return type is required (or allowed) for a constructor. For more about constructors, see §9.4.2 and §9.7.

6.3.4 Using tokens

So, maybe now we can complete our calculator! However, maybe a small amount of planning ahead would be worthwhile. How would we use **Tokens** in the calculator? We can read out input into a vector of **Tokens**:

```
Token get_token();    // read a token from cin

vector<Token> tok;    // we'll put the tokens here

int main()
{
    while (cin) {
        Token t = get_token();
        tok.push_back(t);
    }
    // . . .
}
```

Now we can read an expression first and evaluate later. For example, for **11*12**, we get

'8'	'*'	'8'
11		12

We can look at that to find the multiplication and its operands. Having done that, we can easily perform the multiplication because the numbers 11 and 12 are stored as numeric values and not as strings.

Now let's look at more complex expressions. Given **1+2*3**, **tok** will contain five **Tokens**:

'8'	'+'	'8'	'*'	'8'
1		2		3

Now we could find the multiply operation by a simple loop:

```
for (int i = 0; i<tok.size(); ++i) {
    if (tok[i].kind=='*') {          // we found a multiply!
        double d = tok[i−1].value*tok[i+1].value;
        // now what?
    }
}
```

Yes, but now what? What do we do with that product **d**? How do we decide in which order to evaluate the sub-expressions? Well, **+** comes before ***** so we can't just evaluate from left to right. We could try right-to-left evaluation! That would work for **1+2*3** but not for **1*2+3**. Worse still, consider **1+2*3+4**. This example has to be evaluated "inside out": **1+(2*3)+4**. And how will we handle parentheses, as we eventually will have to do? We seem to have hit a dead end. We need to back off, stop programming for a while, and think about how we read and understand an input string and evaluate it as an arithmetic expression.

So, this first enthusiastic attempt to solve the problem (writing a calculator) ran out of steam. That's not uncommon for first tries, and it serves the important role of helping us understand the problem. In this case, it even gave us the useful notion of a token, which itself is an example of the notion of a (*name,value*) pair that we will encounter again and again. However, we must always make sure that such relatively thoughtless and unplanned "coding" doesn't steal too much time. We should do very little programming before we have done at least a bit of analysis (understanding the problem) and design (deciding on an overall structure of a solution).

TRY THIS

On the other hand, why shouldn't we be able to find a simple solution to this problem? It doesn't seem to be all that difficult. If nothing else, trying would give us a better appreciation of the problem and the eventual solution. Consider what you might do right away. For example, look at the input **12.5+2**. We could tokenize that, decide that the expression was simple, and compute the answer. That may be a bit messy, but straightforward, so maybe we could proceed in this direction and find something that's good enough! Consider what to do if we found both a **+** and a ***** in the line **2+3*4**? That too can be handled by "brute force." How would we deal with a complicated expression, such as **1+2*3/4%5+(6−7*(8))**? And how would we deal with errors, such as **2+*3** and **2&3**? Consider this for a while, maybe doodling a bit on a piece of paper trying to outline possible solutions and interesting or important input expressions.

6.3.5 Back to the drawing board

Now, we will look at the problem again and try not to dash ahead with another half-baked solution. One thing that we did discover was that having the program (calculator) evaluate only a single expression was tedious. We would like to be able to compute several expressions in a single invocation of our program; that is, our pseudo code grows to

```
while (not_finished) {
        read_a_line
        calculate          // do the work
        write_result
}
```

Clearly this is a complication, but when we think about how we use calculators, we realize that doing several calculations is very common. Could we let the user invoke our program several times to do several calculations? We could, but program startup is unfortunately (and unreasonably) slow on many modern operating systems, so we'd better not rely on that.

As we look at this pseudo code, our early attempts at solutions, and our examples of use, several questions – some with tentative answers – arise:

1. If we type in **45+5/7**, how do we find the individual parts **45**, **+**, **5**, **/**, and **7** in the input? (Tokenize!)

2. What terminates an input expression? A newline, of course! (Always be suspicious of "of course": "of course" is not a reason.)

3. How do we represent **45+5/7** as data so that we can evaluate it? Before doing the addition we must somehow turn the characters **4** and **5** into the integer value **45** (i.e., **4*10+5**). (So tokenizing is part of the solution.)

4. How do we make sure that **45+5/7** is evaluated as **45+(5/7)** and not as **(45+5)/7**?

5. What's the value of **5/7**? About **.71**, but that's not an integer. Based on experience with calculators, we know that people would expect a floating-point result. Should we also allow floating-point inputs? Sure!

6. Can we have variables? For example, could we write

   ```
   v=7
   m=9
   v*m
   ```

   Good idea, but let's wait until later. Let's first get the basics working.

Possibly the most important decision here is the answer to question 6. In §7.8, you'll see that if we had said yes we'd have almost doubled the size of the initial project. That would have more than doubled the time needed to get the initial version running. Our guess is that if you really are a novice, it would have at least quadrupled the effort needed and most likely pushed the project beyond your patience. It is most important to avoid "feature creep" early in a project. Instead, always first build a simple version, implementing the essential features only. Once you have something running, you can get more ambitious. It is far easier to build a program in stages than all at once. Saying yes to question 6 would have had yet another bad effect: it would have made it hard to resist the temptation to add further "neat features" along the line. How about adding the usual mathematical functions? How about adding loops? Once we start adding "neat features" it is hard to stop.

From a programmer's point of view, questions 1, 3, and 4 are the most bothersome. They are also related, because once we have found a **45** or a **+**, what do we do with them? That is, how do we store them in our program? Obviously, tokenizing is part of the solution, but only part.

What would an experienced programmer do? When we are faced with a tricky technical question, there often is a standard answer. We know that people have been writing calculator programs for at least as long as there have been computers taking symbolic input from a keyboard. That is at least for 50 years. There has to be a standard answer! In such a situation, the experienced programmer consults colleagues and/or the literature. It would be silly to barge on, hoping to beat 50 years of experience in a morning.

6.4 Grammars

There is a standard answer to the question of how to make sense of expressions: first input characters are read and assembled into tokens (as we discovered). So if you type in

    45+11.5/7

the program should produce a list of tokens representing

    45
    +
    11.5
    /
    7

A token is a sequence of characters that represents something we consider a unit, such as a number or an operator.

After tokens have been produced, the program must ensure that complete expressions are understood correctly. For example, we know that **45+11.5/7** means **45+(11.5/7)** and not **(45+11.5)/7**, but how do we teach the program that useful rule (division "binds tighter" than addition)? The standard answer is that we write a *grammar* defining the syntax of our input and then write a program that implements the rules of that grammar. For example:

```
// a simple expression grammar:

Expression:
    Term
    Expression "+" Term      // addition
    Expression "−" Term      // subtraction
Term:
    Primary
    Term "*" Primary         // multiplication
    Term "/" Primary         // division
    Term "%" Primary         // remainder (modulo)
Primary:
    Number
    "(" Expression ")"       // grouping
Number:
    floating-point-literal
```

This is a set of simple rules. The last rule is read "A **Number** is a **floating-point-literal**." The next-to-last rule says, "A **Primary** is a **Number** or '(' followed by an **Expression** followed by ')'." The rules for **Expression** and **Term** are similar; each is defined in terms of one of the rules that follow.

As seen in §6.3.2, our tokens — as borrowed from the C++ definition — are

- **floating-point-literal** (as defined by C++, e.g., **3.14**, **0.274e2**, or **42**)
- **+, −, *, /, %** (the operators)
- **(,)** (the parentheses)

From our first tentative pseudo code to this approach using tokens and a grammar is actually a huge conceptual jump. It's the kind of jump we hope for but rarely manage without help. This is what experience, the literature, and Mentors are for.

At first glance, a grammar probably looks like complete nonsense. Technical notation often does. However, please keep in mind that it is a general and elegant (as you will eventually appreciate) notation for something you have been able to do since middle school (or earlier). You have no problem calculating **1−2*3** and

1+2–3 and **3*2+4/2**. It seems hardwired in your brain. However, could you explain how you do it? Could you explain it well enough for someone who had never seen conventional arithmetic to grasp? Could you do so for every combination of operators and operands? To articulate an explanation in sufficient detail and precisely enough for a computer to understand, we need a notation – and a grammar is a most powerful and conventional tool for that.

How do you read a grammar? Basically, given some input, you start with the "top rule," **Expression**, and search through the rules to find a match for the tokens as they are read. Reading a stream of tokens according to a grammar is called *parsing*, and a program that does that is often called a *parser* or a *syntax analyzer*. Our parser reads the tokens from left to right, just like we type them and read them. Let's try something really simple: Is **2** an expression?

1. An **Expression** must be a **Term** or end with a **Term**. That **Term** must be a **Primary** or end with a **Primary**. That **Primary** must start with a (or be a **Number**. Obviously, **2** is not a (, but a **floating-point-literal**, which is a **Number**, which is a **Primary**.

2. That **Primary** (the **Number 2**) isn't preceded by a /, *, or %, so it is a complete **Term** (rather than the end of a /, *, or % expression).

3. That **Term** (the **Primary 2**) isn't preceded by a + or –, so it is a complete **Expression** (rather than the end of a + or – expression).

So yes, according to our grammar, **2** is an expression. We can illustrate the progression through the grammar like this:

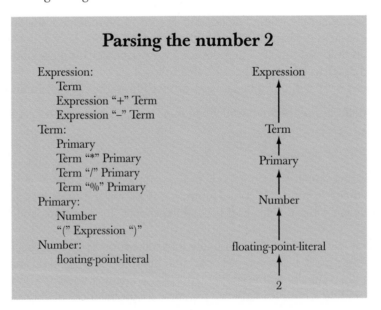

Parsing the number 2

```
Expression:                          Expression
    Term                                  ↑
    Expression "+" Term                   |
    Expression "–" Term                   |
Term:                                    Term
    Primary                               ↑
    Term "*" Primary                   Primary
    Term "/" Primary                      ↑
    Term "%" Primary                      |
Primary:                              Number
    Number                                ↑
    "(" Expression ")"                    |
Number:                          floating-point-literal
    floating-point-literal                ↑
                                          |
                                          2
```

This represents the path we followed through the definitions. Retracing our path, we can say that **2** is an **Expression** because **2** is a **floating-point-literal**, which is a **Number**, which is a **Primary**, which is a **Term**, which is an **Expression**.

Let's try something a bit more complicated: Is **2+3** an **Expression**? Naturally, much of the reasoning is the same as for **2**:

1. An **Expression** must be a **Term** or end with a **Term**, which must be a **Primary** or end with a **Primary**, and a **Primary** must start with a (or be a **Number**. Obviously **2** is not a (, but it is a **floating-point-literal**, which is a **Number**, which is a **Primary**.

2. That **Primary** (the **Number 2**) isn't preceded by a /, *, or %, so it is a complete **Term** (rather than the end of a /, *, or % expression).

3. That **Term** (the **Primary 2**) is followed by a **+**, so it is the end of the first part of an **Expression** and we must look for the **Term** after the **+**. In exactly the same way as we found that **2** was a **Term**, we find that **3** is a **Term**. Since **3** is not followed by a **+** or a **–** it is a complete **Term** (rather than the first part of a **+** or **–** **Expression**). Therefore, **2+3** matches the **Expression + Term** rule and is an **Expression**.

Again, we can illustrate this reasoning graphically (again leaving out the **floating-point-literal** to **Number** rule to simplify):

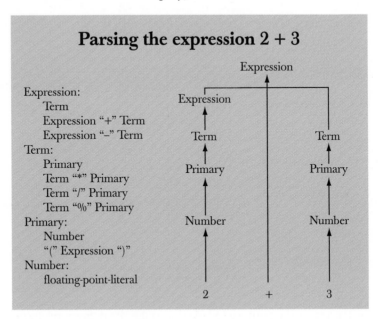

This represents the path we followed through the definitions. Retracing our path, we can say that **2+3** is an **Expression** because **2** is a term which is an **Expression**, **3** is a **Term**, and an **Expression** followed by **+** followed by a **Term** is an **Expression**.

The real reason we are interested in grammars is that they can solve our problem of how to correctly parse expressions with both + and *, so let's try **45+11.5*7**. However, "playing computer" following the rules in detail as we did above is tedious, so let's skip some of the intermediate steps that we have already gone through for **2** and **2+3**. Obviously, **45**, **11.5**, and **7** are all **floating-point-literals** which are **Numbers**, which are **Primarys**, so we can ignore all rules below **Primary**. So we get:

1. **45** is an **Expression** followed by a **+**, so we look for a **Term** to finish the **Expression+Term** rule.

2. **11.5** is a **Term** followed by *, so we look for a **Primary** to finish the **Term*Primary** rule.

3. **7** is **Primary**, so **11.5*7** is a **Term** according to the **Term*Primary** rule. Now we can see that **45+11.5*7** is an **Expression** according to the **Expression*Term** rule. In particular, it is an **Expression** that first does the multiplication **11.5*7** and then the addition **45+11.5*7**, just as if we had written **45+(11.5*7)**.

Again, we can illustrate this reasoning graphically (again leaving out the **floating-point-literal** to **Number** rule to simplify):

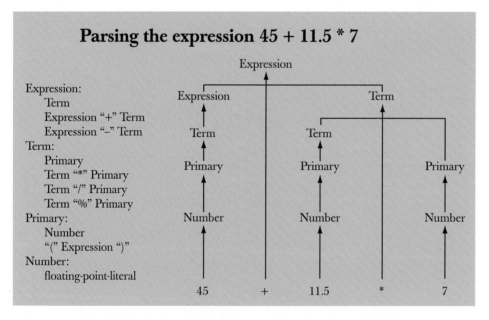

Parsing the expression 45 + 11.5 * 7

Again, this represents the path we followed through the definitions. Note how the **Term * Primary** rule ensures that **11.5** is multiplied by **7** rather than added to **45**.

You may find this logic hard to follow at first, but many humans do read grammars, and simple grammars are not hard to understand. However, we were not really trying to teach *you* to understand **2+2** or **45+11.5*7**. Obviously, you knew that already. We were trying to find a way for the computer to "understand" **45+11.5*7** and all the other complicated expressions you might give it to evaluate. Actually, complicated grammars are not fit for humans to read, but computers are good at it. They follow such grammar rules quickly and correctly with the greatest of ease. Following precise rules is exactly what computers are good at.

6.4.1 A detour: English grammar

If you have never before worked with grammars, we expect that your head is now spinning. In fact, it may be spinning even if you have seen a grammar before, but take a look at the following grammar for a very small subset of English:

```
Sentence :
    Noun Verb                     // e.g., C++ rules
    Sentence Conjunction Sentence  // e.g., Birds fly but fish swim

Conjunction :
    "and"
    "or"
    "but"

Noun :
    "birds"
    "fish"
    "C++"

Verb :
    "rules"
    "fly"
    "swim"
```

A sentence is built from parts of speech (e.g., nouns, verbs, and conjunctions). A sentence can be parsed according to these rules to determine which words are nouns, verbs, etc. This simple grammar also includes semantically meaningless sentences such as "C++ fly and birds rules," but fixing that is a different matter belonging in a far more advanced book.

Many have been taught/shown such rules in middle school or in foreign language class (e.g., English classes). These grammar rules are very fundamental. In fact, there are serious neurological arguments for such rules being hardwired into our brains!

Now look at a parsing tree as we used above for expressions, but used here for simple English:

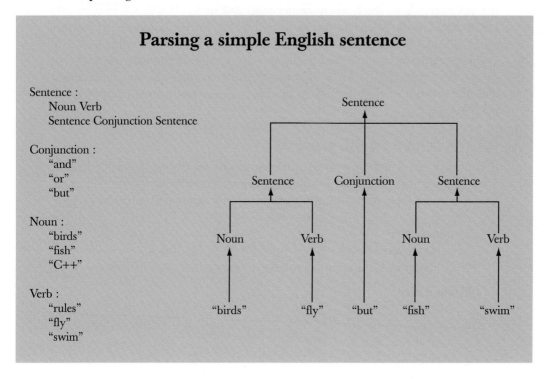

Parsing a simple English sentence

Sentence :
    Noun Verb
    Sentence Conjunction Sentence

Conjunction :
    "and"
    "or"
    "but"

Noun :
    "birds"
    "fish"
    "C++"

Verb :
    "rules"
    "fly"
    "swim"

This is not all that complicated. If you had trouble with §6.4 then please go back and re-read it from the beginning; it may make more sense the second time through!

6.4.2 Writing a grammar

How did we pick those expression grammar rules? "Experience" is the honest answer. The way we do it is simply the way people usually write expression grammars. However, writing a simple grammar is pretty straightforward: we need to know how to

1. Distinguish a rule from a token
2. Put one rule after another (*sequencing*)
3. Express alternative patterns (*alternation*)
4. Express a repeating pattern (*repetition*)
5. Recognize the grammar rule to start with

Different textbooks and different parser systems use different notational conventions and different terminology. For example, some call tokens *terminals* and rules *non-terminals* or *productions*. We simply put tokens in (double) quotes and start with the first rule. Alternatives are put on separate lines. For example:

```
List:
      "{" Sequence "}"
Sequence:
      Element
      Element " ," Sequence
Element:
      "A"
      "B"
```

So a **Sequence** is either an **Element** or an **Element** followed by a **Sequence** using a comma for separation. An **Element** is either the letter **A** or the letter **B**. A **List** is a **Sequence** in "curly brackets." We can generate these **Lists** (how?):

```
{ A }
{ B }
{ A,B }
{A,A,A,A,B }
```

However, these are not lists (why not?):

```
{ }
A
{ A,A,A,A,B
{A,A,C,A,B }
{ A B C }
{A,A,A,A,B, }
```

This sequence rule is not one you learned in kindergarten or have hardwired into your brain, but it is still not rocket science. See §7.4 and §7.8.1 for examples of how we work with a grammar to express syntactic ideas.

6.5 Turning a grammar into code

There are many ways of getting a computer to follow a grammar. We'll use the simplest one: we simply write one function for each grammar rule and use our type **Token** to represent tokens. A program that implements a grammar is often called a *parser*.

6.5.1 Implementing grammar rules

To implement our calculator, we need four functions: one to read tokens plus one for each rule in our grammar:

get_token()	// read characters and compose tokens
	// uses cin
expression()	// deal with + and −
	// calls term() and get_token()
term()	// deal with *, /, and %
	// calls primary() and get_token()
primary()	// deal with numbers and parentheses
	// calls expression() and get_token()

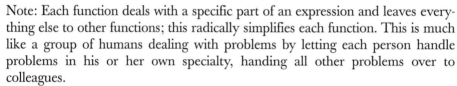

Note: Each function deals with a specific part of an expression and leaves everything else to other functions; this radically simplifies each function. This is much like a group of humans dealing with problems by letting each person handle problems in his or her own specialty, handing all other problems over to colleagues.

What should these functions actually do? Each function should call other grammar functions according to the grammar rule it is implementing and **get_token()** where a token is required in a rule. For example, when **primary()** tries to follow the **(Expression)** rule, it must call

get_token()	// to deal with (and)
expression()	// to deal with Expression

What should such parsing functions return? How about the answer we really wanted? For example, for **2+3**, **expression()** could return **5**. After all, the information is all there. That's what we'll try! Doing so will save us from answering one of the hardest questions from our list: "How do I represent **45+5/7** as data so that I can evaluate it?" Instead of storing a representation of **45+5/7** in memory, we simply evaluate it as we read it from input. This little idea is really a major breakthrough! It will keep the program at a quarter of the size it would have been had we had **expression()** return something complicated for later evaluation. We just saved ourselves about 80% of the work.

The "odd man out" is **get_token()**: because it deals with tokens, not expressions, it can't return the value of a sub-expression. For example, **+** and **(** are not expressions. So, it must return a **Token**. We conclude that we want

```
// functions to match the grammar rules:
Token get_token()    // read characters and compose tokens
```

```
double expression()    // deal with + and −
double term()          // deal with *, /, and %
double primary()       // deal with numbers and parentheses
```

6.5.2 Expressions

Let's first write **expression()**. The grammar looks like this:

> **Expression:**
>   **Term**
>   **Expression '+' Term**
>   **Expression '−' Term**

Since this is our first attempt to turn a set of grammar rules into code, we'll proceed through a couple of false starts. That's the way it usually goes with new techniques, and we learn useful things along the way. In particular, a novice programmer can learn a lot from looking at the dramatically different behavior of similar pieces of code. Reading code is a useful skill to cultivate.

6.5.2.1 Expressions: first try

Looking at the **Expression '+' Term** rule, we try first calling **expression()**, then looking for + (and −) and then **term()**:

```
double expression()
{
        double left = expression();    // read and evaluate an Expression
        Token t = get_token();         // get the next token
        switch (t.kind) {              // see which kind of token it is
        case '+':
                return left + term();  // read and evaluate a Term,
                                       // then do an add

        case '−':
                return left − term();  // read and evaluate a Term,
                                       // then do a subtraction

        default:
                return left;           // return the value of the Expression
        }
}
```

It looks good. It is almost a trivial transcription of the grammar. It is quite simple, really: first read an **Expression** and then see if it is followed by a + or a −, and if it is, read the **Term**.

Unfortunately, that doesn't really make sense. How do we know where the expression ends so that we can look for a + or a −? Remember, our program reads left to right and can't peek ahead to see if a + is coming. In fact, this **expression()** will never get beyond its first line: **expression()** starts by calling **expression()** which starts by calling **expression()** and so on "forever." This is called an *infinite recursion* and will in fact terminate after a short while when the computer runs out of memory to hold the "never-ending" sequence of calls of **expression()**. The term *recursion* is used to describe what happens when a function calls itself. Not all recursions are infinite, and recursion is a very useful programming technique (see §8.5.8).

6.5.2.2 Expressions: second try

So what do we do? Every **Term** is an **Expression**, but not every **Expression** is a **Term**; that is, we could start looking for a **Term** and look for a full **Expression** only if we found a + or a −. For example:

```
double expression()
{
        double left = term();         // read and evaluate a Term
        Token t = get_token();        // get the next token
        switch (t.kind) {             // see which kind of token that is
        case '+':
                return left + expression();   // read and evaluate an Expression,
                                              // then do an add
        case '-':
                return left – expression();   // read and evaluate an Expression,
                                              // then do a subtraction
        default:
                return left;          // return the value of the Term
        }
}
```

This actually − more or less − works. We have tried it in the finished program and it parses every correct expression we throw at it (and no illegal ones). It even correctly evaluates most expressions. For example, **1+2** is read as a **Term** (with the value 1) followed by + followed by an **Expression** (which happens to be a **Term** with the value 2) and gives the answer **3**. Similarly, **1+2+3** gives **6**. We could go on for quite a long time about what works, but to make a long story short: How about **1−2−3**? This **expression()** will read the **1** as a **Term**, then proceed to read **2−3** as an **Expression** (consisting of the **Term 2** followed by the **Expression 3**). It will then subtract the value of **2−3** from **1**. In other words, it will evaluate **1−(2−3)**. The value of **1−(2−3)** is **2** (positive two). However, we were taught (in primary school or even earlier) that **1−2−3** means **(1−2)−3** and therefore has the value **−4** (negative four).

So we got a very nice program that just didn't do the right thing. That's dangerous. It is especially dangerous because it gives the right answer in many cases. For example, **1+2+3** gives the right answer (**6**) because **1+(2+3)** equals (**1+2)+3**. What fundamentally, from a programming point of view, did we do wrong? We should always ask ourselves this question when we have found an error. That way we might avoid making the same mistake again, and again, and again.

Fundamentally, we just looked at the code and guessed. That's rarely good enough! We have to understand what our code is doing and we have to be able to explain why it does the right thing.

Analyzing our errors is often also the best way to find a correct solution. What we did here was to define **expression()** to first look for a **Term** and then, if that **Term** is followed by a + or a –, look for an **Expression**. This really implements a slightly different grammar:

> **Expression:**
> > **Term**
> > **Term '+' Expression**   // addition
> > **Term '–' Expression**   // subtraction

The difference from our desired grammar is exactly that we wanted **1–2–3** to be the **Expression 1–2** followed by – followed by the **Term 3**, but what we got here was the **Term 1** followed by – followed by the **Expression 2–3**; that is, we wanted **1–2–3** to mean (**1–2)–3** but we got **1–(2–3)**.

Yes, debugging can be tedious, tricky, and time-consuming, but in this case we are really working through rules you learned in primary school and learned to avoid without too much trouble. The snag is that we have to teach the rules to a computer – and a computer is a far slower learner than you are.

Note that we could have defined **1–2–3** to mean **1–(2–3)** rather than (**1–2)–3** and avoided this discussion altogether. Often, the trickiest programming problems come when we must match conventional rules that were established by and for humans long before we started using computers.

6.5.2.3 Expressions: third time lucky

So, what now? Look again at the grammar (the correct grammar in §6.5.2): any **Expression** starts with a **Term** and such a **Term** can be followed by a + or a –. So, we have to look for a **Term**, see if it is followed by a + or a –, and keep doing that until there are no more plusses or minuses. For example:

```
double expression()
{
        double left = term();         // read and evaluate a Term
        Token t = get_token();        // get the next token
```

```
        while ( t.kind=='+' || t.kind=='-') {    // look for a + or a –
                if (t.kind == '+')
                        left += term();             // evaluate Term and add
                else
                        left -= term();             // evaluate Term and subtract
                t = get_token();
        }
        return left;        // finally: no more + or –; return the answer
}
```

This is a bit messier: we had to introduce a loop to keep looking for plusses and minuses. We also got a bit repetitive: we test for **+** and **–** twice and twice call **get_token()**. Because it obscures the logic of the code, let's just get rid of the duplication of the test for **+** and **–**:

```
double expression()
{
        double left = term();        // read and evaluate a Term
        Token t = get_token();       // get the next token
        while(true) {
                switch(t.kind) {
                case '+':
                        left += term();        // evaluate Term and add
                        t = get_token();
                        break;
                case '-':
                        left -= term();        // evaluate Term and subtract
                        t = get_token();
                        break;
                default:
                        return left;           // finally: no more + or –; return the answer
                }
        }
}
```

Note that – except for the loop – this is actually rather similar to our first try (§6.5.3.1). What we have done is to remove the mention of **expression()** within **expression()** and replace it with a loop. In other words, we translated the **Expression** in the grammar rules for **Expression** into a loop looking for a **Term** followed by a **+** or a **–**.

6.5.3 Terms

The grammar rule for **Term** is very similar to the **Expression** rule:

Term:
> **Primary**
> **Term '*' Primary**
> **Term '/' Primary**
> **Term '%' Primary**

Consequently, the code should be very similar also. Here is a first try:

```
double term()
{
    double left = primary();
    Token t = get_token();
    while(true) {
        switch (t.kind) {
        case '*':
            left *= primary();
            t = get_token();
            break;
        case '/':
            left /= primary();
            t = get_token();
            break;
        case '%':
            left %= primary();
            t = get_token();
            break;
        default:
            return left;
        }
    }
}
```

Unfortunately, this doesn't compile: the remainder operation (%) is not defined for floating-point numbers. The compiler kindly tells us so. When we answered question 4 above – "Should we also allow floating-point inputs?" – with a confident "Sure!" we actually hadn't thought the issue through and fell victim to *feature creep*. That *always* happens! So what do we do about it? We could at runtime check that both operands of % are integers and give an error if they are not. Or we could simply leave % out of our calculator. Let's take the simplest choice for now. We can always add % later; see §7.5.

After we eliminate the % case, the function works: terms are correctly parsed and evaluated. However, an experienced programmer will notice an undesirable detail that makes **term()** unacceptable. What would happen if you entered **2/0**? You can't divide by zero. If you try, the computer hardware will detect it and terminate your program with a somewhat unhelpful error message. An inexperienced programmer will discover this the hard way. So, we'd better check and give a decent error message:

```
double term()
{
      double left = primary();
      Token t = get_token();
      while(true) {
            switch (t.kind) {
            case '*':
                  left *= primary();
                  t = get_token();
                  break;
            case '/':
            {     double d = primary();
                  if (d == 0) error("divide by zero");
                  left /= d;
                  t = get_token();
                  break;
            }
            default:
                  return left;
            }
      }
}
```

Why did we put the statements handling / into a block? The compiler insists. If you want to define and initialize variables within a **switch**-statement, you must place them inside a block.

6.5.4 Primary expressions

The grammar rule for primary expressions is also simple:

```
Primary:
      Number
      '(' Expression ')'
```

The code that implements it is a bit messy because there are more opportunities for syntax errors:

```
double primary()
{
    Token t = get_token();
    switch (t.kind) {
    case '(':     // handle '(' expression ')'
            {     double d = expression();
                  t = get_token();
                  if (t.kind != ')') error("')' expected");
                  return d;
            }
    case '8':                   // we use '8' to represent a number
            return t.value;     // return the number's value
    default:
            error("primary expected");
    }
}
```

Basically there is nothing new compared to **expression()** and **term()**. We use the same language primitives, the same way of dealing with **Token**s, and the same programming techniques.

6.6 Trying the first version

To run these calculator functions, we need to implement **get_token()** and provide a **main()**. The **main()** is trivial: we just keep calling **expression()** and printing out its result:

```
int main()
try {
    while (cin)
            cout << expression() << '\n';
    keep_window_open();
}
catch (exception& e) {
    cerr << e.what() << endl;
    keep_window_open ();
    return 1;
}
catch (...) {
    cerr << "exception \n";
    keep_window_open ();
    return 2;
}
```

The error handling is the usual "boilerplate" (§5.6.3). Let us postpone the description of the implementation of **get_token**() to §6.8 and test this first version of the calculator.

TRY THIS

This first version of the calculator program (including **get_token**()) is available as file **calculator00.cpp**. Get it to run and try it out.

Unsurprisingly, this first version of the calculator doesn't work quite as we expected. So we shrug and ask, "Why not?" or rather, "So, why does it work the way it does?" and "What does it do?" Type a **2** followed by a newline. No response. Try another newline to see if it's asleep. Still no response. Type a **3** followed by a newline. No response! Type a **4** followed by a newline. It answers **2**! Now the screen looks like this:

```
2

3
4
2
```

We carry on by typing **5+6+7**. The program responds with a **5**, so that the screen looks like this:

```
2

3
4
2
5+6+7
5
```

Unless you have programmed before, you are most likely very puzzled! In fact, even an experienced programmer might be puzzled. What's going on here? At this point, you try to get out of the program. How do you do this? We "forgot" to program an exit command, but an error will cause the program to exit, so you type an **x** and the program prints **Bad token** and exits. Finally, something worked as planned!

However, we forgot to distinguish between input and output on the screen. Before we try to solve the main puzzle, let's just fix the output to better see what we are doing. Adding an **=** to indicate output will do for now:

while (cin) cout << "= " << expression() << '\n';   // version 1

Now, entering the exact sequence of characters as before, we get

    2

    3
    4
    = 2
    5+6+7
    = 5
    x
    Bad token

Strange! Try to figure out what the program did. We tried another few examples, but let's just look at this. This is a puzzle:

Why didn't the program respond after the first **2** and **3** and the newlines?

Why did the program respond with **2**, rather than **4**, after we entered **4**?

Why did the program answer **5**, rather than **18**, after **5+6+7**?

There are many possible ways of proceeding from such mysterious results. We'll examine some of those in the next chapter, but here, let's just think. Could the program be doing bad arithmetic? That's most unlikely; the value of **4** isn't **2**, and the value of **5+6+7** is **18** rather than **5**. Consider what happens when we enter **1 2 3 4+5 6+7 8+9 10 11 12** followed by a newline. We get

    1 2 3 4+5 6+7 8+9 10 11 12
    = 1
    = 4
    = 6
    = 8
    = 10

Huh? No **2** or **3**. Why **4** and not **9** (that is, **4+5**)? Why **6** and not **13** (that is, **6+7**)? Look carefully: the program is outputting every third token! Maybe the program "eats" some of our input without evaluating it? It does. Consider **expression()**:

```
double expression()
{
        double left = term();          // read and evaluate a Term
        Token t = get_token();         // get the next token
        while(true) {
                switch(t.kind) {
```

```
                    case '+':
                            left += term();        // evaluate Term and add
                            t = get_token();
                            break;
                    case '-':
                            left -= term();        // evaluate Term and subtract
                            t = get_token();
                            break;
                    default:
                            return left;           // finally: no more + or -; return the answer
                    }
            }
    }
```

When the **Token** returned by **get_token()** is not a '+' or a '-' we just return. We don't use that token and we don't store it anywhere for any other function to use later. That's not smart. Throwing away input without even determining what it is can't be a good idea. A quick look shows that **term()** has exactly the same problem. That explains why our calculator ate two tokens for each that it used.

Let us modify **expression()** so that it doesn't "eat" tokens. Where would we put that next token (**t**) when the program doesn't need it? We could think of many elaborate schemes, but let's jump to the obvious answer ("obvious" once you see it): that token is going to be used by some other function that is reading tokens from the input, so let's put the token back into the input stream so that it can be read again by some other function! Actually, you can put characters back into an **istream**, but that's not really what we want. We want to deal with tokens, not mess with characters. What we want is an input stream that deals with tokens and that you can put an already read token back into.

So, assume that we have a stream of tokens – a "**Token_stream**" – called **ts**. Assume further that a **Token_stream** has a member function **get()** that returns the next token and a member function **putback(t)** that puts a token **t** back into the stream. We'll implement that **Token_stream** in §6.8 as soon as we have had a look at how it needs to be used. Given **Token_stream**, we can rewrite **expression()** so that it puts a token that it does not use back into the **Token_stream**:

```
double expression()
{
        double left = term();      // read and evaluate a Term
        Token t = ts.get();        // get the next Token from the Token stream

        while(true) {
                switch(t.kind) {
```

```
            case '+':
                    left += term();    // evaluate Term and add
                    t = ts.get();
                    break;
            case '-':
                    left -= term();        // evaluate Term and subtract
                    t = ts.get();
                    break;
            default:
                    ts.putback(t);     // put t back into the token stream
                    return left;       // finally: no more + or -; return the answer
            }
        }
    }
```

In addition, we must make the same change to **term()**:

```
    double term()
    {
        double left = primary();
        Token t = ts.get();         // get the next Token from the Token stream

        while(true) {
            switch (t.kind) {
            case '*':
                    left *= primary();
                    t = ts.get();
                    break;
            case '/':
            {       double d = primary();
                    if (d == 0) error("divide by zero");
                    left /= d;
                    t = ts.get();
                    break;
            }
            default:
                    ts.putback(t);     // put t back into the Token stream
                    return left;
            }
        }
    }
```

For our last parser function, **primary()**, we need just to change **get_token()** to **ts.get()**; **primary()** uses every token it reads.

6.7 Trying the second version

So, we are ready to test our second version. Type **2** followed by a newline. No response. Try another newline to see if it's asleep. Still no response. Type a **3** followed by a newline and it answers **2**. Try **2+2** followed by a newline and it answers **3**. Now your screen looks like this:

```
2

3
=2
2+2
=3
```

Hmm. Maybe our introduction of **putback()** and its use in **expression()** and **term()** didn't fix the problem. Let's try another test:

```
2 3 4 2+3 2*3
= 2
= 3
= 4
= 5
```

Yes! These are correct answers! But the last answer (**6**) is missing. We still have a token-look-ahead problem. However, this time the problem is not that our code "eats" characters, but that it doesn't get any output for an expression until we enter the following expression. The result of an expression isn't printed immediately; the output is postponed until the program has seen the first token of the next expression. Unfortunately, the program doesn't see that token until we hit Return after the next expression. The program isn't really wrong; it is just a bit slow responding.

How can we fix this? One obvious solution is to require a "print command." So, let's accept a semicolon after an expression to terminate it and trigger output. And while we are at it, let's add an "exit command" to allow for graceful exit. The character **q** (for "quit") would do nicely for an exit command. In **main()**, we have

```
while (cin) cout << "=" << expression() << '\n';    // version 1
```

We can change that to the messier but more useful

```
double val = 0;
while (cin) {
        Token t = ts.get();

        if (t.kind == 'q') break;        // 'q' for "quit"
        if (t.kind == ';')               // ';' for "print now"
                cout << "=" << val << '\n';
        else
                ts.putback(t);
        val = expression();
}
```

Now the calculator is actually usable. For example, we get

```
2;
= 2
2+3;
= 5
3+4*5;
= 23
q
```

At this point we have a good initial version of the calculator. It's not quite what we really wanted, but we have a program that we can use as the base for making a more acceptable version. Importantly, we can now correct problems and add features one by one while maintaining a working program as we go along.

6.8 Token streams

Before further improving our calculator, let us show the implementation of **Token_stream**. After all, nothing – nothing at all – works until we get correct input. We implemented **Token_stream** first of all but didn't want too much of a digression from the problems of calculation before we had shown a minimal solution.

Input for our calculator is a sequence of tokens, just as we showed for **(1.5+4)*11** above (§6.5.1). What we need is something that reads characters from the standard input, **cin**, and presents the program with the next token when it asks for it. In addition, we saw that we – that is, our calculator program – often read a token too many, so that we must be able to put it back for later use. This is typical and fundamental; when you see **1.5+4** reading strictly left to right, how

could you know that the number **1.5** had been completely read without reading
the **+**? Until we see the **+** we might be on our way to reading **1.55555**. So, we
need a "stream" that produces a token when we ask for one using **get()** and
where we can put a token back into the stream using **putback()**. Everything we
use in C++ has a type, so we have to start by defining the type **Token_stream**.

You probably noticed the **public:** in the definition of **Token** above. There, it
had no apparent reason. For **Token_stream**, we need it and must explain its function. A C++ user-defined type often consists of two parts: the public interface (labeled "**public:**") and the implementation details (labeled "**private:**"). The idea is to
separate what a user of a type needs for convenient use from the details that we
need in order to implement the type, but that we'd rather not have users mess with:

```
class Token_stream {
public:
        // user interface
private:
        // implementation details
        // (not directly accessible to users of Token_stream)
};
```

Obviously, users and implementers are often just us "playing different roles," but
making the distinction between the (public) interface meant for users and the
(private) implementation details used only by the implementer is a powerful tool
for structuring code. The public interface should contain (only) what a user
needs, which is typically a set of functions, including constructors to initialize objects. The private implementation contains what is necessary to implement those
public functions, typically data and functions dealing with messy details that the
users need not know about and shouldn't directly use.

Let's elaborate the **Token_stream** type a bit. What does a user want from it?
Obviously, we want **get()** and **putback()** functions – that's why we invented the
notion of a token stream. The **Token_stream** is to make **Token**s out of characters
that it reads for input, so we need to be able to make a **Token_stream** and to define it to read from **cin**. Thus, the simplest **Token_stream** looks like this:

```
class Token_stream {
public:
        Token_stream();          // make a Token_stream that reads from cin
        Token get();             // get a Token
        void putback(Token t);   // put a Token back
private:
        // implementation details
};
```

That's all a user needs to use a **Token_stream**. Experienced programmers will wonder why **cin** is the only possible source of characters, but we decided to take our input from the keyboard. We'll revisit that decision in a Chapter 7 exercise.

Why do we use the "verbose" name **putback()** rather than the logically sufficient **put()**? We wanted to emphasize the asymmetry between **get()** and **putback()**; this is an input stream, not something that you can also use for general output. Also, **istream** has a **putback()** function: consistency in naming is a useful property of a system. It helps people remember and helps people avoid errors.

We can now make a **Token_stream** and use it:

```
Token_stream ts;        // a Token_stream called ts
Token t = ts.get();     // get next Token from ts
// . . .
ts.putback(t);          // put the Token t back into ts
```

That's all we need to write the rest of the calculator.

6.8.1 Implementing Token_stream

Now, we need to implement those three **Token_stream** functions. How do we represent a **Token_stream**? That is, what data do we need to store in a **Token_stream** for it to do its job? We need space for any token we put back into the **Token_stream**. To simplify, let's say we can put back at most one token at a time. That happens to be sufficient for our program (and for many, many similar programs). That way, we just need space for one **Token** and an indicator of whether that space is full or empty:

```
class Token_stream {
public:
    Token_stream();          // make a Token_stream that reads from cin
    Token get();             // get a Token (get() is defined elsewhere)
    void putback(Token t);   // put a Token back
private:
    bool full;               // is there a Token in the buffer?
    Token buffer;            // here is where we keep a Token put back using putback()
};
```

Now we can define ("write") the three member functions. The constructor and **putback()** are easy, because they do so little, so we will define those first.

The constructor just sets **full** to indicate that the buffer is **empty**:

```
Token_stream::Token_stream()
    :full(false), buffer(0)    // no Token in buffer
```

```
{
}
```

When we define a member of a class outside the class definition itself, we have to mention which class we mean the member to be a member of. We use the notation

  class_name :: *member_name*

for that. In this case, we define **Token_stream**'s constructor. A constructor is a member with the same name as its class.

Why would we define a member outside its class? The main answer is clarity: the class definition (primarily) states what the class can do. Member function definitions are implementations that specify how things are done. We prefer to put them "elsewhere" where they don't distract. Our ideal is to have every logical entity in a program fit on a screen. Class definitions typically do that if the member function definitions are placed elsewhere, but not if they are placed within the class definition ("in-class").

We initialize the class members in a member initializer list (§6.3.3); **full(false)** sets a **Token_stream**'s member **full** to false and **buffer(0)** initializes the member **buffer** with a "dummy token" we invented just for that purpose. The definition of **Token** (§6.5.1) says that every **Token** must be initialized, so we couldn't just ignore **Token_stream::buffer**.

The **putback()** member function puts its argument back into the **Token_stream**'s buffer:

```
void Token_stream::putback(Token t)
{
        buffer = t;     // copy t to buffer
        full = true;    // buffer is now full
}
```

The keyword **void** (meaning "nothing") is used to indicate that **putback()** doesn't return a value. If we wanted to make sure that we didn't try to use **putback()** twice without reading what we put back in between (using **get()**), we could add a test:

```
void Token_stream::putback(Token t)
{
        if (full) error("putback() into a full buffer");
        buffer = t;     // copy t to buffer
        full = true;    // buffer is now full
}
```

The test of **full** checks the precondition "There is no Token in the buffer."

6.8.2 Reading tokens

All the real work is done by **get()**. If there isn't already a **Token** in **Token_stream::
buffer**, **get()** must read characters from **cin** and compose them into **Tokens**:

```
Token Token_stream::get()
    {
    if (full) {          // do we already have a Token ready?
            // remove Token from buffer
            full=false;
            return buffer;
    }

    char ch;
    cin >> ch;           // note that >> skips whitespace (space, newline, tab, etc.)

    switch (ch) {
    case ';':            // for "print"
    case 'q':            // for "quit"
    case '(': case ')': case '+': case '-': case '*': case '/': case '%':
            return Token(ch);        // let each character represent itself
    case '.':
    case '0': case '1': case '2': case '3': case '4':
    case '5': case '6': case '7': case '8': case '9':
    {   cin.putback(ch);             // put digit back into the input stream
        double val;
        cin >> val;                  // read a floating-point number
        return Token('8',val);       // let '8' represent "a number"
    }
    default:
            error("Bad token");
    }
}
```

Let's examine **get()** in detail. First we check if we already have a **Token** in the
buffer. If so, we can just return that:

```
if (full) {          // do we already have a Token ready?
        // remove Token from buffer
        full=false;
        return buffer;
}
```

Only if **full** is **false** (that is, there is no token in the buffer) do we need to mess with characters. In that case, we read a character and deal with it appropriately. We look for parentheses, operators, and numbers. Any other character gets us the call of **error()** that terminates the program:

```
default:
        error("Bad token");
```

The **error()** function is described in §5.6.3 and we make it available in **std_lib_facilities.h**.

We had to decide how to represent the different kinds of **Tokens**; that is, we had to choose values for the member **kind**. For simplicity and ease of debugging, we decided to let the **kind** of a **Token** be the parentheses and operators themselves. This leads to extremely simple processing of parentheses and operators:

```
case '(': case ')': case '+': case '-': case '*': case '/':
        return Token(ch);          // let each character represent itself
```

To be honest, we had forgotten **';'** for "print" and **'q'** for "quit" in our first version. We didn't add them until we needed them for our second solution.

6.8.3 Reading numbers

Now we just have to deal with numbers. That's actually not that easy. How do we really find the value of **123**? Well, that's **100+20+3**, but how about **12.34**, and should we accept scientific notation, such as **12.34e5**? We could spend hours or days to get this right, but fortunately, we don't have to. Input streams know what C++ literals look like and how to turn them into values of type **double**. All we have to do is to figure out how to tell **cin** to do that for us inside **get()**:

```
case '.':
case '0': case '1': case '2': case '3': case '4': case '5': case '6': case '7':
case '8':case '9':
        {     cin.putback(ch);        // put digit back into the input stream
              double val;
              cin >> val;             // read a floating-point number
              return Token('8',val);  // let '8' represent "a number"
        }
```

We – somewhat arbitrarily – chose **'8'** to represent "a number" in a **Token**.

How do we know that a number is coming? Well, if we guess from experience or look in a C++ reference (e.g., Appendix A), we find that a numeric literal must start with a digit or . (the decimal point). So, we test for that. Next, we want to let **cin** read the number, but we have already read the first character (a digit or dot), so just letting **cin** loose on the rest will give a wrong result. We could try to combine the value of the first character with the value of "the rest" as read by **cin**; for example, if someone typed **123**, we would get **1** and **cin** would read **23** and we'd have to add **100** to **23**. Yuck! And that's a trivial case. Fortunately (and not by accident), **cin** works much like **Token_stream** in that you can put a character back into it. So instead of doing any messy arithmetic, we just put the initial character back into **cin** and then let **cin** read the whole number.

Please note how we again and again avoid doing complicated work and instead find simpler solutions – often relying on library facilities. That's the essence of programming: the continuing search for simplicity. Sometimes that's – somewhat facetiously – expressed as "Good programmers are lazy." In that sense (and only in that sense), we should be "lazy"; why write a lot of code if we can find a way of writing far less?

6.9 Program structure

Sometimes, the proverb says, it's hard to see the forest for the trees. Similarly, it is easy to lose sight of a program when looking at all its functions, classes, etc. So, let's have a look at the program with its details omitted:

```
#include "std_lib_facilities.h"

class Token { /* . . . */ };
class Token_stream { /* . . . */ };

Token_stream::Token_stream() :full(false), buffer(0) { /* . . . */ }
void Token_stream::putback(Token t) { /* . . . */ }
Token Token_stream::get() { /* . . . */ }

Token_stream ts;        // provides get() and putback()
double expression();     // declaration so that primary() can call expression()

double primary() { /* . . . */ }    // deal with numbers and parentheses
double term() { /* . . . */ }       // deal with *, /, and %
double expression()   { /* . . . */ }    // deal with + and –

int main() { /* . . . */ }        // main loop and deal with errors
```

The order of the declarations is important. You cannot use a name before it has been declared, so **ts** must be declared before **ts.get()** uses it, and **error()** must be declared before the parser functions because they all use it. There is an interesting loop in the call graph: **expression()** calls **term()** which calls **primary()** which calls **expression()**.

We can represent that graphically (leaving out calls to **error()** — everyone calls **error()**):

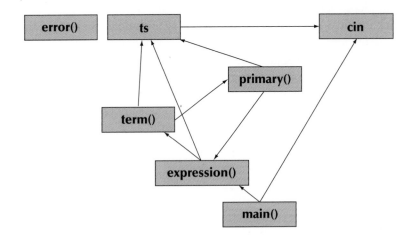

This means that we can't just define those three functions: there is no order that allows us to define every function before it is used. We need at least one declaration that isn't also a definition. We chose to declare ("forward declare") **expression()**.

But does this work? It does, for some definition of "work." It compiles, runs, correctly evaluates expressions, and gives decent error messages. But does it work in a way that we like? The unsurprising answer is "Not really." We tried the first version in §6.6 and removed a serious bug. This second version (§6.7) is not much better. But that's fine (and expected). It is good enough for its main purpose, which is to be something that we can use to verify our basic ideas and get feedback from. As such, it is a success, but try it: it'll (still) drive you nuts!

TRY THIS

Get the calculator as presented above to run, see what it does, and try to figure out why it works as it does.

Drill

This drill involves a series of modifications of a buggy program to turn it from something useless into something reasonably useful.

1. Take the calculator from the file **calculator02buggy.cpp**. Get it to compile. You need to find and fix a few bugs. Those bugs are not in the text in the book.
2. Change the character used as the exit command from q to x.
3. Change the character used as the print command from ; to =.
4. Add a greeting line in **main**():

   > **"Welcome to our simple calculator.**
   > **Please enter expressions using floating-point numbers."**

5. Improve that greeting by mentioning which operators are available and how to print and exit.
6. Find the three logic errors deviously inserted in **calculator02buggy.cpp** and remove them so that the calculator produces correct results.

Review

1. What do we mean by "Programming is understanding"?
2. The chapter details the creation of a calculator program. Write a short analysis of what the calculator should be able to do.
3. How do you break a problem up into smaller manageable parts?
4. Why is creating a small, limited version of a program a good idea?
5. Why is feature creep a bad idea?
6. What are the three main phases of software development?
7. What is a "use case"?
8. What is the purpose of testing?
9. According to the outline in the chapter, describe the difference between a **Term**, an **Expression**, a **Number**, and a **Primary**.
10. In the chapter, an input was broken down into its component **Terms**, **Expressions**, **Primarys**, and **Numbers**. Do this for **(17+4)/(5−1)**.
11. Why does the program not have a function called **number**()?
12. What is a token?
13. What is a grammar? A grammar rule?
14. What is a class? What do we use classes for?
15. What is a constructor?
16. In the expression function, why is the default for the **switch**-statement to "put back" the token?

17. What is "look-ahead"?
18. What does **putback()** do and why is it useful?
19. Why is the remainder (modulus) operation, %, difficult to implement in the **term()**?
20. What do we use the two data members of the **Token** class for?
21. Why do we (sometimes) split a class's members into **private** and **public** members?
22. What happens in the **Token_stream** class when there is a token in the buffer and the **get()** function is called?
23. Why were the **';'** and **'q'** characters added to the **switch**-statement in the **get()** function of the **Token_stream** class?
24. When should we start testing our program?
25. What is a "user-defined type"? Why would we want one?
26. What is the interface to a C++ "user-defined type"?
27. Why do we want to rely on libraries of code?

Terms

analysis	grammar	prototype
class	implementation	pseudo code
class member	interface	**public**
data member	member function	syntax analyzer
design	parser	token
divide by zero	**private**	use case

Exercises

1. If you haven't already, do the **Try this** exercises from this chapter.
2. Add the ability to use {} as well as () in the program, so that {(4+5)*6} / (3+4) will be a valid expression.
3. Add a factorial operator: use a suffix ! operator to represent "factorial." For example, the expression 7! means 7 * 6 * 5 * 4 * 3 * 2 * 1. Make ! bind tighter than * and /; that is, **7*8!** means **7*(8!)** rather than **(7*8)!**. Begin by modifying the grammar to account for a higher-level operator. To agree with the standard mathematical definition of factorial, let **0!** evaluate to **1**.
4. Define a class **Name_value** that holds a string and a value. Give it a constructor (a bit like **Token**). Rework exercise 19 in Chapter 4 to use a **vector<Name_value>** instead of two **vectors**.
5. Add the article **the** to the "English" grammar in §6.4.1, so that it can describe sentences such as "The birds fly but the fish swim."

6. Write a program that checks if a sentence is correct according to the "English" grammar in §6.4.1. Assume that every sentence is terminated by a full stop (.) surrounded by whitespace. For example, **birds fly but the fish swim .** is a sentence, but **birds fly but the fish swim** (terminating dot missing) and **birds fly but the fish swim.** (no space before dot) are not. For each sentence entered, the program should simply respond "OK" or "not OK." Hint: Don't bother with tokens; just read into a **string** using **>>**.

7. Write a grammar for logical expressions. A logical expression is much like an arithmetic expression except that the operators are **!** (not), **~** (complement), **&** (and), **|** (or), and **^** (exclusive or). **!** and **~** are prefix unary operators. A **^** binds tighter than a **|** (just as * binds tighter than +) so that **x|y^z** means **x|(y^z)** rather than **(x|y)^z**. The & operator binds tighter than **^** so that **x^y&z** means **x^(y&z)**.

8. Redo the "Bulls and Cows" game from exercise 12 in Chapter 5 to use four letters rather than four digits.

9. Write a program that reads digits and composes them into integers. For example, **123** is read as the characters 1, 2, and 3. The program should output "**123 is 1 hundred and 2 tens and 3 ones**". The number should be output as an **int** value. Handle numbers with one, two, three, or four digits. Hint: To get the integer value 5 of the character **'5'** subtract **'0'**, that is, **'5'–'0'==5**.

10. A permutation is an ordered subset of a set. For example, say you wanted to pick a combination to a vault. There are 60 possible numbers, and you need three different numbers for the combination. There are $P(60,3)$ permutations for the combination, where P is defined by the formula

$$P(a,b) = \frac{a!}{(a-b)!},$$

where ! is used as a suffix factorial operator. For example, 4! is 4*3*2*1. Combinations are similar to permutations, except that the order of the objects doesn't matter. For example, if you were making a "banana split" sundae and wished to use three different flavors of ice cream out of five that you had, you wouldn't care if you used a scoop of vanilla at the beginning or the end; you would still have used vanilla. The formula for combinations is:

$$C(a,b) = \frac{P(a-b)}{b!}.$$

Design a program that asks users for two numbers, asks them whether they want to calculate permutations or combinations, and prints out the result. This will have several parts. Do an analysis of the above requirements. Write exactly what the program will have to do. Then, go into the design phase. Write pseudo code for the program, and break it into sub-components. This program should have error checking. Make sure that all erroneous inputs will generate good error messages.

Postscript

Making sense of input is one of the fundamental programming activities. Every program somehow faces that problem. Making sense of something directly produced by a human is among the hardest problems. For example, many aspects of voice recognition are still a research problem. Simple variations of this problem, such as our calculator, cope by using a grammar to define the input.

7

Completing a Program

"It ain't over till the fat lady sings."

—Opera proverb

Writing a program involves gradually refining your ideas of what you want to do and how you want to express it. In Chapter 6, we produced the initial working version of a calculator program. Here, we'll refine it. Completing the program — that is, making it fit for users and maintainers — involves improving the user interface, doing some serious work on error handling, adding a few useful features, and restructuring the code for ease of understanding and modification.

7.1 Introduction

When your program first starts running "reasonably," you're probably about halfway finished. For a large program or a program that could do harm if it misbehaved, you will be nowhere near halfway finished. Once the program "basically works," the real fun begins! That's when we have enough working code to experiment with ideas.

In this chapter, we will guide you through the considerations a professional programmer might have trying to improve the calculator from Chapter 6. Note that the questions asked about the program and the issues considered here are far more interesting than the calculator itself. What we do is to give an example of how real programs evolve under the pressure of requirements and constraints and of how a programmer can gradually improve code.

7.2 Input and output

If you look back to the beginning of Chapter 6, you'll find that we decided to prompt the user with

    Expression:

and to report back answers with

    Result:

In the heat of getting the program to run, we forgot all about that. That's pretty typical. We can't think of everything all the time, so when we stop to reflect, we find that we have forgotten something.

For some programming tasks, the initial requirements cannot be changed. That's usually too rigid a policy and leads to programs that are unnecessarily poor solutions to the problems that they are written to solve. So, let's consider what we would do, assuming that we can change the specification of what exactly the program should do. Do we really want the program to write **Expression:** and **Result:**? How would we know? Just "thinking" rarely helps. We have to try and see what works best.

2+3; 5*7; 2+9;

currently gives

> **= 5**
> **= 35**
> **= 11**

If we added **Expression:** and **Result:**, we'd get

> **Expression: 2+3; 5*7; 2+9;**
> **Result : 5**
> **Expression: Result: 35**
> **Expression: Result: 11**
> **Expression:**

We are sure that some people will like one style and others will like the other. In such cases, we can consider giving people a choice, but for this simple calculator that would be overkill, so we must decide. We think that writing **Expression:** and **Result:** is a bit too "heavy" and distracting. Using those, the actual expressions and results are only a minor part of what appears on the screen, and since expressions and results are what matters, nothing should distract from them. On the other hand, unless we somehow separate what the user types from what the computer outputs, the result can be confusing. During initial debugging, we added = as a result indicator. We would also like a short "prompt" to indicate that the program wants input. The > character is often used as a prompt:

> **> 2+3;**
> **= 5**
> **> 5*7;**
> **= 35**
> **>**

This looks much better, and we can get it by a minor change to the main loop of **main()**:

```
double val = 0;
while (cin) {
        cout << "> ";    // print prompt
```

```
        Token t = ts.get();
        if (t.kind == 'q') break;
        if (t.kind == ';')
                cout << "= " << val << '\n';      // print result
        else
                ts.putback(t);
        val = expression();
}
```

Unfortunately, the result of putting several expressions on a line is still messy:

```
> 2+3; 5*7; 2+9;
= 5
> = 35
> = 11
>
```

The basic problem is that we didn't think of multiple expressions on a line when we started out (at least we pretended not to). What we want is

```
> 2+3; 5*7; 2+9;
= 5
= 35
= 11
>
```

This looks right, but unfortunately there is no really obvious way of achieving it. We first looked at **main()**. Is there a way to write out **>** only if it is not immediately followed by a **=**? We cannot know! We need to write **>** before the **get()**, but we do not know if **get()** actually reads new characters or simply gives us a **Token** from characters that it had already read from the keyboard. In other words, we would have to mess with **Token_stream** to make this final improvement.

For now, we decide that what we have is good enough. If we find that we have to modify **Token_stream**, we'll revisit this decision. However, it is unwise to make major structural changes to gain a minor advantage, and we haven't yet thoroughly tested the calculator.

7.3 Error handling

The first thing to do once you have a program that "basically works" is to try to break it; that is, we try to feed it input in the hope of getting it to misbehave. We say "hope" because the challenge here is to find as many errors as possible, so

that you can fix them before anybody else finds them. If you go into this exercise with the attitude that "my program works and I don't make errors!" you won't find many bugs and you'll feel bad when you do find one. You'd be playing head games with yourself! The right attitude when testing is "I'll break it! I'm smarter than any program – even my own!" So, we feed the calculator a mix of correct and incorrect expressions. For example:

```
1+2+3+4+5+6+7+8
1–2–3–4
!+2
;;;
(1+3;
(1+);
1*2/3%4+5–6;
();
1+;
+1
1++;
1/0
1/0;
1++2;
–2;
–2;;;;
1234567890123456;
'a';
q
1+q
1+2; q
```

TRY THIS

Feed a few such "problematic" expressions to the calculator and try to figure out in how many ways you can get it to misbehave. Can you get it to crash, that is, to get it past our error handling and give a machine error? We don't think you can. Can you get it to exit without a useful error message? You can.

Technically, this is known as *testing*. There are people who do this – break programs – for a living. Testing is a very important part of software development and can actually be fun. Chapter 26 examines testing in some detail. One big question is: "Can we test the program systematically, so that we find all of the errors?" There is no general answer to this question; that is, there is no answer that holds for all programs. However, you can do rather well for many programs when you approach testing seriously. You try to create test cases systematically, and just in case your strategy for selecting tests isn't complete, you do some "unreasonable" tests, such as

Mary had a little lamb
srtvrqtiewcbet7rewaewre–wqcntrretewru754389652743nvcqnwq;
!@#$%^&*()~:;

Once, when testing compilers, I got into the habit of feeding email reporting compiler errors straight to the compiler – mail headers, user's explanation, and all. That wasn't "sensible" because "nobody would do that." However, a program ideally catches all errors, not just the sensible ones, and soon that compiler was very resilient against "strange input."

The first really annoying thing we noticed when testing the calculator was that the window closed immediately after inputs such as

```
+1;
()
!+2
```

A little thought (or some tracing of the program's execution) shows that the problem is that the window is closed immediately after the error message has been written. This happens because our mechanism for keeping a window alive was to wait for you to enter a character. However, in all three cases above, the program detected an error before it had read all of the characters, so that there was a character left on the input line. The program can't tell such "leftover" characters from a character entered in response to the **Enter a character to close window** prompt. That "leftover" character then closed the window.

We could deal with that by modifying **main()** (see §5.6.3):

```
catch (runtime_error& e) {
    cerr << e.what() << endl;
    // keep_window_open():
    cout << "Please enter the character ~ to close the window\n";
    char ch;
    while(cin >> ch)    // keep reading until we find a ~
        if (ch=='~') return 1;
    return 1;
}
```

Basically, we replaced **keep_window_open()** with our own code. Note that we still have our problem if a ~ happens to be the next character to be read after an error, but that's rather unlikely.

When we encountered this problem we wrote a version of **keep_window_open()** that takes a string as its argument and closes the window only when you enter that string after getting the prompt, so a simpler solution is:

```
catch (runtime_error& e) {
        cerr << e.what() << endl;
        keep_window_open("~~");
        return 1;
}
```

Now examples such as

```
+1
!1~~
()
```

will cause the calculator to give the proper error messages, then say

Please enter ~~ to exit

and not exit until you enter the string ~~.

The calculator takes input from the keyboard. That makes testing tedious: each time we make an improvement, we have to type in a lot of test cases (yet again!) to make sure we haven't broken anything. It would be much better if we could store our test cases somewhere and run them with a single command. Some operating systems (notably Unix) make it trivial to get **cin** to read from a file without modifying the program, and similarly to divert the output from **cout** to a file. If that's not convenient, we must modify the program to use a file (see Chapter 10).

Now consider:

```
1+2; q
```

and

```
1+2 q
```

We would like both to print the result (**3**) and then exit the program. Curiously enough,

```
1+2 q
```

does that, but the apparently cleaner

    1+2; q

elicits a **Primary expected** error. Where would we look for this error? In **main()** where ; and **q** are handled, of course. We added those "print" and "quit" commands rather quickly to get the calculator to work (§6.6). Now we are paying for that haste. Consider again:

```
double val = 0;
while (cin) {
        cout << "> ";
        Token t = ts.get();
        if (t.kind == 'q') break;
        if (t.kind == ';')
                cout << "= " << val << '\n';
        else
                ts.putback(t);
        val = expression();
}
```

If we find a semicolon, we straightaway proceed to call **expression()** without checking for **q**. The first thing that expression does is to look for a **primary()**, and now it finds **q**. The letter **q** isn't a primary so we get our error message. So, we should test for **q** after testing for a semicolon. While we were at it, we felt the need to simplify the logic a bit, so the complete **main()** reads:

```
int main()
try
{
    while (cin) {
            cout << "> ";
            Token t = ts.get();
            while (t.kind == ';') t=ts.get();     // eat ';'
            if (t.kind == 'q') {
                    keep_window_open();
                    return 0;
            }
            ts.putback(t);
            cout << "= " << expression() << endl;
    }
    keep_window_open();
    return 0;
}
```

```
catch (exception& e) {
    cerr << e.what() << endl;
    keep_window_open("~~");
    return 1;
}
catch (...) {
    cerr << "exception \n";
    keep_window_open("~~");
    return 2;
}
```

This makes for reasonably robust error handling. So we can start considering what else we can do to improve the calculator.

7.4 Negative numbers

If you tested the calculator, you found that it couldn't handle negative numbers elegantly. For example, this is an error:

   –1/2

We have to write

   (0–1)/2

That's not acceptable.

Finding such problems during late debugging and testing is common. Only now do we have the opportunity to see what our design really does and get the feedback that allows us to refine our ideas. When planning a project, it is wise to try to preserve time and flexibility to benefit from the lessons we learn here. All too often, "release 1.0" is shipped without needed refinements because a tight schedule or a rigid project management strategy prevents "late" changes to the specification; "late" addition of "features" is especially dreaded. In reality, when a program is good enough for simple use by its designers but not yet ready to ship, it isn't "late" in the development sequence; it's the earliest time when we can benefit from solid experience with the program. A realistic schedule takes that into account.

In this case, we basically need to modify the grammar to allow unary minus. The simplest change seems to be in **Primary**. We have

```
Primary:
    Number
    "(" Expression ")"
```

and we need something like

```
Primary:
      Number
      "(" Expression ")"
      "-" Primary
      "+" Primary
```

We added unary plus because that's what C++ does. When we have unary minus, someone always tries unary plus and it's easier just to implement that than to explain why it is useless. The code that implements **Primary** becomes

```
double primary()
{
      Token t = ts.get();
      switch (t.kind) {
      case '(':    // handle '(' expression ')'
            {
                  double d = expression();
                  t = ts.get();
                  if (t.kind != ')') error("')' expected");
                  return d;
            }
      case '8':                 // we use '8' to represent a number
            return t.value;     // return the number's value
      case '-':
            return - primary();
      case '+':
            return primary();
      default:
            error("primary expected");
      }
}
```

That's so simple that it actually worked the first time.

7.5 Remainder: %

When we first analyzed the ideals for a calculator, we wanted the remainder (modulo) operator: %. However, it is not defined for floating-point numbers, so we backed off. Now we can consider it again. It should be simple:

1. We add % as a **Token**.
2. We convert the **doubles** to **ints** so that we can use % on those **ints**.

Here is the added code in **term()**:

```
case '%':
        {       double d = term();
                int i1 = int(left);
                int i2 = int(d);
                return i1%i2;
        }
```

The **int(d)** is an explicit notation for turning the **double** into an **int** by truncating (that is, by throwing away whatever was after the decimal point). Unfortunately, it's redundant (see §3.9.2), but we prefer to indicate that we know a conversion is happening, that is, that we didn't just accidentally and implicitly convert a **double** to an **int**. This works in that we now get the correct results for integer operands. For example:

```
> 2%3;
= 0
> 3%2;
= 1
> 5%3;
= 2
```

How should we handle operands that are not integers? What should be the result of

```
> 6.7%3.3;
```

There is no really good answer, so we'll prohibit the use of % on a floating-point argument. We check if the floating-point operands have fractional parts and give an error message if they do. Here is the resulting **term()**:

```
double term()
{
        double left = primary();
        Token t = ts.get();             // get the next token from Token_stream

        while(true) {
                switch (t.kind) {
```

```
        case '*':
            left *= term();
            t = ts.get();
            break;
        case '/':
        {   double d = term();
            if (d == 0) error("divide by zero");
            left /= d;
            t = ts.get();
            break;
        }
        case '%':
        {   double d = term();
            int i1 = int(left);
            if (i1 != left) error ("left-hand operand of % not int");
            int i2 = int(d);
            if (i2 != d) error ("right-hand operand of % not int");
            if (i2 == 0) error("%: divide by zero");
            left = i1%i2;
            t = ts.get();
            break;
        }
        default:
            ts.putback(t);        // put t back into the Token_stream
            return left;
        }
    }
}
```

What we do here is to use **!=** to check if the **double** to **int** conversion changed the value. If not, all is well and we can use %.

The problem of ensuring **int** operands for % is a variant of the narrowing problem (§3.9.2 and §5.6.4), so we could solve it using **narrow_cast**:

```
case '%':
{   int i1 = narrow_cast<int>(left);
    int i2 = narrow_cast<int>(term());
    f (i2 == 0) error("%: divide by zero");
    left = i1%i2;
    t = ts.get();
    break;
}
```

That's certainly shorter, and arguably clearer, but it doesn't give quite as good error messages.

7.6 Cleaning up the code

We have made several changes to the code. They are, we think, all improvements, but the code is beginning to look a bit messy. Now is a good time to review the code to see if we can make it clearer and shorter, add and improve comments, etc. In other words, we are not finished with the program until we have it in a state suitable for someone else to take over maintenance. Except for the almost total absence of comments, the calculator code really isn't that bad, but let's do a bit of cleanup.

7.6.1 Symbolic constants

Looking back, we find the use of **'8'** to indicate a **Token** containing a numeric value odd. It doesn't really matter what value is used to indicate a number **Token** as long as the value is distinct from all other values indicating different kind of **Token**s. However, the code looks a bit odd and we had to keep reminding ourselves in comments:

```
case '8':              // we use '8' to represent a number
        return t.value;    // return the number's value
case '–':
        return – primary();
```

To be honest, we also made a few mistakes, typing **'0'** rather than **'8'**, because we forgot which value we had chosen to use. In other words, using **'8'** directly in the code manipulating **Token**s was sloppy, hard to remember, and error-prone; **'8'** is one of those "magic constants" we warned against in §4.3.1. What we should have done was to introduce a symbolic name for the constant we used to represent number:

```
const char number = '8';    // t.kind==number means that t is a number Token
```

The **const** modifier simply tells the compiler that we are defining a number that is not supposed to change: **number='0'** would cause the compiler to give an error message. Given that definition of **number**, we don't have to use **'8'** explicitly anymore. The code fragment from **primary** above now becomes:

```
case number:
        return t.value;    // return the number's value
case '–':
        return – primary();
```

This requires no comment. We should not say in comments what can be clearly and directly said in code. Repeated comments explaining something are often an indication that the code should be improved.

Similarly, the code in **Token_stream::get()** that recognizes numbers becomes

```
case '.':
case '0': case '1': case '2': case '3': case '4':
case '5': case '6': case '7': case '8': case '9':
    {      cin.putback();         // put digit back into the input stream
           double val;
           cin >> val;            // read a floating-point number
           return Token(number,val);
    }
```

We could consider symbolic names for all tokens, but that seems overkill. After all, '(' and '+' are about as obvious a notation for (and + as anyone could come up with. Looking through the tokens, only ';' for "print" (or "terminate expression") and 'q' for "quit" seem arbitrary. Why not 'p' and 'e'? In a larger program, it is only a matter of time before such obscure and arbitrary notation becomes a cause of a problem, so we introduce

```
const char quit = 'q';     // t.kind==quit means that t is a quit Token
const char print = ';';    // t.kind==print means that t is a print Token
```

Now we can write **main()**'s loop like this:

```
while (cin) {
    cout << "> ";
    Token t = ts.get();
    while (t.kind == print) t=ts.get();
    if (t.kind == quit) {
        keep_window_open();
        return 0;
    }
    ts.putback(t);
    cout << "= " << expression() << endl;
}
```

Introducing symbolic names for "print" and "quit" makes the code easier to read. In addition, it doesn't encourage someone reading **main()** to make assumptions about how "print" and "quit" are represented on input. For example, it should come as no surprise if we decide to change the representation of "quit" to 'e' (for "exit"). That would now require no change in **main()**.

Now the strings ">_" and "=_" stand out. Why do we have these "magical" literals in the code? How would a new programmer reading **main()** guess their purpose? Maybe we should add a comment? Adding a comment might be a good idea, but introducing a symbolic name is more effective:

```
const string prompt = "> ";
const string result = "= ";      // used to indicate that what follows is a result
```

Should we want to change the prompt or the result indicator, we can just modify those **const**s. The loop now reads

```
while (cin) {
        cout << prompt;
        Token t = ts.get();
        while (t.kind ==print) t=ts.get();
        if (t.kind == quit) {
                keep_window_open();
                return 0;
        }
        ts.putback(t);
        cout << result << expression() << endl;
}
```

7.6.2 Use of functions

The functions we use should reflect the structure of our program, and the names of the functions should identify the logically separate parts of our code. Basically, our program so far is rather good in this respect: **expression()**, **term()**, and **primary()** directly reflect our understanding of the expression grammar, and **get()** handles the input and token recognition. Looking at **main()**, though, we notice that it does two logically separate things:

1. **main()** provides general "scaffolding": start the program, end the program, and handle "fatal" errors.
2. **main()** handles the calculation loop.

Ideally, a function performs a single logical action (§4.5.1). Having **main()** perform both of these actions obscures the structure of the program. The obvious solution is to separate out the calculation loop in a separate function **calculate()**:

```
void calculate()         // expression evaluation loop
{
```

```
    while (cin) {
            cout << prompt;
            Token t = ts.get();
            while (t.kind == print) t=ts.get();     // first discard all "prints"
            if (t.kind == quit) return;             // quit
            ts.putback(t);
            cout << result << expression() << endl;
    }
}

int main()
try {
    calculate();
    keep_window_open();         // cope with Windows console mode
    return 0;
}
catch (runtime_error& e) {
    cerr << e.what() << endl;
    keep_window_open("~~");
    return 1;
}
catch (. . .) {
    cerr << "exception \n";
    keep_window_open("~~");
    return 2;
}
```

This reflects the structure much more directly and is therefore easier to understand.

7.6.3 Code layout

Looking through the code for ugly code, we find

```
switch (ch) {
case 'q': case ';': case '%': case '(': case ')': case '+': case '-': case '*': case '/':
    return Token(ch);         // let each character represent itself
```

This wasn't too bad before we added 'q', ';', and '%', but now it's beginning to become obscure. Code that is hard to read is where bugs can more easily hide. And yes, a potential bug lurks here! Using one line per case and adding a couple of comments help. So, **Token_stream**'s get() becomes

```
Token Token_stream::get()
    // read characters from cin and compose a Token
{
    if (full) {        // check if we already have a Token ready
        full=false;
        return buffer;
    }

    char ch;
    cin >> ch;        // note that >> skips whitespace (space, newline, tab, etc.)

    switch (ch) {
    case quit:
    case print:
    case '(':
    case ')':
    case '+':
    case '-':
    case '*':
    case '/':
    case '%':
        return Token(ch);        // let each character represent itself
    case '.':                    // a floating-point-literal can start with a dot
    case '0': case '1': case '2': case '3': case '4':
    case '5': case '6': case '7': case '8': case '9':        // numeric literal
    {   cin.putback(ch);        // put digit back into the input stream
        double val;
        cin >> val;             // read a floating-point number
        return Token(number,val);
    }
    default:
        error("Bad token");
    }
}
```

We could of course have put each digit case on a separate line also, but that didn't seem to buy us any clarity. Also, doing so would prevent **get()** from being viewed in its entirety on a screen at once. Our ideal is for each function to fit on the screen; one obvious place for a bug to hide is in the code that we can't see because it's off the screen horizontally or vertically. Code layout matters.

Note also that we changed the plain **'q'** to the symbolic name **quit**. This improves readability and also guarantees a compile-time error if we should make the mistake of choosing a value for **quit** that clashes with another token name.

When we clean up code, we might accidentally introduce errors. Always retest the program after cleanup. Better still, do a bit of testing after each set of minor improvements so that if something went wrong you can still remember exactly what you did. Remember: Test early and often.

7.6.4 Commenting

We added a few comments as we went along. Good comments are an important part of writing code. We tend to forget about comments in the heat of programming. When you go back to the code to clean it up is an excellent time to look at each part of the program to see if the comments you originally wrote are

1. Still valid (you might have changed the code since you wrote the comment)
2. Adequate for a reader (they usually are not)
3. Not so verbose that they distract from the code

To emphasize that last concern: what is best said in code should be said in code. Avoid comments that repeat an action that's perfectly clear to someone who knows the programming language. For example:

```
x = b+c;        // add b and c and assign the result to x
```

You'll find such comments in this book, but only when we are trying to explain the use of a language feature that might not yet be familiar to you.

Comments are for things that code expresses poorly. An example is intent: code says what it does, not what it was intended to do (§5.9.1). Look at the calculator code. There is something missing: the functions show how we process expressions and tokens, but there is no indication (except the code) what we meant expressions and tokens to be. The grammar is a good candidate for something to put in comments or into some documentation of the calculator.

```
/*
        Simple calculator

        Revision history:

                Revised by Bjarne Stroustrup May 2007
                Revised by Bjarne Stroustrup August 2006
                Revised by Bjarne Stroustrup August 2004
                Originally written by Bjarne Stroustrup
                        (bs@cs.tamu.edu) Spring 2004.

        This program implements a basic expression calculator.
        Input from cin; output to cout.
```

The grammar for input is:

```
Statement:
        Expression
        Print
        Quit

Print:
        ;

Quit:
        q

Expression:
        Term
        Expression + Term
        Expression – Term
Term:
        Primary
        Term * Primary
        Term / Primary
        Term % Primary
Primary:
        Number
        ( Expression )
    – Primary
    + Primary
Number:
        floating-point-literal
```

Input comes from cin through the Token_stream called ts.

```
*/
```

Here we used the block comment, which starts with a /* and continues until a */. In a real program, the revision history would contain indications of what corrections and improvements were made.

Note that the comments are not the code. In fact, this grammar simplifies a bit: compare the rule for **Statement** with what really happens (e.g., have a peek at the code in the following section). The comment fails to explain the loop in **calculate()** that allows us to do several calculations in a single run of the program. We'll return to that problem in §7.8.1.

7.7 Recovering from errors

Why do we exit when we find an error? That seemed simple and obvious at the time, but why? Couldn't we just write an error message and carry on? After all, we often make little typing errors and such an error doesn't mean that we have decided not to do a calculation. So let's try to recover from an error. That basically means that we have to catch exceptions and continue after we have cleaned up any messes that were left behind.

Until now, all errors have been represented as exceptions and handled by **main()**. If we want to recover from errors, **calculate()** must catch exceptions and try to clean up the mess before trying to evaluate the next expression:

```
void calculate()
{
    while (cin)
    try {
        cout << prompt;
        Token t = ts.get();
        while (t.kind == print) t=ts.get();    // first discard all "prints"
        if (t.kind == quit) return;            // quit
        ts.putback(t);
        cout << result << expression() << endl;
    }
    catch (exception& e) {
        cerr << e.what() << endl;              // write error message
        clean_up_mess();
    }
}
```

We simply made the **while**-loop's block into a **try**-block that writes an error message and cleans up the mess. Once that's done, we carry on as always.

What would "clean up the mess" entail? Basically, getting ready to compute again after an error has been handled means making sure that all our data is in a good and predictable state. In the calculator, the only data we keep outside an individual function is the **Token_stream**. So what we need to do is to ensure that we don't have tokens related to the aborted calculation sitting around to confuse the next calculation. For example,

```
1++2*3; 4+5;
```

will cause an error, and **2*3; 4+5** will be left in the **Token_stream**'s buffer after the second **+** has triggered an exception. We have two choices:

1. Purge all tokens from the **Token_stream.**
2. Purge all tokens from the current calculation from the **Token_stream.**

The first choice discards all (including **4+5;**), whereas the second choice just discards **2*3;**, leaving **4+5** to be evaluated. Either could be a reasonable choice and either could surprise a user. As it happens, both are about equally simple to implement. We chose the second alternative because it simplifies testing.

So we need to read input until we find a semicolon. This seems simple. We have **get()** to do our reading for us so we can write a **clean_up_mess()** like this:

```
void clean_up_mess()        // naive
{
    while (true) {          // skip until we find a print
        Token t = ts.get();
        if (t.kind == print) return;
    }
}
```

Unfortunately, that doesn't work all that well. Why not? Consider this input:

```
1@z; 1+3;
```

The @ gets us into the **catch**-clause for the **while**-loop. Then, we call **clean_up_mess()** to find the next semicolon. Then, **clean_up_mess()** calls **get()** and reads the **z**. That gives another error (because **z** is not a token) and we find ourselves in **main()**'s **catch(...)** handler, and the program exits. Oops! We don't get a chance to evaluate **1+3**. Back to the drawing board!

We could try more elaborate **trys** and **catches**, but basically we are heading into an even bigger mess. Errors are hard to handle, and errors during error handling are even worse than other errors. So, let's try to devise some way to flush characters out of a **Token_stream** that couldn't possibly throw an exception. The only way of getting input into our calculator is **get()**, and that can — as we just discovered the hard way — throw an exception. So we need a new operation. The obvious place to put that is in **Token_stream**:

```
class Token_stream {
public:
    Token_stream();             // make a Token_stream that reads from cin
    Token get();                // get a Token
    void putback(Token t);      // put a Token back
    void ignore(char c);        // discard characters up to and including a c
```

```
    private:
        bool full;        // is there a Token in the buffer?
        Token buffer;     // here is where we keep a Token put back using putback()
};
```

This **ignore()** function needs to be a member of **Token_stream** because it needs to look at **Token_stream**'s buffer. We chose to make "the thing to look for" an argument to **ignore()** – after all, the **Token_stream** doesn't have to know what the calculator considers a good character to use for error recovery. We decided that argument should be a character because we don't want to risk composing **Tokens** – we saw what happened when we tried that. So we get

```
void Token_stream::ignore(char c)
    // c represents the kind of Token
{
    // first look in buffer:
    if (full && c==buffer.kind) {
        full = false;
        return;
    }
    full = false;

    // now search input:
    char ch = 0;
    while (cin>>ch)
        if (ch==c) return;
}
```

This code first looks at the buffer. If there is a **c** there, we are finished after discarding that **c**; otherwise, we need to read characters from **cin** until we find a **c**.

We can now write **clean_up_mess()** rather simply:

```
void clean_up_mess()
{
    ts.ignore(print);
}
```

Dealing with errors is always tricky. It requires much experimentation and testing because it is extremely hard to imagine what errors can occur. Trying to make a program foolproof is always a very technical activity; amateurs typically don't care. Quality error handling is one mark of a professional.

7.8 Variables

Having worked on style and error handling, we can return to looking for improvements in the calculator functionality. We now have a program that works quite well; how can we improve it? The first wish list for the calculator included variables. Having variables gives us better ways of expressing longer calculations. Similarly, for scientific calculations, we'd like built-in named values, such as **pi** and **e**, just as we have on scientific calculators.

Adding variables and constants is a major extension to the calculator. It will touch most parts of the code. This is the kind of extension that we should not embark on without good reason and sufficient time. Here, we add variables and constants because it gives us a chance to look over the code again and try out some more programming techniques.

7.8.1 Variables and definitions

Obviously, the key to both variables and built-in constants is for the calculator program to keep (*name,value*) pairs so that we can access the value given the name. We can define a **Variable** like this:

```
class Variable {
public:
        string name;
        double value;
        Variable (string n, double v) :name(n), value(v) { }
};
```

We will use the **name** member to identify a **Variable** and the **value** member to store the value corresponding to that **name**. The constructor is supplied simply for notational convenience.

How can we store **Variable**s so that we can search for a **Variable** with a given **name** string to find its value or to give it a new value? Looking back over the programming tools we have encountered so far, we find only one good answer: a **vector** of **Variable**s:

```
vector<Variable> var_table;
```

We can put as many **Variable**s as we like into the vector **var_table** and search for a given name by looking at the vector elements one after another. We can write a **get_value()** function that looks for a given **name** string and returns its corresponding **value**:

```
double get_value(string s)
      // return the value of the Variable named s
{
      for (int i = 0; i<var_table.size(); ++i)
            if (var_table[i].name == s) return var_table[i].value;
      error("get: undefined variable ", s);
}
```

The code really is quite simple: go through every **Variable** in **var_table** (starting with the first element and continuing until the last) and see if its **name** matches the argument string **s**. If that is the case, return its **value**.

Similarly, we can define a **set_value()** function to give a **Variable** a new **value**:

```
void set_value(string s, double d)
      // set the Variable named s to d
{
      for (int i = 0; i<var_table.size(); ++i)
            if (var_table[i].name == s) {
                  var_table[i].value = d;
                  return;
            }
      error("set: undefined variable ", s);
}
```

We can now read and write "variables" represented as **Variable**s in **var_table**. How do we get a new **Variable** into **var_table**? What does a user of our calculator have to write to define a new variable and later to get its value? We could consider C++'s notation

```
double var = 7.2;
```

That would work, but all variables in this calculator hold **double** values, so saying "double" would be redundant. Could we make do with

```
var = 7.2;
```

Possibly, but then we would be unable to tell the difference between the declaration of a new variable and a spelling mistake:

```
var1 = 7.2;      // define a new variable called var1
var1 = 3.2;      // define a new variable called var2
```

Oops! Clearly, we meant **var2 = 3.2;** but we didn't say so (except in the comment). We could live with this, but we'll follow the tradition in languages, such as C++, that distinguish declarations (with initializations) from assignments. We could use **double**, but for a calculator we'd like something short, so – drawing on another old tradition – we choose the keyword **let**:

> **let var = 7.2;**

The grammar would be

> **Calculation:**
> > **Statement**
> > **Print**
> > **Quit**
> > **Calculation Statement**
>
> **Statement:**
> > **Declaration**
> > **Expression**
>
> **Declaration:**
> > **"let" Name "=" Expression**

Calculation is the new top production (rule) of the grammar. It expresses the loop (in **calculate()**) that allows us to do several calculations in a run of the calculator program. It relies on the **Statement** production to handle expressions and declarations. We can handle a statement like this:

```
double statement()
{
      Token t = ts.get();
      switch (t.kind) {
      case let:
            return declaration();
      default:
            ts.putback(t);
            return expression();
      }
}
```

We can now use **statement()** instead of **expression()** in **calculate()**:

```
void calculate()
{
    while (cin)
    try {
        cout << prompt;
        Token t = ts.get();
        while (t.kind == print) t=ts.get();     // first discard all "prints"
        if (t.kind == quit) return;             // quit
        ts.putback(t);
        cout << result << statement() << endl;
    }
    catch (exception& e) {
        cerr << e.what() << endl;               // write error message
        clean_up_mess();
    }
}
```

We now have to write **declaration()**. What should it do? It should make sure that what comes after a **let** is a **Name** followed by a **=** followed by an **Expression**. That's what our grammar says. What should it do with the **name**? We should add a **Variable** with that **name** string and the value of the expression to our **vector<Variable>** called **var_table**. Once that's done we can retrieve the value using **get_value()** and change it using **set_value()**. However, before writing this, we have to decide what should happen if we define a variable twice. For example:

```
let v1 = 7;
let v1 = 8;
```

We chose to consider such a redefinition an error. Typically, it is simply a spelling mistake. Instead of what we wrote, we probably meant

```
let v1 = 7;
let v2 = 8;
```

There are logically two parts to defining a **Variable** with the name **var** with the value **val**:

1. Check whether there already is a **Variable** called **var** in **var_table**.
2. Add (**var**,**val**) to **var_table**.

We have no use for uninitialized variables. We defined the functions **is_declared()** and **define_name()** to represent those two logically separate operations:

```
bool is_declared(string var)
      // is var already in var_table?
{
      for (int i = 0; i<var_table.size(); ++i)
            if (var_table[i].name == var) return true;
      return false;
}


double define_name(string var, double val)
      // add (var,val) to var_table
{
      if (is_declared(var)) error(var," declared twice");
      var_table.push_back(Variable(var,val));
      return val;
}
```

Adding a new **Variable** to a **vector<Variable>** is easy; that's what **vector**'s **push_back()** member function does:

```
var_table.push_back(Variable(var,val));
```

The **Variable(var,val)** makes the appropriate **Variable** and **push_back()** then adds that **Variable** to the end of **var_table**. Given that, and assuming that we can handle **let** and **name** tokens, **declaration()** is straightforward to write:

```
double declaration()
      // assume we have seen "let"
      // handle: name = expression
      // declare a variable called "name" with the initial value "expression"
{
      Token t = ts.get();
      if (t.kind != name) error ("name expected in declaration");
      string var_name = t.name;

      Token t2 = ts.get();
      if (t2.kind != '=') error("= missing in declaration of ", var_name);

      double d = expression();
      define_name(var_name,d);
      return d;
}
```

Note that we returned the value stored in the new variable. That's useful when the initializing expression is nontrivial. For example:

let v = d/(t2−t1);

This declaration will define **v** and also print its value. Additionally, printing the value of a declared variable simplifies the code in **calculate()** because every **statement()** returns a value. General rules tend to keep code simple, whereas special cases tend to lead to complications.

This mechanism for keeping track of **Variable**s is what is often called a *symbol table* and could be radically simplified by the use of a standard library **map**; see §21.6.1.

7.8.2 Introducing names

This is all very good, but unfortunately, it doesn't quite work. By now, that shouldn't come as a surprise. Our first cut never − well, hardly ever − works. Here, we haven't even finished the program − it doesn't yet compile. We have no '=' token, but that's easily handled by adding a case to **Token_stream::get()** (§7.6.3). But how do we represent **let** and **name** as tokens? Obviously, we need to modify **get()** to recognize these tokens. How? Here is one way:

```
const char name = 'a';        // name token
const char let = 'L';         // declaration token
const string declkey = "let"; // declaration keyword

Token Token_stream::get()
{
    if (full) { full=false; return buffer; }
    char ch;
    cin >> ch;
    switch (ch) {
        // as before
    default:
        if (isalpha(ch)) {
            cin.putback(ch);
            string s;
            cin>>s;
            if (s == declkey) return Token(let);  // declaration keyword
            return Token(name,s);
        }
        error("Bad token");
    }
}
```

Note first of all the call **isalpha(ch)**. This call answers the question "Is **ch** a letter?"; **isalpha()** is part of the standard library that we get from **std_lib_facilities.h**. For more character classification functions, see §11.6. The logic for recognizing names is the same as that for recognizing numbers: find a first character of the right kind (here, a letter), then put it back using **putback()** and read in the whole name using **>>**.

Unfortunately, this doesn't compile; we have no **Token** that can hold a string, so the compiler rejects **Token(name,s)**. Fortunately, that's easily fixed by adding that possibility to the definition of **Token**:

```
struct Token {
        char kind;
        double value;
        string name;
        Token(char ch) :kind(ch), value(0) { }
        Token(char ch, double val) :kind(ch), value(val) { }
        Token(char ch, string n) :kind(ch), name(n) { }
};
```

We chose **'L'** as the representation of the **let** token and the string **let** as our keyword. Obviously, it would be trivial to change that keyword to **double**, var, **#**, or whatever by changing the string **declkey** that we compare **s** to.

Now we try the program again. If you type this, you'll see that it all works:

```
let x = 3.4;
let y = 2;
x + y * 2;
```

However, this doesn't work:

```
let x = 3.4;
let y = 2;
x+y*2;
```

What's the difference between those two examples? Have a look to see what happens.

The problem is that we were sloppy with our definition of **Name**. We even "forgot" to define our **Name** production in the grammar (§7.8.2). What characters can be part of a name? Letters? Certainly. Digits? Certainly, as long as they are not the starting character. Underscores? Eh? The + character? Well? Eh? Look at the code again. After the initial letter we read into a **string** using **>>**. That accepts every character until it sees whitespace. So, for example, **x+y*2;** is a single name — even the trailing semicolon is read as part of the name. That's unintended and unacceptable.

What must we do instead? First we must specify precisely what we want a name to be and then we must modify **get()** to do that. Here is a workable specification of a name: a sequence of letters and digits starting with a letter. Given this definition,

a
ab
a1
Z12
asdsddsfdfdasfdsa434RTHTD12345dfdsa8fsd888fadsf

are names and

1a
as_s
#
as*
a car

are not. Except for leaving out the underscore, this is C++'s rule. We can implement that in the default case of **get()**:

```
default:
    if (isalpha(ch)) {
        string s;
        s += ch;
        while (cin.get(ch) && (isalpha(ch) || isdigit(ch))) s+=ch;
        cin.putback(ch);
        if (s == declkey) return Token(let);   // declaration keyword
        return Token(name,s);
    }
    error("Bad token");
```

Instead of reading directly into the **string s**, we read characters and put those into **s** as long as they are letters or digits. The **s+=ch** statement adds (appends) the character **ch** to the end of the string **s**. The curious statement

while (cin.get(ch) && (isalpha(ch) || isdigit(ch))) s+=ch;

reads a character into **ch** (using **cin**'s member function **get()**) and checks if it is a letter or a digit. If so, it adds **ch** to **s** and reads again. The **get()** member function works just like **>>** except that it doesn't by default skip whitespace.

7.8.3 Predefined names

Now that we have names, we can easily predefine a few common ones. For example, if we imagine that our calculator will be used for scientific calculations, we'd want **pi** and **e**. Where in the code would we define those? In **main()** before the call of **calculate()** or in **calculate()** before the loop. We'll put them in **main()** because those definitions really aren't part of any calculation:

```
int main()
try {
        // predefine names:
        define_name("pi",3.1415926535);
        define_name("e",2.7182818284);

        calculate();

        keep_window_open();        // cope with Windows console mode
        return 0;
}
catch (exception& e) {
        cerr << e.what() << endl;
        keep_window_open("~~");
        return 1;
}
catch (...) {
        cerr << "exception \n";
        keep_window_open("~~");
        return 2;
}
```

7.8.4 Are we there yet?

Not really. We have made so many changes that we need to test everything again, clean up the code, and review the comments. Also, we could do more definitions. For example, we "forgot" to provide an assignment operator (see exercise 2), and if we have an assignment we might want to distinguish between variables and constants (exercise 3).

Initially, we backed off from having named variables in our calculator. Looking back over the code that implements them, we may have two possible reactions:

1. Implementing variables wasn't all that bad; it took only about three dozen lines of code.

2. Implementing variables was a major extension. It touched just about every function and added a completely new concept to the calculator. It increased the size of the calculator by 45% and we haven't even implemented assignment!

In the context of a first program of significant complexity, the second reaction is the correct one. More generally, it's the right reaction to any suggestion that adds something like 50% to a program in terms of both size and complexity. When that has to be done, it is more like writing a new program based on a previous one than anything else, and it should be treated that way. In particular, if you can build a program in stages as we did with the calculator, and test it at each stage, you are far better off doing so than trying to do the whole program all at once.

 Drill

1. Starting from the file **calculator08buggy.cpp**, get the calculator to compile.
2. Go through the entire program and add appropriate comments.
3. As you commented, you found errors (deviously inserted especially for you to find). Fix them; they are not in the text of the book.
4. Testing: prepare a set of inputs and use them to test the calculator. Is your list pretty complete? What should you look for? Include negative values, 0, very small, very large, and "silly" inputs.
5. Do the testing and fix any bugs that you missed when you commented.
6. Add a predefined name **k** meaning **1000**.
7. Give the user a square root function **sqrt()**, for example, **sqrt(2+6.7)**. Naturally, the value of **sqrt(x)** is the square root of **x**; for example, **sqrt(9)** is **3**. Use the standard library **sqrt()** function that is available through the header **std_lib_facilities.h**. Remember to update the comments, including the grammar.
8. Catch attempts to take the square root of a negative number and print an appropriate error message.
9. Allow the user to use **pow(x,i)** to mean "Multiply **x** with itself **i** times"; for example, **pow(2.5,3)** is **2.5*2.5*2.5**. Require **i** to be an integer using the technique we used for %.
10. Change the "declaration keyword" from **let** to **#**.
11. Change the "quit keyword" from **q** to **exit**. That will involve defining a string for "quit" just as we did for "let" in §7.8.2.

Review

1. What is the purpose of working on the program after the first version works? Give a list of reasons.

2. Why does "**1+2; q**" typed into the calculator not quit after it receives an error?

3. Why did we choose to make a constant character called **number**?

4. We split **main()** into two separate functions. What does the new function do and why did we split **main()**?

5. Why do we split code into multiple functions? State principles.

6. What is the purpose of commenting and how should it be done?

7. What does **narrow_cast** do?

8. What is the use of symbolic constants?

9. Why do we care about code layout?

10. How do we handle % (remainder) of floating-point numbers?

11. What does **is_declared**() do and how does it work?

12. The input representation for **let** is more than one character. How is it accepted as a single token in the modified code?

13. What are the rules for what names can and cannot be in the calculator program?

14. Why is it a good idea to build a program incrementally?

15. When do you start to test?

16. When do you retest?

17. How do you decide what should be a separate function?

18. What is the use of symbolic constants?

19. Why do you add comments?

20. What should be in comments and what should not?

21. When do we consider a program finished?

Terms

code layout	maintenance	scaffolding
commenting	recovery	symbolic constant
error handling	revision history	testing
feature creep		

Exercises

1. Allow underscores in the calculator's names.

2. Provide an assignment operator, **=**, so that you can change the value of a variable after you introduce it using **let**.

3. Provide named constants that you really can't change the value of. Hint: You have to add a member to **Variable** that distinguishes between constants and variables and check for it in **set_value()**. If you want to let the user define constants (rather than just having **pi** and **e** defined as constants), you'll have to add a notation to let the user express that, for example, **const pi = 3.14;**.

4. The **get_value()**, **set_value()**, **is_declared()**, and **declare_name()** functions all operate on the global variable **var_table**. Define a class called **Symbol_table** with a member **var_table** of type **vector<Variable>** and member functions **get()**, **set()**, **is_declared()**, and **declare()**. Rewrite the calculator to use a variable of type **Symbol_table**.

5. Modify **Token_stream::get()** to return **Token(print)** when it sees a new-line. This implies looking for whitespace characters and treating newline (**'\n'**) specially. You might find the standard library function **isspace(ch)**, which returns true if **ch** is a whitespace character, useful.

6. Part of what every program should do is to provide some way of helping its user. Have the calculator print out some instructions for how to use the calculator if the user presses the H key.

7. Change the **q** and **h** commands to be **quit** and **help**, respectively.

8. The grammar in §7.6.4 is incomplete (we did warn you against overreliance on comments); it does not define sequences of statements, such as **4+4; 5–6;** and it does not incorporate the grammar changes outlined in §7.8. Fix that grammar. Also add whatever you feel is needed to that comment as the first comment of the calculator program and its overall comment.

9. Define a class **Table** that contains a **vector<Variable>** and provides member functions **get()**, **set()**, and **declare()**. Replace the **var_table** in the calculator with a **Table** called **symbol_table**.

10. Suggest three improvements (not mentioned in this chapter) to the calculator. Implement one of them.

11. Modify the calculator to operate on **ints** (only); give errors for overflow and underflow.

12. Implement an assignment operator, so that we can change the value of a variable after its initialization. Discuss why that can be useful and how it can be a source of problems.

13. Revisit two programs you wrote for the exercises in Chapter 4 or 5. Clean up that code according to the rules outlined in this chapter. See if you find any bugs in the process.

Postscript

As it happens, we have now seen a simple example of how a compiler works. The calculator analyzes input broken down into tokens and understood according to a grammar. That's exactly what a compiler does. After analyzing its output a compiler then produces a representation (object code) that we can later execute. The calculator immediately executes the expressions it has analyzed; programs doing that are called interpreters rather than compilers.

8

Technicalities: Functions, etc.

"No amount of genius can overcome obsession with detail."

—Traditional

In this chapter and the next, we change our focus from programming to our main tool for programming: the C++ programming language. We present language-technical details to give a slightly broader view of C++'s basic facilities and to provide a more systematic view of those facilities. These chapters also act as a review of many of the programming notions presented so far and provide an opportunity to explore our tool without adding new programming techniques or concepts.

8.1 Technicalities

Given a choice, we'd much rather talk about programming than about programming language features; that is, we consider how to express ideas as code far more interesting than the technical details of the programming language that we use to express those ideas. To pick an analogy from natural languages: we'd much rather discuss the ideas in a good novel and the way those ideas are expressed than study the grammar and vocabulary of English. What matters are ideas and how those ideas can be expressed in code, not the individual language features.

However, we don't always have a choice. When you start programming, your programming language is a foreign language for which you need to look at "grammar and vocabulary." This is what we will do in this chapter and the next, but please don't forget:

- Our primary study is programming.
- Our output is programs/systems.
- A programming language is (only) a tool.

Keeping this in mind appears to be amazingly difficult. Many programmers come to care passionately about apparently minor details of language syntax and semantics. In particular, too many get the mistaken belief that the way things are done in their first programming language is "the one true way." Please don't fall into that trap. C++ is in many ways a very nice language, but it is not perfect; neither is any other programming language.

Most design and programming concepts are universal, and many such concepts are widely supported by popular programming languages. That means that the fundamental ideas and techniques we learn in a good programming course carry over from language to language. They can be applied – with varying degrees of ease – in all languages. The language technicalities, however, are specific to a given language. Fortunately, programming languages do not develop in a vacuum, so much of what you learn here will have reasonably obvious counterparts in other languages. In particular, C++ belongs to a group of languages that also includes C (Chapter 27), Java, and C#, so quite a few technicalities are shared with those languages.

Note that when we are discussing language-technical issues, we deliberately use nondescriptive names, such as **f**, **g**, **X**, and **y**. We do that to emphasize the technical nature of such examples, to keep those examples very short, and to try to avoid confusing you by mixing language technicalities and genuine program logic. When you see nondescriptive names (such as should never be used in real code), please focus on the language-technical aspects of the code. Technical examples typically contain code that simply illustrates language rules. If you compiled and ran them, you'd get many "variable not used" warnings, and few such technical program fragments would do anything sensible.

Please note that what we write here is not a complete description of C++'s syntax and semantics – not even for the facilities we describe. The ISO C++ standard is 756 pages of dense technical language and *The C++ Programming Language* by Stroustrup is 1000+ pages of text aimed at experienced programmers. We do not try to compete with those in completeness and comprehensiveness; we compete with them in comprehensibility and value for time spent reading.

8.2 Declarations and definitions

A *declaration* is a statement that introduces a name into a scope (§8.4)

- specifying a type for what is named (e.g., a variable or a function)
- optionally, specifying an initializer (e.g., an initializer value or a function body)

For example:

```
int a = 7;                  // an int variable
const double cd = 8.7;      // a double-precision floating-point constant
double sqrt(double);        // a function taking a double argument
                            // and returning a double result
vector<Token> v;            // a vector-of-Tokens variable
```

Before a name can be used in a C++ program, it must be declared. Consider:

```
int main()
{
        cout << f(i) << '\n';
}
```

The compiler will give at least three "undeclared identifier" errors for this: **cout**, **f**, and **i** are not declared anywhere in this program fragment. We can get **cout** declared by including the header **std_lib_facilities.h**, which contains its declaration:

```
#include "std_lib_facilities.h"    // we find the declaration of cout in here

int main()
{
    cout << f(i) << '\n';
}
```

Now, we get only two "undefined" errors. As you write real-word programs, you'll find that most declarations are found in headers. That's where we define interfaces to useful facilities defined "elsewhere." Basically, a declaration defines how something can be used; it defines the interface of a function, variable, or class. Please note one obvious but invisible advantage of this use of declarations: we didn't have to look at the details of how **cout** and its **<<** operators were defined; we just **#included** their declarations. We didn't even have to look at their declarations; from textbooks, manuals, code examples, or other sources, we just know how **cout** is supposed to be used. The compiler reads the declarations in the header that it needs to "understand" our code.

However, we still have to declare **f** and **i**. We could do that like this:

```
#include "std_lib_facilities.h"    // we find the declaration of cout in here

int f(int);    // declaration of f

int main()
{
    int i = 7;    // declaration of i
    cout << f(i) << '\n';
}
```

This will compile because every name has been declared, but it will not link (§2.4) because we have not defined **f()**; that is, nowhere have we specified what **f()** actually does.

A declaration that (also) fully specifies the entity declared is called a *definition*. For example:

```
int a = 7;
vector<double> v;
double sqrt(double d) { /* . . . */ }
```

Every definition is (by definition ☺) also a declaration, but only some declarations are also definitions. Here are some examples of declarations that are not definitions; each must be matched by a definition elsewhere in the code:

```
double sqrt(double);      // no function body here
extern int a;             // "extern plus no initializer" means "not definition"
```

When we contrast definitions and declarations, we follow convention and use *declarations* to mean "declarations that are not definitions" even though that's slightly sloppy terminology.

A definition specifies exactly what a name refers to. In particular, a definition of a variable sets aside memory for that variable. Consequently, you can't define something twice. For example:

```
double sqrt(double d) { /* . . . */ }   // definition
double sqrt(double d) { /* . . . */ }   // error: double definition

int a;     // definition
int a;     // error: double definition
```

In contrast, a declaration that isn't also a definition simply tells how you can use a name; it is just an interface and doesn't allocate memory or specify a function body. Consequently, you can declare something as often as you like as long as you do so consistently:

```
int x = 7;          // definition
extern int x;       // declaration
extern int x;       // another declaration

double sqrt(double);                    // declaration
double sqrt(double d) { /* . . . */ }   // definition
double sqrt(double);                    // another declaration of sqrt
double sqrt(double);                    // yet another declaration of sqrt

int sqrt(double);                       // error: inconsistent declarations of sqrt
```

Why is that last declaration an error? Because there cannot be two functions called **sqrt** taking an argument of type **double** and returning different types (**int** and **double**).

The **extern** keyword used in the second declaration of **x** simply states that this declaration of **x** isn't a definition. It is rarely useful. We recommend that you don't use it, but you'll see it in other people's code, especially code that uses too many global variables (see §8.4 and §8.6.2).

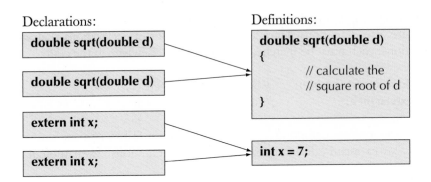

Why does C++ offer both declarations and definitions? The declaration/definition distinction reflects the fundamental distinction between what we need to use something (an interface) and what we need for that something to do what it is supposed to (an implementation). For a variable, a declaration supplies the type but only the definition supplies the object (the memory). For a function, a declaration again provides the type (argument types plus return type) but only the definition supplies the function body (the executable statements). Note that function bodies are stored in memory as part of the program, so it is fair to say that function and variable definitions consume memory, whereas declarations don't.

The declaration/definition distinction allows us to separate a program into many parts that can be compiled separately. The declarations allow each part of a program to maintain a view of the rest of the program without bothering with the definitions in other parts. As all declarations (including the one definition) must be consistent, the use of names in the whole program will be consistent. We'll discuss that further in §8.3. Here, we'll just remind you of the expression parser from Chapter 6: **expression()** calls **term()** which calls **primary()** which calls **expression()**. Since every name in a C++ program has to be declared before it is used, there is no way we could just define those three functions:

```
double expression();     // just a declaration, not a definition

double primary()
{
    // . . .
    expression();
    // . . .
}

double term()
{
    // . . .
```

```
        primary();
        // . . .
}

double expression()
{
        // . . .
        term();
        // . . .
}
```

We can order those four functions any way we like; there will always be one call to a function defined below it. Somewhere, we need a "forward" declaration. Therefore, we declared **expression()** before the definition of **primary()** and all is well. Such cyclic calling patterns are very common.

Why does a name have to be declared before it is used? Couldn't we just require the language implementation to read the program (just as we do) and find the definition to see how a function must be called? We could, but that would lead to "interesting" technical problems, so we decided against that. The C++ definition requires declaration before use (except for class members; see §9.4.4). After all, this is already the convention for ordinary (non-program) writing: when you read a textbook, you expect the author to define terminology before using it; otherwise, you have to guess or go to the index all the time. The "declaration before use" rule simplifies reading for both humans and compilers. In a program, there is a second reason that "declare before use" is important. In a program of thousands of lines (maybe hundred of thousands of lines), most of the functions we want to call will be defined "elsewhere." That "elsewhere" is often a place we don't really want to know about. Having to know the declarations only of what we use saves us (and the compiler) from looking through huge amounts of program text.

8.2.1 Kinds of declarations

There are many kinds of entities that a programmer can define in C++. The most interesting are

- Variables
- Constants
- Functions (see §8.5)
- Namespaces (see §8.7)
- Types (classes and enumerations; see Chapter 9)
- Templates (see Chapter 19)

8.2.2 Variable and constant declarations

The declaration of a variable or a constant specifies a name, a type, and optionally an initializer. For example:

```
int a;              // no initializer
double d = 7;       // initializer using the = syntax
vector<int> vi(10); // initializer using the () syntax
```

You can find the complete grammar in *The C++ Programming Language* by Stroustrup or in the ISO C++ standard.

Constants have the same declaration syntax as variables. They differ in having **const** as part of their type and requiring an initializer:

```
const int x = 7;    // initializer using the = syntax
const int x2(9);    // initializer using the () syntax
const int y;        // error: no initializer
```

The reason for requiring an initializer for a **const** is obvious: how could a **const** be a constant if it didn't have a value? It is almost always a good idea to initialize variables also; an uninitialized variable is a recipe for obscure bugs. For example:

```
void f(int z)
{
        int x;      // uninitialized
        // . . . no assignment to x here . . .
        x = 7;      // give x a value
        // . . .
}
```

This looks innocent enough, but what if the first . . . included a use of **x**? For example:

```
void f(int z)
{
        int x;      // uninitialized
        // . . . no assignment to x here . . .
        if (z>x) {
                // . . .
        }
        // . . .
        x = 7;      // give x a value
        // . . .
}
```

Because **x** is uninitialized, executing **z>x** would be undefined behavior. The comparison **z>x** could give different results on different machines and different results in different runs of the program on the same machine. In principle, **z>x** might cause the program to terminate with a hardware error, but most often that doesn't happen. Instead we get unpredictable results.

Naturally, we wouldn't do something like that deliberately, but if we don't consistently initialize variables it will eventually happen by mistake. Remember, most "silly mistakes" (such as using an uninitialized variable before it has been assigned to) happen when you are busy or tired. Compilers try to warn, but in complicated code — where such errors are most likely to occur — compilers are not smart enough to catch all such errors. There are people who are not in the habit of initializing their variables, often because they learned to program in languages that didn't allow or encourage consistent initialization; so you'll see examples in other people's code. Please just don't add to the problem by forgetting to initialize the variables you define yourself.

8.2.3 Default initialization

You might have noticed that we often don't provide an initializer for **strings**, **vectors**, etc. For example:

```
vector<string> v;
string s;
while (cin>>s) v.push_back(s);
```

This is not an exception to the rule that variables must be initialized before use. What is going on here is that we have defined **string** and **vector** to be initialized with a default value whenever we don't supply one explicitly. Thus, **v** is empty (it has no elements) and **s** is the empty string ("") before we reach the loop. The mechanism for guaranteeing default initialization is called a *default constructor*; see §9.7.3.

Unfortunately, the language doesn't allow us to make such guarantees for built-in types. A global variable is default initialized to 0, but you should minimize the use of global values. The most useful variables, local variables and class members, are uninitialized unless you provide an initializer (or a default constructor). You have been warned!

8.3 Header files

How do we manage our declarations and definitions? After all, they have to be consistent, and in real-world programs there can be tens of thousands of declarations; programs with hundreds of thousands of declarations are not rare. Typically, when we write a program, most of the definitions we use are not written by us. For example, the implementations of **cout** and **sqrt()** were written by someone else many years ago. We just use them.

The key to managing declarations of facilities defined "elsewhere" in C++ is the header. Basically, a *header* is a collection of declarations, typically defined in a file, so a header is also called a *header file*. Such headers are then **#include**d in our source files. For example, we might decide to improve the organization of the source code for our calculator (Chapters 6 and 7) by separating out the token management. We could define a header file **token.h** containing declarations needed to use **Token** and **Token_stream**:

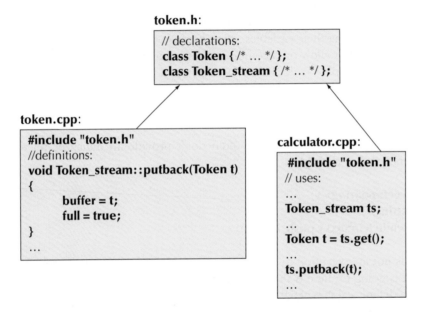

token.h:

```
// declarations:
class Token { /* ... */ };
class Token_stream { /* ... */ };
```

token.cpp:

```
#include "token.h"
//definitions:
void Token_stream::putback(Token t)
{
        buffer = t;
        full = true;
}
...
```

calculator.cpp:

```
#include "token.h"
// uses:
...
Token_stream ts;
...
Token t = ts.get();
...
ts.putback(t);
...
```

The declarations of **Token** and **Token_stream** are in the header **token.h**. Their definitions are in **token.cpp**. The **.h** suffix is the most common for C++ headers, and the **.cpp** suffix is the most common for C++ source files. Actually, the C++ language doesn't care about file suffixes, but some compilers and most program development environments insist, so please use this convention for your source code.

In principle, **#include "file.h"** simply copies the declarations from **file.h** into your file at the point of the **#include**. For example, we could write a header **f.h**:

```
// f.h
int f(int);
```

and include it in our file **f.cpp**:

```
// f.cpp
#include "f.h"
int g(int i)
{
      return f(i);
}
```

When compiling **f.cpp** the compiler would do the **#include** and compile

```
int f(int);
int g(int i)
{
      return f(i);
}
```

Since **#include**s logically happen before anything else a compiler does, handling **#include**s is part of what is called *preprocessing* (§A.17).

To ease consistency checking, we **#include** a header both in source files that use its declarations and in source files that provide definitions for those declarations. That way, the compiler catches errors as soon as possible. For example, imagine that the implementer of **Token_stream::putback()** made mistakes:

```
Token Token_stream::putback(Token t)
{
      buffer.push_back(t);
      return t;
}
```

This looks innocent enough. Fortunately, the compiler catches the mistakes because it sees the (**#include**d) declaration of **Token_stream::putback()**. Comparing that declaration with our definition, the compiler finds that **putback()** should not return a **Token** and that **buffer** is a **Token**, rather than a **vector<Token>**, so we can't use **push_back()**. Such mistakes occur when we work on our code to improve it, but don't quite get a change consistent throughout a program.

Similarly, consider these mistakes:

```
Token t = ts.gett();      // error: no member gett
// ...
ts.putback();             // error: argument missing
```

The compiler would immediately give errors; the header **token.h** gives it all the information it needs for checking.

Our **std_lib_facilities.h** header contains declarations for the standard library facilities we use, such as **cout**, **vector**, and **sqrt**(), together with a couple of simple utility functions, such as **error**(), that are not part of the standard library. In §12.8 we show how to use the standard library headers directly.

A header will typically be included in many source files. That means that a header should only contain declarations that can be duplicated in several files (such as function declarations, class definitions, and definitions of numeric constants).

8.4 Scope

A *scope* is a region of program text. A name is declared in a scope and is valid (is "in scope") from the point of its declaration until the end of the scope in which it was declared. For example:

```
void f()
{
    g();        // error: g() isn't (yet) in scope
}

void g()
{
    f();        // OK: f() is in scope
}

void h()
{
    int x = y;        // error: y isn't (yet) in scope
    int y = x;        // OK: x is in scope
    g();              // OK: g() is in scope
}
```

Names in a scope can be seen from within scopes nested within it. For example, the call of **f**() is within the scope of **g**() which is "nested" in the global scope. The global scope is the scope that's not nested in any other. The rule that a name must be declared before it can be used still holds, so **f**() cannot call **g**().

There are several kinds of scopes that we use to control where our names can be used:

- The *global scope*: the area of text outside any other scope
- A *namespace scope*: a named scope nested in the global scope or in another namespace; see §8.7
- A *class scope*: the area of text within a class; see §9.2

- A *local scope:* between { . . . } braces of a block or in a function argument list
- A *statement scope:* e.g., in a **for**-statement

The main purpose of a scope is to keep names local, so that they won't interfere with names declared elsewhere. For example:

```
void f(int x)        // f is global; x is local to f
{
        int z = x+7;    // z is local
}

int g(int x)         // g is global; x is local to g
{
        int f = x+2;    // f is local
        return 2*f;
}
```

Or graphically:

Global scope:

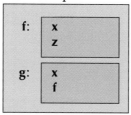

Here f()'s **x** is different from g()'s **x**. They don't "clash" because they are not in the same scope: f()'s **x** is local to **f** and g()'s **x** is local to **g**. Two incompatible declarations in the same scope are often referred to as a *clash*. Similarly, the **f** defined and used within g() is (obviously) not the function f().

Here is a logically equivalent but more realistic example of the use of local scope:

```
int max(int a, int b)          // max is global; a and b are local
{
        return (a>=b) ? a : b;
}

int abs(int a)                 // not max()'s a
{
        return (a<0) ? –a : a;
}
```

You find **max()** and **abs()** in the standard library, so you don't have to write them yourself. The **?:** construct is called an *arithmetic if* or a *conditional expression*. The value of **(a>=b)?a:b** is **a** if **a>=b** and **b** otherwise. A conditional expression saves us from writing long-winded code like this:

```
int max(int a, int b)          // max is global; a and b are local
{
        int m;                 // m is local
        if (a>=b)
                m = a;
        else
                m = b;
        return m;
}
```

So, with the noticeable exception of the global scope, a scope keeps names local. For most purposes, locality is good, so keep names as local as possible. When I declare my variables, functions, etc. within functions, classes, namespace, etc., they won't interfere with yours. Remember: real programs have *many* thousands of named entities. To keep such programs manageable, most names have to be local.

Here is a larger technical example illustrating how names go out of scope at the end of statements and blocks (including function bodies):

```
// no r, i, or v here
class My_vector {
        vector<int> v;          // v is in class scope
public:
        int largest()
        {
                int r = 0;             // r is local (smallest nonnegative int)
                for (int i = 0; i<v.size(); ++i)
                        r = max(r,abs(v[i]));   // i is in the for's statement scope
                // no i here
                return r;
        }
        // no r here
};
// no v here

int x;        // global variable — avoid those where you can
int y;
```

```
int f()
{
    int x;      // local variable
    x = 7;      // the local x
    {
        int x = y;      // local x initialized by global y
        ++x;            // the x from the previous line
    }
    ++x;    // the x from the first line of f()
    return x;
}
```

Whenever you can, avoid such complicated nesting and hiding. Remember: "Keep it simple!"

The larger the scope of a name is, the longer and more descriptive its name should be: x, y, and f are horrible as global names. The main reason that you don't want global variables in your program is that it is hard to know which functions modify them. In large programs, it is basically impossible to know which functions modify a global variable. Imagine that you are trying to debug a program and you find that a global variable has an unexpected value. Who gave it that value? Why? What functions write to that value? How would you know? The function that wrote a bad value to that variable may be in a source file you have never seen! A good program will have only very few (say, one or two), if any, global variables. For example, the calculator in Chapters 6 and 7 had two global variables: the token stream, **ts**, and the symbol table, **names**.

Note that most C++ constructs that define scopes nest:

- Functions within classes: member functions (see §9.4.2)

```
class C {
public:
    void f();
    void g()        // a member function can be defined within its class
    {
        // ...
    }
    // ...
};

void C::f()     // a member definition can be outside its class
{
    // ...
}
```

This is the most common and useful case.

• Classes within classes: member classes (also called nested classes)

```
class C {
public:
    struct M {
        // . . .
    };
    // . . .
};
```

This tends to be useful only in complicated classes; remember that the ideal is to keep classes small and simple.

• Classes within functions: local classes

```
void f()
{
    class L {
        // . . .
    };
    // . . .
}
```

Avoid this; if you feel the need for a local class, your function is probably far too long.

• Functions within functions: local functions (also called nested functions)

```
void f()
{
    void g()    // illegal
    {
        // . . .
    }
    // . . .
}
```

This is not legal in C++; don't do it. The compiler will reject it.

• Blocks within functions and other blocks: nested blocks

```
void f(int x, int y)
{
    if (x>y) {
        // . . .
    }
    else {
        // . . .
        {
```

```
                                    // . . .
                          }
                          // . . .
                }
          }
```

Nested blocks are unavoidable, but be suspicious of complicated nesting: it can easily hide errors.

C++ also provides a language feature, **namespace**, exclusively for expressing scoping; see §8.7.

Note our consistent indentation to indicate nesting. Without consistent indentation, nested constructs become unreadable. For example:

```
// dangerously ugly code
struct X {
void f(int x) {
struct Y {
int f() { return 1; } int m; };
int m;
m=x; Y m2;
return f(m2.f()); }
int m; void g(int m) {
if (m) f(m+2); else {
g(m+2); }}
X() { } void m3() {
}

void main() {
X a; a.f(2);}
};
```

Hard-to-read code usually hides bugs. When you use an IDE, it tries to automatically make your code properly indented (according to some definition of "properly"), and there exist "code beautifiers" that will reformat a source code file for you (often offering you a choice of formats). However, the ultimate responsibility for your code being readable rests with you.

8.5 Function call and return

Functions are the way we represent actions and computations. Whenever we want to do something that is worthy of a name, we write a function. The C++ language gives us operators (such as + and *) with which we can produce new values from operands in expressions, and statements (such as **for** and **if**) with which we can control the order of execution. To organize code made out of these primitives, we have functions.

To do its job, a function usually needs arguments, and many functions return a result. This section focuses on how arguments are specified and passed.

8.5.1 Declaring arguments and return type

Functions are what we use in C++ to name and represent computations and actions. A function declaration consists of a return type followed by the name of the function followed by a list of formal arguments in parentheses. For example:

```
double fct(int a, double d);            // declaration of fct (no body)
double fct(int a, double d) { return a*d; }   // definition of fct
```

A definition contains the function body (the statements to be executed by a call), whereas a declaration that isn't a definition just has a semicolon. Formal arguments are often called *parameters*. If you don't want a function to take arguments, just leave out the formal arguments. For example:

```
int current_power();       // current_power doesn't take an argument
```

If you don't want to return a value from a function, give **void** as its return type. For example:

```
void increase_power(int level);       // increase_power doesn't return a value
```

Here, **void** means "doesn't return a value" or "return nothing."

You can name a parameter or not as it suits you in both declarations and definitions. For example:

```
// search for s in vs;
// vs[hint] might be a good place to start the search
// return the index of a match; −1 indicates "not found"
int my_find(vector<string> vs, string s, int hint);    // naming arguments

int my_find(vector<string>, string, int);              // not naming arguments
```

In declarations, formal argument names are not logically necessary, just very useful for writing good comments. From a compiler's point of view, the second declaration of **my_find()** is just as good as the first: it has all the information necessary to call **my_find()**.

Usually, we name all the arguments in the definition. For example:

```
int my_find(vector<string> vs, string s, int hint)
// search for s in vs starting at hint
{
        if (hint<0 || vs.size()<=hint) hint = 0;
        for (int i = hint; i<vs.size(); ++i)      // search starting from hint
            if (vs[i]==s) return i;
        if (0<hint) {        // if we didn't find s search before hint
            for (int i = 0; i<hint; ++i)
                    if (vs[i]==s) return i;
        }
        return –1;
}
```

The **hint** complicates the code quite a bit, but the **hint** was provided under the assumption that users could use it to good effect by knowing roughly where in the **vector** a **string** will be found. However, imagine that we had used **my_find()** for a while and then discovered that callers rarely used **hint** well, so that it actually hurt performance. Now we don't need **hint** anymore, but there is lots of code "out there" that calls **my_find()** with a **hint.** We don't want to rewrite that code (or can't because it is someone else's code), so we don't want to change the declaration(s) of **my_find()**. Instead, we just don't use the last argument. Since we don't use it we can leave it unnamed:

```
int my_find(vector<string> vs, string s, int)      // 3rd argument unused
{
        for (int i = 0; i<vs.size(); ++i)
            if (vs[i]==s) return i;
        return –1;
}
```

You can find the complete grammar for function definitions in *The C++ Programming Language* by Stroustrup or in the ISO C++ standard.

8.5.2 Returning a value

We return a value from a function using a return statement:

```
T f()      // f() returns a T
{
        V v;
        // . . .
        return v;
}

T x = f();
```

Here, the value returned is exactly the value we would have gotten by initializing a variable of type **T** by a value of type **V**:

```
V v;
// . . .
T t(v);        // initialize t with v
```

That is, value return is a form of initialization. A function declared to return a value must return a value. In particular, it is an error to "fall through the end of the function":

```
double my_abs(int x)      // warning: buggy code
{
        if (x < 0)
                return –x;
        else if (x > 0)
                return x;
}        // error: no value returned if x is 0
```

Actually, the compiler probably won't notice that we "forgot" the case **x==0**. In principle it could, but few compilers are that smart. For complicated functions, it can be impossible for a compiler to know whether or not you return a value, so be careful. Here, "being careful" means to make really sure that you have a return statement or an **error()** for every possible way out of the function.

For historical reasons, **main()** is a special case. Falling through the bottom of **main()** is equivalent to returning the value **0**, meaning "successful completion" of the program.

In a function that does not return a value, we can use **return** without a value to cause a return from the function. For example:

```
void print_until_s(const vector<string> v, const string quit)
{
        for(int i=0; i<v.size(); ++i) {
                if (v[i]==quit) return;
                cout << v[i] << '\n';
        }
}
```

As you can see, it is acceptable to "drop through the bottom" of a **void** function. This is equivalent to a **return;**.

8.5.3 Pass-by-value

The simplest way of passing an argument to a function is to give the function a copy of the value you use as the argument. An argument of a function f() is a local variable in f() that's initialized each time f() is called. For example:

```
// pass-by-value (give the function a copy of the value passed)
int f(int x)
{
        x = x+1;        // give the local x a new value
        return x;
}

int main()
{
        int xx = 0;
        cout << f(xx) << endl;        // write: 1
        cout << xx << endl;           // write: 0; f() doesn't change xx

        int yy = 7;
        cout << f(yy) << endl;        // write: 8
        cout << yy << endl;           // write: 7; f() doesn't change yy
}
```

Since a copy is passed, the **x=x+1** in f() does not change the values **xx** and **yy** passed in the two calls. We can illustrate a pass-by-value argument passing like this:

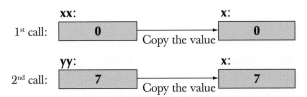

Pass-by-value is pretty straightforward and its cost is the cost of copying the value.

8.5.4 Pass-by-const-reference

Pass-by-value is simple, straightforward, and efficient when we pass small values, such as an **int**, a **double**, or a **Token** (§6.3.2). But what if a value is large, such as an image (often, several million bits), a large table of values (say, thousands of integers), or a long string (say, hundreds of characters)? Then, copying can be costly. We should not be obsessed by cost, but doing unnecessary work can be embarrassing because it is an indication that we didn't directly express our idea of what we wanted. For example, we could write a function to print out a **vector** of floating-point numbers like this:

```
void print(vector<double> v)      // pass-by-value; appropriate?
{
    cout << "{ ";
    for (int i = 0; i<v.size(); ++i) {
        cout << v[i];
        if (i!=v.size()-1) cout << ", ";
    }
    cout << " }\n";
}
```

We could use this **print()** for **vector**s of all sizes. For example:

```
void f(int x)
{
    vector<double> vd1(10);          // small vector
    vector<double> vd2(1000000);     // large vector
    vector<double> vd3(x);           // vector of some unknown size
    // . . . fill vd1, vd2, vd3 with values . . .
    print(vd1);
    print(vd2);
    print(vd3);
}
```

This code works, but the first call of **print()** has to copy ten **doubles** (probably 80 bytes), the second call has to copy a million **doubles** (probably 8 megabytes), and we don't know how much the third call has to copy. The question we must ask ourselves here is: "Why are we copying anything at all?" We just wanted to print the **vector**s, not to make copies of their elements. Obviously, there has to be a way for us to pass a variable to a function without copying it. As an analogy, if you were given the task to make a list of books in a library, the librarians wouldn't ship you a copy of the library building and all its contents; they would send you the address of the library, so that you could go and look at the books. So, we need a way of giving our **print()** function "the address" of the **vector** to **print()** rather than the copy of the **vector**. Such an "address" is called a *reference* and is used like this:

```
void print(const vector<double>& v)        // pass-by-const-reference
{
    cout << "{ ";
    or (int i = 0; i<v.size(); ++i) {
        cout << v[i];
        if (i!=v.size()-1) cout << ", ";
    }
    cout << " }\n";
}
```

The & means "reference" and the **const** is there to stop **print()** modifying its argument by accident. Apart from the change to the argument declaration, all is the same as before; the only change is that instead of operating on a copy, **print()** now refers back to the argument through the reference. Note the phrase "refer back"; such arguments are called references because they "refer" to objects defined elsewhere. We can call this **print()** exactly as before:

```
void f(int x)
{
    vector<double> vd1(10);         // small vector
    vector<double> vd2(1000000);    // large vector
    vector<double> vd3(x);          // vector of some unknown size
    // . . . fill vd1, vd2, vd3 with values . . .
    print(vd1);
    print(vd2);
    print(vd3);
}
```

We can illustrate that graphically:

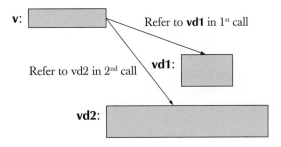

A **const** reference has the useful property that we can't accidentally modify the object passed. For example, if we made a silly error and tried to assign to an element from within **print()**, the compiler would catch it:

```
void print(const vector<double>& v)        // pass-by-const-reference
{
    // . . .
    v[i] = 7;    // error: v is a const (is not mutable)
    // . . .
}
```

Pass-by-**const**-reference is a useful and popular mechanism. Consider again the **my_find()** function (§8.5.1) that searches for a **string** in a **vector** of **strings**. Pass-by-value could be unnecessarily costly:

```
int my_find(vector<string> vs, string s);        // pass-by-value: copy
```

If the **vector** contained thousands of **strings**, you might notice the time spent even on a fast computer. So, we could improve **my_find()** by making it take its arguments by **const** reference:

```
// pass-by-const-reference: no copy, read-only access
int my_find(const vector<string>& vs, const string& s);
```

8.5.5 Pass-by-reference

But what if we did want a function to modify its arguments? Sometimes, that's a perfectly reasonable thing to wish for. For example, we might want an **init()** function that assigned values to vector elements:

```
void init(vector<double>& v)      // pass-by-reference
{
    for (int i = 0; i<v.size(); ++i) v[i] = i;
}

void g(int x)
{
    vector<double> vd1(10);           // small vector
    vector<double> vd2(1000000);      // large vector
    vector<double> vd3(x);            // vector of some unknown size

    init(vd1);
    init(vd2);
    init(vd3);
}
```

Here, we wanted **init()** to modify the argument vector, so we did not copy (did not use pass-by-value) nor declare the reference **const** (did not use pass-by-**const**-value), but simply passed a "plain reference" to the **vector**.

Let us consider references from a more technical point of view. A reference is a construct that allows a user to declare a new name for an object. For example, **int&** is a reference to an **int**, so we can write

```
int i = 7;

int& r = i;      // r is a reference to i
r = 9;           // i becomes 9
i = 10;
cout << r << ' ' << i << '\n';    // write: 10 10
```

That is, any use of **r** is really a use of **i**.

References can be useful as shorthand. For example, we might have a

```
vector< vector<double> > v;      // vector of vector of double
```

and we need to refer to some element **v[f(x)][g(y)]** several times. Clearly, **v[f(x)][g(y)]** is a complicated expression that we don't want to repeat more often than we have to. If we just need its value, we could write

```
double val = v[f(x)][g(y)];         // val is the value of v[f(x)][g(y)]
```

and use **val** repeatedly. But what if we need to both read from **v[f(x)][g(y)]** and write to **v[f(x)][g(y)]**? Then, a reference comes in handy:

```
double& var = v[f(x)][g(y)];        // var is a reference to v[f(x)][g(y)]
```

Now we can read and write **v[f(x)][g(y)]** through **var.** For example:

```
var = var/2+sqrt(var);
```

This key property of references, that a reference can be a convenient shorthand for some object, is what makes them useful as arguments. For example:

```
// pass-by-reference (let the function refer back to the variable passed)
int f(int& x)
{
        x = x+1;
        return x;
}
```

```
int main()
{
      int xx = 0;
      cout << f(xx) << endl;        // write: 1
      cout << xx << endl;           // write: 1; f() changed the value of xx

      int yy = 7;
      cout << f(yy) << endl;        // write: 8
      cout << yy << endl;           // write: 8; f() changed the value of yy
}
```

We can illustrate a pass-by-reference argument passing like this:

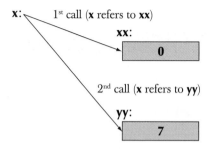

Compare this to the similar example in §8.5.3.

Pass-by-reference is clearly a very powerful mechanism: we can have a function operate directly on any object to which we pass a reference. For example, swapping two values is an immensely important operation in many algorithms, such as sorting. Using references, we can write a function that swaps **doubles** like this:

```
void swap(double& d1, double& d2)
{
      double temp = d1;      // copy d1's value to temp
      d1 = d2;               // copy d2's value to d2
      d2 = temp;             // copy d1's old value to d2
}

int main()
{
      double x = 1;
      double y = 2;
      cout << "x == " << x << " y== " << y << '\n';    // write: x==1 y==2
      swap(x,y);
      cout << "x == " << x << " y== " << y << '\n';    // write: x==2 y==1
}
```

```
void f()
{
    vector<int> vx;
    vector<int> vy;
    // read vx and vy from input
    larger(vx,vy);
    // . . .
}
```

Using pass-by-reference arguments is the only reasonable choice for a function like **larger()**.

It is usually best to avoid functions that modify several objects. In theory, there are always alternatives, such as returning a class object holding several values. However, there are a lot of programs "out there" expressed in terms of functions that modify one or more arguments, so you are likely to encounter them. For example, in Fortran – the major programming language used for numerical calculation for about 50 years – all arguments are passed by reference. Many numeric programmers copy Fortran designs and call functions written in Fortran. Such code often uses pass-by-reference or pass-by-**const**-reference.

If we use a reference simply to avoid copying, we use a **const** reference. Consequently, when we see a non-**const**-reference argument, we assume that the function changes the value of its argument; that is, when we see a pass-by-non-**const**-reference we assume that not only can that function modify the argument passed, but that it will, so that we have to look extra carefully at the call to make sure that it does what we expect it to.

8.5.7 Argument checking and conversion

Passing an argument is the initialization of the function's formal argument with the actual argument specified in the call. Consider:

```
void f(T x);
f(y);
T x=y;      // initialize x with y (see §8.2.2)
```

The call **f(y)** is legal whenever the initialization **T x=y;** is, and when it is legal both **x**'s get the same value. For example:

```
void f(double);

void g(int y)
{
    f(y);
    double x(y);
}
```

Note that to initialize **x** with **y**, we have to convert an **int** to a **double**. The same happens in the call of f(). The **double** value received by f() is the same as the one stored in **x**.

Conversions are often useful, but occasionally they give surprising results (see §3.9.2). Consequently, we have to be careful with them. Passing a **double** as an argument to a function that requires an **int** is rarely a good idea:

```
void ff(int);

void gg(double x)
{
        ff(x);     // how would you know if this makes sense?
}
```

If you really mean to truncate a **double** value to an **int**, say so explicitly:

```
void ggg(double x)
{
        int x1 = x;      // truncate x
        int x2 = int(x);

        ff(x1);
        ff(x2);

        ff(x);           // truncate x
        ff(int(x));
}
```

That way, the next programmer to look at this code can see that you thought about the problem.

8.5.8 Function call implementation

But how does a computer really do a function call? The **expression()**, **term()**, and **primary()** functions from Chapters 6 and 7 are perfect for illustrating this except for one detail: they don't take any arguments, so we can't use them to explain how arguments are passed. But wait! They *must* take some input; if they didn't, they couldn't do anything useful. They do take an implicit argument: they use a **Token_stream** called **ts** to get their input; **ts** is a global variable. That's a bit sneaky. We can improve these functions by letting them take a **Token_stream&** argument. Here they are with a **Token_stream&** parameter added and everything that doesn't concern function call implementation removed.

First, **expression()** is completely straightforward; it has one argument (**ts**) and two local variables (**left** and **t**):

```
double expression(Token_stream& ts)
{
    double left = term(ts);
    Token t = ts.get();
    // . . .
}
```

Second, **term()** is much like **expression()**, except that it has an additional local variable (**d**) that it uses to hold the result of a divisor for '/':

```
double term(Token_stream& ts)
{
    double left = primary(ts);
    Token t = ts.get();
    // . . .
            case '/':
            {
                    double d = primary(ts);
                    // . . .
            }
        // . . .
}
```

Third, **primary()** is much like **term()** except that it doesn't have a local variable **left**:

```
double primary(Token_stream& ts)
{
    Token t = ts.get ();
    switch (t.kind) {
    case '(':
            {   double d = expression(ts);
                // . . .
            }
            // . . .
        }
}
```

Now they don't use any "sneaky global variables" and are perfect for our illustration: they have an argument, they have local variables, and they call each other. You may want to take the opportunity to refresh your memory of what the complete **expression()**, **term()**, and **primary()** looks like, but the salient features as far as function call is concerned are presented here.

When a function is called, the language implementation sets aside a data structure containing a copy of all its parameters and local variables. For example, when **expression()** is first called, the compiler ensures that a structure like this is created:

Call of **expression()**:

ts
left
t
Implementation stuff

The "implementation stuff" varies from implementation to implementation, but that's basically the information that the function needs to return to its caller and to return a value to its caller. Such a data structure is called a *function activation record,* and each function has its own detailed layout of its activation record. Note that from the implementation's point of view, a parameter is just another local variable.

So far, so good, and now **expression()** calls **term()**, so the compiler ensures that an activation record for this call of **term()** is generated:

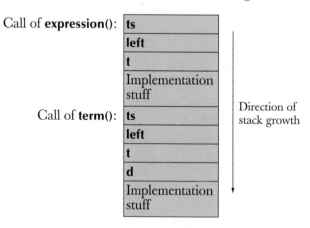

Call of **expression()**:

ts
left
t
Implementation stuff

Call of **term()**:

ts
left
t
d
Implementation stuff

Direction of stack growth

Note that **term()** has an extra variable **d** that needs to be stored, so we set aside space for that in the call even though the code may never get around to using it. That's OK. For reasonable functions (such as every function we directly or indirectly use in this book), the run-time cost of laying down a function activation record doesn't depend on how big it is. The local variable **d** will be initialized only if we execute its **case '/'**.

Now **term()** calls **primary()** and we get

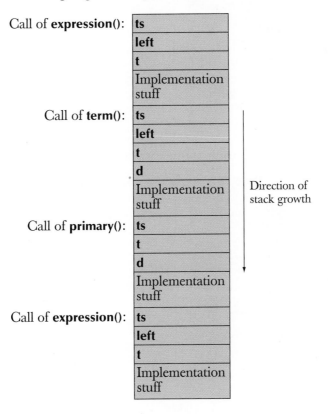

This is starting to get a bit repetitive, but now **primary()** calls **expression()**:

So this call of **expression()** gets its own activation record, different from the first call of **expression()**. That's good or else we'd be in a terrible mess, since **left** and **t** will be different in the two calls. A function that directly or (as here) indirectly calls itself is called *recursive*. As you see, recursive functions follow naturally from the implementation technique we use for function call and return (and vice versa).

So, each time we call a function the *stack of activation records,* usually just called the *stack,* grows with one record. Conversely, when the function returns, its record is no longer used. For example, when that last call of **expression()** returns to **primary()**, the stack will revert to this:

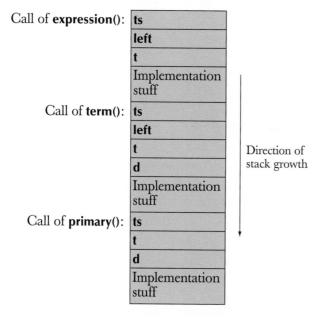

And when that call of **primary()** returns to **term()**, we get back to

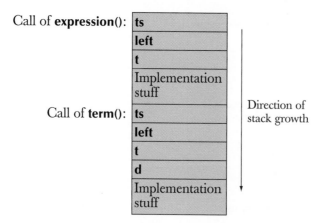

And so on. The stack, also called the *call stack,* is a data structure that grows and shrinks at one end according to the rule: first in, first out.

Please remember that the details of how a call stack is implemented and used vary from C++ implementation to C++ implementation, but the basics are as outlined here. Do you need to know how function calls are implemented to use them? Of course not; you have done well enough before this implementation subsection, but many programmers like to know and many use phrases like "activation record" and "call stack," so it's better to know what they mean.

8.6 Order of evaluation

The evaluation of a program – also called the execution of a program – proceeds through the statements according to the language rules. When this "thread of execution" reaches the definition of a variable, the variable is constructed; that is, memory is set aside for the object and the object is initialized. When the variable goes out of scope, the variable is destroyed; that is, the object it refers to is in principle removed and the compiler can use its memory for something else. For example:

```cpp
string program_name = "silly";
vector<string> v;                        // v is global

void f()
{
    string s;                            // s is local to f
    while (cin>>s && s!="quit") {
        string stripped;                 // stripped is local to the loop
        string not_letters;
        for (int i=0; i<s.size(); ++i)   // i has statement scope
            if (isalpha(s[i]))
                stripped += s[i];
            else
                not_letters += s[i];
        v.push_back(stripped);
        // . . .
    }
    // . . .
}
```

Global variables, such as **program_name** and **v**, are initialized before the first statement of **main()** is executed. They "live" until the program terminates, and then they are destroyed. They are constructed in the order in which they are defined (that is, **program_name** before **v**) and destroyed in the reverse order (that is, **v** before **program_name**).

When someone calls **f()**, first **s** is constructed; that is, **s** is initialized to the empty string. It will live until we return from **f()**.

Each time we enter the block that is the body of the **while**-loop, **stripped** and **not_letters** are constructed. Since **stripped** is defined before **not_letters**, **stripped** is constructed before **not_letters**. They live until the end of the loop, where they are destroyed in the reverse order of construction (that is, **not_letters** before **stripped**) before the condition is reevaluated. So, if ten strings are seen before we encounter the string **quit**, **stripped** and **not_letters** will each be constructed and destroyed ten times.

Each time we reach the **for**-loop, **i** is constructed. Each time we exit the **for**-loop, **i** is destroyed before we reach the **v.push_back(stripped);** statement.

Please note that compilers (and linkers) are clever beasts and they are allowed to − and do − optimize code as long as the results are equivalent to what we have described here. In particular, compilers are clever at not allocating and deallocating memory more often than is really necessary.

8.6.1 Expression evaluation

The order of evaluation of sub-expressions is governed by rules designed to please an optimizer rather than to make life simple for the programmer. That's unfortunate, but you should avoid complicated expressions anyway, and there is a simple rule that can keep you out of trouble: if you change the value of a variable in an expression, don't read or write it twice in that same expression. For example:

```
v[i] = ++i;                      // don't: undefined order of evaluation
v[++i] = i;                      // don't: undefined order of evaluation
int x = ++i + ++i;              // don't: undefined order of evaluation
cout << ++i << ' ' << i << '\n'; // don't: undefined order of evaluation
f(++i,++i);                      // don't: undefined order of evaluation
```

Unfortunately, not all compilers warn if you write such bad code; it's bad because you can't rely on the results being the same if you move your code to another computer, use a different compiler, or use a different optimizer setting. Compilers really differ for such code; just don't do it.

Note in particular that **=** (assignment) is considered just another operator in an expression, so there is no guarantee that the left-hand side of an assignment is evaluated before the right-hand side. That's why **v[++i] = i** is undefined.

8.6.2 Global initialization

Global variables (and namespace variables; see §8.7) in a single translation unit are initialized in the order in which they appear. For example:

```
// file f1.cpp
int x1 = 1;
int y1 = x1+2;        // y1 becomes 3
```

This initialization logically takes place "before the code in **main**() is executed."

Using a global variable in anything but the most limited circumstances is usu-ally not a good idea. We have mentioned the problem of the programmer having no really effective way of knowing which parts of a large program read and/or write a global variable (§8.4). Another problem is that the order of initialization of global variables in different translation units is not defined. For example:

```
// file f2.cpp
extern int y1;
int y2 = y1+2;        // y2 becomes 2 or 5
```

Such code is to be avoided for several reasons: it uses global variables, it gives the global variables short names, and it uses complicated initialization of the global variables. If the globals in file **f1.cpp** are initialized before the globals in **f2.cpp**, **y2** will be initialized to **5** (as a programmer might naively and reasonably expect). However, if the globals in file **f2.cpp** are initialized before the globals in **f1.cpp**, **y2** will be initialized to **2** (because the memory used for global variables is initialized to **0** before complicated initialization is attempted). Avoid such code, and be very suspicious when you see global variables with nontrivial initializers; consider any initializer that isn't a constant expression complicated.

But what do you do if you really need a global variable (or constant) with a complicated initializer? A plausible example would be that we wanted a default value for a **Date** type we were providing for a library supporting business trans-actions:

```
const Date default_date(1970,1,1);     // the default date is January 1, 1970
```

How would we know that **default_date** was never used before it was initialized? Basically, we can't know, so we shouldn't write that definition. The technique that we use most often is to call a function that returns the value. For example:

```
const Date default_date()       // return the default Date
{
     return Date(1970,1,1);
}
```

This constructs the **Date** every time we call **default_date**(). That is often fine, but if **default_date**() is called often and it is expensive to construct **Date**, we'd like to construct the **Date** once only. That is done like this:

```
const Date& default_date()
{
       static const Date dd(1970,1,1);        // initialize dd first time we get here
       return dd;
}
```

A **static** local variable is initialized (constructed) only the first time its function is called. Note that we returned a reference to eliminate unnecessary copying and, in particular, we returned a **const** reference to prevent the called function from accidentally changing the value. The arguments about how to pass an argument (§8.5.6) also apply to returning values.

8.7 Namespaces

We use blocks to organize code within a function (§8.4). We use classes to organize functions, data, and types into a type (Chapter 9). A function and a class both do two things for us:

- They allow us to define a number of "entities" without worrying that their names clash with other names in our program.
- They give us a name to refer to what we have defined.

What we lack so far is something to organize classes, functions, data, and types into an identifiable and named part of a program without defining a type. The language mechanism for such grouping of declarations is a *namespace*. For example, we might like to provide a graphics library with classes called **Color**, **Shape**, **Line**, **Function**, and **Text** (see Chapter 13):

```
namespace Graph_lib {
      struct Color { /* . . . */ };
      struct Shape { /* . . . */ };
      struct Line : Shape { /* . . . */ };
      struct Function : Shape { /* . . . */ };
      struct Text : Shape { /* . . . */ };
      // . . .
      int gui_main() { /* . . . */ }
}
```

Most likely somebody else in the world has used those names, but now that doesn't matter. You might define something called **Text**, but our **Text** doesn't interfere. **Graph_lib::Text** is one of our classes and your **Text** is not. We have a problem only if you have a class or a namespace called **Graph_lib** with **Text** as its member. **Graph_lib** is a slightly ugly name; we chose it because the "pretty and obvious" name **Graphics** had a greater chance of already being used somewhere.

Let's say that your **Text** was part of a text manipulation library. The same logic that made us put our graphics facilities into namespace **Graph_lib** should make you put your text manipulation facilities into a namespace called something like **TextLib**:

```
namespace TextLib {
    class Text { /* . . . */ };
    class Glyph { /* . . . */ };
    class Line { /* . . . */ };
    // . . .
}
```

Had we both used the global namespace, we could have been in real trouble. Someone trying to use both our libraries would have had really bad name clashes for **Text** and **Line**. Worse, if we both had users for our libraries we would not have been able to change our names, such as **Line** and **Text**, to avoid clashes. We avoided that problem by using namespaces; that is, our **Text** is **Graph_lib::Text** and yours is **TextLib::Text**. A name composed of a namespace name (or a class name) and a member name combined by **::** is called a *fully qualified name*.

8.7.1 using declarations and using directives

Writing fully qualified names can be tedious. For example, the facilities of the C++ standard library are defined in namespace **std** and can be used like this:

```
#include<string>          // get the string library
#include<iostream>        // get the iostream library

int main()
{
    std::string name;
    std::cout << "Please enter your first name\n";
    std::cin >> name;
    std::cout << "Hello, " << name << '\n';
}
```

Having seen the standard library **string** and **cout** thousands of times, we don't really want to have to refer to them by their "proper" fully qualified names **std::string** and **std::cout** all the time. A solution is to say that "by **string**, I mean **std::string**," "by **cout**, I mean **std::cout**," etc.:

```
using std::string;      // string means std::string
using std::cout;        // cout means std::cout
// . . .
```

That construct is called a **using** declaration; it is the programming equivalent to using plain "Greg" to refer to Greg Hansen, when there are no other Gregs in the room.

Sometimes, we prefer an even stronger "shorthand" for the use of names from a namespace: "If you don't find a declaration for a name in this scope, look in **std**." The way to say that is to use a **using** directive:

```
using namespace std;    // make names from std directly accessible
```

So we get this common style:

```
#include<string>        // get the string library
#include<iostream>      // get the iostream library
using namespace std;    // make names from std directly accessible

int main()
{
    string name;
    cout << "Please enter your first name\n";
    cin >> name;
    cout << "Hello, " << name << '\n';
}
```

The **cin** is **std::cin**, the **string** is **std::string**, etc. As long as you use **std_lib_facilities.h**, you don't need to worry about standard headers and the **std** namespace.

It is usually a good idea to avoid using directives for any namespace except for a namespace, such as **std**, that's extremely well known in an application area. The problem with overuse of **using** directives is that you lose track of which names come from where, so that you again start to get name clashes. Explicit qualification with namespace names and **using** declarations doesn't suffer from that problem. So, putting a namespace directive in a header file (so that users can't avoid it) is a very bad habit. However, to simplify our initial code we did place a **using** directive for **std** in **std_lib_facilities.h**. That allowed us to write

```
#include "std_lib_facilities.h"

int main()
{
```

```
        string name;
        cout << "Please enter your first name\n";
        cin >> name;
        cout << "Hello, " << name << '\n';
}
```

We promise never to do that for any namespace except **std**.

Drill

1. Create three files: **my.h**, **my.cpp**, and **use.cpp**. The header file **my.h** contains

   ```
   extern int foo;
   void print_foo();
   void print(int);
   ```

   The source code file **my.cpp** #includes **my.h** and **std_lib_facilities.h**, defines **print_foo()** to print the value of **foo** using **cout**, and **print(int i)** to print the value of **i** using **cout**.

   The source code file **use.cpp** #includes **my.h**, defines **main()** to set the value of **foo** to **7** and print it using **print_foo()**, and to print the value of **99** using **print()**. Note that **use.cpp** does not #include **std_lib_facilities.h** as it doesn't directly use any of those facilities.

   Get these files compiled and run. On Windows, you need to have both **use.cpp** and **my.cpp** in a project and use { **char cc; cin>>cc;** } in **use.cpp** to be able to see your output.

2. Write three functions swap_v(int,int), swap_r(int&,int&), and swap_cr(const int&, const int&). Each should have the body

   ```
   { int temp; temp = a, a=b; b=temp; }
   ```

   where **a** and **b** are the names of the arguments.

   Try calling each swap like this

   ```
   int x = 7;
   int y =9;
   swap_?(x,y);    // replace ? by v, r, or cr
   swap_?(7,9);
   const int cx = 7;
   const int cy = 9;
   swap_?(cx,cy);
   swap_?(7.7,9.9);
   ```

```
double dx = 7.7;
double dy = 9.9;
swap_?(dx,dy);
swap_?(dx,dy);
```

Which calls compiled, and why? After each swap that compiled, print the value of the arguments after the call to see if they were actually swapped. If you are surprised by a result, consult §8.6.

3. Write a program using a single file containing three namespaces X, Y, and Z so that the following **main()** works correctly:

```
int main()
{
        X::var = 7;
        X::print();        // print X's var
        using namespace Y;
        var = 9;
        print();           // print Y's var
        {    using Z::var;
             using Z::print;
             var = 11;
             print();      // print Z's var
        }
        print();           // print Y's var
        X::print();        // print X's var
}
```

Each namespace needs to define a variable called **var** and a function called **print()** that outputs the appropriate **var** using **cout**.

Review

1. What is the difference between a declaration and a definition?
2. How do we syntactically distinguish between a function declaration and a function definition?
3. How do we syntactically distinguish between a variable declaration and a variable definition?
4. Why can't you use the functions in the calculator program from Chapter 6 without declaring them first?
5. Is **int a;** a definition or just a declaration?
6. Why is it a good idea to initialize variables as they are declared?
7. What can a function declaration consist of?

8. What good does indentation do?
9. What are header files used for?
10. What is the scope of a declaration?
11. What kinds of scope are there? Give an example of each.
12. What is the difference between a class scope and local scope?
13. Why should a programmer minimize the number of global variables?
14. What is the difference between pass-by-value and pass-by-reference?
15. What is the difference between pass-by-reference and pass-by-**const**-reference?
16. What is a **swap()**?
17. Would you ever define a function with a **vector<double>**-by-value parameter?
18. Give an example of undefined order of evaluation. Why can undefined order of evaluation be a problem?
19. What do **x&&y** and **x||y**, respectively, mean?
20. Which of the following is standard-conforming C++: functions within functions, functions within classes, classes within classes, classes within functions?
21. What goes into an activation record?
22. What is a call stack and why do we need one?
23. What is the purpose of a namespace?
24. How does a namespace differ from a class?
25. What is a **using** declaration?
26. Why should you avoid **using** directives in a header?
27. What is namespace **std**?

Terms

activation record	function definition	pass-by-value
argument	global scope	recursion
argument passing	header file	**return**
call stack	initializer	return value
class scope	local scope	scope
const	**namespace**	statement scope
declaration	namespace scope	technicalities
definition	nested block	undeclared identifier
extern	parameter	**using** declaration
forward declaration	pass-by-**const**-reference	**using** directive
function	pass-by-reference	

Exercises

1. Modify the calculator program from Chapter 7 to make the input stream an explicit parameter (as shown in §8.5.8). Also give the **Token_stream** constructor and **istream&** parameter so that when we figure out how to make our own **istreams** (e.g., attached to files), we can use the calculator for those.

2. Write a function **print()** that prints a **vector** of **ints** to **cout**. Give it two arguments: a string for "labeling" the output and a **vector**.

3. Create a **vector** of Fibonacci numbers and print them using the function from exercise 2. To create the **vector**, write a function, **fibonacci(x,y,v,n)**, where integers **x** and **y** are **ints**, **v** is an empty **vector<int>**, and **n** is the number of elements to put into **v**; **v[0]** will be **x** and **v[1]** will be **y**. A Fibonacci number is one that is part of a sequence where each element is the sum of the two previous ones. For example, starting with 1 and 2, we get 1, 2, 3, 6, 9, 15, 24, ... Your **fibonacci()** function should make such a series starting with its **x** and **y** arguments.

4. An **int** can hold integers only up to a maximum number. Find an approximation of that maximum number by using **fibonacci()**.

5. Write two functions that reverse the order of elements in a **vector<int>**. For example, 1, 3, 5, 7, 9 becomes 9, 7, 5, 3, 1. The first reverse function should produce a new **vector** with the reversed sequence, leaving its original **vector** unchanged. The other reverse function should reverse the elements of its **vector** without using any other **vectors** (hint: **swap**).

6. Write versions of the functions from exercise 5, but with a **vector<string>**.

7. Read five names into a **vector<string> name**, then prompt the user for the ages of the people named and store the ages in a **vector<double> age**. Then print out the five (**name[i],age[i]**) pairs. Sort the names (**sort(name.begin(), name.end())**) and print out the (**name[i],age[i]**) pairs. The tricky part here is to get the **age vector** in the correct order to match the sorted **name vector**. Hint: Before sorting **age**, take a copy and use that to make a copy of **age** in the right order after sorting **age**. Then, do that exercise again but allowing an arbitrary number of names.

8. Write a simple function **randint()** that produces a pseudo-random number in the range [0:MAXINT]. Hint: Knuth, *The Art of Computer Programming, Volume 2*.

9. Write a function that – using **randint()** from the previous exercise – computes a pseudo-random integer in the range [a:b]: **rand_in_range(int a, int b)**. Note: This function is very useful for writing simple games.

10. Write a function that given two **vector<double>**s **price** and **weight** computes a value (an "index") that is the sum of all **price[i]*weight[i]**. Note that we must have **weight.size()<=price.size()**.

11. Write a function **maxv()** that returns the largest element of a **vector** argument.

12. Write a function that finds the smallest and the largest element of a **vector** argument and also computes the mean and the median. Do not use global variables. Either return a **struct** containing the results or pass them back through reference arguments. Which of the two ways of returning several result values do you prefer and why?

13. Improve **print_until_s()** from §8.5.2. Test it. What makes a good set of test cases? Give reasons. Then, write a **print_until_ss()** that prints until it sees a second occurrence of its **quit** argument.

14. Write a function that takes a **vector<string>** argument and returns a **vector<int>** containing the number of characters in each **string**. Also find the longest and the shortest **string** and the lexicographically first and last **string**. How many separate functions would you use for these tasks? Why?

15. Can we declare a non-reference function argument **const** (e.g., **void f(const int);**)? What might that mean? Why might we want to do that? Why don't people do that often? Try it; write a couple of small programs to see what works.

Postscript

We could have put much of this chapter (and much of the next) into an appendix. However, you'll need most of the facilities described here in Part II of this book. You'll also encounter most of the problems that these facilities were invented to help solve very soon. Most simple programming projects that you might undertake will require you to solve such problems. So, to save time and minimize confusion, a somewhat systematic approach is called for, rather than a series of "random" visits to manuals and appendices.

9

Technicalities:
Classes, etc.

"Remember, things take time."

—Piet Hein

In this chapter, we keep our focus on our main tool for programming: the C++ programming language. We present language technicalities, mostly related to user-defined types, that is, to classes and enumerations. Much of the presentation of language features takes the form of the gradual improvement of a **Date** type. That way, we also get a chance to demonstrate some useful class design techniques.

9.1 User-defined types

The C++ language provides you with some built-in types, such as **char**, **int**, and **double** (§A.8). A type is called built-in if the compiler knows how to represent objects of the type and which operations can be done on it (such as **+** and *****) without being told by declarations supplied by a programmer in source code.

Types that are not built-in are called *user-defined types* (UDTs). They can be standard library types − available to all C++ programmers as part of every ISO Standard C++ implementation − such as **string**, **vector**, and **ostream** (Chapter 10), or types that we build for ourselves, such as **Token** and **Token_stream** (§6.5 and §6.6). As soon as we get the necessary technicalities under our belt, we'll build graphics types such as **Shape**, **Line**, and **Text** (Chapter 13). The standard library types are as much a part of the language as the built-in types, but we still consider them user-defined because they are built from the same primitives and with the same techniques as the types we built ourselves; the standard library builders have no special privileges or facilities that you don't have. Like the built-in types, most user-defined types provide operations. For example, **vector** has [ ] and **size()** (§4.6.1, §B.4.8), **ostream** has **<<**, **Token_stream** has **get()** (§6.8), and **Shape** has **add(Point)** and **set_color()** (§14.2).

Why do we build types? The compiler does not know all the types we might like to use in our programs. It couldn't, because there are far too many useful types − no language designer or compiler implementer could know them all. We invent new ones every day. Why? What are types good for? Types are good for directly representing ideas in code. When we write code, the ideal is to represent our ideas directly in our code so that we, our colleagues, and the compiler can understand what we wrote. When we want to do integer arithmetic, **int** is a great help; when we want to manipulate text, **string** is a great help; when we want to manipulate calculator input, **Token** and **Token_stream** are a great help. The help comes in two forms:

a day by simply adding **1** to its member **d** is a time bomb: when **today** is the last day of the month the increment yields an invalid date. The worst aspect of this "very bad code" is that it doesn't look bad.

This kind of thinking leads to a demand for an initialization function that can't be forgotten and for operations that are less likely to be overlooked. The basic tool for that is *member functions*, that is, functions declared as members of the class within the class body. For example:

```
// simple Date
// guarantee initialization with constructor
// provide some notational convenience
struct Date {
      int y, m, d;                  // year, month, day
      Date(int y, int m, int d);    // check for valid date and initialize
      void add_day(int n);          // increase the Date by n days
};
```

A member function with the same name as its class is special. It is called a *constructor* and will be used for initialization ("construction") of objects of the class. It is an error – caught by the compiler – to forget to initialize a class that has a constructor that requires an argument, and there is a special convenient syntax for doing such initialization:

```
Date my_birthday;              // error: my_birthday not initialized
Date today(12,24,2007);        // oops! run-time error
Date last(2000, 12, 31);       // OK (colloquial style)
Date christmas = Date(1976,12,24);     // also OK (verbose style)
```

The attempt to declare **my_birthday** fails because we didn't specify the required initial value. The attempt to declare **today** will pass the compiler, but the checking code in the constructor will catch the illegal date at run time (12/24/2007 – there is no day 2007 of the 24th month of year 12).

The definition of **last** provides the initial value – the arguments required by **Date**'s constructor – in parentheses immediately after the name of the variable. That's the most common style of initialization of variables of a class that has a constructor requiring arguments. We can also use the more verbose style where we explicitly create an object (here, **Date(1976,12,24)**) and then use that to initialize the variable using the = initializer syntax. Unless you actually like typing, you'll soon tire of that.

We can now try to use our newly defined variables:

```
last.add_day(1);
add_day(2);            // error: what date?
```

Note that the member function **add_day()** is called for a particular **Date** using the dot member-access notation. We'll show how to define member functions in §9.4.4.

9.4.3 Keep details private

We still have a problem: What if someone forgets to use the member function **add_day()**? What if someone decides to change the month directly? After all, we "forgot" to provide a facility for that:

```
Date birthday(1960,12,31);     // December 31, 1960
++birthday.d;                  // ouch! invalid date

Date today(1970,2,3);
today.m = 14;                  // ouch! invalid date
```

As long as we leave the representation of **Date** accessible to everybody, somebody will — by accident or design — mess it up; that is, someone will do something that produces an invalid value. In this case, we created a **Date** with a value that doesn't correspond to a day on the calendar. Such invalid objects are time bombs; it is just a matter of time before someone innocently uses the invalid value and gets a run-time error or — usually worse — produces a bad result.

Such concerns lead us to conclude that the representation of **Date** should be inaccessible to users except through the public member functions that we supply. Here is a first cut:

```
// simple Date (control access)
class Date {
     int y, m, d;                // year, month, day
public:
     Date(int y, int m, int d);  // check for valid date and initialize
     void add_day(int n);        // increase the Date by n days
     int month() { return m; }
     int day() { return d; }
     int year() { return y; }
};
```

We can use it like this:

```
Date birthday(1970, 12, 30);        // OK
birthday.m = 14;                    // error: Date::m is private
cout << birthday.month() << endl;   // we provided a way to read m
```

The notion of a "valid **Date**" is an important special case of the idea of a valid value. We try to design our types so that values are guaranteed to be valid; that is, we hide the representation, provide a constructor that creates only valid objects, and design all member functions to expect valid values and leave only valid values behind when they return. The value of an object is often called its *state*, so the idea of a valid value is often referred to as a *valid state* of an object.

The alternative is for us to check for validity every time we use an object, or just hope that nobody left an invalid value lying around. Experience shows that "hoping" can lead to "pretty good" programs. However, producing "pretty good" programs that occasionally produce erroneous results and occasionally crash is no way to win friends and respect as a professional. We prefer to write code that can be demonstrated to be correct.

A rule for what constitutes a valid value is called an *invariant*. The invariant for **Date** ("A **Date** must represent a day in the past, present, or future") is unusually hard to state precisely: remember leap years, the Georgian calendar, time zones, etc. However, for simple realistic uses of **Date**s we can do it. For example, if we are analyzing internet logs, we need not be bothered with the Georgian, Julian, or Mayan calendars. If we can't think of a good invariant, we are probably dealing with plain data. If so, use a **struct**.

9.4.4 Defining member functions

So far, we have looked at **Date** from the point of view of an interface designer and a user. But sooner or later, we have to implement those member functions. First, here is a subset of the **Date** class reorganized to suit the common style of providing the public interface first:

```
// simple Date (some people prefer implementation details last)
class Date {
public:
        Date(int y, int m, int d);   // constructor: check for valid date and initialize
        void add_day(int n);         // increase the Date by n days
        int month();
        // . . .
private:
        int y, m, d;        // year, month, day
};
```

People put the public interface first because the interface is what most people are interested in. In principle, a user need not look at the implementation details. In reality, we are typically curious and have a quick look to see if the implementation looks reasonable and if the implementer used some technique that we could learn from. However, unless we are the implementers, we do tend to spend much more time with the public interface. The compiler doesn't care about the order of class members; it takes the declarations in any order you care to present them.

When we define a member outside its class, we need to say which class it is a member of. We do that using the *class_name*::*member_name* notation:

```
Date::Date(int yy, int mm, int dd)    // constructor
       :y(yy), m(mm), d(dd)           // note: member initializers
{
}

void Date::add_day(int n)
{
      // . . .
}

int month()    // oops: we forgot Date::
{
      return m;     // not the member function, can't access m
}
```

The **:y(yy), m(mm), d(dd)** notation is how we initialize members. We could have written

```
Date::Date(int yy, int mm, int dd)         // constructor
{
      y = yy;
      m = mm;
      d = dd;
}
```

but then we would in principle first have default initialized the members and then assigned values to them. We would then also open the possibility of accidentally using a member before it was initialized. The **:y(yy), m(mm), d(dd)** notation more directly expresses our intent. The distinction is exactly the same as the one between

```
int x;       // first define the variable x
// . . .
x = 2;       // later assign to x
```

and

    int x = 2;   // define and immediately initialize with 2

For consistency, it is even possible to express that last initialization using the "argument"/parenthesis notation:

    int x(2);   // initialize x with 2
    Date sunday(2004,8,29);   // initialize sunday with (2004,8,29)

We can also define member functions right in the class definition:

```
// simple Date (some people prefer implementation details last)
class Date {
public:
        Date(int yy, int mm, int dd)
             :y(yy), m(mm), d(dd)
        {
             // . . .
        }

        void add_day(int n)
        {
             // . . .
        }

        int month() { return m; }

        // . . .
private:
        int y, m, d;    // year, month, day
};
```

The first thing we notice is that the class declaration became larger and "messier." In this example, the code for the constructor and **add_day**() could be a dozen or more lines each. This makes the class declaration several times larger and makes it harder to find the interface among the implementation details. Consequently, we don't define large functions within a class declaration.

    However, look at the definition of **month**(). That's straightforward and shorter than the version that places **Date::month**() out of the class declaration. For such short, simple functions, we might consider writing the definition right in the class declaration.

Note that **month()** can refer to **m** even though **m** is defined after (below) **month()**. A member can refer to another member of its class independently of where in the class that other member is declared. The rule that a name must be declared before it is used is relaxed within the limited scope of a class.

Writing the definition of a member function within the class definition has two effects:

- The function will be *inlined*; that is, the compiler will try to generate code for a call to the inline function without using a function call to get to that code. This can be a significant performance advantage for functions, such as **month()**, that hardly do anything but are used a lot.

- All uses of the class will have to be recompiled whenever we make a change to the body of an inlined function. If the function body is out of the class declaration, recompilation of users is needed only when the class declaration is itself changed. Not recompiling when the body is changed can be a huge advantage in large programs.

The obvious rule of thumb is: Don't put member function bodies in the class declaration unless you know that you need the performance boost from inlining tiny functions. Large functions, say five lines of code, don't benefit from inlining. We rarely inline a function that consists of more than one or two expressions.

9.4.5 Referring to the current object

Consider a simple use of the **Date** class so far:

```
class Date {
    // . . .
    int month() { return m; }
    // . . .
private:
    int y, m, d;    // year, month, day
};

void f(Date d1, Date d2)
{
    cout << d1.month() << ' ' << d2.month() << '\n';
}
```

How does **Date::month()** know to print out **d1.m** in the first call and **d2.m** in the second? Look again at **Date::month()**; its declaration specifies no function argument! How does **Date::month()** know for which object it was called? A class member function, such as **Date::month()**, has an implicit argument which it uses to identify the object for which it is called. So in the first call, **m** correctly refers to **d1.m** and in the second call it refers to **d2.m**. See §17.10 for more uses of this implicit argument.

9.4.6 Reporting errors

What do we do when we find an invalid date? Where in the code do we look for invalid dates? From §5.6, we know that the answer to the first question is "Throw an exception," and the obvious place to look is where we first construct a **Date**. If we don't create invalid **Date**s and also write our member functions correctly, we will never have a **Date** with an invalid value. So, we'll prevent users from ever creating a **Date** with an invalid state:

```
// simple Date (prevent invalid dates)
class Date {
public:
        class Invalid { };            // to be used as exception
        Date(int y, int m, int d);    // check for valid date and initialize
        // . . .
private:
        int y, m, d;        // year, month, day
        bool check();       // return true if date is valid
};
```

We put the testing of validity into a separate **check()** function because checking for validity is logically distinct from initialization and because we might want to have several constructors. As you can see, we can have private functions as well as private data:

```
Date::Date(int yy, int mm, int dd)
        : y(yy), m(mm), d(dd)         // initialize data members
{
        if (!check()) throw Invalid();    // check for validity
}

bool Date::check()    // return true if date is valid
{
        if (m<1 || 12<m) return false;
        // . . .
}
```

Given that definition of **Date**, we can write:

```
void f(int x, int y)
try {
      Date dxy(2004,x,y);
      cout << dxy << '\n';        // see §9.8 for a declaration of <<
      dxy.add_day(2);
}
catch(Date::Invalid) {
      error("invalid date");      // error() defined in §5.6.3
}
```

We now know that **<<** and **add_date()** will have a valid **Date** on which to operate.

Before completing the evolution of our **Date** class in §9.7, we'll take a detour to describe a couple of general language facilities that we'll need to do that well: enumerations and operator overloading.

9.5 Enumerations

An **enum** (an *enumeration*) is a very simple user-defined type, specifying its set of values (its *enumerators*) as symbolic constants. For example:

```
enum Month {
      jan=1, feb, mar, apr, may, jun, jul, aug, sep, oct, nov, dec
};
```

The "body" of an enumeration is simply a list of its enumerators. You can give a specific value for an enumerator, as we did for **jan** here, or leave it to the compiler to pick a suitable value. If you leave it to the compiler to pick, it'll give each enumerator the value of the previous enumerator plus one. Thus, our definition of **Month** gave the months consecutive values starting with **1**. We could equivalently have written

```
enum Month {
      jan=1, feb=2, mar=3, apr=4, may=5, jun=6,
      jul=7, aug=8, sep=9, oct=10, nov=11, dec=12
};
```

However, that's tedious and opens the opportunity for errors. In fact, we made two typing errors before getting this latest version right; it is better to let the compiler do simple, repetitive "mechanical" things. The compiler is better at such tasks than we are, and it doesn't get bored.

If we don't initialize the first enumerator, the count starts with 0. For example:

```
enum Day {
        monday, tuesday, wednesday, thursday, friday, saturday, sunday
};
```

Here **monday==0** and **sunday==6**. In practice, starting with **0** is often a good choice.

We can use our **Month** like this:

```
Month m = feb;
m = 7;                    // error: can't assign an int to a Month
int n = m;                // OK: we can get the numeric value of a Month
Month mm = Month(7);      // convert int to Month (unchecked)
```

Note that a **Month** is a separate type. It has an implicit conversion to **int**, but there is no implicit conversion from **int** to **Month**. This makes sense because every **Month** has an equivalent integer value, but most **ints** do not have a **Month** equivalent. For example, we really do want this initialization to fail:

```
Month bad = 9999;     // error: can't convert an int to a Month
```

If you insist on using the **Month(9999)** notation, on your head be it! In many cases, C++ will not try to stop a programmer from doing something potentially silly when the programmer explicitly insists; after all, the programmer might actually know better.

Unfortunately, we cannot define a constructor for an enumeration to check initializer values, but it is trivial to write a simple checking function:

```
Month int_to_month(int x)
{
        if (x<jan || dec<x) error("bad month");
        return Month(x);
}
```

Given that, we can write

```
void f(int m)
{
        Month mm = int_to_month(m);
        // . . .
}
```

What do we use enumerations for? Basically, an enumeration is useful whenever we need a set of related named integer constants. That happens all the time when we try to represent sets of alternatives (**up**, **down**; **yes**, **no**, **maybe**; **on**, **off**; **n**, **ne**, **e**, **se**, **s**, **sw**, **w**, **nw**) or distinctive values (**red**, **blue**, **green**, **yellow**, **maroon**, **crimson**, **black**).

Note that an enumerator is *not* in the scope of its enumeration type; it is in the same scope as the name of its enumeration type. For example:

```
enum Traffic_sign { red, yellow, green };
int var = red;          // note: not Traffic_sign::red
```

This can cause problems. Imagine the potential for confusion if you have short popular names, such as **red**, **on**, **ne**, and **dec**, as global names. For example, does **ne** mean "northeast" or "not equal"? Does **dec** mean "decimal" or "December"? This is the kind of problem we warned against in §3.7, and we can easily get such problems if we define an **enum** with short, convenient enumerator names in the global scope. In fact, we immediately get this problem when we try to use our **Month** enumeration together with **iostreams** because there is a "manipulator" called **dec** for "decimal" (see §11.2.1). To avoid such problems, we often prefer to define enumerations in more limited scopes, such as within a class. That also allows us to be explicit about what an enumerator value refers to, such as **Month::jan** and **Color::red**. We present the technique for doing that in §9.7.1. If we absolutely need global names, we try to minimize the chance of name clashes by using longer names, by using unusual names (or unusual spellings), and by capitalization. However, our preferred solution is to make names as local as is reasonable.

9.6 Operator overloading

You can define almost all C++ operators for class or enumeration operands. That's often called *operator overloading*. We use it when we want to provide conventional notation for a type we design. For example:

```
enum Month {
        Jan=1, Feb, Mar, Apr, May, Jun, Jul, Aug, Sep, Oct, Nov, Dec
};

Month operator++(Month& m)              // prefix increment operator
{
        m = (m==Dec) ? Jan : Month(m+1);    // "wrap around"
        return m;
}
```

The **?** **:** construct is an "arithmetic if": **m** becomes **Jan** if (**m==Dec**) and **Month(m+1)** otherwise. It is a reasonably elegant way of expressing the fact that months "wrap around" after December. The **Month** type can now be used like this:

```
Month m = Sep;
++m;        // m becomes Oct
++m;        // m becomes Nov
++m;        // m becomes Dec
++m;        // m becomes Jan ("wrap around")
```

You might not think that incrementing a **Month** is common enough to warrant a special operator. That may be so, but how about an output operator? We can define one like this:

```
vector<string> month_tbl;

ostream& operator<<(ostream& os, Month m)
{
        return os << month_tbl[m];
}
```

This assumes that **month_tbl** has been initialized somewhere so that (for example) **month_tbl[Mar]** is **"March"** or some other suitable name for that month; see §10.11.3.

You can define just about any operator provided by C++ for your own types, but only existing operators, such as +, –, *, /, %, [], (), ^, !, &, <, <=, >, and >=. You cannot define your own operators; you might like to have ** or $= as operators in your program, but C++ won't let you. You can define operators only with their conventional number of operands; for example, you can define unary –, but not unary <= (less than or equal), and binary +, but not binary ! (not). Basically, the language allows you to use the existing syntax for the types you define, but not to extend that syntax.

An overloaded operator must have at least one user-defined type as operand:

```
int operator+(int,int);     // error: you can't overload built-in +
Vector operator+(const Vector&, const Vector &);     // OK
Vector operator+=(const Vector&, int);     // OK
```

It is generally a good idea not to define operators for a type unless you are really certain that it makes a big positive change to your code. Also, define operators only with their conventional meaning: + should be addition, binary * multiplication, [] access, () call, etc. This is just advice, not a language rule, but it is good advice: conventional use of operators, such as + for addition, can significantly help us understand a program. After all, such use is the result of hundreds of years of experience with mathematical notation. Conversely, obscure operators and unconventional use of operators can be a significant distraction and a source of errors. We will not elaborate on this point. Instead, in the following chapters, we will simply use operator overloading in a few places where we consider it appropriate.

Note that the most interesting operators to overload aren't +, −, *, and / as people often assume, but =, ==, !=, <, [], and ().

9.7 Class interfaces

We have argued that the public interface and the implementation parts of a class should be separated. As long as we leave open the possibility of using **structs** for types that are "plain old data," few professionals would disagree. However, how do we design a good interface? What distinguishes a good public interface from a mess? Part of that answer can be given only by example, but there are a few general principles that we can list and which are given some support in C++:

- Keep interfaces complete.
- Keep interfaces minimal.
- Provide constructors.
- Support copying (or prohibit it) (see §14.2.4).
- Use types to provide good argument checking.
- Identify nonmodifying member functions (see §9.7.4).
- Free all resources in the destructor (see §17.5).

See also §5.5 (how to detect and report run-time errors).

The first two principles can be summarized as "Keep the interface as small as possible, but no smaller." We want our interface to be small because a small interface is easy to learn and easy to remember, and the implementer doesn't waste a lot of time implementing unnecessary and rarely used facilities. A small interface also means that when something is wrong, there are only a few functions to check to find the problem. On average, the more public member functions, the harder it is to find bugs — and please don't get us started on the complexities of debugging classes with public data. But of course, we want a complete interface; otherwise, it would be useless. We couldn't use an interface that didn't allow us to do all we really needed.

Let's look at the other — less abstract and more directly supported — ideals.

9.7.1 Argument types

When we defined the constructor for **Date** in §9.4.3, we used three **ints** as the arguments. That caused some problems:

```
Date d1(4,5,2005);      // oops: year 4, day 2005
Date d2(2005,4,5);      // April 5 or May 4?
```

The first problem (an illegal day of the month) is easily dealt with by a test in the constructor. However, the second (a month vs. day-of-the-month confusion) can't be caught by code written by the user. The second problem is simply that the conventions for writing month and day-in-month differ; for example, 4/5 is April 5 in the United States and May 4 in England. Since we can't calculate our way out of this, we must do something else. The obvious solution is to use the type system:

```
// simple Date (use Month type)
class Date {
public:
    enum Month {
        jan=1, feb, mar, apr, may, jun, jul, aug, sep, oct, nov, dec
    };

    Date(int y, Month m, int d);    // check for valid date and initialize
    // . . .
private:
    int y;          // year
    Month m;
    int d;          // day
};
```

When we use a **Month** type, the compiler will catch us if we swap month and day, and using an enumeration as the **Month** type also gives us symbolic names to use. It is usually easier to read and write symbolic names than to play around with numbers, and therefore less error-prone:

```
Date dx1(1998, 4, 3);           // error: 2nd argument not a Month
Date dx2(1998, 4, Date::mar);   // error: 2nd argument not a Month
Date dx2(4, Date::mar, 1998);   // oops: run-time error: day 1998
Date dx2(Date::mar, 4, 1998);   // error: 2nd argument not a Month
Date dx3(1998, Date::mar, 30);  // OK
```

This takes care of most "accidents." Note the use of the qualification of the enumerator **mar** with the class name **Date**: **Date::mar**. This is the way we say that it's **Date**'s **mar**. We don't say **Date.mar** because **Date** isn't an object (it's a type) and **mar** isn't a data member (it's an enumerator — a symbolic constant). Use **::** after a class name (or a namespace name; §8.7) and **.** (dot) after an object name.

When we have a choice, we catch errors at compile time rather than at run time. We prefer for the compiler to find the error rather than for us to try to figure out exactly where in the code a problem occurred. Also, errors caught at compile time don't require checking code to be written and executed.

Thinking like that, could we catch the swap of the day of the month and the year also? We could, but the solution is not as simple or as elegant as for **Month**; after all, there was a year 4 and you might want to represent it. Even if we restricted ourselves to modern times there would probably be too many relevant years for us to list them all in an enumeration.

Probably the best we could do (without knowing quite a lot about the intended use of **Date**) would be something like this:

```cpp
class Year {        // year in [min:max) range
      static const int min = 1800;
      static const int max = 2200;
public:
      class Invalid { };
      Year(int x) : y(x) { if (x<min || max<x) throw Invalid(); }
      int year() { return y; }
private:
      int y;
};

class Date {
public:
      enum Month {
            jan=1, feb, mar, apr, may, jun, jul, aug, sep, oct, nov, dec
      };

      Date(Year y, Month m, int d);     // check for valid date and initialize
      // . . .
private:
      Year y;
      Month m;
      int d;        // day
};
```

Now we get

```
Date dx1(Year(1998), 4, 3);              // error: 2nd argument not a Month
Date dx2(Year(1998), 4, Date::mar);      // error: 2nd argument not a Month
Date dx2(4, Date::mar, Year(1998));      // error: 1st argument not a Year
Date dx2(Date::mar, 4, Year(1998));      // error: 2nd argument not a Month
Date dx3(Year(1998), Date::mar, 30);     // OK
```

This weird and unlikely error would still not be caught until run time:

```
Date dx2(Year(4), Date::mar, 1998);      // run-time error: Year::Invalid
```

Is the extra work and notation to get years checked worthwhile? Naturally, that depends on the constraints on the kind of problem you are solving using **Date**, but in this case we doubt it and won't use class **Year** as we go along.

When we program, we always have to ask ourselves what is good enough for a given application. We usually don't have the luxury of being able to search "forever" for the perfect solution after we have already found one that is good enough. Search further, and we might even come up with something that's so elaborate that it is worse than the simple early solution. This is one meaning of the saying "The best is the enemy of the good" (Voltaire).

Note the use of **static const** in the definitions of **min** and **max**. This is the way we define symbolic constants of integer types within classes. For a class member, we use **static** to make sure that there is just one copy of the value in the program, rather than one per object of the class.

9.7.2 Copying

We always have to create objects; that is, we must always consider initialization and constructors. Arguably they are the most important members of a class: to write them, you have to decide what it takes to initialize an object and what it means for a value to be valid (what is the invariant?). Just thinking about initialization will help you avoid errors.

The next thing to consider is often: Can we copy our objects? And if so, how do we copy them?

For **Date** or **Month**, the answer is that we obviously want to copy objects of that type and that the meaning of *copy* is trivial: just copy all of the members. Actually, this is the default case. So as long as you don't say anything else, the compiler will do exactly that. For example, if you copy a **Month** as an initializer or right-hand side of an assignment, all its members are copied:

```
Date holiday(1978, Date::jul, 4);        // initialization
Date d2 = holiday;
Date d3 = Date(1978, Date::jul, 4);
```

```
holiday = Date(1978, Date::dec, 24);       // assignment
d3 = holiday;
```

This will all work as expected. The **Date(1978, Date::dec, 24)** notation makes the appropriate unnamed **Date** object, which you can then use appropriately. For example:

```
cout << Date(1978, Date::dec, 24);
```

This is a use of a constructor that acts much as a literal for a class type. It often comes in as a handy alternative to first defining a variable or **const** and then using it once.

What if we don't want the default meaning of copying? We can either define our own (see §18.2) or make the copy constructor and copy assignment private (see §14.2.4).

9.7.3 Default constructors

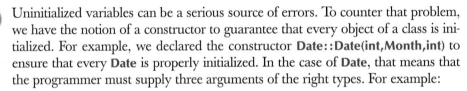

Uninitialized variables can be a serious source of errors. To counter that problem, we have the notion of a constructor to guarantee that every object of a class is initialized. For example, we declared the constructor **Date::Date(int,Month,int)** to ensure that every **Date** is properly initialized. In the case of **Date**, that means that the programmer must supply three arguments of the right types. For example:

```
Date d1;                    // error: no initializer
Date d2(1998);              // error: too few arguments
Date d3(1,2,3,4);           // error: too many arguments
Date d4(1,"jan",2);         // error: wrong argument type
Date d5(1,Date::jan,2);     // OK: use the three-argument constructor
Date d6 = d5;               // OK: use the copy constructor
```

Note that even though we defined a constructor for **Date**, we can still copy **Date**s.

Many classes have a good notion of a default value; that is, there is an obvious answer to the question "What value should it have if I didn't give it an initializer?" For example:

```
string s1;                  // default value: the empty string ""
vector<string> v1;          // default value: the empty vector; no elements
vector<string> v2(10);      // vector of 10 default strings
```

This looks reasonable. It even works the way the comments indicate. That is achieved by giving **vector** and **string** *default constructors* that implicitly provide the desired initialization.

For a type **T**, **T()** is the notation for the default value, as defined by the default constructor, so we could write

```
string s1 = string();              // default value: the empty string ""
vector<string> v1 = vector<string>();   // default value:
                                   // the empty vector; no elements
vector<string> v2(10,string());    // vector of 10 default strings
```

However, we prefer the equivalent and colloquial

```
string s1;              // default value: the empty string ""
vector<string> v1;      // default value: the empty vector; no elements
vector<string> v2(10);  // vector of 10 default strings
```

For built-in types, such as **int** and **double**, the default constructor notation means **0**, so **int()** is a complicated way of saying **0**, and **double()** a long-winded way of saying **0.0**.

Beware of a nasty syntax problem with the () notation for initializers:

```
string s1("Ike");    // string initialized to "Ike"
string s2();         // function taking no argument returning a string
```

Using a default constructor is not just a matter of looks. Imagine that we could have an uninitialized **string** or **vector**.

```
string s;
for (int i=0, i<s.size(), ++i)  // oops: loop an undefined number of times
        toupper(s[i]);   // oops: modify the contents of a random memory location

vector<string> v;
v.push_back("bad");        // oops: write to random address
```

If the values of **s** and **v** were genuinely undefined, **s** and **v** would have no notion of how many elements they contained or (using the common implementation techniques; see §17.5) where those elements were supposed to be stored. The results would be use of random addresses – and that can lead to the worst kind of errors. Basically, without a constructor, we cannot establish an invariant – we cannot ensure that the values in those variables are valid (§9.4.3). We must insist that such variables are initialized. We could insist on an initializer and then write:

```
string s1 = "";
vector<string> v1(0);
vector<string> v2(10,"");    // vector of 10 empty strings
```

But we don't think that's particularly pretty. For **string**, `""` is rather obvious for "empty string." For **vector**, **0** isn't too obscure for "empty vector." However, for many types, it is not easy to find a reasonable notation for a default value. For many types, it is better to define a constructor that gives meaning to the creation of an object without an explicit initializer. Such a constructor takes no arguments and is called a *default constructor*.

There isn't an obvious default value for dates. That's why we didn't define a default constructor for **Date** so far, but let's provide one (just to show we can):

```
class Date {
public:
        // . . .
        Date();      // default constructor
        // . . .
private:
        int y;
        Month m;
        int d;
};
```

We have to pick a default date. The first day of the 21st century might be a reasonable choice:

```
Date::Date()
        :y(2001), m(Date::jan), d(1)
{
}
```

If we didn't like to build the default value right into the constructor code, we could use a constant (or a variable). To avoid a global variable and its associated initialization problems, we use the technique from §8.6.2:

```
Date& default_date()
{
        static Date dd(2001,Date::jan,1);
        return dd;
}
```

We used **static** to get a variable (**dd**) that is created only once, rather than each time **default_date()** is called, and initialized the first time **default_date()** is called. Given **default_date()**, it is trivial to define a default constructor for **Date**:

```
Date::Date()
    :y(default_date().year()),
    m(default_date().month()),
    d(default_date().day())
{
}
```

Note that the default constructor does not need to check its value; the constructor for **default_date** already did that. Given this default **Date** constructor, we can now have vectors of **Dates**:

```
vector<Date> birthdays(10);
```

Without the default constructor, we would have had to be explicit:

```
vector<Date> birthdays(10,default_date());
```

9.7.4 const member functions

Some variables are meant to be changed – that's why we call them "variables" – but some are not; that is, we have "variables" representing immutable values. Those, we typically call *constants* or just **const**s. Consider:

```
void some_function(Date& d, const Date& start_of_term)
{
    int a = d.day();                   // OK
    int b = start_of_term.day();       // should be OK (why?)
    d.add_day(3);                      // fine
    start_of_term.add_day(3);          // error
}
```

Here we intend **d** to be mutable, but **start_of_term** to be immutable; it is not acceptable for **some_function()** to change **start_of_term**. How would the compiler know that? It knows because we told it by declaring **start_of_term const**. So far, so good, but then why is it OK to read the **day** of **start_of_term** using **day()**? As the definition of **Date** stands so far, **start_of_term.day()** is an error because the compiler does not know that **day()** doesn't change its **Date**. We never told it, so the compiler assumes that **day()** may modify its **Date** and reports an error.

We can deal with this problem by classifying operations on a class as modifying and nonmodifying. That's a pretty fundamental distinction that helps us understand a class, but it also has a very practical importance: operations that do not modify the object can be invoked for **const** objects. For example:

```
class Date {
public:
    // . . .
    int day() const;          // const member: can't modify the object
    Month month() const;      // const member: can't modify the object
    int year() const;         // const member: can't modify the object

    void add_day(int n);      // non-const member: can modify the object
    void add_month(int n);    // non-const member: can modify the object
    void add_year(int n);     // non-const member: can modify the object
private:
    int y;          // year
    Month m;
    int d;          // day of month
};

Date d(2000, Date::jan, 20);
const Date cd(2001, Date::feb, 21);

cout << d.day() << " – " << cd.day() << endl;  // OK
d.add_day(1);       // OK
cd.add_day(1);      // error: cd is a const
```

We use **const** right after the argument list in a member function declaration to indicate that the member function can be called for a **const** object. Once we have declared a member function **const**, the compiler holds us to our promise not to modify the object. For example:

```
int Date::day() const
{
    ++d;     // error: attempt to change object from const member function
    return d;
}
```

Naturally, we don't usually try to "cheat" in this way. What the compiler provides for the class implementer is primarily protection against accident, which is particularly useful for more complex code.

9.7.5 Members and "helper functions"

When we design our interfaces to be minimal (though complete), we have to leave out lots of operations that are merely useful. A function that can be simply, elegantly, and efficiently implemented as a freestanding function (that is, as a nonmember function) should be implemented outside the class. That way, a bug in that function cannot directly corrupt the data in a class object. Not accessing the representation is important because the usual debug technique is "round up the usual suspects"; that is, when something goes wrong with a class, we first look at the functions that directly access the representation: one of those almost certainly did it. If there are a dozen such functions we will be much happier than if there were 50.

Fifty functions for a **Date** class! You must wonder if we are kidding. We are not: a few years ago I surveyed a number of commercially used **Date** libraries and found them full of functions like **next_Sunday()**, **next_workday()**, etc. Fifty is not an unreasonable number for a class designed for the convenience of the users rather than for ease of comprehension, implementation, and maintenance.

Note also that if the representation changes, only the functions that directly access the representation need to be rewritten. That's another strong practical reason for keeping interfaces minimal. In our **Date** example, we might decide that an integer representing the number of days since January 1, 1900, is a much better representation for our uses than (year,month,day). Only the member functions would have to be changed.

Here are some examples of *helper functions*:

```
Date next_Sunday(const Date& d)
{
      // access d using d.day(), d.month(), and d.year()
      // make new Date to return
}

Date next_weekday(const Date& d) { /* . . . */ }

bool leapyear(int y) { /* . . . */ }

bool operator==(const Date& a, const Date& b)
{
      return a.year()==b.year()
            && a.month()==b.month()
            && a.day()==b.day();
}

bool operator!=(const Date& a, const Date& b)
{
      return !(a==b);
}
```

Helper functions are also called *convenience functions, auxiliary functions,* and many other things. The distinction between these functions and other nonmember functions is logical; that is, "helper function" is a design concept, not a programming language concept. The helper functions often take arguments of the classes that they are helpers of. There are exceptions, though: note **leapyear()**. Often, we use namespaces to identify a group of helper functions; see §8.7:

```
namespace Chrono {
        class Date { /* . . . */ };
        bool is_date(int y, Date::Month m, int d);        // true for valid date
        Date next_Sunday(const Date& d) { /* . . . */ }
        Date next_weekday(const Date& d) { /* . . . */ }
        bool leapyear(int y) { /* . . . */ }     // see exercise 10
        bool operator==(const Date& a, const Date& b) { /* . . . */ }
        // . . .
}
```

Note the **==** and **!=** functions. They are typical helpers. For many classes, **==** and **!=** make obvious sense, but since they don't make sense for all classes, the compiler can't write them for you the way it writes the copy constructor and copy assignment.

Note also that we introduced a helper function **is_date()**. That function replaces **Date::check()** because checking whether a date is valid is largely independent of the representation of a **Date**. For example, we don't need to know how **Date** objects are represented to know that "January 30, 2008" is a valid date and "February 30, 2008" is not. There still may be aspects of a date that might depend on the representation (e.g., can we represent "January 30, 1066"?), but (if necessary) **Date**'s constructor can take care of that.

9.8 The Date class

So, let's just put it all together and see what that **Date** class might look like when we combine all of the ideas/concerns. Where a function's body is just a . . . comment, the actual implementation is tricky (please don't try to write those just yet). First we place the declarations in a header **Chrono.h**:

```
// file Chrono.h

namespace Chrono {

class Date {
```

```
public:
    enum Month {
        jan=1, feb, mar, apr, may, jun, jul, aug, sep, oct, nov, dec
    };

    class Invalid { };     // to throw as exception

    Date(int y, Month m, int d);    // check for valid date and initialize
    Date();                         // default constructor
    // the default copy operations are fine

    // nonmodifying operations:
    int day() const { return d; }
    Month month() const { return m; }
    int year() const { return y; }

    // modifying operations:
    void add_day(int n);
    void add_month(int n);
    void add_year(int n);
private:
    int y;
    Month m;
    int d;
};

bool is_date(int y, Date::Month m, int d);     // true for valid date

bool leapyear(int y);     // true if y is a leap year

bool operator==(const Date& a, const Date& b);
bool operator!=(const Date& a, const Date& b);

ostream& operator<<(ostream& os, const Date& d);

istream& operator>>(istream& is, Date& dd);

} // Chrono
```

The definitions go into **Chrono.cpp**:

```cpp
// Chrono.cpp

namespace Chrono {

// member function definitions:

Date::Date(int yy, Month mm, int dd)
    : y(yy), m(mm), d(dd)
{
    if (!is_date(yy,mm,dd)) throw Invalid();
}

Date& default_date()
{
    static Date dd(2001,Date::jan,1);    // start of 21st century
    return dd;
}

Date::Date()
    :y(default_date().year()),
    m(default_date().month()),
    d(default_date().day())
{
}

void Date:: add_day(int n)
{
    // . . .
}

void Date::add_month(int n)
{
    // . . .
}

void Date::add_year(int n)
{
    if (m==feb && d==29 && !leapyear(y+n)) {    // beware of leap years!
        m = mar;        // use March 1 instead of February 29
        d = 1;
    }
    y+=n;
}
```

```
// helper functions:

bool is_date(int y, Date::Month m, int d)
{
      // assume that y is valid

      if (d<=0) return false;          // d must be positive

      int days_in_month = 31;      // most months have 31 days

      switch (m) {
      case Date::feb:          // the length of February varies
            days_in_month = (leapyear(y))?29:28;
            break;
      case Date::apr: case Date::jun: case Date::sep: case Date::nov:
            days_in_month = 30;      // the rest have 30 days
            break;
      }

      if (days_in_month<d) return false;

      return true;
}

bool leapyear(int y)
{
      // see exercise 10
}

bool operator==(const Date& a, const Date& b)
{
      return a.year()==b.year()
            && a.month()==b.month()
            && a.day()==b.day();
}

bool operator!=(const Date& a, const Date& b)
{
      return !(a==b);
}

ostream& operator<<(ostream& os, const Date& d)
{
```

```cpp
        return os << '(' << d.year()
                 << ',' << d.month()
                 << ',' << d.day() << ')';
}

istream& operator>>(istream& is, Date& dd)
{
    int y, m, d;
    char ch1, ch2, ch3, ch4;
    is >> ch1 >> y >> ch2 >> m >> ch3 >> d >> ch4;
    if (!is) return is;
    if (ch1!='(' || ch2!=',' || ch3!=',' || ch4!=')') {    // oops: format error
        is.clear(ios_base::failbit);                       // set the fail bit
        return is;
    }

    return is;
}

enum Day {
    sunday, monday, tuesday, wednesday, thursday, friday, saturday
};

Day day_of_week(const Date& d)
{
    // . . .
}

Date next_Sunday(const Date& d)
{
    // ...
}

Date next_weekday(const Date& d)
{
    // . . .
}

} // Chrono
```

The functions implementing >> and << for **Date** will be explained in detail in §10.7 and 10.8.

Drill

This drill simply involves getting the sequence of versions of **Date** to work. For each version define a **Date** called **today** initialized to June 25, 1978. Then, define a **Date** called **tomorrow** and give it a value by copying **today** into it and increasing its day by one using **add_day()**. Finally, output **today** and **tomorrow** using a << defined as in §9.8.

Your check for a valid date may be very simple. However, don't accept a month that is not in the [1,12] range or day of the month that is not in the [1,31] range. Test each version with at least one invalid date (e.g., 2004, 13, –5).

1. The version from §9.4.1
2. The version from §9.4.2
3. The version from §9.4.3
4. The version from §9.7.1
5. The version from §9.7.4

Review

1. What are the two parts of a class, as described in the chapter?
2. What is the difference between the interface and the implementation in a class?
3. What are the limitations and problems of the original **Date struct** that is created in the chapter?
4. Why is a constructor used for the **Date** type instead of an **init_day()** function?
5. What is an invariant? Give examples.
6. When should functions be put in the class definition, and when should they be defined outside the class? Why?
7. When should operator overloading be used in a program? Give a list of operators that you might want to overload (each with a reason).
8. Why should the public interface to a class be as small as possible?
9. What does adding **const** to a member function do?
10. Why are "helper functions" best placed outside the class definition?

Terms

built-in types	enumeration	invariant
class	enumerator	representation
const	helper function	**struct**
constructor	implementation	structure
destructor	inlining	user-defined types
enum	interface	valid state

Exercises

1. List sets of plausible operations for the examples of real-world objects in §9.1 (such as toaster).

2. Design and implement a **Name_pairs** class holding (name,age) pairs where name is a **string** and age is a **double**. Represent that as a **vector<string>** (called **name**) and a **vector<double>** (called **age**) member. Provide an input operation **read_names()** that reads a series of names. Provide a **read_ages()** operation that prompts the user for an age for each name. Provide a **print()** operation that prints out the (**name[i]**,**age[i]**) pairs (one per line) in the order determined by the **name** vector. Provide a **sort()** operation that sorts the **name** vector in alphabetical order and reorganizes the age **vector** to match. Implement all "operations" as member functions. Test the class (of course: test early and often).

3. Replace **Name_pair::print()** with a (global) **operator<<** and define **==** and **!=** for **Name_pairs**.

4. Look at the headache-inducing last example of §8.4. Indent it properly and explain the meaning of each construct. Note that the example doesn't do anything meaningful; it is pure obfuscation.

5. This exercise and the next few require you to design and implement a **Book** class, such as you can imagine as part of software for a library. Class **Book** should have members for the ISBN, title, author, and copyright date. Also store data on whether or not the book is checked out. Create functions for returning those data values. Create functions for checking a book in and out. Do simple validation of data entered into a **Book**; for example, accept ISBNs only of the form **n-n-n-x** where **n** is an integer and **x** is a digit or a letter.

6. Add operators for the **Book** class. Have the **==** operator check whether the ISBN numbers are the same for two books. Have **!=** also compare the ISBN numbers. Have a **<<** print out the title author, and ISBN on separate lines.

7. Create an enumerated type for the **Book** class called **Genre**. Have the types be fiction, nonfiction, periodical, biography, children. Give each book a **Genre** and make appropriate changes to the **Book** constructor and member functions.

8. Create a **Patron** class for the library. The class will have a user's name, library card number, and library fees (if owed). Have functions that access these methods, as well as a function to set the fee of the user. Have a helper method that returns a Boolean (**bool**) depending on whether or not the user owes a fee.

9. Create a **Library** class. Include vectors of **Books** and **Patrons**. Include a **struct** called **Transaction**. Have it include a **Book**, a **Patron**, and a **Date**

from the chapter. Make a vector of **Transaction**s. Create functions to add books to the library, add patrons to the library, and check out books. Whenever a user checks out a book, have the library make sure that both the user and the book are in the library. If they aren't, report an error. Then check to make sure that the user owes no fees. If the user does, report an error. If not, create a **Transaction**, and place it in the vector of **Transaction**s. Also create a method that will return a vector that contains the names of all **Patron**s who owe fees.

10. Implement **leapyear()** from §9.8.

11. Design and implement a set of useful helper function for the **Date** class with functions such as **next_workday()** (assume that any day that is not a Saturday or a Sunday is a workday) and **week_of_year()** (assume that week 1 is the week with January 1 in it and that the first day of a week is a Sunday).

12. Change the representation of a **Date** to be the number of days since January 1, 1970 (known as day 0), represented as a **long**, and re-implement the functions from §9.8. Be sure to reject dates outside the range we can represent that way (feel free to reject days before day 0, i.e., no negative days).

13. Design and implement a rational number class, **Rational**. A rational number has two parts: a numerator and a denominator, for example, 5/6 (five-sixths, also known as approximately .83333). Look up the definition if you need to. Provide assignment, addition, subtraction, multiplication, division, and equality operators. Also, provide a conversion to **double**. Why would people want to use a **Rational** class?

14. Design and implement a **Money** class for calculations involving dollars and cents where arithmetic has to be accurate to the last cent using the 4/5 rounding rule (.5 of a cent rounds up; anything less than .5 rounds down). Represent a monetary amount as a number of cents in a **long**, but input and output as dollars and cents, e.g., $123.45. Do not worry about amounts that don't fit into a **long**.

15. Refine the **Money** class by adding a currency (given as a constructor argument). Accept a floating-point initializer as long as it can be exactly represented as a **long**. Don't accept illegal operations. For example, **Money*Money** doesn't make sense, and **USD1.23+DKK5.00** makes sense only if you provide a conversion table defining the conversion factor between U.S. dollars (USD) and Danish kroner (DKK).

16. Give an example of a calculation where a **Rational** gives a mathematically better result than **Money**.

17. Give an example of a calculation where a **Rational** gives a mathematically better result than **double**.

Postscript

There is a lot to user-defined types, much more than we have presented here. User-defined types, especially classes, are the heart of C++ and the key to many of the most effective design techniques. Most of the rest of the book is about the design and use of classes. A class – or a set of classes – is the mechanism through which we represent our concepts in code. Here we primarily introduced the language-technical aspects of classes; elsewhere we focus on how to elegantly express useful ideas as classes.

Part II

Input and Output

Input and Output Streams

> "Science is what we have learned about
> how to keep from fooling ourselves."
>
> — **Richard P. Feynman**

In this chapter and the next, we present the C++ standard
library facilities for handling input and output from a variety
of sources: I/O streams. We show how to read and write files,
how to deal with errors, how to deal with formatted input, and
how to provide and use I/O operators for user-defined types.
This chapter focuses on the basic model: how to read and write
individual values, and how to open, read, and write whole files.
The final example illustrates the kinds of considerations that go
into a larger piece of code. The next chapter addresses details.

10.1 Input and output

Without data, computing is pointless. We need to get data into our program to do interesting computations and we need to get the results out again. In §4.1, we mentioned the bewildering variety of data sources and targets for output. If we don't watch out, we'll end up writing programs that can receive input only from a specific source and deliver output only to a specific output device. That may be acceptable (and sometimes even necessary) for specialized applications, such as a digital camera or a sensor for an engine fuel injector, but for more common tasks, we need a way to separate the way our program reads and writes from the actual input and output devices used. If we had to directly address each kind of device, we'd have to change our program each time a new screen or disk came on the market, or limit our users to the screens and disks we happen to like. That would be absurd.

Most modern operating systems separate the detailed handling of I/O devices into device drivers and then access the device drivers through an I/O library that makes I/O from/to different sources appear as similar as possible. Generally, the device drivers are deep in the operating system where most users don't see them, and the I/O library provides an abstraction of I/O so that the programmer doesn't have to think about devices and device drivers:

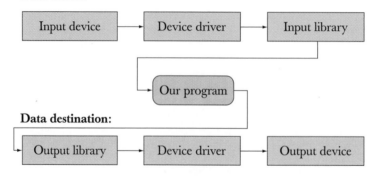

When a model like this is used, all input and all output can be seen as streams of bytes (characters) handled by the input/output library. Our job as programmers of an application then becomes

1. To set up I/O streams to the appropriate data sources and destinations
2. To read and write from/to those streams

The details of how our characters are actually transmitted to/from the devices are dealt with by the I/O library and the device drivers. In this chapter and the next, we'll see how I/O consisting of streams of formatted data is done using the C++ standard library.

From the programmer's point of view there are many different kinds of input and output. One classification is

- Streams of (many) data items (usually to/from files, network connections, recording devices, or display devices)
- Interactions with a user at a keyboard
- Interactions with a user through a graphical interface (outputting objects, receiving mouse clicks, etc.)

This classification isn't the only classification possible, and the distinction between the three kinds of I/O isn't as clear as it might appear. For example, if a stream of output characters happens to be an HTTP document aimed at a browser, the result looks remarkably like user interaction and can contain graphical elements. Conversely, the results of interactions with a GUI (graphical user interface) may be presented to a program as a sequence of characters. However, this classification fits our tools: the first two kinds of I/O are provided by the C++ standard library I/O streams and supported rather directly by most operating systems. We have been using the iostream library since Chapter 1 and will focus on that for this and the next chapter. The graphical output and graphical user interactions are served by a variety of different libraries, and we will focus on that kind of I/O in Chapters 12 to 16.

10.2 The I/O stream model

The C++ standard library provides the type **istream** to deal with streams of input and the type **ostream** to deal with streams of output. We have used the standard **istream** called **cin** and the standard **ostream** called **cout**, so we know the basics of how to use this part of the standard library (usually called the iostream library).

An **ostream**

- Turns values of various types into character sequences
- Sends those characters "somewhere" (such as to a console, a file, the main memory, or another computer)

We can represent an **ostream** graphically like this:

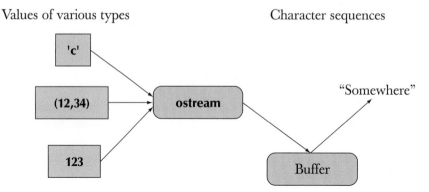

The buffer is a data structure that the **ostream** uses internally to store the data you give it while communicating with the operating system. If you notice a "delay" between your writing to an **ostream** and the characters appearing at their destination, it's usually because they are still in the buffer. Buffering is important for performance, and performance is important if you deal with large amounts of data.

An **istream**

- Turns character sequences into values of various types
- Gets those characters from somewhere (such as a console, a file, the main memory, or another computer)

We can represent an **istream** graphically like this:

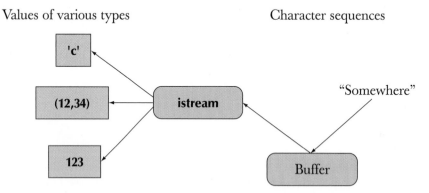

As with an **ostream**, an **istream** uses a buffer to communicate with the operating system. With an **istream**, the buffering can be quite visible to the user. When you use an **istream** that is attached to a keyboard, what you type is left in the buffer until you hit Enter (return/newline) and you can use the erase (Backspace) key "to change your mind" (until you hit Enter).

One of the major uses of output is to produce data for humans to read. Think of email messages, scholarly articles, web pages, billing records, business reports, contact lists, tables of contents, equipment status readouts, etc. Therefore, **ostream**s provide many features for formatting text to suit various tastes. Similarly, much input is written by humans or is formatted to make it easy for humans to read it. Therefore, **istream**s provide features for reading the kind of output produced by **ostream**s. We'll discuss formatting in §11.2 and how to read non-character input in §11.3.2. Most of the complexity related to input has to do with how to handle errors. To be able to give more realistic examples, we'll start by discussing how the iostream model relates to files of data.

10.3 Files

We typically have much more data than can fit in the main memory of our computer, so we store most of it on disks or other large-capacity storage devices. Such devices also have the desirable property that data doesn't disappear when the power is turned off – the data is persistent. At the most basic level, a file is simply a sequence of bytes numbered from 0 upward:

A file has a format; that is, it has a set of rules that determine what the bytes mean. For example, if we have a text file, the first 4 bytes will be the first four characters. On the other hand, if we have a file that uses a binary representation of integers, those very same first 4 bytes will be taken to be the (binary) representation of the first integer (see §11.3.2). The format serves the same role for files on disk as types serve for objects in main memory. We can make sense of the bits in a file if (and only if) we know its format (see §11.2–3).

For a file, an **ostream** converts objects in main memory into streams of bytes and writes them to disk. An **istream** does the opposite; that is, it takes a stream of bytes from disk and composes objects from them:

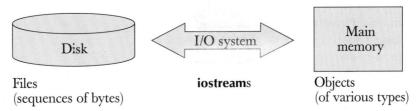

Most of the time, we assume that these "bytes on disk" are in fact characters in our usual character set. That is not always so, but we can get an awfully long way with that assumption, and other representations are not that hard to deal with. We also talk as if all files were on disks (that is, on rotating magnetic storage). Again, that's not always so (think of flash memory), but at this level of programming the actual storage makes no difference. That's one of the beauties of the file and stream abstractions.

To read a file, we must

1. Know its name
2. Open it (for reading)
3. Read in the characters
4. Close it (though that is typically done implicitly)

To write a file, we must

1. Name it
2. Open it (for writing) or create a new file of that name
3. Write out our objects
4. Close it (though that is typically done implicitly)

We already know the basics of reading and writing because an **ostream** attached to a file behaves exactly as **cout** for what we have done so far, and an **istream** attached to a file behaves exactly as **cin** for what we have done so far. We'll present operations that can only be done for files later (§11.3.3), but for now we'll just see how to open files and then concentrate on operations and techniques that apply to all **ostream**s and all **istream**s.

10.4 Opening a file

If you want to read from a file or write to a file you have to open a stream specifically for that file. An **ifstream** is an **istream** for reading from a file, an **ofstream** is an **ostream** for writing to a file, and an **fstream** is an **iostream** that can be used for both reading and writing. Before a file stream can be used it must be attached to a file. For example:

```
cout << "Please enter input file name: ";
string name;
cin >> name;
ifstream ist(name.c_str());       // ist is an input stream for the file named name
if (!ist) error("can't open input file ",name);
```

Defining an **ifstream** with a name string opens the file of that name for reading. The function **c_str()** is a member of **string** that produces a low-level C-style string from a C++ string. Such C-style strings are required by many system interfaces. The test of **!ist** checks that the file was properly opened. After that, we can read from the file exactly as we would from any other **istream**. For example, assuming that the input operator, **>>**, was defined for a type **Point**, we could write

```
vector<Point> points;
Point p;
while (ist>>p) points.push_back(p);
```

Output to files is handled in a similar fashion by **ofstream**s. For example:

```
cout << "Please enter name of output file: ";
string oname;
cin >> oname;
ofstream ost(oname.c_str());   // ost is an output stream for a file named name
if (!ost) error("can't open output file ",oname);
```

Defining an **ofstream** with a name string opens the file with that name for writing. The test of **!ost** checks that the file was properly opened. After that, we can write to the file exactly as we would to any other **ostream**. For example:

```
for (int i=0; i<points.size(); ++i)
ost << '(' << points[i].x << ',' << points[i].y << ")\n";
```

When a file stream goes out of scope its associated file is closed. When a file is closed its associated buffer is "flushed"; that is, the characters from the buffer are written to the file.

It is usually best to open files early in a program before any serious computation has taken place. After all, it is a waste to do a lot of work just to find that we can't complete it because we don't have anywhere to write our results.

Opening the file implicitly as part of the creation of an **ostream** or an **istream** and relying on the scope of the stream to take care of closing the file is the ideal. For example:

```
void fill_from_file(vector<Point>& points, string& name)
{
        ifstream ist(name.c_str());      // open file for reading
        if (!ist) error("can't open input file ",name);
        // . . . use ist . . .
        // the file is implicitly closed when we leave the function
}
```

You can also perform explicit **open()** and **close()** operations (§B.7.1). However, relying on scope minimizes the chances of someone trying to use a file stream before it has been attached to a stream or after it was closed. For example:

```
ifstream ifs;
// . . .
ifs >> foo;                     // won't succeed: no file opened for ifs
// . . .
ifs.open(name,ios_base::in);    // open file named name for reading
// . . .
ifs.close();                    // close file
// . . .
ifs >> bar;                     // won't succeed: ifs' file was closed
// . . .
```

In real-world code the problems would typically be much harder to spot. Fortunately, you can't open a file stream a second time without first closing it. For example:

```
fstream fs;
fs.open("foo", ios_base::in) ;   // open for input
// close() missing
fs.open("foo", ios_base::out);   // won't succeed: ifs is already open
if (fs) error("impossible");
```

Don't forget to test a stream after opening it.

Why would you use **open()** or **close()** explicitly? Well, occasionally the lifetime of a connection to a file isn't conveniently limited by a scope so you have to. But that's rare enough for us not to have to worry about it here. More to the point, you'll find such use in code written by people using styles from languages and libraries that don't have the scoped idiom used by **iostreams** (and the rest of the C++ standard library).

As we'll see in Chapter 11, there is much more to files, but for now we know enough to use them as a data source and a destination for data. That'll allow us to write programs that would be unrealistic if we assumed that a user had to directly type in all the input. From a programmer's point of view, a great advantage of a file is that you can repeatedly read it during debugging until your program works correctly.

10.5 Reading and writing a file

Consider how you might read a set of results of some measurements from a file and represent them in memory. This might be the temperature readings from a weather station:

```
0  60.7
1  60.6
2  60.3
3  59.22
...
```

This data file contains a sequence of (hour of day,temperature) pairs. The hours are numbered **0** to **23** and the temperatures are in Fahrenheit. No further formatting is assumed; that is, the file does not contain any special header information (such as where the reading was taken), units for the values, punctuation (such as parentheses around each pair of values), or termination indicator. This is the simplest case.

We could represent a temperature reading by a **Reading** type:

```
struct Reading {              // a temperature reading
      int hour;               // hour after midnight [0:23]
      double temperature;     // in Fahrenheit
      Reading(int h, double t) :hour(h), temperature(t) { }
};
```

Given that, we could read like this:

```
vector<Reading> temps;   // store the readings here
int hour;
double temperature;
while (ist >> hour >> temperature) {
      if (hour < 0 || 23 <hour) error("hour out of range");
      temps.push_back(Reading(hour,temperature));
}
```

This is a typical input loop. The **istream** called **ist** could be an input file stream (**ifstream**) as shown in the previous section, (an alias for) the standard input stream (**cin**), or any other kind of **istream**. For code like this, it doesn't matter exactly from where the **istream** gets its data. All that our program cares about is that **ist** is an **istream** and that the data has the expected format. The next section addresses the interesting question of how to detect errors in the input data and what we can do after detecting a format error.

Writing to a file is usually simpler than reading from one. Again, once a stream is initialized we don't have to know exactly what kind of stream it is. In particular, we can use the output file stream (**ofstream**) from the section above just like any other **ostream**. For example, we might want to output the readings with each pair of values in parentheses:

```
for (int i=0; i<temps.size(); ++i)
      ost << '(' << temps[i].hour << ',' << temps[i].temperature << ")\n";
```

The resulting program would then be reading the original temperature reading file and producing a new file with the data in (hour,temperature) format.

Because the file streams automatically close their files when they go out of scope, the complete program becomes

```
#include "std_lib_facilities.h"

struct Reading {                    // a temperature reading
        int hour;                   // hour after midnight [0:23]
        double temperature;         // in Fahrenheit
        Reading(int h, double t) :hour(h), temperature(t) { }
};

int main()
{
        cout << "Please enter input file name: ";
        string name;
        cin >> name;
        ifstream ist(name.c_str());        // ist reads from the file named "name"
        if (!ist) error("can't open input file ",name);

        cout << "Please enter name of output file: ";
        cin >> name;
        ofstream ost(name.c_str());        // ost writes to a file named "name"
        if (!ost) error("can't open output file ",name);

        vector<Reading> temps;             // store the readings here
        int hour;
        double temperature;
        while (ist >> hour >> temperature) {
                if (hour < 0 || 23 <hour) error("hour out of range");
                temps.push_back(Reading(hour,temperature));
        }

        for (int i=0; i<temps.size(); ++i)
                ost << '(' << temps[i].hour << ','
                        << temps[i].temperature << ")\n";
}
```

10.6 I/O error handling

When dealing with input we must expect errors and deal with them. What kind of errors? And how? Errors occur because humans make mistakes (misunderstanding instructions, mistyping, letting the cat walk on the keyboard, etc.), because files fail to meet specifications, because we (as programmers) have the wrong expectations, etc. The possibilities for input errors are limitless! However, an **istream** reduces all to four possible cases, called the *stream state*:

Stream states	
good()	The operations succeeded.
eof()	We hit end of input ("end of file").
fail()	Something unexpected happened.
bad()	Something unexpected and serious happened.

Unfortunately, the distinction between **fail()** and **bad()** is not precisely defined and subject to varying opinions among programmers defining I/O operations for new types. However, the basic idea is simple: If an input operation encounters a simple format error, it lets the stream **fail()**, assuming that you (the user of our input operation) might be able to recover. If, on the other hand, something really nasty, such as a bad disk read, happens, the input operation lets the stream go **bad()**, assuming that there is nothing much you can do except to abandon the attempt to get data from that stream. This leaves us with this general logic:

```
int i = 0;
cin >> i;
if (!cin) {    // we get here (only) if an input operation failed
    if (cin.bad()) error("cin is bad");  // stream corrupted: let's get out of here!
    if (cin.eof()) {
        // no more input
        // this is often how we want a sequence of input operations to end
    }
    if (cin.fail()) {       // stream encountered something unexpected
        cin.clear();        // make ready for more input
        // somehow recover
    }
}
```

The **!cin** can be read as "**cin** is not good" or "Something went wrong with **cin**" or "The state of **cin** is not **good()**." It is the opposite of "The operation succeeded." Note the **cin.clear()** where we handle **fail()**. When a stream has failed, we might be able to recover. To try to recover, we explicitly take the stream out of the **fail()** state, so that we can look at characters from it again; **clear()** does that – after **cin.clear()** the state of **cin** is **good()**.

Here is an example of how we might use the stream state. Consider how to read a sequence of integers that may be terminated by the character * or an "end of file" (Ctrl+Z on Windows, Ctrl+D on Unix) into a **vector**. For example:

1 2 3 4 5 *

This could be done using a function like this:

```
void fill_vector(istream& ist, vector<int>& v, char terminator)
        // read integers from ist into v until we reach eof() or terminator
{
        int i = 0;
        while (ist >> i) v.push_back(i);
        if (ist.eof()) return;      // fine: we found the end of file

        if (ist.bad()) error("ist is bad");    // stream corrupted; let's get out of here!
        if (ist.fail()) {  // clean up the mess as best we can and report the problem
                ist.clear();        // clear stream state,
                                    // so that we can look for terminator
                char c;
                ist>>c;             // read a character, hopefully terminator
                if (c != terminator) {   // unexpected character
                        ist.unget();        // put that character back
                        ist.clear(ios_base::failbit);    // set the state to fail()
                }
        }
}
```

Note that when we didn't find the terminator, we still returned. After all, we may have collected some data and the caller of **fill_vector()** may be able to recover from a **fail()**. Since we cleared the state to be able to examine the character, we have to set the stream state back to **fail()**. We do that with **ist.clear(ios_base::failbit)**. Note this potentially confusing use of **clear()**: **clear()** with an argument actually sets the **iostream** state flags (bits) mentioned and (only) clears flags not mentioned. By setting the state to **fail()**, we indicate that we encountered a format error, rather than something more serious. We put the character back into **ist** using **unget()**; the caller of **fill_vector()** might have a use for it. The **unget()** function is a shorter version of **putback()** that relies on the stream remembering which character it last produced, so that you don't have to mention it.

If you called **fill_vector()** and want to know what terminated the read, you can test for **fail()** and **eof()**. You could also catch the **runtime_error** exception thrown by **error()**, but it is understood that getting more data from **istream** in the bad() state is unlikely. Most callers won't bother. This implies that in almost all cases the only thing we want to do if we encounter bad() is to throw an exception. To make life easier, we can tell an **istream** to do that for us:

```
// make ist throw if it goes bad
ist.exceptions(ist.exceptions()|ios_base::badbit);
```

The notation may seem odd, but the effect is simply that from that statement onward, **ist** will throw the standard library exception **ios_base::failure** if it goes bad(). We need to execute that **exceptions()** call only once in a program. That'll allow us to simplify all input loops by ignoring bad():

```
void fill_vector(istream& ist, vector<int>& v, char terminator)
        // read integers from ist into v until we reach eof() or terminator
{
        int i = 0;
        while (ist >> i) v.push_back(i);
        if (ist.eof()) return;      // fine: we found the end of file

        // not good() and not bad() and not eof(), ist must be fail()
        ist.clear();      // clear stream state
        char c;
        ist>>c;           // read a character, hopefully terminator

        if (c != terminator) {      // ouch: not the terminator, so we must fail
                ist.unget();              // maybe my caller can use that character
                ist.clear(ios_base::failbit);      // set the state to fail()
        }
}
```

The **ios_base** that appears here and there is the part of an **iostream** that holds constants such as **badbit**, exceptions such as **failure**, and other useful stuff. You refer to them using the :: operator, for example, **ios_base::badbit** (see §10.6 and §B.7.2). We don't plan to go into the iostream library in that much detail; it could take a whole course to explain all of **iostream**s. For example, **iostream**s can handle different character sets, implement different buffering strategies, and also contain facilities for formatting monetary amounts in various languages; we once had a bug report relating to the formatting of Ukrainian currency. You can read up on whatever bits you need to know about if you need to; see *The C++ Programming Language* by Stroustrup, and Langer, *Standard C++ IOStreams and Locales*.

You can test an **ostream** for exactly the same states as an **istream**: good(), fail(), eof(), and bad(). However, for the kinds of programs we write here, errors are much rarer for output than for input, so we don't do it as often. For programs where output devices have a more significant chance of being unavailable, filled, or broken, we would test after each output operation just as we test after each input operation.

10.7 Reading a single value

So, we know how to read a series of values ending with the end of file or a terminator. We'll show more examples as we go along, but let's just have a look at the ever popular idea of repeatedly asking for a value until an acceptable one is entered. This example will allow us to examine several common design choices. We'll discuss these alternatives through a series of alternative solutions to the simple problem of "how to get an acceptable value from the user." We start with an unpleasantly messy obvious "first try" and proceed through a series of improved versions. Our fundamental assumption is that we are dealing with interactive input where a human is typing input and reading the messages from the program. Let's ask for an integer in the range 1 to 10 (inclusive):

```
cout << "Please enter an integer in the range 1 to 10 (inclusive):\n";
int n = 0;
while (cin>>n) {                  // read
      if  (1<=n && n<=10) break;   // check range
      cout << "Sorry "
            << n << " is not in the [1:10] range; please try again\n";

}
```

This is pretty ugly, but it "sort of works." If you don't like using the **break** (§A.6), you can combine the reading and the range checking:

```
cout << "Please enter an integer in the range 1 to 10 (inclusive):\n";
int n = 0;
while (cin>>n && !(1<=n && n<=10))      // read and check range
      cout << "Sorry "
            << n << " is not in the [1:10] range; please try again\n";
```

However, that's just a cosmetic change. Why does it only "sort of work"? It works if the user carefully enters integers. If the user is a poor typist and hits **t** rather than **6** (**t** is just below **6** on most keyboards), the program will leave the loop without changing the value of **n**, so that **n** will have an out-of-range value. We wouldn't call that quality code. A joker (or a diligent tester) might also send an "end of file" from the keyboard (Ctrl+Z on a Windows machine and Ctrl+D on a Unix machine). Again, we'd leave the loop with **n** out of range. In other words, to get a robust read we have to deal with three problems:

1. The user typing an out-of-range value
2. Getting no value (end of file)
3. The user typing something of the wrong type (here, not an integer)

What do we want to do in those three cases? That's often the question when writing a program: what do we really want? Here, for each of those three errors, we have three alternatives:

1. Handle the problem in the code doing the read.
2. Throw an exception to let someone else handle the problem (potentially terminating the program).
3. Ignore the problem.

As it happens, those are three very common alternatives for dealing with an error condition. Thus, this is a good example of the kind of thinking we have to do about errors.

It is tempting to say that the third alternative, ignoring the problem, is always unacceptable, but that would be patronizing. If I'm writing a trivial program for my own use, I can do whatever I like, including forgetting about error checking with potential nasty results. However, for a program that I might want to use for more than a few hours after I wrote it, I would probably be foolish to leave such errors, and if I want to share that program with anyone, I should not leave such holes in the error checking in the code. Please note that we deliberately use the first-person singular here; "we" would be misleading. We do not consider alternative 3 acceptable even when just two people are involved.

The choice between alternatives 1 and 2 is genuine; that is, in a given program there can be good reasons to choose either way. First we note that in most programs there is no local and elegant way to deal with no input from a user sitting at the keyboard: after the input stream is closed, there isn't much point in asking the user to enter a number. We could reopen **cin** (using **cin.clear()**), but the user is unlikely to have closed that stream by accident (how would you hit Ctrl+Z by accident?). If the program wants an integer and finds "end of file," the part of the program trying to read the integer must usually give up and hope that some other part of the program can cope; that is, our code requesting input from the user must throw an exception. This implies that the choice is not between throwing exceptions and handling problems locally, but a choice of which problems (if any) we should handle locally.

10.7.1 Breaking the problem into manageable parts

Let's try handling both an out-of-range input and an input of the wrong type locally:

```
cout << "Please enter an integer in the range 1 to 10 (inclusive):\n";
int n = 0;
```

```
while (true) {
    cin >> n;
    if (cin) {          // we got an integer; now check it
        if (1<=n && n<=10) break;
        cout << "Sorry "
            << n << " is not in the [1:10] range; please try again\n";
    }
    else if (cin.fail()) {      // we found something that wasn't an integer
        cin.clear();            // set the state back to good();
                                // we want to look at the characters
        cout << "Sorry, that was not a number; please try again\n";
        char ch;
        while (cin>>ch && !isdigit(ch)) ;     // throw away non-digits
        if (!cin) error("no input");      // we didn't find a digit: give up
        cin.unget();   // put the digit back, so that we can read the number
    }
    else {
        error("no input");      // eof or bad: give up
    }
}
// if we get here n is in [1:10]
```

This is messy, and rather long-winded. In fact, it is so messy that we could not recommend that people write such code each time they needed an integer from a user. On the other hand, we do need to deal with the potential errors because people do make them, so what can we do? The reason that the code is messy is that code dealing with several different concerns is all mixed together:

- Reading values
- Prompting the user for input
- Writing error messages
- Skipping past "bad" input characters
- Testing the input against a range

The way to make code clearer is often to separate logically distinct concerns into separate functions. For example, we can separate out the code for recovering after seeing a "bad" (i.e., unexpected) character:

```
void skip_to_int()
{
    if (cin.fail()) {          // we found something that wasn't an integer
        cin.clear();           // we'd like to look at the characters
        char ch;
```

```
        while (cin>>ch){    // throw away non-digits
            if (isdigit(ch)) {
                cin.unget();   // put the digit back,
                               // so that we can read the number
                return;
            }
        }
    }
    error("no input");     // eof or bad: give up
}
```

Given the **skip_to_int()** "utility function," we can write

```
cout << "Please enter an integer in the range 1 to 10 (inclusive):\n";
int n = 0;
while (true) {
    if (cin>>n) {       // we got an integer; now check it
        if (1<=n && n<=10) break;
        cout << "Sorry " << n
            << " is not in the [1:10] range; please try again\n";
    }
    else {
        cout << "Sorry, that was not a number; please try again\n";
        skip_to_int();
    }
}
// if we get here n is in [1:10]
```

This code is better, but it is still too long and too messy to use many times in a program. We'd never get it consistently right, except after (too) much testing.

What operation would we really like to have? One plausible answer is "a function that reads an **int**, any **int**, and another that reads an **int** of a given range":

```
int get_int();                 // read an int from cin
int get_int(int low, int high);   // read an int in [low:high] from cin
```

If we had those, we would at least be able to use them simply and correctly. They are not that hard to write:

```
int get_int()
{
    int n = 0;
    while (true) {
```

```
        if (cin >> n) return n;
        cout << "Sorry, that was not a number; please try again\n";
        skip_to_int();
    }
}
```

Basically, **get_int()** stubbornly keeps reading until it finds some digits that it can interpret as an integer. If we want to get out of **get_int()**, we must supply an integer or end of file (and end of file will cause **get_int()** to throw an exception).

Using that general **get_int()**, we can write the range-checking **get_int()**:

```
int get_int(int low, int high)
{
    cout << "Please enter an integer in the range "
        << low << " to " << high << " (inclusive):\n";

    while (true) {
        int n = get_int();
        if (low<=n && n<=high) return n;
        cout << "Sorry "
            << n << " is not in the [" << low << ':' << high
            << "] range; please try again\n";
    }
}
```

This **get_int()** is as stubborn as the other. It keeps getting **int**s from the non-range **get_int()** until the **int** it gets is in the expected range.

We can now reliably read integers like this:

```
int n = get_int(1,10);
cout << "n: " << n << endl;

int m = get_int(2,300);
cout << "m: " << m << endl;
```

Don't forget to catch exceptions somewhere, though, if you want decent error messages for the (probably rare) case when **get_int()** really couldn't read a number for us.

10.7.2 Separating dialog from function

The **get_int()** functions still mix up reading with writing messages to the user. That's probably good enough for a simple program, but in a large program we might want to vary the messages written to the user. We might want to call **get_int()** like this:

```
int strength = get_int(1,10, "enter strength", "Not in range, try again");
cout << "strength: " << strength << endl;

int altitude = get_int(0,50000,
                "Please enter altitude in feet",
                "Not in range, please try again");
cout << "altitude: " << altitude << "f above sea level\n";
```

We could implement that like this:

```
int get_int(int low, int high, const string& greeting, const string& sorry)
{
        cout << greeting << ": [" << low << ':' << high << "]\n";

        while (true) {
                int n = get_int();
                if (low<=n && n<=high) return n;
                cout << sorry << ": [" << low << ':' << high << "]\n";
        }
}
```

It is hard to compose arbitrary messages, so we "stylized" the messages. That's often acceptable, and composing really flexible messages, such as are needed to support many natural languages (e.g., Arabic, Bengali, Chinese, Danish, English, and French), is not a task for a novice.

Note that our solution is still incomplete: the **get_int()** without a range still "blabbers." The deeper point here is that "utility functions" that we use in many parts of a program shouldn't have messages "hardwired" into them. Further, library functions that are meant for use in many programs shouldn't write to the user at all – after all, the library writer may not even know that the program in which the library runs is used on a machine with a human watching. That's one reason that our **error()** function doesn't just write an error message (§5.6.3); in general, we wouldn't know where to write.

10.8 User-defined output operators

Defining the output operator, <<, for a given type is typically trivial. The main design problem is that different people might prefer the output to look different, so it is hard to agree on a single format. However, even if no single output format is good enough for all uses, it is often a good idea to define << for a user-defined type. That way, we can at least trivially write out objects of the type during debugging and early development. Later, we might provide a more sophisticated << that allows a user to provide formatting information. Also, if we want output that looks different from what a << provides, we can simply bypass the << and write out the individual parts of the user-defined type the way we happen to like them in our application.

Here is a simple output operator for **Date** from §9.8 that simply prints the year, month, and day comma-separated in parentheses:

```
ostream& operator<<(ostream& os, const Date& d)
{
        return os << '(' << d.year()
                << ',' << d.month()
                << ',' << d.day() << ')';
}
```

This will print August 30, 2004, as **(2004,8,30)**. This simple list-of-elements representation is what we tend to use for types with a few members unless we have a better idea or more specific needs.

In §9.6, we mention that a user-defined operator is handled by calling its function. Here we can see an example of how that's done. Given the definition of << for **Date**, the meaning of

```
cout << d1;
```

where **d1** is a **Date** is the call

```
operator<<(cout,d1);
```

Note how **operator<<()** takes an **ostream&** as its first argument and returns it again as its return value. That's the way the output stream is passed along so that you can "chain" output operations. For example, we could output two dates like this:

```
cout << d1 << d2;
```

This will be handled by first resolving the first << and after that the second <<:

```
cout << d1 << d2;    // means operator<<(cout,d1) << d2;
                     // means operator<<(operator<<(cout,d1),d2);
```

That is, first output **d1** to **cout** and then output **d2** to the output stream that is the result of the first output operation. In fact, we can use any of those three variants to write out **d1** and **d2**. We know which one is easier to read, though.

10.9 User-defined input operators

Defining the input operator, **>>**, for a given type and input format is basically an exercise in error handling. It can therefore be quite tricky.

Here is a simple input operator for the **Date** from §9.8 that will read dates as written by the operator **<<** defined above:

```
istream& operator>>(istream& is, Date& dd)
{
      int y, m, d;
      char ch1, ch2, ch3, ch4;
      is >> ch1 >> y >> ch2 >> m >> ch3 >> d >> ch4;
      if (!is) return is;
      if (ch1!='(' || ch2!=',' || ch3!=',' || ch4!=')') {   // oops: format error
            is.clear(ios_base::failbit);
            return is;
      }
      dd = Date(y,Date::Month(m),d);     // update dd
      return is;
}
```

This **>>** will read items like **(2004,8,20)** and try to make a **Date** out of those three integers. As ever, input is harder to deal with than output. There is simply more that can – and often does – go wrong with input than with output.

If this **>>** doesn't find something in the (*integer* , *integer* , *integer*) format, it will leave the stream in a not-good state (**fail**, **eof**, or **bad**) and leave the target **Date** unchanged. The **clear()** member function is used to set the state of the **istream**. Obviously, **ios_base::failbit** puts the stream into the **fail()** state. Leaving the target **Date** unchanged in case of a failure to read is the ideal; it tends to lead to cleaner code. The ideal is for an **operator>>()** not to consume (throw away) any characters that it didn't use, but that's too difficult in this case: we might have read lots of characters before we caught a format error. As an example, consider **(2004, 8, 30}**. Only when we see the final **}** do we know that we have a format error on our hands and we cannot in general rely on putting back many characters. One character **unget()** is all that's universally guaranteed. If this **operator>>()** reads an invalid **Date**, such as **(2004,8,32)**, **Date**'s constructor will throw an exception, which will get us out of this **operator>>()**.

10.10 A standard input loop

In §10.5, we saw how we could read and write files. However, that was before we looked more carefully at errors (§10.6), so the input loop simply assumed that we could read a file from its beginning until end of file. That can be a reasonable assumption, because we often apply separate checks to ensure that a file is valid. However, we often want to check our reads as we go along. Here is a general strategy, assuming that **ist** is an **istream**:

```
My_type var;
while (ist>>var) {        // read until end of file
        // maybe check that var is valid
        // do something with var
}
// we can rarely recover from bad; don't try unless you really have to:
if (ist.bad()) error("bad input stream");
if (ist.fail()) {
        // was it an acceptable terminator?
}
// carry on: we found end of file
```

That is, we read a sequence of values into variables and when we can't read any more values, we check the stream state to see why. As in §10.6, we can improve this a bit by letting the **istream** throw an **exception** of type **failure** if it goes bad. That saves us the bother of checking for it all the time:

```
// somewhere: make ist throw an exception if it goes bad:
ist.exceptions(ist.exceptions()|ios_base::badbit);
```

We could also decide to designate a character as a terminator:

```
My_type var;
while (ist>>var) {        // read until end of file
        // maybe check that var is valid
        // do something with var
}
if (ist.fail()) {        // use '|' as terminator and/or separator
        ist.clear();
        char ch;
        if (!(ist>>ch && ch=='|')) error("bad termination of input");
}
// carry on: we found end of file or a terminator
```

If we don't want to accept a terminator − that is, to accept only end of file as the end; we simply delete the test before the call of **error()**. However, terminators are very useful when you read files with nested constructs, such as a file of monthly readings containing daily readings, containing hourly readings, etc., so we'll keep considering the possibility of a terminating character.

Unfortunately, that code is still a bit messy. In particular, it is tedious to repeat the terminator test if we read a lot of files. We could write a function to deal with that:

```
// somewhere: make ist throw if it goes bad:
ist.exceptions(ist.exceptions()|ios_base::badbit);

void end_of_loop(istream& ist, char term, const string& message)
{
    if (ist.fail()) {       // use term as terminator and/or separator
        ist.clear();
        char ch;
        if (ist>>ch && ch==term) return;     // all is fine
        error(message);
    }
}
```

This reduces the input loop to

```
My_type var;
while (ist>>var) {        // read until end of file
    // maybe check that var is valid

    // do something with var
}
end_of_loop(ist,'|',"bad termination of file");     // test if we can continue

// carry on: we found end of file or a terminator
```

The **end_of_loop()** does nothing unless the stream is in the **fail()** state. We consider that simple enough and general enough for many purposes.

10.11 Reading a structured file

Let's try to use this "standard loop" for a concrete example. As usual, we'll use the example to illustrate widely applicable design and programming techniques. Assume that you have a file of temperature readings that has been structured like this:

- A file holds years (of months of readings).
    - A year starts with { **year** followed by an integer giving the year, such as **1900**, and ends with }.

- A year holds months (of days of readings).
  - A month starts with { **month** followed by a three-letter month name, such as **jan**, and ends with }.
- A reading holds a time and a temperature.
  - A reading starts with a (followed by day of the month, hour of the day, and temperature and ends with a).

For example:

```
{ year 1990 }
{year 1991 { month jun }}
{ year 1992 { month jan ( 1 0 61.5) } { month feb (1 1 64) (2 2 65.2) } }
{year 2000
        { month feb (1 1 68 ) (2 3 66.66 ) ( 1 0 67.2)}
        {month dec (15 15 −9.2 ) (15 14 −8.8) (14 0 −2) }

}
```

This format is somewhat peculiar. File formats often are. There is a move toward more regular and hierarchically structured files (such as HTML and XML files) in the industry, but the reality is still that we can rarely control the input format offered by the files we need to read. The files are the way they are, and we just have to read them. If a format is too awful or files contain too many errors, we can write a format conversion program to produce a format that suits our main program better. On the other hand, we can typically choose the in-memory representation of data to suit our needs, and we can often pick output formats to suit needs and tastes.

So, let's assume that we have been given the temperature reading format above and have to live with it. Fortunately, it has self-identifying components, such as years and months (a bit like HTML or XML). On the other hand, the format of individual readings is somewhat unhelpful. For example, there is no information that could help us if someone flipped a day-of-the-month value with an hour of day or if someone produced a file with temperatures in Celsius and the program expected them in Fahrenheit or vice versa. We just have to cope.

10.11.1 In-memory representation

How should we represent this data in memory? The obvious first choice is three classes, **Year**, **Month**, and **Reading**, to exactly match the input. **Year** and **Month** are obviously useful when manipulating the data; we want to compare temperatures of different years, calculate monthly averages, compare different months of a year, compare the same month of different years, match up temperature readings with sunshine records and humidity readings, etc. Basically, **Year** and **Month** match the way we think about temperatures and weather in general: **Month** holds a month's worth of information and **Year** holds a year's worth of information. But what about **Reading**? That's a low-level notion matching some piece of hardware (a sensor). The data of a **Reading** (day of month, hour of day, temperature) is "odd" and makes sense only within a **Month**. It is also unstructured: we have no promise that readings come in day-of-the-month or hour-of-the-day order. Basically, whenever we want to do anything of interest with the readings we have to sort them.

For representing the temperature data in memory, we make these assumptions:

- If we have any readings for a month, then we tend to have lots of readings for that month.
- If we have any readings for a day, then we tend to have lots of readings for that day.

When that's the case, it makes sense to represent a **Year** as a vector of 12 **Month**s, a **Month** as a vector of about 30 **Day**s, and a **Day** as 24 temperatures (one per hour). That's simple and easy to manipulate for a wide variety of uses. So, **Day**, **Month**, and **Year** are simple data structures, each with a constructor. Since we plan to create **Month**s and **Day**s as part of a **Year** before we know what temperature readings we have, we need to have a notion of "not a reading" for an hour of a day for which we haven't (yet) read data.

  const int not_a_reading = –7777; *// less than absolute zero*

Similarly, we noticed that we often had a month without data, so we introduced the notion "not a month" to represent that directly, rather than having to search through all the days to be sure that no data was lurking somewhere:

  const int not_a_month = –1;

The three key classes then become

```
struct Day {
    vector<double> hour;
    Day();       // initialize hours to "not a reading"
};

Day::Day()
    : hour(24)
{
    for (int i = 0; i<hour.size(); ++i) hour[i]=not_a_reading;
}
```

```
struct Month {        // a month of temperature readings
     int month;            // [0:11] January is 0
     vector<Day> day;  // [1:31] one vector of readings per day
     Month()               // at most 31 days in a month (day[0] wasted)
          :month(not_a_month), day(32) { }
};
```

```
struct Year {   // a year of temperature readings, organized by month
     int year;                      // positive == A.D.
     vector<Month> month;  // [0:11] January is 0
     Year() :month(12) { }      // 12 months in a year
};
```

Each class is basically a simple **vector** of "parts," and **Month** and **Year** have an identifying member **month** and **year**, respectively.

There are several "magic constants" here (for example, **24**, **32**, and **12**). We try to avoid such literal constants in code. These are pretty fundamental (the number of months in a year rarely changes) and will not be used in the rest of the code. However, we left them in the code primarily so that we could remind you of the problem with "magic constants"; symbolic constants are almost always preferable (§7.6.1). Using **32** for the number of days in a month definitely requires explanation; **32** is obviously "magic" here.

10.11.2 Reading structured values

The **Reading** class will be used only for reading input and is even simpler:

```
struct Reading {
     int day;
     int hour;
     double temperature;
};
```

```
istream& operator>>(istream& is, Reading& r)
// read a temperature reading from is into r
// format: ( 3 4 9.7 )
// check format, but don't bother with data validity
{
     char ch1;
     if (is>>ch1 && ch1!='(') {      // could it be a Reading?
          is.unget();
```

```
                is.clear(ios_base::failbit);
                return is;
        }

        char ch2;
        int d;
        int h;
        double t;
        is >> d >> h >> t >> ch2;
        if (!is || ch2!=')') error("bad reading");       // messed-up reading
        r.day = d;
        r.hour = h;
        r.temperature = t;
        return is;
}
```

Basically, we check if the format begins plausibly, and if it doesn't we set the file state to **fail()** and return. This allows us to try to read the information in some other way. On the other hand, if we find the format wrong after having read some data so that there is no real chance of recovering, we bail out with **error()**.

The **Month** input operation is much the same, except that it has to read an arbitrary number of **Readings** rather than a fixed set of values (as **Reading**'s **>>** did):

```
istream& operator>>(istream& is, Month& m)
// read a month from is into m
// format: { month feb . . . }
{
        char ch = 0;
        if (is >> ch && ch!='{') {
                is.unget();
                is.clear(ios_base::failbit);   // we failed to read a Month
                return is;
        }

        string month_marker;
        string mm;
        is >> month_marker >> mm;
        if (!is || month_marker!="month") error("bad start of month");
        m.month = month_to_int(mm);

        Reading r;
```

```
        int duplicates = 0;
        int invalids = 0;
        while (is >> r) {
                if (is_valid(r)) {
                        if (m.day[r.day].hour[r.hour] != not_a_reading)
                                ++duplicates;
                        m.day[r.day].hour[r.hour] = r.temperature;
                }
                else
                        ++invalids;
        }
        if (invalids) error("invalid readings in month",invalids);
        if (duplicates) error("duplicate readings in month", duplicates);
        end_of_loop(is,'}',"bad end of month");
        return is;
}
```

We'll get back to **month_to_int()** later; it converts the symbolic notation for a month, such as **jun**, to a number in the [0:11] range. Note the use of **end_of_loop()** from §10.10 to check for the terminator. We keep count of invalid and duplicate **Readings**; someone might be interested.

Month's >> does a quick check that a **Reading** is plausible before storing it:

```
const int implausible_min = −200;
const int implausible_max = 200;

bool is_valid(const Reading& r)
// a rough test
{
        if (r.day<1 || 31<r.day) return false;
        if (r.hour<0 || 23<r.hour) return false;
        if (r.temperature<implausible_min|| implausible_max<r.temperature)
                return false;
        return true;
}
```

Finally, we can read **Years**. **Year**'s >> is similar to **Month**'s >>:

```
istream& operator>>(istream& is, Year& y)
// read a year from is into y
// format: { year 1972 . . . }
{
```

```
        char ch;
        is >> ch;
        if (ch!='{') {
                is.unget();
                is.clear(ios::failbit);
                return is;
        }

        string year_marker;
        int yy;
        is >> year_marker >> yy;
        if (!is || year_marker!="year") error("bad start of year");
        y.year = yy;

        while(true) {
                Month m;      // get a clean m each time around
                if(!(is >> m)) break;
                y.month[m.month] = m;
        }

        end_of_loop(is,'}',"bad end of year");
        return is;
}
```

We would have preferred "boringly similar" to just "similar," but there is a significant difference. Have a look at the read loop. Did you expect something like the following?

```
Month m;
while (is >> m)
        y.month[m.month] = m;
```

You probably should have, because that's the way we have written all the read loops so far. That's actually what we first wrote, and it's wrong. The problem is that **operator>>(istream& is, Month& m)** doesn't assign a brand-new value to **m**; it simply adds data from **Readings** to **m**. Thus, the repeated **is>>m** would have kept adding to our one and only **m**. Oops! Each new month would have gotten all the readings from all previous months of that year. We need a brand-new, clean **Month** to read into each time we do **is>>m**. The easiest way to do that was to put the definition of **m** inside the loop so that it would be initialized each time around. The alternatives would have been for **operator>>(istream& is, Month& m)** to assign an empty month to **m** before reading into it, or for the loop to do that:

```
Month m;
while (is >> m) {
    y.month[m.month] = m;
    m = Month();    // "reinitialize" m
}
```

Let's try to use it:

```
// open an input file:
cout << "Please enter input file name\n";
string name;
cin >> name;
ifstream ifs(name.c_str());
if (!ifs) error("can't open input file",name);

ifs.exceptions(ifs.exceptions()|ios_base::badbit);     // throw for bad()

// open an output file:
cout << "Please enter output file name\n";
cin >> name;
ofstream ofs(name.c_str());
if (!ofs) error("can't open output file",name);

// read an arbitrary number of years:
vector<Year> ys;
while(true) {
    Year y;          // get a freshly initialized Year each time around
    if (!(ifs>>y)) break;
    ys.push_back(y);
}
cout << "read " << ys.size() << " years of readings\n";

for (int i = 0; i<ys.size(); ++i) print_year(ofs,ys[i]);
```

We leave **print_year()** as an exercise.

10.11.3 Changing representations

To get **Month**'s **>>** to work, we need to provide a way of reading symbolic representations of the month. For symmetry, we'll provide a matching write using a symbolic representation. The tedious way would be to write an **if**-statement convert:

```
if (s=="jan")
    m = 1;
```

```
    else if (s=="feb")
        m = 2;
...
```

This is not just tedious; it also builds the names of the months into the code. It would be better to have those in a table somewhere so that the main program could stay unchanged even if we had to change the symbolic representation. We decided to represent the input representation as a **vector<string>** plus an initialization function and a lookup function:

```
vector<string> month_input_tbl;    // month_input_tbl[0]=="jan"

void init_input_tbl(vector<string>& tbl)
// initialize vector of input representations
{
    tbl.push_back("jan");
    tbl.push_back("feb");
    tbl.push_back("mar");
    tbl.push_back("apr");
    tbl.push_back("may");
    tbl.push_back("jun");
    tbl.push_back("jul");
    tbl.push_back("aug");
    tbl.push_back("sep");
    tbl.push_back("oct");
    tbl.push_back("nov");
    tbl.push_back("dec");
}

int month_to_int(string s)
// is s the name of a month? If so return its index [0:11] otherwise –1
{
    for (int i=0; i<12; ++i) if (month_input_tbl[i]==s) return i;
    return –1;
}
```

In case you wonder: the C++ standard library does provide a simpler way to do this. See §21.6.1 for a **map<string,int>**.

When we want to produce output, we have the opposite problem. We have an **int** representing a month and would like a symbolic representation to be printed. Our solution is fundamentally similar, but instead of using a table to go from **string** to **int**, we use one to go from **int** to **string**:

```
vector<string> month_print_tbl;    // month_print_tbl[0]=="January"
```

```
void init_print_tbl(vector<string>& tbl)
// initialize vector of output representations
{
        tbl.push_back("January");
        tbl.push_back("February");
        tbl.push_back("March");
        tbl.push_back("April");
        tbl.push_back("May");
        tbl.push_back("June");
        tbl.push_back("July");
        tbl.push_back("August");
        tbl.push_back("September");
        tbl.push_back("October");
        tbl.push_back("November");
        tbl.push_back("December");
}

string int_to_month(int i)
// months [0:11]
{
        if (i<0 || 12<=i) error("bad month index");
        return month_print_tbl[i];
}
```

For this to work, we need to call the initialization functions somewhere, such as at the beginning of **main()**:

```
// first initialize representation tables:
init_print_tbl(month_print_tbl);
init_input_tbl(month_input_tbl);
```

So, did you actually read all of that code and the explanations? Or did your eyes glaze over and skip to the end? Remember that the easiest way of learning to write good code is to read a lot of code. Believe it or not, the techniques we used for this example are simple, but not trivial to discover without help. Reading data is fundamental. Writing loops correctly (initializing every variable used correctly) is fundamental. Converting between representations is fundamental. That is, you *will* learn to do such things. The only questions are whether you'll learn to do them well and whether you learn the basic techniques before losing too much sleep.

Drill

1. Start a program to work with points, discussed in §10.4. Begin by defining the data type **Point** that has two coordinate members **x** and **y**.
2. Using the code and discussion in §10.4, prompt the user to input seven (*x,y*) pairs. As the data is entered, store it in a vector of **Points** called **original_points**.
3. Print the data in **original_points** to see what it looks like.
4. Open an **ofstream** and output each point to a file named **mydata.txt**. On Windows, we suggest the **.txt** suffix to make it easier to look at the data with an ordinary text editor (such as WordPad).
5. Close the **ofstream** and then open an **ifstream** for **mydata.txt**. Read the data from **mydata.txt** and store it in a new **vector** called **processed_points**.
6. Print the data elements from both **vectors**.
7. Compare the two **vectors** and print **Something's wrong!** if the number of elements or the values of elements differ.

Review

1. When dealing with input and output, how is the variety of devices dealt with in most modern computers?
2. What, fundamentally, does an **istream** do?
3. What, fundamentally, does an **ostream** do?
4. What, fundamentally, is a file?
5. What is a file format?
6. Name four different types of devices that can require I/O for a program.
7. What are the four steps for reading a file?
8. What are the four steps for writing a file?
9. Name and define the four stream states.
10. Discuss how the following input problems can be resolved:
    a. The user typing an out-of-range value
    b. Getting no value (end of file)
    c. The user typing something of the wrong type
11. In what way is input usually harder than output?
12. In what way is output usually harder than input?
13. Why do we (often) want to separate input and output from computation?
14. What are the two most common uses of the **istream** member function **clear()**?
15. What are the usual function declarations for **<<** and **>>** for a user-defined type **X**?

Terms

bad()	good()	ostream
buffer	ifstream	output device
clear()	input device	output operator
close()	input operator	stream state
device driver	iostream	structured file
eof()	istream	terminator
fail()	ofstream	unget()
file	open()	

Exercises

1. Write a program that produces the sum of all the numbers in a file of whitespace-separated integers.
2. Write a program that creates a file of data in the form of the temperature **Reading** type defined in §10.5. Fill the file with at least 50 temperature readings. Call this program **store_temps.cpp** and the file it creates **raw_temps.txt**.
3. Write a program that reads the data from **raw_temps.txt** created in exercise 2 into a vector and then calculates the mean and median temperatures in your data set. Call this program **temp_stats.cpp**.
4. Modify the **store_temps.cpp** program from exercise 2 to include a temperature suffix **c** for Celsius or **f** for Fahrenheit temperatures. Then modify the **temp_stats.cpp** program to test each temperature, converting the Celsius readings to Fahrenheit before putting them into the vector.
5. Write the function **print_year()** mentioned in §10.11.2.
6. Define a **Roman_int** class for holding Roman numerals (as **ints**) with **<<** and **>>**. Provide **Roman_int** with an **as_int()** member that returns the **int** value, so that if **r** is a **Roman_int**, we can write **cout << "Roman" << r << " equals " << r.as_int() << '\n';**.
7. Make a version of the calculator from Chapter 7 that accepts Roman numerals rather than the usual Arabic ones, for example, **XXI + CIV == CXXV**.
8. Write a program that accepts two file names and produces a new file that is the contents of the first file followed by the contents of the second; that is, the program concatenates the two files.
9. Write a program that takes two files containing sorted whitespace-separated words and merges them, preserving order.
10. Add a command **from x** to the calculator from Chapter 7 that makes it take input from a file **x**. Add a command **to y** to the calculator that makes it write its output (both standard output and error output) to file **y**. Write a collection of test cases based on ideas from §7.3 and use that to test the calculator. Discuss how you would use these commands for testing.

11. Write a program that produces the sum of all the whitespace-separated integers in a text file. For example, "**bears: 17 elephants 9 end**" should output **26**.
12. Write a program that given a file name and a word outputs each line that contains that word together with the line number. Hint: **getline()**.

Postscript

Much of computing involves moving lots of data from one place to another, for example, copying text from a file to a screen or moving music from a computer onto an MP3 player. Often, some transformation of the data is needed on the way. The iostream library is a way of handling many such tasks where the data can be seen as a sequence (a stream) of values. Input and output can be a surprisingly large part of common programming tasks. This is partly because we (or our programs) need a lot of data and partly because the point where data enters a system is a place where lots of errors can happen. So, we must try to keep our I/O simple and try to minimize the chances that bad data "slips through" into our system.

11

Customizing
Input and Output

"Keep it simple:
as simple as possible,
but no simpler."

—Albert Einstein

In this chapter, we concentrate on how to adapt the general iostream framework presented in Chapter 10 to specific needs and tastes. This involves a lot of messy details dictated by human sensibilities to what they read and also practical constraints on the uses of files. The final example shows the design of an input stream for which you can specify the set of separators.

11.1 Regularity and irregularity

The iostream library – the input/output part of the ISO C++ standard library – provides a unified and extensible framework for input and output of text. By "text" we mean just about anything that can be represented as a sequence of characters. Thus, when we talk about input and output we can consider the integer **1234** as text because we can write it using the four characters **1**, **2**, **3**, and **4**.

So far, we have treated all input sources as equivalent. Sometimes, that's not enough. For example, files differ from other input sources (such as communications connections) in that we can address individual bytes. Similarly, we worked on the assumption that the type of an object completely determined the layout of its input and output. That's not quite right and wouldn't be sufficient. For example, we often want to specify the number of digits used to represent a floating-point number on output (its precision). This chapter presents a number of ways in which we can tailor input and output to our needs.

As programmers, we prefer regularity; treating all in-memory objects uniformly, treating all input sources equivalently, and imposing a single standard on the way to represent objects entering and exiting the system give the cleanest, simplest, most maintainable, and often the most efficient code. However, our programs exist to serve humans, and humans have strong preferences. Thus, as programmers we must strive for a balance between program complexity and accommodation of users' personal tastes.

11.2 Output formatting

People care a lot about apparently minor details of the output they have to read. For example, to a physicist **1.25** (rounded to two digits after the dot) can be very different from **1.24670477**, and to an accountant **(1.25)** can be legally different from (**1.2467**) and totally different from **1.25** (in financial documents, parentheses are sometimes used to indicate losses, that is, negative values). As programmers, we aim at making our output as clear and as close as possible to the expectations of the "consumers" of our program. Output streams (**ostreams**) provide a variety of ways for formatting the output of built-in types. For user-defined types, it is up to the programmer to define suitable << operations.

There seems to be an infinite number of details, refinements, and options for output and quite a few for input. Examples are the character used for the decimal point (usually dot or comma), the way to output monetary values, a way to represent true as the word **true** (or **vrai** or **sandt**) rather than the number **1** when output, ways to deal with non-ASCII character sets (such as Unicode), and a way to limit the number of characters read into a string. These facilities tend to be uninteresting until you need them, so we'll leave their description to manuals and specialized works such as Langer, *Standard C++ IOStreams and Locales*; Chapter 21 and Appendix D of *The C++ Programming Language* by Stroustrup; and §22 and §27 of the ISO C++ standard. Here we'll present the most frequently useful features and a few general concepts.

11.2.1 Integer output

Integer values can be output as octal (the base-8 number system), decimal (our usual base-10 number system), and hexadecimal (the base-16 number system). If you don't know about these systems, read §A.1.2.1 before proceeding here. Most output uses decimal. Hexadecimal is popular for outputting hardware-related information. The reason is that a hexadecimal digit exactly represents a 4-bit value. Thus, two hexadecimal digits can be used to present the value of an 8-bit byte, four hexadecimal digits give the value of 2 bytes (that's often a half word), and eight hexadecimal digits can present the value of 4 bytes (that's often the size of a word or a register). When C++'s ancestor C was first designed (in the 1970s), octal was popular for representing bit patterns, but now it's rarely used.

We can specify the output (decimal) value **1234** to be decimal, hexadecimal (often called "hex"), and octal:

```
cout << 1234 << "\t(decimal)\n"
     << hex << 1234 << "\t(hexadecimal)\n"
     << oct << 1234 << "\t(octal)\n";
```

The '\t' character is "tab" (short for "tabulation character"). This prints

```
1234    (decimal)
4d2     (hexadecimal)
2322    (octal)
```

The notations **<< hex** and **<< oct** do not output values. Instead, **<< hex** informs the stream that any further integer values should be displayed in hexadecimal and **<< oct** informs the stream that any further integer values should be displayed in octal. For example:

```
cout << 1234 << '\t' << hex << 1234 << '\t' << oct << 1234 << '\n';
cout << 1234 << '\n';        // the octal base is still in effect
```

This produces

```
1234    4d2    2322
2322                         // integers will continue to show as octal until changed
```

Note that the last output is octal; that is, **oct**, **hex**, and **dec** (for decimal) persist ("stick," "are sticky") – they apply to every integer value output until we tell the stream otherwise. Terms such as **hex** and **oct** that are used to change the behavior of a stream are called *manipulators*.

TRY THIS

> Output your birth year in decimal, hexadecimal, and octal form. Label each value. Line up your output in columns using the tab character. Now output your age.

Seeing values of a base different from 10 can often be confusing. For example, unless we tell you otherwise, you'll assume that **11** represents the (decimal) number 11, rather than 9 (**11** in octal) or 17 (**11** in hexadecimal). To alleviate such problems, we can ask the **ostream** to show the base of each integer printed. For example:

```
cout << 1234 << '\t' << hex << 1234 << '\t' << oct << 1234 << '\n';
cout << showbase << dec;    // show bases
cout << 1234 << '\t' << hex << 1234 << '\t' << oct << 1234 << '\n';
```

This prints

```
1234    4d2    2322
1234    0x4d2  02322
```

So, decimal numbers have no prefix, octal numbers have the prefix **0**, and hexadecimal values have the prefix **0x** (or **0X**). This is exactly the notation for integer literals in C++ source code. For example:

This prints (note the rounding)

```
1234.57      1234.567890   1.234568e+003
1234.6 1234.56789    1.23457e+003
1234.5679    1234.56789000       1.23456789e+003
```

The precision is defined as:

Floating-point precision	
general	precision is the total number of digits
scientific	precision is the number of digits after the decimal point
fixed	precision is the number of digits after the decimal point

Use the default (**general** format with precision 6) unless there is a reason not to. The usual reason not to is "Because we need greater accuracy of the output."

11.2.5 Fields

Using scientific and fixed formats, a programmer can control exactly how much space a value takes up on output. That's clearly useful for printing tables, etc. The equivalent mechanism for integer values is called *fields*. You can specify exactly how many character positions an integer value or string value will occupy using the "set field width" manipulator **setw()**. For example:

```
cout << 123456                          // no field used
     <<'|'<< setw(4) << 123456 << '|'   // 123456 doesn't fit in a 4-char field
     << setw(8) << 123456 << '|'        // set field width to 8
     << 123456 << "\n";                 // field sizes don't stick
```

This prints

```
123456|123456|  123456|123456|
```

Note first the two spaces before the third occurrence of **123456**. That's what we would expect for a six-digit number in an eight-character field. However, **123456** did not get truncated to fit into to a four-character field. Why not? **|1234|** or **|3456|** might be considered plausible outputs for the four-character field. However, that would have completely changed the value printed without any warning to the poor reader that something had gone wrong. The **ostream** doesn't do that; instead it breaks the output format. Bad formatting is almost always preferable to "bad output data." In the most common uses of fields (such as printing out a table), the "overflow" is visually very noticeable, so that it can be corrected.

Fields can also be used for floating-point numbers and strings. For example:

```
cout << 12345 <<'|'<< setw(4) << 12345 << '|'
    << setw(8) << 12345 << '|' << 12345 << "\n";
cout << 1234.5 <<'|'<< setw(4) << 1234.5 << '|'
    << setw(8) << 1234.5 << '|' << 1234.5 << "\n";
cout << "asdfg" <<'|'<< setw(4) << "asdfg" << '|'
    << setw(8) << "asdfg" << '|' << "asdfg" << "\n";
```

This prints

```
12345|12345|  12345|12345|
1234.5|1234.5|  1234.5|1234.5|
asdfg|asdfg|  asdfg|asdfg|
```

Note that the field width "doesn't stick." In all three cases, the first and the last values are printed in the default "as many characters as it takes" format. In other words, unless you set the field width immediately before an output operation, the notion of "field" is not used.

TRY THIS

Make a simple table including the last name, first name, telephone number, and email address for yourself and at least five of your friends. Experiment with different field widths until you are satisfied that the table is well presented.

11.3 File opening and positioning

As seen from C++, a file is an abstraction of what the operating system provides. As described in §10.3, a file is simply a sequence of bytes numbered from 0 upward:

The question is how we access those bytes. Using **iostreams**, this is largely determined when we open a file and associate a stream with it. The properties of a stream determine what operations we can perform after opening the file, and their meaning. The simplest example of this is that if we open an **istream** for a file, we can read from the file, whereas if we open a file with an **ostream**, we can write to it.

11.3.1 File open modes

You can open a file in one of several modes. By default, an **ifstream** opens its file for reading and an **ofstream** opens its file for writing. That takes care of most common needs. However, you can choose between several alternatives:

Filestream open modes	
ios_base::app	append (i.e., add to the end of the file)
ios_base::ate	"at end" (open and seek to end)
ios_base::binary	binary mode — beware of system-specific behavior
ios_base::in	for reading
ios_base::out	for writing
ios_base::trunc	truncate file to 0-length

A file mode is optionally specified after the name of the file. For example:

```
ofstream of1(name1);     // defaults to ios_base::out
ifstream if1(name2);     // defaults to ios_base::in

ofstream ofs(name, ios_base::app);              // ofstreams are by default out
fstream fs("myfile", ios_base::in|ios_base::out);     // both in and out
```

The | in that last example is the "bitwise or" operator (§A.5.5) that can be used to combine modes as shown. The **app** option is popular for writing log files where you always add to the end.

In each case, the exact effect of opening a file may depend on the operating system, and if an operating system cannot honor a request to open a file in a certain way, the result will be a stream that is not in the **good()** state:

```
if (!fs)   // oops: we couldn't open that file that way
```

The most common reason for a failure to open a file for reading is that the file doesn't exist (at least not with the name we used):

```
ifstream ifs("redungs");
if (!ifs)      // error: can't open "readings" for reading
```

In this case, we guess that a spelling error might be the problem.

Note that typically, an operating system will create a new file if you try to open a nonexistent file for output, but (fortunately) not if you try to open a non-existent file for input:

```
ofstream ofs("no-such-file");           // create new file called no-such-file
ofstream ifs("no-file-of-this-name");   // error: ifs will be not be good()
```

11.3.2 Binary files

In memory, we can represent the number 123 as an integer value or as a string value. For example:

```
int n = 123;
string s = "123";
```

In the first case, **123** is stored as a (binary) number in an amount of memory that is the same as for all other **int**s (4 bytes, that is, 32 bits, on a PC). Had we chosen the value **12345** instead, the same 4 bytes would have been used. In the second case, **123** is stored as a string of three characters. Had we chosen the string value **"12345"** it would have used five characters (plus the fixed overhead for managing a **string**). We could illustrate this like this (using the ordinary decimal and character representation, rather than the binary representation actually used within the computer):

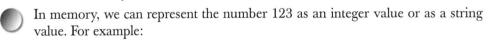

| 123 as characters: | 1 | 2 | 3 | ? | ? | ? | ? | ? |

| 12345 as characters: | 1 | 2 | 3 | 4 | 5 | ? | ? | ? |

| 123 as binary: | 123 | |

| 12345 as binary: | 12345 | |

When we use a character representation, we must use some character to represent the end of a number in memory, just as we do on paper: 123456 is one number and 123 456 are two numbers. On "paper," we use the space character to represent the end of the number. In memory, we could do the same:

| 123456 as characters: | 1 | 2 | 3 | 4 | 5 | 6 | | ? |

| 123 456 as characters: | 1 | 2 | 3 | | 4 | 5 | 6 | |

The distinction between storing fixed-sized binary representation (e.g., an **int**) and variable-sized character string representation (e.g., a **string**) also occurs in files. By default, **iostreams** deal with character representations; that is, an **istream** reads a sequence of characters and turns it into an object of the desired type. An

ostream takes an object of a specified type and transforms it into a sequence of characters which it writes out. However, it is possible to request **istream** and **ostream** to simply copy bytes to and from files. That's called *binary I/O* and is requested by opening a file with the mode **ios_base::binary**. Here is an example that reads and writes binary files of integers. The key lines that specifically deal with "binary" are explained below:

```
int main()
{
        // open an istream for binary input from a file:
        cout << "Please enter input file name\n";
        string name;
        cin >> name;
        ifstream ifs(name.c_str(),ios_base::binary);    // note: stream mode
            // "binary" tells the stream not to try anything clever with the bytes
        if (!ifs) error("can't open input file ", name);

        // open an ostream for binary output to a file:
        cout << "Please enter output file name\n";
        cin >> name;
        ofstream ofs(name.c_str(),ios_base::binary);        // note: stream mode
            .// "binary" tells the stream not to try anything clever with the bytes
        if (!ofs) error("can't open output file ",name);

        vector<int> v;

        // read from binary file:
        int i;
        while (ifs.read(as_bytes(i),sizeof(int)))       // note: reading bytes
            v.push_back(i);

        // . . . do something with v . . .

        // write to binary file:
        for(int i=0; i<v.size(); ++i)
            ofs.write(as_bytes(v[i]),sizeof(int));      // note: writing bytes
        return 0;
}
```

We open the files using **ios_base::binary** as the stream mode:

```
ifstream ifs(name.c_str(), ios_base::binary);

ofstream ofs(name.c_str(), ios_base::binary);
```

In both cases, we chose the trickier, but often more compact, binary representation. When we move from character-oriented I/O to binary I/O we give up our usual >> and << operators. Those operators specifically turn values into character sequences using the default conventions (e.g., the string **"asdf"** turns into the characters **a, s, d, f** and the integer **123** turns into the characters **1, 2, 3**). If we wanted that, we wouldn't need to say **binary** – the default would suffice. We use **binary** only if we (or someone else) thought that we somehow could do better than the default. We use **binary** to tell the stream not to try anything clever with the bytes.

What "cleverness" might we do to an **int**? The obvious is to store a 4-byte **int** in 4 bytes; that is, we can look at the representation of the **int** in memory (a sequence of 4 bytes) and transfer those bytes to the file. Later, we can read those bytes back the same way and reassemble the **int**:

```
ifs.read(as_bytes(i),sizeof(int))        // note: reading bytes
ofs.write(as_bytes(v[i]),sizeof(int))    // note: writing bytes
```

The **ostream write()** and the **istream read()** both take an address (supplied here by **as_byte()**) and a number of bytes (characters) which we obtained by using the operator **sizeof**. That address should refer to the first byte of memory holding the value we want to read or write. For example, if we had an **int** with the value **1234**, we would get the 4 bytes (using hexadecimal notation) **00, 00, 04, d2**:

The **as_bytes()** function is needed to get the address of the first byte of an object's representation. It can – using language facilities yet to be explained (§17.8 and §19.3) – be defined like this:

```
template<class T>
char* as_bytes(T& i)        // treat a T as a sequence of bytes
{
    void* addr = &i;                // get the address of the first byte
                                    // of memory used to store the object
    return static_cast<char*>(addr);    // treat that memory as bytes
}
```

The (unsafe) type conversion using **static_cast** is necessary to get to the "raw bytes" of a variable. The notion of addresses will be explored in some detail in Chapters 17 and 18. Here, we just show how to treat any object in memory as a sequence of bytes for the use of **read()** and **write()**.

This binary I/O is messy, somewhat complicated, and error-prone. However, as programmers we don't always have the freedom to choose file formats, so occasionally we must use binary I/O simply because that's the format someone chose for the files we need to read or write. Alternatively, there may be a good logical reason for choosing a non-character representation. A typical example is an image or a sound file, for which there is no reasonable character representation: a photograph or a piece of music is basically just a bag of bits.

The character I/O provided by default by the iostream library is portable, human readable, and reasonably supported by the type system. Use it when you have a choice and don't mess with binary I/O unless you really have to.

11.3.3 Positioning in files

Whenever you can, just read and write files from the beginning to the end. That's the easiest and least error-prone way. Many times, when you feel that you have to make a change to a file, the better solution is to produce a new file containing the change.

However, if you must, you can use positioning to select a specific place in a file for reading or writing. Basically, every file that is open for reading has a "read/get position" and every file that is open for writing has a "write/put position":

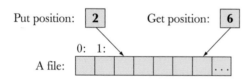

This can be used like this:

```
fstream fs(name.c_str());    // open for input and output
if (!fs) error("can't open ",name);

fs.seekg(5);    // move reading position (g for "get") to 5 (the 6th character)
char ch;
fs>>ch;         // read and increment reading position
cout << "character 6 is " << ch << '(' << int(ch) << ")\n";

fs.seekp(1);    // move writing position (p for "put") to 1
fs<<'y';        // write and increment writing position
```

Please be careful: there is next to no run-time error checking when you use positioning. In particular, it is undefined what happens if you try to seek (using seekg() or seekp()) beyond the end of a file, and operating systems really do differ in what happens then.

11.4 String streams

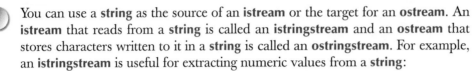

You can use a **string** as the source of an **istream** or the target for an **ostream**. An **istream** that reads from a **string** is called an **istringstream** and an **ostream** that stores characters written to it in a **string** is called an **ostringstream**. For example, an **istringstream** is useful for extracting numeric values from a **string**:

```
double str_to_double(string s)
        // if possible, convert characters in s to floating-point value
{
        istringstream is(s);     // make a stream so that we can read from s
        double d;
        is >> d;
        if (!is) error("double format error: ",s);
        return d;
}

double d1 = str_to_double("12.4");                          // testing
double d2 = str_to_double("1.34e−3");
double d3 = str_to_double("twelve point three");     // will call error()
```

If we try to read beyond the end of a **stringstream**'s string, the **stringstream** will go into **eof()** state. This means that we can use "the usual input loop" for a **stringstream**; a string stream really is a kind of **istream**.

Conversely, an **ostringstream** can be useful for formatting output for a system that requires a simple string argument, such as a GUI system (see §16.5). For example:

```
void my_code(string label, Temperature temp)
{
        // ...
        ostringstream os;     // stream for composing a message
        os << setw(8) << label << ": "
               << fixed << setprecision(5) << temp.temp << temp.unit;
        someobject.display(Point(100,100), os.str().c_str());
        // ...
}
```

The **str()** member function of **ostringstream** returns the **string** composed by output operations to an **ostringstream**. The **c_str()** is a member function of **string** that returns a C-style string as required by many system interfaces.

The **stringstreams** are generally used when we want to separate actual I/O from processing. For example, a **string** argument for **str_to_double()** will usually originate in a file (e.g., a web log) or from a keyboard. Similarly, the message we composed in **my_code()** will eventually end up written to an area of a screen. For example, in §11.7, we use a **stringstream** to filter undesirable characters out of our input. Thus, **stringstream**s can be seen as a mechanism for tailoring I/O to special needs and tastes.

A simple use of an **ostream** is to construct strings by concatenation. For example:

```
int seq_no = get_next_number();        // get the number of a log file
ostringstream name;
name << "myfile" << seq_no;            // e.g., myfile17
ofstream logfile(name.str().c_str());  // e.g., open myfile17
```

Usually, we initialize an **istringstream** with a **string** and then read the characters from that **string** using input operations. Conversely, we typically initialize an **ostringstream** to the empty **string** and then fill it using output operations. There is a more direct way of accessing characters in a **stringstream** that is sometimes useful: **ss.str()** returns a copy of **ss**'s string, and **ss.str(s)** sets in **ss**'s string to a copy of **s**. §11.7 shows an example where **ss.str(s)** is essential.

11.5 Line-oriented input

A **>>** operator reads into objects of a given type according to that type's standard format. For example, when reading into an **int**, **>>** will read until it encounters something that's not a digit, and when reading into a **string**, **>>** will read until it encounters whitespace. The standard library **istream** library also provides facilities for reading individual characters and whole lines. Consider:

```
string name;
cin >> name;                // input: Dennis Ritchie
cout << name << '\n';       // output: Dennis
```

What if we wanted to read everything on that line at once and decide how to format it later? That could be done using the function **getline()**. For example:

```
string name;
getline(cin,name);          // input: Dennis Ritchie
cout << name << '\n';       // output: Dennis Ritchie
```

Now we have the whole line. Why would we want that? A good answer would be "Because we want to do something that can't be done by **>>**." Often, the answer is a poor one: "Because the user typed a whole line." If that's the best you can think of, stick to **>>**, because once you have the line entered, you usually have to parse it somehow. For example:

```
string first_name;
string second_name;
stringstream ss(name);
ss>>first_name;          // input Dennis
ss>>second_name;         // input Ritchie
```

Reading directly into **first_name** and **second_name** would have been simpler.

One common reason for wanting to read a whole line is that the definition of whitespace isn't always appropriate. Sometimes, we want to consider a newline as different from other whitespace characters. For example, a text communication with a game might consider a line a sentence, rather than relying on conventional punctuation:

go left until you see a picture on the wall to your right
remove the picture and open the door behind it. take the bag from there

In that case, we'd first read a whole line and then extract individual words from that.

```
string command;
getline(cin,command);    // read the line

stringstream ss(command);
vector<string> words;
string s;
while (ss>>s) words.push_back(s);    // extract the individual words
```

On the other hand, had we had a choice, we would most likely have preferred to rely on some proper punctuation rather than a line break.

11.6 Character classification

Usually, we read integers, floating-point numbers, words, etc. as defined by format conventions. However, we can — and sometimes must — go down a level of abstraction and read individual characters. That's more work, but when we read individual characters, we have full control over what we are doing. Consider tokenizing an expression (§7.8.2). For example, we want **1+4*x<=y/z*5** to be separated into the eleven tokens

$1 + 4 * x <= y / z * 5$

We could use >> to read the numbers, but trying to read the identifiers as strings would cause **x<=y** to be read as one string (since < and = are not whitespace characters) and **z*** to be read as one string (since * isn't a whitespace character either). Instead, we could write

```
char ch;
while (cin.get(ch)) {
    if (isspace(ch)) {      // if ch is whitespace
        // do nothing (i.e., skip whitespace)
    }
    if (isdigit(ch)) {
        // read a number
    }
    else if (isalpha(ch)) {
        // read an identifier
    }
    else {
        // deal with operators
    }
}
```

The **istream::get()** function reads a single character into its argument. It does not skip whitespace. Like **>>**, **get()** returns a reference to its **istream** so that we can test its state.

When we read individual characters, we usually want to classify them: Is this character a digit? Is this character uppercase? And so forth. There is a set of standard library functions for that:

Character classification	
isspace(c)	Is **c** whitespace (' ', '\t', '\n', etc.)?
isalpha(c)	Is **c** a letter ('a'..'z', 'A'..'Z') (note: not '_')?
isdigit(c)	Is **c** a decimal digit ('0'..'9')?
isxdigit(c)	Is **c** a hexadecimal digit (decimal digit or 'a'..'f' or 'A'..'F')?
isupper(c)	Is **c** an uppercase letter?
islower(c)	Is **c** a lowercase letter?
isalnum(c)	Is **c** a letter or a decimal digit?
iscntrl(c)	Is **c** a control character (ASCII 0..31 and 127)?
ispunct(c)	Is **c** not a letter, digit, whitespace, or invisible control character?
isprint(c)	Is **c** printable (ASCII ' '..'~')?
isgraph(c)	Is **c** isalpha()|isdigit()|ispunct() (note: not space)?

Note the way that classifications can be combined using the "or" operator (|). For example, **isalnum(c)** means **isalpha(c)|isdigit(c)**; that is, "Is **c** either a letter or a digit?"

In addition, the standard library provides two useful functions for getting rid of case differences:

Character case	
toupper(c)	**c** or **c**'s uppercase equivalent
tolower(c)	**c** or **c**'s lowercase equivalent

These are useful when you want to ignore case differences. For example, in input from a user **Right**, **right**, and **rigHT** most likely mean the same thing (**rigHT** most likely being the result of an unfortunate hit on the Caps Lock key). After applying **tolower()** to each character in each of those strings, we get **right** for each. We can do that for an arbitrary **string**:

```
void tolower(string& s)      // put s into lower case
{
      for (int i=0; i<s.length(); ++i) s[i] = tolower(s[i]);
}
```

We use pass-by-reference (§8.5.5) to actually change the **string**. Had we wanted to keep the old string we could have written a function to make a lowercase copy. Prefer **tolower()** to **toupper()** because that works better for text in some natural languages, such as German, where not every lowercase character has an uppercase equivalent.

11.7 Using nonstandard separators

This section provides a semi-realistic example of the use of **iostreams** to solve a real problem. When we read strings, words are by default separated by whitespace. Unfortunately, **istream** doesn't offer a facility for us to define what characters make up whitespace or in some other way directly change how **>>** reads a string. So, what do we do if we need another definition of whitespace? Consider the example from §4.6.3 where we read in "words" and compared them. Those words were whitespace-separated, so if we read

As planned, the guests arrived; then,

We would get the "words"

As
planned,
the
guests
arrived;
then,

This is not what we'd find in a dictionary: "planned," and "arrived;" are not words. They are words plus distracting and irrelevant punctuation characters. For most purposes we must treat punctuation just like whitespace. How might we get rid of such punctuation? We could read characters, remove the punctuation characters – or turn them into whitespace – and then read the "cleaned-up" input again:

```
string line;
getline(cin,line);              // read into line
for (int i=0; i<line.size(); ++i) // replace each punctuation character
                                    by a space
    switch(line[i]) {
    case ';': case '.': case ',': case '?': case '!':
        line[i] = ' ';
    }

stringstream ss(line);          // make an istream ss reading from line
vector<string> vs;
string word;
while (ss>>word)                // read words without punctuation characters
    vs.push_back(word);
```

Using that to read the line we get the desired

As
planned
the
guests
arrived
then

Unfortunately, the code above is messy and rather special-purpose. What would we do if we had another definition of punctuation? Let's provide a more general and useful way of removing unwanted characters from an input stream. What would that be? What would we like our user code to look like? How about

```
ps.whitespace(";:,.");    // treat semicolon, colon, comma, and dot as whitespace
string word;
while (ps>>word) vs.push_back(word);
```

How would we define a stream that would work like **ps**? The basic idea is to read words from an ordinary input stream and then treat the user-specified "whitespace" characters as whitespace; that is, we do not give "whitespace" characters to the user, we just use them to separate words. For example,

as.not

should be the two words

as
not

We can define a class to do that for us. It must get characters from an **istream** and have a **>>** operator that works just like **istream**'s except that we can tell it which characters it should consider to be whitespace. For simplicity, we will not provide a way of treating existing whitespace characters (space, newline, etc.) as non-whitespace; we'll just allow a user to specify additional "whitespace" characters. Nor will we provide a way to completely remove the designated characters from the stream; as before, we will just turn them into whitespace. Let's call that class **Punct_stream**:

```
class Punct_stream {      // like an istream, but the user can add to
                          // the set of whitespace characters
public:
    Punct_stream(istream& is)
        : source(is), sensitive(true) { }

    void whitespace(const string& s)     // make s the whitespace set
        { white = s; }
    void add_white(char c) { white += c; }      // add to the whitespace set
    bool is_whitespace(char c);         // is c in the whitespace set?

    void case_sensitive(bool b) { sensitive = b; }
    bool is_case_sensitive() { return sensitive; }

    Punct_stream& operator>>(string& s);
    operator bool();
```

```
    private:
        istream& source;          // character source
        istringstream buffer;     // we let buffer do our formatting
        string white;             // characters considered "whitespace"
        bool sensitive;           // is the stream case-sensitive?
};
```

The basic idea is – just as in the example above – to read a line at a time from the **istream**, convert "whitespace" characters into spaces, and then use the **stringstream** to do formatting. In addition to dealing with user-defined white-space, we have given **Punct_stream** a related facility: if we ask it to, using **case_sensitive()**, it can convert case-sensitive input into non-case-sensitive input. For example, if we ask, we can get a **Punct_stream** to read

Man bites dog!

as

man
bites
dog

Punct_stream's constructor takes the **istream** to be used as a character source and gives it the local name **source**. The constructor also defaults the stream to the usual case-sensitive behavior. We can make a **Punct_stream** that reads from **cin** regarding semicolon, colon, and dot as whitespace, and that turns all characters into lower case:

```
    Punct_stream ps(cin);         // ps reads from cin
    ps.whitespace(";:.");         // semicolon, colon, and dot are also whitespace
    ps.case_sensitive(false);     // not case-sensitive
```

Obviously, the most interesting operation is the input operator **>>**. It is also by far the most difficult to define. Our general strategy is to read a whole line from the **istream** into a string (called **line**). We then convert all of "our" whitespace characters to the space character (' '). That done, we put the line into the **istringstream** called **buffer**. Now we can use the usual whitespace-separating **>>** to read from **buffer**. The code looks a bit more complicated than this because we simply try reading from the **buffer** and try to fill it only when we find it empty:

```
    Punct_stream& Punct_stream::operator>>(string& s)
    {
```

```
        while (!(buffer>>s)) {      // try to read from buffer
            if (buffer.bad() || !source.good()) return *this;
            buffer.clear();

            string line;
            getline(source,line);  // get a line from source

            // do character replacement as needed:
            for (int i =0; i<line.size(); ++i)
                if (is_whitespace(line[i]))
                        line[i]= ' ';                 // to space
                else if (!sensitive)
                        line[i] = tolower(line[i]); // to lower case

            buffer.str(line);                         // put string into stream
        }
        return *this;
    }
```

Let's consider this bit by bit. Consider first the somewhat unusual

```
    while (!(buffer>>s)) {
```

If there are characters in the **istringstream** called **buffer** the read **buffer>>s** will work, and **s** will receive a "whitespace"-separated word; then there is nothing more to do. That will happen as long as there are characters in **buffer** for us to read. However, when **buffer>>s** fails — that is, if **!(buffer>>s)** — we must replenish **buffer** from **source**. Note that the **buffer>>s** read is in a loop; after we have tried to replenished **buffer**, we need to try another read, so we get

```
    while (!(buffer>>s)) {      // try to read from buffer
        if (buffer.bad() || !source.good()) return *this;
        buffer.clear();

        // replenish buffer
    }
```

If **buffer** is **bad()** or the source has a problem, we give up; otherwise, we clear **buffer** and try again. We need to clear **buffer** because we get into that "replenish loop" only if a read failed, typically because we hit **eof()** for **buffer**; that is, there were no more characters in **buffer** for us to read. Dealing with stream state is always messy and it is often the source of subtle errors that require tedious debugging. Fortunately the rest of the replenish loop is pretty straightforward:

```
string line;
getline(source,line);   // get a line from source

// do character replacement as needed:
for (int i =0; i<line.size(); ++i)
     if (is_whitespace(line[i]))
          line[i]= ' ';                 // to space
     else if (!sensitive)
          line[i] = tolower(line[i]); // to lower case

buffer.str(line);                       // put string into stream
```

We read a line into **buffer.** Then we look at each character of that line to see if we need to change it. The **is_whitespace()** function is a member of **Punct_stream**, which we'll define later. The **tolower()** function is a standard library function doing the obvious, such as turning **A** into **a** (see §11.6).

Once we have a properly processed **line**, we need to get it into our **istring-stream.** That's what **buffer.str(line)** does; it can be read as "Set the **stringstream buffer's string** to **line.**"

Note that we "forgot" to test the state of **source** after reading from it using **getline()**. We don't need to because we will eventually reach the **!source.good()** test at the top of the loop.

As ever, we return a reference to the stream itself, ***this,** as the result of **>>**; see §17.10.

Testing for whitespace is easy; we just compare a character to each character of the string that holds our whitespace set:

```
bool Punct_stream::is_whitespace(char c)
{
     for (int i = 0; i<white.size(); ++i) if (c==white[i]) return true;
     return false;
}
```

Remember that we left the **istringstream** to deal with the usual whitespace characters (e.g., newline and space) in the usual way, so we don't need to do anything special about those.

This leaves one mysterious function:

```
Punct_stream::operator bool()
{
     return !(source.fail() || source.bad()) && source.good();
}
```

The conventional use of an **istream** is to test the result of **>>**. For example:

> **while (ps>>s) { /* . . . */ }**

That means that we need a way of looking at the result of **ps>>s** as a Boolean value. The result of **ps>>s** is a **Punct_stream**, so we need a way of implicitly turning a **Punct_stream** into a **bool**. That's what **Punct_stream**'s **operator bool()** does. A member function called **operator bool()** defines a conversion to **bool**. In particular, it returns **true** if the operation on the **Punct_stream** succeeded.

Now we can write our program.

```
int main()
        // given text input, produce a sorted list of all words in that text
        // ignore punctuation and case differences
        // eliminate duplicates from the output
{
        Punct_stream ps(cin);
        ps.whitespace(";:,.?!()\"{}<>/&$@#%^*|~"); // note \" means " in string
        ps.case_sensitive(false);

        cout << "please enter words\n";
        vector<string> vs;
        string word;
        while (ps>>word) vs.push_back(word);   // read words

        sort(vs.begin(),vs.end());            // sort in lexicographical order
        for (int i=0; i<vs.size(); ++i)       // write dictionary
                if (i==0 || vs[i]!=vs[i−1]) cout << vs[i] << endl;
}
```

This will produce a properly sorted list of words from input. The test

> **if (i==0 || vs[i]!=vs[i−1])**

will suppress duplicates. Feed this program the input

> **There are only two kinds of languages: languages that people complain about, and languages that people don't use.**

and it will output

> **and**
> **are**
> **complain**

don't
languages
of
only
people
that
there
two
use

Why did we get **don't** and not **dont**? We left the single quote out of the **white-space**() call.

Caution: **Punct_stream** behaves like an **istream** in many important and useful ways, but it isn't really an **istream**. For example, we can't ask for its state using **rd-state**(), **eof**() isn't defined, and we didn't bother providing a **>>** that reads integers. Importantly, we cannot pass a **Punct_stream** to a function expecting an **istream**. Could we define a **Punct_istream** that really is an **istream**? We could, but we don't yet have the programming experience, the design concepts, and the language facilities required to pull off that stunt (if you – much later – want to return to this problem, you have to look up stream buffers in an expert-level guide or manual).

Did you find **Punct_stream** easy to read? Did you find the explanations easy to follow? Do you think you could have written it yourself? If you were a genuine novice a few days ago, the honest answer is likely to be "No, no, no!" or even "NO, no! Nooo!! – Are you crazy?" We understand – and the answer to the last question/outburst is "No, at least we think not." The purpose of the example is

- To show a somewhat realistic problem and solution
- To show what can be achieved with relatively modest means
- To provide an easy-to-use solution to an apparently easy problem
- To illustrate the distinction between the interface and the implementation

To become a programmer, you need to read code, and not just carefully polished solutions to educational problems. This is an example. In another few days or weeks, this will become easy for you to read, and you will be looking at ways to improve the solution.

One way to think of this example is as equivalent to a teacher having dropped some genuine English slang into an English-for-beginners course to give a bit of color and enliven the proceedings.

11.8 And there is so much more

The details of I/O seem infinite. They probably are, since they are limited only by human inventiveness and capriciousness. For example, we have not considered the complexity implied by natural languages. What is written as **12.35** in English will be conventionally represented as **12,35** in most other European languages. Naturally, the C++ standard library provides facilities for dealing with that and many other natural-language-specific aspects of I/O. How do you write Chinese characters? How do you compare strings written using Malayalam characters? There are answers, but they are far beyond the scope of this book. If you need to know, look in more specialized or advanced books (such as Langer, *Standard C++ IOStreams and Locales,* and Stroustrup, *The C++ Programming Language*) and in library and system documentation. Look for *locale*; that's the term usually applied to facilities for dealing with natural language differences.

Another source of complexity is buffering: the standard library **iostreams** rely on a concept called **streambuf**. For advanced work — whether for performance or functionality — with **iostreams** these **istreambufs** are unavoidable. If you feel the need to define your own **iostreams** or to tune **iostreams** to new data sources/sinks, see Chapter 21 of *The C++ Programming Language* by Stroustrup or your system documentation.

When using C++, you may also encounter the C standard **printf()**/**scanf()** family of I/O functions. If you do, look them up in §27.6, §B.10.2, or in the excellent C textbook by Kernighan and Ritchie (*The C Programming Language*) or one of the innumerable sources on the web. Each language has its own I/O facilities; they all vary, most are quirky, but most reflect (in various odd ways) the same fundamental concepts that we have presented in Chapters 10 and 11.

The standard library I/O facilities are summarized in Appendix B.

The related topic of graphical user interfaces (GUIs) is described in Chapters 12–16.

Drill

1. Start a program called **Test_output.cpp**. Declare an integer **birth_year** and assign it the year you were born.
2. Output your **birth_year** in decimal, hexadecimal, and octal form.
3. Label each value with the name of the base used.
4. Did you line up your output in columns using the tab character? If not, do it.
5. Now output your age.
6. Was there a problem? What happened? Fix your output to decimal.
7. Go back to 2 and cause your output to show the base for each output.
8. Try reading as octal, hexadecimal, etc.:

```
cin >> a >>oct >> b >> hex >> c >> d;
cout << a << '\t'<< b << '\t'<< c << '\t'<< d << '\n' ;
```

Run this code with the input

1234 1234 1234 1234

Explain the results.

9. Write some code to print the number **1234567.89** three times, first using **general**, then **fixed**, then **scientific** forms. Which output form presents the user with the most accurate representation? Explain why.

10. Make a simple table including last name, first name, telephone number, and email address for yourself and at least five of your friends. Experiment with different field widths until you are satisfied that the table is well presented.

Review

1. Why is I/O tricky for a programmer?
2. What does the notation **<< hex** do?
3. What are hexadecimal numbers used for in computer science? Why?
4. Name some of the options you may want to implement for formatting integer output.
5. What is a manipulator?
6. What is the prefix for decimal? For octal? For hexadecimal?
7. What is the default output format for floating-point values?
8. What is a field?
9. Explain what **setprecision()** and **setw()** do.
10. What is the purpose of file open modes?
11. Which of the following manipulators does not "stick": **hex, scientific, setprecision, showbase, setw**?
12. What is the difference between character I/O and binary I/O?
13. Give an example of when it would probably be beneficial to use a binary file instead of a text file.
14. Give two examples where a **stringstream** can be useful.
15. What is a file position?
16. What happens if you position a file position beyond the end of file?
17. When would you prefer line-oriented input to type-specific input?
18. What does **isalnum(c)** do?

Terms

binary	hexadecimal	octal
character classification	irregularity	output formatting
decimal	line-oriented input	regularity
file positioning	manipulator	**scientific**
fixed	nonstandard separator	**setprecision**
general	**noshowbase**	showbase

Exercises

1. Write a program that reads a text file and converts its input to all lower case, producing a new file.

2. Write a program that removes all vowels from a file ("disemvowels"). For example, **Once upon a time!** becomes **nc pn tm!**. Surprisingly often, the result is still readable; try it on your friends.

3. Write a program called **multi_input.cpp** that prompts the user to enter several integers in any combination of octal, decimal, or hexadecimal, using the **0** and **0x** base suffixes; interprets the numbers correctly; and converts them to decimal form. Then your program should output the values in properly spaced columns like this:

0x4	hexadecimal	converts to	67	decimal
0123	octal	converts to	83	decimal
65	decimal	converts to	65	decimal

4. Write a program that reads strings and for each string outputs the character classification of each character, as defined by the character classification functions presented in §11.6. Note that a character can have several classifications (e.g., **x** is both a letter and an alphanumeric).

5. Write a program that replaces punctuation with whitespace. For example, " - don't use the as-if rule." becomes "   dont use the asif rule ".

6. Modify the program from the previous exercise so that it replaces **don't** with **do not**, **can't** with **cannot**, etc.; leaves hyphens within words intact (so that we get "   do not use the as-if rule "); and converts all characters to lower case.

7. Use the program from the previous exercise to make a dictionary (as an alternative to the approach in §11.7). Run the result on a multi-page text file, look at the result, and see if you can improve the program to make a better dictionary.

8. Split the binary I/O program from §11.3.2 into two: one program that converts an ordinary text file into binary and one program that reads binary and converts it to text. Test these programs by comparing a text file with what you get by converting it to binary and back.

9. Write a function **vector<string> split(const string& s)** that returns a **vector** of whitespace-separated substrings from the argument **s**.

10. Write a function **vector<string> split(const string& s, const string& w)** that returns a **vector** of whitespace-separated substrings from the argument **s**, where whitespace is defined as "ordinary whitespace" plus the characters in **w**.

11. Reverse the order of characters in a text file. For example, **asdfghjkl** becomes **lkjhgfdsa**. Hint: "file open modes."

12. Reverse the order of words (defined as whitespace-separated strings) in a file. For example, **Norwegian Blue parrot** becomes **parrot Blue Norwegian**. You are allowed to assume that all the strings from the file will fit into memory at once.

13. Write a program that reads a text file and writes out how many characters of each character classification (§11.6) are in the file.

14. Write a program that reads a file of whitespace-separated numbers and outputs a file of numbers using scientific format and precision 8 in four fields of 20 characters per line.

15. Write a program to read a file of whitespace-separated numbers and output them in order (lowest value first), one value per line. Write a value only once, and if it occurs more than once write the count of its occurrences on its line. For example, "**7 5 5 7 3 117 5**" should give

3
5   3
7   2
117

Postscript

Input and output are messy because our human tastes and conventions have not followed simple-to-state rules and straightforward mathematical laws. As programmers, we are rarely in a position to dictate that our users depart from their preferences, and when we are, we should typically be less arrogant than to think that we can provide a simple alternative to conventions built up over time. Consequently, we must expect, accept, and adapt to a certain messiness of input and output while still trying to keep our programs as simple as possible – but no simpler.

A Display Model

"The world was black and white then.
[It] didn't turn color
until sometime in the 1930s."

—Calvin's dad

This chapter presents a display model (the output part of GUI), giving examples of use and fundamental notions such as screen coordinates, lines, and color. **Line**, **Lines**, **Polygon**s, **Axis**, and **Text** are examples of **Shape**s. A **Shape** is an object in memory that we can display and manipulate on a screen. The next two chapters will explore these classes further, with Chapter 13 focusing on their implementation and Chapter 14 on design issues.

12.1 Why graphics?

Why do we spend four chapters on graphics and one on GUIs (graphical user interfaces)? After all, this is a book about programming, not a graphics book. There is a huge number of interesting software topics that we don't discuss, and we can at best scratch the surface on the topic of graphics. So, "Why graphics?" Basically, graphics is a subject that allows us to explore several important areas of software design, programming, and programming language facilities:

- *Graphics are useful.* There is much more to programming than graphics and much more to software than code manipulated through a GUI. However, in many areas good graphics are either essential or very important. For example, we wouldn't dream of studying scientific computing, data analysis, or just about any quantitative subject without the ability to graph data. Chapter 15 gives simple (but general) facilities for graphing data.

- *Graphics are fun.* There are few areas of computing where the effect of a piece of code is as immediately obvious and – when finally free of bugs – as pleasing. We'd be tempted to play with graphics even if it wasn't useful!

- *Graphics provide lots of interesting code to read.* Part of learning to program is to read lots of code to get a feel for what good code is like. Similarly, the way to become a good writer of English involves reading a lot of books, articles, and quality newspapers. Because of the direct correspondence between what we see on the screen and what we write in our programs, simple graphics code is more readable than most kinds of code of similar complexity. This chapter will prove that you can read graphics code after a few minutes of introduction; Chapter 13 will demonstrate how you can write it after another couple of hours.

- *Graphics are a fertile source of design examples.* It is actually hard to design and implement a good graphics and GUI library. Graphics are a very rich source of concrete and practical examples of design decisions and design techniques. Some of the most useful techniques for designing classes, designing functions, separating software into layers (of abstraction), and constructing libraries can be illustrated with a relatively small amount of graphics and GUI code.

- *Graphics provide a good introduction to what is commonly called object-oriented programming and the language features that support it.* Despite rumors to the contrary, object-oriented programming wasn't invented to be able to do graphics (see Chapter 22), but it was soon applied to that, and graphics provide some of the most accessible examples of object-oriented designs.

- *Some of the key graphics concepts are nontrivial.* So they are worth teaching, rather than leaving it to your own initiative (and patience) to seek out information. If we did not show how graphics and GUI were done, you might consider them "magic," thus violating one of the fundamental aims of this book.

12.2 A display model

The iostream library is oriented toward reading and writing streams of characters as they might appear in a list of numeric values or a book. The only direct supports for the notion of graphical position are the newline and tab characters. You can embed notions of color and two-dimensional positions, etc., in a one-dimensional stream of characters. That's what layout (typesetting, "markup") languages such as Troff, Tex, Word, HTTP, and XML (and their associated graphical packages) do. For example:

```
<hr>
<h2>
Organization
</h2>
This list is organized in three parts:
<ul>
    <li><b>Proposals</b>, numbered EPddd, . . .</li>
    <li><b>Issues</b>, numbered EIddd, . . .</li>
    <li><b>Suggestions</b>, numbered ESddd, . . .</li>
</ul>
<p>We try to . . .
<p>
```

This is a piece of HTML specifying a header (**<h2>** . . . **</h2>**) a list (**<ul>** . . . **</ul>**) with list items (**<il>** . . . **</il>**) and a paragraph (**<p>**). We left out most of the actual text because it is irrelevant here. The point is that you can express layout notions in plain text, but the connection between the characters written and what appears on the screen is indirect, governed by a program that interprets those "markup" commands. Such techniques are fundamentally simple and immensely useful (just about everything you read has been produced using them), but they also have their limitations.

In this chapter and the next four, we present an alternative: a notion of graphics and of graphical user interfaces that is directly aimed at a computer screen. The fundamental concepts are inherently graphical (and two-dimensional, adapted to the rectangular area of a computer screen), such as coordinates, lines, rectangles, and circles. The aim from a programming point of view is a direct correspondence between the objects in memory and the images on the screen.

The basic model is as follows: We compose objects with basic objects provided by a graphics system, such as lines. We "attach" these graphics objects to a window object, representing our physical screen. A program that we can think of as the display itself, as "a display engine," as "our graphics library," as "the GUI library," or even (humorously) as "the small gnome writing on the back of the screen" then takes the objects we have added to our window and draws them on the screen:

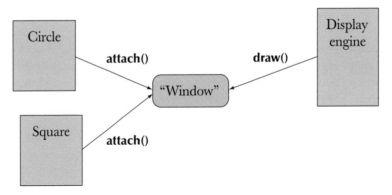

The "display engine" draws lines on the screen, places strings of text on the screen, colors areas of the screen, etc. For simplicity, we'll use the phrase "our GUI library" or even "the system" for the display engine even though our GUI library does much more than just drawing the objects. In the same way that our code lets the GUI library do most of the work for us, the GUI library delegates much of its work to the operating system.

12.3 A first example

Our job is to define classes from which we can make objects that we want to see on the screen. For example, we might want to draw a graph as a series of connected lines. Here is a small program presenting a very simple version of that:

```
#include "Simple_window.h"        // get access to our window library
#include "Graph.h"                // get access to our graphics library facilities

int main()
{
        using namespace Graph_lib;   // our graphics facilities are in Graph_lib

        Point tl(100,100);            // to become top left corner of window

        Simple_window win(tl,600,400,"Canvas");   // make a simple window

        Polygon poly;                 // make a shape (a polygon)

        poly.add(Point(300,200));    // add a point
        poly.add(Point(350,100));    // add another point
        poly.add(Point(400,200));    // add a third point

        poly.set_color(Color::red);   // adjust properties of poly

        win.attach (poly);            // connect poly to the window

        win.wait_for_button();        // give control to the display engine
}
```

When we run this program, the screen looks something like this:

Let's go through the program line by line to see what was done. First we include the headers for our graphics interface libraries:

```
#include "Simple_window.h"     // get access to our window library
#include "Graph.h"             // get access to our graphics library facilities
```

Then, in **main()**, we start by telling the compiler that our graphics facilities are to be found in **Graph_lib**:

```
using namespace Graph_lib;     // our graphics facilities are in Graph_lib
```

Then, we define a point that we will use as the top left corner of our window:

```
Point tl(100,100);    // to become top left corner of window
```

Next, we create a window on the screen:

```
Simple_window win(tl,600,400,"Canvas");      // make a simple window
```

We use a class representing a window in our **Graph_lib** interface library called **Simple_window**. The name of this particular **Simple_window** is **win**; that is, **win** is a variable of class **Simple_window**. The initializer list for **win** starts with the point to be used as the top left corner, **tl**, followed by **600** and **400**. Those are the width and height, respectively, of the window, as displayed on the screen, measured in pixels. We'll explain in more detail later, but the main point here is that we specify a rectangle by giving its width and height. The string **Canvas** is used to label the window. If you look, you can see the word **Canvas** in the top left corner of the window's frame.

On our screen, the window appeared in a position chosen by the GUI library. In §13.7.2, we'll show how to choose a particular position, but for now, we'll just take what our library picks; that's often just right anyway.

Next, we put an object in the window:

```
Polygon poly;                  // make a shape (a polygon)

poly.add(Point(300,200));      // add a point
poly.add(Point(350,100));      // add another point
poly.add(Point(400,200));      // add a third point
```

We define a polygon, **poly**, and then add points to it. In our graphics library, a **Polygon** starts empty and we can add as many points to it as we like. Since we added three points, we get a triangle. A point is simply a pair of values giving the *x* and *y* (horizontal and vertical) coordinates within a window.

Just to show off, we then color the lines of our polygon red:

poly.set_color(Color::red);   // adjust properties of poly

Finally, we attach **poly** to our window, **win**:

win.attach(poly);   // connect poly to the window

If the program wasn't so fast, you would notice that so far nothing had happened to the screen: nothing at all. We created a window (an object of class **Simple_window**, to be precise), created a polygon (called **poly**), painted that polygon red (**Color:: red**), and attached it to the window (called **win**), but we have not yet asked for that window to be displayed on the screen. That's done by the final line of the program:

win.wait_for_button();   // give control to the display engine

To get a GUI system to display objects on the screen, you have to give control to "the system." Our **wait_for_button()** does that, and it also waits for you to "press" ("click") the "Next" button of our **Simple_window** before proceeding. This gives you a chance to look at the window before the program finishes and the window disappears. When you press the button, the program terminates, closing the window.

In isolation, our window looks like this:

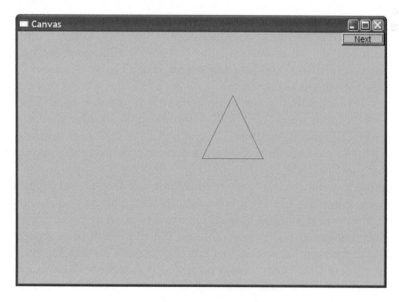

You'll notice that we "cheated" a bit. Where did that button labeled "Next" come from? We built it into our **Simple_window** class. In Chapter 16, we'll move from

Simple_window to "plain" **Window**, which has no potentially spurious facilities built in, and show how we can write our own code to control interaction with a window.

For the next three chapters, we'll simply use that "Next" button to move from one "display" to the next when we want to display information in stages ("frame by frame").

You are so used to the operating system putting a frame around each window that you might not have noticed it specifically. However, the pictures in this and the following chapters were produced on a Microsoft Windows system, so you get the usual three buttons on the top right "for free." This can be useful: if your program gets in a real mess (as it surely will sometimes during debugging), you can kill it by hitting the × button. When you run your program on another system, a different frame will be added to fit that system's conventions. Our only contribution to the frame is the label (here, **Canvas**).

12.4 Using a GUI library

In this book, we will not use the operating system's graphical and GUI (graphical user interface) facilities directly. Doing so would limit our programs to run on a single operating system and would also force us to deal directly with a lot of messy details. As with text I/O, we'll use a library to smooth over operating system differences, I/O device variations, etc. and to simplify our code. Unfortunately, C++ does not provide a standard GUI library the way it provides the standard stream I/O library, so we use one of the many available C++ GUI libraries. So as not to tie you directly into one of those GUI libraries, and to save you from hitting the full complexity of a GUI library all at once, we use a set of simple interface classes that can be implemented in a couple of hundred lines of code for just about any GUI library.

The GUI toolkit that we are using (indirectly for now) is called FLTK (Fast Light Tool Kit, pronounced "full tick") from www.fltk.org. Our code is portable wherever FLTK is used (Windows, Unix, Mac, Linux, etc.). Our interface classes can also be re-implemented using other toolkits, so code using them is potentially even more portable.

The programming model presented by our interface classes is far simpler than what common toolkits offer. For example, our complete graphics and GUI interface library is about 600 lines of C++ code, whereas the extremely terse FLTK documentation is 370 pages. You can download that from www.fltk.org, but we don't recommend you do that just yet. You can do without that level of detail for a while. The general ideas presented in Chapters 12–16 can be used with any popular GUI toolkit. We will of course explain how our interface classes map to FLTK so that you will (eventually) see how you can use that (and similar toolkits) directly, if necessary.

We can illustrate the parts of our "graphics world" like this:

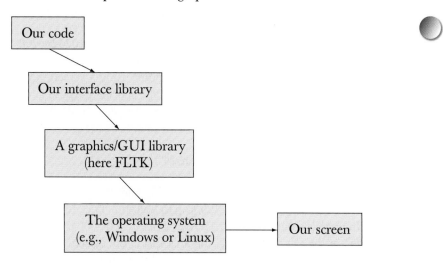

Our interface classes provide a simple and user-extensible basic notion of two-dimensional shapes with limited support for the use of color. To drive that, we present a simple notion of GUI based on "callback" functions triggered by the use of user-defined buttons, etc. on the screen (Chapter 16).

12.5 Coordinates

A computer screen is a rectangular area composed of pixels. A pixel is a tiny spot that can be given some color. The most common way of modeling a screen in a program is as a rectangle of pixels. Each pixel is identified by an x (horizontal) coordinate and a y (vertical) coordinate. The x coordinates start with 0, indicating the leftmost pixel, and increase (toward the right) to the rightmost pixel. The y coordinates start with 0, indicating the topmost pixel, and increase (toward the bottom) to the lowest pixel:

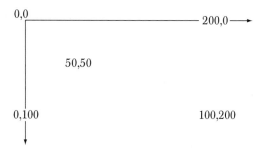

Please note that *y* coordinates "grow downward." Mathematicians, in particular, find this odd, but screens (and windows) come in many sizes, and the top left point is about all that they have in common.

The number of pixels available depends on the screen: 1024-by-768, 1280-by-1024, 1450-by-1050, and 1600-by-1200 are common screen sizes.

In the context of interacting with a computer using a screen, a window is a rectangular region of the screen devoted to some specific purpose and controlled by a program. A window is addressed exactly as a screen. Basically, we see a window as a small screen. For example, when we said

> **Simple_window win(tl,600,400,"Canvas");**

we requested a rectangular area 600 pixels wide and 400 pixels high that we can address 0–599 (left to right) and 0–399 (top to bottom). The area of a window that you can draw on is commonly referred to as a *canvas*. The 600-by-400 area refers to "the inside" of the window, that is, the area inside the system-provided frame; it does not include the space the system uses for the title bar, quit button, etc.

12.6 Shapes

Our basic toolbox for drawing on the screen consists of about a dozen classes:

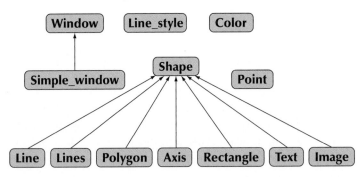

An arrow indicates that the class pointing can be used where the class pointed to is required. For example, a **Polygon** can be used where a **Shape** is required; that is, a **Polygon** is a kind of **Shape**.

We will start out presenting and using

- **Simple_window, Window**
- **Shape, Text, Polygon, Line, Lines, Rectangle, Function,** etc.
- **Color, Line_style, Point**
- **Axis**

Later (Chapter 16), we'll add GUI (user interaction) classes:

- **Button, In_box, Menu**, etc.

We could easily add many more classes (for some definition of "easy"), such as

- **Spline, Grid, Block_chart, Pie_chart**, etc.

However, defining or describing a complete GUI framework with all its facilities is beyond the scope of this book.

12.7 Using Shape primitives

In this section, we will walk you through some of the primitive facilities of our graphics library: **Simple_window, Window, Shape, Text, Polygon, Line, Lines, Rectangle, Color, Line_style, Point, Axis**. The aim is to give you a broad view of what you can do with those facilities, but not yet a detailed understanding of any of those classes. In the next chapters, we explore the design of each.

We will now walk through a simple program, explaining the code line by line and showing the effect of each on the screen. When you run the program you'll see how the image changes as we add shapes to the window and modify existing shapes. Basically, we are "animating" the progress through the code by looking at the program as it is executed.

12.7.1 Graphics headers and main

First, we include the header files defining our interface to the graphics and GUI facilities:

```
#include "Window.h"    // a plain window
#include "Graph.h"
```

or

```
#include "Simple_window.h"    // if we want that "Next" button
#include "Graph.h"
```

As you probably guessed, **Window.h** contains the facilities related to windows and **Graph.h** the facilities related to drawing shapes (including text) into windows. These facilities are defined in the **Graph_lib** namespace. To simplify notation we use a namespace directive to make the names from **Graph_lib** directly available in our program:

```
using namespace Graph_lib;
```

As usual, **main**() contains the code we want to execute (directly or indirectly) and deals with exceptions:

```
int main ()
try
{
        // . . . here is our code . . .


}
catch(exception& e) {
        // some error reporting
        return 1;
}
catch(...) {
        // some more error reporting
        return 2;
}
```

12.7.2 An almost blank window

We will not discuss error handling here (see Chapter 5, in particular, §5.6.3), but go straight to the graphics within **main**():

```
Point tl(100,100);    // top left corner of our window

Simple_window win(tl,600,400,"Canvas");
        // screen coordinate tl for top left corner
        // window size(600*400)
        // title: Canvas
win.wait_for_button();      // display!
```

This creates a **Simple_window**, that is, a window with a "Next" button, and displays it on the screen. Obviously, we need to have **#included** the header **Simple_window.h** rather than **Window.h** to get **Simple_window**. Here we are specific about where on the screen the window should go: its top left corner goes at **Point(100,100)**. That's near, but not too near, the top left corner of the screen. Obviously, **Point** is a class with a constructor that takes a pair of integers and interprets them as an (x, y) coordinate pair. We could have written

```
Simple_window win(Point(100,100),600,400,"Canvas");
```

However, we want to use the point (100,100) several times so it is more convenient to give it a symbolic name. The 600 is the width and 400 is the height of the window, and **Canvas** is the label we want put on the frame of the window.

To actually get the window drawn on the screen, we have to give control to the GUI system. We do this by calling **win.wait_for_button**() and the result is:

In the background of our window, we see a laptop screen (somewhat cleaned up for the occasion). For people who are curious about irrelevant details, we can tell you that I took the photo standing near the Picasso library in Antibes looking across the bay to Nice. The black console window partially hidden behind is the one running our program. Having a console window is somewhat ugly and unnecessary, but it has the advantage of giving us an effective way of killing our window if a partially debugged program gets into an infinite loop and refuses to go away. If you look carefully, you'll notice that we have the Microsoft C++ compiler running, but you could just as well have used some other compiler (such as Borland or GNU).

For the rest of the presentation we will eliminate the distractions around our window and just show that window by itself:

The actual size of the window (in inches) depends on the resolution of your screen. Some screens have bigger pixels than other screens.

12.7.3 Axis

An almost blank window isn't very interesting, so we'd better add some information. What would we like to display? Just to remind you that graphics is not all fun and games, we will start with something serious and somewhat complicated: an axis. A graph without axes is usually a disgrace. You just don't know what the data represents without axes. Maybe you explained it all in some accompanying text, but it is far safer to add axes; people often don't read the explanation and often a nice graphical representation gets separated from its original context. So, a graph needs axes:

```
Axis xa(Axis::x, Point(20,300), 280, 10, "x axis");      // make an Axis
                    // an Axis is a kind of Shape
                    // Axis::x means horizontal
                    // starting at (20,300)
                    // 280 pixels long
                    // 10 "notches"
                    // label the axis "x axis"
win.attach(xa);                     // attach xa to the window, win
win.set_label("Canvas #2");         // relabel the window
win.wait_for_button();              // display!
```

The sequence of actions is: make the axis object, add it to the window, and finally display it:

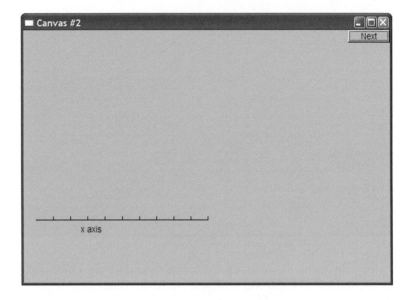

We can see that an **Axis::x** is a horizontal line. We see the required number of "notches" (10) and the label "x axis." Usually, the label will explain what the axis and the notches represent. Naturally, we chose to place the *x* axis somewhere near the bottom of the window. In real life, we'd represent the height and width by symbolic constants so that we could refer to "just above the bottom" as something like **y_max-bottom_margin** rather than by a "magic constant," such as **300** (§4.3.1, §15.6.2).

To help identify our output we relabeled the screen to **Canvas #2** using **Window**'s member function **set_label()**.

Now, let's add a *y* axis:

```
Axis ya(Axis::y, Point(20,300), 280, 10, "y axis");
ya.set_color(Color::cyan);              // choose a color
ya.label.set_color(Color::dark_red);    // choose a color for the text
win.attach(ya);
win.set_label("Canvas #3");
win.wait_for_button();     // display!
```

Just to show off some facilities, we colored our *y* axis cyan and our label dark red.

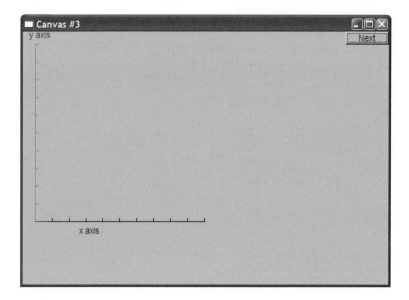

We don't actually think that it is a good idea to use different colors for *x* and *y* axes. We just wanted to show you how you can set the color of a shape and of individual elements of a shape. Using lots of color is not necessarily a good idea. In particular, novices tend to use color with more enthusiasm than taste.

12.7.4 Graphing a function

What next? We now have a window with axes, so it seems a good idea to graph a function. We make a shape representing a sine function and attach it:

```
Function sine(sin,0,100,Point(20,150),1000,50,50);    // sine curve
        // plot sin() in the range [0:100) with (0,0) at (20,150)
        // using 1000 points; scale x values *50, scale y values *50

win.attach(sine);
win.set_label("Canvas #4");
win.wait_for_button();
```

Here, the **Function** named **sine** will draw a sine curve using the standard library function **sin()** to generate values. We explain details about how to graph functions in §15.3. For now, just note that to graph a function we have to say where it starts (a **Point**) and for what set of input values we want to see it (a range), and we need to give some information about how to squeeze that information into our window (scaling):

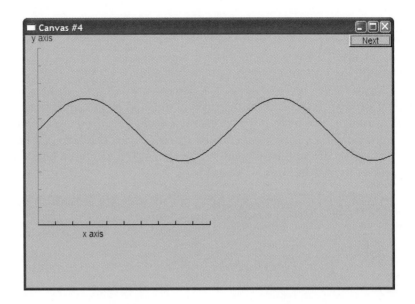

Note how the curve simply stops when it hits the edge of the window. Points drawn outside our window rectangle are simply ignored by the GUI system and never seen.

12.7.5 Polygons

A graphed function is an example of data presentation. We'll see much more of that in Chapter 15. However, we can also draw different kinds of objects in a window: geometric shapes. We use geometric shapes for graphical illustrations, to indicate user interaction elements (such as buttons), and generally to make our presentations more interesting. A **Polygon** is characterized by a sequence of points, which the **Polygon** class connects by lines. The first line connects the first point to the second, the second line connects the second point to the third, and the last line connects the last point to the first:

```
sine.set_color(Color::blue);      // we changed our mind about sine's color

Polygon poly;                     // a polygon; a Polygon is a kind of Shape
poly.add(Point(300,200));         // three points make a triangle
poly.add(Point(350,100));
poly.add(Point(400,200));

poly.set_color(Color::red);
```

```
poly.set_style(Line_style::dash);
win.attach(poly);
win.set_label("Canvas #5");
win.wait_for_button();
```

This time we change the color of the sine curve (**sine**) just to show how. Then, we add a triangle, just as in our first example from §12.3, as an example of a polygon. Again, we set a color, and finally, we set a style. The lines of a **Polygon** have a "style." By default that is solid, but we can also make those lines dashed, dotted, etc. as needed (see §13.5). We get

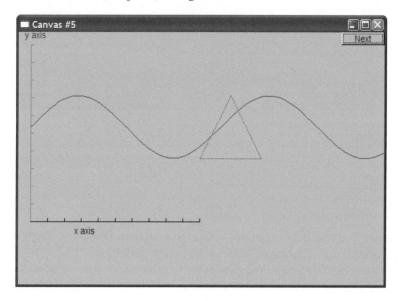

12.7.6 Rectangles

A screen is a rectangle, a window is a rectangle, and a piece of paper is a rectangle. In fact, an awful lot of the shapes in our modern world are rectangles (or at least rectangles with rounded corners). There is a reason for this: a rectangle is the simplest shape to deal with. For example, it's easy to describe (top left corner plus width plus height, or top left corner plus bottom right corner, or whatever), it's easy to tell whether a point is inside a rectangle or outside it, and it's easy to get hardware to draw a rectangle of pixels fast.

So, most higher-level graphics libraries deal better with rectangles than with other closed shapes. Consequently, we provide **Rectangle** as a class separate from the **Polygon** class. A **Rectangle** is characterized by its top left corner plus a width and height:

```
Rectangle r(Point(200,200), 100, 50);     // top left corner, width, height
win.attach(r);
win.set_label("Canvas #6");
win.wait_for_button();
```

From that, we get

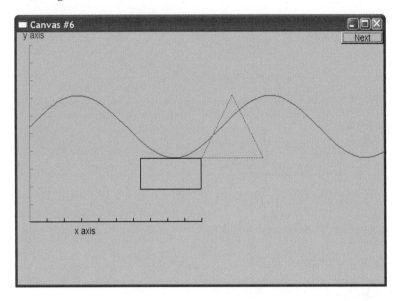

Please note that making a polyline with four points in the right places is not enough to make a **Rectangle**. It is easy to make a **Closed_polyline** that looks like a **Rectangle** on the screen (you can even make an **Open_polyline** that looks just like a **Rectangle**); for example:

```
Closed_polyline poly_rect;
poly_rect.add(Point(100,50));
poly_rect.add(Point(100,50));
poly_rect.add(Point(200,100));
poly_rect.add(Point(100,100));
```

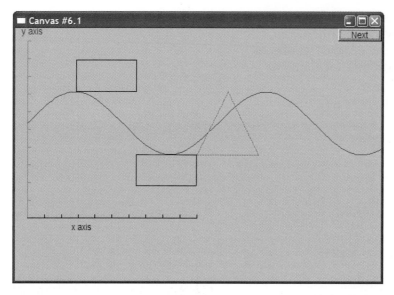

In fact, the *image* on the screen of such a **poly_rect** *is* a rectangle. However, the **poly_rect** object in memory is not a **Rectangle** and it does not "know" anything about rectangles. The simplest way to prove that is to add another point:

> **poly_rect.add(Point(50,75));**

No rectangle has five points:

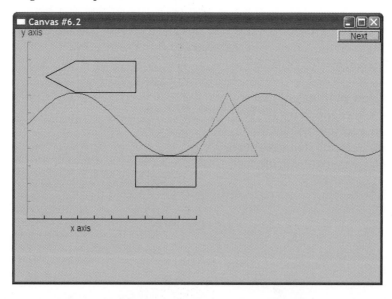

It is important for our reasoning about our code that a **Rectangle** doesn't just happen to look like a rectangle on the screen; it maintains the fundamental guarantees of a rectangle (as we know them from geometry). We write code that depends on a **Rectangle** really being a rectangle on the screen and staying that way.

12.7.7 Fill

We have been drawing our shapes as outlines. We can also "fill" a rectangle with color:

```
r.set_fill_color(Color::yellow);      // color the inside of the rectangle
poly.set_style(Line_style(Line_style::dash,4));
poly_rect.set_style(Line_style(Line_style::dash,2));
win.set_label("Canvas #7");
win.wait_for_button();
```

We also decided that we didn't like the line style of our triangle (**poly**), so we set its line style to "fat (thickness four times normal) dashed." Similarly, we changed the style of **poly_rect** (now no longer looking like a rectangle):

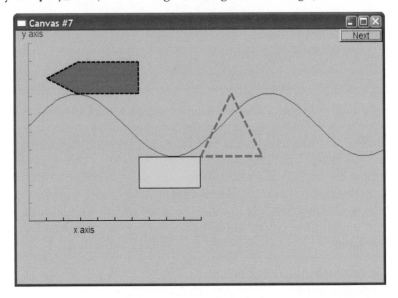

If you look carefully at **poly_rect**, you'll see that the outline is printed on top of the fill.

It is possible to fill any closed shape (see §13.9). Rectangles are just special in how easy (and fast) they are to fill.

12.7.8 Text

Finally, no system for drawing is complete without a simple way of writing text – drawing each character as a set of lines just doesn't cut it. We label the window itself, and axes can have labels, but we can also place text anywhere using a **Text** object:

```
Text t(Point(150,150), "Hello, graphical world! ");
win.attach(t);
win.set_label("Canvas #8");
win.wait_for_button();
```

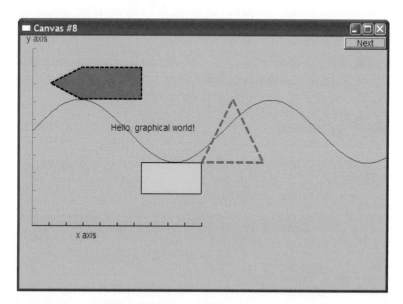

From the primitive graphics elements you see in this window, you can build displays of just about any complexity and subtlety. For now, just note a peculiarity of the code in this chapter: there are no loops, no selection statements, and all data was "hardwired" in. The output was just composed of primitives in the simplest possible way. Once we start composing these primitives using data and algorithms, things will start to get interesting.

We have seen how we can control the color of text: the label of an **Axis** (§12.7.3) is simply a **Text** object. In addition, we can choose a font and set the size of the characters:

```
t.set_font(Font::times_bold);
t.set_font_size(20);
win.set_label("Canvas #9");
win.wait_for_button();
```

We enlarged the characters of the **Text** string **Hello, graphical world!** to point size 20 and chose the Times font in bold:

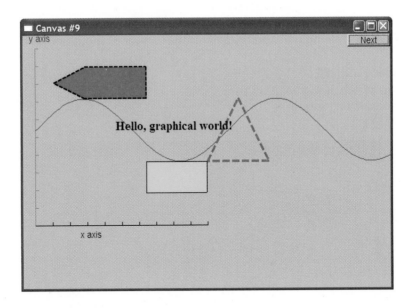

12.7.9 Images

We can also load images from files:

```
Image ii(Point(100,50),"image.jpg");     // 400*212-pixel jpg
win.attach(ii);
win.set_label("Canvas #10");
win.wait_for_button();
```

As it happens, the file called **image.jpg** is a photo of two planes breaking the sound barrier:

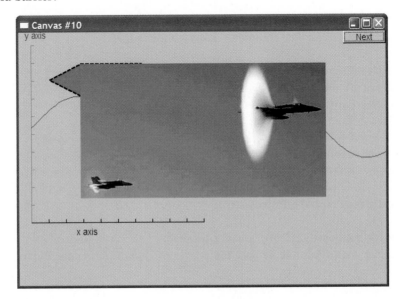

That photo is relatively large and we placed it right on top of our text and shapes. So, to clean up our window a bit, let us move it a bit out of the way:

```
ii.move(100,200);
win.set_label("Canvas #11");
win.wait_for_button();
```

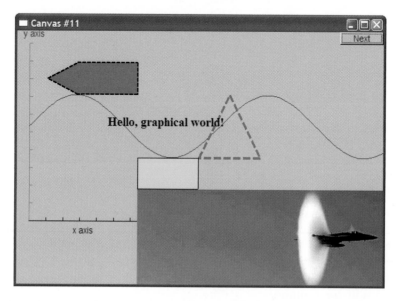

Note how the parts of the photo that didn't fit in the window are simply not represented. What would have appeared outside the window is "clipped" away.

12.7.10 And much more

And here, without further comment, is some more code:

```
Circle c(Point(100,200),50);
Ellipse e(Point(100,200), 75,25);
e.set_color(Color::dark_red);
Mark m(Point(100,200),'x');

ostringstream oss;
oss << "screen size: " << x_max() << "*" << y_max()
    << "; window size: " << win.x_max() << "*" << win.y_max();
Text sizes(Point(100,20),oss.str());

Image cal(Point(225,225),"snow_cpp.gif");      // 320*240-pixel gif
cal.set_mask(Point(40,40),200,150);            // display center part of image
```

```
win.attach(c);
win.attach(m);
win.attach(e);

win.attach(sizes);
win.attach(cal);
win.set_label("Canvas #12");
win.wait_for_button();
```

Can you guess what this code does? Is it obvious?

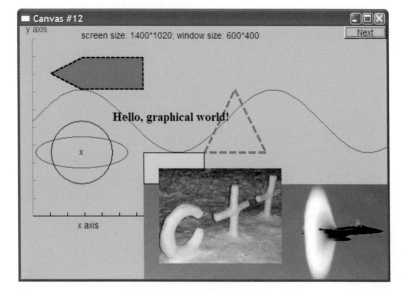

The connection between the code and what appears on the screen is direct. If you don't yet see how that code caused that output, it soon will become clear. Note the way we used a **stringstream** (§11.4) to format the text object displaying sizes.

12.8 Getting this to run

We have seen how to make a window and how to draw various shapes in it. In the following chapters, we'll see how those **Shape** classes are defined and show more ways of using them.

Getting this program to run requires more than the programs we have presented so far. In addition to our code in **main()**, we need to get the interface library code compiled and linked to our code, and finally, nothing will run unless the FLTK library (or whatever GUI system we use) is installed and correctly linked to ours.

One way of looking at the program is that it has four distinct parts:

- Our program code (**main()**, etc.)
- Our interface library (**Window, Shape, Polygon**, etc.)
- The FLTK library
- The C++ standard library

Indirectly, we also use the operating system. Leaving out the OS and the standard library, we can illustrate the organization of our graphics code like this:

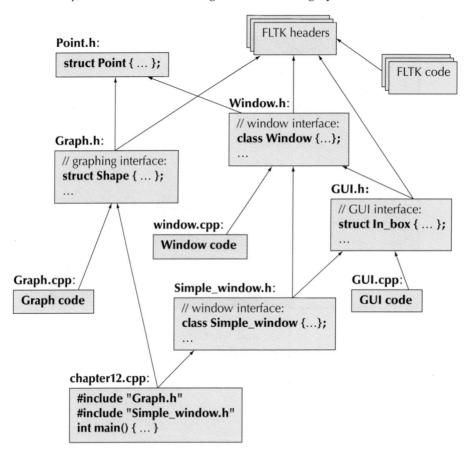

Appendix D explains how to get all of this to work together.

12.8.1 Source files

Our graphics and GUI interface library consists of just five header files and three code files:

- Headers:

    - **Point.h**
    - **Window.h**
    - **Simple_window.h**
    - **Graph.h**
    - **GUI.h**

- Code files:

    - **Window.cpp**
    - **Graph.cpp**
    - **GUI.cpp**

Until Chapter 16, you can ignore the GUI files.

Drill

The drill is the graphical equivalent to the "Hello, World!" program. Its purpose is to get you acquainted with the simplest graphical output tools.

1. Get an empty **Simple_window** with the size 600 by 400 and a label **My window** compiled, linked, and run. Note that you have to link the FLTK library as described in Appendix D; **#include Graph.h**, **Window.h**, and **GUI.h** in your code; and include **Graph.cpp** and **Window.cpp** in your project.
2. Now add the examples from §12.7 one by one, testing between each added subsection example.
3. Go through and make one minor change (e.g., in color, in location, or in number of points) to each of the subsection examples.

Review

1. Why do we use graphics?
2. When do we try not to use graphics?
3. Why is graphics interesting for a programmer?
4. What is a window?
5. In which namespace do we keep our graphics interface classes (our graphics library)?
6. What header files do you need to do basic graphics using our graphics library?

7. What is the simplest window to use?
8. What is the minimal window?
9. What's a window label?
10. How do you label a window?
11. How do screen coordinates work? Window coordinates? Mathematical coordinates?
12. What are examples of simple "shapes" that we can display?
13. What command attaches a shape to a window?
14. Which basic shape would you use to draw a hexagon?
15. How do you write text somewhere in a window?
16. How would you put a photo of your best friend in a window (using a program you wrote yourself)?
17. You made a **Window** object, but nothing appears on your screen. What are some possible reasons for that?
18. You have made a shape, but it doesn't appear in the window. What are some possible reasons for that?

Terms

color	graphics	JPEG
coordinates	GUI	line style
display	GUI library	software layer
fill color	HTTP	window
FLTK	image	XML

Exercises

We recommend that you use **Simple_window** for these exercises.

1. Draw a rectangle as a **Rectangle** and as a **Polygon**. Make the lines of the **Polygon** red and the lines of the **Rectangle** blue.
2. Draw a 100-by-30 **Rectangle** and place the text "Howdy!" inside it.
3. Draw your initials 150 pixels high. Use a thick line. Draw each initial in a different color.
4. Draw a checkers board: 8-by-8 alternating white and red squares.
5. Draw a red ¼-inch frame around a rectangle that is three-quarters the height of your screen and two-thirds the width.
6. What happens when you draw a **Shape** that doesn't fit inside its window? What happens when you draw a **Window** that doesn't fit on your screen? Write two programs that illustrate these two phenomena.
7. Draw a two-dimensional house seen from the front, the way a child would: with a door, two windows, and a roof with a chimney. Feel free to add details; maybe have "smoke" come out of the chimney.

8. Draw the Olympic five rings. If you can't remember the colors, look them up.
9. Display an image on the screen, e.g., a photo of a friend. Label the image both with a title on the window and with a caption in the window.
10. Draw the file diagram from §12.8.
11. Draw a series of regular polygons, one inside the other. The innermost should be an equilateral triangle, enclosed by a square, enclosed by a pentagon, etc. For the mathematically adept only: let all the points of each N-polygon touch sides of the (N+1)-polygon.
12. A superellipse is a two-dimensional shape defined by the equation

$$\left|\frac{x}{a}\right|^m + \left|\frac{y}{b}\right|^n = 1; \qquad m, n > 0.$$

Look up *superellipse* on the web to get a better idea of what such shapes look like. Write a program that draws "starlike" patterns by connecting points on a superellipse. Take **a**, **b**, **m**, **n**, and **N** as arguments. Select **N** points on the superellipse defined by **a**, **b**, **m**, and **n**. Make the points equally spaced for some definition of "equal." Connect each of those **N** points to one or more other points (if you like you can make the number of points connect to another argument or just use **N−1**, i.e., all the other points).
13. Find a way to add color to the superellipse shapes from the previous exercise. Make some lines one color and other lines another color or other colors.

Postscript

The ideal for program design is to have our concepts directly represented as entities in our program. So, we often represent ideas by classes, real-world entities by objects of classes, and actions and computations by functions. Graphics is a domain where this idea has an obvious application. We have concepts, such as circles and polygons, and we represent them in our program as class **Circle** and class **Polygon**. Where graphics is unusual is that when writing a graphics program, we also have the opportunity to see objects of those classes on the screen; that is, the state of our program is directly represented for us to observe – in most applications we are not that lucky. This direct correspondence between ideas, code, and output is what makes graphics programming so attractive. Please do remember, though, that graphics are just illustrations of the general idea of using classes to directly represent concepts in code. That idea is far more general and useful: just about anything we can think of can be represented in code as a class, an object of a class, or a set of classes.

13

Graphics Classes

"A language that doesn't change the way you think isn't worth learning."

—Traditional

Chapter 12 gave an idea of what we could do in terms of graphics using a set of simple interface classes, and how we can do it. This chapter presents many of the classes offered. The focus here is on the design, use, and implementation of individual interface classes such as **Point**, **Color**, **Polygon**, and **Open_polyline** and their uses. The following chapter will present ideas for designing sets of related classes and will also present more implementation techniques.

13.1 Overview of graphics classes

Graphics and GUI libraries provide lots of facilities. By "lots" we mean hundreds of classes, often with dozens of functions applying to each. Reading a description, manual, or documentation is a bit like looking at an old-fashioned botany text-book listing details of thousands of plants organized according to obscure classi-fying traits. It is daunting! It can also be exciting – looking at the facilities of a modern graphics/GUI library can make you feel like a child in a candy store, but it can be hard to figure out where to start and what is really good for you.

One purpose of our interface library is to reduce the shock delivered by the complexity of a full-blown graphics/GUI library. We present just two dozen classes with hardly any operations. Yet they allow you to produce useful graphi-cal output. A closely related goal is to introduce key graphics and GUI concepts through those classes. Already, you can write programs displaying results as sim-ple graphics. After this chapter, your range of graphics programs will have in-creased to exceed most people's initial requirements. After Chapter 14, you'll understand most of the design techniques and ideas involved so that you can deepen your understanding and extend your range of graphical expression as needed. You can do so either by adding to the facilities described here or by adopting another C++ graphics/GUI library.

The key interface classes are:

Graphics interface classes	
Color	used for lines, text, and filling shapes
Line_style	used to draw lines
Point	used to express locations on a screen and within a **Window**

Graphics interface classes (*continued*)	
Line	a line segment as we see it on the screen, defined by its two end **Point**s
Open_polyline	a sequence of connected line segments defined by a sequence of **Point**s
Closed_polyline	like an **Open_polyline**, except that a line segment connects the last **Point** to the first
Polygon	a **Closed_polyline** where no two line segments intersect
Text	a string of characters
Lines	a set of line segments defined by pairs of **Point**s
Rectangle	a common shape optimized for quick and convenient display
Circle	a circle defined by a center and a radius
Ellipse	an ellipse defined by a center and two axes
Function	a function of one variable graphed in a range
Axis	a labeled axis
Mark	a point marked by a character (such as **x** or **o**)
Marks	a sequence of points indicated by marks (such as **x** and **o**)
Marked_polyline	an **Open_polyline** with its points indicated by marks
Image	the contents of an image file

Chapter 15 examines **Function** and **Axis**. Chapter 16 presents the main GUI interface classes:

GUI interface classes	
Window	an area of the screen in which we display our graphics objects
Simple_window	a window with a "Next" button
Button	a rectangle, usually labeled, in a window that we can press to run one of our functions
In_box	a box, usually labeled, in a window into which a user can type a string
Out_box	a box, usually labeled, in a window into which our program can write a string
Menu	a vector of **Button**s

The source code is organized into files like this:

Graphics interface source files	
Point.h	Point
Graph.h	all other graphics interface classes
Window.h	Window
Simple_window.h	Simple_window
GUI.h	Button and the other GUI classes
Graph.cpp	definitions of functions from Graph.h
Window.ccp	definitions of functions from Window.h
GUI.cpp	definitions of functions from GUI.h

In addition to the graphics classes, we present a class that happens to be useful for holding collections for **Shapes** or **Widgets**:

A container of Shapes or Widgets	
Vector_ref	a vector with an interface that makes it convenient for holding unnamed elements

When you read the following sections, please don't move too fast. There is little that isn't pretty obvious, but the purpose of this chapter isn't just to show you some pretty pictures – you see prettier pictures on your computer screen or television every day. The main points of this chapter are

- To show the correspondence between code and the pictures produced.
- To get you used to reading code and thinking about how it works.
- To get you to think about the design of code – in particular to think about how to represent concepts as classes in code. Why do those classes look the way they do? How else could they have looked? We made many, many design decisions, most of which could reasonably have been made differently, in some cases radically differently.

So please don't rush. If you do, you'll miss something important and you might then find the exercises unnecessarily hard.

13.2 Point and Line

The most basic part of any graphic system is the point. To define *point* is to define how we organize our geometric space. Here, we use a conventional, computer-oriented layout of two-dimensional points defined by (x, y) integer coordinates. As described in §12.5, x coordinates go from **0** (representing the left-hand side of the screen) to **max_x()** (representing the right-hand side of the screen); y coordinates go from **0** (representing the top of the screen) to **max_y()** (representing the bottom of the screen).

As defined in **Point.h**, **Point** is simply a pair of **ints** (the coordinates):

```
struct Point {
    int x, y;
    Point(int xx, int yy) : x(xx), y(yy) { }
    Point() :x(0), y(0) { }
};


bool operator==(Point a, Point b) { return a.x==b.x && a.y==b.y; }
bool operator!=(Point a, Point b) { return !(a==b); }
```

In **Graph.h**, we find **Shape**, which we describe in detail in Chapter 14, and **Line**:

```
struct Line : Shape {            // a Line is a Shape defined by two Points
    Line(Point p1, Point p2);    // construct a Line from two Points
};
```

A **Line** is a kind of **Shape**. That's what ": **Shape**" means. **Shape** is called a *base class* for **Line** or simply a *base* of **Line**. Basically, **Shape** provides the facilities needed to make the definition of **Line** simple. Once we have a feel for the particular shapes, such as **Line** and **Open_polyline**, we'll explain what that implies (Chapter 14).

A **Line** is defined by two **Points**. Leaving out the "scaffolding" (**#includes**, etc. as described in §12.3), we can create lines and cause them to be drawn like this:

```
// draw two lines

Simple_window win1(Point(100,100),600,400,"two lines");

Line horizontal(Point(100,100),Point(200,100));    // make a horizontal line
Line vertical(Point(150,50),Point(150,150));       // make a vertical line

win1.attach(horizontal);    // attach the lines to the window
win1.attach(vertical);

win1.wait_for_button();     // display!
```

Executing that, we get

As a user interface designed for simplicity, **Line** works quite well. You don't need to be Einstein to guess that

> **Line vertical(Point(150,50),Point(150,150));**

creates a (vertical) line from (150,50) to (150,150). There are, of course, implementation details, but you don't have to know those to make **Line**s. The implementation of **Line**'s constructor is correspondingly simple:

```
Line::Line(Point p1, Point p2)      // construct a line from two points
{
        add(p1);       // add p1 to this shape
        add(p2);       // add p2 to this shape
}
```

That is, it simply "adds" two points. Adds to what? And how does a **Line** get drawn in a window? The answer lies in the **Shape** class. As we'll describe in Chapter 14, **Shape** can hold points defining lines, knows how to draw lines defined by pairs of **Point**s, and provides a function **add()** that allows an object to add to its **Shape**. The key point (*sic!*) here is that defining **Line** is trivial. Most of the implementation work is done by "the system" so that we can concentrate on writing simple classes that are easy to use.

From now on we'll leave out the definition of the **Simple_window** and the calls of **attach()**. Those are just more "scaffolding" that we need for a complete program but that adds little to the discussion of specific **Shapes**.

13.3 Lines

As it turns out, we rarely draw just one line. We tend to think in terms of objects consisting of many lines, such as triangles, polygons, paths, mazes, grids, bar graphs, mathematical functions, graphs of data, etc. One of the simplest such "composite graphical object classes" is **Lines**:

```
struct Lines : Shape {      // related lines
    void draw_lines() const;
    void add(Point p1, Point p2);      // add a line defined by two points
};
```

A **Lines** object is simply a collection of lines, each defined by a pair of **Points**. For example, had we considered the two lines from the **Line** example in §13.2 as part of a single graphical object, we could have defined them like this:

```
Lines x;
x.add(Point(100,100), Point(200,100));      // first line: horizontal
x.add(Point(150,50), Point(150,150));      // second line: vertical
```

This gives output that is indistinguishable (to the last pixel) from the **Line** version:

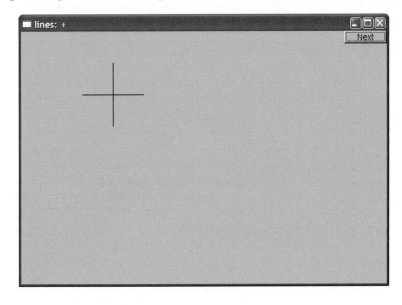

The only way we can tell that this is a different window is that we labeled them differently.

The difference between a set of **Line** objects and a set of lines in a **Lines** object is completely one of our view of what's going on. By using **Lines**, we have expressed our opinion that the two lines belong together and should be manipulated together. For example, we can change the color of all lines that are part of a **Lines** object with a single command. On the other hand, we can give lines that are individual **Line** objects different colors. As a more realistic example, consider how to define a grid. A grid consists of a number of evenly spaced horizontal and vertical lines. However, we think of a grid as one "thing," so we define those lines as part of a **Lines** object, which we call **grid**:

```
int x_size = win3.x_max();      // get the size of our window
int y_size = win3.y_max();
int x_grid = 80;
int y_grid = 40;

Lines grid;
for (int x=x_grid; x<x_size; x+=x_grid)
        grid.add(Point(x,0),Point(x,y_size));      // vertical line
for (int y = y_grid; y<y_size; y+=y_grid)
        grid.add(Point(0,y),Point(x_size,y));      // horizontal line
```

Note how we get the dimension of our window using **x_max()** and **y_max()**. This is also the first example where we are writing code that computes which objects we want to display. It would have been unbearably tedious to define this grid by defining one named variable for each grid line. From that code, we get

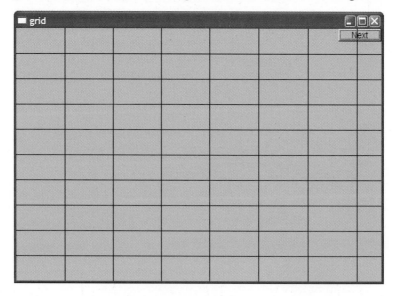

Let's return to the design of **Lines**. How are the member functions of class **Lines** implemented? **Lines** provides just two operations. The **add()** function simply adds a line defined by a pair of points to the set of lines to be displayed:

```
void Lines::add(Point p1, Point p2)
{
     Shape::add(p1);
     Shape::add(p2);
}
```

Yes, the **Shape::** qualification is needed because otherwise the compiler would see **add(p1)** as an (illegal) attempt to call **Lines**' **add()** rather than **Shape**'s **add()**.

The **draw_lines()** function draws the lines defined using **add()**:

```
void Lines::draw_lines() const
{
     if (color().visibility())
          for (int i=1; i<number_of_points(); i+=2)
               fl_line(point(i-1).x,point(i-1).y,point(i).x,point(i).y);
}
```

That is, **Lines::draw_lines()** takes two points at a time (starting with points 0 and 1) and draws the line between them using the underlying library's line-drawing function (**fl_draw()**). Visibility is a property of the **Lines**' **Color** object (§13.4), so we have to check that the lines are meant to be visible before drawing them.

As we explain in Chapter 14, **draw_lines()** is called by "the system." We don't need to check that the number of points is even – **Lines**' **add()** can add only pairs of points. The functions **number_of_points()** and **point()** are defined in class **Shape** (§14.2) and have their obvious meaning. These two functions provide read-only access to a **Shape**'s points. The member function **draw_lines()** is defined to be **const** (see §9.7.4) because it doesn't modify the shape.

We didn't supply **Lines** with a constructor because the model of starting out with no points and then **add()**ing points as needed is more flexible than any constructor could be. We could have provided constructors for simple cases (such as 1, 2, and 3 lines) or for an arbitrary number of lines, but there didn't seem to be a real need. If in doubt, don't add functionality. You can always add to a design if need is demonstrated, but you can rarely remove facilities from code that has found its way into use.

13.4 Color

Color is the type we use to represent color. We can use **Color** like this:

```
grid.set_color(Color::red);
```

This colors the lines defined in **grid** red so that we get

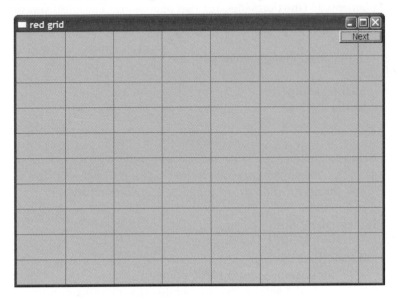

Color defines the notion of a color and gives symbolic names to a few of the more common colors:

```
struct Color {
     enum Color_type {
          red=FL_RED,
          blue=FL_BLUE,
          green=FL_GREEN,
          yellow=FL_YELLOW,
          white=FL_WHITE,
          black=FL_BLACK,
          magenta=FL_MAGENTA,
          cyan=FL_CYAN,
          dark_red=FL_DARK_RED,
          dark_green=FL_DARK_GREEN,
          dark_yellow=FL_DARK_YELLOW,
          dark_blue=FL_DARK_BLUE,
          dark_magenta=FL_DARK_MAGENTA,
          dark_cyan=FL_DARK_CYAN
     };

     enum Transparency { invisible = 0, visible=255 };

     Color(Color_type cc) :c(Fl_Color(cc)), v(visible) { }
```

```
        Color(Color_type cc, Transparency vv) :c(Fl_Color(cc)), v(vv) { }
        Color(int cc) :c(Fl_Color(cc)), v(visible) { }
        Color(Transparency vv) :c(Fl_Color()), v(vv) { }      // default color

        int as_int() const { return c; }

        char visibility() const { return v; }
        void set_visibility(Transparency vv) { v=vv; }
    private:
        char v;      // invisible and visible for now
        Fl_Color c;
    };
```

The purpose of **Color** is

- To hide the implementation's notion of color, FLTK's **Fl_Color** type
- To give the color constants a scope
- To provide a simple version of transparency (visible and invisible)

You can pick colors

- From the list of named colors, for example, **Color::dark_blue**.
- By picking from a small "palette" of colors that most screens display well by specifying a value in the range 0–255; for example, **Color(99)** is a dark green. For a code example, see §13.9.
- By picking a value in the RGB (red, green, blue) system, which we will not explain here. Look it up if you need it. In particular, a search for "RGB color" on the web gives many sources, such as www.hypersolutions.org/rgb.html and www.pitt.edu/~nisg/cis/web/cgi/rgb.html. See also exercises 13 and 14.

Note the use of constructors to allow **Color**s to be created either from the **Color_type** or from a plain **int**. The member **c** is initialized by each constructor. You could argue that **c** is too short and too obscure a name to use, but since it is used only within the small scope of **Color** and not intended for general use, that's probably OK. We made the member **c** private to protect it from direct use from our users. For our representation of the data member **c** we use the FLTK type **Fl_Color** that we don't really want to expose to our users. However, looking at a color as an **int** representing its RGB (or other) value is very common, so we supplied **as_int()** for that. Note that **as_int()** is a **const** member because it doesn't actually change the **Color** object that it is used for.

The transparency is represented by the member **v** which can hold the values **Transparency::visible** and **Transparency::invisible**, with their obvious meaning. It may surprise you that an "invisible color" can be useful, but it can be most useful to have part of a composite shape invisible.

13.5 Line_style

When we draw several lines in a window, we can distinguish them by color, by style, or by both. A line style is the pattern used to outline the line. We can use **Line_style** like this:

> grid.set_style(Line_style::dot);

This displays the lines in **grid** as a sequence of dots rather than a solid line:

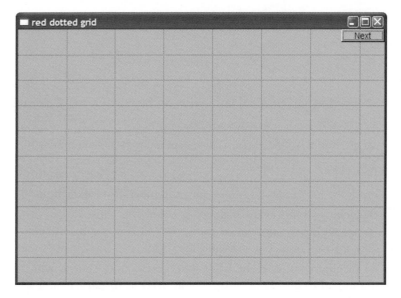

That "thinned out" the grid a bit, making it more discreet. By adjusting the width (thickness) we can adjust the grid lines to suit our taste and needs.

The **Line_style** type looks like this:

```
struct Line_style {
    enum Line_style_type {
        solid=FL_SOLID,                        // -------
        dash=FL_DASH,                          // - - - -
        dot=FL_DOT,                            // .......
        dashdot=FL_DASHDOT,                    // - . - .
        dashdotdot=FL_DASHDOTDOT,              // -..-..
    };

    Line_style(Line_style_type ss) :s(ss), w(0) { }
    Line_style(Line_style_type lst, int ww) :s(lst), w(ww) { }
    Line_style(int ss) :s(ss), w(0) { }
```

```
        int width() const { return w; }
        int style() const { return s; }
    private:
        int s;
        int w;
};
```

The programming techniques for defining **Line_style** are exactly the same as the ones we used for **Color**. Here, we hide the fact that FLTK uses plain **int**s to represent line styles. Why is something like that worth hiding? Because it is exactly such a detail that might change as a library evolves. The next FLTK release might very well have a **Fl_linestyle** type, or we might retarget our interface classes to some other GUI library. In either case, we wouldn't like to have our code and our users' code littered with plain **int**s that we just happened to know represent line styles.

Most of the time, we don't worry about style at all; we just rely on the default (default width and solid lines). This default line width is defined by the constructors in the cases where we don't specify one explicitly. Setting defaults is one of the things that constructors are good for, and good defaults can significantly help users of a class.

Note that **Line_style** has two "components": the style proper (e.g., use dashed or solid lines) and width (the thickness of the line used). The width is measured in integers. The default width is 1. We can request a fat dashed line like this:

   grid.set_style(Line_style(Line_style::dash,2));

This produces

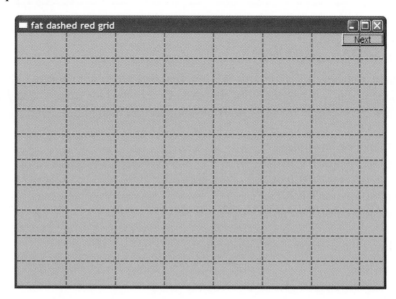

Note that color and style apply to all lines of a shape. That is one of the advantages of grouping many lines into a single graphics object, such as a **Lines**, **Open_polyline**, or **Polygon**. If we want to control the color or style for lines separately, we must define them as separate **Lines**. For example:

```
horizontal.set_color(Color::red);
vertical.set_color(Color::green);
```

This gives us

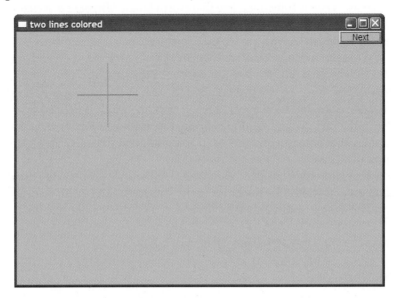

13.6 Open_polyline

An **Open_polyline** is a shape that is composed of a series of connected line segments defined by a series of points. *Poly* is the Greek word for "many," and *polyline* is a fairly conventional name for a shape composed of many lines. For example:

```
Open_polyline opl;
opl.add(Point(100,100));
opl.add(Point(150,200));
opl.add(Point(250,250));
opl.add(Point(300,200));
```

This draws the shape that you get by connecting the points:

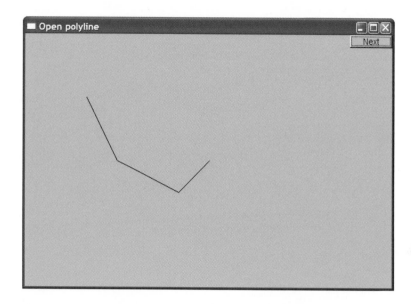

Basically, an **Open_polyline** is a fancy word for what we encountered in kindergarten playing "Connect the Dots."

Class **Open_polyline** is defined like this:

```
struct Open_polyline : Shape {      // open sequence of lines
    void add(Point p) { Shape::add(p); }
};
```

Yes, that's the complete definition. There is literally nothing to **Open_polyline** except its name and what it inherits from **Shape**. **Open_polyline**'s add() function is there simply to allow the users of an **Open_polyline** to access the **add()** from **Shape** (that is, **Shape::add()**). We don't even need to define a **draw_lines()** because **Shape** by default interprets the **Points** add()ed as a sequence of connected lines.

13.7 Closed_polyline

A **Closed_polyline** is just like an **Open_polyline**, except that we also draw a line from the last point to the first. For example, we could use the same points we used for the **Open_polyline** in §13.6 for a **Closed_polyline**:

```
Closed_polyline cpl;
cpl.add(Point(100,100));
cpl.add(Point(150,200));
cpl.add(Point(250,250));
cpl.add(Point(300,200));
```

The result is (of course) identical to that of §13.6 except for that final closing line:

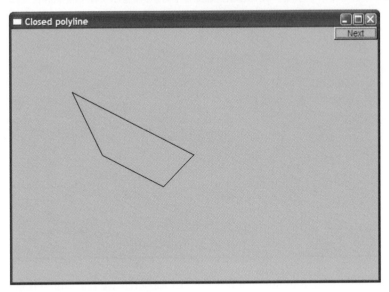

The definition of **Closed_polyline** is

```
struct Closed_polyline : Open_polyline {    // closed sequence of lines
     void draw_lines() const;
};

void Closed_polyline::draw_lines() const
{
     Open_polyline::draw_lines();    // first draw the "open polyline part"
     // then draw closing line:
     if (color().visibility())
          fl_line(point(number_of_points()–1).x,
                      point(number_of_points()–1).y,
                      point(0).x,
                      point(0).y);
}
```

Closed_polyline needs its own **draw_lines()** to draw that closing line connecting the last point to the first. Fortunately, we only have to do the little detail where **Closed_polyline** differs from what **Shape** offers. That's important and is sometimes called "programming by difference." We need to program only what's different about our derived class (here, **Closed_polyline**) compared to what a base class (here, **Open_polyline**) offers.

So how do we draw that closing line? We use the FLTK line-drawing function **fl_line()**. It takes four **ints** representing two points. So, here the underlying graphics library is again used. Note, however, that – as in every other case – the mention of

FLTK is kept within the implementation of our class rather than being exposed to our users. No user code needs to mention **fl_line()** or to know about interfaces where points appear implicitly as integer pairs. If we wanted to, we could replace FLTK with another GUI library with very little impact on our users' code.

13.8 Polygon

A **Polygon** is very similar to a **Closed_polyline**. The only difference is that for **Polygons** we don't allow lines to cross. For example, the **Closed_polyline** above is a polygon, but we can add another point:

    cpl.add(Point(100,250));

The result is

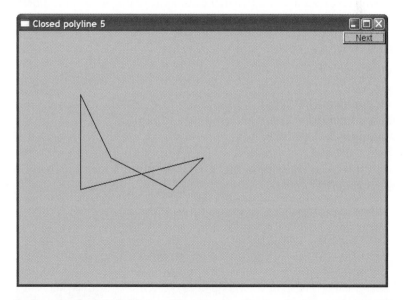

According to classical definitions, this **Closed_polyline** is not a polygon. How do we define **Polygon** so that we correctly capture the relationship to **Closed_poly-line** without violating the rules of geometry? The presentation above contains a strong hint. A **Polygon** is a **Closed_polyline** where lines do not cross. Alternatively, we could emphasize the way a shape is built out of points and say that a **Polygon** is a **Closed_polyline** where we cannot add a **Point** that defines a line segment that intersects one of the existing lines of the **Polygon**.

Given that idea, we define **Polygon** like this:

```
struct Polygon : Closed_polyline {  // closed sequence of nonintersecting lines
    void add(Point p);
    void draw_lines() const;
};
```

```
void Polygon::add(Point p)
{
        // check that the new line doesn't intersect existing lines
        Shape::add(p);
}
```

Here we inherit **Closed_polyline**'s definition of **draw_lines()**, thus saving a fair bit of work and avoiding duplication of code. Unfortunately, we have to check each **add()**. That yields an inefficient (order N-squared) algorithm – defining a **Polygon** with N points requires $N*(N-1)/2$ call of **intersect()**. In effect, we have made the assumption that **Polygon** class will be used for polygons of a low number of points. For example, creating a **Polygon** with 24 **Point**s involves $24*(24-1)/2 == 276$ calls of **intersect()**. That's probably acceptable, but if we wanted a polygon with 2000 points it would cost us about 2,000,000 calls, and we might look for a better algorithm, which might require a modified interface.

Anyway, we can create a polygon like this:

```
Polygon poly;
poly.add(Point(100,100));
poly.add(Point(150,200));
poly.add(Point(250,250));
poly.add(Point(300,200));
```

Obviously, this creates a **Polygon** that (to the last pixel) is identical to our original **Closed_polyline**:

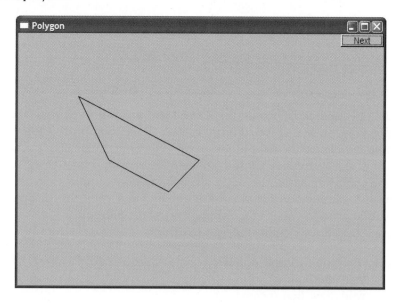

Ensuring that a **Polygon** really represents a polygon turned out to be surprisingly messy. The check for intersection that we left out of **Polygon::add()** is arguably the most complicated in the whole graphics library. If you are interested in fiddly coordinate manipulation of geometry, have a look at the code. And even then we are not done. Consider trying to make a **Polygon** with only two **Points**. We'd better protect against that:

```
void Polygon::draw_lines() const
{
        if (number_of_points() < 3) error("less than 3 points in a Polygon");
        Closed_polyline::draw_lines();
}
```

The trouble is that **Polygon**'s invariant "the points represent a polygon" can't be verified until all points have been defined; that is, we are not – as strongly recommended – establishing **Polygon**'s invariant in its constructor. Placing the "at least three points" check in **Polygon::draw_lines()** is a fairly disreputable trick. See also exercise 18.

13.9 Rectangle

The most common shape on a screen is a rectangle. The reasons for that are partly cultural (most of our doors, windows, pictures, walls, bookcases, pages, etc. are also rectangular) and partly technical (keeping a coordinate within rectangular space is simpler than for any other shaped space). Anyway, rectangles are so common that GUI systems support them directly rather than treating them simply as polygons that happen to have four corners and right angles.

```
struct Rectangle : Shape {
        Rectangle(Point xy, int hh, int ww);
        Rectangle(Point x, Point y);
        void draw_lines() const;

        int height() const { return h; }
        int width() const { return w; }
private:
        int h;    // height
        int w;    // width
};
```

We can specify a rectangle by two points (top left and bottom right) or by one point (top left) and a width and a height. The constructors can be defined like this:

```
Rectangle::Rectangle(Point xy, int ww, int hh)
    : w(ww), h(hh)
{
    if (h<=0 || w<=0)
        error("Bad rectangle: non-positive side");
    add(xy);
}

Rectangle::Rectangle(Point x, Point y)
    :w(y.x–x.x), h(y.y–x.y)
{
    if (h<=0 || w<=0)
        error("Bad rectangle: non-positive width or height");
    add(x);
}
```

Each constructor initializes the members **h** and **w** appropriately (using the member initialization syntax; see §9.4.4) and stores away the top left corner point in the **Rectangle**'s base **Shape** (using **add()**). In addition, it does a simple sanity check: we don't really want **Rectangles** with negative width or height.

One of the reasons that some graphics/GUI systems treat rectangles as special is that the algorithm for determining which pixels are inside a rectangle is far simpler – and therefore far faster – than for other shapes, such as **Polygons** and **Circles**. Consequently, the notion of "fill color" – that is, the color of the space inside the rectangle – is more commonly used for rectangles than for other shapes. We can set the fill color in a constructor or by the operation **set_fill_color()** (provided by **Shape** together with the other services related to color):

```
Rectangle rect00(Point(150,100),200,100);
Rectangle rect11(Point(50,50),Point(250,150));
Rectangle rect12(Point(50,150),Point(250,250));    // just below rect11
Rectangle rect21(Point(250,50),200,100);           // just to the right of rect11
Rectangle rect22(Point(250,150),200,100);          // just below rect21

rect00.set_fill_color(Color::yellow);
rect11.set_fill_color(Color::blue);
rect12.set_fill_color(Color::red);
rect21.set_fill_color(Color::green);
```

This produces

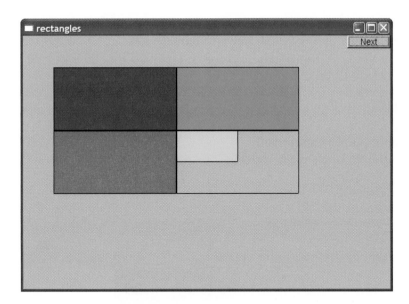

When you don't have a fill color, the rectangle is transparent; that's how you can see a corner of the yellow **rect00**.

We can move shapes around in a window (§14.2.3). For example:

```
rect11.move(400,0);          // to the right of rect21
rect11.set_fill_color(Color::white);
win12.set_label("rectangles 2");
```

This produces

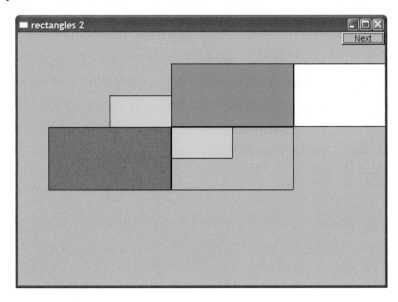

Note how only part of the white **rect11** fits in the window. What doesn't fit is "clipped"; that is, it is not shown anywhere on the screen.

Note also how shapes are placed one on top of another. This is done just like you would put sheets of paper on a table. The first one you put will be on the bottom. Our **Window** (§E.3) provides a simple way of reordering shapes. You can tell a window to put a shape on top (using **Window::put_on_top()**). For example:

```
win12.put_on_top(rect00);
win12.set_label("rectangles 3");
```

This produces

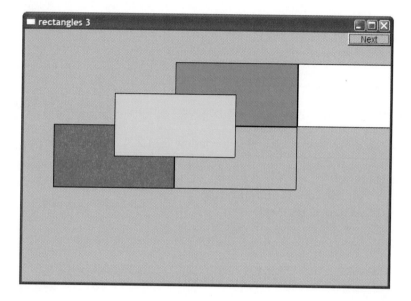

Note that we can see the lines that make up the rectangles even though we have filled (all but one of) them. If we don't like those outlines, we can remove them:

```
rect00.set_color(Color::invisible);
rect11.set_color(Color::invisible);
rect12.set_color(Color::invisible);
rect21.set_color(Color::invisible);
rect22.set_color(Color::invisible);
```

We get

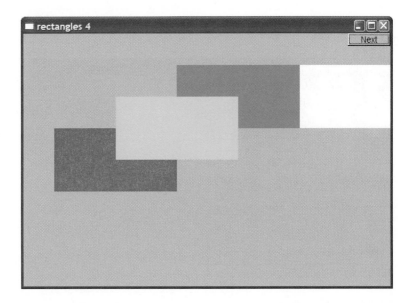

Note that with both fill color and line color set to **invisible, rect22** can no longer be seen.

Because it has to deal with both line color and fill color, **Rectangle**'s **draw_lines()** is a bit messy:

```
void Rectangle::draw_lines() const
{
    if (fill_color().visibility()) {        // fill
        fl_color(fill_color().as_int());
        fl_rectf(point(0).x,point(0).y,w,h);
    }

    if (color().visibility()) {              // lines on top of fill
        fl_color(color().as_int());
        fl_rect(point(0).x,point(0).y,w,h);
    }
}
```

As you can see, FLTK provides functions for drawing rectangle fill (**fl_rectf()**) and rectangle outlines (**fl_rect()**). By default, we draw both (with the lines/outline on top).

13.10 Managing unnamed objects

So far, we have named all our graphical objects. When we want lots of objects, this becomes infeasible. As an example, let us draw a simple color chart of the 256 colors in FLTK's palette; that is, let's make 256 colored squares and draw them in a 16-by-16 matrix that shows how colors with similar color values relate. First, here is the result:

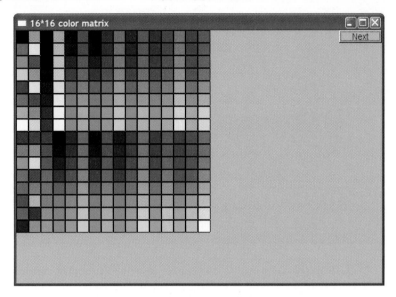

Naming those 256 squares would not only be tedious, it would be silly. The obvious "name" of the top left square is its location in the matrix (0,0), and any other square is similarly identified ("named") by a coordinate pair (i, j). What we need for this example is the equivalent of a matrix of objects. We thought of using a **vector<Rectangle>**, but that turned out to be not quite flexible enough. For example, it can be useful to have a collection of unnamed objects (elements) that are not all of the same type. We discuss that flexibility issue in §14.3. Here, we'll just present our solution: a vector type that can hold named and unnamed objects:

```
template<class T> class Vector_ref {
public:
    // ...
    void push_back(T&);      // add a named object
    void push_back(T*);      // add an unnamed object

    T& operator[](int i);        // subscripting: read and write access
    const T& operator[](int i) const;

    int size() const;
};
```

The way you use it is very much like a standard library **vector**:

```
Vector_ref<Rectangle> rect;
```

```
Rectangle x(Point(100,200),Point(200,300));
rect.push_back(x);     // add named

rect.push_back(new Rectangle(Point(50,60),Point(80,90)));   // add unnamed

for (int i=0; i<rect.size(); ++i) rect[i].move(10,10);    // use rect
```

We explain the **new** operator in Chapter 17, and the implementation of **Vector_ref**
is presented in Appendix E. For now, it is sufficient to know that we can use it to
hold unnamed objects. Operator **new** is followed by the name of a type (here, **Rectangle**) optionally followed by an initializer list (here, **(Point(50,60),Point(80,90))**).
Experienced programmers will be relieved to hear that we did not introduce a
memory leak in this example.

Given **Rectangle** and **Vector_ref**, we can play with colors. For example, we
can write a simple color chart of the 256 colors shown above:

```
Vector_ref<Rectangle> vr;

for (int i = 0; i<16; ++i)
    for (int j = 0; j<16; ++j) {
        vr.push_back(new Rectangle(Point(i*20,j*20),20,20));
        vr[vr.size()-1].set_fill_color(i*16+j);
        win20.attach(vr[vr.size()-1]);
    }
```

We make a **Vector_ref** of 256 **Rectangles**, organized graphically in the **Window** as
an 8-by-8 matrix. We give the **Rectangles** the colors 0, 1, 2, 3, 4, and so on. After
each **Rectangle** is created, we attach it to the window, so that it will be displayed:

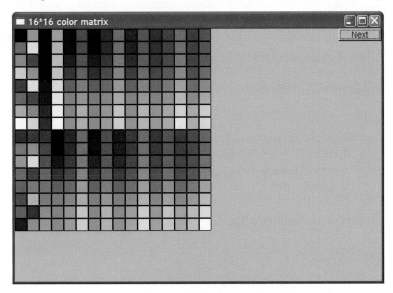

13.11 Text

Obviously, we want to be able to add text to our displays. For example, we might want to label our "odd" **Closed_polyline** from §13.8:

```
Text t(Point(200,200),"A closed polyline that isn't a polygon");
t.set_color(Color::blue);
```

We get

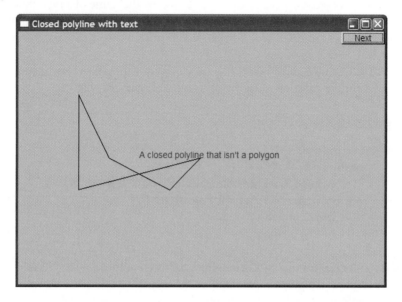

Basically, a **Text** object defines a line of text starting at a **Point**. The **Point** will be the bottom left corner of the text. The reason for restricting the string to be a single line is to ensure portability across systems. Don't try to put in a newline character; it may or may not be represented as a newline in your window. String streams (§11.4) are useful for composing **strings** for display in **Text** objects (examples in §12.7.7 and §12.7.8). **Text** is defined like this:

```
struct Text : Shape {
        // the point is the bottom left of the first letter
        Text(Point x, const string& s)
                : lab(s), fnt(fl_font()), fnt_sz(fl_size())
                { add(x); }

        void draw_lines() const;
```

```
            void set_label(const string& s) { lab = s; }
            string label() const { return lab; }

            void set_font(Font f) { fnt = f; }
            Font font() const { return Font(fnt); }

            void set_font_size(int s) { fnt_sz = s; }
            int font_size() const { return fnt_sz; }
    private:
            string lab;      // label
            Font fnt;
            int fnt_sz;
    };
```

Text has its own **draw_lines()** because only the **Text** class knows how its string is stored:

```
void Text::draw_lines() const
{
        fl_draw(lab.c_str(),point(0).x,point(0).y);
}
```

The color of the characters is determined exactly like the lines in shapes composed of lines (such as **Open_polyline** and **Circle**), so you can choose a color using **set_color()** and see what color is currently used by **color()**. The character size and font are handled analogously. There is a small number of predefined fonts:

```
class Font {        // character font
public:
        enum Font_type {
                helvetica=FL_HELVETICA,
                helvetica_bold=FL_HELVETICA_BOLD,
                helvetica_italic=FL_HELVETICA_ITALIC,
                helvetica_bold_italic=FL_HELVETICA_BOLD_ITALIC,
                courier=FL_COURIER,
                courier_bold=FL_COURIER_BOLD,
                courier_italic=FL_COURIER_ITALIC,
                courier_bold_italic=FL_COURIER_BOLD_ITALIC,
                times=FL_TIMES,
                times_bold=FL_TIMES_BOLD,
                times_italic=FL_TIMES_ITALIC,
```

```
            times_bold_italic=FL_TIMES_BOLD_ITALIC,
            symbol=FL_SYMBOL,
            screen=FL_SCREEN,
            screen_bold=FL_SCREEN_BOLD,
            zapf_dingbats=FL_ZAPF_DINGBATS
    };

    Font(Font_type ff) :f(ff) { }
    Font(int ff) :f(ff) { }

    int as_int() const { return f; }
private:
    int f;
};
```

The style of class definition used to define **Font** is the same as we used to define **Color** (§13.4) and **Line_style** (§13.5).

13.12 Circle

Just to show that the world isn't completely rectangular, we provide class **Circle** and class **Ellipse**. A **Circle** is defined by a center and a radius:

```
struct Circle : Shape {
    Circle(Point p, int rr);    // center and radius

    void draw_lines() const;

    Point center() const ;
    int radius() const { return r; }
    void set_radius(int rr) { r=rr; }
private:
    int r;
};
```

We can use **Circle** like this:

```
Circle c1(Point(100,200),50);
Circle c2(Point(150,200),100);
Circle c3(Point(200,200),150);
```

This produces three circles of different sizes aligned with their centers in a horizontal line:

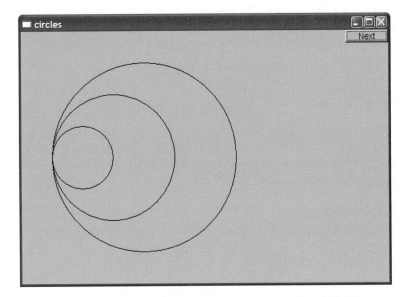

The main peculiarity of **Circle**'s implementation is that the point stored is not the center, but the top left corner of the square bounding the circle. We could have stored either but chose the one FLTK uses for its optimized circle-drawing routine. That way, **Circle** provides another example of how a class can be used to present a different (and supposedly nicer) view of a concept than its implementation:

```
Circle::Circle(Point p, int rr)        // center and radius
    :r(rr)
{
    add(Point(p.x-r,p.y-r));     // store top left corner
}

Point Circle::center() const
{
    return Point(point(0).x+r, point(0).y+r);
}

void Circle::draw_lines() const
{
    if (color().visibility())
    fl_arc(point(0).x,point(0).y,r+r,r+r,0,360);
}
```

Note the use of **fl_arc()** to draw the circle. The initial two arguments specify the top left corner, the next two arguments specify the width and the height of the smallest rectangle that encloses the circle, and the final two arguments specify the beginning and end angle to be drawn. A circle is drawn by going the full 360 degrees, but we can also use **fl_arc()** to write parts of a circle (and parts of an ellipse); see exercise 1.

13.13 Ellipse

An ellipse is similar to **Circle** but is defined with both a major and a minor axis, instead of a radius; that is, to define an ellipse, we give the center's coordinates, the distance from the center to a point on the *x* axis, and the distance from the center to a point on the *y* axis:

```
struct Ellipse : Shape {
        Ellipse(Point p, int w, int h);    // center, max and min distance from center

        void draw_lines() const;

        Point center() const;
        Point focus1() const;
        Point focus2() const;

        void set_major(int ww) { w=ww; }
        int major() const { return w; }

        void set_minor(int hh) { h=hh; }
        int minor() const { return h; }
private:
        int w;
        int h;
};
```

We can use **Ellipse** like this:

```
Ellipse e1(Point(200,200),50,50);
Ellipse e2(Point(200,200),100,50);
Ellipse e3(Point(200,200),100,150);
```

This gives us three ellipses with a common center but different-sized axes:

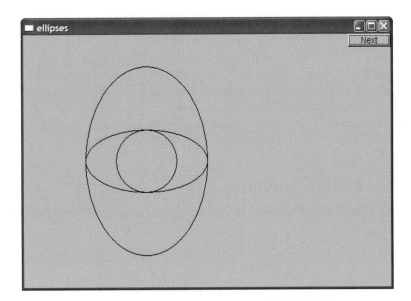

Note that an **Ellipse** with **major()==minor()** looks exactly like a circle.

Another popular view of an ellipse specifies two foci plus a sum of distances from a point to the foci. Given an **Ellipse**, we can compute a focus. For example:

```
Point Ellipse::focus1() const
{
        return Point(center().x+sqrt(double(w*w-h*h)),center().y);
}
```

Why is a **Circle** not an **Ellipse**? Geometrically, every circle is an ellipse, but not every ellipse is a circle. In particular, a circle is an ellipse where the two foci are equal. Imagine that we defined our **Circle** to be an **Ellipse**. We could do that at the cost of needing an extra value in its representation (a circle is defined by a point and a radius; an ellipse needs a center and a pair of axes). We don't like space overhead where we don't need it, but the primary reason for our **Circle** not being an **Ellipse** is that we couldn't define it so without somehow disabling **set_major()** and **set_minor()**. After all, it would not be a circle (as a mathematician would recognize it) if we could use **set_major()** to get **major()!=minor()** – at least it would no longer be a circle after we had done that. We can't have an object that is of one type sometimes (i.e., when **major()!=minor()**) and another type some other time (i.e., when **major()==minor()**). What we can have is an object (an **Ellipse**) that can look like a circle sometimes. A **Circle**, on the other hand, never morphs into an ellipse with two unequal axes.

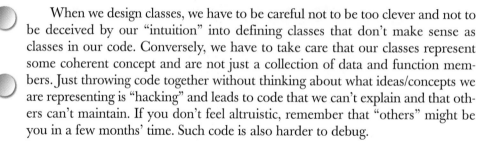

When we design classes, we have to be careful not to be too clever and not to be deceived by our "intuition" into defining classes that don't make sense as classes in our code. Conversely, we have to take care that our classes represent some coherent concept and are not just a collection of data and function members. Just throwing code together without thinking about what ideas/concepts we are representing is "hacking" and leads to code that we can't explain and that others can't maintain. If you don't feel altruistic, remember that "others" might be you in a few months' time. Such code is also harder to debug.

13.14 Marked_polyline

We often want to "label" points on a graph. One way of displaying a graph is as an open polyline, so what we need is an open polyline with "marks" at the points. A **Marked_polyline** does that. For example:

```
Marked_polyline mpl("1234");
mpl.add(Point(100,100));
mpl.add(Point(150,200));
mpl.add(Point(250,250));
mpl.add(Point(300,200));
```

This produces

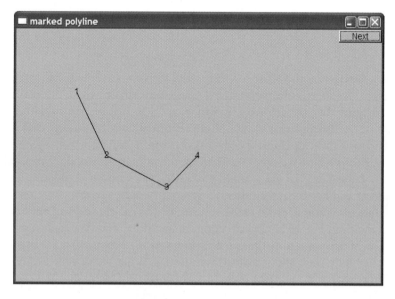

The definition of **Marked_polyline** is

We can select part of that image and add a photo of Rita as seen from space (**rita.jpg**):

```
Image rita(Point(0,0),"rita.jpg");
Image path(Point(0,0),"rita_path.gif");
path.set_mask(Point(50,250),600,400);     // select likely landfall

win.attach(path);
win.attach(rita);
```

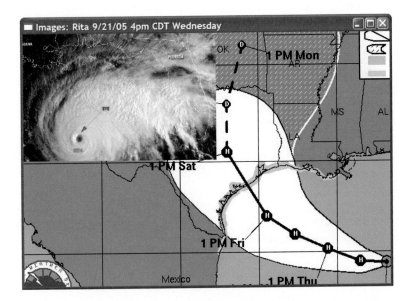

The **set_mask()** operation selects a sub-picture of an image to be displayed. Here, we selected a (600,400)-pixel image from **rita_path.gif** (loaded as **path**) with its top leftmost point at **path**'s point (50,600). Selecting only part of an image for display is so common that we chose to support it directly.

Shapes are laid down in the order they are attached, like pieces of paper on a desk, so we got **path** "on the bottom" simply by attaching it before **rita**.

Images can be encoded in a bewildering variety of formats. Here we deal with only two of the most common, JPEG and GIF:

```
struct Suffix {
        enum Encoding { none, jpg, gif };
};
```

In our graphics interface library, we represent an image in memory as an object of class **Image**:

```
struct Image : Shape {
    Image(Point xy, string file_name, Suffix::Encoding e = Suffix::none);
    ~Image() { delete p; }
    void draw_lines() const;
    void set_mask(Point xy, int ww, int hh)
        { w=ww; h=hh; cx=xy.x; cy=xy.y; }
private:
    int w,h;      // define "masking box" within image relative to
                  // position (cx,cy)
    int cx,cy;
    Fl_Image* p;
    Text fn;
};
```

The **Image** constructor tries to open a file with the name given to it. Then it tries to create a picture using the encoding specified as an optional argument or (more often) as a file suffix. If the image cannot be displayed (e.g., because the file wasn't found), the **Image** displays a **Bad_image**. The definition of **Bad_image** looks like this:

```
struct Bad_image : Fl_Image {
    Bad_image(int h, int w) : Fl_Image(h,w,0) { }
    void draw(int x,int y, int, int, int, int) { draw_empty(x,y); }
};
```

The handling of images within a graphics library is quite complicated, but the main complexity of our graphics interface class **Image** is in the file handling in the constructor:

```
// somewhat overelaborate constructor
// because errors related to image files can be such a pain to debug
Image::Image(Point xy, string s, Suffix::Encoding e)
    :w(0), h(0), fn(xy,"")
{
    add(xy);

    if (!can_open(s)) {      // can we open s?
        fn.set_label("cannot open \""+s+'\"');
```

```
                    p = new Bad_image(30,20);     // the "error image"
                    return;
            }

            if (e == Suffix::none) e = get_encoding(s);

            switch(e) {         // check if it is a known encoding
            case Suffix::jpg:
                    p = new Fl_JPEG_Image(s.c_str());
                    break;
            case Suffix::gif:
                    p = new Fl_GIF_Image(s.c_str());
                    break;
            default:    // unsupported image encoding
                    fn.set_label("unsupported file type \""+s+'\"');
                    p = new Bad_image(30,20); // the "error image"
            }
    }
```

We use the suffix to pick the kind of object we create to hold the image (a
Fl_JPEG_Image or a **Fl_GIF_Image**). We create that implementation object using
new and assign it to a pointer. This is an implementation detail (see Chapter 17
for a discussion of operator **new** and pointers) related to the organization of
FLTK and is of no fundamental importance here.

Now, we just have to implement **can_open()** to test if we can open a named
file for reading:

```
bool can_open(const string& s)
        // check if a file named s exists and can be opened for reading
{
        ifstream ff(s.c_str());
        return ff;
}
```

Opening a file and then closing it again is a fairly clumsy, but effective, way of
portably separating errors related to "can't open the file" from errors related to
the format of the data in the file.

You can look up the **get_encoding()** function, if you like. It simply looks for a
suffix and looks up that suffix in a table of known suffixes. That lookup table is a
standard library **map** (see Chapter 18).

Drill

1. Make an 800-by-1000 **Simple_window**.
2. Put an 8-by-8 grid on the leftmost 800-by-800 part of that window (so that each square is 100 by 100).
3. Make the eight squares on the diagonal starting from the top left corner red (use **Rectangle**).
4. Find a 200-by-200-pixel image (JPEG or GIF) and place three copies of it on the grid (each image covering four squares). If you can't find an image that is exactly 200 by 200, use **set_mask()** to pick a 200-by-200 section of a larger image. Don't obscure the red squares.
5. Add a 100-by-100 image. Have it move around from square to square when you click the "Next" button. Just put **wait_for_button()** in a loop with some code that picks a new square for your image.

Review

1. Why don't we "just" use a commercial or open-source graphics library directly?
2. About how many classes from our graphics interface library do you need to do simple graphic output?
3. What are the header files needed to use the graphics interface library?
4. What classes define closed shapes?
5. Why don't we just use **Line** for every shape?
6. What do the arguments to **Point** indicate?
7. What are the components of **Line_style**?
8. What are the components of **Color**?
9. What is RBG?
10. What are the differences between two **Lines** and a **Lines** containing two lines?
11. What properties can you set for every **Shape**?
12. How many sides does a **Closed_polyline** defined by five **Points** have?
13. What do you see if you define a **Shape** but don't attach it to a **Window**?
14. How does a **Rectangle** differ from a **Polygon** with four **Points** (corners)?
15. How does a **Polygon** differ from a **Closed_polyline**?
16. What's on top: fill or outline?
17. Why didn't we bother defining a **Triangle** class (after all, we did define **Rectangle**)?
18. How do you move a **Shape** to another place in a **Window**?
19. How do you label a **Shape** with a line of text?
20. What properties can you set for a text string in a **Text**?

21. What is a font and why do we care?
22. What is **Vector_ref** for and how do we use it?
23. What is the difference between a **Circle** and an **Ellipse**?
24. What happens if you try to display an **Image** given a file name that doesn't refer to a file containing an image?
25. How do you display part of an image?

Terms

closed shape	image	point
color	image encoding	polygon
ellipse	invisible	polyline
fill	JPEG	unnamed object
font	line	**Vector_ref**
font size	line style	visible
GIF	open shape	

Exercises

For each "define a class" exercise, display a couple of objects of the class to demonstrate that they work.

1. Define a class **Arc**, which draws a part of an ellipse. Hint: fl_arc().
2. Draw a box with rounded corners. Define a class **Box**, consisting of four lines and four arcs.
3. Define a class **Arrow**, which draws a line with an arrowhead.
4. Define functions **n()**, **s()**, **e()**, **w()**, **center()**, **ne()**, **se()**, **sw()**, and **nw()**. Each takes a **Rectangle** argument and returns a **Point**. These functions define "connection points" on and in the rectangle. For example, **nw(r)** is the northwest (top left) corner of a **Rectangle** called **r**.
5. Define the functions from exercise 4 for a **Circle** and an **Ellipse**. Place the connection points on or outside the shape but not outside the bounding rectangle.
6. Write a program that draws a class diagram like the one in §12.6. It will simplify matters if you start by defining a **Box** class that is a rectangle with a text label.
7. Make an RGB color chart (e.g., see www.1netcentral.com/rgb-color-chart.html).
8. Define a class **Hexagon** (a hexagon is a regular six-sided polygon). Use the center and the distance from the center to a corner point as constructor arguments.
9. Tile a part of a window with **Hexagon**s (use at least eight hexagons).

10. Define a class **Regular_polygon**. Use the center, the number of sides (>2), and the distance from the center to a corner as constructor arguments.

11. Draw a 300-by-200-pixel ellipse. Draw a 400-pixel-long x axis and a 300-pixel-long y axis through the center of the ellipse. Mark the foci. Mark a point on the ellipse that is not on one of the axes. Draw the two lines from the foci to the point.

12. Draw a circle. Move a mark around on the circle (let it move a bit each time you hit the "Next" button).

13. Draw the color matrix from §13.10, but without lines around each color.

14. Define a right triangle class. Make an octagonal shape out of eight right triangles of different colors.

15. "Tile" a window with small right triangles.

16. Do the previous exercise, but with hexagons.

17. Do the previous exercise, but using hexagons of a few different colors.

18. Define a class **Poly** that represents a polygon but checks that its points really do make a polygon in its constructor. Hint: You'll have to supply the points to the constructor.

19. Define a class **Star**. One parameter should be the number of points. Draw a few stars with differing numbers of points, differing line colors, and differing fill colors.

Postscript

Chapter 12 showed how to be a user of classes. This chapter moves us one level up the "food chain" of programmers: here we become tool builders in addition to being tool users.

Graphics Class Design

"Functional, durable, beautiful."

—Vitruvius

T he purpose of the graphics chapters is dual: we want to
provide useful tools for displaying information, but we also
use the family of graphical interface classes to illustrate general
design and implementation techniques. In particular, this chapter
presents some ideas of interface design and the notion of inheritance. Along the way, we have to take a slight detour to examine
the language features that most directly support object-oriented
programming: class derivation, virtual functions, and access control. We don't believe that design can be discussed in isolation
from use and implementation, so our discussion of design is
rather concrete. Maybe you'd better think of this chapter as
"Graphics Class Design and Implementation."

14.1 Design principles

What are the design principles for our graphics interface classes? First: What kind of question is that? What are "design principles" and why do we need to look at those instead of getting on with the serious business of producing neat pictures?

14.1.1 Types

Graphics is an example of an application domain. So, what we are looking at here is an example of how to present a set of fundamental application concepts and facilities to programmers (like us). If the concepts are presented confusingly, inconsistently, incompletely, or in other ways poorly represented in our code, the difficulty of producing graphical output is increased. We want our graphics classes to minimize the effort of a programmer trying to learn and to use them.

Our ideal of program design is to represent the concepts of the application domain directly in code. That way, if you understand the application domain, you understand the code and vice versa. For example:

- **Window** – a window as presented by the operating system
- **Line** – a line as you see it on the screen
- **Point** – a coordinate point
- **Color** – as you see it on the screen
- **Shape** – what's common for all shapes in our graphics/GUI view of the world

The last example, **Shape**, is different from the rest in that it is a generalization, a purely abstract notion. We never see just a shape on the screen; we see a particular shape, such as a line or a hexagon. You'll find that reflected in the definition of our types: try to make a **Shape** variable and the compiler will stop you.

The set of our graphics interface classes is a library; the classes are meant to be used together and in combination. They are meant to be used as examples to follow when you define classes to represent other graphical shapes and as building blocks for such classes. We are not just defining a set of unrelated classes, so we can't make design decisions for each class in isolation. Together, our classes present a view of how to do graphics. We must ensure that this view is reasonably elegant and coherent. Given the size of our library and the enormity of the domain of graphical applications, we cannot hope for completeness. Instead, we aim for simplicity and extensibility.

In fact, no class library directly models all aspects of its application domain. That's not only impossible; it is also pointless. Consider writing a library for displaying geographical information. Do you want to show vegetation? National, state, and other political boundaries? Road systems? Railroads? Rivers? Highlight social and economic data? Seasonal variations in temperature and humidity? Wind patterns in the atmosphere above? Airline routes? Mark the locations of schools? The locations of fast-food "restaurants"? Local beauty spots? "All of that!" may be a good answer for a comprehensive geographical application, but it is not an answer for a single display. It may be an answer for a library supporting such geographical applications, but it is unlikely that such a library could also cover other graphical applications such as freehand drawing, editing photographic images, scientific visualization, and aircraft control displays.

So, as ever, we have to decide what's important to us. In this case, we have to decide which kind of graphics/GUI we want to do well. Trying to do everything is a recipe for failure. A good library directly and cleanly models its application domain from a particular perspective, emphasizes some aspects of the application, and deemphasizes others.

The classes we provide here are designed for simple graphics and simple graphical user interfaces. They are primarily aimed at users who need to present data and graphical output from numeric/scientific/engineering applications. You can build your own classes "on top of" ours. If that is not enough, we expose sufficient FLTK details in our implementation for you to get an idea of how to use that (or a similar "full-blown" graphics/GUI library) directly, should you so desire. However, if you decide to go that route, wait until you have absorbed Chapters 17 and 18. Those chapters contain information about pointers and memory management that you need for successful direct use of most graphics/GUI libraries.

One key decision is to provide a lot of "little" classes with few operations. For example, we provide **Open_polyline**, **Closed_polyline**, **Polygon**, **Rectangle**, **Marked_polyline**, **Marks**, and **Mark** where we could have provided a single class (possibly called "polyline") with a lot of arguments and operations that allowed us to specify which kind of polyline an object was and possibly even mutate a polyline from one kind to another. The extreme of this kind of thinking would be to provide every kind of shape as part of a single class **Shape**. We think that using many small classes most closely and most usefully models our domain of graphics. A single class providing "everything" would leave the user messing with data and options without a framework to help understanding, debugging, and performance.

14.1.2 Operations

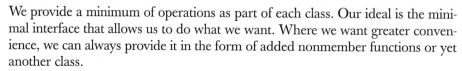

We provide a minimum of operations as part of each class. Our ideal is the minimal interface that allows us to do what we want. Where we want greater convenience, we can always provide it in the form of added nonmember functions or yet another class.

We want the interfaces of our classes to show a common style. For example, all functions performing similar operations in different classes have the same name, take arguments of the same types, and where possible require those arguments in the same order. Consider the constructors: if a shape requires a location, it takes a **Point** as its first argument:

```
Line ln(Point(100,200),Point(300,400));
Mark m(Point(100,200),'x');        // display a single point as an "x"
Circle c(Point(200,200),250);
```

All functions that deal with points use class **Point** to represent them. That would seem obvious, but many libraries exhibit a mixture of styles. For example, imagine a function for drawing a line. We could use one of two styles:

```
void draw_line(Point p1, Point p2);          // from p1 to p2 (our style)
void draw_line(int x1, int y1, int x2, int y2);   // from (x1,y1) to (x2,y2)
```

We could even allow both, but for consistency, improved type checking, and improved readability we use the first style exclusively. Using **Point** consistently also saves us from confusion between coordinate pairs and the other common pair of integers: width and height. For example, consider:

```
draw_rectangle(Point(100,200), 300, 400);   // our style
draw_rectangle (100,200,300,400);           // alternative
```

The first call draws a rectangle with a point, width, and height. That's reasonably easy to guess, but how about the second call? Is that a rectangle defined by points (100,200) and (300,400)? A rectangle defined by a point (100,200), a width 300, and a height 400? Something completely different (though plausible to someone)? Using the **Point** type consistently avoids such confusion.

Incidentally, if a function requires a width and a height, they are always presented in that order (just as we always give an x coordinate before a y coordinate). Getting such little details consistent makes a surprisingly large difference to the ease of use and the avoidance of run-time errors.

Logically identical operations have the same name. For example, every function that adds points, lines, etc. to any kind of shape is called **add()**, and any function that draws lines is called **draw_lines()**. Such uniformity helps us remember (by offering fewer details to remember) and helps us when we design new classes ("just do the usual"). Sometimes, it even allows us to write code that works for many different types, because the operations on those types have an identical pattern. Such code is called *generic*; see Chapters 19–21.

14.1.3 Naming

Logically different operations have different names. Again, that would seem obvious, but consider: why do we "attach" a **Shape** to a **Window**, but "add" a **Line** to a **Shape**? In both cases, we "put something into something," so shouldn't that similarity be reflected by a common name? No. The similarity hides a fundamental difference. Consider:

```
Open_polyline opl;
opl.add(Point(100,100));
opl.add(Point(150,200));
opl.add(Point(250,250));
```

Here, we copy three points into **opl**. The shape **opl** does not care about "our" points after a call to **add()**; it keeps its own copies. In fact, we rarely keep copies of the points — we leave that to the shape. On the other hand, consider:

```
win.attach(opl);
```

Here, we create a connection between the window **win** and our shape **opl**; **win** does not make a copy of **opl** — it keeps a reference to **opl**. So, it is our responsibility to keep **opl** valid as long as **win** uses it. That is, we must not exit **opl**'s scope while **win** is using **opl**. We can update **opl** and the next time **win** comes to draw **opl** our changes will appear on the screen. We can illustrate the difference between **attach()** and **add()** graphically:

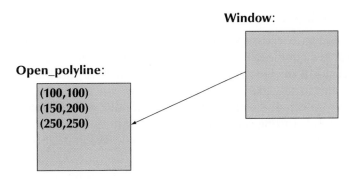

Basically, **add**() uses pass-by-value (copies) and **attach**() uses pass-by-reference (shares a single object). We could have chosen to copy graphical objects into **Windows**. However, that would have given a different programming model, which we would have indicated by using **add**() rather than **attach**(). As it is, we just "attach" a graphics object to a **Window**. That has important implications. For example, we can't create an object, attach it, allow the object to be destroyed, and expect the resulting program to work:

```
void f(Simple_window& w)
{
        Rectangle r(Point(100,200),50,30);
        w.attach(r);
}       // oops, the lifetime of r ends here

int main()
{
        Simple_window win(Point(100,100),600,400,"My window");
        // . . .
        f(win);        // asking for trouble
        // . . .
        win.wait_for_button();
}
```

By the time we have exited from **f**() and reached **wait_for_button**(), there is no **r** for the **win** to refer to and display. In Chapter 17, we'll show how to create objects within a function and have them survive after the return from the function. Until then, we must avoid attaching objects that don't survive until the call of **wait_for_button**(). We have **Vector_ref** (§13.10, §E.4) to help with that.

Note that had we declared **f**() to take its **Window** as a **const** reference argument (as recommended in §8.5.6), the compiler would have prevented our mistake: we can't **attach(r)** to a **const Window** because **attach**() needs to make a change to the **Window** to record the **Window**'s interest in **r**.

14.1.4 Mutability

When we design a class, "Who can modify the data (representation)?" and "How?" are key questions that we must answer. We try to ensure that modification to the state of an object is done only by its own class. The **public/private** distinction is key to this, but we'll show examples where a more flexible/subtle mechanism (**protected**) is employed. This implies that we can't just give a class a data member, say a **string** called **label**; we must also consider if it should be possible to modify it after construction, and if so, how. We must also decide if code other than our class's member functions need to read the value of **label**, and if so, how. For example:

```
struct Circle {
      // . . .
private:
      int r;    // radius
};


Circle c(Point(100,200),50);
c.r = -9;     // OK? No — compile-time error: Circle::r is private
```

As you might have noticed in Chapter 13, we decided to prevent direct access to most data members. Not exposing the data directly gives us the opportunity to check against "silly" values, such as a **Circle** with a negative radius. For simplicity of implementation, we take only limited advantage of this opportunity, so do be careful with your values. The decision not to consistently and completely check reflects a desire to keep the code short for presentation and the knowledge that if a user (you, us) supplies "silly" values the result is simply a messed-up image on the screen and not corruption of precious data.

We treat the screen (seen as a set of **Windows**) purely as an output device. We can display new objects and remove old ones, but we never ask "the system" for information that we don't (or couldn't) know ourselves from the data structures we have built up representing our images.

14.2 Shape

Class **Shape** represents the general notion of something that can appear in a **Window** on a screen:

- It is the notion that ties our graphical objects to our **Window** abstraction, which in turn provides the connection to the operating system and the physical screen.
- It is the class that deals with color and the style used to draw lines. To do that it holds a **Line_style** and a **Color** (for lines and for fill).
- It can hold a sequence of **Points** and has a basic notion of how to draw them.

Experienced designers will recognize that a class doing three things probably has problems with generality. However, here, we need something far simpler than the most general solution.

We'll first present the complete class and then discuss its details:

```
class Shape {      // deals with color and style and holds sequence of lines
public:
      void draw() const;                // deal with color and draw lines
      virtual void move(int dx, int dy); // move the shape +=dx and +=dy

      void set_color(Color col);
      Color color() const;

      void set_style(Line_style sty);
      Line_style style() const;

      void set_fill_color(Color col);
      Color fill_color() const;

      Point point(int i) const;          // read-only access to points
      int number_of_points() const;

      virtual ~Shape() { }
protected:
      Shape();
      virtual void draw_lines() const;  // draw the appropriate lines
      void add(Point p);                // add p to points
      void set_point(int i, Point p);   // points[i]=p;
private:
      vector<Point> points;             // not used by all shapes
      Color lcolor;                     // color for lines and characters
      Line_style ls;
      Color fcolor;                     // fill color

      Shape(const Shape&);              // prevent copying
      Shape& operator=(const Shape&);
};
```

This is a relatively complex class designed to support a wide variety of graphics classes and to represent the general concept of a shape on the screen. However, it still has only four data members and 15 functions. Furthermore, those functions are all close to trivial so that we can concentrate on design issues. For the rest of this section we will go through the members one by one and explain their role in the design.

14.2.1 An abstract class

Consider first **Shape**'s constructor:

```
protected:
      Shape();
```

The constructor is **protected**. That means that it can only be used directly from classes derived from **Shape** (using the **:Shape** notation). In other words, **Shape** can only be used as a base for classes, such as **Line** and **Open_polyline**. The purpose of that "**protected:**" is to ensure that we don't make **Shape** objects directly. For example:

```
Shape ss;      // error: cannot construct Shape
```

Shape is designed to be a base class only. In this case, nothing particularly nasty would happen if we allowed people to create **Shape** objects directly, but by limiting use, we keep open the possibility of modifications to **Shape** that would render it unsuitable for direct use. Also, by prohibiting the direct creation of **Shape** objects, we directly model the idea that we cannot have/see a general shape, only particular shapes, such as **Circle** and **Closed_polyline**. Think about it! What does a shape look like? The only reasonable response is the counter question "What shape?" The notion of a shape that we represent by **Shape** is an abstract concept. That's an important and frequently useful design notion, so we don't want to compromise it in our program. Allowing users to directly create **Shape** objects would do violence to our ideal of classes as direct representations of concepts. The constructor is defined like this:

```
Shape::Shape()
      : lcolor(fl_color()),     // default color for lines and characters
      ls(0),                    // default style
      fcolor(Color::invisible)  // no fill
{
}
```

It is a default constructor, so it sets the members to their default. Here again, the underlying library used for implementation, FLTK, "shines through." However, FLTK's notions of color and style are not mentioned directly by the uses. They are only part of the implementation of our **Shape**, **Color**, and **Line_style** classes. The **vector<Points>** defaults to an empty vector.

A class is *abstract* if it can be used only as a base class. The other – more common – way of achieving that is called a *pure virtual function*; see §14.3.5. A class that can be used to create objects — that is, the opposite of an abstract class — is called a *concrete* class. Note that *abstract* and *concrete* are simply technical words for an everyday distinction. We might go to the store to buy a camera. However, we can't just ask for a camera and take it home. What brand of camera? Which particular model camera? The word *camera* is a generalization; it refers to an abstract notion. An Olympus E-3 refers to a specific kind of camera, which we (in exchange for a large amount of cash) might acquire a particular instance of: a particular camera with a unique serial number. So, "camera" is much like an abstract (base) class; "Olympus E-3" is much like a concrete (derived) class, and the actual camera in my hand (if I bought it) would be much like an object.

The declaration

```
virtual ~Shape() { }
```

defines a virtual destructor. We won't use that for now, so we leave the explanation to §17.5.2, where we show a use.

14.2.2 Access control

Class **Shape** declares all data members private:

```
private:
        vector<Point> points;
        Color lcolor;
        Line_style ls;
        Color fcolor;
```

Since the data members of **Shape** are declared private, we need to provide access functions. There are several possible styles for doing this. We chose one that we consider simple, convenient, and readable. If we have a member representing a property **X**, we provide a pair of functions **X()** and **set_X()** for reading and writing, respectively. For example:

```
void Shape::set_color(Color col)
{
        lcolor = col;

}

Color Shape::color() const
{
        return lcolor;
}
```

The main inconvenience of this style is that you can't give the member variable the same name as its readout function. As ever, we chose the most convenient names for the functions because they are part of the public interface. It matters far less what we call our private variables. Note the way we use **const** to indicate that the readout functions do not modify their **Shape** (§9.7.4).

Shape keeps a vector of **Point**s, called **points**, that a **Shape** maintains in support of its derived classes. We provide the function **add()** for adding **Point**s to **points**:

```
void Shape::add(Point p)          // protected
{
        points.push_back(p);
}
```

Naturally, **points** start out empty. We decided to provide **Shape** with a complete functional interface rather than giving users – even member functions of classes derived from **Shape** – direct access to data members. To some, providing a functional interface is a no-brainer, because they feel that making any member of a class public is bad design. To others, our design seems overly restrictive because we don't allow direct write access to the members to all members of derived classes.

A shape derived from **Shape**, such as **Circle** and **Polygon**, knows what its points mean. The base class **Shape** does not "understand" the points; it only stores them. Therefore, the derived classes need control over how points are added. For example:

- **Circle** and **Rectangle** do not allow a user to add points; that just wouldn't make sense. What would be a rectangle with an extra point? (§12.7.6)
- **Lines** allows only pairs of points to be added (and not an individual point; §13.3).
- **Open_polyline** and **Marks** allow any number of points to be added.
- **Polygon** allows a point to be added only by an **add()** that checks for intersections (§13.8).

We made **add()** **protected** (that is, accessible from a derived class only) to ensure that derived classes take control over how points are added. Had **add()** been **public** (everybody can add points) or **private** (only **Shape** can add points), this close match of functionality to our idea of shapes would not have been possible.

Similarly, we made **set_point()** **protected**. In general, only a derived class can know what a point means and whether it can be changed without violating an invariant. For example, if we have a **Regular_hexagon** class defined as a set of six points, changing just a single point would make the resulting figure "not a regular hexagon." On the other hand, if we changed one of the points of a rectangle, the result would still be a rectangle. In fact, we didn't find a need for **set_points()** in our example classes and code, so **set_point()** is there, just to ensure that the rule that we can read and set every attribute of a **Shape** holds. For example, if we wanted a **Mutable_rectangle**, we could derive it from **Rectangle** and provide operations to change the points.

We made the vector of **Points**, **points**, private to protect it against undesired modification. To make it useful, we also need to provide access to it:

```
void Shape::set_point(int i, Point p)        // not used; not necessary so far
{
        points[i] = p;
}

Point Shape::point(int i) const
{
        return points[i];
}

int Shape::number_of_points() const
{
        return points.size();
}
```

In derived class member functions, these functions are used like this:

```
void Lines::draw_lines() const
        // draw lines connecting pairs of points
{
        for (int i=1; i<number_of_points(); i+=2)
                fl_line(point(i−1).x,point(i−1).y,point(i).x,point(i).y);
}
```

You might worry about all those trivial access functions. Are they not inefficient? Do they slow down the program? Do they increase the size of the program? No, they will all be compiled away ("inlined") by the compiler. Calling **number_of_points()** will take up exactly as many bytes of memory and execute exactly as many instructions as calling **points.size()** directly.

These access control considerations and decisions are important. We could have provided this close-to-minimal version of **Shape**:

```
struct Shape {        // close-to-minimal definition — too simple — not used
        Shape();
        void draw() const;        // deal with color and call draw_lines
```

```
        virtual void draw_lines() const;   // draw the appropriate lines
        virtual void move(int dx, int dy); // move the shape +=dx and +=dy

        vector<Point> points;              // not used by all shapes
        Color lcolor;
        Line_style ls;
        Color fcolor;
    };
```

What value did we add by those extra 12 member functions and two lines of access specifications (**private:** and **protected:**)? The basic answer is that protecting the representation ensures that it doesn't change in ways unanticipated by a class designer so that we can write better classes with less effort. This is the argument about "invariants" (§9.4.3). Here, we'll point out such advantages as we define classes derived from **Shape**. One simple example is that earlier versions of **Shape** used

```
    Fl_Color lcolor;
    int line_style;
```

This turned out to be too limiting (an **int** line style doesn't elegantly support line width, and **Fl_Color** doesn't accommodate invisible) and led to some messy code. Had these two variables been public and used in a user's code, we could have improved our interface library only at the cost of breaking that code (because it mentioned the names **line_color** and **line_style**).

In addition, the access functions often provide notational convenience. For example, **s.add(p)** is easier to read and write than **s.points.push_back(p)**.

14.2.3 Drawing shapes

We have now described almost all but the real heart of class **Shape**:

```
    void draw() const;                    // deal with color and call draw_lines
    virtual void draw_lines() const;      // draw the lines appropriately
```

Shape's most basic job is to draw shapes. We could not remove all other functionality from **Shape** and leave it with no data of its own without doing major conceptual harm (see §14.4); drawing is **Shape**'s essential business. It does so using FLTK and the operating system's basic machinery, but from a user's point of view, it provides just two functions:

- **draw()** applies style and color and then calls **draw_lines()**.
- **draw_lines()** puts pixels on the screen.

The **draw()** function doesn't use any novel techniques. It simply calls FLTK functions to set the color and style to what is specified in the **Shape**, calls **draw_lines()**

to do the actual drawing on the screen, and then tries to restore the color and shape to what they were before the call:

```
void Shape::draw() const
{
    Fl_Color oldc = fl_color();
    // there is no good portable way of retrieving the current style
    fl_color(lcolor.as_int());              // set color
    fl_line_style(ls.style(),ls.width());   // set style
    draw_lines();
    fl_color(oldc);        // reset color (to previous)
    fl_line_style(0);      // reset line style to default
}
```

Unfortunately, FLTK doesn't provide a way of obtaining the current style, so the style is just set to a default. That's the kind of compromise we sometimes have to accept as the cost of simplicity and portability. We didn't think it worthwhile to try to implement that facility in our interface library.

Note that **Shape::draw()** doesn't handle fill color or the visibility of lines. Those are handled by the individual **draw_line()** functions that have a better idea of how to interpret them. In principle, all color and style handling could be delegated to the individual **draw_line()** functions, but that would be quite repetitive.

Now consider how we might handle **draw_lines()**. If you think about it for a bit, you'll realize that it would be hard for a **Shape** function to draw all that needs to be drawn for every kind of shape. To do so would require that every last pixel of each shape should somehow be stored in the **Shape** object. If we kept the **vector<Point>** model, we'd have to store an awful lot of points. Worse, "the screen" (that is, the graphics hardware) already does that – and does it better.

To avoid that extra work and extra storage, **Shape** takes another approach: it gives each **Shape** (that is, each class derived from **Shape**) a chance to define what it means to draw it. A **Text**, **Rectangle**, or **Circle** class may each have a clever way of drawing itself. In fact, most such classes do. After all, such classes "know" exactly what they are supposed to represent. For example, a **Circle** is defined by a point and a radius, rather than, say, a lot of line segments. Generating the required bits for a **Circle** from the point and radius if and when needed isn't really all that hard or expensive. So **Circle** defines its own **draw_lines()** which we want to call instead of **Shape**'s **draw_lines()**. That's what the **virtual** in the declaration of **Shape::draw_lines()** means:

```
struct Shape {
    // . . .
```

```
        virtual void draw_lines() const;    // let each derived class define its
                                            // own draw_lines() if it so chooses
        // . . .
};

    struct Circle : Shape {
        // . . .
        void draw_lines() const;    // "override" Shape::draw_lines()
        // . . .
    };
```

So, **Shape**'s **draw_lines()** must somehow invoke one of **Circle**'s functions if the **Shape** is a **Circle** and one of **Rectangle**'s functions if the **Shape** is a **Rectangle**. That's what the word **virtual** in the **draw_lines()** declaration ensures: if a class derived from **Shape** has defined its own **draw_lines()** (with the same type as **Shape**'s **draw_lines()**), that **draw_lines()** will be called rather than **Shape**'s **draw_lines()**. Chapter 13 shows how that's done for **Text**, **Circle**, **Closed_polyline**, etc. Defining a function in a derived class so that it can be used through the interfaces provided by a base is called *overriding*.

Note that despite its central role in **Shape**, **draw_lines()** is **protected**; it is not meant to be called by "the general user" − that's what **draw()** is for − but simply as an "implementation detail" used by **draw()** and the classes derived from **Shape**.

This completes our display model from §12.2. The system that drives the screen knows about **Window**. **Window** knows about **Shape** and can call **Shape**'s **draw()**. Finally, **draw()** invokes the **draw_lines()** for the particular kind of shape. A call of **gui_main()** in our user code starts the display engine.

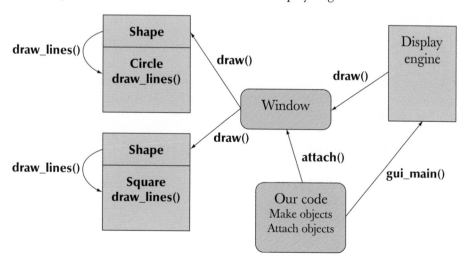

What **gui_main()**? So far, we haven't actually seen **gui_main()** in our code. Instead we use **wait_for_button()**, which invokes the display engine in a more simple-minded manner.

Shape's **move()** function simply moves every point stored relative to the current position:

```
void Shape::move(int dx, int dy)        // move the shape +=dx and +=dy
{
        for (int i = 0; i<points.size(); ++i) {
                points[i].x+=dx;
                points[i].y+=dy;
        }
}
```

Like **draw_lines()**, **move()** is virtual because a derived class may have data that needs to be moved and that **Shape** does not know about. For example, see **Axis** (§12.7.3 and §15.4).

The **move()** function is not logically necessary for **Shape**; we just provided it for convenience and to provide another example of a virtual function. Every kind of **Shape** that has points that it didn't store in its **Shape** must define its own **move()**.

14.2.4 Copying and mutability

The **Shape** class declared the copy constructor and the copy assignment operator private:

```
private:
        Shape(const Shape&);             // prevent copying
        Shape& operator=(const Shape&);
```

The effect is that only members of **Shape** can copy objects of **Shape** using the default copy operations. That is a common idiom for preventing accidental copying. For example:

```
void my_fct(const Open_polyline& op, const Circle& c)
{
        Open_polyline op2 = op;   // error: Shape's copy constructor is private
        vector<Shape> v;
        v.push_back(c);                   // error: Shape's copy constructor is private
```

```
// . . .
    op = op2;                        // error: Shape's assignment is private
}
```

But copying is useful in so many places! Just look at that **push_back()**; without copying, it is hard even to use **vectors** (**push_back()** puts a *copy* of its argument into its **vector**). Why would anyone make trouble for programmers by preventing copying? You prohibit the default copy operations for a type if they are likely to cause trouble. As a prime example of "trouble," look at **my_fct()**. We cannot copy a **Circle** into a **Shape**-sized element "slot" in **v**; a **Circle** has a radius but **Shape** does not so **sizeof(Shape)<sizeof(Circle)**. If that **v.push_back(c)** were allowed, the **Circle** would be "sliced" and any future use of the resulting **Shape** element would most likely lead to a crash; the **Circle** operations would assume a radius member (**r**) that hadn't been copied:

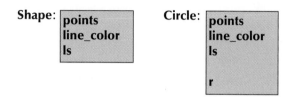

The copy construction of **op2** and the assignment to **op** suffer from exactly the same problem. Consider:

```
Marked_polyline mp("x");
Circle c(p,10);
my_fct(mp,c);     // the Open_polyline argument refers to a Marked_polyline
```

Now the copy operations of the **Open_polyline** would "slice" **mp**'s **string** member **mark** away.

Basically, class hierarchies plus pass-by-reference and default copying do not mix. When you design a class that is meant to be a base class in a hierarchy, disable its copy constructor and copy assignment as was done for **Shape**.

Slicing (yes, that's really a technical term) is not the only reason to prevent copying. There are quite a few concepts that are best represented without copy operations. Remember that the graphics system has to remember where a **Shape** is stored to display it to the screen. That's why we "attach" **Shapes** to a **Window**, rather than copy. The **Window** would know nothing about a copy, so a copy would in a very real sense not be as good as its original.

If we want to copy objects of types where the default copy operations have been disabled, we can write an explicit function to do the job. Such a copy function is often called **clone()**. Obviously, you can write a **clone()** only if the functions for reading members are sufficient for expressing what is needed to construct a copy, but that is the case for all **Shapes**.

14.3 Base and derived classes

Let's take a more technical view of base and derived classes; that is, let us for this section (only) change the focus of discussion from programming, application design, and graphics to programming language features. When designing our graphics interface library, we relied on three key language mechanisms:

- *Derivation:* a way to build one class from another so that the new class can be used in place of the original. For example, **Circle** is derived from **Shape**, or in other words, "a **Circle** is a kind of **Shape**" or "**Shape** is a base of **Circle**." The derived class (here, **Circle**) gets all of the members of its base (here, **Shape**) in addition to its own. This is often called *inheritance* because the derived class "inherits" all of the members of its base. In some contexts, a derived class is called a *subclass* and a base class is called a *superclass*.

- *Virtual functions:* the ability to define a function in a base class and have a function of the same name and type in a derived class called when a user calls the base class function. For example, when **Window** calls **draw_lines()** for a **Circle**, it is the **Circle**'s **draw_lines()** that is executed, rather than **Shape**'s own **draw_lines()**. This is often called *run-time polymorphism, dynamic dispatch,* or *run-time dispatch* because the function called is determined at run time based on the type of the object used.

- *Private and protected members:* We kept the implementation details of our classes private to protect them from direct use that could complicate maintenance. That's often called *encapsulation*.

The use of inheritance, run-time polymorphism, and encapsulation is the most common definition of *object-oriented programming*. Thus, C++ directly supports object-oriented programming in addition to other programming styles. For example, in Chapters 20–21, we'll see how C++ supports generic programming. C++ borrowed – with explicit acknowledgments – its key mechanisms from Simula67, the first language to directly support object-oriented programming (see Chapter 22).

That was a lot of technical terminology! But what does it all mean? And how does it actually work on our computers? Let's first draw a simple diagram of our graphics interface classes showing their inheritance relationships:

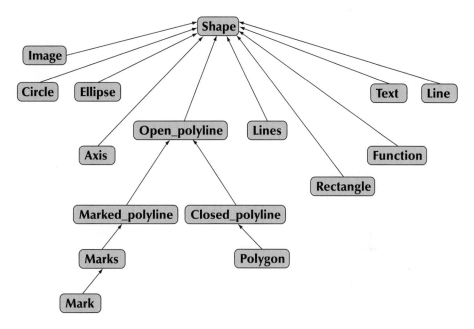

The arrows point from a derived class to its base. Such diagrams help visualize class relationships and often decorate the blackboards of programmers. Compared to commercial frameworks this is a tiny "class hierarchy" with only 16 classes, and only in the case of **Open_polyline**'s many descendants is the hierarchy more than one deep. Clearly the common base (**Shape**) is the most important class here, even though it represents an abstract concept so that we never directly make a shape.

14.3.1 Object layout

How are objects laid out in memory? As we saw in §9.4.1, members of a class define the layout of objects: data members are stored one after another in memory. When inheritance is used, the data members of a derived class are simply added after those of a base. For example:

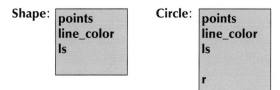

A **Circle** has the data members of a **Shape** (after all, it is a kind of **Shape**) and can be used as a **Shape**. In addition, **Circle** has "its own" data member **r** placed after the inherited data members.

To handle a virtual function call, we need (and have) one more piece of data in a **Shape** object: something to tell which function is really invoked when we call **Shape**'s **draw_lines()**. The way that is usually done is to add the address of a table of functions. This table is usually referred to as the **vtbl** (for "virtual table" or "virtual function table") and its address is often called the **vptr** (for "virtual pointer"). We discuss pointers in Chapters 17–18; here, they act like references. A given implementation may use different names for **vtbl** and **vptr**. Adding the **vptr** and the **vtbls** to the picture we get

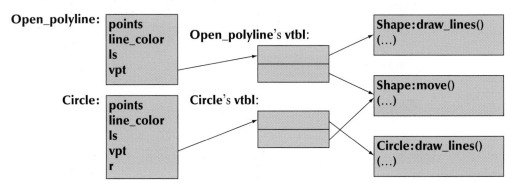

Since **draw_lines()** is the first virtual function, it gets the first slot in the **vtbl**, followed by that of **move()**, the second virtual function. A class can have as many virtual functions as you want it to have; its **vtbl** will be as large as needed (one slot per virtual function). Now when we call **x.draw_lines()**, the compiler generates a call to the function found in the **draw_lines()** slot in the **vtbl** for **x**. Basically, the code just follows the arrows on the diagram. So if **x** is a **Circle**, **Circle::draw_lines()** will be called. If **x** is of a type, say **Open_polyline**, that uses the **vtbl** exactly as **Shape** defined it, **Shape::draw_lines()** will be called. Similarly, **Circle** didn't define its own **move()** so **x.move()** will call **Shape::move()** if **x** is a **Circle**. Basically, code generated for a virtual function call simply finds the **vptr**, uses that to get to the right **vtbl**, and calls the appropriate function there. The cost is about two memory accesses plus the cost of an ordinary function call. This is simple and fast.

Shape is an abstract class so you can't actually have an object that's just a **Shape**, but an **Open_polyline** will have exactly the same layout as a "plain shape" since it doesn't add a data member or define a virtual function. There is just one **vtbl** for each class with a virtual function, not one for each object, so the **vtbls** tend not to add significantly to a program's object code size.

Note that we didn't draw any non-virtual functions in this picture. We didn't need to because there is nothing special about the way such functions are called and they don't increase the size of objects of their type.

Defining a function of the same name and type as a virtual function from a base class (such as **Circle::draw_lines()**) so that the function from the derived class is put into the **vtbl** instead of the version from the base is called *overriding*. For example, **Circle::draw_lines()** overrides **Shape::draw_lines()**.

Why are we telling you about **vtbls** and memory layout? Do you need to know about that to use object-oriented programming? No. However, many people strongly prefer to know how things are implemented (we are among those), and when people don't understand something, myths spring up. We have met people who were terrified of virtual functions "because they were expensive." Why? How expensive? Compared to what? Where would the cost matter? We explain the implementation model for virtual functions so that you won't have such fears. If you need a virtual function call (to select among alternatives at run time) you can't code the functionality to be any faster or to use less memory using other language features. You can see that for yourself.

14.3.2   Deriving classes and defining virtual functions

We specify that a class is to be a derived class by mentioning a base after the class name. For example:

```
struct Circle : Shape { /* . . . */ };
```

By default, the members of a **struct** are public (§9.3), and that will include public members of a base. We could equivalently have said

```
class Circle : public Shape { public: /* . . . */ };
```

These two declarations of **Circle** are completely equivalent, but you can have many long and fruitless discussions with people about which is better. We are of the opinion that time can be spent more productively on other topics.

Beware of forgetting **public** when you need it. For example:

```
class Circle : Shape { public: /* . . . */ };   // probably a mistake
```

This would make **Shape** a private base of **Circle**, making **Shape**'s public functions inaccessible for a **Circle**. That's unlikely to be what you meant. A good compiler will warn about this likely error. There are uses for private base classes, but those are beyond the scope of this book.

A virtual function must be declared **virtual** in its class declaration, but if you place the function definition outside the class, the keyword **virtual** is neither required nor allowed out there. For example:

```
struct Shape {
        // . . .
        virtual void draw_lines() const;
        virtual void move();
        // . . .
};
```

```
virtual void Shape::draw_lines() const { /* . . . */ }      // error
void Shape::move() { /* . . . */ }                           // OK
```

14.3.3 Overriding

When you want to override a virtual function, you must use exactly the same name and type as in the base class. For example:

```
struct Circle : Shape {
        void draw_lines(int) const;    // probably a mistake (int argument?)
        void drawlines() const;        // probably a mistake (misspelled name?)
        void draw_lines();             // probably a mistake (const missing?)
        // . . .
};
```

Here, the compiler will see three functions that are independent of **Shape:: draw_lines()** (because they have a different name or a different type) and won't override it. A good compiler will warn about these likely mistakes. There is nothing you can or must say in an overriding function to ensure that it actually overrides a base class function.

The **draw_lines()** example is real and can therefore be hard to follow in all details, so here is a purely technical example that illustrates overriding:

```
struct B {
        virtual void f() const { cout << "B::f "; }
        void g() const { cout << "B::g "; }           // not virtual
};
```

```
struct D : B {
        void f() const { cout << "D::f "; }           // overrides B::f
        void g() { cout << "D::g "; }
};
```

```
struct DD : D {
        void f() { cout << "DD::f "; }        // doesn't override D::f (not const)
        void g() const { cout << "DD::g "; }
};
```

Here, we have a small class hierarchy with (just) one virtual function **f()**. We can try using it. In particular, we can try to call **f()** and the non-virtual **g()**, which is a function that doesn't know what type of object it had to deal with except that it is a **B** (or something derived from **B**):

```
void call(const B& b)
        // a D is a kind of B, so call() can accept a D
        // a DD is a kind of D and a D is a kind of B, so call() can accept a DD
{
        b.f();
        b.g();
}

int main()
{
        B b;
        D d;
        DD dd;

        call(b);
        call(d);
        call(dd);

        b.f();
        b.g();

        d.f();
        d.g();

        dd.f();
        dd.g();
}
```

You'll get

B::f B::g D::f B::g D::f B::g B::f B::g D::f D::g DD::f DD::g

When you understand why, you'll know the mechanics of inheritance and virtual functions.

14.3.4 Access

C++ provides a simple model of access to members of a class. A member of a class can be

- *Private:* If a member is **private**, its name can be used only by members of the class in which it is declared.

- *Protected:* If a member is **protected**, its name can be used only by members of the class in which it is declared and members of classes derived from that.
- *Public:* If a member is **public**, its name can be used by all functions.

Or graphically:

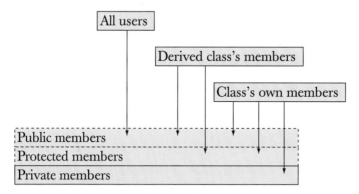

A base can also be **private**, **protected**, or **public**:

- If a base of class **D** is **private**, its **public** and **protected** member names can be used only by members of **D**.
- If a base of class **D** is **protected**, its **public** and **protected** member names can be used only by members of **D** and members of classes derived from **D**.
- If a base is **public**, its name can be used by all functions.

These definitions ignore the concept of "friend" and a few minor details, which are beyond the scope of this book. If you want to become a language lawyer you need to study Stroustrup, *The Design and Evolution of C++* and *The C++ Programming Language*, and the 2003 ISO C++ standard. We don't recommend becoming a language lawyer (someone knowing every little detail of the language definition); being a programmer (a software developer, an engineer, a user, whatever you prefer to call someone who actually uses the language) is much more fun and typically much more useful to society.

14.3.5 Pure virtual functions

An abstract class is a class that can be used only as a base class. We use abstract classes to represent concepts that are abstract; that is, we use abstract classes for concepts that are generalizations of common characteristics of related entities. Thick books of philosophy have been written trying to precisely define *abstract concept* (or *abstraction* or *generalization* or . . .). However you define it philosophically, the notion of an abstract concept is immensely useful. Examples are "animal" (as opposed to any particular kind of animal), "device driver" (as oppose to the driver for any particular kind of device), and "publication" (as opposed to any particular kind of book or magazine). In programs, abstract classes usually define interfaces to groups of related classes (*class hierarchies*).

In §14.2.1, we saw how to make a class abstract by declaring its constructor **protected**. There is another – and much more common – way of making a class abstract: state that one or more of its virtual functions needs to be overridden in a derived class. For example:

```
class B {    // abstract base class
public:
        virtual void f() =0;  // pure virtual function
        virtual void g() =0;
};


B b;      // error: B is abstract
```

The curious **=0** notation says that the virtual functions **B::f()** and **B::g()** are "pure"; that is, they must be overridden in some derived class. Since **B** has pure virtual functions, we cannot create an object of class **B**. Overriding the pure virtual functions solves this "problem":

```
class D1 : public B {
public:
        void f();
        void g();
};


D1 d1;     // OK
```

Note that unless all pure virtual functions are overridden, the resulting class is still abstract:

```
class D2 : public B {
public:
        void f();
        // no g()
};


D2 d2;      // error: D2 is (still) abstract
```

```
class D3 : public D2 {
public:
     void g();
};

D3 d3;     // ok
```

Classes with pure virtual functions tend to be pure interfaces; that is, they tend to have no data members (the data members will be in the derived classes) and consequently have no constructors (if there are no data members to initialize, a constructor is unlikely to be needed).

14.4 Benefits of object-oriented programming

When we say that **Circle** is derived from **Shape**, or that **Circle** is a kind of **Shape**, we do so to obtain (either or both)

- *Interface inheritance:* A function expecting a **Shape** (usually as a reference argument) can accept a **Circle** (and can use a **Circle** through the interface provided by **Shape**).

- *Implementation inheritance:* When we define **Circle** and its member functions, we can take advantage of the facilities (such as data and member functions) offered by **Shape**.

A design that does not provide interface inheritance (that is, a design for which an object of a derived class cannot be used as an object of its public base class) is a poor and error-prone design. For example, we might define a class called **Never_do_this** with **Shape** as its public base. Then we could override **Shape::draw()** with a function that didn't draw the shape, but instead moved its center 100 pixels to the left. That "design" is fatally flawed because even though **Never_do_this** provides the interface of a **Shape**, its implementation does not maintain the semantics (meaning, behavior) required of a **Shape**. Never do that!

Interface inheritance gets its name because its benefits come from code using the interface provided by a base class ("an interface"; here, **Shape**) and not having to know about the derived classes ("implementations"; here, classes derived from **Shape**).

Implementation inheritance gets its name because the benefits come from the simplification in the implementation of derived classes (e.g., **Circle**) provided by the facilities offered by the base class (here, **Shape**).

Note that our graphics design critically depends on interface inheritance: the "graphics engine" calls **Shape::draw()** which in turn calls **Shape**'s virtual function **draw_lines()** to do the real work of putting images on the screen. Neither the "graphics engine" nor indeed class **Shape** knows which kinds of shapes exist. In particular, our "graphics engine" (FLTK plus the operating system's graphics facilities) was written and compiled years before our graphics classes! We just define particular shapes and **attach()** them to **Window**s as **Shape**s (**Window::attach()** takes a **Shape&** argument; see §E.3). Furthermore, since class **Shape** doesn't know about your graphics classes, you don't need to recompile **Shape** each time you define a new graphics interface class.

In other words, we can add new **Shape**s to a program without modifying existing code. This is a holy grail of software design/development/maintenance: extension of a system without modifying it. There are limits to which changes we can make without modifying existing classes (e.g., **Shape** offers a rather limited range of services), and the technique doesn't apply well to all programming problems (see, for example, Chapters 17–19 where we define **vector**; inheritance has little to offer for that). However, interface inheritance is one of the most powerful techniques for designing and implementing systems that are robust in the face of change.

Similarly, implementation inheritance has much to offer, but it is no panacea. By placing useful services in **Shape**, we save ourselves the bother of repeating work over and over again in the derived classes. That can be most significant in real-world code. However, it comes at the cost that any change to the interface of **Shape** or any change to the layout of the data members of **Shape** necessitates a recompilation of all derived classes and their users. For a widely used library, such recompilation can be simply infeasible. Naturally, there are ways of gaining most of the benefits while avoiding most of the problems; see §14.3.5.

✓ Drill

Unfortunately, we can't construct a drill for the understanding of general design principles, so here we focus on the language features that support object-oriented programming.

1. Define a class **B1** with a virtual function **vf()** and a non-virtual function **f()**. Define both of these functions within class **B1**. Implement each function to output its name (e.g. "**B1::vf()**"). Make the functions public. Make a **B1** object and call each function.
2. Derive a class **D1** from **B1** and override **vf()**. Make a **D1** object and call **vf()** and **f()** for it.
3. Define a reference to **B1** (a **B1&**) and initialize that to the **D1** object you just defined. Call **vf()** and **f()** for that reference.
4. Now define a function called **f()** for **D1** and repeat 1–3. Explain the results.
5. Add a pure virtual function called **pvf()** to **B1** and try to repeat 1–4. Explain the result.
6. Define a class **D2** derived from **D1** and override **pvf()** in **D2**. Make an object of class **D2** and invoke **f()**, **vf()**, and **pvf()** for it.

7. Define a class **B2** with a pure virtual function **pvf()**. Define a class **D21** with a **string** data member and a member function that overrides **pvf()**; **D21::pvf()** should output the value of the **string**. Define a class **D22** that is just like **D21** except that its data member is an **int**. Define a function **f()** that takes a **B2&** argument and calls **pvf()** for its argument. Call **f()** with a **D21** and a **D22**.

Review

1. What is an application domain?
2. What are ideals for naming?
3. What can we name?
4. What services does a **Shape** offer?
5. How does an abstract class differ from a class that is not abstract?
6. How can you make a class abstract?
7. What is controlled by access control?
8. What good can it do to make a data member **private**?
9. What is a virtual function and how does it differ from a non-virtual function?
10. What is a base class?
11. What makes a class derived?
12. What do we mean by object layout?
13. What can you do to make a class easier to test?
14. What is an inheritance diagram?
15. What is the difference between a **protected** member and a **private** one?
16. What members of a class can be accessed from a class derived from it?
17. How does a pure virtual function differ from other virtual functions?
18. Why would you make a member function virtual?
19. Why would you make a virtual member function pure?
20. What does overriding mean?
21. How does interface inheritance differ from implementation inheritance?
22. What is object-oriented programming?

Terms

abstract class	mutability	pure virtual function
access control	object layout	subclass
base class	object-oriented	superclass
derived class	polymorphism	virtual function
dispatch	private	virtual function call
encapsulation	protected	virtual function table
inheritance	public	

Exercises

1. Define two classes **Smiley** and **Frowny**, which are both derived from class **Circle** and have two eyes and a mouth. Next, derive classes from **Smiley** and **Frowny**, which add an appropriate hat to each.
2. Try to copy a **Shape**. What happens?
3. Define an abstract class and try to define an object of that type. What happens?
4. Define a class **Immobile_Circle**, which is just like **Circle** but can't be moved.
5. Define a **Striped_rectangle** where instead of fill, the rectangle is "filled" by drawing one-pixel-wide horizontal lines across the inside of the rectangle (say, draw every second line like that). You may have to play with the width of lines and the line spacing to get a pattern you like.
6. Define a **Striped_circle** using the technique from **Striped_rectangle**.
7. Define a **Striped_closed_polyline** using the technique from **Striped_rectangle** (this requires some algorithmic inventiveness).
8. Define a class **Octagon** to be a regular octagon. Write a test that exercises all of its functions (as defined by you or inherited from **Shape**).
9. Define a **Group** to be a container of **Shape**s with suitable operations applied to the various members of the **Group**. Hint: **Vector_ref**. Use a **Group** to define a checkers (draughts) board where pieces can be moved under program control.
10. Define a class **Pseudo_window** that looks as much like a **Window** as you can make it without heroic efforts. It should have rounded corners, a label, and control icons. Maybe you could add some fake "contents," such as an image. It need not actually do anything. It is acceptable (and indeed recommended) to have it appear within a **Simple_window**.
11. Define a **Binary_tree** class derived from **Shape**. Give the number of levels as a parameter (**levels==0** means no nodes, **levels==1** means one node, **levels==2** means one top node with two sub-nodes, **levels==3** means one top node with two sub-nodes each with two sub-nodes, etc.). Let a node be represented by a small circle. Connect the nodes by lines (as is conventional). P.S. In computer science, trees grow downward from a top node (amusingly, but logically, often called the root).
12. Modify **Binary_tree** to draw its nodes using a virtual function. Then, derive a new class from **Binary_tree** that overrides that virtual function to use a different representation for a node (e.g., a triangle).
13. Modify **Binary_tree** to take a parameter (or parameters) to indicate what kind of line to use to connect the nodes (e.g., an arrow pointing down or a red arrow pointing up). Note how this exercise and the last use two alternative ways of making a class hierarchy more flexible and useful.

14. Add an operation to **Binary_tree** that adds text to a node. You may have to modify the design of **Binary_tree** to implement this elegantly. Choose a way to identify a node; for example, you might give a string **"lrrlr"** for navigating left, right, right, left, and right down a binary tree (the root node would match both an initial **l** and an initial **r**).

15. Most class hierarchies have nothing to do with graphics. Define a class **Iterator** with a pure **virtual** function **next()** that returns a **double***. Now derive **Vector_iterator** and **List_iterator** from **Iterator** so that **next()** for a **Vector_iterator** yields a pointer to the next element of a **vector<double>** and **List_iterator** does the same for a **list<double>**. You initialize a **Vector_iterator** with a **vector<double>** and the first call of **next()** yields a pointer to its first element, if any. If there is no next element, return 0. Test this by using a function **void print(Iterator&)** to print the elements of a **vector<double>** and a **list<double>**.

16. Define a class **Controller** with four virtual functions **on()**, **off()**, **set_level(int)**, and **show()**. Derive at least two classes from **Controller**. One should be a simple test class where **show()** prints out whether the class is set to on or off and what is the current level. The second derived class should somehow control the line color of a **Shape**; the exact meaning of "level" is up to you. Try to find a third "thing" to control with such a **Controller** class.

17. The exceptions defined in the C++ standard library, such as **exception**, **runtime_exception**, and **out_of_range** (§5.6.3), are organized into a class hierarchy (with a useful virtual function **what()** returning a string supposedly explaining what went wrong). Search your information sources for the C++ standard exception class hierarchy and draw a class hierarchy diagram of it.

Postscript

The ideal for software is not to build a single program that does everything. The ideal is to build a lot of classes that closely reflect our concepts and that work together to allow us to build our applications elegantly, with minimal effort (relative to the complexity of our task), with adequate performance, and with confidence that the results produced are correct. Such programs are comprehensible and maintainable in a way that code that was simply thrown together to get a particular job done as quickly as possible is not. Classes, encapsulation (as supported by **private** and **protected**), inheritance (as supported by class derivation), and run-time polymorphism (as supported by **virtual** functions) are among our most powerful tools for structuring systems.

15

Graphing Functions
and Data

"The best is the enemy of the good."

—Voltaire

If you are in any empirical field, you need to graph data. If you
are in any field that uses math to model phenomena, you need
to graph functions. This chapter discusses basic mechanisms for
such graphics. As usual, we show the use of the mechanisms and
also discuss their design. The key examples are graphing a function of one argument and displaying values read from a file.

15.1 Introduction

Compared to the professional software systems you'll use if such visualization becomes your main occupation, the facilities presented here are primitive. Our primary aim is not elegance of output, but understanding of how such graphical output can be produced and of the programming techniques used. You'll find the design techniques, programming techniques, and basic mathematical tools presented here of longer-term value than the graphics facilities presented. Therefore, please don't skim too quickly over the code fragments – they contain more of interest than just the shapes they compute and draw.

15.2 Graphing simple functions

Let's start. Let's look at examples of what we can draw and what code it takes to draw them. In particular, look at the graphics interface classes used. Here, first, are a parabola, a horizontal line, and a sloping line:

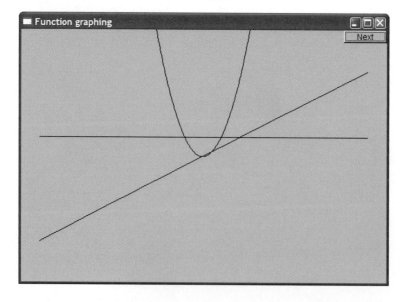

Actually, since this chapter is about graphing functions, that horizontal line isn't just a horizontal line; it is what we get from graphing the function

```
double one(double) { return 1; }
```

This is about the simplest function we could think of: it is a function of one argument that for every argument returns **1**. Since we don't need that argument to compute the result, we need not name it. For every **x** passed as an argument to **one()** we get the **y** value **1**; that is, the line is defined by **(x,y)==(x,1)** for all **x**.

Like all beginning mathematical arguments, this is somewhat trivial and pedantic, so let's look at a slightly more complicated function:

```
double slope(double x) { return x/2; }
```

This is the function that generated the sloping line. For every **x**, we get the **y** value **x/2**. In other words, **(x,y)==(x,x/2)**. The point where the two lines cross is **(2,1)**.

Now we can try something more interesting, the square function that seems to reappear regularly in this book:

```
double square(double x) { return x*x; }
```

If you remember your high school geometry (and even if you don't), this defines a parabola with its lowest point at **(0,0)** and symmetric on the *y* axis. In other words, **(x,y)==(x,x*x)**. So, the lowest point where the parabola touches the sloping line is **(0,0)**.

Here is the code that drew those three functions:

```
const int xmax = 600;        // window size
const int ymax = 400;

const int x_orig = xmax/2;   // position of (0,0) is center of window
const int y_orig = ymax/2;
const Point orig(x_orig,y_orig);

const int r_min = -10;       // range [-10:11)
const int r_max = 11;

const int n_points = 400;    // number of points used in range

const int x_scale = 30;      // scaling factors
const int y_scale = 30;

Simple_window win(Point(100,100),xmax,ymax,"Function graphing");
```

```
Function s(one,r_min,r_max,orig,n_points,x_scale,y_scale);
Function s2(slope,r_min,r_max,orig,n_points,x_scale,y_scale);
Function s3(square,r_min,r_max,orig,n_points,x_scale,y_scale);

win.attach(s);
win.attach(s2);
win.attach(s3);
win.wait_for_button();
```

First, we define a bunch of constants so that we won't have to litter our code with "magic numbers." Then, we make a window, define the functions, attach them to the window, and finally give control to the graphics system to do the actual drawing.

All of this is repetition and "boilerplate" except for the definitions of the three **Functions**, **s**, **s2**, and **s3**:

```
Function s(one,r_min,r_max,orig,n_points,x_scale,y_scale);
Function s2(slope,r_min,r_max,orig,n_points,x_scale,y_scale);
Function s3(square,r_min,r_max,orig,n_points,x_scale,y_scale);
```

Each **Function** specifies how its first argument (a function of one **double** argument returning a **double**) is to be drawn in a window. The second and third arguments give the range of **x** (the argument to the function to be graphed). The fourth argument (here, **orig**) tells the **Function** where the origin **(0,0)** is to be located within the window.

If you think that the many arguments are confusing, we agree. Our ideal is to have as few arguments as possible, because having many arguments confuses and provides opportunities for bugs. However, here we need them. We'll explain the last three arguments later (§15.3). First, however, let's label our graphs:

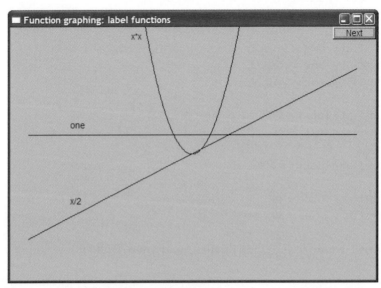

We always try to make our graphs self-explanatory. People don't always read the surrounding text and good diagrams get moved around, so that the surrounding text is "lost." Anything we put in as part of the picture itself is most likely to be noticed and – if reasonable – most likely to help the reader understand what we are displaying. Here, we simply put a label on each graph. The code for "labeling" was three **Text** objects (see §13.11):

```
Text ts(Point(100,y_orig−40),"one");
Text ts2(Point(100,y_orig+y_orig/2−20),"x/2");
Text ts3(Point(x_orig−100,20),"x*x");
win.set_label("Function graphing: label functions");
win.wait_for_button();
```

From now on in this chapter, we'll omit the repetitive code for attaching shapes to the window, labeling the window, and waiting for the user to hit "Next."

However, that picture is still not acceptable. We noticed that **x/2** touched **x*x** at **(0,0)** and that **one** crosses **x/2** at **(2,1)** but that's far too subtle; we need axes to give the reader an unsubtle clue about what's going on:

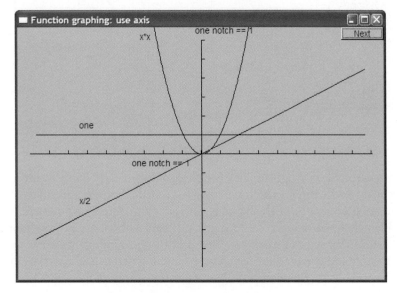

The code for the axes was two **Axis** objects (§15.4):

```
const int xlength = xmax−40;  // make the axis a bit smaller than the window
const int ylength = ymax−40;

Axis x(Axis::x,Point(20,y_orig), xlength, xlength/x_scale, "one notch == 1");
Axis y(Axis::y,Point(x_orig, ylength+20),
        ylength, ylength/y_scale, "one notch == 1");
```

Using **xlength/x_scale** as the number of notches ensures that a notch represents the values 1, 2, 3, etc. Having the axes cross at **(0,0)** is conventional. If you prefer them along the left and bottom edges as is conventional for the display of data (see §15.6), you can of course do that instead. Another way of distinguishing the axes from the data is to use color:

```
x.set_color(Color::red);
y.set_color(Color::red);
```

And we get

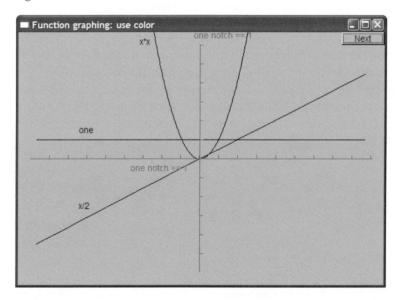

This is acceptable, though for aesthetic reasons, we'd probably want a bit of empty space at the top to match what we have at the bottom and sides. It might also be a better idea to push the label for the *x* axis further to the left. We left these blemishes, so that we could mention them — there are always more aesthetic details that we can work on. One part of a programmer's art is to know when to stop and use the time saved on something better (such as learning new techniques or sleep). Remember: "The best is the enemy of the good."

15.3 Function

The **Function** graphics interface class is defined like this:

```
struct Function : Shape {
        // the function parameters are not stored
```

> **Function(Fct f, double r1, double r2, Point orig,**
> **int count = 100, double xscale = 25, double yscale = 25);**
> **};**

Function is a **Shape** with a constructor that generates a lot of line segments and stores them in its **Shape** part. Those line segments approximate the values of function **f**. The values of **f** are calculated **count** times for values equally spaced in the **[r1:r2)** range:

> **Function::Function(Fct f, double r1, double r2, Point xy,**
> **int count, double xscale, double yscale)**
> // graph f(x) for x in [r1:r2) using count line segments with (0,0) displayed at xy
> // x coordinates are scaled by xscale and y coordinates scaled by yscale
> {
>   **if (r2−r1<=0) error("bad graphing range");**
>   **if (count <=0) error("non-positive graphing count");**
>   **double dist = (r2−r1)/count;**
>   **double r = r1;**
>   **for (int i = 0; i<count; ++i) {**
>   **add(Point(xy.x+int(r*xscale),xy.y−int(f(r)*yscale)));**
>   **r += dist;**
>   **}**
> }

The **xscale** and **yscale** values are used to scale the *x* coordinates and the *y* coordinates, respectively. We typically need to scale our values to make them fit appropriately into a drawing area of a window.

Note that a **Function** object doesn't store the values given to its constructor, so we can't later ask a function where its origin is, redraw it with different scaling, etc. All it does is to store points (in its **Shape**) and draw itself on the screen. If we wanted the flexibility to change a **Function** after construction, we would have to store the values we wanted to change (see exercise 2).

15.3.1 Default arguments

Note the way the **Function** constructor arguments **xscale** and **yscale** were given initializers in the declaration. Such initializers are called *default arguments* and their values are used if a caller doesn't supply values. For example:

> **Function s(one, r_min, r_max,orig, n_points, x_scale, y_scale);**
> **Function s2(slope, r_min, r_max, orig, n_points, x_scale);**   // no yscale
> **Function s3(square, r_min, r_max, orig, n_points);**   // no xscale, no yscale
> **Function s4(sqrt, orig, r_min, r_max);**   // no count, no xscale, no yscale

This is equivalent to

```
Function s(one, r_min, r_max, orig, n_points, x_scale, y_scale);
Function s2(slope, r_min, r_max,orig, n_points, x_scale, 25);
Function s3(square, r_min, r_max, orig, n_points, 25, 25);
Function s4(sqrt, orig, r_min, r_max, 100, 25, 25);
```

Default arguments are used as an alternative to providing several overloaded functions. Instead of defining one constructor with three default arguments, we could have defined four constructors:

```
struct Function : Shape {        // alternative, not using default arguments
      Function(Fct f, double r1, double r2, Point orig,
                  int count, double xscale, double yscale);
      // default scale of y:
      Function(Fct f, double r1, double r2, Point orig,
                  int count, double xscale);
      // default scale of x and y:
      Function(Fct f, double r1, double r2, Point orig, int count);
      // default count and default scale of x or y:
      Function(Fct f, double r1, double r2, Point orig);
};
```

It would have been more work to define four constructors, and with the four-constructor version, the nature of the default is hidden in the constructor definitions rather than being obvious from the declaration. Default arguments are frequently used for constructors but can be useful for all kinds of functions. You can only define default arguments for trailing arguments. For example:

```
struct Function : Shape {
      Function(Fct f, double r1, double r2, Point orig,
                  int count = 100, double xscale, double yscale);     // error
};
```

If an argument has a default argument, all subsequent arguments must also have one:

```
struct Function : Shape {
      Function(Fct f, double r1, double r2, Point orig ,
                  int count = 100, double xscale=25, double yscale=25);
};
```

Sometimes, picking good default arguments is easy. Examples of that are the default for string (the empty **string**) and the default for **vector** (the empty **vector**).

In other cases, such as **Function**, choosing a default is less easy; we found the ones we used after a bit of experimentation and a failed attempt. Remember, you don't have to provide default arguments, and if you find it hard to provide one, just leave it to your user to specify that argument.

15.3.2 More examples

We added a couple more functions, a simple cosine (**cos**) from the standard library, and − just to show how we can compose functions − a sloping cosine that follows the **x/2** slope:

double sloping_cos(double x) { return cos(x)+slope(x); }

Here is the result:

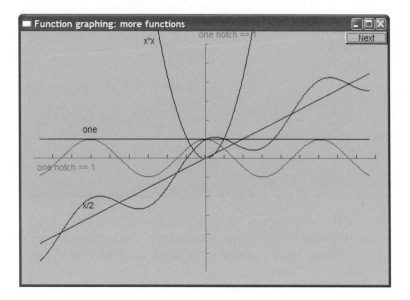

The code is

```
Function s4(cos,r_min,r_max,orig,400,20,20);
s4.set_color(Color::blue);
Function s5(sloping_cos, r_min,r_max,orig,400,20,20);
x.label.move(-160,0);
x.notches.set_color(Color::dark_red);
```

In addition to adding those two functions, we also moved the x axis's label and (just to show how) slightly changed the color of its notches.

Finally, we graph a log, an exponential, a sine, and a cosine:

Function f1(log,0.000001,r_max,orig,200,30,30);   // log() logarithm, base e
Function f2(sin,r_min,r_max,orig,200,30,30);   // sin()
f2.set_color(Color::blue);
Function f3(cos,r_min,r_max,orig,200,30,30);   // cos()
Function f4(exp,r_min,r_max,orig,200,30,30);   // exp() exponential e^x

Since **log(0)** is undefined (mathematically, minus infinity), we started the range for **log** at a small positive number. The result is

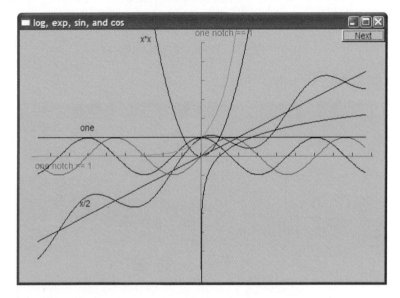

Rather than labeling those functions we used color.

Standard mathematical functions, such as **cos()**, **sin()**, and **sqrt()**, are declared in the standard library header **<cmath>**. See §24.8 and §B.9.2 for lists of the standard mathematical functions.

15.4 Axis

We use **Axis** wherever we present data (e.g., §15.6.4) because a graph without information that allows us to understand its scale is most often suspect. An **Axis** consists of a line, a number of "notches" on that line, and a text label. The **Axis** constructor computes the axis line and (optionally) the lines used as notches on that line:

```
struct Axis : Shape {
      enum Orientation { x, y, z };
      Axis(Orientation d, Point xy, int length,
           int number_of_notches=0, string label = "");
```

```
    void draw_lines() const;
    void move(int dx, int dy);
    void set_color(Color c);

    Text label;
    Lines notches;
};
```

The **label** and **notches** objects are left public so that a user can manipulate them. For example, you can give the notches a different color from the line and **move()** the **label** to a more convenient location. **Axis** is an example of an object composed of several semi-independent objects.

The **Axis** constructor places the lines and adds the "notches" if **number_of_notches** is greater than zero:

```
Axis::Axis(Orientation d, Point xy, int length, int n, string lab)
    :label(Point(0,0),lab)
{
    if (length<0) error("bad axis length");
    switch (d){
    case Axis::x:
    {    Shape::add(xy);                    // axis line
         Shape::add(Point(xy.x+length,xy.y));

         if (1<n) {       // add notches
             int dist = length/n;
             int x = xy.x+dist;
             for (int i = 0; i<n; ++i) {
                 notches.add(Point(x,xy.y),Point(x,xy.y−5));
                 x += dist;
             }
         }

         label.move(length/3,xy.y+20);      // put the label under the line
         break;
    }
    case Axis::y:
    {    Shape::add(xy);     // a y axis goes up
         Shape::add(Point(xy.x,xy.y−length));

         if (1<n) {       // add notches
             int dist = length/n;
             int y = xy.y−dist;
```

```
            for (int i = 0; i<n; ++i) {
                notches.add(Point(xy.x,y),Point(xy.x+5,y));
                y -= dist;
            }
        }

        label.move(xy.x−10,xy.y−length−10);      // put the label at top
        break;
    }
    case Axis::z:
        error("z axis not implemented");
    }
}
```

Compared to much real-world code, this constructor is very simple, but please have a good look at it because it isn't quite trivial and it illustrates a few useful techniques. Note how we store the line in the **Shape** part of the **Axis** (using **Shape::add()**) but the notches are stored in a separate object (**notches**). That way, we can manipulate the line and the notches independently; for example, we can give each its own color. Similarly, a label is placed in a fixed position relative to its axes, but since it is a separate object, we can always move it to a better spot. We use the enumeration **Orientation** to provide a convenient and non-error-prone notation for users.

Since an **Axis** has three parts, we must supply functions for when we want to manipulate an **Axis** as a whole. For example:

```
void Axis::draw_lines() const
{
    Shape::draw_lines();
    notches.draw();    // the notches may have a different color from the line
    label.draw();      // the label may have a different color from the line
}
```

We use **draw()** rather than **draw_lines()** for **notches** and **label** to be able to use the color stored in them. The line is stored in the **Axis::Shape** itself and uses the color stored there.

We can set the color of the line, the notches, and the label individually, but stylistically it's usually better not to, so we provide a function to set all three to the same:

```
void Axis::set_color(Color c)
{
    Shape::set_color(c);
    notches.set_color(c);
    label.set_color(c);
}
```

Similarly, **Axis::move()** moves all the parts of the **Axis** together:

```
void Axis::move(int dx, int dy)
{
    Shape::move(dx,dy);
    notches.move(dx,dy);
    label.move(dx,dy);
}
```

15.5 Approximation

Here we give another small example of graphing a function: we "animate" the calculation of an exponential function. The purpose is to help you get a feel for mathematical functions (if you haven't already), to show the way graphics can be used to illustrate computations, to give you some code to read, and finally to warn about a common problem with computations.

One way of computing an exponential function is to compute the series

$$e^x == 1 + x + x^2/2! + x^3/3! + x^4/4! + \ldots$$

The more terms of this sequence we calculate, the more precise our value of e^x becomes; that is, the more terms we calculate, the more digits of the result will be mathematically correct. What we will do is to compute this sequence and graph the result after each term. The exclamation point here is used with the common mathematical meaning: factorial; that is, we graph these functions in order:

```
exp0(x) = 0       // no terms
exp1(x) = 1       // one term
exp2(x) = 1+x     // two terms; pow(x,1)/fac(1)==x
exp3(x) = 1+x+pow(x,2)/fac(2)
exp4(x) = 1+x+pow(x,2)/fac(2)+pow(x,3)/fac(3)
exp5(x) = 1+x+pow(x,2)/fac(2)+pow(x,3)/fac(3)+pow(x,4)/fac(4)
...
```

Each function is a slightly better approximation of e^x than the one before it. Here, **pow(x,n)** is the standard library function that returns x^n. There is no factorial function in the standard library, so we must define our own:

```
int fac(int n)      // factorial(n); n!
{
    int r = 1;
    while (n>1) {
        r*=n;
        --n;
    }
}
```

```
        return r;
    }
```

For an alternative implementation of **fac()**, see exercise 1. Given **fac()**, we can compute the *n*th term of the series like this:

```
double term(double x, int n) { return pow(x,n)/fac(n); }    // nth term of series
```

Given **term()**, calculating the exponential to the precision of **n** terms is now easy:

```
double expe(double x, int n)        // sum of n terms for x
{
    double sum = 0;
    for (int i=0; i<n; ++i) sum+=term(x,i);
    return sum;
}
```

How can we graph this? From a programming point of view, the difficulty is that our graphing class, **Function**, takes a function of one argument and **expe()** takes two arguments. Given C++, as we have seen it so far, there is no really elegant solution to this problem, so for now, we'll use a simple and inelegant solution (but see exercise 3). We can take the precision, **n**, out of the argument list and make it a variable:

```
int expN_number_of_terms = 10;

double expN(double x)
{
    return expe(x,expN_number_of_terms);
}
```

Now **expN(x)** calculates an exponential to the precision determined by the value of **expN_number_of_terms**. Let's use that to produce some graphics. First, we'll provide some axes and the "real" exponential, the standard library **exp()**, so that we can see how close our approximation using **expN()** is:

```
Function real_exp(exp,r_min,r_max,orig,200,x_scale,y_scale);
real_exp.set_color(Color::blue);
```

Then, we can loop through a series of approximations increasing the number of terms of our approximation, **n**, each time around:

```
for (int n = 0; n<50; ++n) {
    ostringstream ss;
    ss << "exp approximation; n==" << n ;
    win.set_label(ss.str().c_str());
    expN_number_of_terms = n;
    // get next approximation:
    Function e(expN,r_min,r_max,orig,200,x_scale,y_scale);
    win.attach(e);
    win.wait_for_button();
    win.detach(e);
}
```

Note the final **detach(e)** in that loop. The scope of the **Function** object **e** is the block of the **for**-statement. Each time we enter that block we get a new **Function** called **e** and each time we exit the block that **e** goes away, to be replaced by the next. The window must not remember the old **e** because it will have been destroyed. Thus, **detach(e)** ensures that the window does not try to draw a destroyed object.

This first gives a window with just the axes and the "real" exponential rendered in blue:

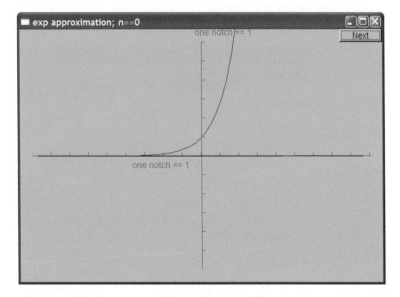

We see that **exp(0)** is **1** so that our blue "real exponential" crosses the *y* axis in **(0,1)**.

If you look carefully, you'll see that we actually drew the zero term approximation (**exp0(x)==0**) as a black line right on top of the *x* axis. Hitting "Next," we get the approximation using just one term. Note that we display the number of terms used in the approximation in the window label:

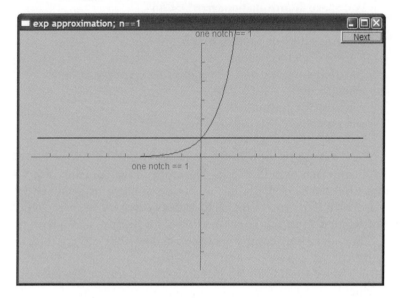

That's the function **exp1(x)==1**, the approximation using just one term of the sequence. It matches the exponential perfectly at **(0,1)**, but we can do better:

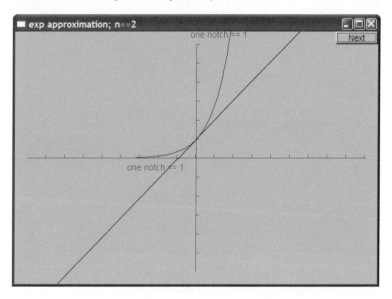

With two terms (**1+x**), we get the diagonal crossing the y axis at **(0,1)**. With three terms (**1+x+pow(x,2)/fac(2)**), we can see the beginning of a convergence:

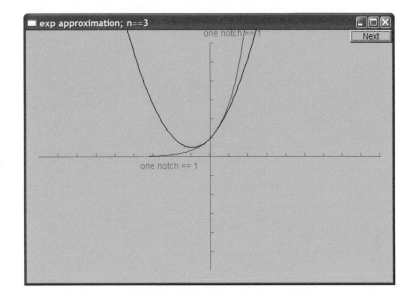

With ten terms we are doing rather well, especially for values larger than –3:

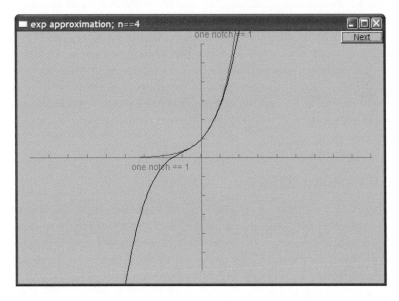

If we don't think too much about it, we might believe that we could get better and better approximations simply by using more and more terms. However, there are limits, and after 13 terms something strange starts to happen. First, the approximations start to get slightly worse, and at 18 terms vertical lines appear:

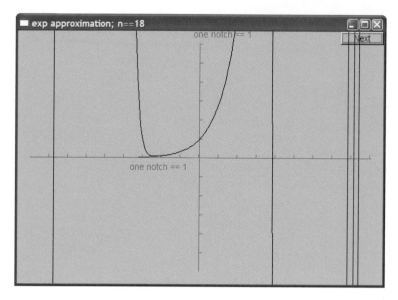

Remember, floating-point arithmetic is not pure math. Floating-point numbers are simply as good an approximation to real numbers as we can get with a fixed number of bits. What happened was that our calculation started to produce values that couldn't be represented as **doubles** so that our results started to diverge from the mathematically correct answers. For more information, see Chapter 24.

This last picture is also a good illustration of the principle that "it looks OK" isn't the same as "tested." Before giving a program to someone else to use, first test it beyond what at first seems reasonable. Unless you know better, running a program slightly longer or with slightly different data could lead to a real mess — as in this case.

15.6 Graphing data

Displaying data is a highly skilled and highly valued craft. When done well, it combines technical and artistic aspects and can add significantly to our understanding of complex phenomena. However, that also makes graphing a huge area that for the most part is unrelated to programming techniques. Here, we'll just show a simple example of displaying data read from a file. The data shown represents the age groups of Japanese people over almost a century. The data to the right of the 2008 line is a projection:

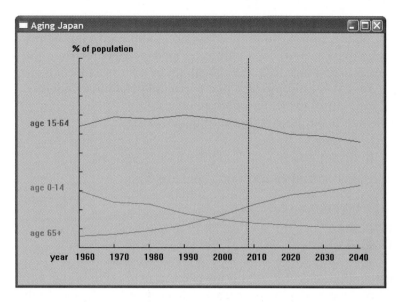

We'll use this example to discuss the programming problems involved in presenting such data:

- Reading a file
- Scaling data to fit the window
- Displaying the data
- Labeling the graph

We will not go into artistic details. Basically, this is "graphs for geeks," not "graphical art." Clearly, you can do better artistically when you need to.

Given a set of data, we must consider how best to display it. To simplify, we will only deal with data that is easy to display using two dimensions, but that's a huge part of the data most people deal with. Note that bar graphs, pie charts, and similar popular displays really are just two-dimensional data displayed in a fancy way. Three-dimensional data can often be handled by producing a series of two-dimensional images, by superimposing several two-dimensional graphs onto a single window (as done in the "Japanese age" example), or by labeling individual points with information. If we want to go beyond that, we'll have to write new graphics classes or adopt another graphics library.

So, our data is basically pairs of values, such as **(year,number of children)**. If we have more data, such as **(year,number of children, number of adults,number of elderly)**, we simply have to decide which pair of values – or pairs of values – we want to draw. In our example, we simply graphed **(year,number of children)**, **(year,number of adults)**, and **(year,number of elderly)**.

There are many ways of looking at a set of **(x,y)** pairs. When considering how to graph such a set it is important to consider whether one value is in some way a function of the other. For example, for a (**year,steel production**) pair it would be quite reasonable to consider the steel production a function of the year and display the data as a continuous line. **Open_polyline** (§13.6) is the obvious choice for graphing such data. If **y** should not be seen as a function of **x**, for example (**gross domestic product per person,population of country**), **Marks** (§13.15) can be used to plot unconnected points.

Now, back to our Japanese age distribution example.

15.6.1 Reading a file

The file of age distributions consists of lines like this:

```
( 1960 : 30 64 6  )
(1970 : 24 69 7 )
(1980 : 23 68 9 )
```

The first number after the colon is the percentage of children (age 0–14) in the population, the second is the percentage of adults (age 15–64), and the third is the percentage of the elderly (age 65+). Our job is to read those. Note that the formatting of the data is slightly irregular. As usual, we have to deal with such details.

To simplify that task, we first define a type **Distribution** to hold a data item and an input operator to read such data items:

```
struct Distribution {
      int year, young, middle, old;
};

istream& operator>>(istream& is, Distribution& d)
      // assume format: ( year : young middle old )
{
      char ch1 = 0;
      char ch2 = 0;
      char ch3 = 0;
      Distribution dd;

      if (is >> ch1 >> dd.year
            >> ch2 >> dd.young >> dd.middle >> dd.old
            >> ch3) {
            if (ch1!= '(' || ch2!=':' || ch3!=')') {
                  is.clear(ios_base::failbit);
                  return is;
            }
      }
}
```

```
            else
                    return is;
            d = dd;
            return is;
    }
```

This is a straightforward application of the ideas from Chapter 10. If this code isn't clear to you, please review that chapter. We didn't need to define a **Distribution** type and a **>>** operator. However, it simplifies the code compared to a brute-force approach of "just read the numbers and graph them." Our use of **Distribution** splits the code up into logical parts to help comprehension and debugging. Don't be shy about introducing types "just to make the code clearer." We define classes to make the code correspond more directly to the way we think about the concepts in our code. Doing so even for "small" concepts that are used only very locally in our code, such as a line of data representing the age distribution for a year, can be most helpful.

Given **Distribution**, the read loop becomes

```
string file_name = "japanese-age-data.txt";
ifstream ifs(file_name.c_str());
if (!ifs) error("can't open ",file_name);

// . . .

Distribution d;
while (ifs>>d) {
        if (d.year<base_year || end_year<d.year)
                error("year out of range");
        if (d.young+d.middle+d.old != 100)
                error("percentages don't add up");
        // . . .
}
```

That is, we try to open the file **japanese-age-data.txt** and exit the program if we don't find that file. It is often a good idea *not* to "hardwire" a file name into the source code the way we did here, but we consider this program an example of a small "one-off" effort, so we don't burden the code with facilities that are more appropriate for long-lived applications. On the other hand, we did put **japanese-age-data.txt** into a named **string** variable so the program is easy to modify if we want to use it – or some of its code – for something else.

The read loop checks that the year read is in the expected range and that the percentages add up to 100. That's a basic sanity check for the data. Since **>>** checks the format of each individual data item, we didn't bother with further checks in the main loop.

15.6.2 General layout

So what do we want to appear on the screen? You can see our answer at the beginning of §15.6. The data seems to ask for three **Open_polylines** – one for each age group. These graphs need to be labeled, and we decided to write a "caption" for each line at the left-hand side of the window. In this case, that seemed clearer than the common alternative: to place the label somewhere along the line itself. In addition, we use color to distinguish the graphs and associate their labels.

We want to label the *x* axis with the years. The vertical line through the year 2008 indicates where the graph goes from hard data to projected data.

We decided to just use the window's label as the title for our graph.

Getting graphing code both correct and good-looking can be surprisingly tricky. The main reason is that we have to do a lot of fiddly calculations of sizes and offsets. To simplify that, we start by defining a set of symbolic constants that defines the way we use our screen space:

```
const int xmax = 600;      // window size
const int ymax = 400;

const int xoffset = 100;   // distance from left-hand side of window to y axis
const int yoffset = 60;    // distance from bottom of window to x axis

const int xspace = 40;     // space beyond axis
const int yspace = 40;

const int xlength = xmax-xoffset-xspace;      // length of axes
const int ylength = ymax-yoffset-yspace;
```

Basically this defines a rectangular space (the window) with another rectangle (defined by the axes) within it:

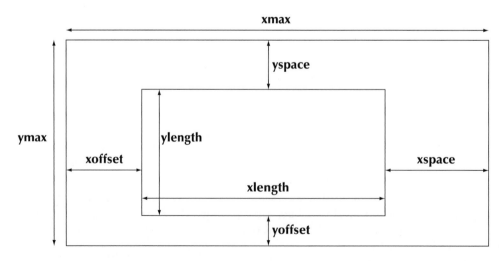

We find that without such a "schematic view" of where things are in our window and the symbolic constants that define it, we get lost and become frustrated when our output doesn't reflect our wishes.

15.6.3 Scaling data

Next we need to define how to fit our data into that space. We do that by scaling the data so that it fits into the space defined by the axes. To do that we need the scaling factors that are the ratio between the data range and the axis range:

```
const int base_year = 1960;
const int end_year = 2040;

const double xscale = double(xlength)/(end_year−base_year);
const double yscale = double(ylength)/100;
```

We want our scaling factors (**xscale** and **yscale**) to be floating-point numbers – or our calculations could be subject to serious rounding errors. To avoid integer division, we convert our lengths to **double** before dividing (§4.3.3).

We can now place a data point on the *x* axis by subtracting its base value (**1960**), scaling with **xscale**, and adding the **xoffset**. A *y* value is dealt with similarly. We find that we can never remember to do that quite right when we try to do that repeatedly. It may be a trivial calculation, but it is fiddly and verbose. To simplify the code and minimize that chance of error (and minimize frustrating debugging), we define a little class to do the calculation for us:

```
class Scale {   // data value to coordinate conversion
        int cbase;          // coordinate base
        int vbase;          // base of values
        double scale;
public:
        Scale(int b, int vb, double s) :cbase(b), vbase(vb), scale(s) { }
        int operator()(int v) const { return cbase + (v−vbase)*scale; }
};
```

We want a class because the calculation depends on three constant values that we wouldn't like to unnecessarily repeat. Given that, we can define

```
Scale xs(xoffset,base_year,xscale);
Scale ys(ymax−yoffset,0,−yscale);
```

Note how we make the scaling factor for **ys** negative to reflect the fact that *y* coordinates grow downward whereas we usually prefer higher values to be represented by higher points on a graph. Now we can use **xs** to convert a year to an *x* coordinate. Similarly, we can use **xy** to convert a percentage to a *y* coordinate.

15.6.4 Building the graph

Finally, we have all the prerequisites for writing the graphing code in a reasonably elegant way. We start creating a window and placing the axes:

```
Window win(Point(100,100),xmax,ymax,"Aging Japan");

Axis x(Axis::x, Point(xoffset,ymax−yoffset), xlength,
        (end_year−base_year)/10,
        "year    1960    1970    1980    1990    "
        "2000     2010    2020    2030    2040");
x.label.move(−100,0);

Axis y(Axis::y, Point(xoffset,ymax−yoffset), ylength, 10,"% of population");

Line current_year(Point(xs(2008),ys(0)),Point(xs(2008),ys(100)));
current_year.set_style(Line_style::dash);
```

The axes cross at **Point(xoffset,ymax−yoffset)** representing **(1960,0)**. Note how the notches are placed to reflect the data. On the *y* axis, we have ten notches each representing 10% of the population. On the *x* axis, each notch represents ten years, and the exact number of notches is calculated from **base_year** and **end_year** so that if we change that range, the axis would automatically be recalculated. This is one benefit of avoiding "magic constants" in the code. The label on the *x* axis violates that rule: it is simply the result of fiddling with the label string until the numbers were in the right position under the notches. To do better, we would have to look to a set of individual labels for individual "notches."

Please note the curious formatting of the label string. We used two adjacent string literals:

```
"year    1960    1970    1980    1990    "
"2000     2010    2020    2030    2040"
```

Adjacent string literals are concatenated by the compiler, so that's equivalent to

```
"year    1960    1970    1980    1990    2000    2010    2020    2030    2040"
```

That can be a useful "trick" for laying out long string literals to make our code more readable.

The **current_line** is a vertical line that separates hard data from projected data. Note how **xs** and **ys** are used to place and scale the line just right.

Given the axes, we can proceed to the data. We define three **Open_polylines** and fill them in the read loop:

```
Open_polyline children;
Open_polyline adults;
Open_polyline aged;

Distribution d;
while (ifs>>d) {
    if (d.year<base_year || end_year<d.year) error("year out of range");
    if (d.young+d.middle+d.old != 100)
        error("percentages don't add up");
    int x = xs(d.year);
    children.add(Point(x,ys(d.young)));
    adults.add(Point(x,ys(d.middle)));
    aged.add(Point(x,ys(d.old)));
}
```

The use of **xs** and **xy** makes scaling and placement of the data trivial. "Little classes," such as **Scale**, can be immensely important for simplifying notation and avoiding unnecessary repetition – thereby increasing readability and increasing the likelihood of correctness.

To make the graphs more readable, we label each and apply color:

```
Text children_label(Point(20,children.point(0).y),"age 0-14");
children.set_color(Color::red);
children_label.set_color(Color::red);

Text adults_label(Point(20,adults.point(0).y),"age 15-64");
adults.set_color(Color::blue);
adults_label.set_color(Color::blue);

Text aged_label(Point(20,aged.point(0).y),"age 65+");
aged.set_color(Color::dark_green);
aged_label.set_color(Color::dark_green);
```

Finally, we need to attach the various **Shapes** to the **Window** and start the GUI system (§14.2.3):

```
win.attach(children);
win.attach(adults);
win.attach(aged);

win.attach(children_label);
win.attach(adults_label);
win.attach(aged_label);
```

```
win.attach(x);
win.attach(y);
win.attach(current_year);

gui_main();
```

All the code could be placed inside **main()**, but we prefer to keep the helper classes **Scale** and **Distribution** outside together with **Distribution**'s input operator.

In case you have forgotten what we were producing, here is the output again:

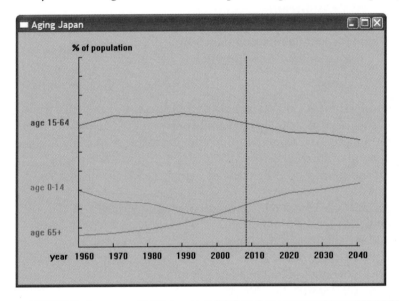

 ## Drill

Function graphing drill:

1. Make an empty 600-by-600 **Window** labeled "Function graphs."
2. Note that you'll need to make a project with the properties specified in the "installation of FLTK" note from the course website.
3. You'll need to move **Graph.cpp** and **Window.cpp** into your project.
4. Add an *x* axis and a *y* axis each of length 400, labeled "1 $==$ 20 pixels" and with a notch every 20 pixels. The axes should cross at (300,300).
5. Make both axes red.

In the following, use a separate **Shape** for each function to be graphed:

1. Graph the function **double one(double x) { return 1; }** in the range [–10,11] with (0,0) at (300,300) using 400 points and no scaling (in the window).
2. Change it to use *x* scale 20 and *y* scale 20.
3. From now on use that range, scale, etc. for all graphs.
4. Add **double slope(double x) { return x/2; }** to the window.
5. Label the slope with a **Text "x/2"** at a point just above its bottom left end point.
6. Add **double square(double x) { return x*x; }** to the window.
7. Add a cosine to the window (don't write a new function).
8. Make the cosine blue.
9. Write a function **sloping_cos()** that adds a cosine to **slope()** (as defined above) and add it to the window.

Class definition drill:

1. Define a **struct Person** containing a **string** name and an **int** age.
2. Define a variable of type **Person**, initialize it with "Goofy" and 63, and write it to the screen (**cout**).
3. Define an input (**>>**) and an output (**<<**) operator for **Person**; read in a **Person** from the keyboard (**cin**) and write it out to the screen (**cout**).
4. Give **Person** a constructor initializing **name** and **age**.
5. Make the representation of **Person** private, and provide **const** member functions **name()** and **age()** to read the name and age.
6. Modify **>>** and **<<** to work with the redefined **Person**.
7. Modify the constructor to check that **age** is [0:150) and that **name** doesn't contain any of the characters ; : " ' [ ] * & ^ % $ # @ !. Use **error()** in case of error. Test.
8. Read a sequence of **Person**s from input (**cin**) into a **vector<Person>**; write them out again to the screen (**cout**). Test with correct and erroneous input.
9. Change the representation of **Person** to have **first_name** and **second_name** instead of **name**. Make it an error not to supply both a first and a second name. Be sure to fix **>>** and **<<** also. Test.

Review

1. What is a function of one argument?
2. When would you use a (continuous) line to represent data? When do you use (discrete) points?
3. What function (mathematical formula) defines a slope?
4. What is a parabola?

5. How do you make an *x* axis? A *y* axis?
6. What is a default argument and when would you use one?
7. How do you add functions together?
8. How do you color and label a graphed function?
9. What do we mean when we say that a series approximates a function?
10. Why would you sketch out the layout of a graph before writing the code to draw it?
11. How would you scale your graph so that the input will fit?
12. How would you scale the input without trial and error?
13. Why would you format your input rather than just having the file contain "the numbers"?
14. How do you plan the general layout of a graph? How do you reflect that layout in your code?

Terms

approximation	function	screen layout
default argument	scaling	

Exercises

1. Here is another way of defining a factorial function:

   ```
   int fac(int n) { return n>1 ? n*fac(n−1) : 1; } // factorial n!
   ```

   It will do **fac(4)** by first deciding that since **4>1** it must be **4*fac(3)**, and that's obviously **4*3*fac(2)**, which again is **4*3*2*fac(1)**, which is **4*3*2*1**. Try to see that it works. A function that calls itself is said to be *recursive*. The alternative implementation in §15.5 is called *iterative* because it iterates through the values (using **while**). Verify that the recursive **fac()** works and gives the same results as the iterative **fac()** by calculating the factorial of 0, 1, 2, 3, 4, up until and including 20. Which implementation of **fac()** do you prefer, and why?

2. Define a class **Fct** that is just like **Function** except that it stores its constructor arguments. Provide **Fct** with "reset" operations, so that you can use it repeatedly for different ranges, different functions, etc.

3. Modify **Fct** from the previous exercise to take an extra argument to control precision or whatever. Make the type of that argument a template parameter for extra flexibility.

4. Graph a sine (**sin()**), a cosine (**cos()**), the sum of those **sin(x)+cos(x)**, and the sum of the squares of those **sin(x)*sin(x)+cos(x)*cos(x)** on a single graph. Do provide axes and labels.

5. "Animate" (as in §15.5) the series **1–1/3+1/5–1/7+1/9–1/11– . . . .** It is known as Leibniz's series and converges to pi/4.

6. Design and implement a bar graph class. Its basic data is a **vector<double>** holding N values, and each value should be represented by a "bar" that is as a rectangle where the height represents the value.

7. Elaborate the bar graph class to allow labeling of the graph itself and its individual bars. Allow the use of color.

8. Here is a collection of heights in centimeters together with the number of people in a group of that height (rounded to the nearest 5cm): (170,7), (175,9), (180,23), (185,17), (190,6), (195,1). How would you graph that data? If you can't think of anything better, do a bar graph. Remember to provide axes and labels. Place the data in a file and read it from that file.

9. Find another data set of heights (an inch is about 2.54cm) and graph them with your program from the previous exercise. For example, search the web for "height distribution" or "height of people in the United States" and ignore a lot of rubbish or ask your friends for their heights. Ideally, you don't have to change anything for the new data set. Calculating the scaling from the data is a key idea. Reading in labels from input also helps minimize changes when you want to reuse code.

10. What kind of data is unsuitable for a line graph or a bar graph? Find an example and find a way of displaying it (e.g., as a collection of labeled points).

11. Find the average maximum temperatures for each month of the year for two or more locations (e.g., Cambridge, England, and Cambridge, Massachusetts; there are lots of towns called "Cambridge") and graph them together. As ever, be careful with axes, labels, use of color, etc.

Postscript

Graphical representation of data is important. We simply understand a well-crafted graph better than the set of numbers that was used to make it. Most people, when they need to draw a graph, use someone else's code – a library. How are such libraries constructed and what do you do if you don't have one handy? What are the fundamental ideas underlying "an ordinary graphing tool"? Now you know: it isn't magic or brain surgery. We covered only two-dimensional graphs; three-dimensional graphing is also very useful in science, engineering, marketing, etc. and can be even more fun. Explore it someday!

Graphical User Interfaces

> "Computing is not about
> computers any more.
> It is about living."

> **—Nicholas Negroponte**

A graphical user interface (GUI) allows a user to interact with a program by pressing buttons, selecting from menus, entering data in various ways, and displaying textual and graphical entities on a screen. That's what we are used to when we interact with our computers and with websites. In this chapter, we show the basics of how code can be written to define and control a GUI application. In particular, we show how to write code that interacts with entities on the screen using callbacks. Our GUI facilities are built "on top of" system facilities. The low-level features and interfaces are presented in Appendix E, which uses features and techniques presented in Chapters 17 and 18. Here we focus on usage.

16.1 User interface alternatives

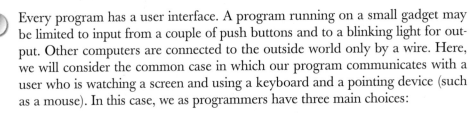

Every program has a user interface. A program running on a small gadget may be limited to input from a couple of push buttons and to a blinking light for output. Other computers are connected to the outside world only by a wire. Here, we will consider the common case in which our program communicates with a user who is watching a screen and using a keyboard and a pointing device (such as a mouse). In this case, we as programmers have three main choices:

- *Use console input and output:* This is a strong contender for technical/professional work where the input is simple and textual, consisting of commands and short data items (such as file names and simple data values). If the output is textual, we can display it on the screen or store it in files. The C++ standard library **iostreams** (Chapters 10–11) provide suitable and convenient mechanisms for this. If graphical output is needed, we can use a graphics display library (as shown in Chapters 12–15) without making dramatic changes to our programming style.

- *Use a graphical user interface (GUI) library:* This is what we do when we want our user interaction to be based on the metaphor of manipulating objects on the screen (pointing, clicking, dragging and dropping, hovering, etc.). Often (but not always), that style goes together with a high degree of graphically displayed information. Anyone who has used a modern computer knows examples where that is convenient. Anyone who wants to match the "feel" of Windows/Mac applications must use a GUI style of interaction.

- *Use a web browser interface:* For that, we need to use a markup (layout) language, such as HTML or XML, and usually a scripting language. Showing how to do this is beyond the scope of this book, but it is often the ideal for applications that require remote access. In that case, the communication between the program and the screen is again textual (using streams of characters). A browser is a GUI application that translates some of that text into graphical elements and translates the mouse clicks, etc. into textual data that can be sent back to the program.

To many, the use of GUI is the essence of modern programming, and sometimes the interaction with objects on the screen is considered the central concern of programming. We disagree: GUI is a form of I/O, and separation of the main logic of an application from I/O is among our major ideals for software. Wherever possible, we prefer to have a clean interface between our main program logic and the parts of the program we use to get input and produce output. Such a separation allows us to change the way a program is presented to a user, to port our programs to use different I/O systems, and – most importantly – to think about the logic of the program and its interaction with users separately.

That said, GUI is important and interesting from several perspectives. This chapter explores both the ways we can integrate graphical elements into our applications and how we can keep interface concerns from dominating our thinking.

16.2 The "Next" button

How did we provide that "Next" button that we used to drive the graphics examples in Chapters 12–15? There, we do graphics in a window using a button. Obviously, that is a simple form of GUI programming. In fact, it is so simple that some would argue that it isn't "true GUI." However, let's see how it was done because it will lead directly into the kind of programming that everyone recognizes as GUI programming.

Our code in Chapters 12–15 is conventionally structured like this:

```
// create objects and/or manipulate objects, display them in Window win:
win.wait_for_button();
```

```
// create objects and/or manipulate objects, display them in Window win:
win.wait_for_button();
```

```
// create objects and/or manipulate objects, display them in Window win:
win.wait_for_button();
```

Each time we reach **wait_for_button()**, we can look at our objects on the screen until we hit the button to get the output from the next part of the program. From the point of view of program logic, this is no different from a program that writes lines of output to a screen (a console window), stopping now and then to receive input from the keyboard. For example:

```
// define variables and/or compute values, produce output
cin >> var;    // wait for input

// define variables and/or compute values, produce output
cin >> var;    // wait for input

// define variables and/or compute values, produce output
cin >> var;    // wait for input
```

From an implementation point of view, these two kinds of programs are quite different. When your program executes **cin>>var**, it stops and waits for "the system" to bring back characters you typed. However, the system (the graphical user interface system) that looks after your screen and tracks the mouse as you use it works on a rather different model: the GUI keeps track of where the mouse is and what the user is doing with the mouse (clicking, etc.). When your program wants an action, it must

- Tell the GUI what to look for (e.g., "Someone clicked the 'Next' button")
- Tell what is to be done when someone does that
- Wait until the GUI detects an action that the program is interested in

What is new and different here is that the GUI does not just return to our program; it is designed to respond in different ways to different user actions, such as clicking on one of many buttons, resizing windows, redrawing the window after it has been obscured by another, and popping up pop-up menus.

For starters, we just want to say, "Please wake me up when someone clicks my button"; that is, "Please continue executing my program when someone clicks the mouse button and the cursor is in the rectangular area where the image of my button is displayed." This is just about the simplest action we could imagine. However, such an operation isn't provided by "the system" so we wrote one ourselves. Seeing how that is done is the first step in understanding GUI programming.

16.3 A simple window

Basically, "the system" (which is a combination of a GUI library and the operating system) continuously tracks where the mouse is and whether its buttons are pressed or not. A program can express interest in an area of the screen and ask "the system" to call a function when "something interesting" happens. In this particular case, we ask the system to call one of our functions (a "callback function") when the mouse button is clicked "on our button." To do that we must

- Define a button
- Get it displayed

- Define a function for the GUI to call
- Tell the GUI about that button and that function
- Wait for the GUI to call our function

Let's do that. A button is part of a **Window**, so (in **Simple_window.h**) we define our class **Simple_window** to contain a member **next_button**:

```
struct Simple_window : Graph_lib::Window {
    Simple_window(Point xy, int w, int h, const string& title );

    void wait_for_button();        // simple event loop
private:
    Button next_button;        // the "Next" button
    bool button_pushed;        // implementation detail

    static void cb_next(Address, Address);        // callback for next_button
    void next();    // action to be done when next_button is pressed
};
```

Obviously, **Simple_window** is derived from **Graph_lib**'s **Window**. All our windows must be derived directly or indirectly from **Graph_lib::Window** because it is the class that (through FLTK) connects our notion of a window with the system's window implementation. For details of **Window**'s implementation, see §E.3.

Our button is initialized in **Simple_window**'s constructor:

```
Simple_window::Simple_window(Point xy, int w, int h, const string& title)
    :Window(xy,w,h,title),
    next_button(Point(x_max()−70,0), 70, 20, "Next", cb_next),
    button_pushed(false)
{
    attach(next_button);
}
```

Unsurprisingly, **Simple_window** passes its location (**xy**), size (**w,h**), and title (**title**) on to **Graph_lib**'s **Window** to deal with. Next, the constructor initializes **next_button** with a location (**Point(x_max()−70,0)**; that's roughly the top right corner), a size (**70,20**), a label (**"Next"**), and a "callback" function (**cb_next**). The first four parameters exactly parallel what we do for a **Window**: we place a rectangular shape on the screen and label it.

Finally, we **attach()** our **next_button** to our **Simple_window**; that is, we tell the window that it must display the button in its position and make sure that the GUI system knows about it.

The **button_pushed** member is a pretty obscure implementation detail; we use it to keep track of whether the button has been pushed since last we executed **next()**. In fact, just about everything here is implementation details, and therefore declared **private**. Ignoring the implementation details, we see:

```
struct Simple_window : Graph_lib::Window {
        Simple_window(Point xy, int w, int h, const string& title );

        wait_for_button();      // simple event loop

        // . . .
};
```

That is, a user can make a window and wait for its button to be pushed.

16.3.1 A callback function

The function **cb_next()** is the new and interesting bit here. This is the function that we want the GUI system to call when it detects a click on our button. Since we give the function to the GUI for the GUI to "call back to us," it's commonly called a *callback* function. We indicate **cb_next()**'s intended use with the prefix **cb_** for "callback." That's just to help us — no language or library requires that naming convention. Obviously, we chose the name **cb_next** because it is to be the callback for our "Next" button. The definition of **cb_next** is an ugly piece of "boilerplate."

Before showing that code, let's consider what is going on here:

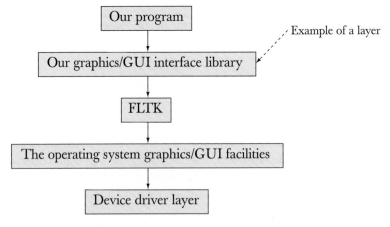

Our program runs on top of several "layers" of code. It uses our graphics library that we implement using the FLTK library, which is implemented using operating system facilities. In a system, there may be even more layers and sub-layers. Somehow, a click detected by the mouse's device driver has to cause our function

cb_next() to be called. We pass the address of **cb_next()** and the address of our **Simple_window** down through the layers of software; some code "down there" then calls **cb_next()** when the "Next" button is pressed.

The GUI system (and the operating system) can be used by programs written in a variety of languages, so it cannot impose some nice C++ style on all users. In particular, it does not know about our **Simple_window** class or our **Button** class. In fact, it doesn't know about classes or member functions at all. The type required for a callback function is chosen so that it is usable from the lowest level of programming, including C and assembler. A callback function returns no value and takes two addresses as its arguments. We can declare a C++ member function that obeys those rules like this:

```
static void cb_next(Address, Address);    // callback for next_button
```

The keyword **static** is there to make sure that **cb_next()** can be called as an ordinary function, that is, not as a C++ member function invoked for a specific object. Having the system call a proper C++ member function would have been much nicer. However, the callback interface has to be usable from many languages, so this is what we get: a **static** member function. The **Address** arguments specify that **cb_next()** takes arguments that are addresses of "something in memory." C++ references are unknown to most languages, so we can't use those. The compiler isn't told what the types of those "somethings" are. We are close to the hardware here and don't get the usual help from the language. "The system" will invoke a callback function with the first argument being the address of the GUI entity ("**Widget**") for which the callback was triggered. We won't use that first argument, so we don't bother to name it. The second argument is the address of the window containing that **Widget**; for **cb_next()**, that will be our **Simple_window**. We can use that information like this:

```
void Simple_window::cb_next(Address, Address pw)
// call Simple_window::next() for the window located at pw
{
        reference_to<Simple_window>(pw).next();
}
```

The **reference_to<Simple_window>(pw)** tells the compiler that the address in **pw** is to be considered the address of a **Simple_window**; that is, we can use **reference_to<Simple_window>(pw)** as a reference to a **Simple_window**. In Chapters 17 and 18, we will return to the issue of addressing memory. In §E.1, we present the (by then, trivial) definition of **reference_to**. For now, we are just glad that we finally obtained a reference to our **Simple_window** so that we can access our data and functions exactly as we like and are used to. Finally, we get out of this system-dependent code as quickly as possible by calling our member function **next()**.

We could have written all the code we wanted to execute in **cb_next()**, but we – like most good GUI programmers – prefer to keep messy low-level stuff separate from our nice user code, so we handle a callback with two functions:

- **cb_next()** simply maps the system conventions for a callback into a call to an ordinary member function (**next()**).

- **next()** does what we want done (without having to know about the messy conventions of callbacks).

The fundamental reason for using two functions here is the general principle that "a function should perform a single logical action": **cb_next()** gets us out of the low-level system-dependent part of the system and **next()** performs our desired action. Whenever we want a callback (from "the system") to one of our windows, we define such a pair of functions; for example, see §16.5–7. Before going further, let's repeat what is going on here:

- We define our **Simple_window**.
- **Simple_window**'s constructor registers its **next_button** with the GUI system.
- When we click the image of **next_button** on the screen, the GUI calls **cb_next()**.
- **cb_next()** converts the low-level system information into a call of our member function **next()** for our window.
- **next()** performs whatever action we want done in response to the button click.

That's a rather elaborate way of getting a function called. But remember that we are dealing with the basic mechanism for communicating an action of a mouse (or other hardware device) to a program. In particular:

- There are typically many programs running.
- The program is written long after the operating system.
- The program is written long after the GUI library.
- The program can be written in a language that is different from that used in the operating system.
- The technique deals with all kinds of interactions (not just our little button push).
- A window can have many buttons; a program can have many windows.

However, once we understand how **next()** is called, we basically understand how to deal with every action in a program with a GUI interface.

16.3.2 A wait loop

So, in this − our simplest case − what do we want done by **Simple_window**'s **next()** each time the button is "pressed"? Basically, we want an operation that stops the execution of our program at some point, giving us a chance to see what has been done so far. And, we want **next()** to restart our program after that wait:

```
// create some objects and/or manipulate some objects, display them in a window
win.wait_for_button();      // next() causes the program to proceed from here
// create some objects and/or manipulate some objects
```

Actually, that's easily done. Let's first define **wait_for_button()**:

```
void Simple_window::wait_for_button()
      // modified event loop:
      // handle all events (as per default), quit when button_pushed becomes true
      // this allows graphics without control inversion
{

      while (!button_pushed) Fl::wait();
      button_pushed = false;
      Fl::redraw();
}
```

Like most GUI systems, FLTK provides a function that stops a program until something happens. The FLTK version is called **wait()**. Actually, **wait()** takes care of lots of things because our program gets woken up whenever anything that affects it happens. For example, when running under Microsoft Windows, it is the job of a program to redraw its window when it is being moved or becomes unobscured after having been hidden by another window. It is also the job of the **Window** to handle resizing. The **Fl::wait()** handles all of these tasks in the default manner. Each time **wait()** has dealt with something, it returns to give our code a chance to do something.

So, when someone clicks our "Next" button, **wait()** calls **cb_next()** and returns (to our "wait loop"). To proceed in **wait_for_button()**, **next()** just has to set the Boolean variable **button_pushed** to **true**. That's easy:

```
void Simple_window::next()
{
      button_pushed = true;
}
```

Of course we also need to define **button_pushed** somewhere:

```
bool button_pushed = false;
```

After waiting, **wait_for_button()** needs to reset **button_pushed** and **redraw()** the window to make sure that any changes we made can be seen on the screen. So that's what it did.

16.4 Button and other Widgets

We define a button like this:

```
struct Button : Widget {
        Button(Point xy, int w, int h, const string& label, Callback cb);
        void attach(Window&);
};
```

So, a **Button** is a **Widget** with a location (**xy**), a size (**w,h**), a text label (**label**), and a callback (**cb**). Basically, anything that appears on a screen with an action (e.g., a callback) associated is a **Widget**.

16.4.1 Widgets

Yes, *widget* really is a technical term. A more descriptive, but less evocative, name for a widget is a *control*. We use widgets to define forms of interaction with a program through a GUI (graphical user interface). Our **Widget** interface class looks like this:

```
class Widget {
        // Widget is a handle to an Fl_widget — it is *not* an Fl_widget
        // we try to keep our interface classes at arm's length from FLTK
public:
        Widget(Point xy, int w, int h, const string& s, Callback cb);

virtual void move(int dx,int dy);
        virtual void hide();
        virtual void show();
        virtual void attach(Window&) = 0;

        Point loc;
        int width;
        int height;
        string label;
        Callback do_it;

protected:
        Window* own;        // every Widget belongs to a Window
        Fl_Widget* pw;      // connection to the FLTK Widget
};
```

A **Widget** has two interesting functions that we can use for **Button** (and also for any other class derived from **Widget**, e.g., a **Menu**; see §16.7):

- **hide()** makes the **Widget** invisible.
- **show()** makes the **Widget** visible again.

A **Widget** starts out visible.

Just like a **Shape**, we can **move()** a **Widget** in its **Window**, and we must **attach()** it to a **Window** before it can be used. Note that we declared **attach()** to be a pure virtual function (§14.3.5): every class derived from **Widget** must define what it means for it to be attached to a **Window**. In fact, it is in **attach()** that the system-level widgets are created. The **attach()** function is called from **Window** as part of its implementation of **Window**'s own **attach()**. Basically, connecting a window and a widget is a delicate little dance where each has to do its own part. The result is that a window knows about its widgets and that each widget knows about its window:

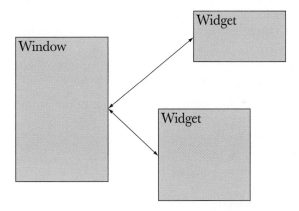

Note that a **Window** doesn't know what kind of **Widget**s it deals with. As described in §14.4–5, we are using basic object-oriented programming to ensure that a **Window** can deal with every kind of **Widget**. Similarly, a **Widget** doesn't know what kind of **Window** it deals with.

We have been slightly sloppy, leaving data members accessible. The **own** and **pw** members are strictly for the implementation of derived classes so we have declared them **protected**.

The definitions of **Widget** and of the widgets we use here (**Button**, **Menu**, etc.) are found in **GUI.h**.

16.4.2 Buttons

A **Button** is the simplest **Widget** we deal with. All it does is to invoke a callback when we click on it:

```
class Button : public Widget {
public:
    Button(Point xy, int ww, int hh, const string& s, Callback cb)
        :Widget(xy,ww,hh,s,cb) { }

    void attach(Window& win);
};
```

That's all. The **attach()** function contains all the (relatively) messy FLTK code. We have banished the explanation to Appendix E (not to be read until after Chapters 17 and 18). For now, please just note that defining a simple **Widget** isn't particularly difficult.

We do not deal with the somewhat complicated and messy issue of how buttons (and other **Widgets**) look on the screen. The problem is that there is a near infinity of choices and that some styles are mandated by certain systems. Also, from a programming technique point of view, nothing really new is needed for expressing the looks of buttons. If you get desperate, we note that placing a **Shape** on top of a button doesn't affect the button's ability to function – and you know how to make a shape look like anything at all.

16.4.3 In_box and Out_box

We provide two **Widgets** for getting text in and out of our program:

```
struct In_box : Widget {
    In_box(Point xy, int w, int h, const string& s)
        :Widget(xy,w,h,s,0) { }
    int get_int();
    string get_string();

    void attach(Window& win);
};

struct Out_box : Widget {
    Out_box(Point xy, int w, int h, const string& s)
        :Widget(xy,w,h,s,0) { }
    void put(int);
    void put(const string&);

    void attach(Window& win);
};
```

An **In_box** can accept text typed into it, and we can read that text as a string using **get_string()** or as an integer using **get_int()**. If you want to know if text has been entered, you can read using **get_string()** and see if you get the empty string:

```
string s = some_inbox.get_string();
if (s =="") {
      // deal with missing input
}
```

An **Out_box** is used to present some message to a user. In analogy to **In_box**, we can **put()** either integers or strings. §16.5 gives examples of the use of **In_box** and **Out_box**.

We could have provided **get_floating_point()**, **get_complex()**, etc., but we did not bother because you can take the string, stick it into a **stringstream**, and do any input formatting you like that way (§11.4).

16.4.4 Menus

We offer a very simple notion of a menu:

```
struct Menu : Widget {
      enum Kind { horizontal, vertical };
      Menu(Point xy, int w, int h, Kind kk, const string& label);
      Vector_ref<Button> selection;
      Kind k;
      int offset;
      int attach(Button& b);          // attach button to Menu
      int attach(Button* p);          // attach new button to Menu

      void show()                     // show all buttons
      {
            for (unsigned int i = 0; i<selection.size(); ++i)
                  selection[i].show();
      }
      void hide();                    // hide all buttons
      void move(int dx, int dy);      // move all buttons

      void attach(Window& win);       // attach all buttons to Window win
};
```

A **Menu** is basically a vector of buttons. As usual, the **Point xy** is the top left corner. The width and height are used to resize buttons as they are added to the menu. For examples, see §16.5 and §16.7. Each menu button ("a menu item") is an independent **Widget** presented to the **Menu** as an argument to **attach()**. In turn, **Menu** provides an **attach()** operation to attach all of its **Button**s to a **Window**. The **Menu** keeps track of its **Button**s using a **Vector_ref** (§13.10, §E.4). If you want a "pop-up" menu, you have to make it yourself; see §16.7.

16.5 An example

To get a better feel for the basic GUI facilities, consider the window for a simple application involving input, output, and a bit of graphics:

This program allows a user to display a sequence of lines (an open polyline; §13.6) specified as a sequence of coordinate pairs. The idea is that the user repeatedly enters (x,y) coordinates in the "next x" and "next y" boxes; after each pair the user hits the "next point" button.

Initially, the "current (x,y)" box is empty and the program waits for the user to enter the first coordinate pair. That done, the starting point appears in the "current (x,y)" box, and each new coordinate pair entered results in a line being drawn: A line from the current point (which has its coordinates displayed in the "current (x,y)" box) to the newly entered (x,y) is drawn, and that (x,y) becomes the new current point.

This draws an open polyline. When the user tires of this activity, there is the "quit" button for exiting. That's pretty straightforward, and the program exercises several useful GUI facilities: text input and output, line drawing, and multiple buttons. The window above shows the result after entering two coordinate pairs; after seven we can get this:

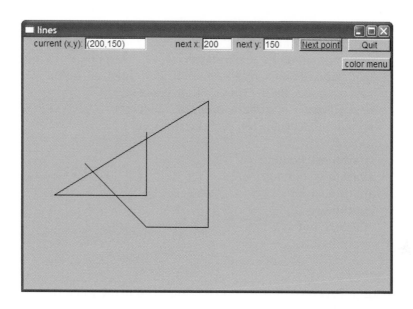

Let's define a class for representing such windows. It is pretty straightforward:

```
struct Lines_window : Window {
    Lines_window(Point xy, int w, int h, const string& title );
    Open_polyline lines;
private:
    Button next_button;        // add (next_x,next_y) to lines
    Button quit_button;
    In_box next_x;
    In_box next_y;
    Out_box xy_out;

    static void cb_next(Address, Address);    // callback for next_button
    void next();
    static void cb_quit(Address, Address);    // callback for quit_button
    void quit();
};
```

The line is represented as an **Open_polyline**. The buttons and boxes are declared (as **Buttons**, **In_boxes**, and **Out_boxes**) and for each button a member function implementing the desired action is defined together with its "boilerplate" callback function.

Lines_window's constructor initializes everything:

```
Lines_window::Lines_window(Point xy, int w, int h, const string& title)
    :Window(xy,w,h,title),
    next_button(Point(x_max()–150,0), 70, 20, "Next point", cb_next),
    quit_button(Point(x_max()–70,0), 70, 20, "Quit", cb_quit),
    next_x(Point(x_max()–310,0), 50, 20, "next x:"),
    next_y(Point(x_max()–210,0), 50, 20, "next y:"),
    xy_out(Point(100,0), 100, 20, "current (x,y):")
{

    attach(next_button);
    attach(quit_button);
    attach(next_x);
    attach(next_y);
    attach(xy_out);
    attach(lines);
}
```

That is, each widget is constructed and then attached to the window.
    Dealing with the "Quit" button is trivial:

```
void Lines_window::cb_quit(Address, Address pw)        // "the usual"
{
    reference_to<Lines_window>(pw).quit();
}

void Lines_window::quit()
{
    hide();        // curious FLTK idiom for delete window
}
```

This is just "the usual": a callback function (here, **cb_quit()**) that forwards to the
function (here, **quit()**) that does the real work. Here the real work is to delete the
Window. That's done using the curious FLTK idiom of simply hiding it.
    All the real work is done in the "Next point" button. Its callback function is
just the usual:

```
void Lines_window::cb_next(Address, Address pw)        // "the usual"
{
    reference_to<Lines_window>(pw).next();
}
```

The **next()** function defines what the "Next point" button actually does: it reads a
pair of coordinates, updates the **Open_polyline**, updates the position readout,
and redraws the window:

```
void Lines_window::next()
{
        int x = next_x.get_int();
        int y = next_y.get_int();

        lines.add(Point(x,y));

        // update current position readout:
        stringstream ss;
        ss << '(' << x << ',' << y << ')';
        xy_out.put(ss.str());

        redraw();
}
```

That's all pretty obvious. We get integer coordinates from the **In_box**es using **get_int()**. We use a **stringstream** to format the string to be put into the **Out_box**; the **str()** member function lets us get to the string within the **stringstream**. The final **redraw()** here is needed to present the results to the user; until a **Window**'s **redraw()** is called, the old image remains on the screen.

So what's odd and different about this program? Let's see its **main()**:

```
#include "GUI.h"

int main()
try {
        Lines_window win(Point(100,100),600,400,"lines");
        return gui_main();
}
catch(exception& e) {
        cerr << "exception: " << e.what() << '\n';
        return 1;
}
catch (...) {
        cerr << "Some exception\n";
        return 2;
}
```

There is basically nothing there! The body of **main()** is just the definition of our window, **win**, and a call to a function **gui_main()**. There is not another function, **if**, **switch**, or loop − nothing of the kind of code we saw in Chapters 6 and 7 − just a definition of a variable and a call to the function **gui_main()**, which is itself just a call of FLTK's **run()**. Looking further, we can find that **run()** is simply the infinite loop:

```
while(wait());
```

Except for a few implementation details postponed to Appendix E, we have seen all of the code that makes our lines program run. We have seen all of the fundamental logic. So what happens?

16.6 Control inversion

What happened was that we moved the control of the order of execution from the program to the widgets: whichever widget the user activates, runs. For example, click on a button and its callback runs. When that callback returns, the program settles back, waiting for the user to do something else. Basically, **wait()** tells "the system" to look out for the widgets and invoke the appropriate callbacks. In theory, **wait()** could tell you, the programmer, which widget requested attention and leave it to you to call the appropriate function. However, in FLTK and most other GUI systems, **wait()** simply invokes the appropriate callback, saving you the bother of writing code to select it.

A "conventional program" is organized like this:

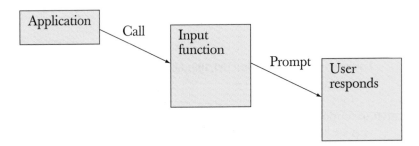

A "GUI program" is organized like this:

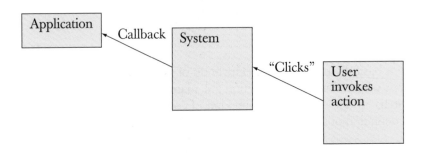

One implication of this "control inversion" is that the order of execution is completely determined by the actions of the user. This complicates both program organization and debugging. It is hard to imagine what a user will do and hard to imagine every possible effect of a random sequence of callbacks. This makes systematic testing a nightmare (see Chapter 26). The techniques for dealing with that are beyond the scope of this book, but we encourage you to be extra careful with code driven by users through callbacks. In addition to the obvious control flow problems, there are also problems of visibility and difficulties with keeping track of which widget is connected to what data. To minimize hassle, it is essential to keep the GUI portion of a program simple and to build a GUI program incrementally, testing at each stage. When working on a GUI program, it is almost essential to draw little diagrams of the objects and their interactions.

How does the code triggered by the various callbacks communicate? The simplest way is for the functions to operate on data stored in the window, as was done in the example in §16.5. There, the **Lines_window**'s **next()** function, invoked by pressing the "Next point" button, reads data from the **In_boxes** (**next_x** and **next_y**) and updates the **lines** member variable and the **Out_box** (**xy_out**). Obviously, a function invoked by a callback can do anything: it could open files, connect to the web, etc. However, for now, we'll just consider the simple case in which we hold our data in a window.

16.7 Adding a menu

Let's explore the control and communication issues raised by "control inversion" by providing a menu for our "lines" program. First, we'll simply provide a menu that allows the user to change the color of all lines in the **lines** member variable. We add the menu **color_menu** and its callbacks:

```
struct Lines_window : Window {
        Lines_window(Point xy, int w, int h, const string& title);

        Open_polyline lines;
        Menu color_menu;

        static void cb_red(Address, Address);      // callback for red button
        static void cb_blue(Address, Address);     // callback for blue button
        static void cb_black(Address, Address);    // callback for black button

        // the actions:
        void red_pressed() { change(Color::red); }
        void blue_pressed() { change(Color::blue); }
        void black_pressed() { change(Color::black); }
```

```
    void change(Color c) { lines.set_color(c); }

    // . . . as before . . .
};
```

Writing all of those almost identical callback functions and "action" functions is tedious. However, it is conceptually simple, and offering something that's significantly simpler to type in is beyond the scope of this book. When a menu button is pressed, it changes the lines to the requested color.

Having defined the **color_menu** member, we need to initialize it:

```
Lines_window::Lines_window(Point xy, int w, int h, const string& title)
    :Window(xy,w,h,title),
    // . . . as before . . .
    color_menu(Point(x_max()–70,40),70,20,Menu::vertical,"color")
{
    // . . . as before . . .
    color_menu.attach(new Button(Point(0,0),0,0,"red",cb_red));
    color_menu. attach(new Button(Point(0,0),0,0,"blue",cb_blue));
    color_menu. attach(new Button(Point(0,0),0,0,"black",cb_black));
    attach(color_menu);
}
```

The buttons are dynamically attached to the menu (using **attach()**) and can be removed and/or replaced as needed. **Menu::attach()** adjusts size and location of the button and attaches them to the window. That's all, and we get:

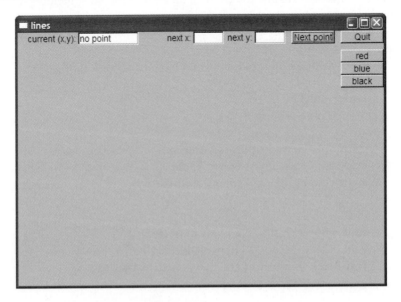

Having played with this for a while, we decided that what we really wanted was a "pop-up menu"; that is, we didn't want to spend precious screen space on a menu except when we are using it. So, we added a "color menu" button. When we press that, up pops the color menu, and when we have made a selection, the menu is again hidden and the button appears.

Here first is the window after we have added a few lines:

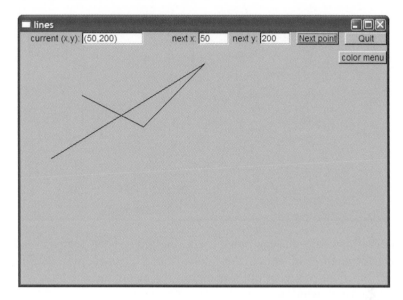

We see the new "color menu" button and some (black) lines. Press "color menu" and the menu appears:

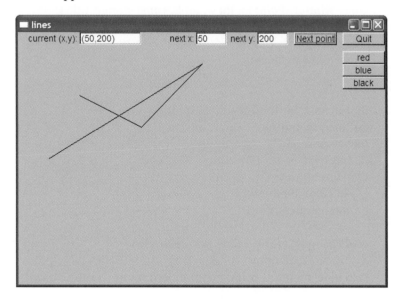

Note that the "color menu" button is now hidden. We don't need it until we are finished with the menu. Press "blue" and we get:

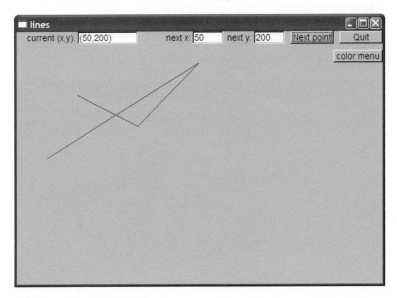

The lines are now blue and the "color menu" button has reappeared.

To achieve this we added the "color menu" button and modified the "pressed" functions to adjust the visibility of the menu and the button. Here is the complete **Lines_window** after all our modifications:

```
struct Lines_window : Window {
        Lines_window(Point xy, int w, int h, const string& title );
private:
        // data:
        Open_polyline lines;

        // widgets:
        Button next_button;   // add (next_x,next_y) to lines
        Button quit_button;   // end program
        In_box next_x;
        In_box next_y;
        Out_box xy_out;
        Menu color_menu;
        Button menu_button;

        void change(Color c) { lines.set_color(c); }

        void hide_menu() { color_menu.hide(); menu_button.show(); }
```

```
// actions invoked by callbacks:
void red_pressed() { change(Color::red); hide_menu(); }
void blue_pressed() { change(Color::blue); hide_menu(); }
void black_pressed() { change(Color::black); hide_menu(); }
void menu_pressed() { menu_button.hide(); color_menu.show(); }
void next();
void quit();

// callback functions:
static void cb_red(Address, Address);
static void cb_blue(Address, Address);
static void cb_black(Address, Address);
static void cb_menu(Address, Address);
static void cb_next(Address, Address);
static void cb_quit(Address, Address);
};
```

Note how all but the constructor is private. Basically, that window class is the
program. All that happens, happens through its callbacks, so no code from outside the window is needed. We sorted the declarations a bit hoping to make the
class more readable. The constructor provides arguments to all of its sub-objects
and attaches them to the window:

```
Lines_window::Lines_window(Point xy, int w, int h, const string& title)
    :Window(xy,w,h,title),
    color_menu(Point(x_max()-70,30),70,20,Menu::vertical,"color"),
    menu_button(Point(x_max()-80,30), 80, 20, "color menu", cb_menu),
    next_button(Point(x_max()-150,0), 70, 20, "Next point", cb_next),
    quit_button(Point(x_max()-70,0), 70, 20, "Quit", cb_quit),
    next_x(Point(x_max()-310,0), 50, 20, "next x:"),
    next_y(Point(x_max()-210,0), 50, 20, "next y:"),
    xy_out(Point(100,0), 100, 20, "current (x,y):")
{
    attach(next_button);
    attach(quit_button);
    attach(next_x);
    attach(next_y);
    attach(xy_out);
    xy_out.put("no point");
    color_menu.attach(new Button(Point(0,0),0,0,"red",cb_red));
    color_menu. attach(new Button(Point(0,0),0,0,"blue",cb_blue));
    color_menu. attach(new Button(Point(0,0),0,0,"black",cb_black));
    attach(color_menu);
```

```
        color_menu.hide();
        attach(menu_button);
        attach(lines);
}
```

Note that the initializers are in the same order as the data member definitions.
That's the proper order in which to write the initializers. In fact, member initializers are always executed in the order their data members were declared. Some
compilers (helpfully) give a warning if a base or member constructor is specified
out of order.

16.8 Debugging GUI code

Once a GUI program starts working it is often quite easy to debug: what you see
is what you get. However, there is often a most frustrating period before the first
shapes and widgets start appearing in a window or even before a window appears on the screen. Try this **main()**:

```
int main()
{
        Lines_window (Point(100,100),600,400,"lines");
        return gui_main();
}
```

Do you see the error? Whether you see it or not, you should try it; the program
will compile and run, but instead of the **Lines_window** giving you a chance to
draw lines, you get at most a flicker on the screen. How do you find errors in
such a program?

- By carefully using well-tried program parts (classes, function, libraries)
- By simplifying all new code, by slowly "growing" a program from its
  simplest version, by carefully looking over the code line for line
- By checking all linker settings
- By comparing to already working programs
- By explaining the code to a friend

The one thing that you will find it hard to do is to trace the execution of the
code. If you have learned to use a debugger, you have a chance, but just inserting
"output statements" will not work in this case – the problem is that no output appears. Even debuggers will have problems because there are several things going
on at once ("multi-threading") – your code is not the only code trying to interact
with the screen. Simplification of the code and a systematic approach to understanding the code are key.

So what was the problem? Here is the correct version (from §16.5):

```
int main()
{
    Lines_window win(Point(100,100),600,400,"lines");
    return gui_main();
}
```

We "forgot" the name of the **Lines_window**, **win**. Since we didn't actually need that name that seemed reasonable, but the compiler then decided that since we didn't use that window, it could immediately destroy it. Oops! That window existed for something on the order of a millisecond. No wonder we missed it.

Another common problem is to put one window *exactly* on top of another. This obviously (or rather not at all obviously) looks as if there is only one window. Where did the other window go? We can spend significant time looking for nonexistent bugs in the code. The same problem can occur if we put one shape on top of another.

Finally – to make matters still worse – exceptions don't always work as we would like them to when we use a GUI library. Since our code is managed by a GUI library, an exception we throw may never reach our handler – the library or the operating system may "eat" it (that is, they may rely on error-handling mechanisms that differ from C++ exceptions and may indeed be completely oblivious of C++).

Common problems found during debugging include **Shapes** and **Widgets** not showing because they were not attached and objects misbehaving because they have gone out of scope. Consider how a programmer might factor out the creation and attachment of buttons in a menu:

```
// helper function for loading buttons into a menu
void load_disaster_menu(Menu& m)
{
    Point orig(0,0);
    Button b1(orig,0,0,"flood",cb_flood);
    Button b2(orig,0,0,"fire",cb_fire);
    // . . .
    m.attach(b1);
    m.attach(b2);
    // . . .
}

int main()
{
    // . . .
```

```
        Menu disasters(Point(100,100),60,20,Menu::horizontal,"disasters");
        load_disaster_menu(disasters);
        win.attach(disasters);
        // . . .
    }
```

This will not work. All those buttons are local to the **load_disaster_menu** function and attaching them to a menu will not change that. An explanation can be found in §18.5.4 (*Don't return a pointer to a local variable*), and an illustration of the memory layout for local variables is presented in §8.5.8. The essence of the story is that after **load_disaster_menu()** has returned, those local objects have been destroyed and the **disasters** menu refers to nonexistent (destroyed) objects. The result is likely to be surprising and not pretty. The solution is to use unnamed objects created by **new** instead of named local objects:

```
    // helper function for loading buttons into a menu
    void load_disaster_menu(Menu& m)
    {
        Point orig(0,0);
        m.attach(new Button(orig,0,0,"flood",cb_flood));
        m.attach(new Button(orig,0,0,"fire",cb_fire));
        // . . .
    }
```

The correct solution is even simpler than the (all too common) bug.

Drill

1. Make a completely new project with linker settings for FLTK (as described in Appendix D).
2. Using the facilities of **Graph_lib**, type in the line-drawing program from §16.5 and get it to run.
3. Modify the program to use a pop-up menu as described in §16.7 and get it to run.
4. Modify the program to have a second menu for choosing line styles and get it to run.

Review

1. Why would you want a graphical user interface?
2. When would you want a non-graphical user interface?

3. What is a software layer?
4. Why would you want to layer software?
5. What is the fundamental problem when communicating with an operating system from C++?
6. What is a callback?
7. What is a widget?
8. What is another name for widget?
9. What does the acronym FLTK mean?
10. How do you pronounce FLTK?
11. What other GUI toolkits have you heard of?
12. Which systems use the term *widget* and which prefer *control*?
13. What are examples of widgets?
14. When would you use an inbox?
15. What is the type of the value stored in an inbox?
16. When would you use a button?
17. When would you use a menu?
18. What is control inversion?
19. What is the basic strategy for debugging a GUI program?
20. Why is debugging a GUI program harder than debugging an "ordinary program using streams for I/O"?

Terms

button	dialog box	visible/hidden
callback	GUI	waiting for input
console I/O	menu	wait loop
control	software layer	widget
control inversion	user interface	

Exercises

1. Make a **My_window** that's a bit like **Simple_window** except that it has two buttons, **next** and **quit**.
2. Make a window (based on **My_window**) with a 4-by-4 checkerboard of square buttons. When pressed, a button performs a simple action, such as printing its coordinates in an output box, or turns a slightly different color (until another button is pressed).
3. Place an **Image** on top of a **Button**; move both when the button is pushed. Use this random number generator to pick a new location for the "image button":

   int rint(int low, int high) { return low+rand()%(high−low); }

   It returns a random **int** in the range [**low**,**high**).

4. Make a menu with items that make a circle, a square, an equilateral triangle, and a hexagon, respectively. Make an input box (or two) for giving a coordinate pair, and place the shape made by pressing a menu item at that coordinate. Sorry, no drag and drop.

5. Write a program that draws a shape of your choice and moves it to a new point each time you click "Next." The new point should be determined by a coordinate pair read from an input stream.

6. Make an "analog clock," that is, a clock with hands that move. You get the time of day from the operating system through a library call. A major part of this exercise is to find the functions that give you the time of day and a way of waiting for a short period of time (e.g., a second for a clock tick) and to learn to use them based on the documentation you found. Hint: **clock()**, **sleep()**.

7. Using the techniques developed in the previous exercises, make an image of an airplane "fly around" in a window. Have a "start" and a "stop" button.

8. Provide a currency converter. Read the conversion rates from a file on startup. Enter an amount in an input window and provide a way of selecting currencies to convert to and from (e.g., a pair of menus).

9. Modify the calculator from Chapter 7 to get its input from an input box and return its results in an output box.

10. Provide a program where you can choose among a set of functions (e.g., **sin()** and **log()**), provide parameters for those functions, and then graph them.

Postscript

GUI is a huge topic. Much of it has to do with style and compatibility with existing systems. Furthermore, much has to do with a bewildering variety of widgets (such as a GUI library offering many dozens of alternative button styles) that would make a traditional botanist feel quite at home. However, little of that has to do with fundamental programming techniques, so we won't proceed in that direction. Other topics, such as scaling, rotation, morphing, three-dimensional objects, shadowing, etc., require sophistication in graphical and/or mathematical topics which we don't assume here.

One thing you should be aware of is that most GUI systems provide a "GUI builder" that allows you to design your window layouts graphically and attach callbacks and actions to buttons, menus, etc. specified graphically. For many applications, such a GUI builder is well worth using to reduce the tedium of writing "scaffolding code" such as our callbacks. However, always try to understand how the resulting programs work. Sometimes, the generated code is equivalent to what you have seen in this chapter. Sometimes more elaborate and/or expensive mechanisms are used.

Part III

Data and Algorithms

17

Vector and Free Store

"Use **vector** as the default!"

— **Alex Stepanov**

This chapter and the next four describe the containers and algorithms part of the C++ standard library, traditionally called the STL. We describe the key facilities from the STL and some of their uses. In addition, we present the key design and programming techniques used to implement the STL and some low-level language features used for that. Among those are pointers, arrays, and free store. The focus of this chapter and the next two is the design and implementation of the most common and most useful STL container: **vector**.

17.1 Introduction

The most useful container in the C++ standard library is **vector**. A **vector** provides a sequence of elements of a given type. You can refer to an element by its index (subscript), extend the **vector** by using **push_back()**, ask a **vector** for the number of its elements using **size()**, and have access to the **vector** checked against attempts to access out-of-range elements. The standard library **vector** is a convenient, flexible, efficient (in time and space), statically type-safe container of elements. The standard **string** has similar properties, as have other useful standard container types, such as **list** and **map**, which we will describe in Chapter 20. However, a computer's memory doesn't directly support such useful types. All that the hardware *directly* supports is sequences of bytes. For example, for a **vector<double>**, the operation **v.push_back(2.3)** adds **2.3** to a sequence of **doubles** and increases the element count of **v** (**v.size()**) by 1. At the lowest level, the computer knows nothing about anything as sophisticated as **push_back()**; all it knows is how to read and write a few bytes at a time.

In this and the following two chapters, we show how to build **vector** from the basic language facilities available to every programmer. Doing so allows us to illustrate useful concepts and programming techniques, and to see how they are expressed using C++ language features. The language facilities and programming techniques we encounter in the **vector** implementation are generally useful and very widely used.

Once we have seen how **vector** is designed, implemented, and used, we can proceed to look at other standard library containers, such as **map**, and examine the elegant and efficient facilities for their use provided by the C++ standard library (Chapters 20 and 21). These facilities, called algorithms, save us from programming common tasks involving data ourselves. Instead, we can use what is available as part of every C++ implementation to ease the writing and testing of our libraries. We have already seen and used one of the standard library's most useful algorithms: **sort**().

We approach the standard library **vector** through a series of increasingly sophisticated **vector** implementations. First, we build a very simple **vector**. Then, we see what's undesirable about that **vector** and fix it. When we have done that a few times, we reach a **vector** implementation that is roughly equivalent to the standard library **vector** − shipped with your C++ compiler, the one that you have been using in the previous chapters. This process of gradual refinement closely mirrors the way we typically approach a new programming task. Along the way, we encounter and explore many classical problems related to the use of memory and data structures. The basic plan is this:

- *Chapter 17 (this chapter):* How can we deal with varying amounts of memory? In particular, how can different **vectors** have different numbers of elements and how can a single **vector** have different numbers of elements at different times? This leads us to examine free store (heap storage), pointers, casts (explicit type conversion), and references.

- *Chapter 18:* How can we copy **vectors**? How can we provide a subscript operation for them? We also introduce arrays and explore their relation to pointers.

- *Chapter 19:* How can we have **vectors** with different element types? And how can we deal with out-of-range errors? To answer those questions, we explore the C++ template and exception facilities.

In addition to the new language facilities and techniques that we introduce to handle the implementation of a flexible, efficient, and type-safe vector, we will also (re)use many of the language facilities and programming techniques we have already seen. Occasionally, we'll take the opportunity to give those a slightly more formal and technical definition.

So, this is the point at which we finally get to deal directly with memory. Why do we have to? Our **vector** and **string** are extremely useful and convenient; we can just use those. After all, containers, such as **vector** and **string**, are designed to insulate us from some of the unpleasant aspects of real memory. However, unless we are content to believe in magic, we must examine the lowest level of memory management. Why shouldn't you "just believe in magic"? Or − to put a more positive spin on it − why shouldn't you "just trust that the implementers of **vector** knew what they were doing"? After all, we don't suggest that you examine the device physics that allows our computer's memory to function.

Well, we are programmers (computer scientists, software developers, or whatever) rather than physicists. Had we been studying device physics, we would have had to look into the details of computer memory design. However, since we are studying programming, we must look into the detailed design of programs. In theory, we could consider the low-level memory access and management facilities "implementation details" just as we do the device physics. However, if we did that, you would not just have to "believe in magic"; you would be unable to implement a new container (should you need one, and that's not uncommon). Also, you would be unable to read huge amounts of C and C++ code that directly uses memory. As we will see over the next few chapters, pointers (a low-level and direct way of referring to an object) are also useful for a variety of reasons not related to memory management. It is not easy to use C++ well without sometimes using pointers.

More philosophically, I am among the large group of computer professionals who are of the opinion that if you lack a basic and practical understanding of how a program maps onto a computer's memory and operations, you will have problems getting a solid grasp of higher-level topics, such as data structures, algorithms, and operating systems.

17.2 vector basics

We start our incremental design of **vector** by considering a very simple use:

```
vector<double> age(4);     // a vector with 4 elements of type double
age[0]=0.33;
age[1]=22.0;
age[2]=27.2;
age[3]=54.2;
```

Obviously, this creates a **vector** with four elements of type **double** and gives those four elements the values **0.33, 22.0, 27.2,** and **54.2**. The four elements are numbered 0, 1, 2, 3. The numbering of elements in C++ standard library containers always starts from 0 (zero). Numbering from 0 is very common, and it is a universal convention among C++ programmers. The number of elements of a **vector** is called its size. So, the size of **age** is 4. The elements of a **vector** are numbered (indexed) from 0 to size−1. For example, the elements of **age** are numbered **0** to **age.size()−1**. We can represent **age** graphically like this:

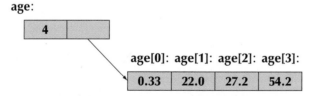

How do we make this "graphical design" real in a computer's memory? How do we get the values stored and accessed like that? Obviously, we have to define a class and we want to call this class **vector**. Furthermore, it needs a data member to hold its size and one to hold its elements. But how do we represent a set of elements where the number of elements can vary? We could use a standard library **vector**, but that would — in this context — be cheating: we are building a **vector** here.

So, how do we represent that arrow in the drawing above? Consider doing without it. We could define a fixed-sized data structure:

```
class vector {
      int size, age0, age1, age2, age3;
      // . . .
};
```

Ignoring some notational details, we'll have something like this:

	age:			
size:	**age[0]**:	**age[1]**:	**age[2]**:	**age[3]**:
4	0.33	22.0	27.2	54.2

That's simple and nice, but the first time we try to add an element with **push_back()** we are sunk: we have no way of adding an element; the number of elements is fixed to four in the program text. We need something more than a data structure holding a fixed number of elements. Operations that change the number of elements of a **vector**, such as **push_back()**, can't be implemented if we defined **vector** to have a fixed number of elements. Basically, we need a data member that points to the set of elements so that we can make it point to a different set of elements when we need more space. We need something like the memory address of the first element. In C++, a data type that can hold an address is called a *pointer* and is syntactically distinguished by the suffix *, so that **double*** means "pointer to **double**." Given that, we can define our first version of a **vector** class:

```
// a very simplified vector of doubles (like vector<double>)
class vector {
      int sz;                 // the size
      double* elem;           // pointer to the first element (of type double)
public:
      vector(int s);          // constructor: allocate s doubles,
                              // let elem point to them
                              // store s in sz
      int size() const { return sz; }     // the current size
};
```

Before proceeding with the **vector** design, let us study the notion of "pointer" in some detail. The notion of "pointer" — together with its closely related notion of "array" — is key to C++'s notion of "memory."

17.3 Memory, addresses, and pointers

A computer's memory is a sequence of bytes. We can number the bytes from 0 to the last one. We call such "a number that indicates a location in memory" an *address*. You can think of an address as a kind of integer value. The first byte of memory has the address 0, the next the address 1, and so on. We can visualize a megabyte of memory like this:

Everything we put in memory has an address. For example:

```
int var = 17;
```

This will set aside an "**int**-sized" piece of memory for **var** somewhere and put the value **17** into that memory. We can also store and manipulate addresses. An object that holds an address value is called a *pointer*. For example, the type needed to hold the address of an **int** is called a "pointer to **int**" or an "**int** pointer" and the notation is **int***:

```
int* ptr = &var;        // ptr holds the address of var
```

The "address of" operator, unary **&**, is used to get the address of an object. So, if **var** happens to start at address 4096 (also known as 2^{12}), **ptr** will hold the value 4096:

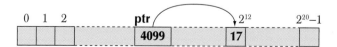

Basically, we view our computer's memory as a sequence of bytes numbered from 0 to the memory size minus 1. On some machines that's a simplification, but as an initial programming model of the memory, it will suffice.

Each type has a corresponding pointer type. For example:

```
char ch = 'c';
char* pc = &ch;         // pointer to char

int ii = 17;
int* pi = &ii;          // pointer to int
```

If we want to see the value of the object pointed to, we can do that using the "contents of" operator, unary *. For example:

```
cout << "pc==" << pc << "; contents of pc==" << *pc << "\n";
cout << "pi==" << pi << "; contents of pi==" << *pi << "\n";
```

The output for *pc will be the character c and the output for *pi will be the integer 17. The output for pc and pi will vary depending on where the compiler allocated our variables ch and ii in memory. The notation used for the pointer value (address) may also vary depending on which conventions your system uses; hexadecimal notation (§A.2.1.1) is popular for pointer values.

The *contents of* operator (often called the *dereference* operator) can also be used on the left-hand side of an assignment:

```
*pc = 'x';      // OK: you can assign 'x' to the char pointed to by pc
*pi = 27;       // OK: an int* points to an int so *pi is an int
*pi = *pc;      // OK: you can assign a char (pc) to an int (pi)
```

Note that even though a pointer value can be printed as an integer, a pointer is not an integer. "What does an **int** point to?" is not a well-formed question; **ints** do not point, pointers do. A pointer type provides the operations suitable for addresses, whereas **int** provides the (arithmetic and logical) operations suitable for integers. So pointers and integers do not implicitly mix:

```
int i = pi;     // error: can't assign an int* to an int
pi = 7;         // error: can't assign an int to an int*
```

Similarly, a pointer to **char** (a **char***) is not a pointer to **int** (an **int***). For example:

```
pc = pi;        // error: can't assign an int* to a char*
pi = pc;        // error: can't assign a char* to an int*
```

Why is it an error to assign **pc** to **pi**? Consider one answer: a **char** is usually much smaller than an **int**, so consider this:

```
char ch1 = 'a';
char ch2 = 'b';
char ch3 = 'c';
char ch4 = 'd';
int* pi = &ch3;      // point to ch, a char-sized piece of memory
                     // error: we cannot assign a char* to an int*
                     // but let's pretend we could
*pi = 12345;         // write to an int-sized piece of memory
*pi = 67890;
```

Exactly how the compiler allocates variables in memory is implementation defined, but we might very well get something like this:

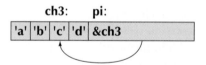

Now, had the compiler allowed the code, we would have been writing **12345** to the memory starting at **&ch3**. That would definitely have changed the value of some nearby memory, such as **ch2** or **ch4**. If we were really unlucky (which is likely), we would have overwritten part of **pi** itself! In that case, the next assignment ***pi=67890** would place **67890** in some completely different part of memory. Be glad that such assignment is disallowed, but this is one of the very few protections offered by the compiler at this low level of programming.

In the unlikely case that you really need to convert an **int** to a pointer or to convert one pointer type to another, you have to use **reinterpret_cast**; see §17.8.

We are really close to the hardware here. This is not a particularly comfortable place to be for a programmer. We have only a few primitive operations available and hardly any support from the language or the standard library. However, we had to get here to know how higher-level facilities, such as **vector**, are implemented. We need to understand how to write code at this level because not all code can be "high-level" (see Chapter 25). Also, we might better appreciate the convenience and relative safety of the higher levels of software once we have experienced their absence. Our aim is always to work at the highest level of abstraction that is possible given a problem and the constraints on its solution. In this chapter and in Chapters 18–19, we show how to get back to a more comfortable level of abstraction by implementing a **vector**.

17.3.1 The sizeof operator

So how much memory does an **int** really take up? A pointer? The operator **sizeof** answers such questions:

```
cout << "the size of char is " << sizeof(char) << ' ' << sizeof ('a') << '\n';
cout << "the size of int is " << sizeof(int) << ' ' << sizeof (2+2) << '\n';
int* p = 0;
cout << "the size of int* is " << sizeof(int*) << ' ' << sizeof (p) << '\n';
```

As you can see, we can apply **sizeof** either to a type name or to an expression; for a type, **sizeof** gives the size of an object of that type and for an expression it gives the size of the type of the result. The result of **sizeof** is a positive integer and the unit is **sizeof(char)**, which is defined to be **1**. Typically, a **char** is stored in a byte, so **sizeof** reports the number of bytes.

TRY THIS

Execute the example above and see what you get. Then extend the example to determine the size of **bool**, **double**, and some other type.

The size of a type is *not* guaranteed to be the same on every implementation of C++. These days, **sizeof(int)** is typically 4 on a laptop or desktop machine. With an 8-bit byte, that means that an **int** is 32 bits. However, embedded-systems processors with 16-bit **ints** and high-performance architectures with 64-bit **ints** are common.

How much memory is used by a **vector**? We can try

```
vector<int> v(1000);
cout << "the size of vector<int>(1000) is " << sizeof (v) << '\n';
```

The output will be something like

```
the size of vector<int>(1000) is 20
```

The explanation will become obvious over this chapter and the next (see also §19.2.1), but clearly, **sizeof** is not counting the elements.

17.4 Free store and pointers

Consider the implementation of **vector** from the end of §17.2. From where does the **vector** get the space for the elements? How do we get the pointer **elem** to point to them? When you start a C++ program, the compiler sets aside memory for your code (sometimes called *code storage* or *text storage*) and for the global variables you define (called *static storage*). It also sets aside some memory to be used when you call functions, and they need space for their arguments and local variables (that's called *stack storage* or *automatic storage*). The rest of the computer's memory is potentially available for other uses; it is "free." We can illustrate that graphically:

memory layout:

The C++ language makes this "free store" (also called the *heap*) available through an operator called **new**. For example:

    double* p = new double[4];   // allocate 4 doubles on the free store

This asks the C++ run-time system to allocate 4 **doubles** on the free store and return a pointer to the first **double** to us. We use that pointer to initialize our pointer variable **p**. We can represent this graphically:

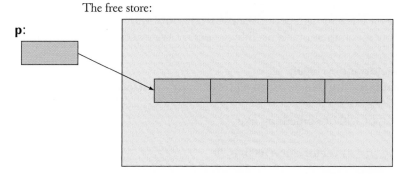

The free store:

p:

The **new** operator returns a pointer to the object it creates. If it created several objects (an array), it returns a pointer to the first of those objects. If that object is of type **X**, the pointer returned by **new** is of type **X***. For example:

    char* q = new double[4];   // error: double* assigned to char*

That **new** returns a pointer to a **double** and a **double** isn't a **char**, so we should not (and cannot) assign it to the pointer to **char** variable **q**.

17.4.1 Free-store allocation

We request memory to be *allocated* on the *free store* by the **new** operator:

- The **new** operator returns a pointer to the allocated memory.
- A pointer value is the address of the first byte of the memory.
- A pointer points to an object of a specified type.
- A pointer does *not* know how many elements it points to.

The **new** operator can allocate individual elements or sequences (arrays) of elements. For example:

    int* pi = new int;   // allocate one int
    int* qi = new int[4];   // allocate 4 ints (an array of 4 ints)

double* pd = new double;   // allocate one double
double* qd = new double[n];   // allocate n doubles (an array of n doubles)

Note that the number of objects allocated can be a variable. That's important because that allows us to select how many objects we allocate at run time. If **n** is **2**, we get

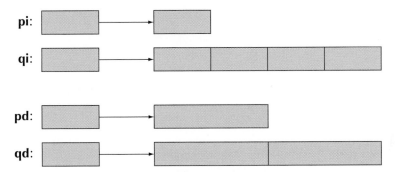

Pointers to objects of different types are different types. For example:

pi = pd;   // error: can't assign a double* to an int*
pd = pi;   // error: can't assign an int* to a double*

Why not? After all, we can assign an **int** to a **double** and a **double** to an **int**. The reason is the [ ] operator. It relies on the size of the element type to figure out where to find an element. For example, **qi[2]** is two **int** sizes further on in memory than **qi[0]**, and **qd[2]** is two **double** sizes further on in memory than **qd[0]**. If the size of an **int** is different from the size of **double**, as it is on many computers, we could get some rather strange results if we allowed **qi** to point to the memory allocated for **qd**.

That's the "practical explanation." The theoretical explanation is simply "Allowing assignment of pointers to different types would allow type errors."

17.4.2 Access through pointers

In addition to using the dereference operator * on a pointer, we can use the subscript operator [ ]. For example:

double* p = new double[4];   // allocate 4 doubles on the free store
double x = *p;   // read the (first) object pointed to by p
double y = p[2];   // read the 3rd object pointed to by p

Unsurprisingly, the subscript operator counts from 0 just like **vector**'s subscript operator, so **p[2]** refers to the third element; **p[0]** is the first element so **p[0]** means exactly the same as ***p**. The [ ] and * operators can also be used for writing:

```
*p = 7.7;            // write to the (first) object pointed to by p
p[2] = 9.9;          // write to the 3rd object pointed to by p
```

A pointer points to an object in memory. The "contents of" operator (also called the *dereference* operator) allows us to read and write the object pointed to by a pointer **p**:

```
double x = *p;       // read the object pointed to by p
*p = 8.8;            // write to the object pointed to by p
```

When applied to a pointer, the [ ] operator treats memory as a sequence of objects (of the type specified by the pointer declaration) with the first one pointed to by a pointer **p**:

```
double x = p[3];     // read the 4th object pointed to by p
p[3] = 4.4;          // write to the 4th object pointed to by p
double y = p[0];     // p[0] is the same as *p
```

That's all. There is no checking, no implementation cleverness, just simple access to our computer's memory:

p[0]:	p[1]:	p[2]:	p[3]:
8.8		9.9	4.4

This is exactly the simple and optimally efficient mechanism for accessing memory that we need to implement a **vector**.

17.4.3 Ranges

The major problem with pointers is that a pointer doesn't "know" how many elements it points to. Consider:

```
double* pd = new double[3];
pd[2] = 2.2;
pd[4] = 4.4;
pd[-3] = -3.3;
```

Does **pd** have a third element **pd[2]**? Does it have a fifth element **pd[4]**? If we look at the definition of **pd**, we find that the answers are yes and no, respectively. However, the compiler doesn't know that; it does not keep track of pointer values. Our code will simply access memory as if we had allocated enough memory. It will even access **pd[−3]** as if the location three **doubles** before what **pd** points to was part of our allocation:

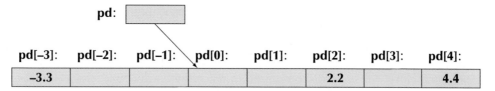

We have no idea what the memory locations marked **pd[–3]** and **pd[4]** are used for. However, we do know that they weren't meant to be used as part of our array of three **doubles** pointed to by **pd**. Most likely, they are parts of other objects and we just scribbled all over those. That's not a good idea. In fact, it is typically a disastrously poor idea: "disastrous" as in "My program crashes mysteriously" or "My program gives wrong output." Try saying that aloud; it doesn't sound nice at all. We'll go a long way to avoid that. Out-of-range access is particularly nasty because apparently unrelated parts of a program are affected. An out-of-range read gives us a "random" value that may depend on some completely unrelated computation. An out-of-range write can put some object into an "impossible" state or simply give it a totally unexpected and wrong value. Such writes typically aren't noticed until long after they occurred, so they are particularly hard to find. Worse still: run a program with an out-of-range error twice with slightly different input and it may give different results. Bugs of this kind ("transient bugs") are some of the most difficult bugs to find.

We have to ensure that such out-of-range access doesn't happen. One of the reasons we use **vector** rather than directly using memory allocated by **new** is that a **vector** knows its size so that it (or we) can easily prevent out-of-range access.

One thing that can make it hard to prevent out-of-range access is that we can assign one **double*** to another **double*** independently of how many objects each points to. A pointer really doesn't know how many objects it points to. For example:

```
double* p = new double;          // allocate a double
double* q = new double[1000];    // allocate 1000 doubles

q[700] = 7.7;        // fine
q = p;               // let q point to the same as p
double d = q[700];   // out-of-range access!
```

Here, in just three lines of code, **q[700]** refers to two different memory locations, and the last use is an out-of-range access and a likely disaster.

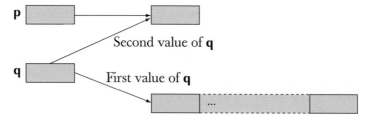

By now, we hope that you are asking, "But why can't pointers remember the size?" Obviously, we could design a "pointer" that did exactly that – a **vector** is almost that, and if you look through the C++ literature and libraries, you'll find many "smart pointers" that compensate for weaknesses of the low-level built-in pointers. However, somewhere we need to reach the hardware level and understand how objects are addressed – and a machine address does not "know" what it addresses. Also, understanding pointers is essential for understanding lots of real-world code.

17.4.4 Initialization

As ever, we would like to ensure that an object has been given a value before we use it; that is, we want to be sure that our pointers are initialized and also that the objects they point to have been initialized. Consider:

```
double* p0;                  // uninitialized: likely trouble
double* p1 = new double;     // get (allocate) an uninitialized double
double* p2 = new double(5.5); // get a double initialized to 5.5
double* p3 = new double[5];  // get (allocate) 5 uninitialized doubles
```

Obviously, declaring **p0** without initializing it is asking for trouble. Consider:

```
*p0 = 7.0;
```

This will assign **7.0** to some location in memory. We have no idea which part of memory that will be. It could be harmless, but never, never ever, rely on that. Sooner or later, we get the same result as for an out-of-range access: "My program crashed mysteriously" or "My program gives wrong output." A scary percentage of serious problems with old-style C++ programs ("C-style programs") is caused by access through uninitialized pointers and out-of-range access. We must do all we can to avoid such access, partly because we aim at professionalism, partly because we don't care to waste our time searching for that kind of error. There are few activities as frustrating and tedious as tracking down this kind of bug. It is much more pleasant and productive to prevent bugs than to hunt for them.

Memory allocated by **new** is not initialized for built-in types. If you don't like that for a single object, you can specify value, as we did for **p2**: *p2 is **5.5**. Note the use of ( ) for initialization. This contrasts to the use of [ ] to indicate "array."

There is no facility for specifying an initializer for an array of objects of built-in types allocated by **new**. For arrays, we have to do some work ourselves if we don't like the default initializer. For example:

```
double* p4 = new double[5];
for (int i = 0; i<5; ++i) p4[i] = i;
```

Now **p4** points to objects of type **double** containing the values **0.0, 1.0, 2.0, 3.0,** and **4.0.**

As usual, we should worry about uninitialized objects and make sure we give them a value before we read them. Beware that compilers often have a "debug mode" where they by default initialize every variable to a predictable value (usually 0). That implies that when turning off the debug features to ship a program, when running an optimizer, or simply when compiling on a different machine, a program with uninitialized variables may suddenly run differently. Don't get caught with an uninitialized variable.

When we define our own types, we have better control of initialization. If a type **X** has a default constructor, we get:

```
X* px1 = new X;        // one default-initialized X
X* px2 = new X[17];    // 17 default-initialized Xs
```

If a type **Y** has a constructor, but not a default constructor, we have to explicitly initialize:

```
Y* py1 = new Y;        // error: no default constructor
Y* py2 = new Y[17];    // error: no default constructor
Y* py3 = new Y(13);    // OK: initialized to Y(13)
```

17.4.5 The null pointer

If you have no other pointer to use for initializing a pointer, use **0** (zero):

```
double* p0 = 0;        // the null pointer
```

When assigned to a pointer, the value zero is called the *null pointer,* and often we test whether a pointer is valid (i.e., whether it points to something) by checking whether it is **0**. For example:

```
if (p0 != 0)    // consider p0 valid
```

This is not a perfect test, because **p0** may contain a "random" value that happens to be nonzero or the address of an object that has been **deleted** (see §17.4.6). However, that's often the best we can do. We don't actually have to mention 0 explicitly because an **if**-statement really checks whether its condition is nonzero:

```
if (p0)    // consider p0 valid; equivalent to p0!=0
```

We prefer this shorter form, considering it a more direct expression of the idea "**p0** is valid," but opinions vary.

We need to use the null pointer when we have a pointer that sometimes points to an object and sometimes not. That's rarer than many people think; consider: if you don't have an object for a pointer to point to, why did you define that pointer? Couldn't you wait until you have an object?

17.4.6 Free-store deallocation

The **new** operator allocates ("gets") memory from the free store. Since a computer's memory is limited, it is usually a good idea to return memory to the free store once we are finished using it. That way, the free store can reuse that memory for a new allocation. For large programs and for long-running programs such freeing of memory for reuse is essential. For example:

```
double* calc(int res_size, int max)      // leaks memory
{
     double* p = new double[max];
     double* res = new double[res_size];
     // use p to calculate results to be put in res
     return res;
}


double* r = calc(100,1000);
```

As written, each call of **calc()** "leaks" the **double**s allocated for **p**. For example, the call **calc(100,1000)** will render the space needed for **100 double**s unusable for the rest of the program.

The operator for returning memory to the free store is called **delete**. We apply **delete** to a pointer returned by **new** to make the memory available to the free store for future allocation. The example now becomes

```
double* calc(int res_size, int max)
     // the caller is responsible for the memory allocated for res
{
     double* p = new double[max];
     double* res = new double[res_size];
     // use p to calculate results to be put in res
     delete[] p;      // we don't need that memory anymore: free it
     return res;
}

double* r = calc(100,1000);
// use r
delete[] r;       // we don't need that memory anymore: free it
```

Incidentally, this example demonstrates one of the major reasons for using free store: we can create objects in a function and pass them back to a caller.

There are two forms of **delete**:

- **delete p** frees the memory for an individual object allocated by **new**.
- **delete[] p** frees the memory for an array of objects allocated by **new**.

It is the programmer's tedious job to use the right version.

Deleting an object twice is a bad mistake. For example:

```
int* p = new int(5);
delete p;          // fine: p points to an object created by new
// . . . no use of p here . . .
delete p;          // error: p points to memory owned by the free-store manager
```

There are two problems with the second **delete p**:

- You don't own the object pointed to anymore so the free-store manager may have changed its internal data structure in such a way that it can't correctly execute **delete p** again.
- The free-store manager may have "recycled" the memory pointed to by **p** so that **p** now points to another object; deleting that other object (owned by some other part of the program) will cause errors in your program.

Both problems occur in a real program; they are not just theoretical possibilities.

Deleting the null pointer doesn't do anything (because the null pointer doesn't point to an object), so deleting the null pointer is harmless. For example:

```
int* p = 0;
delete p;          // fine: no action needed
delete p;          // also fine (still no action needed)
```

Why do we have to bother with freeing memory? Can't the compiler figure out when we don't need a piece of memory anymore and just recycle it without human intervention? It can. That's called *automatic garbage collection* or just *garbage collection*. Unfortunately, automatic garbage collection is not cost-free and not ideal for all kinds of applications. If you really need automatic garbage collection, you can plug a garbage collector into your C++ program. Good garbage collectors are available (see www.research.att.com/~bs/C++.html). However, in this book we assume that you have to deal with your own "garbage," and we show how to do so conveniently and efficiently.

When is it important not to leak memory? A program that needs to run "forever" can't afford any memory leaks. An operating system is an example of a program that "runs forever," and so are most embedded systems (see Chapter 25). A library should not leak memory because someone might use it as part of a system that shouldn't leak memory. In general, it is simply a good idea not to leak. Many programmers consider leaks as proof of sloppiness. However, that's slightly over-stating the point. When you run a program under an operating system (Unix, Windows, whatever), all memory is automatically returned to the system at the end of the program. It follows that if you know that your program will not use more memory than is available, you might reasonably decide to "leak" until the operating system does the deallocation for you. However, if you decide to do that, be sure that your memory consumption estimate is correct, or people will have good reason to consider you sloppy.

17.5 Destructors

Now we know how to store the elements for a **vector**. We simply allocate suffi-cient space for the elements on the free store and access them through a pointer:

```
// a very simplified vector of doubles
class vector {
        int sz;              // the size
        double* elem;        // a pointer to the elements
public:
        vector(int s)                   // constructor
                :sz(s),                 // initialize sz
                elem(new double[s])     // initialize elem
                {
                        for (int i=0; i<s; ++i) elem[i]=0;   // initialize elements
                }
        int size() const { return sz; }    // the current size
        // . . .
};
```

So, **sz** is the number of elements. We initialize it in the constructor and a user of **vector** can get the number of elements by calling **size()**. Space for the elements is allocated using **new** in the constructor, and the pointer returned from the free store is stored in the member pointer **elem**.

Note that we initialize the elements to their default value (**0.0**). The standard library **vector** does that, so we thought it best to do the same from the start.

Unfortunately, our first primitive **vector** leaks memory. In the constructor, it allocates memory for the elements using **new**. To follow the rule stated in §17.4, we must make sure that this memory is freed using **delete**. Consider:

```
void f(int n)
{
    vector v(n);        // allocate n doubles
    // . . .
}
```

When we leave **f()**, the elements created on the free store by **v** are not freed. We could define a **clean_up()** operation for **vector** and call that:

```
void f2(int n)
{
    vector v(n);        // define a vector (which allocates another n ints)
    // . . . use v . . .
    v.clean_up();       // clean_up() deletes elem
}
```

That would work. However, one of the most common problems with free store is that people forget to **delete**. The equivalent problem would arise for **clean_up()**; people would forget to call it. We can do better than that. The basic idea is to have the compiler know about a function that does the opposite of a constructor, just as it knows about the constructor. Inevitably, such a function is called a *destructor*. In the same way that a constructor is implicitly called when an object of a class is created, a destructor is implicitly called when an object goes out of scope. A constructor makes sure that an object is properly created and initialized. Conversely, a destructor makes sure that an object is properly cleaned up before it is destroyed. For example:

```
// a very simplified vector of doubles
class vector {
    int sz;             // the size
    double* elem;       // a pointer to the elements
public:
    vector(int s)                         // constructor
        :sz(s), elem(new double[s])       // allocate memory
    {
        for (int i=0; i<s; ++i) elem[i]=0;  // initialize elements
    }

    ~vector()                             // destructor
        { delete[] elem; }                // free memory
    // . . .
};
```

Given that, we can write

```
void f3(int n)
{
    int* p = new int[n];     // allocate n ints
    vector v(n);             // define a vector (which allocates another n ints)
    // . . . use p and v . . .
    delete[] p;              // deallocate the ints
}  // vector automatically cleans up after v
```

Suddenly, that **delete**[] looks rather tedious and error-prone! Given **vector**, there is no reason to allocate memory using **new** just to deallocate it using **delete**[] at the end of a function. That's what **vector** does and does better. In particular, a **vector** cannot forget to call its destructor to deallocate the memory used for the elements.

We are not going to go into great detail about the uses of destructors here, but they are great for handling resources that we need to first acquire (from somewhere) and later give back: files, threads, locks, etc. Remember how **iostreams** clean up after themselves? They flush buffers, close files, free buffer space, etc. That's done by their destructors. Every class that "owns" a resource needs a destructor.

17.5.1 Generated destructors

If a member of a class has a destructor, then that destructor will be called when the object containing the member is destroyed. For example:

```
struct Customer {
    string name;
    vector<string> addresses;
    // . . .
};

void some_fct()
{
    Customer fred;
    // initialize fred
    // use fred
}
```

When we exit **some_fct**(), so that **fred** goes out of scope, **fred** is destroyed; that is, the destructors for **name** and **addresses** are called. This is obviously necessary for destructors to be useful and is sometimes expressed as "The compiler generated a destructor for **Customer**, which calls the members' destructors." That is indeed often how the obvious and necessary guarantee that destructors are called is implemented.

The destructors for members – and for bases – are implicitly called from a derived class destructor (whether user-defined or generated). Basically, all the rules add up to: "Destructors are called when the object is destroyed" (by going out of scope, by **delete**, etc.).

17.5.2 Destructors and free store

Destructors are conceptually simple but are the foundation for many of the most effective C++ programming techniques. The basic idea is simple:

- Whatever resources a class object needs to function, it acquires in a constructor.

- During the object's lifetime it may release resources and acquire new ones.

- At the end of the object's lifetime, the destructor releases all resources still owned by the object.

The matched constructor/destructor pair handling free-store memory for **vector** is the archetypical example. We'll get back to that idea with more examples in §19.5. Here, we will examine an important application that comes from the use of free-store and class hierarchies in combination. Consider:

```
Shape* fct()
{
        Text tt(Point(200,200),"Annemarie");
        // . . .
        Shape* p = new Text(Point(100,100),"Nicholas");
        return p;
}

void f()
{
        Shape* q = fct();
        // . . .
        delete q;
}
```

This looks fairly plausible – and it is. It all works, but let's see how, because that exposes an elegant, important, simple technique. Inside **fct()**, the **Text** object **tt** is properly destroyed at the exit from **fct()**. **Text** has a **string** member, which obviously needs to have its destructor called – **string** handles its memory acquisition and release exactly like **vector**. For **tt**, that's easy; the compiler just calls **Text**'s generated destructor as described in §17.5.1. But what about the **Text** object that was returned from **fct()**? The calling function **f()** has no idea that **q** points to a **Text**; all it knows is that it points to a **Shape**. Then how does **delete p** get to call **Text**'s destructor?

In §14.2.1, we breezed past the fact that **Shape** has a destructor. In fact, **Shape** has a **virtual** destructor. That's the key. When we say **delete p**, **delete** looks at **p**'s type to see if it needs to call a destructor, and if so it calls it. So, **delete p** calls **Shape**'s destructor **~Shape()**. But **~Shape()** is **virtual**, so – using the virtual call mechanism (§14.3.1) – that call invokes the destructor of **Shape**'s derived class, in this case **~Text()**. Had **Shape::~Shape()** not been **virtual**, **Text::~Text()** would not have been called and **Text**'s **string** member wouldn't have been properly destroyed.

As a rule of thumb: if you have a class with a **virtual** function, it needs a **virtual** destructor. The reason is:

1. If a class has a **virtual** function it is likely to be used as a base class, and
2. If it is a base class its derived class is likely to be allocated using **new**, and
3. If a derived class object is allocated using **new** and manipulated through a pointer to its base, then
4. It is likely to be **delete**d through a pointer to its base

Note that destructors are invoked implicitly or indirectly through **delete**. They are not called directly. That saves a lot of tricky work.

TRY THIS

Write a little program using base classes and members where you define the constructors and destructors to output a line of information when they are called. Then, create a few objects and see how their constructors and destructors are called.

17.6 Access to elements

For **vector** to be usable, we need a way to read and write elements. For starters, we can provide simple **get()** and **set()** member functions:

```
// a very simplified vector of doubles
class vector {
        int sz;                 // the size
        double* elem;           // a pointer to the elements
public:
        vector(int s) :sz(s), elem(new double[s]) { }    // constructor
        ~vector() { delete[] elem; }                     // destructor
```

```
        int size() const { return sz; }                    // the current size

        double get(int n) { return elem[n]; }              // access: read
        void set(int n, double v) { elem[n]=v; }           // access: write
};
```

Both **get()** and **set()** access the elements using the [ ] operator on the **elem** pointer:
elem[n].

Now we can make a **vector** of **doubles** and use it:

```
vector v(5);
for (int i=0; i<v.size(); ++i) {
        v.set(i,1.1*i);
        cout << "v[" << i << "]==" << v.get(i) << '\n';
}
```

This will output

```
v[0]==0
v[1]==1.1
v[2]==2.2
v[3]==3.3
v[4]==4.4
```

This is still an overly simple **vector**, and the code using **get()** and **set()** is rather
ugly compared to the usual subscript notation. However, we aim to start small and
simple and then grow our programs step by step, testing along the way. As ever,
this strategy of growth and repeated testing minimizes errors and debugging.

17.7 Pointers to class objects

The notion of "pointer" is general, so we can point to just about anything we can
place in memory. For example, we can use pointers to **vectors** exactly as we use
pointers to **chars**:

```
vector* f(int s)
{
        vector* p = new vector(s);      // allocate a vector on free store
        // fill *p
        return p;
}
```

```
void ff()
{
    vector* q = f(4);
    // use *q
    delete q;                    // free vector on free store
}
```

Note that when we **delete** a **vector**, its destructor is called. For example:

```
vector* p = new vector(s);      // allocate a vector on free store
delete p;                       // deallocate
```

Creating the **vector** on the free store, the **new** operator

- First allocates memory for a **vector**
- Then invokes the **vector**'s constructor to initialize that **vector**; the constructor allocates memory for the **vector**'s elements and initializes those elements

Deleting the **vector**, the **delete** operator

- First invokes the **vector**'s destructor; the destructor invokes the destructors for the elements (if they have destructors) and then deallocates the memory used for the **vector**'s elements
- Then deallocates the memory used for the **vector**

Note how nicely that works recursively (see §8.5.8). Using the real (standard library) **vector** we can also do:

```
vector< vector<double> >* p = new vector<vector<double> > (10);
delete p;
```

Here **delete p** invokes the destructor for **vector< vector<double> >**; this destructor in turn invokes the destructor for its **vector<double>** elements, and all is neatly cleaned up, leaving no object undestroyed and leaking no memory.

Because **delete** invokes destructors (for types, such as **vector**, that have one), **delete** is often said to destroy objects, not just deallocate them.

As usual, please remember that a "naked" **new** outside a constructor is an opportunity to forget to **delete** it. Unless you have a good (that is, really simple, such as **Vector_ref** from §13.10 and §E.4) strategy for deleting objects, try to keep **new**s in constructors and **delete**s in destructors.

So far, so good, but how do we access the members of a **vector**, given only a pointer? Note that all classes support the operator **.** (dot) for accessing members, given the name of an object:

```
vector v(4);
int x = v.size();
double d = v.get(3);
```

Similarly, all classes support the operator −> (arrow) for accessing members, given a pointer to an object:

```
vector* p = new vector(4);
int x = p−>size();
double d = p−>get(3);
```

Like . (dot), −> (arrow) can be used for both data members and function members. Since built-in types, such as **int** and **double**, have no members, −> doesn't apply to built-in types. Dot and arrow are often called *member access operators.*

17.8 Messing with types: void* and casts

Using pointers and free-store-allocated arrays, we are very close to the hardware. Basically, our operations on pointers (initialization, assignment, *, and []) map directly to machine instructions. At this level, the language offers only a bit of notational convenience and the compile-time consistency offered by the type system. Occasionally, we have to give up even that last bit of protection.

Naturally, we don't want to make do without the protection of the type system, but sometimes there is no logical alternative (e.g., we need to interact with another language that doesn't know about C++'s types). There are also an unfortunate number of cases where we need to interface with old code that wasn't designed with static type safety in mind. For that, we need two things:

- A type of pointer that points to memory without knowing what kinds of objects reside in that memory
- An operation to tell the compiler what kind of type to assume (without proof) for memory pointed to by one of those pointers

The type **void*** means "pointer to some memory that the compiler doesn't know the type of." We use **void*** when we want to transmit an address between pieces of code that really don't know each other's types. Examples are the "address" arguments of a callback function (§16.3.1) and the lowest level of memory allocators (such as the implementation of the **new** operator).

There are no objects of type **void**, but as we have seen, we use **void** to mean "no value returned":

```
void v;      // error: there are no objects of type void
void f();    // f() returns nothing — f() does not return an object of type void
```

A pointer to any object type can be assigned to a **void***. For example:

```
void* pv1 = new int;          // OK: int* converts to void*
void* pv2 = new double[10];   // OK: double* converts to void*
```

Since the compiler doesn't know what a **void*** points to, we must tell it:

```
void f(void* pv)
{
      void* pv2 = pv;     // copying is OK (copying is what void*s are for)
      double* pd = pv;    // error: cannot convert void* to double*
      *pv = 7;            // error: cannot dereference a void*
                          // (we don't know what type of object it points to)
      pv[2] = 9;          // error: cannot subscript a void*
      int* pi = static_cast<int*>(pv);    // OK: explicit conversion
      // . . .
}
```

A **static_cast** can be used to explicitly convert between related pointer types, such as **void*** and **double*** (§A.5.7). The name "**static_cast**" is a deliberately ugly name for an ugly (and dangerous) operation – use it only when absolutely necessary. You shouldn't find it necessary very often – if at all. An operation such as **static_cast** is called an *explicit type conversion* (because that's what it does) or colloquially a *cast* (because it is used to support something that's broken).

C++ offers two casts that are potentially even nastier than **static_cast**:

- **reinterpret_cast** can cast between unrelated types, such as **int** and **double***.
- **const_cast** can "cast away **const**."

For example:

```
Register* in = reinterpret_cast<Register*>(0xff);

void f(const Buffer* p)
{
      Buffer* b = const_cast<Buffer*>(p);
      // . . .
}
```

The first example is the classical necessary and proper use of a **reinterpret_cast**. We tell the compiler that a certain part of memory (the memory starting with location **0xFF**) is to be considered a **Register** (presumably with special semantics). Such code is necessary when you write things like device drivers.

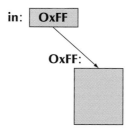

In the second example, **const_cast** strips the **const** from the **const Buffer*** called **p**. Presumably, we know what we are doing.

At least **static_cast** can't mess with the pointer/integer distinction or with "**const**-ness," so prefer **static_cast** if you feel the need for a cast. When you think you need a cast, reconsider: Is there a way to write the code without the cast? Is there a way to redesign that part of the program so that the cast is not needed? Unless you are interfacing to other people's code or to hardware, there usually is a way. If not, expect subtle and nasty bugs. Don't expect code using **reinterpret_cast** to be portable.

17.9 Pointers and references

You can think of a reference as an automatically dereferenced immutable pointer or as an alternative name for an object. Pointers and references differ in these ways:

- Assignment to a pointer changes the pointer's value (not the pointed-to value).
- To get a pointer you generally need to use **new** or **&**.
- To access an object pointed to by a pointer you use * or [ ].
- Assignment to a reference changes what the reference refers to (not the reference itself).
- You cannot make a reference refer to a different object after initialization.
- Assignment of references does deep copy (assigns to the referred-to object); assignment of pointers does not (assigns to the pointer object itself).
- Beware of null pointers.

For example:

```
int x = 10;
int* p = &x;        // you need & to get a pointer
*p = 7;             // use * to assign to x through p
int x2 = *p;        // read x through p
int* p2 = &x2;      // get a pointer to another int
p2 = p;             // p2 and p both point to x
p = &x2;            // make p point to another object
```

The equivalent example for references is

```
int y = 10;
int& r = y;      // the & is in the type, not in the initializer
r = 7;           // assign to y through r (no * needed)
int y2 = r;      // read y through r (no * needed)
int& r2 = y2;    // get a reference to another int
r2 = r;          // the value of y is assigned to y2
r = &y2;         // error: you can't change the value of a reference
                 // (no assignment of an int* to an int&)
```

Note the last example; it is not just this construct that will fail – there is no way to get a reference to refer to a different object after initialization. If you need to point to something different, use a pointer. For ideas of how to use pointers, see §17.9.3.

A reference and a pointer are both implemented by using a memory address. They just use that address differently to provide you – the programmer – slightly different facilities.

17.9.1 Pointer and reference parameters

When you want to change the value of a variable to a value computed by a function, you have three choices. For example:

```
int incr_v(int x) { return x+1; }    // compute a new value and return it
void incr_p(int* p) { ++*p; }        // pass a pointer
                                     // (dereference it and increment the result)
void incr_r(int& r) { ++r; }         // pass a reference
```

How do you choose? We think returning the value often leads to the most obvious (and therefore least error-prone) code; that is:

```
int x = 2;
x = incr_v(x);    // copy x to incr_v(); then copy the result out and assign it
```

We prefer that style for small objects, such as an **int**. However, passing a value back and forth is not always feasible. For example, we might be writing a function that modifies a huge data structure, such as a **vector** of 10,000 **ints**; we can't copy those 40,000 bytes (at least twice) with acceptable efficiency.

How do we choose between using a reference argument and using a pointer argument? Unfortunately, either way has both attractions and problems, so again the answer is less than clear-cut. You have to make a decision based on the individual function and its likely uses.

Using a pointer argument alerts the programmer that something might be changed. For example:

```
int x = 7;
incr_p(&x)     // the & is needed
incr_r(x);
```

The need to use **&** in **incr_p(&x)** alerts the user that **x** might be changed. In contrast, **incr_r(x)** "looks innocent." This leads to a slight preference for the pointer version.

On the other hand, if you use a pointer as a function argument, the function has to beware that someone might call it with a null pointer, that is, with a pointer with the value zero. For example:

```
incr_p(0);     // crash: incr_p() will try to dereference 0
int* p = 0;
incr_p(p);     // crash: incr_p() will try to dereference 0
```

This is obviously nasty. The person who writes **incr_p()** can protect against this:

```
void incr_p(int* p)
{
        if (p==0) error("null pointer argument to incr_p()");
        ++*p;   // dereference the pointer and increment the object pointed to
}
```

But now **incr_p()** suddenly doesn't look as simple and attractive as before. Chapter 5 discusses how to cope with bad arguments. In contrast, users of a reference (such as **incr_r()**) are entitled to assume that a reference refers to an object.

If "passing nothing" (passing no object) is acceptable from the point of view of the semantics of the function, we must use a pointer argument. Note: That's not the case for an increment operation – hence the need for throwing an exception for **p==0**.

So, the real answer is: "The choice depends on the nature of the function":

- For tiny objects prefer pass-by-value.
- For functions where "no object" (represented by **0**) is a valid argument use a pointer parameter (and remember to test for **0**).
- Otherwise, use a reference parameter.

See also §8.5.6.

17.9.2 Pointers, references, and inheritance

In §14.3, we saw how a derived class, such as **Circle**, could be used where an object of its public base class **Shape** was required. We can express that idea in terms of pointers or references: a **Circle*** can be implicitly converted to a **Shape*** because **Shape** is a public base of **Circle**. For example:

```
void rotate(Shape* s, int n);      // rotate *s n degrees

Shape* p = new Circle(Point(100,100),40);
Circle c(Point(200,200),50);
rotate(&c,45);
```

And similarly for references:

```
void rotate(Shape& s, int n);      // rotate s n degrees

Shape& r = c;
rotate(c,75);
```

This is crucial for most object-oriented programming techniques (§14.3–4).

17.9.3 An example: lists

Lists are among the most common and useful data structures. Usually, a list is made out of "links" where each link holds some information and pointers to other links. This is one of the classical uses of pointers. For example, we could represent a short list of Norse gods like this:

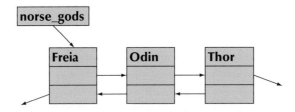

A list like this is called a *doubly-linked list* because given a link, we can find both the predecessor and the successor. A list where we can find only the successor is called a *singly-linked list*. We use doubly-linked lists when we want to make it easy to remove an element. We can define these links like this:

```
struct Link {
    string value;
```

```
      Link* prev;
      Link* succ;
      Link(const string& v, Link* p = 0, Link* s = 0)
            : value(v), prev(p), succ(s) { }
};
```

That is, given a **Link**, we can get to its successor using the **succ** pointer and to its predecessor using the **prev** pointer. We use the null pointer to indicate that a **Link** doesn't have a successor or a predecessor. We can build our list of Norse gods like this:

```
Link* norse_gods = new Link("Thor",0,0);
norse_gods = new Link("Odin",norse_gods,0);
norse_gods->succ->prev = norse_gods;
norse_gods = new Link("Freia",norse_gods,0);
norse_gods->succ->prev = norse_gods;
```

We built that list by creating the **Link**s and tying them together as in the picture: first Thor, then Odin as the predecessor of Thor, and finally Freia as the predecessor of Odin. You can follow the pointer to see that we got it right, so that each **succ** and **prev** points to the right god. However, the code is obscure because we didn't explicitly define and name an insert operation:

```
Link* insert(Link* p, Link* n)      // insert n before p (incomplete)
{
      n->succ = p;          // p comes after n
      p->prev->succ = n;    // n comes after what used to be p's predecessor
      n->prev = p->prev;    // p's predecessor becomes n's predecessor
      p->prev = n;          // n becomes p's predecessor
      return n;
}
```

This works provided that **p** really points to a **Link** and that the **Link** pointed to by **p** really has a predecessor. Please convince yourself that this really is so. When thinking about pointers and linked structures, such as a list made out of **Link**s, we invariably draw little box-and-arrow diagrams on paper to verify that our code works for small examples. Please don't be too proud to rely on this effective low-tech design technique.

That version of **insert()** is incomplete because it doesn't handle the cases where **n**, **p**, or **p->prev** is **0**. We add the appropriate tests for the null pointer and get the messier, but correct, version:

```
Link* insert(Link* p, Link* n)        // insert n before p; return n
{
        if (n==0) return p;
        if (p==0) return n;
        n->succ = p;              // p comes after n
        if (p->prev) p->prev->succ = n;
        n->prev = p->prev;   // p's predecessor becomes n's predecessor
        p->prev = n;             // n becomes p's predecessor
        return n;
}
```

Given that, we could write

```
Link* norse_gods = new Link("Thor");
norse_gods = insert(norse_gods,new Link("Odin"));
norse_gods = insert(norse_gods,new Link("Freia"));
```

Now all the error-prone fiddling with the **prev** and **succ** pointers has disappeared from sight. Pointer fiddling is tedious and error-prone and *should* be hidden in well-written and well-tested functions. In particular, many errors in conventional code come from people forgetting to test pointers against **0** – just as we (deliberately) did in the first version of **insert()**.

Note that we used default arguments (§15.3.1, §A.9.2) to save users from mentioning predecessors and successors in every constructor use.

17.9.4 List operations

The standard library provides a **list** class, which we will describe in §20.4. It hides all link manipulation, but here we will elaborate on our notion of list based on the **Link** class to get a feel for what goes on "under the covers" of list classes and see more examples of pointer use.

What operations does our **Link** class need to allow its users to avoid "pointer fiddling"? That's to some extent a matter of taste, but here is a useful set:

- The constructor
- **insert**: insert before an element
- **add**: insert after an element
- **erase**: remove an element
- **find**: find a **Link** with a given value
- **advance**: get the *n*th successor

We could write these operations like this:

```
Link* add(Link* p, Link* n)      // insert n after p; return n
{
      // much like insert (see exercise 11)
}


Link* erase(Link* p)        // remove *p from list; return p's successor
{
      if (p==0) return 0;
      if (p->succ) p->succ->prev = p->prev;
      if (p->prev) p->prev->succ = p->succ;
      return p->succ;
}


Link* find(Link* p, const string& s)     // find s in list;
                                         // return 0 for "not found"
{
      while(p) {
            if (p->value == s) return p;
            p = p->succ;
      }
      return 0;
}


Link* advance(Link* p, int n)      // move n positions in list
                                   // return 0 for "not found"
      // positive n moves forward, negative backward
{
      if (p==0) return 0;
      if (0<n) {
            while (n--) {
                  if (p->succ == 0) return 0;
                  p = p->succ;
            }
      }
      if (n<0) {
            while (n++) {
                  if (p->prev == 0) return 0;
                  p = p->prev;
            }
      }
      return p;
}
```

Note the use of the postfix **n++**. This form of increment ("post-increment") yields the value before the increment as its value.

17.9.5 List use

As a little exercise, let's build two lists:

```
Link* norse_gods = new Link("Thor");
norse_gods = insert(norse_gods,new Link("Odin"));
norse_gods = insert(norse_gods,new Link("Zeus"));
norse_gods = insert(norse_gods,new Link("Freia"));

Link* greek_gods = new Link("Hera");
greek_gods = insert(greek_gods,new Link("Athena"));
greek_gods = insert(greek_gods,new Link("Mars"));
greek_gods = insert(greek_gods,new Link("Poseidon"));
```

"Unfortunately," we made a couple of mistakes: Zeus is a Greek god, rather than a Norse god, and the Greek god of war is Ares, not Mars (Mars is his Latin/Roman name). We can fix that:

```
Link* p = find(greek_gods, "Mars");
if (p) p->value = "Ares";
```

Note how we were cautious about **find**() returning a **0**. We think that we know that it can't happen in this case (after all, we just inserted Mars into **greek_gods**), but in a real example someone might change that code.

Similarly, we can move Zeus into his correct Pantheon:

```
Link* p = find(norse_gods,"Zeus");
if (p) {
    erase(p);
    insert(greek_gods,p);
}
```

Did you notice the bug? It's quite subtle (unless you are used to working directly with links). What if the **Link** we **erase**() is the one pointed to by **norse_gods**? Again, that doesn't actually happen here, but to write good, maintainable code, we have to take that possibility into account:

```
Link* p = find(norse_gods, "Zeus");
if (p) {
    if (p==norse_gods) norse_gods = p->succ;
```

```
        erase(p);
        greek_gods = insert(greek_gods,p);
    }
```

While we were at it, we also corrected the second bug: when we insert Zeus *before* the first Greek god, we need to make **greek_gods** point to Zeus's **Link**. Pointers are extremely useful and flexible, but subtle.

Finally, let's print out those lists:

```
    void print_all(Link* p)
    {
        cout << "{ ";
        while (p) {
            cout << p->value;
            if (p=p->succ) cout << ", ";
        }
        cout << " }";
    }

    print_all(norse_gods);
    cout<<"\n";

    print_all(greek_gods);
    cout<<"\n";
```

This should give

```
    { Freia, Odin, Thor }
    { Zeus, Poseidon, Ares, Athena, Hera }
```

17.10 The this pointer

Note that each of our list functions takes a **Link*** as its first argument and accesses data in that object. That's the kind of function that we often make member functions. Could we simplify **Link** (or link use) by making the operations members? Could we maybe make the pointers private so that only the member functions have access to them? We could:

```
    class Link {
    public:
        string value;
```

```
Link(const string& v, Link* p = 0, Link* s = 0)
     : value(v), prev(p), succ(s) { }

Link* insert(Link* n) ;          // insert n before this object
Link* add(Link* n) ;             // insert n after this object
Link* erase() ;                  // remove this object from list
Link* find(const string& s);     // find s in list
const Link* find(const string& s) const;   // find s in list

Link* advance(int n) const;      // move n positions in list

Link* next() const { return succ; }
Link* previous() const { return prev; }
private:
Link* prev;
Link* succ;
};
```

This looks promising. We defined the operations that don't change the state of a
Link into **const** member functions. We added (nonmodifying) **next()** and **previous()**
functions so that users could iterate over lists (of **Link**s) — those are needed now that
direct access to **succ** and **prev** is prohibited. We left the value as a public member because (so far) we have no reason not to; it is "just data."

Now let's try to implement **Link::insert()** by copying our previous global
insert() and modifying it suitably:

```
Link* Link::insert(Link* n)      // insert n before p; return n
{
    Link* p = this;              // pointer to this object
    if (n==0) return p;          // nothing to insert
    if (p==0) return n;          // nothing to insert into
    n->succ = p;                 // p comes after n
    if (p->prev) p->prev->succ = n;
    n->prev = p->prev;           // p's predecessor becomes n's predecessor
    p->prev = n;                 // n becomes p's predecessor
    return n;
}
```

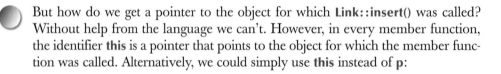

But how do we get a pointer to the object for which **Link::insert()** was called?
Without help from the language we can't. However, in every member function,
the identifier **this** is a pointer that points to the object for which the member function was called. Alternatively, we could simply use **this** instead of **p**:

```
Link* Link::insert(Link* n)      // insert n before this object; return n
{
        if (n==0) return this;
        if (this==0) return n;
        n->succ = this;            // this object comes after n
        if (this->prev) this->prev->succ = n;
        n->prev = this->prev;      // this object's predecessor
                                   // becomes n's predecessor
        this->prev = n;            // n becomes this object's predecessor
        return n;
}
```

This is a bit verbose, but we don't need to mention **this** to access a member, so we can abbreviate:

```
Link* Link::insert(Link* n)      // insert n before this object; return n
{
        if (n==0) return this;
        if (this==0) return n;
        n->succ = this;      // this object comes after n
        if (prev) prev->succ = n;
        n->prev = prev;      // this object's predecessor becomes n's predecessor
        prev = n;            // n becomes this object's predecessor
        return n;
}
```

In other words, we have been using the **this** pointer – the pointer to the current object – implicitly every time we accessed a member. It is only when we need to refer to the whole object that we need to mention it explicitly.

Note that **this** has a specific meaning: it points to the object for which a member function is called. It does not point to any old object. The compiler ensures that we do not change the value of **this** in a member function. For example:

```
struct S {
        // . . .
        void mutate(S* p)
        {
                this = p;   // error: "this" is immutable
                // . . .
        }
};
```

17.10.1 More link use

Having dealt with the implementation issues, we can see how the use now looks:

```
Link* norse_gods = new Link("Thor");
norse_gods = norse_gods->insert(new Link("Odin"));
norse_gods = norse_gods->insert(new Link("Zeus"));
norse_gods = norse_gods->insert(new Link("Freia"));

Link* greek_gods = new Link("Hera");
greek_gods = greek_gods->insert(new Link("Athena"));
greek_gods = greek_gods->insert(new Link("Mars"));
greek_gods = greek_gods->insert(new Link("Poseidon"));
```

That's very much like before. As before, we correct our "mistakes." Correct the name of the god of war:

```
Link* p = greek_gods->find("Mars");
if (p) p->value = "Ares";
```

Move Zeus into his correct Pantheon:

```
Link* p2 = norse_gods->find("Zeus");
if (p2) {
    if (p2==norse_gods) norse_gods = p2->next();
    p2->erase();
    greek_gods = greek_gods->insert(p2);
}
```

Finally, let's print out those lists:

```
void print_all(Link* p)
{
    cout << "{ ";
    while (p) {
        cout << p->value;
        if (p=p->next()) cout << ", ";
    }
    cout << " }";
}
```

```
print_all(norse_gods);
cout<<"\n";

print_all(greek_gods);
cout<<"\n";
```

This should again give

> { Freia, Odin, Thor }
> { Zeus, Poseidon, Ares, Athena, Hera }

So, which version do you like better: the one where **insert()**, etc. are member functions or the one where they are freestanding functions? In this case the differences don't matter much, but see §9.7.5.

One thing to observe here is that we still don't have a list class, only a link class. That forces us to keep worrying about which pointer is the pointer to the first element. We can do better than that – by defining a class **List** – but designs along the lines presented here are very common. The standard library **list** is presented in §20.4.

 Drill

This drill has two parts. The first exercises/builds your understanding of free-store-allocated arrays and contrasts arrays with **vectors**:

1. Allocate an array of ten **ints** on the free store using **new**.
2. Print the values of the ten **ints** to **cout**.
3. Deallocate the array (using **delete[]**).
4. Write a function **print_array10(ostream& os, int* a)** that prints out the values of **a** (assumed to have ten elements) to **os**.
5. Allocate an array of ten **ints** on the free store; initialize it with the values 100, 101, 102, etc.; and print out its values.
6. Allocate an array of 11 **ints** on the free store; initialize it with the values 100, 101, 102, etc.; and print out its values.
7. Write a function **print_array(ostream& os, int* a, int n)** that prints out the values of **a** (assumed to have **n** elements) to **os**.
8. Allocate an array of 20 ints on the free store; initialize it with the values 100, 101, 102, etc.; and print out its values.
9. Did you remember to delete the arrays? (If not, do it.)
10. Do 5, 6, and 8 using a **vector** instead of an array and a **print_vector()** instead of **print_array()**.

The second part focuses on pointers and their relation to arrays. Using **print_array()** from the last drill:

1. Allocate an **int**, initialize it to 7, and assign its address to a variable **p1**.
2. Print out the value of **p1** and of the **int** it points to.
3. Allocate an array of seven **ints**; initialize it to 1, 2, 4, 8, etc.; and assign its address to a variable **p2**.
4. Print out the value of **p2** and of the array it points to.
5. Declare an **int*** called **p3** and initialize it with **p2**.
6. Assign **p1** to **p2**.
7. Assign **p3** to **p2**.
8. Print out the values of **p1** and **p2** and of what they point to.
9. Deallocate all the memory you allocated from the free store.
10. Allocate an array of ten **ints**; initialize it to 1, 2, 4, 8, etc.; and assign its address to a variable **p1**.
11. Allocate an array of ten **ints**, and assign its address to a variable **p2**.
12. Copy the values from the array pointed to by **p1** into the array pointed to by **p2**.
13. Repeat 10–12 using a **vector** rather than an array.

Review

1. Why do we need data structures with varying numbers of elements?
2. What four kinds of storage do we have for a typical program?
3. What is free store? What other name is commonly used for it? What operators support it?
4. What is a dereference operator and why do we need one?
5. What is an address? How are memory addresses manipulated in C++?
6. What information about a pointed-to object does a pointer have? What useful information does it lack?
7. What can a pointer point to?
8. What is a leak?
9. What is a resource?
10. How can we initialize a pointer?
11. What is a null pointer? When do we need to use one?
12. When do we need a pointer (instead of a reference or a named object)?
13. What is a destructor? When do we want one?
14. When do we want a **virtual** destructor?
15. How are destructors for members called?
16. What is a cast? When do we need to use one?
17. How do we access a member of a class through a pointer?
18. What is a doubly-linked list?
19. What is **this** and when do we need to use it?

Terms

address	destructor	pointer
address of: **&**	free store	range
allocation	link	resource leak
cast	list	subscripting
container	member access: **->**	subscript: **[ ]**
contents of: *****	member destructor	**this**
deallocation	memory	type conversion
delete	memory leak	**virtual** destructor
delete[]	**new**	**void***
dereference	null pointer	

Exercises

1. What is the output format of pointer values on your implementation? Hint: Don't read the documentation.
2. How many bytes are there in an **int**? In a **double**? In a **bool**? Do not use **sizeof** except to verify your answer.
3. Write a function, **void to_lower(char* s)**, that replaces all uppercase characters in the C-style string **s** with their lowercase equivalents. For example, "**Hello, World!**" becomes "**hello, world!**" Do not use any standard library functions. A C-style string is a zero-terminated array of characters, so if you find a **char** with the value **0** you are at the end.
4. Write a function, **char* strdup(const char*)**, that copies a C-style string into memory it allocates on the free store. Do not use any standard library functions.
5. Write a function, **char* findx(const char* s, const char* x)**, that finds the first occurrence of the C-style string **x** in **s**.
6. This chapter does not say what happens when you run out of memory using **new**. That's called *memory exhaustion*. Find out what happens. You have two obvious alternatives: look for documentation, or write a program with an infinite loop that allocates but never deallocates. Try both. Approximately how much memory did you manage to allocate before failing?
7. Write a program that reads characters from **cin** into an array that you allocate on the free store. Read individual characters until an exclamation mark (**!**) is entered. Do not use a **std::string**. Do not worry about memory exhaustion.
8. Do exercise 7 again, but this time read into a **std::string** rather than to memory you put on the free store (**string** knows how to use the free store for you).

9. Which way does the stack grow: up (toward higher addresses) or down (toward lower addresses)? Which way does the free store initially grow (that is, before you use **delete**)? Write a program to determine the answers.

10. Look at your solution of exercise 7. Is there any way that input could get the array to overflow; that is, is there any way you could enter more characters than you allocated space for (a serious error)? Does anything reasonable happen if you try to enter more characters than you allocated? Look up **realloc()** and use it to extend your allocation if needed.

11. Complete the "list of gods" example from §17.10.1 and run it.

12. Why did we define two versions of **find()**?

13. Modify the **Link** class from §17.10.1 to hold a value of a **struct God**. **struct God** should have members of type **string**: name, mythology, vehicle, and weapon. For example, **God("Zeus", "Greek", "", "lightning")** and **God("Odin", "Norse", "Eight-legged flying horse called Sleipner", "")**. Write a **print_all()** function that lists gods with their attributes one per line. Add a member function **add_ordered()** that places its **new** element in its correct lexicographical position. Using the **Link**s with the values of type **God**, make a list of gods from three mythologies; then move the elements (gods) from that list to three lexicographically ordered lists – one for each mythology.

14. Could the "list of gods" example from §17.10.1 have been written using a singly-linked list; that is, could we have left the **prev** member out of **Link**? Why might we want to do that? For what kind of examples would it make sense to use a singly-linked list? Re-implement that example using only a singly-linked list.

Postscript

Why bother with messy low-level stuff like pointers and free store when we can simply use **vector**? Well, one answer is that someone has to design and implement **vector** and similar abstractions, and we'd like to know how that's done. There are programming languages that don't provide facilities equivalent to pointers and thus dodge the problems with low-level programming. Basically, programmers of such languages delegate the tasks that involve direct access to hardware to C++ programmers (and programmers of other languages suitable for low-level programming). Our favorite reason, however, is simply that you can't really claim to understand computers and programming until you have seen how software meets hardware. People who don't know about pointers, memory addresses, etc. often have the strangest ideas of how their programming language facilities work; such wrong ideas can lead to code that's "interestingly poor."

Vectors and Arrays

"Caveat emptor!"

—Good advice

This chapter describes how vectors are copied and accessed through subscripting. To do that, we discuss copying in general and consider **vector**'s relation to the lower-level notion of arrays. We present arrays' relation to pointers and consider the problems arising from their use. We also present the five essential operations that must be considered for every type: construction, default construction, copy construction, copy assignment, and destruction.

18.1 Introduction

To get into the air, a plane has to accelerate along the runway until it moves fast enough to "jump" into the air. While the plane is lumbering along the runway, it is little more than a particularly heavy and awkward truck. Once in the air, it soars to become an altogether different, elegant, and efficient vehicle. It is in its true element.

In this chapter, we are in the middle of a "run" to gather enough programming language features and techniques to get away from the constraints and difficulties of plain computer memory. We want to get to the point where we can program using types that provide exactly the properties we want based on logical needs. To "get there" we have to overcome a number of fundamental constraints related to access to the bare machine, such as the following:

- An object in memory is of fixed size.

- An object in memory is in one specific place.

- The computer provides only a few fundamental operations on such objects (such as copying a word, adding the values from two words, etc.).

Basically, those are the constraints on the built-in types and operations of C++ (as inherited from C; see §22.2.5 and Chapter 27). In Chapter 17, we saw the beginnings of a **vector** type that controls all access to its elements and provides us with operations that seem "natural" from the point of view of a user, rather than from the point of view of hardware.

This chapter focuses on the notion of copying. This is an important but rather technical point: What do we mean by copying a nontrivial object? To what extent are the copies independent after a copy operation? What copy operations are there? How do we specify them? And how do they relate to other fundamental operations, such as initialization and cleanup?

Inevitably, we get to discuss how memory is manipulated when we don't have higher-level types such as **vector** and **string**. We examine arrays and pointers, their relationship, their use, and the traps and pitfalls of their use. This is essential information to anyone who gets to work with low-level uses of C++ or C code.

Please note that the details of **vector** are peculiar to **vectors** and the C++ ways of building new higher-level types from lower-level ones. However, every "higher-level" type (**string, vector, list, map**, etc.) in every language is somehow built from the same machine primitives and reflects a variety of resolutions to the fundamental problems described here.

18.2 Copying

Consider our **vector** as it was at the end of Chapter 17:

```
class vector {
        int sz;                 // the size
        double* elem;           // a pointer to the elements
public:
        vector(int s)                                   // constructor
                :sz(s), elem(new double[s]) { }         // allocates memory
        ~vector()                                       // destructor
                { delete[] elem; }                      // deallocates memory
        // . . .
};
```

Let's try to copy one of these vectors:

```
void f(int n)
{
        vector v(3);        // define a vector of 3 elements
        v.set(2,2.2);       // set v[2] to 2.2
        vector v2 = v;      // what happens here?
        // . . .
}
```

Ideally, **v2** becomes a copy of **v** (that is, = makes copies); that is, **v2.size()==v.size()** and the **v2[i]==v[i]** for all **i**'s in the range [**0:v.size**()). Furthermore, all memory is returned to the free store upon exit from **f**(). That's what the standard library **vector** does (of course), but it's not what happens for our still-far-too-simple **vector**. Our task is to improve our **vector** to get it to handle such examples correctly, but first let's figure out what our current version actually does. Exactly what does it do wrong? How? And why? Once we know that, we can probably fix the problems. More importantly, we have a chance to recognize and avoid similar problems when we see them in other contexts.

The default meaning of copying for a class is "Copy all the data members." That often makes perfect sense. For example, we copy a **Point** by copying its co-ordinates. But for a pointer member, just copying the members causes problems. In particular, for the **vector**s in our example, it means that after the copy, we have **v.sz==v2.sz** and **v.elem==v2.elem** so that our **vector**s look like this:

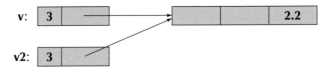

That is, **v2** doesn't have a copy of **v**'s elements; it shares **v**'s elements. We could write

```
v.set(1,99);          // set v[1] to 99
v2.set(0,88);         // set v2[0] to 88
cout << v.get(0) << ' ' << v2.get(1);
```

The result would be the output **88 99**. That wasn't what we wanted. Had there been no "hidden" connection between **v** and **v2**, we would have gotten the output **0 0**, because we never wrote to **v[0]** or to **v2[1]**. You could argue that the behavior we got is "interesting," "neat!" or "sometimes useful," but that is not what we intended or what the standard library **vector** provides. Also, what happens when we return from **f()** is an unmitigated disaster. Then, the destructors for **v** and **v2** are implicitly called; **v**'s destructor frees the storage used for the elements using

```
delete[] elem;
```

and so does **v2**'s destructor. Since **elem** points to the same memory location in both **v** and **v2**, that memory will be freed twice with likely disastrous results (§17.4.6).

18.2.1 Copy constructors

So, what do we do? We'll do the obvious: provide a copy operation that copies the elements and make sure that this copy operation gets called when we initialize one **vector** with another.

Initialization of objects of a class is done by a constructor. So, we need a constructor that copies. Such a constructor is obviously called a *copy constructor*. It is defined to take as its argument a reference to the object from which to copy. So, for class **vector** we need

```
vector(const vector&);
```

This constructor will be called when we try to initialize one **vector** with another. We pass by reference because we (obviously) don't want to copy the argument of the constructor that defines copying. We pass by **const** reference because we don't want to modify our argument (§8.5.6). So we refine **vector** like this:

```
class vector {
      int sz;
      double* elem;
      void copy(const vector& arg);      // copy elements from arg into *elem
public:
      vector(const vector&) ;            // copy constructor: define copy
      // . . .
};
```

The **copy**() simply copies the elements from an argument vector:

```
void vector::copy(const vector& arg)
      // copy elements [0:arg.sz–1]
{
      for (int i = 0; i<arg.sz; ++i) elem[i] = arg.elem[i];
}
```

The **copy**() member function assumes that there are **sz** elements available both in its argument **arg** and in the **vector** it is copying into. To help make sure that's true, we make **copy**() private. Only functions that are part of the implementation of **vector** can call **copy**(). These functions need to make sure that the sizes match.

The copy constructor sets the number of elements (**sz**) and allocates memory for the elements (initializing **elem**) before copying element values from the argument **vector**:

```
vector:: vector(const vector& arg)
// allocate elements, then initialize them by copying
      :sz(arg.sz), elem(new double[arg.sz])
{
      copy(arg);
}
```

Given this copy constructor, consider again our example:

> **vector v2 = v;**

This definition will initialize **v2** by a call of **vector**'s copy constructor with **v** as its argument. Again given a **vector** with three elements, we now get

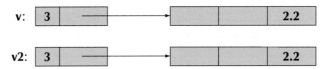

Given that, the destructor can do the right thing. Each set of elements is correctly freed. Obviously, the two **vectors** are now independent so that we can change the value of elements in **v** without affecting **v2** and vice versa. For example:

> **v.set(1,99);** *// set v[1] to 99*
> **v2.set(0,88);** *// set v2[0] to 88*
> **cout << v.get(0) <<' '<< v2.get(1);**

This will output **0 0**.
 Instead of saying

> **vector v2 = v;**

we could equally well have said

> **vector v2(v);**

When **v** (the initializer) and **v2** (the variable being initialized) are of the same type and that type has copying conventionally defined, those two notations mean exactly the same and you can use whichever notation you like better.

18.2.2 Copy assignments

We handle copy construction (initialization), but we can also copy **vectors** by assignment. As with copy initialization, the default meaning of copy assignment is memberwise copy, so with **vector** as defined so far, assignment will cause a double deletion (exactly as shown for copy constructors in §18.2.1) plus a memory leak. For example:

> **void f2(int n)**
> **{**
>   **vector v(3);** *// define a vector*

```
        v.set(2,2.2);
        vector v2(4);
        v2 = v;                 // assignment: what happens here?
        // . . .
}
```

We would like **v2** to be a copy of **v** (and that's what the standard library **vector** does), but since we have said nothing about the meaning of assignment of our **vector**, the default assignment is used; that is, the assignment is a memberwise copy so that **v2**'s **sz** and **elem** become identical to **v**'s **sz** and **elem**, respectively. We can illustrate that like this:

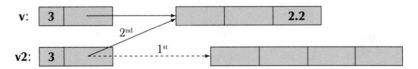

When we leave **f2()**, we have the same disaster as we had when leaving **f()** in §18.2 before we added the copy constructor: the elements pointed to by both **v** and **v2** are freed twice (using **delete[]**). In addition, we have leaked the memory initially allocated for **v2**'s four elements. We "forgot" to free those. The remedy for this copy assignment is fundamentally the same as for the copy initialization (§18.2.1). We define an assignment that copies properly:

```
class vector {
        int sz;
        double* elem;
        void copy(const vector& arg);      // copy elements from arg into *elem
public:
        vector& operator=(const vector&) ;    // copy assignment
        // . . .
};

vector& vector::operator=(const vector& a)
        // make this vector a copy of a
{
        double* p = new double[a.sz];    // allocate new space
        copy(a);                // copy elements
        delete[] elem;          // deallocate old space
        elem = p;               // now we can reset elem
        sz = a.sz;
        return *this;           // return a self-reference (see §17.10)
}
```

Assignment is a bit more complicated than construction because we must deal with the old elements. Our basic strategy is to make a copy of the elements from the source **vector**:

```
double* p = new double[a.sz];        // allocate new space
copy(a);
```

Then we free the old elements from the target **vector**:

```
delete[] elem;                       // deallocate old space
```

Finally, we let **elem** point to the new elements:

```
elem = p;                            // now we can reset elem
sz = a.sz;
```

We can represent the result graphically like this:

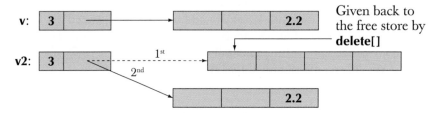

We now have a **vector** that doesn't leak memory and doesn't free (**delete[]**) any memory twice.

When implementing the assignment, you could consider simplifying the code by freeing the memory for the old elements before creating the copy, but it is usually a very good idea not to throw away information before you know that you can replace it. Also, if you did that, strange things would happen if you assigned a **vector** to itself:

```
vector v(10);
v=v;      // self-assignment
```

Please check that our implementation handles that case correctly (if not with optimal efficiency).

18.2.3 Copy terminology

Copying is an issue in most programs and in most programming languages. The basic issue is whether you copy a pointer (or reference) or copy the information pointed to (referred to):

- *Shallow copy* copies only a pointer so that the two pointers now refer to the same object. That's what pointers and references do.
- *Deep copy* copies what a pointer points to so that the two pointers now refer to distinct objects. That's what **vectors**, **strings**, etc. do. We define copy constructors and copy assignments when we want deep copy for objects of our classes.

Here is an example of shallow copy:

```
int* p = new int(77);
int* q = p;      // copy the pointer p
*p = 88;         // change the value of the int pointed to by p and q
```

We can illustrate that like this:

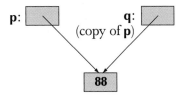

In contrast, we can do a deep copy:

```
int* p = new int(77);
int* q = new int(*p);   // allocate a new int, then copy the value pointed to by p
*p = 88;                // change the value of the int pointed to by p
```

We can illustrate that like this:

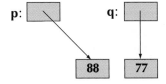

Using this terminology, we can say that the problem with our original **vector** was that it did a shallow copy, rather than copying the elements pointed to by its **elem** pointer. Our improved **vector**, like the standard library **vector**, does a deep copy by allocating new space for the elements and copying their values. Types that provide shallow copy (like pointers and references) are said to have *pointer semantics* or *reference semantics* (they copy addresses). Types that provide deep copy (like **string** and **vector**) are said to have *value semantics* (they copy the values pointed to). From a user perspective, types with value semantics behave as if no pointers were involved – just values that can be copied. One way of thinking of types with value semantics is that they "work just like integers" as far as copying is concerned.

18.3 Essential operations

We have now reached the point where we can discuss how to decide which constructors a class should have, whether it should have a destructor, and whether you need to provide a copy assignment. There are five essential operations to consider:

- Constructors from one or more arguments
- Default constructor
- Copy constructor (copy object of same type)
- Copy assignment (copy object of same type)
- Destructor

Usually we need one or more constructors that take arguments needed to initialize an object. For example:

```
string s("Triumph");       // initialize s to the character string "Triumph"
vector<double> v(10);      // make v a vector of 10 doubles
```

As you can see, the meaning/use of an initializer is completely up to the constructor. The standard **string**'s constructor uses a character string as an initial value, whereas the standard **vector**'s constructor uses an integer as the initial number of elements. Usually we use a constructor to establish an invariant (§9.4.3). If we can't define a good invariant for a class that its constructors can establish, we probably have a poorly designed class or a plain data structure.

Constructors that take arguments are as varied as the classes they serve. The remaining operations have more regular patterns.

How do we know if a class needs a default constructor? We need a default constructor if we want to be able to make objects of the class without specifying an initializer. The most common example is when we want to put objects of a class into a standard library **vector**. The following works only because we have default values for **int**, **string**, and **vector<int>**:

```
vector<double> vi(10);       // vector of 10 doubles, each initialized to 0.0
vector<string> vs(10);       // vector of 10 strings, each initialized to ""
vector<vector< int> > vvi(10); // vector of 10 vectors, each initialized to vector()
```

So, having a default constructor is often useful. The question then becomes: "When does it make sense to have a default constructor?" An answer is: "When we can establish the invariant for the class with a meaningful and obvious default value." For value types, such as **int** and **double**, the obvious value is **0** (for **double**, that becomes **0.0**). For **string**, the empty **string**, **""**, is the obvious choice. For

vector, the empty **vector** serves well. For every type **T**, **T**() is the default value, if a default exists. For example, **double**() is **0.0**, **string**() is **""**, **and vector<int>**() is the empty **vector** of **int**s.

A class needs a destructor if it acquires resources. A resource is something you "get from somewhere" and that you must give back once you have finished using it. The obvious example is memory that you get from the free store (using **new**) and have to give back to the free store (using **delete** or **delete[]**). Our **vector** acquires memory to hold its elements, so it has to give that memory back; therefore, it needs a destructor. Other resources that you might encounter as your programs increase in ambition and sophistication are files (if you open one, you also have to close it), locks, thread handles, and sockets (for communication with processes and remote computers).

Another sign that a class needs a destructor is simply that it has members that are pointers or references. If a class has a pointer or a reference member, it often needs a destructor and copy operations.

A class that needs a destructor almost always also needs a copy constructor and a copy assignment. The reason is simply that if an object has acquired a resource (and has a pointer member pointing to it), the default meaning of copy (shallow, memberwise copy) is almost certainly wrong. Again, **vector** is the classic example.

In addition, a base class for which a derived class may have a destructor needs a **virtual** destructor (§17.5.2).

18.3.1 Explicit constructors

A constructor that takes a single argument defines a conversion from its argument type to its class. This can be most useful. For example:

```
class complex {
public:
        complex(double);       // defines double-to-complex conversion
        complex(double,double);
        // . . .
};

        complex z1 = 3.14;     // OK: convert 3.14 to (3.14,0)
        complex z2 = complex(1.2, 3.4);
```

However, implicit conversions should be used sparingly and with caution, because they can cause unexpected and undesirable effects. For example, our **vector**, as defined so far, has a constructor that takes an **int**. This implies that it defines a conversion from **int** to **vector**. For example:

```
class vector {
     // . . .
     vector(int);
     // . . .
};

vector v = 10;        // odd: makes a vector of 10 doubles
v = 20;               // eh? Assigns a new vector of 20 doubles to v

void f(const vector&);
f(10);                // eh? Calls f with a new vector of 10 doubles
```

It seems we are getting more than we have bargained for. Fortunately, it is simple to suppress this use of a constructor as an implicit conversion. A constructor defined **explicit** provides only the usual construction semantics and not the implicit conversions. For example:

```
class vector {
     // . . .
     explicit vector(int);
     // . . .
};

vector v = 10;        // error: no int-to-vector<double> conversion
v = 20;               // error: no int-to-vector<double> conversion
vector v0(10);        // OK

void f(const vector<double>&);
f(10);                // error: no int-to-vector<double> conversion
f(vector<double>(10));   // OK
```

To avoid surprising conversions, we – and the standard – define **vector**'s single-argument constructors to be **explicit**. It's a pity that constructors are not explicit by default; if in doubt, make any constructor that can be invoked with a single argument **explicit**.

18.3.2 Debugging constructors and destructors

Constructors and destructors are invoked at well-defined and predictable points of a program's execution. However, we don't always write explicit calls, such as **vector(2)**; rather we do something, such as declaring a **vector**, passing a **vector** as a by-value argument, or creating a **vector** on the free store using **new**. This can cause confusion for people who think in terms of syntax. There is not just a single syntax that triggers a constructor. It is simpler to think of constructors and destructors this way:

```
        double operator[](int n) const;    // for const vectors
};
```

We obviously couldn't return a **double&** from the **const** version, so we returned a **double** value. We could equally well have returned a **const double &**, but since a **double** is a small object there would be no point in returning a reference (§8.5.6) so we decided to pass it back by value. We can now write:

```
    void ff(const vector& cv, vector& v)
    {
        double d = cv[1];    // fine (uses the const [])
        cv[1] = 2.0;         // error (uses the const [])
        double d = v[1];     // fine (uses the non-const [])
        v[1] = 2.0;          // fine (uses the non-const [])
    }
```

Since **vectors** are often passed by **const** reference, this **const** version of **operator[]()** is an essential addition.

18.5 Arrays

For a while, we have used *array* to refer to a sequence of objects allocated on the free store. We can also allocate arrays elsewhere as named variables. In fact, they are common

- As global variables (but global variables are most often a bad idea)
- As local variables (but arrays have serious limitations there)
- As function arguments (but an array doesn't know its own size)
- As class members (but member arrays can be hard to initialize).

Now, you might have detected that we have a not-so-subtle bias in favor of **vectors** over arrays. Use **vector** where you have a choice – and you have a choice in most contexts. However, arrays existed long before **vectors** and are roughly equivalent to what is offered in other languages (notably C), so you must know arrays, and know them well, to be able to cope with older code and with code written by people who don't appreciate the advantages of **vector**.

So, what is an array? How do we define an array? How do we use an array? An *array* is a homogeneous sequence of objects allocated in contiguous memory; that is, all elements of an array have the same type and there are no gaps between the objects of the sequence. The elements of an array are numbered from 0 upward. In a declaration, an array is indicated by "square brackets":

```
    const int max = 100;
    int gai[max];              // a global array (of 100 ints); "lives forever"
```

```
void f(int n)
{
        char lac[20];        // local array; "lives" until the end of scope
        int lai[60];
        double lad[n];       // error: array size not a constant
        // . . .
}
```

Note the limitation: the number of elements of a named array must be known at compile time. If you want the number of elements to be a variable, you must put it on the free store and access it through a pointer. That's what **vector** does with its array of elements.

Just like the arrays on free store, we access named arrays using the subscript and dereference operators ([ ] and *). For example:

```
void f2()
{
        char lac[20];        // local array; "lives" until the end of scope

        lac[7] = 'a';
        *lac = 'b';          // equivalent to lac[0]='b'

        lac[-2] = 'b';       // huh?
        lac[200] = 'c';      // huh?
}
```

This function compiles, but we know that "compiles" doesn't mean "works correctly." The use of [ ] is obvious, but there is no range checking, so **f2()** compiles, and the result of writing to **lac[-2]** and **lac[200]** is (as for all out-of-range access) usually disastrous. Don't do it. Arrays do not range check. Again, we are dealing directly with physical memory here; don't expect "system support."

But couldn't the compiler see that **lac** has just 20 elements so that **lac[200]** is an error? A compiler could, but as far as we know no production compiler does. The problem is that keeping track of array bounds at compile time is impossible in general, and catching errors in the simplest cases (like the one above) only is not very helpful.

18.5.1 Pointers to array elements

A pointer can point to an element of an array. Consider:

```
double ad[10];
double* p = &ad[5];    // point to ad[5]
```

We now have a pointer **p** to the **double** known as **ad[5]**:

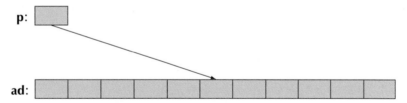

We can subscript and dereference that pointer:

```
*p =7;
p[2] = 6;
p[−3] = 9;
```

We get

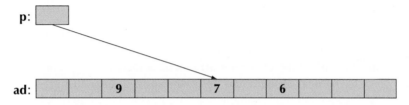

That is, we can subscript the pointer with both positive and negative numbers. As long as the resulting element is in range, all is well. However, access outside the range of the array pointed into is illegal (as with free-store-allocated arrays; see §17.4.3). Typically, access outside an array is not detected by the compiler and (sooner or later) is disastrous.

Once a pointer points into an array, addition and subscripting can be used to make it point to another element of the array. For example:

```
p += 2;        // move p 2 elements to the right
```

We get

And

```
p −= 5;        // move p 5 elements to the left
```

We get

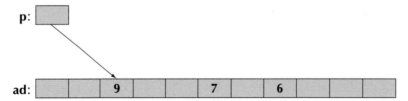

Using **+**, **−**, **+=**, and **−=** to move pointers around is called *pointer arithmetic*. Obviously, if we do that, we have to take great care to ensure that the result is not a pointer to memory outside the array:

```
p += 1000;          // insane: p points into an array with just 10 elements
double d = *p;      // illegal: probably a bad value
                    // (definitely an unpredictable value)
*p = 12.34;         // illegal: probably scrambles some unknown data
```

Unfortunately, not all bad bugs involving pointer arithmetic are that easy to spot. The best policy is usually simply to avoid pointer arithmetic.

The most common use of pointer arithmetic is incrementing a pointer (using **++**) to point to the next element and decrementing a pointer (using **−−**) to point to the previous element. For example, we could print the value of **ad**'s elements like this:

```
for (double* p = &ad[0]; p<&ad[10]; ++p) cout << *p << '\n';
```

Or backward:

```
for (double* p = &ad[9]; p>=&ad[0]; --p) cout << *p << '\n';
```

This use of pointer arithmetic is not uncommon. However, we find the last ("backward") example quite easy to get wrong. Why **&ad[9]** and not **&ad[10]**? Why **>=** and not **>**? These examples could equally well (and equally efficiently) be done using subscripting. Such examples could be done equally well using subscripting into a **vector**, which is more easily range checked.

Note that most real-world uses of pointer arithmetic involve a pointer passed as a function argument. In that case, the compiler doesn't have a clue how many elements are in the array pointed into: you are on your own. That is a situation we prefer to stay away from whenever we can.

Why does C++ have (allow) pointer arithmetic at all? It can be such a bother and doesn't provide anything new once we have subscripting. For example:

```
double* p1 = &ad[0];
double* p2 = p1+7;
double* p3 = &p1[7];
if (p2 != p3) cout << "impossible!\n";
```

Mainly, the reason is historical. These rules were crafted for C decades ago and can't be removed without breaking a lot of code. Partly, there can be some convenience gained using pointer arithmetic in some important low-level applications, such as memory managers.

18.5.2 Pointers and arrays

The name of an array refers to all the elements of the array. Consider:

```
char ch[100];
```

The size of **ch**, **sizeof(ch)**, is 100. However, the name of an array turns into ("decays to") a pointer with the slightest excuse. For example:

```
char* p = ch;
```

Here **p** is initialized to **&ch[0]** and **sizeof(p)** is something like 4 (not 100).

This can be useful. For example, consider a function **strlen()** that counts the number of characters in a zero-terminated array of characters:

```
int strlen(const char* p)      // similar to the standard library strlen()
{
    int count = 0;
    while (*p) { ++count; ++p; }
    return count;
}
```

We can now call this with **strlen(ch)** as well as **strlen(&ch[0])**. You might point out that this is a very minor notational advantage, and we'd have to agree.

One reason for having array names convert to pointers is to avoid accidentally passing large amounts of data by value. Consider:

```
int strlen(const char a[])      // similar to the standard library strlen()
{
    int count = 0;
    while (a[count]) { ++count; }
    return count;
}
```

```
char lots [100000];

void f()
{
    int nchar = strlen(lots);
    // . . .
}
```

Naively (and quite reasonably), you might expect this call to copy the 100,000 characters specified as the argument to **strlen()**, but that's not what happens. Instead, the argument declaration **char p[]** is considered equivalent to **char* p** and the call **strlen(lots)** is considered equivalent to **strlen(&lots[0])**. This saves you from an expensive copy operation, but it should surprise you. Why should it surprise you? Because in every other case, when you pass an object and don't explicitly declare an argument to be passed by reference (§8.5.3–6), that object is copied.

Note that the pointer you get from treating the name of an array as a pointer to its first element is a value and not a variable, so you cannot assign to it:

```
char ac[10];
ac = new char [20];        // error: no assignment to array name
&ac[0] = new char [20];    // error: no assignment to pointer value
```

Finally! A problem that the compiler will catch!

As a consequence of this implicit array-name-to-pointer conversion, you can't even copy arrays using assignment:

```
int x[100];
int y[100];
// . . .
x = y;             // error
int z[100] = y;    // error
```

This is consistent, but often a bother. If you need to copy an array, you must write some more elaborate code to do so. For example:

```
for (int i=0; i<100; ++i) x[i]=y[i];    // copy 100 ints
memcpy(x,y,100*sizeof(int));            // copy 100*sizeof(int) bytes
copy(y,y+100, x);                       // copy 100 ints
```

Note that the C language doesn't support anything like **vector**, so in C, you must use arrays extensively. This implies that a lot of C++ code uses arrays (§27.1.2). In particular, C-style strings (zero-terminated arrays of characters; see §27.5) are very common.

If we want assignment, we have to use something like **vector**. The **vector** equivalent to the copying code above is

```
vector<int> x(100);
vector<int> y(100);
// . . .
x = y;      // copy 100 ints
```

18.5.3 Array initialization

Arrays have one significant advantage over vectors and other user-defined containers: the C++ language provides notational support for the initialization of arrays. For example:

```
char ac[] = "Beorn";      // array of 6 chars
```

Count those characters. There are five, but **ac** becomes an array of six characters because the compiler adds a terminating zero character at the end of a string literal:

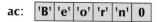

ac: | 'B' | 'e' | 'o' | 'r' | 'n' | 0 |

A zero-terminated string is the norm in C and many systems. We call such a zero-terminated array of characters a *C-style string*. All string literals are C-style strings. For example:

```
char* pc = "Howdy";      // pc points to an array of 6 chars
```

Graphically:

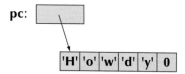

pc:

'H' 'o' 'w' 'd' 'y' 0

Note that the **char** with the numeric value **0** is not the character **'0'** or any other letter or digit. The purpose of that terminating zero is to allow functions to find the end of the string. Remember: An array does not know its size. Relying on the terminating zero convention, we can write

```
int strlen(const char* p)      // similar to the standard library strlen()
{
    int n = 0;
    while (p[n]) ++n;
    return n;
}
```

Actually, we don't have to define **strlen()** because it is a standard library function defined in the **<string.h>** header (§27.5, §B.10.3). Note that **strlen()** counts the characters, but not the terminating **0**; that is, you need *n*+1 **chars** to store *n* characters in a C-style string.

Only character arrays can be initialized by literal strings, but all arrays can be initialized by a list of values of their element type. For example:

```
int ai[] = { 1, 2, 3, 4, 5, 6 };           // array of 6 ints
int ai2[100] = { 0,1,2,3,4,5,6,7,8,9 };    // the last 90 elements are initialized to 0
double ad[100] = { };                       // all elements initialized to 0.0
char chars[] = { 'a', 'b', 'c' };           // no terminating 0!
```

Note that the number of elements of **ai** is six (not seven) and the number of elements for **chars** is three (not four) — the "add a **0** at the end" rule is for literal character strings only. If an array isn't given a size, that size is deduced from the initializer list. That's a rather useful feature. If there are fewer initializer values than array elements (as in the definitions of **ai2** and **ad**), the remaining elements are initialized by the element type's default value.

18.5.4 Pointer problems

Like arrays, pointers are often overused and misused. Often, the problems people get themselves into involve both pointers and arrays, so we'll summarize the problems here. In particular, all serious problems with pointers involve trying to access something that isn't an object of the expected type, and many of those problems involve access outside the bounds of an array. Here we will consider

- Access through the null pointer
- Access through an uninitialized pointer
- Access off the end of an array
- Access to a deallocated object
- Access to an object that has gone out of scope

In all cases, the practical problem for the programmer is that the actual access looks perfectly innocent; it is "just" that the pointer hasn't been given a value that makes the use valid. Worse (in the case of a write through the pointer), the problem may manifest itself only a long time later when some apparently unrelated object has been corrupted. Let's consider examples:

Don't access through the null pointer:

```
int* p = 0;
*p = 7;       // ouch!
```

Obviously, in real-world programs, this typically occurs when there is some code in between the initialization and the use. In particular, passing **p** to a function or receiving it as the result from a function are common examples. We prefer not to pass null pointers around, but if you have to, test for the null pointer before use:

```
int* p = fct_that_can_return_a_0();
if (p == 0) {
        // do something
}
else {
        // use p
        *p = 7;
}
```

and

```
void fct_that_can_receive_a_0(int* p)
{
        if (p == 0) {
                // do something
        }
        else {
                // use p
                *p = 7;
        }
}
```

Using references (§17.9.1) and using exceptions to signal errors (§5.6 and §19.5) are the main tools for avoiding null pointers.

Do initialize your pointers:

```
int* p;
*p = 9;     // ouch!
```

In particular, don't forget to initialize pointers that are class members.

Don't access nonexistent array elements:

```
int a[10];
int* p = &a[10];
*p = 11;        // ouch!
a[10] = 12;     // ouch!
```

Be careful with the first and last elements of a loop, and try not to pass arrays around as pointers to their first elements. Instead use **vectors**. If you really must use an array in more than one function (passing it as an argument), then be extra careful and pass its size along.

Don't access through a deleted pointer:

```
int* p = new int(7);
// . . .
delete p;
// . . .
*p = 13;    // ouch!
```

The **delete p** or the code after it may have scribbled all over *p or used it for something else. Of all of these problems, we consider this one the hardest to systematically avoid. The most effective defense against this problem is not to have "naked" **news** that require "naked" **deletes**: use **new** and **delete** in constructors and destructors or use a container, such as **Vector_ref** (§E.4), to handle **deletes**.

Don't return a pointer to a local variable:

```
int* f()
{
    int x = 7;
    // . . .
    return &x;
}

// . . .

int* p = f();
// . . .
*p = 15;    // ouch!
```

The return from **f()** or the code after it may have scribbled all over *p or used it for something else. The reason for that is that the local variables of a function are allocated (on the stack) upon entry to the function and deallocated again at the exit from the function. In particular, destructors are called for local variables of classes with destructors (§17.5.1). Compilers could catch most problems related to returning pointers to local variables, but few do.

Consider a logically equivalent example:

```
vector& ff()
{
    vector x(7);
```

```
        // . . .
        return x;
}       // the vector x is destroyed here

// . . .

vector& p = ff();
// . . .
p[4] = 15;      // ouch!
```

Quite a few compilers catch this variant of the return problem.

It is common for programmers to underestimate these problems. However, many experienced programmers have been defeated by the innumerable variations and combinations of these simple array and pointer problems. The solution is not to litter your code with pointers, arrays, **news**, and **deletes**. If you do, "being careful" simply isn't enough in realistically sized programs. Instead, rely on vectors, RAII ("Resource Acquisition Is Initialization"; see §19.5), and other systematic approaches to the management of memory and other resources.

18.6 Examples: palindrome

Enough technical examples! Let's try a little puzzle. A *palindrome* is a word that is spelled the same from both ends. For example, *anna*, *petep*, and *malayalam* are palindromes, whereas *ida* and *homesick* are not. There are two basic ways of determining whether a word is a palindrome:

- Make a copy of the letters in reverse order and compare that copy to the original.
- See if the first letter is the same as the last, then see if the second letter is the same as the second to last, and keep going until you reach the middle.

Here, we'll take the second approach. There are many ways of expressing this idea in code depending on how we represent the word and how we keep track of how far we have come with the comparison of characters. We'll write a little program that tests whether words are palindromes in a few different ways just to see how different language features affect the way the code looks and works.

18.6.1 Palindromes using string

First, we try a version using the standard library **string** with **int** indices to keep track of how far we have come with our comparison:

```
bool is_palindrome(const string& s)
{
        int first = 0;              // index of first letter
```

```
    int last = s.length()–1;      // index of last letter
    while (first < last) {          // we haven't reached the middle
        if (s[first]!=s[last]) return false;
        ++first;    // move forward
        --last;     // move backward
    }
    return true;
}
```

We return **true** if we reach the middle without finding a difference. We suggest that you look at this code to convince yourself that it is correct when there are no letters in the string, just one letter in the string, an even number of letters in the string, and an odd number of letters in the string. Of course, we should not just rely on logic to see that our code is correct. We should also test. We can exercise **is_palindrome()** like this:

```
int main()
{
    string s;
    while (cin>>s) {
        cout << s << " is";
        if (!is_palindrome(s)) cout << " not";
        cout << " a palindrome\n";
    }
}
```

Basically, the reason we are using a **string** is that "**string**s are good for dealing with words." It is simple to read a whitespace-separated word into a string, and a **string** knows its size. Had we wanted to test **is_palindrome()** with strings containing whitespace, we could have read using **getline()** (§11.5). That would have shown *ah ha* and *as df fd sa* to be palindromes.

18.6.2 Palindromes using arrays

What if we didn't have **string**s (or **vector**s), so that we had to use an array to store the characters? Let's see:

```
bool is_palindrome(const char s[], int n)
    // s points to the first character of an array of n characters
{
    int first = 0;              // index of first letter
    int last = n–1;             // index of last letter
```

```
        while (first < last) {        // we haven't reached the middle
            if (s[first]!=s[last]) return false;
            ++first;    // move forward
            --last;     // move backward
        }
        return true;
    }
```

To exercise **is_palindrome()**, we first have to get characters read into the array. One way to do that safely (i.e., without risk of overflowing the array) is like this:

```
    istream& read_word(istream& is, char* buffer, int max)
        // read at most max−1 characters from is into buffer
    {
        is.width(max);      // read at most max−1 characters in the next >>
        is >> buffer;       // read whitespace-terminated word,
                            // add zero after the last character read into p
        return is;
    }
```

Setting the **istream**'s width appropriately prevents buffer overflow for the next **>>** operation. Unfortunately, it also means that we don't know if the read terminated by whitespace or by the buffer being full (so that we need to read more characters). Also, who remembers the details of the behavior of **width()** for input? The standard library **string** and **vector** are really better as input buffers because they expand to fit the amount of input. The terminating 0 character is needed because most popular operations on arrays of characters (C-style strings) assume 0 termination. Using **read_word()** we can write

```
    int main()
    {
        const int max = 128;
        char s[max];
        while (read_word(cin,s,max)) {
            cout << s << " is";
            if (!is_palindrome(s,strlen(s))) cout << " not";
            cout << " a palindrome\n";
        }
    }
```

The **strlen(s)** call returns the number of characters in the array after the call of **read_word()**, and **cout<<s** outputs the characters in the array up to the terminating **0**.

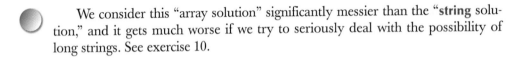

We consider this "array solution" significantly messier than the "**string** solution," and it gets much worse if we try to seriously deal with the possibility of long strings. See exercise 10.

18.6.3 Palindromes using pointers

Instead of using indices to identify characters, we could use pointers:

```
bool is_palindrome(const char* first, const char* last)
        // first points to the first letter, last to the last letter
{
        while (first < last) {          // we haven't reached the middle
                if (*first!=*last) return false;
                ++first;     // move forward
                --last;      // move backward
        }
        return true;
}
```

Note that we can actually increment and decrement pointers. Increment makes a pointer point to the next element of an array and decrement makes a pointer point to the previous element. If the array doesn't have such a next element or previous element, you have a serious uncaught out-of-range error. That's another problem with pointers.

We call this **is_palindrome()** like this:

```
int main()
{
        const int max = 128;
        char s[max];
        while (read_word(cin,s,max)) {
                cout << s << " is";
                if (!is_palindrome(&s[0],&s[strlen(s)–1])) cout << " not";
                cout << " a palindrome\n";
        }
}
```

Just for fun, we rewrite **is_palindrome()** like this:

```
bool is_palindrome(const char* first, const char* last)
        // first points to the first letter, last to the last letter
{
```

```
        if (first<last) {
                if (*first!=*last) return false;
                return is_palindrome(++first,--last);
        }
        return true;
}
```

This code becomes obvious when we rephrase the definition of *palindrome*: a word is a palindrome if the first and the last characters are the same and if the substring you get by removing the first and the last characters is a palindrome.

 ## Drill

In this chapter, we have two drills: one to exercise arrays and one to exercise **vectors** in roughly the same manner. Do both and compare the effort involved in each.

Array drill:

1. Define a global **int** array **ga** of ten **int**s initialized to 1, 2, 4, 8, 16, etc.
2. Define a function **f()** taking an **int** array argument and an **int** argument indicating the number of elements in the array.
3. In **f()**:
   a. Define a local **int** array **la** of ten **int**s.
   b. Copy the values from **ga** into **la**.
   c. Print out the elements of **la**.
   d. Define a pointer **p** to **int** and initialize it with an array allocated on the free store with the same number of elements as the argument array.
   e. Copy the values from the argument array into the free-store array.
   f. Print out the elements of the free-store array.
   g. Deallocate the free-store array.
4. In **main()**:
   a. Call **f()** with **ga** as its argument.
   b. Define an array **aa** with ten elements, and initialize it with the first ten factorial values (1, 2*1, 3*2*1, 4*3*2*1, etc.).
   c. Call **f()** with **aa** as its argument.

Standard library vector drill:

1. Define a global **vector<int> gv**; initialize it with ten **int**s, 1, 2, 4, 8, 16, etc.
2. Define a function **f()** taking a **vector<int>** argument.
3. In **f()**:
   a. Define a local **vector<int> lv** with the same number of elements as the argument vector.

    b. Copy the values from **gv** into **lv**.

    c. Print out the elements of **lv**.

    d. Define a local **vector<int> lv2**; initialize it to be a copy of the argument array.

    e. Print out the elements of **lv2**.

4. In **main()**:

    a. Call **f()** with **gv** as its argument.

    b. Define a **vector<int> vv,** and initialize it with the first ten factorial values (1, 2*1, 3*2*1, 4*3*2*1, etc.).

    c. Call **f()** with **vv** as its argument.

Review

1. What does "Caveat emptor!" mean?
2. What is the default meaning of copying for class objects?
3. When is the default meaning of copying of class objects appropriate? When is it inappropriate?
4. What is a copy constructor?
5. What is a copy assignment?
6. What is the difference between copy assignment and copy initialization?
7. What is shallow copy? What is deep copy?
8. How does the copy of a **vector** compare to its source?
9. What are the five "essential operations" for a class?
10. What is an **explicit** constructor? Where would you prefer one over the (default) alternative?
11. What operations may be invoked implicitly for a class object?
12. What is an array?
13. How do you copy an array?
14. How do you initialize an array?
15. When should you prefer a pointer argument over a reference argument? Why?
16. What is a C-style string?
17. What is a palindrome?

Terms

array	deep copy	**explicit** constructor
array initialization	default constructor	palindrome
copy assignment	essential operations	shallow copy
copy constructor		

Exercises

1. Write a function, **char* strdup(const char*)**, that copies a C-style string into memory it allocates on the free store. Do not use any standard library functions. Do not use subscripting; use the dereference operator * instead.

2. Write a function, **char* findx(const char* s, const char* x)**, that finds the first occurrence of the C-style string **x** in **s**. Do not use any standard library functions. Do not use subscripting; use the dereference operator * instead.

3. Write a function, **int strcmp(const char* s1, const char* s2)**, that compares C-style strings. Let it return a negative number if **s1** is lexicographically before **s2**, zero if **s1** equals **s2**, and a positive number if **s1** is lexicographically after **s2**. Do not use any standard library functions. Do not use subscripting; use the dereference operator * instead.

4. Consider what happens if you give **strdup()**, **findx()**, and **strcmp()** an argument that is not a C-style string. Try it! First figure out how to get a **char*** that doesn't point to a zero-terminated array of characters and then use it (never do this in real – non-experimental – code; it can create havoc). Try with free-store-allocated and stack-allocated "fake C-style strings." If the results still look reasonable, turn off debug mode. Redesign and re-implement those three functions so that they take another argument giving the maximum number of elements allowed in argument strings. Then, test that with correct C-style strings and "bad" strings.

5. Write a function, **string cat_dot(const string& s1, const string& s2)**, that concatenates two strings with a dot in between. For example, **cat_dot("Niels", "Bohr")** will return a string containing **Niels.Bohr**.

6. Modify **cat_dot()** from the previous exercise to take a string to be used as the separator (rather than dot) as its third argument.

7. Write versions of the **cat_dot()**s from the previous exercises to take C-style strings as arguments and return a free-store-allocated C-style string as the result. Do not use standard library functions or types in the implementation. Test these functions with several strings. Be sure to free (using **delete**) all the memory you allocated from free store (using **new**). Compare the effort involved in this exercise with the effort involved for exercises 5 and 6.

8. Rewrite all the functions in §18.6 to use the approach of making a backward copy of the string and then comparing; for example, take **"home"**, generate **"emoh"**, and compare those two strings to see that they are different, so *home* isn't a palindrome.

9. Consider the memory layout in §17.3. Write a program that tells the order in which static storage, the stack, and the free store are laid out in memory. In which direction does the stack grow: upward toward higher addresses or downward toward lower addresses? In an array on free store, are elements with higher indices allocated at higher or lower addresses?

10. Look at the "array solution" to the palindrome problem in §18.6.2. Fix it to deal with long strings by (a) reporting if an input string was too long and (b) allowing an arbitrarily long string. Comment on the complexity of the two versions.

11. Look up (e.g., on the web) *skip list* and implement that kind of list. This is not an easy exercise.

12. Implement a version of the game "Hunt the Wumpus." "Hunt the Wumpus" (or just "Wump") is a simple (non-graphical) computer game originally invented by Gregory Yob. The basic premise is that a rather smelly monster lives in a dark cave consisting of connected rooms. Your job is to slay the wumpus using bow and arrow. In addition to the wumpus, the cave has two hazards: bottomless pits and giant bats. If you enter a room with a bottomless pit, it's the end of the game for you. If you enter a room with a bat, the bat picks you up and drops you into another room. If you enter the room with the wumpus or he enters yours, he eats you. When you enter a room you will be told if a hazard is nearby:

    "I smell the wumpus": It's in an adjoining room.

    "I feel a breeze": One of the adjoining rooms is a bottomless pit.

    "I hear a bat": A giant bat is in an adjoining room.

    For your convenience, rooms are numbered. Every room is connected by tunnels to three other rooms. When entering a room, you are told something like "You are in room 12; there are tunnels to rooms 1, 13, and 4; move or shoot?" Possible answers are **m13** ("Move to room 13") and **s13–4–3** ("Shoot an arrow through rooms 13, 4, and 3"). The range of an arrow is three rooms. At the start of the game, you have five arrows. The snag about shooting is that it wakes up the wumpus and he moves to a room adjoining the one he was in – that could be your room.

    Probably the trickiest part of the exercise is to make the cave by selecting which rooms are connected with which other rooms. You'll probably want to use a random number generator (e.g., **randint()** from **std_lib_facilities.h**) to make different runs of the program use different caves and to move around the bats and the wumpus. Hint: Be sure to have a way to produce a debug output of the state of the cave.

Postscript

The standard library **vector** is built from lower-level memory management facilities, such as pointers and arrays, and its primary role is to help us avoid the complexities of those facilities. Whenever we design a class, we must consider initialization, copying, and destruction.

Vector, Templates, and Exceptions

"Success is never final."

—Winston Churchill

This chapter completes the design and implementation of the most common and most useful STL container: **vector**. Here, we show how to implement containers where the number of elements can vary, how to specify containers where the element type is a parameter, and how to deal with range errors. As usual, the techniques used are generally applicable, rather than simply restricted to the implementation of **vector**, or even to the implementation of containers. Basically, we show how to deal safely with varying amounts of data of a variety of types. In addition, we add a few doses of realism as design lessons. The techniques rely on templates and exceptions, so we show how to define templates and give the basic techniques for resource management that are the keys to good use of exceptions.

19.1 The problems

At the end of Chapter 18, our **vector** reached the point where we can

- Create **vectors** of double-precision floating-point elements (objects of class **vector**) with whatever number of elements we want
- Copy our **vectors** using assignment and initialization
- Rely on **vectors** to correctly release their memory when they go out of scope
- Access **vector** elements using the conventional subscript notation (on both the right-hand side and the left-hand side of an assignment)

That's all good and useful, but to reach the level of sophistication we expect (based on experience with the standard library **vector**), we need to address three more concerns:

- How do we change the size of a **vector** (change the number of elements)?
- How do we catch and report out-of-range **vector** element access?
- How do we specify the element type of a **vector** as an argument?

For example, how do we define **vector**, so that this is legal:

```
vector<double> vd;              // elements of type double
double d;
while(cin>>d) vd.push_back(d);  // grow vd to hold all the elements

vector<char> vc(100);           // elements of type char
```

```
int n;
cin>>n;
vc.resize(n);                        // make vc have n elements
```

Obviously, it is nice and useful to have **vectors** that allow this, but why is it important from a programming point of view? What makes it interesting to someone collecting useful programming techniques for future use? We are using two kinds of flexibility. We have a single entity, the **vector**, for which we can vary two things:

- The number of elements
- The type of elements

Those kinds of variability are useful in rather fundamental ways. We always collect data. Looking around my desk, I see piles of bank statements, credit card bills, and phone bills. Each of those is basically a list of lines of information of various types: strings of letters and numeric values. In front of me lies a phone; it keeps lists of phone numbers and names. In the bookcases across the room, there is shelf after shelf of books. Our programs tend to be similar: we have containers of elements of various types. We have many different kinds of containers (**vector** is just the most widely useful), and they contain information such as phone numbers, names, transaction amounts, and documents. Essentially all the examples from my desk and my room originated in some computer program or another. The obvious exception is the phone: it *is* a computer, and when I look at the numbers on it I'm looking at the output of a program just like the ones we're writing. In fact, those numbers may very well be stored in a **vector<Number>**.

Obviously, not all containers have the same number of elements. Could we live with a **vector** that had its size fixed by its initial definition; that is, could we write our code without **push_back()**, **resize()**, and equivalent operations? Sure we could, but that would put an unnecessary burden on the programmer: the basic trick for living with fixed-size containers is to move the elements to a bigger container when the number of elements grows too large for the initial size. For example, we could read into a **vector** without ever changing the size of a **vector** like this:

```
// read elements into a vector without using push_back:
vector<double>* p = new vector<double>(10);
int n = 0;        // number of elements
double d;
while(cin >> d) {
      if (n==p->size()) {
            vector<double>* q = new vector<double>(p->size()*2);
            copy(p->begin(), p->end(), q->begin());
```

```
            delete p;
            p = q;
    }
    (*p)[n] = d;
    ++n;
}
```

That's not pretty. Are you convinced that we got it right? How can you be sure? Note how we suddenly started to use pointers and explicit memory management. What we did was to imitate the style of programming we have to use when we are "close to the machine," using only the basic memory management techniques dealing with fixed-size objects (arrays; see §18.5). One of the reasons to use containers, such as **vector**, is to do better than that; that is, we want **vector** to handle such size changes internally to save us — its users — the bother and the chance to make mistakes. In other words, we prefer containers that can grow to hold the exact number of elements we happen to need. For example:

```
vector<double> d;
double d;
while(cin>>d) vd.push_back(d);
```

Are such changes of size common? If they are not, facilities for changing size are simply minor conveniences. However, such size changes are very common. The most obvious example is reading an unknown number of values from input. Other examples are collecting a set of results from a search (we don't in advance know how many results there will be) and removing elements from a collection one by one. Thus, the question is not whether we should handle size changes for containers, but how.

Why do we bother with changing sizes at all? Why not "just allocate enough space and be done with it!"? That appears to be the simplest and most efficient strategy. However, it is that only if we can reliably allocate enough space without allocating grossly too much space — and we can't. People who try that tend to have to rewrite code (if they carefully and systematically checked for overflows) and deal with disasters (if they were careless with their checking).

Obviously, not all **vectors** have the same type of elements. We need **vectors** of **doubles**, temperature readings, records (of various kinds), **strings**, operations, GUI buttons, shapes, dates, pointers to windows, etc. The possibilities are endless.

There are many kinds of containers. This is an important point, and because it has important implications it should be not be accepted without thought. Why can't all containers be **vectors**? If we could make do with a single kind of container (e.g., **vector**), we could dispense with all the concerns about how to program it and just make it part of the language. If we could make do with a single kind of container, we needn't bother learning about different kinds of containers; we'd just use **vector** all the time.

Well, data structures are the key to most significant applications. There are many thick and useful books about how to organize data, and much of that information could be described as answers to the question "How do I best store my data?" So, the answer is that we need many different kinds of containers, but it is too large a subject to adequately address here. However, we have already used **vectors** and **strings** (a **string** is a container of characters) extensively. In the next chapters, we will see **lists**, **maps** (a **map** is a tree of pairs of values), and matrices. Because we need many different containers, the language features and programming techniques needed to build and use containers are widely useful. If fact, the techniques we use to store and access data are among the most fundamental and most useful for all nontrivial forms of computing.

At the most basic memory level, all objects are of a fixed size and no types exist. What we do here is to introduce language facilities and programming techniques that allow us to provide containers of objects of various types for which we can vary the number of elements. This gives us a fundamentally useful degree of flexibility and convenience.

19.2 Changing size

What facilities for changing size does the standard library **vector** offer? It provides three simple operations. Given

```
vector<double> v(n); // v.size()==n
```

we can change its size in three ways:

```
v.resize(10);        // v now has 10 elements

v.push_back(7);      // add an element with the value 7 to the end of v
                     // v.size() increases by 1

v = v2;              // assign another vector; v is now a copy of v2
                     // v.size() now equals v2.size()
```

The standard library **vector** offers more operations that can change a **vector**'s size, such as **erase()** and **insert()** (§B.4.7), but here we will just see how we can implement those three operations for our **vector**.

19.2.1 Representation

In §19.1, we show the simplest strategy for changing size: just allocate space for the new number of elements and copy the old elements into the new space. However, if you resize often, that's inefficient. In practice, if we change the size once, we usually do so many times. In particular, we rarely see just one **push_back()**.

So, we can optimize our programs by anticipating such changes in size. In fact, all **vector** implementations keep track of both the number of elements and an amount of "free space" reserved for "future expansion." For example:

```
class vector {
        int sz;              // number of elements
        double* elem;        // address of first element
        int space;           // number of elements plus "free space"/"slots"
                             // for new elements ("the current allocation")
public:
        // . . .
};
```

We can represent this graphically like this:

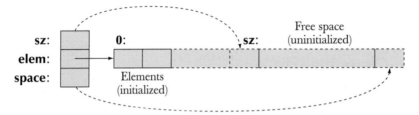

Since we count elements starting with **0**, we represent **sz** (the number of elements) as referring to one beyond the last element and **space** as referring to one beyond the last allocated slot. The pointers shown are really **elem+sz** and **elem+space**.

When a vector is first constructed, **space** is 0:

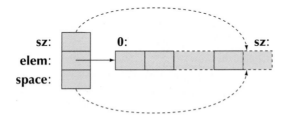

We don't start allocating extra slots until we begin changing the number of elements. Typically, **space==sz**, so there is no memory overhead unless we use **push_back()**.

The default constructor (creating a **vector** with no elements) sets all three members to 0:

```
vector::vector() :sz(0), elem(0), space(0) { }
```

That gives

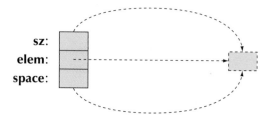

That one-beyond-the-end element is completely imaginary. The default constructor does no free-store allocation and occupies minimal storage (but see exercise 16).

Please note that our **vector** illustrates techniques that can be used to implement a standard vector (and other data structures), but a fair amount of freedom is given to standard library implementations so that **std::vector** on your system may use different techniques.

19.2.2 reserve and capacity

The most fundamental operation when we change sizes (that is, when we change the number of elements) is **vector::reserve()**. That's the operation we use to add space for new elements:

```
void vector::reserve(int newalloc)
{
    if (newalloc<=space) return;          // never decrease allocation
    double* p = new double[newalloc];     // allocate new space
    for (int i=0; i<sz; ++i) p[i] = elem[i];  // copy old elements
    delete[] elem;                         // deallocate old space
    elem = p;
    space = newalloc;
}
```

Note that we don't initialize the elements of the reserved space. After all, we are just reserving space; using that space for elements is the job of **push_back()** and **resize()**.

Obviously the amount of free space available in a **vector** can be of interest to a user, so we (like the standard) provide a member function for obtaining that information:

```
int vector::capacity() const { return space; }
```

That is, for a **vector** called **v**, **v.capacity()**–**v.size()** is the number of elements we could **push_back()** to **v** without causing reallocation.

19.2.3 resize

Given **reserve()**, implementing **resize()** for our **vector** is fairly simple. We have to handle several cases:

- The new size is larger than the old allocation.
- The new size is larger than the old size, but smaller than or equal to the old allocation.
- The new size is equal to the old size.
- The new size is smaller than the old size.

Let's see what we get:

```
void vector::resize(int newsize)
     // make the vector have newsize elements
     // initialize each new element with the default value 0.0
{
     reserve(newsize);
     for (int i=sz; i<newsize; ++i) elem[i] = 0;      // initialize new elements
     sz = newsize;
}
```

We let **reserve()** do the hard work of dealing with memory. The loop initializes new elements (if there are any).

We didn't explicitly deal with any cases here, but you can verify that all are handled correctly nevertheless.

TRY THIS

What cases do we need to consider (and test) if we want to convince ourselves that this **resize()** is correct? How about **newsize == 0**? How about **newsize == –77**?

19.2.4 push_back

When we first think of it, **push_back()** may appear complicated to implement, but given **reserve()** it is quite simple:

```
void vector::push_back(double d)
     // increase vector size by one; initialize the new element with d
{
     if (space==0) reserve(8);                   // start with space for 8 elements
     else if (sz==space) reserve(2*space);    // get more space
     elem[sz] = d;       // add d at end
     ++sz;                    // increase the size (sz is the number of elements)
}
```

In other words, if we have no spare space, we double the size of the allocation. In practice that turns out to be a very good choice for the vast majority of uses of **vector**, and that's the strategy used by most implementations of the standard library **vector**.

19.2.5 Assignment

We could have defined vector assignment in several different ways. For example, we could have decided that assignment was legal only if the two vectors involved had the same number of elements. However, in §18.2.2 we decided that vector assignment should have the most general and arguably the most obvious meaning: after assignment **v1=v2**, the vector **v1** is a copy of **v2**. Consider:

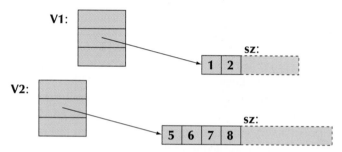

Obviously, we need to copy the elements, but what about the spare space? Do we "copy" the "free space" at the end? We don't: the new **vector** will get a copy of the elements, but since we have no idea how that new **vector** is going to be used, we don't bother with extra space at the end:

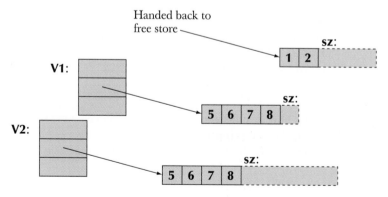

The simplest implementation of that is:

- Allocate memory for a copy.
- Copy the elements.
- Delete the old allocation.
- Set the **sz**, **elem**, and **space** to the new values.

Like this:

```
vector& vector::operator=(const vector& a)
        // like copy constructor, but we must deal with old elements
{
        double* p = new double[a.sz];           // allocate new space
        for (int i = 0; i<a.sz; ++i) p[i] = a.elem[i]; // copy elements
        delete[] elem;                          // deallocate old space
        space = sz = a.sz;                      // set new size
        elem = p;                               // set new elements
        return *this;                           // return self-reference
}
```

By convention, an assignment operator returns a reference to the object assigned to. The notation for that is *this, which is explained in §17.10.

This implementation is correct, but when we look at it a bit we realize that we do a lot of redundant allocation and deallocation. What if the **vector** we assign to has more elements than the one we assign? What if the **vector** we assign to has the same number of elements as the **vector** we assign? In many applications, that last case is very common. In either case, we can just copy the elements into space already available in the target **vector**:

```
vector& vector::operator=(const vector& a)
{
        if (this==&a) return *this;    // self-assignment, no work needed

        if (a.sz<=space) {          // enough space, no need for new allocation
                for (int i = 0; i<a.sz; ++i) elem[i] = a.elem[i];    // copy elements
                sz = a.sz;
                return *this;
        }

        double* p = new double[a.sz];           // allocate new space
        for (int i = 0; i<a.sz; ++i) p[i] = a.elem[i]; // copy elements
        delete[] elem;                          // deallocate old space
        space = sz = a.sz;                      // set new size
        elem = p;                               // set new elements
        return *this;                           // return a self-reference
}
```

Here, we first test for self-reference (e.g., **v=v**); in that case, we just do nothing. That test is logically redundant but sometimes a significant optimization. It does, however, show a common use of the **this** pointer checking if the argument **a** is the same object as the object for which a member function (here, **operator=()**) was called. Please convince yourself that this code actually works if we remove the **this==&a** line. The **a.sz<=space** is also just an optimization. Please convince yourself that this code actually works if we remove the **a.sz<=space** case.

19.2.6 Our vector so far

Now we have an almost real **vector** of **doubles**:

```
// an almost real vector of doubles:
class vector {
/*
        invariant:
                for 0<=n<sz elem[n] is element n
                sz<=space;
                if sz<space there is space for (space–sz) doubles after elem[sz–1]
*/
        int sz;                 // the size
        double* elem;           // pointer to the elements (or 0)
        int space;              // number of elements plus number of free slots
public:
        vector() : sz(0), elem(0), space(0) { }
        vector(int s) :sz(s), elem(new double[s]), space(s)
        {
                for (int i=0; i<sz; ++i) elem[i]=0;     // elements are initialized
        }

        vector(const vector&);                  // copy constructor
        vector& operator=(const vector&);       // copy assignment

        ~vector() { delete[] elem; }            // destructor

        double& operator[ ](int n) { return elem[n]; }      // access
        const double& operator[](int n) const { return elem[n]; }

        int size() const { return sz; }
        int capacity() const { return space; }

        void resize(int newsize);               // growth
        void push_back(double d);
        void reserve(int newalloc);
};
```

Note how it has the essential operations (§18.3): constructor, default constructor, copy operations, destructor. It has an operation for accessing data (subscripting: []) and for providing information about that data (**size()** and **capacity()**), and for controlling growth (**resize()**, **push_back()**, and **reserve()**).

19.3 Templates

But we don't just want **vector**s of **double**s; we want to freely specify the element type for our **vector**s. For example:

```
vector<double>
vector<int>
vector<Month>
vector<Window*>              // vector of pointers to Windows
vector< vector<Record> >     // vector of vectors of Records
vector<char>
```

To do that, we must see how to define templates. We have used templates from day one, but until now we haven't had a need to define one. The standard library provides what we have needed so far, but we mustn't believe in magic, so we need to examine how the designers and implementers of the standard library provided facilities such as the **vector** type and the **sort()** function (§21.1, §B.5.4). This is not just of theoretical interest, because — as usual — the tools and techniques used for the standard library are among the most useful for our own code. For example, in Chapters 21 and 22, we show how templates can be used for implementing the standard library containers and algorithms. In Chapter 24, we show how to design matrices for scientific computation.

Basically, a *template* is a mechanism that allows a programmer to use types as parameters for a class or a function. The compiler then generates a specific class or function when we later provide specific types as arguments.

19.3.1 Types as template parameters

We want to make the element type a parameter to **vector**. So we take our **vector** and replace **double** with **T** where **T** is a parameter that can be given "values" such as **double**, **int**, **string**, **vector<Record>**, and **Window***. The C++ notation for introducing a type parameter **T** is **template<class T>** prefix, meaning "for all types T." For example:

```
// an almost real vector of Ts:
template<class T> class vector {       // read "for all types T" (just like in math)
    int sz;          // the size
```

```
          T* elem;        // a pointer to the elements
          int space;      // size+free_space
    public:
          vector() : sz(0), elem(0), space(0) { }
          vector(int s);

          vector(const vector&);                  // copy constructor
          vector& operator=(const vector&);       // copy assignment

          ~vector() { delete[] elem; }            // destructor

          T& operator[](int n) { return elem[n]; }   // access: return reference
          const T& operator[](int n) const { return elem[n]; }

          int size() const { return sz; }         // the current size
          int capacity() const { return space; }

          void resize(int newsize);               // growth
          void push_back(const T& d);
          void reserve(int newalloc);
    };
```

That's just our vector of **doubles** from §19.2.6 with **double** replaced by the template parameter **T**. We can use this class template **vector** like this:

```
    vector<double> vd;           // T is double
    vector<int> vi;              // T is int
    vector<double*> vpd;         // T is double*
    vector< vector<int> > vvi;   // T is vector<int>, in which T is int
```

One way of thinking about what a compiler does when we use a template is that it generates the class with the actual type (the template argument) in place of the template parameter. For example, when the compiler sees **vector<char>** in the code, it (somewhere) generates something like this:

```
    class vector_char {
          int sz;         // the size
          char* elem;     // a pointer to the elements
          int space;      // size+free_space
    public:
          vector_char();
          vector_char(int s);
```

```
    vector_char(const vector_char&);            // copy constructor
    vector_char& operator=(const vector_char &); // copy assignment

    ~vector_char ();                            // destructor

    char& operator[] (int n);                   // access: return reference
    const char& operator[] (int n) const;

    int size() const;                           // the current size
    int capacity() const;

    void resize(int newsize);                   // growth
    void push_back(const char& d);
    void reserve(int newalloc);
};
```

For **vector<double>**, the compiler generates roughly the **vector** (of **double**) from
§19.2.6 (using a suitable internal name meaning **vector<double>**).

Sometimes, we call a class template a *type generator*. The process of generating
types (classes) from a class template given template arguments is called *specialization* or *template instantiation*. For example, **vector<char>** and **vector<Poly_line*>** are
said to be specializations of **vector**. In simple cases, such as our **vector**, instantiation is a pretty simple process. In the most general and advanced cases, template
instantiation is horrendously complicated. Fortunately for the user of templates,
that complexity is in the domain of the compiler writer, not the template user.
Template instantiation (generation of template specializations) takes place at compile time or link time, not at run time.

Naturally, we can use member functions of such a class template. For example:

```
    void fct(vector<string>& v)
    {
        int n = v.size();
        v.push_back("Norah");
        // . . .
    }
```

When such a member function of a class template is used, the compiler generates the
appropriate function. For example, when the compiler sees **v.push_back("Norah")**, it
generates a function

```
    void vector<string>::push_back(const string& d) { /* . . . */ }
```

from the template definition

> **template<class T> void vector<T>::push_back(const T& d) { /* . . . */ };**

That way, there is a function for **v.push_back("Norah")** to call. In other words, when you need a function for a given argument type, the compiler will write it for you based on its template.

Instead of writing **template<class T>**, you can write **template<typename T>**. The two constructs mean exactly the same thing, but some prefer **typename** "because it is clearer" and "because nobody gets confused by **typename** thinking that you can't use a built-in type, such as **int**, as a template argument." We are of the opinion that **class** already means type, so it makes no difference. Also, **class** is shorter.

19.3.2 Generic programming

Templates are the basis for generic programming in C++. In fact, the simplest definition of "generic programming" in C++ is "using templates." That definition is a bit too simpleminded, though. We should not define fundamental programming concepts in terms of programming language features. Programming language features exist to support programming techniques — not the other way around. As with most popular notions, there are many definitions of "generic programming." We think that the most useful simple definition is

> *Generic programming:* Writing code that works with a variety of types presented as arguments, as long as those argument types meet specific syntactic and semantic requirements.

For example, the elements of a **vector** must be of a type that we can copy (by copy construction and copy assignment), and in Chapters 20 and 21 we will see templates that require arithmetic operations on their arguments. When what we parameterize is a class, we get a *class template,* what is often called a *parameterized type* or a *parameterized class.* When what we parameterize is a function, we get a *function template,* what is often called a *parameterized function* and sometimes also called an *algorithm.* Thus, generic programming is sometimes referred to as "algorithm-oriented programming"; the focus of the design is more the algorithms than the data types they use.

Since the notion of parameterized types is so central to programming, let's explore the somewhat bewildering terminology a bit further. That way we have a chance not to get too confused when we meet such notions in other contexts.

This form of generic programming relying on explicit template parameters is often called *parametric polymorphism.* In contrast, the polymorphism you get from using class hierarchies and virtual functions is called *ad hoc polymorphism* and that style of programming is called *object-oriented programming* (§14.3–4). The reason that both styles of programming are called *polymorphism* is that each style relies on the programmer to present many versions of a concept by a single interface. *Polymorphism* is Greek for "many shapes," referring to the many different types you can manipulate through a common interface. In the **Shape** examples from Chapters 16–19 we literally accessed many shapes (such as **Text**, **Circle**, and **Polygon**) through the interface defined by **Shape**. When we use **vectors**, we use many **vectors** (such as **vector<int>**, **vector<double>**, and **vector<Shape*>**) through the interface defined by the **vector** template.

There are several differences between object-oriented programming (using class hierarchies and virtual functions) and generic programming (using templates). The most obvious is that the choice of function invoked when you use generic programming is determined by the compiler at compile time, whereas for object-oriented programming, it is not determined until run time. For example:

```
v.push_back(x);     // put x into the vector v
s.draw();           // draw the shape s
```

For **v.push_back(x)** the compiler will determine the element type for **v** and use the appropriate **push_back()**, but for **s.draw()** the compiler will indirectly call some **draw()** function (using **s**'s **vtbl**; see §14.3.1). This gives object-oriented programming a degree of freedom that generic programming lacks, but leaves run-of-the-mill generic programming more regular, easier to understand, and better performing (hence the "ad hoc" and "parametric" labels).

To sum up:

- *Generic programming:* supported by templates, relying on compile-time resolution
- *Object-oriented programming:* supported by class hierarchies and virtual functions, relying on run-time resolution

Combinations of the two are possible and useful. For example:

```
void draw_all(vector<Shape*>& v)
{
    for (int i=0; i<v.size(); ++i) v[i]->draw();
}
```

Here we call a virtual function (**draw()**) on a base class (**Shape**) using a virtual function – that's certainly object-oriented programming. However, we also kept **Shape***s in a **vector**, which is a parameterized type, so we also used (simple) generic programming.

So – assuming you have had your fill of philosophy for now – what do people actually use templates for? For unsurpassed flexibility and performance,

- Use templates where performance is essential (e.g., numerics and hard real time; see Chapters 24 and 25).
- Use templates where flexibility in combining information from several types is essential (e.g., the C++ standard library; see Chapters 20–21).

Templates have many useful properties, such as great flexibility and near-optimal performance, but unfortunately they are not perfect. As usual, the benefits have corresponding weaknesses. For templates, the main problem is that the flexibility and performance come at the cost of poor separation between the "inside" of a template (its definition) and its interface (its declaration). This manifests itself in poor error diagnostics – often spectacularly poor error messages. Sometimes, these error messages come much later in the compilation process than we would prefer.

When compiling a use of a template, the compiler "looks into" the template and also into the template argument types. It does so to get the information to generate optimal code. To have all that information available, current compilers tend to require that a template must be fully defined wherever it is used. That includes all of its member functions and all template functions called from those. Consequently, template writers tend to place template definitions in header files. This is not actually required by the standard, but until improved implementations are widely available, we recommend that you do so for your own templates: place the definition of any template that is to be used in more than one translation unit in a header file.

Initially, write only very simple templates yourself and proceed carefully to gain experience. One useful development technique is to do as we did for **vector**: First develop and test a class using specific types. Once that works, replace the specific types with template parameters. Use template-based libraries, such as the C++ standard library, for generality, type safety, and performance. Chapters 20 and 21 are devoted to the containers and algorithms of the standard library and will give you examples of the use of templates.

19.3.3 Containers and inheritance

There is one kind of combination of object-oriented programming and generic programming that people always try, but it doesn't work: attempting to use a container of objects of a derived class as a container of objects of a base class. For example:

```
vector<Shape> vs;
vector<Circle> vc;
```

```
vs = vc;          // error: vector<Shape> required
void f(vector<Shape>&);
f(vc);            // error: vector<Shape> required
```

But why not? After all, you say, I can convert a **Circle** to a **Shape**! Actually, no, you can't. You can convert a **Circle*** to a **Shape*** and a **Circle&** to a **Shape&**, but we deliberately disabled assignment of **Shape**s, so that you wouldn't have to wonder what would happen if you put a **Circle** with a radius into a **Shape** variable that doesn't have a radius (§14.2.4). What would have happened – had we allowed it – would have been what is called "slicing" and is the class object equivalent to integer truncation (§3.9.2).

So we try again using pointers:

```
vector<Shape*> vps;
vector<Circle*> vpc;
vps = vpc;        // error: vector<Shape*> required
void f(vector<Shape*>&);
f(vpc);           // error: vector<Shape*> required
```

Again, the type system resists; why? Consider what **f()** might do:

```
void f(vector<Shape*>& v)
{
      v.push_back(new Rectangle(Point(0,0),Point(100,100)));
}
```

Obviously, we can put a **Rectangle*** into a **vector<Shape*>**. However, if that **vector<Shape*>** was elsewhere considered to be a **vector<Circle*>**, someone would get a nasty surprise. In particular, had the compiler accepted the example above, what would a **Rectangle*** be doing in **vpc**? Inheritance is a powerful and subtle mechanism and templates do not implicitly extend its reach. There are ways of using templates to express inheritance, but they are beyond the scope of this book. Just remember that "**D** is a **B**" does not imply "**C<D>** is a **C<B>**" for an arbitrary template **C** – and we should value that as a protection against accidental type violations. See also §25.4.4.

19.3.4 Integers as template parameters

Obviously, it is useful to parameterize classes with types. How about parameterizing classes with "other things," such as integer values and string values? Basically, any kind of argument can be useful, but we'll consider only type and integer parameters. Other kinds of parameters are less frequently useful, and C++'s support for other kinds of parameters is such that their use requires quite detailed knowledge of language features.

Consider an example of the most common use of an integer value as a template argument, a container where the number of elements is known at compile time:

```
template<class T, int N> struct array {
        T elem[N];                              // hold elements in member array

        // rely on the default constructors, destructor, and assignment

        T& operator[] (int n);          // access: return reference
        const T& operator[] (int n) const;

        T* data() { return elem; }      // conversion to T*
        const T* data() const { return elem; }

        int size() const { return N; }
};
```

We can use **array** (see also §20.7) like this:

```
array<int,256> gb;        // 256 integers
array<double,6> ad = { 0.0, 1.1, 2.2, 3.3, 4.4, 5.5 };    // note the initializer!
const int max = 1024;

void some_fct(int n)
{
        array<char,max> loc;
        array<char,n> oops;   // error: the value of n not known to compiler
        // . . .
        array<char,max> loc2 = loc;      // make backup copy
        // . . .
        loc = loc2;                      // restore
        // . . .
}
```

Clearly, **array** is very simple – much simpler and less powerful than **vector** – so why would anyone want to use an **array** rather than a **vector**? One answer is "efficiency." We know the size of an **array** at compile time, so the compiler can allocate static memory (for global objects, such as **gb**) and stack memory (for local objects, such as **loc**) rather than using the free store. When we do range checking, the checks can be against constants (the size parameter N). For most programs the efficiency improvement is insignificant, but if you are writing a crucial system component, such as a network driver, even a small difference can matter.

More importantly, some programs simply can't be allowed to use free store. Such programs are typically embedded systems programs and/or safety-critical programs (see Chapter 25). In such programs, **array** gives us many of the advantages of **vector** without violating a critical restriction (no free-store use).

Let's ask the opposite question: not "Why can't we just use **vector**?" but "Why not just use built-in arrays?" As we saw in §18.5, arrays can be rather ill behaved: they don't know their own size, they convert to pointers at the slightest provocation, they don't copy properly; **array** doesn't have those problems. For example:

```
double* p = ad;            // error: no implicit conversion to pointer
double* q = ad.data();     // OK: explicit conversion

template<class C> void printout(const C& c)
{
    for (int i = 0; i<c.size(); ++i) cout << c[i] <<'\n';
}
```

This **printout()** can be called by an **array** as well as a **vector**:

```
printout(ad);         // call with array
vector<int> vi;
// . . .
printout(vi);         // call with vector
```

This is a simple example of generic programming applied to data access. It works because the interface used for **array** and **vector** (**size()** and subscripting) is the same. Chapters 20 and 21 will explore this style of programming in some detail.

19.3.5 Template argument deduction

For a class template, you specify the template arguments when you create an object of some specific class. For example:

```
array<char,1024> buf;      // for buf, T is char and N is 1024
array<double,10> b2;       // for b2, T is double and N is 10
```

For a function template, the compiler usually deduces the template arguments from the function arguments. For example:

```
template<class T, int N> void fill(array<T,N>& b, const T& val)
{
    for (int i = 0; i<N; ++i) b[i] = val;
}
```

```
void f()
{
        fill(buf, 'x');         // for fill(), T is char and N is 1024
                                // because that's what buf has
        fill(b2,0.0);           // for fill(), T is double and N is 10
                                // because that's what b2 has

}
```

Technically, **fill(buf,'x')** is shorthand for **fill<char,1024>(buf,'x')**, and **fill(b2,0)** is shorthand for **fill<double,10>(b2,0)**, but fortunately we don't often have to be that specific. The compiler figures it out for us.

19.3.6 Generalizing vector

When we generalized **vector** from a class "**vector** of **double**" to a template "**vector** of **T**," we didn't review the definitions of **push_back()**, **resize()**, and **reserve()**. We must do that now because as they are defined in §19.2.2 and §19.2.3 they make assumptions that are true for **doubles**, but not true for all types that we'd like to use as **vector** element types:

- How do we handle a **vector<X>** where **X** doesn't have a default value?
- How do we ensure that elements are destroyed when we are finished with them?

Must we solve those problems? We could say, "Don't try to make **vectors** of types without default values" and "Don't use **vectors** for types with destructors in ways that cause problems." For a facility that is aimed at "general use," such restrictions are annoying to users and give the impression that the designer hasn't thought the problem through or doesn't really care about users. Often, such suspicions are correct, but the designers of the standard library didn't leave these warts in place. To mirror the standard library **vector**, we must solve these two problems.

We can handle types without a default by giving the user the option to specify the value to be used when we need a "default value":

template<class T> void vector<T>::resize(int newsize, T def = T());

That is, use **T()** as the default value unless the user says otherwise. For example:

```
vector<double> v1;
v1.resize(100);         // add 100 copies of double(), that is, 0.0
v1.resize(200, 0.0);    // add 100 copies of 0.0 — mentioning 0.0 is redundant
v1.resize(300, 1.0);    // add 100 copies of 1.0
```

```
struct No_default {
    No_default(int);    // the only constructor for No_default
    // . . .
};

vector<No_default> v2(10);       // error: tries to make 10 No_default()s
vector<No_default> v3;
v3.resize(100, No_default(2));   // add 100 copies of No_default(2)
v3.resize(200);                  // error: tries to make 100 No_default()s
```

The destructor problem is harder to address. Basically, we need to deal with something really awkward: a data structure consisting of some initialized data and some uninitialized data. So far, we have gone a long way to avoid uninitialized data and the programming errors that usually accompany it. Now – as implementers of **vector** – we have to face that problem so that we – as users of **vector** – don't have to in our applications.

First, we need to find a way of getting and manipulating uninitialized storage. Fortunately, the standard library provides a class **allocator**, which provides uninitialized memory. A slightly simplified version looks like this:

```
template<class T> class allocator {
public:
    // . . .
    T* allocate(int n);           // allocate space for n objects of type T
    void deallocate(T* p, int n); // deallocate n objects of type T starting at p

    void construct(T* p, const T& v);  // construct a T with the value v in p
    void destroy(T* p);                // destroy the T in p
};
```

Should you need the full story, have a look in *The C++ Programming Language*, **<memory>** (§B.1.1), or the standard. However, what is presented here shows the four fundamental operators that allow us to

- Allocate memory of a size suitable to hold an object of type **T** without initializing
- Construct an object of type **T** in uninitialized space
- Destroy an object of type **T**, thus returning its space to the uninitialized state
- Deallocate uninitialized space of a size suitable for an object of type **T**

Unsurprisingly, an **allocator** is exactly what we need for implementing **vector<T>::reserve()**. We start by giving **vector** an allocator parameter:

```
template<class T, class A = allocator<T> > class vector {
    A alloc;      // use allocate to handle memory for elements
    // . . .
};
```

Except for providing an allocator – and using the standard one by default instead of using **new** – all is as before. As users of **vector**, we can ignore allocators until we find ourselves needing a **vector** that manages memory for its elements in some unusual way. As implementers of **vector** and as students trying to understand fundamental problems and learn fundamental techniques, we must see how a vector can deal with uninitialized memory and present properly constructed objects to its users. The only code affected is **vector** member functions that directly deal with memory, such as **vector<T>::reserve()**:

```
template<class T, class A>
void vector<T,A>::reserve(int newalloc)
{
    if (newalloc<=space) return;        // never decrease allocation
    T* p = alloc.allocate(newalloc);    // allocate new space
    for (int i=0; i<sz; ++i) alloc.construct(&p[i],elem[i]);  // copy
    for (int i=0; i<sz; ++i) alloc.destroy(&elem[i]);         // destroy
    alloc.deallocate(elem,space);       // deallocate old space
    elem = p;
    space = newalloc;
}
```

We move an element to the new space by constructing a copy in uninitialized space and then destroying the original. We can't use assignment because for types such as **string**, assignment assumes that the target area has been initialized.

Given **reserve()**, **vector<T,A>::push_back()** is simple to write:

```
template<class T, class A>
void vector<T,A>::push_back(const T& val)
{
    if (space==0) reserve(8);              // start with space for 8 elements
    else if (sz==space) reserve(2*space);  // get more space
    alloc.construct(&elem[sz],val);        // add val at end
    ++sz;                                  // increase the size
}
```

Similarly, **vector<T,A>::resize()** is not too difficult:

```
template<class T, class A>
void vector<T,A>::resize(int newsize, T val = T())
{
    reserve(newsize);
    for (int i=sz; i<newsize; ++i) alloc.construct(&elem[i],val); // construct
    for (int i = newsize; i<sz; ++i) alloc.destroy(&elem[i]);      // destroy
    sz = newsize;
}
```

Note that because some types do not have a default constructor, we again provide the option to supply a value to be used as an initial value for new elements.

The other new thing here is the destruction of "surplus elements" in the case where we are resizing to a smaller vector. Think of the destructor as turning a typed object into "raw memory."

"Messing with allocators" is pretty advanced stuff, and tricky. Leave it alone until you are ready to become an expert.

19.4 Range checking and exceptions

We look at our **vector** so far and find (with horror?) that access isn't range checked. The implementation of **operator[]** is simply

```
template<class T, class A> T& vector<T,A>::operator[](int n)
{
    return elem[n];
}
```

So, consider:

```
vector<int> v(100);
v[-200] = v[200];       // oops!
int i;
cin>>i;
v[i] = 999;             // maul an arbitrary memory location
```

This code compiles and runs, accessing memory not owned by our **vector**. This could mean big trouble! In a real program, such code is unacceptable. Let's try to improve our **vector** to deal with this problem. The simplest approach would be to add a checked access operation, called **at()**:

```
struct out_of_range { /* . . . */ };        // class used to report range access errors

template<class T, class A = allocator<T> > class vector {
      // . . .
      T& at(int n);                    // checked access
      const T& at(int n) const;        // checked access

      T& operator[](int n);            // unchecked access
      const T& operator[](int n) const; // unchecked access
      // . . .
};

template<class T, class A > T& vector<T,A>::at(int n)
{
      if (n<0 || sz<=n) throw out_of_range();
      return elem[n];
}

template<class T, class A > T& vector<T,A>::operator[](int n)    // as before
{
      return elem[n];
}
```

Given that, we could write

```
void print_some(vector<int>& v)
{
      int i = −1;
      cin >> i;
      while(i!= −1) try {
            cout << "v[" << i << "]==" << v.at(i) << "\n";
      }
      catch(out_of_range) {
            cout << "bad index: " << i << "\n";
      }
}
```

Here, we use **at**() to get range-checked access and we catch **out_of_range** in case of an illegal access.

The general idea is to use subscripting with [] when we know that we have a valid index and **at**() when we might have an out-of-range index.

19.4.1 An aside: design considerations

So far, so good, but why didn't we just add the range check to **operator[]()**? Well, the standard library **vector** provides checked **at()** and unchecked **operator[]()** as shown here. Let's try to explain how that makes some sense. There are basically four arguments:

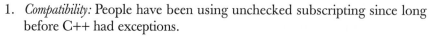

1. *Compatibility:* People have been using unchecked subscripting since long before C++ had exceptions.
2. *Efficiency:* You can build a checked-access operator on top an optimally fast unchecked-access operator, but you cannot build an optimally fast access operator on top of a checked-access operator.
3. *Constraints:* In some environments, exceptions are unacceptable.
4. *Optional checking:* The standard doesn't actually say that you can't range check **vector**, so if you want checking, use an implementation that checks.

19.4.1.1 Compatibility

People really, really don't like to have their old code break. For example, if you have a million lines of code, it could be a very costly affair to rework it all to use exceptions correctly. We can argue that the code would be better for the extra work, but then we are not the ones who have to pay (in time or money). Furthermore, maintainers of existing code usually argue that unchecked code may be unsafe in principle, but their particular code has been tested and used for years and all the bugs have already been found. We can be skeptical about that argument, but again nobody who hasn't had to make such decisions about real code should be too judgmental. Naturally, there was no code using the standard library **vector** before it was introduced into the C++ standard, but there were many millions of lines of code that used very similar **vector**s that (being pre-standard) didn't use exceptions. Much of that code was later modified to use the standard.

19.4.1.2 Efficiency

Yes, range checking can be a burden in extreme cases, such as buffers for network interfaces and matrices in high-performance scientific computations. However, the cost of range checking is rarely a concern in the kind of "ordinary computing" that most of us spend most of our time on. Thus, we recommend and use a range-checked implementation of **vector** whenever we can.

19.4.1.3 Constraints

Again, the argument holds for some programmers and some applications. In fact, it holds for a whole lot of programmers and shouldn't be lightly ignored. However, if you are starting a new program in an environment that doesn't involve hard real time (see §25.2.1), prefer exception-based error handling and range-checked **vector**s.

19.4.1.4 Optional checking

The ISO C++ standard simply states that out-of-range **vector** access is not guaranteed to have any specific semantics, and that such access should be avoided. It is perfectly standards-conforming to throw an exception when a program tries an out-of-range access. So, if you like **vector** to throw and don't need to be concerned by the first three reasons for a particular application, use a range-checked implementation of **vector**. That's what we are doing for this book.

The long and the short of this is that real-world design can be messier than we would prefer, but there are ways of coping.

19.4.2 A confession: macros

Like our **vector**, most implementations of the standard library **vector** don't guarantee to range check the subscript operator ([ ]) but provide **at()** that checks. So where did those **std::out_of_range** exceptions in our programs come from? Basically, we chose "option 4" from §19.4.1: a **vector** implementation is not obliged to range check [ ], but it is not prohibited from doing so either, so we arranged for checking to be done. What you might have been using is our debug version, called **Vector**, which does check [ ]. That's what we use when we develop code. It cuts down on errors and debug time at little cost to performance:

```
struct Range_error : out_of_range {    // enhanced vector range error reporting
    int index;
    Range_error(int i) :out_of_range("Range error"), index(i) { }
};

template<class T> struct Vector : public std::vector<T> {
    typedef typename std::vector<T>::size_type size_type;

    Vector() { }
    Vector(size_type n) :std::vector<T>(n) {}
    Vector(size_type n, const T& v) :std::vector<T>(n,v) {}

    T& operator[](unsigned int i)   // rather than return at(i);
    {
        if (i<0||this->size()<=i) throw Range_error(i);
        return std::vector<T>::operator[](i);
    }

    const T& operator[](unsigned int i) const
    {
        if (i<0||this->size()<=i) throw Range_error(i);
        return std::vector<T>::operator[](i);
    }
};
```

We use **Range_error** to make the offending index available for debugging. The **typedef** introduces a convenient synonym; see §20.5.

This **Vector** is very simple, arguably too simple, but it has been useful in debugging nontrivial programs. The alternative is to use a systematically checked implementation of the complete standard library **vector** – in fact, that *may* indeed be what you have been using; we have no way of knowing exactly what degree of checking your compiler and library provide (beyond what the standard guarantees).

In **std_lib_facilities.h**, we use the nasty trick (a macro substitution) of redefining **vector** to mean **Vector**:

```
// disgusting macro hack to get a range-checked vector:
#define vector Vector
```

That means that whenever you wrote **vector**, the compiler saw **Vector**. This trick is nasty because what you see looking at the code is not what the compiler sees. In real-world code, macros are a significant source of obscure errors (§27.8, §A.17).

We did the same to provide range-checked access for **string**.

Unfortunately, there is no standard, portable, and clean way of getting range checking from an implementation of **vector**'s [ ]. It is, however, possible to do a much cleaner and more complete job of a range-checked **vector** (and **string**) than we did. However, that usually involves replacement of a vendor's standard library implementation, adjusting installation options, or messing with standard library source code. None of those options is appropriate for a beginner's first week of programming – and we used **string** in Chapter 2.

19.5 Resources and exceptions

So, **vector** can throw exceptions, and we recommend that when a function cannot perform its required action, it throws an exception to tell that to its callers (Chapter 5). Now is the time to consider what to do when we write code that must deal with exceptions thrown by **vector** operations and other functions that we call. The naive answer – "Use a **try**-block to catch the exception, write an error message, and then terminate the program" – is too crude for most nontrivial systems.

One of the fundamental principles of programming is that if we acquire a resource, we must – somehow, directly or indirectly – return it to whatever part of the system manages that resource. Examples of resources are

- Memory
- Locks
- Fine handles
- Thread handles
- Sockets
- Windows

Basically, we define a resource as something that is acquired and must be given back (released) or reclaimed by some "resource manager." The simplest example is free-store memory that we acquire using **new** and return to the free store using **delete**. For example:

```
void suspicious(int s, int x)
{
        int* p = new int[s];      // acquire memory
        // . . .
        delete[] p;               // release memory
}
```

As we saw in §17.4.6, we have to remember to release the memory, and that's not always easy to do. When we add exceptions to the picture, resource leaks can become common; all it takes is ignorance or some lack of care. In particular, we view code, such as **suspicious**(), that explicitly uses **new** and assigns the resulting pointer to a local variable with great suspicion.

19.5.1 Potential resource management problems

One reason for suspicion of apparently innocuous pointer assignments such as

```
int* p = new int[s];     // acquire memory
```

is that it can be hard to verify that the **new** has a corresponding **delete**. At least **suspicious**() has a **delete[] p;** statement that might release the memory, but let's imagine a few things that might cause that release not to happen. What could we put in the . . . part to cause a memory leak? The problematic examples we find should give you cause for thought and make you suspicious of such code. They should also make you appreciate the simple and powerful alternative to such code.

Maybe **p** no longer points to the object when we get to the **delete**:

```
void suspicious(int s, int x)
{
        int* p = new int[s];      // acquire memory
        // . . .
        if (x) p = q;             // make p point to another object
        // . . .
        delete[] p;               // release memory
}
```

We put that **if (x)** there to be sure that you couldn't know whether we had changed the value of **p**. Maybe we never get to the **delete**:

```
void suspicious(int s, int x)
{
    int* p = new int[s];      // acquire memory
    // . . .
    if (x) return;
    // . . .
    delete[] p;               // release memory
}
```

Maybe we never get to the **delete** because we threw an exception:

```
void suspicious(int s, int x)
{
    int* p = new int[s];      // acquire memory
    vector<int> v;
    // . . .
    if (x) p[x] = v.at(x);
    // . . .
    delete[] p;               // release memory
}
```

It is this last possibility that concerns us most here. When people first encounter this problem, they tend to consider it a problem with exceptions rather than a resource management problem. Having misclassified the root cause, they come up with a solution that involves catching the exception:

```
void suspicious(int s, int x) // messy code
{
    int* p = new int[s];      // acquire memory
    vector<int> v;
    // . . .
    try {
        if (x) p[x] = v.at(x);
        // . . .
    } catch (...) {           // catch every exception
        delete[] p;           // release memory
        throw;                // re-throw the exception
    }
    // . . .
    delete[] p;               // release memory
}
```

This solves the problem at the cost of some added code and a duplication of the resource release code (here, **delete[] p;**). In other words, this solution is ugly; worse, it doesn't generalize well. Consider acquiring more resources:

```
void suspicious(vector<int>& v, int s)
{
    int* p = new int[s];
    vector<int>v1;
    // . . .
    int* q = new int[s];
    vector<double> v2;
    // . . .
    delete[] p;
    delete[] q;
}
```

Note that if **new** fails to find free-store memory to allocate, it will throw the standard library exception **bad_alloc**. The **try... catch** technique works for this example also, but you'll need several **try**-blocks, and the code is repetitive and ugly. We don't like repetitive and ugly code because "repetitive" translates into code that is a maintenance hazard, and "ugly" translates into code that is hard to get right, hard to read, and a maintenance hazard.

TRY THIS

Add **try**-blocks to this last example to ensure that all resources are properly released in all cases where an exception might be thrown.

19.5.2 Resource acquisition is initialization

Fortunately, we don't need to plaster our code with complicated **try... catch** statements to deal with potential resource leaks. Consider:

```
void f(vector<int>& v, int s)
{
    vector<int> p(s);
    vector<int> q(s);
    // . . .
}
```

This is better. More importantly, it is *obviously* better. The resource (here, free-store memory) is acquired by a constructor and released by the matching destructor.

We actually solved this particular "exception problem" when we solved the memory leak problems for vectors. The solution is general; it applies to all kinds of resources: acquire a resource in the constructor for some object that manages it, and release it again in the matching destructor. Examples of resources that are usually best dealt with in this way include database locks, sockets, and I/O buffers (**iostreams** does it for you). This technique is usually referred to by the awkward phrase "Resource Acquisition Is Initialization," abbreviated to RAII.

Consider the example above. Whichever way we leave **f()**, the destructors for **p** and **q** are invoked appropriately: since **p** and **q** aren't pointers, we can't assign to them, a **return** statement will not prevent the invocation of destructors, and neither will throwing an exception. This general rule holds: when the thread of execution leaves a scope, the destructors for every fully constructed object and sub-object are invoked. An object is considered constructed when its constructor completes. Exploring the detailed implications of those two statements might cause a headache, but they simply mean that constructors and destructors are invoked as needed.

In particular, use **vector** rather than explicit **new** and **delete** when you need a nonconstant amount of storage within a scope.

19.5.3 Guarantees

What can we do where we can't keep the **vector** within a single scope (and its sub-scopes)? For example:

```
vector<int>* make_vec()     // make a filled vector
{
        vector<int>* p = new vector<int>;   // we allocate on free store
        // . . . fill the vector with data; this may throw an exception . . .
        return p;
}
```

This is an example of a common kind of code: we call a function to construct a complicated data structure and return that data structure as the result. The snag is that if an exception is thrown while "filling" the **vector**, **make_vec()** leaks that **vector**. An unrelated problem is that if the function succeeds, someone will have to **delete** the object returned by **make_vec()** (see §17.4.6).

We can add a **try**-block to deal with the possibility of a **throw**:

```
vector<int>* make_vec()     // make a filled vector
{
        vector<int>* p = new vector<int>;   // we allocate on free store
        try {
                // fill the vector with data; this may throw an exception
                return p;
        }
```

```
        catch (...) {
                delete p;        // do our local cleanup
                throw;           // re-throw to allow our caller to deal with the fact
                                 // that some_function() couldn't do what was
                                 // required of it
        }
}
```

This **make_vec()** function illustrates a very common style of error handling: it tries to do its job and if it can't, it cleans up any local resources (here the **vector** on the free store) and indicates failure by throwing an exception. Here, the exception thrown is one that some other function (**vector::at()**) threw; **make_vec()** simply re-throws it using **throw;**. This is a simple and effective way of dealing with errors and can be used systematically.

- *The basic guarantee:* The purpose of the **try ... catch** code is to ensure that **make_vec()** either succeeds or throws an exception without having leaked any resources. That's often called the *basic guarantee*. All code that is part of a program that we expect to recover from an exception **throw** should provide the basic guarantee. All standard library code provides the basic guarantee.

- *The strong guarantee:* If, in addition to providing the basic guarantee, a function also ensures that all observable values (all values not local to the function) are the same after failure as they were when we called the function, that function is said to provide the *strong guarantee*. The strong guarantee is the ideal when we write a function: either the function succeeded at doing everything it was asked to do or else nothing happened except that an exception was thrown to indicate failure.

- *The no-throw guarantee:* Unless we could do simple operations without any risk of failing and throwing an exception, we would not be able to write code to meet the basic guarantee and the strong guarantee. Fortunately, essentially all built-in facilities in C++ provide the no-throw guarantee: they simply can't throw. To avoid throwing, simply avoid **throw** itself, **new**, and **dynamic_cast** of reference types (§A.5.7).

The basic guarantee and the strong guarantee are most useful for thinking about correctness of programs. RAII is essential for implementing code written according to those ideals simply and with high performance. For more detailed information see Appendix E of *The C++ Programming Language*.

Naturally, we should always avoid undefined (and usually disastrous) operations, such as dereferencing 0, dividing by 0, and accessing an array beyond its range. Catching exceptions does not save you from violations of the fundamental language rules.

19.5.4 auto_ptr

So, **make_vec()** is a useful kind of function that obeys the basic rules for good resource management in the presence of exceptions. It provides the basic guarantee – as all good functions should when we want to recover from exception throws. Unless something nasty is done with nonlocal data in the "fill the vector with data" part, it even provides the strong guarantee. However, that **try**... **catch** code is still ugly. The solution is obvious: somehow we must use RAII; that is, we need to provide an object to hold that **vector<int>** so that it can delete the **vector** if an exception occurs. In **<memory>**, the standard library provides the **auto_ptr** for that:

```
vector<int>* make_vec()     // make a filled vector
{
        auto_ptr< vector<int> > p(new vector<int>);     // allocate on free store
        // fill the vector with data; this may throw an exception
        return p.release();       // return the pointer held by p
}
```

An **auto_ptr** is simply an object that holds a pointer for you within a function. We immediately initialize it with the object we got from **new**. You can use **–>** and ***** on an **auto_ptr** exactly like a pointer (e.g., **p–> at(2)** or **(*p).at(2)**), so we think of **auto_ptr** as a kind of pointer. However, don't copy an **auto_ptr** without first reading the **auto_ptr** documentation; the semantics of **auto_ptr** are different from those of every other type you have seen. The **release()** operation tells the **auto_ptr** to give us our ordinary pointer back, so that we can return that pointer and so that the **auto_ptr** doesn't destroy the object pointed to when we return. If you feel tempted to use **auto_ptr** in more interesting ways (e.g., to copy one), resist that temptation. Holding a pointer to guarantee deletion at the end of a scope is what **auto_ptr** is for, and other uses require you to master some rather specialized skills. This **auto_ptr** is a very specialized facility to handle examples like this last version of **make_vec()** simply and efficiently. In particular, **auto_ptr** allows us to repeat our recommendation to look upon explicit **try**-blocks with suspicion; most can be replaced by some variant of the "Resource Acquisition Is Initialization" technique.

19.5.5 RAII for vector

Even using a smart pointer, such as **auto_ptr**, may seem to be a bit ad hoc. How can we be sure that we have spotted all pointers that require protection? How can we be sure that we have released all pointers to objects that should not be destroyed at the end of a scope? Consider **reserve()** from §19.3.5:

```
template<class T, class A>
void vector<T,A>::reserve(int newalloc)
{
        if (newalloc<=space) return;                    // never decrease allocation
        T* p = alloc.allocate(newalloc);                // allocate new space

        for (int i=0; i<sz; ++i) alloc.construct(&p[i],elem[i]);     // copy

        for (int i=0; i<sz; ++i) alloc.destroy(&elem[i]);           // destroy

        alloc.deallocate(elem,space);                   // deallocate old space
        elem = p;
        space = newalloc;
}
```

Note that the copy operation for an old element, **alloc.construct(&p[i],elem[i])**, might throw an exception. So, **p** is an example of the problem we warned about in §19.5.1. Ouch! We could apply the **auto_ptr** solution. A better solution is to step back and realize that "memory for a vector" is a resource; that is, we can define a class **vector_base** to represent the fundamental concept we have been using all the time, the picture with the three elements defining a vector's memory use:

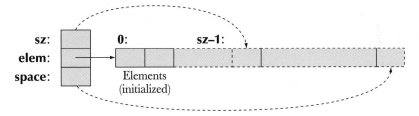

In code, that is (after adding the allocator for completeness)

```
template<class T, class A>
struct vector_base {
        A alloc;        // allocator
        T* elem;        // start of allocation
        int sz;         // number of elements
        int space;      // amount of allocated space

        vector_base(const A& a, int n)
                : alloc(a), elem(a.allocate(n)), sz(n), space(n) { }
        ~vector_base() { alloc.deallocate(elem,space); }
};
```

Note that **vector_base** deals with memory rather than (typed) objects. Our **vector** implementation can use that to hold objects of the desired element type. Basically, **vector** is simply a convenient interface to **vector_base**:

```
template<class T, class A = allocator<T> >
class vector : private vector_base<T,A> {
public:
     // . . .
};
```

We can then rewrite **reserve()** to something simpler and more correct:

```
template<class T, class A>
void vector<T,A>::reserve(int newalloc)
{
     if (newalloc<=space) return;              // never decrease allocation
     vector_base<T,A> b(alloc,newalloc);       // allocate new space
     for (int i=0; i<sz; ++i) alloc.construct(&b.elem[i],elem[i]);    // copy
     for (int i=0; i<sz; ++i) alloc.destroy(&elem[i]);       // destroy old
     swap< vector_base<T,A> >(*this,b);        // swap representations
}
```

When we exit **reserve()**, the old allocation is automatically freed by **vector_base**'s destructor — even if that exit is caused by the copy operation throwing an exception. The **swap()** function is a standard library algorithm (from **<algorithm>**) that exchanges the value of two objects. We used **swap< vector_base<T,A> >(*this,b)** rather than the simpler **swap(*this,b)** because ***this** and **b** are of different types (**vector** and **vector_base**, respectively), so we had to be explicit about which swap specialization we wanted.

TRY THIS

Modify **reserve** to use **auto_ptr**. Remember to release before returning. Compare that solution to the **vector_base** one. Consider which is easier to write and which is easier to get correct.

Drill

1. Define **template<class T> struct S { T val; };**.
2. Add a constructor, so that you can initialize with a **T**.
3. Define variables of types **S<int>**, **S<char>**, **S<double>**, **S<string>**, and **S< vector<int> >**; initialize them with values of your choice.
4. Read those values and print them.
5. Add a function template **get()** that returns a reference to **val**.
6. Put the definition of **get()** outside the class.
7. Make **val** private.
8. Do 4 again using **get()**.
9. Add a **set()** function template so that you can change **val**.
10. Replace **get()** and **set()** with an **operator[ ]**.
11. Provide **const** and non-**const** versions of **operator[]**.
12. Define a function **template<class T> read_val(T& v)** that reads from **cin** into **v**.
13. Use **read_val()** to read into each of the variables from 3 except the **S< vector<int> >** variable.
14. Bonus: Define **template<class T> ostream& operator<<(ostream&, vector<T>&)** so that **read_val()** will also handle the **S< vector<int> >** variable.

Remember to test after each step.

Review

1. Why would we want to change the size of a **vector**?
2. Why would we want to have different element types for different **vectors**?
3. Why don't we just always define a **vector** with a large enough size for all eventualities?
4. How much spare space do we allocate for a new vector?
5. When must we copy **vector** elements to a new location?
6. Which **vector** operations can change the size of a **vector** after construction?
7. What is the value of a **vector** after a copy?
8. Which two operations define copy for **vector**?
9. What is the default meaning of copy for class objects?
10. What is a template?
11. What are the two most useful types of template arguments?
12. What is generic programming?
13. How does generic programming differ from object-oriented programming?

14. How does **array** differ from **vector**?
15. How does **array** differ from the built-in array?
16. How does **resize()** differ from **reserve()**?
17. What is a resource? Define and give examples.
18. What is a resource leak?
19. What is RAII? What problem does it address?
20. What is **auto_ptr** good for?

Terms

#define	macro	specialization
at()	**push_back()**	strong guarantee
auto_ptr	RAII	template
basic guarantee	**resize()**	template parameter
exception	resource	**this**
guarantees	re-throw	**throw;**
instantiation	self-assignment	

Exercises

For each exercise, create and test (with output) a couple of objects of the defined classes to demonstrate that your design and implementation actually do what you think they do. Where exceptions are involved, this can require careful thought about where errors can occur.

1. Write a template function that adds a **vector** of elements of an object of any type to which elements can be added.
2. Write a template function that takes a **vector<T> vt** and a **vector<U> vu** as arguments and returns the sum of all **vt[i]*vu[i]**s.
3. Write a template class **Pair** that can hold a pair of values of any type. Use this to implement a simple symbol table like the one we used in the calculator (§7.8).
4. Modify class **Link** from §17.9.3 to be a template with the type of value as the template argument. Then redo exercise 13 from Chapter 17 with **Link<God>**.
5. Define a class **Int** having a single member of class **int**. Define constructors, assignment, and operators +, −, *, / for it. Test it, and improve its design as needed (e.g., define operators << and >> for convenient I/O).
6. Repeat the previous exercise, but with a class **Number<T>** where **T** can be any numeric type. Try adding % to **Number** and see what happens when you try to use % for **Number<double>** and **Number<int>**.
7. Try your solution to exercise 2 with some **Numbers**.

8. Implement an allocator (§19.3.6) using the basic allocation functions **malloc()** and **free()** (§B.10.4). Get **vector** as defined by the end of §19.4 to work for a few simple test cases.

9. Re-implement **vector::operator=()** (§19.2.5) using an allocator (§19.3.6) for memory management.

10. Implement a simple **auto_ptr** supporting only a constructor, destructor, **->**, *****, and **release()**. In particular, don't try to implement an assignment or a copy constructor.

11. Design and implement a **counted_ptr<T>** that is a type that holds a pointer to an object of type **T** and a pointer to a "use count" (an **int**) shared by all counted pointers to the same object of type **T**. The use count should hold the number of counted pointers pointing to a given **T**. Let the **counted_ptr**'s constructor allocate a **T** object and a use count on the free store. Give the **counted_ptr** an initial value for the **T**. When the last **counted_ptr** for a **T** is destroyed, **counted_ptr**'s destructor should **delete** the **T**. Give the **counted_ptr** operations that allow us to use it as a pointer. This is an example of a "smart pointer" used to ensure that an object doesn't get destroyed until after its last user has stopped using it. Write a set of test cases for **counted_ptr** using it as an argument in calls, container elements, etc.

12. Define a **File_handle** class with a constructor that takes a string argument (the file name), opens the file in the constructor, and closes it in the destructor.

13. Write a **Tracer** class where its constructor prints a string and its destructor prints a string. Give the strings as constructor arguments. Use it to see where RAII management objects will do their job (i.e., experiment with **Tracer**s as local objects, member objects, global objects, objects allocated by **new**, etc.). Then add a copy constructor and a copy assignment so that you can use **Tracer** objects to see when copying is done.

14. Provide a GUI interface and a bit of graphical output to the "Hunt the Wumpus" game from the exercises in Chapter 18. Take the input in an input box and display a map of the part of the cave currently known to the player in a window.

15. Modify the program from the previous exercise to allow the user to mark rooms based on knowledge and guesses, such as "maybe bats" and "bottomless pit."

16. Sometimes, it is desirable that an empty **vector** be as small as possible. For example, someone might use **vector< vector< vector<int> > >** a lot, but have most element vectors empty. Define a vector so that **sizeof(vector<int>)==sizeof(int*)**, that is, so that the **vector** itself consists only of a pointer to a representation consisting of the elements, the number of elements, and the **space** pointer.

Postscript

Templates and exceptions are immensely powerful language features. They support programming techniques of great flexibility — mostly by allowing people to separate concerns, that is, to deal with one problem at a time. For example, using templates, we can define a container, such as **vector**, separately from the definition of an element type. Similarly, using exceptions, we can write the code that detects and signals an error separately from the code that handles that error. The third major theme of this chapter, changing the size of a **vector**, can be seen in a similar light: **push_back()**, **resize()**, and **reserve()** allow us to separate the definition of a **vector** from the specification of its size.

Containers and Iterators

"Write programs that do one thing
and do it well. Write programs
to work together."

—Doug McIlroy

This chapter and the next present the STL, the containers
and algorithms part of the C++ standard library. The STL
is an extensible framework for dealing with data in a C++ program. After a first simple example, we present the general ideals
and the fundamental concepts. We discuss iteration, linked-list
manipulation, and STL containers. The key notions of sequence
and iterator are used to tie containers (data) together with algorithms (processing). This chapter lays the groundwork for the
general, efficient, and useful algorithms presented in the next
chapter. As an example, it also presents a framework for text editing as a sample application.

20.1 Storing and processing data

Before looking into dealing with larger collections of data items, let's consider a simple example that points to ways of handling a large class of data-processing problems. Jack and Jill are each measuring vehicle speeds, which they record as floating-point values. Jack was brought up as a C programmer and stores his values in an array, whereas Jill stores hers in a **vector**. Now we'd like to use their data in our program. How might we do this?

We could have Jack's and Jill's programs write out the values to a file and then read them back into our program. That way, we are completely insulated from their choices of data structures and interfaces. Often, such isolation is a good idea, and if that's what we decide to do we can use the techniques from Chapters 10–11 for input and a **vector<double>** for our calculations.

But, what if using files isn't a good option for the task we want to do? Let's say that the data-gathering code is designed to be invoked as a function call to deliver a new set of data every second. Once a second, we call Jack's and Jill's functions to deliver data for us to process:

```
double* get_from_jack(int* count);   // Jack puts doubles into an array and
                                     // returns the number of elements in *count
vector<double>* get_from_jill();     // Jill fills the vector

void fct()
{
        int jack_count = 0;
        double* jack_data = get_from_jack(&jack_count);
        vector<double>* jill_data = get_from_jill();
        // . . . process . . .
        delete[] jack_data;
        delete jill_data;
}
```

The assumption is that the data is stored on the free store and that we should delete it when we are finished using it. Another assumption is that we can't rewrite Jack's and Jill's code, or wouldn't want to.

20.1.1 Working with data

Clearly, this is a somewhat simplified example, but it is not dissimilar to a vast number of real-world problems. If we can handle this example elegantly, we can handle a huge number of common programming problems. The fundamental problem here is that we don't control the way in which our "data suppliers" store the data they give us. It's our job to either work with the data in the form in which we get it or to read it and store it the way we like better.

What do we want to do with that data? Sort it? Find the highest value? Find the average value? Find every value over 65? Compare Jill's data with Jack's? See how many readings there were? The possibilities are endless, and when writing a real program we will simply do the computation required. Here, we just want to do something to learn how to handle data and do computations involving lots of data. Let's first do something really simple: find the element with the highest value in each data set. We can do that by inserting this code in place of the ". . . process . . ." comment in **fct()**:

```
// . . .
double h = -1;
double* jack_high;    // jack_high will point to the element with the highest value
double* jill_high;    // jill_high will point to the element with the highest value

for (int i=0; i<jack_count; ++i)
    if (h< jack_data[i])
        jack_high = &jack_data [i];    // save address of largest element

h = -1;
for (int i=0; i< jill_data ->size(); ++i)
    if (h<(*jill_data)[i])
        jill_high = &(*jill_data)[i];    // save address of largest element

cout << "Jill's max: " << *jill_high
     << "; Jack's max: " << *jack_high;

// . . .
```

Note the ugly notation we use to access Jill's data: (*jill_data)[i]. The function from_jill() returns a pointer to a **vector**, a **vector<double>***. To get to the data, we first have to dereference the pointer to get to the **vector**, *jill_data, then we can subscript that. However, *jill_data[i] isn't what we want; that means *(jill_data[i]) because [ ] binds tighter than *, so we need the parentheses around *jill_data and get (*jill_data)[i].

TRY THIS

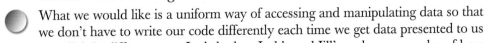

If you were able to change Jill's code, how would you redesign its interface to get rid of the ugliness?

20.1.2 Generalizing code

What we would like is a uniform way of accessing and manipulating data so that we don't have to write our code differently each time we get data presented to us in a slightly different way. Let's look at Jack's and Jill's code as examples of how we can make our code more abstract and uniform.

Obviously, what we do for Jack's data strongly resembles what we do for Jill's. However, there are some annoying differences: **jack_count** vs. **jill_data–>size()** and **jack_data[i]** vs. **(*jill_data)[i]**. We could eliminate the latter difference by introducing a reference:

```
vector<double>& v = *jill_data;
for (int i=0; i<v.size(); ++i)
        if (h<v[i]) jill_high = &v[i];
```

This is tantalizingly close to the code for Jack's data. What would it take to write a function that could do the calculation for Jill's data as well as for Jack's? We can think of several ways (see exercise 3), but for reasons of generality which will become clear over the next two chapters, we chose a solution based on pointers:

```
double* high(double* first, double* last)
// return a pointer to the element in [first,last) that has the highest value
{
        double h = -1;
        double* high;
        for(double* p = first; p!=last; ++p)
                if (h<*p) high = p;
        return high;
}
```

Given that, we can write

```
double* jack_high = high(jack_data,jack_data+jack_count);
vector<double>& v = *jill_data;
double* jill_high = high(&v[0],&v[0]+v.size());
```

This looks better. We don't introduce so many variables and we write the loop and the loop body only once (in **high()**). If we want to know the highest values, we can look at *__jack_high__ and *__jill_high__. For example:

```
cout << "Jill's max: " << *jill_high
     << "; Jack's max: " << *jack_high;
```

Note that **high()** relies on a vector storing its elements in an array, so that we can express our "find highest element" algorithm in terms of pointers into an array.

TRY THIS

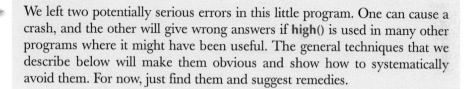

We left two potentially serious errors in this little program. One can cause a crash, and the other will give wrong answers if **high()** is used in many other programs where it might have been useful. The general techniques that we describe below will make them obvious and show how to systematically avoid them. For now, just find them and suggest remedies.

This **high()** function is limited in that it is a solution to a single specific problem:

- It works for arrays only. We rely on the elements of a **vector** being stored in an array, but there are many more ways of storing data, such as lists and maps (see §20.4 and §21.6.1).
- It can be used for **vectors** and arrays of **doubles**, but not for arrays or **vectors** with other element types, such as **vector<double*>** and **char[10]**.
- It finds the element with the highest value, but there are many more simple calculations that we want to do on such data.

Let's explore how we can support this kind of calculation on sets of data in far greater generality.

Please note that by deciding to express our "find highest element" algorithm in terms of pointers, we "accidentally" generalized it to do more than we required: we can — as desired — find the highest element of an array or a **vector**, but we can also find the highest element in part of an array or in part of a **vector**. For example:

```
// . . .
vector<double>& v = *jill_data;
double* middle = &v[0]+v.size()/2;
double* high1 = high(&v[0], middle);           // max of first half
double* high2 = high(middle, &v[0]+v.size());  // max of second half
// . . .
```

Here **high1** will point to the element with the largest value in the first half of the vector and **high2** will point to the element with the largest value in the second half. Graphically, it will look something like this:

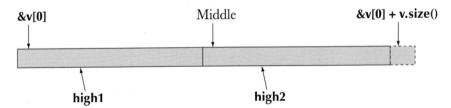

We used pointer arguments for **high()**. That's a bit low-level and can be error-prone. We suspect that for many programmers, the obvious function for finding the element with the largest value in a **vector** would look like this:

```
double* find_highest(vector<double>& v)
{
        double h = -1;
        double* high = 0;
        for (int i=0; i<v.size(); ++i)
                if (h<v[i]) high = &v[i];
        return high;
}
```

However, that wouldn't give us the flexibility we "accidentally" obtained from **high()** – we can't use **find_highest()** to find the element with the highest value in part of a **vector**. We actually achieved a practical benefit from writing a function that could be used for both arrays and **vectors** by "messing with pointers." We will remember that: generalization can lead to functions that are useful for more problems.

20.2 STL ideals

The C++ standard library provides a framework for dealing with data as sequences of elements, called the STL. STL is usually said to be an acronym for "standard template library." The STL is the part of the ISO C++ standard library that provides containers (such as **vector**, **list**, and **map**) and generic algorithms (such as **sort**, **find**, and **accumulate**). Thus we can – and do – refer to facilities, such as **vector**, as being part of both "the STL" and "the standard library." Other standard library features, such as **ostream** (Chapter 10) and C-style string functions (§B.10.3), are not part of the STL. To better appreciate and understand the STL, we will first consider the problems we must address when dealing with data and the ideals we have for a solution.

There are two major aspects of computing: the computation and the data. Sometimes we focus on the computation and talk about if-statements, loops, functions, error handling, etc. At other times, we focus on the data and talk about arrays, vectors, strings, files, etc. However, to get useful work done we need both. A large amount of data is incomprehensible without analysis, visualization, and searching for "the interesting bits." Conversely, we can compute as much as we like, but it's going to be tedious and sterile unless we have some data to tie our computation to something real. Furthermore, the "computation part" of our program has to elegantly interact with the "data part."

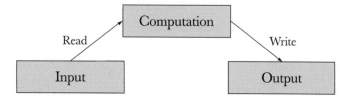

When we talk about data in this way, we think of lots of data: dozens of **Shapes**, hundreds of temperature readings, thousands of log records, millions of points, billions of web pages, etc.; that is, we talk about processing containers of data, streams of data, etc. In particular, this is not a discussion of how best to choose a couple of values to represent a small object, such as a complex number, a temperature reading, or a circle. For such types, see Chapters 9, 11, and 14.

Consider some simple examples of something we'd like to do with "a lot of data":

- Sort the words in dictionary order.
- Find a number in a phone book, given a name.
- Find the highest temperature.
- Find all values larger than 8800.
- Find the first occurrence of the value 17.
- Sort the telemetry records by unit number.
- Sort the telemetry records by time stamp.
- Find the first value larger than "Petersen."
- Find the largest amount.
- Find the first difference between two sequences.
- Compute the pair-wise product of the elements of two sequences.
- Find the highest temperature for each day in a month.
- Find the top ten best sellers in the sales records.
- Count the number of occurrences of "Stroustrup" on the web.
- Compute the sum of the elements.

Note that we can describe each of these tasks without actually mentioning how the data is stored. Clearly, we must be dealing with something like lists, vectors, files, input streams, etc. for these tasks to make sense, but we don't have to know the details about how the data is stored (or gathered) to talk about what to do with it. What is important is the type of the values or objects (the element type), how we access those values or objects, and what we want to do with them.

These kinds of tasks are very common. Naturally, we want to write code performing such tasks simply and efficiently. Conversely, the problems for us as programmers are:

- There is an infinite variation of data types ("kinds of data").
- There is a bewildering number of ways to store collections of data elements.
- There is a huge variety of tasks we'd like to do with collections of data.

To minimize the effect of these problems, we'd like our code to take advantage of commonalities among types, among the ways of storing data, and among our processing tasks. In other words, we want to generalize our code to cope with these kinds of variations. We really don't want to hand-craft each solution from scratch; that would be a tedious waste of time.

To get an idea of what support we would like for writing our code, consider a more abstract view of what we do with data:

- Collect data into containers

  - Such as **vector**, **list**, and array

- Organize data

  - For printing
  - For fast access

- Retrieve data items

  - By index (e.g., the 42nd element)
  - By value (e.g., the first record with the "age field" 7)
  - By properties (e.g., all records with the "temperature field" >32 and <100)

- Modify a container

  - Add data
  - Remove data
  - Sort (according to some criteria)

- Perform simple numeric operations (e.g., multiply all elements by 1.7)

We'd like to do these things without getting sucked into a swamp of details about differences among containers, differences in ways of accessing elements, and differences among element types. If we can do that, we'll have come a long way toward our goal of simple and efficient use of large amounts of data.

Looking back at the programming tools and techniques from the previous chapters, we note that we can (already) write programs that are similar independently of the data type used:

- Using an **int** isn't all that different from using a **double**.
- Using a **vector<int>** isn't all that different from using a **vector<string>**.
- Using an array of **double** isn't all that different from using a **vector<double>**.

We'd like to organize our code so that we have to write new code only when we want to do something really new and different. In particular, we'd like to provide code for common programming tasks so that we don't have to rewrite our solution each time we find a new way of storing the data or find a slightly different way of interpreting the data.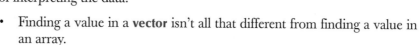

- Finding a value in a **vector** isn't all that different from finding a value in an array.
- Looking for a **string** ignoring case isn't all that different from looking at a **string** considering uppercase letters different from lowercase ones.
- Graphing experimental data with exact values isn't all that different from graphing data with rounded values.
- Copying a file isn't all that different from copying a **vector**.

We want to build on these observations to write code that's

- Easy to read
- Easy to modify
- Regular
- Short
- Fast

To minimize our programming work, we would like

- Uniform access to data
  - Independently of how it is stored
  - Independently of its type

- Type-safe access to data
- Easy traversal of data
- Compact storage of data

- Fast

  - Retrieval of data
  - Addition of data
  - Deletion of data

- Standard versions of the most common algorithms

  - Such as copy, find, search, sort, sum, . . .

The STL provides that, and more. We will look at it not just as a very useful set of facilities, but also as an example of a library designed for maximal flexibility and performance. The STL was designed by Alex Stepanov to provide a framework for general, correct, and efficient algorithms operating on data structures. The ideal was the simplicity, generality, and elegance of mathematics.

The alternative to dealing with data using a framework with clearly articulated ideals and principles is for each programmer to craft each program out of the basic language facilities using whatever ideas seem good at the time. That's a lot of extra work. Furthermore, the result is often an unprincipled mess; rarely is the result a program that is easily understood by people other than its original designer, and only by chance is the result code that we can use in other contexts.

Having considered the motivation and the ideals, let's look at the basic definitions of the STL, and then finally get to the examples that'll show us how to approximate those ideals — to write better code for dealing with data and to do so with greater ease.

20.3 Sequences and iterators

The central concept of the STL is the sequence. From the STL point of view, a collection of data is a sequence. A sequence has a beginning and an end. We can traverse a sequence from its beginning to its end, optionally reading or writing the value of each element. We identify the beginning and the end of a sequence by a pair of iterators. An *iterator* is an object that identifies an element of a sequence. We can think of a sequence like this:

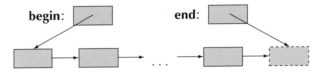

Here, **begin** and **end** are iterators; they identify the beginning and the end of the sequence. An STL sequence is what is usually called "half-open"; that is, the element identified by **begin** is part of the sequence, but the **end** iterator points one beyond the end of the sequence. The usual mathematical notation for such sequences (ranges) is [begin:end). The arrows from one element to the next indicate that if we have an iterator to one element we can get an iterator to the next.

What is an iterator? An iterator is a rather abstract notion:

- An iterator points to (refers to) an element of a sequence (or one beyond the last element).
- You can compare two iterators using == and !=.
- You can refer to the value of the element pointed to by an iterator using the unary * operator ("dereference" or "contents of").
- You can get an iterator to the next element by using ++.

For example, if **p** and **q** are iterators to elements of the same sequence:

Basic standard iterator operations	
p==q	true if and only if **p** and **q** point to the same element or both point to one beyond the last element
p!=q	!(p==q)
***p**	refers to the element pointed to by **p**
***p=val**	writes to the element pointed to by **p**
val=*p	reads from the element pointed to by **p**
++p	makes **p** refer to the next element in the sequence or to one beyond the last element

Clearly, the idea of an iterator is related to the idea of a pointer (§17.4). In fact, a pointer to an element of an array is an iterator. However, many iterators are not just pointers; for example, we could define a range-checked iterator that throws an exception if you try to make it point outside its [**begin:end**) sequence or tries to dereference **end**. It turns out that we get enormous flexibility and generality from having iterator as an abstract notion rather than as a specific type. This chapter and the next will give several examples.

TRY THIS

Write a function **void copy(int* f1, int* e1, int* f2)** that copies the elements of an array of **ints** defined by [**f1:e1**) into another [**f2:f2+(e1–f1)**). Use only the iterator operations mentioned above (not subscripting).

Iterators are used to connect our code (algorithms) to our data. The writer of the code knows about the iterators (and not about the details of how the iterators actually get to the data), and the data provider supplies iterators rather than exposing details about how the data is stored to all users. The result is pleasingly simple and offers an important degree of independence between algorithms and containers. To quote Alex Stepanov: "The reason STL algorithms and containers work so well together is that they don't know anything about each other." Instead, both understand about sequences defined by pairs of iterators.

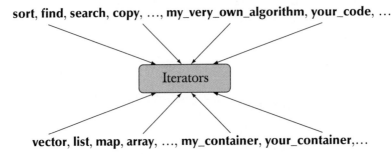

In other words, my code no longer has to know about the bewildering variety of ways of storing and accessing data; it just has to know about iterators. Conversely, if I'm a data provider, I no longer have to write code to serve a bewildering variety of users; I just have to implement an iterator for my data. At the most basic level, an iterator is defined by just the *, ++, ==, and != operators. That makes them simple and fast.

The STL framework consists of about ten containers and about 60 algorithms connected by iterators (see Chapter 21). In addition, many organizations and individuals provide containers and algorithms in the style of the STL. The STL is probably the currently best-known and most widely used example of generic programming (§19.3.2). If you know the basic concepts and a few examples, you can use the rest.

20.3.1 Back to the example

Let's see how we can express the "find the element with the largest value" problem using the STL notion of a sequence:

```
template<class Iterator >
Iterator high(Iterator first, Iterator last)
// return an iterator to the element in [first:last) that has the highest value
{
        Iterator high = first;
        for (Iterator p = first; p!=last; ++p)
            if (*high<*p) high = p;
        return high;
}
```

Note that we eliminated the local variable **h** that we had used to hold the highest value seen so far. When we don't know the name of the actual type of the elements of the sequence, the initialization by −**1** seems completely arbitrary and odd. That's because it was arbitrary and odd! It was also an error waiting to happen: in our example −**1** worked only because we happened not to have any negative velocities. We knew that "magic constants," such as −**1**, are bad for code maintenance (§4.3.1, §7.6.1, §10.11.1, etc.). Here, we see that they can also limit the utility of a function and can be a sign of incomplete thought about the solution; that is, "magic constants" can be − and often are − a sign of sloppy thinking.

Note that this "generic" **high()** can be used for any element type that can be compared using **<**. For example, we could use **high()** to find the lexicographically last string in a **vector<string>** (see exercise 7).

The **high()** template function can be used for any sequence defined by a pair of iterators. For example, we can exactly replicate our example program:

```
double* get_from_jack(int* count);   // Jack puts doubles into an array and
                                     // returns the number of elements in *count
vector<double>* get_from_jill();     // Jill fills the vector

void fct()
{
      int jack_count = 0;
      double* jack_data = get_from_jack(&jack_count);
      vector<double>* jill_data = get_from_jill();

      double* jack_high = high(jack_data,jack_data+jack_count);
      vector<double>& v = *jill_data;
      double* jill_high = high(&v[0],&v[0]+v.size());
      cout << "Jill's high " << *jill_high << "; Jack's high " << *jack_high;
      // . . .
      delete[] jack_data;
      delete jill_data;
}
```

For the two calls here, the **Iterator** template argument type for **high()** is **double***. Apart from (finally) getting the code for **high()** correct, there is apparently no difference from our previous solution. To be precise, there is no difference in the code that is executed, but there is a most important difference in the generality of our code. The templated version of **high()** can be used for every kind of sequence that can be described by a pair of iterators. Before looking at the detailed conventions of the STL and the useful standard algorithms that it provides to save us from writing common tricky code, let's consider a couple of more ways of storing collections of data elements.

TRY THIS

We again left a serious error in that program. Find it, fix it, and suggest a general remedy for that kind of problem.

20.4 Linked lists

 Consider again the graphical representation of the notion of a sequence:

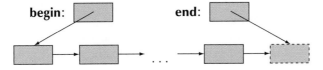

Compare it to the way we visualize a **vector** in memory:

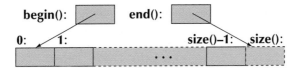

Basically, the subscript **0** identifies the same element as does the iterator **v.begin()**, and the subscript **v.size()** identifies the one-beyond-the-last element also identified by the iterator **v.end()**.

    The elements of the **vector** are consecutive in memory. That's not required by STL's notion of a sequence, and it so happens that there are many algorithms where we would like to insert an element in between two existing elements without moving those existing elements. The graphical representation of the abstract notion suggests the possibility of inserting elements (and of deleting elements) without moving other elements. The STL notion of iterators supports that.

    The data structure most directly suggested by the STL sequence diagram is called a *linked list*. The arrows in the abstract model are usually implemented as pointers. An element of a linked list is part of a "link" consisting of the element and one or more pointers. A linked list where a link has just one pointer (to the next link) is called a *singly-linked list* and a list where a link has pointers to both the previous and the next link is called a *doubly-linked list*. We will sketch the implementation of a doubly-linked list, which is what the C++ standard library provides under the name of **list**. Graphically, it can be represented like this:

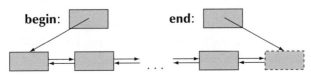

This can be represented in code as

```
template<class Elem> struct Link {
    Link* prev;    // previous link
    Link* succ;    // successor (next) link
    Elem val;      // the value
};

template<class Elem> struct list {
    Link<Elem>* first;
    Link<Elem>* last;    // one beyond the last link
};
```

The layout of a **Link** is

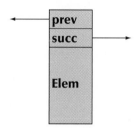

There are many ways of implementing linked lists and presenting them to users. A description of the standard library version can be found in Appendix B. Here, we'll just outline the key properties of a list – you can insert and delete elements without disturbing existing elements – show how we can iterate over a list, and give an example of list use.

When you try to think about lists, we strongly encourage you to draw little diagrams to visualize the operations you are considering. Linked-list manipulation really is a topic where a picture is worth 1K words.

20.4.1 List operations

What operations do we need for a list?

- The operations we have for **vector** (constructors, size, etc.), except subscripting
- Insert (add an element) and erase (remove an element)
- Something that can be used to refer to elements and to traverse the list: an iterator

In the STL, that iterator type is a member of its class, so we'll do the same:

```
template<class Elem> class list {
    // representation and implementation details
public:
    class iterator;        // member type: iterator

    iterator begin();      // iterator to first element
    iterator end( );       // iterator to one beyond last element

    iterator insert(iterator p, const Elem& v); // insert v into list after p
    iterator erase(iterator p);                  // remove p from the list

    void push_back(const Elem& v);       // insert v at end
    void push_front(const Elem& v);      // insert v at front
    void pop_front();      // remove the first element
    void pop_back();       // remove the last element

    Elem& front();         // the first element
    Elem& back();          // the last element

    // . . .
};
```

Just as "our" **vector** is not the complete standard library **vector**, this **list** is not the complete definition of the standard library **list**. There is nothing wrong with this **list**; it simply isn't complete. The purpose of "our" **list** is to convey an understanding of what linked lists are, how a **list** might be implemented, and how to use the key features. For more information see Appendix B or an expert-level C++ book.

The iterator is central in the definition of an STL **list**. Iterators are used to identify places for insertion and elements for removal (erasure). They are also used for "navigating" through a list rather than using subscripting. This use of iterators is very similar to the way we used pointers to traverse arrays and vectors in §20.1 and §20.3.1. This style of iterators is the key to the standard library algorithms (§21.1–3).

Why not subscripting for **list**? We could subscript a list, but it would be a surprisingly slow operation: **lst[1000]** would involve starting from the first element and then visiting each link along the way until we reached element number **1000**. If we want to do that, we can do it ourselves (or use **advance()**; see §20.6.2). Consequently, the standard library **list** doesn't provide the innocuous-looking subscript syntax.

We made **list**'s iterator type a member (a nested class) because there was no reason for it to be global. It is used only with **lists**. Also, this allows us to name every container's iterator type **iterator**. In the standard library, we have **list<T>::iterator**, **vector<T>::iterator**, **map<K,V>::iterator**, and so on.

20.4.2 Iteration

The list iterator must provide *, ++, ==, and !=. Since the standard library list is a doubly-linked list, it also provides –– for iterating "backward" toward the front of the list:

```
template<class Elem> class list<Elem>::iterator {
      Link<Elem>* curr;        // current link
public:
      iterator(Link* p) :curr(p) { }

      iterator& operator++() {curr = curr->succ; return *this; } // forward
      iterator& operator--() { curr = curr->prev; return *this; } // backward
      Elem& operator*() { return val; } // get value (dereference)

      bool operator==(const iterator& b) const { return curr==b.curr; }
      bool operator!= (const iterator& b) const { return curr!=b.curr; }
};
```

These functions are short and simple, and obviously efficient: there are no loops, no complicated expressions, and no "suspicious" function calls. If the implementation isn't clear to you, just have a quick look at the diagrams above. This **list** iterator is just a pointer to a link with the required operations. Note that even though the implementation (the code) for a **list<Elem>::iterator** is very different from the simple pointer we have used as an iterator for **vectors** and arrays, the meaning (the semantics) of the operations is identical. Basically, the **List iterator** provides suitable ++, ––, *, ==, and != for a **Link** pointer.

    Now look at **high()** again:

```
template<class Iterator >
Iterator high(Iterator first, Iterator last)
// return an iterator to the element in [first,last) that has the highest value
{
      Iterator high = first;
      for (Iterator p = first; p!=last; ++p)
            if (*high<*p) high = p;
      return high;
}
```

We can use it for a **list**:

```
void f()
{
      list<int> lst;
```

```
        int x;
        while (cin >> x) lst.push_front(x);

        list<int>::iterator p = high(lst.begin(), lst.end());
        cout << "the highest value was " << *p << endl;
    }
```

Here, the "value" of the **Iterator** argument is **list<int>::iterator**, and the implementation of **++**, *****, and **!=** has changed dramatically from the array case, but the
meaning is still the same. The template function **high()** still traverses the data
(here a **list**) and finds the highest value. We can insert an element anywhere in a
list, so we used **push_front()** to add elements at the front just to show that we
could. We could equally well have used **push_back()** as we do for **vectors**.

TRY THIS

> The standard library **vector** doesn't provide **push_front()**. Why not? Imple-
> ment **push_front()** for **vector** and compare it to **push_back()**.

Now, finally, is the time to ask, "But what if the **list** is empty?" In other words,
"What if **lst.begin()==lst.end()**?" In that case, ***p** will be an attempt to dereference the one-beyond-the-last element, **lst.end()**: disaster! Or – potentially worse
– the result could be a random value that might be mistaken for a correct answer.

The last formulation of the question strongly hints at the solution: we can
test whether a list is empty by comparing **begin()** and **end()** – in fact, we can test
whether any STL sequence is empty by comparing its beginning and end:

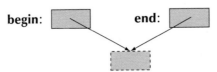

That's the deeper reason for having **end** point one beyond the last element rather
than at the last element: the empty sequence is not a special case. We dislike special cases because – by definition – we have to remember to write special-case
code for them.

In our example, we could use that like this:

```
        list<int>::iterator p = high(lst.begin(), lst.end());
        if (p==lst.end())        // did we reach the end?
                cout << "The list is empty";
        else
                cout << "the highest value is " << *p << endl;
```

We use this kind of test systematically with STL algorithms.

Because the standard library provides a list, we won't go further into the implementation here. Instead, we'll have a brief look at what lists are good for (see exercises 12–14 if you are interested in list implementation details).

20.5 Generalizing vector yet again

Obviously, from the examples in §20.3–4, the standard library vector has an **iterator** member type and **begin()** and **end()** member functions (just like **std::list**). However, we did not provide those for our **vector** in Chapter 19. What does it really take for different containers to be used more or less interchangeably in the STL generic programming style presented in §20.3? First, we'll outline the solution (ignoring allocators to simplify) and then explain it:

```
template<class T> class vector {
public:
        typedef unsigned long size_type;
        typedef T value_type;
        typedef T* iterator;
        typedef const T* const_iterator;

        // . . .

        iterator begin();
        const_iterator begin() const;
        iterator end();
        const_iterator end() const;

        size_type size();

        // . . .
};
```

A **typedef** creates an alias for a type; that is, for our **vector**, **iterator** is a synonym, another name, for the type we chose to use as our iterator: **T***. Now, for a **vector** called **v**, we can write

```
vector<int>::iterator p = find(v.begin(), v.end(),32);
```

and

```
for (vector<int>::size_type i = 0; i<v.size(); ++i) cout << v[i] << '\n';
```

The point is that to write that, we don't actually have to know what types are named by **iterator** and **size_type**. In particular, the code above, because it is expressed in terms of **iterator** and **size_type**, will work with **vectors** where **size_type** is not an **unsigned long** (as it is not on many embedded systems processors) and where **iterator** is not a plain pointer, but a class (as it is on many popular C++ implementations).

The standard defines **list** and the other standard containers similarly. For example:

```
template<class Elem> class list {
public:
        class Link;
        typedef unsigned long size_type;
        typedef Elem value_type;
        class iterator;     // see §20.4.2
        class const_iterator;     // like iterator,
                                  // but not allowing writes to elements

        // . . .

        iterator begin();
        const_iterator begin() const;
        iterator end();
        const_iterator end() const;

        size_type size();

        // . . .
};
```

That way, we can write code that does not care whether it uses a **list** or a **vector**. All the standard library algorithms are defined in terms of these member type names, such as **iterator** and **size_type**, so that they don't unnecessarily depend on the implementations of containers or exactly which kind of container they operate on (see Chapter 21).

20.6 An example: a simple text editor

The essential feature of a list is that you can add and remove elements without moving other elements of the list. Let's try a simple example that illustrates that. Consider how to represent the characters of a text document in a simple text editor. The representation should make operations on the document simple and reasonably efficient.

Which operations? Let's assume that a document will fit in your computer's main memory. That way, we can choose any representation that suits us and simply convert it to a stream of bytes when we want to store it in a file. Similarly, we can read a stream of bytes from a file and convert those to our in-memory representation. That decided, we can concentrate on choosing a convenient in-memory representation. Basically, there are five things that our representation must support well:

- Constructing it from a stream of bytes from input
- Inserting one or more characters
- Deleting one or more characters
- Searching for a string
- Generating a stream of bytes for output to a file or a screen

The simplest representation would be a **vector<char>**. However, to add or delete a character we would have to move every following character in the document. Consider:

> **This is he start of a very long document.**
> **There are lots of . . .**

We could add the **t** needed to get

> **This is the start of a very long document.**
> **There are lots of . . .**

However, if those characters were stored in a single **vector<char>**, we'd have to move every character from **h** onward one position to the right. That could be a lot of copying. In fact, for a 70,000-character-long document (such as this chapter, counting spaces), we would on average have to move 35,000 characters to insert or delete a character. The resulting real-time delay is likely to be noticeable and annoying to users. Consequently, we "break down" our representation into "chunks" so that we can change part of the document without moving a lot of characters around. We represent a document as a list of "lines," **list<Line>**, where a **Line** is a **vector<char>**. For example:

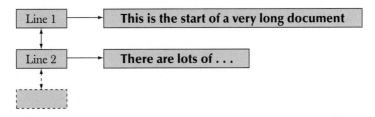

Now, when we inserted that **t**, we only had to move the rest of the characters on that line. Furthermore, when we need to, we can add a new line without moving any characters. For example, we could insert **"This is a new line."** after **"document."** to get

> **This is the start of a very long document.**
> **This is a new line.**
> **There are lots of . . .**

All we needed to do was to insert a new "line" in the middle:

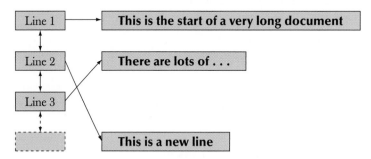

The logical reason that it is important to be able to insert new links in a list without moving existing links is that we might have iterators pointing to those links or pointers (and references) pointing to the objects in those links. Such iterators and pointers are unaffected by insertions or deletions of lines. For example, a word processor may keep a **vector<list<Line>::iterator>** holding iterators to the beginning of every title and subtitle in the current **Document**:

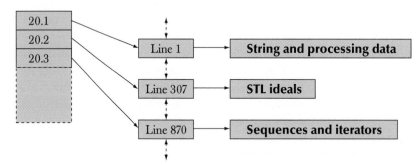

We can add lines to "paragraph 20.2" without invalidating the iterator to "paragraph 20.3."

In conclusion, we use a **list** of lines rather than a **vector** of lines or a **vector** of all the characters for both logical and performance reasons. Please note that situations where these reasons apply are rather rare so that the "by default, use **vector**" rule of thumb still holds. You need a specific reason to prefer a **list** over a **vector** – even if you think of your data as a list of elements! (See §20.7.) A list is a logical concept that you can represent in your program as a (linked) **list** or as a **vector**. The closest STL analog to our everyday concept of a list (e.g., a to-do list, a list of groceries, or a schedule) is a sequence, and most sequences are best represented as **vectors**.

20.6.1 Lines

How do we decide what's a "line" in our document? There are three obvious choices:

1. Rely on newline indicators (e.g., '\n') in user input.
2. Somehow parse the document and use some "natural" punctuation (e.g., .).
3. Split any line that grows beyond a given length (e.g., 50 characters) into two.

There are undoubtedly also some less obvious choices. For simplicity, we use alternative 1 here.

We will represent a document in our editor as an object of class **Document**. Stripped of all refinements, our document type looks like this:

```
typedef vector<char> Line;     // a line is a vector of characters

struct Document {
    list<Line> line;     // a document is a list of lines
                         // line[i] is the ith line
    Document() { line.push_back(Line()); }
};
```

Every **Document** starts out with a single empty line: **Document**'s constructor makes an empty line and pushes it into the list of lines.

Reading and splitting into lines can be done like this:

```
istream& operator>>(istream& is, Document& d)
{
    char ch;
    while (is>>ch) {
        d.line.back().push_back(ch);     // add the character
        if (ch=='\n')
            d.line.push_back(Line());     // add another line
    }
    return is;
}
```

Both **vector** and **list** have a member function **back()** that returns a reference to the last element. To use it, you have to be sure that there really is a last element for **back()** to refer to – don't use it on an empty container. That's why we defined an empty **Document** to have one empty **Line**. Note that we store every character from input, even the newline characters ('**\n**'). Storing those newline characters greatly simplifies output, but you have to be careful how you define a character count (just counting characters will give a number that includes space and newline characters).

20.6.2 Iteration

If the document was just a **vector<char>** it would be simple to iterate over it. How do we iterate over a list of lines? Obviously, we can iterate over the list using **list<Line>::iterator**. However, what if we wanted to visit the characters one after another without any fuss about line breaks? We could provide an iterator specifically designed for our **Document**:

```
class Text_iterator {    // keep track of line and character position within a line
    list<Line>::iterator ln;
    Line::iterator pos;
public:
    // start the iterator at line ll's character position pp:
    Text_iterator(list<Line>::iterator ll, Line::iterator pp)
        :ln(ll), pos(pp) { }

    char& operator*() { return *pos; }
    Text_iterator& operator++();

    bool operator==(const Text_iterator& other) const
        { return ln==other.ln && pos==other.pos; }
    bool operator!=(const Text_iterator& other) const
        { return !(*this==other); }
};

Text_iterator& Text_iterator::operator++()
{
    if (pos==(*ln).end()) {
        ++ln;                      // proceed to next line
        pos = (*ln).begin();
    }
    ++pos;                         // proceed to next character
    return *this;
}
```

As we have seen (§17.2, §18.5), arrays are useful and necessary for dealing with memory at the lowest possible level and for interfacing with code written in C (§27.1.2, §27.5). Apart from that, **vector** is preferred because it is easier to use, more flexible, and safer.

TRY THIS

What does that list of differences mean in real code? For each array of **char**, **vector<char>**, **list<char>**, and **string**, define one with the value "Hello", pass it to a function as an argument, write out the number of characters in the string passed, try to compare it to "Hello" in that function (to see if you really did pass "Hello"), and compare the argument to "Howdy" to see which would come first in a dictionary. Copy the argument into another variable of the same type.

TRY THIS

Do the previous **Try this** for an array of **int**, **vector<int>**, and **list<int>** each with the value { 1, 2, 3, 4, 5 }.

20.7.1 insert and erase

The standard library **vector** is our default choice for a container. It has most of the desired features, so we use alternatives only if we have to. Its main problem is its habit of moving elements when we do list operations (**insert()** and **erase()**); that can be costly when we deal with **vectors** with many elements or **vectors** of large elements. Don't be too worried about that, though. We have been quite happy reading half a million floating-point values into a vector using **push_back()** – measurements confirmed that pre-allocation didn't make a noticeable difference. Always measure before making significant changes in the interest of performance; even for experts, guessing about performance is very hard.

As pointed out in §20.6, moving elements also implies a logical constraint: don't hold iterators or pointers to elements of a **vector** when you do list operations (such as **insert()**, **erase()**, and **push_back()**): if an element moves, your iterator or pointer will point to the wrong element or to no element at all. This is the principal advantage of **lists** (and **maps**; see §21.6) over **vectors**. If you need a collection of large objects or of objects that you point to from many places in a program, consider using a **list**.

Let's compare **insert()** and **erase()** for a **vector** and a **list**: First we take an example designed only to illustrate the key points:

```
vector<int>::iterator p = v.begin();      // take a vector
++p; ++p; ++p;                            // point to its 3rd element
vector<int>::iterator q = p;
++q;                                      // point to its 4th element
```

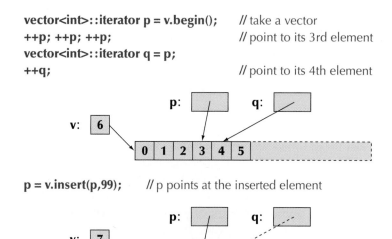

```
p = v.insert(p,99);      // p points at the inserted element
```

Note that **q** is now invalid. The elements may have been reallocated as the size of the vector grew. If **v** had spare capacity, so that it grew in place, **q** most likely points to the element with the value **3** rather than the element with the value **4**, but don't try to take advantage of that.

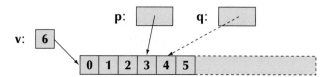

```
p = v.erase(p);          // p points at the element after the erased one
```

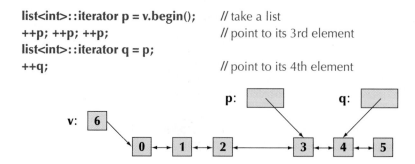

That is, an **insert()** followed by an **erase()** of the inserted element leaves us back where we started, but with **q** invalidated. However, in between, we moved all the elements after the insertion point, and maybe all elements were relocated as **v** grew.

To compare, we'll do exactly the same with a **list**:

```
list<int>::iterator p = v.begin();        // take a list
++p; ++p; ++p;                            // point to its 3rd element
list<int>::iterator q = p;
++q;                                      // point to its 4th element
```

p = v.insert(p,99);   // p points at the inserted element

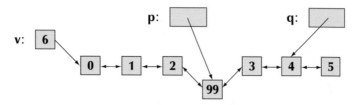

Note that **q** still points to the element with the value **4**.

p = v.erase(p);   // p points at the element after the erased one

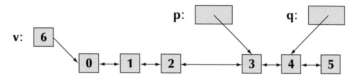

Again we find ourselves back where we started. However, for **list** as opposed to for **vector**, we didn't move any elements and **q** was valid at all times.

A **list<char>** takes up at least three times as much memory as the other three alternatives – on a PC a **list<char>** uses 12 bytes per element; a **vector<char>** uses 1 byte per element. For large numbers of characters, that can be significant.

In what way is a **vector** superior to a **string**? Looking at the lists of their properties, it seems that a **string** can do all that a **vector** can, and more. That's part of the problem: since **string** has to do more things, it is harder to optimize. In fact, **vector** tends to be optimized for "memory operations" such as **push_back()**, whereas **string** tends not to be. Instead, **string** tends to be optimized for handling of copying, for dealing with short strings, and for interaction with C-style strings. In the text editor example, we chose **vector** because we were using **insert()** and **delete()**. That is a performance reason, though. The major logical difference is that you can have a **vector** of just about any element type. We have a choice only when we are thinking about characters. In conclusion, prefer **vector** to **string** unless you need string operations, such as concatenation or reading whitespace-separated words.

20.8 Adapting our vector to the STL

After adding **begin()**, **end()**, and the **typedefs** in §20.5, **vector** now just lacks **insert()** and **erase()** to be as close an approximation of **std::vector** as we need it to be:

```
template<class T, class A = allocator<T> > class vector {
    int sz;        // the size
    T* elem;       // a pointer to the elements
```

```
    int space;      // number of elements plus number of free space "slots"
    A alloc;        // use allocate to handle memory for elements
public:
    // . . . all the other stuff from Chapter 19 and §20.5 . . .
    typedef T* iterator;    // Elem* is the simplest possible iterator

    iterator insert(iterator p, const T& val);
    iterator erase(iterator p);
};
```

We again used a pointer to the element type, **T***, as the iterator type. That's the simplest possible solution. We left providing a range-checked iterator as an exercise (exercise 18).

Typically, people don't provide list operations, such as **insert()** and **erase()**, for data types that keep their elements in contiguous storage, such as **vector**. However, list operations, such as **insert()** and **erase()**, are immensely useful and surprisingly efficient for short **vectors** or small numbers of elements. We have repeatedly seen the usefulness of **push_back()**, which is another operation traditionally associated with lists.

Basically, we implement **vector<T>::erase()** by copying all elements after the element we erase (remove, delete). Using the definition of **vector** from §19.3.6 with the additions above, we get

```
template<class T, class A>
vector<T,A>::iterator vector<T,A>::erase(iterator p)
{
    if (p==end()) return p;
    for (iterator pos = p+1; pos!=end(); ++pos)
        *(pos−1) = *pos;        // copy element "one position to the left"
    alloc.destroy(&*pos);       // destroy surplus copy of last element
    −−sz;
    return p;
}
```

It is easier to understand such code if you look at a graphical representation:

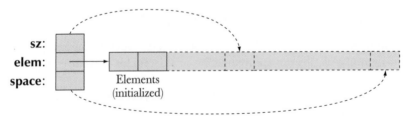

The code for **erase()** is quite simple, but it may be a good idea to try out a couple of examples by drawing them on paper. Is the empty **vector** correctly handled? Why do we need the **p==end()** test? What if we erased the last element of a **vector**? Would this code have been easier to read if we had used the subscript notation?

Implementing **vector<T,A>::insert()** is a bit more complicated:

```
template<class T, class A>
vector<T,A>::iterator vector<T,A>::insert(iterator p, const T& val)
{
        int index = p−begin();
        if (size()==capacity()) reserve(2*size());    // make sure we have space

        // first copy last element into uninitialized space:
        alloc.construct(elem+sz,*back());
        ++sz;
        iterator pp = begin()+index;        // the place to put val
        for (iterator pos = end()−1; pos!=pp; −−pos)
                *pos = *(pos−1);        // copy elements one position to the right
        *(begin()+offset) = val;    // "insert" val
        return pos;
}
```

Please note:

- An iterator may not point outside its sequence, so we use pointers, such as **elem+space**, for that. That's one reason that allocators are defined in terms of pointers and not iterators.

- When we use **reserve()**, the elements may be moved to a new area of memory. Therefore, we must remember the index of the element to be erased, rather than the iterator to it. When **vector** reallocates its elements, iterators into that **vector** become invalid – you can think of them as pointing to the old memory.

- Our use of the allocator argument, **A**, is intuitive, but inaccurate. If you should ever need to implement a container, you'll have to do some careful reading of the standard.

- It is subtleties like these that make us avoid dealing with low-level memory issues whenever we can. Naturally, the standard library **vector** – and all other standard library containers – get that kind of important semantic detail right. That's one reason to prefer the standard library over "home brew."

For performance reasons, you wouldn't use **insert()** and **erase()** in the middle of a 100,000-element **vector**; for that, **lists** (and **maps**; see §21.6) are better. However, the insert() and erase() operations are available for all **vectors**, and their performance is unbeatable when you are just moving a few words of data – or even a few dozen words – because modern computers are really good at this kind of copying; see exercise 20. Avoid (linked) **lists** for representing a list of a few small elements.

20.9 Adapting built-in arrays to the STL

We have repeatedly pointed out the weaknesses of the built-in arrays: they implicitly convert to pointers at the slightest provocation, they can't be copied using assignment, they don't know their own size (§18.5.2), etc. We have also pointed out their main strength: they model physical memory almost perfectly.

To get the best of both worlds, we can build an **array** container that provides the benefits of arrays without the weaknesses. A version of **array** was introduced into the standard as part of a Technical Report. Since a feature from a TR is not required to be part of every implementation, **array** may not be part of the implementation you use. However, the idea is simple and useful:

```
template <class T, int N>    // not quite the standard array
struct array {
        typedef T value_type;
        typedef T* iterator;
        typedef T* const_iterator;
        typedef unsigned int size_type;      // the type of a subscript

        T elems[N];
        // no explicit construct/copy/destroy needed

        iterator begin() { return elems; }
        const_iterator begin() const { return elems; }
        iterator end() { return elems+N; }
        const_iterator end() const { return elems+N; }

        size_type size() const;

        T& operator[](int n) { return elems[n]; }
        const T& operator[](int n) const { return elems[n]; }

        const T& at(int n) const;      // range-checked access
        T& at(int n);                  // range-checked access

        T * data() { return elems; }
        const T * data() const { return elems; }
};
```

This definition isn't complete or completely standards-conforming, but it will give you the idea. It will also give you something to use if your implementation doesn't yet provide the standard **array**. If available, it is in **<array>**. Note that because **array<T,N>** "knows" that its size is **N**, we can (and do) provide assignment, **==**, **!=**, etc. just as for **vector**.

As an example, let's use an array with the STL version of **high()** from §20.4.2:

```
void f()
{
    array<double,6> a = { 0.0, 1.1, 2.2, 3.3, 4.4, 5.5 };
    array<double,6>::iterator p = high(a.begin(), a.end());
    cout << "the highest value was " << *p << endl;
}
```

Note that we did not think of **array** when we wrote **high()**. Being able to use **high()** for an **array** is a simple consequence of following standard conventions for both.

20.10 Container overview

The STL provides quite a few containers:

Standard containers	
vector	a contiguously allocated sequence of elements; use it as the default container
list	a doubly-linked list; use it when you need to insert and delete elements without moving existing elements
deque	a cross between a list and a vector; don't use it until you have expert-level knowledge of algorithms and machine architecture
map	a balanced ordered tree; use it when you need to access elements by value (see §21.6.1–3)
multimap	a balanced ordered tree where there can be multiple copies of a key; use it when you need to access elements by value (see §21.6.1–3)
unordered_map	a hash table; an optimized version of **map**; use for large maps when you need high performance and can devise a good hash function (see §21.6.4)

Standard containers (*continued*)	
unordered_multimap	a hash table where there can be multiple copies of a key; an optimized version of **multimap**; use it for large maps when you need high performance and can devise a good hash function (see §21.6.4)
set	a balanced ordered tree; use it when you need to keep track of individual values (see §21.6.5)
multiset	a balanced ordered tree where there can be multiple copies of a key; use it when you need to keep track of individual values (see §21.6.5)
unordered_set	like **unordered_map**, but just with values, not (key,value) pairs
unordered_multiset	like **unordered_multimap**, but just with values, not (key,value) pairs
array	a fixed-size array that doesn't suffer most of the problems related to the built-in arrays (see §20.6)

You can look up incredible amounts of additional information on these containers and their use in books and online documentation. Here are a few quality information sources:

Austern, Matt, ed. "Technical Report on C++ Standard Library Extensions," ISO/IEC PDTR 19768. (Colloquially known as TR1.)

Austern, Matthew H. *Generic Programming and the STL.* Addison-Wesley, 1999. ISBN 0201309564.

Koenig, Andrew, ed. *The C++ Standard.* Wiley, 2003. ISBN 0470846747. (Not suitable for novices.)

Lippman, Stanley B., Josée Lajoie, and Barbara E. Moo. *The C++ Primer.* Addison-Wesley, 2005. ISBN 0201721481. (Use only the 4th edition.)

Musser, David R., Gillmer J. Derge, and Atul Saini. *STL Tutorial and Reference Guide: C++ Programming with the Standard Template Library, Second Edition.* Addison-Wesley, 2001. ISBN 0201379236.

Stroustrup, Bjarne. *The C++ Programming Language.* Addison-Wesley, 2000. ISBN 0201700735.

The documentation for the SGI implementation of the STL and the iostream library: www.sgi.com/tech/stl. Note that they also provide complete code.

The documentation of the Dinkumware implementation of the standard library: www.dinkumware.com/manuals/default.aspx. (Beware of several library versions.)

The documentation of the Rogue Wave implementation of the standard library: www2.roguewave.com/support/docs/index.cfm.

Do you feel cheated? Do you think we should explain all about containers and their use to you? That's just not possible. There are too many standard facilities, too many useful techniques, and too many useful libraries for you to absorb them all at once. Programming is too rich a field for anyone to know all facilities and techniques – it can also be a noble art. As a programmer, you must acquire the habit of seeking out new information about language facilities, libraries, and techniques. Programming is a dynamic and rapidly developing field, so just being content with what you know and are comfortable with is a recipe for being left behind. "Look it up" is a perfectly reasonable answer to many problems, and as your skills grow and mature, it will more and more often be the answer.

On the other hand, you will find that once you understand **vector**, **list**, and **map** and the standard algorithms presented in Chapter 21, you'll find other STL and STL-style containers easy to use. You'll also find that you have the basic knowledge to understand non-STL containers and code using them.

What is a container? You can find the definition of an STL container in all of the sources above. Here we will just give an informal definition. An STL container

- Is a sequence of elements [**begin()**:**end()**).
- Container operations copy elements. Copying can be done with assignment or a copy constructor.
- Names its element type **value_type**.
- Has iterator types called **iterator** and **const_iterator**. Iterators provide *, ++ (both prefix and postfix), ==, and != with the appropriate semantics. The iterators for **list** also provide -- for moving backward in the sequence; that's called a *bidirectional iterator*. The iterators for **vector** also provide --, [ ], +, and – and are called *random-access iterators*. (See §20.10.1.)
- Provides **insert()** and **erase()**, **front()** and **back()**, **push_back()** and **pop_back()**, **size()**, etc.; **vector** and **map** also provide subscripting (e.g., operator [ ]).
- Provides comparison operators (==, !=, <, <=, >, and >=) that compare the elements. Containers use lexicographical ordering for <, <=, >, and >=; that is, they compare the elements in order starting with the first.

The aim of this list is to give you an overview. For more detail see Appendix B. For a more precise specification and complete list, see *The C++ Programming Library* or the standard.

Some data types provide much of what is required from a standard container, but not all. We sometimes refer to those as "almost containers." The most interesting of those are:

"Almost containers"	
T[n] built-in array	no **size()** or other member functions; prefer a container, such as **vector**, **string**, or **array**, over a built-in array when you have a choice
string	holds only characters but provides operations useful for text manipulation, such as concatenation (**+** and **+=**); prefer the standard string to other strings
valarray	a numerical vector with vector operations, but with many restrictions to encourage high-performance implementations; use only if you do a lot of vector arithmetic

In addition, many people and many organizations have produced containers that meet the standard container requirements, or almost do so.

If in doubt, use **vector**. Unless you have a solid reason not to, use **vector**.

20.10.1 Iterator categories

We have talked about iterators as if all iterators are interchangeable. They are interchangeable if you do only the simplest operations, such as traversing a sequence once reading each value once. If you want to do more, such as iterating backward or subscripting, you need one of the more advanced iterators.

Iterator categories	
input iterator	We can iterate forward using **++** and read element values using *****. This is the kind of iterator that **istream** offers; see §21.7.2. If **(*p).m** is valid, **p–>m** can be used as a shorthand.
output iterator	We can iterate forward using **++** and write element values using *****. This is the kind of iterator that **ostream** offers; see §21.7.2.
forward iterator	We can iterate forward repeatedly using **++** and read and write (unless the elements are **const**, of course) element values using *****. If **(*p).m** is valid, **p–>m** can be used as a shorthand.
bidirectional iterator	We can iterate forward (using **++**) and backward (using **––**) and read and write (unless the elements are **const**) element values using *****. This is the kind of iterator that **list**, **map**, and **set** offer. If **(*p).m** is valid, **p–>m** can be used as a shorthand.

Iterator categories (*continued*)	
random-access iterator	We can iterate forward (using **++**) and backward (using **--**) and read and write (unless the elements are **const**) element values using * or [ ]. We can subscript and add an integer to a random-access iterator using **+** and subtract an integer using **–**. We can find the distance between two random-access iterators to the same sequence by subtracting one from the other. This is the kind of iterator that **vector** offers. If (***p).m** is valid, **p–>m** can be used as a shorthand.

From the operations offered, we can see that wherever we can use an output iterator or an input iterator, we can use a forward iterator. A bidirectional iterator is also a forward iterator and a random-access iterator is also a bidirectional iterator. Graphically, we can represent the iterator categories like this:

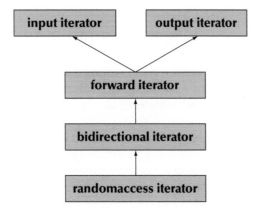

Note that since the iterator categories are not classes, this hierarchy is not a class hierarchy implemented using derivation.

Drill

1. Define an array of **ints** with the ten elements { 0, 1, 2, 3, 4, 5, 6, 7, 8, 9 }.
2. Define a **vector<int>** with those ten elements.
3. Define a **list<int>** with those ten elements.
4. Define a second array, vector, and list, each initialized as a copy of the first array, vector, and list, respectively.
5. Increase the value of each element in the array by 2; increase the value of each element in the vector by 3; increase the value of each element in the list by 5.

6. Write a simple **copy()** operation,

    template<class Iter1, class Iter2> copy(Iter1 f1, Iter1 e1, Iter2 f2);

    that copies **[f1,e1)** to **[f2,f2+(e1–f1))** just like the standard library copy function. Note that if **f1==e1** the sequence is empty, so that there is nothing to copy.
7. Use your **copy()** to copy the array into the vector and to copy the list into the array.
8. Use the standard library **find()** to see if the vector contains the value 3 and print out its position if it does; use **find()** to see if the list contains the value 27 and print out its position if it does. The "position" of the first element is 0, the position of the second element is 1, etc. Note that if **find()** returns the end of the sequence, the value wasn't found.

Remember to test after each step.

Review

1. Why does code written by different people look different? Give examples.
2. What are simple questions we ask of data?
3. What are a few different ways of storing data?
4. What basic operations can we do to a collection of data items?
5. What are some ideals for the way we store our data?
6. What is an STL sequence?
7. What is an STL iterator? What operations does it support?
8. How do you move an iterator to the next element?
9. How do you move an iterator to the previous element?
10. What happens if you try to move an iterator past the end of a sequence?
11. What kinds of iterators can you move to the previous element?
12. Why is it useful to separate data from algorithms?
13. What is the STL?
14. What is a linked list? How does it fundamentally differ from a vector?
15. What is a link (in a linked list)?
16. What does **insert()** do? What does **erase()** do?
17. How do you know if a sequence is empty?
18. What operations does an iterator for a **list** provide?
19. How do you iterate over a container using the STL?
20. When would you use a **string** rather than a **vector**?
21. When would you use a **list** rather than a **vector**?
22. What is a container?
23. What should **begin()** and **end()** do for a container?
24. What containers does the STL provide?
25. What is an iterator category? What kinds of iterators does the STL offer?
26. What operations are provided by a random-access iterator, but not a bidirectional iterator?

Terms

algorithm	empty sequence	sequence
array container	**end()**	singly-linked list
begin()	**erase()**	**size_type**
container	**insert()**	STL
contiguous	iteration	**typedef**
doubly-linked list	iterator	**value_type**
element	linked list	

Exercises

1. If you haven't already, do all **Try this** exercises in the chapter.
2. Get the Jack-and-Jill example from §20.1.2 to work. Use input from a couple of small files to test it.
3. Look at the palindrome examples (§18.6); redo the Jack-and-Jill example from §20.1.2 using that variety of techniques.
4. Find and fix the errors in the Jack-and-Jill example from §20.3.1 by using STL techniques throughout.
5. Define an input and an output operator (**>>** and **<<**) for **vector**.
6. Write a find-and-replace operation for **Documents** based on §20.6.2.
7. Find the lexicographical last string in an unsorted **vector<string>**.
8. Define a function that counts the number of characters in a **Document**.
9. Define a program that counts the number of words in a **Document**. Provide two versions: one that defines "word" as "a whitespace-separated sequence of characters" and one that defines "word" as "a sequence of consecutive alphabetic characters." For example, with the former definition, **alpha.numeric** and **as12b** are both single words, whereas with the second definition they are both two words.
10. Define a version of the word-counting program where the user can specify the set of whitespace characters.
11. Given a **list<int>** as a (by-reference) parameter, make a **vector<double>** and copy the elements of the list into it. Verify that the copy was complete and correct. Then print the elements sorted in order of increasing value.
12. Complete the definition of **list** from §20.4.1–2 and get the **high()** example to run. Allocate a **Link** to represent one past the end.
13. We don't really need a "real" one-past-the-end **Link** for a **list**. Modify your solution to the previous exercise to use **0** to represent a pointer to the (nonexistent) one-past-the-end **Link** (**list<Elem>::end()**); that way, the size of an empty list can be equal to the size of a single pointer.
14. Define a singly-linked list, **slist**, in the style of **std::list**. Which operations from **list** could you reasonably eliminate from **slist** because it doesn't have back pointers?

15. Define a **pvector** to be like a **vector** of pointers except that it contains pointers to objects and its destructor **delete**s each object.

16. Define an **ovector** that is like **pvector** except that the [ ] and * operators return a reference to the object pointed to by an element rather than the pointer.

17. Define an **ownership_vector** that hold pointers to objects like **pvector**, but provides a mechanism for the user to decide which objects are owned by the vector (i.e., which objects are **delete**d by the destructor). Hint: This exercise is simple if you were awake for Chapter 13.

18. Define a range-checked iterator for **vector** (a random-access iterator).

19. Define a range-checked vector for **list** (a bidirectional iterator).

20. Run a small timing experiment to compare the cost of using **vector** and **list**. You can find an explanation of how to time a program in §26.6.1. Generate N random **int** values in the range [0:N). As each **int** is generated, insert it into a **vector<int>** (which grows by one element each time). Keep the **vector** sorted; that is, a value is inserted after every previous value that is less than or equal to the new value and before every previous value that is larger than the new value. Now do the same experiment using a **list<int>** to hold the **int**s. For which N is the **list** faster than the **vector**? Try to explain your result. This experiment was first suggested by John Bentley.

Postscript

If we have N kinds of containers of data and M things we'd like to do with them, we can easily end up writing $N*M$ pieces of code. If the data is of K different types, we could even end up with $N*M*K$ pieces of code. The STL addresses this proliferation by having the element type as a parameter (taking care of the K factor) and by separating access to data from algorithms. By using iterators to access data in any kind of container from any algorithm, we can make do with $N+M$ algorithms. This is a huge simplification. For example, if we have 12 containers and 60 algorithms, the brute-force approach would require 720 functions, whereas the STL strategy requires only 60 functions and 12 definitions of iterators: we just saved ourselves 90% of the work. In addition, the STL provides conventions for defining algorithms that simplify writing correct code and composable code, so the saving is greater still.

Algorithms and Maps

"In theory, practice is simple."

—Trygve Reenskaug

This chapter completes our presentation of the fundamental ideas of the STL and our survey of the facilities it offers. Here, we focus on algorithms. Our primary aim is to introduce you to about a dozen of the most useful ones, which will save you days, if not months, of work. Each is presented with examples of its uses and of programming techniques that it supports. Our second aim here is to give you sufficient tools to write your own – elegant and efficient – algorithms if and when you need more than what the standard library and other available libraries have to offer. In addition, we introduce three more containers: **map**, **set**, and **unordered_map**.

21.1 Standard library algorithms

The standard library offers about 60 algorithms. All are useful for someone sometimes; we focus on some that are often useful for many and on some that are occasionally very useful for someone:

Selected standard algorithms	
r=find(b,e,v)	**r** points to the first occurrence of **v** in [**b**:**e**).
r=find_if(b,e,p)	**r** points to the first element **x** in [**b**:**e**) so that **p(x)** is **true**.
x=count(b,e,v)	**x** is the number of occurrences of **v** in [**b**:**e**).
x=count_if(b,e,p)	**x** is the number of elements in [**b**:**e**) so that **p(x)** is **true**.
sort(b,e)	Sort [**b**:**e**) using **<**.
sort(b,e,p)	Sort [**b**:**e**) using **p**.
copy(b,e,b2)	Copy [**b**:**e**) to [**b2**:**b2**+(**e**−**b**)); there had better be enough elements after **b2**.
unique_copy(b,e,b2)	Copy [**b**:**e**) to [**b2**:**b2**+(**e**−**b**)); don't copy adjacent duplicates.
merge(b,e,b2,e2,r)	Merge two sorted sequences [**b2**:**e2**) and [**b**:**e**) into [**r**:**r**+(**e**−**b**)+(**e2**−**b2**)) .
r=equal_range(b,e,v)	**r** is the subsequence of the sorted range [**b**:**e**) with the value **v**, basically, a binary search for **v**.

Selected standard algorithms (*continued*)	
equal(b,e,b2)	Do all elements of [**b:e**) and [**b2:b2+(e−b)**) compare equal?
x=accumulate(b,e,i)	**x** is the sum of **i** and the elements of [**b:e**).
x=accumulate(b,e,i,op)	Like the other **accumulate**, but with the "sum" calculated using **op**.
x=inner_product(b,e,b2,i)	**x** is the inner product of [**b:e**) and [**b2:b2+(e−b)**).
x=inner_product(b,e,b2,i,op,op2)	Like the other **inner_product**, but with **op** and **op2** instead of + and *.

By default, comparison for equality is done using == and ordering is done based on < (less-than). The standard library algorithms are found in **<algorithm>**. For more information, see §B.5 and the sources listed in §20.7. These algorithms take one or more sequences. An input sequence is defined by a pair of iterators; an output sequence is defined by an iterator to its first element. Typically an algorithm is parameterized by one or more operations that can be defined as function objects or as functions. The algorithms usually report "failure" by returning the end of an input sequence. For example, **find(b,e,v)** returns **e** if it doesn't find **v**.

21.2 The simplest algorithm: find()

Arguably, the simplest useful algorithm is **find()**. It finds an element with a given value in a sequence:

```
template<class In, class T>
In find(In first, In last, const T& val)
// find the first element in [first,last) that equals val
{
        while (first!=last && *first != val) ++first;
        return first;
}
```

Let's have a look at the definition of **find()**. Naturally, you can use **find()** without knowing exactly how it is implemented − in fact, we have used it already (e.g., §20.6.2). However, the definition of **find()** illustrates many useful design ideas, so it is worth looking at.

First of all, **find()** operates on a sequence defined by a pair of iterators. We are looking for the value **val** in the half-open sequence [**first:last**). The result returned by **find()** is an iterator. That result points either to the first element of the sequence with the value **val** or to **last**. Returning an iterator to the one-beyond-the-last element of a sequence is the most common STL way of reporting "not found." So we can use **find()** like this:

```
void f(vector<int>& v, int x)
{
      vector<int>::iterator p = find(v.begin(),v.end(),x);
      if (p!=v.end()) {
            // we found x in v
      }
      else {
            // no x in v
      }
      // . . .
}
```

Here, as is common, the sequence consists of all the elements of a container (an STL **vector**). We check the returned iterator against the end of our sequence to see if we found our value.

We now know how to use **find()** and therefore also how to use a bunch of other algorithms that follow the same conventions as **find()**. Before proceeding with more uses and more algorithms, let's just have a closer look at that definition:

```
template<class In, class T>
In find(In first, In last, const T& val)
      // find the first element in [first,last) that equals val
{
      while (first!=last && *first != val) ++first;
      return first;
}
```

Did you find that loop obvious at first glance? We didn't. It is actually minimal, efficient, and a direct representation of the fundamental algorithm. However, until you have seen a few examples, it is not obvious. Let's write it "the pedestrian way" and see how that version compares:

```
template<class In, class T>
In find(In first, In last, const T& val)
      // find the first element in [first,last) that equals val
{
```

```
        for (In p = first; p!=last; ++p)
                if (*p == val) return p;
        return last;
    }
```

These two definitions are logically equivalent, and a really good compiler will generate the same code for both. However, in reality many compilers are not good enough to eliminate that extra variable (**p**) and to rearrange the code so that all the testing is done in one place. Why worry and explain? Partly, because the style of the first (and preferred) version of **find()** has become very popular, and you must understand it to read other people's code; partly, because performance matters exactly for small, frequently used functions that deal with lots of data.

TRY THIS

Are you sure those two definitions are logically equivalent? How would you be sure? Try constructing an argument for their being equivalent. That done, try both on some data. A famous computer scientist (Don Knuth) once said, "I have only proven the algorithm correct, not tested it." Even mathematical proofs can contain errors. To be confident, you need to both reason and test.

21.2.1 Some generic uses

The **find()** algorithm is generic. That means that it can be used for different data types. In fact, it is generic in two ways; it can be used for

- Any STL-style sequence
- Any element type

Here are some examples (consult the diagrams in §20.4 if you get confused):

```
    void f(vector<int>& v, int x)        // works for vector of int
    {
        vector<int>::iterator p = find(v.begin(),v.end(),x);
        if (p!=v.end()) { /* we found x */ }
        // . . .
    }
```

Here, the iteration operations used by **find()** are those of a **vector<int>::iterator**; that is, **++** (in **++first**) simply moves a pointer to the next location in memory (where the next element of the **vector** is stored) and * (in ***first**) dereferences such a pointer. The iterator comparison (in **first!=last**) is a pointer comparison, and the value comparison (in ***first!=val**) simply compares two integers.

Let's try with a **list**:

```
void f(list<string>& v, string x)          // works for list of string
{
        list<string>::iterator p = find(v.begin(),v.end(),x);
        if (p!=v.end()) { /* we found x */ }
        // . . .
}
```

Here, the iteration operations used by **find()** are those of a **list<string>::iterator**. The operators have the required meaning, so that the logic is the same as for the **vector<int>** above. The implementation is very different, though; that is, **++** (in **++first**) simply follows a pointer in the **Link** part of the element to where the next element of the **list** is stored, and ***** (in ***first**) finds the value part of a **Link**. The iterator comparison (in **first!=last**) is a pointer comparison of **Link***s and the value comparison (in ***first!=val**) compares **string**s using **string**'s **!=** operator.

So, **find()** is extremely flexible: as long as we obey the simple rules for iterators, we can use **find()** to find elements for any sequence we can think of and for any container we care to define. For example, we can use **find()** to look for a character in a **Document** as defined in §20.6:

```
void f(Document& v, char x)          // works for Document of char
{
        Text_iterator p = find(v.begin(),v.end(),x);
        if (p!=v.end()) { /* we found x */ }
        // . . .
}
```

This kind of flexibility is the hallmark of the STL algorithms and makes them more useful than most people imagine when they first encounter them.

21.3 The general search: find_if()

We don't actually look for a specific value all that often. More often, we are interested in finding a value that meets some criteria. We could get a much more useful **find** operation if we could define our search criteria ourselves. Maybe we want to find a value larger than **42**. Maybe we want to compare strings without taking case (upper case vs. lower case) into account. Maybe we want to find the first odd value. Maybe we want to find a record where the address field is **"17 Cherry Tree Lane"**.

The standard algorithm that searches based on a user-supplied criterion is find_if():

```
template<class In, class Pred>
In find_if(In first, In last, Pred pred)
{
        while (first!=last && !pred(*first)) ++first;
        return first;
}
```

Obviously (when you compare the source code), it is just like **find()** except that it uses **!pred(*first)** rather than ***first!=val**; that is, it stops searching once the predicate **pred()** succeeds rather than when an element equals a value.

A predicate is a function that returns **true** or **false**. Clearly, **find_if()** requires a predicate that takes one argument so that it can say **pred(*first)**. We can easily write a predicate that checks some property of a value, such as "Does the string contain the letter x?" "Is the value larger than 42?" "Is the number odd?" For example, we can find the first odd value in a vector of **ints** like this:

```
bool odd(int x) { return x%2; }    // % is the modulo operator

void f(vector<int>& v)
{
        vector<int>::iterator p = find_if(v.begin(), v.end(), odd);
        if (p!=v.end()) { /* we found an odd number */ }
        // . . .
}
```

For that call of **find_if()**, **find_if()** calls **odd()** for each element until it finds the first odd value.

Similarly, we can find the first element of a list with a value larger than 42 like this:

```
bool larger_than_42(int x) { return x>42; }

void f(list<double>& v)
{
        list<double>::iterator p = find_if(v.begin(), v.end(), larger_than_42);
        if (p!=v.end()) { /* we found a value > 42 */ }
        // . . .
}
```

This last example is not very satisfying, though. What if we next wanted to find an element larger than 41? We would have to write a new function. Find an element larger than 19? Write yet another function. There has to be a better way!

If we want to compare to an arbitrary value **v**, we need somehow to make **v** an implicit argument to **find_if()**'s predicate. We could try (choosing **v_val** as a name that is less likely to clash with other names)

```
int v_val;          // the value to which larger_than_v() compares its argument
bool larger_than_v(int x) { return x>v_val; }

void f(list<double>& v, int x)
{
        v_val = 31;      // set v_val to 31 for the next call of larger_than_v
        list<double>::iterator p = find_if(v.begin(), v.end(), larger_than_v);
        if (p!=v.end()) { /* we found a value > 31 */ }

        v_val = x;   // set v_val to x for the next call of larger_than_v
        list<double>::iterator q = find_if(v.begin(), v.end(), larger_than_v);
        if (q!=v.end()) { /* we found a value > x*/ }

        // . . .

}
```

Yuck! We are convinced that people who write such code will eventually get what they deserve, but we pity their users and anyone who gets to maintain their code. Again: there has to be a better way!

TRY THIS

Why are we so disgusted with that use of **v**? Give at least three ways this could lead to obscure errors. List three applications in which you'd particularly hate to find such code.

21.4 Function objects

So, we want to pass a predicate to **find_if()**, and we want that predicate to compare elements to a value we specify as some kind of argument. In particular, we want to write something like this:

```
void f(list<double>& v, int x)
{
        list<double>::iterator p = find_if(v.begin(), v.end(), Larger_than(31));
        if (p!=v.end()) { /* we found a value > 31 */ }

        list<double>::iterator q = find_if(v.begin(), v.end(), Larger_than(x));
        if (q!=v.end()) { /* we found a value > x */ }

        // . . .
}
```

Obviously, **Larger_than** must be something that

- We can call as a predicate, e.g., **pred(*first)**
- Can store a value, such as **31** or **x**, for use when called

For that we need a "function object," that is, an object that can behave like a func- tion. We need an object because objects can store data, such as the value with which to compare. For example:

```
class Larger_than {
        int v;
public:
        Larger_than(int vv) : v(vv) { }              // store the argument
        bool operator()(int x) const { return x>v; } // compare
};
```

Interestingly, this definition makes the example above work as specified. Now we just have to figure out why it works. When we say **Larger_than(31)** we (obviously) make an object of class **Larger_than** holding **31** in its data member **v**. For example:

```
find_if(v.begin(),v.end(),Larger_than(31))
```

Here, we pass that object to **find_if()** as its parameter called **pred**. For each element of **v**, **find_if()** makes a call

```
pred(*first)
```

This invokes the call operator, called **operator()**, for our function object using the argument *first. The result is a comparison of the element's value, *first, with **31**.

What we see here is that function call can be seen as an operator, the "( ) op- erator," just like any other operator. The "( ) operator" is also called the *function call operator* and the *application operator.* So ( ) in **pred(*first)** is given a meaning by **Larger_than::operator()**, just as subscripting in **v[i]** is given a meaning by **vector::operator[ ]**.

21.4.1 An abstract view of function objects

We have here a mechanism that allows for a "function" to "carry around" data that it needs. Clearly, function objects provide us with a very general, powerful, and convenient mechanism. Consider a more general notion of a function object:

```
class F {        // abstract example of a function object
        S s;  // state
public:
        F(const S& ss) :s(ss) { /* establish initial state */ }
        T operator() (const S& ss) const
        {
                // do something with ss to s
                // return a value of type T (T is often void, bool, or S)
        }

        const S& state() const { return s; }    // reveal state
        void reset(const S& ss) { s = ss; }      // reset state
};
```

An object of class **F** holds data in its member **s**. If needed, a function object can have many data members. Another way of saying that something holds data is that it "has state." When we create an **F**, we can initialize that state. Whenever we want to, we can read that state. For **F**, we provided an operation, **state()**, to read that state and another, **reset()**, to write it. However, when we design a function object we are free to provide any way of accessing its state that we consider appropriate. And, of course, we can directly or indirectly call the function object using the normal function call notation. We defined **F** to take a single argument when it is called, but we can define function objects with as many parameters as we need.

Use of function objects is the main method of parameterization in the STL. We use function objects to specify what we are looking for in searches (§21.3), for defining sorting criteria (§21.4.2), for specifying arithmetic operations in numerical algorithms (§21.5), for defining what it means for values to be equal (§21.8), and for much more. The use of function objects is a major source of flexibility and generality.

Function objects are usually very efficient. In particular, passing a small function object by value to a template function typically leads to optimal performance. The reason is simple, but surprising to people more familiar with passing functions as arguments: typically, passing a function object leads to significantly smaller and faster code than passing a function! This is true only if the object is small (something like zero, one, or two words of data) or passed by reference and if the function call operator is small (e.g., a simple comparison using <) and defined to be inline (e.g., has its definition within its class itself). Most of the examples in this chapter – and in this book – follow this pattern. The basic reason for the high performance of small and simple function objects is that they preserve sufficient type information for compilers to generate optimal code. Even older compilers with unsophisticated optimizers can generate a simple "greater-than" machine instruction for the comparison in **Larger_than** rather than calling a function. Calling a function typically takes 10 to 50 times longer than executing a simple comparison operation. In addition, the code for a function call is several times larger than the code for a simple comparison.

21.4.2 Predicates on class members

As we have seen, standard algorithms work well with sequences of elements of basic types, such as **int** and **double**. However, in some application areas, containers of class values are far more common. Consider an example that is key to applications in many areas, sorting a record by several criteria:

```
struct Record {
        string name;        // standard string for ease of use
        char addr[24];      // old style to match database layout
        // . . .
};

vector<Record> vr;
```

Sometimes we want to sort **vr** by name, and sometimes we want to sort it by address. Unless we can do both elegantly and efficiently, our techniques are of limited practical interest. Fortunately, doing so is easy. We can write

```
// . . .
sort(vr.begin(), vr.end(), Cmp_by_name());    // sort by name
// . . .
sort(vr.begin(), vr.end(), Cmp_by_addr());    // sort by addr
// . . .
```

Cmp_by_name is a function object that compares two **Record**s by comparing their **name** members. **Cmp_by_addr** is a function object that compares two **Record**s by comparing their **addr** members. To allow the user to specify such comparison criteria, the standard library **sort** algorithm takes an optional third argument specifying the sorting criteria. **Cmp_by_name**() creates a **Cmp_by_name** for **sort**() to use to compare **Record**s. That looks OK – meaning that we wouldn't mind maintaining code that looked like that. Now all we have to do is to define **Cmp_by_name** and **Cmp_by_addr**:

```
// different comparisons for Record objects:

struct Cmp_by_name {
     bool operator()(const Record& a, const Record& b) const
          { return a.name < b.name; }
};

struct Cmp_by_addr {
     bool operator()(const Record& a, const Record& b) const
          { return strncmp(a.addr, b.addr, 24) < 0; }    // !!!
};
```

The **Cmp_by_name** class is pretty obvious. The function call operator, **operator**()(), simply compares the **name** strings using the standard **string**'s < operator. However, the comparison in **Cmp_by_addr** is ugly. That is because we chose an ugly representation of the address: an array of 24 characters (not zero terminated). We chose that partly to show how a function object can be used to hide ugly and error-prone code and partly because this particular representation was once presented to me as a challenge: "an ugly and important real-world problem that the STL can't handle." Well, the STL could. The comparison function uses the standard C (and C++) library function **strncmp**() that compares fixed-length character arrays returning a negative number if the second "string" comes lexicographically after the first. Look it up should you ever need to do such an obscure comparison (e.g., §B.10.3).

21.5 Numerical algorithms

Most of the standard library algorithms deal with data management issues: they copy, sort, search, etc. data. However, a few help with numerical computations. These numerical algorithms can be important when you compute, and they serve as examples of how you can express numerical algorithms within the STL framework.

There are just four STL-style standard library numerical algorithms:

Numerical algorithms	
x=accumulate(b,e,i)	Add a sequence of values; e.g., for {a,b,c,d} produce a+b+c+d. The type of the result **x** is the type of the initial value **i**.
x=inner_product(b,e,b2,i)	Multiply pairs of values from two sequences and sum the results; e.g., for {a,b,c,d} and {e,f,g,h} produce a*e+b*f+c*g+d*h. The type of the result **x** is the type of the initial value **i**.
r=partial_sum(b,e,r)	Produce the sequence of sums of the first n elements of a sequence; e.g., for {a,b,c,d} produce {a, a+b, a+b+c, a+b+c+d}.
r=adjacent_difference(b,e,b2,r)	Produce the sequence of differences between elements of a sequence; e.g., for {a,b,c,d} produce {a,b–a,c–b,d–c}.

They are found in **<numeric>**. We'll describe the first two here and leave it for you to explore the other two if you feel the need.

21.5.1 Accumulate

The simplest and most useful numerical algorithm is **accumulate()**. In its simplest form, it adds a sequence of values:

```
template<class In, class T> T accumulate(In first, In last, T init)
{
        while (first!=last) {
                init = init + *first;
                ++first;
        }
        return init;
}
```

Given an initial value, **init**, it simply adds every value in the [**first:last**) sequence to it and returns the sum. The variable in which the sum is computed, **init**, is often referred to as the *accumulator*. For example:

```
int a[] = { 1, 2, 3, 4, 5 };
cout << accumulate(a, a+sizeof(a)/sizeof(int), 0);
```

This will print 15, that is, 0+1+2+3+4+5 (0 is the initial value). Obviously, **accumulate()** can be used for all kinds of sequences:

```
void f(vector<double>& vd, int* p, int n)
{
        double sum = accumulate(vd.begin(), vd.end(), 0.0);
        int sum2 = accumulate(p,p+n,0);
}
```

The type of the result (the sum) is the type of the variable that **accumulate()** uses to hold the accumulator. This gives a degree of flexibility that can be important. For example:

```
void f(int* p, int n)
{
        int s1 = accumulate(p, p+n, 0);          // sum into an int
        long sl = accumulate(p, p+n, long(0));   // sum the ints into a long
        double s2 = accumulate(p, p+n, 0.0);     // sum the ints into a double
}
```

A **long** has more significant digits than an **int** on some computers. A **double** can represent larger (and smaller) numbers than an **int**, but possibly with less precision. We'll revisit the role of range and precision in numerical computations in Chapter 24.

Using the variable in which you want the result as the initializer is a popular idiom for specifying the type of the accumulator:

```
void f(vector<double>& vd, int* p, int n)
{
        double s1 = 0;
        s1 = accumulate(vd.begin(), vd.end(), s1);
        int s2 = accumulate(vd.begin(), vd.end(), s2);    // oops
        float s3 = 0;
        accumulate(vd.begin(), vd.end(), s3);             // oops
}
```

Do remember to initialize the accumulator and to assign the result of **accumulate()** to the variable. In this example, **s2** was used as an initializer before it was itself initialized; the result is therefore undefined. We passed **s3** to **accumulate()** (pass-by-value; see §8.5.3), but the result is never assigned anywhere; that compilation is just a waste of time.

21.5.2 Generalizing accumulate()

So, the basic three-argument **accumulate()** adds. However, there are many other useful operations, such as multiply and subtract, that we might like to do on a sequence, so the STL offers a second four-argument version of **accumulate()** where we can specify the operation to be used:

```
template<class In, class T, class BinOp>
T accumulate(In first, In last, T init, BinOp op)
{
        while (first!=last) {
                init = op(init, *first);
                ++first;
        }
        return init;
}
```

Any binary operation that accepts two arguments of the accumulator's type can be used here. For example:

```
array<double,4> a = { 1.1, 2.2, 3.3, 4.4 };      // see §20.9
cout << accumulate(a.begin(),a.end(), 1.0, multiplies<double>());
```

This will print 35.1384, that is, 1.0*1.1*2.2*3.3*4.4 (1.0 is the initial value). The binary operator supplied here, **multiplies<double>()**, is a standard library function object that multiplies; **multiplies<double>** multiplies **doubles**, **multiplies<int>** multiplies **ints**, etc. There are other binary function objects: **plus** (it adds), **minus** (it subtracts), **divides**, and **modulus** (it takes the remainder). They are all defined in **<functional>** (§B.6.2).

Note that for products of floating-point numbers, the obvious initial value is **1.0**.

As in the **sort()** example (§21.4.2), we are often interested in data within class objects, rather than just plain built-in types. For example, we might want to calculate the total cost of items given the unit prices and number of units:

```
struct Record {
        double unit_price;
        int units;               // number of units sold
        // . . .
};
```

We can let the **accumulate**'s operator extract the **units** from a **Record** element as well as multiplying it to the accumulator value:

```
double price(double v, const Record& r)
{
        return v + r.unit_price * r.units;   // calculate price and accumulate
}
```

```
void f(const vector<Record>& vr)
{
        double total = accumulate(vr.begin(), vr.end(), 0.0, price);
        // . . .
}
```

We were "lazy" and used a function, rather than a function object, to calculate the price — just to show that we could do that also. We tend to prefer function objects

- If they need to store a value between calls, or
- If they are so short that inlining can make a difference (at most a handful of primitive operations)

In this example, we might have chosen a function object for the second reason.

TRY THIS

Define a **vector<Record>**, initialize it with four records of your choice, and compute their total price using the functions above.

21.5.3 Inner product

Take two vectors, multiply each pair of elements with the same subscript, and add all of those sums. That's called the *inner product* of the two vectors and is a most useful operation in many areas (e.g., physics and linear algebra; see §24.6). If you prefer code to words, here is the STL version:

```
template<class In, class In2, class T>
T inner_product(In first, In last, In2 first2, T init)
        // note: this is the way we multiply two vectors (yielding a scalar)
{
        while(first!=last) {
                init = init + (*first) * (*first2);      // multiply pairs of elements
                ++first;
                ++first2;
        }
        return init;
}
```

This generalizes the notion of inner product to any kind of sequence of any type of element. As an example, consider a stock market index. The way that works is to take a set of companies and assign each a "weight." For example, in the Dow Jones Industrial index Alcoa had a weight of 2.4808 when last we looked. To get the current value of the index, we multiply each company's share price with its weight and add all the resulting weighted prices together. Obviously, that's the inner product of the prices and the weights. For example:

```
// calculate the Dow Jones Industrial index:
vector<double> dow_price;         // share price for each company
dow_price.push_back(81.86);
dow_price.push_back(34.69);
dow_price.push_back(54.45);
// . . .

list<double> dow_weight;          // weight in index for each company
dow_weight.push_back(5.8549);
dow_weight.push_back(2.4808);
dow_weight.push_back(3.8940);
// . . .

double dji_index = inner_product(  // multiply (weight,value) pairs and add
        dow_price.begin(), dow_price.end(),
        dow_weight.begin(),
        0.0);

cout << "DJI value " << dji_index << '\n';
```

Note that **inner_product()** takes two sequences. However, it takes only three arguments: only the beginning of the second sequence is mentioned. The second sequence is supposed to have at least as many elements as the first. If not, we have a run-time error. As far as **inner_product()** is concerned, it is OK for the second sequence to have more elements than the first; those "surplus elements" will simply not be used.

The two sequences need not be of the same type, nor do they need to have the same element types. To illustrate this point, we used a **vector** to hold the prices and a **list** to hold the weights.

21.5.4 Generalizing inner_product()

The **inner_product()** can be generalized just as **accumulate()** was. For **inner_product()** we need two extra arguments, though: one to combine the accumulator with the new value, exactly as for **accumulate()**, and one for combining the element value pairs:

```
template<class In, class In2, class T, class BinOp, class BinOp2 >
T inner_product(In first, In last, In2 first2, T init, BinOp op, BinOp2 op2)
{
    while(first!=last) {
        init = op(init, op2(*first, *first2));
        ++first;
        ++first2;
    }
    return init;
}
```

In §21.6.3, we return to the Dow Jones example and use this generalized **inner_product()** as part of a more elegant solution.

21.6 Associative containers

After **vector**, the most useful standard library container is probably the **map**. A **map** is an ordered sequence of (key,value) pairs in which you can look up a value based on a key; for example, **my_phone_book["Nicholas"]** could be the phone number of Nicholas. The only potential competitor to **map** in a popularity contest is **unordered_map** (see §21.6.4), and that's a **map** optimized for keys that are strings. Data structures similar to **map** and **unordered_map** are known under many names, such as *associative arrays*, *hash tables*, and *red-black trees*. Popular and useful concepts always seem to have many names. In the standard library, we collectively call all such data structures *associative containers*.

The standard library provides eight associative containers:

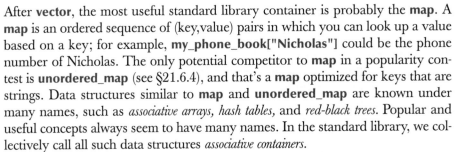

Associative containers	
map	an ordered container of (key,value) pairs
set	an ordered container of keys
unordered_map	an unordered container of (key,value) pairs
unordered_set	an unordered container of keys
multimap	a **map** where a key can occur multiple times
multiset	a **set** where a key can occur multiple times
unordered_multimap	an **unordered_map** where a key can occur multiple times
unordered_multiset	an **unordered_set** where a key can occur multiple times

These containers are found in **<map>**, **<set>**, **<unordered_map>**, and **<unordered_set>**.

21.6.1 Maps

Consider a conceptually simple task: make a list of the number of occurrences of words in a text. The obvious way of doing this is to keep a list of words we have seen together with the number of times we have seen each. When we read a new word, we see if we have already seen it; if we have, we increase its count by one; if not, we insert it in our list and give it the value 1. We could do that using a **list** or a **vector**, but then we would have to do a search for each word we read. That could be slow. A **map** stores its keys in a way that makes it easy to see if a key is present, thus making the searching part of our task trivial:

```
int main()
{
    map<string,int> words;      // keep (word,frequency) pairs

    string s;
    while (cin>>s) ++words[s]; // note: words is subscripted by a string

    typedef map<string,int>::const_iterator Iter;
    for (Iter p = words.begin(); p!=words.end(); ++p)
        cout << p->first << ": " << p->second << '\n';
}
```

The really interesting part of the program is **++words[s]**. As we can see from the first line of **main()**, **words** is a **map** of (**string,int**) pairs; that is, **words** maps **strings** to **ints**. In other words, given a **string**, **words** can give us access to its corresponding **int**. So, when we subscript **words** with a **string** (holding a word read from our input), **words[s]** is a reference to the **int** corresponding to **s**. Let's look at a concrete example:

```
words["sultan"]
```

If we have not seen the string **"sultan"** before, **"sultan"** will be entered into **words** with the default value for an **int**, which is **0**. Now, **words** has an entry (**"sultan",0**). It follows that if we haven't seen **"sultan"** before, **++words["sultan"]** will associate the value **1** with the string **"sultan"**. In detail: the **map** will discover that **"sultan"** wasn't found, insert a (**"sultan",0**) pair, and then **++** will increment that value, yielding **1**.

Now look again at the program: **++words[s]** takes every "word" we get from input and increases its value by one. The first time a new word is seen, it gets the value **1**. Now the meaning of the loop is clear:

```
while (cin>>s) ++words[s];
```

This reads every (whitespace-separated) word on input and computes the number of occurrences for each. Now all we have to do is to produce the output. We can iterate though a **map**, just like any other STL container. The elements of a **map<string,int>** are of type **pair<string,int>**. The first member of a **pair** is called **first** and the second member **second**, so the output loop becomes

```
typedef map<string,int>::const_iterator Iter;
for (Iter p = words.begin(); p!=words.end(); ++p)
        cout << p->first << ": " << p->second << '\n';
```

The **typedef** (§20.5 and §A.16) is just for notational convenience and readability.

As a test, we can feed the opening statements of the first edition of *The C++ Programming Language* to our program:

> C++ is a general purpose programming language designed to make programming more enjoyable for the serious programmer. Except for minor details, C++ is a superset of the C programming language. In addition to the facilities provided by C, C++ provides flexible and efficient facilities for defining new types.

We get the output

```
C: 1
C++: 3
C,: 1
Except: 1
In: 1
a: 2
addition: 1
and: 1
by: 1
defining: 1
designed: 1
details,: 1
efficient: 1
enjoyable: 1
facilities: 2
flexible: 1
for: 3
general: 1
is: 2
```

language: 1
language.: 1
make: 1
minor: 1
more: 1
new: 1
of: 1
programmer.: 1
programming: 3
provided: 1
provides: 1
purpose: 1
serious: 1
superset: 1
the: 3
to: 2
types.: 1

If we don't like to distinguish between upper- and lowercase letters or would like to eliminate punctuation, we can do so: see exercise 13.

21.6.2 map overview

So what is a **map**? There is a variety of ways of implementing maps, but the STL map implementations tend to be balanced binary search trees; more specifically, they are red-black trees. We will not go into details, but now you know the technical terms, so you can look them up in the literature or on the web, should you want to know more.

A tree is built up from nodes (in a way similar to a list being built from links; see §20.4). A **Node** holds a key, its corresponding value, and pointers to two descendant **Node**s.

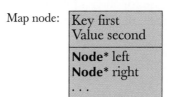

Here is the way a **map<Fruit,int>** might look in memory assuming we had inserted (Kiwi,100), (Quince,0), (Plum,8), (Apple,7), (Grape,2345), and (Orange,99) into it:

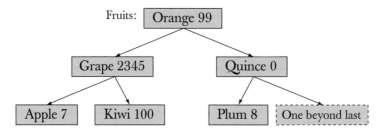

Given that the name of the **Node** member that holds the key value is **first**, the basic rule of a binary search tree is

left–>first<first && first<right–>first

That is, for every node,

- Its left sub-node has a key that is less than the node's key, and
- The node's key is less than the key of its right sub-node

You can verify that this holds for each node in the tree. That allows us to search "down the tree from its root." Curiously enough, in computer science literature trees grow downward from their roots. In the example, the root node is (Orange, 99). We just compare our way down the tree until we find what we are looking for or the place where it should have been. A tree is called *balanced* when (as in the example above) each sub-tree has approximately as many nodes as every other sub-tree that's equally far from the root. Being balanced minimizes the average number of nodes we have to visit to reach a node.

A **Node** may also hold some more data which the map will use to keep its tree of nodes balanced. A tree is balanced when each node has about as many descendants to its left as to its right. If a tree with N nodes is balanced, we have to at most look at $\log_2(N)$ nodes to find a node. That's much better than the average of $N/2$ nodes we have to examine if we had the keys in a list and searched from the beginning (the worst case for such a linear search is N). (See also §21.6.4.) For example, have a look at an unbalanced tree:

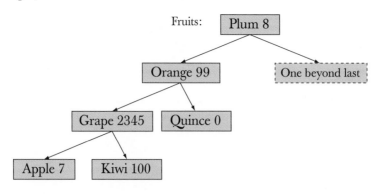

This tree still meets the criteria that the key of every node is greater than that of its left sub-node and less than that of its right sub-node:

left–>first<first && first<right–>first

However, this version of the tree is unbalanced, so we now have three "hops" to reach Apple and Kiwi, rather than the two we had in the balanced tree. For trees of many nodes the difference can be very significant, so the trees used to implement **maps** are balanced.

We don't have to understand about trees to use **map**. It is just reasonable to assume that professionals understand at least the fundamentals of their tools. What we do have to understand is the interface to **map** provided by the standard library. Here is a slightly simplified version:

```
template<class Key, class Value, class Cmp = less<Key> > class map {
    // . . .
    typedef pair<Key,Value> value_type;   // a map deals in (Key,Value) pairs

    typedef sometype1 iterator;          // probably a pointer to a tree node
    typedef sometype2 const_iterator;

    iterator begin();             // points to first element
    iterator end();               // points one beyond the last element

    Value& operator[](const Key& k);   // subscript with k

    iterator find(const Key& k);       // is there an entry for k?

    void erase(iterator p);               // remove element pointed to by p
    pair<iterator, bool> insert(const value_type&); // insert a (key,value) pair
    // . . .
};
```

You can find the real version in **<map>**. You can imagine the iterator to be a **Node***, but you cannot rely on your implementation using that specific type to implement **iterator**.

The similarity to the interfaces for **vector** and **list** (§20.5 and §B.4) is obvious. The main difference is that when you iterate, the elements are pairs – of type **pair<Key,Value>**. That type is another useful STL type:

```
template<class T1, class T2> struct pair {
    typedef T1 first_type;
    typedef T2 second_type;
```

```
        T1 first;
        T2 second;

        pair() :first(T1()), second(T2()) { }
        pair(const T1& x, const T2& y) :first(x), second(y) { }
        template<class U, class V>
                pair(const pair<U,V>& p) :first(p.first), second(p.second) { }
};

template<class T1, class T2>
pair<T1,T2> make_pair(T1 x, T2 y)
{
        return pair<T1,T2>(x,y);
}
```

We copied the complete definition of **pair** and its useful helper function **make_pair()** from the standard.

Note that when you iterate over a **map**, the elements will come in the order defined by the key. For example, if we iterated over the fruits in the example, we would get

(Apple,7) (Grape,100) (Kiwi,2345) (Orange,99) (Plum,8) (Quince,0)

The order in which we inserted those fruits doesn't matter.

The **insert()** operation has an odd return value, which we most often ignore in simple programs. It is a pair of an iterator to the (key,value) element and a **bool** which is **true** if the (key,value) pair was inserted by this call of **insert()**. If the key was already in the map, the insertion fails and the **bool** is **false**.

Note that you can define the meaning of the order used by a map by supplying a third argument (**Cmp** in the map declaration). For example:

map<string, double, No_case> m;

No_case defines case-insensitive compare; see §21.8. By default the order is defined by **less<Key>**, meaning less-than.

21.6.3 Another map example

To better appreciate the utility of **map**, let's return to the Dow Jones example from §21.5.3. The code there was correct if and only if all weights appear in the same position in their **vector** as their corresponding name. That's implicit and could easily be the source of an obscure bug. There are many ways of attacking that problem, but one attractive one is to keep each weight together with its company's ticker symbol, e.g., ("AA",2.4808). A "ticker symbol" is an abbreviation of a company name used where a terse representation is needed. Similarly we can keep the company's ticker symbol together with its share price, e.g., ("AA",34.69). Finally, for those of us who don't regularly deal with the U.S. stock market, we can keep the company's ticker symbol together with the company name, e.g., ("AA","Alcoa Inc."); that is, we could keep three maps of corresponding values.

First we make the (symbol,price) map:

```
map<string,double> dow_price;
        // Dow Jones Industrial index (symbol,price);
        // for up-to-date quotes see www.djindexes.com
dow_price["MMM"] = 81.86;
dow_price ["AA"] = 34.69;
dow_price ["MO"] = 54.45;
// . . .
```

The (symbol,weight) map:

```
map<string,double> dow_weight;  // Dow (symbol,weight)

dow_weight.insert(make_pair("MMM", 5.8549));
dow_weight.insert(make_pair("AA",2.4808));
dow_weight.insert(make_pair("MO",3.8940));
// . . .
```

We used **insert()** and **make_pair()** to show that the elements of a **map** really are **pairs**. The example also illustrates the value of notation; we find the subscript notation easier to read and – less important – easier to write.

The (symbol,name) map:

```
map<string,string> dow_name;      // Dow (symbol,name)
dow_name["MMM"] = "3M Co.";
dow_name["AA"] = "Alcoa Inc.";
dow_name["MO"] = "Altria Group Inc.";
// . . .
```

Given those maps, we can conveniently extract all kinds of information. For example:

```
double alcoa_price = dow_price ["AAA"];        // read values from a map
double boeing_price = dow_price ["BA"];

if (dow_price.find("INTC") != dow_price.end())    // find an entry in a map
        cout << "Intel is in the Dow\n";
```

Iterating through a map is easy. We just have to remember that the key is called **first** and the value is called **second**:

```
typedef map<string,double>::const_iterator Dow_iterator;

// write price for each company in the Dow index:
for (Dow_iterator p = dow_price.begin(); p!=dow_price.end(); ++p) {
        const string& symbol = p->first;     // the "ticker" symbol
                cout << symbol << '\t'
                << p->second << '\t'
                << dow_name[symbol] << '\n';
}
```

We can even do some computation directly using maps. In particular, we can calculate the index, just as we did in §21.5.3. We have to extract share values and weights from their respective maps and multiply them. We can easily write a function for doing that for any two **map<string,double>**s:

```
double weighted_value(
        const pair<string,double>& a,
        const pair<string,double>& b
                    )  // extract values and multiply
{
        return a.second * b.second;
}
```

Now we just plug that function into the generalized version of **inner_product()** and we have the value of our index:

```
double dji_index =
        inner_product(dow_price.begin(), dow_price.end(), // all companies
                    dow_weight.begin(),     // their weights
                    0.0,                    // initial value
                    plus<double>(),         // add (as usual)
                    weighted_value);        // extract values and weights
                                            // and multiply
```

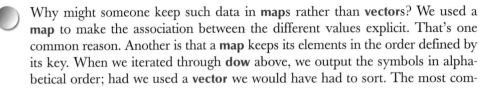

Why might someone keep such data in **maps** rather than **vectors**? We used a **map** to make the association between the different values explicit. That's one common reason. Another is that a **map** keeps its elements in the order defined by its key. When we iterated through **dow** above, we output the symbols in alphabetical order; had we used a **vector** we would have had to sort. The most common reason to use a **map** is simply that we want to look up values based on the key. For large sequences, finding something using **find()** is far slower than looking it up in a sorted structure, such as a **map**.

TRY THIS

Get this little example to work. Then add a few companies of your own choice, with weights of your choice.

21.6.4 unordered_map

To find an element in a **vector**, **find()** needs to examine all the elements from the beginning to the element with the right value or to the end. On average, the cost is proportional to the length of the **vector** (N); we call that cost $O(N)$.

To find an element in a **map**, the subscript operator needs to examine all the elements of the tree from the root to the element with the right value or to a leaf. On average the cost is proportional to the depth of the tree. A balanced binary tree holding N elements has a maximum depth of $\log_2(N)$; the cost is $O(\log_2(N))$. $O(\log_2(N))$ – that is, cost proportional to $\log_2(N)$ – is actually pretty good compared to $O(N)$:

N	15	128	1023	16,383
$\log_2(N)$	4	7	10	14

The actual cost will depend on how soon in our search we find our values and how expensive comparisons and iterations are. It is usually somewhat more expensive to chase pointers (as the **map** lookup does) than to increment a pointer (as **find()** does in a **vector**).

For some types, notably integers and character strings, we can do even better than a **map**'s tree search. We will not go into details, but the idea is that given a key, we compute an index into a **vector**. That index is called a *hash value* and a container that uses this technique is typically called a *hash table*. The number of possible keys is far larger than the number of slots in the hash table. For example, we often use a hash function to map from the billions of possible strings into an index for a **vector** with 1000 elements. This can be tricky, but it can be handled well and is especially useful for implementing large **map**s. The main virtue of a hash table is that on average the cost of a lookup is (near) constant and independent of the number of elements in the table, that is, $O(1)$. Obviously, that can be a significant advantage for large maps, say a map of 500,000 web addresses. For more information about hash lookup, you can look at the documentation for **unordered_map** (available on the web) or just about any basic text on data structures (look for *hash table* and *hashing*).

We can illustrate lookup in an (unsorted) vector, a balanced binary tree, and a hash table graphically like this:

- Lookup in unsorted **vector**:

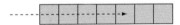

- Lookup in **map** (balanced binary tree):

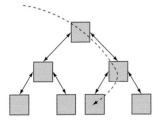

- Lookup in **unordered_map** (hash table):

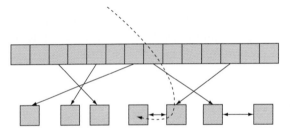

The STL **unordered_map** is implemented using a hash table, just as the STL **map** is implemented using a balanced binary tree, and an STL **vector** is implemented using an array. Part of the utility of the STL is to fit all of these ways of storing and accessing data into a common framework together with algorithms. The rule of thumb is:

- Use **vector** unless you have a good reason not to.
- Use **map** if you need to look up based on a value (and if your key type has a reasonable and efficient less-than operation).
- Use **unordered_map** if you need to do a lot of lookup in a large map and you don't need an ordered traversal (and if you can find a good hash function for your key type).

Here, we will not describe **unordered_map** in any detail. You can use an **unordered_map** with a key of type **string** or **int** exactly like a **map**, except that when you iterate over the elements, the elements will not be ordered. For example, we could rewrite part of the Dow Jones example from §21.6.3 like this:

```
unordered_map<string,double> dow_price;

typedef unordered_map<string,double>::const_iterator Dow_iterator;

for (Dow_iterator p = dow_price.begin(); p!=dow_price.end(); ++p) {
    const string& symbol = p->first;    // the "ticker" symbol
        cout << symbol << '\t'
        << p->second << '\t'
        << dow_name[symbol] << '\n';
}
```

Lookup in **dow** might now be faster. However, that would not be significant because there are only 30 companies in that index. Had we been keeping the prices of all the companies on the New York Stock Exchange, we might have noticed a performance difference. We will, however, notice a logical difference: the output from the iteration will now not be in alphabetical order.

The unordered maps are new in the context of the C++ standard and not yet quite "first-class members," as they are defined in a Technical Report rather than in the standard proper. They are widely available, though, and where they are not you can often find their ancestors, called something like **hash_map**.

TRY THIS

Write a small program using **#include<unordered_map>**. If that doesn't work, **unordered_map** wasn't shipped with your C++ implementation. If you really need **unordered_map**, you have to download one of the available implementations (e.g., see www.boost.org).

21.6.5 Sets

We can think of a **set** as a map where we are not interested in the values, or rather as a map without values. We can visualize a set node like this:

Set node:

Key first
Node* left
Node* right

We can represent the **set** of fruits used in the **map** example (§21.6.2) like this:

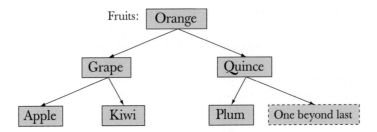

What are sets useful for? As it happens, there are lots of problems that require us to remember if we have seen a value. Keeping track of which fruits are available (independently of price) is one example; building a dictionary is another. A slightly different style of usage is having a set of "records"; that is, the elements are objects that potentially contain "lots of" information – we simply use a member as the key. For example:

```
struct Fruit {
        string name;
        int count;
        double unit_price;
        Date last_sale_date;
        // . . .
};

struct Fruit_order {
        bool operator()(const Fruit& a, const Fruit& b) const
        {
                return a.name<b.name;
        }
};

set<Fruit, Fruit_order> inventory;
```

Here again, we see how using a function object can significantly increase the range of problems for which an STL component is useful.

Since **set** doesn't have a value type, it doesn't support subscripting (**operator[]()**) either. We must use "list operations," such as **insert()** and **erase()**, instead. Unfortunately, **map** and **set** don't support **push_back()** either – the reason is obvious: the **set** and not the programmer determines where the new value is inserted. Instead use **insert()**. For example:

```
inventory.insert(Fruit("quince",5));
inventory.insert(Fruit("apple", 200, 0.37));
```

One advantage of **set** over **map** is that you can use the value obtained from an iterator directly. Since there is no (key,value) pair as for **map** (§21.6.3), the dereference operator gives a value of the element type:

```
typedef set<Fruit>::const_iterator SI;
for (SI p = inventory.begin(), p!=inventory.end(); ++p) cout << *p << '\n';
```

Assuming, of course, that you have defined **<<** for **Fruit**.

21.7 Copying

In §21.2, we deemed **find()** "the simplest useful algorithm." Naturally, that point can be argued. Many simple algorithms are useful – even some that are trivial to write. Why bother to write new code when you can use what others have written and debugged for you, however simple? When it comes to simplicity and utility, **copy()** gives **find()** a run for its money. The STL provides three versions of copy:

Copy operations	
copy(b,e,b2)	Copy [b:e) to [b2:b2+(e−b)).
unique_copy(b,e,b2)	Copy [b:e) to [b2:b2+(e−b)); suppress adjacent copies.
copy_if(b,e,b2,p)	Copy [b:e) to [b2:b2+(e−b)), but only elements that meet the predicate **p**.

21.7.1 Copy

The basic copy algorithm is defined like this:

```
template<class In, class Out> Out copy(In first, In last, Out res)
{
    while (first!=last) {
        *res = *first;  // copy element
        ++res;
        ++first;
    }
    return res;
}
```

Given a pair of iterators, **copy()** copies a sequence into another sequence specified by an iterator to its first element. For example:

```
void f(vector<double>& vd, list<int>& li)
    // copy the elements of a list of ints into a vector of doubles
{
    if (vd.size() < li.size()) error("target container too small");
    copy(li.begin(), li.end(), vd.begin());
    // . . .
}
```

Note that the type of the input sequence of **copy()** can be different from the type of the output sequence. That's a useful generality of STL algorithms: they work for all kinds of sequences without making unnecessary assumptions about their implementation. We remembered to check that there was enough space in the output sequence to hold the elements we put there. It's the programmer's job to check such sizes. STL algorithms are programmed for maximal generality and optimal performance; they do not (by default) do range checking or other potentially expensive tests to protect their users. At times, you'll wish they did, but when you want checking, you can add it as we did above.

21.7.2 Stream iterators

You will have heard the phrases "copy to output" and "copy from input." That's a nice and useful way of thinking of some forms of I/O, and we can actually use **copy** to do exactly that.

Remember that a sequence is something

- With a beginning and an end
- Where we can get to the next element using **++**
- Where we can get the value of the current element using *****

We can easily represent input and output streams that way. For example:

```
ostream_iterator<string> oo(cout);      // assigning to *oo is to write to cout

*oo = "Hello, ";        // meaning cout << "Hello, "
++oo;                   // "get ready for next output operation"
*oo = "World!\n";       // meaning cout << "World!\n"
```

You can imagine how this could be implemented. The standard library provides an **ostream_iterator** type that works like that; **ostream_iterator<T>** is an iterator that you can use to write values of type **T**.

Similarly, the standard library provides the type **istream_iterator<T>** for reading values of type **T**:

```
istream_iterator<string> ii(cin);   // reading *ii is to read a string from cin

string s1 = *ii;        // meaning cin>>s1
++ii;                   // "get ready for the next input operation"
string s2 = *ii;        // meaning cin>>s2
```

Using **ostream_iterator** and **istream_iterator**, we can use **copy()** for our I/O. For example, we can make a "quick and dirty" dictionary like this:

```
int main()
{
    string from, to;
    cin >> from >> to;                          // get source and target file names

    ifstream is(from.c_str());                  // open input stream
    ofstream os(to.c_str());                    // open output stream

    istream_iterator<string> ii(is);            // make input iterator for stream
    istream_iterator<string> eos;               // input sentinel
    ostream_iterator<string> oo(os,"\n");       // make output iterator for stream

    vector<string> b(ii,eos);                   // b is a vector initialized from input
    sort(b.begin() ,b.end());                   // sort the buffer
    copy(b.begin() ,b.end() ,oo);               // copy buffer to output
}
```

The iterator **eos** is the stream iterator's representation of "end of input." When an **istream** reaches end of input (often referred to as **eof**), its **istream_iterator** will equal the default **istream_iterator** (here called **eos**).

Note that we initialized the **vector** by a pair of iterators. As the initializers for a container, a pair of iterators **(a,b)** means "Read the sequence [a:b) into the container." Naturally, the pair of iterators that we used was **(ii,eos)** – the beginning and end of input. That saves us from explicitly using **>>** and **push_back()**. We strongly advise against the alternative

```
vector<string> b(max_size);     // don't guess about the amount of input!
copy(ii,eos,b.begin());
```

People who try to guess the maximum size of input usually find that they have underestimated, and serious problems emerge – for them or for their users – from the resulting buffer overflows. Such overflows are also a source of security problems.

TRY THIS

First get the program as written to work and test it with a small file of, say, a few hundred words. Then try the *emphatically not recommended* version that guesses about the size of input and see what happens when the input buffer **b** overflows. Note that the worst-case scenario is that the overflow led to nothing bad in your particular example, so that you would be tempted to ship it to users.

In our little program, we read in the words and then sorted them. That seemed an obvious way of doing things at the time, but why should we put words in "the wrong place" so that we later have to sort? Worse yet, we find that we store a word and print it as many times as it appears in the input.

We can solve the latter problem by using **unique_copy()** instead of **copy()**. A **unique_copy()** simply doesn't copy repeated identical values. For example, using plain **copy()** the program will take

> **the man bit the dog**

and produce

> **bit**
> **dog**
> **man**
> **the**
> **the**

If we used **unique_copy()**, the program would write

> **bit**
> **dog**
> **man**
> **the**

Where did those newlines come from? Outputting with separators is so common that the **ostream_iterator**'s constructor allows you to (optionally) specify a string to be printed after each value:

> **ostream_iterator<string> oo(os,"\n");**   // make output iterator for stream

Obviously, a newline is a popular choice for output meant for humans to read, but maybe we prefer spaces as separators? We could write

```
ostream_iterator<string> oo(os," ");        // make output iterator for stream
```

This would give us the output

bit dog man the

21.7.3 Using a set to keep order

There is an even easier way of getting that output; use a **set** rather than a **vector**:

```
int main()
{
    string from, to;
    cin >> from >> to;                      // get source and target file names

    ifstream is(from.c_str());              // make input stream
    ofstream os(to.c_str());                // make output stream

    istream_iterator<string> ii(is);        // make input iterator for stream
    istream_iterator<string> eos;           // input sentinel
    ostream_iterator<string> oo(os," ");    // make output iterator for stream

    set<string> b(ii,eos);                  // b is a set initialized from input
    copy(b.begin() ,b.end() ,oo);           // copy buffer to output
}
```

When we insert values into a **set**, duplicates are ignored. Furthermore, the elements of a **set** are kept in order so no sorting is needed. With the right tools, most tasks are easy.

21.7.4 copy_if

The **copy()** algorithm copies unconditionally. The **unique_copy()** algorithm suppresses adjacent elements with the same value. The third copy algorithm copies only elements for which a predicate is true:

```
template<class In, class Out, class Pred>
Out copy_if(In first, In last, Out res, Pred p)
        // copy elements that fulfill the predicate
```

```
        {
                while (first!=last) {
                        if (p(*first)) *res++ = *first;
                        ++first;
                }
                return res;
        }
```

Using our **Larger_than** function object from §21.4, we can find all elements of a sequence larger than **6** like this:

```
        void f(const vector<int>& v)
                // copy all elements with a value larger than 6
        {
                vector<int> v2(v.size());
                copy_if(v.begin(), v.end(), v2.begin(), Larger_than(6));
                // . . .
        }
```

Thanks to a mistake I made, this algorithm is missing from the 1998 ISO Standard. This mistake has now been remedied, but you can still find implementations without **copy_if**. If so, just use the definition from this section.

21.8 Sorting and searching

Often, we want our data ordered. We can achieve that either by using a data structure that maintains order, such as **map** and **set**, or by sorting. The most common and useful sort operation in the STL is the **sort()** that we have already used several times. By default, **sort()** uses < as the sorting criterion, but we can also supply our own criteria:

```
        template<class Ran> void sort(Ran first, Ran last);
        template<class Ran, class Cmp> void sort(Ran first, Ran last, Cmp cmp);
```

As an example of sorting based on a user-specified criterion, we'll show how to sort strings without taking case into account:

```
        struct No_case {
                bool operator()(const string& x, const string& y) const
                {
```

```
                    for (int i = 0; i<x.length(); ++i) {
                        if (i == y.length()) return false;      // y<x
                        char xx = tolower(x[i]);
                        char yy = tolower(y[i]);
                        if (xx<yy) return true;                 // x<y
                        if (yy<xx) return false;                // y<x
                    }
                    return true;          // x<y (fewer characters in x)
                }
        };

        void sort_and_print(vector<string>& vc)
        {
            sort(vc.begin(),vc.end(),No_case());

            for (vector<string>::const_iterator p = vc.begin(); p!=vc.end(); ++p)
                cout << *p << '\n';
        }
```

Once a sequence is sorted, we no longer need to search from the beginning using **find**(); we can use the order to do a binary search. Basically, a binary search works like this:

Assume that we are looking for the value x; look at the middle element:

- If the element's value equals x, we found it!
- If the element's value is less than x, any element with value x must be to the right, so we look at the right half (doing a binary search on that half).
- If the value of x is less than the element's value, any element with value x must be to the left, so we look at the left half (doing a binary search on that half).
- If we have reached the last element (going left or right) without finding x, then there is no element with that value.

For longer sequences, a binary search is much faster than **find**() (which is a linear search). The standard library algorithms for binary search are **search**() and **equal_range**(). What do we mean by "longer"? It depends, but ten elements are usually sufficient to give **search**() an advantage over **find**(). For a sequence of 1000 elements, **search**() will be something like 200 times faster than **find**(); see §21.6.4.

The **binary_search** algorithm comes in two variants:

```
template<class Ran, class T>
bool binary_search(Ran first, Ran last, const T& val);
```

```
template<class Ran, class T, class Cmp>
bool binary_search(Ran first, Ran last, const T& val, Cmp cmp);
```

These algorithms require and assume that their input sequence is sorted. If it isn't, "interesting things," such as infinite loops, might happen. A **binary_search()** simply tells us whether a value is present:

```
void f(vector<string>& vs)      // vs is sorted
{
        if (binary_search(vs.begin(),vs.end(),"starfruit")) {
                // we have a starfruit
        }

        // . . .
}
```

So, **binary_search()** is ideal when all we care about is whether a value is in a sequence or not. If we care about the element we find, we can use **lower_bound()**, **upper_bound()**, or **equal_range()** (§23.4, §B.5.4). In the cases where we care which element is found, the reason is usually that it is an object containing more information than just the key, that there can be many elements with the same key, or that we want to know which element met a search criterion.

Drill

After each operation (as defined by a line of this drill) print the **vector.**
1. Define a **struct Item { string name; int iid; double value; /* . . . */ };** and make a **vector<Item>**, **vi**, and fill it with ten items from a file.
2. Sort **vi** by name.
3. Sort **vi** by iid.
4. Sort **vi** by value; print it in order of decreasing value (i.e., largest value first).
5. Insert **Item("horse shoe",99,12.34)** and **Item("Canon S400", 9988,499.95).**
6. Remove (erase) two **Items** identified by **name** from **vi.**
7. Remove (erase) two **Items** identified by **iid** from **vi.**
8. Repeat the exercise with a **list<Item>** rather than a **vector<Item>.**

Now try a **map:**
1. Define a **map<string,int>** called **msi.**
2. Insert ten (name,value) pairs into it, e.g., **msi["lecture"]=21.**

3. Output the (name,value) pairs to **cout** in some format of your choice.
4. Erase the (name,value) pairs from **msi**.
5. Write a function that reads value pairs from **cin** and places them in **msi**.
6. Read ten pairs from input and enter them into **msi**.
7. Write the elements of **msi** to **cout**.
8. Output the sum of the (integer) values in **msi**.
9. Define a **map<int,string>** called **mis**.
10. Enter the values from **msi** into **mis**; that is, if **msi** has an element ("lecture",21), **mis** should have an element (21,"lecture").
11. Output the elements of **mis** to **cout**.

More **vector** use:

1. Read some floating-point values (at least 16 values) from a file into a **vector<double>** called **vd**.
2. Output **vd** to **cout**.
3. Make a vector **vi** of type **vector<int>** with the same number of elements as **vd**; copy the elements from **vd** into **vi**.
4. Output the pairs of (**vd[i],vi[i]**) to **cout**, one pair per line.
5. Output the sum of the elements of **vd**.
6. Output the difference between the sum of the elements of **vd** and the sum of the elements of **vi**.
7. There is a standard library algorithm called **reverse** that takes a sequence (pair of iterators) as arguments; reverse **vd**, and output **vd** to **cout**.
8. Compute the mean value of the elements in **vd**; output it.
9. Make a new **vector<double>** called **vd2** and copy all elements of **vd** with values lower than (less than) the mean into **vd2**.
10. Sort **vd**; output it again.

Review

1. What are examples of useful STL algorithms?
2. What does **find()** do? Give at least five examples.
3. What does **count_if()** do?
4. What does **sort(b,e)** use as its sorting criterion?
5. How does an STL algorithm take a container as an input argument?
6. How does an STL algorithm take a container as an output argument?
7. How does an STL algorithm usually indicate "not found" or "failure"?
8. What is a function object?
9. In which ways does a function object differ from a function?
10. What is a predicate?
11. What does **accumulate()** do?
12. What does **inner_product()** do?

13. What is an associative container? Give at least three examples.
14. Is **list** an associative container? Why not?
15. What is the basic ordering property of binary tree?
16. What (roughly) does it mean for a tree to be balanced?
17. How much space per element does a **map** take up?
18. How much space per element does a **vector** take up?
19. Why would anyone use an **unordered_map** when an (ordered) **map** is available?
20. How does a **set** differ from a **map**?
21. How does a **multi_map** differ from a **map**?
22. Why use a **copy()** algorithm when we could "just write a simple loop"?
23. What is a binary search?

Terms

accumulate()	**find()**	searching
algorithm	**find_if()**	sequence
application: ()	function object	**set**
associative container	generic	**sort()**
balanced tree	hash function	sorting
binary_search()	**inner_product()**	stream iterator
copy()	**lower_bound()**	**unique_copy()**
copy_if()	**map**	**unordered_map**
equal_range()	predicate	**upper_bound()**

Exercises

1. Go through the chapter and do all **Try this** exercises that you haven't already done.
2. Find a reliable source of STL documentation and list every standard library algorithm.
3. Implement **count()** yourself. Test it.
4. Implement **count_if()** yourself. Test it.
5. What would we have to do if we couldn't return **end()** to indicate "not found"? Redesign and reimplement **find()** and **count()** to take iterators to the first and last elements. Compare the results to the standard versions.
6. In the Fruit example in §21.6.5, we copy **Fruits** into the **set**. What if we didn't want to copy the **Fruits**? We could have a **set<Fruit*>** instead. However, to do that, we'd have to define a comparison operation for that set. Implement the Fruit example using a **set<Fruit*, Fruit_comparison>**. Discuss the differences between the two implementations.

7. Write a binary search function for a **vector<int>** (without using the standard one). You can choose any interface you like. Test it. How confident are you that your binary search function is correct? Now write a binary search function for a **list<string>**. Test it. How much do the two binary search functions resemble each other? How much do you think they would have resembled each other if you had not known about the STL?

8. Take the word-frequency example from §21.6.1 and modify it to output its lines in order of frequency (rather than in lexicographical order). An example line would be **3: C++** rather than **C++: 3**.

9. Define an **Order** class with (customer) name, address, data, and **vector<Purchase>** members. **Purchase** is a class with a (product) **name**, **unit_price**, and **count** members. Define a mechanism for reading and writing **Orders** to and from a file. Define a mechanism for printing **Orders**. Create a file of at least ten **Orders**, read it into a **vector<Order>**, sort it by name (of customer), and write it back out to file. Create another file of at least ten **Orders** of which about a third are the same as in the first file, read it into a **list<Order>**, sort it by address (of customer), and write it back out to file. Merge the two files into a third using **std::merge()**.

10. Compute the total value of the orders in the two files from the previous exercise. The value of an individual **Purchase** is (of course) its **unit_price*count**.

11. Provide a GUI interface for entering **Orders** into files.

12. Provide a GUI interface for querying a file of **Orders**; e.g., "Find all orders from **Joe**," "Find the total value of orders in file **Hardware**," and "List all orders in file **Clothing**." Hint: First design a non-GUI interface; then, build the GUI on top of that.

13. Write a program to "clean up" a text file for use in a word query program; that is, replace punctuation with whitespace, put words into lower case, replace *don't* with *do not* (etc.), and remove plurals (e.g., *ships* becomes *ship*). Don't be too ambitious. For example, it is hard to determine plurals in general, so just remove an *s* if you find both *ship* and *ships*. Use that program on a real-world text file with at least 5000 words (e.g., a research paper).

14. Write a program (using the output from the previous exercise) to answer questions such as: "How many occurrences of *ship* are there in a file?" "Which word occurs most frequently?" "Which is the longest word in the file?" "Which is the shortest?" "List all words starting with *s*." "List all four-letter words."

15. Provide a GUI for the program from the previous exercise.

Postscript

The STL is the part of the ISO C++ standard library concerned with containers
and algorithms. As such it provides very general, flexible, and useful basic tools.
It can save us a lot of work: reinventing the wheel can be fun, but it is rarely productive. Unless there are strong reasons not to, use the STL containers and basic
algorithms. What is more, the STL is an example of generic programming, showing how concrete problems and concrete solutions can give rise to a collection of
powerful and general tools. If you need to manipulate data – and most programmers do – the STL provides an example, a set of ideas, and an approach that
often can help.

Part IV

Broadening the View

Ideals and History

> "When someone says,
> 'I want a programming language
> in which I need only say what I wish done,'
> give him a lollipop."

—Alan Perlis

This chapter is a very brief and very selective history of programming languages and the ideals they have been designed to serve. The ideals and the languages that express them are the basis for professionalism. Because C++ is the language we use in this book, we focus on C++ and languages that influenced C++. The aim is to give a background and a perspective to the ideas presented in this book. For each language, we present its designer or designers: a language is not just an abstract creation, but a concrete solution designed by individuals in response to problems they faced at the time.

22.1 History, ideals, and professionalism

"History is bunk," Henry Ford famously declared. The contrary opinion has been widely quoted since antiquity: "He who does not know history is condemned to repeat it." The problem is to choose which parts of history to know and which parts to discard: "95% of everything is bunk" is another relevant quote (with which we concur, though 95% is probably an underestimate). Our view of the relation of history to current practice is that there can be no professionalism without some understanding of history. If you know too little of the background of your field, you are gullible because the history of any field of work is littered with plausible ideas that didn't work. The "real meat" of history is ideas and ideals that have proved their worth in practical use.

We would have loved to talk about the origins of key ideas in many more languages and in all kinds of software, such as operating systems, databases, graphics, networking, the web, scripting, etc., but you'll have to find those important and useful areas of software and programming elsewhere. We have barely enough space to scratch the surface of the ideals and history of programming languages.

The ultimate aim of programming is always to produce useful systems. In the heat of discussions about programming techniques and programming languages, that's easily forgotten. Don't forget that! If you need a reminder, take another look at Chapter 1.

22.1.1 Programming language aims and philosophies

What is a programming language? What is a programming language supposed to do for us? Popular answers to "What is a programming language?" include

- A tool for instructing machines
- A notation for algorithms
- A means of communication among programmers
- A tool for experimentation

- A means of controlling computerized devices
- A way of expressing relationships among concepts
- A means of expressing high-level designs

Our answer is "All of the above – and more!" Clearly, we are thinking about general-purpose programming languages here, as we will throughout this chapter. In addition, there are special-purpose languages and domain-specific languages serving narrower and typically more precisely defined aims.

What properties of a programming language do we consider desirable?

- Portability
- Type safety
- Precisely defined
- High performance
- Ability to concisely express ideas
- Anything that eases debugging
- Anything that eases testing
- Access to all system resources
- Platform independence
- Runs on all platforms
- Stability over decades
- Prompt improvements in response to changes in application areas
- Ease of learning
- Small
- Support for popular programming styles (e.g., object-oriented programming and generic programming)
- Whatever helps analysis of programs
- Lots of facilities
- Supported by a large community
- Supportive of novices (students, learners)
- Comprehensive facilities for experts (e.g., infrastructure builders)
- Lots of software development tools available
- Lots of software components available (e.g., libraries)
- Supported by an open software community
- Supported by major platform vendors (Microsoft, IBM, etc.)

Unfortunately, we can't have all this at the same time. That's sad because every one of these "properties" is objectively a good thing: each provides benefits, and a language that doesn't provide them imposes added work and complications on its users. The reason we can't have it all is equally fundamental: several of the properties are mutually exclusive. For example, you cannot be 100% platform independent and also access all system resources; a program that accesses a resource that is not available on every platform cannot run everywhere. Similarly, we obviously want a language (and the tools and libraries we need to use it) that is small and easy to learn, but that can't be achieved while providing comprehensive support for programming on all kinds of systems and for all kinds of application areas.

This is where ideals become important. Ideals are what guide the technical choices and trade-offs that every language, library, tool, and program designer must make. Yes, when you write a program you are a designer and must make design choices.

22.1.2 Programming ideals

The preface of *The C++ Programming Language* starts, "C++ is a general purpose programming language designed to make programming more enjoyable for the serious programmer." Say what? Isn't programming all about delivering products? About correctness, quality, and maintainability? About time-to-market? About supporting software engineering? That, too, of course, but we shouldn't forget the programmer. Consider another example: Don Knuth said, "The best thing about the Alto is that it doesn't run faster at night." The Alto was a computer from the Xerox Palo Alto Research Center (PARC) that was one of the first "personal computers," as opposed to the shared computers for which there was a lot of competition for daytime access.

Our tools and techniques for programming exist to make a programmer, a human, work better and produce better results. Please don't forget that. So what guidelines can we articulate to help a programmer produce the best software with the least pain? We have made our ideals explicit throughout the book so this section is basically a summary.

The main reason we want our code to have a good structure is that the structure is what allows us to make changes without excessive effort. The better the structure, the easier it is to make a change, find and fix a bug, add a new feature, port it to a new architecture, make it run faster, etc. That's exactly what we mean by "good."

For the rest of this section, we will

- Revisit what we are trying to achieve, that is, what we want from our code

- Present two general approaches to software development and decide that a combination is better than either alternative by itself

- Consider key aspects of program structure as expressed in code:

  - Direct expression of ideas

- Abstraction level
- Modularity
- Consistency and minimalism

Ideals are meant to be used. They are tools for thinking, not simply fancy phrases to trot out to please managers and examiners. Our programs are meant to approximate our ideals. When we get stuck in a program, we step back to see if our problems come from a departure from some ideal; sometimes that helps. When we evaluate a program (preferably before we ship it to users), we look for departures from the ideals that might cause problems in the future. Apply ideals as widely as possible, but remember that practical concerns (e.g., performance and simplicity) and weaknesses in a language (no language is perfect) will often prevent you from achieving more than a good approximation of the ideals.

Ideals can guide us when making specific technical decisions. For example, we can't just make every single decision about interfaces for a library individually and in isolation (§14.1). The result would be a mess. Instead we must go back to our first principles, decide what is important about this particular library, and then produce a consistent set of interfaces. Ideally, we would articulate our design principles and trade-offs for that particular design in the documentation and in comments in the code.

During the start of a project, review the ideals and see how they relate to the problems and the early ideas for their solution. This can be a good way to get ideas and to refine ideas. Later in the design and development process, when you are stuck, step back and see where your code has most departed from the ideals – this is where the bugs are most likely to lurk and the design problems are most likely to occur. This is an alternative to the default technique of repetitively looking in the same place and trying the same techniques to find the bug. "The bug is always where you are not looking – or you would have found it already."

22.1.2.1 What we want

Typically, we want

- *Correctness:* Yes, it can be difficult to define what we mean by "correct," but doing so is an important part of the complete job. Often, others define for us what is correct for a given project, but then we have to interpret what they say.
- *Maintainability:* Every successful program will be changed over time; it will be ported to new hardware and software platforms, it will be extended with new facilities, and new bugs will be found that must be fixed. The sections below about ideals for program structure address this ideal.
- *Performance:* Performance ("efficiency") is a relative term. Performance has to be adequate for the program's purpose. It is often claimed that efficient code is necessarily low-level and that concerns with a good, high-level

structure of the code cause inefficiency. On the contrary, we find that acceptable performance is often achieved though adherence to the ideals and approaches we recommend. The STL is an example of code that is simultaneously abstract and very efficient. Poor performance can as easily arise from an obsession with low-level details as it can from disdain for such details.

- *On-time delivery:* Delivering the perfect program a year late is usually not good enough. Obviously, people expect the impossible, but we need to deliver quality software in a reasonable time. There is a myth that "completed on time" implies shoddiness. On the contrary, we find that emphasis on good structure (e.g., resource management, invariants, and interface design), design for testability, and use of appropriate libraries (often designed for a specific application or application area) is a good way to meet deadlines.

This leads to a concern for structure in our code:

- If there is a bug in a program (and every large program has bugs), it is easier to find in a program with a clear structure.

- If a program needs to be understood by a new person or needs to be modified in some way, a clear structure is comprehensible with far less effort than a mess of low-level details.

- If a program hits a performance problem, it is often easier to tune a high-level program (one that is a good approximation of the ideals and has a well-defined structure) than a low-level or messy one. For starters, the high-level one is more likely to be understandable. Second, the high-level one is often ready for testing and tuning long before the low-level one.

Note the point about a program being understandable. Anything that helps us understand a program and helps us reason about it is good. Fundamentally, regularity is better than irregularity – as long as the regularity is not achieved through oversimplification.

22.1.2.2 General approaches

There are two approaches to writing correct software:

- *Bottom-up:* Compose the system using only components proved to be correct.

- *Top-down:* Compose the system out of components assumed to contain errors and catch all errors.

Interestingly, the most reliable systems combine these two – apparently contrary – approaches. The reason for that is simple: for a large real-world system, neither approach will deliver the needed correctness, adaptability, and maintainability:

- We can't build and "prove" enough basic components to eliminate all sources of errors.

- We can't completely compensate for the flaws of buggy basic components (libraries, subsystems, class hierarchies, etc.) when combining them in the final system.

However, a combination of approximations to the two approaches can deliver more than either in isolation: we can produce (or borrow or buy) components that are sufficiently good, so that the problems that remain can be compensated for by error handling and systematic testing. Also, if we keep building better components, a larger part of a system can be constructed from them, reducing the amount of "messy ad hoc code" needed.

Testing is an essential part of software development. It is discussed in some detail in Chapter 26. Testing is the systematic search for errors. "Test early and often" is a popular slogan. We try to design our programs to simplify testing and to make it harder for errors to "hide" in messy code.

22.1.2.3 Direct expression of ideas

When we express something – be it high-level or low-level – the ideal is to express it directly in code, rather than though work-arounds. The fundamental ideal of representing our ideas directly in code has a few specific variants:

- *Represent ideas directly in code.* For example, it is better to represent an argument as a specific type (e.g., **Month** or **Color**) than as a more general one (e.g., **int**).

- *Represent independent ideas independently in code.* For example, with a few exceptions, the standard **sort()** can sort any standard container of any element type; the concepts of sorting, sorting criteria, container, and element type are independent. Had we built a "**vector** of objects allocated on the free store where the elements are of a class derived from **Object** with a **before()** member function defined for use by **vector::sort()**" we would have a far less general **sort()** because we made assumptions about storage, class hierarchy, available member functions, ordering, etc.

- *Represent relationships among ideas directly in code.* The most common relationships that can be directly represented are inheritance (e.g., a **Circle** is a kind of **Shape**) and parameterization (e.g., a **vector<T>** represents what's common for all vectors independently of a particular element type).

- *Combine ideas expressed in code freely – where and only where combinations make sense.* For example, **sort()** allows us to use a variety of element types and a variety of containers, but the elements must support **<** (if they do not, we use the **sort()** with an extra argument specifying the comparison criteria), and the containers we sort must support random-access iterators.

- *Express simple ideas simply.* Following the ideals listed above can lead to overly general code. For example, we may end up with class hierarchies with a more complicated taxonomy (inheritance structure) than anyone needs or with seven parameters to every (apparently) simple class. To avoid every user having to face every possible complication, we try to provide simple versions that deal with the most common or most important cases. For example, we have a **sort(b,e)** that implicitly sorts using less-than in addition to the general version **sort(b,e,op)** that sorts using **op**. If we could (and we will be able to in C++0x; see §22.2.8), we'd also provide versions **sort(c)** for sorting a standard container using less-than and **sort(c,op)** for sorting a standard container using **op**.

22.1.2.4 Abstraction level

We prefer to *work at the highest feasible level of abstraction*; that is, our ideal is to express our solutions in as general a way as possible.

For example, consider how to represent entries for a phone book (as we might keep it on a PDA or a cell phone). We could represent a set of (name,value) pairs as a **vector<pair<string,Value_type>>**. However, if we essentially always accessed that set using a name, **map<string,Value_type>** would be a higher level of abstraction, saving us the bother of writing (and debugging) access functions. On the other hand, **vector<pair<string,Value_type>>** is itself a higher level of abstraction than two arrays, **string[max]** and **Value_type[max]**, where the relationship between the string and its value is implicit. The lowest level of abstraction would be something like an **int** (number of elements) plus two **void***s (pointing to some form of representation, known to the programmer but not to the compiler). In our example, every suggestion so far could be seen as too low-level because it focuses on the representation of the pair of values, rather than their function. We could move closer to the application by defining a class that directly reflected a use. For example, we could write our application code using a class **Phonebook** with an interface designed for convenient use. That **Phonebook** class could be implemented using any one of the representations suggested.

The reason for preferring the higher level of abstraction (when we have an appropriate abstraction mechanism and if our language supports it with acceptable efficiency) is that such formulations are closer to the way we think about our problems and solutions than solutions that have been expressed at the level of computer hardware.

The reason given for dropping to a lower level of abstraction is typically "efficiency." This should be done only when really needed (§25.2.2). Using a lower-level (more primitive) language feature does not necessarily give better performance. Sometimes, it eliminates optimization opportunities. For example, using a **Phonebook** class, we have a choice of implementations, say, between **string[max]** plus **Value_type[max]** and **map<string,Value_type>**. For some applications the former is more efficient and for others the latter is. Naturally, performance would not be a major concern in an application involving only your personal directory. However, this kind of trade-off becomes interesting when we have to keep track of – and manipulate – millions of entries. More seriously, after a while, the use of low-level features soaks up the programmer's time so that opportunities for improvements (performance or otherwise) are missed because of lack of time.

22.1.2.5 Modularity

Modularity is an ideal. We want to compose our systems out of "components" (functions, classes, class hierarchies, libraries, etc.) that we can build, understand, and test in isolation. Ideally, we also want to design and implement such components so that they can be used in more than one program ("reused"). *Reuse* is the building of systems out of previously tested components that have been used elsewhere – and the design and use of such components. We have touched upon this in our discussions of classes, class hierarchies, interface design, and generic programming. Much of what we say about "programming styles" (in §22.1.3) relates to the design, implementation, and use of potentially "reusable" components. Please note that not every component can be used in more than one program; some code is simply too specialized and is not easily improved to be usable elsewhere.

Modularity in code should reflect important logical distinctions in the application. We do not "increase reuse" simply by putting two completely separate classes A and B into a "reusable component" called C. By providing the union of A's and B's interfaces, the introduction of C complicates our code:

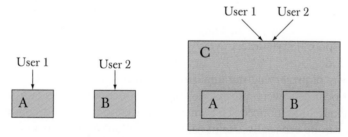

Here, User 1 and User 2 both use C. Unless you look into C, you might think that User 1 and User 2 gained benefits from sharing a popular component. Benefits from sharing ("reuse") would (in this case, wrongly) be assumed to include better testing, less total code, larger user base, etc. Unfortunately, except for a bit of oversimplification, this is not a particularly rare phenomenon.

What would help? Maybe a common interface to A and B could be provided:

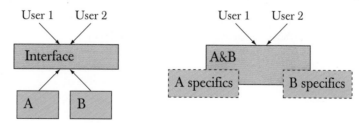

These diagrams are intended to suggest inheritance and parameterization, respectively. In both cases, the interface provided must be smaller than a simple union of A's and B's interfaces for the exercise to be worthwhile. In other words, A and B have to have a fundamental commonality for users to benefit from. Note how we again came back to interfaces (§9.7, §25.4.2) and by implication to invariants (§9.4.3).

22.1.2.6 Consistency and minimalism

Consistency and minimalism are primarily ideals for expressing ideas. So we might dismiss them as being about appearance. However, it is really hard to present a messy design elegantly, so demands of consistency and minimalism can be used as design criteria and affect even the most minute details of a program:

- Don't add a feature if you are in doubt about its utility.
- Do give similar facilities similar interfaces (and names), but only if the similarity is fundamental.
- Do give different facilities different names (and possibly different interface style), but only if the differences are fundamental.

Consistent naming, interface style, and implementation style help maintenance. When code is consistent, a new programmer doesn't have to learn a new set of conventions for every part of a large system. The STL is an example (Chapters 20–21, §B.4–6). When such consistency is impossible (for example, for ancient code or code in another language), it can be an idea to supply an interface that matches the style of the rest of the program. The alternative is to let the foreign ("strange," "poor") style infect every part of a program that needs to access the offending code.

One way of preserving minimalism and consistency is to carefully (and consistently) document every interface. That way, inconsistencies and duplication are more likely to be noticed. Documenting pre-conditions, post-conditions, and invariants can be especially useful as can careful attention to resource management and error reporting. A consistent error-handling and resource management strategy is essential for simplicity (§19.5).

To some programmers, the key design principle is KISS ("Keep It Simple, Stupid"). We have even heard it claimed that KISS is the only worthwhile design principle. However, we prefer less evocative formulations, such as "Keep simple things simple" and "Keep it simple: as simple as possible, but no simpler." The latter is a quote from Albert Einstein, which reflects that there is a danger of simplifying beyond the point where it makes sense, thus damaging the design. The obvious question is, "Simple for whom and compared to what?"

22.1.3 Styles/paradigms

When we design and implement a program, we aim for a consistent style. C++
supports four major styles that can be considered fundamental:

- Procedural programming
- Data abstraction
- Object-oriented programming
- Generic programming

These are sometimes (somewhat pompously) called "programming paradigms."
There are many more "paradigms," such as functional programming, logic programming, rule-based programming, constraints-based programming, and as-
pect-oriented programming. However, C++ doesn't support those directly, and
we just can't cover everything in a single beginner's book, so we'll leave those to
"future work" together with the mass of details that we must leave out about the
paradigms/styles we do cover:

- *Procedural programming:* the idea of composing a program out of functions
  operating on arguments. Examples are libraries of mathematical functions, such as **sqrt()** and **cos()**. C++ supports this style of programming
  through the notion of functions (Chapter 8). The ability to choose to
  pass arguments by value, by reference, and by **const** reference can be
  most valuable. Often, data is organized into data structures represented
  as **structs**. Explicit abstraction mechanisms (such as private data members or member functions of a class) are not used. Note that this style of
  programming – and functions – is an integral part of every other style.

- *Data abstraction:* the idea of first providing a set of types suitable for an application area and then writing the program using those. Matrices provide a classical example (§24.3–6). Explicit data hiding (e.g., the use of
  private data members of a class) is heavily used. The standard **string** and
  vector are popular examples, which show the strong relationship between data abstraction and parameterization as used by generic programming. This is called "abstraction" because a type is used through an
  interface, rather than by directly accessing its implementation.

- *Object-oriented programming:* the idea of organizing types into hierarchies to
  express their relationships directly in code. The classical example is the
  Shape hierarchy from Chapter 14. This is obviously valuable when the
  types really have fundamental hierarchical relationships. However, there
  has been a strong tendency to overuse; that is, people built hierarchies of
  types that do not belong together for fundamental reasons. When people
  derive, ask why. What is being expressed? How does the base/derived
  distinction help me in this particular case?

• *Generic programming:* the idea of taking concrete algorithms and "lifting" them to a higher level of abstraction by adding parameters to express what can be varied without changing the essence of an algorithm. The **high()** example from Chapter 20 is a simple example of lifting. The **find()** and **sort()** algorithms from the STL are classical algorithms expressed in very general forms using generic programming. See Chapters 20–21 and the following example.

All together now! Often, people talk about programming styles ("paradigms") as if they were simple disjointed alternatives: either you use generic programming or you use object-oriented programming. If your aim is to express solutions to problems in the best possible way, you will use a combination of styles. By "best," we mean easy to read, easy to write, easy to maintain, and sufficiently efficient. Consider an example: the classical "**Shape** example" originated with Simula (§22.2.6) and is usually seen as an example of object-oriented programming. A first solution might look like this:

```
void draw_all(vector<Shape*>& v)
{
        for(int i = 0; i<v.size(); ++i) v[i]->draw();
}
```

This does indeed look "rather object-oriented." It critically relies on a class hierarchy and on the virtual function call finding the right **draw()** function for every given **Shape**; that is, for a **Circle**, it calls **Circle::draw()** and for an **Open_polyline**, it calls **Open_polyline::draw()**. But the **vector<Shape*>** is basically a generic programming construct: it relies on a parameter (the element type) that is resolved at compile time. We could emphasize that by using a simple standard library algorithm to express the iteration over all elements:

```
void draw_all(vector<Shape*>& v)
{
        for_each(v.begin(),v.end(),mem_fun(&Shape::draw));
}
```

The third argument of **for_each()** is a function to be called for each element of the sequence specified by the first two arguments (§B.5.1). Now, that third function call is assumed to be an ordinary function (or a function object) called using the **f(x)** syntax, rather than a member function, called by the **p->f()** syntax. So, we use the standard library function **mem_fun()** (§B.6.2) to say that we really want to call a member function (the virtual function **Shape::draw()**). The point is that **for_each()** and **mem_fun()**, being templates, really aren't very "OO-like"; they clearly belong to what we usually consider generic programming. More interesting still, **mem_fun()** is a freestanding (template) function returning a class object. In other words, it can easily be classified as plain data abstraction (no inheritance) or even procedural programming (no data hiding). So, we could claim that this one line of code uses key aspects of all of the four fundamental styles supported by C++.

But why would we write the second version of the "draw all **Shapes**" example? It fundamentally does the same as the first version; it even takes a few more characters to write it in that way! We could argue that expressing the loop using **for_each**() is "more obvious and less error-prone" than writing out the **for**-loop, but for many that's not a terribly convincing argument. A better one is that "**for_each**() says what is to be done (iterate over a sequence) rather than how it is to be done." However, for most people the convincing argument is simply that "it's useful": it points the way to a generalization (in the best generic programming tradition) that allows us to solve more problems. Why are the shapes in a **vector**? Why not a **list**? Why not a general sequence? So we can write a third (and more general) version:

```
template<class Iter> void draw_all(Iter b, Iter e)
{
        for_each(b,e,mem_fun(&Shape::draw));
}
```

This will now work for all kinds of sequences of shapes. In particular, we can even call it for the elements of an array of **Shapes**:

```
Point p(0,100);
Point p2(50,50);
Shape* a[] = { new Circle(p,50), new Triangle(p,p2,Point(25,25)) };
draw_all(a,a+2);
```

For lack of a better term, we call programming using the most appropriate mix of styles *multi-paradigm programming*.

22.2 Programming language history overview

In the very beginning, programmers chiseled the zeros and ones into stones by hand! Well, almost. Here, we'll start (almost) from the beginning and quickly introduce some of the major developments in the history of programming languages as they relate to programming using C++.

There are a lot of programming languages. The rate of language invention is at least 2000 a decade, and the rate of "language death" is about the same. Here, we cover almost 60 years by briefly mentioning ten languages. For more information, see http://research.ihost.com/hopl/HOPL.html. There, you can find links to all the articles of the three ACM SIGPLAN HOPL (History of Programming

Languages) conferences. These are extensively peer-reviewed papers – and therefore far more trustworthy and complete than the average web source of information. The languages we discuss here were all represented at HOPL. Note that if you type the full title of a famous paper into a web search engine, there is a good chance that you'll find the paper. Also, most computer scientists mentioned here have home pages where you can find much information about their work.

Our presentation of a language in this chapter is necessarily very brief: each language mentioned – and hundreds not mentioned – deserves a whole book. We are also very selective in what we mention about a language. We hope you take this as a challenge to learn more rather than thinking, "So that's all there is to language X!" Remember, every language mentioned here was a major accomplishment and made an important contribution to our world. There is just no way we could do justice to these language in this short space – but not mentioning any would be worse. We would have liked to supply a bit of code for each language, but sorry, this is not the place for such a project (see exercises 5 and 6).

Far too often, an artifact (e.g., a programming language) is presented as simply what it is or as the product of some anonymous "development process." This misrepresents history: typically – especially in the early and formative years – a language is the result of the ideals, work, personal tastes, and external constraints on one or (typically) more individuals. Thus, we emphasize key people associated with the languages. IBM, Bell Labs, Cambridge University, etc. do not design languages; individuals from such organizations do – typically in collaboration with friends and colleagues.

Please note a curious phenomenon that often skews our view of history. Photographs of famous scientists and engineers are most often taken when they are famous and distinguished, members of national academies, Fellows of the Royal Society, Knights of St. John, recipients of the Turing Award, etc. – in other words, when they are decades older than when they did their most spectacular work. Almost all were/are among the most productive members of their profession until late in life. However, when you look back to the birth of your favorite language features and programming techniques, try to imagine a young man (there are still far too few women in science and engineering) trying to figure out if he has sufficient cash to invite a girlfriend out to a decent restaurant or a parent trying to decide if a crucial paper can be submitted to a conference at a time and place that can be combined with a vacation for a young family. The gray beards, balding heads, and dowdy clothes come much later.

22.2.1 The earliest languages

When – starting in 1948 – the first "modern" stored-program electronic computers appeared, each had its own language. There was a one-to-one correspondence between the expression of an algorithm (say, a calculation of a planetary orbit) and instructions for a specific machine. Obviously, the scientist (the users were most often scientists) had notes with mathematical formulas, but the program was a list of machine instructions. The first primitive lists were decimal or octal numbers – exactly matching their representation in the computer's memory. Later, assemblers and "auto codes" appeared; that is, people developed languages where machine instructions and machine facilities (such as registers) had symbolic names. So, a programmer might write "LD R0 123" to load the contents of the memory with the address 123 into register 0. However, each machine had its own set of instructions and its own language.

David Wheeler from the University of Cambridge Computer Laboratory is the obvious candidate for representing programming language designers of that time. In 1948, he wrote the first real program ever to run on a stored-program computer (the "table of squares" program we saw in §4.4.2.1). He is one of about ten people who have a claim on having written the first compiler (for a machine-specific "auto code"). He invented the function call (yes, even something so apparently simple needs to have been invented at some point). He wrote a brilliant paper on how to design libraries in 1951; that paper was at least 20 years ahead of its time! He was co-author with Maurice Wilkes (look him up) and D. J. Gill of the first book about programming. He received the first Ph.D. in computer science (from Cambridge in 1951) and later made major contributions to hardware (cache architectures and early local-area networks) and algorithms (e.g., the TEA encryption algorithm [§25.5.6] and the "Burrows-Wheeler transform" [the compression algorithm used in bzip2]). David Wheeler happens to have been Bjarne Stroustrup's Ph.D. thesis adviser – computer science is a young discipline. David Wheeler did some of his most important work as a grad student. He worked on to become a professor at Cambridge and a Fellow of the Royal Society.

References

Burrows, M., and David Wheeler. "A Block Sorting Lossless Data Compression Algorithm." Technical Report 124, Digital Equipment Corporation, 1994.

Bzip2 link: www.bzip.org/.

Cambridge Ring website: http://koo.corpus.cam.ac.uk/projects/earlyatm/cr82.

Campbell-Kelly, Martin. "David John Wheeler." *Biographical Memoirs of Fellows of the Royal Society,* Vol. 52, 2006. (His technical biography.)

EDSAC: http://en.wikipedia.org/wiki/EDSAC.

Knuth, Donald. *The Art of Computer Programming.* Addison-Wesley, 1968, and many revisions. Look for "David Wheeler" in the index of each volume.

TEA link: http://en.wikipedia.org/wiki/Tiny_Encryption_Algorithm.

Wheeler, D. J. "The Use of Sub-routines in Programmes." Proceedings of the 1952 ACM National Meeting. (That's the library design paper from 1951.)

Wilkes, M. V., D. Wheeler, and D. J. Gill. *Preparation of Programs for an Electronic Digital Computer.* Addison-Wesley Press, 1951; 2nd edition, 1957. The first book on programming.

22.2.2 The roots of modern languages

Here is a chart of important early languages:

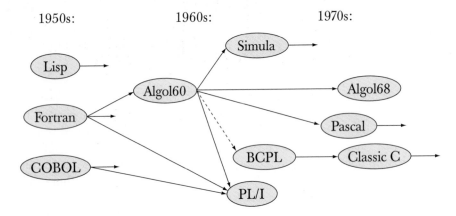

These languages are important partly because they were (and in some cases still are) widely used or because they became the ancestors to important modern languages – often direct descendants with the same name. In this section, we address the three early languages – Fortran, COBOL, and Lisp – to which most modern languages trace their ancestry.

22.2.2.1 Fortran

The introduction of Fortran in 1956 was arguably the most significant step in the development of programming languages. "Fortran" stands for "Formula Translation," and the fundamental idea was to generate efficient machine code from a notation designed for people rather than machines. The model for the Fortran notation was what scientists and engineers wrote when solving problems using mathematics, rather than the machine instructions provided by the (then very new) electronic computers.

From a modern perspective, Fortran can be seen as the first attempt to directly represent an application domain in code. It allowed programmers to write linear algebra much as they found it in textbooks. Fortran provided arrays, loops, and standard mathematical functions (using the standard mathematical notation, such as **x+y** and **sin(x)**). There was a standard library of mathematical functions, mechanisms for I/O, and a user could define additional functions and libraries.

The notation was largely machine independent so that Fortran code could often be moved from computer to computer with only minor modification. This was a *huge* improvement over the state of the art. Therefore, Fortran is considered the first high-level programming language.

It was considered essential that the machine code generated from the Fortran source code was close to optimally efficient: machines were room-sized and enormously expensive (many times the yearly salary of a team of good programmers), they were (by modern standards) ridiculously slow (such as 100,000 instructions/second), and they had absurdly small memories (such as 8K bytes). However, people were fitting useful programs into those machines, and an improvement in notation (leading to better programmer productivity and portability) could not be allowed to get in the way of that.

Fortran was hugely successful in its target domain of scientific and engineering calculations and has been under continuous evolution ever since. The main versions of the Fortran language are II, IV, 77, 90, 95, 03. It is still debated whether Fortran77 or Fortran90 is more widely used today.

The first definition of and implementation of Fortran were done by a team at IBM led by John Backus: "We did not know what we wanted and how to do it. It just sort of grew." How could he have known? Nothing like that had been done before, but along the way they developed or discovered the basic structure of compilers: lexical analysis, syntax analysis, semantic analysis, and optimization. To this day Fortran leads in the optimization of numerical computations. One thing that emerged (after the initial Fortran) was a notation for specifying grammars: the Backus-Naur Form (BNF). It was first used for Algol60 (§22.2.3.1) and is now used for most modern languages. We use a version of BNF for our grammars in Chapters 6 and 7.

Much later, John Backus pioneered a whole new branch of programming languages ("functional programming"), advocating a mathematical approach to programming as opposed to the machine view based on reading and writing memory locations. Note that pure math does not have the notion of assignment, or even actions. Instead you "simply" state what must be true given a set of conditions. Some of the roots of functional programming are in Lisp (§22.2.2.3), and some of the ideas from functional programming are reflected in the STL (Chapter 21).

References

Backus, John. "Can Programming Be Liberated from the von Neumann Style?" *Communications of the ACM,* 1977. (His Turing award lecture.)

Backus, John. "The History of FORTRAN I, II, and III." *ACM SIGPLAN Notices,* Vol. 13 No. 8, 1978. Special Issue: History of Programming Languages Conference.

Hutton, Graham. *Programming in Haskell.* Cambridge University Press, 2007. ISBN 0521692695.

ISO/IEC 1539. *Programming Languages – Fortran.* (The "Fortran 95" standard.)

Paulson, L. C. *ML for the Working Programmer.* Cambridge University Press, 1991. ISBN 0521390222.

22.2.2.2 COBOL

COBOL ("The Common Business-Oriented Language") was (and sometimes still is) for business programmers what Fortran was (and sometimes still is) for scientific programmers. The emphasis was on data manipulation:

- Copying
- Storing and retrieving (record keeping)
- Printing (reports)

Calculation/computation was (often correctly in COBOL's core application domains) seen as a minor matter. It was hoped/claimed that COBOL was so close to "business English" that managers could program and programmers would soon become redundant. That is a hope we have heard frequently repeated over the years by managers keen on cutting the cost of programming. It has never been even remotely true.

COBOL was initially designed by a committee (CODASYL) in 1959–60 at the initiative of the U.S. Department of Defense and a group of major computer manufacturers to address the needs of business-related computing. The design built directly on the FLOW-MATIC language invented by Grace Hopper. One of her contributions was the use of a close-to-English syntax (as opposed to the mathematical notation pioneered by Fortran and still dominant today). Like Fortran – and like all successful languages – COBOL underwent continuous evolution. The major revisions were 60, 61, 65, 68, 70, 80, 90, and 04.

Grace Murray Hopper had a Ph.D. in mathematics from Yale University. She worked for the U.S. Navy on the very first computers during World War II. She returned to the navy after a few years in the early computer industry:

"Rear Admiral Dr. Grace Murray Hopper (U.S. Navy) was a remarkable woman who grandly rose to the challenges of programming the first computers. During her lifetime as a leader in the field of software development concepts, she contributed to the transition from primitive programming techniques to the use of sophisticated compilers. She believed that 'we've always done it that way' was not necessarily a good reason to continue to do so."

—Anita Borg, at the "Grace Hopper Celebration of Women in Computing" conference, 1994

Grace Murray Hopper is often credited with being the first person to call an error in a computer a "bug." She certainly was among the early users of the term and documented a use:

As can be seen, that bug was real (a moth), and it affected the hardware directly. Most modern bugs appear to be in the software and have less graphical appeal.

References

A biography of G. M. Hopper: http://tergestesoft.com/~eddysworld/hopper.htm.
ISO/IEC 1989:2002. *Information Technology – Programming Languages – COBOL.*
Sammet, Jean E. "The Early History of COBOL." *ACM SIGPLAN Notices,* Vol. 13
    No. 8, 1978. Special Issue: History of Programming Languages Conference.

22.2.2.3 Lisp

Lisp was originally designed in 1958 by John McCarthy at MIT for linked-list and symbolic processing (hence its name: "LISt Processing"). Initially Lisp was (and is often still) interpreted, as opposed to compiled. There are dozens (most likely hundreds) of Lisp dialects. In fact, it is often claimed that "Lisp has an implied plural." The current most popular dialects are Common Lisp and Scheme. This family of languages has been (and is) the mainstay of artificial intelligence (AI) research (though delivered products have often been in C or C++). One of the main sources of inspiration for Lisp was the (mathematical notion of) lambda calculus.

Fortran and COBOL were specifically designed to help deliver solutions to real-world problems in their respective application areas. The Lisp community was much more concerned with programming itself and the elegance of programs. Often these efforts were successful. Lisp was the first language to separate its definition from the hardware and base its semantics on a form of math. If Lisp had a specific application domain, it is far harder to define precisely: "AI" or "symbolic computation" don't map as clearly into common everyday tasks as "business processing" and "scientific programming." Ideas from Lisp (and from the Lisp community) can be found in many more modern languages, notably the functional languages.

John McCarthy's B.S. was in mathematics from the California Institute of Technology and his Ph.D. was in mathematics from Princeton University. You may notice that there are a lot of math majors among the programming language designers. After his memorable work at MIT, McCarthy moved to Stanford in 1962 to help found the Stanford AI lab. He is widely credited for inventing the term *artificial intelligence* and made many contributions to that field.

References

Abelson, Harold, and Gerald J. Sussman. *Structure and Interpretation of Computer Programs, Second Edition.* MIT Press, 1996. ISBN 0262011530.

ANSI INCITS 226-1994 (formerly ANSI X3.226:1994). *American National Standard for Programming Language − Common LISP.*

McCarthy, John. "History of LISP." *ACM SIGPLAN Notices,* Vol. 13 No. 8, 1978. Special Issue: History of Programming Languages Conference.

Steele, Guy L. Jr. *Common Lisp: The Language.* Digital Press, 1990. ISBN 1555580416.

Steele, Guy L. Jr., and Richard Gabriel. "The Evolution of Lisp." Proceedings of the ACM History of Programming Languages Conference (HOPL-2). *ACM SIGPLAN Notices,* Vol. 28 No. 3, 1993.

22.2.3 The Algol family

In the late 1950s, many felt that programming was getting too complicated, too ad hoc, and too unscientific. They felt that the variety of programming languages was unnecessarily great and that those languages were put together with insufficient concern for generality and sound fundamental principles. This is a sentiment that has surfaced many times since then, but a group of people came together under the auspices of IFIP (the International Federation of Information Processing), and in just a couple of years they created a new language that revolutionized the way we think about languages and their definition. Most modern languages − including C++ − owe much to this effort.

22.2.3.1 Algol60

The "ALGOrithmic Language," Algol, which resulted from the efforts of the IFIP 2.1 group, was a breakthrough of modern programming language concepts:

- Lexical scope
- Use of grammar to define the language
- Clear separation of syntactic and semantic rules
- Clear separation of language definition and implementation
- Systematic use of (static, i.e., compile-time) types
- Direct support for structured programming

The very notion of a "general-purpose programming language" came with Algol. Before that, languages were scientific (e.g., Fortran), business (e.g., COBOL), list manipulation (e.g., Lisp), simulation, etc. Of these languages, Algol60 is most closely related to Fortran.

Unfortunately, Algol60 never reached major nonacademic use. It was seen as "too weird" by many in the industry, "too slow" by Fortran programmers, "not supportive of business processing" by COBOL programmers, "not flexible enough" by Lisp programmers, "too academic" by most people in the industry (including the managers who controlled investment in tools), and "too European" by many Americans. Most of the criticisms were correct. For example, the Algol60 report didn't define any I/O mechanism! However, similar criticisms could have been leveled at just about any contemporary language — and Algol set the new standard for many areas.

One problem with Algol60 was that no one knew how to implement it. That problem was solved by a team of programmers led by Peter Naur (the editor of the Algol60 report) and Edsger Dijkstra:

Peter Naur was educated (as an astronomer) at the University of Copenhagen and worked at the Technical University of Copenhagen (DTH) and for the Danish computer manufacturer Regnecentralen. He learned programming early (1950–51) in the Computer Laboratory in Cambridge, England (Denmark didn't have computers that early) and later had a distinguished career spanning the academia/industry gulf. He was co-inventor of BNF (the"Backus-Naur Form") used to describe grammars and a very early proponent of formal reasoning about programs (Bjarne Stroustrup first – in 1971 or so – learned the use of invariants from Peter Naur's technical articles). Naur consistently maintained a thoughtful perspective on computing, always considering the human aspects of programming. In fact, his later work could reasonably be considered part of philosophy (except that he considers conventional academic philosophy utter nonsense). He was the first professor of Datalogi at the University of Copenhagen (the Danish term *datalogi* is best translated as "informatics"; Peter Naur hates the term *computer science* as a misnomer – computing is not primarily about computers).

Edsger Dijkstra was another of computer science's all-time greats. He studied physics in Leyden but did his early work in computing in Mathematisch Centrum in Amsterdam. He later worked in quite a few places, including Eindhoven University of Technology, Burroughs Corporation, and the University of Texas (Austin). In addition to his seminal work on Algol, he was a pioneer and strong proponent of the use of mathematical logic in programming, algorithms, and one of the designers and implementers of THE operating system – one of the first operating systems to systematically deal with concurrency. THE stands for "Technische Hogeschool Eindhoven" – the university where Edsger Dijkstra worked at the time. Arguably, his most famous paper was "Go-To Statement Considered Harmful," which convincingly demonstrated the problems with unstructured control flows.

The Algol family tree is impressive:

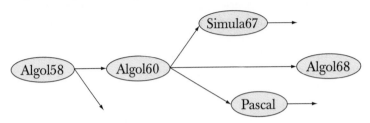

Note Simula67 and Pascal. These languages are the ancestors to many (probably most) modern languages.

References

Dijkstra, Edsger W. "Algol 60 Translation: An Algol 60 Translator for the x1 and Making a Translator for Algol 60." Report MR 35/61. Mathematisch Centrum (Amsterdam), 1961.

Dijkstra, Edsger. "Go-To Statement Considered Harmful." *Communications of the ACM,* Vol. 11 No. 3, 1968.

Lindsey, C. H. "The History of Algol68." Proceedings of the ACM History of Programming Languages Conference (HOPL-2). *ACM SIGPLAN Notices,* Vol. 28 No. 3, 1993.

Naur, Peter, ed. "Revised Report on the Algorithmic Language Algol 60." A/S Regnecentralen (Copenhagen), 1964.

Naur, Peter. "Proof of Algorithms by General Snapshots." *BIT,* Vol. 6, 1966, pp. 310–16. Probably the first paper on how to prove programs correct.

Naur, Peter. "The European Side of the Last Phase of the Development of ALGOL 60." *ACM SIGPLAN Notices,* Vol. 13 No. 8, 1978. Special Issue: History of Programming Languages Conference.

Perlis, Alan J. "The American Side of the Development of Algol." *ACM SIGPLAN Notices,* Vol. 13 No. 8, 1978. Special Issue: History of Programming Languages Conference.

van Wijngaarden, A., B. J. Mailloux, J. E. L. Peck, C. H. A. Koster, M. Sintzoff, C. H. Lindsey, L. G. L. T. Meertens, and R. G. Fisker, eds. *Revised Report on the Algorithmic Language Algol 68* (Sept. 1973). Springer-Verlag, 1976.

22.2.3.2 Pascal

The Algol68 language mentioned in the Algol family tree was a large and ambitious project. Like Algol60, it was the work of "the Algol committee" (IFIP working group 2.1), but it took "forever" to complete and many were impatient and doubtful that something useful would ever come from that project. One member of the Algol committee, Niklaus Wirth, decided simply to design and implement his own successor to Algol. In contrast to Algol68, that language, called Pascal, was a simplification of Algol60.

Pascal was completed in 1970 and was indeed simple and somewhat inflexible as a result. It was often claimed to be intended just for teaching, but early papers describe it as an alternative to Fortran on the supercomputers of the day. Pascal was indeed easy to learn, and after a very portable implementation became available it became very popular as a teaching language, but it proved to be no threat to Fortran.

Pascal was the work of Professor Niklaus Wirth (photos from 1969 and 2004) of the Technical University of Switzerland in Zurich (ETH). His Ph.D. (in electrical engineering and computer science) is from the University of California at Berkeley, and he maintains a lifelong connection with California. Professor Wirth is the closest thing the world has had to a professional language designer. Over a period of 25 years, he designed and implemented

- Algol W
- PL/360
- Euler
- Pascal
- Modula
- Modula-2
- Oberon
- Oberon-2
- Lola (a hardware description language)

Niklaus Wirth describes this as his unending quest for simplicity. His work has been most influential. Studying that series of languages is a most interesting exercise. Professor Wirth is the only person ever to present two languages at HOPL.

In the end, pure Pascal proved to be too simple and rigid for industrial success. In the 1980s, it was saved from extinction primarily through the work of

Anders Hejlsberg. Anders Hejlsberg was one of the three founders of Borland. He first designed and implemented Turbo Pascal (providing, among other things, more flexible argument-passing facilities) and later added a C++-like object model (but with just single inheritance and a nice module mechanism). He was educated at the Technical University in Copenhagen, where Peter Naur occasionally lectured − it's sometimes a very small world. Anders Hejlsberg later designed Delphi for Borland and C# for Microsoft.

The (necessarily simplified) Pascal family tree looks like this:

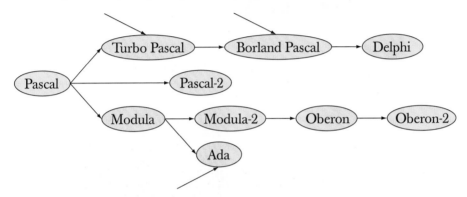

References

Borland/Turbo Pascal. http://en.wikipedia.org/wiki/Turbo_Pascal.

Hejlsberg, Anders, Scott Wiltamuth, and Peter Golde. *The C# Programming Language, Second Edition.* Microsoft .NET Development Series. ISBN 0321334434.

Wirth, Niklaus. "The Programming Language Pascal." *Acta Informatics,* Vol. 1 Fasc 1, 1971.

Wirth, Niklaus. "Design and Implementation of Modula." *Software−Practice and Experience,* Vol. 7 No. 1, 1977.

Wirth, Niklaus. "Recollections about the Development of Pascal." Proceedings of the ACM History of Programming Languages Conference (HOPL-2). *ACM SIGPLAN Notices,* Vol. 28 No. 3, 1993.

Wirth, Niklaus. *Modula-2 and Oberon.* Proceedings of the Third ACM SIGPLAN Conference on the History of Programming Languages (HOPL-III). San Diego, CA, 2007. http://portal.acm.org/toc.cfm?id=1238844.

22.2.3.3 Ada

The Ada programming language was designed to be a language for all the programming needs of the U.S. Department of Defense. In particular, it was to be a language in which to deliver reliable and maintainable code for embedded systems programming. Its most obvious ancestors are Pascal and Simula (see

§22.2.6). The leader of the group that designed Ada was Jean Ichbiah – a past chairman of the Simula Users' Group. The Ada design emphasized

- Data abstraction (but no inheritance until 1995)
- Strong static type checking
- Direct language support concurrency

The design of Ada aimed to be the embodiment of software engineering in programming languages. Consequently, the U.S. DoD did not design the language; it designed an elaborate process for designing the language. A huge number of people and organizations contributed to the design process, which progressed through a series of competitions, to produce the best specification and next to produce the best language embodying the ideas of the winning specification. This immense 20-year project (1975–98) was from 1980 managed by a department called AJPO (Ada Joint Program Office).

In 1979, the resulting language was named after Lady Augusta Ada Lovelace (a daughter of Lord Byron, the poet). Lady Lovelace could be claimed to have been the first programmer of modern times (for some definition of "modern") because she had worked with Charles Babbage (the Lucasian Professor of Mathematics in Cambridge – that's Newton's chair!) on a revolutionary mechanical computer in the 1840s. Unfortunately, Babbage's machine was unsuccessful as a practical tool.

Thanks to the elaborate process, Ada has been considered the ultimate design-by-committee language. The lead designer of the winning design team, Jean Ichbiah from the French company Honeywell Bull, emphatically denied that. However, I suspect (based on discussion with him) that he could have designed a better language, had he not been so constrained by the process.

Ada's use was mandated for military applications by the DoD for many years, leading to the saying "Ada, it's not just a good idea, it's the law!" Initially, the use of Ada was just "mandated," but when many projects received "waivers" to use other languages (typically C++), the U.S. Congress passed a law requiring the use of Ada in most military applications. That law was later rescinded in the face of commercial and technical realities. Bjarne Stroustrup is one of the very few people to have had his work banned by the U.S. Congress.

That said, we insist that Ada is a much better language than its reputation would indicate. We suspect that if the U.S. DoD had been less heavy-handed about its use and the exact way in which it was to be used (standards for application development processes, software development tools, documentation, etc.), it could have become noticeably more successful. To this day, Ada is important in aerospace applications and similar advanced embedded systems application areas.

Ada became a military standard in 1980, an ANSI standard in 1983 (the first implementation was done in 1983 – three years *after* the first standard!), and an ISO standard in 1987. The ISO standard was extensively (but of course compatibly) revised for a 1995 ISO standard. Notable improvements included more flexibility in the concurrency mechanisms and support for inheritance.

References

Barnes, John. *Programming in Ada 2005*. Addison-Wesley, 2006. ISBN 0321340787.

Consolidated Ada Reference Manual, consisting of the international standard (ISO/IEC 8652:1995). *Information Technology – Programming Languages – Ada*, as updated by changes from *Technical Corrigendum 1* (ISO/IEC 8652:1995:TC1:2000).

Official Ada homepage: www.usdoj.gov/crt/ada/.

Whitaker, William A. *ADA – The Project: The DoD High Order Language Working Group*. Proceedings of the ACM History of Programming Languages Conference (HOPL-2). *ACM SIGPLAN Notices*, Vol. 28 No. 3, 1993.

22.2.4 Simula

Simula was developed in the early to mid-1960s by Kristen Nygaard and Ole-Johan Dahl at the Norwegian Computing Center and Oslo University. Simula is indisputably a member of the Algol family of languages. In fact, Simula is almost completely a superset of Algol60. However, we choose to single out Simula for special attention because it is the source of most of the fundamental ideas that today are referred to as "object-oriented programming." It was the first language to provide inheritance and virtual functions. The words *class* for "user-defined type" and *virtual* for a function that can be overridden and called through the interface provided by a base class come from Simula.

Simula's contribution is not limited to language features. It came with an articulated notion of object-oriented design based on the idea of modeling real-world phenomena in code:

- Represent ideas as classes and class objects.
- Represent hierarchical relations as class hierarchies (inheritance).

Thus, a program becomes a set of interacting objects rather than a monolith.

Kristen Nygaard – the co-inventor (with Ole-Johan Dahl, to the left, wearing glasses) of Simula 67 – was a giant by most measures (including height), with an intensity and generosity to match. He conceived of the fundamental ideas of object-oriented programming and design, notably inheritance, and pursued their implications over decades. He was never satisfied with simple, short-term, and shortsighted answers. He had a constant social involvement that lasted over decades. He can be given a fair bit of credit for Norway staying out of the European Union, which he saw as a potential centralized and bureaucratic nightmare that would be insensitive to the needs of a small country at the far edge of the Union – Norway. In the mid-1970s Kristen Nygaard spent significant time in the computer science department of the University of Aarhus, Denmark (where, at the time, Bjarne Stroustrup was studying for his master's degree).

Kristen Nygaard's master's degree is in mathematics from the University of Oslo. He died in 2002, just a month before he was (together with his lifelong friend Ole-Johan Dahl) to receive the ACM's Turing Award, arguably the highest professional honor for a computer scientist.

Ole-Johan Dahl was a more conventional academic. He was very interested in specification languages and formal methods. In 1968, he became the first full professor of informatics (computer science) at Oslo University.

In August 2000 Dahl and Nygaard were made Commanders of the Order of Saint Olav by the King of Norway. Even true geeks can gain recognition in their hometown!

References

Birtwistle, G., O-J. Dahl, B. Myhrhaug, and K. Nygaard: *SIMULA Begin*. Student-litteratur (Lund. Sweden), 1979. ISBN 9144062125.

Holmevik, J. R. "Compiling SIMULA: A Historical Study of Technological Genesis." *IEEE Annals of the History of Computing*, Vol. 16 No. 4, 1994, pp. 25–37.

Kristen Nygaard's homepage: http://heim.ifi.uio.no/~kristen/.

Krogdahl, S. "The Birth of Simula." Proceedings of the HiNC 1 Conference in Trondheim, June 2003 (IFIP WG 9.7, in cooperation with IFIP TC 3).

Nygaard, Kristen, and Ole-Johan Dahl. "The Development of the SIMULA Languages." *ACM SIGPLAN Notices*, Vol. 13 No. 8, 1978. Special Issue: History of Programming Languages Conference.

SIMULA Standard. *DATA processing – Programming languages – SIMULA*. Swedish Standard, Stockholm, Sweden (1987). ISBN 9171622349.

22.2.5 C

In 1970, it was "well known" that serious systems programming – in particular the implementation of an operating system – had to be done in assembly code and could not be done portably. That was much as the situation had been for scientific programming before Fortran. Several individuals and groups set out to challenge that orthodoxy. In the long run, the C programming language (Chapter 27) was by far the most successful of those efforts.

Dennis Ritchie designed and implemented the C programming language in Bell Telephone Laboratories' Computer Science Research Center in Murray Hill, New Jersey. The beauty of C is that it is a deliberately simple programming language sticking very close to the fundamental aspects of hardware. Most of the current complexities (most of which reappear in C++ for compatibility reasons) were added after his original design and in several cases over Dennis Ritchie's objections. Part of C's success was its early wide availability, but its real strength was its direct mapping of language features to hardware facilities (see §25.4–5). Dennis Ritchie has succinctly described C as "a strongly typed, but weakly checked language"; that is, C has a static (compile-time) type system, and a program that uses an object in a way that differs from its definition is not legal. However, a C compiler can't check that. That made sense when the C compiler had to run in 48K bytes of memory. Soon after C came into use, people devised a program, called lint, that separately from the compiler verified conformance to the type system.

Together with Ken Thompson, Dennis Ritchie is the co-inventor of Unix, easily the most influential operating system of all times. C was – and is – associated with the Unix operating system and through that with Linux and the open-source movement.

Dennis Ritchie is retired from Lucent Bell Labs. For 40 years he worked in Bell Laboratories' Computer Science Research Center. He is a graduate of Harvard University (physics); his Ph.D. is in applied mathematics from Harvard University.

In the early years, 1974–1979, many people in Bell Labs influenced the design of C and its adoption. Doug McIlroy was everybody's favorite critic, discussion partner, and ideas man. He influenced C, C++, Unix, and much more.

Brian Kernighan is a programmer and writer extraordinaire. Both his code and his prose are models of clarity. The style of this book is in part derived from the tutorial sections of his masterpiece, *The C Programming Language* (known as "K&R" after its co-authors Brian Kernighan and Dennis Ritchie).

It is not enough to have good ideas; to be useful on a large scale, those ideas have to be reduced to their simplest form and articulated clearly in a way that is accessible to large numbers of people in their target audience. Verbosity is among the worst enemies of such presentation of ideas; so is obfuscation and over-abstraction. Purists often scoff at the results of such popularization and prefer "original results" presented in a way accessible only to experts. We don't: getting a nontrivial, but valuable, idea into the head of a novice is difficult, essential to the growth of professionalism, and valuable to society at large.

Over the years, Brian Kernighan has been involved with many influential programming and publishing projects. Two examples are AWK – an early scripting language named by the initials of its authors (Aho, Weinberger, and Kernighan) – and AMPL, "A Mathematical Programming Language."

Brian Kernighan is currently a professor at Princeton University; he is of course an excellent teacher, specializing in making otherwise complex topics clear. For more than 30 years he worked in Bell Laboratories' Computer Science Research Center. Bell Labs later became AT&T Bell Labs and later still split into AT&T Labs and Lucent Bell Labs. He is a graduate of the University of Toronto (physics); his Ph.D. is in electrical engineering from Princeton University.

The C language family tree looks like this:

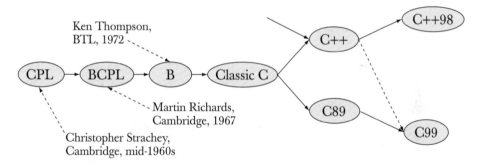

The origins of C lay in the never-completed CPL project in England, the BCPL (Basic CPL) language that Martin Richards did while visiting MIT on leave from Cambridge University, and an interpreted language, called B, done by Ken Thompson. Later, C was standardized by ANSI and the ISO and there were a lot of influences from C++ (e.g., function argument checking and **const**s).

CPL was a joint project between Cambridge University and Imperial College in London. Initially, the project had been done in Cambridge, so "C" officially stood for "Cambridge." When Imperial College became a partner, the official explanation of the "C" became "Combined." In reality (or so we are told), it always stood for "Christopher" after Christopher Strachey, CPL's main designer.

References

Brian Kernighan's home page: http://cm.bell-labs.com/cm/cs/who/bwk.
Dennis Ritchie's home page: http://cm.bell-labs.com/cm/cs/who/dmr.
ISO/IEIC 9899:1999. *Programming Languages – C.* (The C standard.)

Kernighan, Brian, and Dennis Ritchie. *The C Programming Language*. Prentice Hall, 1978. Second Edition, 1989. ISBN 0131103628.

A list of members of the Bell Labs' Computer Science Research Center: http://cm.bell-labs.com/cm/cs/alumni.html.

Ritchards, Martin. *BCPL – The Language and Its Compiler*. Cambridge University Press, 1980. ISBN 0521219655.

Ritchie, Dennis. "The Development of the C Programming Language. Proceedings of the ACM History of Programming Languages Conference (HOPL-2). *ACM SIGPLAN Notices,* Vol. 28 No. 3, 1993.

Salus, Peter. *A Quarter Century of UNIX*. Addison-Wesley, 1994. ISBN 0201547775.

22.2.6 C++

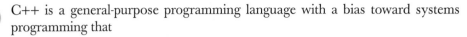

C++ is a general-purpose programming language with a bias toward systems programming that

- Is a better C
- Supports data abstraction
- Supports object-oriented programming
- Supports generic programming

It was originally designed and implemented by Bjarne Stroustrup in Bell Telephone Laboratories' Computer Science Research Center in Murray Hill, New Jersey, that is, down the corridor from Dennis Ritchie, Brian Kernighan, Ken Thompson, Doug McIlroy, and other Unix greats.

Bjarne Stroustrup received a master's degree (in mathematics with computer science) from the university in his hometown, Århus in Denmark. Then he went to Cambridge, where he got his Ph.D. (in computer science) working for David Wheeler. The main contributions of C++ were to

- Make abstraction techniques affordable and manageable for mainstream projects
- Pioneer the use of object-oriented and generic programming techniques in application areas where efficiency is a premium

Before C++, these techniques (often sloppily lumped together under the label of "object-oriented programming") were mostly unknown in the industry. As with scientific programming before Fortran and systems programming before C, it was "well known" that these techniques were too expensive for real-world use and also too complicated for "ordinary programmers" to master.

The work on C++ started in 1979 and led to a commercial release in 1985. After its initial design and implementation, Bjarne Stroustrup developed it further together with friends at Bell Labs and elsewhere until its standardization officially started in 1990. Since then, the definition of C++ has been developed by first ANSI (the national standards body for the United States) and since 1991 by ISO (the international standards organization). Bjarne Stroustrup has taken a major part in that effort as the chairman of the key subgroup in charge of new language features. The first international standard (C++98) was ratified 1998 and the second is in the works (C++0x).

The most significant development in C++ after its initial decade of growth was the STL – the standard library's facilities for containers and algorithms. It was the outcome of work – primarily by Alexander Stepanov – over decades aiming at producing the most general and efficient software, inspired by the beauty and utility of mathematics.

Alex Stepanov is the inventor of the STL and a pioneer of generic programming. He is a graduate of the University of Moscow and has worked on robotics, algorithms, and more, using a variety of languages (including Ada, Scheme, and C++). Since 1979, he has worked in U.S. academia and industry, notably at GE Labs, AT&T Bell Labs, Hewlett-Packard, Silicon Graphics, and Adobe.

The C++ family tree looks like this:

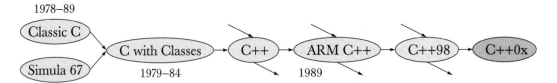

"C with Classes" was Bjarne Stroustrup's initial synthesis of C and Simula ideas. It died immediately following the implementation of its successor, C++.

Language discussions often focus on elegance and advanced features. However, C and C++ didn't become two of the most successful languages in the history of computing that way. Their strengths were flexibility, performance, and stability. Major software systems live over decades, often exhaust their hardware resources, and often suffer completely unexpected changes of requirements. C and C++ have been able to thrive in that environment. Our favorite Dennis Ritchie quote is, "Some languages are designed to prove a point; others are designed to solve a problem." By "others," he primarily meant C. Bjarne Stroustrup is fond of saying, "Even I knew how to design a prettier language than C++." The aim for C++ — as for C — was not abstract beauty (though we strongly appreciate that when we can get it), but utility.

I have often regretted not being able to use C++0x features in this book. It would have simplified many examples and explanations. However, **unordered_map** (§21.6.4), **array** (§20.9), and **regexp** (§23.5–9) are examples from the C++0x standard library. C++0x will also feature better checking of templates, simpler and more general initialization, and in places a more robust notation. See my HOPL-III paper.

References

Alexander Stepanov's publications: www.stepanovpapers.com.

Bjarne Stroustrup's home page: www.research.att.com/~bs.

ISO/IEC 14882:2003. *Programming Languages – C++*. (The C++ standard.)

Stroustrup, Bjarne. "A History of C++: 1979–1991. Proceedings of the ACM History of Programming Languages Conference (HOPL-2). *ACM SIGPLAN Notices,* Vol. 28 No. 3, 1993.

Stroustrup, Bjarne. *The Design and Evolution of C++.* Addison-Wesley, 1994. ISBN 0201543303.

Stroustrup, Bjarne. *The C++ Programming Language (Special Edition).* Addison-Wesley, 2000. ISBN 0201700735.

Stroustrup, Bjarne. "C and C++: Siblings"; "C and C++: A Case for Compatibility"; and "C and C++: Case Studies in Compatibility." *The C/C++ Users Journal.* July, Aug., and Sept. 2002.

Stroustrup, Bjarne. "Evolving a Language in and for the Real World: C++ 1991–2006. Proceedings of the Third ACM SIGPLAN Conference on the History of Programming Languages (HOPL-III). San Diego, CA, 2007. http://portal.acm.org/toc.cfm?id=1238844.

22.2.7 Today

What programming languages are currently used and for what? That's a *really* hard question to answer. The family tree of current languages is – even in a most abbreviated form – somewhat crowded and messy:

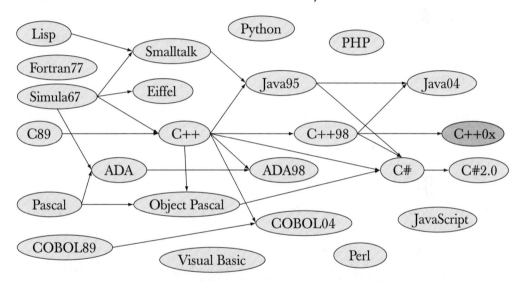

In fact, most of the statistics we find on the web (and elsewhere) are hardly better than rumors because they measure things that are only weakly correlated with use, such as number of web postings containing the name of a programming language, compiler shipments, academic papers, books sales, etc. All such measures favor the new over the established. Anyway, what is a programmer? Someone who uses a programming language every day? How about a student who writes small programs just to learn? A professor who just talks about programming? A physicist who writes a program almost every year? Is a professional programmer who – almost by definition – uses several programming languages every week counted many times or just once? We have seen each of these questions answered each way for different statistics.

However, we feel obliged to give you an opinion, so in 2008 there are about 10 million professional programmers in the world. For that opinion we rely on

IDC (a data-gathering firm), discussions with publishers and compiler suppliers, and various web sources. Feel free to quibble, but we know the number is larger than 1 million and less than 100 million for any halfway reasonable definition of "programmer." Which language do they use? Ada, C, C++, C#, COBOL, Fortran, Java, PERL, PHP, and Visual Basic probably (just probably) account for significantly more than 90% of all programs.

In addition to the languages mentioned here, we could list dozens or even hundreds more. Apart from trying to be fair to interesting or important languages, we see no point. Please seek out information yourself as needed. A professional knows several languages and learns new ones as needed. There is no "one true language" for all people and all applications. In fact, all major systems we can think of use more than one language.

22.2.8 Information sources

Each individual language description above has a reference list. These are references covering several languages:

More language designer links/photos
www.angelfire.com/tx4/cus/people/.

A few examples of languages
http://dmoz.org/Computers/Programming/Languages/.

Textbooks
Scott, Michael L. *Programming Language Pragmatics*. Morgan Kaufmann, 2000. ISBN 1558604421.

Sebesta, Robert W. *Concepts of Programming Languages*. Addison-Wesley, 2003. ISBN 0321193628.

History books
Bergin, T. J., and R. G. Gibson, eds. *History of Programming Languages – II*. Addison-Wesley, 1996. ISBN 0201895021.

Hailpern, Brent, and Barbara G. Ryder, eds. Proceedings of the Third ACM SIGPLAN Conference on the History of Programming Languages (HOPL-III). San Diego, CA, 2007. http://portal.acm.org/toc.cfm?id=1238844.

Lohr, Steve. *Go To: The Story of the Math Majors, Bridge Players, Engineers, Chess Wizards, Maverick Scientists and Iconoclasts—The Programmers Who Created the Software Revolution*. Basic Books, 2002. ISBN 9780465042265.

Sammet, Jean. *Programming Languages: History and Fundamentals*. Prentice-Hall, 1969. ISBN 0137299885.

Wexelblat, Richard L., ed. *History of Programming Languages*. Academic Press, 1981. ISBN 0127450408.

Review

1. What are some uses of history?
2. What are some uses of a programming language? List examples.
3. List some fundamental properties of programming languages that are objectively good.
4. What do we mean by abstraction? By higher level of abstraction?
5. What are our four high-level ideals for code?
6. List some potential advantages of high-level programming.
7. What is reuse and what good might it do?
8. What is procedural programming? Give a concrete example.
9. What is data abstraction? Give a concrete example.
10. What is object-oriented programming? Give a concrete example.
11. What is generic programming? Give a concrete example.
12. What is multi-paradigm programming? Give a concrete example.
13. When was the first program run on a stored-program computer?
14. What work made David Wheeler noteworthy?
15. What was the primary contribution of John Backus's first language?
16. What was the first language designed by Grace Murray Hopper?
17. In which field of computer science did John McCarthy primarily work?
18. What were Peter Naur's contributions to Algol60?
19. What work made Edsger Dijkstra noteworthy?
20. What languages did Niklaus Wirth design and implement?
21. What languages did Anders Hejlsberg design?
22. What was Jean Ichbiah's role in the Ada project?
23. What style of programming did Simula pioneer?
24. Where (outside Oslo) did Kristen Nygaard teach?
25. What work made Ole-Johan Dahl noteworthy?
26. Ken Thompson was the main designer of which operating system?
27. What work made Doug McIlroy noteworthy?
28. What is Brian Kernighan's most famous book?
29. Where did Dennis Ritchie work?
30. What work made Bjarne Stroustrup noteworthy?
31. What languages did Alex Stepanov use trying to design the STL?
32. List ten languages not described in §22.2.
33. Scheme is a dialect of which language?
34. What are C++'s two most prominent ancestors?
35. What does the C in C++ stand for?
36. Is Fortran an acronym? If so, what for?
37. Is COBOL an acronym? If so, what for?
38. Is Lisp an acronym? If so, what for?
39. Is Pascal an acronym? If so, what for?
40. Is Ada an acronym? If so, what for?
41. Which is the best programming language?

Terms

In this chapter "Terms" are really languages, people, and organizations.

- Languages:
  - Ada
  - Algol
  - BCPL
  - C
  - C++
  - COBOL
  - Fortran
  - Lisp
  - Pascal
  - Scheme
  - Simula

- People:
  - Charles Babbage
  - John Backus
  - Ole-Johan Dahl
  - Edsger Dijkstra
  - Anders Hejlsberg
  - Grace Murray Hopper
  - Jean Ichbiah
  - Brian Kernighan
  - John McCarthy
  - Doug McIlroy
  - Peter Naur
  - Kristen Nygaard
  - Dennis Ritchie
  - Alex Stepanov
  - Bjarne Stroustrup
  - Ken Thompson
  - David Wheeler
  - Niklaus Wirth

- Organizations:
  - Bell Laboratories
  - Borland
  - Cambridge University (England)
  - ETH (Swiss Federal Technical University)
  - IBM
  - MIT
  - Norwegian Computer Center
  - Princeton University
  - Stanford University
  - Technical University of Copenhagen
  - U.S. Department of Defense
  - U.S. Navy

Exercises

1. Define *programming*.
2. Define *programming language*.
3. Go through the book and look at the chapter vignettes. Which ones were from computer scientists? Write one paragraph summarizing what each of those scientists contributed.
4. Go through the book and look at the chapter vignettes. Which ones were not from computer scientists? Identify the country of origin and field of work of each.
5. Write a "Hello, World!" program in each of the languages mentioned in this chapter.
6. For each language mentioned in this chapter, look at a popular textbook and see what is used as the first complete program. Write that program in all of the other languages. Warning: This could easily be a 100-program project.
7. We have obviously "missed" many important languages. In particular, we essentially had to cut all developments after C++. Make a list of five modern languages that you think ought to be covered and write a page and a half – along the lines of the languages sections in this chapter – on three of those.
8. What is C++ used for and why? Write a 10- to 20-page report.
9. What is C used for and why? Write a 10- to 20-page report.
10. Pick one language (not C or C++) and write a 10- to 20-page description of its origins, aims, and facilities. Give plenty of concrete examples. Who uses it and for what?
11. Who currently holds the Lucasian Chair in Cambridge?
12. Of the language designers mentioned in this chapter, who has a degree in mathematics? Who does not?
13. Of the language designers mentioned in this chapter, who has a Ph.D.? In which field? Who does not have a Ph.D.?
14. Of the language designers mentioned in this chapter, who has received the Turing Award? What is that? Find the actual Turing Award citations for the winners mentioned here.
15. Write a program that, given a file of (name,year) pairs, such as (Algol,1960) and (C,1974), graphs the names on a timeline.
16. Modify the program from the previous exercise so that it reads a file of (name,year,(ancestors)) tuples, such as (Fortran,1956,()), (Algol,1960,(Fortran)), and (C++,1985,(C,Simula)), and graphs them on a timeline with arrows from ancestors to descendants. Use this program to draw improved versions of the diagrams in §22.2.2 and §22.2.7.

Postscript

Obviously, we have only scratched the surface of both the history of programming languages and of the ideals that fuel the quest for better software. We consider history and ideals sufficiently important to feel really bad about that. We hope to have conveyed some of our excitement and some idea of the immensity of the quest for better software and better programming as it manifest itself though the design and implementation of programming languages. That said, please remember that programming – the development of quality software – is the fundamental and important topic; a programming language is just a tool for that.

Text Manipulation

"Nothing is so obvious that it's obvious....
The use of the word 'obvious' indicates
the absence of a logical argument."

—Errol Morris

This chapter is mostly about extracting information from text. We store lots of our knowledge as words in documents, such as books, email messages, or "printed" tables, just to later have to extract it into some form that is more useful for computation. Here, we review the standard library facilities most used in text processing: **string**s, **iostream**s, and **map**s. Then, we introduce regular expressions (**regex**s) as a way of expressing patterns in text. Finally, we show how to use regular expressions to find and extract specific data elements, such as ZIP codes (postal codes), from text and to verify the format of text files.

23.1 Text

We manipulate text essentially all the time. Our books are full of text, much of what we see on our computer screens is text, and our source code is text. Our communication channels (of all sorts) overflow with words. Everything that is communicated between two humans could be represented as text, but let's not go overboard. Images and sound are usually best represented as images and sound (i.e., just bags of bits), but just about everything else is fair game for program text analysis and transformation.

We have been using **iostreams** and **strings** since Chapter 3, so here, we'll just briefly review those libraries. Maps (§23.4) are particularly useful for text processing, so we present an example of their use for email analysis. After this review, this chapter is concerned with searching for patterns in text using regular expressions (§23.3–10).

23.2 Strings

A **string** contains a sequence of characters and provides a few useful operations, such as adding a character to a **string**, giving the length of the **string**, and concatenating **strings**. Actually, the standard **string** provides quite a few operations, but most are useful only when you have to do fairly complicated text manipulation at a low level. Here, we just mention a few of the more useful. You can look up their details (and the full set of **string** operations) in a manual or expert-level textbook should you need them. They are found in **<string>** (note: not **<string.h>**):

Selected **string operations**	
s1 = s2	Assign **s2** to **s1**; **s2** can be a **string** or a C-style **string**.
s += x	Add **x** at end; **x** can be a character, a **string**, or a C-style string.
s[i]	Subscripting.
s1+s2	Concatenation; the characters in the resulting **string** will be a copy of those from **s1** followed by a copy of those from **s2**.
s1==s2	Comparison of **string** values; **s1** or **s2**, but not both, can be a C-style string. Also != .
s1<s2	Lexicographical comparison of **string** values; **s1** or **s2**, but not both, can be a C-style string. Also <=, >, and >=.
s.size()	Number of characters in **s**.
s.length()	Number of characters in **s**.
s.c_str()	C-style version of characters in **s**.
s.begin()	Iterator to first character.
s.end()	Iterator to one beyond the end of **s**.
s.insert(pos,x)	Insert **x** before **s[pos]**; **x** can be a character, a **string**, or a C-style string. **s** expands to make room for the characters from **x**.
s.append(pos,x)	Insert **x** after **s[pos]**; **x** can be a character, a **string**, or a C-style string. **s** expands to make room for the characters from **x**.
s.erase(pos)	Remove the character in **s[pos]**. **s**'s size decreases by 1.
pos = s.find(x)	Find **x** in **s**; **x** can be a character, a **string**, or a C-style string; **pos** is the index of the first character found, or **npos** (a position off the end of **s**).
in>>s	Read a whitespace-separated word into **s** from **in**.
getline(in,s)	Read a line into **s** from **in**.
out<<s	Write from **s** to **out**.

The I/O operations are explained in Chapters 10 and 11 and summarized in §23.3. Note that the input operations into a **string** expand the **string** as needed, so that overflow cannot happen.

The **insert()** and **append()** operations move characters to make room for new characters. The **erase()** operation moves characters "forward" in the **string** to make sure that no gap is left where we erased a character.

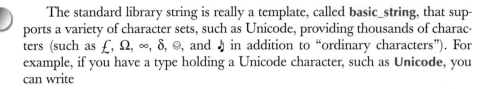

The standard library string is really a template, called **basic_string**, that supports a variety of character sets, such as Unicode, providing thousands of characters (such as £, Ω, ∞, δ, ☺, and ♪ in addition to "ordinary characters"). For example, if you have a type holding a Unicode character, such as **Unicode**, you can write

> **basic_string<Unicode> a_unicode_string;**

The standard string, **string**, which we have been using, is simply the **basic_string** of an ordinary **char**:

> **typedef basic_string<char> string;**   // string means basic_string<char>

We do not cover Unicode characters or Unicode strings here, but if you need them you can look them up, and you'll find that they can be handled (by the language, by **string**, by **iostreams**, and by regular expressions) much as ordinary characters and strings. If you need to use Unicode characters, it is best to ask someone experienced for advice; to be useful, your code has to follow not just the language rules but also some system conventions.

In the context of text processing, it is important that just about anything can be represented as a string of characters. For example, here on this page, the number **12.333** is represented as a string of six characters (surrounded by whitespace). If we read this number, we must convert those characters to a floating-point number before we can do arithmetic operations on the number. This leads to a need to convert values to **strings** and **strings** to values. In §11.4, we saw how to turn an integer into a **string** using a **stringstream**. This technique can be generalized to any type that has a << operator:

```
template<class T> string to_string(const T& t)
{
        ostringstream os;
        os << t;
        return os.str();
}
```

For example:

```
string s1 = to_string(12.333);
string s2 = to_string(1+5*6–99/7);
```

The value of **s1** is now **"12.333"** and the value of **s2** is **"17"**. In fact, **to_string()** can be used not just for numeric values, but for any class **T** with a << operator.

The opposite conversion, from **strings** to numeric values, is about as easy, and as useful:

```
struct bad_from_string : std::bad_cast
    // class for reporting string cast errors
{
    const char* what() const     // override bad_cast's what()
    {
        return "bad cast from string";
    }
};

template<class T> T from_string(const string& s)
{
    istringstream is(s);
    T t;
    if (!(is >> t)) throw bad_from_string();
    return t;
}
```

For example:

```
double d = from_string<double>("12.333");

void do_something(const string& s)
try
{
    int i = from_string<int>(s);
    // . . .
}
catch (bad_from_string e) {
    error ("bad input string",s);
}
```

The added complication of **from_string()** compared to **to_string()** comes because a **string** can represent values of many types. This implies that we must say which type of value we want to extract from a **string**. It also implies that the **string** we are looking at may not hold a representation of a value of the type we expect. For example:

```
int d = from_string<int>("Mary had a little lamb");     // oops!
```

So there is a possibility of error, which we have represented by the exception **bad_from_string**. In §23.9, we demonstrate how **from_string()** (or an equivalent function) is essential for serious text processing because we need to extract numeric values from text fields. In §16.4.3, we saw how an equivalent function **get_int()** was used in GUI code.

Note how **to_string()** and **from_string()** are similar in function. In fact, they are roughly inverses of each other; that is (ignoring details of whitespace, rounding, etc.), for every "reasonable type **T**" we have

>   **s==to_string(from_string<T>(s))**   *// for all s*

and

>   **t==from_string<T>(to_string(t))**   *// for all t*

Here, "reasonable" means that **T** should have a default constructor, a **>>** operator, and a matching **<<** operator defined.

Note also how the implementations of **to_string()** and **from_string()** both use a **stringstream** to do all the hard work. This observation has been used to define a general conversion operation between any two types with matching **<<** and **>>** operations:

```
struct bad_lexical_cast : std::bad_cast
{
        const char* what() const { return "bad cast"; }
};

template<typename Target, typename Source>
Target lexical_cast(Source arg)
{
        std::stringstream interpreter;
        Target result;

        if (!(interpreter << arg)              // read arg into stream
            || !(interpreter >> result)         // read result from stream
            || !(interpreter >> std::ws).eof()) // stuff left in stream?
                throw bad_lexical_cast();

        return result;
}
```

The curious and clever **!(interpreter>>std::ws).eof()** reads any whitespace that might be left in the **stringstream** after we have extracted the result. Whitespace is allowed, but there should be no more characters in the input and we can check that by seeing if we are at "end of file." So if we are trying to read an **int** from a **string** using **lexical_cast**, **"123"** and **"123 "** will succeed, but **"123 5"** will not because of that last 5.

This rather elegant, though oddly named, **lexical_cast** is provided by the boost library, which we will use for regular expression matching in §23.6–9. It will also be part of future versions of the C++ standard.

23.3 I/O streams

Considering the connection between strings and other types, we get to I/O streams. The I/O stream library doesn't just do input and output; it also performs conversions between string formats and types in memory. The standard library I/O streams provide facilities for reading, writing, and formatting strings of characters. The **iostream** library is described in Chapters 10 and 11, so here we'll just summarize:

Stream I/O	
in >> x	Read from **in** into **x** according to **x**'s type.
out << x	Write **x** to **out** according to **x**'s type.
in.get(c)	Read a character from **in** into **c**.
getline(in,s)	Read a line from **in** into the string **s**.

The standard streams are organized into a class hierarchy (§14.3):

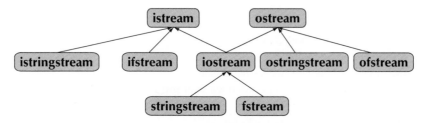

Together, these classes supply us with the ability to do I/O to and from files and strings (and anything that can be made to look like a file or a string, such as a keyboard and a screen; see Chapter 10). As described in Chapters 10 and 11, the **iostreams** provide fairly elaborate formatting facilities. The arrows indicate inheritance (see §14.3), so that, for example, a **stringstream** can be used as an **iostream** or as an **istream** or as an **ostream**.

Like **string**, **iostreams** can be used with larger character sets such as Unicode, much like ordinary characters. Please again note that if you need to use Unicode I/O, it is best to ask someone experienced for advice; to be useful, your code has to follow not just the language rules but also some system conventions.

23.4 Maps

Associative arrays (maps, hash tables) are key (pun intended) to a lot of text processing. The reason is simply that when we process text, we collect information, and that information is often associated with text strings, such as names, addresses, postal codes, Social Security numbers, job titles, etc. Even if some of those text strings could be converted into numeric values, it is often more convenient and simpler to treat them as text and use that text for identification. The word-counting example (§21.6) is a good simple example. If you don't feel comfortable using **map**s, please reread §21.6 before proceeding.

Consider email. We often search and analyze email messages and email logs – usually with the help of some program (e.g., Thunderbird or Outlook). Mostly, those programs save us from seeing the complete source of the messages, but all the information about who sent, who received, where the message went along the way, and much more is presented to the programs as text in a message header. That's a complete message. There are thousands of tools for analyzing the headers. Most use regular expressions (as described in §23.5–9) to extract information and some form of associative arrays to associate related messages. For example, we often search a mail file to collect all messages with the same sender, the same subject, or containing information on a particular topic.

Here, we will use a very simplified mail file to illustrate some of the techniques for extracting data from text files. The headers are real RFC2822 headers from www.faqs.org/rfcs/rfc2822.html. Consider:

```
xxx
xxx
----
From: John Doe <jdoe@machine.example>
To: Mary Smith <mary@example.net>
Subject: Saying Hello
Date: Fri, 21 Nov 1997 09:55:06 -0600
Message-ID: <1234@local.machine.example>

This is a message just to say hello.
So, "Hello".
----
From: Joe Q. Public <john.q.public@example.com>
To: Mary Smith <@machine.tld:mary@example.net>, , jdoe@test  .example
Date: Tue, 1 Jul 2003 10:52:37 +0200
Message-ID: <5678.21-Nov-1997@example.com>

Hi everyone.
----
```

> To: "Mary Smith: Personal Account" <smith@home.example>
> From: John Doe <jdoe@machine.example>
> Subject: Re: Saying Hello
> Date: Fri, 21 Nov 1997 11:00:00 −0600
> Message−ID: <abcd.1234@local.machine.tld>
> In−Reply−To: <3456@example.net>
> References: <1234@local.machine.example> <3456@example.net>
>
> This is a reply to your reply.
> −−−−
>
> −−−−

Basically, we have abbreviated the file by throwing most of the information away and eased the analysis by terminating each message by a line containing just −−−− (four dashes). We will write a small "toy application" that finds all messages sent by "John Doe" and write out their "Subject." If we can do that, we can do many interesting things.

First, we must consider whether we want random access to the data or just to analyze it as it streams by in an input stream. We choose the former because in a real program, we would probably be interested in several senders or in several pieces of information from a given sender. Also, it's actually the harder of the two tasks, so it will allow us to examine more techniques. In particular, we get to use iterators again.

Our basic idea is to read a complete mail file into a structure (which we call a **Mail_file**). This structure will hold all the lines of the mail file (in a **vector<string>**) and indicators of where each individual message starts and ends (in a **vector<Message>**):

Mail file:

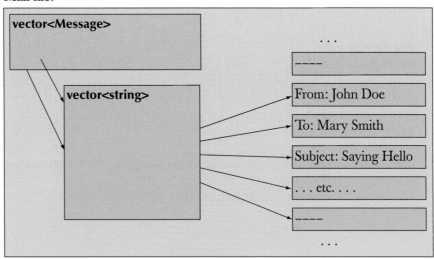

To this, we will add iterators and **begin**() and **end**() functions, so that we can iterate through the lines and through the messages in the usual way. This "boilerplate" will allow us convenient access to the messages. Given that, we will write our "toy application" to gather all the messages from each sender so that they are easy to access together:

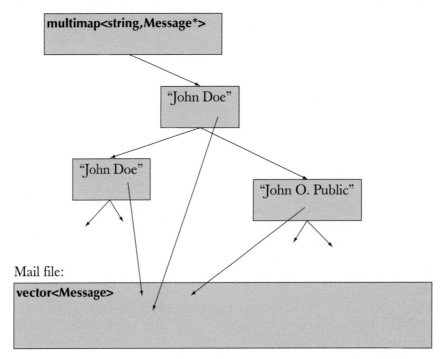

Finally, we will write out all the subject headers of messages from "John Doe" to illustrate a use of the access structures we have created.

We use many of the basic standard library facilities:

```
#include<string>
#include<vector>
#include<map>
#include<fstream>
#include<iostream>
using namespace std;
```

We define a **Message** as a pair of iterators into a **vector<string>** (our vector of lines):

```
typedef vector<string>::const_iterator Line_iter;
```

```
    class Message { // a Message points to the first and the last lines of a message
        Line_iter first;
        Line_iter last;
public:
        Message(Line_iter p1, Line_iter p2) :first(p1), last(p2) { }
        Line_iter begin() const { return first; }
        Line_iter end() const { return last; }
        // . . .
};
```

We define a **Mail_file** as a structure holding lines of text and messages:

```
    typedef vector<Message>::const_iterator Mess_iter;

    struct Mail_file {    // a Mail_file holds all the lines from a file
                          // and simplifies access to messages
        string name;           // file name
        vector<string> lines;  // the lines in order
        vector<Message> m;     // Messages in order

        Mail_file(const string& n);  // read file n into lines

        Mess_iter begin() const { return m.begin(); }
        Mess_iter end() const { return m.end(); }
};
```

Note how we added iterators to the data structures to make it easy to systematically traverse them. We are not actually going to use standard library algorithms here, but if we wanted to, the iterators are there to allow it.

To find information in a message and extract it, we need two helper functions:

```
    // find the name of the sender in a Message;
    // return true if found
    // if found, place the sender's name in s:
    bool find_from_addr(const Message* m, string& s);

    // return the subject of the Message, if any, otherwise "":
    string find_subject(const Message* m);
```

Finally, we can write some code to extract information from a file:

```
int main()
{
      Mail_file mfile("my-mail-file.txt");      // initialize mfile from a file

      // first gather messages from each sender together in a multimap:

      multimap<string, const Message*> sender;

      for (Mess_iter p = mfile.begin(); p!=mfile.end(); ++p) {
            const Message& m = *p;
            string s;
            if (find_from_addr(&m,s))
                  sender.insert(make_pair(s,&m));
      }

      // now iterate through the multimap
      // and extract the subjects of John Doe's messages:
      typedef multimap<string, const Message*>::const_iterator MCI;
      pair<MCI,MCI> pp = sender.equal_range("John Doe");
      for(MCI p = pp.first; p!=pp.second; ++p)
            cout << find_subject(p->second) << '\n';
}
```

Let us examine the use of maps in detail. We used a **multimap** (§20.10, §B.4) because we wanted to gather many messages from the same address together in one place. The standard library **multimap** does that (makes it easy to access elements with the same key). Obviously (and typically), we have two parts to our task:

- Build the map.
- Use the map.

We build the **multimap** by traversing all the messages and inserting them into the **multimap** using **insert()**:

```
for (Mess_iter p = mfile.begin(); p!=mfile.end(); ++p) {
      const Message& m = *p;
      string s;
      if (find_from_addr(&m,s))
            sender.insert(make_pair(s,&m));
}
```

What goes into a map is a (key,value) pair, which we make with **make_pair()**. We use our "homemade" **find_from_addr()** to find the name of the sender. We use the empty string to indicate that an address wasn't found.

Why do we introduce the reference **m** and pass its address? Why don't we just use **p** directly and say **find_from_addr(p,s)**? Because even though we know that **Mess_iter** refers to a **Message**, there is no guarantee that it is implemented as a pointer.

Why did we first put the **Messages** in a **vector** and then later build a **multimap**? Why didn't we just put the **Messages** into a **map** immediately? The reason is simple and fundamental:

- First, we build a general structure that we can use for many things.

- Then, we use that for a particular application.

That way, we build up a collection of more or less reusable components. Had we immediately built a **map** in the **Mail_file**, we would have had to redefine it whenever we wanted to do some different task. In particular, our **multimap** (significantly called **senders**) is sorted based on the Address field of a message. Most other applications would not find that order particularly useful: they might be looking at Return fields, Recipients, Copy-to fields, Subject fields, time stamps, etc.

This way of building applications in stages (or *layers,* as the parts are sometimes called) can dramatically simplify the design, implementation, documentation, and maintenance of programs. The point is that each part does only one thing and does it in a straightforward way. On the other hand, doing everything at once would require cleverness. Obviously, our "extracting information from an email header" program was just a tiny example of an application. The value of keeping separate things separate, modularization, and gradually building an application increases with size.

To extract information, we simply find all the entries with the key **"John Doe"** using the **equal_range()** function (§B.4.10). Then we iterate through all the elements in the sequence [first,second) returned by **equal_range()**, extracting the subject by using **find_subject()**:

```
typedef multimap<string, const Message*>::const_iterator MCI;

pair<MCI,MCI> pp = sender.equal_range("John Doe");

for (MCI p = pp.first; p!=pp.second; ++p)
    cout << find_subject(p->second) << '\n';
```

When we iterate over the elements of a **map**, we get a sequence of (key,value) pairs, and as with all **pair**s, the first element (here, the **string** key) is called **first** and the second (here, the **Message** value) is called **second** (§21.6).

23.4.1 Implementation details

Obviously, we need to implement the functions we use. It was tempting to save a tree by leaving this as an exercise, but we decided to make this example complete. The **Mail_file** constructor opens the file and constructs the **lines** and **m** vectors:

```
Mail_file::Mail_file(const string& n)
        // open file named "n"
        // read the lines from "n" into "lines"
        // find the messages in the lines and compose them in m
        // for simplicity assume every message is ended by a "----" line
{
        ifstream in(n.c_str());      // open the file
        if (!in) {
                cerr << "no " << n << '\n';
                exit(1);              // terminate the program
        }

        string s;
        while (getline(in,s)) lines.push_back(s);      // build the vector of lines

        Line_iter first = lines.begin();      // build the vector of Messages
        for (Line_iter p = lines.begin(); p!=lines.end(); ++p) {
                if (*p == "----") {      // end of message
                        m.push_back(Message(first,p));
                        first = p+1;    // ---- not part of message
                }
        }
}
```

The error handling is rudimentary. If this were a program we planned to give to friends to use, we'd have to do better.

TRY THIS

> What would be "better error handling"? Modify **Mail_file**'s constructor to handle likely formatting errors related to the use of "----".

The **find_from_addr()** and **find_subject()** functions are simple placeholders until we can do a better job of identifying information in a file (using regular expressions §23.6–10):

```
int is_prefix(const string& s, const string& p)
    // is p the first part of s?
{
    int n = p.size();
    if (string(s,0,n)==p) return n;
    return 0;
}


bool find_from_addr(const Message* m, string& s)
{
    for(Line_iter p = m->begin(); p!=m->end(); ++p)
        if (int n = is_prefix(*p,"From: ")) {
            s = string(*p,n);
            return true;
        }
    return false;
}


string find_subject(const Message& m)
{
    for(Line_iter p = m.begin(); p!=m.end(); ++p)
        if (int n = is_prefix(*p,"Subject: ")) return string(*p,n);
    return "";
}
```

Note the way we use substrings: **string(s,n)** constructs a string consisting of the tail of **s** from **s[n]** onward (**s[n]..s[s.size()–1]**), whereas **string(s,0,n)** constructs a string consisting of the characters **s[0]..s[n–1]**. Since these operations actually construct new strings and copy characters, they should be used with care where performance matters.

Why are the **find_from_addr()** and **find_subject()** functions so different? For example, one returns a **bool** and the other a **string**. They are different because we wanted to make a point:

- **find_from_addr()** distinguishes between finding an address line with an empty address (**""**) and finding no address line. In the first case, **find_from_addr()** returns **true** (because it found an address) and sets **s** to **""** (because the address just happens to be empty). In the second case, it returns **false** (because there was no address line).

- **find_subject()** returns **""** if there was an empty subject or if there was no subject line.

Is the distinction made by **find_from_addr()** useful? Necessary? We think that the distinction can be useful and that we definitely should be aware of it. It is a distinction that comes up again and again when looking for information in a data file: did we find the field we were looking for and was there something useful in it? In a real program, both the **find_from_addr()** and **find_subject()** functions would have been written in the style of **find_from_addr()** to allow users to make that distinction.

This program is not tuned for performance, but it is probably fast enough for most uses. In particular, it reads its input file only once, and it does not keep multiple copies of the text from that file. For large files, it may be a good idea to replace the **multimap** with an **unordered_multimap**, but unless you measure, you'll never know.

See §21.6 for an introduction to the standard library associative containers (**map**, **multimap**, **set**, **unordered_map**, and **unordered_multimap**).

23.5 A problem

I/O streams and **string** help us read and write sequences of characters, help us store them, and help with basic manipulation. However, it is very common to do operations on text where we need to consider the context of a string or involve many similar strings. Consider a trivial example. Take an email message (a sequence of words) and see if it contains a U.S. state abbreviation and ZIP code (two letters followed by five digits):

```
string s;
while (cin>>s) {
        if (s.size()==7
        && isalpha(s[0]) && isalpha(s[1])
        && isdigit(s[2]) && isdigit(s[3]) && isdigit(s[4])
        && isdigit(s[5]) && isdigit(s[6]))
                cout << "found " << s << '\n';
}
```

Here, **isletter(x)** is **true** if **x** is a **letter** and **isdigit(x)** is **true** if **x** is a digit (see §11.6).
There are several problems with this simple (too simple) solution:

- It's verbose (four lines, eight function calls).
- We miss (intentionally?) every ZIP code number not separated from its context by whitespace (such as **"TX77845"**, **TX77845–1234**, and **ATX77845**).
- We miss (intentionally?) every ZIP code number with a space between the letters and the digits (such as **TX 77845**).

- We accept (intentionally?) every ZIP code number with the letters in lower case (such as **tx77845**).

- If we decided to look for a postal code in a different format (such as **CB3 0FD**), we have to completely rewrite the code.

There has to be a better way! Before revealing that way, let's just consider the problems we would encounter if we decided to stay with the "good old simple way" of writing more code to handle more cases.

- If we want to deal with more than one format, we'd have to start adding **if**-statements or **switch**-statements.

- If we want to deal with upper and lower case, we'd explicitly have to convert (usually to lower case) or add yet another **if**-statement.

- We need to somehow (how?) describe the context of what we want to find. That implies that we must deal with individual characters rather than with strings, and that implies that we lose many of the advantages provided by **iostreams** (§7.8.2).

If you like, you can try to write the code for that, but it is obvious that on this track we are headed for a mess of **if**-statements dealing with a mess of special cases. Even for this simple example, we need to deal with alternatives (e.g., both five- and nine-digit ZIP codes). For many other examples, we need to deal with repetition (e.g., any number of digits followed by an exclamation mark, such as **123!** and **123456!**). Eventually, we would also have to deal with both prefixes and suffixes. As we observed (§11.1–2), people's tastes in output formats are not limited by a programmer's desire for regularity and simplicity. Just think of the bewildering variety of ways people write dates:

2007–06–05
June 5, 2007
jun 5, 2007
12 June 2007
6/5/2007
5/6/07
. . .

At this point – if not earlier – the experienced programmer declares, "There has to be a better way!" (than writing more ordinary code) and proceeds to look for it. The simplest and most popular solution is using what are called *regular expressions*. Regular expressions are the backbone of much text processing, the basis for the Unix grep command (see exercise 8), and an essential part of languages heavily used for such processing (such as AWK, PERL, and PHP).

The regular expressions we will use are implemented by a library that will be part of the next C++ standard (C++0x). It is compatible with the regular expressions in PERL. This makes many explanations, tutorials, and manuals available. For example, see the C++ standard committee's working paper (look for "WG21" on the web), John Maddoc's **boost::regex** documentation, and most PERL tutorials. Here, we will describe the fundamental concepts and some of the most basic and useful ways of using regular expressions.

TRY THIS

The last two paragraphs "carelessly" used several names and acronyms without explanation. Do a bit of web browsing to see what we are referring to.

23.6 The idea of regular expressions

The basic idea of a regular expression is that it defines a pattern that we can look for in a text. Consider how we might concisely describe the pattern for a simple ZIP code, such as **TX77845**. Here is a first attempt:

> **wwddddd**

Here, **w** represents "any letter" and **d** represents "any digit." We use **w** (for "word") because **l** (for "letter") is too easily confused with the digit 1. This notation works for this simple example, but let's try it for the nine-digit ZIP code format (such as **TX77845–5629**). How about:

> **wwddddd–dddd**

That looks OK, but how come that **d** means "any digit" but – means "plain" dash? Somehow, we ought to indicate that **w** and **d** are special: they represent character classes rather than themselves (**w** means "an **a** or a **b** or a **c** or . . ." and **d** means "a **1** or a **2** or a **3** or . . ."). That's too subtle. Let's prefix a letter that is a name of a class of characters with a backslash in the way special characters have always been indicated in C++ (e.g., **\n** is newline in a string literal). This way we get

> **\w\w\d\d\d\d\d–\d\d\d\d**

This is a bit ugly, but at least it is unambiguous, and the backslashes make it obvious that "something unusual is going on." Here, we represent repetition of a character by simply repeating. That can be a bit tedious and is potentially error-prone. Quick: Did we really get the five digits before the dash and four after it right? We did, but nowhere did we actually *say* **5** and **4**, so you had to count to make sure. We could add a count after a character to indicate repetition. For example:

> \w2\d5–\d4

However, we really ought to have some syntax to show that the **2**, **5**, and **4** in that pattern are counts, rather than just the alphanumeric characters **2**, **5**, and **4**. Let's indicate counts by putting them in curly braces:

> \w{2}\d{5}–\d{4}

That makes { special in the same way as \ (backslash) is special, but that can't be helped and we can deal with that.

So far, so good, but we have to deal with two more messy details: the final four digits in a ZIP code are optional. We somehow have to be able to say that we will accept both **TX77845** and **TX77845–5629**. There are two fundamental ways of expressing that:

> \w{2}\d{5} or \w{2}\d{5}–\d{4}

and

> \w{2}\d{5} and optionally –\d{4}

To say that concisely and precisely, we first have to express the idea of grouping (or sub-pattern) to be able to speak about the **\w{2}\d{5}** and **–\d{4}** parts of **\w{2}\d{5}–\d{4}**. Conventionally, we use parentheses to express grouping:

> (\w{2}\d{5})(–\d{4})

Now we have split the pattern into two sub-patterns, so we just have to say what we want to do with them. As usual, the cost of introducing a new facility is to introduce another special character: (is now "special" just like \ and {. Conventionally | is used to express "or" (alternatives) and **?** is used to express something conditional (optional), so we might write:

> (\w{2}\d{5})|(\w{2}\d{5}–\d{4})

and

    (\w{2}\d{5})(–\d{4})?

As with the curly braces in the count notation (e.g., \w{2}), we use the question mark (?) as a suffix. For example, (–\d{4})? means "optionally –\d{4}"; that is, we accept four digits preceded by a dash as a suffix. Actually, we are not using the parentheses around the pattern for the five-digit ZIP code (\w{2}\d{5}) for anything, so we could leave them out:

    \w{2}\d{5}(–\d{4})?

To complete our solution to the problem stated in §23.5, we could add an optional space after the two letters:

    \w{2} ?\d{5}(–\d{4})?

That " ?" looks a bit odd, but of course it's a space character followed by the ?, indicating that the space character is optional. If we wanted to avoid a space being so unobtrusive that it looks like a bug, we could put it in parentheses:

    \w{2}( )?\d{5}((–\d{4})?

If someone considered that still too obscure, we could invent a notation for a whitespace character, such as \s (s for "space"). That way we could write
    \w{2}\s?\d{5}(–\d{4})?

But what if someone wrote two spaces after the letters? As defined so far, the pattern would accept **TX77845** and **TX 77845** but not **TX 77845**. That's a bit subtle. We need to be able to say "zero or more whitespace characters," so we introduce the suffix * to mean "zero or more" and get

    \w{2}\s*\d{5}(–\d{4})?

This makes sense if you followed every step of the logical progression. This notation for patterns is logical and extremely terse. Also, we didn't pick our design choices at random: this particular notation is extremely common and popular. For many text-processing tasks, you need to read and write this notation. Yes, it looks a bit as if a cat walked over the keyboard, and yes, typing a single character wrong (even a space) completely changes the meaning, but please just get used to it. We can't suggest anything dramatically better, and this style of notation has already been wildly popular for more than 30 years since it was first introduced for the Unix grep command – and it wasn't completely new even then.

23.7 Searching with regular expressions

Now, we will use the ZIP code pattern from the previous section to find ZIP codes in a file. The program defines the pattern and then reads a file line by line, searching for the pattern. If the program finds an occurrence of the pattern in a line, it writes out the line number and what it found:

```cpp
#include <boost/regex.hpp>
#include <iostream>
#include <string>
#include <fstream>
using namespace std;

int main()
{
    ifstream in("file.txt");     // input file
    if (!in) cerr << "no file\n";

    boost::regex pat ("\\w{2}\\s*\\d{5}(-\\d{4})?");      // ZIP code pattern
    cout << "pattern: " << pat << '\n';

    int lineno = 0;
    string line;     // input buffer
    while (getline(in,line)) {
        ++lineno;
        boost::smatch matches;        // matched strings go here
        if (boost::regex_search(line, matches, pat))
            cout << lineno << ": " << matches[0] << '\n';
    }
}
```

This requires a bit of a detailed explanation. First consider:

```cpp
#include <boost/regex.hpp>
...
boost::regex pat ("\\w{2}\\s*\\d{5}(-\\d{4})?"); // ZIP code pattern
boost::smatch matches;        // matched strings go here
if (boost::regex_search(line, matches, pat))
```

We are using the boost implementation of the regex library that will soon be part of the standard library. To use that library, you may have to install it. To indicate which facilities are from the **regex** library, we use explicit qualifications with the library's namespace **boost**, e.g., **boost::regex**.

Back to regular expressions! Consider:

```
boost::regex pat ("\\w{2}\\s*\\d{5}(-\\d{4})?");
cout << "pattern: " << pat << '\n';
```

Here we first define a pattern, **pat** (of type **regex**), and then write it to output.
Note that we wrote

```
"\\w{2}\\s*\\d{5}(-\\d{4})?"
```

If you run the program, you'll see the output:

```
pattern: \w{2}\s*\d{5}(-\d{4})?
```

In C++ string literals, backslash is the escape character (§A.2.4), so to get a (single) \ into a literal string we have to write \\.

A **regex** pattern really is a kind of **string**, so we can output it using <<. A **regex** is not *just* a **string**, but the somewhat sophisticated mechanism for pattern matching that is created when you initialize a **regex** (or assign to one) is hidden and beyond the scope of this book. However, once we have initialized a **regex** with our pattern for ZIP codes, we can apply it to each line of our file:

```
boost::smatch matches;
if (boost::regex_search(line, matches, pat))
        cout << lineno << ": " << matches[0] << '\n';
```

The **regex_search(line, matches, pat)** searches the **line** for anything that matches the regular expression stored in **pat**, and if it finds any matches, it stores them in **matches**. Naturally, if no match was found, **regex_search(line, matches, pat)** returns **false**.

The **matches** variable is of type **smatch**. The **s** stands for "sub." Basically, an **smatch** is a vector of sub-matches. The first element, here **matches[0]**, is the complete match. We can treat **matches[i]** as a string if **i<matches.size()**. So if − for a given regular expression − the maximum number of sub-patterns is **N**, we find **matches.size()==N+1**.

So, what is a sub-pattern? A good first answer is, "Anything in parentheses in the pattern." Looking at **"\\w{2}\\s*\\d{5}(-\\d{4})?"**, we see the parentheses around the four-digit extension of the ZIP code. That's the only sub-pattern we see, so we guess (correctly) that **matches.size()==2**. We also guess that we can easily access those last four digits. For example:

```
while (getline(in,line)) {
        boost::smatch matches;
```

```
            if (boost::regex_search(line, matches, pat)) {
                    cout << lineno << ": " << matches[0] << '\n';        // whole match
                    if (1<matches.size() && matches[1].matched)
                            cout  << "\t: " << matches[1] << '\n';        // sub-match
            }
    }
```

Strictly speaking, we didn't have to test **1<matches.size()** because we already had
a good look at the pattern, but we felt like being paranoid (because we have been
experimenting with a variety of patterns in **pat** and they didn't all have just one
sub-pattern). We can ask if a sub-match succeeded by looking at its **matched** member, here **matches[1].matched**. In case you wonder: when **matches[i].matched** is
false, the unmatched sub-pattern **matches[i]** prints as the empty string. Similarly, a
sub-pattern that doesn't exist, such as **matches[17]** for the pattern above, is treated
as an unmatched sub-pattern.

We tried this program with a file containing

address TX77845
ffff tx 77843 asasasaa
ggg TX3456–23456
howdy
zzz TX23456–3456sss ggg TX33456–1234
cvzcv TX77845–1234 sdsas
xxxTx77845xxx
TX12345–123456

and got the output

pattern: "\w{2}\s*\d{5}(–\d{4})?"
1: TX77845
2: tx 77843
5: TX23456–3456
: –3456
6: TX77845–1234
: –1234
7: Tx77845
8: TX12345–1234
: –1234

Note that we

- Did not get fooled by the ill-formatted "ZIP code" on the line with **ggg**
  (what's wrong with that one?)

- Only found the first ZIP code from the line with **zzz** (we only asked for one per line)
- Found the correct suffixes on lines 5 and 6
- Found the ZIP code "hidden" among the **xxx**'s on line 7
- Found (unfortunately?) the ZIP code "hidden" in **TX12345–123456**

23.8 Regular expression syntax

We have seen a rather basic example of regular expression matching. Now is the time to consider regular expressions (in the form they are used in the **regex** library) a bit more systematically and completely.

Regular expressions ("regexps" or "regexs") is basically a little language for expressing patterns of characters. It is a powerful (expressive) and terse language, and as such it can be quite cryptic. After decades of use, there are many subtle features and several dialects. Here, we will just describe a (large and useful) subset of what appears to be the currently most widely used dialect (the PERL one). Should you need more to express what you need to say or to understand the regular expressions of others, go look on the web. Tutorials (of wildly differing quality) and specifications abound. In particular, the **boost::regex** specification and its standard committee equivalent (in WG21 TR1) are easily found.

The library also supports the ECMAscript, POSIX, awk, grep, and egrep notations and a host of search options. This can be extremely useful, especially if you need to match some pattern specified in another language. You can look up those options if you feel the need to go beyond the basic facilities described here. However, remember that "using the most features" is not an aim of good programming. Whenever you can, take pity on the poor maintenance programmer (maybe yourself in a couple of months) who has to read and understand your code: write code that is not unnecessarily clever and avoid obscure features whenever you can.

23.8.1 Characters and special characters

A regular expression specifies a pattern that can be used to match characters from a string. By default, a character in a pattern matches itself in a string. For example, the regular expression (pattern) **"abc"** will match the **abc** in **Is there an abc here?**

The real power of regular expressions comes from "special characters" and character combinations that have special meanings in a pattern:

Characters with special meaning	
.	any single character (a "wildcard")
[	character class
{	count
(	begin grouping
)	end grouping
\	next character has a special meaning
*	zero or more
+	one or more
?	optional (zero or one)
|	alternative (or)
^	start of line; negation
$	end of line

For example,

x.y

matches any three-letter string starting with an **x** and ending with a **y**, such as **xxy**, **x3y**, and **xay**, but not **yxy**, **3xy**, and **xy**.

Note that { . . . }, *, +, and ? are suffix operators. For example, \d+ means "one or more decimal digits."

If you want to use one of the special characters in a pattern, you have to "escape it" using backslash; for example, in a pattern + is the one-or-more operator, but \+ is a plus sign.

23.8.2 Character classes

The most common combinations of characters are represented in a terse form as "special characters":

Special characters for character classes		
\d	a decimal digit	[[:digit:]]
\l	a lowercase character	[[:lower:]]
\s	a space (space, tab, etc.)	[[:space:]]
\u	an uppercase character	[[:upper:]]
\w	a letter (a–z or A–Z) or digit (0–9) or an underscore (_)	[[:alnum:]]

Special characters for character classes (*continued*)		
\D	not \d	[^[:digit:]]
\L	not \l	[^[:lower:]]
\S	not \s	[^[:space:]]
\U	not \u	[^[:upper:]]
\W	not \w	[^[:alnum:]]

Note that an uppercase special character means "not the lowercase version of that special character." In particular, \W means "not a letter" rather than "an uppercase letter."

The entries in the third column (e.g., [[:digit:]]) give an alternative syntax using a longer name.

Like the **string** and **iostream** libraries, the **regex** library can handle large character sets, such as Unicode. As with **string** and **iostream**, we just mention this so that you can look for help and more information should you need it. Dealing with Unicode text manipulation is beyond the scope of this book.

23.8.3 Repeats

Repeating patterns are specified by the suffix operators:

Repetition	
{ n }	exactly *n* times
{ n, }	*n* or more times
{n,m}	at least *n* and at most *m* times
*	zero or more, that is, {0,}
+	one or more, that is, {1,}
?	optional (zero or one), that is, {0,1}

For example,

   Ax*

matches an **A** followed by zero or more **x**s, such as

   A
   Ax

Axx
Axxxxxxxxxxxxxxxxxxxxxxxxxxxxx

If you want at least one occurrence, use + rather than *. For example,

Ax+

matches an **A** followed by one or more **x**s, such as

Ax
Axx
Axxxxxxxxxxxxxxxxxxxxxxxxxxxxxx

but not

A

The common case of zero or one occurrence ("optional") is represented by a question mark. For example,

\d–?\d

matches the two digits with an optional dash between them, such as

1–2
12

but not

1––2

To specify a specific number of occurrences or a specific range of occurrences, use curly braces. For example,

\w{2}–\d{4,5}

matches exactly two letters and a dash (–) followed by four or five digits, such as

Ab–1234
XX–54321
22–54321

but not

Ab−123
?b−1234

Yes, digits are **\w** characters.

23.8.4 Grouping

To specify a regular expression as a sub-pattern, you group it using parentheses. For example:

(\d*:)

This defines a sub-pattern of zero or more digits followed by a colon. A group can be used as part of a more elaborate pattern. For example:

(\d*:)?(\d+)

This specifies an optional and possibly empty sequence of digits followed by a colon followed by a sequence of one or more digits. No wonder people invented a terse and precise way of saying such things!

23.8.5 Alternation

The "or" character (|) specifies an alternative. For example:

Subject: (FW:|Re:)?(.*)

This recognizes an email subject line with an optional **FW:** or **Re:** followed by zero or more characters. For example:

Subject: FW: Hello, world!
Subject: Re:
Subject: Norwegian Blue

but not

SUBJECT: Re: Parrots
Subject FW: No subject!

An empty alternative is not allowed:

(|def)   // error

However, we can specify several alternatives at once:

(bs|Bs|bS|BS)

23.8.6 Character sets and ranges

The special characters provide a shorthand for the most common classes of characters: digits (**\d**); letters, digits, and underscore (**\w**); etc. (§23.7.2). However, it is easy and often useful to define our own. For example:

[\w @]	a word character, a space, or an @
[a–z]	the lowercase characters from **a** to **z**
[a–zA–Z]	upper- or lowercase characters from **a** to **z**
[Pp]	an upper- or lowercase **P**
[\w\–]	a word character or a dash (plain – means range)
[asdfghjkl;']	the characters on the middle line of a U.S. QWERTY keyboard
[.]	a dot
[.[{(*+?^$]	a character with special meaning in a regular expression

In a character class specification – (dash) is used to specify a range, such as **[1–3]** (**1**, **2**, or **3**) and **[w–z]** (**w**, **x**, **y**, or **z**). Please use such ranges carefully: not every language has the same letters and not every letter encoding has the same ordering. If you feel the need for any range that isn't a sub-range of the most common letters and digits of the English alphabet, consult the documentation.

Note that we can use the special characters, such as **\w** (meaning "any word character"), within a character class specification. So, how do we get a backslash (\) into a character class? As usual, we "escape it" with a backslash: ****.

When the first character of a character class specification is ^, that ^ means negation. For example:

[^aeiouy]	not an English vowel
[^\d]	not a digit
[^aeiouy]	an English vowel or a ^

In the last regular expression, the ^ wasn't the first character after the [, so it was just a character, not a negation operator. Regular expressions can be subtle.

An implementation of **regex** also supplies a set of named character classes for use in matching. For example, if you want to match any alphanumeric character (that is, a letter or a digit: **a–z** or **A–Z** or **0–9**) you can do it by the regular expression **[[:alnum:]]**. Here, **alnum** is the name of a set a characters (the set of alphanumeric characters). A pattern for a nonempty quoted string of alphanumeric characters would be **"[[:alnum:]]+"**. To put that regular expression into a string, we have to escape the quotes:

```
string s = "\"[[:alnum:]]+\"";
```

Furthermore, to put that **string** into a **regex**, we must escape the backslashes as well as the quotes and use the () style of initialization because **regex**'s constructor from a **string** is explicit:

```
regex s("\\\"[[:alnum:]]+\\\"");
```

Using regular expressions leads to a lot of notational conventions. Anyway, here is a list of the standard character classes:

Character classes	
alnum	any alphanumeric character
alpha	any alphabetic character
blank	any whitespace character that is not a line separator
cntrl	any control character
d	any decimal digit
digit	any decimal digit
graph	any graphical character
lower	any lowercase character
print	any printable character
punct	any punctuation character
s	any whitespace character
space	any whitespace character
upper	any uppercase character
w	any word character (alphanumeric characters plus the underscore)
xdigit	any hexadecimal digit character

An implementation of **regex** may provide more character classes, but if you decide to use a named class not listed here, be sure to check if it is portable enough for your intended use.

23.8.7 Regular expression errors

What happens if we specify an illegal regular expression? Consider:

```
regex pat1("(|ghi)");     // missing alternative
regex pat2("[c-a]");      // not a range
```

When we assign a pattern to a **regex**, the pattern is checked, and if the regular expression matcher can't use it for matching because it's illegal or too complicated, a **bad_expression** exception is thrown.

Here is a little program that's useful for getting a feel for regular expression matching:

```
#include <boost/regex.hpp>
#include <iostream>
#include <string>
#include <fstream>
#include<sstream>
using namespace std;
using namespace boost;      // if you use the boost implementation

// accept a pattern and a set of lines from input
// check the pattern and search for lines with that pattern

int main()
{
    regex pattern;

    string pat;
    cout << "enter pattern: ";
    getline(cin,pat);           // read pattern

    try {
        pattern = pat;          // this checks pat
        cout << "pattern: " << pattern << '\n';
    }
    catch (bad_expression) {
        cout << pat << " is not a valid regular expression\n";
        exit(1);
    }

    cout << "now enter lines:\n";
    string line;                // input buffer
    int lineno = 0;

    while (getline(cin,line)) {
        ++lineno;
        smatch matches;
```

```
        if (regex_search(line, matches, pattern)) {
                cout << "line " << lineno << ": " << line << '\n';
                for (int i = 0; i<matches.size(); ++i)
                        cout << "\tmatches[" << i << "]: "
                                << matches[i] << '\n';
        }
        else
                cout << "didn't match\n";
    }
}
```

TRY THIS

Get the program to run and use it to try out some patterns, such as **abc, x.*x,** **(.*), \\([^)]*\\),** and **\\w+ \\w+(Jr\\.)?.**

23.9 Matching with regular expressions

There are two basic uses of regular expressions:

• *Searching* for a string that matches a regular expression in an (arbitrarily long) stream of data — **regex_search**() looks for its pattern as a substring in the stream

• *Matching* a regular expression against a string (of known size) — **regex_match**() looks for a complete match of its pattern and the string

The search for ZIP codes in §23.6 was an example of searching. Here, we will examine an example of matching. Consider extracting data from a table like this:

KLASSE	ANTAL DRENGE	ANTAL PIGER	ELEVER IALT
0A	12	11	23
1A	7	8	15
1B	4	11	15
2A	10	13	23
3A	10	12	22
4A	7	7	14
4B	10	5	15
5A	19	8	27
6A	10	9	19

KLASSE	ANTAL DRENGE	ANTAL PIGER	ELEVER IALT
6B	9	10	19
7A	7	19	26
7G	3	5	8
7I	7	3	10
8A	10	16	26
9A	12	15	27
0MO	3	2	5
0P1	1	1	2
0P2	0	5	5
10B	4	4	8
10CE	0	1	1
1MO	8	5	13
2CE	8	5	13
3DCE	3	3	6
4MO	4	1	5
6CE	3	4	7
8CE	4	4	8
9CE	4	9	13
REST	5	6	11
Alle klasser	184	202	386

This table (of the number of students in Bjarne Stroustrup's old primary school in 2007) was extracted from a context (a web page) where it looks nice and is fairly typical of the kind of data we need to analyze:

- It has numeric data fields.
- It has character fields with strings meaningful only to people who understand the context of the table. (Here, that point is emphasized by the use of Danish.)
- The character strings include spaces.
- The "fields" of this data are separated by a "separation indicator," which in this case is a tab character.

We chose this table to be "fairly typical" and "not too difficult," but note one subtlety we must face: we can't actually see the difference between spaces and tab characters; we have to leave that problem to our code.

We will illustrate the use of regular expressions to

- Verify that this table is properly laid out (i.e., every row has the right number of fields)
- Verify that the numbers add up (the last line claims to be the sum of the columns above)

If we can do that, we can do just about anything! For example, we could make a new table where the rows with the same initial digit (indicating the year: first grades start with 1) are merged or see if the number of students is increasing or decreasing over the years in question (see exercises 10–11).

To analyze the table, we need two patterns: one for the header line and one for the rest of the lines:

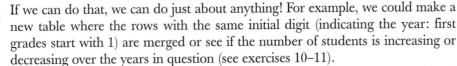

```
regex header( "^[\\w ]+(    [\\w ]+)*$");
regex row( "^[\\w ]+(    \\d+)( \\d+)( \\d+)$");
```

Please remember that we praised the regular expression syntax for terseness and utility; we did not praise it for ease of comprehension by novices. In fact, regular expressions have a well-earned reputation for being a "write-only language." Let us start with the header. Since it does not contain any numeric data, we could just have thrown away that first line, but – to get some practice – let us parse it. It consists of four "word fields" ("alphanumeric fields") separated by tabs. These fields can contain spaces, so we cannot simply use plain \w to specify its characters. Instead, we use [\w], that is, a word character (letter, digit, or underscore) or a space. One or more of those is written [\w]+. We want the first of those at the start of a line, so we get ^([\w]+). The "hat" (^) means "start of line." Each of the rest of the fields can be expressed as a tab followed by some words: ([\w]+). Now we take an arbitrary number of those followed by an end of line: ([\w]+)*$. The dollar sign ($) means "end of line." Now to write that as a C++ string literal, we have to add extra backslashes, and we get

```
"^[\\w ]+(    [\\w ]+)*$"
```

Note how we can't see that the tab characters are really tabs, but in this case they expand in the typesetting so as to reveal themselves.

Now for the more interesting part of the exercise: the pattern for the lines from which we want to extract the numeric data. The first field is as before: ^[\w]+. It is followed by exactly three numeric fields, each preceded by a tab: (\d+), so that we get

```
^[\w ]+(    \d+)(    \d+)(    \d+)$
```

which, after putting it into a string literal, is

```
"^[\\w ]+(    \\d+)(    \\d+)(    \\d+)$"
```

Now all we have to do is to use those patterns. First we will just validate the table layout:

```
int main()
{
    ifstream in("table.txt");    // input file
    if (!in) error("no input file\n");

    string line;    // input buffer
    int lineno = 0;

    regex header( "^[\\w ]+(    [\\w ]+)*$");                    // header line
    regex row( "^[\\w ]+(    \\d+)(    \\d+)(    \\d+)$");        // data line

    if (getline(in,line)) {        // check header line
        smatch matches;
        if (!regex_match(line, matches, header))
            error("no header");
    }
    while (getline(in,line)) {    // check data line
        ++lineno;
        smatch matches;
        if (!regex_match(line, matches, row))
            error("bad line",to_string(lineno));
    }
}
```

For brevity, we left out the **#includes**. We are checking all the characters on each line, so we use **regex_match** rather than **regex_search**. The difference between those two is exactly that **regex_match** must match every character of its input to succeed, whereas **regex_search** looks at the input trying to find a substring that matches. Mistakenly typing **regex_match** when you meant **regex_search** (or vice versa) can be a most frustrating bug to find. However, both of those functions use their "matches" argument identically.

We can now proceed to verify the data in that table. We keep a sum of the number of pupils in the boys ("drenge") and girls ("piger") columns. For each row, we check that last field ("ELEVER IALT") really is the sum of the first two fields. The last row ("Alle klasser") purports to be the sum of the columns above.

To check that, we modify **row** to make the text field a submatch so that we can recognize "Alle klasser":

```
int main()
{
        ifstream in("table.txt");       // input file
        if (!in) error("no input file");

        string line;                    // input buffer
        int lineno = 0;

        regex header( "^[\\w ]+(      [\\w ]+)*$");
        regex row( "^([\\w ]+)(       \\d+)(    \\d+)(    \d+)$");

        if (getline(in,line)) {         // check header line
            boost::smatch matches;
            if (!boost::regex_match(line, matches, header)) {
                error("no header");
            }
        }

        // column totals:
        int boys = 0;
        int girls = 0;

        while (getline(in,line)) {
            ++lineno;
            smatch matches;
            if (!regex_match(line, matches, row))
                cerr << "bad line: " << lineno << '\n';

            if (in.eof()) cout << "at eof\n";

            // check row:
            int curr_boy = from_string<int>(matches[2]);
            int curr_girl = from_string<int>(matches[3]);
            int curr_total = from_string<int>(matches[4]);
            if (curr_boy+curr_girl != curr_total)  error("bad row sum \n");

            if (matches[1]=="Alle klasser") {       // last line
                if (curr_boy != boys) error("boys don't add up\n");
                if (curr_girl != girls) error("girls don't add up\n");
                if (!(in>>ws).eof()) error("characters after total line");
                return 0;
            }
```

```
            // update totals:
            boys += curr_boy;
            girls += curr_girl;
        }

        error("didn't find total line");
    }
```

The last row is semantically different from the other rows – it is their sum. We recognize it by its label ("Alle klasser"). We decided to accept no more non-white-space characters after that last one (using the technique from **lexical_cast** (§23.2)) and to give an error if we did not find it.

We used the **from_string** function from §23.2 to extract an integer value from the data fields. We had already checked that those fields consisted exclusively of digits so we did not have to check that the **string**-to-**int** conversion succeeded.

23.10 References

Regular expressions are a popular and useful tool. They are available in many programming languages and in many formats. They are supported by an elegant theory based on formal languages and by an efficient implementation technique based on state machines. The full generality of regular expressions, their theory, their implementation, and the use of state machines in general are beyond the scope of this book. However, because these topics are rather standard in computer science curricula and because regular expressions are so popular, it is not hard to find more information (should you need it or just be interested).

For more information, see:

Aho, Alfred V., Monica S. Lam, Ravi Sethi, and Jeffrey D. Ullman. *Compilers: Principles, Techniques, and Tools, Second Edition* (usually called "The Dragon Book"). Addison-Wesley, 2007. ISBN 0321547985.

Austern, Matt, ed. "Draft Technical Report on C++ Library Extensions." ISO/IEC DTR 19768, 2005. www.open-std.org/jtc1/sc22/wg21/docs/papers/2005/n1836.pdf.

Boost.org. A repository for libraries meant to work well with the C++ standard library. www.boost.org.

Cox, Russ. "Regular Expression Matching Can Be Simple and Fast (but Is Slow in Java, Perl, PHP, Python, Ruby, . . .)." http://swtch.com/~rsc/regexp/regexp1.html.

Maddoc, J. boost::regex documentation. www.boost.org/libs/regex/doc/index.html.

Schwartz, Randal L., Tom Phoenix, and Brian D. Foy. *Learning Perl, Fourth Edition.* O'Reilly, 2005. ISBN 0596101058.

Drill

1. Find out if **regex** is shipped as part of your standard library. Hint: Try **std::regex** and **tr1::regex**.
2. Get the little program from §23.7.7 to work; that may involve getting **boost::regex** installed on your system (if it isn't already) and figuring out how to set the project and/or command-line options to link to the **regex** library and use the **regex** headers.
3. Use the program from drill 1 to test the patterns from §23.7.

Review

1. Where do we find "text"?
2. What are the standard library facilities most frequently useful for text analysis?
3. Does **insert()** add before or after its position (or iterator)?
4. What is Unicode?
5. How do you convert to and from a **string** representation (to and from some other type)?
6. What is the difference between **cin>>s** and **getline(cin,s)** assuming **s** is a **string**?
7. List the standard streams.
8. What is the key of a **map**? Give examples of useful key types.
9. How do you iterate over the elements of a **map**?
10. What is the difference between a **map** and a **multimap**? Which useful **map** operation is missing for **multimap**, and why?
11. What operations are required for a forward iterator?
12. What is the difference between an empty field and a nonexistent field? Give two examples.
13. Why do we need an escape character to express regular expressions?
14. How do you get a regular expression into a **regex** variable?
15. What does **\w+\s\d{4}** match? Give three examples. What string literal would you use to initialize a **regex** variable with that pattern?
16. How (in a program) do you find out if a string is a valid regular expression?
17. What does **regex_search()** do?
18. What does **regex_match()** do?
19. How do you represent the character dot (**.**) in a regular expression?
20. How do you represent the notion of "at least three" in a regular expression?
21. Is **7** a **\w** character? Is **_** (underscore)?

22. What is the notation for an uppercase character?
23. How do you specify your own character set?
24. How do you extract the value of an integer field?
25. How do you represent a floating-point number as a regular expression?
26. How do you extract a floating-point value from a match?
27. What is a sub-match? How do you access one?

Terms

match	regex_match()	search
multimap	regex_search()	smatch
pattern	regular expression	sub-pattern

Exercises

1. Get the email file example to run; test it using a larger file of your own creation. Be sure to include messages that are likely to trigger errors, such as messages with two address lines, several messages with the same address and/or same subject, and empty messages. Also test the program with something that simply isn't a message according to that program's specification, such as a large file containing no . . . lines.
2. Add a **multimap** and have it hold subjects. Let the program take an input string from the keyboard and print out every message with that string as its subject.
3. Modify the email example from §23.4 to use regular expressions to find the subject and sender.
4. Find a real email message file (containing real email messages) and modify the email example to extract subject lines from sender names taken as input from the user.
5. Find a large email message file (thousands of messages) and then time it as written with a **multimap** and with that **multimap** replaced by an **unordered_multimap**. Note that our application does not take advantage of the ordering of the **multimap**.
6. Write a program that finds dates in a text file. Write out each line containing at least one date in the format **line–number: line**. Start with a regular expression for a simple format, e.g., 12/24/2000, and test the program with that. Then, add more formats.
7. Write a program (similar to the one in the previous exercise) that finds credit card numbers in a file. Do a bit of research to find out what credit card formats are really used.

8. Modify the program from §23.8.7 so that it takes as inputs a pattern and a file name. Its output should be the numbered lines (**line–number: line**) that contain a match of the pattern. If no matches are found, no output should be produced.

9. Using **eof()** (§B.7.2), it is possible to determine which line of a table is the last. Use that to (try to) simplify the table-checking program from §23.9. Be sure to test your program with files that end with empty lines after the table and with files that don't end with a newline at all.

10. Modify the table-checking program from §23.9 to write a new table where the rows with the same initial digit (indicating the year: first grades start with 1) are merged.

11. Modify the table-checking program from §23.9 to see if the number of students is increasing or decreasing over the years in question.

12. Write a program, based on the program that finds lines containing dates (exercise 6), that finds all dates and reformats them to the ISO yyyy/mm/dd format. The program should take an input file and produce an output file that is identical to the input file except for the changed date formatting.

13. Does dot (.) match '\n'? Write a program to find out.

14. Write a program that, like the one in §23.8.7, can be used to experiment with pattern matching by typing in a pattern. However, have it read a file into memory (representing a line break with the newline character, '\n'), so that you can experiment with patterns spanning line breaks. Test it and document a dozen test patterns.

15. Describe a pattern that cannot be expressed as a regular expression.

16. For experts only: Prove that the pattern found in the previous exercise really isn't a regular expression.

Postscript

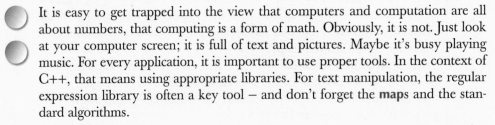

It is easy to get trapped into the view that computers and computation are all about numbers, that computing is a form of math. Obviously, it is not. Just look at your computer screen; it is full of text and pictures. Maybe it's busy playing music. For every application, it is important to use proper tools. In the context of C++, that means using appropriate libraries. For text manipulation, the regular expression library is often a key tool — and don't forget the **maps** and the standard algorithms.

Numerics

"For every complex problem
there is an answer that is
clear, simple, and wrong."

— **H. L. Mencken**

This chapter is an overview of some fundamental language and library facilities supporting numeric computation. We present the basic problems of size, precision, and truncation. The central part of the chapter is a discussion of multidimensional arrays — both C-style and an N-dimensional matrix library. We introduce random numbers as frequently needed for testing, simulation, and games. Finally, we list the standard mathematical functions and briefly introduce the basic functionality of the standard library complex numbers.

24.1 Introduction

For some people, numerics – that is, serious numerical computations – are everything. Many scientists, engineers, and statisticians are in this category. For many people, numerics are sometimes essential. A computer scientist occasionally collaborating with a physicist would be in this category. For most people, a need for numerics – beyond simple arithmetic of integers and floating-point numbers – is rare. The purpose of this chapter is to address language-technical details needed to deal with simple numerical problems. We do not attempt to teach numerical analysis or the finer points of floating-point operations; such topics are far beyond the scope of this book and blend with domain-specific topics in the application areas. Here, we present

- Issues related to the built-in types having fixed size, such as precision and overflow
- Arrays, both the built-in notion of multidimensional arrays and a **Matrix** library that is better suited to numerical computation
- A most basic description of random numbers
- The standard library mathematical functions
- Complex numbers

The emphasis is on the **Matrix** library that makes handling of matrices (multidimensional arrays) trivial.

24.2 Size, precision, and overflow

When we use the built-in types and usual computational techniques, numbers are stored in fixed amounts of memory; that is, the integer types (**int**, **long**, etc.) are only approximations of the mathematical notion of integers (whole numbers) and the floating-point types (**float**, **double**, etc.) are (only) approximations of the mathematical notion of real numbers. This implies that from a mathematical point of view, some computations are imprecise or wrong. Consider:

```
float x = 1.0/333;
float sum = 0;
for (int i=0; i<333; ++i) sum+=x;
cout << setprecision(15) << sum << "\n";
```

Running this, we do not get 1 as someone might naively expect, but rather

0.999999463558197

We expected something like that. What we see here is an effect of a rounding error. A floating-point number has only a fixed number of bits, so we can always "fool it" by specifying a computation that requires more bits to represent a result than the hardware provides. For example, the rational number 1/3 cannot be represented exactly as a decimal number (however many decimals we use). Neither can 1/333, so when we add 333 copies of **x** (the machine's best approximation of 1/333 as a **float**), we get something that is slightly different from 1. Whenever we make significant use of floating-point numbers, rounding errors will occur; the only question is whether the error significantly affects the result.

Always check that your results are plausible. When you compute, you must have some notion of what a reasonable result would look like or you could easily get fooled by some "silly bug" or computation error. Be aware of the possibility of rounding errors and if in doubt, consult an expert or read up on numerical techniques.

TRY THIS

Replace 333 in the example with 10 and run the example again. What result would you expect? What result did you get? You have been warned!

The effects of integers being of fixed size can surface more dramatically. The reason is that floating-point numbers are by definition approximations of (real) numbers, so they tend to lose precision (i.e., lose the least significant bits). Integers, on the other hand, tend to overflow (i.e., lose the most significant bits). That tends to make floating-point errors sneaky (and often unnoticed by novices) and integer errors spectacular (and typically hard not to notice). Remember that we prefer errors to manifest themselves early and spectacularly so that we can fix them.

Consider an integer problem:

```
short int y = 40000;
int i = 1000000;
cout << y << "    " << i*i << "\n";
```

Running this, we got the output

    −25536   −727379968

That was expected. What we see here is the effect of overflow. Integer types represent (relatively) small integers only. There just aren't enough bits to exactly represent every number we need in a way that's amenable to efficient computation. Here, a 2-byte **short** integer could not represent 40,000 and a 4-byte **int** can't represent 1,000,000,000,000. The exact sizes of C++ built-in types (§A.8) depend on the hardware and the compiler; **sizeof(x)** gives you the size of **x** in bytes for a variable **x** or a type **x**. By definition, **sizeof(char)==1**. We can illustrate sizes like this:

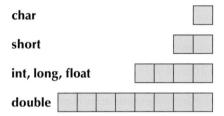

These sizes are for Windows using a Microsoft compiler. C++ supplies integers and floating-point numbers of a variety of sizes, but unless you have a very good reason for something else, stick to **char**, **int**, and **double**. In most (but of course not all) programs, the remaining integer and floating-point types are more trouble than they are worth.

You can assign an integer to a floating-point number. If the integer is larger than the floating-point type can represent, you lose precision. For example:

```
cout << "sizes: " << sizeof(int) << ' ' << sizeof(float) << '\n';
int x = 2100000009;     // large int
float f = x;
cout << x << ' ' << f << endl;
cout << setprecision(15) << x << ' ' << f << '\n';
```

On our machine, this produced

    Sizes: 4 4
    2100000009 2.1e+009

2100000009 2100000000

A **float** and an **int** take up the same amount of space (4 bytes). A **float** is represented as a "mantissa" (typically a value between 0 and 1) and an exponent (mantissa*10^{exponent}), so it cannot represent exactly the largest **int**. (If we tried to, where would we find space for the mantissa after we had taken the space needed for the exponent?) As it should, **f** represented **2100000009** as approximately correct as it could. However, that last **9** was too much for it to represent exactly – and that was of course why we chose that number.

On the other hand, when you assign a floating-point number to an integer, you get truncation; that is, the fractional part – the digits after the decimal point – is simply thrown away. For example:

```
float f = 2.8;
int x = f;
cout << x << ' ' << f << '\n';
```

The value of **x** will be **2**. It will not be **3** as you might imagine if you are used to "4/5 rounding rules." C++ **float**-to-**int** conversions truncate rather than round.

When you calculate, you must be aware of possible overflow and truncation. C++ will not catch such problems for you. Consider:

```
void f(int i, double fpd)
{
        char c = i;          // yes: chars really are very small integers
        short s = i;         // beware: an int may not fit in a short int
        i = i+1;             // what if i was the largest int?
        long lg = i*i;       // beware: a long may not be any larger than an int
        float fps = fpd;     // beware: a large double may not fit in a float
        i = fpd;             // truncates: e.g., 5.7 –> 5
        fps = i;             // you can lose precision (for very large int values)
}

void g()
{
        char ch = 0;
        for (int i = 0; i<500; ++i)
                cout << int(ch++) << '\t';
}
```

If in doubt, check, experiment! Don't just despair and don't just read the documentation. Unless you are experienced, it is easy to misunderstand the highly technical documentation related to numerics.

TRY THIS

Run g(). Modify f() to print out **c**, **s**, **i**, etc. Test it with a variety of values.

The representation of integers and their conversions will be examined further in §25.5.3. When we can, we prefer to limit ourselves to a few data types. That can help minimize confusion. For example, by not using **float** in a program, but only **double**, we eliminate the possibility of **double**-to-**float** conversion problems. In fact, we prefer to limit our use to **int**, **double**, and **complex** (see §24.8) for computation, **char** for characters, and **bool** for logical entities. We deal with the rest of the arithmetic types only when we have to.

24.2.1 Numeric limits

In **<limits>**, **<limits.h>**, and **<float.h>**, each C++ implementation specifies properties of the built-in types, so that programmers can use those properties to check against limits, set sentinels, etc. These values are listed in §B.9.1 and can be critically important to low-level tool builders. If you think you need them, you are probably too close to hardware, but there are other uses. For example, it is not uncommon to be curious about aspects of the language implementation, such as "How big is an **int**?" or "Are **char**s signed?" Trying to find the definite and correct answers in the system documentation can be difficult, and the standard only specifies minimum requirements. However, a program giving the answer is trivial to write:

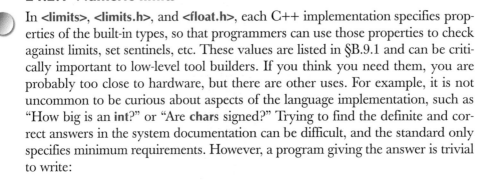

```
cout << "number of bytes in an int: " << sizeof(int) << '\n';
cout << "largest int: " << INT_MAX << endl;
cout << "smallest int value: " << numeric_limits<int>::min() << '\n';

if (numeric_limits<char>::is_signed)
        cout << "char is signed\n";
else
        cout << "char is unsigned\n";

cout << "char with min value: " << numeric_limits<char>::min() << '\n';
cout << "min char value: " << int(numeric_limits<char>::min()) << '\n';
```

When you write code intended to run on several kinds of hardware, it occasionally becomes immensely valuable to have this kind of information available to the program. The alternative would typically be to hand-code the answers into the program, thereby creating a maintenance hazard.

These limits can also be useful when you want to detect overflow.

24.3 Arrays

An *array* is a sequence of elements where we can access an element by its index (position). Another word for that general notion is *vector*. Here we are particularly concerned with arrays where the elements are themselves arrays: multidimensional arrays. A common word for a multidimensional array is *matrix*. The variety of names is a sign of the popularity and utility of the general concept. The standard **vector** (§B.4), **array** (§20.9), and the built-in array (§A.8.2) are one-dimensional. So, what if we need two dimensions (e.g., a matrix)? If we need seven dimensions?

We can visualize one- and two-dimensional arrays like this:

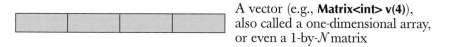

A vector (e.g., **Matrix<int> v(4)**), also called a one-dimensional array, or even a 1-by-N matrix

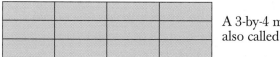

A 3-by-4 matrix (e.g., **Matrix<int,2> m(3,4)**), also called a two-dimensional array

Arrays are fundamental to most computing ("number crunching"). Most interesting scientific, engineering, statistics, and financial computations rely heavily on arrays.

We often refer to an array as consisting of rows and columns:

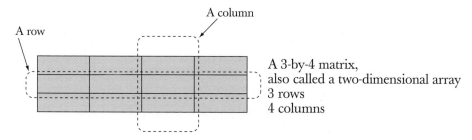

A column

A row

A 3-by-4 matrix, also called a two-dimensional array 3 rows 4 columns

A column is a sequence of elements with the same first (x) coordinate. A row is a set of elements with the same second (y) coordinate.

24.4 C-style multidimensional arrays

The C++ built-in array can be used as a multidimensional array. We simply treat a multidimensional array as an array of arrays, that is, an array with arrays as elements. For example:

```
int ai[4];                  // 1-dimensional array
double ad[3][4];            // 2-dimensional array
char ac[3][4][5];           // 3-dimensional array
ai[1] = 7;
ad[2][3] = 7.2;
ac[2][3][4] = 'c';
```

This approach inherits the virtues and the disadvantages of the one-dimensional array:

- Advantages

    - Direct mapping to hardware
    - Efficient for low-level operations
    - Direct language support

- Problems

    - C-style multidimensional arrays are arrays of arrays (see below).
    - Fixed sizes (i.e., fixed at compile time). If you want to determine a size at run time, you'll have to use free store.
    - Can't be passed cleanly. An array turns into a pointer to its first element at the slightest provocation.
    - No range checking. As usual, an array doesn't know its own size.
    - No array operations, not even assignment (copy).

Built-in arrays are widely used for numeric computation. They are also a *major* source of bugs and complexity. For most people, they are a serious pain to write and debug. Look them up if you are forced to use them (e.g., *The C++ Programming Language,* Appendix C, pp. 836–40). Unfortunately, C++ shares its multidimensional arrays with C, so there is a lot of code "out there" using them.

The most fundamental problem is that you can't pass multidimensional arrays cleanly, so you have to fall back on pointers and explicit calculation of locations in a multidimensional array. For example:

```
void f1(int a[3][5]);              // useful for [3][5] matrices only

void f2(int [ ][5], int dim1);     // 1st dimension can be a variable

void f3(int [5 ][ ], int dim2);    // error: 2nd dimension cannot be a variable

void f4(int[ ][ ], int dim1, int dim2);  // error (and wouldn't work anyway)
```

```
void f5(int* m, int dim1, int dim2)    // odd, but works
{
        for (int i=0; i<dim1; ++i)
                for (int j = 0; j<dim2; ++j) m[i*dim2+j] = 0;
}
```

Here, we pass **m** as an **int*** even though it is a two-dimensional array. As long as the second dimension needs to be a variable (a parameter), there really isn't any way of telling the compiler that **m** is a (**dim1,dim2**) array, so we just pass a pointer to the start of the memory that holds it. The expression **m[i*dim2+j]** really means **m[i,j]**, but because the compiler doesn't know that **m** is a two-dimensional array, we have to calculate the position of **m[i,j]** in memory.

This is too complicated, primitive, and error-prone for our taste. It can also be slow because calculating the location of an element explicitly complicates optimization. Instead of trying to teach you all about it, we will concentrate on a C++ library that eliminates the problems with the built-in arrays.

24.5 The Matrix library

What are the basic "things" we want from an array/matrix aimed at numerical computation?

- "My code should look very much like what I find in my math/engineering textbook text about arrays."

    - Or about vectors, matrices, tensors

- Compile-time and run-time checked.

    - Arrays of any dimension
    - Arrays with any number of elements in a dimension

- Arrays are proper variables/objects.

    - You can pass them around

- Usual array operations:

    - Subscripting: ( )
    - Slicing: [ ]
    - Assignment: =
    - Scaling operations (+=, −=, *=, %=, etc.)
    - Fused vector operations (e.g., **res[i] = a[i]*c+b[2]**)
    - Dot product (**res** = sum of a[i]*b[i]; also known as the **inner_product**)

- Basically, transforms conventional array/vector notation into the code you would laboriously have had to write yourself (and runs at least as efficiently as that).

- You can extend it yourself as needed (no "magic" was used in its implementation).

The **Matrix** library does that and only that. If you want more, such as advanced array functions, sparse arrays, control over memory layout, etc., you must write it yourself or (preferably) use a library that better approximates your needs. However, many such needs can be served by building algorithm and data structures on top of **Matrix**. The **Matrix** library is not part of the ISO C++ standard library. You find it on the course site as **Matrix.h**. It defines its facilities in namespace **Numeric_lib**. We chose the name "matrix" because "vector" and "array" are even more overused in C++ libraries. The plural of *matrix* is *matrices* (with *matrixes* as a rarer form). Where "**Matrix**" refers to a C++ language entity, we will use **Matrix**es as the plural to avoid confusion. The implementation of the **Matrix** library uses advanced techniques and will not be described here.

24.5.1 Dimensions and access

Consider a simple example:

```
#include "Matrix.h"
using namespace Numeric_lib;

void f(int n1, int n2, int n3)
{
        Matrix<double,1> ad1(n1);       // elements are doubles; one dimension
        Matrix<int,1> ai1(n1);          // elements are ints; one dimension
        ad1(7) = 0;                     // subscript using ( ) — Fortran style
        ad1[7] = 8;                     // [ ] also works — C style

        Matrix<double,2> ad2(n1,n2);    // 2-dimensional
        Matrix<double,3> ad3(n1,n2,n3); // 3-dimensional
        ad2(3,4) = 7.5;                 // true multidimensional subscripting
        ad3(3,4,5) = 9.2;
}
```

So, when you define a **Matrix** (an object of a **Matrix** class), you specify the element type and the number of dimensions. Obviously, **Matrix** is a template, and the element type and the number of dimensions are template parameters. The result of giving a pair of arguments to **Matrix** (e.g., **Matrix<double,2>**) is a type (a class) of which you can define objects by supplying arguments (e.g., **Matrix<double,2>**

ad2(n1,n2)); those arguments specify the dimensions. So, **ad2** is a two-dimensional array with dimensions **n1** and **n2**, also known as an **n1**-by-**n2** matrix. To get an element of the declared element type from a one-dimensional **Matrix**, you subscript with one index; to get an element of the declared element type from a two-dimensional **Matrix**, you subscript with two indices; and so on.

Like built-in arrays, and **vectors**, our **Matrix** indices are zero-based (rather than 1-based like Fortran arrays); that is, the elements of a **Matrix** are numbered [0,max), where max is the number of elements.

This is simple and "straight out of the textbook." If you have problems with this, you need to look at an appropriate math textbook, not a programmer's manual. The only "cleverness" here is that you can leave out the number of dimensions for a **Matrix**: "one-dimensional" is the default. Note also that we can use [ ] for subscripting (C and C++ style) or ( ) for subscripting (Fortran style). Having both allows us to better deal with multiple dimensions. The [x] subscript notation always takes a single subscript, yielding the appropriate row of the **Matrix**; if **a** is an n-dimensional **Matrix**, a[x] is an $n-1$-dimensional **Matrix**. The (x,y,z) subscript notation takes one or more subscripts, yielding the appropriate element of the **Matrix**; the number of subscripts must equal the number of dimensions.

Let's see what happens when we make mistakes:

```
void f(int n1, int n2, int n3)
{
        Matrix<int,0> ai0;          // error: no 0D matrices

        Matrix<double,1> ad1(5);
        Matrix<int,1> ai(5);
        Matrix<double,1> ad11(7);

        ad1(7) = 0;      // Matrix_error exception (7 is out of range)
        ad1 = ai;        // error: different element types
        ad1 = ad11;      // Matrix_error exception (different dimensions)

        Matrix<double,2> ad2(n1);   // error: length of 2nd dimension missing
        ad2(3) = 7.5;               // error: wrong number of subscripts
        ad2(1,2,3) = 7.5;           // error: wrong number of subscripts

        Matrix<double,3> ad3(n1,n2,n3);
        Matrix<double,3> ad33(n1,n2,n3);
        ad3 = ad33;          // OK: same element type, same dimensions
}
```

We catch mismatches between the declared number of dimensions and their use at compile time. Range errors we catch at run time and throw a **Matrix_error** exception.

The first dimension is the row and the second the column, so we index a 2D matrix (two-dimensional array) with (row,column). We can also use the [row][column] notation because subscripting a 2D matrix with a single index gives the 1D matrix that is the row. We can visualize that like this:

This **Matrix** will be laid out in memory in "row-first" order:

A **Matrix** "knows" its dimensions, so we can address the elements of a **Matrix** passed as an argument very simply:

```
void init(Matrix<int,2>& a)  // initialize each element to a characteristic value
{
    for (int i=0; i<a.dim1(); ++i)
        for (int j = 0; j<a.dim2(); ++j)
            a(i,j) = 10*i+j;
}

void print(const Matrix<int,2>& a)  // print the elements of a row by row
{
    for (int i=0; i<a.dim1(); ++i) {
        for (int j = 0; j<a.dim2(); ++j)
            cout << a(i,j) <<'\t';
        cout << '\n';
    }
}
```

So, **dim1()** is the number of elements in the first dimension, **dim2()** the number of elements in the second dimension, and so on. The type of the elements and the number of dimensions are part of the **Matrix** type, so we cannot write a function that takes any **Matrix** as an argument (but we could write a template to do that):

```
void init(Matrix& a);   // error: element type and number of dimensions missing
```

Note that the **Matrix** library doesn't supply matrix operations, such as adding two 4D **Matrix**es or multiplying a 2D **Matrix** with a 1D **Matrix**. Doing so elegantly and efficiently is currently beyond the scope of this library. Matrix libraries of a variety of designs could be built on top of the **Matrix** library (see exercise 12).

24.5.2 1D Matrix

What can we do to the simplest **Matrix**, the 1D (one-dimensional) **Matrix**?

We can leave the number of dimensions out of a declaration because 1D is the default:

```
Matrix<int,1> a1(10);      // a1 is a 1D Matrix of ints
Matrix<int> a(10);         // means Matrix<int,1> a(10);
```

So, **a** and **a1** are of the same type (**Matrix<int,1>**). We can ask for the size (the number of elements) and the dimension (the number of elements in a dimension). For a 1D **Matrix**, those are the same.

```
a.size();      // number of elements in Matrix
a.dim1();      // number of elements in 1st dimension
```

We can ask for the elements as laid out in memory, that is, a pointer to the first element:

```
int* p = a.data();      // extract data as a pointer to an array
```

This is useful for passing **Matrix** data to C-style functions taking pointer arguments. We can subscript:

```
a(i);      // ith element (Fortran style), but range checked
a[i];      // ith element (C style), range checked
a(1,2);    // error: a is a 1D Matrix
```

It is common for algorithms to refer to part of a **Matrix**. Such a "part" is called a **slice()** (a sub-**Matrix** or a range of elements) and we provide two versions:

```
a.slice(i);      // the elements from the a[i] to the last
a.slice(i,n);    // the n elements from the a[i] to a[i+n−1]
```

Subscripts and slices can be used on the left-hand side of an assignment as well as on the right. They refer to the elements of their **Matrix** without making copies of them. For example:

a.slice(4,4) = a.slice(0,4);   // assign first half of a to second half

For example, if **a** starts out as

{ 1 2 3 4 5 6 7 8 }

we get

{ 1 2 3 4 1 2 3 4 }

Note that the most common slices are the "initial elements" of a **Matrix** and the "last elements"; that is, **a.slice(0,j)** is the range **[0:j)** and **a.slice(j)** is the range **[j:a.size())**. In particular, the example above is most easily written

a.slice(4) = a.slice(0,4);   // assign first half of a to second half

That is, the notation favors the common cases. You can specify **i** and **n** so that **a.slice(i,n)** is outside the range of **a**. However, the resulting slice will refer only to the elements actually in **a**. For example, **a.slice(i,a.size())** refers to the range **[i:a.size())**, and **a.slice(a.size())** and **a.slice(a.size(),2)** are empty **Matrix**es. This happens to be a useful convention for many algorithms. We borrowed that convention from math. Obviously, **a.slice(i,0)** is an empty **Matrix**. We wouldn't write that deliberately, but there are algorithms that are simpler if **a.slice(i,n)** where **n** happens to be **0** is an empty **Matrix** (rather than an error we have to avoid).

We have the usual (for C++ objects) copy operations that copy all elements:

Matrix<int> a2 = a;   // copy initialization
a = a2;   // copy assignment

We can apply a built-in operation to each element of a **Matrix**:

a *= 7;   // scaling: a[i]*=7 for each i (also +=, -=, /=, etc.)
a = 7;   // a[i]=7 for each i

This works for every assignment and every composite assignment operator (=, +=, -=, /=, *=, %=, ^=, &=, |=, >>=, <<=) provided the element type supports that operator. We can also apply a function to each element of a **Matrix**:

a.apply(f);   // a[i]=f(a[i]) for each element a[i]
a.apply(f,7);   // a[i]=f(a[i],7) for each element a[i]

The composite assignment operators and **apply()** modify the elements of their **Matrix** argument. If we instead want to create a new **Matrix** as the result, we can use

  b = apply(abs,a); // make a new Matrix with b(i)==abs(a(i))

This **abs** is the standard library's absolute value function (§24.8). Basically, **apply(f,x)** relates to **x.apply(f)** as + relates to +=. For example:

  b = a*7;   // b[i] = a[i]*7 for each i
  a *= 7;   // a[i] = a[i]*7 for each i
  y = apply(f,x); // y[i] = f(x[i]) for each i
  x.apply(f);   // x[i] = f(x[i]) for each i

Here we get **a==b** and **x==y**.

  In Fortran, this second **apply** is called a "broadcast" function and is typically written **f(x)** rather than **apply(f,x)**. To make this facility available for every function **f** (rather than just a selected few functions as in Fortran), we need a name for the "broadcast" operation, so we (re)use **apply**.

  In addition, to match the two-argument version of the member **apply**, **a.apply(f,x)**, we provide

  b = apply(f,a,x); // b[i]=f(a[i],x) for each i

For example:

  double scale(double d, double s) { return d*s; }
  b = apply(scale,a,7); // b[i] = a[i]*7 for each i

Note that the "freestanding" **apply()** takes a function that produces a result from its argument; **apply()** then uses those results to initialize the resulting **Matrix**. Typically it does not modify the **Matrix** to which it is applied. The member **apply()** differs in that it takes a function that modifies its argument; that is, it modifies elements of the **Matrix** to which it is applied. For example:

  void scale_in_place(double& d, double s) { d *= s; }
  b.apply(scale_in_place,7); // b[i] *= 7 for each i

We also supply a couple of the most useful functions from traditional numerics libraries:

  Matrix<int> a3 = scale_and_add(a,8,a2); // fused multiply and add
  int r = dot_product(a3,a);   // dot product

The **scale_and_add()** operation is often referred to as *fused multiply-add* or simply *fma*; its definition is **result(i)=arg1(i)*arg2+arg3(i)** for each **i** in the **Matrix**. The dot product is also known as the **inner_product** and is described in §21.5.3; its definition is **result+=arg1(i)*arg2(i)** for each **i** in the **Matrix** where **result** starts out as 0.

One-dimensional arrays are very common; you can represent one as a built-in array, a **vector**, or a **Matrix**. You use **Matrix** if you need the matrix operations provided, such as ***=**, or if the **Matrix** has to interact with higher-dimensional **Matrix**es.

You can explain the utility of a library like this as "It matches the math better" or "It saves you from writing all those loops to do things for each element." Either way, the resulting code is significantly shorter and there are fewer opportunities to make mistakes writing it. The **Matrix** operations – such as copy, assignment to all elements, and operations on all elements – each save us from reading or writing a loop (and from wondering if we got the loop exactly right).

Matrix supports two constructors for copying data from a built-in array into a **Matrix**. For example:

```
void some_function(double* p, int n)
{
        double val[] = { 1.2, 2.3, 3.4, 4.5 };
        Matrix<double> data(p,n);
        Matrix<double> constants(val);
        // . . .
}
```

These are often useful when we have our data delivered in terms of arrays or **vector**s from parts of a program not using **Matrix**es.

Note that the compiler is able to deduce the number of elements of an initialized array, so we don't have to give the number of elements when we define **constants** – it is **4**. On the other hand, the compiler doesn't know the number of elements given only a pointer, so for **data** we have to specify both the pointer (**p**) and the number of elements (**n**).

24.5.3 2D Matrix

The general idea of the **Matrix** library is that **Matrix**es of different dimensions really are quite similar, except where you need to be specific about dimensions, so most of what we said about a 1D **Matrix** applies to a 2D **Matrix**:

```
Matrix<int,2> a(3,4);

int s = a.size();        // number of elements
int d1 = a.dim1();       // number of elements in a row
int d2 = a.dim2();       // number of elements in a column
int* p = a.data();       // extract data as a pointer to a C-style array
```

We can ask for the total number of elements and the number of elements of each dimension. We can get a pointer to the elements as they are laid out in memory as a matrix.

We can subscript:

```
a(i,j);         // (i,j)th element (Fortran style), but range checked
a[i];           // ith row (C style), range checked
a[i][j];        // (i,j)th element (C style)
```

For a 2D **Matrix**, subscripting with **[i]** yields the 1D **Matrix** that is the ist row. This means that we can extract rows and pass them to operations and functions that require a 1D **Matrix** or even a built-in array (**a[i].data()**). Note that **a(i,j)** may be faster than **a[i][j]**, though that will depend a lot on the compiler and optimizer.

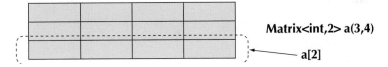

We can take slices:

```
a.slice(i);     // the rows from the a[i] to the last
a.slice(i,n);   // the rows from the a[i] to the a[i+n−1]
```

a.slice(0,2)

Matrix<int,2> a(3,4)

a[2].slice(2)

Note that a slice of a 2D **Matrix** is itself a 2D **Matrix** (possibly with fewer rows).

The distributed operations are the same as for 1D **Matrix**es. These operations don't care how we organize the elements; they just apply to all elements in the order those elements are laid down in memory:

```
Matrix<int,2> a2 = a;   // copy initialization
a = a2;                 // copy assignment
a *= 7;                 // scaling (and +=, −=, /=, etc.)
a.apply(f);             // a(i,j)=f(a(i,j)) for each element a(i,j)
a.apply(f,7);           // a(i,j)=f(a(i,j),7) for each element a(i,j)
b=apply(f,a);           // make a new Matrix with b(i,j)==f(a(i,j))
b=apply(f,a,7);         // make a new Matrix with b(i,j)==f(a(i,j),7)
```

It turns out that swapping rows is often useful, so we supply that:

> **a.swap_rows(7,9);**   // swap rows a[7] <-> a[9]

There is no **swap_columns()**. If you need it, write it yourself (exercise 11). Because of the row-first layout, rows and columns are not completely symmetrical concepts. This asymmetry also shows up in that **[i]** yields a row (and we have not provided a column selection operator). In that **(i,j,k)**, the first index, **i**, selects the row. The asymmetry also reflects deep mathematical properties.

There seems to be an infinite number of "things" that are two-dimensional and thus obvious candidates for applications of 2D **Matrix**es:

```
enum Piece { none, pawn, knight, queen, king, bishop, rook };
Matrix<Piece,2> board(8,8);               // a chessboard

const int white_start_row = 0;
const int black_start_row = 7;

Piece init_pos[] = {rook, knight, bishop, queen, king, bishop, knight, rook};
Matrix<Piece> start_row(init_pos);        // initialize elements from init_pos
Matrix<Piece> clear_row(8) ;              // 8 elements of the default value
```

The initialization of **clear_row** takes advantage of **none==0** and that elements are by default initialized to **0**. We would have liked to write

```
Matrix<Piece> start_row
        = {rook, knight, bishop, queen, king, bishop, knight, rook};
```

However, that won't work until the next version of C++ (C++0x), so we must use the trick of initializing an array (here, **init_pos**) and use that to initialize the **Matrix**. We can use **start_row** and **clear_row** like this:

```
board[white_start_row] = start_row;       // reset white pieces
for (int i = 1; i<7; ++i) board[i] = clear_row;   // clear middle of the board
board[black_start_row] = start_row;       // reset black pieces
```

Note when we extract a row, using **[i]**, we get an lvalue (§4.3); that is, we can assign to the result of **board[i]**.

24.5.4 Matrix I/O

The **Matrix** library provides *very* simple I/O for 1D and 2D **Matrix**es:

> **Matrix<double> a(4);**

The goal is to find values for the unknowns that simultaneously satisfy the n equations. These equations can compactly be expressed in terms of a matrix and two vectors:

$$\mathbf{Ax} = \mathbf{b}$$

Here, $\mathbf{A}$ is the square n-by-n matrix defined by the coefficients:

$$\mathbf{A} = \begin{bmatrix} a_{1,1} & \cdots & a_{1,n} \\ \vdots & \vdots & \vdots \\ a_{n,1} & \cdots & a_{n,n} \end{bmatrix}$$

The vectors $\mathbf{x}$ and $\mathbf{b}$ are the vectors of unknowns and constants, respectively:

$$\mathbf{x} = \begin{bmatrix} x_1 \\ \vdots \\ x_n \end{bmatrix}, \quad \text{and} \quad \mathbf{b} = \begin{bmatrix} b_1 \\ \vdots \\ b_n \end{bmatrix}$$

This system may have zero, one, or an infinite number of solutions, depending on the coefficients of the matrix $\mathbf{A}$ and the vector $\mathbf{b}$. There are various methods for solving linear systems. We use a classic scheme, called Gaussian elimination (see Freeman and Phillips, *Parallel Numerical Algorithms*; Stewart, *Matrix Algorithms, Volume I*; and Wood, *Introduction to Numerical Analysis*). First, we transform $\mathbf{A}$ and $\mathbf{b}$ so that $\mathbf{A}$ is an upper-triangular matrix. By upper-triangular, we mean all the coefficients below the diagonal of $\mathbf{A}$ are zero. In other words, the system looks like this:

$$\begin{bmatrix} a_{1,1} & \cdots & a_{1,n} \\ 0 & \ddots & \vdots \\ 0 & 0 & a_{n,n} \end{bmatrix} \begin{bmatrix} x_1 \\ \vdots \\ x_n \end{bmatrix} = \begin{bmatrix} b_1 \\ \vdots \\ b_n \end{bmatrix}$$

This is easily done. A zero for position $a(i,j)$ is obtained by multiplying the equation for row i by a constant so that $a(i,j)$ equals another element in column j, say $a(k,j)$. That done, we just subtract the two equations and $a(i,j) == 0$ and the other values in row i change appropriately.

If we can get all the diagonal coefficients to be nonzero, then the system has a unique solution, which can be found by "back substitution." The last equation is easily solved:

$$a_{n,n} x_n = b_n$$

Obviously, $x[n]$ is $b[n]/a(n,n)$. That done, eliminate row n from the system and proceed to find the value of $x[n-1]$, and so on, until the value for $x[1]$ is computed.

For each n, we divide by $a(n,n)$ so the diagonal values must be nonzero. If that does not hold, the back substitution method fails, meaning that the system has zero or an infinite number of solutions.

24.6.1 Classical Gaussian elimination

Now let us look at the C++ code to express this. First, we'll simplify our notation by conventionally naming the two **Matrix** types that we are going to use:

```
typedef Numeric_lib::Matrix<double, 2> Matrix;
typedef Numeric_lib::Matrix<double, 1> Vector;
```

Next we will express our desired computation:

```
Vector classical_gaussian_elimination(Matrix A, Vector b)
{
        classical_elimination(A, b);
        return back_substitution(A, b);
}
```

That is, we make copies of our inputs **A** and **b** (using call by value), call a function to solve the system, and then calculate the result to return by back substitution. The point is that our breakdown of the problem and our notation for the solution are right out of the textbook. To complete our solution, we have to implement **classical_elimination**() and **back_substitution**(). Again, the solution is in the textbook:

```
void classical_elimination(Matrix& A, Vector& b)
{
        const Index n = A.dim1();

        // traverse from 1st column to the next-to-last
        // filling zeros into all elements under the diagonal:
        for (Index j = 0; j<n−1; ++j) {
                const double pivot = A(j, j);
                if (pivot == 0) throw Elim_failure(j);

                // fill zeros into each element under the diagonal of the ith row:
                for (Index i = j+1; i<n; ++i) {
                        const double mult = A(i, j) / pivot;
                        A[i].slice(j) = scale_and_add(A[j].slice(j), −mult, A[i].slice(j));
                        b(i) −= mult * b(j);      // make the corresponding change to b
                }
        }
}
```

The "pivot" is the element that lies on the diagonal of the row we are currently dealing with. It must be nonzero because we need to divide by it; if it is zero we give up by throwing an exception:

```
Vector back_substitution(const Matrix& A, const Vector& b)
{
    const Index n = A.dim1();
    Vector x(n);

    for (Index i = n – 1; i >= 0; ––i) {
        double s = b(i)–dot_product(A[i].slice(i+1),x.slice(i+1));

        if (double m = A(i, i))
            x(i) = s / m;
        else
            throw Back_subst_failure(i);
    }

    return x;
}
```

24.6.2 Pivoting

We can avoid the divide-by-zero problem and also achieve a more robust solution by sorting the rows to get zeros and small values away from the diagonal. By "more robust" we mean less sensitive to rounding errors. However, the values change as we go along placing zeros under the diagonal, so we have to also re-order to get small values away from the diagonal as we go along (that is, we can't just reorder the matrix and then use the classical algorithm):

```
void elim_with_partial_pivot(Matrix& A, Vector& b)
{
    const Index n = A.dim1();

    for (Index j = 0; j < n; ++j) {
        Index pivot_row = j;

        // look for a suitable pivot:
        for (Index k = j + 1; k < n; ++k)
            if (abs(A(k, j)) > abs(A(pivot_row, j))) pivot_row = j;

        // swap the rows if we found a better pivot:
        if (pivot_row != j) {
            A.swap_rows(j, pivot_row);
            std::swap(b(j), b(pivot_row));
        }
```

```
// elimination:
for (Index i = j + 1; i < n; ++i) {
        const double pivot = A(j, j);
        if (pivot==0) error("can't solve: pivot==0");
        const double mult = A(i, j)/pivot;
        A[i].slice(j) = scale_and_add(A[j].slice(j), −mult, A[i].slice(j));
        b(i) −= mult * b(j);
    }
    }
}
```

We use **swap_rows()** and **scale_and_multiply()** to make the code more conventional and to save us from writing an explicit loop.

24.6.3 Testing

Obviously, we have to test our code. Fortunately, there is a simple way to do that:

```
void solve_random_system(Index n)
{
    Matrix A = random_matrix(n);    // see §24.7
    Vector b = random_vector(n);

    cout << "A = " << A << endl;
    cout << "b = " << b << endl;

    try {
        Vector x = classical_gaussian_elimination(A, b);
        cout << "classical elim solution is x = " << x << endl;
        Vector v = A * x;
        cout << " A * x = " << v << endl;
    }
    catch(const exception& e) {
        cerr << e.what() << std::endl;
    }
}
```

We can get to the **catch** clause in three ways:

- A bug in the code (but, being optimists, we don't think there are any)
- An input that trips up **classical_elimination** (we should have used **elim_with_partial_pivot**)
- Rounding errors

However, our test is not as realistic as we'd like because genuinely random matrices are unlikely to cause problems for **classical_elimination**.

To verify our solution, we print out **A*x**, which had better equal **b** (or close enough for our purpose, given rounding errors). The likelihood of rounding errors is the reason we didn't just do

```
if (A*x!=b) error("substitution failed");
```

Because floating-point numbers are just approximations to real numbers, we have to accept approximately correct answers. In general, using **==** and **!=** on the result of a floating-point computation is best avoided: floating point is inherently an approximation.

The **Matrix** library doesn't define multiplication of a matrix with a vector, so we did that for this program:

```
Vector operator*(const Matrix& m, const Vector& u)
{
    const Index n = m.dim1();
    Vector v(n);
    for (Index i = 0; i < n; ++i) v(i) = dot_product(m[i], u);
    return v;
}
```

Again, a simple **Matrix** operation did most of the work for us. The **Matrix** output operations came from **MatrixIO.h** as described in §24.5.3. The **random_matrix()** and **random_vector()** functions are simple uses of random numbers (§24.7) and are left as an exercise. **Index** is a **typedef** (§A.15) for the index type used by the **Matrix** library. We brought it into scope with a **using** declaration:

```
using Numeric_lib::Index;
```

24.7 Random numbers

If you ask people for a random number, most say 7 or 17, so it has been suggested that those are the "most random" numbers. People essentially never give the answer 0. Zero is seen to be such a nice round number that it is not perceived as "random" and could therefore be deemed the "least random" number. From a mathematical point of view this is utter nonsense: it is not an individual number that is random. What we often need, and what we often refer to as random numbers, is a sequence of numbers that conform to some distribution and where you cannot easily predict the next number in the sequence given the previous ones.

Such numbers are most useful in testing (that's one way of generating a lot of test cases), in games (that is one way of making sure that the next run of the game differs from the previous run), and in simulations (we can make a simulated entity behave in a "random" fashion within the limits of its parameters).

As a practical tool and a mathematical problem, random numbers reach a high degree of sophistication to match their real-world importance. Here, we will just touch the basics as needed for simple testing and simulation. In **<cstdlib>**, the standard library provides

```
int rand();                  // returns values in the range [0:RAND_MAX]
RAND_MAX                     // the largest value that rand() can produce
void srand(unsigned int);    // seed the random number generator
```

Repeated calls of **rand()** produce a pseudo-random sequence of **int**s uniformly distributed in the range **[0:RAND_MAX]**. We call the sequence of values pseudo-random because it is generated by a mathematical formula so that it repeats itself after a while (i.e., it is predictable and not perfectly random). In particular, if we call **rand()** repeatedly in a program, it will give the same sequence every time the program is run. That's extremely useful for debugging. When we want different sequences, we call **srand()** with different values. For each different argument to **srand()**, we get a different sequence from **rand()**.

For example, consider the function **random_vector()** that was used in §24.6.3. A call **random_vector(n)** produces a **Matrix<double,1>** with **n** elements with random values in the range **[0:n]**:

```
Vector random_vector(Index n)
{
    Vector v(n);

    for (Index i = 0; i < n; ++i)
        v(i) = 1.0 * n * rand() / RAND_MAX;

    return v;
}
```

Note the use of **1.0** to make sure that we use floating-point arithmetic. It would be embarrassing if we had used integer division with **RAND_MAX** and always gotten the value **0**.

Getting an integer in a specific range, such as **[0:max)**, is harder. Most people's first attempt looks like this:

```
int val = rand()%max;
```

This used to be a really bad idea because this simply picks off the low-order bits of the random number and those bits are not properly randomized by many traditional random number generators. Today, it appears to be better on many systems, but for portable code, "hide" the random number calculation in a function:

```
int rand_int(int max) { return rand()%max; }

int rand_int(int min, int max) { return rand_int(max–min)+min; }
```

That way, you can replace the definition of **rand_int()** if you find a poor implementation of **rand()**. For industrial-strength software or if you need a nonuniform distribution, use one of the quality random number libraries that are widely available, such as **Boost::random**. To get an idea of the quality of your system's random number generator, do exercise 10.

24.8 The standard mathematical functions

The standard mathematical functions (**cos**, **sin**, **log**, etc.) are provided by the standard library. Their declarations are found in **<cmath>**.

Standard mathematical functions	
abs(x)	absolute value
ceil(x)	smallest integer >= x
floor(x)	largest integer <= x
sqrt(x)	square root; **x** must be nonnegative
cos(x)	cosine
sin(x)	sine
tan(x)	tangent
acos(x)	arccosine; result is nonnegative
asin(x)	arcsine; result nearest to 0 returned
atan(x)	arctangent
sinh(x)	hyperbolic sine
cosh(x)	hyperbolic cosine
tanh(x)	hyperbolic tangent
exp(x)	base-e exponential
log(x)	natural logarithm, base-e; **x** must be positive
log10(x)	base-10 logarithm

The standard mathematical functions are provided for types **float, double, long double**, and **complex** (§24.9) arguments. If you do floating-point computations, you'll find these functions useful. If you need more details, documentation is widely available; your online documentation would be a good place to start.

If a standard mathematical function cannot produce a mathematically valid result, it sets the variable **errno**. For example:

```
errno = 0;
double s2 = sqrt(−1);
if (errno) cerr << "something went wrong with something somewhere";
if (errno == EDOM)        // domain error
      cerr << "sqrt() not defined for negative argument";
pow(very_large,2);        // not a good idea
if (errno==ERANGE)        // range error
      cerr << "pow(" << very_large << ",2) too large for a double";
```

If you do serious mathematical computations you must check **errno** to ensure that it is still **0** after you get your result. If not, something went wrong. Look at your manual or online documentation to see which mathematical functions can set **errno** and which values they use for **errno**.

As indicated in the example, a nonzero **errno** simply means "Something went wrong." It is not uncommon for functions not in the standard library to set **errno** in case of error, so you have to look more carefully at the value of **errno** to get an idea of exactly what went wrong. If you test **errno** immediately after a standard library function and if you made sure that **errno==0** before calling it, you can rely on the values as we did with **EDOM** and **ERANGE** in the example. **EDOM** is set for a domain error (i.e., a problem with the result). **ERANGE** is set for a range error (i.e., a problem with the arguments).

Error handling based on **errno** is somewhat primitive. It dates from the first (1975 vintage) C mathematical functions.

24.9 Complex numbers

Complex numbers are widely used in scientific and engineering computations. We assume that if you need them, you will know about their mathematical properties, so we'll just show you how complex numbers are expressed in the ISO C++ standard library. You find the declaration of complex numbers and their associated standard mathematical functions in **<complex>**:

```
template<class Scalar> class complex {
      // a complex is a pair of scalar values, basically a coordinate pair
      Scalar re, im;
```

```
public:
        complex(const Scalar & r, const Scalar & i) :re(r), im(i) { }
        complex(const Scalar & r) :re(r),im(Scalar ()) { }
        complex() :re(Scalar ()), im(Scalar ()) { }

        Scalar real() { return re; }      // real part
        Scalar imag() { return im; }      // imaginary part

        // operators: = += −= *= /=
};
```

The standard library **complex** is guaranteed to be supported for scalar types **float**, **double**, and **long double**. In addition to the members of **complex** and the standard mathematical functions (§24.8), **<complex>** offers a host of useful operations:

Complex operators	
z1+z2	addition
z1−z2	subtraction
z1*z2	multiplication
z1/z2	division
z1==z2	equality
z1!=z2	inequality
norm(z)	the square of **abs(z)**
conj(z)	conjugate: if **z** is **{re,im}**, then **conj(z)** is **(re,−im)**
polar(x,y)	make a complex given polar coordinates (rho,theta)
real(z)	real part
imag(z)	imaginary part
abs(z)	also known as rho
arg(z)	also known as theta
out << z	complex output
in >> z	complex input

Note: **complex** does not provide **<** or **%**.

Use **complex<T>** exactly like a built-in type, such as **double**. For example:

```
typedef complex<double> dcmplx;      // sometimes complex<double>
                                     // gets verbose
```

```
void f(dcmplx z, vector<dcmplx>& vc)
{
    dcmplx z2 = pow(z,2);
    dcmplx z3 = z2*9.3+vc[3];
    dcmplx sum = accumulate(vc.begin(), vc.end(), dcmplx());
    // . . .
}
```

Remember that not all operations that we are used to from **int** and **double** are defined for a **complex**. For example:

if (z2<z3)   // error: there is no < for complex numbers

Note that the representation (layout) of the C++ standard library complex numbers is compatible with their corresponding types in C and Fortran.

24.10 References

Basically, the issues discussed in this chapter, such as rounding errors, **Matrix** operations, and complex arithmetic, are of no interest and make no sense in isolation. We simply describe (some of) the support provided by C++ to people with the need and knowledge of mathematical concepts and techniques to do numerical computations.

   In case you are a bit rusty in those areas or simply curious, we can recommend some information sources:

The MacTutor History of Mathematics archive, http://www-gap.dcs.st-and.ac.uk/
   ~history
   • A great link for anyone who likes math or simply needs to use math
   • A great link for someone who would like to see the human side of mathematics; for example, who is the only major mathematician to win an Olympic medal?
      • Famous mathematicians: biographies, accomplishments
      • Curio
   • Famous curves
   • Famous problems
   • Mathematical topics
      • Algebra
      • Analysis
      • Numbers and number theory

- Geometry and topology
- Mathematical physics
- Mathematical astronomy
  - The history of mathematics
  - . . .

Freeman, T. L., and Chris Phillips. *Parallel Numerical Algorithms*. Prentice Hall, 1992.

Gullberg, Jan. *Mathematics – From the Birth of Numbers*. W. W. Norton, 1996. ISBN 039304002X. One of the most enjoyable books on basic and useful mathematics. A (rare) math book that you can read for pleasure and also use to look up specific topics, such as matrices.

Knuth, Donald E. *The Art of Computer Programming, Volume 2: Seminumerical Algorithms, Third Edition*. Addison-Wesley, 1998. ISBN: 0201896842.

Stewart, G. W. *Matrix Algorithms, Volume I: Basic Decompositions*. SIAM, 1998. ISBN 0898714141.

Wood, Alistair. *Introduction to Numerical Analysis*. Addison-Wesley, 1999. ISBN 020194291X.

 Drill

1. Print the size of a **char**, a **short**, an **int**, a **long**, a **float**, a **double**, an **int***, and a **double*** (use **sizeof**, not **<limits>**).
2. Print out the size as reported by **sizeof** of **Matrix<int> a(10)**, **Matrix<int> b(10)**, **Matrix<double> c(10)**, **Matrix<int,2> d(10,10)**, **Matrix<int,3> e(10, 10,10)**.
3. Print out the number of elements of each of the **Matrix**es from 2.
4. Write a program that takes **ints** from **cin** and outputs the **sqrt()** of each **int**, or "no square root" if **sqrt(x)** is illegal for some **x** (i.e., check your **sqrt()** return values).
5. Read ten floating-point values from input and put them into a **Matrix<double>**. **Matrix** has no **push_back()** so be careful to handle an attempt to enter a wrong number of **doubles**. Print out the **Matrix**.
6. Compute a multiplication table for **[0,n)*[0,m)** and represent it as a 2D **Matrix**. Take **n** and **m** from **cin** and print out the table nicely (assume that **m** is small enough that the results fit on a line).
7. Read ten **complex<double>**s from **cin** (yes, **cin** supports **>>** for **complex**) and put them into a **Matrix**. Calculate and output the sum of the ten complex numbers.
8. Read six **ints** into a **Matrix<int,2> m(2,3)** and print them out.

Review

1. Who uses numerics?
2. What is precision?
3. What is overflow?
4. What is a common size of a **double**? Of an **int**?
5. How can you detect overflow?
6. Where do you find numeric limits, such as the largest **int**?
7. What is an array? A row? A column?
8. What is a C-style multidimensional array?
9. What are the desirable properties of language support (e.g., a library) for matrix computation?
10. What is a dimension of a matrix?
11. How many dimensions can a matrix have (in theory/math)?
12. What is a slice?
13. What is a broadcast operation? List a few.
14. What is the difference between Fortran-style and C-style subscripting?
15. How do you apply an operation to each element of a matrix? Give examples.
16. What is a fused operation?
17. Define *dot product*.
18. What is linear algebra?
19. What is Gaussian elimination?
20. What is a pivot? (In linear algebra? In "real life"?)
21. What makes a number random?
22. What is a uniform distribution?
23. Where do you find the standard mathematical functions? For which argument types are they defined?
24. What is the imaginary part of a complex number?
25. What is the square root of −1?

Terms

array	Fortran	scaling
C	fused operation	size
column	imaginary	**sizeof**
complex number	**Matrix**	slicing
dimension	multidimensional	subscripting
dot product	random number	uniform distribution
element-wise operation	real	
errno	row	

Exercises

1. The function arguments **f** for **a.apply(f)** and **apply(f,a)** are different. Write a **double()** function for each and use each to double the elements of an array { **1 2 3 4 5** }. Define a single **double()** function that can be used for both **a.apply(double)** and **apply(double,a)**. Explain why it could be a bad idea to write every function to be used by **apply()** that way.

2. Do exercise 1 again, but with function objects, rather than functions. Hint: **Matrix.h** contains examples.

3. Expert level only (this cannot be done with the facilities described in this book): Write an **apply(f,a)** that can take a **void (T&)**, a **T (const T&)**, and their function object equivalents. Hint: **Boost::bind**.

4. Get the Gaussian elimination program to work; that is, complete it, get it to compile, and test it with a simple example.

5. Try the Gaussian elimination program with **A=={ {0 1} {1 0} }** and **b=={ 5 6 }** and watch it fail. Then, try **elim_with_partial_pivot()**.

6. In the Gaussian elimination example, replace the vector operations **dot_product()** and **scale_and_add()** with loops. Test, and comment on the clarity of the code.

7. Rewrite the Gaussian elimination program without using the **Matrix** library; that is, use built-in arrays or **vector**s instead of **Matrix**es.

8. Animate the Gaussian elimination.

9. Rewrite the nonmember **apply()** functions to return a **Matrix** of the return type of the function applied; that is, **apply(f,a)** should return a **Matrix<R>** where **R** is the return type of **f**. Warning: The solution requires information about templates not available in this book.

10. How random is your **rand()**? Write a program that takes two integers **n** an **d** as inputs and calls **randint(n) d** times, recording the result. Output the number of draws for each of [**0:n**) and "eyeball" how similar the counts are. Try with low values for **n** and with low values for **d** to see if drawing only a few random numbers causes obvious biases.

11. Write a **swap_columns()** to match **swap_rows()** from §24.5.3. Obviously, to do that you have to read and understand some of the existing **Matrix** library code. Don't worry too much about efficiency: it is not possible to get **swap_columns()** to run as fast as **swap_rows()**.

12. Implement

```
Matrix<double> operator*(Matrix<double,2>&,Matrix<double>&);
```

and

```
Matrix<double,N> operator+(Matrix<double,N>&,Matrix<double,N>&)
```

If you need to, look up the mathematical definitions in a textbook.

Postscript

If you don't feel comfortable with mathematics, you probably didn't like this chapter and you'll probably choose a field of work where you are unlikely to need the information presented here. On the other hand, if you do like mathematics, we hope that you appreciate how closely the fundamental concepts of mathematics can be represented in code.

Embedded Systems Programming

> " 'Unsafe' means 'Somebody may die.' "
>
> **—Safety officer**

We present a view of embedded systems programming; that is, we discuss topics primarily related to writing programs for "gadgets" that do not look like conventional computers with screens and keyboards. We focus on the principles, programming techniques, language facilities, and coding standards needed to work "close to the hardware." The main language issues addressed are resource management, memory management, pointer and array use, and bit manipulation. The emphasis is on safe use and on alternatives to the use of the lowest-level features. We do not attempt to present specialized machine architectures or direct access to hardware devices; that is what specialized literature and manuals are for. As an example, we present the implementation of an encryption/decryption algorithm.

25.1 Embedded systems

Most computers in the world are not immediately recognizable as computers. They are simply a part of a larger system or "gadget." For example:

- *Cars:* A modern car may have many dozens of computers, controlling the fuel injection, monitoring engine performance, adjusting the radio, controlling the brakes, watching for underinflated tires, controlling the windshield wipers, etc.

- *Telephones:* A mobile telephone contains at least two computers; typically one of those is specialized for signal processing.

- *Airplanes:* A modern airplane contains computers for everything from running the passenger entertainment system to wiggling the wing tips for optimal flight properties.

- *Cameras:* There are cameras with five processors and for which each lens even has its own separate processor.

- *Credit cards* (of the "smart card" variety)

- *Medical equipment monitors and controllers* (e.g., CAT scanners)

- *Elevators* (lifts)

- *PDAs* (Personal Digital Assistant)

- *Printer controllers*

- *Sound systems*

- *MP3 players*

- *Kitchen appliances* (such as rice cookers and bread machines)
- *Telephone switches* (typically consisting of thousands of specialized computers)
- *Pump controllers* (for water pumps and oil pumps, etc.)
- *Welding robots:* some for use in tight or dangerous places where a human welder cannot go
- *Wind turbines:* some capable of generating megawatts of power and 70m (210ft) tall
- *Sea-wall gate controllers*
- *Assembly-line quality monitors*
- *Bar code readers*
- *Car assembly robots*
- *Centrifuge controllers* (as used in many medical analysis processes)
- *Disk-drive controllers*

These computers are parts of larger systems. Such "large systems" usually don't look like computers and we don't usually think of them as computers. When we see a car coming down the street, we don't say, "Look, there's a distributed computer system!" Well, the car is *also* a distributed computer system, but its operation is so integrated with the mechanical, electronic, and electrical parts that we can't really consider the computers in isolation. The constraints on their computations (in time and space) and the very definition of program correctness cannot be separated from the larger system. Often, an embedded computer controls a physical device, and the correct behavior of the computer is defined as the correct operation of the physical device. Consider a large marine diesel engine:

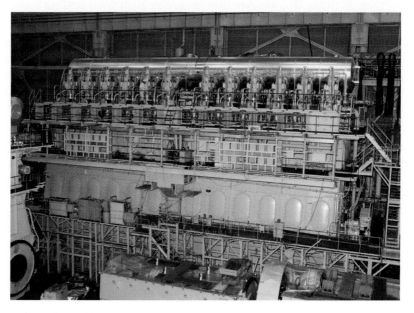

Note the man at the head of cylinder number 5. This is a big engine, the kind of engine that powers the largest ships. If an engine like this fails, you'll read about it on the front page of your morning newspaper. On this engine, a cylinder control system, consisting of three computers, sits on each cylinder head. Each cylinder control system is connected to the engine control system (another three computers) through two independent networks. The engine control system is then connected to the control room where the machine engineers can communicate with it through a specialized GUI system. The complete system can also be remotely monitored via radio (through satellites) from a shipping-line control center. For more examples, see Chapter 1.

So, from a programmer's point of view, what's special about the programs running in the computers that are parts of that engine? More generally, what are examples of concerns that become prominent for various kinds of embedded systems that we don't typically have to worry too much about for "ordinary programs"?

- Often, *reliability is critical:* Failure can be spectacular, expensive (as in "billions of dollars"), and potentially lethal (for the people on board a wreck or the animals in its environment).

- Often, *resources (memory, processor cycles, power) are limited:* That's not likely to be a problem on the engine computer, but think of cell phones, sensors, PDAs, computers on board space probes, etc. In a world where dual-processor 2GHz laptops with 2GB of memory are common, a critical computer in an airplane or a space probe may have just 60MHz and 256KB, and a small gadget just sub-1MHz and a few hundred words of RAM. Computers made resilient to environmental hazards (vibration, bumps, unstable electricity supplies, heat, cold, humidity, workers stepping on them, etc.) are typically far slower than what powers a student's laptop.

- Often, *real-time response is essential:* If the fuel injector misses an injection cycle, bad things can happen to a very complex system generating 100,000Hp; miss a few cycles – that is, fail to function correctly for a second or so – and strange things can start happening to propellers that can be up to 33ft (10m) in diameter and weigh up to 130 tons. You really don't want that to happen.

- Often, *a system must function uninterrupted for years:* Maybe the system is running in a communications satellite orbiting the earth, or maybe the system is just so cheap and exists in so many copies that any significant repair rate would ruin its maker (think of MP3 players, credit cards with embedded chips, and automobile fuel injectors). In the United States, the mandated reliability criterion for backbone telephone switches is 20 minutes of downtime in 20 years (don't even think of taking such a switch down each time you want to change its program).

- Often, *hands-on maintenance is infeasible or very rare:* You can take a large ship into a harbor to service the computers every second year or so when other parts of the ship require service and the necessary computer specialists are available in the right place at the right time. Unscheduled, hands-on maintenance is infeasible (no bugs are allowed while the ship is in a major storm in the middle of the Pacific). You simply can't send someone to repair a space probe in orbit around Mars.

Few systems suffer all of these constraints, and any system that suffers even one is the domain of experts. Our aim is not to make you an "instant expert"; attempting to do that would be quite silly and very irresponsible. Our aim is to acquaint you with the basic problems and the basic concepts involved in their solution so that you can appreciate some of the skills needed to build such systems. Maybe you could become interested in acquiring such valuable skills. People who design and implement embedded systems are critical to many aspects of our technological civilization. This is an area where a professional can do a lot of good.

Is this relevant to novices? To C++ programmers? Yes and yes. There are many more embedded systems processors than there are conventional PCs. A huge fraction of programming jobs relate to embedded systems programming, so your first real job may involve embedded systems programming. Furthermore, the list of examples of embedded systems that started this section is drawn from what I have personally seen done using C++.

25.2 Basic concepts

Much programming of computers that are parts of an embedded system can be just like other programming, so most of the ideas presented in this book apply. However, the emphasis is often different: we must adjust our use of programming language facilities to the constraints of the task, and often we must manipulate our hardware at the lowest level:

- *Correctness:* This is even more important than usual. "Correctness" is not just an abstract concept. In the context of an embedded system, what it means for a program to be correct becomes not just a question of producing the correct results, but also producing them at the right time, in the right order, and using only an acceptable set of resources. Ideally, the details of what constitutes correctness are carefully specified, but often such a specification can be completed only after some experimentation. Often, critical experiments can be performed only after the complete system (of which the computer running the program is a part) has been built. Completely specifying correctness for an embedded system can at the same time be extremely difficult and extremely important. Here, "extremely difficult" can mean "impossible given the time and resources available"; we must try our best using all available tools and techniques. Fortunately, the range of specification, simulation, testing, and other techniques in a given area can be quite impressive. Here, "extremely important" can mean "failure leads to injury or ruin."

• *Fault tolerance:* We must be careful to specify the set of conditions that a program is supposed to handle. For example, for an ordinary student program, you might find it unfair if we kicked the cord out of the power supply during a demonstration. Losing power is not among the conditions an ordinary PC application is supposed to deal with. However, losing power is not uncommon for embedded systems, and some are expected to deal with that. For example, a critical part of a system may have dual power sources, backup batteries, etc. Worse, "But I assumed that the hardware worked correctly" is no excuse for some applications. Over a long time and over a large range of conditions, hardware simply doesn't work correctly. For example, some telephone switches and some aerospace applications are written based on the assumption that sooner or later some bit in the computer's memory will just "decide" to change its value (e.g., from 0 to 1). Alternatively, it may "decide" that it likes the value 1 and ignore attempts to change that 1 to a 0. Such erroneous behavior happens eventually if you have enough memory and use it for a long enough time. It happens sooner if you expose the memory to hard radiation, such as you find beyond the earth's atmosphere. When we work on a system (embedded or not), we have to decide what kind of tolerance to hardware failure we must provide. The usual default is to assume that hardware works as specified. As we deal with more critical systems, that assumption must be modified.

• *No downtime:* Embedded systems typically have to run for a long time without changes to the software or intervention by a skilled operator with knowledge of the implementation. "A long time" can be days, months, years, or the lifetime of the hardware. This is not unique for embedded systems, but it is a difference from the vast majority of "ordinary applications" and from all examples and exercises in this book (so far). This "must run forever" requirement implies an emphasis on error handling and resource management. What is a "resource"? A resource is something of which a machine has only a limited supply; from a program you acquire a resource through some explicit action ("acquire the resource," "allocate") and return it ("release," "free," "deallocate") to the system explicitly or implicitly. Examples of resources are memory, file handles, network connections (sockets), and locks. A program that is part of a long-running system must release every resource it requires except a few that it permanently owns. For example, a program that forgets to close a file every day will on most operating systems not survive for more than about a month. A program that fails to deallocate 100 bytes every day will waste more than 32K a year – that's enough to crash a small gadget after a few months. The nasty thing about such resource "leaks" is that the program will work perfectly for months before it suddenly ceases to function. If a program will crash, we prefer it to crash as soon as possible so that we can remedy the problem. In particular, we prefer it to crash long before it is given to users.

- *Real-time constraints:* We can classify an embedded system as *hard real time* if a certain response must occur before a deadline. If a response must occur before a deadline most of the time, but we can afford an occasional time overrun, we classify the system as *soft real time*. Examples of soft real time are a controller for a car window and a stereo amplifier. A human will not notice a fraction of a second's delay in the movement of the window, and only a trained listener would be able to hear a millisecond's delay in a change of pitch. An example of hard real time is a fuel injector that has to "squirt" at exactly the right time relative to the movement of the piston. If the timing is off by even a fraction of a millisecond, performance suffers and the engine starts to deteriorate; a major timing problem could completely stop the engine, possibly leading to accident or disaster.

- *Predictability:* This is a key notion in embedded systems code. Obviously, the term has many intuitive meanings, but here – in the context of programming embedded systems – we will use a specialized technical meaning: an operation is *predictable* if it takes the same amount of time to execute every time it is executed on a given computer, and if all such operations take the same amount of time to execute. For example, when **x** and **y** are integers, **x+y** takes the same amount of time to execute every time and **xx+yy** takes the same amount of time when **xx** and **yy** are two other integers. Usually, we can ignore minor variations in execution speed related to machine architecture (e.g., differences caused by caching and pipelining) and simply rely on there being a fixed, constant upper limit on the time needed. Operations that are not predictable (in this sense of the word) can't be used in hard real-time systems and must be used with great care in all real-time systems. A classical example of an unpredictable operation is a linear search of a list (e.g., **find()**) where the number of elements is unknown and not easily bounded. Only if we can reliably predict the number of elements or at least the maximum number of elements does such a search become acceptable in a hard real-time system; that is, to *guarantee* a response within a given fixed time we must be able to – possibly aided by code analysis tools – calculate the time needed for every possible code sequence leading up to the deadline.

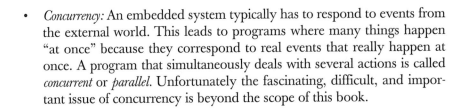

- *Concurrency:* An embedded system typically has to respond to events from the external world. This leads to programs where many things happen "at once" because they correspond to real events that really happen at once. A program that simultaneously deals with several actions is called *concurrent* or *parallel.* Unfortunately the fascinating, difficult, and important issue of concurrency is beyond the scope of this book.

25.2.1 Predictability

From the point of view of predictability, C++ is pretty good, but it isn't perfect. All facilities in the C++ language (including virtual function calls) are predictable, except

- Free-store allocation using **new** and **delete** (see §25.3)
- Exceptions (§19.5)
- **dynamic_cast** (§A.5.7)

These facilities must be avoided for hard real-time applications. The problems with **new** and **delete** are described in detail in §25.3; those are fundamental. Note that the standard library **string** and the standard containers (**vector**, **map**, etc.) indirectly use free store, so they are not predictable either. The problem with **dynamic_cast** is a problem with current implementations but is not fundamental.

The problem with exceptions is that when looking at a particular **throw**, the programmer cannot – without looking at large sections of code – know how long it will take to find a matching **catch** or even if there is such a **catch**. In an embedded systems program, there had better be a **catch** because we can't rely on a C++ programmer sitting ready to use the debugger. The problems with exceptions can in principle be dealt with by a tool that for each **throw** tells you exactly which **catch** will be invoked and how long it will take the **throw** to get there, but currently, that's a research problem, so if you need predictability, you'll have to make do with error handling based on return codes and other old-fashioned and tedious, but predictable, techniques.

25.2.2 Ideals

When writing an embedded systems program there is a danger that the quest for performance and reliability will lead the programmer to regress to exclusively using low-level language facilities. That strategy is workable for individual small pieces of code. However, it can easily leave the overall design a mess, make it difficult to be confident about correctness, and increase the time and money needed to build a system.

As ever, our ideal is to work at the highest level of abstraction that is feasible given the constraints on our problem. Don't get reduced to writing glorified assembler code! As ever, represent your ideas as directly in code as you can (given all constraints). As ever, try hard to write the clearest, cleanest, most maintainable code. Don't optimize until you have to. Performance (in time or space) is often essential for an embedded system, but trying to squeeze performance out of every little piece of code is misguided. Also, for many embedded systems the key is to be correct and fast enough; beyond "fast enough" the system simply idles until another action is needed. Trying to write every few lines of code to be as efficient as possible takes a lot of time, causes a lot of bugs, and often leads to missed opportunities for optimization as algorithms and data structures get hard to understand and hard to change. For example, that "low-level optimization" approach often leads to missed opportunities for memory optimization because almost similar code appears in many places and can't be shared because of incidental differences.

John Bentley – famous for his highly efficient code – offers two "laws of optimization":

- First law: Don't do it.
- Second law (for experts only): Don't do it yet.

Before optimizing, make sure that you understand the system. Only then can you be confident that it is – or can become – correct and reliable. Focus on algorithms and data structures. Once an early version of the system runs, carefully measure and tune it as needed. Fortunately, pleasant surprises are not uncommon: clean code sometimes runs fast enough and doesn't take up excessive memory space. Don't count on that, though; measure. Unpleasant surprises are not uncommon either.

25.2.3 Living with failure

Imagine that we are to design and implement a system that may not fail. By "not fail" let's say that we mean "will run without human intervention for a month." What kind of failures must we protect against? We can exclude dealing with the sun going nova and probably also with the system being trampled by an elephant. However, in general we cannot know what might go wrong. For a specific system, we can and must make assumptions about what kinds of errors are more common than others. Examples:

- Power surges/failure
- Connector vibrating out of its socket
- System hit by falling debris crushing a processor
- Falling system (disk might be destroyed by impact)
- X-rays causing some memory bits to change value in ways impossible according to the language definition

Transient errors are usually the hardest to find. A *transient error* is one that happens "sometimes" but not every time a program is run. For example, we have heard of a processor that misbehaved only when the temperature exceeded 130°F (54°C). It was never supposed to get that hot; however, it did when the system was (unintentionally and occasionally) covered up on the factory floor, never in the lab while being tested.

Errors that occur away from the lab are the hardest to fix. You will have a hard time imagining the design and implementation effort involved in letting the JPL engineers diagnose software and hardware failures on the Mars Rovers (twenty minutes away from the lab for a signal traveling at the speed of light) and update the software to fix a problem once understood.

Domain knowledge – that is, knowledge about a system, its environment, and its use – is essential for designing and implementing a system with a good resilience against errors. Here, we will touch only upon generalities. Note that every "generality" we mention here has been the subject of thousands of papers and decades of research and development.

- *Prevent resource leaks:* Don't leak. Be specific about what resources your program uses and be sure you conserve them (perfectly). Any leak will kill your system or subsystem eventually. The most fundamental resources are time and memory. Typically, a program will also use other resources, such as locks, communication channels, and files.

- *Replicate:* If a system critically needs a hardware resource (e.g., a computer, an output device, a wheel) to function, then the designer is faced with a basic choice: should the system contain several copies of the critical resource? We can either accept failure if the hardware breaks or provide a spare and let the software switch to using the spare. For example, the fuel injector controllers for the marine diesel engine are triplicated computers connected by duplicate networks. Note that "the spare" need not be identical to the original (e.g., a space probe may have a primary strong antenna and a weaker backup). Note also that "the spare" can typically be used to boost performance when the system works without a problem.

- *Self-check:* Know when the program (or hardware) is misbehaving. Hardware components (e.g., storage devices) can be very helpful in this respect, monitoring themselves for errors, correcting minor errors, and reporting major failures. Software can check for consistency of its data structures, check invariants (§9.4.3), and rely on internal "sanity checks" (assertions). Unfortunately, self-checking can itself be unreliable, and care must be taken that reporting an error doesn't itself cause an error – it is really hard to completely check error checking.

- *Have a quick way out of misbehaving code:* Make systems modular. Base error handling on modules: each module has a specific task to do. If a module decides it can't do its task, it can report that to some other module. Keep the error handling within a module simple (so that it is more likely to be correct and efficient), and have some other module responsible for serious errors. A good reliable system is modular and multi-level. At each level, serious errors are reported to a module at the next level – in the end, maybe to a person. A module that has been notified of a serious error (one that another module couldn't handle itself) can then take appropriate action – maybe involving a restart of the module that detected the error or running with a less sophisticated (but more robust) "backup" module. Defining exactly what "a module" is for a given system is part of the overall system design, but you can think of it as a class, a library, a program, or all the programs on a computer.

- *Monitor subsystems* in case they can't or don't notice a problem themselves. In a multi-level system higher levels can monitor lower levels. Many systems that really aren't allowed to fail (e.g., the marine engines or space station controllers) have three copies of critical subsystems. This triplication is not done just to have two spares, but also so that disagreements about which subsystem is misbehaving can be settled by 2-to-1 votes. Triplication is especially useful where a multi-level organization is difficult (i.e., at the highest level of a system or subsystem that may not fail).

We can design as much as we like and be as careful with the implementation as we know how to, but the system will still misbehave. Before delivering a system to users, it must be systematically and thoroughly tested; see Chapter 26.

25.3 Memory management

The two most fundamental resources in a computer are time (to execute instructions) and space (memory to hold data and code). In C++, there are three ways to allocate memory to hold data (§17.4, §A.4.2):

- *Static memory:* allocated by the linker and persists as long as the program runs
- *Stack (automatic) memory:* allocated when we call a function and freed when we return from the function
- *Dynamic (heap) memory:* allocated by **new** and freed for possible reuse by **delete**

Let's consider these from the perspective of embedded systems programming. In particular, we will consider memory management from the perspective of tasks where predictability (§25.2.1) is considered essential, such as hard real-time programming and safety-critical programming.

Static memory poses no special problem in embedded systems programming: all is taken care of before the program starts to run and long before a system is deployed.

Stack memory can be a problem because it is possible to use too much of it, but this is not hard to take care of. The designers of a system must determine that for no execution of the program will the stack grow over an acceptable limit. This usually means that the maximum nesting of function calls must be limited; that is, we must be able to demonstrate that a chain of calls (e.g., **f1** calls **f2** calls . . . calls **fn**) will never be too long. In some systems, that has caused a ban on recursive calls. Such a ban can be reasonable for some systems and for some recursive functions, but it is not fundamental. For example, I *know* that **factorial(10)** will call **factorial** at most ten times. However, an embedded systems programmer might very well prefer an iterative implementation of **factorial** (§15.5) to avoid any doubt or accident.

Dynamic memory allocation is usually banned or severely restricted; that is, **new** is either banned or its use restricted to a startup period, and **delete** is banned. The basic reasons are

- *Predictability:* Free-store allocation is not predictable; that is, it is not guaranteed to be a constant time operation. Usually, it is not: in many implementations of **new**, the time needed to allocate a new object can increase dramatically after many objects have been allocated and deallocated.

- *Fragmentation:* The free store may fragment; that is, after allocating and deallocating objects the remaining unused memory may be "fragmented" into a lot of little "holes" of unused space that are useless because each hole is too small to hold an object of the kind used by the application. Thus, the size of useful free store can be far less than the size of the initial free store minus the size of the allocated objects.

The next section explains how this unacceptable state of affairs can arise. The bottom line is that we must avoid programming techniques that use both **new** and **delete** for hard real-time or safety-critical systems. The following sections explain how we can systematically avoid problems with the free store using stacks and pools.

25.3.1 Free-store problems

What's the problem with **new**? Well, really it's a problem with **new** and **delete** used together. Consider the result of this sequence of allocations and deallocations:

```
Message* get_input(Device&);        // make a Message on the free store

while(/* . . . */) {
    Message* p = get_input(dev);
    // . . .
    Node* n1 = new Node(arg1,arg2);
    // . . .
```

```
        delete p;
        Node* n2 = new Node (arg3,arg4);
        // . . .
    }
```

Each time around the loop we create two **Node**s, and in the process of doing so we create a **Message** and delete it again. Such code would not be unusual as part of building a data structure based on input from some "device." Looking at this code, we might expect to "consume" **2*sizeof(Node)** bytes of memory (plus free-store overhead) each time around the loop. Unfortunately, it is not guaranteed that the "consumption" of memory is restricted to the expected and desired **2*sizeof(Node)** bytes. In fact, it is unlikely to be the case.

Assume a simple (though not unrealistic) memory manager. Assume also that a **Message** is a bit larger than a **Node**. We can visualize the use of free space like this, using orange for the **Message**, green for the **Node**s, and plain white for "a hole" (that is, "unused space"):

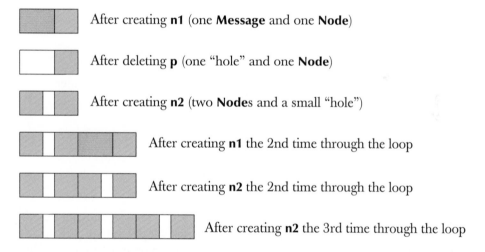

After creating **n1** (one **Message** and one **Node**)

After deleting **p** (one "hole" and one **Node**)

After creating **n2** (two **Node**s and a small "hole")

After creating **n1** the 2nd time through the loop

After creating **n2** the 2nd time through the loop

After creating **n2** the 3rd time through the loop

So, we are leaving behind some unused space ("a hole") on the free store each time we execute the loop. That may be just a few bytes, but if we can't use those holes it will be as bad as a memory leak — and even a small leak will eventually kill a long-running program. Having the free space in our memory scattered in many "holes" too small for allocating new objects is called *memory fragmentation*. Basically, the free-store manager will eventually use up all "holes" that are big enough to hold the kind of objects that the program uses, leaving only holes that are too small to be useful. This is a serious problem for essentially all long-running programs that use **new** and **delete** extensively; it is not uncommon to find unusable fragments taking up most of the memory. That usually dramatically increases the time needed to execute **new** as it has to search through lots of objects and fragments for a suitably sized chunk of memory. Clearly this is not the kind of behavior we can accept for an embedded system. This can also be a serious problem in naively designed non-embedded systems.

Why can't "the language" or "the system" deal with this? Alternatively, can't we just write our program to not create such "holes"? Let's first examine the most obvious solution to having all those little useless "holes" in our memory: let's move the **Node**s so that all the free space gets compacted into one contiguous area that we can use to allocate more objects.

Unfortunately, "the system" can't do that. The reason is that C++ code refers directly to objects in memory. For example, the pointers **n1** and **n2** contain real memory addresses. If we moved the objects pointed to, those addresses would no longer point to the right objects. Assume that we (somewhere) keep pointers to the nodes we created. We could represent the relevant part of our data structure like this:

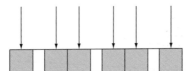

Nodes with pointers to nodes

Now we compact memory by moving an object so that all the unused memory is in one place:

After compacting

Unfortunately, we now have made a mess of those pointers by moving the objects they pointed to without updating the pointers. Why don't we just update the pointers when we move the objects? We could write a program to do that, but only if we knew the details of the data structure. In general, "the system" (the C++ run-time support system) has no idea where the pointers are; that is, given an object, the question "Which pointers in the program point to this object right now?" has no good answer. Even if that problem could be easily solved, this approach (known as *compacting garbage collection*) is not always the right one. For example, to work well, it typically requires more than twice the memory that the program ever needs to be able to keep track of pointers and to move objects around in. That extra memory may not be available on an embedded system. In addition, an efficient compacting garbage collector is hard to make predictable.

We could of course answer that "Where are the pointers?" question for our own data structures and compact those. That would work, but a simpler approach is to avoid fragmentation in the first place. In the example here, we could simply have allocated both **Nodes** before allocating the message:

```
while( . . . ) {
        Node* n1 = new Node;
        Node* n2 = new Node;
        Message* p = get_input(dev);
        // . . . store information in nodes . . .
        delete p;
        // . . .
}
```

However, rearranging code to avoid fragmentation isn't easy in general. Doing so reliably is at best very difficult and often incompatible with other rules for good code. Consequently, we prefer to restrict the use of free store to ways that don't cause fragmentation in the first place. Often, preventing a problem is better than solving it.

TRY THIS

> Complete the program above and print out the addresses and sizes of the objects created to see if and how "holes" appear on your machine. If you have time, you might draw memory layouts like the ones above to better visualize what's going on.

25.3.2 Alternatives to general free store

So, we mustn't cause fragmentation. What do we do then? The first simple observation is that **new** cannot by itself cause fragmentation; it needs **delete** to create the holes. So we start by banning **delete**. That implies that once an object is allocated, it will stay part of the program forever.

In the absence of **delete**, is **new** predictable; that is, do all **new** operations take the same amount of time? Yes, in all common implementations, but it is not actually guaranteed by the standard. Usually, an embedded system has a startup sequence of code that establishes the system as "ready to run" after initial power-up or restart. During that period, we can allocate memory any way we like up to an allowed maximum. We could decide to use **new** during startup. Alternatively (or additionally) we could set aside global (static) memory for future use. For reasons of program structure, global data is often best avoided, but it can be sensible to use that language mechanism to pre-allocate memory. The exact rules for this should be laid down in a coding standard for a system (see §25.6).

There are two data structures that are particularly useful for predictable memory allocation:

- *Stacks:* A stack is a data structure where you can allocate an arbitrary amount of memory (up to a given maximum size) and deallocate the last allocation (only); that is, a stack can grow and shrink only at the top. There can be no fragmentation, because there can be no "hole" between two allocations.

- *Pools:* A pool is a collection of objects of the same size. We can allocate and deallocate objects as long as we don't allocate more objects than the pool can hold. There can be no fragmentation because all objects are of the same size.

For both stacks and pools, both allocation and deallocation are predictable and fast.

So, for a hard real-time or critical system we can define stacks and pools as needed. Better yet, we ought to be able to use stacks and pools as specified, implemented, and tested by someone else (as long as the specification meets our needs).

Note that the C++ standard containers (**vector**, **map**, etc.) and the standard **string** are not to be used because they indirectly use **new**. You can build (buy or borrow) "standard-like" containers to be predictable, but the default ones that come with your implementation are not constrained for embedded systems use.

Note that embedded systems typically have very stringent reliability requirements, so whatever solution we choose, we must make sure not to compromise our programming style by regressing into using lots of low-level facilities directly. Code that is full of pointers, explicit conversions, etc. is unreasonably hard to guarantee as correct.

25.3.3 Pool example

A *pool* is a data structure from which we can allocate objects of a given type and later deallocate (free) such objects. A pool contains a maximum number of objects; that number is specified when the pool is created. Using green for "allocated object" and blue for "space ready for allocation as an object," we can visualize a pool like this:

Pool:

A **Pool** can be defined like this:

```
template<class T, int N>class Pool {     // Pool of N objects of type T
public:
    Pool();                     // make pool of N Ts
    T* get();                   // get a T from the pool; return 0 if no free Ts
    void free(T*);              // return a T given out by get() to the pool
    int available() const;      // number of free Ts
```

private:
　　　// space for T[N] and data to keep track of which Ts are allocated
　　　// and which are not (e.g., a list of free objects)
};

Each **Pool** object has a type of elements and a maximum number of objects. We can use a **Pool** like this:

```
Pool<Small_buffer,10> sb_pool;
Pool<Status_indicator,200> indicator_pool;

Small_buffer* p = sb_pool.get();
// . . .
sb_pool.free(p);
```

It is the job of the programmer to make sure that a pool is never exhausted. The exact meaning of "make sure" depends on the application. For some systems, the programmer must write the code such that **get()** is never called unless there is an object to allocate. On other systems, a programmer can test the result of **get()** and take some remedial action if that result is **0**. A characteristic example of the latter is a telephone system engineered to handle at most 100,000 calls at a time. For each call, some resource, such as a dial buffer, is allocated. If the system runs out of dial buffers (e.g., **dial_buffer_pool.get()** returns **0**), the system refuses to set up new connections (and may "kill" a few existing calls to create capacity). The would-be caller can try again later.

Naturally, our **Pool** template is only one variation of the general idea of a pool. For example, where the restraints on memory allocation are less Draconian, we can define pools where the number of elements is specified in the constructor or even pools where the number of elements can be changed later if we need more objects than initially specified.

25.3.4 Stack example

A *stack* is a data structure from which we can allocate chunks of memory and deallocate the last allocated chunk. Using green for "allocated memory" and blue for "space ready for allocation," we can visualize a stack like this:

As indicated, this stack "grows" toward the right.

We could define a stack of objects, just as we defined a pool of objects:

```
template<class T, int N> class Stack {          // stack of Ts
    // . . .
};
```

However, most systems have a need for allocation of objects of varying sizes. A stack can do that whereas a pool cannot, so we'll show how to define a stack from which we allocate "raw" memory of varying sizes rather than fixed-sized objects:

```
template<int N>class Stack {       // stack of N bytes
public:
    Stack();                       // make an N-byte stack
    void* get(int n);              // allocate n bytes from the stack;
                                   // return 0 if no free space
    void free();                   // return the last value returned by get() to the stack
    int available() const;         // number of available bytes
private:
    // space for char[N] and data to keep track of what is allocated
    // and what is not (e.g., a top-of-stack pointer)
};
```

Since **get()** returns a **void*** pointing to the required number of bytes, it is our job to convert that memory to the kinds of objects we want. We can use such a stack like this:

```
Stack<50*1024> my_free_store;   // 50K worth of storage to be used as a stack

void* pv1 = my_free_store.get(1024);
int* buffer = static_cast<int*>(pv1);

void* pv2 = my_free_store.get(sizeof(Connection));
Connection* pconn = new(pv2) Connection(incoming,outgoing,buffer);
```

The use of **static_cast** is described in §17.8. The **new(pv2)** construct is a "placement **new**." It means "Construct an object in the space pointed to by **pv2**." It doesn't allocate anything. The assumption here is that the type **Connection** has a constructor that will accept the argument list **(incoming,outgoing,buffer)**. If that's not the case, the program won't compile.

Naturally, our **Stack** template is only one variation of the general idea of a stack. For example, where the restraints on memory allocation are less Draconian, we can define stacks where the number of bytes available for allocation is specified in the constructor.

25.4 Addresses, pointers, and arrays

Predictability is a need of some embedded systems; reliability is a concern of all. This leads to attempts to avoid language features and programming techniques that have proved error-prone (in the context of embedded systems programming, if not necessarily everywhere). Careless use of pointers is the main suspect here. Two problem areas stand out:

- Explicit (unchecked and unsafe) conversions
- Passing pointers to array elements

The former problem can typically be handled simply by severely restricting the use of explicit type conversions (casts). The pointer/array problems are more subtle, require understanding, and are best dealt with using (simple) classes or library facilities (such as **array**, §20.9). Consequently, this section focuses on how to address the latter problems.

25.4.1 Unchecked conversions

Physical resources (e.g., control registers for external devices) and their most basic software controls typically exist at specific addresses in a low-level system. We have to enter such addresses into our programs and give a type to such data. For example:

Device_driver* p = reinterpret_cast<Device_driver*>(0xffb8);

See also §17.8. This is the kind of programming you do with a manual or online documentation open. The correspondence between a hardware resource – the address of the resource's register(s) (expressed as an integer, often a hexadecimal integer) – and pointers to the software that manipulates the hardware resource is brittle. You have to get it right without much help from the compiler (because it is not a programming language issue). Usually, a simple (nasty, completely unchecked) **reinterpret_cast** from an **int** to a pointer type is the essential link in the chain of connections from an application to its nontrivial hardware resources.

Where explicit conversions (**reinterpret_cast**, **static_cast**, etc.; see §A.5.7) are not essential, avoid them. Such conversions (casts) are necessary far less frequently than is typically assumed by programmers whose primary experience is with C and C-style C++.

25.4.2 A problem: dysfunctional interfaces

As mentioned (§18.5.1), an array is often passed to a function as a pointer to an element (often, a pointer to the first element). Thereby, they "lose" their size, so that the receiving function cannot directly tell how many elements are pointed to, if any. This is a cause of many subtle and hard-to-fix bugs. Here, we examine examples of those array/pointer problems and present an alternative. We start with an example of a very poor (but unfortunately not rare) interface and proceed to improve it. Consider:

```
void poor(Shape* p, int sz)     // poor interface design
{
        for (int i = 0; i<sz; ++i) p[i].draw();
}

void f(Shape* q, vector<Circle>& s0)     // very bad code
{
        Polygon s1[10];
        Shape s2[10];
        // initialize
        Shape* p1 = new Rectangle(Point(0,0),Point(10,20));
        poor(&s0[0],s0.size());     // #1 (pass the array from the vector)
        poor(s1,10);                // #2
        poor(s2,20);                // #3
        poor(p1,1);                 // #4
        delete p1;
        p1 = 0;
        poor(p1,1);                 // #5
        poor(q,max);                // #6
}
```

The function **poor()** is an example of poor interface design: it provides an interface that provides the caller ample opportunity for mistakes but offers the implementer essentially no opportunity to defend against such mistakes.

TRY THIS

Before reading further, try to see how many errors you can find in **f()**. Specifically, which of the calls of **poor()** could cause the program to crash?

At first glance, the calls look fine, but this is the kind of code that costs a programmer long nights of debugging and gives a quality engineer nightmares.

1. Passing the wrong element type, e.g., **poor(&s0[0],s0.size())**. Also, **s0** might be empty, in which case **&s0[0]** is wrong.

2. Use of a "magic constant" (here, correct): **poor(s1,10)**. Also, wrong element type.

3. Use of a "magic constant" (here, incorrect): **poor(s2,20)**.

4. Correct (easily verified): first call **poor(p1,1)**.

5. Passing a null pointer: second call **poor(p1,1)**.

6. May be correct: **poor(q,max)**. We can't be sure from looking at this code fragment. To see if **q** points to an array with at least **max** elements, we have to find the definitions of **q** and **max** and determine their values at our point of use.

In each case, the errors are simple. We are not dealing with some subtle algorithmic or data structure problem. The problem is that **poor()**'s interface, involving an array passed as a pointer, opens the possibility of a collection of problems. You may appreciate how the problems were obscured by our use of "technical" unhelpful names, such as **p1** and **s0**. However, mnemonic, but misleading, names can make such problems even harder to spot.

In theory, a compiler could catch a few of these errors (such as the second call of **poor(p1,1)** where **p1==0**), but realistically we are saved from disaster for this particular example only because the compiler catches the attempt to define objects of the abstract class **Shape**. However, that is unrelated to **poor()**'s interface problems, so we should not take too much comfort from that. In the following, we use a variant of **Shape** that is not abstract so as not to get distracted from the interface problems.

How come the **poor(&s0[0],s0.size())** call is an error? The **&s0[0]** refers to the first element of an array of **Circles**; it is a **Circle***. We expect a **Shape*** and we pass a pointer to an object of a class derived from **Shape** (here, a **Circle***). That's obviously acceptable: we need that conversion so that we can do object-oriented programming, accessing objects of a variety of types through their common interface (here, **Shape**) (§14.2). However, **poor()** doesn't just use that **Shape*** as a pointer; it uses it as an array, subscripting its way through that array:

```
for (int i = 0; i<sz; ++i) p[i].draw();
```

That is, it looks at the objects starting at memory locations **&p[0]**, **&p[1]**, **&p[2]**, etc.:

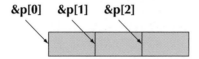

In terms of memory addresses, these pointers are **sizeof(Shape)** apart (§17.3.1). Unfortunately for **poor()**'s caller, **sizeof(Circle)** is larger than **sizeof(Shape)**, so that the memory layout can be visualized like this:

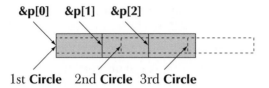

&p[0] &p[1] &p[2]

1st **Circle**   2nd **Circle** 3rd **Circle**

That is, **poor()** is calling **draw()** with a pointer into the middle of the **Circle**s! This is likely to lead to immediate disaster (crash).

The call **poor(s1,10)** is sneakier. It relies on a "magic constant" so it is immediately suspect as a maintenance hazard, but there is a deeper problem. The only reason the use of an array of **Polygon**s doesn't immediately suffer the problem we saw for **Circle**s is that a **Polygon** didn't add data members to its base class **Shape** (whereas **Circle** did; see §13.8 and §13.12); that is, **sizeof(Shape)==sizeof(Polygon)** and − more generally − a **Polygon** has the same memory layout as a **Shape**. In other words, we were "just lucky"; a slight change in the definition of **Polygon** will cause a crash. So **poor(s1,10)** works, but it is a bug waiting to happen. This is emphatically not quality code.

What we see here is the implementation reason for the general language rule that "a **D** is a **B**" does not imply "a **Container<D>** is a **Container<B>**" (§19.3.3). For example:

```
class Circle : public Shape { /* . . . */ };

void fv(vector<Shape>&);
void f(Shape &);

void g(vector<Circle>& vd, Circle & d)
{
       f(d);        // OK: implicit conversion from Circle to Shape
       f(vd);       // error: no conversion from vector<Circle> to vector<Shape>
}
```

OK, so the use of **poor()** is very bad code, but can such code be considered embedded systems code; that is, should this kind of problem concern us in areas where safety or performance matters? Can we dismiss it as a hazard for programmers of non-critical systems and just tell them, "Don't do that"? Well, many modern embedded systems rely critically on a GUI, which is almost always organized in the object-oriented manner of our example. Examples include the iPod user interface, the interfaces of some cell phones, and operator's displays on "gadgets" up to and including airplanes. Another example is that controllers of similar gadgets (such as a variety of electric motors) can constitute a classical class hierarchy. In other words, this kind of code − and in particular, this kind of function declaration – is exactly the kind of code we should worry about. We need a safer way of passing information about collections of data without causing other significant problems.

So, we don't want to pass a built-in array to a function as a pointer plus a size. What do we do instead? The simplest solution is to pass a reference to a container, such as a **vector**. The problems we saw for

    void poor(Shape* p, int sz);

simply cannot occur for

    void general(vector<Shape>&);

If you are programming where **std::vector** (or the equivalent) is acceptable, simply use **vector** (or the equivalent) consistently in interfaces; never pass a built-in array as a pointer plus a size.

If you can't restrict yourself to **vector** or equivalents, you enter a territory that is more difficult and the solutions there involve techniques and language features that are not simple – even though the use of the class (**Array_ref**) we provide is straightforward.

25.4.3 A solution: an interface class

Unfortunately, we cannot use **std::vector** in many embedded systems because it relies on free store. We can solve that problem either by having a special implementation of **vector** or (more easily) by using a container that behaves like a **vector** but doesn't do memory management. Before outlining such an interface class, let's consider what we want from it:

- It is a reference to objects in memory (it does not own objects, allocate objects, delete objects, etc.).
- It "knows" its size (so that it is potentially range checked).
- It "knows" the exact type of its elements (so that it cannot be the source of type errors).
- It is as cheap to pass (copy) as a (pointer,count) pair.
- It does *not* implicitly convert to a pointer.
- It is easy to express a subrange of the range of elements described by an interface object.
- It is as easy to use as built-in arrays.

We will only be able to approximate "as easy to use as built-in arrays." We don't want it to be so easy to use that errors start to become likely.

Here is one such class:

```
template<class T>
class Array_ref {
public:
    Array_ref(T* pp, int s) :p(pp), sz(s) { }

    T& operator[ ](int n) { return p[n]; }
    const T& operator[ ](int n) const { return p[n]; }

    bool assign(Array_ref a)
    {
        if (a.sz!=a) return false;
        for (int i=0; i<sz; ++i) { p[i]=a.p[i]; }
    }

    void reset(Array_ref a) { reset(a.p,a.sz); }
    void reset(T* pp, int s) { p=pp; sz=s; }

    int size() const { return sz; }

    // default copy operations:
    //      Array_ref doesn't own any resources
    //      Array_ref has reference semantics
private:
    T* p;
    int sz;
};
```

Array_ref is close to minimal:

- No **push_back()** (that would require free store) and no **at()** (that would require exceptions).
- **Array_ref** is a form of reference, so copying simply copies (**p,sz**).
- By initializing with different arrays, we can have **Array_refs** that are of the same type but have different sizes.
- By updating (**p,size**) using **reset()**, we can change the size of an existing **Array_ref** (many algorithms require specification of subranges).
- No iterator interface (but that could be easily added if we needed it). In fact, an **Array_ref** is in conception very close to a range described by two iterators.

An **Array_ref** does not own its elements; it does no memory management; it is simply a mechanism for accessing and passing a sequence of elements. In that, it differs from the standard library **array** (§20.9).

To ease the creation of **Array_refs**, we supply a few useful helper functions:

```
template<class T> Array_ref<T> make_ref(T* pp, int s)
{
        return (pp) ? Array_ref<T>(pp,s) : Array_ref<T>(0,0);
}
```

If we initialize an **Array_ref** with a pointer, we have to explicitly supply a size. That's an obvious weakness because it provides us with an opportunity to give the wrong size. It also gives us an opportunity to use a pointer that is a result of an implicit conversion of an array of a derived class to a pointer to a base class, such as **Polygon[10]** to **Shape*** (the original horrible problem from §25.4.2), but sometimes we simply have to trust the programmer.

We decided to be careful about null pointers (because they are a common source of problems), and we took a similar precaution for empty **vectors**:

```
template<class T> Array_ref<T> make_ref(vector<T>& v)
{
        return (v.size()) ? Array_ref<T>(&v[0],v.size()) : Array_ref<T>(0,0);
}
```

The idea is to pass the **vector**'s array of elements. We concern ourselves with **vector** here even though it is often not suitable in the kind of system where **Array_ref** can be useful. The reason is that it shares key properties with containers that can be used there (e.g., pool-based containers; see §25.3.3).

Finally, we deal with built-in arrays where the compiler knows the size:

```
template <class T, int s> Array_ref<T> make_ref(T (&pp)[s])
{
        return Array_ref<T>(pp,s);
}
```

The curious **T(&pp)[s]** notation declares the argument **pp** to be a reference to an array of **s** elements of type **T**. That allows us to initialize an **Array_ref** with an array, remembering its size. We can't declare an empty array, so we don't have to test for zero elements:

```
Polygon ar[0];      // error: no elements
```

Given **Array_ref**, we can try to rewrite our example:

```
void better(Array_ref<Shape> a)
{
    for (int i = 0; i<a.size(); ++i) a[i].draw();
}

void f(Shape* q, vector<Circle>& s0)
{
    Polygon s1[10];
    Shape s2[20];
    // initialize
    Shape* p1 = new Rectangle(Point(0,0),Point(10,20));
    better(make_ref(s0));      // error: Array_ref<Shape> required
    better(make_ref(s1));      // error: Array_ref<Shape> required
    better(make_ref(s2));      // OK (no conversion required)
    better(make_ref(p1,1));    // OK: one element
    delete p1;
    p1 = 0;
    better(make_ref(p1,1));    // OK: no elements
    better(make_ref(q,max));   // OK (if max is OK)
}
```

We see improvements:

- The code is simpler. The programmer rarely has to think about sizes, but when necessary they are in a specific place (the creation of an **Array_ref**), rather than scattered throughout the code.

- The type problem with the **Circle[]**-to-**Shape[]** and **Polygon[]**-to-**Shape[]** conversions is caught.

- The problems with the wrong number of elements for **s1** and **s2** are implicitly dealt with.

- The potential problem with **max** (and other element counts for pointers) becomes more visible – it's the only place we have to be explicit about size.

- We deal implicitly and systematically with null pointers and empty **vector**s.

25.4.4 Inheritance and containers

But what if we wanted to treat a collection of **Circle**s as a collection of **Shape**s, that is, if we really wanted **better()** (which is a variant of our old friend **draw_all()**; see §19.3.2, §22.1.3) to handle polymorphism? Well, basically, we can't. In §19.3.3 and §25.4.2, we saw that the type system has very good reasons for refusing to accept a **vector<Circle>** as a **vector<Shape>**. For the same reason, it refuses to accept an **Array_ref<Circle>** as an **Array_ref<Shape>**. If you have a problem remembering why, it might be a good idea to reread §19.3.3, because the point is pretty fundamental even though it can be inconvenient.

Furthermore, to preserve run-time polymorphic behavior, we have to manipulate our polymorphic objects through pointers (or references): the dot in **p[i].draw()** in **better()** was a giveaway. We should have expected problems with polymorphism the second we saw that dot rather than an arrow (–>).

So what can we do? First we *must* use pointers (or references) rather than objects directly, so we'll try to use **Array_ref<Circle*>**, **Array_ref<Shape*>**, etc. rather than **Array_ref<Circle>**, **Array_ref<Shape>**, etc.

However, we still cannot convert an **Array_ref<Circle*>** to an **Array_ref<Shape*>** because we might then proceed to put elements into the **Array_ref<Shape*>** that are not **Circle***s. But there is a loophole:

- Here, we don't want to modify our **Array_ref<Shape*>**; we just want to draw the **Shape**s! This is an interesting and useful special case: our argument against the **Array_ref<Circle*>**-to-**Array_ref<Shape*>** conversion doesn't apply to a case where we don't modify the **Array_ref<Shape*>**.

- All arrays of pointers have the same layout (independently of what kinds of objects they point to), so we don't get into the layout problem from §25.4.2.

That is, there would be nothing wrong with treating an **Array_ref<Circle*>** as an *immutable* **Array_ref<Shape*>**. So, we "just" have to find a way to treat an **Array_ref<Circle*>** as an immutable **Array_ref<Shape*>**. Consider:

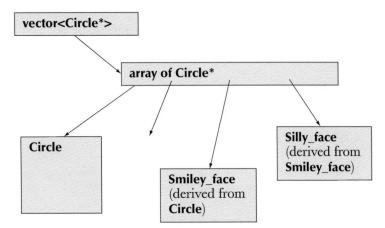

There is no logical problem treating that array of **Circle*** as an immutable array of **Shape*** (from an **Array_ref**).

We seem to have strayed into expert territory. In fact, this problem is genuinely tricky and is unsolvable with the tools supplied so far. However, let's see what it takes to produces a close-to-perfect alternative to our dysfunctional – but all too popular – interface style (pointer plus element count; see §25.4.2). Please remember: Don't go into "expert territory" just to prove how clever you are. Most often, it is a better strategy to find a library where some experts have done the design, implementation, and testing for you.

First, we rework **better()** to something that uses pointers and guarantees that we don't "mess with" the argument container:

```
void better2(const Array_ref<Shape*const> a)
{
        for (int i = 0; i<a.size(); ++i)
                if (a[i])
                        a[i]–>draw();
}
```

We are now dealing with pointers, so we should check for null pointers. To make sure that **better2()** doesn't modify our arrays and vectors in unsafe ways through **Array_ref**, we added a couple of **const**s. The first **const** ensures that we do not apply modifying (mutating) operations, such as **assign()** and **reset()**, on our **Array_ref**. The second **const** is placed after the * to indicate that we want a constant pointer (rather than a pointer to constants); that is, we don't want to modify the element pointers even if we have operations available for that.

Next, we have to solve the central problem: how do we express the idea that **Array_ref<Circle*>** can be converted

- To something like **Array_ref<Shape*>** (that we can use in **better2()**)
- But only to an immutable version of **Array_ref<Shape*>**

We can do that by adding a conversion operator to **Array_ref**:

```
template<class T>
class Array_ref {
public:
        // as before

        template<class Q>
        operator const Array_ref<const Q>()
        {
                // check implicit conversion of elements:
                static_cast<Q>(*static_cast<T*>(0));
```

```
        // cast Array_ref:
        return Array_ref<const Q>(reinterpret_cast<Q*>(p),sz);
    }

    // as before
};
```

This is headache-inducing, but basically:

- The operator casts to **Array_ref<cost Q>** for every type **Q** provided we can cast an element of **Array_ref<T>** to an element of **Array_ref<Q>** (we don't use the result of that cast; we just check that we can cast the element types).

- We construct a new **Array_ref<const Q>** by using brute force (**reinterpret_cast**) to get a pointer to the desired element type. Brute-force solutions often come at a cost; in this case, never use an **Array_ref** conversion from a class using multiple inheritance (§A.12.4).

- Note that **const** in **Array_ref<const Q>**: that's what ensures that we cannot copy a **Array_ref<const Q>** into a plain old mutable **Array_ref<Q>**.

We did warn you that this was "expert territory" and "headache-inducing." However, this version of **Array_ref** is easy to use (it's only the definition/implementation that is tricky):

```
void f(Shape* q, vector<Circle*>& s2)
{
    Polygon* s1[10];
    Shape* s2[20];
    // initialize
    Shape* p1 = new Rectangle(Point(0,0),10);
    better2(make_ref(s0));    // OK: converts to Array_ref<Shape*const>
    better2(make_ref(s1));    // OK: converts to Array_ref<Shape*const>
    better2(make_ref(s2));    // OK (no conversion needed)
    better2(make_ref(p1,1));  // error
    better2(make_ref(q,max)); // error
}
```

The attempts to use pointers result in errors because they are **Shape***s whereas **better2()** expects an **Array_ref<Shape*>**; that is, **better2()** expects something that holds pointers rather than a pointer. If we want to pass pointers to **better2()**, we have to put them into a container (e.g., a built-in array or a **vector**) and pass that. For an individual pointer, we could use the awkward **make_ref(&p1,1)**. However, there is no solution for arrays (with more than one element) that doesn't involve creating a container of pointers to objects.

In conclusion, we can create simple, safe, easy-to-use, and efficient interfaces to compensate for the weaknesses of arrays. That was the major aim of this section. "Every problem is solved by another indirection" (quote by David Wheeler) has been proposed as "the first law of computer science." That was the way we solved this interface problem.

25.5 Bits, bytes, and words

We have talked about hardware memory concepts, such as bits, bytes, and words, before, but in general programming those are not the ones we think much about. Instead we think in terms of objects of specific types, such as **double**, **string**, **Matrix**, and **Simple_window**. Here, we will look at a level of programming where we have to be more aware of the realities of the underlying memory.

If you are uncertain about your knowledge of binary and hexadecimal representations of integers, this may be a good time to review §A.2.1.1.

25.5.1 Bits and bit operations

Think of a byte as a sequence of 8 bits:

Note the convention of numbering bits in a byte from the right (the least significant bit) to the left (the most significant bit). Now think of a word as a sequence of 4 bytes:

3:	2:	1:	0:
0xff	0x10	0xde	0xad

Again, we number right to left, that is, least significant byte to most significant byte. These pictures oversimplify what is found in the real world: there have been computers where a byte was 9 bits (but we haven't seen one for a decade), and machines where a word is 2 bytes are not rare. However, as long as you remember to check your systems manual before taking advantage of "8 bits" and "4 bytes," you should be fine.

In code meant to be portable, use **<limits>** (§24.2.1) to make sure your assumptions about sizes are correct.

How do we represent a set of bits in C++? The answer depends on how many bits we need and what kinds of operations we want to be convenient and efficient. We can use the integer types as sets of bits:

- **bool** – 1 bit, but takes up a whole byte of space
- **char** – 8 bits
- **short** – 16 bits
- **int** – typically 32 bits, but many embedded systems have 16-bit **int**s
- **long int** – 32 bits or 64 bits

The sizes quoted are typical, but different implementations may have different sizes, so if you need to know, test. In addition, the standard library provides ways of dealing with bits:

- **std::vector<bool>** – when we need more than 8*sizeof(long) bits
- **std::bitset** – when we need more than 8*sizeof(long) bits
- **std::set** – an unordered collection of named bits (see §21.6.5)
- A file: lots of bits (see §25.5.6)

Furthermore, we can use two language features to represent bits:

- Enumerations (**enum**s); see §9.5
- Bitfields; see §25.5.5

This variety of ways to represent "bits" reflects the fact that ultimately everything in computer memory is a set of bits, so people have felt the urge to provide a variety of ways of looking at bits, naming bits, and doing operations on bits. Note that the built-in facilities all deal with a set of a fixed number of bits (e.g., 8, 16, 32, and 64) so that the computer can do logical operations on them at optimal speed using operations provided directly by hardware. In contrast, the standard library facilities all provide an arbitrary number of bits. This may limit performance, but don't prejudge efficiency issues: the library facilities can be – and often are – optimized to run well if you pick a number of bits that maps well to the underlying hardware.

Let's first look at the integers. For these, C++ basically provides the bitwise logical operations that the hardware directly implements. These operations apply to each bit of their operands:

Bitwise operations		
|	or	Bit **n** of x|y is 1 if bit **n** of **x** or bit **n** of **y** is 1.
&	and	Bit **n** of x&y is 1 if bit **n** of **x** and bit **n** of **y** is 1.
^	exclusive or	Bit **n** of x^y is 1 if bit **n** of **x** or bit **n** of **y** is 1 but not if both are 1.
<<	left shift	Bit **n** of x<<s is bit **n+s** of **x**.
>>	right shift	Bit **n** of x>>s is bit **n−s** of **x**.
~	complement	Bit **n** of ~x is the opposite of bit **n** of **x**.

You might find the inclusion of "exclusive or" (^, sometimes called "xor") as a fundamental operation odd. However, that's the essential operation in much graphics and encryption code.

The compiler won't confuse a bitwise logical << for an output operator, but you might. To avoid confusion, remember that an output operator takes an **ostream** as its left-hand operand, whereas a bitwise logical operator takes an integer as its left-hand operand.

Note that & differs from && and | differs from || by operating individually on every bit of its operands (§A.5.5), producing a result with as many bits as its operands. In contrast, && and || just return **true** or **false**.

Let's try a couple of examples. We usually express bit patterns using hexadecimal notation. For a half byte (4 bits) we have

Hex	Bits		Hex	Bits
0x0	0000		0x8	1000
0x1	0001		0x9	1001
0x2	0010		0xa	1010
0x3	0011		0xb	1011
0x4	0100		0xc	1100
0x5	0101		0xd	1101
0x6	0110		0xe	1110
0x7	0111		0xf	1111

For numbers up to 9 we could have used decimal, but using hexadecimal helps us to remember that we are thinking about bit patterns. For bytes and words, hexadecimal becomes really useful. The bits in a byte can be expressed as two hexadecimal digits. For example:

Hex byte	Bits
0x00	0000 0000
0x0f	0000 1111
0xf0	1111 0000
0xff	1111 1111
0xaa	1010 1010
0x55	0101 0101

So, using **unsigned** (§25.5.3) to keep things as simple as possible, we can write

unsigned char a = 0xaa;
unsigned char x0 = ~a;   // complement of a

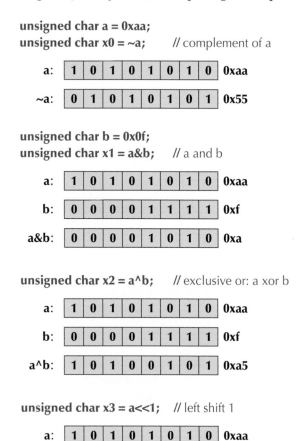

Note that a 0 is "shifted in" from beyond bit 7 to fill up the byte. The leftmost bit (bit 7) simply disappears.

unsigned char x4 == a>>2; // right shift 2

a:	1	0	1	0	1	0	1	0	0xaa
a>>2:	0	0	1	0	1	0	1	0	0x2a

Note that a 0 is "shifted in" from beyond bit 0 to fill up the byte. The rightmost 2 bits (bit 1 and bit 0) simply disappear.

We can draw bit patterns like this and it is good to get a feel for bit patterns, but it soon becomes tedious. Here is a little program that converts integers to their bit representation:

```
int main()
{
    int i;
    while (cin>>i)
        cout << dec << i << "=="
            << hex << "0x" << i << "=="
            << bitset<8*sizeof(int)>(i) << '\n';
}
```

To print the individual bits of the integer, we use a standard library **bitset**:

> **bitset<8*sizeof(int)>(i)**

A **bitset** is a fixed number of bits. In this case, we use the number of bits in an **int** − **8*sizeof(int)** − and initialize that **bitset** with our integer **i**.

TRY THIS

> Get the bits example to work and try out a few values to develop a feel for binary and hexadecimal representations. If you get confused about the representation of negative values, just try again after reading §25.5.3.

25.5.2 bitset

The standard library template class **bitset** from **<bitset>** is used to represent and manipulate sets of bits. Each **bitset** is of a fixed size, specified at construction:

```
bitset<4> flags;
bitset<128> dword_bits;
bitset<12345> lots;
```

A **bitset** is by default initialized to "all zeros" but is typically given an initializer; **bitset** initializers can be unsigned integers or strings of zeros and ones. For example:

```
bitset<4> flags = 0xb;
bitset<128> dword_bits(string("1010101010101010"));
```

```
bitset<12345> lots;
```

Here **lots** will be all zeros, and **dword_bits** will have 112 zeros followed by the 16 bits we explicitly specified. If you try to initialize with a string that has characters different from **'0'** and **'1'**, a **std::invalid_argument** exception is thrown:

```
string s;
cin>>s;
bitset<12345> my_bits(s);    // may throw std::invalid_argument
```

We can use the usual bit manipulation operators for **bitsets**. Assume that **b1**, **b2**, and **b3** are **bitsets**:

```
b1 = b2&b3;    // and
b1 = b2|b3;    // or
b1 = b2^b3;    // xor
b1 = ~b2;      // complement
b1 = b2<<2;    // shift left
b1 = b2>>3;    // shift right
```

Basically, for bit operations (bitwise logical operations), a **bitset** acts like an **unsigned int** (§25.5.3) of an arbitrary, user-specified size. What you can do to an **unsigned int** (with the exception of arithmetic operations), you can do to a **bitset**. In particular, **bitsets** are useful for I/O:

```
cin>>b;                    // read a bitset from input
cout<<bitset<8>('c');      // output the bit pattern for the character 'c'
```

When reading into a **bitset**, an input stream looks for zeros and ones. Consider:

```
10121
```

This is read as **101** leaving **21** unread in the stream.

As for a byte and a word, the bits of a **bitset** are numbered right to left (from the least significant bit toward the most significant), so that, for example, the numerical value of bit 7 is 2^7:

7:	6:	5:	4:	3:	2:	1:	0:
1	0	1	0	0	1	1	1

For **bitsets**, the numbering is not just a convention because a **bitset** supports subscripting of bits. For example:

```
int main()
{
    const int max = 10;
    bitset<max> b;
    while (cin>>b) {
        cout << b << '\n';
        for (int i =0; i<max; ++i) cout << b[i];      // reverse order
        cout << '\n';
    }
}
```

If you need a more complete picture of **bitsets**, look them up in your online doc-umentation, a manual, or an expert-level textbook.

25.5.3 Signed and unsigned

Like most languages, C++ supports both signed and unsigned integers. Un-signed integers are trivial to represent in memory: bit0 means 1, bit1 means 2, bit2 means 4, and so on. However, signed integers pose a problem: how do we distinguish between positive and negative numbers? C++ gives the hardware de-signers some freedom of choice, but almost all implementations use the two's complement representation. The leftmost (most significant bit) is taken as the "sign bit":

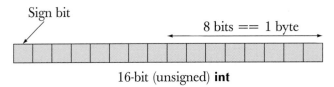

16-bit (unsigned) **int**

If the sign bit is 1, the number is negative. Almost universally, the two's comple-ment representation is used. To save paper, we consider how we would represent signed numbers in a 4-bit integer:

Positive:	0	1	2	4	7
	0000	0001	0010	0100	0111
Negative:	1111	1110	1101	1011	1000
	–1	–2	–3	–5	–8

The bit pattern for –(x+1) can be described as the complement of the bits in **x** (also known as ~x; see §25.5.1).

So far, we have just used signed integers (e.g., **int**). A slightly better set of rules would be:

- Use signed integers (e.g., **int**) for numbers.
- Use unsigned integers (e.g., **unsigned int**) for sets of bits.

That's not a bad rule of thumb, but it's hard to stick to because some people prefer unsigned integers for some forms of arithmetic and we sometimes need to use their code. In particular, for historical reasons going back to the early days of C when **int**s were 16 bits and every bit mattered, **v.size()** for a **vector** is an unsigned integer. For example:

```
vector<int> v;
// . . .
for (int i = 0; i<v.size(); ++i) cout << v[i] << '\n';
```

A "helpful" compiler may warn us that we are mixing signed (i.e., **i**) and unsigned (i.e., **v.size()**) values. Mixing signed and unsigned variables could lead to disaster. For example, the loop variable **i** might overflow; that is, **v.size()** might be larger than the largest signed **int**. Then, **i** would reach the highest value that could represent a positive integer in a signed **int** (the number of bits in an **int** minus 1 to the power of two, minus 1, e.g., $2^{15}-1$). Then, the next **++** couldn't yield the next-highest integer and would instead result in a negative value. The loop would never terminate! Each time we reached the largest integer, we would start again from the smallest negative **int** value. So for 16-bit **int**s that loop is a (probably very serious) bug if **v.size()** is 32*1024 or larger; for 32-bit **int**s the problem occurs if **i** reaches 2*1024*1024*1024.

So, technically, most of the loops in this book have been sloppy and could have caused problems. In other words, for an embedded system, we should either have verified that the loop could never reach the critical point or replaced it with a different form of loop. To avoid this problem we can use either the **size_type** provided by **vector** or iterators:

```
for (vector<int>::size_type i = 0; i<v.size(); ++i) cout << v[i] << '\n';

for (vector<int>::iterator p = v.begin(); p!=v.end(); ++p) cout << *p << '\n';
```

The **size_type** is guaranteed to be unsigned, so the first (unsigned integer) form has one more bit to play with than the **int** version above. That can be significant, but it still gives only a single bit of range (doubling the number of iterations that can be done). The loop using iterators has no such limitation.

TRY THIS

The following example may look innocent, but it is an infinite loop:

```
void infinite()
{
        unsigned char max = 160;        // very large
        for (signed char i=0; i<max; ++i) cout << int(i) << '\n';
}
```

Run it and explain why.

Basically, there are two reasons for using unsigned integers as integers, as opposed to using them simply as sets of bits (i.e., not using +, −, *, and /):

- To gain that extra bit of precision
- To express the logical property that the integer can't be negative

The former is what programmers get out of using an unsigned loop variable.

The problem with using both signed and unsigned types is that in C++ (as in C) they convert to each other in surprising and hard-to-remember ways. Consider:

```
unsigned int ui = −1;
int si = ui;
int si2 = ui+2;
unsigned ui2 = ui+2;
```

Surprisingly, the first initialization succeeds and **ui** gets the value 4294967295, which is the unsigned 32-bit integer with the same representation (bit pattern) as the signed integer −1 ("all ones"). Some people consider that neat and use −1 as shorthand for "all ones"; others consider that a problem. The same conversion rule applies from unsigned to signed, so **si** gets the value −1. As we would expect, **si2** becomes 1 (−1+2 == 1), and so does **ui2**. The result for **ui2** ought to surprise you for a second: why should 4294967295+2 be 1? Look at 4294967295 as a hexadecimal number (**0xffffffff**) and things become clearer: 4294967295 is the largest unsigned 32-bit integer, so 4294967297 cannot be represented as a 32-bit integer − unsigned or not. So we say either that 4294967295+2 overflowed or (more precisely) that unsigned integers support modular arithmetic; that is, arithmetic on 32-bit integers is modulo-32 arithmetic.

Is everything clear so far? Even if it is, we hope we have convinced you that playing with that extra bit of precision in an unsigned integer is playing with fire. It can be confusing and is therefore a potential source of errors.

What happens if an integer overflows? Consider:

```
Int i = 0;
while (++i) print(i);    // print i as an integer followed by a space
```

What sequence of values will be printed? Obviously, this depends on the definition of **Int** (no, for once, the use of the capital *I* isn't a typo). For an integer type with a limited number of bits, we will eventually overflow. If **Int** is unsigned (e.g., **unsigned char**, **unsigned int**, or **unsigned long long**), the **++** is modulo arithmetic, so after the largest number that can be represented we get 0 (and the loop terminates). If **Int** is a signed integer (e.g., **signed char**), the numbers will suddenly turn negative and start working their way back up to 0 (where the loop will terminate). For example, for a **signed char**, we will see 1 2 . . . 126 127 –128 –127 . . . –2 –1.

What happens if an integer overflows? The answer is that we proceed as if we had enough bits, but throw away whichever part of the result doesn't fit in the integer into which we store our result. That strategy will lose us the leftmost (most significant) bits. That's the same effect we see when we assign:

```
int si = 257;       // doesn't fit into a char
char c = si;         // implicit conversion to char
unsigned char uc = si;
signed char sc = si;
print(si); print(c); print(uc); print(sc); cout << '\n';

si = 129;            // doesn't fit into a signed char
c = si;
uc = si;
sc = si;
print(si); print(c); print(uc); print(sc);
```

We get

```
257   1       1       1
129   –127     129     –127
```

The explanation of this result is that 257 is two more than will fit into 8 bits (255 is "8 ones") and 129 is two more than can fit into 7 bits (127 is "7 ones") so the sign bit gets set. Aside: This program shows that **char**s on our machine are unsigned (**c** behaves as **uc** and differs from **sc**).

TRY THIS

Draw out the bit patterns on a piece of paper. Using paper, then figure out what the answer would be for **si**=128. Then run the program to see if your machine agrees.

An aside: Why did we introduce that **print()** function? We could try:

```
cout << i << ' ';
```

However, if **i** was a **char**, we would then output it as a character rather as an integer value. So, to treat all integer types uniformly, we defined

```
template<class T> void print(T i) { cout << i << '\t'; }
```

```
void print(char i) { cout << int(i) << '\t'; }
```

```
void print(signed char i) { cout << int(i) << '\t'; }
```

```
void print(unsigned char i) { cout << int(i) << '\t'; }
```

To conclude: You can use unsigned integers exactly as signed integers (including ordinary arithmetic), but avoid that when you can because it is tricky and error-prone.

- Try never to use unsigned just to get another bit of precision.
- If you need one extra bit, you'll soon need another.

Unfortunately, you can't completely avoid unsigned arithmetic:

- Subscripting for standard library containers uses unsigned.
- Some people like unsigned arithmetic.

25.5.4 Bit manipulation

Why do we actually manipulate bits? Well, most of us prefer not to. "Bit fiddling" is low-level and error-prone, so when we have alternatives, we take them. However, bits are both fundamental and very useful, so many of us can't just pretend they don't exist. This may sound a bit negative and discouraging, but that's deliberate. Some people really *love* to play with bits and bytes, so it is worth remembering that bit fiddling is something you do when you must (quite possibly having some fun in the process), but bits shouldn't be everywhere in your code. To quote John Bentley: "People who play with bits will be bitten" and "People who play with bytes will be bytten."

So, when do we manipulate bits? Sometimes the natural objects of our application simply are bits, so that some of the natural operations in our application domain are bit operations. Examples of such domains are hardware indicators ("flags"), low-level communications (where we have to extract values of various types out of byte streams), graphics (where we have to compose pictures out of several levels of images), and encryption (see the next section).

For example, consider how to extract (low-level) information from an integer (maybe because we wanted to transmit it as bytes, the way binary I/O does):

```
void f(short val)      // assume 16-bit, 2-byte short integer
{
        unsigned char left = val&0xff;          // leftmost (least significant) byte
        unsigned char right = (val>>8)&0xff;    // rightmost (most significant) byte
        // . . .
        bool negative = val&0x8000;             // sign bit
        // . . .
}
```

Such operations are common. They are known as "shift and mask." We "shift" (using << or >>) to place the bits we want to consider to the rightmost (least significant) part of the word where they are easy to manipulate. We "mask" using and (&) together with a bit pattern (here **0xff**) to eliminate (set to zero) the bits we do not want in the result.

When we want to name bits, we often use enumerations. For example:

```
enum Printer_flags {
        acknowledge=1,
        paper_empty=1<<1,
        busy=1<<2,
        out_of_black=1<<3,
        out_of_color=1<<4,
        // . . .
};
```

This defines each enumerator to have exactly the value that its name indicates:

out_of_color	16	0x10	0001 0000
out_of_black	8	0x8	0000 1000
busy	4	0x4	0000 0100
paper_empty	2	0x2	0000 0010
acknowledge	1	0x1	0000 0001

Such values are useful because they can be combined independently:

```
unsigned char x = out_of_color | out_of_black;   // x becomes 24 (16+8)
x |= paper_empty;                                // x becomes 26 (24+2)
```

Note how |= can be read as "set a bit" (or as "set some bits"). Similarly, & can be read as "Is a bit set?" For example:

```
if (x& out_of_color) {      // is out_of_color set? (yes, it is)
// . . .
}
```

We can still use & to mask:

```
unsigned char y = x &(out_of_color | out_of_black);      // x becomes 24
```

Now **y** has a copy of the bits from **x**'s positions 4 and 3 (**out_of_color** and **out_of_black**).

It is very common to use an **enum** as a set of bits. When doing that, we need a conversion to get the result of a bitwise logical operation "back into" the **enum**. For example:

```
Flags z = Printer_flags(out_of_color | out_of_black); // the cast is necessary
```

The reason that the cast is needed is that the compiler cannot know that the result of **out_of_color | out_of_black** is a valid value for a **Flags** variable. The compiler's skepticism is warranted: after all, no enumerator has a value 24 (**out_of_color | out_of_black**), but in this case, we know the assignment to be reasonable (but the compiler does not).

25.5.5 Bitfields

As mentioned, the hardware interface is one area where bits occur frequently. Typically, an interface is defined as a mixture of bits and numbers of various sizes. These "bits and numbers" are typically named and occur in specific positions of a word, often called a *device register*. C++ has a specific language facility to deal with such fixed layouts: *bitfields*. Consider a page number as used in the page manager deep in an operating system. Here is a diagram from an operating system manual:

position:	31:	9:	6:	3:	2:	1:	0:
PPN:	22	3	3	1	1	1	1
name:	PFN	unused	CCA	dirty nonreachable		global valid	

The 32-bit word is used as two numeric fields (one of 22 bits and one of 3 bits) and four flags (1 bit each). The sizes and positions of these pieces of data are fixed. There is even an unused (and unnamed) "field" in the middle. We can express this as a **struct**:

```
struct PPN {  // R6000 Physical Page Number
        unsigned int PFN : 22 ;       // Page Frame Number
        int : 3 ;                     // unused
        unsigned int CCA : 3 ;        // Cache Coherency Algorithm
        bool nonreachable : 1 ;
        bool dirty : 1 ;
        bool valid : 1 ;
        bool global : 1 ;
};
```

We had to read the manual to see that **PFN** and **CCA** should be interpreted as unsigned integers, but otherwise we could write out that **struct** directly from the diagram. Bitfields fill a word left to right. You give the number of bits as an integer value after a colon. You can't specify an absolute position (e.g., bit 8). If you "consume" more bits with bitfields than a word can hold, the fields that don't fit are put into the next word. Hopefully, that's what you want. Once defined, a bitfield is used exactly like other variables:

```
void part_of_VM_system(PPN * p )
{
     // . . .
     if (p–>dirty) { // contents changed
            // copy to disk
            p–>dirty = 0 ;
     }
     // . . .
}
```

Bitfields primarily save you the bother of shifting and masking to get to information placed in the middle of a word. For example, given a **PPN** called **pn** we could extract the **CCA** like this:

```
unsigned int x = pn.CCA;          // extract CCA
```

Had we used an **int** called **pni** to represent the same bits, we could instead have written:

```
unsigned int y = (pni>>4)&0x7;       // extract CCA
```

That is, shift **pn** right so that the **CCA** is the leftmost bit, then mask all other bits off with the **0x7** (i.e., last three bits set). If you look at the machine code, you'll most likely find that the generated code is identical for those two lines.

The "acronym soup" (**CCA, PPN, PFN**) is typical of code at this level and makes little sense out of context.

25.5.6 An example: simple encryption

As an example of manipulation of data at the level of the data's representation as bits and bytes, let us consider a simple encryption algorithm: the Tiny Encryption Algorithm (TEA). It was originally written by David Wheeler of Cambridge University (§22.2.1). It is small but the protection against undesired decryption is excellent.

Don't look too hard at the code (unless you really want to and are willing to risk a headache). We present the code simply to give you the flavor of some real-world and useful bit manipulation code. If you want to make a study of encryption, you need a separate textbook for that. For more information and variants of the algorithm in other languages, see http://en.wikipedia.org/wiki/Tiny_Encryption_Algorithm and the TEA website of Professor Simon Shepherd, Bradford University, England. The code is not meant to be self-explanatory (no comments!).

The basic idea of enciphering/deciphering (also know as encryption/decryption) is simple. I want to send you some text, but I don't want others to read it. Therefore, I transform the text in a way that renders it unreadable to people who don't know exactly how I modified it – but in such a way that you can reverse my transformation and read the text. That's called enciphering. To encipher I use an algorithm (which we must assume an uninvited listener knows) and a string called the "key." You and I both have the key (and we hope that the uninvited listener does not). When you get the enciphered text, you decipher it using the "key"; that is, you re-constitute the "clear text" that I sent.

TEA takes as argument an array of two unsigned **longs** (**v[0],v[1]**) representing eight characters to be enciphered, an array of two unsigned **longs** (**w[0],w[1]**) into which the enciphered output is written, and an array of four unsigned **longs** (**k[0]..k[3]**), which is the key:

```
void encipher(
        const unsigned long *const v,
        unsigned long *const w,
        const unsigned long * const k)
{

        unsigned long y = v[0];
        unsigned long z = v[1];
        unsigned long sum = 0;
        unsigned long delta = 0x9E3779B9;
        unsigned long n = 32;
```

```
    while(n-- > 0) {
        y += (z << 4 ^ z >> 5) + z ^ sum + k[sum&3];
        sum += delta;
        z += (y << 4 ^ y >> 5) + y ^ sum + k[sum>>11 & 3];
    }
    w[0]=y; w[1]=z;
}
```

Note how all data is unsigned so that we can perform bitwise operations on it without fear of surprises caused by special treatment related to negative numbers. Shifts (<< and >>), exclusive or (^), and bitwise and (&) do the essential work with an ordinary (unsigned) addition thrown in for good measure. This code is specifically written for a machine where there are 4 bytes in a **long**. The code is littered with "magic" constants (e.g., it assumes that **sizeof(long)** is 4). That's generally not a good idea, but this particular piece of software fits on a single sheet of paper. As a mathematical formula, it fits on the back of an envelope or – as originally intended – in the head of a programmer with a good memory. David Wheeler wanted to be able to encipher things while he was traveling without bringing notes, a laptop, etc. In addition to being small, this code is also fast. The variable **n** determines the number of iterations: the higher the number of iterations, the stronger the encryption. To the best of our knowledge, for **n==32** TEA has never been broken.

Here is the corresponding deciphering function:

```
void decipher(
    const unsigned long *const v,
    unsigned long *const w,
    const unsigned long * const k)
{
    unsigned long y = v[0];
    unsigned long z = v[1];
    unsigned long sum = 0xC6EF3720;
    unsigned long delta = 0x9E3779B9;
    unsigned long n = 32;
    // sum = delta<<5, in general sum = delta * n
    while(n-- > 0) {
        z -= (y << 4 ^ y >> 5) + y ^ sum + k[sum>>11 & 3];
        sum -= delta;
        y -= (z << 4 ^ z >> 5) + z ^ sum + k[sum&3];
    }
    w[0]=y; w[1]=z;
}
```

We can use TEA like this to produce a file to be sent over an unsafe connection:

```cpp
int main()     // sender
{
        const int nchar = 2*sizeof(long);    // 64 bits
        const int kchar = 2*nchar;           // 128 bits

        string op;
        string key;
        string infile;
        string outfile;
        cout << "please enter input file name, output file name, and key:\n";
        cin >> infile >> outfile >> key;
        while (key.size()<kchar) key += '0';    // pad key
        ifstream inf(infile.c_str());
        ofstream outf(outfile.c_str());
        if (!inf || !outf) error("bad file name");

        const unsigned long* k =
                reinterpret_cast<const unsigned long*>(key.data());

        unsigned long outptr[2];
        char inbuf[nchar];
        unsigned long* inptr = reinterpret_cast<unsigned long*>(inbuf);
        int count = 0;

        while (inf.get(inbuf[count])) {
                outf << hex;      // use hexadecimal output
                if (++count == nchar) {
                        encipher(inptr,outptr,k);
                        // pad with leading zeros:
                        outf << setw(8) << setfill('0') << outptr[0] << ' '
                                << setw(8) << setfill('0') << outptr[1] << ' ';
                        count = 0;
                }
        }

        if (count) {    // pad
                while(count != nchar) inbuf[count++] = '0';
                encipher(inptr,outptr,k);
                outf << outptr[0] << ' ' << outptr[1] << ' ';
        }
}
```

The essential piece of code is the while loop; the rest is just support. The while loop reads characters into the input buffer, **inbuf**, and every time it has eight characters as needed by TEA it passes them to **encipher()**. TEA doesn't care about characters; in fact, it has no idea what it is enciphering. For example, you could encipher a photo or a phone conversation. All TEA cares about is that it is given 64 bits (two unsigned **long**s) so that it can produce a corresponding 64 bits. So, we take a pointer to the **inbuf** and cast it to an unsigned **long*** and pass that to TEA. We do the same for the key; TEA will use the first 128 bits (four unsigned **long**s) of the key, so we "pad" the user's input to be sure that there are 128 bits. The last statement pads the text with zeros to make up the multiple of 64 bits (8 bytes) required by TEA.

How do we transmit the enciphered text? We have a free choice, but since it is "just bits" rather than ASCII or Unicode characters, we can't really treat it as ordinary text. Binary I/O (see §11.3.2) would be an option, but here we decided to output the output words as hexadecimal numbers:

```
5b8fb57c 806fbcce 2db72335 23989d1d 991206bc 0363a308
8f8111ac 38f3f2f3 9110a4bb c5e1389f 64d7efe8 ba133559
4cc00fa0 6f77e537 bde7925f f87045f0 472bad6e dd228bc3
a5686903 51cc9a61 fc19144e d3bcde62 4fdb7dc8 43d565e5
f1d3f026 b2887412 97580690 d2ea4f8b 2d8fb3b7 936cfa6d
6a13ef90 fd036721 b80035e1 7467d8d8 d32bb67e 29923fde
197d4cd6 76874951 418e8a43 e9644c2a eb10e848 ba67dcd8
7115211f dbe32069 e4e92f87 8bf3e33e b18f942c c965b87a
44489114 18d4f2bc 256da1bf c57b1788 9113c372 12662c23
eeb63c45 82499657 a8265f44 7c866aae 7c80a631 e91475e1
5991ab8b 6aedbb73 71b642c4 8d78f68b d602bfe4 d1eadde7
55f20835 1a6d3a4b 202c36b8 66a1e0f2 771993f3 11d1d0ab
74a8cfd4 4ce54f5a e5fda09d acbdf110 259a1a19 b964a3a9
456fd8a3 1e78591b 07c8f5a2 101641ec d0c9d7e1 60dbeb11
b9ad8e72 ad30b839 201fc553 a34a79c4 217ca84d 30f666c6
d018e61c d1c94ea6 6ca73314 cd60def1 6e16870e 45b94dc0
d7b44fcd 96e0425a 72839f71 d5b6427c 214340f9 8745882f
0602c1a2 b437c759 ca0e3903 bd4d8460 edd0551e 31d34dd3
c3f943ed d2cae477 4d9d0b61 f647c377 0d9d303a ce1de974
f9449784 df460350 5d42b06c d4dedb54 17811b5f 4f723692
14d67edb 11da5447 67bc059a 4600f047 63e439e3 2e9d15f7
4f21bbbe 3d7c5e9b 433564f5 c3ff2597 3a1ea1df 305e2713
9421d209 2b52384f f78fbae7 d03c1f58 6832680a 207609f3
9f2c5a59 ee31f147 2ebc3651 e017d9d6 d6d60ce2 2be1f2f9
eb9de5a8 95657e30 cad37fda 7bce06f4 457daf44 eb257206
418c24a5 de687477 5c1b3155 f744fbff 26800820 92224e9d
43c03a51 d168f2d1 624c54fe 73c99473 1bce8fbb 62452495
5de382c1 1a789445 aa00178a 3e583446 dcbd64c5 ddda1e73
```

```
fa168da2  60bc109e  7102ce40  9fed3a0b  44245e5d  f612ed4c
b5c161f8  97ff2fc0  1dbf5674  45965600  b04c0afa  b537a770
9ab9bee7  1624516c  0d3e556b  6de6eda7  d159b10e  71d5c1a6
b8bb87de  316a0fc9  62c01a3d  0a24a51f  86365842  52dabf4d
372ac18b  9a5df281  35c9f8d7  07c8f9b4  36b6d9a5  a08ae934
239efba5  5fe3fa6f  659df805  faf4c378  4c2048d6  e8bf4939
31167a93  43d17818  998ba244  55dba8ee  799e07e7  43d26aef
d5682864  05e641dc  b5948ec8  03457e3f  80c934fe  cc5ad4f9
0dc16bb2  a50aa1ef  d62ef1cd  f8fbbf67  30c17f12  718f4d9a
43295fed  561de2a0
```

TRY THIS

The key was **bs**; what was the text?

Any security expert will tell you that it is a dumb idea to store clear text and enciphered files together and also express an opinion about padding, about using a two-letter key, etc., but this is a programming book, rather than a book on computer security.

We tested the programs by reading the enciphered text and getting the original back. When writing a program, it is always nice to be able to conduct a simple test of correctness.

Here is the central part of the deciphering program:

```
unsigned long inptr[2];
char outbuf[nchar+1];
outbuf[nchar]=0;   // terminator
unsigned long* outptr = reinterpret_cast<unsigned long*>(outbuf);
inf.setf(ios_base::hex ,ios_base::basefield);        // use hexadecimal input

while (inf>>inptr[0]>>inptr[1]) {
    decipher(inptr,outptr,k);
    outf<<outbuf;
}
```

Note the use of

```
inf.setf(ios_base::hex ,ios_base::basefield);
```

to read the hexadecimal numbers. For decryption, it's the output buffer, **outbuf**, that we treat as bits using a cast.

R102: All code shall conform to ISO/IEC 14882:2003(E) standard C++.
Reason: Language extensions or variations from ISO/IEC 14882 are likely to be less stable, to be less well specified, and to limit portability.

Preprocessor rules

R200: No macros shall be used except for source control using **#ifdef** and **#ifndef**.
Reason: Macros don't obey scope and type rules. Macro use is not obvious when visually examining source text.

R201: **#include** shall be used only to include header (***.h**) files.
Reason: **#include** is used to access interface declarations – not implementation details.

R202: All **#include** directives shall precede all non-preprocessor declarations.
Reason: An **#include** in the middle of a file is more likely to be overlooked by a reader and to cause inconsistencies from a name resolved differently in different places.

R203: Header files (***.h**) shall not contain non-**const** variable definitions or non-inline non-template function definitions.
Reason: Header files should contain interface declarations – not implementation details. However, constants are often seen as part of the interface, some very simple functions need to be inline (and therefore in headers) for performance, and current template implementations require complete template definitions in headers.

Naming and layout

R300: Indentations shall be used and be consistent within the same source file.
Reason: Readability and style.

R301: Each new statement starts on a new line.
Reason: Readability.
Example:

```
int a = 7; x = a+7; f(x,9);      // violation
int a = 7;   // OK
x = a+7;     // OK
f(x,9);      // OK
```

Example:

```
if (p<q) cout << *p;      // violation
```

Example:

```
if (p<q)
    cout << *p;    // OK
```

R302: Identifiers should be given descriptive names.

Identifiers may contain common abbreviations and acronyms.

When used conventionally, **x, y, i, j,** etc. are descriptive.

Use the **number_of_elements** style rather than the **numberOfElements** style.

Hungarian notation shall not be used.

Type, template, and namespace names (only) start with a capital letter.

Avoid excessively long names.

Example: **Device_driver** and **Buffer_pool**.
Reason: Readability.
Note: Identifiers starting with an underscore are reserved to the language implementation by the C++ standard and thus banned.
Exception: When calling an approved library, the names from that library may be used.
Exception: Macro names used for **#include** guards.

R303: Identifiers shall not differ only by

- A mixture of case
- The presence/absence of the underscore character
- The interchange of the letter *O* with the number 0 or the letter *D*
- The interchange of the letter *I* with the number 1 or the letter *l*
- The interchange of the letter *S* with the number 5
- The interchange of the letter *Z* with the number 2
- The interchange of the letter *n* with the letter *h*

Example: **Head** and **head** // violation
Reason: Readability.

R304: No identifier shall be in all capital letters and underscores.
Example: **BLUE** and **BLUE_CHEESE** // violation
Reason: All capital letters are widely used for macros that may be used in **#include** files for approved libraries.

Function and expression rules

r400: Identifiers in an inner scope should not be identical to identifiers in an outer scope.

Example:
> **int var = 9; { int var = 7; ++var; }**   // violation: var hides var

Reason: Readability.

R401: Declarations shall be declared in the smallest possible scope.
Reason: Keeping initialization and use close minimizes chances of confusion; letting a variable go out of scope releases its resources.

R402: Variables shall be initialized.
Example:
> **int var;**   // violation: var is not initialized

Reason: Uninitialized variables are a common source of errors.
Exception: An array or a container that is immediately filled from input need not be initialized.

R403: Casts shall not be used.
Reason: Casts are a common source of errors.
Exception: **dynamic_cast** may be used.
Exception: New-style casts may be used to convert hardware addresses into pointers and **void*** received from sources external to a program (e.g., a GUI library) into pointers of a proper type.

R404: Built-in arrays shall not be used in interfaces; that is, a pointer as function argument shall be assumed to point to a single element. Use **Array_ref** to pass arrays.
Reason: An array is passed as a pointer and its number of elements is not carried along to the called function. Also, the combination of implicit array-to-pointer conversion and implicit derived-to-base conversion can lead to memory corruption.

Class rules

R500: Use **class** for classes with no public data members. Use **struct** for classes with no private data members. Don't use classes with both public and private data members.
Reason: Clarity.

r501: If a class has a destructor or a member of pointer or reference type, it must have a copy constructor and a copy assignment defined or prohibited.
Reason: A destructor usually releases a resource. The default copy semantics rarely does "the right thing" for pointer and reference members or for a class with a destructor.

R502: If a class has a virtual function it must have a virtual destructor.
Reason: A class has a virtual function so that it can be used through a base class interface. A function that knows an object only through that base class may delete it and derived classes need a chance to clean up (in their destructors).

r503: A constructor that accepts a single argument must be declared **explicit**.
Reason: To avoid surprising implicit conversions.

Hard real-time rules

R800: Exceptions shall not be used.
Reason: Not predictable.

R801: new shall be used only during startup.
Reason: Not predictable.
Exception: placement-**new** (with the standard meaning) may be used for memory allocated from stacks.

R802: delete shall not be used.
Reason: Not predictable; can cause fragmentation.

R803: dynamic_cast shall not be used.
Reason: Not predictable (assuming common implementation technique).

R804: The standard library containers, except **std::array**, shall not be used.
Reason: Not predictable (assuming common implementation technique).

Critical systems rules

R900: Increment and decrement operations shall not be used as sub-expressions.
Example:

```
int x = v[++i];     // violation
```

Example:

```
++i;
int x = v[i];       // OK
```

Reason: Such an increment might be overlooked.

R901: Code should not depend on precedence rules below the level of arithmetic expressions.
Example:

```
x = a*b+c;  // OK
```

Example:

```
if( a<b || c<=d)     // violation: parenthesize (a<b) and (c<=d)
```

Reason: confusion about precedence has been repeatedly found in code written by programmers with a weak C/C++ background.

We left gaps in the numbering so that we could add new rules without changing the numbering of existing ones and still have the general classification recognized through the numbering. It is very common for rules to become known by their number, so that renumbering would be resisted by the users.

25.6.3 Real coding standards

There are lots of C++ coding standards. Most are corporate and not widely available. In many cases, that's probably a good thing except possibly for the programmers of those corporations. Here is a list of standards that — when used appropriately in areas to which they apply — can do some good:

Henricson, Mats, and Erik Nyquist. *Industrial Strength C++: Rules and Recommendations.* Prentice Hall, 1996. ISBN 0131209655. A set of rules written in a telecommunications company. Unfortunately, these rules are somewhat dated: the book was published before the ISO C++ standard. In particular, templates don't enter the picture to the extent they would have had these rules been written today.

Lockheed Martin Corporation. "Joint Strike Fighter Air Vehicle Coding Standards for the System Development and Demonstration Program." Document Number 2RDU00001 Rev C. December 2005. Colloquially known as "JSF++"; a set of rules written at Lockheed-Martin Aero for air vehicle (read "airplane") software. These rules really were written by and for programmers who produce software upon which human lives depend. www.research.att.com/~bs/JSF-AV-rules.pdf.

Programming Research. High-integrity C++ Coding Standard Manual Version 2.4. www.programmingresearch.com.

Sutter, Herb, and Andrei Alexandrescu. *C++ Coding Standards: 101 Rules, Guidelines, and Best Practices.* Addison-Wesley, 2004. ISBN 0321113586. This is more of a "meta coding standard"; that is, instead of specific rules it has guidance on which rules are good and why.

Note that there is no substitute for knowing your application area, your programming language, and the relevant programming technique. For most applications — and certainly for most embedded systems programming — you also need to know your operating system and/or hardware architecture. If you need to use C++ for low-level coding, have a look at the ISO C++ committee's report on performance (ISO/IEC TR 18015, www.research.att.com/~bs/performanceTR.pdf); by "performance" they/we primarily mean "embedded systems programming."

Language dialects and proprietary languages abound in the embedded systems world, but whenever you can, use standardized language (such as ISO C++), tools, and libraries. That will minimize your learning curve and increase the likelihood that your work will last.

Drill

1. Run this:

   ```
   int v = 1; for (int i = 0; i<sizeof(v)*8; ++i) { cout << v << ' '; v <<=1; }
   ```

2. Run that again with **v** declared to be an **unsigned int**.
3. Using hexadecimal literals, define **short unsigned int**s:

   a. With every bit set
   b. The lowest (least significant bit) set
   c. The highest (most significant bit) set
   d. The lowest byte all set
   e. The highest byte all set
   f. Every second bit set (and the lowest bit 1)
   g. Every second bit set (and the lowest bit 0)

4. Print each as a decimal and as a hexidecimal.
5. Do 3 and 4 using bit manipulation operations (|, &, <<) and (only) the literals 1 and 0.

Review

1. What is an embedded system? Give ten examples, out of which at least three should not be among those mentioned in this chapter.
2. What is special about embedded systems? Give five concerns that are common.
3. Define predictability in the context of embedded systems.
4. Why can it be hard to maintain and repair an embedded system?
5. Why can it be a poor idea to optimize a system for performance?
6. Why do we prefer higher levels of abstraction to low-level code?
7. What are transient errors? Why do we particularly fear them?
8. How can we design a system to survive failure?
9. Why can't we prevent every failure?
10. What is domain knowledge? Give examples of application domains.
11. Why do we need domain knowledge to program embedded systems?
12. What is a subsystem? Give examples.
13. From a C++ language point of view, what are the three kinds of storage?
14. When would you like to use free store?
15. Why is it often infeasible to use free store in an embedded system?
16. When can you safely use **new** in an embedded system?

17. What is the potential problem with **std::vector** in the context of embedded systems?
18. What is the potential problem with exceptions in the context of embedded systems?
19. What is a recursive function call? Why do some embedded systems programmers avoid them? What do they use instead?
20. What is memory fragmentation?
21. What is a garbage collector (in the context of programming)?
22. What is a memory leak? Why can it be a problem?
23. What is a resource? Give examples.
24. What is a resource leak and how can we systematically prevent it?
25. Why can't we easily move objects from one place in memory to another?
26. What is a stack?
27. What is a pool?
28. Why doesn't the use of stacks and pools lead to memory fragmentation?
29. Why is **reinterpret_cast** necessary? Why is it nasty?
30. Why are pointers dangerous as function arguments? Give examples.
31. What problems can arise from using pointers and arrays? Give examples.
32. What are alternatives to using pointers (to arrays) in interfaces?
33. What is "the first law of computer science"?
34. What is a bit?
35. What is a byte?
36. What is the usual number of bits in a byte?
37. What operations do we have on sets of bits?
38. What is an "exclusive or" and why is it useful?
39. How can we represent a set (sequence, whatever) of bits?
40. How do we conventionally number bits in a word?
41. How do we conventionally number bytes in a word?
42. What is a word?
43. What is the usual number of bits in a word?
44. What is the decimal value of **0xf7**?
45. What sequence of bits is **0xab**?
46. What is a **bitset** and when would you need one?
47. How does an **unsigned int** differ from a **signed int**?
48. When would you prefer an **unsigned int** to a **signed int**?
49. How would you write a loop if the number of elements to be looped over was very high?
50. What is the value of an **unsigned int** after you assign **−3** to it?
51. Why would we want to manipulate bits and bytes (rather than higher-level types)?
52. What is a bitfield?
53. For what are bitfields used?

54. What is encryption (enciphering)? Why do we use it?
55. Can you encrypt a photo?
56. What does TEA stand for?
57. How do you write a number to output in hexadecimal notation?
58. What is the purpose of coding standards? List reasons for having them.
59. Why can't we have a universal coding standard?
60. List some properties of a good coding standard.
61. How can a coding standard do harm?
62. Make a list of at least ten coding rules that you like (have found useful)? Why are they useful?
63. Why do we avoid ALL_CAPITAL identifiers?

Terms

address	encryption	pool
bit	exclusive or	predictability
bitfield	gadget	real time
bitset	garbage collector	resource
coding standard	hard real time	soft real time
embedded system	leak	**unsigned**

Exercises

1. If you haven't already, do the **Try this** exercises in this chapter.
2. Make a list of words that can be spelled with hexadecimal notation. Read 0 as *o*, read 1 as *l*, read 2 as *to*, etc. For example, Fool and Beef. Kindly eliminate vulgarities from the list before submitting it for grading.
3. Initialize a 32-bit signed integer with the bit patterns and print the result: all zeros, all ones, alternating ones and zeros (starting with a leftmost one), alternating zeros and ones (starting with a leftmost zero), the 110011001100 . . . pattern, the 001100110011 . . . pattern, the pattern of all-one bytes and all-zero bytes starting with an all-ones byte, the pattern of all-one bytes and all-zero bytes starting with an all-zeros byte. Repeat that exercise with a 32-bit unsigned integer.
4. Add the bitwise logical operators &, |, ^, and ~ to the calculator from Chapter 7.
5. Write an infinite loop. Execute it.
6. Write an infinite loop that is hard to recognize as an infinite loop. A loop that isn't really infinite because it terminates after completely consuming some resource is acceptable.
7. Write out the hexadecimal values from 0 to 400; write out the hexadecimal values from –200 to 200.
8. Write out the numerical values of each character on your keyboard.

9. Without using any standard headers (such as **<limits>**) or documentation, compute the number of bits in an **int** and determine whether **char** is signed or unsigned on your implementation.

10. Look at the bitfield example from §25.5.5. Write an example that initializes a **PPN**, then reads and print each field value, then changes each field value (by assigning to the field), and prints the result. Repeat this exercise, but store the **PPN** information in a 32-bit unsigned integer and use bit manipulation operators (§25.5.4) to access the bits in the word.

11. Repeat the previous exercise, but keep the bits in a **bitset<32>**.

12. Write out the clear text of the example from §25.5.6.

13. Use TEA (§25.5.6) to communicate "securely" between two computers. Email is minimally acceptable.

14. Implement a simple vector that can hold at most N elements allocated from a pool. Test it for $N==1000$ and integer elements.

15. Measure the time (§26.6.1) it takes to allocate 10,000 objects of random sizes in the [1000:0]-byte range using **new**; then measure the time it takes to deallocate them using **delete**. Do this twice, once deallocating in the reverse order of allocation and once deallocating in random order. Then, do the equivalent for allocating 10,000 objects of size 500 bytes from a pool and freeing them. Then, do the equivalent of allocating 10,000 objects of random sizes in the [1000:0]-byte range on a stack and then free them (in reverse order). Compare the measurements. Do each measurement at least three times to make sure the results are consistent.

16. Formulate 20 coding style rules (don't just copy those in §25.6). Apply them to a program of more than 300 lines that you recently wrote. Write a short (a page or two) comment on the experience of applying those rules. Did you find errors in the code? Did the code get clearer? Did some code get less clear? Now modify the set of rules based on this experience.

17. In §25.23–4 we provided a class **Array_ref** claimed to make access to elements of an array simpler and safer. In particular, we claimed to handle inheritance correctly. Try a variety of ways to get a **Rectangle*** into a **vector<Circle*>** using an **Array_ref<Shape*>** but no casts or other operations involving undefined behavior. This ought to be impossible.

Postscript

So, is embedded systems programming basically "bit fiddling"? Not at all, especially if you deliberately try to minimize bit fiddling as a potential problem with correctness. However, somewhere in a system bits and bytes have "to be fiddled"; the question is just where and how. In most systems, the low-level code can and should be localized. Many of the most interesting systems we deal with are embedded, and some of the most interesting and challenging programming tasks are in this field.

Testing

> "I have only proven the code correct,
> not tested it."

—Donald Knuth

This chapter covers testing and design for correctness. These are huge topics, so we can only scratch their surfaces. The emphasis is on giving some practical ideas and techniques for testing units, such as functions and classes, of a program. We discuss the use of interfaces and the selection of tests to run against them. We emphasize the importance of designing systems to simplify testing and the use of testing from the earliest stages of development. Proving programs correct and dealing with performance problems are also briefly considered.

26.1 What we want

Let's try a simple experiment. Write a binary search. Do it now. Don't wait until the end of the chapter. Don't wait until after the next section. It's important that you try. Now! A binary search is a search in a sorted sequence that starts at the middle:

- If the middle element is equal to what we are searching for, we are finished.

- If the middle element is less than what we are searching for, we look at the right-hand half, doing a binary search on that.

- If the middle element is greater than what we are searching for, we look at the left-hand half, doing a binary search on that.

- The result is an indicator of whether the search was successful and something that allows us to modify the element, if found, such as an index, a pointer, or an iterator.

Use less-than ($<$) as the comparison (sorting) criterion. Feel free to use any data structure you like, any calling conventions you like, and any way of returning the result that you like, but do write the search code yourself. In this rare case, using someone else's function is counterproductive, even with proper acknowledgment. In particular, don't use the standard library algorithm (**binary_search** or **equal_range**) that would have been your first choice in most situations. Take as much time as you like.

So now you have written your binary search function. If not, go back to the previous paragraph. How do you know that your search function is correct? If you haven't already, write down why you are convinced that this code is correct. How confident are you about your reasoning? Are there parts of your argument that might be weak?

That was a trivially simple piece of code. It implemented a very regular and well-known algorithm. Your compiler is on the order of 200K lines of code, your operating system is 10M to 50M lines of code, and the safety-critical code in the airplane you'll fly on for your next vacation or conference is 500K to 2M lines of code. Does that make you feel comfortable? How do the techniques you used for your binary search function scale to real-world software sizes?

Curiously, given all that complex code, most software works correctly most of the time. We do not count anything running on a game-infested consumer PC as "critical." Even more importantly, safety-critical software works correctly just about all of the time. We cannot recall an example of a plane or a car crashing because of a software failure over the last decade. Stories about bank software getting seriously confused by a check for $0.00 are now very old; such things essentially don't happen anymore. Yet software is written by people like you. You know that you make mistakes; we all do, so how do "they" get it right?

The most fundamental answer is that "we" have figured out how to build reliable systems out of unreliable parts. We try hard to make every program, every class, and every function correct, but we typically fail our first attempt at that. Then we debug, test, and redesign to find and remove as many errors as possible. However, in any nontrivial system, some bugs will still be hiding. We know that, but we can't find them − or rather, we can't find them with the time and effort we are able and willing to expend. Then, we redesign the system yet again to recover from unexpected and "impossible" events. The result can be systems that are spectacularly reliable. Note that such reliable systems may still harbor errors − they usually do − and still occasionally work less well than we would like. However, they don't crash and always deliver minimally acceptable service. For example, a phone system may not manage to connect every call when demand is exceptionally high, but it never fails to connect many calls.

Now, we could be philosophical and discuss whether an unexpected error that we have conjectured and catered for is really an error, but let's not. It is more profitable and productive for systems builders "just" to figure how to make our systems more reliable.

26.1.1 Caveat

Testing is a huge topic. There are several schools of thought about how testing should be done and different industries and application areas have different traditions and standards for testing. That's natural − you really don't need the same reliability standard for video games and avionics software − but it leads to confusing differences in terminology and tools. Treat this chapter as a source of ideas for your personal projects and as a source of ideals if you encounter testing of major systems. The testing of major systems involves a variety of combinations of tools and organizational structures that it would make little sense to try to describe here.

26.2 Proofs

Wait a minute! Why don't we just prove that our programs are correct, rather than fussing around with tests? As Edsger Dijkstra succinctly pointed out, "Testing can reveal the presence of errors, not their absence." This leads to an obvious desire to prove programs correct "much as mathematicians prove theorems."

Unfortunately, proving nontrivial programs correct is beyond the state of the art (outside very constrained applications domains), the proofs themselves can contain errors (as can the ones mathematicians produce), and the whole field of program proving is an advanced topic. So, we try as hard as we can to structure our programs so that we can reason about them and convince ourselves that they are correct. However, we also test (§26.3) and try to organize our code to be resilient against remaining errors (§26.4).

26.3 Testing

In §5.11, we described testing as "a systematic way to search for errors." Let's look at techniques for doing that.

People distinguish between *unit testing* and *system testing*. A "unit" is something like a function or a class that is a part of a complete program. If we test such units in isolation, we know where to look for the cause of problems when we find an error; any error will be in the unit that we are testing (or in the code we use to conduct the tests). This contrasts with system testing, where we test a complete system and all we know is that an error is "somewhere in the system." Typically, errors found in system testing – once we have done a good job at unit testing – relate to undesirable interactions between units. They are harder to find than errors within individual units and often more expensive to fix.

Obviously, a unit (say, a class) can be composed of other units (say, functions and other classes), and systems (say, an electronic commerce system) can be composed of other systems (say, a database, a GUI, a networking system, and an order validation system), so the distinction between unit testing and systems testing isn't as clear as you might have thought, but the general idea is that by testing our units well, we save ourselves work – and our end users pain.

One way of looking at testing is that any nontrivial system is built out of units, and these units are themselves built out of smaller units. So, we start testing the smallest units, then we test the units composed from those, and we work our way up until we have tested the whole system; that is, "the system" is just the largest unit (until we use that as a unit for some yet larger system).

So, let's first consider how to test a unit (such as a function, a class, a class hierarchy, or a template). Testers distinguish between white-box testing (where you can look at the detailed implementation of what you are testing) and black-box testing (where you can look only at the interface of what you are testing). We will not make a big deal of this distinction; by all means read the implementation of what you test. But remember that someone might later come and rewrite that implementation, so try not to depend on anything that is not guaranteed in the interface. In fact, when testing anything, the basic idea is to throw anything we can at its interface to see if it responds reasonably.

Mentioning that someone (maybe yourself) might change the code after you tested it brings us to regression testing. Basically, whenever you make a change, you have to retest to make sure that you have not broken anything. So when you have improved a unit, you rerun its unit tests, and before you give the complete system to someone else (or use it for something real yourself), you run the complete system test.

Running such complete tests of a system is often called *regression testing* because it usually includes running tests that have previously found errors to see if these errors are still fixed. If not, the program has "regressed" and needs to be fixed again.

26.3.1 Regression tests

Building up a large collection of tests that have been useful for finding errors in the past is a major part of building an effective test suite for a system. Assume that you have users; they will send you bugs. Never throw away a bug report! Professionals use bug-tracking systems to ensure that. Anyway, a bug report demonstrates either an error in the system or an error in a user's understanding of the system. Either way it is useful.

Usually, a bug report contains far too much extraneous information, and the first task of dealing with it is to produce the smallest program that exhibits the reported problem. This often involves cutting away most of the code submitted: in particular, we try to eliminate the use of libraries and application code that does not affect the error. Finding that minimal test program often helps us localize the bug in the system's code, and that minimal program is what is added to the regression test suite. The way we find that minimal program is to keep removing code until the error disappears – and then reinsert the last bit of code we removed. This we do until we run out of candidates for removal.

Just running hundreds (or tens of thousands) of tests produced from old bug reports may not seem very systematic, but what we are really doing here is to systematically use the experience of users and developers. The regression test suite is a major part of a developer group's institutional memory. For a large system, we simply can't rely on having the original developers available to explain details of the design and implementation. The regression suite is what keeps a system from mutating away from what the developers and users have agreed to be its proper behavior.

26.3.2 Unit tests

OK. Enough words for now! Let's try a concrete example: let's test a binary search. Here is the specification from the ISO standard (§25.3.3.4):

```
template<class ForwardIterator, class T>
bool binary_search(ForwardIterator first , ForwardIterator last ,
                   const T& value );


template<class ForwardIterator, class T, class Compare>
bool binary_search(ForwardIterator first , ForwardIterator last ,
                   const T& value , Compare comp );
```

Requires: The elements e of [first ,last) are partitioned with respect to the expressions e < value and !(value < e) or comp (e, value) and !comp (value, e). Also, for all elements e of [first , last), e < value implies !(value < e) or comp (e, value) implies !comp (value, e).

Returns: true if there is an iterator i in the range [first ,last) that satisfies the corresponding conditions: !(*i < value) && !(value < *i) or comp (*i, value) == false && comp (value , *i) == false.

Complexity: At most log(last − first) + 2 comparisons.

Nobody said that a formal specification (well, semiformal) was easy to read for the uninitiated. However, if you actually did the exercise of designing and implementing a binary search that we strongly suggested at the beginning of the chapter, you have a pretty good idea of what a binary search does and how to test it. This (standard) version takes a pair of forward iterators (§20.10.1) and a value as arguments and returns **true** if the value is in the range defined by the iterators. The iterators must define a sorted sequence. The comparison (sorting) criterion is <. We'll leave the second version of **binary_search** that takes a comparison criterion as an extra argument as an exercise.

Here, we will deal only with errors that are not caught by the compiler, so examples like these are somebody else's problem:

```
binary_search(1,4,5);          // error: an int is not a forward iterator
vector<int> v(10);
binary_search(v.begin(),v.end(),"7");   // error: can't search for a string
                                         // in a vector of ints
binary_search(v.begin(),v.end());       // error: forgot the value
```

How can we *systematically* test **binary_search()**? Obviously we can't just try every possible argument for it, because every possible argument would be every possible sequence of every possible type of value − that would be an infinite number of tests! So, we must choose tests and to choose, we need some principles for making a choice:

- Test for *likely mistakes* (find the most errors).
- Test for *bad mistakes* (find the errors with the worst potential consequences).

By "bad," we mean errors that would have the direst consequences. In general, that's a fuzzy notion, but it can be made precise for a specific program. For example, for a binary search considered in isolation, all errors are about equally bad, but if we used that **binary_search** in a program where all answers were carefully double-checked, getting a wrong answer from **binary_search** might be far more acceptable than having it not return because it went into an infinite loop. In that case, we would spend greater effort tricking **binary_search** into an infinite (or very long) loop than we would trying to trick it into giving a wrong answer. Note our use of "tricking" here. Testing is — among other things — an exercise in applying creative thinking to the problem of "how can we get this code to misbehave?" The best testers are not just systematic, but also quite devious (in a good cause, of course).

26.3.2.1 Testing strategy

How do we go about breaking **binary_search**? We start by looking at **binary_search**'s requirements, that is, what it assumes about its inputs. Unfortunately, from our perspective as testers, it is clearly stated that **[first,last)** must be a sorted sequence; that is, it is the caller's job to ensure that, so we can't fairly try to break **binary_search** by giving it unsorted input or a **[first,last)** where **last<first**. Note that the requirements for **binary_search** do not say what it will do if we give it input that doesn't meet its requirements. Elsewhere in the standard, it says that it may throw an exception in that case, but it is not required to. These facts are good to remember for when we test uses of **binary_search**, though, because a caller failing to establish the requirements of a function, such as **binary_search**, is a likely source of errors.

We can imagine the following kinds of errors for **binary_search**:

- Never returned (e.g., infinite loop)
- Crash (e.g., bad dereference, infinite recursion)
- Value not found even though it was in the sequence
- Value found even though it wasn't in the sequence

In addition, we remember the following "opportunities" for user errors:

- The sequence is not sorted (e.g., {2,1,5,−7,2,10}).
- The sequence is not a valid sequence (e.g., **binary_search(&a[100], &a[50],77)**).

How might an implementer have made a mistake (for testers to find) for a simple call **binary_search(p1,p2,v)**? Errors often occur for "special cases." In particular, when considering sequences (of any sort), we always look for the beginning and the end. In particular, the empty sequence should always be tested. So, let's consider a few arrays of integers that are properly ordered as required:

```
{ 1,2,3,5,8,13,21 }              // an "ordinary sequence"
{ }                              // the empty sequence
{ 1 }                            // just one element
{ 1,2,3,4 }                      // even number of elements
{ 1,2,3,4,5 }                    // odd number of elements
{ 1, 1, 1, 1, 1, 1, 1 }          // all elements equal
{ 0,1,1,1,1,1,1,1,1,1,1,1,1 }    // different element at end
{ 0,0,0,0,0,0,0,0,0,0,0,0,0,1 }  // different element at end
```

Some test sequences are best generated by a program:

- **vector<int> v1;**
  for (int i=0; i<100000000; ++i) v.push_back(i); // a very large sequence
- Some sequences with a random number of elements
- Some sequences with random elements (but still ordered)

This is not as systematic as we'd have liked. After all, we "just picked" some sequences. However, we used some fairly general rules of thumb that often are useful when dealing with sets of values; consider:

- The empty set
- Small sets
- Large sets
- Sets with extreme distributions
- Sets where "what is of interest" happens near the end
- Sets with duplicate elements
- Sets with even and with odd numbers of elements
- Sets generated using random numbers

We use the random sequences just to see if we can get lucky (i.e., find an error) with something we didn't think about. It's a brute-force technique, but relatively cheap in terms of our time.

Why "odd and even"? Well, lots of algorithms partition their input sequences, e.g., into the first half and the last half, and maybe the programmer considered only the odd or the even case. More generally, when we partition a sequence, the point where we split it becomes the end of a subsequence, and we know that errors are likely near ends of sequences.

In general, we look for

- Extreme cases (large, small, strange distributions of input, etc.)
- Boundary conditions (anything near a limit)

What that really means, depends on the particular program we are testing.

26.3.2.2 A simple test harness

We have two categories of tests: tests that should succeed (e.g., searching for a value that's in a sequence) and tests that should fail (e.g., searching for a value in an empty sequence). For each of our sequences, let's construct some succeeding and some failing tests. We will start from the simplest and most obvious and proceed to improve until we have something that's good enough for our **binary_search** example:

```
int a[] = { 1,2,3,5,8,13,21 };
if (binary_search(a,a+sizeof(a)/sizeof(*a),1) == false) cout << "failed";
if (binary_search(a,a+sizeof(a)/sizeof(*a),5) == false) cout << "failed";
if (binary_search(a,a+sizeof(a)/sizeof(*a),8) == false) cout << "failed";
if (binary_search(a,a+sizeof(a)/sizeof(*a),21) == false) cout << "failed";
if (binary_search(a,a+sizeof(a)/sizeof(*a),-7) == true) cout << "failed";
if (binary_search(a,a+sizeof(a)/sizeof(*a),4) == true) cout << "failed";
if (binary_search(a,a+sizeof(a)/sizeof(*a),22) == true) cout << "failed";
```

This is repetitive and tedious, but it will do for a start. In fact, many simple tests are nothing but a long list of calls like this. This naive approach has the virtue of being extremely simple. Even the newest member of the test team can add a new test to the set. However, we can usually do better. For example, when something failed here, we are not told which test failed. That's unacceptable. So:

```
int a[] = { 1,2,3,5,8,13,21 };
if (binary_search(a,a+sizeof(a)/sizeof(*a),1) == false) cout << "1 failed";
if (binary_search(a,a+sizeof(a)/sizeof(*a),5) == false) cout << "2 failed";
if (binary_search(a,a+sizeof(a)/sizeof(*a),8) == false) cout << "3 failed";
if (binary_search(a,a+sizeof(a)/sizeof(*a),21) == false) cout << "4 failed";
if (binary_search(a,a+sizeof(a)/sizeof(*a),-7) == true) cout << "5 failed";
if (binary_search(a,a+sizeof(a)/sizeof(*a),4) == true) cout << "6 failed";
if (binary_search(a,a+sizeof(a)/sizeof(*a),22) == true) cout << "7 failed";
```

Assuming that we will eventually have dozens of tests, this will make a huge difference. For testing real-world systems, we often have many thousands of tests, so being precise about what test failed is essential.

Before going further, note another example of (semi-systematic) testing technique: we tested with correct values, choosing some from the ends of the sequence and some from "the middle." For this sequence we could have tried all values, but typically that's not a realistic option. For the failing values, we chose one from each end and one in the middle. Again, this is not perfectly systematic, but we begin to see a pattern that is useful whenever we deal with sequences of values or ranges of values – and that's very common.

What's wrong with these initial tests?

- We write the same things repeatedly.
- We number the tests manually.
- The output is very minimal (not very helpful).

After looking at this for a while, we decided to keep our tests as data in a file. Each test would contain an identifying label, a value to be looked up, a sequence, and an expected result. For example:

```
{ 27 7 { 1 2 3 5 8 13 21} 0 }
```

This is test number **27**. It looks for **7** in the sequence { **1,2,3,5,8,13,21** } expecting the result **0** (meaning **false**). Why do we put the test inputs in a file rather than placing them right into the text of the test program? Well, in this case we could have typed the tests straight into the program text, but having a lot of data in a source code file can be messy, and often, we use programs to generate test cases. Machine-generated test cases are typically in data files. Also, we can now write a test program that we can run with a variety of files of test cases:

```
struct Test {
      string label;
      int val;
      vector<int> seq;
      bool res;
};

istream& operator>>(istream& is, Test& t);   // use the described format

int test_all()
{
      int error_count = 0;
      Test t;
      while (cin>>t) {
            bool r = binary_search( t.seq.begin(), t.seq.end(), t.val);
```

```
                    if (r !=t.res) {
                         cout << "failure: test " << t.label
                             << " binary_search: "
                             << t.seq.size() << " elements, val==" << t.val
                             << " -> " << t.res << '\n';
                         ++error_count;
                    }
              }
          return error_count;
     }

     int main()
     {
          int errors = test_all();
          cout << "number of errors: " << errors << "\n";
     }
```

Here is some test input using the sequences we listed above:

```
{ 1.1 1 { 1,2,3,5,8,13,21 } 1 }
{ 1.2 5 { 1,2,3,5,8,13,21 } 1 }
{ 1.3 8 { 1,2,3,5,8,13,21 } 1 }
{ 1.4 21 { 1,2,3,5,8,13,21 } 1 }
{ 1.5 −7 { 1,2,3,5,8,13,21 } 0 }
{ 1.6 4 { 1,2,3,5,8,13,21 } 0 }
{ 1.7 22 { 1,2,3,5,8,13,21 } 0 }

{ 2 1 { } 0 }

{ 3.1 1 { 1 } 1 }
{ 3.2 0 { 1 } 0 }
{ 3.3 2 { 1 } 0 }
```

Here we see why we used a string label rather than a number: that way we can "number" our tests using a more flexible system – here using a decimal system to indicate separate tests for the same sequence. A more sophisticated format would eliminate the need to repeat a sequence in our test data file.

26.3.2.3 Random sequences

When we choose values to be used in testing, we try to outwit the implementers (who are often ourselves) and to use values that focus on areas where we know bugs can hide (e.g., complicated sequences of conditions, the ends of sequences, loops, etc.). However, that's also what we did when we tried to write and debug the code. So, we might repeat a logical mistake from the design when we design the tests and completely miss a problem. This is one reason it is a good idea to have someone different from the developer(s) involved with designing the tests. We have one technique that occasionally helps with that problem: just generate (a lot of) random values. For example, here is a function that writes a test description to **cout** using **rand_int()** from §24.7:

```
void make_test(const string& lab, int n, int base, int spread)
    // write a test description with the label lab to cout
    // generate a sequence of n elements starting at base
    // the average distance between elements is spread
{
    cout << "{ " << lab << " " << n << " { ";
    vector<int> v;
    int elem = base;
    for (int i = 0; i<n; ++i) {        // make elements
        elem+= rand_int(spread);
        v.push_back(elem);
    }

    int val = base+ rand_int(elem−base);        // make search value
    bool found = false;
    for (int i = 0; i<n; ++i) {        // print elements and see if val is found
        if (v[i]==val) found = true;
        cout << v[i] << " ";
    }
    cout << "} " << found << " }\n";
}
```

Note that we did not use **binary_search** to see if the random **val** was in the random sequence. We can't use what we are testing to determine the correct value of a test.

Actually, **binary_search** isn't a particularly suitable example of the brute-force random number approach to testing. We doubt that this will find any bugs that are not picked up by our "hand-crafted" tests, but often this technique is useful. Anyway, let's make a few random tests:

```
int no_of_tests = rand_int(100);        // make about 50 tests
for (int i = 0; i<no_of_tests; ++i) {
    string lab = "rand_test_";
    make_test(lab+to_string(i),        // to_string from §23.2
```

```
        rand_int(500),        // number of elements
        0,                    // base
        rand_int(50));        // spread
}
```

Generated tests based on random numbers are particularly useful when we need to test the cumulative effects of many operations where the result of an operation depends on how earlier operations were handled, that is, when a system has state; see §5.2.

The reason that random numbers are not all that useful for **binary_search** is that each search of a sequence is independent of all other searches of that sequence. That of course assumes that the implementation of **binary_search** hasn't done something terminally stupid, such as modifying its sequence. We have a better test for that (exercise 5).

26.3.3 Algorithms and non-algorithms

We have used **binary_search**() as an example. It's a proper algorithm with

- Well-specified requirements on its inputs
- A well-specified effect on its inputs (in this case, no effects)
- No dependencies on objects that are not its explicit inputs
- Without serious constraints imposed by the environment (e.g., no specified time, space, or resource-sharing requirements)

It has obvious and explicitly stated pre- and post-conditions (§5.10). In other words, it's a tester's dream. Often, we are not so lucky: we have to test messy code that (at best) is defined by a somewhat sloppy English text and a couple of diagrams.

Wait a minute! Are we indulging in sloppy logic here? How can we talk about correctness and testing when we don't have a precise specification of what the code is supposed to do? The problem is that much of what needs to be done in software is not easy to specify in perfectly clear mathematical terms. Also, in many cases where it in theory could be specified like that, the math is beyond the abilities of the programmers who write and test the code. So we are left with the ideal of perfectly precise specifications and a reality of what someone (such as us) can manage under real-world conditions and time pressures.

So, assume that you have a messy function that you have to test. By "messy" we mean:

- *Inputs:* Its requirements on its (explicit or implicit) inputs are not specified quite as well as we would like.
- *Outputs:* Its (explicit or implicit) outputs are not specified quite as well as we would like.

- *Resources:* Its use of resources (time, memory, files, etc.) are not specified quite as well as we would like.

By "explicit or implicit" we mean that we have to look not just at the formal parameter and the return value, but also on any effects on global variables, **iostreams**, files, free-store memory allocation, etc. So, what can we do? First of all, such a function is almost certainly too long — or we could have stated its requirements and effects more clearly. Maybe we are talking about a function that is five pages long or uses "helper functions" in complicated and non-obvious ways. You may think that five pages is a lot for a function. It is, but we have seen much, much longer functions than that. Unfortunately, they are not uncommon.

If it is our code and if we had time, we would first of all try to break such a "messy function" up into smaller functions that each come closer to our ideals of a well-specified function and first test those. However, here we will assume that our aim is to test the software — that is, to systematically find as many errors as possible — rather than (just) fixing bugs as we find them.

So, what do we look for? Our job as testers is to find errors. Where are bugs likely to hide? What characterizes code that is likely to contain bugs?

- Subtle dependencies on "other code": look for use of global variables, non-**const**-reference arguments, pointers, etc.
- Resource management: look for memory management (**new** and **delete**), file use, locks, etc.
- Look for loops: check end conditions (as for **binary_search()**).
- **if**-statements and switches (often referred to as "branching"): look for errors in their logic.

Let's look at examples of each.

26.3.3.1 Dependencies

Consider this nonsense function:

```
int do_dependent(int a, int& b)        // messy function
      // undisciplined dependencies
{
      int val ;
      cin>>val;
      vec[val] += 10;
      cout << a;
      b++;
      return b;
}
```

To test **do_ dependent**(), we can't just synthesize sets of arguments and see what it does with them. We have to take into account that it uses the global variables **cin**, **cout**, and **vec**. That's pretty obvious in this little nonsense function, but in real code this may be hidden in a larger amount of code. Fortunately, there is software that can help us find such dependencies. Unfortunately, it is not always easily available or widely used. Assuming that we don't have analysis software to help us, we go through the function line by line, listing all its dependencies.

To test **do_ dependent**(), we have to consider

- Its inputs:
    - The value of **a**
    - The value of **b** and the value of the **int** referenced by **b**
    - The input from **cin** (into **val**) and the state of **cin**
    - The state of **cout**
    - The value of **vec**, in particular, the value of **vec[val]**

- Its outputs:
    - The return value
    - The value of the **int** referenced by **b** (we incremented it)
    - The state of **cin** (beware of stream state and format state)
    - The state of **cout** (beware of stream state and format state)
    - The state of **vec** (we assigned to **vec[val]**)
    - Any exceptions that **vec** might have thrown (**vec[val]** might be out of range)

This is a long list. In fact, that list is longer that the function itself. This goes a long way toward explaining our dislike of global variables and our concerns about non-**const** references (and pointers). There really is something very nice about a function that just reads its arguments and produces a result as a return value: we can easily understand and test it.

Once the inputs and outputs are identified, we are basically back to the **binary_search**() case. We simply generate tests with input values (for explicit and implicit inputs) to see if they give the desired outputs (considering both implicit and explicit outputs). With **do_ dependent**(), we would probably start with a very large **val** and a negative **val**, to see what happens. It looks as if **vec** had better be a range-checked vector (or we can very simply generate really bad errors). We would of course check what the documentation said about all those inputs and outputs, but with a messy function like that we have little hope of the specification being complete and precise, so we will just break the functions (i.e., find errors) and start asking questions about what is correct. Often, such testing and questions should lead to a redesign.

26.3.3.2 Resource management

Consider this nonsense function:

```
void do_resources1(int a, int b, const char* s)  // messy function
        // undisciplined resource use
{
        FILE* f = fopen(s,"r");       // open file (C style)
        int* p = new int[a];          // allocate some memory
        if (b<=0) throw Bad_arg();    // maybe throw an exception
        int* q = new int[b];          // allocate some more memory
        delete[] p;                   // deallocate the memory pointed to by p
}
```

To test **do_resources1()**, we have to consider whether every resource acquired has been properly disposed of, that is, whether every resource has been either released or passed to some other function.

Here, it is obvious that

- The file named **s** is not closed
- The memory allocated for **p** is leaked if **b<=0** or if the second **new** throws
- The memory for **q** is leaked if **0<b**

In addition, we should always consider the possibility that an attempt at opening a file might fail. To get this miserable result, we deliberately used a very old-fashioned programming style (**fopen()** is the standard C way of opening files). We could have made the job for testers more straightforward by writing

```
void do_resources2(int a, int b, const char* s)  // less messy function
{
        ifstream is(s);               // open file
        vector<int>v1(a);             // create vector (owning memory)
        if (b<=0) throw Bad_arg();    // maybe throw an exception
        vector<int> v2(b);            // create another vector (owning memory)
}
```

Now every resource is owned by an object with a destructor that will release it. Considering how we could write a function more simply (more cleanly) is sometimes a good way to get ideas for testing. The "Resource Acquisition Is Initialization" (RAII) technique from §19.5.2 provides a general strategy for this kind of resource management problem.

Please note that resource management is not just checking that every piece of memory allocated is deleted. Sometimes we receive resources from elsewhere (e.g., as an argument), and sometimes we pass resources out of a function (e.g., as a return value). It can be quite hard to determine what is right about such cases. Consider:

```
FILE* do_resources3(int a, int* p, const char* s)        // messy function
    // undisciplined resource passing
{
        FILE* f = fopen(s,"r");
        delete p;
        delete var;
        var = new int[27];
        return f;
}
```

Is it right for **do_resources3**() to pass the (supposedly) opened file back as the return value? Is it right for **do_resources3**() to delete the memory passed to it as the argument **p**? We also added a really sneaky use of the global variable **var** (obviously a pointer). Basically, passing resources in and out of functions is common and useful, but to know if it is correct requires knowledge of a resource management strategy. Who owns the resource? Who is supposed to delete/release it? The documentation should clearly and simply answer those questions. (Dream on.) In either case, passing of resources is a fertile area for bugs and a tempting target for testing.

Note how we (deliberately) complicated the resource management example by using a global variable. Things can get really messy when we start to mix the sources of likely bugs. As programmers, we try to avoid that. As testers, we look for such examples as easy pickings.

26.3.3.3 Loops

We have looked at loops when we discussed **binary_search**(). Basically most errors occur at the ends:

- Is everything properly initialized when we start the loop?
- Do we correctly end with the last case (often the last element)?

Here is an example where we get it wrong:

```
int do_loop(vector<int>& v)         // messy function
    // undisciplined loop
{
        int i;
        int sum;
        while(i<=vec.size()) sum+=v[i];
        return sum;
}
```

There are three obvious errors. (What are they?) In addition, a good tester will immediately spot the opportunity for an overflow where we are adding to **sum**:

- Many loops involve data and might cause some sort of overflow when they are given large inputs.

A famous and particularly nasty loop error, the buffer overflow, falls into the category that can be caught by systematically asking the two key questions about loops:

```
char buf[MAX];      // fixed-size buffer

char* read_line()   // dangerously sloppy
{
      int i = 0;
      char ch;
      while(cin.get(ch) && ch!='\n') buf[i++] = ch;
      buf[i+1] = 0;
      return buf;
}
```

Of course, *you* wouldn't write something like that! (Why not? What's so wrong with **read_line()**?) However, it is sadly common and comes in many variations, such as

```
// dangerously sloppy:
gets(buf);          // read a line into buf
scanf("%s",buf);    // read a line into buf
```

Look up **gets()** and **scanf()** in your documentation and avoid them like the plague. By "dangerous," we mean that such buffer overflows are a staple of "cracking" – that is, break-ins – on computers. Some implementations now warn against **gets()** and its cousins for exactly this reason.

26.3.3.4 Branching

Obviously, when we have to make a choice, we may make the wrong choice. This makes **if**-statements and **switch**-statements good targets for testers. There are two major problems to look for:

- Are all possibilities covered?
- Are the right actions associated with the right possibilities?

Consider this nonsense function:

```
void do_branch1(int x, int y)    // messy function
    // undisciplined use of if
{
    if (x<0) {
        if (y<0)
            cout << "very negative\n";
        else
            cout << "somewhat negative\n";
    }
    else if (x>0) {
        if (y<0)
            cout << "very positive\n";
        else
            cout << "somewhat positive\n";
    }
}
```

The most obvious error here is that we "forgot" the case where **x** is 0. When testing against zero (or for positive and negative values), zero is often forgotten or lumped with the wrong case (e.g., considered negative). Also, there is a more subtle (but not uncommon) error lurking here: the actions for **(x>0 && y<0)** and **(x>0 && y>=0)** have "somehow" been reversed. This happens a lot with cut-and-paste editing.

The more complicated the use of **if**-statements is, the more likely such errors become. From a tester's point of view, we look at such code and try to make sure that every branch is tested. For **do_branch1()** the obvious test set is

```
do_branch1(-1,-1);
do_branch1(-1, 1);
do_branch1(1,-1);
do_branch1(1,1);
do_branch1(-1,0);
do_branch1(0,-1);
do_branch1(1,0);
do_branch1(0,1);
do_branch1(0,0);
```

Basically, that's the brute-force "try all the alternatives" approach after we noticed that **do_branch1()** tested against 0 using **<** and **>**. To catch the wrong actions for positive values of **x**, we have to combine the calls with their desired output.

Dealing with **switch**-statements is fundamentally similar to dealing with **if**-statements.

```
void do_branch1(int x, int y)   // messy function
        // undisciplined use of switch
{
     if (y<0 && y<=3)
             switch (x) {
             case 1:
                   cout << "one\n";
                   break;
             case 2:
                   cout << "two\n";
             case 3:
                   cout << "three\n";
             }
}
```

Here we have made four classical mistakes:

- We range checked the wrong variable (**y** instead of **x**).
- We forgot a break statement leading to a wrong action for **x==2**.
- We forgot a default case (thinking we had taken care of that with the **if**-statement).
- We wrote **y<0** when we meant to say **0<y**.

As testers, we always look for unhandled cases. Please note that "just fixing the problem" is not enough. It may reappear when we are not looking. As testers, we want to write tests that systematically catch errors. If we just fixed this simple code, we may very well get our fix wrong so that it either doesn't solve the problem or introduces new and different errors. The purpose of looking at the code is not really to spot errors (though that's always useful), but to design a suitable set of tests that will catch all errors (or, more realistically, will catch many errors).

Note that loops have an implicit "**if**": they test whether we have reached the end. Thus loops are also branching statements. When we look at programs containing branching, the first question is always, "Have we covered (tested) every branch?" Surprisingly that is not always possible in real code (because in real code, a function is called as needed by other functions and not necessarily in all possible ways). Consequently, a common question for testers is, "What is your code coverage?" and the answer had better be, "We tested most branches," followed by an explanation of why the remaining branches are hard to reach. 100% coverage is the ideal.

26.3.4 System tests

Testing any significant system is a skilled job. For example, the testing of the computers that control telephone systems takes place in specially constructed rooms with racks full of computers simulating the traffic of tens of thousands of people. Such systems cost millions and are the work of teams of very skilled engineers. After it is deployed, a main telephone switch is supposed to work continuously for 20 years with at most 20 minutes of downtime (for any reason, including power failures, flooding, and earthquakes). We will not go into detail here − it would be easier to teach a physics freshman to calculate course corrections for a Mars probe − but we'll try to give you some ideas that could be useful for a smaller project or for understanding the testing of a larger system.

First of all, please remember that the purpose of testing is to find errors, especially potentially frequent and potentially serious errors. It is not simply to write and run the largest number of tests. This implies that some understanding of the system being tested is highly desirable. Even more than for unit testing, effective system testing relies on knowledge of the application (domain knowledge). Developing a system takes more than just knowledge of programming language issues and computer science; it requires an understanding of the application areas and of the people who use the applications. This is something we find important for motivating us to work with code: we get to see so many interesting applications and meet interesting people.

For a complete system to be tested, it has to be built out of all of its parts (units). This can take significant time, so many system tests are run just once a day (often at night while the developers are supposed to be asleep) after all unit tests have been done. Regression tests are a key component here. The areas of a program in which we are most likely to find errors are new code and areas of code where errors were found earlier. So running the collection of old tests (the regression tests) is essential; without those a large system will never become stable. We would introduce new bugs as fast as we removed old ones.

Note that we take it for granted that when we fix a few errors, we accidentally introduce a few new ones. We hope the number of new bugs is lower than the number of old ones that we removed, and that the consequences of the new ones are less severe. However, at least until we have rerun our regression tests and added new tests for our new code, we must assume that our system is broken (by our bug fixes).

26.3.4.1 Testing GUIs

Imagine sitting in front of a screen trying to be systematic about testing a program with an elaborate graphical user interface. Where do I click the mouse? In what order? What values do I enter? In what order? For any significant program, this is hopeless. There are so many possibilities that we could consider hiring a whole bunch of pigeons to peck at the screen at random (they work for bird feed!). Hiring large numbers of "ordinary novice users" and seeing where they "peck" is indeed not uncommon and also necessary, but it is not a systematic strategy. Any real solution has to involve some repeatable sequence of tests. This typically involves designing an interface to the application that bypasses the GUI.

Why is it necessary to sit a human in front of a GUI application and "peck"? The reason is simply that testers cannot anticipate every action that a devious, clumsy, naive, sophisticated, or hurried user can make. Even with the best and most systematic testing, we still need real people to try out the system. Experience shows that for any significant system real users will do things that even experienced designers, implementers, and testers have failed to anticipate. Or as a programmer's proverb has it, "As soon as you build a foolproof system, nature produces a better fool."

So, the ideal for testing is that the GUI simply composes calls to some well-defined interface to the "main program"; that is, the GUI simply provides I/O, and any significant processing is done in isolation from I/O. Doing this implies that we can provide a different (non-graphical) interface:

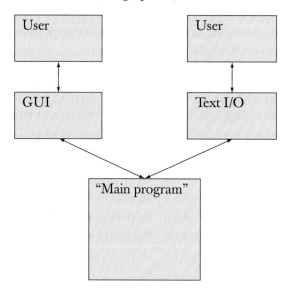

That allows us to write or generate scripts for the "main program" just as we did for our unit testing (§26.3.2). Then we can test the "main program" in isolation from the GUI:

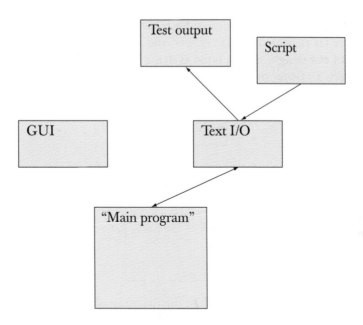

Interestingly, this also allows us to semi-systematically test the GUI: we can run scripts using the text I/O and watch the effect on the GUI (assuming that we send the output from the main program to the GUI as well as the text-I/O interface). More radically, we might bypass the "main application" while we test the GUI by providing text commands that go "directly" to the GUI through a little text-to-GUI-command "translator":

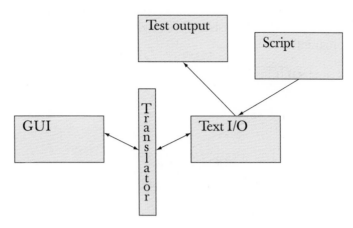

This illustrates two important aspects of good testing:

- Parts of a system should (as far as possible) be testable in isolation. Only "units" with clearly defined interfaces are testable in isolation.
- Tests should (as far as possible) be repeatable. Essentially no test that involves a human is repeatable.

This is also an example of the "design for testing" that we have alluded to: some programs are far easier to test than others, and if we think about testing from the very onset of our design, we can build systems that are better organized and easier to test (§26.2). Better organized? Consider:

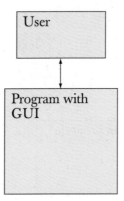

This diagram is obviously simpler than the diagrams above. We can start building this system with less forethought – just use our favorite GUI library wherever in the code we need to communicate with the user. It will probably also require less code than our hypothetical application with both text and graphical I/O. How then can our application using an explicit interface and more parts be better organized than a "simple and straightforward" application where the GUI logic is dispersed throughout the code?

Well, to have two interfaces, we need to carefully define the interface between the "main program" and I/O. In fact, we have to define a common I/O interface layer (similar to the "translator" we used to test the GUI in isolation from the "main program":

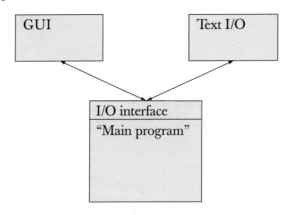

We have seen an example of this: the graphical interface classes in Chapters 13–16 provided an example. They isolate a "main program" (that is, the code you wrote) from the "off-the-shelf" GUI system: FLTK, Windows, Linux's GUI, whatever. With this design we can use any I/O system.

Is this important? We think it is immensely so. First, it helps testing, and without systematic testing it is hard to be serious about correctness. Second, it offers portability. Consider the following scenario: You have started a small company and written your initial application for an Apple because you happen to like that computer. Now, your company is getting successful, and you notice that most of your potential customers run their programs on Windows machines and non-Mac Linux systems. What do you do? With the "simple" organization of the code with (Apple Mac) GUI commands scattered throughout your code, you must rewrite everything. That's OK, because it (relying on ad hoc testing) probably has many hidden errors. But consider the alternative where the "main program" kept the GUI at arm's length (to simplify systematic testing). Now you simply interface another GUI to your interface classes (the "translator" on the diagram) and keep most code unchanged across systems:

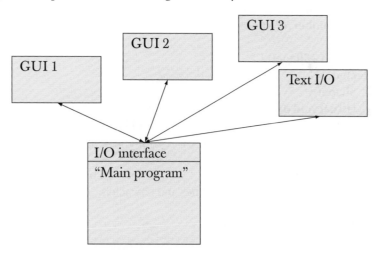

Actually, this design is an example of the use of "thin" explicit interfaces to explicitly separate parts of a program. It is similar to the use of "layers" that we saw in §12.4. Testing really reinforces the desire to have a program partitioned into clearly delimited parts (with interfaces that we can use for testing).

26.3.5 Testing classes

Testing a class is technically unit testing, but since there are typically several member functions and some state involved, testing a class takes on aspects of system testing. This is even more true if the class we are trying to test is a base class, so that we have to consider it in several contexts (as defined by different derived classes). Consider the **Shape** class from §14.2:

```
class Shape {      // deals with color and style, and holds sequence of lines
public:
        void draw() const;                      // deal with color and draw lines
        virtual void move(int dx, int dy);      // move the shape +=dx and +=dy

        void set_color(Color col);
        Color color() const;

        void set_style(Line_style sty);
        Line_style style() const;

        void set_fill_color(Color col);
        Color fill_color() const;

        Point point(int i) const;               // read-only access to points
        int number_of_points() const;

        virtual ~Shape() { }
protected:
        Shape();
        virtual void draw_lines() const;        // draw the appropriate lines
        void add(Point p);                      // add p to points
        void set_point(int i,Point p);          // points[i]=p;
private:
        vector<Point> points;                   // not used by all shapes
        Color lcolor;      // color for lines and characters
        Line_style ls;
        Color fcolor;      // fill color

        Shape(const Shape&);                     // prevent copying
        Shape& operator=(const Shape&);
};
```

How would we go about testing that? Let's first consider what (from a testing point of view) makes **Shape** different from **binary_search**:

- **Shape** has several functions.
- A **Shape** has a mutable state (we can add points, change color, etc.); that is, the effect of one function can affect the behavior of another function.

- **Shape** has **virtual** functions; that is, the behavior of a **Shape** depends on what (if any) class has been derived from it.
- **Shape** is not an algorithm.
- A change to a **Shape** can have an effect on the screen.

The last point is really nasty. This basically means that we have to have a human sit and watch to see if a **Shape** behaves as intended. This is not conducive to systematic, repeatable, and affordable testing. As mentioned in §26.3.4.1, we'll often go out of our way to avoid that. However, for now, we will assume an alert watcher who'll note if the image on the screen deviates from what was required.

Note an important detail: a user can add points, but not remove them. A user or a **Shape** can read points, but not change them. From the point of view of testing, anything that does not (or at least isn't supposed to) change eases our work.

What can we test and what can't we test? To test **Shape**, we must try to test in isolation and in combination with a couple of derived classes. However, to test that **Shape** works correctly for a particular derived class, we have to test that derived class.

We note that basically a **Shape** has a state (value) defined by four data members:

```
vector<Point> points;
Color lcolor;      // color for lines and characters
Line_style ls;
Color fcolor;      // fill color
```

All we can do to a **Shape** is to make changes to those and see what happens. Fortunately, the only way to change the data members is through the interface defined by the member functions.

The simplest **Shape** is a **Line**, so we start (using the most naive style) by making one and then making all the changes we can:

```
Line ln(Point(10,10), Point(100, 100));
ln.draw();                 // see if it appears

// check the points:
if (ln.number_of_points() != 2) cerr << "wrong number of points";
if (ln.point(0)!=Point(10,10)) cerr<< "wrong point 1";
if (ln.point(1)!=Point(100,100)) cerr<< "wrong point 2";

for (int i=0; i<10; ++i) {     // see if it moves
    ln.move(i+5,i+5);
    ln.draw();
}
```

```
for (int i=0; i<10; ++i) {        // see if it moves back to where it started
     ln.move(i−5,i−5);
     ln.draw();
}
if (point(0)!=Point(10,10)) cerr<< "wrong point 1 after move";
if (point(1)!=Point(100,100)) cerr<< "wrong point 2 after move";

for (int i = 0; i<100; ++i) {    // see if the color changes correctly
     ln.set_color(Color(i*100));
     if (ln.color() != i*100) cerr << "bad set_color";
     ln.draw();
}

for (int i = 0; i<100; ++i) {    // see if the style changes correctly
     ln.set_style(Line_style(i*5));
     if (ln.style() != i*5) cerr << "bad set_style";
     ln.draw();
}
```

In principle, this tests creation, movement, color, and style. In reality, we need to pick our test cases far more carefully (and deviously), just as we did for **binary_search**. Again, we will almost certainly conclude that reading in a description of what tests to run from a file is a better solution and we'll find a better way of reporting errors.

Also, we'll find that no human can keep up with the changes to the **Shape**, so we have just two alternatives. We can

- Slow down the program so that a human can keep up
- Find a representation of the **Shape** that we can have a program read and analyze

What is almost completely missing so far is testing of **add(Point)**. For that, we'd probably use an **Open_polyline**.

26.3.6 Finding assumptions that do not hold

The specification of **binary_search** clearly stated that the sequence in which we search must be sorted. That deprived us of many opportunities for sneaky unit tests. But obviously there are opportunities for writing bad code that we have not devised tests to detect (except for the system tests). Can we use our understanding of a system's "units" (functions, classes, etc.) to devise better tests?

Unfortunately, the simplest answer is no. As pure testers, we cannot change the code, but to detect violations of an interface's requirements (pre-conditions), someone must either check before each call or as part of the implementation of each call (see §5.5). However, if we are testing our own code, we can insert such tests. If we are testers and the people who write the code will listen to us (that's not always the case), we can tell them about the unchecked requirements and have them ensure that they are checked.

Consider again **binary_search**: we couldn't test that the input sequence **[first:last)** really was a sequence and that it was sorted (§26.3.2.2). However, we could write a function that does check:

```
template<class Iter, class T>
bool b2(Iter first, Iter last, const T& value)
{
        // check if [first:last) is a sequence:
        if (last<first) throw Bad_sequence();

        // check if the sequence is ordered:
        if (2<last−first)
                for (Iter p = first+1; p<last; ++p)
                        if (*p<*(p−1)) throw Not_ordered();

        // all's OK, call binary_search:
        return binary_search(first,last,value);
}
```

Now, there are reasons why **binary_search** isn't written with such tests, including these:

- The test for **last<first** can't be done for a forward iterator; for example, the iterator for **std::list** does not have a < (§B.3.2). In general, there is no really good way of testing that a pair of iterators defines a sequence (starting to iterate from **first** hoping to meet **last** is not a good idea).
- Scanning the sequence to check that the values are ordered is far more expensive than executing **binary_search** itself (the real purpose of **binary_search** is not to have to blindly walk through the sequence looking for a value the way **std::find** does).

So what could we do? We could replace **binary_search** with **b2** when we are testing (only for calls to **binary_search** with random-access iterators, though). Alternatively, we could have the implementer of **binary_search** insert code that a tester could enable:

```
template<class Iter, class T>        // warning: contains pseudo code
bool binary_search (Iter first, Iter last, const T& value)
{
      if (test enabled) {
            if (Iter is a random access iterator) {
                  // check if [first:last) is a sequence:
                  if (last<first) throw Bad_sequence();
            }

            // check if the sequence is ordered:
            if (first!=last) {
                  Iter prev = first;
                  for (Iter p = ++first; p!=last; ++p, ++ prev)
                        if (*p<*prev) throw Not_ordered();
            }
      }

      // now do binary_search
}
```

Since the meaning of **test enabled** depends on how testing of code is arranged (for a specific system in a specific organization), we have left it as pseudo code: when testing your own code, you could simply have a **test_enabled** variable. We also left the **Iter is a random access iterator** test as pseudo code because we haven't explained "iterator traits." Should you really need such a test, look up *iterator traits* in a more advanced C++ textbook.

26.4 Design for testing

When we start writing a program, we know that we would like it to eventually be complete and correct. We also know that to achieve that, we must test it. Consequently, we try to design for correctness and testing from day one. In fact, many good programmers have as their slogan "Test early and often" and don't write any code before they have some idea about how they would go about testing it. Thinking about testing early helps to avoid errors in the first place (as well as helping to find them later). We subscribe to that philosophy. Some programmers even write unit tests before they implement a unit.

The example in §26.3.2.1 and the examples in §26.3.3 illustrate these key notions:

- Use well-defined interfaces so that you can write tests for the use of these interfaces.

- Have a way of representing operations as text so that they can be stored, analyzed, and replayed. This also applies to output operations.

- Embed tests of unchecked assumptions (assertions) in the calling code to catch bad arguments before system testing.
- Minimize dependencies and keep dependencies explicit.
- Have a clear resource management strategy.

Philosophically, this could be seen as enabling unit-testing techniques for subsystems and complete systems.

If performance didn't matter, we could leave the test of the (otherwise) unchecked assumptions (requirements, pre-conditions) enabled all the time. However, there are usually reasons why they are not systematically checked. For example, we saw how checking whether a sequence is sorted is both complicated and far more expensive than using **binary_sort**. Consequently, it is a good idea to design a system that allows us to selectively enable and disable such checks. For many systems, it is a good idea to leave a fair number of the cheaper checks enabled even in the final (shipping) version: sometimes "impossible" things happen and we would prefer to know about them from a specific error message rather than from a simple crash.

26.5 Debugging

Debugging is an issue of technique and attitude. Of these, attitude is the more important. Please revisit Chapter 5. Note how debugging and testing differ. Both catch bugs, but debugging is much more ad hoc and typically concerned with removing known bugs and implementing features. Whatever we can do to make debugging more like testing should be done. It is a slight exaggeration to say that we love testing, but we definitely hate debugging. Good early unit testing and design for testing help minimize debugging.

26.6 Performance

Having a program correct is not enough for it to be useful. Even assuming that it has sufficient facilities to make it useful, it must also provide appropriate performance. A good program is "efficient enough"; that is, it will run in an acceptable time given the resources available. Note that absolute efficiency is uninteresting, and an obsession with getting a program to run fast can seriously damage development by complicating code (leading to more bugs and more debugging) and making maintenance (including porting and performance tuning) more difficult and costly.

So, how can we know that a program (or a unit of a program) is "efficient enough"? In the abstract we cannot know, and for many programs the hardware is so fast that the question doesn't arise. We have seen products shipped that were compiled in debug mode (i.e., running about 25 times slower than necessary) to enable better diagnostics for errors occurring after deployment (this can happen to even the best code when it has to coexist with code developed "elsewhere").

Consequently, the answer to the "Is it efficient enough?" question is: "Measure how long interesting test cases take." To do that, you obviously have to know your end users well enough to have an idea of what they would consider "interesting" and how much time such interesting uses can acceptably take. Logically, we simply clock our tests with a stopwatch and check that none consumes an unreasonable amount of time. This becomes practical when we use functions such as **clock()** (§26.6.1) to do the timing for us, and we can automatically compare the time taken by tests with estimates of what is reasonable. Alternatively (or additionally) we can record how long tests take and compare them to earlier tests runs. This way we get a form of regression test for performance.

Some of the worst performance bugs are caused by poor algorithms and can be found by testing. One reason for testing with large sets of data is to expose inefficient algorithms. As an example, assume that an application has to make sums of the elements in rows of a matrix (using the **Matrix** library from Chapter 24). Someone supplied an appropriate function:

```
double row_sum(Matrix<double,2> m, int n);       // sum of elements in m[n]
```

Now someone uses that to generate a **vector** of sums where **v[n]** is the sum of the elements of the first **n** rows:

```
double row_accum(Matrix<double,2> m, int n)    // sum of elements in m[0:n]
{
    double s = 0;
    for (int i=0; i<n; ++n) s+=row_sum(m,i);
    return s;
}
```

```
// compute accumulated sums of rows of m:
vector<double> v;
for (int i = 0; i<m.dim1(); ++i) v.push_back(row_accum(m,i+1));
```

You can imagine this to be part of a unit test or executed as part of the application exercised by a system test. In either case, you will notice something strange if the matrix ever gets really large: basically, the time needed goes up with the square of the size of **m**. Why? What we did was to add all the elements of the first row, then we added all the elements in the second row (revisiting all the elements of the first row), then we added all the elements in the third row (revisiting all the elements of the first and second rows), etc.

If you think this example was bad, consider what would have happened if the **row_sum()** had had to access a database to get its data. Reading from disk is many thousands of times slower than reading from main memory.

Now, you may complain: "Nobody would write something that stupid!" Sorry, but we have seen much worse, and usually a poor algorithm (from the performance point of view) is not that easy to spot when buried in application code. Did you spot the performance problem when you first glanced at the code? A problem can be quite hard to spot unless you are specifically looking for that particular kind of problem. Here is a simple real-world example found in a server:

```
for (int i=0; i<strlen(s); ++i) { /* do something with s[i] */ }
```

Often, **s** was a string with about 20K characters.

Not all performance problems have to do with poor algorithms. In fact (as we pointed out in §26.3.3), much of the code we write does not classify as proper algorithms. Such "non-algorithmic" performance problems typically fall under the broad classification of "poor design." They include

- Repeated recalculation of information (e.g., the row-summing problem above)

- Repeated checking of the same fact (e.g., checking that an index is in range each time it is used in a loop or checking an argument repeatedly as it is passed unchanged from function to function)

- Repeated visits to the disk (or to the web)

Note the (repeated) *repeated*. Obviously, we mean "unnecessarily repeated," but the point is that unless you do something many times, it will not have an impact on performance. We are all for thorough checking of function arguments and loop variables, but if we do the same check a million times for the same values, those redundant checks just might hurt performance. If we – by measurement – find that performance is hurt, we will try to see if we can remove a repeated action. Don't do that unless you are sure that performance is really a problem. Premature optimization is the source of many bugs and much wasted time.

26.6.1 Timing

How do you know if a piece of code is fast enough? How do you know how long an operation takes? Well, in many cases where it matters, you can simply look at a clock (stopwatch, wall clock, or wristwatch). That's not scientific or accurate, but if that's not feasible, you can often conclude that the program was fast enough. It is not good to be obsessed with performance.

If you need to measure smaller increments of time or if you can't sit around with a stopwatch, you need to get your computer to help you; it knows the time and can give it to you. For example, on a Unix system, simply prefixing a command with **time** will make the system print out the time taken. You might use **time** to figure out how long it takes to compile a C++ source file **x.cpp.** Normally, you compile it like this:

> **g++ x.cpp**

To get that compilation timed, you just add **time**:

> **time g++ x.cpp**

This will compile **x.cpp** and also print the time taken on the screen. This is a simple and effective way of timing small programs. Remember to always do several timing runs because "other activities" on your machine might interfere. If you get roughly the same answer three times, you can usually trust the result.

But what if you want to measure something that takes just milliseconds? What if you want to do your own, more detailed, measurements of a part of a program? You use the standard library function **clock()** to measure the time used by a function **do_something()** like this:

```
#include <ctime>
#include <iostream>
using namespace std;

int main()
{
    int n = 10000000;            // repeat do_something() n times

    clock_t t1 = clock();        // start time
    if (t1 == clock_t(-1)) {     // clock_t(-1) means "clock() didn't work"
        cerr << "sorry, no clock\n";
        exit(1);
    }

    for (int i = 0; i<n; i++) do_something();   // timing loop

    clock_t t2 = clock();        // end time
    if (t2 == clock_t(-1)) {
        cerr << "sorry, clock overflow\n";
        exit(2);
    }
```

```
        cout << "do_something() " << n << " times took "
            << double(t2–t1)/CLOCKS_PER_SEC << " seconds"
            << " (measurement granularity: "
            << CLOCKS_PER_SEC << " of a second)\n";
}
```

The **clock()** function returns a result of type **clock_t**. The explicit conversion **double(t2–t1)** before dividing is necessary because **clock_t** might be an integer. Exactly when the **clock()** starts running is implementation defined; **clock()** is meant to measure time intervals within a single run of a program. For the values **t1** and **t2** returned by **clock()**, **double(t2–t1)/CLOCKS_PER_SEC** is the system's best approximation of the time in seconds between the two calls. You'll find **CLOCKS_PER_SEC** ("clock ticks per second") in **<ctime>**.

If **clock()** isn't provided for a processor or if a time interval is too long to measure, **clock()** returns **clock_t(–1)**.

The **clock()** function is meant to measure intervals from a fraction of a second to a few seconds. For example, if (as is not uncommon) **clock_t** is a 32-bit signed **int** and **CLOCKS_PER_SEC** is **1000000**, we can use **clock()** to measure from 0 to just over 2000 seconds (about half an hour) in microseconds.

Again, don't believe any time measurement that you cannot repeat with roughly the same result three times. What does "roughly the same" mean? "Within 10%" is a reasonable answer. Remember that modern computers are *fast:* 1,000,000,000 instructions per second is common. This implies that you won't be able to measure anything unless you can repeat it tens of thousands of times or it does something really slow, such as writing to disk or accessing the web. In the latter case, you just have to get it to repeat a few hundred times, but you have to worry that so much is going on that you might not understand the results.

26.7 References

Stone, Debbie, Caroline Jarrett, Mark Woodroffe, and Shailey Minocha. *User Interface Design and Evaluation*. Morgan Kaufmann, 2005. ISBN 0120884364.

Whittaker, James A. *How to Break Software: A Practical Guide to Testing*. Addison-Wesley, 2003. ISBN 0321194330.

Drill

Get the test of **binary_search** to run:

1. Implement the input operator for **Test** from §26.3.2.2.
2. Complete a file of tests for the sequences from §26.3:
   a. { 1,2,3,5,8,13,21}   // an "ordinary sequence"
   b. { }
   c. { 1 }
   d. { 1,2,3,4 }   // even number of elements
   e. {1,2,3,4,5 }   // odd number of elements
   f. { 1, 1, 1, 1, 1, 1, 1 }   // all elements equal
   g. { 0,1,1,1,1,1,1,1,1,1,1,1,1 }   // different element at end
   h. { 0,0,0,0,0,0,0,0,0,0,0,0,0,1 }   // different element at end

3. Based on §26.3.1.3, complete a program that generates
   a. A very large sequence (what would you consider very large, and why?)
   b. Ten sequences with a random number of elements
   c. Ten sequences with 0, 1, 2 . . . 9 random elements (but still ordered)

4. Repeat these tests for sequences of strings, such as { **Bohr Darwin Einstein Lavoisier Newton Turing** }.

Review

1. Make a list of applications, each with a brief explanation of the worst thing that can happen if there is a bug; e.g., airplane control – crash: 231 people dead; $500M equipment loss.
2. Why don't we just prove our programs correct?
3. What's the difference between unit testing and system testing?
4. What is regression testing and why is it important?
5. What is the purpose of testing?
6. Why doesn't **binary_search** just check its requirements?
7. If we can't check for all possible errors, what kinds of errors do we primarily look for?
8. Where are bugs most likely to occur in code manipulating a sequence of elements?
9. Why is it a good idea to test for large values?
10. Why do we often represent tests as data rather than as code?
11. Why and when would we use lots of tests based on random values?
12. Why is it hard to test a program using a GUI?
13. What is needed to test a "unit" in isolation?
14. What is the connection between testability and portability?

15. What makes testing a class harder than testing a function?
16. Why is it important that tests be repeatable?
17. What can a tester do when finding that a "unit" relies on unchecked assumptions (pre-conditions)?
18. What can a designer/implementer do to improve testing?
19. How does testing differ from debugging?
20. When does performance matter?
21. Give two (or more) examples of how to (easily) create bad performance problems.

Terms

assumptions	post-condition	test coverage
black-box testing	pre-condition	test harness
branching	proof	testing
clock()	regression	timing
design for testing	resource usage	unit test
inputs	state	white-box testing
outputs	system test	

Exercises

1. Run your **binary search** algorithm from §26.1 with the tests presented in §26.2.1.
2. Modify the testing of **binary_search** to deal with arbitrary element types. Then, test it with **string** sequences and floating-point sequences.
3. Repeat the exercise in §26.2.1 with the version of **binary_search** that takes a comparison criterion. Make a list of new opportunities for errors introduced by that extra argument.
4. Devise a format for test data so that you can define a sequence once and run several tests against it.
5. Add a test to the set of **binary_search** tests to try to catch the (unlikely) error of a **binary_search** modifying the sequence.
6. Modify the calculator from Chapter 7 minimally to let it take input from a file and produce output to a file (or use your operating system's facilities for redirecting I/O). Then devise a reasonably comprehensive test for it.
7. Test the "simple text editor" from §20.6.
8. Add a text-based interface to the graphics interface library from Chapters 12–15. For example, the string **Circle(Point(0,1),15)** should generate a call **Circle(Point(0,1),15)**. Use this text interface to make a "kid's drawing" of a two-dimensional house with a roof, two windows, and a door.

9. Add a text-based output format for the graphics interface library. For example, when a call **Circle(Point(0,1),15)** is executed, a string like **Circle(Point(0,1),15)** should be produced on an output stream.

10. Use the text-based interface from exercise 9 to write a better test for the graphical interface library.

11. Time the sum example from §26.6 with **m** being square matrices with dimensions 100, 10,000, 1,000,000, and 10,000,000. Use random element values in the range [–10:10). Rewrite the calculation of **v** to use a more efficient (not $O(n^2)$) algorithm and compare the timings.

12. Write a program that generates random floating-point numbers and sort them using **std::sort()**. Measure the time used to sort 500,000 **doubles** and 5,000,000 **doubles**.

13. Repeat the experiment in the previous exercise, but with random strings of lengths in the [0:100) range.

14. Repeat the previous exercise, except using a **map** rather than a **vector** so that we don't need to sort.

Postscript

As programmers, we dream about writing beautiful programs that just work – preferably the first time we try them. The reality is different: it is hard to get programs right, and it is hard to get them to stay right as we (and our colleagues) work to improve them. Testing – including design for testing – is a major way of ensuring that the systems we ship actually work. Whenever we reach the end of a day in our highly technological world, we really ought to give a kind thought to the (often forgotten) testers.

The C Programming Language

"C is a strongly typed,
weakly checked,
programming language."

—Dennis Ritchie

This chapter is a brief overview of the C programming language and its standard library from the point of view of someone who knows C++. It lists the C++ features missing from C and gives examples of how a C programmer can cope without those. C/C++ incompatibilities are presented, and C/C++ interoperability is discussed. Examples of I/O, list manipulation, memory management, and string manipulation are included as illustration.

27.1 C and C++: siblings

The C programming language was designed and implemented by Dennis Ritchie at Bell Labs and popularized by the book *The C Programming Language* by Brian Kernighan and Dennis Ritchie (colloquially known as "K&R"), which is arguably still the best introduction to C and one of the great books on programming (§22.2.5). The text of the original definition of C++ was an edit of the text of the 1980 definition of C, supplied by Dennis Ritchie. After this initial branch, both languages evolved further. Like C++, C is now defined by an ISO standard.

We see C primarily as a subset of C++. Thus, from a C++ point of view, the problem of describing C boils down to two issues:

- Describe where C isn't a subset of C++.

- Describe which C++ features are missing in C and which facilities and techniques can be used to compensate.

Historically, modern C and modern C++ are siblings. Both are direct descendants of "Classic C," the dialect of C popularized by the first edition of Kernighan and Ritchie's *The C Programming Language* plus structure assignment and enumerations:

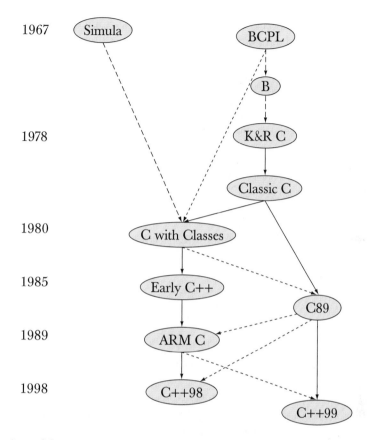

The version of C that is used almost exclusively today is C89 (as described in the second edition of K&R), and that's what we are describing here. There is still some Classic C in use and a few examples of C99, but those should not cause you any problems when you know C++ and C89.

Both C and C++ were "born" in the Computer Science Research Center of Bell Labs in Murray Hill, New Jersey (for a while, my office was a couple of doors down and across the corridor from those of Dennis Ritchie and Brian Kernighan):

Both languages are now defined/controlled by ISO standards committees. For each, many supported implementations are in use. Often, an implementation supports both languages with the desired language chosen by a compiler switch or a source file suffix. Both are available on more platforms than any other language. Both were primarily designed for and are now heavily used for hard system programming tasks, such as

- Operating system kernels
- Device drivers
- Embedded systems
- Compilers
- Communications systems

There are no performance differences between equivalent C and C++ programs.

Like C++, C is very widely used. Taken together, the C/C++ community is the largest software development community on earth.

27.1.1 C/C++ compatibility

It is not uncommon to hear references to "C/C++." However, there is no such language, and the use of "C/C++" is typically a sign of ignorance. We use "C/C++" only in the context of C/C++ compatibility issues and when talking about the large shared C/C++ technical community.

C++ is largely, but not completely, a superset of C. With a few very rare exceptions, constructs that are both C and C++ have the same meaning (semantics) in both languages. C++ was designed to be "as close as possible to C, but no closer":

- For ease of transition
- For coexistence

Most incompatibilities relate to C++'s stricter type checking.

An example of a program that is legal C but not C++ is one that uses a C++ keyword that is not a C keyword as an identifier (see §27.3.2):

```
int class(int new, int bool);     /* C, but not C++ */
```

Examples where the semantics differ for a construct that is legal in both languages are harder to find, but here is one:

```
int s = sizeof('a');               /* sizeof(int), often 4 in C and 1 in C++ */
```

The type of a character literal, such as 'a', is **int** in C and **char** in C++. However, for a **char** variable **ch** we have **sizeof(ch)==1** in both languages.

Information related to compatibility and language differences is not exactly exciting. There are no new neat programming techniques to learn. You might like **printf()** (§27.6), but with that possible exception (and some feeble attempts at geek humor), this chapter is bone dry. Its purpose is simple: to allow you to read and write C if you need to. This includes pointing out the hazards that are obvious to experienced C programmers, but typically unexpected by C++ programmers. We hope you can learn to avoid those hazards with minimal grief.

Most C++ programmers will have to deal with C code at some point or another, just as most C programmers will have to deal with C++ code. Much of what we describe in this chapter will be familiar to most C programmers, but some will be considered "expert level." The reason for that is simple: not everyone agrees about what is "expert level" and we just describe what is common in real-world code. Maybe understanding compatibility issues can be a cheap way of gaining an unfair reputation as a "C expert." But do remember: real expertise is in the use of a language (in this case C), rather than in understanding esoteric language rules (as are exposed by considering compatibility issues).

References

ISO/IEC 9899:1999. *Programming Languages – C.* This defines C99; most implementations implement C89 (often with a few extensions).

ISO/IEC 14882:2003-04-01 (second edition). *Programming Languages – C++.* From a programmer's point of view, this standard is identical to the 1997 version.

Kernighan, Brian W., and Dennis M. Ritchie. *The C Programming Language.* Addison-Wesley, 1988. ISBN 0131103628.

Stroustrup, Bjarne. "Learning Standard C++ as a New Language." *C/C++ Users Journal,* May 1999.

Stroustrup, Bjarne. "C and C++: Siblings"; "C and C++: A Case for Compatibility"; and "C and C++: Case Studies in Compatibility." *The C/C++ Users Journal,* July, Aug., and Sept. 2002.

The papers by Stroustrup are most easily found on my publications home page.

27.1.2 C++ features missing from C

From a C++ perspective, C (i.e., C89) lacks a lot of features, such as

- Classes and member functions
  - Use **struct** and global functions.

- Derived classes and virtual functions
  - Use **structs**, global functions, and pointers to functions (§27.2.3).
- Templates and inline functions
  - Use macros (§27.8).
- Exceptions
  - Use error codes, error return values, etc.
- Function overloading
  - Give each function a distinct name.
- **new/delete**
  - Use **malloc()/free()** and separate initialization/cleanup code.
- References
  - Use pointers.
- **const** in constant expressions
  - Use macros.
- Declarations in **for**-statements and declarations as statements
  - Place all declarations at the top of a block or introduce a new block for each set of definitions.
- **bool**
  - Use **int**.
- **static_cast**, **reinterpret_cast**, and **const_cast**
  - Use C-style casts, e.g., **(int)a** rather than **static<int>(a)**.
- *//* comments
  - Use */* ... *//* comments.

Lots of useful code is written in C, so this list should remind us that no one language feature is absolutely necessary. Most language features – even most C language features – are there for the convenience (only) of the programmer. After all, given sufficient time, cleverness, and patience, every program can be written in assembler. Note that because C and C++ share a machine model that is very close to the real machine, they are well suited to emulate varieties of programming styles.

The rest of this chapter explains how to write useful programs without those features. Our basic advice for using C is:

- Emulate the programming techniques that the C++ features were designed to support with the facilities provided by C.
- When writing C, write in the C subset of C++.
- Use compiler warning levels that ensure function argument checking.
- Use lint for large programs (see §27.2.2).

Many of the details of C/C++ incompatibilities are rather obscure and technical. However, to read and write C, you don't actually have to remember most of those:

- The compiler will remind you when you are using a C++ feature that is not in C.
- If you follow the rules above, you are unlikely to encounter anything that means something different in C from what it means in C++.

With the absence of all those C++ facilities, some facilities gain importance in C:

- Arrays and pointers
- Macros
- **typedef**
- **sizeof**
- Casts

We give examples of a few such uses in this chapter.

I introduced the // comments into C++ from C's ancestor BCPL when I got really fed up with typing /* . . . */ comments. The // comments are accepted by most C dialects including C99, so it is probably safe just to use them. Here, we will use /* . . . */ exclusively in examples meant to be C. C99 introduced a few more C++ features (as well as a few features that are incompatible with C++), but here we will stick to C89, because that's far more widely used.

27.1.3 The C standard library

Naturally, a C++ library facility that depends on classes and templates is not available in C. This includes

- **vector**
- **map**
- **set**
- **string**
- The STL algorithms: e.g., **sort()**, **find()**, and **copy()**
- **iostreams**
- **regex**

For these, there are often C libraries based on arrays, pointers, and functions to help compensate. The main parts of the C standard library are

- **<stdlib.h>**: general utilities (e.g., **malloc()** and **free()**; see §27.4)
- **<stdio.h>**: standard I/O; see §27.6
- **<string.h>**: C-style string manipulation and memory manipulation; see §27.5
- **<math.h>**: standard floating-point mathematical functions; see §24.8
- **<errno.h>**: error codes for **<math.h>**; see §24.8
- **<limits.h>**: sizes of integer types; see §24.2
- **<time.h>**: date and time; see §26.6.1
- **<assert.h>**: debug assertions; see §27.9
- **<ctype.h>**: character classification; see §11.6
- **<stdbool.h>**: Boolean macros

For a complete description, see a good C textbook, such as K&R. All of these libraries (and header files) are also available in C++.

27.2 Functions

In C:

- There can be only one function of a given name.
- Function argument type checking is optional.
- There are no references (and therefore no pass-by-reference).
- There are no member functions.
- There are no inline functions (except in C99).
- There is an alternative function definition syntax.

Apart from that, things are much as you are used to in C++. Let us explore what that means.

27.2.1 No function name overloading
Consider:

```
void print(int);        /* print an int */
void print(const char*);   /* print a string */   /* error! */
```

The second declaration is an error because there cannot be two functions with the same name. So you'll have to invent a suitable pair of names:

```
void print_int(int);              /* print an int */
void print_string(const char*);   /* print a string */
```

This is occasionally claimed to be a virtue: now you can't accidentally use the wrong function to print an **int**! Clearly we don't buy that argument, and the lack of overloaded functions does make generic programming ideas awkward to implement because generic programming depends on semantically similar functions having the same name.

27.2.2 Function argument type checking

Consider:

```
int main()
{
    f(2);
}
```

A C compiler will accept this: you don't have to declare a function before you call it (though you can and should). There may be a definition of f() somewhere. That f() could be in another translation unit, but if it isn't, the linker will complain.

Unfortunately, that definition in another source file might look like this:

```
/* other_file.c: */

int f(char* p)
{
    int r = 0;
    while (*p++) r++;
    return r;
}
```

The linker will not report that error. You will get a run-time error or some random result.

How do we manage problems like that? Consistent use of header files is a practical answer. If every function you call or define is declared in a header that is consistently **#include**d whenever needed, we get checking. However, in large programs that can be hard to achieve. Consequently, most C compilers have options that give warnings for calls of undeclared functions: use them. Also, from the earliest days of C, there have been programs that can be used to check for all kinds of consistency problems. They are usually called *lint*. Use a lint for every nontrivial C program. You will find that lint pushes you toward a style of C usage that is rather similar to using a subset of C++. One of the observations that led to the design of C++ was that the compiler could easily check much (but not all) of what lint checked.

You can ask to have function arguments checked in C. You do that simply by declaring a function with its argument types specified (just as in C++). Such a declaration is called a *function prototype*. However, beware of function declarations that do not specify arguments; those are *not* function prototypes and do not imply function argument checking:

```
int g(double);      /* prototype — like C++ function declaration */
int h();            /* not a prototype — the argument types are unspecified */


void my_fct()
{
    g();            /* error: missing argument */
    g("asdf");      /* error: bad argument type */
    g(2);           /* OK: 2 is converted to 2.0 */
    g(2,3);         /* error: one argument too many */

    h();            /* OK by the compiler! May give unexpected results */
    h("asdf");      /* OK by the compiler! May give unexpected results */
    h(2);           /* OK by the compiler! May give unexpected results */
    h(2,3);         /* OK by the compiler! May give unexpected results */

}
```

The declaration of **g()** specifies no argument type. This does not mean that **g()** doesn't accept arguments; it means "Accept any set of arguments and hope they are correct for the called function." Again, a good compiler warns and lint will catch the problem.

C++	C equivalent
void f(); // preferred	**void f(void);**
void f(void);	**void f(void);**
void f(. . .); // accept any arguments	**void f();** /* accept any arguments */

There is a special set of rules for converting arguments where no function prototype is in scope. For example, **chars** and **shorts** are converted to **ints**, and **floats** are converted to **doubles**. If you need to know, say, what happens to a **long**, look it up in a good C textbook. Our recommendation is simple: don't call functions without prototypes.

Note that even though the compiler will allow an argument of the wrong type to be passed, such as a **char*** to a parameter of type **int**, the use of such an argument of a wrong type is an error. As Dennis Ritchie said, "C is a strongly typed, weakly checked, programming language."

27.2.3 Function definitions

You can define functions exactly as in C++ and such definitions are function prototypes:

```
double square(double d)
{
    return d*d;
}

void ff()
{
    double x = square(2);        /* OK: convert 2 to 2.0 and call */
    double y = square();         /* argument missing */
    double y = square("Hello");  /* error: wrong argument type */
    double y = square(2,3);      /* error: too many arguments */
}
```

A definition of a function with no arguments is not a function prototype:

```
void f() { /* do something */ }

void g()
{
    f(2);    /* OK in C; error in C++ */
}
```

Having

```
void f();        /* no argument type specified */
```

mean "f() can take any number of arguments of any type" seemed really strange. In response, I invented a new notation where "nothing" was explicitly stated using the keyword **void** (*void* is a four-letter word meaning "nothing"):

```
void f(void);  /* no arguments accepted */
```

I soon regretted that, though, since that looks odd and is completely redundant when argument type checking is uniformly applied. Worse, Dennis Ritchie (the father of C) and Doug McIlroy (the ultimate arbiter of taste in the Bell Labs Computer Science Research Center; see §22.2.5) both called it "an abomination." Unfortunately, that abomination became very popular in the C community. Don't use it in C++, though, where it is not only ugly, but also logically redundant.

C also provides a second, Algol60-style function definition, where the parameter types are (optionally) specified separately from their names:

```
int old_style(p,b,x) char* p; char b;
{
     /* ... */
}
```

This "old-style definition" predates C++ and is not a prototype. By default, an argument without a declared type is an **int**. So, **x** is an **int** parameter of **old_style()**. We can call **old_style()** like this:

```
old_style();                      /* OK: all arguments missing */
old_style("hello", 'a', 17);      /* OK: all arguments are of the right type */
old_style(12, 13, 14);            /* OK: 12 is the wrong type, */
                                  /* but maybe old_style() won't use p */
```

The compiler should accept these calls (but would warn, we hope, for the first and third).

Our recommendation about function argument checking:

- Use function prototypes consistently (use header files).
- Set compiler warning levels so that argument type errors are caught.
- Use (some) lint.

The result will be code that's also C++.

27.2.4 Calling C from C++ and C++ from C

You can link files compiled with a C compiler together with files compiled with a C++ compiler provided the two compilers were designed for that. For example, you can link object files generated from C and C++ using your GNU C and C++ compiler (GCC) together. You can also link object files generated from C and C++ using your Microsoft C and C++ compiler (MSC++) together. This is common and useful because it allows you to use a larger set of libraries than would be available in just one of those two languages.

C++ provides stricter type checking than C. In particular, a C++ compiler and linker check that two functions **f(int)** and **f(double)** are consistently defined and used – even in different source files. A linker for C doesn't do that kind of checking. To call a function defined in C from C++ and to have a function defined in C++ called from C, we need to tell the compiler what we are doing:

```
// calling C function from C++:

extern "C" double sqrt(double);     // link as a C function

void my_c_plus_plus_fct()
{
        double sr = sqrt(2);
}
```

Basically **extern "C"** tells the compiler to use C linker conventions. Apart from that, all is normal from a C++ point of view. In fact, the C++ standard **sqrt(double)** usually is the C standard library **sqrt(double)**. Nothing is required from the C program to make a function callable from C++ in this way. C++ simply adapts to the C linkage convention.

We can also use **extern "C"** to make a C++ function callable from C:

```
// C++ function callable from C:

extern "C" int call_f(S* p, int i)
{
        return p->f(i);
}
```

In a C program, we can now call the member function **f()** indirectly, like this:

```
/* call C++ function from C: */

int call_f(S* p, int i);
struct S* make_S(int,const char*);

void my_c_fct(int i)
{
        /* ... */
        struct S* p = make_S(x, "foo");
        int x = call_f(p,i);
        /* ... */
}
```

No mention of C++ is needed (or possible) in C for this to work.

The benefit of this interoperability is obvious: code can be written in a mix of C and C++. In particular, a C++ program can use libraries written in C, and C programs can use libraries written in C++. Furthermore, most languages (notably Fortran) have an interface for calling to/from C.

In the examples above, we assumed that C and C++ could share the class object pointed to by **p**. That is true for most class objects. In particular, if you have a class like this,

```
// in C++:
class complex {
        double re, im;
public:
        // all the usual operations
};
```

you can get away with passing a pointer to an object to and from C. You can even access **re** and **im** in a C program using a declaration:

```
/* in C: */
struct complex {
        double re, im;
        /* no operations */
};
```

The rules for layout in any language can be complex, and the rules for layout among languages can even be hard to specify. However, you can pass built-in types between C and C++ and also classes (**struct**s) without virtual functions. If a class has **virtual** functions, you should just pass pointers to its objects and leave the actual manipulation to C++ code. The **call_f()** was an example of this: **f()** might be **virtual** and then that example would illustrate how to call a virtual function from C.

Apart from sticking to the built-in types, the simplest and safest sharing of types is a **struct** defined in a common C/C++ header file. However, that strategy seriously limits how C++ can be used, so we don't restrict ourselves to it.

27.2.5 Pointers to functions

What can we do in C if we want to use object-oriented techniques (§14.2–4)? Basically, we need an alternative to **virtual** functions. For most people, the first idea that springs to mind is to use a **struct** with a "type field" that describes what kind of shape a given object represents. For example:

```
struct Shape1 {
      enum Kind { circle, rectangle } kind;
      /* . . . */
};

void draw(struct Shape1* p)
{
      switch (p->kind) {
      case circle:
            /* draw as circle */
            break;
      case rectangle:
            /* draw as rectangle */
            break;
      }
}

int f(struct Shape1* pp)
{
      draw(pp);
      /* . . . */
}
```

This works. There are two snags, though:

- For each "pseudo-virtual" function (such as **draw()**), we have to write a new **switch**-statement.

- Each time we add a new shape, we have to modify every "pseudo-virtual" function (such as **draw()**) by adding a case to the **switch**-statement.

The second problem is quite nasty because it means that we can't provide our "pseudo-virtual" functions as part of a library, because our users will have to modify those functions quite often. The most effective alternative involves pointers to functions:

```
typedef void (*Pfct0)(struct Shape2*);
typedef void (*Pfct1int)(struct Shape2*,int);

struct Shape2 {
      Pfct0 draw;
      Pfct1int rotate;
      /* . . . */
};
```

```
void draw(struct Shape2* p)
{
     (p–>draw)(p);
}

void rotate(struct Shape2* p, int d)
{
     (p–>rotate)(p,d);
}
```

This **Shape2** can be used just like **Shape1**.

```
int f(struct Shape2* pp)
{
     draw(pp);
     /* . . . */
}
```

With a little extra work, an object need not hold one pointer to a function for each pseudo-virtual function. Instead, it can hold a pointer to an array of pointers to functions (much as **virtual** functions are implemented in C++). The main problem with using such schemes in real-world programs is to get the initialization of all those pointers to functions right.

27.3 Minor language differences

This section gives examples of minor C/C++ differences that could trip you up if you have never heard of them. Few seriously impact programming in that the differences have obvious work-arounds.

27.3.1 struct tag namespace

In C, the names of **struct**s (there is no **class** keyword) are in a separate namespace from other identifiers. Therefore, every name of a **struct** (called a *structure tag*) must be prefixed with the keyword **struct**. For example:

```
struct pair { int x,y; };
pair p1;         /* error: no identifier "pair" in scope */
struct pair p2;  /* OK */
int pair = 7;    /* OK: the struct tag pair is not in scope */
struct pair p3;  /* OK: the struct tag pair is not hidden by the int */
pair = 8;        /* OK: "pair" refers to the int */
```

Amazingly enough, thanks to a devious compatibility hack, this also works in C++. Having a variable (or a function) with the same name as a **struct** is a fairly common C idiom, though not one we recommend.

If you don't want to write **struct** in front of every structure name, use a **typedef** (§20.5). The following idiom is common:

```
typedef struct { int x,y; } pair;
pair p1 = { 1, 2 };
```

In general, you'll find **typedef**s more common and more useful in C, where you don't have the option of defining new types with associated operations.

In C, names of nested **struct**s are placed in the same scope as the **struct** in which they are nested. For example:

```
struct S {
    struct T { /* . . . */ };
    /* . . . */
};
```

```
struct T x;     /* OK in C (not in C++) */
```

In C++, you would write

```
S::T x;     // OK in C++ (not in C)
```

Whenever possible, don't nest **struct**s in C: their scope rules differ from what most people naively (and reasonably) expect.

27.3.2 Keywords

Many keywords in C++ are not keywords in C (because C doesn't provide the functionality) and can be used as identifiers in C:

C++ keywords that are not C keywords					
and	and_eq	asm	bitand	bitor	bool
catch	class	compl	const_cast	delete	dynamic_cast
explicit	export	false	friend	inline	mutable
namespace	new	not	not_eq	operator	or
or_eq	private	protected	public	reinterpret_cast	static_cast
template	this	throw	true	try	typeid
typename	using	virtual	wchar_t	xor	xor_eq

Don't use these names as identifiers in C, or your code will not be portable to C++. If you use one of these names in a header file, that header won't be useful from C++.

Some C++ keywords are macros in C:

C++ keywords that are C macros						
and	and_eq	bitand	bitor	bool	compl	false
not	not_eq	or	or_eq	true	wchar_t| xor	xor_eq

In C, they are defined in **<iso646.h>** and **<stdbool.h>** (**bool**, **true**, **false**). Don't take advantage of the fact that they are macros in C.

27.3.3 Definitions

C++ allows definitions in more places than C. For example:

```
for (int i = 0; i<max; ++i) x[i] = y[i];      // definition of i not allowed in C

while (struct S* p = next(q)) {                // definition of p not allowed in C
     /* . . . */
}

void f(int i)
{
     if (i< 0 || max<=i) error("range error");
     int a[max];       // error: declaration after statement not allowed in C
     /* . . . */
}
```

C (C89) doesn't allow declarations as initializers in **for**-statements, as conditions, or after a statement in a block. We have to write something like

```
int i;
for (i = 0; i<max; ++i) x[i] = y[i];

struct S* p;
while (p = next(q)) {
     /* . . . */
}

void f(int i)
{
     if (i< 0 || max<=i) error("range error");
```

```
        {
                int a[max];
                /* . . . */
        }
    }
```

In C++, an uninitialized declaration is a definition; in C, it is just a declaration so that there can be two of them:

```
    int x;
    int x;      /* defines or declares a single integer called x in C; error in C++ */
```

In C++, an entity must be defined exactly once. This gets a bit more interesting if the two **ints** are in different translation units:

```
    /* in file x.c: */
    int x;

    /* in file y.c: */
    int x;
```

No C or C++ compiler will find any fault with either **x.c** or **y.c**. However, if **x.c** and **y.c** are compiled as C++, the linker will give a "double definition" error. If **x.c** and **y.c** are compiled as C, the linker accepts the program and (correctly according to C rules) considers there to be just one **x** that is shared between code in **x.c** and **y.c**. If you want a program where a global variable **x** is shared, say so explicitly:

```
    /* in file x.c: */
    int x = 0;          /* the definition */

    /* in file y.c: */
    extern int x;       /* a declaration, not a definition */
```

Better still, use a header file:

```
    /* in file x.h: */
    extern int x;       /* a declaration, not a definition */

    /* in file x.c: */
    #include "x.h"
    int x = 0;          /* the definition */
```

```
/* in file y.c: */
#include "x.h"
/* the declaration of x is in the header */
```

Better still, avoid the global variable.

27.3.4 C-style casts

In C (and C++), you can explicitly convert a value **v** to a type **T** by this minimal notation:

    (T)v

This "C-style cast" or "old-style cast" is beloved by poor typists and sloppy thinkers because it's minimal and you don't have to know what it takes to make a **T** from **v**. On the other hand, this style of cast is rightfully feared by maintenance programmers because it is just about invisible and leaves no clue about the writer's intent. The C++ casts (*new-style casts* or *template-style casts*; see §A.5.7) were introduced to make explicit type conversion easy to spot (ugly) and specific. In C, you have no choice:

```
int* p = (int*)7;      /* reinterpret bit pattern: reinterpret_cast<int*>(0) */
int x = (int)7.5;      /* truncate double: static_cast<int>(7.5) */

typedef struct S1 { /* ... */ } S1;
typedef struct S2 { /* ... */ } S2;
S1 a;
const S2 b;            /* uninitialized consts are allowed in C */

S1* p = (S1*)&a;       /* reinterpret bit pattern: reinterpret_cast<S1*>(&a) */
S2* q = (S2*)&b;       /* cast away const: const_cast<S2*>(&b) */
S1* r = (S1*)&a;       /* remove const and change type; probably a bug */
```

We hesitate to recommend a macro (§27.8) even in C, but it may be an idea to express intent like this:

```
#define REINTERPRET_CAST(T,v) ((T)(v))
#define CONST_CAST(T,v) ((T)(v))

S1* p = REINTERPRET_CAST (S1*,&a);
S2* q = CONST_CAST(S2*,&b);
```

This does not give the type checking done by **reinterpret_cast** and **const_cast**, but it does make these inherently ugly operations visible and the programmer's intent explicit.

27.3.5 Conversion of void*

In C, a **void*** may be used as the right-hand operand of an assignment to or initialization of a variable of any pointer type; in C++ it may not. For example:

```
void* alloc(size_t x);      /* allocate x bytes */

void f (int n)
{
        int* p = alloc(n*sizeof(int));      /* OK in C; error in C++ */
        /* . . . */
}
```

Here, the **void*** result of **alloc()** is implicitly converted to an **int***. In C++, we would have to rewrite that line to

```
int* p = (int*)alloc(n*sizeof(int));      /* OK in C and C++ */
```

We used the C-style cast (§27.3.4) so that it would be legal in both C and C++.

Why is the **void***-to-**T*** implicit conversion illegal in C++? Because such conversions can be unsafe:

```
void f()
{
        char i = 0;
        char j = 0;
        char* p = &i;
        void* q = p;
        int* pp = q;      /* unsafe; legal in C, error in C++ */
        *pp = -1;      /* overwrite memory starting at &i */
}
```

Here we can't even be sure what memory is overwritten. Maybe **j** and part of **p**? Maybe some memory used to manage the call of **f()** (**f**'s stack frame)? Whatever data is being overwritten here, a call of **f()** is bad news.

Note that (the opposite) conversion of a **T*** to a **void*** is perfectly safe — you can't construct nasty examples like the one above for that — and those are allowed in both C and C++.

Unfortunately, implicit **void***-to-**T*** conversions are common in C and possibly the major C/C++ compatibility problem in real code (see §27.4).

27.3.6 enum

In C, you can assign an **int** to an **enum** without a cast. For example:

```
enum color { red, blue, green };
int x = green;            /* OK in C and C++ */
enum color col = 7;    /* OK in C; error in C++ */
```

One implication of this is that we can use increment (**++**) and decrement (**--**) on variables of enumeration type in C. That can be convenient but does imply a hazard:

```
enum color x = blue;
++x;     /* x becomes green; error in C++ */
++x;     /* x becomes 3; error in C++ */
```

"Falling off the end" of the enumerators may or may not have been what we wanted.

Note that like structure tags, the names of enumerations are in their own namespace, so you have to prefix them with the keyword **enum** each time you use them:

```
color c2 = blue;          /* error in C: color not in scope; OK in C++ */
enum color c3 = red;    /* OK */
```

27.3.7 Namespaces

There are no namespaces (in the C++ sense of the word) in C. So what do you do when you want to avoid name clashes in large C programs? Typically, people use prefixes or suffixes. For example:

```
/* in bs.h: */
typedef struct bs_string { /* ... */ } bs_string;     /* Bjarne's string */
typedef int bs_bool ;                                       /* Bjarne's Boolean type */

/* in pete.h: */
typedef char* pete_string;     /* Pete's string */
typedef char pete_bool ;        /* Pete's Boolean type */
```

This technique is so popular that it is usually a bad idea to use one- or two-letter prefixes.

27.4 Free store

C does not provide the **new** and **delete** operators dealing with objects. To use free store, you use functions dealing with memory. The most important functions are defined in the "general utilities" standard header **<stdlib.h>**:

```
void* malloc(size_t sz);            /* allocate sz bytes */
void free(void* p);                 /* deallocate the memory pointed to by p */
void* calloc(size_t n, size_t sz);  /* allocate n*sz bytes initialized to 0 */
void* realloc(void* p, size_t sz);  /* reallocate the memory pointed to by p
                                           to a space of size sz */
```

The **typedef size_t** is an unsigned type also defined in **<stdlib.h>**.

Why does **malloc()** return a **void***? Because **malloc()** has no idea which type of object you want to put in that memory. Initialization is your problem. For example:

```
struct Pair {
     const char* p;
     int val;
};

struct Pair p2 = {"apple",78};
struct Pair* pp = (struct Pair*) malloc(sizeof(Pair));     /* allocate */
pp->p = "pear";       /* initialize */
pp->val = 42;
```

Note that we cannot write

```
*pp = {"pear", 42};     /* error: not C or C++98 */
```

in either C or C++. However, in C++, we would define a constructor for **Pair** and write

```
Pair* pp = new Pair("pear", 42);
```

In C (but not C++; see §27.3.4), you can leave out the cast before **malloc()**, but we don't recommend that:

```
int* p = malloc(sizeof(int)*n);     /* avoid this */
```

Leaving out the cast is quite popular because it saves some typing and because it catches the rare error of (illegally) forgetting to include **<stdlib.h>** before using

malloc(). However, it can also remove a visual clue that a size was wrongly calculated:

```
p = malloc(sizeof(char)*m);        /* probably a bug — not room for m ints */
```

Don't use **malloc()/free()** in C++ programs; **new/delete** require no casts, deal with initialization (constructors) and cleanup (destructors), report memory allocation errors (through an exception), and are just as fast. Don't **delete** an object allocated by **malloc()** or **free()** an object allocated by **new**. For example:

```
int* p = new int[200];
// . . .
free(p);     // error

X* q = (X*)malloc(n*sizeof(X));
// . . .
delete q;       // error
```

This might work, but it is not portable code. Furthermore, for objects with constructors or destructors, mixing C-style and C++-style free-store management is a recipe for disaster.

The **realloc()** function is typically used for expanding buffers:

```
int max = 1000;
int count = 0;
int c;
char* p = (char*)malloc(max);
while ((c=getchar())!=EOF) {        /* read: ignore chars on eof line */
     if (count==max−1) {            /* need to expand buffer */
          max += max;               /* double the buffer size */
          p = (char*)realloc(p,max);
          if (p==0) quit();
     }
     p[count++] = c;
}
```

For an explanation of the C input operations, see §27.6.2 and §B.10.2.

The **realloc()** function may or may not move the old allocation into newly allocated memory. Don't even think of using **realloc()** on memory allocated by **new**.

Using the C++ standard library, the (roughly) equivalent code is

```
vector<char> buf;
char c;
while (cin.get(c)) buf.push_back(c);
```

Refer to the paper "Learning Standard C++ as a New Language" (see the reference list in §27.1) for a more thorough discussion of input and allocation strategies.

27.5 C-style strings

In C, a string (often called a *C string* or a *C-style string* in C++ literature) is a zero-terminated array of characters. For example:

```
char* p = "asdf";
char s[] = "asdf";
```

In C, we cannot have member functions, we cannot overload functions, and we cannot define an operator (such as ==) for a **struct**. It follows that we need a set of (nonmember) functions to manipulate C-style strings. The C and C++ standard libraries provide such functions in **<string.h>**:

```
size_t strlen(const char* s);              /* count the characters */
char* strcat(char* s1, const char* s2);    /* copy s2 onto the end of s1 */
int strcmp(const char* s1, const char* s2); /* compare lexicographically */
char* strcpy(char* s1,const char* s2);     /* copy s2 into s1 */

char* strchr(const char *s, int c);        /* find c in s */
char* strstr(const char *s1, const char *s2); /* find s2 in s1 */

char* strncpy(char*, const char*, size_t n);  /* strcpy, max n chars */
char* strncat(char*, const char, size_t n);   /* strcat with max n chars */
int strncmp(const char*, const char*, size_t n); /* strcmp with max n chars */
```

This is not the full set, but these are the most useful and most used functions. We will briefly illustrate their use.

We can compare strings. The equality operator (==) compares pointer values; the standard library function **strcmp()** compares C-style string values:

```
const char* s1 = "asdf";
const char* s2 = "asdf";

if (s1==s2) {    /* do s1 and s2 point to the same array? */
                 /* (typically not what you want) */

}
```

```
if (strcmp(s1,s2)==0) {    /* do s1 and s2 hold the same characters? */

}
```

The **strcmp()** function does a three-way comparison of its two arguments. Given the values of **s1** and **s2** above, **strcmp(s1,s2)** will return 0, meaning a perfect match. If **s1** was lexicographically before **s2** it would return a negative number, and if **s1** was lexicographically after **s2** it would return a positive number. The term *lexicographical* means roughly "as in a dictionary." For example:

```
strcmp("dog","dog")==0
strcmp("ape","dodo")<0    /* "ape" comes before "dodo" in a dictionary */
strcmp("pig","cow")>0     /* "pig" comes after "cow" in a dictionary */
```

The value of the pointer comparison **s1==s2** is not guaranteed to be 0 (**false**). An implementation may decide to use the same memory to hold all copies of a character literal, so we would get the answer 1 (**true**). Usually, **strcmp()** is the right choice for comparing C-style strings.

We can find the length of a C-style string using **strlen()**:

```
int lgt = strlen(s1);
```

Note that **strlen()** counts characters excluding the terminating 0. In this case, **strlen(s1)==4** and it takes 5 bytes to store **"asdf"**. This little difference is the source of many off-by-one errors.

We can copy one C-style string (including the terminating 0) into another:

```
strcpy(s1,s2);    /* copy characters from s2 into s1 */
```

It is your job to be sure that the target string (array) has enough space to hold the characters from the source.

The **strncpy()**, **strncat()**, and **strncmp()** functions are versions of **strcpy()**, **strcat()**, and **strcmp()** that will consider a maximum of **n** characters, where **n** is their third argument. Note that if there are more than **n** characters in the source string, **strncpy()** will not copy a terminating 0, so that the result will not be a valid C-style string.

The **strchr()** and **strstr()** functions find their second argument in the string that is their first argument and return a pointer to the first character of the match. Like **find()**, they search from left to right in the string.

It is amazing both how much can be done with these simple functions and how easy it is to make minor mistakes. Consider a simple problem of concatenating a user name with an address, placing the @ character in between. Using **std:string** this can be done like this:

```
string s = id + '@' + addr;
```

Using the standard C-style string function we can write that as

```
char* cat(const char* id, const char* addr)
{
    int sz = strlen(id)+strlen(addr)+2;
    char* res = (char*) malloc(sz);
    strcpy(res,id);
    res[strlen(id)+1] = '@';
    strcpy(res+strlen(id)+2,addr);
    res[sz−1]=0;
    return res;
}
```

Did we get that right? Who will **free()** the string returned from **cat()**?

TRY THIS

Test **cat()**. Why **2**? We left a beginner's performance error in **cat()**; find it and remove it. We "forgot" to comment our code. Add comments suitable for someone who can be assumed to know the standard C-string functions.

27.5.1 C-style strings and const
Consider:

```
char* p = "asdf";
p[2] = 'x';
```

This is legal in C but not in C++. In C++, a string literal is a constant, an immutable value, so **p[2]='x'** (to make the value pointed to **"asxf"**) is illegal. Unfortunately, few compilers will catch the assignment to **p** that leads to the problem. If you are lucky, a run-time error will occur, but don't rely on that. Instead, write

```
const char* p = "asdf";      // now you can't write to "asdf" through p
```

This recommendation applies to both C and C++.

The C **strchr()** has a similar but even harder-to-spot problem. Consider:

```
char* strchr(const char* s, int c); /* find c in constant s (not C++) */

const char aa[] = "asdf";          /* aa is an array of constants */
char* q = strchr(aa, 'd');         /* finds 'd' */
*q = 'x';                          /* change 'd' in a to 'x' */
```

Again, this is illegal in C and C++, but C compilers can't catch it. Sometimes this is referred to as *transmutation*: it turns **const**s into non-**const**s, violating reasonable assumptions about code.

In C++, the problem is solved by the standard library declaring **strchr()** differently:

```
char const* strchr(const char* s, int c);   // find c in constant s
char* strchr(char* s, int c);               // find c in s
```

Similarly for **strstr()**.

27.5.2 Byte operations

In the distant dark ages (the early 1980s), before the invention of **void***, C (and C++) programmers used the string operations to manipulate bytes. Now the basic memory manipulation standard library functions have **void*** parameters and return types to warn users about their direct manipulation of essentially untyped memory:

```
/* copy n bytes from s2 to s1 (like strcpy): */
void* memcpy(void* s1, const void* s2, size_t n);

/* copy n bytes from s2 to s1 ( [s1:s1+n] may overlap with [s2:s2+n] ): */
void* memmove(void* s1, const void* s2, size_t n);

/* compare n bytes from s2 to s1 (like strcmp): */
int memcmp(const void* s1, const void* s2, size_t n);

/* find c (converted to an unsigned char) in the first n bytes of s: */
void* memchr(const void* s, int c, size_t n);

/* copy c (converted to an unsigned char)
   into each of the first n bytes that s points to: */
void* memset(void* s, int c, size_t n);
```

Don't use these functions in C++. In particular, **memset()** typically interferes with the guarantees offered by constructors.

27.5.3 An example: strcpy()

The definition of **strcpy()** is both famous and infamous as an example of the terse style that C (and C++) is capable of:

```
char* strcpy(char* p, const char* q)
{
        while (*p++ = *q++);
        return p;
}
```

We leave to you the explanation of why this actually copies the C-style string **q** into **p**.

TRY THIS

Is this implementation of **strcpy()** correct? Explain why.

If you can't explain why, we won't consider you a C programmer (however competent you are at programming in other languages). Every language has its own idioms, and this is one of C's.

27.5.4 A style issue

We have quietly taken sides in a long-standing, often furiously debated, and largely irrelevant style issue. We declare a pointer like this:

```
char* p;        // p is a pointer to a char
```

and not like this:

```
char *p;        /* p is something that you can dereference to get a char */
```

The placement of the whitespace is completely irrelevant to the compiler, but programmers care. Our style (common in C++) emphasizes the type of the variable being declared, whereas the other style (more common in C) emphasizes the use of the variable. Note that we don't recommend declaring many variables in a single declaration:

```
char c, *p, a[177], *f();        /* legal, but confusing */
```

Such declarations are not uncommon in older code. Instead, use multiple lines and take advantage of the extra horizontal space for comments and initializers:

```
char c = 'a';    /* termination character for input using f() */
char* p = 0;     /* last char read by f() */
char a[177];     /* input buffer */
char* f();       /* read into buffer a; return pointer to first char read */
```

Also, choose meaningful names.

27.6 Input/output: stdio

There are no **iostreams** in C, so we use the C standard I/O defined in **<stdio.h>** and commonly referred to as stdio. The stdio equivalents to **cin** and **cout** are **stdin** and **stdout**. Stdio and **iostream** use can be mixed in a single program (for the same I/O streams), but we don't recommend that. If you feel the need to mix, read up on stdio and **iostreams** (especially **ios_base::sync_with_stdio()**) in an expert-level textbook. See also §B.10.

27.6.1 Output

The most popular and useful function of stdio is **printf()**. The most basic use of **printf()** just prints a (C-style) string:

```
#include<stdio.h>

void f(const char* p)
{
        printf("Hello, World!\n");
        printf(p);
}
```

That's not particularly interesting. The interesting bit is that **printf()** can take an arbitrary number of arguments, and the initial string controls if and how those extra arguments are printed. The declaration of **printf()** in C looks like this:

```
int printf(const char* format, . . . );
```

The . . . means "and optionally more arguments." We can call **printf()** like this:

```
void f1(double d, char* s, int i, char ch)
{
        printf("double %g string %s int %d char %c\n", d, s, i, ch);
}
```

Here, **%g** means "Print a floating-point number using the general format," **%s** means "Print a C-style string," **%d** means "Print an integer using decimal digits," and **%c** means "Print a character." Each such format specifier picks the next so-far-unused argument, so %g prints **d**, %s prints **s**, %d prints **i**, and %c prints **ch**. You can find the full list of **printf()** formats in §B.10.2.

Unfortunately, **printf()** is not type safe. For example:

```
char a[] = { 'a', 'b' };        /* no terminating 0 */

void f2(char* s, int i)
{
        printf("goof %s\n", i);         /* uncaught error */
        printf("goof %d: %s\n", i);     /* uncaught error */
        printf("goof %s\n", a);         /* uncaught error */

}
```

The effect of the last **printf()** is interesting: it prints every byte in memory following **a[1]** until it encounters a 0. That could be a lot of characters.

This lack of type safety is one reason we prefer **iostreams** over stdio even though stdio works identically in C and C++. The other reason is that the stdio functions are not extensible: you cannot extend **printf()** to print values of your own types, the way you can using **iostreams**. For example, there is no way you can define your own **%Y** to print some **struct Y**.

There is a useful version of **printf()** that takes a file descriptor as its first argument:

```
int fprintf(FILE* stream, const char* format, . . . );
```

For example:

```
fprintf(stdout,"Hello, World!\n");   // exactly like printf("Hello, World!\n");
FILE* ff = fopen("My_file","w");     // open My_file for writing
fprintf(ff,"Hello, World!\n");       // write "Hello, World!\n" to My_file
```

File handles are described in §27.6.3.

27.6.2 Input

The most popular stdio functions include

```
int scanf(const char* format, . . . );   /* read from stdin using a format */
int getchar(void);                        /* get a char from stdin */
```

```
int getc(FILE* stream);           /* get a char from stream */
char* gets(char* s);              /* get characters from stdin */
```

The simplest way of reading a string of characters is using **gets()**. For example:

```
char a[12];
gets(a);      /* read into char array pointed to by a until a '\n' is input */
```

Never do that! Consider **gets()** poisoned. Together with its close cousin **scanf("%s")**, **gets()** used to be the root cause of about a quarter of all successful hacking attempts. It is still a major security problem. In the trivial example above, how would you know that at most 11 characters would be input before a newline? You can't know that. Thus, **gets()** almost certainly leads to memory corruption (of the bytes after the buffer), and memory corruption is a major tool of crackers. Don't think that you can guess a maximum buffer size that is "large enough for all uses." Maybe the "person" at the other end of the input stream is a program that does not meet your criteria for reasonableness.

The **scanf()** function reads using a format just as **printf()** writes using a format. Like **printf()** it can be very convenient:

```
void f()
{
    int i;
    char c;
    double d;
    char* s = (char*)malloc(100);
    /* read into variables passed as pointers: */
    scanf("%i %c %g %s", &i, &c, &d, s);
    /* %s skips initial whitespace and is terminated by whitespace */
}
```

Like **printf()**, **scanf()** is not type safe. The format characters and the arguments (all pointers) must match exactly, or strange things will happen at run time. Note also that the %s read into **s** may lead to an overflow. Don't ever use **gets()** or **scanf("%s")**!

So how do we read characters safely? We can use a form of %s that places a limit on the number of characters read. For example:

```
char buf[20];
scanf("%19s",buf);
```

We need space for a terminating 0 (supplied by **scanf()**), so 19 is the maximum number of characters we can read into **buf**. However, that leaves us with the problem of what to do if someone does type more than 19 characters. The "extra" characters will be left in the input stream to be "found" by later input operations.

The problem with **scanf()** implies that it is often prudent and easier to use **getchar()**. The typical way of reading characters with **getchar()** is

```
while((x=getchar())!=EOF) {
    /* . . . */
}
```

EOF is a stdio macro meaning "end of file"; see also §27.4.

The C++ standard library alternative to **scanf("%s")** and **gets()** doesn't suffer from these problems:

```
string s;
cin >> s;          // read a word
getline(cin,s);    // read a line
```

27.6.3 Files

In C (or C++), files can be opened using **fopen()** and closed using **fclose()**. These functions, together with the representation of a file handle, **FILE**, and the **EOF** (end-of-file) macro, are found in **<stdio.h>**:

```
FILE *fopen(const char* filename, const char* mode);
int fclose(FILE *stream);
```

Basically, you use files like this:

```
void f(const char* fn, const char* fn2)
{
    FILE* fi = fopen(fn, "r");      /* open fn for reading */
    FILE* fo = fopen(fn2, "w");     /* open fn for writing */

    if (fi == 0) error("failed to open input file");
    if (fo == 0) error("failed to open output file");

    /* read from file using stdio input functions, e.g., getc() */
    /* write from file using stdio output functions, e.g., fprintf() */

    fclose(fo);
    fclose(fi);
}
```

Consider this: there are no exceptions in C, so how do we make sure that the files are closed whichever error happens?

27.7 Constants and macros

In C, a **const** is never a compile-time constant:

```
const int max = 30;
const int x;    /* const not initialized: OK in C (error in C++) */

void f(int v)
{
      int a1[max];   /* error: array bound not a constant (OK in C++) */
                     /* (max is not allowed in a constant expression!) */
      int a2[x];     /* error: array bound not a constant */

      switch (v) {
      case 1:
           /* ... */
           break;
      case max:      /* error: case label not a constant (OK in C++) */
           /* ... */
           break;
      }
}
```

The technical reason in C (though not in C++) is that a **const** is implicitly accessible from other translation units:

```
/* file x.c: */
const int x;          /* initialize elsewhere */

/* file xx.c: */
const int x = 7;      /* here is the real definition */
```

In C++, that would be two different objects, each called **x** in its own file. Instead of using **const** to represent symbolic constants, C programmers tend to use macros. For example:

```
#define MAX 30
```

```
void f(int v)
{
      int a1[MAX];      /* OK */

      switch (v) {
      case 1:
            /* . . . */
            break;
      case MAX:         /* OK */
            /* . . . */
            break;
      }
}
```

The name of the macro **MAX** is replaced by the characters **30**, which is the value of the macro; that is, the number of elements of **a1** is **30** and the value in the second case label is **30**. We use all capital letters for the **MAX** macro, as is conventional. This naming convention helps minimize errors caused by macros.

27.8 Macros

Beware of macros: in C there are no really effective ways of avoiding macros, but their use has serious side effects because they don't obey the usual C (or C++) scope and type rules. Macros are a form of text substitution. See also §A.17.2.

How do we try to protect ourselves from the potential problems of macros apart from (relying on C++ alternatives and) minimizing their use?

- Give all macros we define **ALL_CAPS** names.
- Don't give anything that isn't a macro an **ALL_CAPS** name.
- Never give a macro a short or "cute" name, such as **max** or **min**.
- Hope that everybody else follows this simple and common convention.

The main uses of macros are

- Definition of "constants"
- Definition of function-like constructs
- "Improvements" to the syntax
- Control of conditional compilation

In addition, there is a wide variety of less common uses.

We consider macros seriously overused, but there are no reasonable and complete alternatives to the use of macros in C programs. It can even be hard to avoid them in C++ programs (especially if you need to write programs that have to be portable to very old compilers or to platforms with unusual constraints).

Apologies to people who consider the techniques described below "dirty tricks" and believe such are best not mentioned in polite company. However, we believe that programming is to be done in the real world and that these (very mild) examples of uses and misuses of macros can save hours of grief for the novice programmer. Ignorance about macros is not bliss.

27.8.1 Function-like macros

Here is a fairly typical function-like macro:

```
#define MAX(x, y) ((x)>=(y)?(x):(y))
```

We use the capital **MAX** to distinguish it from the many functions called **max** (in various programs). Obviously, this is very different from a function: there are no argument types, no block, no return statement, etc., and what are all those parentheses doing? Consider:

```
int aa = MAX(1,2);
double dd = MAX(aa++,2);
char cc = MAX(dd,aa)+2;
```

This expands to

```
int aa = ((1)>=( 2)?(1):(2));
double dd = ((aa++)>=(2)?( aa++):(2));
char cc = ((dd)>=(aa)?(dd):(aa))+2;
```

Had "all the parentheses" not been there, the last expansion would have ended up as

```
char cc = dd>=aa?dd:aa+2;
```

That is, **cc** could easily have gotten a different value from what you would reasonably expect looking at the definition of **cc**. When you define a macro, remember to put every use of an argument as an expression in parentheses.

On the other hand, not all the parentheses in the world could save the second expansion. The macro parameter x was given the value **aa++**, and since x is used twice in **MAX**, **a** can get incremented twice. Don't pass an argument with a side effect to a macro.

As it happens, some genius did define a macro like that and stuck it in a popular header file. Unfortunately, he also called it **max**, rather than **MAX**, so when the C++ standard header defines

```
template<class T> inline T max(T a,T b) { return a<b?b:a; }
```

the **max** gets expanded with the arguments **T a** and **T b**, and the compiler sees

```
template<class T> inline T ((T a)>=( T b)?( T a):( T b)) { return a<b?b:a; }
```

The compiler error messages are "interesting" and not very helpful. In an emergency, you can "undefine" a macro:

```
#undef max
```

Fortunately, that macro was not all that important. However, there are tens of thousands of macros in popular header files; you can't undefine them all without causing havoc.

Not all macro parameters are used as expressions. Consider:

```
#define ALLOC(T,n) ((T*)malloc(sizeof(T)*n))
```

This is a real example that can be very useful for avoiding errors stemming from a mismatch of the intended type of an allocation and its use in a **sizeof**:

```
double* p = malloc(sizeof(int)*10);     /* likely error */
```

Unfortunately, it is nontrivial to write a macro that also catches memory exhaustion. This might do, provided that you define **error_var** and **error()** appropriately somewhere:

```
#define ALLOC(T,n) (error_var = (T*)malloc(sizeof(T)*n), \
                    (error_var==0)\
                    ?(error("memory allocation failure"),0)\
                    :error_var)
```

The lines ending with \ are not a typesetting problem; it is the way you break a macro definition across lines. When writing C++, we prefer to use **new**.

27.8.2 Syntax macros

You can define macros that make the source code look more to your taste. For example:

```
#define forever for(;;)
#define CASE break; case
#define begin {
#define end }
```

We strongly recommend against this. *Many* people have tried this idea. They (or the people who maintain their code) find that

- Many people don't share their idea of what is a better syntax.
- The "improved" syntax is nonstandard and surprising; others get confused.
- There are uses of the "improved" syntax that cause obscure compile-time errors.
- What you see is not what the compiler sees, and the compiler reports errors in the vocabulary it knows (and sees in source code), not in yours.

Don't write syntactic macros to "improve" the look of code. You and your best friends might find it really nice, but experience shows that you'll be a tiny minority in the larger community, so that someone will have to rewrite your code (assuming it survives).

27.8.3 Conditional compilation

Imagine you have two versions of a header file, say, one for Linux and one for Windows. How do you select in your code? Here is a common way:

```
#ifdef WINDOWS
        #include "my_windows_header.h"
#else
        #include "my_linux_header.h"
#endif
```

Now, if someone had defined **WINDOWS** before the compiler sees this, the effect is

```
#include "my_windows_header.h"
```

Otherwise it is

```
#include "my_linux_header.h"
```

The **#ifdef WINDOWS** test doesn't care what **WINDOWS** is defined to be; it just tests that it is defined.

Most major systems (including all operating system variants) have macros defined so that you can check. The check whether you are compiling as C++ or compiling as C is

```
#ifdef __cplusplus
        // in C++
#else
        /* in C */
#endif
```

A similar construct, often called an *include guard,* is commonly used to prevent a header file from being **#include**d twice:

```
/* my_windows_header.h: */
#ifndef MY_WINDOWS_HEADER
#define MY_WINDOWS_HEADER
        /* here is the header information */
#endif
```

The **#ifndef** test checks that something is not defined; i.e., **#ifndef** is the opposite of **#ifdef**. Logically, these macros used for source file control are very different from the macros we use for modifying source code. They just happen to use the same underlying mechanisms to do their job.

27.9 An example: intrusive containers

The C++ standard library containers, such as **vector** and **map**, are non-intrusive; that is, they require no data in the types used as elements. That is how they generalize nicely to essentially all types (built-in or user-defined) as long as those types can be copied. There is another kind of container, an *intrusive container,* that is popular in both C and C++. We will use a non-intrusive list to illustrate C-style use of **struct**s, pointers, and free store.

Let's define a doubly-linked list with nine operations:

```
void init(struct List* lst);          /* initialize lst to empty */
struct List* create();                /* make a new empty list on free store */
void clear(struct List* lst);         /* free all elements of lst */
void destroy(struct List* lst);       /* free all elements of lst, then free lst */

void push_back(struct List* lst, struct Link* p);   /* add p at end of lst */
void push_front(struct List*, struct Link* p);      /* add p at front of lst */

/* insert q before p in lst: */
void insert(struct List* lst, struct Link* p, struct Link* q);
struct Link* erase(struct List* lst, struct Link* p);   /* remove p from lst */

/* return link n "hops" before or after p: */
struct Link* advance(struct Link* p, int n);
```

The idea is to define these operations so that their users need only use **List***s and **Link***s. This implies that the implementation of these functions could be changed radically without affecting those users. Obviously, the naming is influenced by the STL. **List** and **Link** can be defined in the obvious and trivial manner:

```
struct List {
      struct Link* first;
      struct Link* last;
};

struct Link {      /* link for doubly-linked list */
      struct Link* pre;
      struct Link* suc;
};
```

Here is a graphical representation of a **List**:

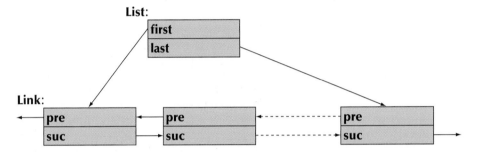

It is not our aim to demonstrate clever representation techniques or clever algorithms, so there are none of those here. However, do note that there is no mention of any data held by the **Links** (the elements of a **List**). Looking back at the functions provided, we note that we are doing something very similar to defining a pair of abstract classes **Link** and **List**. The data for **Links** will be supplied later. **Link*** and **List*** are sometimes called handles to opaque types; that is, giving **Link***s and **List***s to our functions allows us to manipulate elements of a **List** without knowing anything about the internal structure of a **Link** or a **List**.

To implement our **List** functions, we first **#include** some standard library headers:

```
#include<stdio.h>
#include<stdlib.h>
#include<assert.h>
```

C doesn't have namespaces, so we need not worry about **using** declarations or **using** directives. On the other hand, we should probably worry that we have grabbed some very common short names (**Link**, **insert**, **init**, etc.), so this set of functions cannot be used "as is" outside a toy program.

Initializing is trivial, but note the use of **assert()**:

```
void init(struct List* lst)      /* initialize *p to the empty list */
{
    assert(lst);
    lst->first = lst->last = 0;
}
```

We decided not to deal with error handling for bad pointers to lists at run time. By using **assert()**, we simply give a (run-time) system error if a list pointer is null. The "system error" will give the file name and line number of the failed **assert()**; **assert()** is a macro defined in **<assert.h>** and the checking is enabled only during debugging. In the absence of exceptions, it is not easy to know what to do with bad pointers.

The **create()** function simply makes a **List** on the free store. It is a sort of combination of a constructor (**init()** initializes) and **new** (**malloc()** allocates):

```
struct List* create()        /* make a new empty list */
{
    struct List* lst = (struct List*)malloc(sizeof(struct List*));
    init(lst);
    return lst;
}
```

The **clear()** function assumes that all **Link**s are created on the free store and **free()**s them:

```
void clear(struct List* lst)    /* free all elements of lst */
{
    assert(lst);
    {
        struct Link* curr = lst->first;
        while(curr) {
            struct Link* next = curr->suc;
            free(curr);
            curr = next;
        }
        lst->first = lst->last = 0;
    }
}
```

Note the way we traverse using the **suc** member of **Link**. We can't safely access a member of a **struct** object after that object has been **free()**d, so we introduce the variable **next** to hold our position in the **List** while we **free()** a **Link**.

If we didn't allocate all of our **Link**s on the free store, we had better not call **clear()**, or **clear()** will create havoc.

The **destroy()** function is essentially the opposite of **create()**, that is, a sort of combination of a destructor and a **delete**:

```
void destroy(struct List* lst)    /* free all elements of lst; then free lst */
{
      assert(lst);
      clear(lst);
      free(lst);
}
```

Note that we are making no provisions for calling a cleanup function (destructor) for the elements represented by **Link**s. This design is not a completely faithful imitation of C++ techniques or generality — it couldn't and probably shouldn't be.

The **push_back()** function — adding a **Link** as the new last **Link** — is pretty straightforward:

```
void push_back(struct List* lst, struct Link* p)     /* add p at end of lst */
{
      assert(lst);
      {
            struct Link* last = lst->last;
            if (last) {
                  last->suc = p;        /* add p after last */
                  p->pre = last;
            }
            else {
                  lst->first = p;       /* p is the first element */
                  p->pre = 0;
            }
            lst->last = p;              /* p is the new last element */
            p->suc = 0;
      }
}
```

However, we would never have gotten it right without drawing a few boxes and arrows on our doodle pad. Note that we "forgot" to consider the case where the argument **p** was null. Pass 0 instead of a pointer to a **Link** and this code will fail miserably. This is not inherently bad code, but it is *not* industrial strength. Its purpose is to illustrate common and useful techniques (and, in this case, also a common weakness/bug).

The **erase**() function can be written like this:

```
struct Link* erase(struct List* lst, struct Link* p)
/*
    remove p from lst;
    return a pointer to the link after p
*/
{
    assert(lst);
    if (p==0) return 0;      /* OK to erase(0) */

    if (p == lst->first) {
        if (p->suc) {
            lst->first = p->suc;          /* the successor becomes first */
            p->suc->pre = 0;
            return p->suc;
        }
        else {
            lst->first = lst->last = 0;   /* the list becomes empty */
            return 0;
        }
    }
    else if (p == lst->last) {
        if (p->pre) {
            lst->last = p->pre;       /* the predecessor becomes last */
            p->pre->suc = 0;
        }
        else {
            lst->first = lst->last = 0;   /* the list becomes empty */
            return 0;
        }
    }
    else {
        p->suc->pre = p->pre;
        p->pre->suc = p->suc;
        return p->suc;
    }
}
```

We will leave the rest of the functions as an exercise, as we don't need them for our (all too simple) test. However, now we must face the central mystery of this design: Where is the data in the elements of the list? How do we implement a simple list of names represented by a C-style string? Consider:

```
struct Name {
      struct Link lnk;       /* the Link required by List operations */
      char* p;               /* the name string */
};
```

So far, so good, though how we get to use that **Link** member is a mystery; but since we know that a **List** likes its **Links** on the free store, we write a function creating **Names** on the free store:

```
struct Name* make_name(char* n)
{
      struct Name* p = (struct Name*)malloc(sizeof(struct Name));
      p->p = n;
      return p;
}
```

Or graphically:

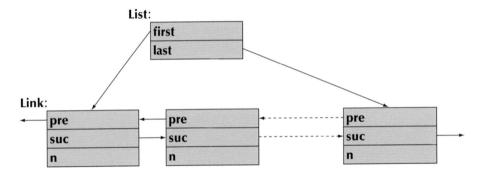

Now let's use that:

```
int main()
{
      struct List names;      /* make a list */
      struct List* curr;
      init(&names);

      /* make a few Names and add them to the list: */
      push_back(&names,(struct Link*)make_name("Norah"));
      push_back(&names,(struct Link*)make_name("Annemarie"));
      push_back(&names,(struct Link*)make_name("Kris"));

      /* remove the second name (with index 1): */
      erase(&names,advance(names.first,1));
```

```
curr = names.first;      /* write out all names */
int count = 0;
for (; curr!=0; curr=curr–>suc) {
    count++;
    printf("element %d: %s\n", count, ((struct Name*)curr)–>p);
}
}
```

So we "cheated." We used a cast to treat a **Name*** as a **Link***. In that way, the user knows about the "library-type" **Link**. However, the "library" doesn't know about the "application-type" **Name**. Is that allowed? Yes, it is: in C (and C++), you can treat a pointer to a **struct** as a pointer to its first element and vice versa.

Obviously, this **List** example is also C++ exactly as written.

TRY THIS

A common refrain among C++ programmers talking with C programmers is, "Everything you can do, I can do better!" So, rewrite the intrusive **List** example in C++, showing how to make it shorter and easier to use without making the code slower or the objects bigger.

Drill

1. Write a "Hello, World!" program in C, compile it, and run it.
2. Define two variables holding "Hello" and "World!" respectively; concatenate them with a space in between; and output them as **Hello, World!**.
3. Define a C function that takes a **char*** parameter **p** and an **int** parameter **x** and print out their values in this format: **p is "foo" and x is 7**. Call it with a few argument pairs.

Review

In the following, assume that by C we mean ISO standard C89.

1. Is C++ a subset of C?
2. Who invented C?
3. Name a highly regarded C textbook.
4. In what organization were C and C++ invented?
5. Why is C++ (almost) compatible with C?
6. Why is C++ only *almost* compatible with C?

7. List a dozen C++ features not present in C.
8. What organization "owns" C and C++?
9. List six C++ standard library components that cannot be used in C.
10. Which C standard library components can be used in C++?
11. How do you achieve function argument type checking in C?
12. What C++ features related to functions are missing in C? List at least three. Give examples.
13. How do you call a C function from C++?
14. How do you call a C++ function from C?
15. Which types are layout compatible between C and C++? (Just) give examples.
16. What is a structure tag?
17. List 20 C++ keywords that are not keywords in C.
18. Is "int x;" a definition in C++? In C?
19. What is a C-style cast and why is it dangerous?
20. What is **void*** and how does it differ in C and C++?
21. How do enumerations differ in C and C++?
22. What do you do in C to avoid linkage problems from popular names?
23. What are the three most common C functions from free-store use?
24. What is the definition of a C-style string?
25. How do == and **strcmp()** differ for C-style strings?
26. How do you copy C-style strings?
27. How do you find the length of a C-style string?
28. How would you copy a large array of **ints**?
29. What's nice about **printf()**? What are its problems/limitations?
30. Why should you never use **gets()**? What can you use instead?
31. How do you open a file for reading in C?
32. What is the difference between **const** in C and **const** in C++?
33. Why don't we like macros?
34. What are common uses of macros?
35. What is an include guard?

Terms

#define	Dennis Ritchie	non-intrusive
#ifdef	**FILE**	opaque type
#ifndef	**fopen()**	overloading
Bell Labs	format string	**printf()**
Brian Kernighan	intrusive	**strcpy()**
C/C++	K&R	structure tag
compatibility	lexicographical	three-way comparison
conditional compilation	linkage	**void**
C-style cast	macro	**void***
C-style string	**malloc()**	

Exercises

For these exercises it may be a good idea to compile all programs with both a C and a C++ compiler. If you use only a C++ compiler, you may accidentally use non-C features. If you use only a C compiler, type errors may remain undetected.

1. Implement versions of **strlen()**, **strcmp()**, and **strcpy()**.
2. Complete the intrusive **List** example in §27.9 and test it using every function.
3. "Pretty up" the intrusive **List** example in §27.9 as best you can to make it convenient to use. Do catch/handle as many errors as you can. It is fair game to change the details of the **struct** definitions, to use macros, whatever.
4. If you didn't already, write a C++ version of the intrusive **List** example in §27.9 and test it using every function.
5. Compare the results of exercises 3 and 4.
6. Change the representation of **Link** and **List** from §27.9 without changing the user interface provided by the functions. Allocate **Links** in an array of links and have the members **first**, **last**, **pre**, and **suc** be **ints** (indices into the array).
7. What are the advantages and disadvantages of intrusive containers compared to C++ standard (non-intrusive) containers? Make lists of pros and cons.
8. What is the lexicographical order on your machine? Write out every character on your keyboard together with its integer value; then, write the characters out in the order determined by their integer value.
9. Using only C facilities, including the C standard library, read a sequence of words from **stdin** and write them to **stdout** in lexicographical order. Hint: The C sort function is called **qsort()**; look it up somewhere. Alternatively, insert the words into an ordered list as you read them. There is no C standard library list.
10. Make a list of C language features adopted from C++ or C with Classes (§27.1).
11. Make a list of C language features *not* adopted by C++.
12. Implement a (C-style **string**, **int**) lookup table with operations such as **find(struct table*, const char*)**, **insert(struct table*, const char*, int)**, and **remove(struct table*, const char*)**. The representation of the table could be an array of a **struct** pair or a pair of arrays (**const char***[] and **int***); you choose. Also choose return types for your functions. Document your design decisions.
13. Write a program that does the equivalent of **string s; cin>>s;** in C; that is, define an input operation that reads an arbitrarily long sequence of whitespace-terminated characters into a zero-terminated array of **chars**.
14. Write a function that takes an array of **ints** as its input and finds the smallest and the largest elements. It should also compute the median and mean. Use a **struct** holding the results as the return value.

15. Simulate single inheritance in C. Let each "base class" contain a pointer to an array of pointers to functions (to simulate virtual functions as freestanding functions taking a pointer to a "base class" object as their first argument); see §27.2.3. Implement "derivation" by making the "base class" the type of the first member of the derived class. For each class, initialize the array of "virtual functions" appropriately. To test the ideas, implement a version of "the old **Shape** example" with the base and derived **draw**() just printing out the name of their class. Use only language features and library facilities available in standard C.

16. Use macros to obscure (simplify the notation for) the implementation in the previous exercise.

Postscript

We did mention that compatibility issues are not all that exciting. However, there is a lot of C code "out there" (billions of lines of code), and if you have to read or write it, this chapter prepares you to do so. Personally, we prefer C++, and the information in this chapter gives part of the reason for that. And please don't underestimate that "intrusive **List**" example – both "intrusive **Lists**" and opaque types are important and powerful techniques (in both C and C++).

Part V
Appendices

Language Summary

> "Be careful what you wish for;
> you might get it."
>
> **—Traditional**

This appendix summarizes key language elements of C++. The summary is very selective and specifically geared to novices who want to explore a bit beyond the sequence of topics in the book. The aim is conciseness, not completeness.

A.1 General

This appendix is a reference. It is not intended to be read from beginning to end like a chapter. It (more or less) systematically describes key elements of the C++ language. It is not a complete reference, though; it is just a summary. Its focus and emphasis were determined by student questions. Often, you will need to look at the chapters for a more complete explanation. This summary does not attempt to equal the precision and terminology of the standard. Instead, it attempts to be accessible. For more information, see Stroustrup, *The C++ Programming Lan-*

guage. The definition of C++ is the ISO C++ standard, but that document is neither intended for nor suitable for novices. Don't forget to use your online documentation. If you look at this appendix while working on the early chapters, expect much to be "mysterious," that is, explained in later chapters.

For standard library facilities, see Appendix B.

The standard for C++ is defined by a committee working under the auspices of the ISO (the international organization for standards) in collaboration with national standards bodies, such as INCITS (United States), BSI (United Kingdom), and AFNOR (France). The current definition is ISO/IEC 14882:2003 *Standard for Programming Language C++.* It is available electronically and as a book (on paper): *The C++ Standard,* published by Wiley, ISBN 0470846747.

A.1.1 Terminology

The C++ standard defines what a C++ program is and what the various constructs mean:

- *Conforming:* A program that is C++ according to the standard is called *conforming* (or colloquially, *legal* or *valid*).

- *Implementation defined:* A program can (and usually does) depend on features (such as the size of an **int** and the numeric value of **'a'**) that are only well defined on a given compiler, operating system, machine architecture, etc. The implementation-defined features are listed in the standard and must be documented in implementation documentation, and many are reflected in standard headers, such as **<limits>** (see §B.1.1). So, being conforming is not the same as being portable to all C++ implementations.

- *Unspecified:* The meaning of some constructs is *unspecified, undefined,* or *not conforming but not requiring a diagnostic.* Obviously, such features are best avoided. This book avoids them. The unspecified features to avoid include

  - Inconsistent definitions in separate source files (use header files consistently; see §8.3)

  - Reading *and* writing the same variable repeatedly in an expression (the main example is **a[i]=++i;**)

  - Many uses of explicit type conversion (casts), especially of **reinterpret_cast**

A.1.2 Program start and termination

A C++ program must have a single global function called **main()**. The program starts by executing **main()**. The return type of **main()** is **int** (**void** is *not* a conforming alternative). The value returned by **main()** is the program's return value to "the system." Some systems ignore that value, but successful termination is indicated by returning zero and failure by returning a nonzero value or by an uncaught exception (but an uncaught exception is considered poor style).

The arguments to **main()** can be implementation defined, but every implementation must accept two versions (though only one per program):

```
int main();                        // no arguments
int main(int argc, char* argv[]);  // argv[] holds argc C-style strings
```

The definition of **main()** need not explicitly return a value. If it doesn't, "dropping through the bottom," it returns a zero. This is the minimal C++ program:

```
int main() { }
```

If you define a global (namespace) scope object with a constructor and a destructor, the constructor will logically be executed "before **main()**" and the destructor logically executed "after **main()**" (technically, executing those constructors is part of invoking **main()** and executing the destructors part of returning from **main()**). Whenever you can, avoid global objects, especially global objects requiring nontrivial construction and destruction.

A.1.3 Comments

What can be said in code, should be. However, C++ offers two comment styles to allow the programmer to say things that are not well expressed as code:

```
// this is a line comment

/*
      this is a
      block comment
*/
```

Obviously, block comments are mostly used for multi-line comments, though some people prefer single-line comments even for multiple lines:

```
// this is a
// multi-line comment
// expressed using three line comments

/* and this is a single line of comment expressed using a block comment */
```

Comments are essential for documenting the intent of code; see also §7.6.4.

A.2 Literals

Literals represent values of various types. For example, the literal **12** represents the integer value "twelve," **"Morning"** represents the character string value *Morning*, and **true** represent the Boolean value *true*.

A.2.1 Integer literals

Integer literals come in three varieties:

- Decimal: a series of decimal digits
  Decimal digits: 0, 1, 2, 3, 4, 5, 6, 7, 8, and 9
- Octal: a series of octal digits starting with 0
  Octal digits: 0, 1, 2, 3, 4, 5, 6, and 7
- Hexadecimal: a series of hexadecimal digits starting with 0x or 0X
  Hexadecimal digits: 0, 1, 2, 3, 4, 5, 6, 7, 8, 9, a, b, c, d, e, f, A, B, C, D, E, and F

A suffix **u** or **U** makes an integer literal **unsigned** (§25.5.3), and a suffix **l** or **L** makes it **long**; for example, **10u** and **123456UL**.

A.2.1.1 Number systems

We usually write out numbers in decimal notation. **123** means **1** hundred plus **2** tens plus **3** ones, or **1*100+2*10+3*1**, or (using **^** to mean "to the power of") **1*10^2+2*10^1+3*10^0**. Another word for *decimal* is *base-10*. There is nothing really special about 10 here. What we have is **1*base^2+2*base^1+3*base^0** where **base==10**. There are lots of theories about why we use base-10. One theory has been "built into" some natural languages: we have ten fingers and each symbol, such as 0, 1, and 2, that directly stands for a value in a positional number system is called a digit. *Digit* is Latin for "finger."

Occasionally, other bases are used. Typically, positive integer values in computer memory are represented in base-2 (it is relatively easy to reliably represent 0 and 1 as physical states in materials), and humans dealing with low-level hardware issues sometimes use base-8 and more often base-16 to refer to the content of memory.

Consider hexadecimal. We need to name the 16 values from 0 to 15. Usually, we use 0, 1, 2, 3, 4, 5, 6, 7, 8, 9, A, B, C, D, E, F, where A has the decimal value 10, B the decimal value 11, and so on:

$$\textbf{A==10, B==11, C==12, D==13, E==14, F==15}$$

We can now write the decimal value **123** as **7B** using the hexadecimal notation. To see that, note that in the hexadecimal system **7B** means **7*16+11**, which is (decimal) **123**. Conversely, hexadecimal **123** means **1*16^2+2*16+3**, which is

1*256+2*16+3, which is (decimal) **291**. If you have never dealt with non-decimal integer representations, we strongly recommend you try converting a few numbers to and from decimal and hexadecimal. Note that a hexadecimal digit has a very simple correspondence to a binary value:

Hexadecimal and binary								
hex	**0**	**1**	**2**	**3**	**4**	**5**	**6**	**7**
binary	0000	0001	0010	0011	0100	0101	0110	0111
hex	**8**	**9**	**A**	**B**	**C**	**D**	**E**	**F**
binary	1000	1001	1010	1011	1100	1101	1110	1111

This goes a long way toward explaining the popularity of hexadecimal notation. In particular, the value of a byte is simply expressed as two hexadecimal digits.

In C++, (fortunately) numbers are decimal unless we specify otherwise. To say that a number is hexadecimal, we prefix **0X** ("*X* for hex"), so **123==0X7B** and **0X123==291**. We can equivalently use a lowercase **x**, so we also have **123==0x7B** and **0x123==291**. Similarly, we can use lowercase **a**, **b**, **c**, **d**, **e**, and **f** for the hexadecimal digits. For example, **123==0x7b.**

Octal is base-8. We need only eight octal digits: **0**, **1**, **2**, **3**, **4**, **5**, **6**, **7**. In C++, base-8 numbers are represented starting with a **0**, so **0123** is not the decimal number **123**, but $1*8^2+2*8+3$, that is, **1*64+2*8+3**, or (decimal) **83**. Conversely, octal **83**, that is, **083**, is **8*8+3**, which is (decimal) **67**. Using C++ notation, we get **0123==83** and **083==67**.

Binary is base-2. We need only two digits, **0** and **1**. We cannot directly represent base-2 numbers as literals in C++. Only base-8 (octal), base-10 (decimal), and base-16 (hexadecimal) are directly supported as literals and as input and output formats for integers. However, binary numbers are useful to know even if we cannot directly represent them in C++ text. For example, (decimal) **123** is

$$1*2^6+1*2^5+1*2^4+1*2^3+0*2^2+1*2+1,$$

which is **1*64+1*32+1*16+1*8+0*4+1*2+1**, which is (binary) **1111011**.

A.2.2 Floating-point-literals

A *floating-point-literal* contains a decimal point (.), an exponent (e.g., **e3**), or a floating-point suffix (**d** or **f**). For example:

```
123        // int (no decimal point, suffix, or exponent)
123.       // double:       123.0
```

```
123.0      // double
.123       // double:      0.123
0.123      // double
1.23e3     // double:      1230.0
1.23e-3    // double:      0.00123
1.23e+3    // double:      1230.0
```

Floating-point-literals have type **double** unless a suffix indicates otherwise. For example:

```
1.23     // double
1.23f    // float
1.23L    // long double
```

A.2.3 Boolean literals

The literals of type **bool** are **true** and **false**. The integer value of **true** is **1** and the integer value of **false** is **0**.

A.2.4 Character literals

A *character literal* is a character enclosed in single quotes, for example, 'a' and '@'. In addition, there are some "special characters":

Name	ASCII name	C++ name
newline	NL	\n
horizontal tab	HT	\t
vertical tab	VT	\v
backspace	BS	\b
carriage return	CR	\r
form feed	FF	\f
alert	BEL	\a
backslash	\	\\
question mark	?	\?
single quote	'	\'
double quote	"	\"
octal number	ooo	\ooo
hexadecimal number	hhh	\xhhh

A special character is represented as its "C++ name" enclosed in single quotes, for example, '\n' (newline) and '\t' (tab).

The character set includes the following visible characters:

abcdefghijklmnopqrstuvwxyz
ABCDEFGHIJKLMNOPQRSTUVWXYZ
0123456789
!@#$%^&*()_+|~`{}[]:";'<>?,./

In portable code, you cannot rely on more visible characters. The value of a character, such as 'a' for a, is implementation dependent (but easily discovered, for example, **cout << int('a')**).

A.2.5 String literals

A *string literal* is a series of characters enclosed in double quotes, for example, **"Knuth"** and **"King Canute"**. A newline cannot be part of a string; instead use the special character \n to represent newline in a string:

```
"King
Canute "         // error: newline in string literal
"King\nCanute"    // OK: correct way to get a newline into a string literal
```

Two string literals separated only by whitespace are taken as a single string literal. For example:

```
"King" "Canute"   // equivalent to "KingCanute" (no space)
```

Note that special characters, such as \n, can appear in string literals.

A.2.6 The pointer literal

There is only one *pointer literal:* the null pointer, **0**. Any constant expression that evaluates to **0** can be used as the null pointer. For example:

```
t* p1 = 0;        // OK: null pointer
int* p2 = 2-2;    // OK: null pointer
int* p3 = 1;      // error: 1 is an int, not a pointer
int z = 0;
int* p4 = z;      // error: z is not a constant
```

What is happening here is that the value **0** is implicitly converted to the null pointer. The null pointer is typically (but not always) represented as an all-zeros bit pattern, just like **0**.

In C++ (but not in C, so beware of C headers), **NULL** is defined to mean **0** so that you can write

```
int* p4 = NULL;      // (given the right definition of NULL) the null pointer
```

In C++0x, the keyword **nullptr** will denote the null pointer. For now, we recommend just using **0** for the null pointer.

A.3 Identifiers

An *identifier* is a sequence of characters starting with a letter or an underscore followed by zero or more (uppercase or lowercase) letters, digits, or underscores:

```
int foo_bar;   // OK
int FooBar;    // OK
int foo bar;    // error: space can't be used in an identifier
int foo$bar;   // error: $ can't be used in an identifier
```

Identifiers starting with an underscore or containing a double underscore are reserved for use by the implementation; don't use them. For example:

```
int _foo;        // don't
int foo_bar;     // OK
int foo__bar;   // don't
int foo_;        // OK
```

A.3.1 Keywords

Keywords are identifiers used by the language itself to express language constructs.

Keywords (reserved identifiers)					
and	and_eq	asm	auto	bitand	bitor
bool	break	case	catch	char	class
compl	const	const_cast	continue	default	delete
do	double	dynamic_cast	else	enum	explicit
export	extern	false	float	for	friend
goto	if	inline	int	long	mutable
namespace	new	not	not_eq	operator	or

Keywords (reserved identifiers) *(continued)*					
or_eq	private	protected	public	register	reinterpret_cast
return	short	signed	sizeof	static	static_cast
struct	switch	template	this	throw	true
try	typedef	typeid	typename	union	unsigned
using	virtual	void	volatile	wchar_t	while
xor	xor_eq				

A.4 Scope, storage class, and lifetime

Every name in C++ (with the lamentable exception of preprocessor names; see §A.17) exists in a scope; that is, the name belongs to a region of text in which it can be used. Data (objects) are stored in memory somewhere; the kind of memory used to store an object is called its *storage class*. The lifetime of an object is from the time it is first initialized until it is finally destroyed.

A.4.1 Scope

There are five kinds of *scopes* (§8.4):

- *Global scope:* A name is in global scope unless it is declared inside some language construct (e.g., a class or a function).
- *Namespace scope:* A name is in a namespace scope if it is defined within a namespace and not inside some language construct (e.g., a class or a function). Technically, the global scope is a namespace scope with "the empty name."
- *Local scope:* A name is in a local scope if it is declared inside a function (this includes function parameters).
- *Class scope:* A name is in a class scope if it is the name of a member of a class.
- *Statement scope:* A name is in a statement scope if it is declared in the (. . .) part of a **for-**, **while-**, **switch-**, or **if**-statement.

The scope of a variable extends (only) to the end of the statement in which it is defined. For example:

```
for (int i = 0; i<v.size(); ++i) {
        // i can be used here
}
if (i < 27)      // the i from the for-statement is not in scope here
```

Class and namespace scopes have names, so that we can refer to a member from "elsewhere." For example:

```
void f();    // in global scope

namespace N {
    void f()        // in namespace scope N
    {
        int v;      // in local scope
        ::f();      // call the global f()
    }
}

void f()
{
    N::f();     // call N's f()
}
```

What would happen if you called **N::f()** or **::f()**? See also §A.15.

A.4.2 Storage class

There are three *storage classes* (§17.4):

- *Automatic storage:* Variables defined in functions (including function parameters) are placed in automatic storage (i.e., "on the stack") unless explicitly declared to be **static**. Automatic storage is allocated when a function is called and deallocated when a call returns; thus, if a function is (directly or indirectly) called by itself, multiple copies of automatic data can exist: one for each call (§8.5.8).

- *Static storage:* Variables declared in global and namespace scope are stored in static storage, as are variables explicitly declared **static** in functions and classes. The linker allocates static storage "before the program starts running."

- *Free store (heap):* Objects created by **new** are allocated in the free store.

For example:

```
vector<int> vg(10);       // constructed once at program start ("before main()")

vector<int>* f(int x)
{
    static vector<int> vs(x);     // constructed in first call of f() only
    vector<int> vf(x+x);          // constructed in each call of f()
```

```
        for (int i=1; i<10; ++i) {
                vector<int> vl(i);        // constructed in each iteration
                // ...
        }       // v1 destroyed here (in each iteration)

        return new vector<int>(vf);      // constructed on free store as a copy of vf
} // vf destroyed here

void ff()
{
        vector<int>* p = f(10);          // get vector from f()
        // ...
        delete p;                        // delete the vector from f
}
```

The statically allocated variables **vg** and **vs** are destroyed at program termination ("after **main()**"), provided they have been constructed.

Class members are not allocated as such. When you allocate an object somewhere, the non-static members are placed there also (with the same storage class as the class object to which they belong).

Code is stored separately from data. For example, a member function is *not* stored in each object of its class; one copy is stored with the rest of the code for the program.

See also §14.3 and §17.4.

A.4.3 Lifetime

Before an object can be (legally) used, it must be initialized. This initialization can be explicit using an initializer or implicit using a constructor or a rule for default initialization of built-in types. The lifetime of an object ends at a point determined by its scope and storage class (e.g., see §17.4 and §B.4.2):

- *Local (automatic) objects* are constructed if/when the thread of execution gets to them and destroyed at end of scope.

- *Temporary objects* are created by a specific sub-expression and destroyed at the end of their full expression. A full expression is an expression that is not a sub-expression of some other expression.

- *Namespace objects and static class members* are constructed at the start of the program ("before **main()**") and destroyed at the end of the program ("after **main()**").

- *Local static objects* are constructed if/when the thread of execution gets to them and (if constructed) destroyed at the end of the program.

- *Free-store objects* are constructed by **new** and optionally destroyed using **delete**.

A temporary variable bound to a reference "lives" as long as the reference. For example:

```
const char* string_tbl[] = { "Mozart", "Grieg", "Haydn", "Chopin" };
const char* f(int i) { return string_tbl[i]; }
void g(string s){}

void h()
{
        const string& r = f(0);     // bind temporary string to r
        g(f(1));                     // make a temporary string and pass it
        string s = f(2);             // initialize s from temporary string
        cout << "f(3): " << f(3)     // make a temporary string and pass it
              <<" s: " << s
              << " r: " << r << '\n';
}
```

The result is

f(3): Chopin s: Haydn r: Mozart

The **string** temporaries generated for the calls **f(1)**, **f(2)**, and **f(3)** are destroyed at the end of the expression in which they were created. However, the temporary generated for **f(0)** is bound to **r** and "lives" until the end of **h()**.

A.5 Expressions

This section summarizes C++'s operators. We use abbreviations that we find mnemonic, such as **m** for a member name, **T** for a type name, **p** for an expression yielding a pointer, **x** for expression, **v** for an lvalue expression, and **lst** for an argument list. The result type of the arithmetic operations is determined by "the usual arithmetic conversions" (§A.5.2.2). The descriptions in this section are of the built-in operators, not of any operator you might define on your own, though when you define your own operators, you are encouraged to follow the semantic rules described for built-in operations (§9.6).

Scope resolution	
N :: m	**m** is in the namespace **N**; **N** is the name of a namespace or a class.
:: m	**m** is in the global namespace.

Note that members can themselves nest, so that you can get **N::C::m**; see also §8.7.

Postfix expressions	
x . m	member access; **x** must be a class object
p –> m	member access; **p** must point to a class object; equivalent to **(*p).m**
p[x]	subscripting; equivalent to ***(p+x)**
f(lst)	function call: call **f** with the argument list **lst**
T(lst)	construction: construct a **T** with the argument list **lst**
v++	(post) increment; the value of **v++** is the value of **v** before incrementing
v––	(post) decrement; the value of **v––** is the value of **v** before decrementing
typeid(x)	run-time type identification for **x**
typeid(T)	run-time type identification for **T**
dynamic_cast<T>(x)	run-time checked conversion of **x** to **T**
static_cast<T>(x)	compile-time checked conversion of **x** to **T**
const_cast<T>(x)	unchecked conversion to add or remove **const** from **x**'s type to get **T**
reinterpret_cast<T>(x)	unchecked conversion of **x** to **T** by reinterpreting the bit pattern of **x**

The **typeid** operator and its uses are not covered in this book; see an expert-level reference. Note that casts do not modify their argument. Instead, they produce a result of their type, which somehow corresponds to the argument value; see §A.5.7.

Unary expressions	
sizeof(T)	the size of a **T** in bytes
sizeof(x)	the size of an object of **x**'s type in bytes
++v	(pre) increment; equivalent to **v+=1**
––v	(pre) decrement; equivalent to **v–=1**
~x	complement of **x**; **~** is a bitwise operation
!x	not **x**; returns **true** or **false**
&v	address of **v**
*p	contents of object pointed to by **p**
new T	make a **T** on the free store
new T(lst)	make a **T** on the free store and initialize it with **lst**
new(lst) T	construct a **T** at location determined by **lst**

Unary expressions (*continued*)	
new(lst) T(lst2)	construct a **T** at location determined by **lst** and initialize it with **lst2**
delete p	free the object pointed to by **p**
delete[] p	free the array of objects pointed to by **p**
(T)x	C-style cast; convert **x** to **T**

Note that the object(s) pointed to by **p** in **delete p** and **delete[] p** must be allocated using **new**; see §A.5.6. Note that **(T)x** is far less specific – and therefore more error-prone – than the more specific cast operators; see §A.5.7.

Member selection	
x.*ptm	the member of **x** identified by the pointer-to-member **ptm**
p−>*ptm	the member of ***p** identified by the pointer-to-member **ptm**

Not covered in this book; see an expert-level reference.

Multiplicative operators	
x*y	Multiply **x** by **y**.
x/y	Divide **x** by **y**.
x%y	Modulo (remainder) of **x** by **y** (not for floating-point types).

The effect of **x/y** and **x%y** is undefined if **y==0**. The effect of **x%y** is implementation defined if **x** or **y** is negative.

Additive operators	
x+y	Add **x** and **y**.
x−y	Subtract **y** from **x**.

Shift operators	
x<<y	Shift **x** left by **y** bit positions.
x>>y	Shift **x** right by **y** bit positions.

For the (built-in) use of >> and << for shifting bits, see §25.5.4. When their left-most operators are **iostreams**, these operators are used for I/O; see Chapters 10 and 11.

Relational operators	
x<y	x less than y; returns a **bool**
x<=y	x less than or equal to y
x>y	x greater than y
x>=y	x greater than or equal to y

The result of a relational operator is a **bool**.

Equality operators	
x==y	x equals y; returns a **bool**
x!=y	x not equal to y

Note that x!=y is !(x==y). The result of an equality operator is a **bool**.

Bitwise and	
x&y	bitwise and of x and y

Note that & (like ^, |, ~, >>, and <<) delivers a set of bits. For example, if **a** and **b** are **unsigned chars**, **a&b** is an **unsigned char** with each bit being the result of applying & to the corresponding bits in **a** and **b**; see §A.5.5.

Bitwise xor	
x^y	bitwise exclusive or of x and y

Bitwise or	
x|y	bitwise or of x and y

Logical and	
x&&y	logical and; returns **true** or **false**; evaluate y only if x is true

Logical or	
x‖y	logical or; returns **true** or **false**; evaluate **y** only if **x** is false

See §A.5.5.

Conditional expression	
x?y:z	if **x** the result is **y**; otherwise the result is **z**

For example:

> **template<class T> T& max(T& a, T& b) { return (a>b)?a:b; }**

The "question mark colon operator" is explained in §8.4.

Assignments	
v=x	assign **x** to **v**; result is the resulting **v**
v*=x	roughly **v=v*(x)**
v/=x	roughly **v=v/(x)**
v%=x	roughly **v=v%(x)**
v+=x	roughly **v=v+(x)**
v−=x	roughly **v=v−(x)**
v>>=x	roughly **v=v>>(x)**
v<<=x	roughly **v=v<<(x)**
v&=x	roughly **v=v&(x)**
v^=x	roughly **v=v^(x)**
v‖=x	roughly **v=v‖(x)**

By "roughly **v=v*(x)**" we mean that **v*=x** has that value except that **v** is evaluated only once. For example **v[++i]*=7+3** means **(++i, v[i]=v[i]*(7+3))** rather than **(v[++i]=v[++i]*(7+3))** (which would be undefined; see §8.6.1).

Throw expression	
throw x	throw the value of **x**

The type of a **throw**-expression is **void**.

Comma expression	
x,y	Execute **x** then **y**; the result is **y**.

Each box holds operators with the same precedence. Operators in higher boxes have higher precedence than operators in lower boxes. For example, **a+b*c** means **a+(b*c)** rather than **(a+b)*c** because * has higher precedence than +. Similarly, ***p++** means ***(p++)**, not **(*p)++**. Unary operators and assignment operators are right-associative; all others are left-associative. For example, **a=b=c** means **a=(b=c)** and **a+b+c** means **(a+b)+c**.

An lvalue is an expression that identifies an object that could in principle be modified (but obviously an lvalue that has a **const** type is protected against modification by the type system) and have its address taken. The complement to lvalue is rvalue, that is, an expression that identifies something that may not be modified or have its address taken, such as a value returned from a function (**&f(x)** is an error because **f(x)** is an rvalue).

A.5.1 User-defined operators

The rules defined here are for built-in types. If a user-defined operator is used, an expression is simply transformed into a call of the appropriate user-defined operator function, and the rules for function call determine what happens. For example:

```
class Mine { /* . . . */ };
bool operator==(Mine, Mine);

void f(Mine a, Mine b)
{
    if (a==b) {      // a==b means operator==(a,b)
        // . . .
    }
}
```

A user-defined type is a class (§A12, Chapter 9) or an enumeration (§A.11, §9.5).

A.5.2 Implicit type conversion

Integral and floating-point types (§A.8) can be mixed freely in assignments and expressions. Wherever possible, values are converted so as not to lose information. Unfortunately, value-destroying conversions are also performed implicitly.

A.5.2.1 Promotions

The implicit conversions that preserve values are commonly referred to as *promotions*. Before an arithmetic operation is performed, *integral promotion* is used to create **ints** out of shorter integer types. This reflects the original purpose of these promotions: to bring operands to the "natural" size for arithmetic operations. In addition, **float** to **double** is considered a promotion.

Promotions are used as part of the usual arithmetic conversions (see §A.5.2.2).

A.5.2.2 Conversions

The fundamental types can be converted into each other in a bewildering number of ways. When writing code, you should always aim to avoid undefined behavior and conversions that quietly throw away information (see §3.9 and §25.5.3). A compiler can warn about many questionable conversions.

- *Integral conversions:* An integer can be converted to another integer type. An enumeration value can be converted to an integer type. If the destination type is **unsigned**, the resulting value is simply as many bits from the source as will fit in the destination (high-order bits are thrown away if necessary). If the destination type is signed, the value is unchanged if it can be represented in the destination type; otherwise, the value is implementation defined. Note that **bool** and **char** are integer types.

- *Floating-point conversions:* A floating-point value can be converted to another floating-point type. If the source value can be exactly represented in the destination type, the result is the original numeric value. If the source value is between two adjacent destination values, the result is one of those values. Otherwise, the behavior is undefined. Note that **float** to **double** is considered a promotion.

- *Pointer and reference conversions:* Any pointer to an object type can be implicitly converted to a **void*** (§17.8, §27.3.5). A pointer (reference) to a derived class can be implicitly converted to a pointer (reference) to an accessible and unambiguous base (§14.3). A constant expression (§A.5, §4.3.1) that evaluates to 0 can be implicitly converted to any pointer type. A **T*** can be implicitly converted to a **const T***. Similarly, a **T&** can be implicitly converted to a **const T&**.

- *Boolean conversions:* Pointers, integrals, and floating-point values can be implicitly converted to **bool**. A nonzero value converts to **true**; a zero value converts to **false**.

- *Floating-integral conversions:* When a floating-point value is converted to an integer value, the fractional part is discarded. In other words, conversion from a floating-point type to an integer type truncates. The behavior is undefined if the truncated value cannot be represented in the destination type. Conversions from integer to floating types are as mathematically correct as the hardware allows. Loss of precision occurs if an integral value cannot be represented exactly as a value of the floating type.

- *Usual arithmetic conversions:* These conversions are performed on the operands of a binary operator to bring them to a common type, which is then used as the type of the result:

  1. If either operand is of type **long double**, the other is converted to **long double**. Otherwise, if either operand is **double**, the other is converted to **double**. Otherwise, if either operand is **float**, the other is converted to **float**. Otherwise, integral promotions are performed on both operands.

  2. Then, if either operand is **unsigned long**, the other is converted to **unsigned long**. Otherwise, if one operand is a **long int** and the other is an **unsigned int**, then if a **long int** can represent all the values of an **unsigned int**, the **unsigned int** is converted to a **long int**; otherwise, both operands are converted to **unsigned long int**. Otherwise, if either operand is **long**, the other is converted to **long**. Otherwise, if either operand is **unsigned**, the other is converted to **unsigned**. Otherwise, both operands are **int**.

Obviously, it is best not to rely too much on complicated mixtures of types, so as to minimize the need for implicit conversions.

A.5.2.3 User-defined conversions

In addition to the standard promotions and conversions, a programmer can define conversions for user-defined types. A constructor that takes a single argument defines a conversion from its argument type to its type. If the constructor is **explicit** (see §18.3.1), the conversion happens only when the programmer explicitly requires the conversion. Otherwise, the conversion can be implicit.

A.5.3 Constant expressions

A *constant expression* is an expression that can be evaluated at compile time and involves only **int** operands. (That's a slight simplification, but good enough for most purposes.) For example:

```
const int a = 2*3;
const int b = a+3;
```

Constant expressions are required in a few places, such as array bounds, case labels, enumerator initializers, and **int** template arguments. For example:

```
int var = 7;
```

```
switch (x) {
case 77:        // OK
case a+2:       // OK
case var:       // error (var is not a constant expression)
        // . . .
};
```

A.5.4 sizeof

In **sizeof(x)**, **x** can be a type or an expression. If **x** is an expression, the value of **sizeof(x)** is the size of the resulting object. If **x** is a type, **sizeof(x)** is the size of an object of type **x**. Sizes are measured in bytes. By definition, **sizeof(char)==1**.

A.5.5 Logical expressions

C++ provides logical operators for integer types:

Bitwise logical operations	
x&y	bitwise and of **x** and **y**
x|y	bitwise or of **x** and **y**
x^y	bitwise exclusive or of **x** and **y**

Logical operations	
x&&y	logical and; returns **true** or **false**; evaluate **y** only if **x** is **true**
x||y	logical or; returns **true** or **false**; evaluate **y** only if **x** is **false**

The bitwise operators do their operation on each bit of their operands, whereas the logical operators (**&&** and **||**) treat a **0** as the value **false** and anything else as the value **true**. The definitions of the operations are:

&	0	1
0	0	0
1	0	1

|	0	1
0	0	1
1	1	1

^	0	1
0	0	1
1	1	0

A.5.6 new and delete

Memory on the free store (dynamic store, heap) is allocated using **new** and deallocated ("freed") using **delete** (for individual objects) or **delete[]** (for an array).

If memory is exhausted, **new** throws a **bad_alloc** exception. A successful **new** operation allocates at least 1 byte and returns a pointer to the allocated object. The type of object allocated is specified after **new**. For example:

```
int* p1 = new int;        // allocate an (uninitialized) int
int* p2 = new int(7);     // allocate an int initialized to 7
int* p3 = new int[100];   // allocate 100 (uninitialized) ints
// . . .
delete p1;      // deallocate individual object
delete p2;
delete[] p3;    // deallocate array
```

If you allocate objects of a built-in type using **new**, they will not be initialized unless you specify an initializer. If you allocate objects of a class with a constructor using **new**, a constructor is called; the default constructor is called unless you specify an initializer (§17.4.4).

A **delete** invokes the destructor, if any, for its operand. Note that a destructor may be virtual (§A.12.3.1).

A.5.7 Casts

There are four type-conversion operators:

Type-conversion operators	
x=dynamic_cast<D*>(p)	Try to convert v into a **D*** (may return 0).
x=dynamic_cast<D&>(*p)	Try to convert *p into a **D&** (may throw **bad_cast**).
x=static_cast<T>(v)	Convert **v** into a **T** if a **T** can be converted into **v**'s type.
x=reinterpret_cast<T>(v)	Convert **v** into a **T** represented by the same bit pattern.
x=const_cast<T>(v)	Convert **v** into a **T** by adding or subtracting **const**.
x=(T)v	C-style cast: do any old cast.
x=T(v)	Functional cast: do any old cast.

The dynamic cast is typically used for class hierarchy navigation where **p** is a pointer to a base class and **D** is derived from that base. It returns **0** if **v** is not a **D***. If you want **dynamic_cast** to throw an exception (**bad_cast**) instead of returning **0**, cast to a reference instead of to a pointer. The dynamic cast is the only cast that relies on run-time checking.

Static cast is used for "reasonably well-behaved conversions," that is, where **v** could have been the result of an implicit conversion from a **T**; see §17.8.

Reinterpret cast is used for reinterpreting a bit pattern. It is not guaranteed to be portable. In fact, it is best to assume that every use of **reinterpret_cast** is nonportable. A typical example is an **int**-to-pointer conversion to get a machine address into a program; see §17.8 and §25.4.1.

The C-style and functional casts can perform any conversion that can be achieved by a **static_cast** or a **reinterpret_cast**, combined with a **const_cast**.

Casts are best avoided. In most cases, consider their use a sign of poor programming. Exceptions to this rule are presented in §17.8 and §25.4.1. The C-style cast and function-style casts have the nasty property that you don't have to understand exactly what the cast is doing (§27.3.4). Prefer the named casts when you cannot avoid an explicit type conversion.

A.6 Statements

Here is a grammar for C++'s statements ($_{opt}$ means "optional"):

> *statement:*
> > *declaration*
> > { *statement-list$_{opt}$* }
> > **try** { *statement-list$_{opt}$* } *handler-list*
> > *expression$_{opt}$* **;**
> > *selection-statement*
> > *iteration-statement*
> > *labeled-statement*
> > *control-statement*

> *selection-statement:*
> > **if** (*condition*) *statement*
> > **if** (*condition*) *statement* **else** *statement*
> > **switch** (*condition*) *statement*

> *iteration-statement:*
> > **while** (*condition*) *statement*
> > **do** *statement* **while** (*expression*) **;**
> > **for** (*for-init-statement condition$_{opt}$* **;** *expression$_{opt}$*) *statement*

> *labeled-statement:*
> > **case** *constant-expression* **:** *statement*
> > **default : ** *statement*
> > **identifier :** *statement*

control-statement:
>**break** ;
>**continue** ;
>**return** *expression$_{opt}$* ;
>**goto** *identifier* ;

statement-list:
>*statement statement-list$_{opt}$*

condition:
>*expression*
>*type-specifier declarator = expression*

for-init-statement:
>*expression$_{opt}$* ;
>*type-specifier declarator = expression* ;

handler-list:
>**catch** (*exception-declaration*) { *statement-list$_{opt}$* }
>*handler-list handler-list$_{opt}$*

Note that a declaration is a statement and that there is no assignment statement or procedure call statement; assignments and function calls are expressions. More information:

- Iteration (**for** and **while**); see §4.4.2.
- Selection (**if**, **switch**, **case**, and **break**); see §4.4.1. A **break** "breaks out of" the nearest enclosing **switch**-statement, **while**-statement, **do**-statement, or **for**-statement; that is, the next statement executed will be the statement following that enclosing statement.
- Expressions; see §A.5, §4.3.
- Declarations; see §A.6, §8.2.
- Exceptions (**try** and **catch**); see §5.6, §19.4.

Here is an example concocted simply to demonstrate a variety of statements (what does it do?):

```
int* f(int p[], int n)
{
    if (p==0) throw Bad_p(n);
    vector<int> v;
    int x;
```

```
        while (cin>>x) {
                if (x==terminator) break;    // exit while loop
                v.push_back(x);
        }
        for (int i = 0; i<v.size() && i<n; ++i) {
                if (v[i]==*p)
                        return p;
                else
                        ++p;
        }
        return 0;
}
```

A.7 Declarations

A *declaration* consists of three parts:

- The name of the entity being declared
- The type of the entity being declared
- The initial value of the entity being declared (optional in most cases)

We can declare

- Objects of built-in types and user-defined types (§A.8)
- User-defined types (classes and enumerations) (§A.10–11, Chapter 9)
- Templates (class templates and function templates) (§A.13)
- Aliases (§A.16)
- Namespaces (§A.15, §8.7)
- Functions (including member functions and operators) (§A.9, Chapter 8)
- Enumerators (values for enumerations) (§A.11, §9.5)
- Macros (§A.17.2, §27.8)

A.7.1 Definitions

A declaration that initializes, sets aside memory, or in other ways provides all the information necessary for using a name in a program is called a *definition*. Each type, object, and function in a program must have exactly one definition. Examples:

```
double f();                  // a declaration
double f() { /* . . . */ };    // (also) a definition
```

```
extern const int x;        // a declaration
int y;                     // (also) a definition
int z = 10;                // a definition with an explicit initializer
```

A **const** must be initialized. This is achieved by requiring an initializer for a **const** unless it has an explicit **extern** in its declaration (so that the initializer must be on its definition elsewhere) or it is of a type with a default constructor (§A.12.3). Class members that are **const**s must be initialized in every constructor using a member initializer (§A.12.3).

A.8 Built-in types

C++ has a host of fundamental types and types constructed from fundamental types using modifiers:

Built-in types	
bool x	**x** is a Boolean (values **true** and **false**).
char x	**x** is a character (usually 8 bits).
short x	**x** is a short **int** (usually 16 bits).
int x	**x** is the default integer type.
float x	**x** is a floating-point number (a "short double").
double x	**x** is a ("double-precision") floating-point number.
void* p	**p** is a pointer to raw memory (memory of unknown type).
T* p	**p** is a pointer to **T**.
T *const p	**p** is a constant (immutable) pointer to **T**.
T a[n]	**a** is an array of **n** **T**s.
T& r	**r** is a reference to **T**.
T f(arguments)	**f** is a function taking **arguments** and returning a **T**.
const T x	**x** is a constant (immutable) version of **T**.
long T x	**x** is a **long T**.
unsigned T x	**x** is an **unsigned T**.
signed T x	**x** is a **signed T**.

Here, **T** indicates "some type," so you can have a **long unsigned int**, a **long double**, an **unsigned char**, and a **const char *** (pointer to constant **char**). However, this system is not perfectly general; for example, there is no **short double** (that would have been a **float**), no **signed bool** (that would have been meaningless), no

short long int (that would have been redundant), and no **long long long long int**. Some compilers anticipate the C++0x standard and accept **long long int** (read that as "very long integer"). A **long long** is guaranteed to hold at least 64 bits.

The *floating-point types* are **float**, **double**, and **long double**. They are C++'s approximation of real numbers.

The *integer types* (sometimes called *integral types*) are **bool**, **char**, **short**, **int**, **long**, and (in C++0x) **long long** and their unsigned variants. Note that an enumeration type or value can often be used where an integer type or value is needed.

The sizes of built-in types are discussed in §3.8, §17.3.1, and §25.5.1. Pointers and arrays are discussed in Chapters 17 and 18. References are discussed in §8.5.4–6.

A.8.1 Pointers

A *pointer* is an address of an object or a function. Pointers are stored in variables of pointer types. A valid object pointer holds the address of an object:

```
int x = 7;
int* pi = &x;       // pi points to x
int xx = *pi;       // *pi is the value of the object pointed to by pi, that is, 7
```

An invalid pointer is a pointer that does not hold the value of an object:

```
int* pi2;           // uninitialized
*pi2 = 7;           // undefined behavior
pi2 = 0;            // the null pointer (pi2 is still invalid)
*pi2 = 7;           // undefined behavior

pi2 = new int(7);   // now pi2 is valid
int xxx = *pi2;     // fine: xxx becomes 7
```

We try to have invalid pointers hold the null pointer (**0**), so that we can test it:

```
if (p2 == 0) {  // "if invalid"
     // don't use *p2
}
```

Or simply

```
if (p2) {       // "if valid"
     // use *p2
}
```

See §17.4 and §18.5.4.

The operations on a (non-**void**) object pointer are:

Pointer operations	
*p	dereference/indirection
p[i]	dereference/subscripting
p=q	assignment and initialization
p==q	equality
p!=q	inequality
p+i	add integer
p−i	subtract integer
p−q	distance: subtract pointers
++p	pre-increment (move forward)
p++	post-increment (move forward)
−−p	pre-decrement (move backward)
p−−	post-decrement (move backward)
p+=i	move forward **i** elements
p−=i	move backward **i** elements

Note that any form of pointer arithmetic (e.g., **++p** and **p+=7**) is allowed only for pointers into an array and that the effect of dereferencing a pointer pointing outside the array is undefined (and most likely not checked by the compiler or the language run-time system).

The only operations on a **void*** pointer are copying (assignment or initialization) and casting (type conversion).

A pointer to function (§27.2.5) can only be copied and called. For example:

```
typedef void (*Handle_type)(int);
void my_handler(int);
Handle_type handle = my_handler;
handle(10);        // equivalent to my_handler(10)
```

A.8.2 Arrays

An *array* is a fixed-length contiguous sequence of objects (elements) of a given type:

```
int a[10];      // 10 ints
```

If an array is global, its elements will be initialized to the appropriate default value for the type. For example, the value of **a[7]** will be **0**. If the array is local (a variable declared in a function) or allocated using **new**, elements of built-in types will be uninitialized and elements of class types will be initialized as required by the class's constructors.

The name of an array is implicitly converted to a pointer to its first element. For example:

```
int* p = a;     // p points to a[0]
```

An array or a pointer to an element of an array can be subscripted using the [ ] operator. For example:

```
a[7] = 9;
int xx = p[6];
```

Array elements are numbered starting with 0; see §18.5.

Arrays are not range checked, and since they are often passed as pointers, the information to range check them is not reliably available to users. Prefer **vector**.

The size of an array is the sum of the sizes of its elements. For example:

```
int a[max];     // sizeof(a)==sizeof(a[0])*max==sizeof(int)*max
```

You can define and use an array of an array (a two-dimensional array), an array of an array of an array, etc. (multidimensional arrays). For example:

```
double da[100][200][300];   // 300 elements of type
                            // 200 elements of type
                            // 100 type double
da[7][9][11] = 0;
```

Nontrivial uses of multidimensional arrays are subtle and error-prone; see §24.4. If you have a choice, prefer a **Matrix** library (such as the one in Chapter 24).

A.8.3 References

A *reference* is an alias (alternative name) for an object:

```
int a = 7;
int& r = a;
r = 8;     // a becomes 8
```

References are most common as function parameters, where they are used to avoid copying:

```
void f(const string& s);
// . . .
f("this string could be somewhat costly to copy, so we use a reference");
```

See §8.5.4–6.

A.9 Functions

A *function* is a named piece of code taking a (possibly empty) set of arguments and optionally returning a value. A function is declared by giving the return type followed by its name followed by the parameter list:

```
char f(string, int);
```

So, **f** is a function taking a **string** and an **int** returning a **char**. If the function is just being declared, the declaration is terminated by a semicolon. If the function is being defined, the argument declaration is followed by the function body:

```
char f(string s, int i) { return s[i]; }
```

The function body must be a block (§8.2) or a **try**-block (§5.6.3).

A function declared to return a value must return a value (using the **return**-statement):

```
char f(string s, int i) { char c = s[i]; }     // error: no value returned
```

The **main**() function is the odd exception to that rule (§A.1.2). Except for **main**(), if you don't want to return a value, declare the function **void**; that is, use **void** as the "return type":

```
void increment(int& x) { ++x; }       // OK: no return value required
```

A function is called using the call operator (application operator), (), with an acceptable list of arguments:

```
char x1 = f(1,2);          // error: f()'s first argument must be a string
string s = "Battle of Hastings";
char x2 = f(s);            // error: f() requires two arguments
char x3 = f(s,2);          // OK
```

For more information about functions, see Chapter 8.

A.9.1 Overload resolution

Overload resolution is the process of choosing a function to call based on a set of arguments. For example:

```
void print(int);
void print(double);
void print(const std::string&);

print(123);     // use print(int)
print(1.23);    // use print(double)
print("123");   // use print(const string&)
```

It is the compiler's job to pick the right function according to the language rules. Unfortunately, in order to cope with complicated examples, the language rules are quite complicated. Here we present a simplified version.

Finding the right version to call from a set of overloaded functions is done by looking for a best match between the type of the argument expressions and the parameters (formal arguments) of the functions. To approximate our notions of what is reasonable, a series of criteria is tried in order:

1. Exact match, that is, match using no or only trivial conversions (for example, array name to pointer, function name to pointer to function, and **T** to **const T**)

2. Match using promotions, that is, integral promotions (**bool** to **int**, **char** to **int**, **short** to **int**, and their unsigned counterparts; see §A.8) and **float** to **double**

3. Match using standard conversions, for example, **int** to **double**, **double** to **int**, **double** to **long double**, **Derived*** to **Base*** (§14.3), **T*** to **void*** (§17.8), **int** to **unsigned int** (§25.5.3)

4. Match using user-defined conversions (§A.5.2.3)

5. Match using the ellipsis **...** in a function declaration (§A.9.3)

If two matches are found at the highest level where a match is found, the call is rejected as ambiguous. The resolution rules are this elaborate primarily to take into account the elaborate rules for built-in numeric types (§A.5.3).

For overload resolution based on multiple arguments, we first find the best match for each argument. If one function is at least as good a match as all other functions for every argument and is a better match than all other functions for one argument, that function is chosen; otherwise the call is ambiguous. For example:

```
void f(int, const string&, double);
void f(int, const char*, int);

f(1,"hello",1);              // OK: call f(int, const char*, int)
f(1,string("hello"),1.0);    // OK: call f(int, const string&, double)
f(1, "hello",1.0);           // error: ambiguous
```

In the last call, the **"hello"** matches **const char*** without a conversion and **const string&** only with a conversion. On the other hand, **1.0** matches **double** without a conversion, but **int** only with a conversion, so neither **f()** is a better match than the other.

If these simplified rules don't agree with what your compiler says and what you thought reasonable, please first consider if your code is more complicated than necessary. If so, simplify your code; if not, consult an expert-level reference.

A.9.2 Default arguments

A general function sometimes needs more arguments than are needed for the most common cases. To handle that, a programmer may provide default arguments to be used if a caller of a function doesn't specify an argument. For example:

```
void f(int, int=0, int=0);
f(1,2,3);
f(1,2);     // calls f(1,2,0)
f(1);       // calls f(1,0,0)
```

Only trailing arguments can be defaulted and left out in a call. For example:

```
void g(int, int =7, int);    // error: default for non-trailing argument
f(1,,1);                     // error: second argument missing
```

Overloading can be an alternative to using default arguments (and vice versa).

A.9.3 Unspecified arguments

It is possible to specify a function without specifying the number or types of its arguments. This is indicated by an ellipsis (...), meaning "and possibly more arguments." For example, here is the declaration of and some calls to what is arguably the most famous C function, **printf()** (§27.6.1, §B.10.2):

```
void printf(const char* format ...);    // takes a format string and maybe more

int x = 'x';
printf("hello, world!");
```

```
printf("print a char '%c'\n",x);    // print the int x as a char
printf("print a string \"%s\"",x);  // shoot yourself in the foot
```

The "format specifiers" in the format string, such as %c and %s, determine if and how further arguments are used. As demonstrated, this can lead to nasty type errors. In C++, unspecified arguments are best avoided.

A.9.4 Linkage specifications

C++ code is often used in the same program as C code; that is, parts of a program are written in C++ (and compiled by a C++ compiler) and other parts in C (and compiled by a C compiler). To ease that, C++ offers *linkage specifications* for the programmer to say that a function obeys C linkage conventions. A C linkage specification can be placed in front of a function declaration:

```
extern "C" void callable_from_C(int);
```

Alternatively it can apply to all declarations in a block:

```
extern "C" {
    void callable_from_C(int);
    int and_this_one_also(double, int*);
    /* . . . */
}
```

For details of use, see §27.2.3.

C doesn't offer function overloading, so you can put a C linkage specification on at most one version of a C++ overloaded function.

A.10 User-defined types

There are two ways for a programmer to define a new (user-defined) type: as a class (**class**, **struct**, or **union**; see §A.12) and as an enumeration (**enum**; see §A.11).

A.10.1 Operator overloading

A programmer can define the meaning of most operators to take operands of one or more user-defined types. It is not possible to change the standard meaning of an operator for built-in types or to introduce a new operator. The name of a user-defined operator ("overloaded operator") is the operator prefixed by the keyword **operator**; for example, the name of a function defining **+** is **operator +**:

```
Matrix operator+(const Matrix&, const Matrix&);
```

For examples, see **std::ostream** (Chapters 10–11), **std::vector** (Chapters 17–19, §B.4), **std::complex** (§B.9.3), and **Matrix** (Chapter 24).

All but the following operators can be user-defined:

?:   .   .*   ::   sizeof   typeid

Functions defining the following operators must be members of a class:

=   [ ]   ()   ->

All other operators can be defined as member functions or as freestanding functions.

Note that every user-defined type has **=** (assignment and initialization), **&** (address of), and **,** (comma) defined by default.

Be restrained and conventional with operator overloading.

A.11 Enumerations

An *enumeration* defines a type with a set of named values (*enumerators*):

```
enum Color { green, yellow, red };
```

By default the value of the first enumerator is 0, so that **green==0**, and the values increase by one, so that **yellow==1** and **red==2**. It is also possible to explicitly define the value of an enumerator:

```
enum Day { Monday=1, Tuesday, Wednesday };
```

Here, we get **Monday==1**, **Tuesday==2**, and **Wednesday==3**.

Note that enumerators are not in the scope of their enumeration but belong to its enclosing scope:

```
int x = green;        // OK
int y = Color::green; // error
```

Enumerators and enumeration values implicitly convert to integers, but integers do not implicitly convert to enumeration types:

```
int x = green;        // OK: implicit Color-to-int conversion
Color c = green;      // OK
c = 2;                // error: no implicit int-to-Color conversion
c = Color(2);         // OK: (unchecked) explicit conversion
int y = c;            // OK: implicit Color-to-int conversion
```

For a discussion of the uses of enumerations, see §9.5.

A.12 Classes

A *class* is a type for which the user defines the representation of its objects and the operations allowed on those objects:

```
class X {
public:
        // user interface
private:
        // implementation
};
```

A variable, function, or type defined within a class declaration is called a *member* of the class. See Chapter 9 for class technicalities.

A.12.1 Member access

A **public** member can be accessed by users; a **private** member can be accessed only by the class's own members:

```
class Date {
public:
        // . . .
        int next_day();
private:
        int y, m, d;
};

void Date::next_day() { return d+1; }      // OK

void f(Date d)
{
        int nd = d.d+1;      // error: Date::d is private
        // . . .
}
```

A **struct** is a class where members are by default **public**:

```
struct S {
        // members (public unless explicitly declared private)
};
```

For more details of member access, including a discussion of **protected**, see §14.3.4.

Members of an object can be accessed through a variable or referenced using the . (dot) operator or through a pointer using the **->** (arrow) operator:

```
struct Date {
        int d, m, y;
        int day() const { return d; } // defined in-class
        int month() const;            // just declared; defined elsewhere
        int year() const;             // just declared; defined elsewhere
};
```

```
Date x;
x.d = 15;               // access through variable
int y = x.day();        // call through variable
Date* p = &x;
p->m = 7;               // access through pointer
int z = p->month();     // call through pointer
```

Members of a class can be referred to using the **::** (scope resolution) operator:

```
int Date::year() const { return y; }   // out-of-class definition
```

Within a member function, we can refer to other members by their unqualified name:

```
struct Date {
        int d, m, y;
        int day() const { return d; }
        // . . .
};
```

Such unqualified names refer to the member of the object for which the member function was called:

```
void f(Date d1, Date d2)
{
        d1.day();       // will access d1.d
        d2.day();       // will access d2.d
        // . . .
}
```

A.12.1.1 The this pointer

If we want to be explicit when referring to the object for which the member function is called, we can use the predefined pointer **this**:

```
struct Date {
    int d, m, y;
    int month() const { return this->m; }
    // . . .
};
```

A member function declared **const** (a **const** member function) cannot modify the value of a member of the object for which it is called:

```
struct Date {
    int d, m, y;
    int month() const { ++m; }  // error: month() is const
    // . . .
};
```

For more information about **const** member functions, see §9.7.4.

A.12.1.2 Friends

A function that is not a member of a class can be granted access to all members through a **friend** declaration. For example:

```
// needs access to Matrix and Vector members:
Vector operator*(const Matrix&, const Vector&);

class Vector {
    friend
    Vector operator*(const Matrix&, const Vector&);  // grant access
    // . . .
};

class Matrix {
    friend
    Vector operator*(const Matrix&, const Vector&);  // grant access
    // . . .
};
```

As shown, this is usually done for functions that need to access two classes. Another use of **friend** is to provide an access function that should not be called using the member access syntax. For example:

```
class Iter {
public:
    int distance_to(const iter& a) const;
    friend int difference(const Iter& a, const Iter& b);
    // . . .
};

void f(Iter& p, Iter& q)
{
    int x = p.distance_to(q);    // invoke using member syntax
    int y = difference(p,q);     // invoke using "mathematical syntax"
    // . . .
}
```

Note that a function declared **friend** cannot also be declared **virtual**.

A.12.2 Class member definitions

Class members that are integer constants, functions, or types can be defined/initialized either *in-class* or *out-of-class*:

```
struct S {
    static const int c = 1;
    static const int c2;

    void f() { }
    void f2();

    struct SS { int a; };
    struct SS2;
};
```

The members that were not defined in-class must be defined "elsewhere":

```
const int S::c2 = 7;

void S::f2() { }

struct S::SS2 { int m; };
```

The **static const int** members are an odd special case. They just define symbolic integer constants and do not take up memory in the object. Non-**static** data members do not require separate definition, cannot be separately defined, and cannot have in-class initializers:

```
struct X {
        int x;
        int y = 7;                         // error: non-static data members
                                           // cannot have in-class initializers
        static int z = 7;                  // error: non-const data members
                                           // cannot have in-class initializers
        static const string ae = "7";      // error: non-integral type
                                           // cannot have in-class initializers
        static const int oe = 7;           // OK: static const integral type
};

        int X::x = 7;   // error: non-static data members cannot be defined out-of-class
```

If you want to ensure initialization of non-**static**, non-**const** data members, do it in constructors.

Function members do not occupy space in an object:

```
struct S {
        int m;
        void f();
};
```

Here, **sizeof(S)==sizof(int)**. That's not actually guaranteed by the standard, but it is true for all implementations we know of. But note that a class with a virtual function has one "hidden" member to allow virtual calls (§14.3.1).

A.12.3 Construction, destruction, and copy

You can define the meaning of initialization for an object of a class by defining one or more *constructors*. A constructor is a member function with the same name as its class and no return type:

```
class Date {
public:
        Date(int yy, int mm, int dd) :y(yy), m(mm), d(dd) { }
        // . . .
private:
        int y,m,d;
};
```

```
Date d1(2006,11,15);    // OK: initialization done by the constructor
Date d2;                // error: no initializers
Date d3(11,15);         // error: bad initializers (three initializers required)
```

Note that data members can be initialized by using an initializer list in the constructor (a base and member initializer list). Members will be initialized in the order in which they are declared in the class.

Constructors are typically used to establish a class's invariant and to acquire resources (§9.4.2–3).

Class objects are constructed "from the bottom up," starting with base class objects (§14.3.1) in declaration order, followed by members in declaration order, followed by the code in the constructor itself. Unless the programmer does something really strange, this ensures that every object is constructed before use.

Unless declared **explicit**, a single-argument constructor defines an implicit conversion from its argument type to its class:

```
class Date {
public:
    Date(string);
    explicit Date(long);    // use an integer encoding of date
    // . . .
};

void f(Date);

Date d1 = "June 5, 1848";    // OK
f("June 5, 1848");           // OK

Date d2 = 2007*12*31+6*31+5;    // error: Date(long) is explicit
f(2007*12*31+6*31+5);           // error: Date(long) is explicit

Date d3(2007*12*31+6*31+5);            // OK
Date d4 = Date(2007*12*31+6*31+5);     // OK
f(Date(2007*12*31+6*31+5));            // OK
```

Unless a class has bases or members that require explicit arguments, and unless the class has other constructors, a default constructor is automatically generated. This default constructor initializes each base or member that has a default constructor (leaving members without default constructors uninitialized). For example:

```
struct S {
    string name, address;
    int x;
};
```

This **S** has an implicit constructor **S()** that initializes **name** and **address**, but not **x**.

A.12.3.1 Destructors

You can define the meaning of an object being destroyed (e.g., going out of scope) by defining a *destructor*. The name of a destructor is ~ (the complement operator) followed by the class name:

```
class Vector { // vector of doubles
public:
      explicit Vector(int s) : sz(s), p(new double[s]) { }   // constructor
      ~Vector() { delete[] p; }                              // destructor
      // . . .
private:
      int sz;
      double* p;
};

void f(int ss)
{
      Vector v(s);
      // . . .
} // v will be destroyed upon exit from f(); Vector's destructor will be called for v
```

Destructors that invoke the destructors of members of a class can be generated by the compiler, and if a class is to be used as a base class, it usually needs a **virtual** destructor; see §17.5.2.

A destructor is typically used to "clean up" and release resources.

Class objects are destructed "from the top down" starting with the code in the destructor itself, followed by members in declaration order, followed by the base class objects in declaration order, that is, in reverse order of construction (§A.12.3.1).

A.12.3.2 Copying

You can define the meaning of *copying* an object of a class:

```
class Vector { // vector of doubles
public:
      explicit Vector(int s) : sz(s), p(new double[s]) { }   // constructor
      ~Vector() { delete[] p; }                              // destructor
      Vector(const Vector&);                                 // copy constructor
      Vector& operator=(const Vector&);                      // copy assignment
      // . . .
```

```
private:
    int sz;
    double* p;
};

void f(int ss)
{
    Vector v(s);
    Vector v2 = v;    // use copy constructor
    // . . .
    v = v2;           // use copy assignment
    // . . .
}
```

By default (that is, unless you define a copy constructor and a copy assignment), the compiler will generate copy operations for you. The default meaning of copy is memberwise copy; see also §14.2.4 and §18.2.

A.12.4 Derived classes

A class can be defined as derived from other classes, in which case it inherits the members of the classes from which it is derived (its base classes):

```
struct B {
    int mb;
    void fb() { };
};

class D : B {
    int md;
    void fd();
};
```

Here **B** has two members, **mb** and **fb()**, whereas **D** has four members, **mb**, **fb()**, **md**, and **fd()**.

Like members, bases can be **public** or **private**:

```
Class DD : public B1, private B2 {
    // . . .
};
```

So, the **public** members of **B1** become **public** members of **DD**, whereas the **public** members of **B2** become **private** members of **DD**. A derived class has no special access to members of its bases, so **DD** does not have access to the **private** members of **B1** or **B2**.

A class with more than one direct base class (such as **DD**) is said to use *multiple inheritance*.

A pointer to a derived class, **D**, can be implicitly converted to a pointer to its base class, **B**, provided **B** is accessible and is unambiguous in **D**. For example:

```
struct B { };
struct B1: B { };      // B is a public base of B1
struct B2: B { };      // B is a public base of B2
struct C { };
struct DD : B1, B2, private C { };


DD* p = new DD;
B1* pb1 = p;  // OK
B* pb = p;      // error: ambiguous: B1::B or B2::B
C* pc = p;      // error: DD::C is private
```

Similarly, a reference to a derived class can be implicitly converted to an unambiguous and accessible base class.

For more information about derived classes, see §14.3. For more information about **protected**, see an expert-level textbook or reference.

A.12.4.1 Virtual functions

A *virtual function* is a member function that defines a calling interface to functions of the same name taking the same argument types in derived classes. When calling a virtual function, the function invoked by the call will be the one defined for the most derived class. The derived class is said to override the virtual function in the base class.

```
class Shape {
public:
     virtual void draw();    // "virtual" means "can be overridden"
     virtual ~Shape() { }    // virtual destructor
     // . . .
};


class Circle : public Shape {
public:
     void draw();  // override Shape::draw
     ~Circle();      // override Shape::~Shape()
     // . . .
};
```

Basically, the virtual functions of a base class (here, **Shape**) define a calling interface for the derived class (here, **Circle**):

```
void f(Shape& s)
{
    // . . .
    s.draw();
}

void g()
{
    Circle c(Point(0,0), 4);
    f(c);      // will call Circle's draw
}
```

Note that **f()** doesn't know about **Circles**, only about **Shapes**. An object of a class with a virtual function contains one extra pointer to allow it to find the set of overriding functions; see §14.3.

Note that a class with virtual functions usually needs a virtual destructor (as **Shape** has); see §17.5.2.

A.12.4.2 Abstract classes

An *abstract class* is a class that can be used only as a base class. You cannot make an object of an abstract class:

```
Shape s;        // error: Shape is abstract

class Circle : public Shape {
public:
    void draw();   // override Shape::draw
    // . . .
};

Circle c(p,20);      // OK: Circle is not abstract
```

The most common way of making a class abstract is to define at least one pure virtual function. A *pure virtual function* is a virtual function that requires overriding:

```
class Shape {
public:
    virtual void draw() = 0;      // =0 means "pure"
    // . . .
};
```

See §14.3.5.

The rarer, but equally effective, way of making a class abstract is to declare all its constructors protected (§14.2.1).

A.12.4.3 Generated operations

When you define a class, it will by default have several operations defined for its objects:

- Default constructor
- Copy operations (copy assignment and copy initialization)
- Destructor

Each is (again by default) defined to apply recursively to each of its base classes and members. Construction is done "bottom-up," that is, base before members. Destruction is done "top-down," that is, members before bases. Members and bases are constructed in order of appearance and destroyed in the opposite order. That way, constructor and destructor code always relies on well-defined base and member objects. For example:

```
struct D : B1, B2 {
    M1 m1;
    M2 m2;
};
```

Assuming that **B1**, **B2**, **M1**, and **M2** are defined, we can now write

```
void f()
{
    D d;            // default initialization
    D d2 = d;       // copy initialization
    d = D();        // default initialization followed by copy assignment
}  // d and d2 are destroyed here
```

For example, the default initialization of **d** invokes four default constructors (in order): **B1::B1()**, **B2::B2()**, **M1::M1()**, and **M2::M2()**. If one of those doesn't exist or can't be called, the construction of **d** fails. The destruction of **d** invokes four destructors (in order): **M2::~M2()**, **M1::~M1()**, **B2::~B2()**, and **B1::~B1()**. If one of those doesn't exist or can't be called, the destruction of **d** fails. Each of these constructors and destructors can be either user-defined or generated.

The implicit (compiler-generated) default constructor is not defined (generated) if a class has a user-defined constructor.

A.12.5 Bitfields

A *bitfield* is a mechanism for packing many small values into a word or to match an externally imposed bit-layout format (such as a device register). For example:

```
struct PPN {
      unsigned int PFN : 22;
      int : 3;                    // unused
      unsigned int CCA;
      bool nonreacheable;
      bool dirty;
      bool valid;
      bool global;
};
```

Packing the bitfields into a word left to right leads to a layout of bits in a word like this (see §25.5.5):

position:	31:		9:	6:	3:	2:	1:	0:
PPN:	22		3	3	1	1	1	1
name:	PFN		unused	CCA	/ dirty / global

nonreachable   valid

A bitfield need not have a name, but if it doesn't, you can't access it.

Surprisingly, packing many small values into a single word does not necessarily save space. In fact, using one of those values often wastes space compared to using a **char** or an **int** to represent even a single bit. The reason is that it takes several instructions (which have to be stored in memory somewhere) to extract a bit from a word and to write a single bit of a word without modifying other bits of a word. Don't try to use bitfields to save space unless you need lots of objects with tiny data fields.

A.12.6 Unions

A *union* is a class where all members are allocated starting at the same address. A union can hold only one element at a time, and when a member is read it must be the same as was last written. For example:

```
union U {
      int x;
      double d;
}

U a;
a.x = 7;
```

```
int x1 = a.x;    // OK
a.d = 7.7;
int x2 = a.x;    // oops
```

The rule requiring consistent reads and writes is not checked by the compiler. You have been warned.

A.13 Templates

A *template* is a class or a function parameterized by a set of types and/or integers:

```
template<class T>
class vector {
public:
      // . . .
      int size() const;
private:
      int sz;
      T* p;
};

template<class T>
int vector<T>::size() const
{
      return sz;
}
```

In a template argument list, **class** means type; **typename** is an equivalent alternative. A member function of a template class is implicitly a template function with the same template arguments as its class.

Integer template arguments must be constant expressions:

```
template<typename T, int sz>
class Fixed_array {
public:
      T a[sz];
      // . . .
      int size() const { return sz; };
};

Fixed_array<char,256> x1;      // OK
int var = 226;
Fixed_array<char,var> x2;      // error: non-const template argument
```

A.13.1 Template arguments

Arguments for a template class are specified whenever its name is used:

```
vector<int> v1;        // OK
vector v2;             // error: template argument missing
vector<int,2> v3;      // error: too many template arguments
vector<2> v4;          // error: type template argument expected
```

Arguments for template functions are typically deduced from the function arguments:

```
template<class T>
T find(vector<T>& v, int i)
{
        return v[i];
}

vector<int> v1;
vector<double> v2;
// . . .
int x1 = find(v1,2);    // find()'s T is int
int x2 = find(v2,2);    // find()'s T is double
```

It is possible to define a template function for which it is not possible to deduce its template arguments from its function arguments. In that case we must specify the missing template arguments explicitly (exactly as for class templates). For example:

```
template<class T, class U> T* make(const U& u) { return new T(u); }
int* pi = make<int>(2);
Node* pn = make<Node>(make_pair("hello",17));
```

This works if a **Node** can be initialized by a **pair<const char *,int>** (§B.6.3). Only trailing template arguments can be left out of an explicit argument specialization (to be deduced).

A.13.2 Template instantiation

A version of a template for a specific set of template arguments is called a *specialization*. The process of generating specializations from a template and a set of arguments is called *template instantiation*. Usually, the compiler generates a specialization from a template and a set of template arguments, but the programmer can also define a specific specialization. This is usually done when a general template is un-suitable for a particular set of arguments. For example:

```
template<class T> struct Compare {    // general compare
    bool operator()(const T& a, const T& b) const
    {
        return a<b;
    }
};


template<> struct Compare<const char*> {    // compare C-style strings
    bool operator()(const char* a, const char* b) const
    {
        return strcmp(a,b)==0;
    }
};


Compare<int> c2;            // general compare
Compare<const char*> c;    // C-style string compare

bool b1 = c2(1,2);            // use general compare
bool b2 = c("asd","dfg");    // use C-style string compare
```

For functions, the rough equivalent is achieved through overloading:

```
template<class T> bool compare(const T& a, const T& b)
{
    return a<b;
}

bool compare (const char* a, const char* b)    // compare C-style strings
{
    return strcmp(a,b)==0;
}

bool b3 = compare(2,3);            // use general compare
bool b4 = compare("asd","dfg");    // use C-style string compare
```

Separate compilation of templates (i.e., keeping declarations only in header files and unique definitions in .cpp files) does not work portably, so if a template needs to be used in several .cpp files, put its complete definition in a header file.

A.13.3 Template member types

A template can have members that are types and members that are not types (such as data members and member functions). This means that in general, it can be hard to tell whether a member name refers to a type or to a non-type. For language-technical reasons, the compiler has to know, so occasionally we must tell it. For that, we use the keyword **typename**. For example:

```
template<class T> struct Vec {
        typedef T value_type;      // a member type
        static int count;          // a data member
        // . . .
};

template<class T> void my_fct(Vec<T>& v)
{
        int x = Vec<T>::count;     // by default members names
                                   // are assumed to refer to non-types
        v.count = 7;               // a simpler way to refer to a non-type member
        typename Vec<T>::value_type xx = x;    // "typename" is needed here
        // . . .
}
```

For more information about templates, see Chapter 19.

A.14 Exceptions

An exception is used (with a **throw** statement) to tell a caller about an error that cannot be handled locally. For example, move **Bad_size** out of **Vector**:

```
struct Bad_size {
        int sz;
        Bad_size(int s) : ss(s) { }
};

class Vector {
        Vector(int s) { if (s<0 || maxsize<s) throw Bad_size(s); }
        // . . .
};
```

Usually, we throw a type that is defined specifically to represent a particular error. A caller can catch an exception:

```
void f(int x)
{
    try {
        Vector v(x);    // may throw
        // . . .
    }
    catch (Bad_size bs) {
        cerr << "Vector with bad size (" << bs.sz << ")\n";
        // . . .
    }
}
```

A "catch all" clause can be used to catch every exception:

```
try {
    // . . .
} catch (...) {  // catch all exceptions
    // . . .
}
```

Usually, the RAII ("Resource Acquisition Is Initialization") technique is better (simpler, easier, more reliable) than using lots of explicit **trys** and **catch**es; see §19.5.

A **throw** without an argument (i.e., **throw;**) re-throws the current exception. For example:

```
try {
    // . . .
} catch (Some_exception& e) {
    // do local cleanup
    throw;      // let my caller do the rest
}
```

You can define your own types for use as exceptions. The standard library defines a few exception types that you can also use; see §B.2.1. Never use a built-in type as an exception (someone else might have done that and your exceptions might be confused with those).

When an exception is thrown, the run-time support system for C++ searches "up the call stack" for a **catch**-clause with a type that matches the type of the object thrown; that is, it looks through **try**-statements in the function that threw, then through the function that called the function that threw, then through the function that called the function that called, etc., until it finds a match. If it doesn't find a match, the program terminates. In each function encountered in this search of a matching **catch**-clause and in each scope on the way, destructors are called to clean up. This process is called *stack unwinding*.

An object is considered constructed once its constructor has completed and will then be destroyed during unwinding or any other exit from its scope. This implies that partially constructed objects (with some members or bases constructed and some not), arrays, and variables in a scope are correctly handled. Subobjects are destroyed if and only if they have been constructed.

Do not throw an exception so that it leaves a destructor. This implies that a destructor should not fail. For example:

> **X::~X() { if (in_a_real_mess()) throw Mess(); }**   // never do this!

The primary reason for this Draconian advice is that if a destructor throws (and doesn't itself catch the exception) during unwinding, we wouldn't know which exception to handle. It is worthwhile to go to great lengths to avoid a destructor exiting by a throw because we know of no systematic way of writing correct code where that can happen. In particular, no standard library facility is guaranteed to work if that happens.

A.15 Namespaces

A *namespace* groups related declarations together and is used to prevent name clashes:

```
int a;

namespace Foo {
        int a;
        void f(int i)
        {
                a+= i;    // that's Foo's a (Foo::a)
        }
}

void f(int);

int main()
{
        a = 7;        // that's the global a (::a)
        f(2);         // that's the global f (::f)
        Foo::f(3);    // that's Foo's f
```

```
        ::f(4);          // that's the global f (::f)
    }
```

Names can be explicitly qualified by their namespace name (e.g., **Foo::f(3)**) or by
:: (e.g., **::f(2)**), indicating the global scope.

All names from a namespace (here, the standard library namespace, **std**) can
be made accessible by a single namespace directive:

```
    using namespace std;
```

Be restrained in the use of **using** directives. The notational convenience offered
by a **using** directive is achieved at the cost of potential name clashes. In particular, avoid **using** directives in header files. A single name from a namespace can be
made available by a namespace declaration:

```
    using Foo::g;
    g(2);     // that's Foo's g (Foo::g)
```

For more information about namespaces, see §8.7.

A.16 Aliases

We can define an *alias* for a name; that is, we can define a symbolic name that
means exactly the same as what it refers to (for most uses of the name):

```
    typedef int* Pint;                          // Pint means pointer to int

    namespace Long_library_name { /* . . . */ }
    namespace Lib = Long_library_name;  // Lib means Long_library_name

    int x = 7;
    int& r = x;                                 // r means x
```

A reference (§8.5.5, §A.8.3) is a run-time mechanism, referring to objects. The
typedef (§20.5, §27.3.1) and **namespace** aliases are compile-time mechanisms, referring to names. In particular, a **typedef** does not introduce a new type, just a
new name for a type. For example:

```
    typedef char* Pchar;      // Pchar is a name for char*
    Pchar p = "Idefix";       // OK: p is a char*
    char* q = p;              // OK: p and q are both char*s
    int x = strlen(p);        // OK: p is a char*
```

A.17 Preprocessor directives

Every C++ implementation includes a *preprocessor*. In principle, the preprocessor runs before the compiler proper and transforms the source code we wrote into what the compiler sees. In reality, this action is integrated into the compiler and uninteresting except when it causes problems. Every line starting with # is a preprocessor directive.

A.17.1 #include

We have used the preprocessor extensively to include headers. For example:

```
#include "file.h"
```

This is a directive that tells the preprocessor to include the contents of **file.h** at the point of the source text where the directive occurs. For standard headers, we can also use < . . . > instead of " . . . ". For example:

```
#include<vector>
```

That is the recommended notation for standard header inclusion.

A.17.2 #define

The preprocessor implements a form of character manipulation called *macro sub-stitution*. For example, we can define a name for a character string:

```
#define FOO bar
```

Now, whenever **FOO** is seen, **bar** will be substituted:

```
int FOO = 7;
int FOOL = 9;
```

Given that, the compiler will see

```
int bar = 7;
int FOOL = 9;
```

Note that the preprocessor knows enough about C++ names not to replace the **FOO** that's part of **FOOL**.
    You can also define macros that take parameters:

```
#define MAX(x,y) (((x)>(y))?(x) : (y))
```

And we can use it like this:

```
int xx = MAX(FOO+1,7);
int yy = MAX(++xx,9);
```

This will expand to

```
int xx = (((bar+1)>( 7))?(bar+1) : (7));
int yy = (((++xx)>( 9))?(++xx) : (9));
```

Note how the parentheses were necessary to get the right result for **FOO+1**. Also note that **xx** was incremented twice in a very non-obvious way. Macros are immensely popular – primarily because C programmers have few alternatives to using them. Common header files define thousands of macros. You have been warned!

If you must use macros, the convention is to name them using **ALL_CAPI-TAL_LETTERS**. No ordinary name should be in all capital letters. Don't depend on others to follow this sound advice. For example, we have found a macro called **max** in an otherwise reputable header file.

See also §27.8.

B

Standard Library Summary

"All complexities should,
if possible,
be buried out of sight."

—David J. Wheeler

This appendix summarizes key C++ standard library facilities. The summary is selective and geared to novices who want to get an overview of the standard library facilities and explore a bit beyond the sequence of topics in the book.

B.1 Overview

This appendix is a reference. It is not intended to be read from beginning to end like a chapter. It (more or less) systematically describes key elements of the C++ standard library. It is not a complete reference, though; it is just a summary with a few key examples. Often, you will need to look at the chapters for a more complete explanation. Note also that this summary does not attempt to equal the precision and terminology of the standard. For more information, see Stroustrup, *The C++ Programming Language*. The complete definition is the ISO C++ standard, but that document is not intended for or suitable for novices. Don't forget to use your online documentation.

What use is a selective (and therefore incomplete) summary? You can quickly look for a known operation or quickly scan a section to see what common operations are available. You may very well have to look elsewhere for a detailed explanation, but that's fine: now you have a clue as to what to look for. Also, this summary contains cross-references to tutorial material in the chapters. This appendix provides a compact overview of standard library facilities. Please do not try to memorize the information here; that's not what it is for. On the contrary, this appendix is a tool that can save you from spurious memorization.

This is a place to look for useful facilities – instead of trying to invent them yourself. Everything in the standard library (and especially everything featured in this appendix) has been useful to large groups of people. A standard library facility is almost certainly better designed, better implemented, better documented, and more portable than anything you could design and implement in a hurry. So when you can, prefer a standard library facility over "home brew." Doing so will also make your code easier for others to understand.

If you are a sensible person, you'll find the sheer mass of facilities intimidating. Don't worry; ignore what you don't need. If you are a "details person," you'll find much missing. However, completeness is what the expert-level guides and your online documentation offer. In either case, you'll find much that will seem mysterious, and possibly interesting. Explore some of it!

B.1.1 Header files

The interfaces to standard library facilities are defined in headers. The list below contains a few headers that are not part of the C++ 1998 ISO standard, but that will be part of the next standard and are widely available. The latter ones are marked "C++0x," and their use may require installation and/or use of a namespace different from **std** (e.g., **tr1** or **boost**). Use this section to gain an overview of what is available and to help guess where a facility might be defined and described:

The STL (containers, iterators, and algorithms)	
<algorithm>	algorithms; **sort()**, **find()**, etc. (§B.5, §21.1)
<array>	fixed-sized array (C++0x) (§20.9)
<bitset>	array of **bool** (§25.5.2)
<deque>	double-ended queue
<functional>	function objects (§B.6.2)
<iterator>	iterators (§B.4.4)
<list>	doubly-linked list (§B.4, §20.4)
<map>	(key,value) **map** and **multimap** (§B.4, §21.6.1–3)
<memory>	allocators for containers
<queue>	**queue** and **priority_queue**
<set>	**set** and **multiset** (§B.4, §21.6.5)

The STL (containers, iterators, and algorithms) (*continued*)

<stack>	**stack**
<unordered_map>	hash maps (C++0x) (§21.6.4)
<unordered_set>	hash sets (C++0x)
<utility>	operators and **pair** (§B.6.3)
<vector>	**vector** (dynamically expandable) (§B.4, §20.8)

I/O streams

<iostream>	I/O stream objects (§B.7)
<fstream>	file streams (§B.7.1)
<sstream>	**string** streams (§B.7.1)
<iosfwd>	declare (but don't define) I/O stream facilities
<ios>	I/O streams base classes
<streambuf>	stream buffers
<istream>	input streams (§B.7)
<ostream>	output streams (§B.7)
<iomanip>	formatting and manipulators (§B.7.6)

String manipulation

<string>	**string** (§B.8.2)
<regex>	regular expressions (C++0x) (Chapter 23)

Numerics

<complex>	complex numbers and arithmetic (§B.9.3)
<random>	random number generation (C++0x)
<valarray>	numeric arrays
<numeric>	generalized numeric algorithms, e.g., **accumulate()** (§B.9.5)
<limits>	numerical limits (§B.9.1)

Utility and language support	
<exception>	exception types (§B.2.1)
<stdexcept>	exception hierarchy (§B.2.1)
<locale>	culture-specific formatting
<typeinfo>	standard type information (from **typeid**)
<new>	allocation and deallocation functions

C standard libraries	
<cstring>	C-style string manipulation (§B.10.3)
<cstdio>	C-style I/O (§B.10.2)
<ctime>	**clock()**, **time()**, etc. (§B.10.5)
<cmath>	standard floating-point math functions (§B.9.2)
<cstdlib>	etc. functions: **abort()**, **abs()**, **malloc()**, **qsort()**, etc. (Chapter 27)
<cerrno>	C-style error handling (§24.8)
<cassert>	assert macro (§27.9)
<clocale>	culture-specific formatting
<climits>	C-style numerical limits (§B.9.1)
<cfloat>	C-style floating-point limits (§B.9.1)
<cstddef>	C language support; **size_t**, etc.
<cstdarg>	macros for variable argument processing
<csetjmp>	**stejmp()** and **longjmp()** (never use those)
<csignal>	signal handling
<cwchar>	wide characters
<cctype>	character type classification (§B.8.1)
<cwctype>	wide character type classification

For each of the C standard library headers, there is also a version without the initial **c** in its name and with a trailing **.h**, such as **<time.h>** for **<ctime>**. The **.h** versions define global names rather than names in namespace **std**.

Some – but not all – of the facilities defined in these headers are described in the sections below and in the chapters. If you need more information, look at your online documentation or an expert-level C++ book.

B.1.2 Namespace std

The standard library facilities are defined in namespace **std**, so to use them, you need an explicit qualification, a **using** declaration, or a **using** directive:

```
std::string s;              // explicit qualification

using std::vector;          // using declaration
vector<int>v(7);

using namespace std;        // using directive
map<string,double> m;
```

In this book, we have used the **using** directive for **std**. Be very frugal with **using** directives; see §A.15.

B.1.3 Description style

A full description of even a simple standard library operation, such as a constructor or an algorithm, can take pages. Consequently, we use an extremely abbreviated style of presentation. For example:

Examples of notation	
p=op(b,e,x)	**op** does something to the range [**b:e**) and **x**, returning **p**.
foo(x)	**foo** does something to **x**, but returns no result.
bar(b,e,x)	Does **x** have something to do with [**b:e**)?

We try to be mnemonic in our choice of identifiers, so **b,e** will be iterators specifying a range, **p** a pointer or an iterator, and **x** some value, all depending on context. In this notation, only the commentary distinguishes no result from a Boolean result, so you can confuse those if you try hard enough. For an operation returning **bool**, the explanation usually ends with a question mark.

Where an algorithm follows the usual pattern of returning the end of an input sequence to indicate "failure," "not found," etc. (§B.3.1), we do not mention that explicitly.

B.2 Error handling

The standard library consists of components developed over a period of almost 40 years. Thus, their style and approaches to error handling are not consistent.

- C-style libraries consist of functions, many of which set **errno** to indicate that an error happened; see §24.8.

- Many algorithms operating on a sequence of elements return an iterator to the one-past-the-last element to indicate "not found" or "failure."

- The I/O streams library relies on a state in each stream to reflect errors and may (if the user requests it) throw exceptions to indicate errors; see §10.6, §B.7.2.

- Some standard library components, such as **vector**, **string**, and **bitset**, throw exceptions to indicate errors.

The standard library is designed so that all facilities obey "the basic guarantee" (see §19.5.3); that is, even if an exception is thrown, no resource (such as memory) is leaked and no invariant for a standard library class is broken.

B.2.1 Exceptions

Some standard library facilities report errors by throwing exceptions:

Standard library exceptions	
bitset	throws **invalid_argument, out_of_range, overflow_error**
dynamic_cast	throws **bad_cast** if it cannot perform a conversion
iostream	throws **ios_base::failure** if exceptions are enabled
new	throws **bad_alloc** if it cannot allocate memory
regex	throws **regex_error**
string	throws **length_error, out_of_range**
typeid	throws **bad_typeid** if it cannot deliver a **type_info**
vector	throws **out_of_range**

These exceptions may be encountered in any code that directly or indirectly uses these facilities. Unless you *know* that no facility is used in a way that could throw an exception, it is a good idea to always catch one of the root classes of the standard library exception hierarchy (such as **exception**) somewhere (e.g., in **main()**).

We strongly recommend that you do not **throw** built-in types, such as **int** and C-style strings. Instead, throw objects of types specifically defined to be used as exceptions. A class derived from the standard library class **exception** can be used for that:

```
class exception {
public:
```

```
        exception();
        exception(const exception&);
        exception& operator=(const exception&);
        virtual ~exception();
        virtual const char* what() const;
    };
```

The **what()** function can be used to obtain a string that is supposed to indicate something about the error that caused the exception.

This hierarchy of standard exception classes may help by providing a classification of exceptions:

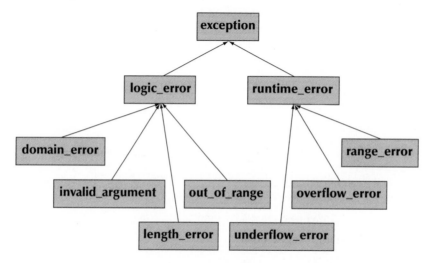

You can define an exception by deriving from a standard library exception like this:

```
struct My_error : runtime_error {
    My_error(int x) : interesting_value(x) { }
    int interesting_value;
    const char* what() const { return "My_error"; }
};
```

B.3 Iterators

Iterators are the glue that ties standard library algorithms to their data. Conversely, you can say that iterators are the mechanism used to minimize an algorithm's dependence on the data structures on which it operates (§20.3):

sort, find, search, copy, …, my_very_own_algorithm, your_code, …

Iterators

vector, list, map, array, …, my_container, your_container,…

B.3.1 Iterator model

An iterator is akin to a pointer in that it provides operations for indirect access (e.g., * for dereferencing) and for moving to a new element (e.g., **++** for moving to the next element). A sequence of elements is defined by a pair of iterators defining a half-open range [**begin:end**):

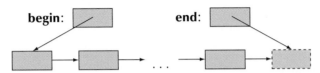

That is, **begin** points to the first element of the sequence and **end** points to one beyond the last element of the sequence. Never read from or write to *end. Note that the empty sequence has **begin==end**; that is, [**p:p**) is the empty sequence for any iterator **p**.

To read a sequence, an algorithm usually takes a pair of iterators (**b,e**) and iterates using **++** until the end is reached:

```
while (b!=e) {    // use != rather than <
      // do something
      ++b;     // go to next element
}
```

Algorithms that search for something in a sequence usually return the end of the sequence to indicate "not found"; for example:

```
p = find(v.begin(),v.end(),x);        // look for x in v
if (p!=v.end()) {
      // x found at p
}
else {
      // x not found in [v.begin():v.end())
}
```

See §20.3.

Algorithms that write to a sequence often are given only an iterator to its first element. In that case, it is the programmer's responsibility not to write beyond the end of that sequence. For example:

```
template<class Iter> void f(Iter p, int n)
{
        while (n>0) *p = --n;
}


vector<int> v(10);
f(v.begin(),v.size());      // OK
f(v.begin(),1000);          // big trouble
```

Some standard library implementations range check – that is, throw an exception – for that last call of f(), but you can't rely on that for portable code; many implementations don't check.

The operations on iterators are:

Iterator operations	
++p	Pre-increment: make **p** refer to the next element in the sequence or to one-beyond-the-last-element ("advance one element"); the resulting value is **p+1**.
p++	Post-increment: make **p** refer to the next element in the sequence or to one-beyond-the-last-element ("advance one element"); the resulting value is **p** (before the increment).
--p	Pre-decrement: make **p** point to previous element ("go back one element"); the resulting value is **p−1**.
p--	Post-decrement: make **p** point to previous element ("go back one element"); the resulting value is **p** (before the decrement).
*p	Access (dereference): ***p** refers to the element pointed to by **p**.
p[n]	Access (subscripting): **p[n]** refers to the element pointed to by **p+n**; equivalent to ***(p+n)**.
p->m	Access (member access); equivalent to **(*p).m**.
p==q	Equality: true if **p** and **q** point to the same element or both point to one-beyond-the-last-element.
p!=q	Inequality: !(p==q).

Iterator operations (*continued*)	
p<q	Does **p** point to an element before what **q** points to?
p<=q	**p<q || p==q**
p>q	Does **p** point to an element after what **q** points to?
p>=q	**p>q || p==q**
p+=n	Advance **n**: make **p** point to the **n**th element after the one it points to.
p−=n	Advance **−n**: make **p** point to the **n**th element before the one it points to.
q=p+n	**q** points to the **n**th element after the one pointed to by **p**.
q=p−n	**q** points to the **n**th element before the one pointed to by **p**; afterward, we have **q+n==p**.
advance(p,n)	Advance: like **p+=n**; **advance()** can be used even if **p** is not a random-access iterator; it may take **n** steps (through a list).
x=difference(p,q)	Difference: like **q−p**; **difference()** can be used even if **p** is not a random-access iterator; it may take **n** steps (through a list).

Note that not every kind of iterator (§B.3.2) supports every iterator operation.

B.3.2 Iterator categories

The standard library provides five kinds of iterators (five "iterator categories"):

Iterator categories	
input iterator	We can iterate forward using **++** and read each element once only using *****. We can compare iterators using **==** and **!=**. This is the kind of iterator that **istream** offers; see §21.7.2.
output iterator	We can iterate forward using **++** and write each element once only using *****. This is the kind of iterator that **ostream** offers; see §21.7.2.
forward iterator	We can iterate forward repeatedly using **++** and read and write (unless the elements are **const**) elements using *****. If it points to a class object, it can use **−>** to access a member.

Iterator categories (*continued*)	
bidirectional iterator	We can iterate forward (using **++**) and backward (using **−−**) and read and write (unless the elements are **const**) elements using *. This is the kind of iterator that **list**, **map**, and **set** offer.
randomaccess iterator	We can iterate forward (using **++** or **+=**) and backward (using **—** or **−=**) and read and write (unless the elements are **const**) elements using * or []. We can subscript, add an integer to a random-access iterator using **+**, and subtract an integer using **−**. We can find the distance between two random-access iterators to the same sequence by subtracting one from the other. We can compare iterators using **<**, **<=**, **>**, and **>=**. This is the kind of iterator that **vector** offers.

Logically, these iterators are organized in a hierarchy (§20.8):

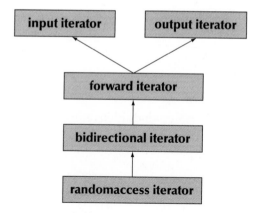

Note that since the iterator categories are not classes, this hierarchy is not a class hierarchy implemented using derivation. If you need to do something advanced with iterator categories, look for **iterator_traits** in an advanced reference.

Each container supplies iterators of a specified category:

- **vector** – random access
- **list** – bidirectional
- **deque** – random access
- **bitset** – none

- **set** – bidirectional
- **multiset** – bidirectional
- **map** – bidirectional
- **multimap** – bidirectional
- **unordered_set** – forward
- **unordered_multiset** – forward
- **unordered_map** – forward
- **unordered_multimap** – forward

B.4 Containers

A container holds a sequence of objects. The elements of the sequence are of the member type called **value_type**. The most commonly useful containers are:

Sequence containers	
array<T,N>	fixed-size array of **N** elements of type **T** (C++0x)
deque<T>	double-ended queue
list<T>	doubly-linked list
vector<T>	dynamic array of elements of type **T**

Associative containers	
map<K,V>	map from **K** to **V**; a sequence of (**K**,**V**) pairs
multimap<K,V>	map from **K** to **V**; duplicate keys allowed
set<K>	set of **K**
multiset<K>	set of **K** (duplicate keys allowed)
unordered_map<K,V>	map from **K** to **V** using a hash function (C++0x)
unordered_multimap<K,V>	map from **K** to **V** using a hash function; duplicate keys allowed (C++0x)
unordered_set<K>	set of **K** using a hash function (C++0x)
unordered_multiset<K>	set of **K** using a hash function; duplicate keys allowed (C++0x)

Container adaptors	
priority_queue\<T>	priority queue
queue\<T>	queue with **push()** and **pop()**
stack\<T>	stack with **push()** and **pop()**

These containers are defined in **\<vector>**, **\<list>**, etc. (see §B.1.1). The sequence containers are contiguously allocated or linked lists of elements of their **value_type** (**T** in the notation used above). The associative containers are linked structures (trees) with nodes of their **value_type** (**pair(K,V)** in the notation used above). The sequence of a **set**, **map**, or **multimap** is ordered by its key values (**K**). The sequence of an **unordered_*** does not have a guaranteed order. A **multimap** differs from a **map** in that a key value may occur many times. Container adaptors are containers with specialized operations constructed from other containers.

If in doubt, use **vector**. Unless you have a solid reason not to, use **vector**.

A container uses an "allocator" to allocate and deallocate memory (§19.3.6). We do not cover allocators here; if necessary, see an expert-level reference. By default, an allocator uses **new** and **delete** when it needs to acquire or release memory for its elements.

Where meaningful, an access operation exists in two versions: one for **const** and one for non-**const** objects (§18.4).

This section lists the common and almost common members of the standard containers. For more details, see Chapter 20. Members that are peculiar to a specific container, such as **list**'s **splice()**, are not listed; see an expert-level reference.

Some data types provide much of what is required from a standard container, but not all. We sometimes refer to those as "almost containers." The most interesting of those are:

"Almost containers"	
T[n] built-in array	no **size()** or other member functions; prefer a container, such as **vector**, **string**, or **array**, over array when you have a choice
string	holds only characters but provides operations useful for text manipulation, such as concatenation (**+** and **+=**); prefer the standard **string** to other strings
valarray	a numerical vector with vector operations, but with many restrictions to encourage high-performance implementations; use only if you do a lot of vector arithmetic

B.4.1 Overview

The operations provided by the standard containers can be summarized like this:

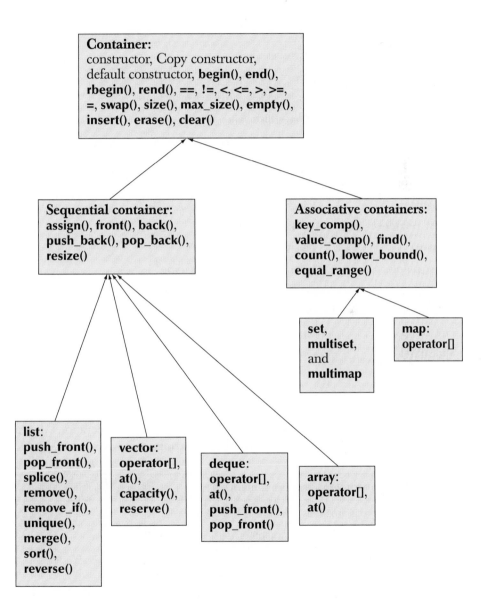

B.4.2 Member types

A container defines a set of member types:

Member types	
value_type	type of element
size_type	type of subscripts, element counts, etc.
difference_type	type of difference between iterators
iterator	behaves like **value_type***
const_iterator	behaves like **const value_type***
reverse_iterator	behaves like **value_type***
const_reverse_iterator	behaves like **const value_type***
reference	**value_type&**
const_reference	**const value_type&**
pointer	behaves like **value_type***
const_pointer	behaves like **const value_type***
key_type	type of key (associative containers only)
mapped_type	type of mapped value (associative containers only)
key_compare	type of comparison criterion (associative containers only)
allocator_type	type of memory manager

B.4.3 Constructors, destructors, and assignments

Containers provide a variety of constructors and assignment operations. For a container called **C** (e.g., **vector<double>** or **map<string,int>**) we have:

Constructors, destructors, and assignment	
C c;	c is an empty container.
C()	Make an empty container.
C c(n);	c initialized with **n** elements with default element value (not for associative containers).
C c(n,x);	c initialized with **n** copies of **x** (not for associative containers).
C c(b,e);	c initialized with elements from [**b:e**).

Constructors, destructors, and assignment (*continued*)	
C c(c2);	**c** is a copy of **c2**.
~C()	Destroy a **C** and all of its elements (usually invoked implicitly).
c1=c2	Copy assignment; copy all elements from **c2** to **c1**; after the assignment **c1==c2**.
c.assign(n,x)	Assign **n** copies of **x** (not for associative containers).
c.assign(b,e)	Assign from [**b**:**e**).

Note that for some containers and some element types, a constructor or an element copy may throw an exception.

B.4.4 Iterators

A container can be viewed as a sequence either in the order defined by the container's **iterator** or in reverse order. For an associative container, the order is based on the container's comparison criterion (by default **<**):

Iterators	
p=c.begin()	**p** points to first element of **c**.
p=c.end()	**p** points to one past last element of **c**.
p=c.rbegin()	**p** points to first element of reverse sequence of **c**.
p=c.rend()	**p** points to one past last element of reverse sequence of **c**.

B.4.5 Element access

Some elements can be accessed directly:

Element access	
c.front()	reference to first element of **c**
c.back()	reference to last element of **c**
c[i]	reference to element **i** of **c**; unchecked access (not for list)
c.at(i)	reference to element **i** of **c**; checked access (**vector** and **deque** only)

Some implementations – especially debug versions – always do range checking, but you cannot portably rely on that for correctness or on the absence of checking for performance. Where such issues are important, examine your implementations.

B.4.6 Stack and queue operations

The standard **vector** and **deque** provide efficient operations at the end (back) of their sequence of elements. In addition, **list** and **deque** provide the equivalent operations on the start (front) of their sequences:

Stack and queue operations	
c.push_back(x)	Add **x** to the end of **c**.
c.pop_back()	Remove last element from **c**.
c.push_front(x)	Add **x** to **c** before first element (**list** and **deque** only).
c.pop_front()	Remove first element from **c** (**list** and **deque** only).

Note that **push_front()** and **push_back()** copy an element into a container. This implies that the size of the container increases (by one). If the copy constructor of the element type can throw an exception, a push can fail.

Note that pop operations do not return a value. Had they done so, a copy constructor throwing an exception could have seriously complicated the implementation. Use **front()** and **back()** (§B.4.5) to access stack and queue elements. We have not recorded the complete set of requirements here; feel free to guess (your compiler will usually tell you if you guessed wrong) and to consult more detailed documentation.

B.4.7 List operations

Containers provide list operations:

List operations	
q=c.insert(p,x)	Add **x** before **p**.
q=c.insert(p,n,x)	Add **n** copies of **x** before **p**.
q=c.insert(p,first,last)	Add elements from [**first**:**last**) before **p**.
q=c.erase(p)	Remove element at **p** from **c**.
q=c.erase(first,last)	Erase [**first**:**last**) of **c**.
c.clear()	Erase all elements of **c**.

For **insert()** functions, the result, **q**, points to the last element inserted. For **erase()** functions, **q** points to the element that followed the last element erased.

B.4.8 Size and capacity

The size is the number of elements in the container; the capacity is the number of elements that a container can hold before allocating more memory:

Size and capacity	
x=c.size()	**x** is the number of elements of **c**.
c.empty()	Is **c** empty?
x=c.max_size()	**x** is the largest possible number of elements of **c**.
x=c.capacity()	**x** is the space allocated for **c** (**vector** and **string** only).
c.reserve(n)	Reserve space for **n** elements for **c** (**vector** and **string** only).
c.resize(n)	Change size of **c** to **n** (**vector**, **string**, **list**, and **deque** only).

When changing the size or the capacity, the elements may be moved to new storage locations. That implies that iterators (and pointers and references) to elements may become invalid (e.g., point to the old element locations).

B.4.9 Other operations

Containers can be copied (see §B.4.3), compared, and swapped:

Comparisons and swap	
c1==c2	Do all corresponding elements of **c1** and **c2** compare equal?
c1!=c2	Do any corresponding elements of **c1** and **c2** compare not equal?
c1<c2	Is **c1** lexicographically before **c2**?
c1<=c2	Is **c1** lexicographically before or equal to **c2**?
c1>c2	Is **c1** lexicographically after **c2**?
c1>=c2	Is **c1** lexicographically after or equal to **c2**?
swap(c1,c2)	Swap elements of **c1** and **c2**.
c1.swap(c2)	Swap elements of **c1** and **c2**.

When comparing containers with an operator (e.g., <), their elements are compared using the equivalent element operator (i.e., <).

B.4.10 Associative container operations

Associative containers provide lookup based on keys:

Associative container operations	
c[k]	Refers to the element with key **k** (containers with unique keys).
p=c.find(k)	**p** points to the first element with key **k**.

Associative container operations (*continued*)	
p=c.lower_bound(k)	**p** points to the first element with key **k**.
p=c.upper_bound(k)	**p** points to the first element with key greater than **k**.
pair(p1,p2)=c.equal_range(k)	[**p1**,**p2**) are the elements with key **k**.
r=c.key_comp()	**r** is a copy of the key-comparison object.
r=c.value_comp()	**r** is a copy of the **mapped_value**-comparison object. If a key is not found, **c.end**() is returned.

The first iterator of the pair returned by **equal_range** is **lower_bound** and the second is **upper_bound**. You can print the value of all elements with the key "**Marian**" in a **multimap<string,int>** like this:

```
string k = "Marian";
typedef multimap<string,int>::iterator MI;
pair<MI,MI> pp = m.equal_range(k);
if (pp.first!=pp.second)
        cout << "elements with value ' " << k << " ':\n";
else
        cout << "no element with value ' " << k << " '\n";
for (MI p = pp.first; p!=pp.second; ++p) cout << p->second << '\n';
```

We could equivalently have used:

```
pair<MI,MI> pp = make_pair(m.lower_bound(k),m.upper_bound(k));
```

However, that would take about twice as long to execute. The **equal_range**, **lower_bound**, and **upper_bound** algorithms are also provided for sorted sequences (§B.5.4). The definition of **pair** is in §B.6.3.

B.5 Algorithms

There are about 60 standard algorithms defined in **<algorithm>**. They all operate on sequences defined by a pair of iterators (for inputs) or a single iterator (for outputs).

When copying, comparing, etc. two sequences, the first is represented by a pair of iterators [**b:e**) but the second by just a single iterator, **b2**, which is considered the start of a sequence holding sufficient elements for the algorithm, for example, as many elements as the first sequence: [**b2:b2+(e−b)**).

Some algorithms, such as **sort**, require random-access iterators, whereas many, such as **find**, only read their elements in order so that they can make do with a forward iterator.

Many algorithms follow the usual convention of returning the end of a sequence to represent "not found." We don't mention that for each algorithm.

B.5.1 Nonmodifying sequence algorithms

A nonmodifying algorithm just reads the elements of a sequence; it does not rearrange the sequence and does not change the value of the elements:

Nonmodifying sequence algorithms	
f=for_each(b,e,f)	Do **f** for each element in [**b**:**e**); return **f**.
p=find(b,e,v)	**p** points to the first occurrence of **v** in [**b**:**e**).
p=find_if(b,e,f)	**p** points to the first element in [**b**:**e**) so that **f**(*****p**).
p=find_first_of(b,e,b2,e2)	**p** points to the first element in [**b**:**e**) so that *****p**==*****q** for some **q** in [**b2**:**e2**).
p=find_first_of(b,e,b2,e2,f)	**p** points to the first element in [**b**:**e**) so that **f**(*****p**,*****q**) for some **q** in [**b2**:**e2**).
p=adjacent_find(b,e)	**p** points to the first **p** in [**b**:**e**) such that *****p**==*****(p+1)**.
p=adjacent_find(b,e,f)	**p** points to the first **p** in [**b**:**e**) such that **f**(*****p**,*****(p+1)**).
equal(b,e,b2)	Do all elements of [**b**:**e**) and [**b2**:**b2+(e−b)**) compare equal?
equal(b,e,b2,f)	Do all elements of [**b**:**e**) and [**b2**:**b2+(e−b)**) compare equal using **f**(*****p**,*****q**) as the test?
pair(p1,p2)=mismatch(b,e,b2)	(**p1**,**p2**) points to the first pair of elements in [**b**:**e**) and [**b2**:**b2+(e−b)**) for which !(*****p1**==*****p2**).
pair(p1,p2)=mismatch(b,e,b2,f)	(**p1**,**p2**) points to the first pair of elements in [**b**:**e**) and [**b2**:**b2+(e−b)**) for which !**f**(*****p1**,*****p2**).
p=search(b,e,b2,e2)	**p** points to the first *****p** in [**b**:**e**) such that *****p** equals an element in [**b2**:**e2**).
p=search(b.e,b2,e2,f)	**p** points to the first *****p** in [**b**:**e**) such that **f**(*****p**,*****q**) for an element *****q** in [**b2**:**e2**).
p=find_end(b,e,b2,e2)	**p** points to the last *****p** in [**b**:**e**) such that *****p** equals an element in [**b2**:**e2**).
p=find_end(b,e,b2,e2,f)	**p** points to the last *****p** in [**b**:**e**) such that **f**(*****p**,*****q**) for an element *****q** in [**b2**:**e2**).
p=search_n(b,e,n,v)	**p** points to the first element of [**b**:**e**) such that each element in [**p**:**p+n**) has the value **v**.
p=search_n(b,e,n,v,f)	**p** points to the first element of [**b**:**e**) such that for each element *****q** in [**p**:**p+n**) we have **f**(*****q**,**v**).
x=count(b,e,v)	**x** is the number of occurrences of **v** in [**b**:**e**).
x=count_if(b,e,v,f)	**x** is the number of elements in [**b**:**e**) so that **f**(*****p**,**v**).

Note that nothing stops the operation passed to **for_each** from modifying elements; that's considered acceptable. Passing an operation that changes the elements it examines to some other algorithm (e.g., **count** or **==**) is not acceptable.

An example (of proper use):

```
bool odd(int x) { return x&1; }

int n_even(const vector<int>& v)     // count the number of even values in v
{
        return v.size()–count_if(v.begin(),v.end(),odd);
}
```

B.5.2 Modifying sequence algorithms

The modifying algorithms (also called *mutating sequence algorithms*) can (and often do) modify the elements of their argument sequences.

Modifying sequence algorithms	
p=transform(b,e,out,f)	Apply *p2=f(*p1) to every *p1 in [b:e] writing to the corresponding *p2 in [out:out+(e–b)); p=out+(e–b)
p=transform(b,e,b2,out,f)	Apply *p3=f(*p1,*p2) to every element in *p1 in [b:e] and the corresponding element *p2 in [b2:b2+(e–b)), writing to *p3 in [out:out+(e–b)); p=out+(e–b)
p=copy(b,e,out)	Copy [b:e] to [out:p).
p=copy_backward(b,e,out)	Copy [b:e] to [out:p) starting with its last element.
p=unique(b,e)	Move elements in [b:e) so that [b:p) has adjacent duplicates removed (== defines "duplicate").
p=unique(b,e,f)	Move elements in [b:e) so that [b:p) has adjacent duplicates removed (f defines "duplicate").
p=unique_copy(b,e,out)	Copy [b:e) to [out:p); don't copy adjacent duplicates.
p=unique_copy(b,e,out,f)	Copy [b:e) to [out:p); don't copy adjacent duplicates (f defines "duplicate").
replace(b,e,v,v2)	Replace elements *q in [b:e) for which *q==v with v2.
replace(b,e,f,v2)	Replace elements *q in [b:e) for which f(*q) with v2.
p=replace_copy(b,e,out,v,v2)	Copy [b:e) to [out:p), replacing elements *q in [b:e) for which *q==v with v2.

Modifying sequence algorithms (*continued*)

---

p=replace_copy(b,e,out,f,v2)	Copy [**b**:**e**) to [**out**:**p**), replacing elements *****q** in [**b**:**e**) for which **f**(*****q**) with **v2**.
p=remove(b,e,v)	Move elements *****q** in [**b**:**e**) so that [**b**:**p**) becomes the elements for which !(*****q==v**).
p=remove(b,e,v,f)	Move elements *****q** in [**b**:**e**) so that [**b**:**p**) becomes the elements for which !**f**(*****q**).
p=remove_copy(b,e,out,v)	Copy elements from [**b**:**e**) for which !(*****q==v**) to [**out**:**p**).
p=remove_copy_if(b,e,out,f)	Copy elements from [**b**:**e**) for which !**f**(*****q,v**) to [**out**:**p**).
reverse(b,e)	Reverse the order of elements in [**b**:**e**).
p=reverse_copy(b,e,out)	Copy [**b**:**e**) into [**out**:**p**) in reverse order.
rotate(b,m,e)	Rotate elements: treat [**b**:**e**) as a circle with the first element right after the last. Move *****b** to *****m** and in general move *****(b+i**) to *****((b+(i+(e−m))%(e−b)**).
p=rotate_copy(b,m,e,out)	Copy [**b**:**e**) into a rotated sequence [**out**:**p**).
random_shuffle(b,e)	Shuffle elements of [**b**:**e**) into a distribution using the default uniform random number generator.
random_shuffle(b,e,f)	Shuffle elements of [**b**:**e**) into a distribution using **f** as a random number generator.

A shuffle algorithm shuffles its sequence much in the way we would shuffle a pack of cards; that is, after a shuffle, the elements are in a random order, where "random" is defined by the distribution produced by the random number generator.

Please note that these algorithms do not know if their argument sequence is a container, so they do not have the ability to add or remove elements. Thus, an algorithm such as **remove** cannot shorten its input sequence by deleting (erasing) elements; instead, it (re)moves the elements it keeps to the front of the sequence:

```
typedef vector<int>::iterator VII;

void print_digits(const string& s, VII b, VII e)
{
    cout << s;
    while (b!=e) { cout << *b; ++b; }
    cout << '\n';
}
```

```
void ff()
{
    int a[] = { 1,1,1, 2,2, 3, 4,4,4, 3,3,3, 5,5,5,5, 1,1,1 };
    vector<int> v(a,a+sizeof(a)/sizeof(int));
    print_digits("all: ",v.begin(), v.end());

    vector<int>::iterator pp = unique(v.begin(),v.end());
    print_digits("head: ",v.begin(),pp);
    print_digits("tail: ",pp,v.end());

    pp=remove(v.begin(),pp,4);
    print_digits("head: ",v.begin(),pp);
    print_digits("tail: ",pp,v.end());
}
```

The resulting output is

```
all:   1112234443335555111
       head: 1234351
       tail:   443335555111
       head: 123351
       tail:   1443335555111
```

B.5.3 Utility algorithms

Technically, these utility algorithms are also modifying sequence algorithms, but we thought it a good idea to list them separately, lest they get overlooked.

Utility algorithms	
swap(x,y)	Swap **x** and **y**.
iter_swap(p,q)	Swap *p and *q.
swap_ranges(b,e,b2)	Swap the elements of [b:e) and [b2:b2+(e−b)).
fill(b,e,v)	Assign **v** to every element of [b:e).
fill_n(b,n,v)	Assign **v** to every element of [b:b+n).
generate(b,e,f)	Assign f() to every element of [b:e).
generate_n(b,n,f)	Assign f() to every element of [b:b+n).
uninitialized_fill(b,e,v)	Initialize all elements in [b:e) with **v**.
uninitialized_copy(b,e,out)	Initialize all elements of [out:out+(e−b)) with the corresponding element from [b:e).

Note that uninitialized sequences should occur only at the lowest level of programming, usually inside the implementation of containers. Elements that are targets of **uninitialized_fill** or **uninitialized_copy** must be of built-in type or uninitialized.

B.5.4 Sorting and searching

Sorting and searching are fundamental and the needs of programmers are quite varied. Comparison is by default done using the < operator and equivalence of a pair of values **a** and **b** is determined by **!(a<b)&&!(b<a)** rather than requiring operator **==**.

Sorting and searching	
sort(b,e)	Sort [**b**:**e**).
sort(b,e,f)	Sort [**b**:**e**) using **f(*p,*q)** as the sorting criterion.
stable_sort(b,e)	Sort [**b**:**e**), maintaining order of equivalent elements.
stable_sort(b,e,f)	Sort [**b**:**e**) using **f(*p,*q)** as the sorting criterion, maintaining order of equivalent elements.
partial_sort(b,m,e)	Sort [**b**:**e**) to get [**b**:**m**) into order; [**m**:**e**) need not be sorted.
partial_sort(b,m,e,f)	Sort [**b**:**e**) using **f(*p,*q)** as the sorting criterion to get [**b**:**m**) into order; [**m**:**e**) need not be sorted.
partial_sort_copy(b,e,b2,e2)	Sort enough of [**b**:**e**) to copy the **e2−b2** first elements to [**b2**:**e2**).
partial_sort_copy(b,e,b2,e2,f)	Sort enough of [**b**:**e**) to copy the **e2−b2** first elements to [**b2**:**e2**); use **f** as the comparison.
nth_element(b,e)	Put the **n**th element of [**b**:**e**) in its proper place.
nth_element(b,e,f)	Put the **n**th element of [**b**:**e**) in its proper place using **f** for comparison.
p=lower_bound(b,e,v)	**p** points to the first occurrence of **v** in [**b**:**e**).
p=lower_bound(b,e,v,f)	**p** points to the first occurrence of **v** in [**b**:**e**) using **f** for comparison.
p=upper_bound(b,e,v)	**p** points to the first value larger than **v** in [**b**:**e**).
p=upper_bound(b,e,v,f)	**p** points to the first value larger than **v** in [**b**:**e**) using **f** for comparison.
binary_search(b,e,v)	Is **v** in the sorted sequence [**b**:**e**)?
binary_search(b,e,v,f)	Is **v** in the sorted sequence [**b**:**e**) using **f** for comparison?
pair(p1,p2)=equal_range(b,e,v)	[**p1**,**p2**) is the subsequence of [**b**:**e**) with the value **v**; basically, a binary search for **v**.

Sorting and searching (*continued*)	
pair(p1,p2)=equal_range(b,e,v,f)	[**p1,p2**) is the subsequence of [**b:e**) with the value **v** using **f** for comparison; basically, a binary search for **v**.
p=merge(b,e,b2,e2,out)	Merge two sorted sequences [**b2:e2**) and [**b:e**) into [**out:p**).
p=merge(b,e,b2,e2,out,f)	Merge two sorted sequences [**b2:e2**) and [**b:e**) into [**out,out+p**) using **f** as the comparison.
inplace_merge(b,m,e)	Merge two sorted subsequences [**b:m**) and [**m:e**) into a sorted sequence [**b:e**).
inplace_merge(b,m,e,f)	Merge two sorted subsequences [**b:m**) and [**m:e**) into a sorted sequence [**b:e**) using **f** as the comparison.
p=partition(b,e,f)	Place elements for which **f(*p1)** in [**b:p**) and other elements in [**p:e**).
p=stable_partition(b,e,f)	Place elements for which **f(*p1)** in [**b:p**) and other elements in [**p:e**), preserving relative order.

For example:

```
vector<int> v;
list<double> lst;
v.push_back(3); v.push_back(1);
v.push_back(4); v.push_back(2);
lst.push_back(0.5); lst.push_back(1.5);
lst.push_back(2); lst.push_back(2.5);     // lst is in order
sort(v.begin(),v.end());                  // put v in order
vector<double> v2;
merge(v.begin(),v.end(),lst.begin(),lst.end(),back_inserter(v2));
for (int i = 0; i<v2.size(); ++i) cout << v2[i] << ", ";
```

For inserters, see §B.6.1. The output is

0.5, 1, 1.5, 2, 2, 2.5, 3, 4,

The **equal_range**, **lower_bound**, and **upper_bound** algorithms are used just like their equivalents for associative containers; see §B.4.10.

B.5.5 Set algorithms

These algorithms treat a sequence as a set of elements and provide the basic set operations. The input sequences are supposed to be sorted and the output sequences are also sorted:

Set algorithms	
includes(b,e,b2,e2)	Are all elements of [**b2**:**e2**) also in [**b**:**e**)?
includes(b,e,b2,e2,f)	Are all elements of [**b2**:**e2**) also in [**b**:**e**) using **f** for comparison?
p=set_union(b,e,b2,e2,out)	Construct a sorted sequence [**out**:**p**) of elements that are in either [**b**:**e**) or [**b2**:**e2**).
p=set_union(b,e,b2,e2,out,f)	Construct a sorted sequence [**out**:**p**) of elements that are in either [**b**:**e**) or [**b2**:**e2**) using **f** for comparison.
p=set_intersection(b,e,b2,e2,out)	Construct a sorted sequence [**out**:**p**) of elements that are in both [**b**:**e**) and [**b2**:**e2**).
p=set_intersection(b,e,b2,e2,out,f)	Construct a sorted sequence [**out**:**p**) of elements that are in both [**b**:**e**) and [**b2**:**e2**) using **f** for comparison.
p=set_difference(b,e,b2,e2,out)	Construct a sorted sequence [**out**:**p**) of elements that are in [**b**:**e**) but not in [**b2**:**e2**).
p=set_difference(b,e,b2,e2,out,f)	Construct a sorted sequence [**out**:**p**) of elements that are in [**b**:**e**) but not in [**b2**:**e2**) using **f** for comparison.
p=set_symmetric_difference(b,e,b2,e2,out)	Construct a sorted sequence [**out**:**p**) of elements that are in [**b**:**e**) or [**b2**:**e2**) but not in both.
p=set_symmetric_difference(b,e,b2,e2,out,f)	Construct a sorted sequence [**out**:**p**) of elements that are in [**b**:**e**) or [**b2**:**e2**) but not in both using **f** for comparison.

B.5.6 Heaps

A heap is a data structure that keeps the element with highest value first. The heap algorithms allow a programmer to treat a random-access sequence as a heap:

Heap operations	
make_heap(b,e)	Make sequence ready to be used as a heap.
make_heap(b,e,f)	Make sequence ready to be used as a heap, using **f** for comparison.
push_heap(b,e)	Add element to heap (in its proper place).
push_heap(b,e,f)	Add element to heap, using **f** for comparison.

Heap operations (*continued*)	
pop_heap(b,e)	Remove largest (first) element from heap.
pop_heap(b,e,f)	Remove element from heap, using **f** for comparison.
sort_heap(b,e)	Sort the heap.
sort_heap(b,e,f)	Sort the heap, using **f** for comparison.

The point of a heap is to provide fast addition of elements and fast access to the element with the highest value. The main use of heaps is to implement priority queues.

B.5.7 Permutations

Permutations are used to generate combinations of elements of a sequence. For example, the permutations of **abc** are **abc**, **acb**, **bac**, **bca**, **cab**, and **cba**.

Permutations	
x=next_permutation(b,e)	Make [**b**:**e**) the next permutation in lexicographical order.
x=next_permutation(b,e,f)	Make [**b**:**e**) the next permutation in lexicographical order, using **f** for comparison.
x=prev_permutation(b,e)	Make [**b**:**e**) the previous permutation in lexicographical order.
x=prev_permutation(b,e,f)	Make [**b**:**e**) the previous permutation in lexicographical order, using **f** for comparison.

The return value (**x**) for **next_permutation** is **false** if [**b**:**e**) already contains the last permutation (**cba** in the example); in that case, it returns the first permutation (**abc** in the example). The return value for **prev_permutation** is **false** if [**b**:**e**) already contains the first permutation (**abc** in the example); in that case, it returns the last permutation (**cba** in the example).

B.5.8 min and max

Value comparisons are useful in many contexts:

min **and max**	
x=max(a,b)	x is the larger of **a** and **b**.
x=max(a,b,f)	x is the larger of **a** and **b** using **f** for comparison.
x=min(a,b)	x is the smaller of **a** and **b**.
x=min(a,b,f)	x is the smaller of **a** and **b** using **f** for comparison.
p= max_element(b,e)	**p** points to the largest element of [**b**:**e**].
p=max_element(b,e,f)	**p** points to the largest element of [**b**:**e**] using **f** for the element comparison.
p=min_element(b,e)	**p** points to the smallest element of [**b**:**e**].
p=min_element(b,e,f)	**p** points to the smallest element of [**b**:**e**] using **f** for the element comparison.
lexicographical_compare(b,e,b2,e2)	Is [**b**:**e**]<[**b2**:**e2**]?
lexicographical_compare(b,e,b2,e2,f)	Is [**b**:**e**]<[**b2**:**e2**], using **f** for the element comparison?

B.6 STL utilities

The standard library provides a few facilities for making it easier to use standard library algorithms.

B.6.1 Inserters

Producing output through an iterator into a container implies that elements pointed to by the iterator and following it can be overwritten. This also implies the possibility of overflow and consequent memory corruption. For example:

```
void f(vector<int>& vi)
{
    fill_n(vi.begin(), 200,7 );     // assign 7 to vi[0]..[199]
}
```

If **vi** has fewer than 200 elements, we are in trouble.

In **<iterator>**, the standard library provides three iterators to deal with this problem by adding (inserting) elements to a container rather than overwriting old elements. Three functions are provided for generating those inserting iterators:

Inserters	
r=back_inserter(c)	*r=x causes a **c.push_back(x)**.
r=front_inserter(c)	*r=x causes a **c.push_front(x)**.
r=inserter(c,p)	*r=x causes a **c.insert(p,x)**.

For **inserter(c,p)**, **p** must be a valid iterator for the container **c**. Naturally, a container grows by one element each time a value is written to it through an insert iterator. When written to, an inserter inserts a new element into a sequence using **push_back(x)**, **c.push_front()**, or **insert()** rather than overwriting an existing element. For example:

```
void g(vector<int>& vi)
{
    fill_n(back_inserter(vi), 200,7 );   // add 200 7s to the end of vi
}
```

B.6.2 Function objects

Many of the standard algorithms take function objects (or functions) as arguments to control the way they work. Common uses are comparison criteria, predicates (functions returning **bool**), and arithmetic operations. In **<functional>**, the standard library supplies a few common function objects.

Predicates	
p=equal_to<T>()	p(x,y) means x==y when x and y are of type **T**.
p=not_equal_to<T>()	p(x,y) means x!=y when x and y are of type **T**.
p=greater<T>()	p(x,y) means x>y when x and y are of type **T**.
p=less<T>()	p(x,y) means x<y when x and y are of type **T**.
p=greater_equal<T>()	p(x,y) means x>=y when x and y are of type **T**.
p=less_equal<T>()	p(x,y) means x<=y when x and y are of type **T**.
p=logical_and<T>()	p(x,y) means x&&y when x and y are of type **T**.
p=logical_or<T>()	p(x,y) means x‖y when x and y are of type **T**.
p=logical_not<T>()	p(x) means !x when x is of type **T**.

For example:

```
vector<int> v;
// . . .
sort(v.begin(),v.end(),greater<int>());      // sort v in decreasing order
```

Note that **logical_and** and **logical_or** always evaluate both their arguments (whereas **&&** and **||** do not).

Arithmetic operations	
f=plus<T>()	**f(x,y)** means **x+y** when **x** and **y** are of type **T**.
f=minus<T>()	**f(x,y)** means **x−y** when **x** and **y** are of type **T**.
f=multiplies<T>()	**f(x,y)** means **x*y** when **x** and **y** are of type **T**.
f=divides<T>()	**f(x,y)** means **x/y** when **x** and **y** are of type **T**.
f=modulus<T>()	**f(x,y)** means **x%y** when **x** and **y** are of type **T**.
f=negate<T>()	**f(x)** means **−x** when **x** is of type **T**.

Adaptors	
f=bind2nd(g,y)	**f(x)** means **g(x,y)**.
f=bind1st(g,x)	**f(y)** means **g(x,y)**.
f=mem_fun(mf)	**f(p)** means **p−>mf()**.
f=mem_fun_ref(mf)	**f(r)** means **r.mf()**.
f=not1(g)	**f(x)** means **!g(x)**.
f=not2(g)	**f(x,y)** means **!g(x,y)**.

B.6.3 pair

In **<utility>**, the standard library provides a few "utility components," including **pair**:

```
template <class T1, class T2>
    struct pair {
        typedef T1 first_type;
        typedef T2 second_type;
        T1 first;
        T2 second;
```

```
        pair();   // default constructor
        pair(const T1& x , const T2& y );

        // copy operations:
        template<class U , class V > pair(const pair<U , V >& p );
};

template <class T1, class T2>
    pair<T1,T2> make_pair(T1 x, T2 y) { return pair<T1,T2>(x,y); }
```

The **make_pair** function makes the use of pairs simple. For example, here is the outline of a function that returns a value and an error indicator:

```
pair<double,error_indicator> my_fct(double d)
{
        errno = 0;      // clear C-style global error indicator
        // do a lot of computation involving d computing x
        error_indicator ee = errno;
        errno = 0;      // clear C-style global error indicator
        return make_pair(x,ee);
}
```

This example of a useful idiom can be used like this:

```
pair<int,error_indicator> res = my_fct(123.456);
if (res.second==0) {
        // use res.first
}
else {
        // oops: error
}
```

B.7 I/O streams

The I/O stream library provides formatted and unformatted buffered I/O of text and numeric values. The definitions for I/O stream facilities are found in <istream>, <ostream>, etc.; see §B.1.1.

An **ostream** converts typed objects to a stream of characters (bytes):

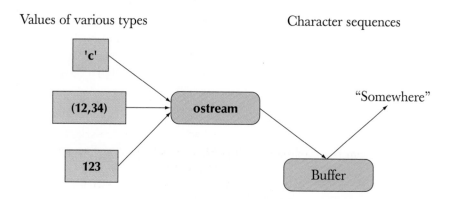

An **istream** converts a stream of characters (bytes) to typed objects:

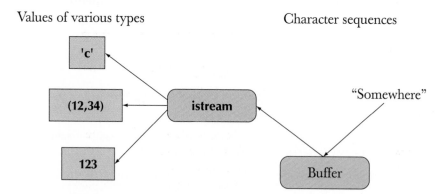

An **iostream** is a stream that can act as both an **istream** and an **ostream**. The buffers in the diagrams are "stream buffers" (**streambufs**). Look them up in an expert-level textbook if you ever need to define a mapping from an **iostream** to a new kind of device, file, or memory.

There are three standard streams:

Standard I/O streams
cout   the standard character output (often by default a screen)
cin   the standard character input (often by default a keyboard)
cerr   the standard character error output (unbuffered)

B.7.1 I/O streams hierarchy

An **istream** can be connected to an input device (e.g., a keyboard), a file, or a **string**. Similarly, an **ostream** can be connected to an output device (e.g., a text window), a file, or a **string**. The I/O stream facilities are organized in a class hierarchy:

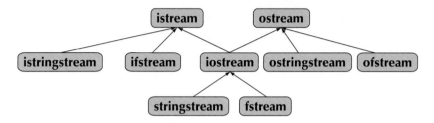

A stream can be opened either by a constructor or by an **open()** call:

Stream types	
stringstream(m)	Make an empty string stream with mode **m**.
stringstream(s,m)	Make a string stream containing **string s** with mode **m**.
fstream()	Make a file stream for later opening.
fstream(s,m)	Open file called **s** with mode **m** and make a file stream to refer to it.
fs.open(s,m)	Open file called **s** with mode **m** and have **fs** refer to it.
fs.is_open()	Is **fs** open?

For file streams, the file name is a C-style string.

You can open a file in one of several modes:

Stream modes	
ios_base::app	append (i.e., add to the end of the file)
ios_base::ate	"at end" (open and seek to end)
ios_base::binary	binary mode — beware of system-specific behavior
ios_base::in	for reading
ios_base::out	for writing
ios_base::trunc	truncate file to 0 length

In each case, the exact effect of opening a file may depend on the operating system, and if an operating system cannot honor a request to open a file in a certain way, the result will be a stream that is not in the **good()** state.

An example:

```
void my_code(ostream& os);      // my code can use any ostream

ostringstream os;               // o for "output"
ofstream of("my_file");
if (!of) error("couldn't open 'my_file' for writing");
my_code(os);                    // use a string
my_code(of);                    // use a file
```

See §11.3.

B.7.2 Error handling

An **iostream** can be in one of four states:

Stream states	
good()	The operations succeeded.
eof()	We hit end of input ("end of file").
fail()	Something unexpected happened (e.g., we looked for a digit and found **'x'**).
bad()	Something unexpected and serious happened (e.g., disk read error).

By using **s.exceptions()**, a programmer can request an **iostream** to throw an exception if it turns from **good()** into another state (see §10.6).

Any operation attempted on a stream that is not in the **good()** state has no effect; it is a "no op."

An **iostream** can be used as a condition. In that case, the condition is true (succeeds) if the state of the **iostream** is **good()**. That is the basis for the common idiom for reading a stream of values:

```
X x;  // an "input buffer" for holding one value of type X
while (cin>>x) {
      // do something with x
}
// we get here when >> couldn't read another X from cin
```

B.7.3 Input operations

Input operations are found in **<istream>** except for the ones reading into a **string**; those are found in **<string>**:

Formatted input	
in >> x	Read from **in** into **x** according to **x**'s type.
getline(in,s)	Read a line from **in** into the string **s**.

Unless otherwise stated, an **istream** operation returns a reference to its **istream**, so that we can "chain" operations, for example, **cin>>x>>y;**.

Unformatted input	
x=in.get()	Read one character from **in** and return its integer value.
in.get(c)	Read a character from **in** into **c**.
in.get(p,n)	Read at most **n** characters from **in** into the array starting at **p**.
in.get(p,n,t)	Read at most **n** characters from **in** into the array starting at **p**; consider **t** a terminator.
in.getline(p,n)	Read at most **n** characters from **in** into the array starting at **p**; remove terminator from **in**.
in.getline(p,n,t)	Read at most **n** characters from **in** into the array starting at **p**; consider **t** a terminator; remove terminator from **in**.
in.read(p,n)	Read at most **n** characters from **in** into the array starting at **p**.
x=in.gcount()	**x** is number of characters read by most recent unformatted input operation on **in**.

The **get()** and **getline()** functions place a **0** at the end of the characters (if any) written to **p[0]** . . . ; **getline()** removes the terminator (**t**) from the input, if found, whereas **get()** does not. A **read(p,n)** does not write a **0** to the array after the characters read. Obviously, the formatted input operators are simpler to use and less error-prone than the unformatted ones.

B.7.4 Output operations

Output operations are found in **<ostream>** except for the ones writing out a **string**; those are found in **<string>**:

Output operations	
out << x	Write **x** to **out** according to **x**'s type.
out.put(c)	Write the character **c** to **out**.
out.write(p,n)	Write the characters **p[0]..p[n−1]** to **out**.

Unless otherwise stated, an **ostream** operation returns a reference to its **ostream**, so that we can "chain" operations, for example, **cout << x<<y;**.

B.7.5 Formatting

The format of stream I/O is controlled by a combination of object type, stream state, locale information (see **<locale>**), and explicit operations. Chapters 10 and 11 explain much of this. Here, we just list the standard manipulators (operations modifying the state of a stream) because they provide the most straightforward way of modifying formatting.

Locales are beyond the scope of this book.

B.7.6 Standard manipulators

The standard library provides manipulators corresponding to the various format states and state changes. The standard manipulators are defined in **<ios>**, **<istream>**, **<ostream>**, **<iostream>**, and **<iomanip>** (for manipulators that take arguments):

I/O manipulators	
s<<boolalpha	Use symbolic representation of **true** and **false** (input and output).
s<<noboolalpha	**s.unsetf(ios_base::boolalpha)**.
s<<showbase	On output prefix **oct** by **0** and **hex** by **0x**.
s<<noshowbase	**s.unsetf(ios_base::showbase)**.
s<<showpoint	Always show decimal point.
s<<noshowpoint	**s.unsetf(ios_base::showpoint)**.
s<<showpos	Show + for positive numbers.
s<<noshowpos	**s.unsetf(ios_base::showpos)**.
s>>skipws	Skip whitespace.
s>>noskipws	**s.unsetf(ios_base::skipws)**.
s<<uppercase	Use uppercase in numeric output, e.g., **1.2E10** and **0X1A2** rather than **1.2e10** and **0x1a2**.

I/O manipulators (*continued*)	
s<<nouppercase	**x** and **e** rather than **X** and **E**.
s<<internal	Pad where marked in formatting pattern.
s<<left	Pad after value.
s<<right	Pad before value.
s<<dec	Integer base is 10.
s<<hex	Integer base is 16.
s<<oct	Integer base is 8.
s<<fixed	Floating-point format dddd.dd.
s<<scientific	Scientific format d.ddddEdd.
s<<endl	Put '\n' and flush.
s<<ends	Put '\0'.
s<<flush	Flush stream.
s>>ws	Eat whitespace.
s<<resetiosflags(f)	Clear flags **f**.
s<<setiosflags(f)	Set flags **f**.
s<<setbase(b)	Output integers in base **b**.
s<<setfill(c)	Make **c** the fill character.
s<<setprecision(n)	Precision is **n** digits.
s<<setw(n)	Next field width is **n** characters.

Each of these operations returns a reference to its first (stream) operand, **s**. For example:

        cout << 1234 << ',' << hex << 1234 << ',' << oct << 1234 << endl;

produces

        1234,4d2,2322

and

        cout << '(' << setw(4) << setfill('#') << 12 << ") (" << 12 << ")\n";

produces

        (##12) (12)

To explicitly set the general output format for floating-point numbers use

> **b.setf(ios_base::fmtflags(0), ios_base::floatfield)**

See Chapter 11.

B.8 String manipulation

The standard library offers character classification operations in **<cctype>**, strings with associated operations in **<string>**, regular expression matching in **<regex>** (C++0x), and support for C-style strings in **<cstring>**.

B.8.1 Character classification

The characters from the basic execution character set can be classified like this:

Character classification	
isspace(c)	Is **c** whitespace (' ', '\t', '\n', etc.)?
isalpha(c)	Is **c** a letter ('a'..'z', 'A'..'Z')? (Note: not '_'.)
isdigit(c)	Is **c** a decimal digit ('0'..'9')?
isxdigit(c)	Is **c** a hexadecimal digit (decimal digit or 'a'..'f' or 'A'..'F')?
isupper(c)	Is **c** an uppercase letter?
islower(c)	Is **c** a lowercase letter?
isalnum(c)	Is **c** a letter or a decimal digit?
iscntrl(c)	Is **c** a control character (ASCII 0..31 and 127)?
ispunct(c)	Is **c** not a letter, digit, whitespace, or invisible control character?
isprint(c)	Is **c** printable (ASCII ' '..'~')?
isgraph(c)	Is **c** **isalpha()|isdigit()|ispunct()**? (Note: not space.)

In addition, the standard library provides two useful functions for getting rid of case differences:

Upper and lower case	
toupper(c)	**c** or **c**'s uppercase equivalent
tolower(c)	**c** or **c**'s lowercase equivalent

Extended character sets, such as Unicode, are supported but are beyond the scope of this book.

B.8.2 String

The standard library string class, **string**, is a specialization of a general string template **basic_string** for the character type **char**; that is, **string** is a sequence of **chars**:

String operations	
s=s2	Assign **s2** to **s**; **s2** can be a string or a C-style string.
s+=x	Append **x** at end of **s**; **x** can be a character, a string, or a C-style string
s[i]	Subscripting.
s+s2	Concatenation; the result is a new string with the characters from **s** followed by the characters from **s2**.
s==s2	Comparison of string values; **s1** or **s2**, but not both, can be a C-style string.
s!=s2	Comparison of string values; **s** or **s2**, but not both, can be a C-style string.
s<s2	Lexicographical comparison of string values; **s** or **s2**, but not both, can be a C-style string.
s<=s2	Lexicographical comparison of string values; **s** or **s2**, but not both, can be a C-style string.
s>s2	Lexicographical comparison of string values; **s** or **s2**, but not both, can be a C-style string.
s>=s2	Lexicographical comparison of string values; **s** or **s2**, but not both, can be a C-style string.
s.size()	Number of characters in **s**.
s.length()	Number of characters in **s**.
s.c_str()	C-style string version (zero terminated) of characters in **s**.
s.begin()	Iterator to first character.
s.end()	Iterator to one beyond the end of **s**.
s.insert(pos,x)	Insert **x** before **s[pos]**; **x** can be a character, a string, or a C-style string.
s.append(pos,x)	Insert **x** after **s[pos]**; **x** can be a character, a string, or a C-style string.
s.erase(pos)	Remove the character in **s[pos]**.
s.push_back(c)	Append the character **c**.
pos=s.find(x)	Find **x** in **s**; **x** can be a character, a string, or a C-style string; **pos** is the index of the first character found, or **npos** (a position off the end of **s**).
in>>s	Read a word into **s** from **in**.

B.8.3 Regular expression matching

The regular expression library is not yet part of the standard library, but it will soon be and it is widely available, so we list it here. See Chapter 23 for more detailed explanations. The main **<regex>** functions are

- *Searching* for a string that matches a regular expression in an (arbitrarily long) stream of data – supported by **regex_search()**
- *Matching* a regular expression against a string (of known size) – supported by **regex_match()**
- *Replacement* of matches – supported by **regex_replace()**; not described in this book; see an expert-level text or manual

The result of a **regex_search()** or a **regex_match()** is a collection of matches, typically represented as an **smatch**:

```
regex row( "^[\\w ]+(          \\d+)( \\d+)( \\d+)$");      // data line

while (getline(in,line)) {      // check data line
    smatch matches;
    if (!regex_match(line, matches, row))
        error("bad line", lineno);

        // check row:
    int field1 = from_string<int>(matches[1]);
    int field2 = from_string<int>(matches[2]);
    int field3 = from_string<int>(matches[3]);
    // . . .
}
```

The syntax of regular expressions is based on characters with special meaning (Chapter 23):

Regular expression special characters	
.	any single character (a "wildcard")
[	character class
{	count
(	begin grouping
)	end grouping
\	next character has a special meaning
*	zero or more
+	one or more

Regular expression special characters (*continued*)

?	optional (zero or one)
|	alternative (or)
^	start of line; negation
$	end of line

Repetition

{ n }	exactly **n** times
{ n, }	**n** or more times
{n,m}	at least **n** and at most **m** times
*	zero or more, that is, **{0,}**
+	one or more, that is, **{1,}**
?	optional (zero or one), that is **{0,1}**

Character classes

alnum	any alphanumeric character or the underscore
alpha	any alphabetic character
blank	any whitespace character that is not a line separator
cntrl	any control character
d	any decimal digit
digit	any decimal digit
graph	any graphical character
lower	any lowercase character
print	any printable character
punct	any punctuation character
s	any whitespace character
space	any whitespace character
upper	any uppercase character
w	any word character (alphanumeric characters)
xdigit	any hexadecimal digit character

Several character classes are supported by shorthand notation:

Character class abbreviations		
\d	a decimal digit	[[:digit:]]
\l	a lowercase character	[[:lower:]]
\s	a space (space, tab, etc.)	[[:space:]]
\u	an uppercase character	[[:upper:]]
\w	a letter, a decimal digit, or an underscore (_)	[[:alnum:]]
\D	not \d	[^[:digit:]]
\L	not \l	[^[:lower:]]
\S	not \s	[^[:space:]]
\U	not \u	[^[:upper:]]
\W	not \w	[^[:alnum:]]

B.9 Numerics

The C++ standard library provides the most basic building blocks for mathematical (scientific, engineering, etc.) calculations.

B.9.1 Numerical limits

Each C++ implementation specifies properties of the built-in types, so that programmers can use those properties to check against limits, set sentinels, etc.

From **<limits>**, we get **numeric_limits <T>** for each built-in or library type **T**. In addition, a programmer can define **numeric_limits<X>** for a user-defined numeric type **X**. For example:

```
class numeric_limits<float> {
public:
        static const bool is_specialized = true;

        static const int radix = 2;     // base of exponent (in this case, binary)
        static const int digits = 24;   // number of radix digits in mantissa
        static const int digits10 = 6;  // number of base-10 digits in mantissa

        static const bool is_signed = true;
        static const bool is_integer = false;
        static const bool is_exact = false;
```

```cpp
    static float min() { return 1.17549435E-38F; }    // example value
    static float max() { return 3.40282347E+38F; }    // example value

    static float epsilon() { return 1.19209290E-07F; }   // example value
    static float round_error() { return 0.5F; }          // example value

    static float infinity() { return /* some value */; }
    static float quiet_NaN() { return /* some value */; }
    static float signaling_NaN() { return /* some value */; }
    static float denorm_min() { return min(); }

    static const int min_exponent = -125;      // example value
    static const int min_exponent10 = -37;     // example value
    static const int max_exponent = +128;      // example value
    static const int max_exponent10 = +38;     // example value

    static const bool has_infinity = true;
    static const bool has_quiet_NaN = true;
    static const bool has_signaling_NaN = true;
    static const float_denorm_style has_denorm = denorm_absent;
    static const bool has_denorm_loss = false;

    static const bool is_iec559 = true;        // conforms to IEC-559
    static const bool is_bounded = true;
    static const bool is_modulo = false;
    static const bool traps = true;
    static const bool tinyness_before = true;

    static const float_round_style round_style = round_to_nearest;
};
```

From <limits.h> and <float.h>, we get macros specifying key properties of integers and floating-point numbers, including:

Limit macros	
CHAR_BIT	number of bits in a **char** (usually 8)
CHAR_MIN	minimum **char** value
CHAR_MAX	maximum **char** value (usually 127 if **char** is signed and 255 if **char** is unsigned)
INT_MIN	smallest **int** value
INT_MAX	largest **int** value

Limit macros (*continued*)	
LONG_MIN	smallest **int** value
LONG_MAX	largest **int** value
FLT_MIN	smallest positive **float** value (e.g., 1.175494351e–38F)
FLT_MAX	largest **float** value (e.g., 3.402823466e+38F)
FLT_DIG	number of decimal digits of precision (e.g., 6)
FLT_MAX_10_EXP	largest decimal exponent (e.g., 38)
DBL_MIN	smallest **double** value
DBL_MAX	largest **double** value (e.g., 1.7976931348623158e+308)
DBL_EPSILON	smallest such that **1.0+DBL_EPSILON != 1.0**

B.9.2 Standard mathematical functions

The standard library provides the most common mathematical functions (defined in **<cmath>** and **<complex>**):

Standard mathematical functions	
abs(x)	absolute value
ceil(x)	smallest integer **>= x**
floor(x)	largest integer **<= x**
sqrt(x)	square root; **x** must be nonnegative
cos(x)	cosine
sin(x)	sine
tan(x)	tangent
acos(x)	arccosine; result is nonnegative
asin(x)	arcsine; result nearest to 0 returned
atan(x)	arctangent
sinh(x)	hyperbolic sine
cosh(x)	hyperbolic cosine
tanh(x)	hyperbolic tangent
exp(x)	base-e exponential
log(x)	natural logarithm, base-e; **x** must be positive
log10(x)	base-10 logarithm

There are versions taking **float**, **double**, **long double**, and **complex** arguments. For each function, the return type is the same as the argument type.

If a standard mathematical function cannot produce a mathematically valid result, it sets the variable **errno**.

B.9.3 Complex

The standard library provides complex number types **complex<float>**, **complex<double>**, and **complex<long double>**. A **complex<Scalar>** where **Scalar** is some other type supporting the usual arithmetic operations usually works but is not guaranteed to be portable.

```
template<class Scalar> class complex {
        // a complex is a pair of scalar values, basically a coordinate pair
        Scalar re, im;
public:
        complex(const Scalar & r, const Scalar & i) :re(r), im(i) { }
        complex(const Scalar & r) :re(r),im(Scalar ()) { }
        complex() :re(Scalar ()), im(Scalar ()) { }

        Scalar real() { return re; }        // real part
        Scalar imag() { return im; }        // imaginary part

        // operators: = += −= *= /=
};
```

In addition to the members of complex, **<complex>** offers a host of useful operations:

Complex operators	
z1+z2	addition
z1−z2	subtraction
z1*z2	multiplication
z1/z2	division
z1==z2	equality
z1!=z2	inequality
norm(z)	the square of **abs(z)**
conj(z)	conjugate: if **z** is {re,im} then **conj(z)** is {re,−im}
polar(x,y)	make a complex given polar coordinates (rho,theta)
real(z)	real part

Complex operators (*continued*)	
imag(z)	imaginary part
abs(z)	also known as rho
arg(z)	also known as theta
out << z	complex output
in >> z	complex input

The standard mathematical functions (see §B.9.2) are also available for complex numbers. Note: **complex** does not provide < or %; see also §24.9.

B.9.4 valarray

The standard **valarray** is a single-dimensional numerical array; that is, it provides arithmetic operations for an array type (much as **Matrix** in Chapter 24) plus support for slices and strides.

B.9.5 Generalized numerical algorithms

These algorithms from **<numeric>** provide general versions of common operations on sequences of numerical values:

Numerical algorithms	
x = accumulate(b,e,i)	**x** is the sum of **i** and the elements of [**b**:**e**).
x = accumulate(b,e,i,f)	Accumulate, but with **f** instead of +.
x = inner_product(b,e,b2,i)	**x** is the inner product of [**b**:**e**) and [**b2**:**b2**+(**e**–**b**)), that is, the sum of **i** and (*p1)*(*p2) for all **p1** in [**b**:**e**) and all corresponding **p2** in [**b2**:**b2**+(**e**–**b**)).
x = inner_product(b,e,b2,i,f,f2)	**inner_product**, but with **f** and **f2** instead of + and *, respectively.
p=partial_sum(b,e,out)	Element **i** of [**out**:**p**) is the sum of elements 0..i of [**b**:**e**).
p=partial_sum(b,e,out,f)	**partial_sum**, using **f** instead of +.
p=adjacent_difference(b,e,out)	Element **i** of [**out**:**p**) is *(**b**+i)–*(**b**+i–1) for i>1; if **e**–**b**>0 then *out is *b.
p=adjacent_difference(b,e,out,f)	**adjacent_difference**, using **f** instead of –.

B.10 C standard library functions

The standard library for the C language is with very minor modifications incorporated into the C++ standard library. The C standard library provides quite a few functions that have proved useful over the years in a wide variety of contexts – especially for relatively low-level programming. Here, we have organized them into a few conventional categories:

- C-style I/O
- C-style strings
- Memory
- Date and time
- Etc.

There are more C standard library functions than we present here; see a good C textbook, such as Kernighan and Ritchie, *The C Programming Language* (K&R), if you need to know more.

B.10.1 Files

The **<stdio>** I/O system is based on "files." A file (a **FILE***) can refer to a file or to one of the standard input and output streams, **stdin**, **stdout**, and **stderr**. The standard streams are available by default; other files need to be opened:

File open and close	
f=fopen(s,m)	Open a file stream for a file named **s** with the mode **m**.
x=fclose(f)	Close file stream **f**; return **0** if successful.

A "mode" is a string containing one or more directives specifying how a file is to be opened:

File modes	
"r"	reading
"w"	writing (discard previous contents)
"a"	append (add at end)
"r+"	reading and writing
"w+"	reading and writing (discard previous contents)
"b"	binary; use together with one or more other modes

There may be (and usually are) more options on a specific system. Some options can be combined; for example, **fopen("foo","rb")** tries to open a file called **foo** for binary reading. The I/O modes should be the same for stdio and **iostreams** (§B.7.1)

B.10.2 The printf() family

The most popular C standard library functions are the I/O functions. However, we recommend **iostreams** because that library is type safe and extensible. The formatted output function, **printf()**, is widely used (also in C++ programs) and widely imitated in other programming languages:

printf	
n=printf(fmt,args)	Print the "format string" **fmt** to **stdout** inserting the arguments **args** as appropriate.
n=fprintf(f,fmt,args)	Print the "format string" **fmt** to file **f**, inserting the arguments **args** as appropriate.
n=sprintf(s,fmt,args)	Print the "format string" **fmt** to the C-style string **s**, inserting the arguments **args** as appropriate.

For each version, **n** is the number of characters written or a negative number if the output failed. The return value from **printf()** is essentially always ignored.

The declaration of **printf()** is

```
int printf(const char* format ...);
```

In other words, it takes a C-style string (typically a string literal) followed by an arbitrary number of arguments of arbitrary type. The meaning of those "extra arguments" is controlled by conversion specifications, such as **%c** (print as character) and **%d** (print as decimal integer), in the format string. For example:

```
int x = 5;
const char* p = "asdf";
printf("the value of x is '%d' and the value of s is '%s'\n",x,s);
```

A character following a % controls the handling of an argument. The first % applies to the first "extra argument" (here, **%d** applies to **x**), the second % to the second "extra argument" (here, **%s** applies to **s**), and so on. In particular, the output of that call to **printf()** is

   the value of x is '5' and the value of s is 'asdf'

followed by a newline.

In general, the correspondence between a % conversion directive and the type to which it is applied cannot be checked, and when it can, it usually is not. For example:

printf("the value of x is '%s' and the value of s is '%d'\n",x,s);   // oops

The set of conversion specifications is quite large and provides a great degree of flexibility (and possibilities for confusion). Following the %, there may be:

- **–** an optional minus sign that specifies left adjustment of the converted value in the field.

- **+** an optional plus sign that specifies that a value of a signed type will always begin with a + or – sign.

- **0** an optional zero that specifies that leading zeros are used for padding of a numeric value. If – or a precision is specified, this 0 is ignored.

- **#** an optional # that specifies that floating-point values will be printed with a decimal point even if no nonzero digits follow, that trailing zeros will be printed, that octal values will be printed with an initial **0**, and that hexadecimal values will be printed with an initial **0x** or **0X**.

- **d** an optional digit string specifying a field width; if the converted value has fewer characters than the field width, it will be blank-padded on the left (or right, if the left-adjustment indicator has been given) to make up the field width; if the field width begins with a zero, zero padding will be done instead of blank padding.

- **.** an optional period that serves to separate the field width from the next digit string.

- *dd* an optional digit string specifying a precision that specifies the number of digits to appear after the decimal point, for **e**- and **f**-conversion, or the maximum number of characters to be printed from a string.

- ***** a field width or precision may be * instead of a digit string. In this case, an integer argument supplies the field width or precision.

- **h** an optional character **h**, specifying that a following **d**, **o**, **x**, or **u** corresponds to a short integer argument.

- **l** an optional character **l** (the letter l), specifying that a following **d**, **o**, **x**, or **u** corresponds to a long integer argument.

- **L** an optional character **L**, specifying that a following **e**, **E**, **g**, **G**, or **f** corresponds to a long **double** argument.

- **%** indicating that the character % is to be printed; no argument is used.

c a character that indicates the type of conversion to be applied. The conversion characters and their meanings are:

d The integer argument is converted to decimal notation.

i The integer argument is converted to decimal notation.

o The integer argument is converted to octal notation.

x The integer argument is converted to hexadecimal notation.

X The integer argument is converted to hexadecimal notation.

f The **float** or **double** argument is converted to decimal notation in the style [–]*ddd.ddd*. The number of *d*'s after the decimal point is equal to the precision for the argument. If necessary, the number is rounded. If the precision is missing, six digits are given; if the precision is explicitly **0** and **#** isn't specified, no decimal point is printed.

e The **float** or **double** argument is converted to decimal notation in the scientific style [–]*d.ddde+dd* or [–]*d.ddde–dd*, where there is one digit before the decimal point and the number of digits after the decimal point is equal to the precision specification for the argument. If necessary, the number is rounded. If the precision is missing, six digits are given; if the precision is explicitly **0** and **#** isn't specified, no digits and no decimal point are printed.

E As **e**, but with an uppercase **E** used to identify the exponent.

g The **float** or **double** argument is printed in style **d**, in style **f**, or in style **e**, whichever gives the greatest precision in minimum space.

G As **g**, but with an uppercase **E** used to identify the exponent.

c The character argument is printed. Null characters are ignored.

s The argument is taken to be a string (character pointer), and characters from the string are printed until a null character or until the number of characters indicated by the precision specification is reached; however, if the precision is **0** or missing, all characters up to a null are printed.

p The argument is taken to be a pointer. The representation printed is implementation dependent.

u The unsigned integer argument is converted to decimal notation.

n The number of characters written so far by the call of **printf()**, **fprintf()**, or **sprintf()** is written to the **int** pointed to by the pointer to **int** argument.

In no case does a nonexistent or small field width cause truncation of a field; padding takes place only if the specified field width exceeds the actual width.

Because C does not have user-defined types in the sense that C++ has, there are no provisions for defining output formats for user-defined types, such as **complex**, **vector**, or **string**.

The C standard output, **stdout**, corresponds to **cout**. The C standard input, **stdin**, corresponds to **cin**. The C standard error output, **stderr**, corresponds to **cerr**. This correspondence between C standard I/O and C++ I/O streams is so close that C-style I/O and I/O streams can share a buffer. For example, a mix of **cout** and **stdout** operations can be used to produce a single output stream (that's not uncommon in mixed C and C++ code). This flexibility carries a cost. For better performance, don't mix stdio and **iostream** operations for a single stream and call **ios_base::sync_with_stdio(false)** before the first I/O operation.

The stdio library provides a function, **scanf()**, that is an input operation with a style that mimics **printf()**. For example:

```
int x;
char s[buf_size];
int i = scanf("the value of x is '%d' and the value of s is '%s'\n",&x,s);
```

Here, **scanf()** tries to read an integer into **x** and a sequence of non-whitespace characters into **s**. Non-format characters specify that the input should contain that character. For example,

```
the value of x is '123' and the value of s is 'string '\n"
```

will read **123** into **x** and **string** followed by a **0** into **s**. If the call of **scanf()** succeeds, the result value (**i** in the call above) will be the number of argument pointers assigned to (hopefully 2 in the example); otherwise, **EOF**. This way of specifying input is error-prone (e.g., what would happen if you forgot the space after **string** on that input line?). All arguments to **scanf()** must be pointers. We strongly recommend against the use of **scanf()**.

So what can we do for input if we are obliged to use stdio? One popular answer is, "Use the standard library function **gets()**":

```
// very dangerous code:
char s[buf_size];
char* p = gets(s);       // read a line into s
```

The call **p=gets(s)** reads characters into **s** until a newline or an end of file is encountered and a **0** character is placed after the last character written to **s**. If an end of file is encountered or if an error occurred, **p** is set to **NULL** (that is, **0**);

otherwise it is set to **s**. Never use **gets(s)** or its rough equivalent (**scanf("%s",s)**)! For years, they were the favorites of virus writers: by providing an input that overflows the input buffer (**s** in the example), a program can be corrupted and a computer potentially taken over by an attacker. The **sprintf()** function suffers similar buffer-overflow problems.

The stdio library also provides simple and useful character read and write functions:

stdio character functions	
x=getc(st)	Read a character from input stream **st**; return the character's integer value; **x==EOF** if end of file or an error occurred.
x=putc(c,st)	Write the character **c** to the output stream **st**; return the integer value of the character written; **x==EOF** if an error occurred.
x=getchar()	Read a character from **stdin**; return the character's integer value; **x==EOF** if end of file or an error occurred.
x=putchar(c)	Write the character **c** to **stdout**; return the integer value of the character written; **x==EOF** if an error occurred.
x=ungetc(c,st)	Put **c** back onto the input stream **st**; return the integer value of the character pushed; **x==EOF** if an error occurred.

Note that the result of these functions is an **int** (not a **char**, or **EOF** couldn't be returned). For example, this is a typical C-style input loop:

```
int ch;   /* not char ch; */
while ((ch=getchar())!=EOF) { /* do something */ }
```

Don't do two consecutive **ungetch()**s on a stream. The result of that is undefined and (therefore) non-portable.

There are more stdio functions; see a good C textbook, such as K&R, if you need to know more.

B.10.3 C-style strings

A C-style string is a zero-terminated array of **char**. This notion of a string is supported by a set of functions defined in **<cstring>** (or **<string.h>**; note: *not* **<string>**) and **<cstdlib>**. These functions operate on C-style strings through **char*** pointers (**const char*** pointers for memory that's only read):

C-style string operations	
x=strlen(s)	Count the characters (excluding the terminating 0).
p=strcpy(s,s2)	Copy **s2** into **s**; [**s:s+n**) and [**s2:s2+n**) may not overlap; **p=s**; the terminating 0 is copied.
p=strcat(s,s2)	Copy **s2** onto the end of **s**; **p=s**; the terminating 0 is copied.
x=strcmp(s, s2)	Compare lexicographically: if **s<s2** then **x** is negative; if **s==s2** then **x==0**; if **s>s2** then **x** is positive.
p=strncpy(s,s2,n)	**strcpy**; max **n** characters; may fail to copy terminating 0; **p=s**.
p=strncat(s,s2,n)	**strcat**; max **n** characters; may fail to copy terminating 0; **p=s**.
x=strncmp(s,s2,n)	**strcmp**; max **n** characters.
p=strchr(s,c)	Make **p** point to the first **c** in **s**.
p=strrchr(s,c)	Make **p** point to the last **c** in **s**.
p=strstr(s,s2)	Make **p** point to the first character of **s** that starts a substring equal to **s2**.
p=strpbrk(s,s2)	Make **p** point to the first character of **s** also found in **s2**.
x=atof(s)	Extract a **double** from **s**.
x=atoi(s)	Extract an **int** from **s**.
x=atol(s)	Extract a **long int** from **s**.
x=strtod(s,p)	Extract a **double** from **s**; set **p** to the first character after the **double**.
x=strtol(s,p)	Extract a **long int** from **s**; set **p** to the first character after the **long**.
x=strtoul(s,p)	Extract an **unsigned long int** from **s**; set **p** to the first character after the **long**.

Note that in C++, **strchr()** and **strstr()** are duplicated to make them type safe (they can't turn a **const char*** into a **char*** the way the C equivalents can); see also §27.5.

An extraction function looks into its C-style string argument for a conventionally formatted representation of a number, such as **"124"** and **" 1.4"**. If no such representation is found, the extraction function returns **0**. For example:

```
int x = atoi("fortytwo");    /* x becomes 0 */
```

B.10.4 Memory

The memory manipulation functions operate on "raw memory" (no type known) through **void*** pointers (**const void*** pointers for memory that's only read):

C-style memory operations	
q=memcpy(p, p2, n)	Copy **n** bytes from **p2** to **p** (like **strcpy**); [**p:p+n**) and [**p2:p2+n**) may not overlap; **q=p**.
q=memmove(p,p2,n)	Copy **n** bytes from **p2** to **p**; **q=p**.
x=memcmp(p,p2,n)	Compare **n** bytes from **p2** to the equivalent **n** bytes from **p** (like **strcmp**).
q=memchr(p,c,n)	Find **c** (converted to an **unsigned char**) in **p[0]..p[n−1]** and let **q** point to that element; **q=0** if **c** is not found.
q=memset(p,c,n)	Copy **c** (converted to an **unsigned char**) into each of **p[0]..[n−1]**; **q=p**.
p=calloc(n,s)	Allocate **n*s** bytes initialized to **0** on free store; **p=0** if **n*s** bytes could not be allocated.
p=malloc(s)	Allocate **s** uninitialized bytes on free store; **p=0** if **s** bytes could not be allocated.
q=realloc(p,s)	Allocate **s** bytes on free store; **p** must be a pointer returned by **malloc()** or **calloc()**; if possible reuse the space pointed to by **p**; if that is not possible copy all bytes in the area pointed to by **p** to a new area; **q=0** if **s** bytes could not be allocated.
free(p)	Deallocate the memory pointed to by **p**; **p** must be a pointer returned by **malloc()**, **calloc()**, or **realloc()**.

Note that **malloc()**, etc. do not invoke constructors and **free()** doesn't invoke destructors. Do not use these functions for types with constructors or destructors. Also, **memset()** should never be used for any type with a constructor.

The **mem*** functions are found in **<cstring>** and the allocation functions in **<cstdlib>**.

See also §27.5.2.

B.10.5 Date and time

In **<ctime>**, you can find several types and functions related to date and time.

Date and time types	
clock_t	an arithmetic type for holding short time intervals (maybe just intervals of a few minutes)
time_t	an arithmetic type for holding long time intervals (maybe centuries)
tm	a **struct** for holding date and time (since year 1900)

struct tm is defined like this:

```
struct tm {
    int tm_sec;    // second of minute [0:61]; 60 and 61 represent leap seconds
    int tm_min;    // minute of hour [0,59]
    int tm_hour;   // hour of day [0,23]
    int tm_mday;   // day of month [1,31]
    int tm_mon;    // month of year [0,11]; 0 means January (note: not [1:12])
    int tm_year;   // year since 1900; 0 means year 1900, and 102 means 2002
    int tm_wday;   // days since Sunday [0,6]; 0 means Sunday
    int tm_yday;   // days since January 1 [0,365]; 0 means January 1
    int tm_isdst;  // hours of Daylight Savings Time
};
```

Date and time functions:

```
clock_t clock();       // number of clock ticks since the start of the program

time_t time(time_t* pt);       // current calendar time
double difftime(time_t t2, time_t t1);   // t2–t1 in seconds

tm* localtime(const time_t* pt);  // local time for the *pt
tm* gmtime(const time_t* pt);  // Greenwich Mean Time (GMT) tm for *pt, or 0

time_t mktime(tm* ptm);        // time_t for *ptm, or time_t(–1)

char* asctime(const tm* ptm);   // C-style string representation for *ptm
char* ctime(const time_t* t) { return asctime(localtime(t)); }
```

An example of the result of a call of **asctime()** is **"Sun Sep 16 01:03:52 1973\n"**.

Here is an example of how **clock** can be used to time a function (**do_something()**):

```
int main(int argc, char* argv[])
{
    int n = atoi(argv[1]);

    clock_t t1 = clock();      // start time
    if (t1 == clock_t(–1)) {   // clock_t(–1) means "clock() didn't work"
        cerr << "sorry, no clock\n";
        exit(1);
    }
```

```
        for (int i = 0; i<n; i++) do_something();   // timing loop

        clock_t t2 = clock();        // end time
        if (t2 == clock_t(−1)) {
            cerr << "sorry, clock overflow\n";
            exit(2);
        }
        cout << "do_something() " << n << " times took "
            << double(t2−t1)/CLOCKS_PER_SEC << " seconds"
            << " (measurement granularity: " << CLOCKS_PER_SEC
            << " of a second)\n";

    }
```

The explicit conversion **double(t2−t1)** before dividing is necessary because **clock_t** might be an integer. For values **t1** and **t2** returned by **clock()**, **double(t2−t1)/CLOCKS_PER_SEC** is the system's best approximation of the time in seconds between the two calls.

If **clock()** isn't provided for a processor or if a time interval was too long to measure, **clock()** returns **clock_t(−1)**.

B.10.6 Etc.

In **<cstdlib>** we find:

Etc. stdlib functions	
abort()	Terminate the program "abnormally."
exit(n)	Terminate the program with value **n**; **n==0** means successful termination.
system(s)	Execute the C-style string as a command (system dependent).
qsort(b,n,s,cmp)	Sort array starting at **b** with **n** elements of size **s** using the comparison function **cmp**.
bsearch(k,b,n,s,cmp)	Search for **k** in the sorted array starting at **b** with **n** elements of size **s** using the comparison function **cmp**.
d=rand()	**d** is a pseudo-random number in the range **[0:RAND_MAX]**.
srand(d)	Start a sequence of pseudo-random numbers using **d** as the seed.

The comparison function (**cmp**) used by **qsort()** and **bsearch()** must have the type

int (*cmp)(const void* p, const void* q);

That is, no type information is known to the sort function that simply "sees" its array as a sequence of bytes. The integer returned is

- Negative if ***p** is considered less than ***q**
- Zero if ***p** is considered equal to ***q**
- Positive if ***p** is considered greater than ***q**

Note that **exit()** and **abort()** do not invoke destructors. If you want destructors called for constructed automatic and static objects (§A.4.2), throw an exception.

For more standard library functions see K&R or some other reputable C language reference.

B.11 Other libraries

Looking through the standard library facilities, you'll undoubtedly have failed to find something you could use. Compared to the challenges faced by programmers and the number of libraries available in the world, the C++ standard library is minute. There are many libraries for

- Graphical user interfaces
- Advanced math
- Database access
- Networking
- XML
- Date and time
- File system manipulation
- 3D graphics
- Animation
- Etc.

However, such libraries are not part of the standard. You can find them by searching the web or by asking friends and colleagues. Please don't get the idea that the only useful libraries are those that are part of the standard library.

C

Getting Started with Visual Studio

> "The universe is not only queerer
> than we imagine,
> it's queerer than we *can* imagine."
>
> **—J. B. S. Haldane**

This appendix explains the steps you have to go through to enter a program, compile it, and have it run using Microsoft Visual Studio.

C.1 Getting a program to run

To get a program to run, you need to somehow place the files together (so that when a file refers to another − e.g., your source file refers to a header file − it finds it). You then need to invoke the compiler and the linker (if nothing else, then to link to the C++ standard library), and finally you need to run (execute) the program. There are several ways of doing that, and different systems (e.g., Windows and Linux) have different conventions and tool sets. However, you can run all of the examples from this book on all major systems using any of the major tool sets. This appendix explains how to do it for one popular system, Microsoft's Visual Studio.

Personally, we find few exercises as frustrating as getting a first program to work on a new and strange system. This is a task for which it makes sense to ask for help. However, if you do get help, be sure that the helper teaches you how to do it, rather than just doing it for you.

C.2 Installing Visual Studio

Visual Studio is an interactive development environment (IDE) for Windows. If Visual Studio is not installed on your computer, you may purchase a copy and follow the instructions that come with it, or download and install the free Visual C++ Express from www.microsoft.com/express/download. The description here is based on Visual Studio 2005. Other versions may differ slightly.

C.3 Creating and running a program

The steps are:

1. Create a new project.
2. Add a C++ source file to the project.
3. Enter your source code.
4. Build an executable file.
5. Execute the program.
6. Save the program.

C.3.1 Create a new project

In Visual Studio, a "project" is a collection of files that together provide what it takes to create and run a program (also called an *application*) under Windows.

1. Open the Visual C++ IDE by clicking the Microsoft Visual Studio 2005 icon, or select it from **Start > Programs > Microsoft Visual Studio 2005 > Microsoft Visual Studio 2005**.
2. Open the **File** menu, point to **New**, and click **Project**.
3. Under **Project Types**, select **Visual C++**.
4. In the **Templates** section, select **Win32 Console Application**.
5. In the **Name** text box type the name of your project, for example, **Hello,World!**.
6. Choose a directory for your project. The default, **C:\Documents and Settings\Your Name\My Documents\Visual Studio 2005 Projects**, is usually a good choice.
7. Click **OK**.
8. The WIN32 Application Wizard should appear.
9. Select **Application Settings** on the left side of the dialog box.
10. Under **Additional Options** select **Empty Project**.
11. Click **Finish**. All compiler settings should now be initialized for your console project.

C.3.2 Use the std_lib_facilities.h header file

For your first programs, we strongly suggest that you use the custom header file **std_lib_facilities.h** from www.stroustrup.com/programming/std_lib_facilities.h.

Place a copy of it in the directory you chose in §C.3.1, step 6. (Note: Save as text, not HTML.) To use it, you need the line

```
#include "../../std_lib_facilities.h"
```

in your program. The "../../" tells the compiler that you placed the header in **C:\Documents and Settings\Your Name\My Documents\Visual Studio 2005 Projects** where it can be used by all of your projects, rather than right next to your source file in a project where you would have to copy it for each project.

C.3.3 Add a C++ source file to the project

You need at least one source file in your program (and often many):

1. Click the **Add New Item** icon on the menu bar (usually the second icon from the left). That will open the **Add New Item** dialog box. Select **Code** under the **Visual C++** category.

2. Select the **C++ File (.cpp)** icon in the template window. Type the name of your program file (**Hello, World!**) in the **Name** text box and click **Add**.

You have created an empty source code file. You are now ready to type your source code program.

C.3.4 Enter your source code

At this point you can either enter the source code by typing it directly into the IDE, or you can copy and paste it from another source.

C.3.5 Build an executable program

When you believe you have properly entered the source code for your program, go to the **Build** menu and select **Build Solution** or hit the triangular icon pointing to the right on the list of icons near the top of the IDE window. The IDE will try to compile and link your program. If it is successful, the message

Build: 1 succeeded, 0 failed, 0 up-to-date, 0 skipped

should appear in the **Output** window. Otherwise a number of error messages will appear. Debug the program to correct the errors and **Build Solution** again.

If you used the triangular icon, the program will automatically start running (executing) if there were no errors. If you used the **Build Solution** menu item, you have to explicitly start the program, as described in §C.3.6.

C.3.6 Execute the program

Once all errors have been eliminated, execute the program by going to the **Debug** menu and selecting **Start Without Debugging**.

C.3.7 Save the program

Under the **File** menu, click **Save All**. If you forget and try to close the IDE, the IDE will remind you.

C.4 Later

The IDE has an apparent infinity of features and options. Don't worry about those early on – or you'll get completely lost. If you manage to mess up a project so that it "behaves oddly," ask an experienced friend for help or build a new project from scratch. Over time, slowly experiment with new features and options.

Installing FLTK

"If the code and the comments disagree,
then both are probably wrong."

—Norm Schryer

T his appendix describes how to download, install, and link to the FLTK graphics and GUI toolkit.

D.1 Introduction

We chose FLTK, the Fast Light Tool Kit (pronounced "full tick"), as the base for our presentation of graphics and GUI issues because it is portable, relatively simple, relatively conventional, and relatively easy to install. We explain how to install FLTK under Microsoft Visual Studio because that's what most of our students use and because it is the hardest. If you use some other system (as some of our students also do), just look in the main folder (directory) of the downloaded files (§D.3) for directions for your favorite system.

Whenever you use a library that is not part of the ISO C++ standard, you (or someone else) have to download it, install it, and correctly use it from your own code. That's rarely completely trivial, and installing FLTK is probably a good exercise – because downloading and installing even the best library can be quite frustrating when you haven't tried before. Don't be too reluctant to ask advice from people who have tried before, but don't just let them do it for you: learn from them.

Note that there might be slight differences in files and procedures from what we describe here. For example, there may be a new version of FLTK or you may be using a different version of Visual Studio from what we describe in §D.4 or a completely different C++ implementation.

D.2 Downloading FLTK

Before doing anything, first see if FLTK is already installed on your machine; see §D.5. If it is not there, the first thing to do is to get the files onto your computer:

1. Go to http://fltk.org. (In an emergency, instead download a copy from our book support website: www.stroustrup.com/Programming/FLTK.)

2. Click **Download** in the navigation menu.

3. Choose **FLTK 1.1.x** in the drop-down and click **Show Download Locations**.

4. Choose a download location and download the .zip file.

The file you get will be in .zip format. That is a compressed format suitable for transmitting lots of files across the net. You'll need a program on your machine to "unzip" it into normal files; on Windows, WinZip and 7-Zip are examples of such programs.

D.3 Installing FLTK

Your main problem in following our instructions is likely to be one of two: something has changed since we wrote and tested them (it happens), or the terminology is alien to you (we can't help with that; sorry). In the latter case, find a friend to translate.

1. Unzip the downloaded file and open the main folder, **fltk-1.1.?**. In a Visual C++ folder (e.g., ~~vc2005 or vcnet~~), open **fltk.dsw**. If asked about updating old project files, choose **Yes to All**.

2. From the **Build** menu, choose **Build Solution**. This may take a few minutes. The source code is being compiled into static link libraries so that you do not have to recompile the FLTK source code any time you make a new project. When the process has finished, close Visual Studio.

3. From the main FLTK directory open the **lib** folder. Copy (not just move/drag) all the **.lib** files except **README.lib** (there should be seven) into **C:\Program Files\Microsoft Visual Studio\Vc\lib**.

4. Go back to the FLTK main directory and copy the **FL** folder into **C:\Program Files\Microsoft Visual Studio\Vc\include**.

Experts will tell you that there are better ways to install than copying into **C:\Program Files\Microsoft Visual Studio\Vc\lib** and **C:\Program Files\Microsoft Visual Studio\Vc\include**. They are right, but we are not trying to make you VS experts. If the experts insist, let them be responsible for showing you the better alternative.

D.4 Using FLTK in Visual Studio

1. Create a new project in Visual Studio with one change to the usual procedure: create a "Win32 project" instead of a "console application" when choosing your project type. Be sure to create an "empty project"; otherwise, some "software wizard" will add a lot of stuff to your project that you are unlikely to need or understand.

2. In Visual Studio, choose **Project** from the main (top) menu, and from the drop-down menu choose **Properties**.

3. In the **Properties** dialog box, in the left menu, click the **Linker** folder. This expands a sub-menu. In this sub-menu, click **Input**. In the **Additional Dependencies** text field on the right, enter the following text:

   fltkd.lib wsock32.lib comctl32.lib fltkjpegd.lib fltkimagesd.lib

   [The following step may be unnecessary because it is now the default.] In the **Ignore Specific Library** text field, enter the following text:

   libcd.lib

4. [This step may be unnecessary because /MDd is now the default.] In the left menu of the same **Properties** window, click **C/C++** to expand a different sub-menu. Click the **Code Generation** sub-menu item. In the right menu, change the **Runtime Library** drop-down to **Multi-threaded Debug DLL (/MDd)**. Click OK to close the **Properties** window.

D.5 Testing if it all worked

Create a single new .cpp file in your newly created project and enter the following code. It should compile without problems.

```
#include <FL/Fl.h>
#include <FL/Fl_Box.h>
#include <FL/Fl_Window.h>

int main()
{
    Fl_Window window(200, 200, "Window title");
    Fl_Box box(0,0,200,200,"Hey, I mean, Hello, World!");
    window.show();
    return Fl::run();
}
```

If it did not work:

- "Compiler error stating a .lib file could not be found": Your problem is most likely in the installation section. Pay attention to step 3, which involves putting the link libraries (.lib) files where your compiler can easily find them.

- "Compiler error stating a .h file could not be opened": Your problem is most likely in the installation section. Pay attention to step 4, which involves putting the header (.h) files where your compiler can easily find them.

- "Linker error involving unresolved external symbols": Your problem is most likely in the project section.

If that didn't help, find a friend to ask.

GUI Implementation

"When you finally understand
what you are doing,
things will go right."

—Bill Fairbank

This appendix presents implementation details of callbacks, **Window**, **Widget**, and **Vector_ref**. In Chapter 16, we couldn't assume the knowledge of pointers and casts needed for a more complete explanation, so we banished that explanation to this appendix.

E.1 Callback implementation

We implemented callbacks like this:

```
void Simple_window::cb_next(Address, Address addr)
    // call Simple_window::next() for the window located at pw
{
    reference_to<Simple_window>(addr).next();
}
```

Once you have understood Chapter 17, it is pretty obvious that an **Address** must be a **void***. And, of course, **reference_to<Simple_window>(addr)** must somehow create a reference to a **Simple_window** from the **void*** called **addr**. However, unless you had previous programming experience, there was nothing "pretty obvious" or "of course" about that before you read Chapter 17, so let's look at the use of addresses in detail.

As described in §A.17, C++ offers a way of giving a name to a type. For example:

```
typedef void* Address;      // Address is a synonym for void*
```

This means that the name **Address** can now be used instead of **void***. Here, we used **Address** to emphasize that an address was passed, and also to hide the fact that **void*** is the name of the type of pointer to an object for which we don't know the type.

So **cb_next()** receives a **void*** called **addr** as an argument and − somehow − promptly converts it to a **Simple_window&**:

```
reference_to<Simple_window>(addr)
```

The **reference_to** is a template function (§A.13):

```
template<class W> W& reference_to(Address pw)
    // treat an address as a reference to a W
```

```
{
        return *static_cast<W*>(pw);
}
```

Here, we used a template function to write ourselves an operation that acts as a cast from a **void*** to a **Simple_window&**. The type conversion, **static_cast**, is described in §17.8.

The compiler has no way of verifying our assertion that **addr** points to a **Simple_window**, but the language rule requires the compiler to trust the programmer here. Fortunately, we are right. The way we know that we are right is that FLTK is handing us back a pointer that we gave to it. Since we knew the type of the pointer when we gave it to FLTK, we can use **reference_to** to "get it back." This is messy, unchecked, and not all that uncommon at the lower levels of a system.

Once we have a reference to a **Simple_window**, we can use it to call a member function of **Simple_window**. For example (§16.3):

```
void Simple_window::cb_next(Address, Address pw)
        // call Simple_window::next() for the window located at pw
{
        reference_to<Simple_window>(pw).next();
}
```

We use the messy callback function **cb_next()** simply to adjust the types as needed to call a perfectly ordinary member function **next()**.

E.2 Widget implementation

Our **Widget** interface class looks like this:

```
class Widget {
        // Widget is a handle to a Fl_widget — it is *not* a Fl_widget
        // we try to keep our interface classes at arm's length from FLTK
public:
        Widget(Point xy, int w, int h, const string& s, Callback cb)
                :loc(xy), width(w), height(h), label(s), do_it(cb)
{ }

        virtual ~Widget() { }        // destructor

        virtual void move(int dx,int dy)
                { hide(); pw->position(loc.x+=dx, loc.y+=dy); show(); }
```

```
        virtual void hide() { pw->hide(); }
        virtual void show() { pw->show(); }

        virtual void attach(Window&) = 0;    // each Widget defines at least
                                             // one action for a window

        Point loc;
        int width;
        int height;
        string label;
        Callback do_it;

    protected:
        Window* own;        // every Widget belongs to a Window
        Fl_Widget* pw;      // a Widget "knows" its Fl_Widget
    };
```

Note that our **Widget** keeps track of its FLTK widget and the **Window** with which it is associated. Note that we need pointers for that because a **Widget** can be associated with different **Window**s during its life. A reference or a named object wouldn't suffice. (Why not?)

It has a location (**loc**), a rectangular shape (**width** and **height**), and a **label**. Where it gets interesting is that it also has a callback function (**do_it**) – it connects a **Widget**'s image on the screen to a piece of our code. The meaning of the operations (**move()**, **show()**, **hide()**, and **attach()**) should be obvious.

Widget has a "half-finished" look to it. It was designed as an implementation class that users should not have to see very often. It is a good candidate for a redesign. We are suspicious about all of those public data members, and "obvious" operations typically need to be reexamined for unplanned subtleties.

Widget has virtual function and can be used as a base class, so it has a **virtual** destructor (§17.5.2).

E.3 Window implementation

When do we use pointers and when do we use references instead? We examine that general question in §8.5.6. Here, we'll just observe that some programmers like pointers and that we need pointers when we want to point to different objects at different times in a program.

So far, we have not shown one of the central classes in our graphics and GUI library, **Window**. The most significant reasons are that it uses a pointer and that its implementation using FLTK requires free store. As found in **Window.h**, here it is:

```
class Window : public Fl_Window {
public:
        // let the system pick the location:
        Window(int w, int h, const string& title);
        // top left corner in xy:
        Window(Point xy, int w, int h, const string& title);

        virtual ~Window() { }

        int x_max() const { return w; }
        int y_max() const { return h; }

        void resize(int ww, int hh) { w=ww, h=hh; size(ww,hh); }

        void set_label(const string& s) { label(s.c_str()); }

        void attach(Shape& s) { shapes.push_back(&s); }
        void attach(Widget&);

        void detach(Shape& s);        // remove w from shapes
        void detach(Widget& w);       // remove w from window
                                      // (deactivates callbacks)

        void put_on_top(Shape& p);    // put p on top of other shapes
protected:
        void draw();
private:
        vector<Shape*> shapes;        // shapes attached to window
        int w,h;                      // window size

        void init();
};
```

So, when we **attach()** a **Shape** we store a pointer in **shapes** so that the **Window** can draw it. Since we can later **detach()** that shape, we need a pointer. Basically, an **attach()**ed shape is still owned by our code; we just give the **Window** a reference to it. **Window::attach()** converts its argument to a pointer so that it can store it. As shown above, **attach()** is trivial; **detach()** is slightly less simple. Looking in **Window.cpp**, we find:

```
void Window::detach(Shape& s)
    // guess that the last attached will be first released
{
    for (unsigned int i = shapes.size(); 0<i; --i)
        if (shapes[i-1]==&s) shapes.erase(&shapes[i-1]);
}
```

The **erase()** member function removes ("erases") a value from a **vector**, decreasing the **vector**'s size by one (§20.7.1).

Window is meant to be used as a base class, so it has a **virtual** destructor (§17.5.2).

E.4 Vector_ref

Basically, **Vector_ref** simulates a **vector** of references. You can initialize it with references or with pointers:

- If an object is passed to **Vector_ref** as a reference, it is assumed to be owned by the caller who is responsible for its lifetime (e.g., the object is a scoped variable).

- If an object is passed to **Vector_ref** as a pointer, it is assumed to be allocated by **new** and it is **Vector_ref**'s responsibility to delete it.

An element is stored as a pointer − not as a copy of the object − into the **Vector_ref** and has reference semantics. For example, you can put a **Circle** into a **Vector_ref<Shape>** without suffering slicing.

```
template<class T> class Vector_ref {
    vector<T*> v;
    vector<T*> owned;
public:
    Vector_ref() {}
    Vector_ref(T* a, T* b = 0, T* c = 0, T* d = 0);

    ~Vector_ref() { for (int i=0; i<owned.size(); ++i) delete owned[i]; }

    void push_back(T& s) { v.push_back(&s); }
    void push_back(T* p) { v.push_back(p); owned.push_back(p); }

    T& operator[](int i) { return *v[i]; }
```

```
    const T& operator[](int i) const { return *v[i]; }

    int size() const { return v.size(); }
};
```

Vector_ref's destructor **delete**s every object passed to it as a pointer.

E.5 An example: manipulating Widgets

Here is a complete program. It exercises many of the **Widget/Window** features. It is only minimally commented. Unfortunately, such insufficient commenting is not uncommon. It is an exercise to get this program to run and to explain it.

Basically, when you run it, it appears to define four buttons:

```
#include "../GUI.h"
using namespace Graph_lib;

class W7 : public Window {
    // four ways to make it appear that a button moves around:
    // show/hide, change location, create new one, and attach/detach
public:
    W7(int h, int w, const string& t);

    Button* p1;          // show/hide
    Button* p2;
    bool sh_left;

    Button* mvp;         // move
    bool mv_left;

    Button* cdp;         // create/destroy
    bool cd_left;

    Button* adp1;        // activate/deactivate
    Button* adp2;
    bool ad_left;

    void sh();           // actions
    void mv();
    void cd();
    void ad();
```

```
        static void cb_sh(Address, Address addr)     // callbacks
                { reference_to<W7>(addr).sh(); }
        static void cb_mv(Address, Address addr)
                { reference_to<W7>(addr).mv(); }
        static void cb_cd(Address, Address addr)
                { reference_to<W7>(addr).cd(); }
        static void cb_ad(Address, Address addr)
                { reference_to<W7>(addr).ad(); }
};
```

However, a **W7** (**Window** experiment number 17) really has six buttons; it just
keeps two hidden:

```
W7::W7(int h, int w, const string& t)
    :Window(h,w,t),
    sh_left(true), mv_left(true), cd_left(true), ad_left(true)
{
    p1 = new Button(Point(100,100),50,20,"show",cb_sh);
    p2 = new Button(Point(200,100),50,20,"hide",cb_sh);

    mvp = new Button(Point(100,200),50,20,"move",cb_mv);

    cdp = new Button(Point(100,300),50,20,"create",cb_cd);

    adp1 = new Button(Point(100,400),50,20,"activate",cb_ad);
    adp2 = new Button(Point(200,400),80,20,"deactivate",cb_ad);

    attach(*p1);
    attach(*p2);
    attach(*mvp);
    attach(*cdp);
    p2->hide();
    attach(*adp1);
}
```

There are four callbacks. Each makes it appear that the button you press disappears and a new one appears. However, this is achieved in four different ways:

```
void W7::sh()        // hide a button, show another
{
    if (sh_left) {
        p1->hide();
        p2->show();
    }
```

```
    else {
            p1->show();
            p2->hide();
    }
    sh_left = !sh_left;
}

void W7::mv()        // move the button
{
    if (mv_left) {
            mvp->move(100,0);
    }
    else {
            mvp->move(-100,0);
    }
    mv_left = !mv_left;
}

void W7::cd()    // delete the button and create a new one
{
    cdp->hide();
    delete cdp;
    string lab = "create";
    int x = 100;
    if (cd_left) {
            lab = "delete";
            x = 200;
    }
    cdp = new Button(Point(x,300), 50, 20, lab, cb_cd);
    attach(*cdp);
    cd_left = !cd_left;
}

void W7::ad()    // detach the button from the window and attach its replacement
{
    if (ad_left) {
            detach(*adp1);
            attach(*adp2);
    }
    else {
            detach(*adp2);
            attach(*adp1);
    }
```

```
        ad_left = !ad_left;
}

int main()
{
        W7 w(400,500,"mole");
        return gui_main();
}
```

This program demonstrates the fundamental ways of adding and subtracting widgets to/from a window — or just appearing to.

Glossary

"Often, a few well-chosen words
are worth a thousand pictures."

—Anonymous

A *glossary* is a brief explanation of words used in a text. This is a rather short glossary of the terms we thought most essential, especially in the earlier stages of learning programming. The index and the "Terms" sections of the chapters might also help. A more extensive glossary, relating specifically to C++, can be found at www.research.att.com/~bs/glossary.html, and there is an incredible variety of specialized glossaries (of greatly varying quality) available on the web. Please note that a term can have several related meanings (so we occasionally list some) and that most terms we list have (often weakly) related meanings in other contexts; for example, we don't define *abstract* as it relates to modern painting, legal practice, or philosophy.

abstract class a class that cannot be directly used to create objects; often used to define an interface to derived classes. A class is made abstract by having a pure virtual function or a protected constructor.

abstraction a description of something that selectively and deliberately ignores (hides) details (e.g., implementation details); selective ignorance.

address a value that allows us to find an object in a computer's memory.

algorithm a procedure or formula for solving a problem; a finite series of computational steps to produce a result.

alias an alternative way of referring to an object; often a name, pointer, or reference.

application a program or a collection of programs that is considered an entity by its users.

approximation something (e.g., a value or a design) that is close to the perfect or ideal (value or design). Often an approximation is a result of trade-offs among ideals.

argument a value passed to a function or a template, in which it is accessed through a parameter.

array a homogeneous sequence of elements, usually numbered, e.g., [0:max).

assertion a statement inserted into a program to state (assert) that something must always be true at this point in the program.

base class a class used as the base of a class hierarchy. Typically a base class has one or more virtual functions.

bit the basic unit of information in a computer. A bit can have the value 0 or the value 1.

bug an error in a program.

byte the basic unit of addressing in most computers. Typically, a byte holds 8 bits.

class a user-defined type that may contain data members, function members, and member types.

code a program or a part of a program; ambiguously used for both source code and object code.

compiler a program that turns source code into object code.

complexity a hard-to-precisely-define notion or measure of the difficulty of constructing a solution to a problem or of the solution itself. Sometimes *complexity* is used to (simply) mean an estimate of the number of operations needed to execute an algorithm.

computation the execution of some code, usually taking some input and producing some output.

concrete class class for which objects can be created.

constant a value that cannot be changed (in a given scope); not mutable.

constructor an operation that initializes ("constructs") an object. Typically a constructor establishes an invariant and often acquires resources needed for an object to be used (which are then typically released by a destructor).

container an object that holds elements (other objects).

correctness a program or a piece of a program is correct if it meets its specification. Unfortunately, a specification can be incomplete or inconsistent, or can fail to meet users' reasonable expectations. Thus, to produce acceptable code, we sometimes have to do more than just follow the formal specification.

cost the expense (e.g., in programmer time, run time, or space) of producing a program or of executing it. Ideally, cost should be a function of complexity.

data values used in a computation.

debugging the act of searching for and removing errors from a program; usually far less systematic than testing.

declaration the specification of a name with its type in a program.

definition a declaration of an entity that supplies all information necessary to complete a program using the entity. Simplified definition: a declaration that allocates memory.

derived class a class derived from one or more base classes.

design an overall description of how a piece of software should operate to meet its specification.

destructor an operation that is implicitly invoked (called) when an object is destroyed (e.g., at the end of a scope). Often, it releases resources.

error a mismatch between reasonable expectations of program behavior (often expressed as a requirement or a users' guide) and what a program actually does.

executable a program ready to be run (executed) on a computer.

feature creep a tendency to add excess functionality to a program "just in case."

file a container of permanent information in a computer.

floating-point number a computer's approximation of a real number, such as 7.93 and 10.78e–3.

function a named unit of code that can be invoked (called) from different parts of a program; a logical unit of computation.

generic programming a style of programming focused on the design and efficient implementation of algorithms. A generic algorithm will work for all argument types that meet its requirements. In C++, generic programming typically uses templates.

header a file containing declarations used to share interfaces between parts of a program.

hiding the act of preventing a piece of information from being directly seen or accessed. For example, a name from a nested (inner) scope can prevent that same name from an outer (enclosing) scope from being directly used.

ideal the perfect version of something we are striving for. Usually we have to make trade-offs and settle for an approximation.

implementation (1) the act of writing and testing code; (2) the code that implements a program.

infinite loop a loop where the termination condition never becomes true. See **iteration**.

infinite recursion a recursion that doesn't end until the machine runs out of memory to hold the calls. In reality, such recursion is never infinite but is terminated by some hardware error.

information hiding the act of separating interface and implementation, thus hiding implementation details not meant for the user's attention and providing an abstraction.

initialize giving an object its first (initial) value.

input values used by a computation (e.g., function arguments and characters typed on a keyboard).

integer a whole number, such as 42 and –99.

interface a declaration or a set of declarations specifying how a piece of code (such as a function or a class) can be called.

invariant something that must be always true at a given point (or points) of a program; typically used to describe the state (set of values) of an object or the state of a loop before entry into the repeated statement.

iteration the act of repeatedly executing a piece of code; see **recursion**.

iterator an object that identifies an element of a sequence.

library a collection of types, functions, classes, etc. implementing a set of facilities (abstractions) meant to be potentially used as part of more that one program.

lifetime the time from the initialization of an object until it becomes unusable (goes out of scope, is deleted, or the program terminates).

linker a program that combines object code files and libraries into an executable program.

literal a notation that directly specifies a value, such as 12 specifying the integer value "twelve."

loop a piece of code executed repeatedly; in C++, typically a **for**-statement or a **while**-statement.

mutable changeable; the opposite of immutable, constant, and variable.

object (1) an initialized region of memory of a known type which holds a value of that type; (2) a region of memory.

object code output from a compiler intended as input for a linker (for the linker to produce executable code).

object file a file containing object code.

object-oriented programming a style of programming focused on the design and use of classes and class hierarchies.

operation something that can perform some action, such as a function and an operator.

output values produced by a computation (e.g., a function result or lines of characters written on a screen).

overflow producing a value that cannot be stored in its intended target.

overload defining two functions or operators with the same name but different argument (operand) types.

override defining a function in a derived class with the same name and argument types as a virtual function in the base class, thus making the function callable through the interface defined by the base class.

paradigm a somewhat pretentious term for design or programming style; often used with the (erroneous) implication that there exists a paradigm that is superior to all others.

parameter a declaration of an explicit input to a function or a template. When called, a function can access the arguments passed through the names of its parameters.

pointer (1) a value used to identify a typed object in memory; (2) a variable holding such a value.

post-condition a condition that must hold upon exit from a piece of code, such as a function or a loop.

pre-condition a condition that must hold upon entry into a piece of code, such as a function or a loop.

program code (possibly with associated data) that is sufficiently complete to be executed by a computer.

programming the art of expressing solutions to problems as code.

programming language a language for expressing programs.

pseudo code a description of a computation written in an informal notation rather than a programming language.

pure virtual function a virtual function that must be overridden in a derived class.

RAII ("Resource Acquisition Is Initialization") a basic technique for resource management based on scopes.

range a sequence of values that can be described by a start point and an end point. For example, [0:5) means the values 0, 1, 2, 3, and 4.

regular expression a notation for patterns in character strings.

recursion the act of a function calling itself; see also **iteration**.

reference (1) a value describing the location of a typed value in memory; (2) a variable holding such a value.

requirement (1) a description of the desired behavior of a program or part of a program; (2) a description of the assumptions a function or template makes of its arguments.

resource something that is acquired and must later be released, such as a file handle, a lock, or memory.

rounding conversion of a value to the mathematically nearest value of a less precise type.

scope the region of program text (source code) in which a name can be referred to.

sequence elements that can be visited in a linear order.

software a collection of pieces of code and associated data; often used interchangeably with **program**.

source code code as produced by a programmer and (in principle) readable by other programmers.

source file a file containing source code.

specification a description of what a piece of code should do.

standard an officially agreed upon definition of something, such as a programming language.

state a set of values.

string a sequence of characters.

style a set of techniques for programming leading to a consistent use of language features; sometimes used in a very restricted sense to refer just to low-level rules for naming and appearance of code.

subtype derived type; a type that has all the properties of a type and possibly more.

supertype base type; a type that has a subset of the properties of a type.

system (1) a program or a set of programs for performing a task on a computer; (2) a shorthand for "operating system," that is, the fundamental execution environment and tools for a computer.

template a class or a function parameterized by one or more types or (compile-time) values; the basic C++ language construct supporting generic programming.

testing a systematic search for errors in a program.

trade-off the result of balancing several design and implementation criteria.

truncation loss of information in a conversion from a type into another that cannot exactly represent the value to be converted.

type something that defines a set of possible values and a set of operations for an object.

uninitialized the (undefined) state of an object before it is initialized.

unit (1) a standard measure that gives meaning to a value (e.g., km for a distance); (2) a distinguished (e.g., named) part of a larger whole.

use case a specific (typically simple) use of a program meant to test its functionality and demonstrate its purpose.

value a set of bits in memory interpreted according to a type.

variable a named object of a given type; contains a value unless uninitialized.

virtual function a member function that can be overridden in a derived class.

word a basic unit of memory in a computer, usually the unit used to hold an integer.

Bibliography

Aho, Alfred V., Monica S. Lam, Ravi Sethi, and Jeffrey D. Ullman. *Compilers: Principles, Techniques, and Tools, Second Edition* (usually called "The Dragon Book"). Addison-Wesley, 2007. ISBN 0321547985.

Andrews, Mike, and James A. Whittaker. *How to Break Software: Functional and Security Testing of Web Applications and Web Services*. Addison-Wesley, 2006. ISBN 0321369440.

Austern, Matthew H. *Generic Programming and the STL: Using and Extending the C++ Standard Template Library*. Addison-Wesley, 1999. ISBN 0201309564.

Austern, Matt, ed. *Draft Technical Report on C++ Standard Library Extensions*. ISO/IEC PDTR 19768. www.open-std.org/jtc1/sc22/wg21/docs/papers/2005/n1836.pdf.

Bergin, Thomas J., and Richard G. Gibson, eds. *History of Programming Languages – Volume 2*. Addison-Wesley, 1996. ISBN 0201895021.

Blanchette, Jasmin, and Mark Summerfield. *C++ GUI Programming with Qt 4*. Prentice Hall, 2006. ISBN 0131872493.

Boost.org. "A Repository for Libraries Meant to Work Well with the C++ Standard Library." www.boost.org.

Cox, Russ. "Regular Expression Matching Can Be Simple and Fast (but Is Slow in Java, Perl, PHP, Python, Ruby, . . .)." http://swtch.com/~rsc/regexp/regexp1.html.

dmoz.org. http://dmoz.org/Computers/Programming/Languages.

Freeman, T. L., and Chris Phillips. *Parallel Numerical Algorithms*. Prentice Hall, 1992. ISBN 0136515975.

Gamma, Erich, Richard Helm, Ralph Johnson, and John M. Vlissides. *Design Patterns: Elements of Reusable Object-Oriented Software*. Addison-Wesley, 1994. ISBN 0201633612.

Goldthwaite, Lois, ed. *Technical Report on C++ Performance*. ISO/IEC PDTR 18015. www.research.att.com/~bs/performanceTR.pdf.

Gullberg, Jan. *Mathematics – From the Birth of Numbers*. W. W. Norton, 1996. ISBN 039304002X.

Hailpern, Brent, and Barbara G. Ryder, eds. *Proceedings of the Third ACM SIGPLAN Conference on the History of Programming Languages (HOPL-III)*. San Diego, CA, 2007. http://portal.acm.org/toc.cfm?id=1238844.

Henricson, Mats, and Erik Nyquist. *Industrial Strength C++: Rules and Recommendations.* Prentice Hall, 1996. ISBN 0131209655.

ISO/IEC 9899:1999. *Programming Languages – C.* The C standard.

ISO/IEC 14882:2003. *Programming Languages – C++.* The C++ standard.

Kernighan, Brian W., and Dennis M. Ritchie. *The C Programming Language.* Prentice Hall, first edition, 1978; second edition, 1988. ISBN 0131103628.

Knuth, Donald E. *The Art of Computer Programming, Volume 2: Seminumerical Algorithms, Third Edition.* Addison-Wesley, 1998. ISBN 0201896842.

Koenig, Andrew, ed. *The C++ Standard.* ISO/IEC 14882:2002. Wiley, 2003. ISBN 0470846747.

Koenig, Andrew, and Barbara E. Moo. *Accelerated C++: Practical Programming by Example.* Addison-Wesley, 2000. ISBN 020170353X.

Langer, Angelika, and Klaus Kreft. *Standard C++ IOStreams and Locales: Advanced Programmer's Guide and Reference.* Addison-Wesley, 2000. ISBN 0201183951.

Lippman, Stanley B., Josée Lajoie, and Barbara E. Moo. *The C++ Primer.* Addison-Wesley, 2005. ISBN 0201721481. (Use only the 4th edition.)

Lockheed Martin Corporation. "Joint Strike Fighter Air Vehicle Coding Standards for the System Development and Demonstration Program." Document Number 2RDU00001 Rev C. December 2005. Colloquially known as "JSF++." www.research.att.com/~bs/JSF-AV-rules.pdf.

Lohr, Steve. *Go To: The Story of the Math Majors, Bridge Players, Engineers, Chess Wizards, Maverick Scientists and Iconoclasts – The Programmers Who Created the Software Revolution.* Basic Books, 2002. ISBN 9780465042265.

Maddoc, J. boost::regexp documentation. www.boost.org and www.boost.org/doc/libs/1_36_0/libs/regex/doc/html/index.html.

Meyers, Scott. *Effective STL: 50 Specific Ways to Improve Your Use of the Standard Template Library.* Addison-Wesley, 2001. ISBN 0201749629.

Meyers, Scott. *Effective C++: 55 Specific Ways to Improve Your Programs and Designs, Third Edition.* Addison-Wesley, 2005. ISBN 0321334876.

Musser, David R., Gillmer J. Derge, and Atul Saini. *STL Tutorial and Reference Guide: C++ Programming with the Standard Template Library, Second Edition.* Addison-Wesley, 2001. ISBN 0201379236.

Programming Research. *High-integrity C++ Coding Standard Manual Version 2.4.* www.programmingresearch.com.

Richards, Martin. *BCPL – The Language and Its Compiler.* Cambridge University Press, 1980. ISBN 0521219655.

Ritchie, Dennis. "The Development of the C Programming Language." *Proceedings of the ACM History of Programming Languages Conference (HOPL-2). ACM SIGPLAN Notices,* Vol. 28 No. 3, 1993.

Salus, Peter. *A Quarter Century of UNIX.* Addison-Wesley, 1994. ISBN 0201547775.

Sammet, Jean. *Programming Languages: History and Fundamentals,* Prentice Hall, 1969. ISBN 0137299885.

Schmidt, Douglas C., and Stephen D. Huston. *C++ Network Programming, Volume 1: Mastering Complexity with ACE and Patterns.* Addison-Wesley, 2002. ISBN 0201604647.

Schmidt, Douglas C., and Stephen D. Huston. *C++ Network Programming, Volume 2: Systematic Reuse with ACE and Frameworks.* Addison-Wesley, 2003. ISBN 0201795256.

Schwartz, Randal L., Tom Phoenix, and Brian D. Foy: *Learning Perl, Fourth Edition*. O'Reilly, 2005. ISBN 0596101058.

Scott, Michael L. *Programming Language Pragmatics*. Morgan Kaufmann, 2000. ISBN 1558604421.

Sebesta, Robert W. *Concepts of Programming Languages, Sixth Edition*. Addison-Wesley, 2003. ISBN 0321193628.

Shepherd, Simon. "The Tiny Encryption Algorithm (TEA)." www.tayloredge.com/reference/Mathematics/TEA-XTEA.pdf and http://143.53.36.235:8080/tea.htm.

Stepanov, Alexander. www.stepanovpapers.com.

Stewart, G. W. *Matrix Algorithms, Volume I: Basic Decompositions*. SIAM, 1998. ISBN 0898714141.

Stone, Debbie, Caroline Jarrett, Mark Woodroffe, and Shailey Minocha. *User Interface Design and Evaluation*. Morgan Kaufmann, 2005. ISBN 0120884364.

Stroustrup, Bjarne. "A History of C++: 1979–1991." *Proceedings of the ACM History of Programming Languages Conference (HOPL-2). ACM SIGPLAN Notices,* Vol. 28 No. 3, 1993.

Stroustrup, Bjarne. *The Design and Evolution of C++*. Addison-Wesley, 1994. ISBN 0201543303.

Stroustrup, Bjarne. "Learning Standard C++ as a New Language." *C/C++ Users Journal,* May 1999.

Stroustrup, Bjarne. *The C++ Programming Language (Special Edition)*. Addison-Wesley, 2000. ISBN 0201700735.

Stroustrup, Bjarne. "C and C++: Siblings"; "C and C++: A Case for Compatibility"; and "C and C++: Case Studies in Compatibility." *The C/C++ Users Journal,* July, Aug., and Sept. 2002.

Stroustrup, Bjarne. "Evolving a Language in and for the Real World: C++ 1991–2006." *Proceedings of the Third ACM SIGPLAN Conference on the History of Programming Languages (HOPL-III)*. San Diego, CA, 2007. http://portal.acm.org/toc.cfm?id=1238844.

Stroustrup, Bjarne. Author's home page, www.research.att.com/~bs.

Sutter, Herb. *Exceptional C++: 47 Engineering Puzzles, Programming Problems, and Solutions*. Addison-Wesley, 2000. ISBN 0201615622.

Sutter, Herb, and Andrei Alexandrescu. *C++ Coding Standards: 101 Rules, Guidelines, and Best Practices*. Addison-Wesley, 2004. ISBN 0321113586.

University of St. Andrews. The MacTutor History of Mathematics archive. http://www-gap.dcs.st-and.ac.uk/~history.

Wexelblat, Richard L., ed. *History of Programming Languages*. Academic Press, 1981. ISBN 0127450408.

Whittaker, James A. *How to Break Software: A Practical Guide to Testing*. Addison-Wesley, 2003. ISBN 0321194330.

Wood, Alistair. *Introduction to Numerical Analysis*. Addison-Wesley, 1999. ISBN 020134291X.

Index

A

D

W

Photo Citations and Credits

Page 787. John Backus 1996. Copyright: Louis Fabian Bachrach. For a collection of pho-tographs of computer pioneers, see Christopher Morgan: *Wizards and their wonders: portraits in computing.* ACM Press. 1997. ISBN 0-89791-960-2

Page 789. Grace Murray Hopper. Source: Computer History Museum.

Page 790. Grace Murray Hopper's bug. Source: Computer History Museum.

Page 791. John C. McCarthy, 1967, at Stanford. Source: Stanford University.

Page 791. John C. McCarthy, 1996. Copyright: Louis Fabian Bachrach.

Page 792. Peter Naur photographed by Brian Randell in Munich in 1968 when they to-gether edited the report that launched the field of Software Engineering. Re-produced by permission from Brian Randell.

Page 792. Peter Naur, from oil painting by Duo Duo Zhuang 1995. Reproduced by per-mission from Erik Frøkjær.

Page 793. Edsger Dijkstra. Source: Wikimedia Commons.

Page 795. Niklaus Wirth. Source: N. Wirth.

Page 795. Niklaus Wirth. Source: N. Wirth.

Page 797. Jean Ichbiah. Source: Ada Information Clearinghouse.

Page 797. Lady Lovelace, 1838. Vintage print. Source: Ada Information Clearinghouse.

Page 799. Kristen Nygaard and Ole-Johan Dahl, circa 1968. Source: University of Oslo.

Page 800. Kristen Nygaard, circa 1996. Source: University of Oslo.

Page 800. Ole-Johan Dahl, 2002. Source: University of Oslo.

Page 801. Dennis M. Ritchie and Ken Thompson, approx. 1978. Copyright: AT&T Bell Labs.

Page 801. Dennis M. Ritchie, 1996. Copyright: Louis Fabian Bachrach.

Page 802. Doug McIlroy, circa 1990. Source: Gerard Holzmann.

Page 802. Brian W. Kernighan, circa 2004. Source: Brian Kernighan.

Page 804. Bjarne Stroustrup, 1996. Source: Bjarne Stroustrup.

Page 805. Alex Stepanov, 2003. Source: Bjarne Stroustrup.

Page 989. AT&T Bell Labs' Murray Hill Research center, approx. 1990. Copyright: AT&T Bell Labs.

Register
Your Book

at informit.com/register

You may be eligible to receive:

- Advance notice of forthcoming editions of the book
- Related book recommendations
- Chapter excerpts and supplements of forthcoming titles
- Information about special contests and promotions throughout the year
- Notices and reminders about author appearances, tradeshows, and online chats with special guests

Contact us

If you are interested in writing a book or reviewing manuscripts prior to publication, please write to us at:

Editorial Department
Addison-Wesley Professional
75 Arlington Street, Suite 300
Boston, MA 02116 USA
Email: AWPro@aw.com

Addison-Wesley

Visit us on the Web: informit.com/aw

LearnIT at InformIT

Go Beyond the Book

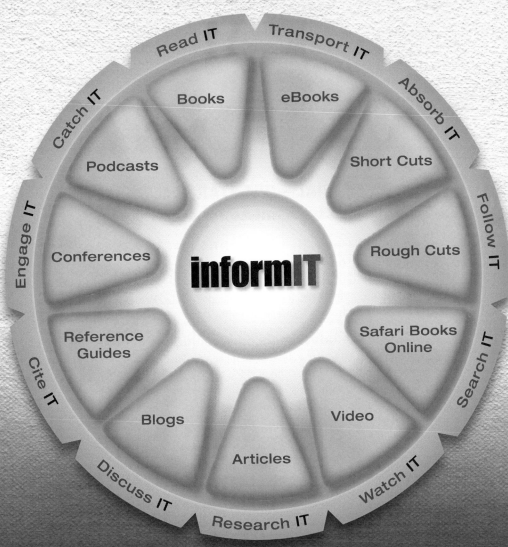

11 WAYS TO LEARN IT at **www.informIT.com/learn**

The online portal of the information technology
publishing imprints of Pearson Education

Addison Wesley   Cisco Press   EXAM/CRAM   IBM Press   que   PRENTICE HALL   SAMS

Try Safari Books Online FREE

Get online access to 5,000+ Books and Videos

Books Online

FREE TRIAL—GET STARTED TODAY!
www.informit.com/safaritrial

Find trusted answers, fast
Only Safari lets you search across thousands of best-selling books from the top technology publishers, including Addison-Wesley Professional, Cisco Press, O'Reilly, Prentice Hall, Que, and Sams.

Master the latest tools and techniques
In addition to gaining access to an incredible inventory of technical books, Safari's extensive collection of video tutorials lets you learn from the leading video training experts.

WAIT, THERE'S MORE!

Keep your competitive edge
With Rough Cuts, get access to the developing manuscript and be among the first to learn the newest technologies.

Stay current with emerging technologies
Short Cuts and Quick Reference Sheets are short, concise, focused content created to get you up-to-speed quickly on new and cutting-edge technologies.